ENCYCLOPEDIA OF ANTIQUES

Encyclopedia of
ANTIQUES

Edited by Arthur Negus

Hamlyn
London · New York · Sydney · Toronto

£8

First published in 1983 by
The Hamlyn Publishing Group Limited
London · New York · Sydney · Toronto
Astronaut House, Feltham, Middlesex, England

The Arthur Negus Guide to English Furniture
© Copyright Robin Butler 1978

The Arthur Negus Guide to English Pottery and Porcelain
© Copyright Bernard Price 1978

The Arthur Negus Guide to British Glass © Copyright J. A. Brooks 1981

The Arthur Negus Guide to British Pewter, Copper and Brass
© Copyright Peter Hornsby 1981

The Arthur Negus Guide to British Silver © Copyright Brand Inglis 1980

The Arthur Negus Guide to English Clocks
© Copyright David Barker 1980

ISBN 0 600 37313 4

Printed in Yugoslavia

Contents

Introduction by Arthur Negus   7
Furniture   9
Author's note   11
Introduction   12
Part one
1   Evolution of objects and design   18
2   Timber and other materials   33
3   The parts of furniture   42
4   Construction   44
5   Quality and condition   64
Part two
6   Individual items   80
7   The market place   164
Glossary   168
Chronology   176
Bibliography   178
Pottery and Porcelain   179
1   An approach to collecting   180
2   Unravelling the mystique   191
3   The influences from abroad   208
4   English pottery   221
5   Josiah Wedgwood   257
6   English porcelain   282
7   The nineteenth century   319
Glossary   345
Bibliography   346
Glass   347
Author's note   349
1   Glass: Its nature and early history   350
2   Styles of eighteenth century drinking glasses   373
3   Irish glass   414
4   Late Georgian glass   426
5   Methods of decorating glassware   450
6   Victorian glassmaking   464
7   Victorian decorative glass   478
8   Copies and fakes   505
9   About collecting   512
Glossary   515
Bibliography   516

Pewter, Copper and Brass 517
1 Collecting base metal 519
2 The metals and processes 524
3 Pewter: the historical background 532
4 What to look for in pewter 542
5 Pewter for kitchen and dining room 561
6 Pewter for drinking 579
7 Pewter in general use 591
8 Scottish, Channel Islands and Irish pewter 597
9 The history of the copper, brass and bronze industry 604
10 What to look for in brass, copper and bronze 617
11 Copper, brass and bronze in cooking 638
12 Lighting and candlesticks 651
13 Keeping warm 669
14 General household uses 675
Appendix: the level of survival 682
Glossary 686

Silver 687
1 The goldsmith's trade 688
2 Hall marks 703
3 Changing styles in British silver 1500-1900 710
4 Cutlery 1500-1900 792
5 Collecting silver 804
6 Provincial goldsmiths 816
Cleaning silver 828
Collections of British silver 829
Glossary of articles 833
Bibliography 838

Clocks 839
Introduction 841
1 Clocks and horological terms 847
2 The clock movement 856
3 Dials and hands 871
4 Clock cases 897
5 Lantern clocks 922
6 Long-case clocks 938
7 Bracket clocks 957
8 Wall clocks 968
9 Mass-produced and novelty clocks 978
10 Some notable clockmakers 986
11 Buying and restoring clocks 1002
Index 1025
Acknowledgements 1037

Introduction by Arthur Negus

When, several years ago The Hamlyn Publishing Group decided to produce a series of collector's reference books, I was delighted to be asked to act as Consultant Editor. In this capacity I was able to assist the publishers in their search for suitable authors, to guide the authors themselves in their treatment of their subject, and finally, to write a Foreword to each of the books.

Now that these various titles (*Furniture*; *Pottery and Porcelain*; *Glass*; *Pewter, Copper and Brass*; *Silver*; and *Clocks*) have been gathered together in one volume I am very pleased to have been asked, once again, to provide an Introduction. I feel I can do no better than to summarize what I said in my prefaces to the individual books.

In *Furniture* Robin Butler imparts, with a wealth of fascinating information, that knowledge – gained through years of practical experience – of woods, of construction and of detail which forms an important part in identifying a piece of furniture as being genuinely old. He teaches us to look inside and underneath, at the flaws and the botched repairs as well as at superb examples of the cabinet-maker's art. I am confident that his work will prove of enormous value to all those interested in the subject.

Bernard Price's approach to *Pottery and Porcelain*, concentrating on and dealing in detail with the different English factories will be of special interest to collectors. He writes not just about the ideal, the perfect specimen firmly behind museum glass, but about pieces which he has handled, with all their imperfections, and about examples which, without too much difficulty or expense, you too may handle and possess. A true enthusiast, he admirably conveys his appreciation of his chosen subject.

Today, when an increasing number of people are beginning to collect glass, attracted by its beauty and its elegance, it is fortunate that in *Glass* John Brooks, that happy combination of expert and enthusiast, is not only able to pass on some of his expertise to the reader but also, I feel, much of his own enjoyment. An abundance of useful information is given in these pages and the illustrations (with the exception of some early rarities) are confined to glassware that is in the hands of private people, thus demonstrating the opportunities that are still open to collectors.

In *Pewter, Copper and Brass*, Peter Hornsby has provided a guide which will appeal to all, both experienced collectors and novices. The history of the subject, methods of production, local and regional styles and the whole range of domestic metalware can be found here, and the author conveys the excitement of collecting as well as his own specialist skills.

We were fortunate in persuading Brand Inglis to write a book on *Silver*: the mysteries of the craft (the Goldsmiths Company and its ancient rules) are explained and the method of producing silver articles described, all in a language easy to understand. The student of silver as well as the amateur collector will find much here to stimulate their interest in a story which begins in medieval times, and covers French Huguenot styles, classically elegant Georgian silver and the development of Art Nouveau.

In *Clocks* David Barker studies the development of the English clockmaking industry from the seventeenth century onwards and explains in simple terms the major mechanical innovations in clock design over that period. The author's knowledge of restoration allows him to discuss in detail the methods of the old clockmakers, the tools and the metals they used, and the kind of solutions they employed in the design of each clock movement. Everything is covered: lantern clocks, long-case clocks, bracket clocks, wall clocks, the movement, the dial and the hands. As a result the reader will be able to fully appreciate the qualities of a clock both as an object d'art and as a working piece of machinery.

Arthur Negus

FURNITURE

ROBIN BUTLER

Author's note

Dear Reader,

During August 1977, Arthur Negus asked me if I would write a book on old English Furniture and, after much hesitation and persuasion, I consented. A friend suggested that I would do well to commit to paper those thoughts I had about the subject but that during the gestation and writing of the book, I should refrain from consulting any reference books whatsoever. This is the product of that sound advice.

I make no pretence that this volume contains the fruit of any original or hitherto unpublished research, nor do I boast any stunning revelations on the subject. Rather, this is my expression of what I have learned from others – my colleagues, friends and particularly my family – and what I have taught myself. I have endeavoured to explain the thought process that I use in the daily execution of my work.

To many people I owe a large debt of gratitude and I must particularly mention Elizabeth Norris, Brian Kern and Sheila Miles. Guy Holland proffered numerous most helpful suggestions and John Gaisford created meaningful prose from a plethora of incoherent ramblings. The book owes a great deal to the photographs, most of which are the highly skilled work of Robert Du Pontet.

It is a sad reflection of our society that by revealing the identities of the owners of the illustrated items, I would render them liable to the attention of thieves and, for this lamentable reason, they remain anonymous. All of them have shown me enormous hospitality and have met the demands I have placed on them with great kindness. Finally I add thanks in abundance to my long-suffering assistant, Suki Osmond.

I do hope you take enjoyment from reading the following pages and if, as a result of your better appreciation of old furniture, you derive greater pleasure from that too, then I shall be a very happy author.

Yours sincerely,
Robin Butler

Introduction

If a group of observers in the year 2000 were to look at a collection of photographs taken by a family in the mid-twentieth century – the snapshot album that many of us treasure – there is a chance that some of those observers would be able to date the album fairly accurately. An engineer would probably date a photo of a motor car to within five years, and a woman interested in fashion could probably make a close estimate by looking at the girls' dresses. Artists would recognise lettering and advertisements – or would they? What about those mirror-posters made today evoking memories of pre-war Ovaltine, Worthington, Rolls-Royce, or Bovril? By the year 2000 these copies will be old themselves and will have accumulated signs of wear comparable to the originals.

The same dilemma confronts furniture experts when they examine an antique. Knowledge of the materials used and the method of construction sometimes permits a confident assessment, but on other occasions the experts will be less fortunate and, despite thorough examination in a good light, will still be left uncertain as to who made the article, where and when. Recently, at a conference of the Furniture History Society, a large group of people were discussing two chests of drawers. Several suggestions were put forward as to the nature of the chests, but the only point on which there was agreement was that *nobody* knew for certain. Yet among these experts were the senior staff from leading British museums as well as dealers, lecturers, authors and collectors.

Fortunately such incidents are rare, and in the following pages I shall lead you through the questions you should be asking yourself when you consider a piece of furniture. The first step is to locate the piece in one of four categories: genuine, reproduction, fake or composite. The *genuine* piece can be defined as an object made at the date that its design would suggest. Thus a chair designed by Thomas Chippendale and made in his workshops in the 1760s is genuine, in exactly the same way as a perspex and stainless steel chair made in the

1960s. However, a chair made by John Smith in 1860 to a 1762 Chippendale design is not genuine, despite its considerable age: it is a *reproduction*.

Reproductions are objects made in the style of an earlier time, even if that style is quite recent. Usually they are sold as such when new, and little or no attempt is made to disguise the fact that the maker is trying to conjure up the feeling of a bygone age. These articles are very often superbly crafted in fine materials. While it is quite acceptable for the polish of a reproduction to be shaded, or even for the surface to be 'distressed', in an attempt to mellow the appearance, this process should not be continued to such a degree that an intelligent, if inexperienced, observer may be excused for thinking that the object is old. Just occasionally, however, the maker tries to simulate the passage of time in his creation, and eventually the point is reached where the intention is to deceive. This type of copy can only be described as a *fake*, and indeed some fakers are so knowledgeable that they can simulate even the finer points known only to the experts. Only considerable experience and advanced science can combat such trickery, and one must be thankful for its rarity.

The fourth and last category of furniture is known as the *composite*. This may be a combination of any, or all, of the above types, individual parts of which have been 'doctored' or 'improved'. During the mid-nineteenth century for example, Renaissance carved oak furniture was highly fashionable. Fragments of original carved panels were often incorporated into lavish Victorian sideboards, and much plain oak furniture of the seventeenth century was newly embellished by the carver's chisel. Hundreds of seventeenth-, and early eighteenth-century oak long-case clocks (unwarrantedly called by the Victorians grandfather clocks) were the subject of such 'improvement' during the nineteenth century.

Also in the composite category can be listed 'part items', such as the top half of a corner cupboard which has been separated from its lower section and hung from the wall as an entity in its own right. Even the stripped pine furniture which is currently very fashionable must be regarded as composite, for nearly all such pieces were originally painted – either to simulate more expensive wood, or in other colours. When the price of furniture was dictated primarily by the cost of materials rather than labour, servants' quarters and humble households were equipped throughout with articles made of pine.

In the course of this book I hope to show you how to place a piece of furniture into one of these four categories. The strongest emphasis will be on observation and on making logical deductions from the available evidence. Antique collectors are like detectives: at any viewing of an auction sale you will notice people pulling out drawers from bureaux and turning chairs upside down, peering at the parts you will never see unless you follow their example. They are looking for the clues which will help them decide what type of item they are looking at – genuine, reproduction, composite or fake. At the same time, I shall be drawing attention to features which allow us to date an item of furniture; and first and foremost among these is the design.

The dating of all domestic art, whether furniture or glass, silver or porcelain, involves committing to memory the *general* shapes of countless different objects. In my definition of the genuine, I mentioned Thomas Chippendale, who designed many chairs of which the majority are similar in general appearance. Plate 1 is an illustration from his book *The Gentleman and Cabinet Maker's Director*. Perhaps you are one of the very few fortunate people who have seen a chair taken exactly from one of these designs; many more readers will have seen chairs similar in feeling and made at almost the same time.

Plate 3 shows two such chairs. The one on the left bears a very strong resemblance to a design in Plate 1, but the chair on the right, although very similar, does not appear in Chippendale's book (nor, for that matter, in the design books of

1 Plate XVI from the 1762 (third) edition of Thomas Chippendale's *Gentleman and Cabinet Maker's Director*, engraved by Miller.

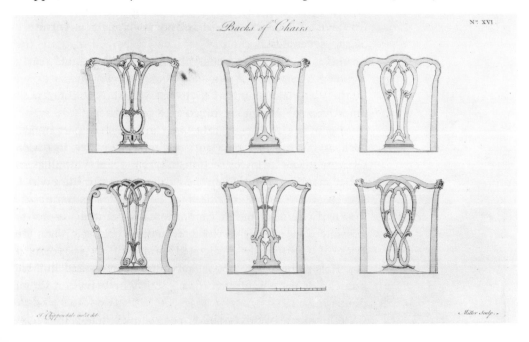

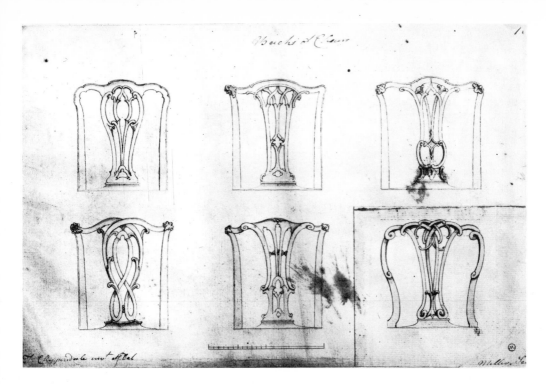

2 The original drawing from which Plate 1 was engraved, now in the Victoria and Albert Museum, London.

any of his contemporaries that I have been able to trace). These are two of perhaps 2000 slightly different chairs, all made at the same time, which are now given the rather nebulous term 'Chippendale'. Thus, while it is important to remember what a 'Chippendale chair' looks like, it is unnecessary to remember each one individually. They all have a resemblance to one another which is quite distinctive; and the same applies to other pieces of furniture.

Quite apart from the designers, external historical factors also affect styles. Furniture historians often mention particular kings and queens, describing items as 'George III' or 'Regency', for the social, financial, religious, artistic and other climates peculiar to each reign seem to have fostered particular aspects of design and craftsmanship. For example, the influx of Huguenot craftsmen during the closing years of the seventeenth century had a profound influence on the evolution of design – not only in furniture but particularly in silver and almost every other form of applied art. It is important to realise, however, that fashions did not change overnight with the death of the ruler, and a piece of furniture described as 'Queen Anne' may well have been made two or three years after the end of her reign. Furniture made after the accession of Queen Victoria, in 1837, is not generally regarded as antique; indeed 1830 is often taken as the latest date for antique. Design

15

changed fundamentally around this time, and the increasing use of machinery in furniture-making signalled the decline of the craftsman.

The evolution of English furniture is a complex subject, and it is quite possible to write a book just on the development of the chair. Readers who require more detailed information should refer to the bibliography at the end of this book, or visit the splendid collections in museums such as the Victoria and Albert in London and Temple Newsam House in Leeds. My main concern has been to give advice which will be useful in the auction room or the dealer's shop, and this book has been written with practical problems constantly in mind.

The first part of the book deals in broad outline with information that the reader will need to know before looking at individual pieces of furniture. The fundamental turning points in furniture design are put into a historical context, and some of the great names are mentioned at this point. Once the reader has grasped the main development in English cabinet-making however, a knowledge of the materials used and construction techniques will be indispensable, and a brief account of both is included. Advice is also given on how to recognise quality in furniture, what to look for in surface and colour, and how to check condition. Some readers may find this section difficult at

3 Two 'Chippendale' chairs, the left hand one bearing a strong resemblance to the centre top row of Plates 1 and 2. The right hand one though very similar, does not appear in the *Director*.

first, but do not despair! Used as reference, its contents will soon fall into place and greatly enhance an understanding of furniture in general and items you buy, in particular.

The second part of the book takes a close look at specific items of furniture, spaced fairly evenly throughout the period from 1600 to 1830. The object of this section is to show the reader how an expert will approach a piece of furniture at auction or in a dealer's showroom. It gives a 'bird's eye' view of the process by which one arrives at a satisfactory definition, avoiding the pitfalls which await the unwary. A brief chapter on the market place, and how best to get value for money when buying or selling furniture, concludes the volume.

Critics will find many omissions in this book – Charles II cane seat furniture, brass-inlaid Regency rosewood, scrolled paperwork, to name just three. I would have liked to include examples of all these, and much more, but space is at a premium. Consequently I have made a deliberate decision to include only those pieces which illustrate a particular design or method of construction. Readers who require a comprehensive reference book – of which many have already been published are advised to consult the bibliography.

My aim has been to encourage the reader not just to admire a piece of furniture as a good example of a particular period in history, but to *think* about it: good and bad quality, to appreciate line and movement, and to notice, perhaps for the first time, the minutiae of design and detail. To this end I have included many photographs showing specific aspects of construction and decoration; but it must be emphasized that these are no real substitute for 'going into the field' and physically examining as many pieces as possible.

Throughout, I have expressed personal opinions about pieces of furniture of which I have an intimate knowledge. It is my sincere hope that my own enthusiasm for these pieces will become manifest, and I can only hope that readers will derive as much satisfaction from handling similar items. In the second section I have included the occasional reproduction, fake and composite article, in an endeavour to give a cross-section of the type of furniture one may encounter in everyday circumstances. Care has been taken to find examples of the humble as well as the grandiose, and I hope that my enthusiasm for modest charm as well as the virtuoso product will be apparent.

If I can stimulate your interest in English antique furniture, and give a glimpse of how much there is to admire and enthuse over, then this book will have achieved its purpose.

Evolution of objects and design

Before the seventeenth century, houses were sparsely furnished, with a very limited variety of articles. The most common items were the coffer, which held everything that today we would put on shelves, or in cupboards and drawers, and the aumbry or hutch. Even chairs were confined to the grander households and reserved for important people; lesser mortals sat on benches or stools. Most tables were of the refectory type and only used at mealtimes, although towards the end of the sixteenth century, a few other tables were being made for games and for placing in smaller rooms such as bed-chambers. The very well-to-do had four-poster beds, which were considered prime status symbols because the drapery was so costly – and this remained true well into the eighteenth century. Rich households may also have boasted portable writing desks and musical instruments.

During the next 100 years, however, these basic forms began to evolve and diverge into the styles we are familiar with today. By about 1620, the dining chair had already emerged: the rear legs of the common stool were simply projected upwards to provide the framework for an upholstered back-rest. The food hutch had been developed into a cupboard designed not only for the reception of food and possessions, but also as a display stand for the family silver and for porcelain, which was beginning to be imported from the Orient. Drawers were incorporated into portable writing desks, and by the end of the seventeenth century the chest of drawers itself became a common object, having first appeared during the 1650s. Travelling desks were kept on top of chests of drawers and tables, for towards the end of the seventeenth century someone decided to marry the two pieces together – resulting in the bureau.

A growing vogue for decoration on furniture coincided with these developments. Some medieval pieces were carved with biblical scenes, or occasionally allegorical subjects; otherwise, the main concession to ornament was iron straps. The most

4 A late sixteenth-century oak chair, the back panelled with a carved cresting rail and the arms and seat rails of cacqueteuse shape. The seat slides forward to reveal a commode (the chamber pot being removed through the cupboard door on the other side).

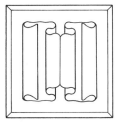

Linenfold

common form of decoration in the late fifteenth and sixteenth centuries was the carving of panels in linenfold. This stylised rendering of drapery was fairly uniform in concept and appears not to have found favour after 1570. Panels carved at this time sometimes had Romayne heads (Plate 5) for alternative decoration.

A technique first used by the Egyptians in the time of Tutankhamun was re-discovered during the sixteenth century: the art of the inlayer. Chests, or coffers, and the headboards of four-poster beds are often decorated with holly and bog oak, the white and black of the inlays contrasting sharply with the brown of the oak or walnut into which they are set.

5 *Left*: A Romayne head, or carved portrait medallion, typifying Renaissance influence, sixteenth-century.

6 *Opposite above*: The inlaid back panel of a writing desk *c.* 1580, typically depicting architectural and geometric designs, probably inspired by Nonesuch Palace. Victoria and Albert Museum.

7 *Opposite below*: Walnut long case clock. The large number of crisp mouldings and intelligent use of halved veneers on the case show its quality. The movement is by George Graham a London clockmaker of the highest calibre.

These decorations often take the form of chevron or chequer lines in a panel, or intersecting triangles and rectangles. Others, on the fronts of coffers and cabinets, depict architecture and, sometimes, the inlay represents Nonesuch Palace, built by Henry VIII and long since destroyed.

During the seventeenth century the use of inlay very soon dropped from favour. Decoration was confined to designs produced by carving or by turning component parts of furniture – such as the legs of chairs and tables – on a lathe. Furniture was first made in this way during the second half of the sixteenth century, and gained importance during the seventeenth century. The flamboyance of the Elizabethan era slowly waned and carving, which was usually confined to gouging, arcading, scrolls and lozenges, became progressively more restrained until the middle of the century.

During the Commonwealth period (1649-60) the Puritan religious influence was so severe that furniture was completely plain, with turning usually the sole concession to decoration. The restoration of the monarchy brought an exuberance unknown since Elizabethan times: carved crowns supported by cherubs abounded. Scrolling and foliage was the

order of the day, and soon even this gave way to marquetry decoration with fruit, flowers and birds in profusion whenever the expense permitted.

The Glorious Revolution of 1688 brought William III from Holland and with him a considerable Dutch influence. William's architect, Daniel Marot, together with the Huguenot craftsmen who came with him, produced designs which were to have a profound effect upon the development of furniture for the next fifty years. The use of new materials, most notably walnut, beechwood and caning for chairs, resulted in new techniques of construction. At the same time, the 'S' scroll became a basic design element for the legs supporting any piece of furniture. Perhaps influenced by designs brought in from the Orient, these were now elongated, and soon developed into the cabriole leg.

The reign of Queen Anne saw a further period of restraint. Carving was abandoned and great importance was attached to symmetry and proportion. Many people consider that the simple furniture of this period is among the finest ever made, with the unadorned cabriole leg the epitome of quiet elegance. The principal timber for fine quality pieces was walnut – cabinet-makers enhanced its attractive natural markings by cross-banding features such as cupboards and drawers and very often offset these with herring-bone or feather banding as well. Walnut particularly lends itself to the production of crisp mouldings both along and across the grain, and maximum advantage was taken of this. However, the harsh winter of 1709 caused havoc with the supplies of walnut and when the governments of producing countries forbade its export in about 1720, the import duties on other foreign timbers were relaxed.

8 *Opposite*: Mahogany
cabinet of architectural form
and with crisp carving from
Temple Newsam House,
Leeds. The door and sides are
panelled with needlework.

Mahogany, imported in bulk after 1725, is characterised by deep tones suitable for furniture of architectural and monumental proportions. The simplicity of the walnut period gave way to ornamental features such as pilaster columns and carved decorated mouldings, such as egg-and-dart, symbolising, life and death (page 170), which were derived from classical architecture. The straight grain and density of mahogany also enabled cabriole legs to be made slightly finer than was possible with walnut, which is softer. Carved decoration on the knee of a walnut cabriole tends to become worn with ordinary household usage, but the same decoration carved in mahogany is more durable. It was not long before cabinet-makers and carvers recognised and took advantage of the qualities of mahogany.

The first half of the eighteenth century saw the growth in Europe of the Baroque, with its emphasis on asymmetry and ornate, curvilinear shapes suggesting movement. The style

9 Detail of Plate 8 showing
the vigour, crispness and
high quality of the carving
on the cabriole knee of the
cabinet. Temple Newsam
House, Leeds.

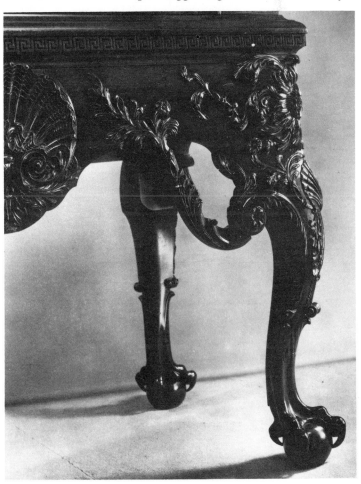

10 *Below*: A Rococo girandole, or looking glass with candlesticks. Note the foliage, scrolls and asymmetric cresting.

11 *Opposite*: Inlaid mahogany cabinet. While the general outline, especially the shape of the upper section, derives from the Rococo, the decorative detail and in particular the anthemion motifs on the glazing inter-sections and the swags on the cornice show a very clear Neo-classical inspiration. Such pieces are often described as transitional, *c.* 1770.

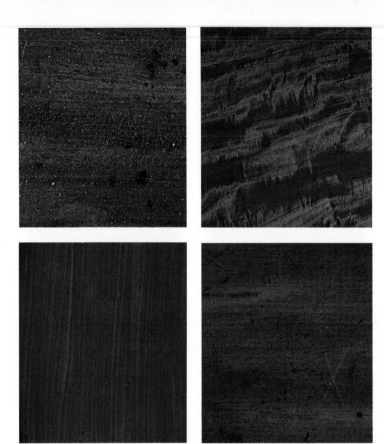

12 Mahogany displays many variations in appearance, these are the four primary categories. *Top left* the very dense and dark Jamaican wood from a piece of furniture *c.* 1730. *Top right* the brilliantly figured Cuban wood from a chest of drawers *c.* 1770. *Bottom left* a San Domingo mahogany of stripy figure and straight grain from a commode *c.* 1790. *Bottom right* the pale, soft, open-grained Honduras mahogany, the staining and scratches are indicative of its porosity and softness, from a table *c.* 1810.

13 On the left is the straight grained ash, rather more orange than typical. The oak in the middle is an old surface, and with difficulty some medullary rays may be seen evenly distributed over it. The right hand section is elm with the characteristically wavy grain and more broadly spaced annual rings. No photograph can hope to show the variety of any one timber and these are merely fairly typical examples.

14 On the left is a West Indian satinwood – note the similarity between this and Cuban mahogany, although visually the satinwood is much lighter and yellower, and tangibly it is a great deal harder and heavier. On the right is East Indian satinwood which always displays a stripy figure. This example, untypically, dated from about 1800 whereas more commonly this wood appears from *c.* 1880 onwards.

15 *Left*: Brazilian rosewood of characteristic honey colour with black streaks. Note that the grain runs straight through the vivid black marks. From a Regency chiffonière *c.* 1810. *Right*: East Indian rosewood is characterised by darker hues than the Brazilian variety and a relative freedom from contrasting black streaks. Newly cut, is almost black; on prolonged exposure to sunlight it fades to honey. This example is half way, and is taken from a piano, *c.* 1910.

16 An intelligent disposition of four pieces of flame, or crotch, figured Cuban mahogany veneer, taken from four consecutive layers of the same tree. From a Pembroke table top *c.* 1770.

17 Although this writing cabinet does not appear in Sheraton's designs, the bowed ends, turned reeded pilaster columns and spinning-top feet typify his designs, as do the oval panels, quartered veneers, ivory escutcheons and knob handles.

never really caught on in England, with a mere handful of admittedly notable exceptions – primarily looking-glasses and console tables *en suite*. Its progeny, the Rococo, however, was an immediate success with asymmetry flourishing amongst foliage, scrolls, icicles and rock-work (from which the name *rococo* is derived). England's most famous exponent of Rococo, Thomas Chippendale, remains a household name. He was a native of Otley in Yorkshire, who served an apprenticeship as a cabinet-maker and moved to London where he set up workshops in St Martin's Lane. In 1754, when he was thirty-six, he produced a book of furniture designs called *The Gentleman and Cabinet Maker's Director* upon which much of his fame still rests. The book served two purposes: first, it informed likely patrons of the styles available for them to choose from; and second, more importantly, it contained working drawings of furniture for cabinet-makers to reproduce his designs – complete with measurements and precise details of mouldings and construction. Chippendale produced furniture to his own designs in the St Martin's Lane work-shops where he employed cabinet-makers, upholsterers and

18 Chippendale mahogany wardrobe with carved decoration. The shape of the lower section is said to be 'bombé'.

29

19 Plate CXXXI from Chippendale's *Director* (third edition). The design is described as a 'Commode Cloths Press'. Much of the inspiration and detail of the wardrobe in Plate 11 is taken from this design.

numerous other tradesmen. He also executed designs to the particular requests of patrons, and many houses such as Harewood, Nostell Priory and Corsham Court retain Chippendale's original bills, which can be correlated with furniture still in the rooms for which it was made. He also supplied carpets, curtains and door furniture (fittings), and today would be called an interior decorator.

During the closing years of the seventeenth century much lacquered furniture had been imported into the country through the East India Company, and interest in the Orient was maintained throughout the eighteenth century. Although Chinese and Japanese lacquering materials were not available in England as they would not travel, work of a lesser quality, commonly called Japanning and popularised by Stalker and Parker, was carried out and a great deal of furniture was made in the Chinese style. Chippendale produced many designs based on Chinese works, which include railings, chairs, cabinets, desks and looking-glasses. Even the thirteen-panel glazed door displays a clear Chinese influence.

By popular demand, and no doubt for sound commercial reasons, Chippendale produced further editions of his book in 1755 and 1762. But Rococo was short-lived in fashionable society and by the time of the last edition, it was already giving way to the Neo-classical. The prime movers of the new style were the brothers Robert and James Adam, who were inspired by their Grand Tour to Italy in the 1750s. Suddenly the outline of furniture became a great deal more simple. The Neo-classic revived the styles of ancient Greece and Rome, where neatness and the symmetrical disposition of set motifs were *de rigueur*. Chief amongst the forms of ornamentation were fluting and oval medallions, anthemion (stylised honeysuckle), sphinx's heads, festoons of garya husks, vases, urns, Greek key patterns, silhouette portraits and the guilloche. The decoration was both carved and inlaid as Neo-classical features still lent themselves to the carver's art, especially the fluting and paterae (Plate 20 and glossary).

Being an astute businessman, Thomas Chippendale realised that his earlier advice was now completely out of date, and soon he was co-operating with the Adam brothers in furnishing great houses such as Osterley. George Hepplewhite was another cabinet-maker who followed Adam's lead. His designs appear in *The Cabinet Maker's and Upholsterer's Guide* which was published in 1788, two years after his death, with second and third editions in 1789 and 1794. Among Hepplewhite's many delightful and utilitarian designs one particularly notices the shield-back dining chair (Plate 100), the splayed bracket foot and the revived slender version of the cabriole leg (Plate 41).

Another gentleman who has given his name to an enormous quantity of furniture is Thomas Sheraton. Little is known of his life, except that he was a Baptist minister. He produced the first part of *The Cabinet Maker's and Upholsterer's Drawing Book* in 1791 with designs which were, to a large extent, variations on Hepplewhite's themes, but more advanced. His book contains extremely detailed instructions on perspective drawing and the construction of furniture. Among the many other people producing design books at this time, Thomas Shearer's influence could be said to equal Sheraton's; his *The Cabinet Maker's London Book of Prices* appeared in 1788. Almost all these design books are available in facsimile editions today.

The monumental furniture of the 1730s and 1740s had given way to the decorated style of the Rococo, containing a great deal less wood and thus becoming much lighter. With Neo-classical furniture, the outline had again become simple, and

20 Wine cooler from Osterley Park House, Middlesex. Of carved wood with gilt and metal details, it typifies the Neo-classical movement as designed by Robert Adam. Note the fluting, paterae, medallions, draped rams' heads, the symmetry and, of course, the urn.

Splayed bracket foot

31

the proportions were further refined, until a period in the 1790s when tables for example stood on the most slender legs. George Hepplewhite's book even advocated the making of chairs without stretchers to unite and strengthen the legs. Moreover, the quality of cabinet-making in fine, London-made pieces was of such a high order that many survive today in almost perfect condition.

Two influential figures of the early nineteenth century were Thomas Hope and George Smith, who revived the Neo-classical and particularly Egyptian styles. The Regency style 1800-20 (which does not quite coincide with the Regency period 1811-20) was an elaboration of outline, though quite different from Rococo or the earlier Elizabethan and Restoration carved form. Egyptian sphinxes, griffins and hairy paws abounded and with the use of rosewood, satinwood, and gilding a conscious break was made from brown mahogany (Plate 93). The death of Nelson in 1805 plunged the whole country into mourning and resulted in numerous pieces of furniture being outlined with ebony stringing, as a black line of mourning. From this period the inclusion of as much wood and carving as possible became a major feature of fine quality furniture.

21 *Above*: A Victorian credenza (side cabinet) of elaborate and degenerate design. The complicated decoration derives from the work of André Charles Boulle, a maître ébéniste of the late seventeenth-century. This work, however, lacks the quality of earlier examples and much of the detail is mechanical in its concept and execution.

Chapter 2
Timber and other materials

Much furniture today is constructed of leather, stainless steel, plastic and even paper. Tables are made from glass and aluminium, while beds may be filled with water and chairs with haricot beans. In the eighteenth century, however, although beds and chairs were stuffed with horsehair, down, straw and flock, and upholstered in cotton, linen, wool or silk, the rigid parts were usually made of wood. Furthermore, many pieces of furniture like tables or wardrobes were made entirely of timber. It is consequently of great importance to recognise the type of wood employed in any particular piece. Knowledge of the various timbers used in cabinet-making may help particularly in dating an article. For example, if someone claims to have a Queen Anne mahogany chair, they are either mistaken or deliberately trying to deceive. Apart from references to the use of mahogany as ballast in ships returning from the West Indies during Charles II's reign (1660-85), it was not used in England until ten years after Queen Anne died in 1714. The earliest known mahogany furniture dates *c*. 1725.

In the next few pages, the woods most widely used will be described, approximately in chronological order of the furniture in which they are likely to be found. For the less well-known woods, the reader is directed to a fuller list in the glossary. First, however, a simplified description of the structure of the tree will prove helpful. I shall concentrate on those aspects by which each variety of timber can be distinguished visually from the others. Before going further, one primary distinction must be made. Pine (or 'deal') is the timber from coniferous (or fir) trees and is known as softwood, as opposed to wood from broad-leafed (or deciduous) trees, which is known as hardwood. Softwood is quite different from hardwood and does not show all the characteristics mentioned in this chapter. It is rarely used in good quality furniture, except for back boards and other secondary purposes.

Outside the tropics, where the growing season extends through most of the year, trees grow at an uneven rate. The period of greatest activity is in spring and to a lesser extent the summer; in the autumn and winter trees hardly grow at all. Each year, as they get taller, they put on girth around already established wood. But because climatic conditions change from year to year, the amount of annual growth will vary. Hence when felled and observed in cross-section, trees exhibit rings of uneven width, called annual rings. These are easily seen because the spring growth tends to be coarser in texture than the fine summer wood, and occasionally a dark line separates each year's growth. When a tree is damaged, by fire for example, it heals the wound by producing a lot of extra wood. This occurs at greater than average speed, and so the annual rings are much broader apart, forming an interesting pattern in the timber.

The bark, which forms the outer 'skin' of the tree, is not used in cabinet-making and need be considered no further. Directly underneath is the sapwood, which is paler in colour than the main heartwood and is also softer. Sapwood is seldom used in furniture because it is less strong and is a favourite meal of the woodworm. With certain woods, however, the distinction between sapwood and heartwood is very difficult, if not impossible, to detect with the naked eye.

Running up the tree and out along its branches are fibrous structures like miniature parcels of tubes, each about as thick as a hair. In cross-section, they appear as a cluster of tiny circles; if the cut is made at an angle, they become oval-shaped; and if along the tubes they appear as open grooves. In theory one could cut a piece of wood with grooves running continuously along it, but since trees do not grow absolutely straight, the grooves usually peter out after less than an inch (25 mm).

These tubes are correctly called tracheids and their disposition on the surface of a piece of wood is referred to as the

Section through timber

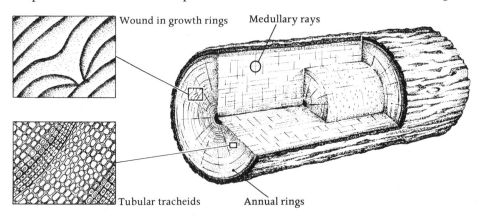

Wound in growth rings   Medullary rays

Tubular tracheids   Annual rings

The grain on this violin back can just be discerned running along the length of the instrument. The markings which run across the width and join in the middle (the back is made in two pieces) are called figure.

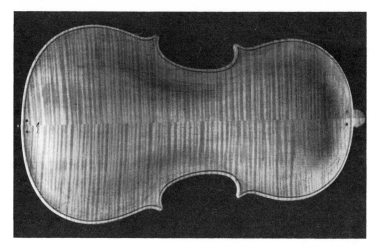

grain. I mentioned that they come in parcels; they grow larger in the spring, and decrease in size as summer progresses. The grain of wood grown in a temperate climate will therefore follow the annual growth rings of the tree, while timber from tropical zones will show a less regular pattern of grain, since the growing season is almost continuous.

A great many types of wood have distinctive patterns or 'figures' which are quite separate from their tracheid arrangement. For example, the grain on the back of a violin runs down its length, in the same direction as the strings. The marking in the wood, however, usually appears to go across the instrument, in a stripy, light-and-dark way that appears to change when the observer and the source of light alter their relative positions. Maple – the wood most commonly used for violin backs – is well known for this particular effect. The same figure appears both in sycamore and mahogany (a totally unrelated tree) and is known – not surprisingly – as fiddleback figure. Other figures occur frequently and have names, such as feather, flame, curl, roe, plum-pudding and bird's eye, which are all self-descriptive.

While tracheids feed a tree along its length, another system – medullary rays – feeds the girth. Seen in the cross-section of a tree, these are dense fibres radiating from the centre. They are sometimes considerably different in shade from the rest of the wood, and can provide a pattern running at an angle to the grain. In most furniture, however, the medullary rays are difficult to discern.

In the eighteenth century and earlier, a tree to be used for cabinet furniture was first felled and the limbs (or larger branches) removed. A hole was drilled in the butt, or trunk, and a chain inserted in it. This was secured and the trunk

35

allowed to soak in a river for a year. On being taken out it was dried slowly – for two years or so. It was then planked and, depending on the thickness of the plank, it was seasoned at the rate of a year per inch of plank thickness. In this way a man laid the foundation for his son's success. Today the soaking is dispensed with and the drying period is reduced to three to five years, but the seasoning remains the same. All this was important to ensure that the wood warped and split as little as possible.

There are two ways of cutting a 'butt' or tree trunk. The usual method is to cut planks parallel to the diameter. This is quick, and produces the maximum width of planks and therefore return for money. Wood cut in this way is said to be 'run of the mill'– hence our cliché meaning ordinary. Timbers such as oak, where the medullary rays can be seen to advantage, are better 'quarter cut'. This method is expensive but gives the maximum practicable number of cuts that are nearly along a radius. In the Middle Ages the riving iron was used to split wood radially, giving planks of narrow triangular cross-section, and just occasionally one sees a piece of furniture made with wood cut in this way (Plate 56).

From Tudor times specialist sawyers travelled the countryside in pairs, moving from one estate to the next. By manoeuvring the butts across a saw-pit they could cut along the length of even the heaviest trees with a long, two-handled saw – the senior man working above the ground, the junior below. It was hard, monotonous work, demanding considerable concentration, and must have been particularly uncomfortable for the man in the pit. Since the beginning of the century pit-saws have been made redundant by the introduction of large band-saws.

More than once a faked piece of furniture has been discovered for what it is by the tell-tale signs of the machine age. Marks left on timber by imperfections in a band-saw blade, which is always power-driven and fed mechanically, Cutting timber

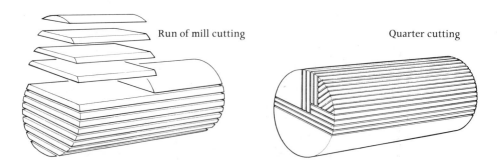

Run of mill cutting   Quarter cutting

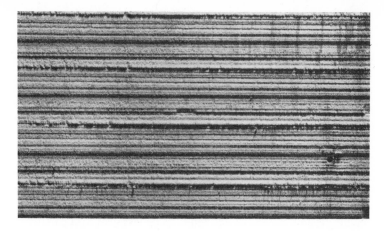

23 Detail of a piece of timber cut with a band-saw. The strong light accentuates the markings, but they will remain visible wherever a band saw has been used.

will be parallel. Marks left by a pit-saw, by contrast, are somewhat irregular. Perhaps the best place to look for pit-saw marks is on the under-side of seventeenth- and early eighteenth-century oak furniture – under gate-leg table tops of that period and under the tops of dressers and cupboards where there has been no need to finish the wood further.

During the Middle Ages and up to the middle of the seventeenth century, furniture was generally made from wood grown close to the place of manufacture. Most English trees which grow large enough to provide planks can be used for furniture making. They include ash, elm, oak, sycamore, chestnut, beech, birch, maple and walnut. With the exception of oak, all are subject, to a greater or lesser degree, to decay either through rot, or through woodworm or other beetles of that family. Furniture-makers and joiners have long been aware of the lasting properties of oak and used this wood for their better quality wares. Consequently, most of the very early furniture which has survived is made of oak.

24 The underside of a gate leg table top showing the irregularity of the marks left by a pit-saw. The consistency of the majority of the saw marks indicates the expertise of the sawyers. The hinge is held in position with hand-made nails, and is itself hand wrought.

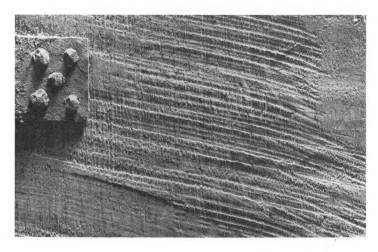

Oak is a heavy wood, ranging in colour from pale straw to that of a brazil-nut shell. The annual rings vary considerably in width and it has very marked medullary rays when quarter-cut – sometimes called 'silver fleck'. On an old surface these usually appear dark, but on freshly cut or re-polished wood they appear many shades lighter than the rest. The medullary rays are also harder and for this reason will occasionally stand proud from surrounding wood. The grain in oak is deep and difficult to fill but otherwise it accepts a polish easily (Plate 17).

Very early furniture is sometimes a mellow, deep straw colour, but late sixteenth- and seventeenth-century pieces tend to be a dark grey-brown, largely due to surface dirt accumulation. Georgian oak tends to be less grey and can even veer towards a reddish-brown, though never as much as mahogany. When used in drawer linings, the lack of light and air keeps oak an ochre hue.

Oak normally exhibits little or no figure. However, when a tree is consistently lopped, growth may accumulate at that point, producing a burr figure known as pollard oak. Another much sought-after variety is so-called brown oak. It has a deeper, red-brown colour, caused by pigment from a large fungus that permeates the whole tree. All oak is hard, and will resist any attempt to depress it with a thumb-nail.

Ash bears a strong resemblance to oak and it can be very difficult to fill but otherwise it accepts a polish easily (Plate 13). ash tends to be coarser and the wood is marginally softer; it is usually possible to depress the wood with a thumb-nail. Ash is also whiter and the grain is usually straighter. Unlike oak, ash is susceptible to attack from woodworm and the presence of the beetle can often be a sure indication. Very little ash furniture survives from the seventeenth century and later it was employed only in more rustic pieces.

Elm completes the trio of frequently used hardwoods that are problematic to identify. Like ash, elm is susceptible to woodworm and has a very similar density. However, it has a more ginger colour and the grain is broader and usually more wavy (Plate 13). The planks into which it is cut are generally larger than with oak or ash, and farmhouse table tops made of a single plank can be up to 3 feet 6 inches (over a metre) wide.

Walnut has a fine grain: the tracheids are small but often extend for an inch or more along the surface. The medullary rays are very rarely discernible. Perhaps the most distinctive feature of walnut, however, is its basic honey colour (Plate 73), ranging from pale through golden to a deep rich hue, with never a trace of red or grey. Nonetheless, walnut can, and often does, have grey to black streaks and can show some interesting figures. The best known is the burr (Plate 76), taken from growths which are usually formed on the trunk of a mature tree. Walnut can also show mottled figures. It is of medium weight and density, but the evenness of grain makes it an easy wood to work on, whether it is for carving or for cutting into veneers.

Walnut was regarded as a first-grade timber for furniture in the seventeenth century and earlier, but relatively little survives from this period, as the wood is highly vulnerable to woodworm. It was frequently used as a veneer during the first quarter of the eighteenth century, but owing to a severe winter which devastated the walnut tree throughout Europe in 1709 it was little used once the seasoned stocks had been exhausted during the 1720s. Cabinet-makers kept back some of their finest walnut, however, and the few pieces of walnut furniture crafted in the 1730s and 1740s are usually of the finest quality. The timber was eventually re-introduced during the mid-nineteenth century.

Red walnut is similar to the common variety except that it never has burr figures and, true to its name, is red-brown in colour. It is also known as Virginia walnut because it comes from that part of the United States. Red walnut is easily mistaken for mahogany, but since it is grown in a temperate climate, the annual growth rings are quite apparent and the grain provides the pattern. All mahogany is tropical, and the grain passes through any surface pattern. Like mahogany, red walnut is resistant to woodworm and occasionally one will notice sapwood which is golden yellow, usually on insignificant or unseen surfaces, such as the top inside of the back leg of a chair, or the underside of stretchers.

Mahogany is a red-brown timber. It was commonly used in Britain from 1724 and was the wood most used in quality cabinet-making for the next 200 years. If a piece of furniture has a reddish hue, there is a strong chance that it will be mahogany. A strong, fine-grained timber, it shows considerable variation in density and its colour ranges from pale honey to dark plum. Mahogany can be divided for convenience into four main categories (Plate 12).

Jamaican wood, of which the earliest mahogany furniture was made, is very dark and heavy. When freshly cut the wood has an almost purple hue, with characteristic white flecks in the grain. When observed on an unrestored piece, it usually accumulates a greenish, grey-black surface almost resembling bronze where it is not polished regularly. It has little figure and on account of its density and the closeness of its grain is well suited to mouldings and carvings, which remain very crisp. It is said that this early mahogany, seldom seen after about 1745, grew only by the coast and that the supply was used up quickly as it was easier to take wood from the coastal areas than to cut inland through dense tropical forests.

When stocks of the very dense Jamaican wood were exhausted, importers turned to the less desirable *Cuban* wood. This varies little in colour except when subjected to prolonged sunlight and is within a few shades of a reddish tan. Cuban mahogany weighs about half to two-thirds as much as Jamaican wood, but compensates for its lack of density by a considerable range of figure. The most common Cuban figure is the flame or crotch, while more unusual and therefore more sought-after figures are plum pudding, roe, fiddle-back and splash.

San Domingo mahogany is also called Spanish mahogany, as it originally came from the Spanish colonies of the West Indies. It was considered of better quality than Cuban wood and is denser and of a slightly darker hue. It exhibits fewer figures, but is often somewhat 'stripy' or 'cloudy'. The grain tends to be straighter than in Cuban wood and is consequently stronger, making this type of mahogany more suitable for use in fine quality legs and other structural parts. Many experts find the difference between Cuban and San Domingo mahoganies very difficult to perceive.

Honduras mahogany, cut from trees on the South American mainland away from the coast, was also known as baywood. It is quite inferior to other mahoganies, being considerably lighter in colour and density. It has few figures, but during the last quarter of the eighteenth century was considered adequate for drawer linings and other non-visible and utilitarian parts of furniture. Cheaper furniture was made entirely of baywood, which was much used after about 1870 when many of the finer woods were exhausted.

Boxwood and ebony can be considered together, because they are used for similar purposes. Boxwood is a very heavy, dense timber with little figure, and is pale yellow or straw in colour. Ebony is also very heavy and hard, but is almost completely black (though in large pieces yellowish figures appear). Both woods are generally cut into long, thin strips of square cross-section; this is called stringing and provides a perfect edging for furniture. It gives both a contrasting colour, to emphasise the outline, and an edge that will withstand wear. For decorative purposes, ebony and boxwood are used together, often in threes, one sandwiching the other. Sometimes boxwood was replaced by holly, which is not so hard, but almost the same colour, or sycamore which is softer still. Similar economies were practised with ebony, but as no cheaper natural black wood is available, stains and even scorching were employed.

There are two types of satinwood, from the West and East Indies respectively. West Indian satinwood bears strong resemblance to mahogany in its figures, but is much heavier and, except when left unpolished for a long time, is distinctly golden yellow. When freshly cut it emits a sickly, sweet smell and is a pale but bright yellow. West Indian satinwood was generally used as a veneer on quality furniture between 1770 and 1810. East Indian satinwood is also a golden yellow colour and is, if anything, even harder and heavier. Its distinguishing feature is a pronounced 'stripy' figure, which 'moves' easily in different lights. It was introduced to Britain late in the eighteenth century, but is seldom found in furniture of that time. However, it was frequently used in 'Sheraton-style' furniture made between 1890 and 1920 and often provides the first clue in recognising these reproductions.

As with satinwood, there are two varieties of rosewood. The most desirable type comes from Brazil and is also known as Rio rosewood. Its colour ranges from coffee to honey, but the most distinctive features of the timber are black streaks, forming patterns which cut across the grain and finish abruptly. Rio rosewood was introduced almost simultaneously with satinwood, during the last quarter of the eighteenth century, and is characteristically found in free-standing quality furniture such as sofa tables, teapoys, small tea caddies and work boxes.

East Indian rosewood, from Ceylon and the eastern seaboard of India, was introduced much earlier, being imported by the East India Company and used in cabinets during Charles II's reign (1660-85). Wood of this period, through oxidisation over a very long time, has acquired a similar colour to the Brazilian variety but lacks the black streaks and figure. East Indian rosewood was re-introduced around 1800 and was used extensively during the first sixty or seventy years of the nineteenth century, both as a veneer and in the solid. When an article of East Indian rosewood furniture has been left in strong sunlight for a prolonged period of time it may acquire a pale golden colour, but it started life almost entirely black and an unoxidised wood or re-polished surface will be very dark indeed. Like its Brazilian counterpart it is very heavy and dense, with a broad grain which is difficult to fill and polish.

Chapter 3

The parts of furniture

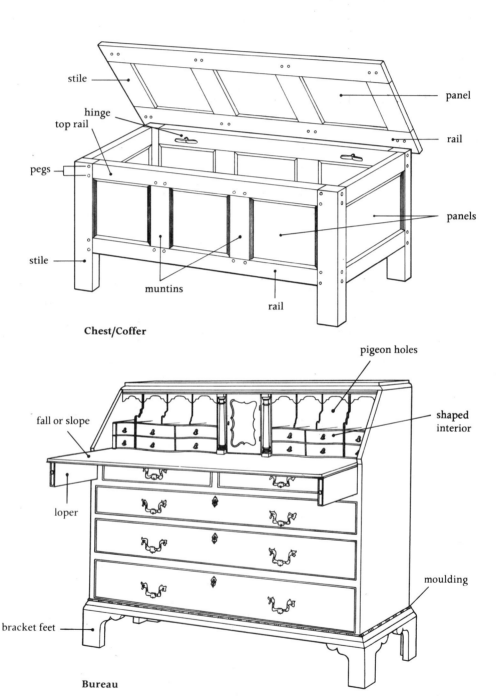

stile

hinge

top rail

pegs

stile

muntins

rail

panel

rail

panels

Chest/Coffer

pigeon holes

fall or slope

loper

shaped
interior

moulding

bracket feet

Bureau

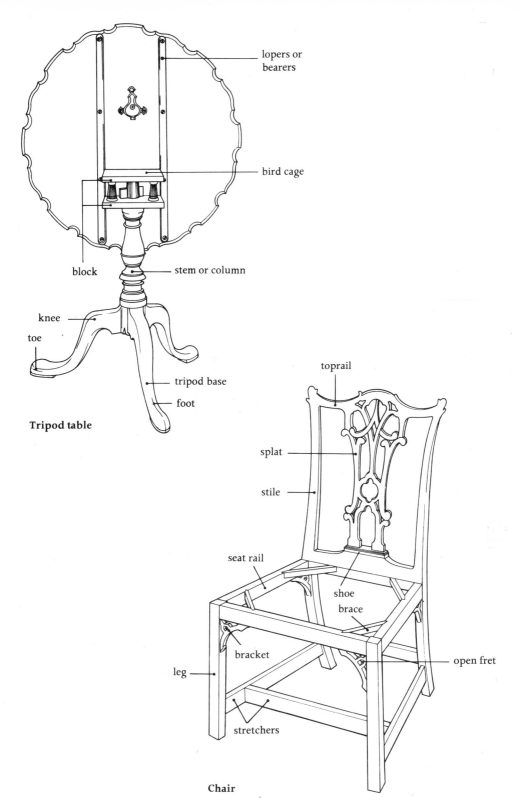

lopers or
bearers

bird cage

block

stem or column

knee

toe

tripod base

foot

Tripod table

toprail

splat

stile

seat rail

shoe

brace

bracket

leg

open fret

stretchers

Chair

Chapter 4

Construction

Over the centuries, the vagaries of fashion and the use of different types of wood brought numerous subtle changes in the methods of furniture construction. The way in which a piece is actually put together will therefore provide valuable clues to the date of its assembly. For example, in the seventeenth century all 'carcase' or 'case' furniture (made to contain cupboards or drawers, as opposed to tables and seat furniture) was made with a panelled construction. This was to cope with the problem of shrinkage, for as timber dries, it shrinks across the width of the grain.

If the average shrinkage is one per cent, then the shrinkage in a board 10 inches (254 mm) wide will be only $\frac{1}{10}$ inch (2.5 mm). This is a negligible amount; but in a piece of wood, or pieces of wood glued together, 10 feet (2.5 m) wide, the shrinkage will be more than an inch (25 mm) – quite impossible to hide in any piece of furniture. By constructing large surfaces from a number of small panels 'floating' in rebates (grooves), the problem can be overcome. In a coffer, for example, the rails, stiles and muntins will all be rebated to hold the panels. When the panels shrink, no gaps appear because the entire width still falls within the rebate.

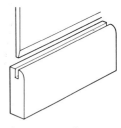

Rebate in a panel

In the seventeenth century glue was not made sufficiently strong to be used in structural joints. Consequently, a system was devised for keeping furniture together without the use of glue, nails (which tend to make wood split and which rust), or screws (which are complicated to make, which also rust, and which were considered suitable only for special purposes). The 'mortise and tenon' joint became the principal method of constructing furniture. The mortise is a rectangular hole cut into one piece of wood (it may not go right through) and the tenon is a tongue cut in the adjoining piece of wood to slot directly into the mortise. In certain parts of England the tenon is called the 'tenant', which is a good way of remembering that the tenon (tenant) lives in the mortise.

Well made, such a joint will hold by itself, but it can easily

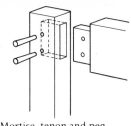

Mortise, tenon and peg

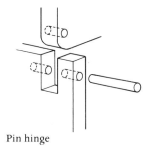

Pin hinge

Wire hinge

Six-board coffer with strap hinge

be knocked apart. In the sixteenth century, to avoid this happening, a hole was drilled right through the mortise and tenon and a piece of green (unseasoned) timber driven in. This green wood was called a peg and was usually about $\frac{1}{4}$ inch (6 mm) in diameter. The timber of houses of that date was held together in the same fashion, the pegs in this case being anything up to an inch (25 mm) across. During the seventeenth century it became the norm to double up on this procedure and two pegs will be found in each member in most furniture, unless the piece of wood holding the tenon is very small.

In panelled furniture of the period, pegs will be found at the junction of each stile and rail. It should be noted that a stile always continues to the top of the joint, and that the rail always tenons into it. A piece of furniture where the rail runs the entire width and the stile tenons into the rail should be regarded with considerable suspicion, but such construction is not entirely unknown. The muntins will, of course, tenon into the rails and will usually be held by pegs, although during the eighteenth century this practice was sometimes dropped. In a coffer the same construction will apply to the top and side panels, and probably the back also. The lid will closely resemble the construction of the front, but will not be carved.

In very early coffers the lid was pin-hinged, but during the late sixteenth century it became fashionable to use wire hinges, which were simply two interlocking loops of wire. Contemporary with both was a third form of hinge, used when more security was desired: the long strap-hinge. This is more like the modern form of hinge, with the stationary section short and broad, and the other part a long, tapered piece of iron, very often with a decorative end. Eventually it was realised that the strap-hinge was the most satisfactory, as its dimensions could be adjusted to suit the needs of both security and decoration. Old strap-hinges were hand wrought, and this will be evident on close inspection.

One variety of coffer required the least knowledge of construction techniques of any piece of furniture: the very simple, long rectangular box known as a six-board coffer. The front and back were fixed to the ends with nails, and the ends projected downwards to form the feet. Wire hinging was common, although strap-hinges are quite often encountered. Until recently coffers were of relatively little value unless they dated from the sixteenth century or earlier. Later items are very numerous, and are a good subject for study as they were not considered worth altering or 'improving'. Although there are now a great many reproductions and fakes in existence, a large proportion are genuine pieces of seventeenth-century oak furniture and a detailed study of the colour, surface, construction and type of timber is to be recommended.

The chest of drawers was constructed in much the same way as a panelled coffer. The stiles were mortised and the rails, which divided the drawers, were tenoned into them. The sides were also panelled and the top was pegged to the rails. Mouldings might be applied at various points on the carcase to give a decorative finish. Tables and chairs were held together in a similar way with pegged mortises and tenons, and the same was true of beds, cradles, stools and cupboards (Plates 4, 52–61), which constitute almost the entire repertoire of the joiner's art – such furniture was often described as 'joyned' or 'joynt'. By 1715 in London, however, or 1740-50 in remote country areas, better glues had been developed and the peg was usually omitted from mortise and tenon joints. It was retained only where considerable stress could be anticipated – for example, at the top of chair legs.

During the last fifteen years of the seventeenth century two other important techniques had been developed. The first was the use of veneers. This merely involves gluing a thin piece of wood (the veneer) on to a thicker piece (the ground). A large area could thus be covered cheaply with fine quality wood, and if two or more pieces of consecutive veneer were taken from the same cut, they could be arranged to form a decorative pattern with their figure. Veneers varied from $\frac{1}{8}$ inch (3 mm) down to as little as $\frac{1}{16}$ inch (1.6 mm) thick, becoming finer as techniques improved. By the early eighteenth century the use of veneers was already widespread. The general rule is that the thicker the veneer the earlier it is. In the eighteenth century veneers were hand sawn and, as techniques improved, the thickness diminished from $\frac{1}{8}$ inch to $\frac{1}{16}$ inch (3 mm to 1.6 mm). By the nineteenth century the machine age enabled the production of mechanically sawn veneers less than $\frac{1}{16}$ inch (1.6 mm), and by the twentieth century veneers were mechanically knife cut to paper thinness.

The second technique was a new way of joining two pieces of wood at right angles, and was known as the dovetail. This joint uses a minimum of glue and was very satisfactory for joining the sides to the top and bottom of a piece of furniture. It was now possible to abandon the long established mortise and tenon, for which the wood always had to be more than an inch (25 mm) thick and often as much as two inches (50 mm). With this new technique the proportions of carcase furniture were radically altered, for it was now possible to have the sides of a

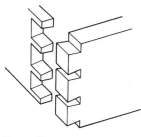

Dovetail

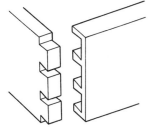

Lapped dovetail

chest of drawers no more than $\frac{3}{4}$ inch (19 mm) thick and strips of wood dividing the drawers could be rebated into them. The drawers could extend to within a fraction of an inch of the side of the object concerned.

The greatest application of the dovetail, however, was in the construction of the drawers themselves, and developments here make the observation of drawers of particular value in dating carcase furniture. Indeed, it is quite possible to date a piece by the construction and material of the drawer alone to within twenty years and sometimes even closer.

Until about 1680 the drawer front was rebated at each end and the sides (linings) were fixed into the rebates with nails. The bottom of the drawer was nailed and rebated into the front and also nailed to the bottom of the linings. The sides had to be at least $\frac{1}{2}$ inch (12.7 mm) and sometimes as much as $\frac{7}{8}$ inch (22 mm) thick, for a groove almost $\frac{1}{2}$ inch (12.7 mm) square was cut right along the drawer, half way up each side. These grooves slid along square wooden runners fixed inside the carcase between the front and back stiles, thus supporting the weight of the drawer. (Curiously enough, this method has enjoyed a revival since the Second World War.) It was customary for the bottom of the drawer to have the grain running from back to front unless the drawer was very wide, in which case it ran from side to side. Drawers in good quality pieces have linings made of oak; pine is more common for rustic pieces, in which case considerable wear will almost certainly be in evidence and one should look for a replacement runner on the upper surface, which takes the weight of the drawer. Oak-lined drawers are known to run quite smoothly even after three or four centuries and, unless the drawer is very deep or has contained heavy things, one would not expect very much wear.

By the 1680s, the dovetail was in common use for better quality drawers. At first the dovetails ran straight through to the front of the drawer and, in order to hide them, a moulding was placed around the front edge. This probably gave rise to the geometrically-panelled chest of drawers with which oak collectors are so familiar – a simple expedient so the cabinet-maker could hide his dovetail joint. At the same time the side drawer-runner became obsolete, for a flat piece of wood fixed to the carcase, reaching from the front to the back, beneath each drawer, proved sufficient to take the weight. The drawer bottoms now had to be fixed to the lining by rebates and glue, for nail heads running on the drawer divide would soon cause damage. With this new construction it was possible to make the drawer linings narrower, first to a bare $\frac{1}{2}$ inch

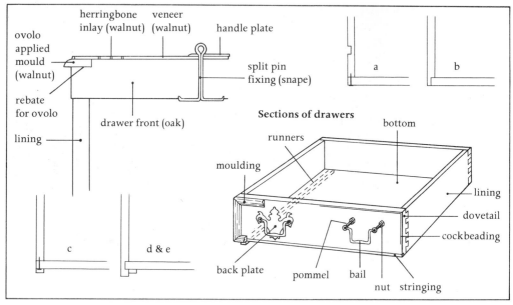

herringbone inlay (walnut)   veneer (walnut)   handle plate

ovolo applied mould (walnut)

split pin fixing (snape)

rebate for ovolo

drawer front (oak)

lining

a   b

Sections of drawers

c   d & e

runners

moulding

bottom

lining

dovetail

cockbeading

back plate   pommel   bail

nut   stringing

25 (a) Drawer, c. 1620. Because the drawer is very wide the grain runs from side to side. Note the front rebate and the sides nailed into the rebate, and the side runner. (b) Veneered drawer front c. 1690. Points to note are the dovetails running right through the drawer front and only covered by the thickness of the veneer. The grain of the drawer bottom runs from back to front. The linings are of quarter-cut oak (with the medullary rays visible) and their tops are flush with the top of the front. The handle is not original. Notice the broad, but well made, dovetails. (Ann Eame was the original owner of this piece, and her name appears in several places.) (c) Drawer from a country-made piece of furniture. The drawer bottoms 'incorrectly' go from side to side. The broad dovetails are crudely put together, do not extend to the front of the drawer and are not hidden by the moulding. The linings

have round tops, and the drawer front stands proud of them. c. 1720. (d) Well-made country drawer, c. 1725. Note the pine drawer linings, broad dovetails and, in contrast, the quality of the original brass handle and mitred cross banding on the drawer front. Note also the ovolo mould to the edge of the drawer and the step down from the drawer front to the linings. (e) Fine quality small drawer, c. 1720. The similarity between this and the previous one is obvious, but note the finer dovetails and the use of oak as a drawer lining. The ovolo mould overhangs the linings and the top edge to form a dust excluder. The quality is also shown in the engraved plate handle, figured drawer front and use of feather banding in addition to cross banding. Note also the fixing of the lock. (f) Drawer c. 1770. The grain on the bottom runs from side to side. Note the finer dovetails, and particularly the use of

c

d

e

f

the cockbead to edge the drawer front. The linings are thin and of quartered oak, notice the scribing line at the end of the dovetails. (g) London-made drawer, *c.* 1800. Note the exceedingly fine dovetails and the drawer front outlined with stringing. The stringing on the top of the drawer front extends to the back of the drawer front, a feature indicating great quality. The grain of the drawer bottom runs from side to side. The wooden handle knob is original and the drawer sides are of Honduras mahogany.

g

(12.7 mm) and over the next 100 years to as narrow as $\frac{1}{8}$ inch (3 mm). This gradual narrowing was progressive, and is a distinct aid in the dating of drawers. During the last years of the seventeenth century it became possible to relinquish the moulding which covered the dovetail, and instead the whole drawer front was veneered.

By 1690-1700 the dovetails no longer extended right through to the veneer and their shape was also changing. Viewed from the side of the drawer, the dovetails had been broad at first, but they gradually became narrower. By the mid-eighteenth century dovetails were ending in a point, and the frequency with which the joints appear along a given length of a drawer side became an indicator of quality. The scribing line, made by the cabinet-maker when preparing to cut his first dovetail, frequently remains for us to see today. It was of course always scribed, never drawn with a pencil.

During the first half of the eighteenth century, when drawer linings were $\frac{1}{4}$–$\frac{3}{8}$ inch (6–9.5 mm) wide, it was customary for the drawer lining to be $\frac{1}{8}$ inch (3 mm) shallower than the drawer front, forming a distinct step down from the top of the drawer front to the top of the drawer lining, and to have the grain of the drawer bottom running from side to side. This was not a firm rule, however, and in several genuine pieces different drawer linings even run from back to front and from side to side within the same piece of furniture.

By about 1720-25, it became the practice to fit the drawer bottom into a rebate $\frac{1}{8}$ inch (3 mm) from the base of the linings and front. The projecting linings then had a strengthening fillet some $\frac{1}{2}$–$\frac{3}{4}$ inch (12-20 mm) wide along their perimeter and the drawer slid along these runners. Usually the fillet was 'mitred' – cut at an angle of 45° – at the back. Drawers of this construction run far more smoothly than the earlier types because the area in contact with the carcase is reduced. Lubricated well with candlewax they will last a great many years with almost no wear at all. However, owners have not always treated their furniture well and the amount of wear on drawer runners may testify to the age of the drawer, or at least indicate whether or not it is a reproduction.

The method of finishing the edge of a drawer front is a further guide to the age of a piece. Mention has been made of the geometrical mouldings applied to the front of furniture during the third quarter of the seventeenth century. When veneers were first used they were usually banded to make a decorative border and the veneer simply ran to the edge of the drawer. A moulding, half round as a rule, was applied to the carcase and thus drew attention to the shape of the drawers. Later this half round was doubled up, yet still the drawer front remained perfectly flat (Plates 59 and 69).

By about 1700-20 it was common to rebate the edge of the drawer front and to apply an ovolo moulding; the joint between the rebate and the moulding was covered with veneer. For a very short while the ovolo mould finished flush with the top and sides of the drawer, but soon it overlapped the carcase so that when the drawer was pressed home it formed an effective dust excluder. By about 1720 the most common of all drawer finishes had been evolved – the cockbead. The drawer front was simply rebated to the depth of $\frac{3}{8}$ inch (9.5 mm) all the way round its perimeter and the rebate, approximately $\frac{1}{8}$ inch (3 mm) wide, was filled with a piece of wood which protruded some $\frac{1}{16}$ inch (1.6 mm) from the drawer and was rounded on the front edge.

During the second half of the eighteenth century drawer linings in quality furniture became progressively finer. Occasionally the decoration on the front of the drawer, if veneered, would form the drawer edge, but the cock bead remained in vogue until after the turn of the century. From about 1770 some good quality furniture had drawer linings made of cedarwood, and from as early as 1740 mahogany was occasionally used for small drawers in the finest pieces and in box toilet mirrors. In the best walnut furniture drawer linings were themselves made of walnut. Channel Island furniture often has linings made of chestnut wood, while Irish pieces frequently have drawers lined in elm and birch. Many Irish chests of drawers have three drawers across the top instead of one or two as in English examples.

By about 1780 it became fashionable to inlay furniture with boxwood and ebony stringing, thus strengthening the edges with very tough and durable timber. In most cases the cock bead gave way to a boxwood stringing; but in the finest London-made examples, the boxwood sometimes covers the entire top of the drawer front. Such pieces may also have $\frac{1}{4}$ inch (6 mm) quarter-round beading along the inside bottom edge (also known as a quadrant dust bead), and if the drawer is wide enough there will be a central muntin as well. This form of construction had itself become common by about 1800.

The earliest form of handle for drawers and cupboards was the wooden knob, although many cupboards were opened and closed with a key only. By the seventeenth century the use of iron handles had become widespread. Their form varied very little for at least fifty years. By the end of the century, however, brass was beginning to be used. The first designs followed continental fashion, often an elongated pear-shaped (or bifurcated scroll) drop with a back plate behind. During the 1690s a six-pointed star was popular.

By 1700 it became fashionable to have a bail handle, simply a 'C' scroll-shaped piece of brass with a lug at either end so it could rotate upon its long axis. Both the bail handle and the earlier pear drop were fixed to the drawer front by a snape which was bent back on the inside of the drawer front and secured. With the bail handle came the introduction of the back plate, which protected the drawer front from being scratched by the hand as the bail was grasped. Early back plates were of shaped outline but not pierced; they were cast with bevelled edges and often decorated with punched circles.

By about 1715, back plates were mostly plain; they tended to be more curvilinear, but still with bevelled edges. The next development, in about 1720, was the piercing of the back plate and at this stage it became larger and more fanciful, though still

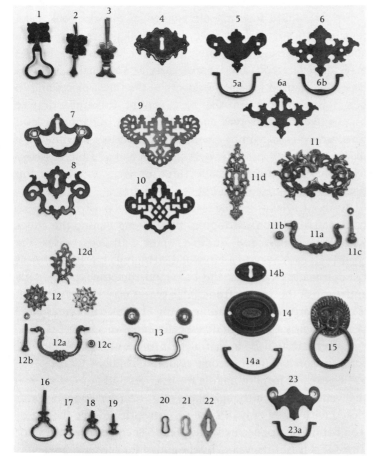

26 Drawer handles

1. Iron drop handle with heart pull and quatrefoil backplate. Iron snape fixing, c. 1650.

2. Brass 'Dutch drop', engraved quatrefoil backplate – note the snapes, c. 1680.

3. Bifurcated drop, gilded hexafoil backplate – thick snapes not original, c. 1690.

4. Escutcheon – gilt punched brass – note solid appearance and bevelled edge.

5 and 5a. Backplate and bail, dull brass bevelled edges – note fluency of curves, c. 1720.

6, 6a, 6b. Backplate, bail and matching escutcheon – very elaborate non-pierced type – note differences between backplate and escutcheon – fixing holes, etc, c. 1730.

7 and 8. Two escutcheon cum backplates (for short drawers with central handle and lock) – early pierced handles bevelled on all edges – usually gilded.

9 and 10. Two more for a similar use to 7 and 8, but note the greater elaboration with 'Chinese Fret' influence.

11, a, b, c, and d. Gilded cast Rococo handle with cast bail. Note the turned pommel and circular nut fixing. The taller escutcheon en suite comes from a bookcase cupboard door, it is not a drawer escutcheon which would match the handle backplate, c. 1755.

12, a, b, c and d. A simple cast and gilt Rococo handle, but the backplate now has two separate rosettes. Escutcheon suitable for cupboards and drawers, c. 1765.

13. The simplicity of the classic swan-neck, c. 1790–1800. (See also Plates 69, 90.)

14. Brass oval plate handle with matching escutcheon.

Note the new shape of the bail with inward facing lugs. Gilded, c. 1800.

15. Sphinx head mask and ring handle. Gilded pressed brass. Alternative versions are lion masks and satyr masks. The pommels are integral with the backplate, c. 1800.

16. Intertwined 'C' scroll handle, probably from a night commode cupboard, c. 1770.

17. Diminutive gilt brass with wood screw, similar to 16. From the small interior drawer of a bureau, c. 1790.

18. Gilt brass pommel and ring from a bureau loper or brushing slide of a chest of drawers. Note hand-made thread to the screw with its abrupt end, c. 1750.

19. Brass knob, c. 1810. Very similar shapes were used about 1720, but notice the tapered, machine-made screw indicating a late date.

20 and 21. Skeleton escutcheons, c. 1760–90.

22. Bone lozenge escutcheon, probably Irish, often found on flamboyant furniture of second-rate quality, c. 1800.

23. Modern reproduction of a type of handle of circa 1730. Note the unfluent curves and gawky outline, the lack of gilding and no bevels on the edge. The oxidisation of the brass looks very 'forced'. Compare marginal differences of the bails with 5 and 6.

plain and bevelled on both the pierced and outside edges. The unadorned handles were cast and were usually approximately $\frac{1}{16}$ inch (1.6 mm) thick, reflecting the simple designs of furniture in that period. By 1740, with the introduction of the Rococo, handles and backplates became more ornate. Chippendale's design book, amongst others, illustrates enormous handles made of cast brass, although flat handles continued to be made to a slightly more complicated design, reflecting Gothick or chinoiserie style.

In about 1770 handles again became simple and perhaps the classic of handle design, the swan-neck, was introduced. The back plate was reduced to plain roundels and the bail, instead of being a simple 'C', developed into a pair of conjoined ogee curves – hence the expression 'swan-neck'. These remained in fashion for a long while, but the Neo-classical style of Adam brought with it a re-introduction of the back plate handle, now in a different form with Neo-classical ornament; the oval was much in demand. Instead of being cast, these handles were usually pressed from fine brass sheets and it was now quite possible to achieve very crisp designs. Oval back plates often depict trophies of acorns, agricultural instruments and even nationalist themes such as the victories of Nelson or the Scottish thistle. Pressed back plates could also be rectangular or shaped rectangular in outline.

Cast handles were still made, and it is interesting that on furniture such as sideboards, whose light cupboard doors may have handles made from pressed brass, the heavy cellaret drawers would be cast in the same design, giving them the additional strength needed. The Neo-classical period also produced the ring handle, replacing the bail with a single loop pivoting about its uppermost point. The wooden knob was reintroduced in about 1790. At first it was used only on small drawers such as those found on music canterburies, drum tables or whatnots. By the 1820s, however, the knob had become very popular and remained in vogue for the rest of the century. The handles on bureau lopers and very small interior drawer fitments were small brass knobs. By the middle of the eighteenth century, they were conjoined 'C' scrolls, but by the century's end again become diminutive brass or ivory knobs.

Seventeenth-century handles were usually held in place, not with nuts and bolts, but with a split pin either of brass or steel and always narrow in cross-section (Plates 25c and e). This 'snape' method had been abandoned by about 1710. It was replaced by the pommel, a piece of metal with a screw at one end and a ball at the other. A hole was drilled through the ball

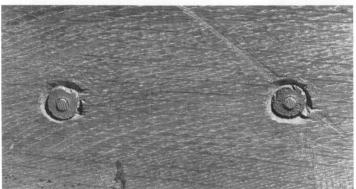

27 Methods of fixing drawer handles. (a) Snape fixing seen from inside the drawer in Plate 25 (c). Snapes are usually longer and are often punched into the wood. (b) Square nut fixing common *c.* 1730-1770. Note the bevelled edge to the hand cut nut and the hand cut thread and pommel. This plate shows the inside of the drawer illustrated in Plate 25(b) and the mark on the right of the handle is a rebate to accommodate the lock, now missing. (c) Circular recessed handle fixing nuts. This variety usually had a slot where a special screw driver was used to secure the nut. The saw mark is probably the work of a ham-fisted restorer and indicates that the handle could have been taken off and replaced at some time.

to accommodate the bail. Apart from early eighteenth-century pommels, where the head is unadorned, these were usually stamped with a circular, turned decoration. They were held in place by a square brass nut with a bevelled edge. By about 1770 the square nut gave way to the circular nut, often with a screw-driver incision. This required the use of a special screw-driver with a notch, to straddle the pommel coming through the nut.

If drawers are used a lot the handles wear out and, as it can be very difficult to find a matching replacement, this can mean replacing the entire set. It is not surprising therefore that relatively few pieces of eighteenth-century English furniture survive with their original handles. During the nineteenth century a considerable amount of furniture was refitted with wooden knob handles and it is only quite recently that the original type of handles have been considered aesthetically worth restoring. When a dealer removes the knobs to replace them with handles appropriate to the design, this usually reveals marks made by the knobs – if not by their fixing, then by their outline. It may even be necessary to make a third set of handle holes, although it is preferable to use the original holes if possible.

Sometimes the restorer is fortunate in that one of the original holes was used for the fixing of a wooden knob, in which case

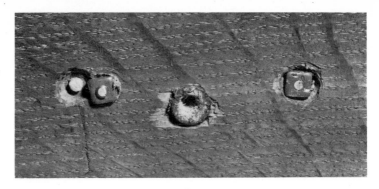

28 Here is evidence of at least three sets of handles having been used. The extreme left hand hole and the right hand hole appear to be original, the left hand one now being filled with a block. The central mark was made by a Victorian wooden knob. This was replaced with another handle using one of the original holes. The wooden knob was sawn off on the front surface of the drawer, but because the replacement handle was not as wide as the original, another hole had to be drilled on the left. Compare these machine-made nuts with the hand-made ones in Plate 27. This whole surface is a clear example of tawdry restoration. (The diagonal marks in the timber are the medullary rays of the oak.)

there may be very little evidence that the piece has had more than one set of handles. Since handles are usually removable, it is often a good idea to take one off if there is any doubt as to whether they are original, and see if there is any sign of holes or marks left by previous sets. On one such occasion I noticed that there were three sets of handle holes at the back of the drawer front, but only one set on the front. This was clear evidence that the piece of furniture had had the drawer fronts re-veneered using old wood.

Locks will be a small help in dating. Seventeenth-century locks tended to be steel, and upwards of 3 inches (76 mm) across and almost square, held in place with nails. They became progressively smaller and by about 1720 were usually a bare 2 inches (51 mm) square on fine domestic furniture, although larger on pieces of massive proportions. By 1740 brass was used as well as steel, being considered more decorative, and locks were held in position with screws, the drawer front being rebated to accept the lock.

The piece of brass that surrounds the key-hole is called an escutcheon, unless it follows the shape of the key-hole and is very narrow indeed, in which case it is simply called a skeleton key-hole or skeleton escutcheon. When a key is inserted in a lock it is very rare for a key to locate on its pin at once without striking the drawer front, and the escutcheon protected the

29 From left to right: Steel lock, *c.* 1720. Brass lock, *c.* 1780 (note the steel wards on the back plate). Steel lock *c.* 1780 (note the long shoot). Bramah lock *c.* 1800 (note the absence of ward marks on the back plate and the name on the top). Victorian lock, *c.* 1880 (note the writing on the top plate – 'Secure patent three lever' – and absence of wards).

drawer from this damage. By about 1770 escutcheons for the first time varied in size from the back plates and became diminutive interpretations of the larger designs.

During the nineteenth century locks were patented, and impressed letters saying 'patent' or 'secure', or even royal cyphers, indicate a late date of manufacture. The drawer itself may be earlier, if it has been refitted at a later date with another lock, but this is a point which should be checked when encountered. Bramah locks were fashionable for good quality furniture, but this company was not founded until 1784 and it is very rare to find one of their locks before about 1800. They became very popular, especially for desks, in the mid-nineteenth century.

The bookcase is one item of carcase furniture which may not have drawers, and we must look elsewhere for indications of quality and date. Most bookcases have adjustable shelves to accommodate different size books. In early examples, strips of wood often no more than $\frac{1}{4}$ inch (6 mm) thick are applied to the sides of the bookcase at regular intervals, and the shelves rest between these fillets. With the introduction of close-grained mahogany it was more common to rebate the sides and the shelves slide into the grooves. The top and bottom of the bookcase itself were normally fixed to the sides with a series of dovetail joints, which give great strength in a lateral direction and form a brace against the outward thrust of the shelves. Both fillets and rebates normally stop short of the top and bottom of the bookcase by about 4-9 inches (102-229 mm). If they run right to the top, this may indicate that the piece has been reduced in height to fit a room with a lower ceiling.

In the early part of the nineteenth century there was a new development. Each side was drilled with two rows of corresponding holes, one at the front and one at the back. Small wooden pegs shaped like button mushrooms were inserted into these holes and these supported the shelves. In some cases metal pegs were used, which were closer in shape to a violin peg, but smaller; the shelves were drilled at each end with a recess which locked on to the peg. This method of support was invisible at a casual glance.

The thirteen-panelled glazed door is a very common way of finishing bureau bookcases and cabinets. The glazing bars should be approximately $\frac{1}{8}$ inch (3 mm) wide and rebate a similar depth into the stiles and rails. Sometimes the rebate is hidden, if the glazing bars are tenoned into the stiles and rails, but this rarely occurred before about 1800. Early glass makers could not produce large sheets of glass, which was made by

30 *Above*: Glazing bars, *c.* 1780. The wide piece on the left hand side is the stile of the cupboard door of the corner cupboard in Plate 93. The thin piece of wood entering it is a glazing bar and can be seen to rebate into the stile. The bevel between the glazing bar, stile and the glass is the putty holding the glass. Old putty becomes rock hard. *Opposite*: Glazing bars, *c.* 1800. A similar section from the bureau bookcase in Plate 95. The stiles stand proud of the glazing bars which mortise into it.

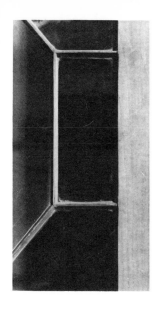

blowing a bubble or cylinder, then cutting this open and laying it flat on a 'table'. The size of a pane was thus determined by the power of the maker's lungs. Such glass is very thin, perhaps $\frac{1}{16}$ inch (1.6 mm), and is never completely flat. It is secured into bookcase doors with putty, which is stained to a dark brown. New putty takes months to harden and restoration, even using old glass from a picture for example, may therefore be noticeable for some considerable time. Expert craftsmen using special materials, however, can readily simulate the appearance of age.

The first mirrors of glass appeared with the restoration of the monarchy in 1660. The plates seldom exceeded 15 inches (380 mm) in any one direction, and were generally surrounded with intricately shaped frames of stump work, bead work, straw work, silver and so on. Looking glasses of the early eighteenth century were also most valuable objects and were still novelties in their time. Any mirror longer than 3 feet (1 m) in any direction had to be made of more than one plate, and until the middle of the eighteenth century it was impossible to make large mirrors with silvered plates. The edge of a plate was usually bevelled, but on old bevels, the angle is very shallow and should hardly be detectable when you run your finger across the apex. The glass will also often be quite striated on the bevel.

Even today bevelling is a long and expensive process, but it is a most satisfactory way of finishing a plate. For about ten years either side of 1700 plates were often decorated with cutting or stars. Early mirrors are thin, and this can be tested by touching the surface with a finger or a sharp object. Observe how far the reflection is from the object. With old glass it should appear little more than $\frac{1}{8}$ inch (3 mm) away, but with modern glass which is often twice as thick the image will appear $\frac{1}{4}$ inch (6 mm) away. The distance of the image will always be double the thickness of the glass.

Moving on from carcase furniture, we find that tables are most readily distinguished by the construction of the legs. These are fixed at their upper ends by an arrangement of rails running between them, and the rails are held together by mortise and tenon joints. If the table dates from the seventeenth century or earlier, the framework will be held together with an arrangement of pegs, and the top will be fixed to the framework in a similar fashion. The only rails not united by a pegged mortise and tenon will be those which are accommodating the drawers.

Glue replaced the use of pegs in the early eighteenth century

Shelf arrangements

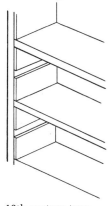

18th-century type

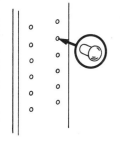

19th-century fixing

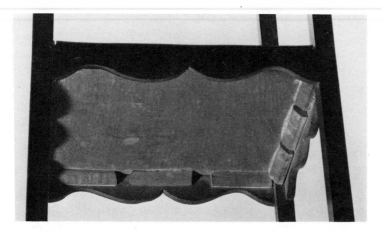

31 Glued blocks on the undersurface of the tray of a whatnot. Note the canted edges and that the surface glue has perished around the perimeter of the blocks.

and from that date it was customary to hold the top with glued blocks: small strips of square timber canted on one edge, with one surface stuck to the top and another to the rail. By the 1740s an alternative method was also being used: the side rail was gouged out to within $\frac{1}{2}$ inch (12.7 mm) of the top and a screw sunk through this recess into the top. Unfortunately (at least for dating purposes) this method of making tables, or a combination of the two, has been used ever since, and it is only in the second half of the twentieth century that resin-based glues have been made in sufficient strength to replace the old form of construction.

Pie-crust table tops and trays are cut and carved from a solid piece of wood, in contrast to modern reproductions where the pie-crust is generally applied afterwards. Trays and little tables which have thin wavy edges or fretted galleries are made with plywood. The wood (mahogany, as a rule) is cut into veneers, two sections going along the grain, sandwiching a cross-grain centre section. The gallery is then rebated into the tray or table top and cut to its wavy shape. The top edge, where the ply

32 The undersurface of a table top, showing the gouge and its screw holding the rail to the top.

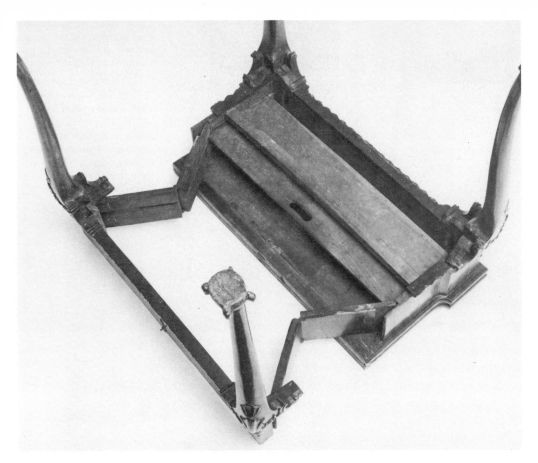

33 The undersurface of a concertina action card table, half opened. When fully extended, the uppermost of the two braces (the one with the handle hole) slides along a rebate to prevent the concertina folding accidentally. Such slides are frequently fitted with a drawer to take cards, gaming chips, etc.

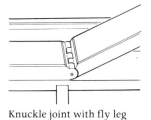

Knuckle joint with fly leg

construction would show, is concealed with a veneer, or else the centre ply is cut away and a stringing line put in its place. The second technique gives considerable strength to such galleries and is a valuable indication that the piece is constructed correctly – that it is genuine, and not copied.

The earliest examples of tea tables and card tables are supported on gate legs. By about 1720 the concertina arrangement was evolved for best quality tables, with a series of hinges enabling the table, when opened, to display a leg at each corner and an apron all the way round. This style had died out by around 1760 and was rarely used again, although I have seen one freak example made of satinwood in about 1790. Most card and tea tables are supported by an arrangement whereby either one or both back legs swing out on a knuckle joint and the top is supported by the upper surface of the legs, sometimes lined with baize. The wood forming the knuckle joint is usually beech and, because this wood is very susceptible to wear and woodworm and because the joint itself is rather unsatisfactory, this part is repaired or replaced frequently. By about 1810,

59

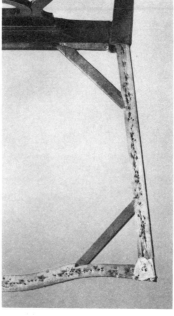

34 *Far left*: A trap-seat chair. Note the rebate in the narrow seat rails, and the small glued blocks flush with the rebate at each angle.

35 *Left*: Beech seat rails for a stuff-over seat. This is slightly unusual in having braces at the back as well. The holes in the seat rails indicate numerous visits to the upholsterer (note also several nail holes in the shoe).

card tables in the Regency style no longer had swinging fly legs and the whole of the frieze remained stationary, while the top pivoted on a joint about two-thirds of the way along its length and folded over the rest of the frieze. These were the only methods of card table support until the 1840s.

With chairs, the seat rails are the most revealing items of construction. There are two ways in which a dining chair may be made. First, it may have a drop-in (or trap) seat, in which case the seat rails will be less than an inch (25 mm) in width and will be rebated to accept the seat. Small blocks will be glued into the corners, giving additional strength to the mortise and tenon joints, but the size of the glued blocks will seldom exceed $\frac{3}{4}$ inch (19 mm) in either direction. Alternatively, the chair may be upholstered by bringing the material down over the seat rail: this is called a stuff-over seat. In this case the chair will have a piece of wood approximately $4\frac{1}{2}$ inches (115 mm) to 6 inches (150 mm) long and $\frac{3}{4}$ inch (19 mm) square rebated into the front and side seat rails. This is known as a corner brace and does not often appear at the rear corners. When upholstered in this way the webbing causes considerable strain on the side rails, which the braces support.

The seat rails in stuff-over chairs are almost always made of beechwood for the simple reason that beech takes upholstery nails very easily, and it is not necessary to replace the seat rails when the chair is re-upholstered. However, beech is highly susceptible to woodworm and it is not uncommon to find an

Regency card table action

eighteenth-century chair which has been re-railed because the original timber had become infested. Braces often drop out when a chair is being upholstered, and it is quite common for an upholsterer to replace them with triangular pieces of wood screwed to the rails. This was a common form of construction in the nineteenth century and might suggest that a chair was made at that time unless one notices marks where braces have once been.

Until the beginning of the nineteenth century, the uprights or stiles on the back of the chair were the one exception to the general rule of furniture that stiles should reach the top. Before this time the top rail of a chair was always mortised and the stiles tenoned into it as was the central splat, which also tenoned into the back seat rail. However, the splat is glued only at the top joint; the bottom end is left floating to allow for shrinkage. The shoe will be rebated to accept the splat, or it may, with a trap seat, be through-tenoned: that is the splat may go right through the shoe, which is glued to back seat rail. With a stuff-over seat the shoe must be removable for the upholstery to pass beneath it. Consequently it is usually tacked on with a nail, and a chair which has been re-upholstered on a number of occasions should have several nail marks where they have been replaced.

With eighteenth-century armchairs, the arms are usually screwed to the seat rails and into the stiles at the back. The screws are countersunk and a small block of wood is used to conceal the hole. If the arm has been strengthened or repaired, this piece of wood will have been removed and since it is made of the same wood as the rest of the chair, the replacement will be obvious. It is impossible to re-use the original piece. Very rarely, the arm is dovetailed rather than screwed into the side seat rail. Stretchers are tenoned into the legs and the outside surface of a stretcher should be flush, or very nearly so, with the outside edge of the leg. Occasionally the stretcher uniting the back legs of a chair is set in slightly from the rear surface. Stretchers may be joined to one another in several ways: sometimes they are rebated, more rarely they are dovetailed or even mitred. In English chairs of the seventeenth century, square stretchers did not run into circular legs, nor did circular stretchers run into square legs, or even into the square sections of turned legs. The same rule applies to stretchers which joined one another.

With both tables and chairs it was sometimes thought decorative to have parts of the leg larger than the rest. For example, Elizabethan tables with bulbous 'cup and cover' legs had a centre section (gadrooned and carved) fatter than the top and bottom. A similar effect is sometimes found in furniture of the 1680s and 1690s: a piece of turning larger than the square piece of wood from which the whole leg is made. In such instances the fatter section is created by gluing four additional pieces of wood on to the square; when dry, the whole piece is put on the lathe and decorated. If this procedure has not been followed the piece must have been made at a later date. The same is true of scroll toes and some turned legs with pad feet (Plate 67). The pad foot often overhangs the outline of the turned leg, despite the fact that the leg tapers towards the ankle. Where the pad foot is broader than the square at the head of the foot, a join should also be visible.

In the cabriole leg, however, the whole was cut from a single piece of wood. As this method was rather extravagant, it was reserved for better quality furniture and, especially in the provinces, furniture was still made with turned legs way into the nineteenth century. The ears (or shoulders as they are sometimes called) on either side of the knee of the cabriole leg are always made separately, and the joint should be clearly visible between leg and ear. This particular part frequently becomes loose and is therefore often replaced; when examining a lowboy, stool, chair, or any object with cabriole legs, one should take care to see that all the ears are original.

Cabriole-leg chairs which were intended to be placed in the centre of a room, say behind a desk, had their back legs carved so that the chair could be viewed from all sides and display an equal degree of quality. Many chairs, however, were designed to be placed around the edge of the room. This is particularly true of the highest quality furniture, which was made for state apartments in large houses, where the most formal arrangements of furniture was obligatory. In such cases the front and sides of the chair will be carved but the back legs will be quite plain.

English furniture is unique in its use of casters. The French produced gilded brass (ormolu) mounts for their furniture, frequently using these as a decorative feature. This was very rare in England, and, apart from the magnificent productions of the expatriates Pierre Langlois and Abraham Roentgen, the sole indigenous exponent was the cabinet-maker John Channon, who moved from Exeter to London in the 1730s and produced some fine examples of ormolu mounted furniture, though perhaps more reminiscent of Teutonic or Scandinavian fashions than of the French. However, the English cabinet-makers did use brass for making casters. Much furniture

Cup and cover leg

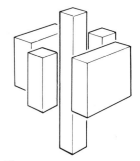

The start

The finish

36 Groups of casters from English furniture. Top row, left to right: modern reproduction with solid brass roller simulating a caster of *c.* 1790. A wooden roller held by iron plate and shackle, *c.* 1730. Brass caster with laminated leather roller, 1775, from the Pembroke table (Plate 97). A large cast brass hairy paw, *c.* 1805. Bottom row, left to right: cast brass caster with circular socket and hollowed roller, *c.* 1800. Cast iron caster with swivelling action of a type fitted to large library chairs and bulky furniture, *c.* 1770. Square box caster with hollowed roller and well shaped shank, *c.* 1790.

produced between 1720 and 1870 had casters fitted, particularly for drawing and reception rooms. Dining chairs were not provided with casters.

The earliest casters were made of wood, frequently laburnum, and were ball-shaped; on large carcase furniture (Plate 85) they were recessed well in from the visible parts of the legs or bracket feet. Most pieces originally fitted with such casters have since had them removed. Laminated leather was the next material used, presumably to keep noise to a minimum, and these rollers were held in a short, brass framework. These early casters were attached to the bottom of the foot or leg by a plate drilled with three countersunk holes, for screw fixing. For lighter pieces, the leather caster continued in use until the 1790s, but the framework was greatly elongated. After this time the roller was almost invariably of brass, but made as light as possible, the inside being cut out; reproductions of this variety usually have solid cylindrical brass rollers which are quite different. At the turn of the century brass casters in the form of a claw or an animal's foot became fashionable.

Around 1775, the square tapered or chamfered leg had given way to the turned leg, which was in widespread use by 1800. The shape of casters had to be changed from the square box and became circular in cross-section: I cannot recall ever having seen a leather roller on such a turned caster. In the nineteenth century legs became fatter and casters followed suit. In mid-century it became customary to make the rollers of white or brown porcelain, which does not wear out so quickly, but on the other hand shatters more easily. Casters of all periods are normally fixed with screws, and the leg is cut in order to accept them. In better designed pieces the caster will be flush with the wood to which it is fitted.

Chapter 5

Quality and condition

The quality of a piece of furniture may be considered in three stages. First there is the quality of the design. Even with two chairs taken from the same plans, one may be of finer interpretation than the other. Second, there is the quality of materials used; and third, there is the quality of workmanship. By and large these three aspects will complement one another perfectly. For example, the chair illustrated here is supremely

37 Profile of the chair in Plate 72, designed with the human anatomy very much in mind.

38 Plan of the same chair showing the bowed lateral outline.

well designed, anatomically correct and aesthetically very attractive. It is made of the finest timber, with the legs and stiles in straight grained wood which lends strength to the finished article, and the splat has an excellent veneer commensurate with the quality of the design – the very fact that it is veneered indicates a high standard of workmanship.

Quality of workmanship can be assessed fairly easily.

39 Detail of the back of the same chair. Note the straight grain of the stiles, the decorative quality of the splat and the fluency of the carved and shaped decoration.

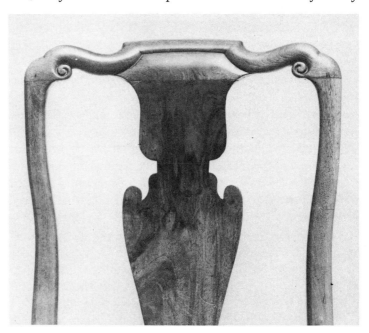

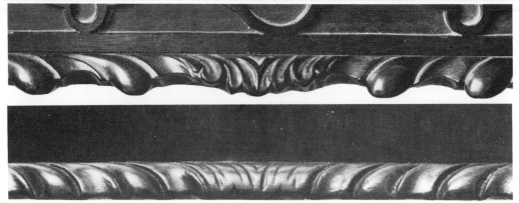

Mouldings, for example, will be complex and crisp in better pieces. Glazing bars in bookcases will be fine and narrow (provided they are made after 1740), and drawer linings will be as thin as the age of the piece permits. In chairs, when viewed from above the back should be bowed to accommodate the round shape of the human back. Similarly, a good quality chair will 'move' when viewed laterally: the back legs should kick down well to give additional stability. In lesser quality chairs, the back may be straight and if the back legs fail to kick out sufficiently the chair will be unstable; consequently the joints are more likely to wear loose.

Quality of design is a more contentious subject. Some people, for example, enthuse wildly over the Regency style of the Brighton Pavilion, while others wax lyrical at the simplicity of early walnut furniture, and others still prefer the Rococo or mother-of-pearl inlaid *papier-mâché* furniture. Yet an experienced observer of old furniture can distinguish a Charles II cane seat-and-back chair from a moderate nineteenth-century copy at a distance. Why exactly the original is thought to be finer in design than the copy lies, I think, outside the scope of this book. That the majority of informed opinion feels this to be the case, however, is quite definite.

In considering quality, it may help to compare the properties of something good, and something *very* good. In Plate 41, the chair on the left is in the French taste, often referred to as French Hepplewhite owing to the fact that George Hepplewhite, in his book of designs, drew a stool and also a console table with legs similar to these. Many people consider that the French Hepplewhite chair represents the pinnacle of achievement in English chair making. There is not a single straight line anywhere in the chair. The design is sound in that such chairs are stable, generally remain in good condition and, despite the fact that they are upholstered in

40 Gadroon mouldings, which only appear on fine quality furniture, require the arts of both cabinet-maker and carver. The lower example shows a typical gadroon mould (from the card table Plate 84), but there is much greater vigour in the upper example, where the crispness of execution displays not only the quality of the original carving, but of the material used.

hard horse hair, are enormously comfortable for very long periods of time.

When I first saw this chair it was still covered in its original upholstery, with brass studs outlining the cartouche shaped back, arm pads and seat rails. The back, too, was originally buttoned in the present manner. Occasionally these chairs have the back outlined in mahogany, but this one, as is often the case, is upholstered all the way round. The arms are shaped to conform in outline with the seat rails, and the upright supports of the arms are carved with moulding and scrolls. The terminals – the end of the arm where one's hand rests – are carved with small garya husks. The arm pads also sit within a raised moulding. The front cabriole legs are carved with a stylised shell upon more garya husks, the ears are in the form of rose paterae and the feet end with a scroll.

The chair on the right, apart from being of generous proportions, is also curvilinear, although the arm terminals are clearly somewhat different. The arm supports are very similar and the legs, while being cabriole, shaped at the knee and ears, are quite plain, but they also terminate in a scroll.

Where then is the difference? The left-hand example is good, as are all French Hepplewhite chairs. They were not the

41 Two mahogany armchairs, *c.* 1775, inspired by the designs of George Hepplewhite and often described as in the 'French taste'.

product of a second rate chair maker. Yet one must admit that the way the arm sits on its support is somewhat unhappy. The cabriole leg is too narrow at the top, too thin at the ankle and fails to flow as smoothly as it should. The timber is broad-grained, and the chair is somewhat light in weight. The right-hand chair by contrast is very heavy and of fine quality timber. The arm sits delightfully on the upright, which itself is most elegantly curved. The cabriole legs, although plain, are the epitome of fine design and, while the other chair looks as if it might give way under a heavy gentleman, this example will accommodate a heavy man with ease for a great many years. A certain depth of upholstery is necessary and the generous proportions of the seat allow a more satisfying proportion of seat depth to size. The curvature at the back is admirable and gives support where it is most needed. It could be argued that the back would be more elegant if the rear legs had shown above the seat, but despite this one small disadvantage, the right-hand chair is enormously superior to the left, which incidentally is one of a pair.

If the design, materials and workmanship of a piece of furniture are all found satisfactory, the next point to be considered is the condition. Obviously the environment in which it has been kept will determine how often it has been subject to the claws of cats or the devastations of young children. The heavy man who always sits at table on the same chair and is given to leaning back will eventually cause damage. However, a well-made mortise and tenon is very strong indeed and will endure enormous abuse almost indefinitely, and in straight grain wainscot oak or Jamaican mahogany one would be most surprised to see such joints broken. A chair in Honduras mahogany will frequently be considerably eroded on the centre stretcher by wear from shoes and boots, but even moderate San Domingo mahogany will stand the wear of shoes for a very long time.

There is a variety of chair made from about 1770 to 1790 in which the splat is longer than the stiles; it is known as the camel-back chair. The top rail is cut from a piece of wood anything up to five inches wide, and this tends to shrink when exposed to central heating. Consequently the joints loosen and sometimes come apart at the top of the stiles, and breakage frequently occurs at this point. This is an example of how a design can prove faulty in adverse conditions. The camel-back was seldom employed by the finest cabinet-makers, although there are some surprising exceptions to this rule.

There are numerous places to look for wear and tear. Drawer

42 *Opposite, above*: Undersurface of an oval-top stool. The decorative scrolled hole in the top is designed for easy transportation. Compare the accumulation of dirt and the patination at that point and also a comparable surface around the edge of the top. Most particularly, however, note the 'dry' surface inside the apron where the stool cannot be touched with normal usage.

43 *Opposite, below*: The underside of the lowboy in Plate 81. Notice the dry, unstained appearance of all the wood, although some dirt has seeped through the planks of the top, and the centre drawer partly removed shows signs of being made of second-hand timber. The drawer runners appear many shades lighter because the timber is newer having been recently abraided. Note the patination and colour of all the surfaces. This is the epitome of an 'honest' piece.

44 A worn drawer runner. Notice how one section of the drawer runner has eroded completely and how the drawer front has protected the last section.

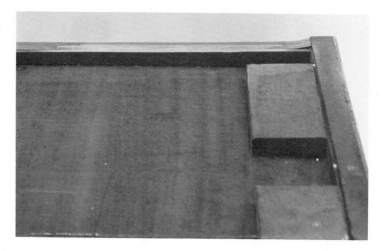

runners in a bureau or chest of drawers will show considerable signs of abrasion, as will the corresponding parts in the carcase. Loop handles, if they are not provided with a back plate, will cause dents in the timber of a drawer front. The human hand leaves traces of dirt and grease in specific places. When a chair is lifted by the person sitting in it, this will occur under the side rails and one should look for signs of dirt at that particular

45 The carcase accommodating the drawer in Plate 44. Notice how the drawer runner has worn grooves at its edge (some of the small marks are caused by grit). The block on the right-hand side mates with a block on the underside of the drawer to prevent it being pushed in too far; this is called a drawer stop.

46 *Opposite*: A fine mahogany tea-kettle stand with a triangular serpentine pie-crust top supported by flying 'C' scrolls. The base includes numerous Rococo carved motifs – claw-and-ball, fish scale, acanthus, gadrooning and beading, and the column is fluted, *c.* 1750. The silver kettle is of comparable quality and was made in London in 1739 by William Kidney.

The repaired junction of a stile and top rail of a chair. Note the direction of the splits along the grain in both members and the crude screwed repairs. Often new wood has been inserted at this joint.

point. When vacant, chairs are usually lifted by the top rail and similar marks may be found on the underside of that. If the chair is rather heavy it may be dragged rather than lifted, and one should look for wear on the rear edge of the back legs. Chairs are seldom dragged sideways and therefore one would not expect much wear in this direction.

Because the junction between the stile and the top rail of a chair is weak, and because this is a place where a chair is frequently handled, it is also one of the first places to become damaged to such an extent that repair becomes necessary. Similarly, the chair may become so worn on its back legs that some form of restoration is necessary. Other places on a chair where a different type of wear takes place include the joints round the seat rails and on chairs made later than 1720 the glue will loosen and the whole chair becomes wobbly. When this happens it is a perfectly straightforward operation to knock the chair apart, clean up the joints and re-glue them. Sometimes, however, owners do not think of this, or perhaps they have only just re-upholstered the chairs when they notice the rails are loose. Instead of doing the job correctly, they drill a hole and try to hold the joints together with screws. This inevitably leads to a messy area of repair.

Another reason for chairs failling into disrepair is the habit owners have of recovering trap seats without first removing the existing cover. I have even seen trap seats upholstered with as many as six covers, one on top of the other. Each layer of material expands the size of the trap seat, and since the recess into which it is forced remains constant in size, undue strain is placed on the seat rails. Eventually, it only needs the weight of a human to force the seat too far in and breakages occur.

Among the weakest points in a chair are the stiles just above the rear legs, and the very tall chairs of the late seventeenth and very early eighteenth centuries are frequently damaged here. Stretcher rails are often thin pieces of wood, since they are merely braces and are not designed to carry any weight; consequently, they are easily broken. More often than not the whole stretcher is replaced, but they are sometimes repaired if they break where the centre stretcher joins them. When examining a set of chairs the experienced observer will pick up each one in turn and examine the top rail for signs of breakage where the seat meets the back, then check for signs of damage to the seat rails as a result of incorrect upholstery, observe the amount of wear on the rear legs and front leg, and carefully check the stretchers.

Minor damage of this kind may be found in numerous places, so the observer must adopt the attitude of a detective and consider where a piece is most likely to have suffered. If signs of ageing occur in some places but not all, danger signals flash for the experienced observer (Plate 43). For example

48 The front corner of a trap-seat chair. The seat has been forced outwards by too many new upholstered covers being placed on top of the old worn ones. The breakage caused here is typical.

a knee-hole desk with only the outer edges of each drawer worn would make one suspect that it was once a chest of drawers; the wide drawers down its length may have been cut and a knee-hole inserted. This is a frequent occurrence, and in such cases one looks for lack of wear in the carcase on the inside edges of each small drawer. A skilled mutilator will try to copy accurately the spacing and quality of the dovetails on the inside of each drawer, but is unlikely to have the perfect match of timber. It is equally unlikely that the signs of wear on the drawer runners and in the carcase can be simulated. Finally, the observer should turn the piece of furniture upside down to see that no alterations have taken place structurally.

Clearly furniture like this is unacceptable to the collector and constitutes a composite article. For many years the straight-front chest of drawers was considered unimportant and of little value, while the knee-hole always enjoyed a healthy market. It is little wonder that many generations of cabinet-makers have converted the one into the other. But when does alteration cease to be repair and cause a piece of furniture to jump suddenly into another category? This question has been the subject of countless debates, but current thinking is that repair should be considered acceptable only when occasioned by fair wear and tear. The enhancement of any piece over its original design is unacceptable to the collector, but it will continue to happen so long as a premium is paid for objects of greater utilitarian and aesthetic merit.

It is important to remember that every piece of furniture was once new, and during what we now regard as the period when antiques were made, cabinet-makers had no need to stain any structural member. Wood turns dark naturally through ageing, oxidisation and the gathering of dirt. The lower surface of any piece of furniture, therefore, should only exhibit evidence of this, and any stain on, say, a chair seat rail, should be regarded with suspicion and is probably the result of some later repair, or an indication that the piece was made at a later date. Having said that, it must be remembered that certain specialist techniques, such as lacquering and gilding, do involve the use of stain.

Most tripod tables have a hingeing top (page 43), which made storage easier and allowed the table to double as a firescreen when the top was folded to its vertical position. If the top revolves, it will be supported by a bird-cage arrangement of two blocks secured by four pillars. The column support of the table passes through a hole in the bottom block and is located by a pin between them. Both this type and the non-rotating

74

49 *Right*: On the left a tripod polescreen of about 1765, carved on the knee and on the vase column. Beside it is a circular tray of about the same date. It is a common malpractice to cut the polescreen below the banner and to place the tray on top to form a low table.

tripods have some lopers or bearers to support the top, unless it is quite small. The column on the non-rotating table will be tenoned into the block, while with the bird-cage type the column will show through the top block and be wedged into position. Since the top is opened and closed frequently both these methods of fixing leave imprints on the undersurface of the table top. If the top has been altered or replaced or if the lopers have been moved, the presence of a previous arrangement will always show.

The tops of tripod tables often mirrored the contemporary taste in trays and *vice versa*, and this has been a source of much trickery. A few years ago trays had little value, as did pole firescreens, but torchères and carved tripod tables have always been highly esteemed. It was therefore common to take a pole screen, reduce the column in height and fix a tray on the top. The only part which would show as new was the block beneath the tray, but as this was often made with beechwood in

genuine pieces and therefore liable to woodworm, its replacement was not unlikely. To a very experienced eye the design will give the game away, but close examination should reveal the scratch marks which every tray inevitably accumulates on its underside.

Other very popular items for which the demand far exceeds supply include low wine tables and similar objects, made to accommodate tea kettles standing on their original burners, known as kettle stands. Like commodes and console tables, these objects were found only in grand houses and were very rare; moreover they had a limited period of manufacture, from around 1720 to 1770. Here again, pole screens with their upper column cut off were frequently fitted with a small tray. These are often 18-23 inches high (457-584 mm), while original tripod or occasional tables stand 27-30 inches (686-762 mm) high.

From about 1880 to 1925 Sheraton-style furniture, in mahogany with satinwood cross-banding, was much in vogue. Many plain pieces of furniture, which were deemed to have an adequate outline, were insufficiently decorated with inlay to be saleable. A glance through art magazines of the first twenty years of this century will show considerable numbers of inlaid sideboards, chests of drawers, wardrobes and so forth. Many of these we accept today for what they are, genuine late eighteenth-century pieces, inlaid and cross-banded at a later date. Except on the square, tapered legs of card tables and sideboards, boxwood stringing lines were not inlaid into solid timber during the Georgian period (you can check whether the timber is solid or not by looking at the grain on the other side).

It is difficult to set a new stringing line in an old piece without marking the surrounding wood, so when examining cross-banded furniture, careful attention should be given to the timber inside the cross-banding. Look for scratches which stop suddenly at the decoration, for these are either the result of the most amazing coincidence, or more likely, show that the cross-banding was put in at a later date. Bear in mind that timbers used for cross-banding are usually much harder and denser than the ground wood, and so a scratch there may not be as deep. It should also be noted that whole pieces of furniture were sometimes stripped and French polished when this redecoration took place. In such instances much of the beauty will have been lost anyway, but re-polishing, particularly with a dark varnish, always gives grounds for suspicion.

The surface and colour of furniture are themselves important indicators. The first consideration of the polisher is to fill the holes and channels made by the grain. Exactly how furniture was finished in the seventeenth century is uncertain, but oak was polished with waxes of several different varieties, primarily a beeswax softened with a medium to allow an even application. Many people today advocate a simple mixture of beeswax and turpentine, and this recipe has no doubt been in use for a very long time. However, it does leave the surface quite sticky, and impossible to polish without the use of further solvents.

If this mixture was used in the seventeenth and early eighteenth centuries, it would account for the darkening of many pieces of early oak furniture by the accumulation of surface dirt. Indeed, a close inspection of any piece of seventeenth-century furniture will almost certainly reveal black deposits on any surface not easily reached with a polishing duster. On the top of a coffer or chest of drawers, for example, the rear third tends to be darker and dirtier than the front, which is more accessible for polishing and dusting. Exactly how seasoned wood behaves over a very prolonged period is uncertain but, judging from the dirty deposits which often accumulate, one may presume that the grain itself exudes sticky substances which attract dust.

Walnut furniture was polished before it left the workshop.

In order to fill the grain and produce a flat surface on which to build a shine, it seems likely that the timber was painted with several coats of very diluted glue – Scotch glue, made from animal bones, hooves and so forth, which is still used today. After the wood was coated, it was rubbed down to a fine surface and then polished with wax. This process appears to have continued for some time, although exactly what sealing and filling substance was employed after the introduction of mahogany is quite uncertain.

By the 1820s it was realised that timber could be sealed with clear varnish. The application of many coats, and the sanding down of the surface between each coat, is called French polish, and during the nineteenth and twentieth centuries thousands of pieces of furniture have been cleaned and subjected to the French polishing process. This is incompatible with the desires of the collector and accordingly, with more widespread knowledge and appreciation of furniture, many such pieces have been re-cleaned and given a surface which the polisher thinks approximates the old one. French polish or varnish should only be removed by an antique restorer, who may use solvents, methylated spirits or any number of other preparations to make the surface ready for re-waxing.

In an old surface one expects to see a certain degree of scratching, bruising and staining, depending on the use to which the piece has been put. Dining tables are an exception, for they were almost invariably covered with cloths until this side of the First World War and one therefore expects a Georgian dining table to be relatively free of staining. The interior of a bureau, however, would be fairly heavily stained with ink and one should also bear in mind that damp or wet iron, left in contact with wood, produces a black stain in reaction with the tannic acid contained in timber. Before the invention of stainless steel and plastic, many vessels were made of iron and one may reasonably expect to see a number of circular black stains on tables and cupboards.

Most people would prefer an old surface to be free from stains, but where they do occur the owner faces a dilemma, as some colours are considered more desirable than others. Perhaps the best way of deciding is to examine the collections in our museums and stately homes or the stocks of leading dealers, who will always be willing to discuss the colour and surface of any item they have in stock. During the latter half of the nineteenth and the beginning of the twentieth centuries it was customary for dealers themselves to clean oak, and one will sometimes find good quality seventeenth-century oak in exceptionally clean condition which has already acquired quite a good surface. Such pieces may even bear the dealer's trade label.

The balance must be drawn between smartness on the one hand and mellowness on the other. In the late eighteenth century satinwood was sometimes inlaid with purpleheart, boxwood and other timbers, to a most bright and garish effect. A look at any modern reproduction will soon make this clear. Over the years, however, the wood in original pieces has oxidised and the surface has been built up with wax, polish, dirt and more polish, and the end result is a great deal more mellow. If such an object passes into the hands of someone who cares very little, and stores it for example in a damp shed, the glory of its former being soon degenerates into something very shabby. If the piece is then resurrected, the effects of its temporary relegation are only too apparent and the new owner must decide whether the shabbiness is preferable to the original gaudy surface.

Where a surface is simply dirty through grime, a mild kitchen abrasive can be used, though with extreme care. Perhaps a safer method is carefully to apply a cloth moistened with a mixture of turpentine, methylated spirit, vinegar and linseed oil. This will loosen the sort of dirt created by greasy hands and dust, and will leave the surface suitable for wax polishing. It will be noticed that the proprietary brands of furniture polish fall into three categories. Those containing silicones cannot be advised for antique furniture which has not been French polished. Wax should be used instead – either the soft polishes containing a high proportion of aromatic oils and solvents, or the harder polishes generally available only at specialist suppliers. The soft wax polishes, if used regularly, will clean even the dirtiest piece of furniture after a few months and are to be commended for general use. Harder waxes are used in workshops, and restorers and dealers will give advice on their use which is generally confined to building up a surface after stripping.

In the preceding pages of this book, I have explained to the reader the main things he will need to know when looking at a piece of furniture: the names of its constituent parts, the materials from which it is made, the evolution of its design, the way it is put together, and factors affecting its quality and condition. In the next section, all these strands will be drawn together in a series of descriptions of individual items of furniture, taken chronologically.

Individual items

We shall start this section of the book with a description of the coffer or chest (or kist, if you live in the North of England) illustrated in Plate 56. It measures 24 inches (610 mm) wide, 20 inches (510 mm) high, and 14 inches (355 mm) deep, and is medieval in form and construction, though it would be an exceedingly rash person who would date such a piece to within even 100 years. The style is perhaps fourteenth century. Such a piece is often referred to in the trade as an ark coffer, because of the canted shape of the top. It is made from oak, riven with a riving iron or froe, and the horizontal members of the lid can be clearly seen to be of long triangular section as one would expect of a split log. All the constituent parts are split and, because the grain of oak is not arrow-straight, the timber undulates along its surface. This is particularly noticeable if one runs one's hand across the surface, and can be seen in the photograph on the rear plank of the top. Save for the cut of the

51 Detail of the end of the coffer in Plate 56 showing its construction.

grooves in the front legs and the cut of each plank to a length, a saw has not been used in its making.

The sides of the coffer simply rest in a rebate in the stiles. The stiles are kept a set distance apart by braces tenoning right through them, and the photograph clearly shows the pegs holding the tenons in place. The tenons, too, can be seen protruding through the front stiles in the photograph. The front board, which accommodates the lock, is tenoned into the stiles. The lid is made of three planks overlapping and rebated into one another, and they in turn are rebated into the thick horizontal members, again each piece being held together with pegs. The hasp is fixed on the inside of the lid, which hinges on pin or peg hinges. The medullary rays or silver fleck can be seen in most sections as the wood was split radially. The colour is pale and faded.

While it is useful to introduce this section of the book with a very early piece of furniture, one should stress that it is most unlikely that any reader would come across a piece of this age outside a museum. Coffers comprise the large proportion of pieces surviving from the medieval period. The more important ecclesiastical counterparts would have been carved with a religious subject enabling one to hazard a reasonable opinion as to the date. But the simplicity of this example, although giving the coffer an enormous amount of appeal, is a stumbling block where accurate dating is concerned.

One of the most prestigious pieces of furniture in the early part of the seventeenth century was the buffet. It was a dual purpose item, often employed for storage, but perhaps its main use was the display of important silver and pewter. Another valuable possession was porcelain from China, and the cupboard illustrated in Plate 52 perhaps originally had a display of blue and white porcelain and silver on the top and on the lower shelf.

The upper section has a pair of cupboard doors flanking a panel, and each door has a central panel framed with stiles and rails which are channel moulded. Each door panel is carved with strap-work and a geometrical arrangement of formal, stylised flowers. The door opens to reveal the cupboard inside, extending behind the central panel, and has a small shelf high up at the back and another shelf behind the overhanging frieze. The central panel between the doors is formed as an arch, with applied mouldings of pieces of wood carved with 'S' scrolls flanking the central arch which is carved with a stylised tree. The Romanesque arch, of which this is an example, was a

52 An oak buffet, or court
cupboard, with turned
supports and carved
decoration dating from about
1630.

veneered form of decoration on more complicated furniture at
this time. It is sometimes carved from a single piece of wood in a
panel, but where a deeper relief effect is required, as here, the
use of applied mouldings is quite correct. Although these
pieces are obviously held on with glue we will note that glue is
not used structurally.

The locks are no longer present, but one can see rebates on
the inside of the door where they were once fitted and this
would indicate that the cupboard perhaps held valuables
rather than food. The frieze is carved with a band of continual
'S' scrolls with foliate terminals. All this is below the
architectural corbels which support the top. The decoration
carries on round the side, and the frieze overhangs the
cupboard doors by some 5 inches (127 mm) at the front, and is
supported by unnecessarily massive turned supports. On
marginally earlier examples the pair of cupboard doors would
have been canted, that is the cupboard section would have
been a half hexagon, whereas earlier still the cupboards would

have been entirely lacking and the piece would have been three shelves. The retention of the supports on the top is therefore quite understandable, if by this time superfluous. Soon afterwards these were done away with, and in eighteenth century examples (mainly from Wales) a pendant turning is considered sufficient decoration (see Plate 61).

Below the waist shelf is a convex moulding above a band of strap-work, part of which forms the drawer illustrated in Plate 25a. The construction of the drawer is fully illustrated in the chapter on drawers. Below all this lies the bottom shelf, set on another band of carving of alternate lunettes and inverted lunettes. The bun feet below that are not original, although they probably date from the latter end of the seventeenth century.

Many variations exist on this theme. Very rarely pieces such as this may have had an additional shelf. Fine sixteenth-century examples have, instead of turned supports, carved heraldic beasts, and sometimes the carving is substituted with geometrical inlays. Because buffets were always considered prestigious, they have always been much in demand. Consequently there are in existence plain cupboards which have been carved in the nineteenth century, and many more examples which are completely made at that time in the style of the seventeenth century.

It has been stated elsewhere that it is very difficult to make firm assertions or rules about furniture making, and this is clearly demonstrated by the bottom rail of this example. The bench in Plate 62 has a similar lunette carving, the design of

53 Carved heraldic beast. This diminutive creature measures 3″ high and comes from a piece of furniture dating from 1608. Larger versions appear instead of turned supports on buffets and refectory tables.

54 Detail of the bottom left hand rail. The abrupt halting of the decoration could give ground for suspicion, but closer inspection reveals that it was done deliberately.

which ends at a logical point at its junction with a stile. The reader would be well advised to reserve judgment therefore about the bottom rail of this example, where a half round is cut abruptly in the middle. Very close examination will reveal, however, that although the decoration terminates in this way it is almost certainly deliberate.

The cupboard or wardrobe illustrated in Plate 55 apparently dates from the first half of the seventeenth century – but does it? The lunette carvings on the top rail of the doors are typical of that period and bear close resemblance to the carvings on the bench (Plate 62) and the buffet (Plate 52). The moulded stiles and rails are equally right for that date, as are the surface and colour. Cupboards of this size and shape were not unknown in the period – but that is as far as the 'rightness' of this piece goes. In fact, it is of twentieth-century manufacture, but constructed of carved room panelling made in the seventeenth century.

The top rail above the doors is carved in such a way that the design finishes correctly at each end, but the top rail of the left-hand door finishes in mid-lunette, and the decoration is in a different design altogether. Seventeenth-century pegs, when they have not been moved, present a very clean edge and almost invariably stand slightly proud of the surrounding surface. Those in the present example have been bashed and hidden and clearly are not original. The centre stile, between the doors, is not even pegged into the top rail, and no seventeenth-century joiner would have made such an omission.

On opening the door, further signs of this lack of authenticity are abundantly clear. The whole of the back is modern stained pine with machine planing marks and, while the base is old, the top has been reconstructed, as have the back, sides and rails. The side panels one would expect to be of equal size, but the top is very weak, and no seventeenth-century joiner would have finished a piece without a cornice complementing the shape and size of the article he was making. Had there ever been one, signs of its fixing would be evident.

For all that, the cupboard is very practical and fits in well with furniture contemporary to the date of its panels. The hinges, while of almost correct design and fixed with hand-wrought nails, are impressed with a nineteenth-century maker's stamp. Pieces like this abound in antique shops and auction rooms. To many people they have the attraction of being both functional and a great deal less expensive than the

55 An oak cupboard or wardrobe, constructed from seventeenth-century room panelling.

real thing. Constructed in the present form the piece was clearly not intended to deceive. The maker constructed a wardrobe to use up some seventeenth-century panelling at his disposal, and this is therefore a composite piece of furniture. Its value is merely that of a practical article, not of an antique, but I think many people would prefer this to a nineteenth-century oak cupboard carved in much the same style.

The court cupboard illustrated in Plate 57, dating from *c.* 1640, is a delightful example because its condition is exemplary; it is unusually small and the carving is both crisp and varied. These attributes weigh heavily in its favour, but it cannot be said to be exceedingly fine because it is neither inlaid nor carved with fabulous beasts – this is perhaps the distinction between something which is eminently collectable and the superlative pieces to be found in our museums.

The top overhangs the upper section and is carved with 'S' scrolls which terminate in a leafy motif. The columns, which in earlier examples would have supported the overhanging top, have now been reduced to a pendant turning, and the upper section is merely a cupboard with one opening door in the centre, flanked by a pair of panels which do not open. The stiles and muntins are carved in exactly the same fashion as the top rail, while the other rails have a simple punched arched motif of small size. The carved panels on either side are in the form of a Norman arch, enclosing a stylised tree. The central door is similarly decorated, but the mitred framing is plain and accommodates the small decorated strap hinges. Below the waist ledge is a rail of fluted decoration, while the stiles, other rails, and muntins are decorated with gouged channel moulding with an arrangement of carved panels flanking the plain door.

The simple carving below is a combination of geometrical and stylised leafy motifs, while the members forming the central cupboard door are plain channel moulded. The hinges are all of the bifurcated strap type, often reproduced at a later date, although these examples are original. The heart-shaped iron handles may once have been elsewhere, but are probably original to the piece. The whole construction is, as one would expect, mortised and tenoned and double pegged. The end panels are quite plain, though the rails are channel moulded like the lower cupboard door. The surface is quite original, though fairly dark, and the timber is oak throughout. Much of the desirability of this piece derives from its very small size: only 50$\frac{1}{2}$ inches (1280 mm) wide by 49 inches (1245 mm) high by 17 inches (432 mm) deep. As with all court cupboards, the inside is floored with boards some $\frac{3}{8}$ inch (9.5 mm) thick running from back to front. It would be most unusual in a piece of this age to come across any other form of construction.

The coffer illustrated in Plate 58 is a good seventeenth-century example. At this time there was a definite pecking order for the decoration of coffers. The first member to receive attention would be the top rail and the front panels would normally be next, although occasionally the stiles and muntin(s) would be

56 A riven oak chest, or ark coffer, of medieval construction.

57 Small oak court cupboard c. 1640, with interesting decoration.

58 A small carved, panelled oak coffer dating from the latter end of the first half of the seventeenth century.

59 *Opposite*: Walnut marquetry escritoire, *c.* 1690, of high quality and showing continental influence on an English design. The large brass escutcheons are original. The handles are substitutes.

decorated while the panels remained plain. Finally the joiner might decorate the side panels in the same order, rail first and then panel. The tops were never more than moulded in any coffer and carving here should be regarded with considerable suspicion.

In the present example the front top rail is carved with the same configuration of lunettes and stylised foliage as the bench in Plate 62 and the cupboard in Plate 55. It is perhaps the most common of all seventeenth-century decoration, but it would be well to note the depth and fineness of the carving and the fact that the colour in the decoration is the same as on the top surface. The panels are carved with stylised tulips, although the foliage is hardly that of a bulb. The tulip was a Stuart emblem and was most common in carved furniture of the period, as well as being found in other forms of decoration such as brass, silver and pottery. The stiles and bottom rail have a rebated channel mould with a slight, incised diaper motif. Very frequently such mouldings would be elaborated with punched star decoration or dots between the crosses, but the present example is plain. The rails are channel moulded, but it will be noticed that the moulding peters out before the central muntin: this is quite common on genuine pieces but seldom appears on reproductions. The side panels on the present example are plain, only the top rail being moulded on its lower edge. The top is equally plain and made from two panels – such

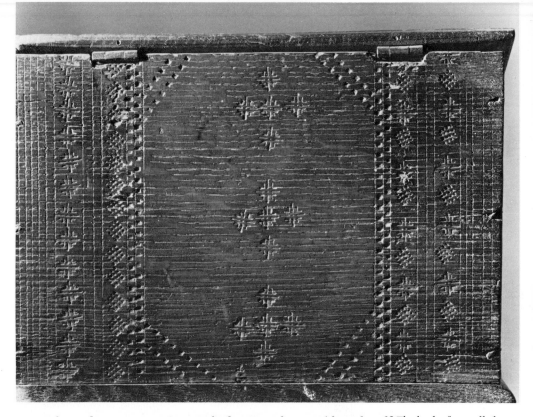

pieces have from two to six panels forming the top (though three or four is the norm). In this instance the muntins are moulded, while the rails are chamfered on their inside edges. The back has a single panel running the entire length of the coffer, which is somewhat unusual, and retains its original wire hinges. These can be seen where they protrude through the lid.

Mention has been made of punched decoration. Carving was the most common form of decoration during the age of oak, although inlay was used during the sixteenth century and for the first few years of the seventeenth. Where small designs were required to run along a stile or rail, punched decoration was often employed. A tool was fashioned by the joiner or his blacksmith with a star, crescent, circle, dot or cross, usually of approximately $\frac{1}{4}$ inch (6 mm) in diameter. This tool was struck with a mallet and left its impression along a line as a shallow decoration.

Almost coinciding with Queen Victoria's accession to the throne in 1837 came a revival of the Gothic – for example, Barry and Pugin started to build the Houses of Parliament in 1840. Gothic designs had been revived before, in the 1760s and

60 The back of a candle box displaying several forms of punched decoration. The front of the box is carved.

90

again in the 1800s, but this latest fashion went to much greater lengths to copy the feeling of the Gothic than the mere adaptation of certain motifs. The fashion blossomed and soon encompassed all forms of medieval, Tudor, renaissance and other early art forms. Anything of oak, carved and purporting to be pre-1700, whether real or genuine, was much esteemed. A great many pieces of furniture were made reproducing earlier styles, while a large quantity of early furniture was redecorated. During the first half of the seventeenth century and later in country areas, a considerable amount of oak furniture had been made which was very plain. In the nineteenth century much of this earlier furniture was 'improved' by carving the panels to sixteenth and seventeenth century patterns. Sometimes the decoration was overtly alteration, on other occasions it was intended to deceive.

The cupboard illustrated in Plate 61 is just such a piece. The

61 Court cupboard dated 1670, but made perhaps as much as 200 years later incorporating earlier sections.

lower half is a simple seventeenth-century cupboard and the channel moulding and gouged decoration are as honest as any set of stiles and rails could be. The panels are also seventeenth century, but their decoration is not. The upper section, carved with dragons which appear to have squirrels' tails, is entirely nineteenth century and largely a pastiche of Victorian ideas of what seventeenth-century furniture should look like. A comparison of the stylised foliage and lozenge carving with genuine pieces is worthwhile, for the difference is difficult to describe in words, and the reader is urged to try to find some examples and make a careful examination. The use of split balusters is slightly incorrect, as they were in fashion in the 1670s whereas the lozenge and foliage decoration is more common on earlier pieces, and it is unusual to have the two forms of decoration in one piece. The addition of snakes is completely wrong and gives the first indication that the whole piece is a fake. The carving of the date, 1670, and the initials A.C. indicates that the piece was intended to deceive when it was made, and it is interesting to note that the lettering of the initials is quite inconceivable for that date.

The amount of information available to the Victorian public was more limited than today, and early reference books show many pieces like this as being genuine. We are fortunate that a great deal more is known today about design and construction than was then and there are very few, if any, knowledgeable people who would now be taken in by this piece. Apart from the actual design, new wood has had to be employed in the construction of the upper section, and this has been stained in order to simulate the colour of the old wood of the lower section. On places where the wood has been handled the stain has rubbed away to reveal much light timber, yet if it had been old wood one would have expected these places to be darker. It is quite impossible to impregnate stain into the wood in such a way that it simulates in depth the colour accumulated by naturally aged wood.

Academics and dealers often dismiss furniture like this as being fake and unworthy of discussion or merit. Yet many thousands of such pieces exist and are for the most part, like this example, wonderfully practical and superbly made. For furnishing a home these items have the added advantage of being inexpensive. The present example is a much treasured family possession, and rightly so. It should not be thought that the analysis above constitutes in any way a denigration; it is merely observing what the article is, and putting its production in a historical context.

62 *Above*: Oak bench,
c. 1640. The sides have
lunette decoration and an
unusual 'H' stretcher
arrangement.

Until 1640 or thereabouts only very important people sat at a
meal on chairs; for the most part seating consisted of stools and
benches. The bench illustrated in Plate 62 is a typical example
dating from the second quarter of the seventeenth century.
The top has a simple thumb moulding running round the edge
and is fixed to the frieze with pegs at intervals of about 18
inches (457 mm). The top is cut from quartered oak and has
occasional black circular marks caused by wet iron containers
being placed upon it. The frieze is carved on all sides with
lunettes, a motif which was most common in the second quarter
of the seventeenth century. It will be noticed that the carving
finishes at each end in a logical fashion and was definitely not
cut from a longer piece.

The table for which this bench was made was no doubt
carved in exactly the same way. However, despite the fact that
the bench is carved on all four sides, it would depend upon its
original position whether the table would have been carved on
one, three, or all four sides. If the table originally sat in the
centre of the room it would have been carved on all four sides,
but if made to sit along the side of a room, it would have been
carved on one side, and possibly on both ends as well, but not
on the side nearest the wall. The wall might have been fitted
with a built-in bench, but otherwise the present example
would have had the pair to match it on the other side of the table.
The table for which this was made was perhaps 18 inches (457
mm) longer than this bench, but it could have been
considerably larger if a number of matching benches were used

93

on each side, for example down the centre of a hall. Very often tables were made for stools as opposed to benches, and sets of up to six or more are known, although it is most uncommon to find sets still in existence.

The turnings forming the legs or stiles of this bench would be diminutive interpretations of the larger legs of the corresponding table, and it can be clearly seen that this turning bears a strong resemblance in feel and proportion to the massive turnings of the buffet illustrated in Plate 52. Most commonly the legs of benches are united by four stretchers, running between each leg. It is most uncommon to find an H stretcher as in the present example, but almost certainly this reflected the style of the table to which it belonged. As one would expect every joint is a pegged mortise and tenon. On examination of the inside surface of the frieze, there is a delightful dryness to the timber which has never been polished and acquired only a surface of dust. Examination there also reveals the pegs showing through in every instance. Perhaps the clearest distinction between a reproduction and an old joint stool or bench can be found in the way the holes were drilled for the pegs. If they are drilled right through and the pegs are visible from the inside of the frieze, then they are constructed in the right way – reproductions are frequently not pegged at all or, if pegged, not right through.

On the end surface of the frieze there is a certain amount of shine, but the surface on the outside top of the frieze is quite shiny although dirty and this is due to an accumulation of dirt and grease where the bench has been handled over the years. The undersurface of the centre stretcher rail betrays clearly the marks of the pit-saw and it is perfectly reasonable that this part should not have been finished. The patination of this bench is exemplary and the only drawback is the lack of turning below the level of the stretchers. Originally there would have been one more turning below the stretcher – a diminutive bun foot. It often happened that furniture of this type originally stood on flagstone floors, with the attendant problem of rising damp. No timber will survive this treatment for long and the estate carpenter was called in periodically to trim each foot so that the bench did not wobble as a result of one foot or more being rotted away.

It was stated earlier that it is more common to find stools than benches. Because such pieces were made by a joiner they are known as joyned or joynt stools, but their construction is identical to that of this bench. They are, however, sometimes called coffin stools. This derives from the practice of resting a coffin on such stools in churches at funerals. But it is more pleasant, and certainly correct, to call them joyned or joynt.

Because of their height and small size joynt stools have for many years been a favourite with collectors and people wishing to furnish their houses. There are few good ones left on the market, and it is common to find that one or more stretchers have been replaced, and that the bun feet are no longer present or have been cut off and replaced. They were always held with six pegs securing the top to the rails, but West Country-made ones had tops held into the stiles with four pegs, but this is an unsatisfactory method of fixing as the shrinkage in the top and the leg will be the same. Once the top becomes loose it will soon become separated from the base and will be subject to considerable damage, if not total loss. The tops were always moulded and are most difficult to fake. Comparison with the surface of each side will soon betray signs of a top having been made at a later date. Even when the frieze was completely plain, it was always moulded on the lower edge. Invariably the legs taper outwards when viewed from the end – that is, the base is wider than the frieze – but viewed from the longer side, the legs will be parallel. Conformity of design and size is truly remarkable, and perhaps some scholar will one day write a thesis on how it came about that joynt stools, whether they were made in Northumberland or Sussex, East Anglia or Cornwall, seem always to be of the same configuration.

Just as the bed was the prime status symbol of the house, the babies of wealthy families were accorded quality furniture in the form of cradles. As with any other piece of furniture of this date, the example shown is of panelled construction, and each panel is carved with a lozenge which incorporates many familiar geometrical motifs and 'S' scrolls. The stiles, rails and muntins are pegged, as one would expect, and the head rail at the back is initialled I.L. and dated 1651. It is thought that many of these cradles had rockers, which could be removed so that the cradle would remain stable when required. A plank of wood could then be inserted between the two wings of the cradle to form a seat. By substituting the seat plank with another piece with a hole cut in it, and placing a chamber pot beneath, the cradle became a miniature commode. The purpose of the trap door now becomes apparent!

The finials at the top of the stiles at the head end show where a lathe was used to turn them, and are of very truncated form. Those at the foot are longer but crude and were for holding the cradle in order to rock it. The base boards are all loose, allowing them to be removed for cleaning. It is most rare for the rockers to be original and indeed the present example has replacements, although at first one might be forgiven for thinking them original. Certainly the colour and type of wood is comparable to the rest of the piece; however, at the tail end the

64 Oak cradle dated 1651, with panels of lozenge carving.

65 Detail of the rocker of the cradle in Plate 64. Note the modern pegs and the holes made by a handle and also the rebate where a lock was once.

upper edges are almost razor sharp and there is no edge in the rest of the piece which bears comparison to this sharpness.

On careful examination the rocker reveals marks at the head where handles have once been, indicating without doubt that this piece of wood was once a drawer front. This does not in itself make the rocker not genuine, as it is known, particularly in the seventeenth century, for joiners to use second-hand timber for making a piece. The mark left by the handle, however, is of the type not used before about 1750 – a hundred years after the cradle purports to have been made – and it is for this reason that one must doubt the rocker's authenticity. The condition of the cradle leaves something to be desired. The colour is rather grey and uninteresting, and the carving is not of enormously high quality. Comparison of the depth and crispness of the carving with that of the buffet illustrated in Plate 52 will leave no doubt about the bold and surehanded carving of a superior craftsman on the buffet – on the cradle the execution is weak and hesitant. The channel moulding on the rails is good, but the feel of the whole piece suggests it was country-made, with no pretention to great quality. Nevertheless the rarity of furniture of this quality and of this date is sufficient to make it a very desirable piece and much sought after by collectors. It is amusing that today cradles are most frequently used as containers for flower arrangements.

The side-table illustrated in Plate 66 measures $26\frac{3}{4}$ inches (670 mm) wide by $19\frac{3}{4}$ inches (490 mm) deep by $26\frac{1}{2}$ inches (670 mm) high. It dates from 1685-90 and is typical of that period in being 'over-hatted' – the top is considerably larger than the framework below. The top, of quarter sawn oak, shows silver

97

fleck or medullary rays and is in two planks. The ends have been cleated in order to show long grain along each side and, as befits an article of sophisticated design and workmanship, the cleats are mitred at the corners. This has resulted in the two planks parting company because of shrinkage, despite the fact that the timber was obviously well seasoned. The top also has a half-round moulding to the edge.

The frieze is fitted with a single drawer, the linings of which are thick and very crudely dovetailed. The bottom of the drawer is made of two planks with the grain running from back to front. The drawer front is a single piece of unadorned oak and retains its original gilt-brass, bifurcated drop handles, attached to the drawer with snapes – brass strips which pass through the drawers and divide in the manner of a split or cotter pin. The lock is missing and the present escutcheon is a Victorian replacement: the dirt mark left around the original escutcheon shows quite clearly.

Below the drawer and running around the frieze is a large astragal mould and the supports are barley-twist columns above vase-shaped turnings. These are good examples of the later barley-twist; ten to fifteen years earlier perhaps, they would have been thicker and with a less extended spiral. The stretcher joining the legs is of fretted curvilinear outline and is mitred at the corners. The table rests on diminutive bun feet.

The cabinet-making and the design are quite sophisticated and, when made, this piece was very much in fashion. At this date, however, quality tables were usually finished with floral or seaweed marquetry and *en suite* with a looking glass and a pair of torchères. The stretcher joining the four legs was often in the form of an elaborate cross.

Despite the replacement of one rear bun foot and the lack of the lock and its escutcheon, this table is in a remarkable state of preservation. The surface has never been scraped or re-polished, and has a fine patination.

One remarkable feature is its size, for the vast majority of tables of this design tend to be approximately one quarter as large again or bigger. This was one of the most fashionable ideas imported from France. A grand house would have an enfilade of rooms, each joining the next, and normally with two windows to each room. Between each pair of windows in the first three rooms, which were large, would be a pier, where it would be customary to have just such a table, probably in marquetry, the style closely resembling the escritoire in Plate 59. A pair of torchères would be made in precisely the same way and a mirror, in the form of a simple rectangular plate surrounded by a large convex moulding surmounted by a cresting would be hung above the table.

Up to the sixteenth century, dining tables were of the refectory type – long and narrow; the sophisticated variation on this theme was the draw-leaf table, in which the length was almost doubled by pulling two half flaps underneath each end. By the seventeenth century, eating had become a more private activity and a form of table evolved to suit a family, called the gate-leg table. This is oval, or sometimes circular, and supported on a framework of eight legs. The four immovable legs stand at each corner, while the others are formed in two pairs, each on a separate framework, and pivoting like gates between the stationary legs. The whole

structure is joined by a frieze beneath the top and a stretcher arrangement a short way off the ground.

The earliest of these tables dates from the first quarter of the seventeenth century and is of massive proportions. Occasionally the gate is part of the end legs, in which case the end leg splits in half down its length; this feature is more common on Dutch pieces and is called a split baluster gateleg. A particularly delightful type is that in which the members are made up of spiral twists (sometimes called barley twists) like the table in Plate 66. Almost invariably the uprights are turned, but it is very common for the horizontal members to be of square section and simply moulded, as in the present example, illustrated in Plate 67. The most common sizes for such tables are between 42 inches (1065 mm) and 54 inches (1370 mm), and the present example measures 48 inches (1220 mm) by 56 inches (1420 mm) when extended. It dates from the 1690s. The top has a thumb moulding at the edge and a similar moulding runs along the rule joints where the flaps meet the 'bed', the part of the top which does not hinge. The thicker the top in early gate-legs, the greater the esteem in which they are held today.

67 Unusually elegant gate-leg ·
table of walnut with turned
supports and rare carved
decoration and 'Spanish'
scroll feet, c. 1690.

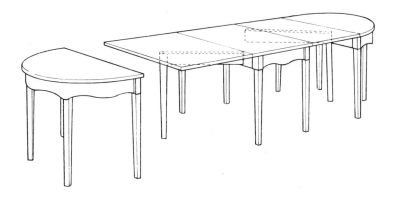

The uprights are turned and tapered, while the frieze is shaped at each end and contains one drawer. The unusual features of the table illustrated are the carved shaped panels where the legs meet the stretchers, and the Spanish scroll feet. These overhang the square section of the main body of the leg, and careful examination of the scroll feet will reveal joints where additional timber has been added. The table is constructed entirely in solid walnut of a somewhat reddish hue, with the exception of the cedarwood frieze at each end. That the cedarwood is original is without doubt because the pegs holding it in position are undisturbed and original. The majority of gate-leg tables one sees on the market today are of oak, and country made. For one to be carved in walnut is an immediate indication of superior quality. That the feet have not worn down, nor been the subject of repair, is both unusual and very desirable.

Unfortunately one leaf has been the subject of more than fair wear and tear and a strip of wood some $4\frac{1}{2}$ inches (114 mm) wide has had to be replaced. It is difficult to imagine why such a large piece of timber has had to be set into a table of this quality. Very often with gate-legs the tip of a flap becomes lost or broken, but for a piece of wood to have to be placed within the flap is almost unaccountable. It is interesting to note that when the restorer inset this piece, he had to clean the surface of the surrounding timber, and coloured the new wood in order to make it match. The restoration is no doubt a great deal more obvious now than it was when it was done, as the colour so applied has since faded, but the rest of the top, with its original surface, has retained its colour. Quite how some former owner managed to lose the drawer also seems inexplicable, but is indeed the case, for the existing drawer is quite new. Closer inspection reveals the application of stain to the wainscot oak, which gives the game away, and the suspicion is confirmed by both the crispness of the edges and the dissimilarity of the wood in the drawer front to that in the rest of the table. One would also expect the top of the drawer linings to be rounded, but they are quite square.

On tables of this nature the most frequent place to find signs of wear and tear is on the edges of the rule joints. When the flaps are in the down position, a gap will appear on the end of the join. When walking past a folded table it is easy for clothing to catch in this tapered gap, and consequently the timber may be subjected to strain and eventually split. Dealers tend to regard tops without any splits in this particular place as an unexpected bonus. Of the four corners on the present example, three have been patched, which is about par for the course.

The reader might well wonder why such a table, with all its faults, has been thought fit to be illustrated. The answer is that it is very rare to find furniture in a completely unrestored state *and* not requiring restoration. The finer the piece of furniture the more rare this is likely to be. In this particular case, the restorer has fortunately not tried to 'improve' upon the original design, but a table with half a flap missing and with a cubby hole where a drawer should be, would clearly have been both useless and ugly. The restoration effected on this gate-leg might well go unnoticed by many people, even in a good light. In bad light they might not be noticed even by an expert.

After the Civil War and the early years of the Restoration of the monarchy in the 1660s, two socially important developments took place. The first was the establishment of a form of postal system on a national scale, with a consequent increase in the number of letters written. The second was the building of a great many fine houses. These concurrent developments resulted in a piece of furniture known as a scriptor, which was also referred to by the French term escritoire. In its simplest form this item had a large panel which could be let down in the front and, when opened, rested horizontally, providing a surface upon which to write, and inside were numerous compartments, and pigeon holes in which to store cor-respondence, household accounts, bills and so on. Earlier ones were often on a stand, perhaps containing one drawer, and were either made of oak, or, in the case of the more elaborate items, were veneered with kingwood oyster veneers. Later ones employed the full range of decorative detail available at the time. The Huguenot immigration brought with it many techniques of which marquetry had perhaps the greatest influence in furniture decoration (Plate 59).

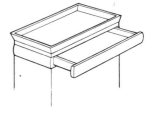

Cushion drawer construction

The configuration of this escritoire is standard; the cornice is a typical arrangement of complex cross-grain mouldings and immediately beneath is a cushion-shaped moulding which, as was customary, forms a drawer. The cushion moulding extends round the side as well as the front of the piece, and therefore the drawer linings are set well back from the edge of the drawer front. The large panel in the front folds down to reveal a symmetrical arrangement of smaller drawers, pigeon holes and a cupboard. Often the cupboard inside opens to reveal a further arrangement of drawers, and it is not uncommon to find a great many secret drawers in a piece of furniture of this type. The let-down front is secured in its opened or writing position by a folding iron stay which is bolted right through the carcase, and is inset with a leather writing surface within a very broad cross-band. The lock is not square, but rectangular, and, in common with good quality locks of that time (and indeed during the next sixty years), has four shoots when activated. Each section of the side is inlaid with an arch, a common feature, but the depiction of a Roman soldier is more unusual. The cross-banding on the ends is very broad and is further outlined with a black and white stringing. The lower section of this piece is a typical arrangement of two short and two long graduated drawers upon an ogee base-mould, and ebonised bun feet. The carcase has a half round moulding of cross-grain timber separating the drawers. The arrangement of marquetry panels is quite typical, indeed it would be most unusual to find panels inlaid in any other form.

Since very similar marquetry flowers to those shown here can be found on furniture of a very diverse nature – clocks, chests of drawers, cabinets, tables, torchères, mirrors, barometers and many more – it is possible that manufacturers sold this in ready-made panels so that the veneer layer could use them at his own discretion. One might also speculate that outworkers of the marquetry cutting trade were able to produce single flowers and leaves and that the marquetry seller assembled these flowers into the design that we see. Carnations, peonies and tulips appear to be the favoured flowers and acanthus leaves feature prominently too. Some marquetry includes ivory, both of a natural colour and stained green. However, the workings of the marquetry cutting industry are comparatively undocumented and would benefit from more research.

Chests of drawers were first made in England in the middle of the seventeenth century. Early examples had the familiar decoration of the period, namely mouldings arranged geo-metrically applied to the fronts of the drawers, and the second drawer from the top was quite deep, usually between 9 inches (228 mm) and 11 inches (279 mm). The drawers below this were usually enclosed by cupboard doors. By 1670 the doors were omitted, leaving all the drawers exposed.

The first departure from geometrical mouldings came with the use of veneers. Before exotic foreign timbers were used to any great extent, native laburnum and walnut was cut into 'oysters' and veneered as is shown on the chest of drawers of c. 1690 in Plate 69. These 'oysters' were taken from the cross-sections of relatively small limbs on the tree. At the same time it was discovered that a pleasing arrangement was achieved by putting the deepest drawer at the bottom and making each drawer upwards progressively shallower. This arrangement has been in continuous use in all better quality pieces until the present time.

To offset the 'oysters', the present example has been outlined with a cross-banding of pear wood on both the drawer

69 Oyster veneered chest of drawers, *c.* 1690, with geometric inlaid top and bun feet. The handles are replacements of *c.* 1770.

fronts and the sides. The ground wood throughout the carcase is pine. On the top the 'oyster' veneers and pear wood have been arranged in a geometrical pattern based on circles in a way that was very typical of the last fifteen years before 1700. In a better-quality piece, parts of the top might have been filled with marquetry of flowers and foliage, and the sides might have been similarly decorated and with pear wood stringing. The drawer fronts might also have had pear wood stringing or panels of marquetry to emphasise the 'oyster' veneers. The marquetry escritoire (Plate 59) shows this form of decoration, as well as marquetry panels at the side and on the drawer fronts. The similarity of thickness and drawer divides and the use of half round mouldings indicate a very similar date, but while the chest is of very good quality the escritoire is superb.

The broad quarter-round moulding of the chest's top and base has a cross-grain veneer as do the half round mouldings between the drawers. These features are common to many pieces of this quality, whether they are chests of drawers, wardrobes, knee-hole desks or any other carcase furniture. The drawer bottoms are rebated into the sides and front, and the drawers slide on the whole bottom surface; the amount of wear is minimal as the load has been spread over a wide area. The drawer linings are held to the front by coarse dovetails

105

running right to the front of the drawer, which are only hidden by the veneer (Plate 25b).

The handles are of good quality, but date from about 1770 and are merely replacements. The original handles were fixed where the inside pommel is now and they probably resembled the bifurcated drops illustrated in Plate 66. The top drawers were probably opened with a key only; the escutcheons would have been of cartouche shape, and probably engraved. The replacement escutcheons, though possibly dating from 1740, are more likely contemporary with the existing handles as they are of a design which remained in fashion for many years, indeed well into the nineteenth century. The elm bun feet, although old, are possibly not original, though perfectly in keeping with the design of the rest of the piece.

This chest of drawers represents the earliest type made in the same way as they are today – a break from the pegged stile and rail type with geometrical mouldings. It is also a very early example of the use of veneers, which indicate a craftsman working to the latest dictates of fashion. The inclusion of oyster veneers gives one the first and strongest indication of date, which is confirmed by the mouldings, timbers and construction of the carcase and drawers. The chest fulfils its utilitarian function as well today as it did when it was made and is of high, though not supreme, quality.

The chair illustrated in Plate 75 is one of a set of six. They date from about 1710 and are made of walnut, beechwood and pine. However the entire visible framework is lacquered red. The back is brilliantly coloured and embossed leather and the top rail is a shaped arch with a foliate cresting centred by a curious double cartouche. The top rail, stiles and bottom rail are all vigorously moulded with complex astragal, part of which forms the moulding which runs around the seat rails. Below the back is a pendant of carved foliage, hatching, and an inverted shell. The seat is also decorated like the back. The cabriole front legs are boldly curved with no loss of proportion for their vigour. (It is so easy for a cabinet-maker to go a little too far in the curve of the cabriole leg which then immediately loses all its appeal.) The upper sections of the cabriole are outlined with a moulded 'C' scroll, the feet are perfectly plain and pad-shaped. The back legs have a turned section above the square bottom member which kicks out in a most pronounced fashion, as one would expect of a fine quality chair. The stretcher arrangement is shaped and moulded whereas the one uniting the rear legs is simply turned.

Several points are of interest here. Such chairs are part of the important furnishings of a state room. Embossed leather, often of Spanish origin, was much sought after and highly prized, and the embossing bears a close resemblance to the decoration of silver of that time and its use as the upholstery on furniture is most rare. The framework of lacquer (a most fashionable and expensive decoration) together with the size and proportions of these chairs indicates their importance. The comparison between these and the walnut chair illustrated in Plate 72 with its veneered back, carved knee and stretchers is most interesting. One forms part of an important set of state furniture, the other is delicate and restrained in design although superbly carved and of fine quality.

This is not a judgment of monetary value, but it does point to the difference between finely crafted domestic furniture and important state items such as the one shown here.

The upper section of the bookcase illustrated in Plate 70 has a shaped mirror door flanked with a pair of pilasters, the heads of which are carved with acanthus, egg-and-dart, and scrolls – an elaborate variation on the Ionic column. The mirror plate has a border of contrasting feather banding and the cornice has a simple cavetto moulding. The door opens to reveal two bookshelves which are adjustable. The lower section has a fall outlined with a double half-round moulding. The centre of the fall is quarter-veneered and is cross-banded and feather banded; it also has a moulding to support a book along its lower edge. It opens to reveal a stepped interior and a recess or well below the writing surface. A pair of lopers support the fall, and below them is a waist moulding. The carcase contains two short and two long graduated drawers outlined by a double half-round moulding on the carcase. The drawers are further outlined with herringbone inlay, and the handles are the engraved plate type with matching escutcheons. The whole piece sits on bun feet beneath a moulding. So far, one might well imagine from the illustration and description that it dates from about 1710, but let us examine the construction in detail.

First, it is correct for the looking-glass plate to be bevelled, but the angle of the bevel is too great. One should scarcely be able to feel a bevel on early eighteenth-century glass. The star cut in the middle of the glass is not quite correct in style for this period, though the idea is right. Also, on putting one's finger nail to the surface of the mirror, the reflection is a full $\frac{1}{4}$ inch (6 mm) from the object, indicating plate glass at least $\frac{1}{8}$ inch (3 mm) thick, too much for a Queen Anne mirror. Looking inside, the

70 A burr ash and walnut bureau bookcase of early eighteenth-century design.

construction is largely correct, but the piece of wood which secures the mirror in place is held with machine-made screws, not hand-made like those of the eighteenth century. The lock is quite original to the door and is stamped 'improved four lever' and is also held with machine-made screws – all decidedly twentieth century!

The inclusion in the design of a bookrest on the fall indicates careful attention to a design of about 1700, but on a genuine piece the cross-banding and the feather banding inside it would be shaped to follow the outline of the bookrest. The lock on the fall of an eighteenth-century bureau seldom measures less than $3\frac{1}{2}$ inches (89 mm) across, while the present example is $2\frac{1}{2}$ inches (63 mm). The handles are a very good imitation of the early eighteenth-century design, but they are marginally too thick and the pommels are secured with machine-made brass nuts. On looking at a modern lock from the back, all one can see is a brass plate, inside which are steel wards which mate with the shape of the key. On eighteenth-century locks, however, the fixing of the steel wards into the brass plate can be seen from the outside. They are not visible on this example (Plate 29).

The use of burr ash as a timber in this piece was an intelligent variation of the burr walnut theme, and certainly lends an air of authenticity, but it is quite definitely a reproduction, and on even closer examination pretends to be nothing else.

Much attractive oak furniture was made after around 1700, but mostly in country areas where craftsmen had not so much ability to make finely crafted joints and were usually without an appreciation of the finer points of design. London cabinet-makers at this time, even by the 1680s, were concentrating their attentions on walnut, which could easily be cut into veneers. Oak furniture was more crudely made and is therefore considered of second-rate manufacture; for this reason oak collectors tend to dismiss anything after about 1700. The sideboard illustrated in Plate 71 may, however, be considered worthy of attention, although it was made as late as 1720. Its size and proportions are delightful, measuring 56 inches (1420 mm) long, 18 inches (460 mm) deep and 30 inches (760 mm) high. It is made entirely of good, dark honey-coloured oak, and where it has not been polished it shades to much darker tones, most noticeable round the ogee (or onion) arches.

The three drawers are thickly lined in oak, with rounded top edges to the linings and with broad, but crude, dovetails. These suggest a date of about 1720, as do the handles which are quite

original (Plate 25c) – this categorical statement is based on the fact that there are no indications in the woodwork that other handles have ever been present. The vase baluster turnings of the legs could be mistaken for a seventeenth-century design, and the mouldings on the drawer edges, beneath the top and round the platform base would be reason to strengthen this argument. The rails and muntins are held by single pegs, and the top is also pegged. However, there is no doubt at all that the drawers are original to its construction and the piece must be dated to its latest feature. The ogee arches between the column supports were also much in vogue in the 1720s and, although it was common to shape the frieze of a sideboard in the seventeenth century, this particular design is eighteenth century. Such pieces were also made with upper sections of shelves, when they were called dressers, and were intended for the display of pewter and pottery. One should look for marks where this section might have been fitted.

Comparison between this piece and the sideboard illustrated in Plate 88 shows how little the design of such objects changed in country areas. One can easily imagine this piece with cupboards below the drawers instead of turned legs and a platform shelf. By the same token one can imagine the sideboard in Plate 88 as standing on legs and a platform base instead of the cupboards. It is interesting that one is able to date these pieces by constructional detail.

The walnut chair illustrated in Plate 72 dates from about 1715-20. The back 'moves' in every conceivable direction to combine aesthetic line with anatomical proportions (Plates 37, 38 and 39). The re-entrant corners are a typical decoration of the period, but the scrolls add a touch of individuality and are repeated on the shoe. The splat is a development of the

72 Walnut side chair, c. 1715–20.

inverted vase, and the front surface, which forms the most important piece of show-wood in the chair, is veneered – a feature found only on the finest examples. The seat rails are quite plain and straightforward and it is interesting to note that pegs have been omitted, indicating the craftsman's confidence that he could break away from former techniques and place his trust in the new glues and the quality of his mortise and tenon joints.

The front seat rail is shaped on its lower edge to complement the curves of the back and the rear seat rail is numbered VIII. Quite correctly, this has been done with a chisel, and each stoke is approximately $\frac{5}{8}$ inch (15.8 mm) long. Chairs were always numbered in this fashion, and should one find numbers or joints numbered with Arabic numerals, then either they were made at a later date, or the chair has been taken apart and reassembled. The front legs are cabriole and the knees are carved with a curious stylised shell, from which hangs a flower and three spots. The feet are in the form of a shoe, and are commonly known as Manx feet. It should be noticed that carving on the knee of a cabriole should always stand proud of the general shape. Plain cabriole legs have been often decorated since they were made, and to do this the carver has to cut into an existing shape. When assessing the originality or otherwise of such a leg, it is important to check that it does stand out from the general shape of the leg or foot.

The centre stretcher here has a ribbed motif, echoing the shell carving on the knee. The rear legs move and swell to accept the stretchers, which must therefore have been an

73 *Opposite*: Unusually finely crafted walnut tallboy, incorporating a secretaire drawer and the sun-burst motif, *c.* 1735.

74 The numbering on the rear seat rail of the chair in Plate 72. Each stroke of the roman numerals is always made by a single blow of a chisel struck by a mallet.

75 *Left*: One of a very important set of six lacquer chairs with embossed leather upholstery and gilt embellishments, *c.* 1715.

76 *Below*: Detail of Plate 85. Note the general colour and variety of grain of the walnut. Pieces of veneer can easily become separated during the gluing of the burr figures to the ground wood, and it was therefore sometimes necessary to patch. Two such patches are visible in the top drawer front.

77 *Opposite*: A very fine mahogany breakfront bookcase, *c.* 1760 owing much to the designs of Thomas Chippendale, and probably made by his firm.

78 Detail of a front leg of the chair in Plate 72. Note the fluency of the carving which stands proud of the surrounding leg shape.

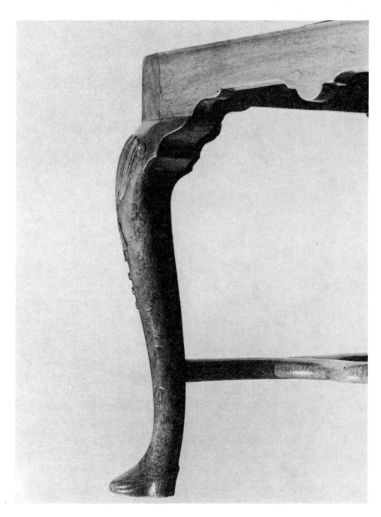

79 Opposite: Important West Indian satinwood commode, inlaid with marquetry decoration in the Neo-classical taste, *c.* 1775.

integral part of the design. In order to accommodate the upholstered drop-in or trap seat, the seat rails are rebated.

Many dealers refer to such chairs as spoonbacks, and because they are generally in walnut they are said to be Queen Anne; however, modern thinking would give more credence to a George I label. They pre-date the broader backed variety, with the top rail becoming lower and the seat rails tending to be bell shaped. A former head of department at the Victoria and Albert Museum once said that he had never seen a finer example than this chair. However, it can be argued that the comparable lacquer chairs were more highly valued when originally made, and it is not unknown for a chair of this date or later to be covered with gesso and gilded. Such a chair would be regarded as being of the highest importance, as would a chair decorated in lacquer, because of the frail nature of the decoration.

In the text accompanying Plates 72 and 75, two chairs with close similarities have already been described. The chair illustrated here in Plate 80 is of the same type, often called Queen Anne, as can be seen from the general outline of the back, the cabriole legs and the stretchers. This example, however, has neither the carved decoration, the veneered splat or the carved legs; it is constructed in solid walnut and the various members are pegged together. It is also lacking the anatomical outline of the others, and the height and width are much less generous.

The arms are perhaps the most interesting features of this chair. Arms of this design were quite unknown in 1720 when this chair was originally made, but the same type are often seen in chairs manufactured in 1800-10. If the reader can imagine the arms removed, the whole chair assumes a more realistic proportion, but even then the back is a good deal smaller than that of the chair in Plate 72. Originally this chair had a drop-in seat, but it has been replaced by a solid seat of oak, and given a loose squab cushion to make this comfortable.

The front legs also look very unfinished at their upper end, for a cabriole leg should have 'ears' to give it a finished appearance. These are fixed separately, as the cabinet-maker would require a piece of wood 6 inches (152 mm) square at least to make the whole cabriole from one piece. During the life of this chair the glue securing the ears to the leg has perished and the ears have been lost. Presumably the cabinet-maker realised that glue was not good enough for major joints and relied on pegs to keep the rest of the chair together. From the surface and polish where the ears should be, it is clear that they parted company a very considerable time ago. Nonetheless, the cabriole legs swell very delightfully to receive the 'H'-shaped stretcher. Notice how the turned section of the stretcher fits into the turned front leg, but the square back leg receives a square section of stretcher.

No part of this chair is less than 175 years old and therefore, in a strict sense, it must certainly be called antique. Whether, because it has been altered and added to during its life, it can be called 'genuine' is another matter. Certainly there is nothing fake or in any way deceiving about it, and undoubtedly the chair has a very considerable charm. It is very typical of a large number of pieces of furniture on the market today.

Bedroom furniture usually includes a chest of drawers as well as cupboards. If one chest is not enough, there are two alternatives – either to have a second chest, or to increase the height of the first chest to such an extent that it becomes virtually one chest upon another. In America such pieces are still called 'chest on chests', but in Britain they are called tallboys. They made their debut at the turn of the eighteenth century, and soon developed into the sophistication of the example illustrated in Plate 73.

As is common, the upper section has three small drawers at the top. Above them is a complicated moulding of general concave outline. The arrangement of drawers is much as one would expect in a chest of drawers, a neat gradation, increasing towards the bottom. The present example is of finely figured walnut, inlaid some $\frac{1}{2}$ inch (12.7 mm) in from each edge with the most delicate arrangement of boxwood and ebony in a chequered design. This is an elegant variation on the more usual herringbone or feather banding theme. The figure of the timber, moreover, is of such interest that it continues right to the edge of the drawer rather than being bordered with a cross-banding, which is more common.

The drawers are fitted with pierced plate handles which retain their original gilding, and escutcheons to match. It will be noted that the handles of the three short drawers on the top incorporate the escutcheon, as do the short drawers below; this is quite normal. The drawers are outlined in cock beading and are lined with finest quarter-cut wainscot oak, $\frac{1}{4}$ inch (6 mm) thick with rounded top edges. The grain of the drawer bottom runs from back to front and the drawers are flanked by a fluted pilaster column on the canted angles. The lower section is marginally wider than the top and the difference is made good on the waist with a cross grained moulding.

The lower section is decorated in much the same way as the upper, but the top drawer opens and hinges downwards to reveal a shaped secretaire interior, fitted with drawers, pigeon holes and a cupboard in much the same way as a bureau. As one would expect of such a very fine article, the small interior drawers are also lined in walnut and the linings are less than an $\frac{1}{8}$ inch (3 mm) thick. The quality of the dovetails is superb, even though they are rather widely spaced. The cupboard and drawers are inlaid like the larger drawers and the cupboard door, with its mirror, is flanked by a pair of simulated pilasters of inlaid boxwood.

The lower section is flanked by a slightly wider pair of pilasters which terminate with an ogee mould at their base, but perhaps one of the most desirable features of this piece is the shape of the bottom drawer and of the bottom moulding to accommodate it. It has been cut at its centre with a niche and inlaid in boxwood and ebony to simulate a sunburst. This motif is repeated on the floor of the secretaire drawer and is one of the most highly prized motifs on walnut furniture. The base-mould, like all the others, is of cross-grain timber, and the whole piece sits on ogee bracket feet of shaped outline.

The ends of the tallboy are well-figured walnut of halved veneers and are finished on both the back and front with cross-banding. More usually such furniture was finished in very plain timber or even in pine. It would be most unusual, however, having seen the quality of the inlays, the sunburst, the inclusion of the secretaire drawer, the ogee bracket feet and the cross grained mouldings to find an end of any less quality. In other words, the consistency of quality is total. It is when the quality varies within a piece that one's suspicions as to its authenticity are aroused.

Plate 81 shows a George II oak lowboy, or three-drawer side-table of about 1730. The top comprises three planks of quarter-cut oak, exhibiting 'silver fleck' or medullary rays. A cross-banding of walnut some $\frac{3}{4}$ inch (19 mm) wide has been let into the edge, which has been moulded. It will be noticed that the top is thinner than on earlier furniture and the moulding exaggerates this effect. The apron, or frieze, is shaped at the

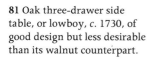

81 Oak three-drawer side table, or lowboy, *c.* 1730, of good design but less desirable than its walnut counterpart.

121

sides with a simple ogee arch (note the similarity with the arches on the oak sideboard in Plate 71), and in the front is fretted around a knee-hole and accommodates three short drawers.

When opened, the drawers reveal thin pine linings with coarse dovetails (Plate 25d); the tops of the linings are round, which is a typical feature of the period. Examination inside shows no signs of this piece ever having had another set of handles: indeed the present set look as if they have never been moved. The brass nuts which hold the pommels of the handles have not been marked by spanners or pliers, and there are no tell-tale scratches on the wood. The drawer fronts are decorated in the same way as the top with cross-banding of walnut on an oak ground, and the cross-banding is mitred at the corners. Outside the banding is a simple quarter-round or ovolo moulding which is flush with the sides of the drawers. The brassplate handles are typical of their period and it will be noticed that they are not quite central, especially in the case of the centre drawer.

This lowboy shows good design and aspects such as the cross-banding indicate that the cabinet-maker was highly skilled, although not necessarily London based. Were the piece of the finest quality it would have been veneered with walnut on all the main surfaces and outlined in herringbone or feather banding as well as cross-banding. The cabriole legs, which end in simple pad feet, would have been solid walnut and the drawer linings, while of similar thickness, would have been wainscot oak, probably with better dovetails (Plate 25e).

Some cross-banding is missing from the left-hand drawer and from the top. However, there is no visible sign of restoration. When the top is examined with a powerful magnifying glass, numerous tiny, and some slightly larger, scratches appear, but not a single one stops at the junction of the oak and the cross-banding. There is therefore no reason for doubting the authenticity of the banding.

In the finest houses, reception rooms were arranged along the exterior walls of the house, with tall windows divided by masonry divisions called piers. These rooms were for formal entertainment, suitable to the social stature of the owners of the house, and it was almost obligatory to furnish them in the prevailing fashion – namely a table at each pier with a looking glass above it. A formal arrangement of seat furniture would have been set about the periphery of such a room and these chairs would be moved as the occasion demanded. Of course,

82 One of a pair of console tables of carved and gilded wood, possibly designed by William Kent, *c.* 1740.

such furniture was rare in the first place, as only the grandest houses were so equipped.

The tables were generally large, with mirrors of corresponding proportions above them, and it is therefore a delight to see such a small pier table as that in Plates 82 and 83. The top is rectangular, with double re-entrant corners, and a moulding all round the edge. The whole table is gilded; the top is decorated in gesso with a symmetrical pattern of foliage and acorns, scrolls and strapwork, scallop shells and garya husks, all in low relief against a hatched background. The frieze is below a carved acanthus moulding and is decorated with Vitruvian scrolls, with foliage at the corners and a scallop shell in the centre. The main support is a vigorously modelled eagle carved in the round and perched on a plinth, carved in sympathy with the top with acanthus foliage, and on a base moulding of unequal guilloche, with flowerhead paterae within the circles.

The table dates from about 1740 and is the product of a specialist maker. With further research it might be feasible to attribute this to the workshops of Gumley, Grendey or Moore. Even now, fine houses often retain records of such purchases, including the maker of the original furniture. These archives

provide a fascinating source of reference for academics studying furniture, as it is sometimes possible to ascribe a maker to a piece of furniture about which very little had previously been known. In the same room as the present example (which is one of a pair), there is another pair with several characteristics in common with it. It is known that William Kent worked in the house and a design attribution to him may be plausible.

The card table shown in Plate 84 dates from about 1745, and exhibits some of the best and worst features of antique furniture. Whether its merits outweigh its shortcomings is a matter of where one draws the line and this I will leave the reader to decide. The rectangular top is of plain San Domingo mahogany and opens to reveal a baize-lined interior. Each corner projects from the rectangular outline, and is recessed to accommodate a mahogany square on which a candlestick would stand to illuminate the game. In many tables of similar design, a shallow bowl-shaped depression, about 3 inches (76 mm) deep and 2 inches (51 mm) wide, would be adjacent to

83 Detail of the top of the console in Plate 82. This elaborate decoration rendered the table quite useless for any purpose other than decoration.

124

each candlestick square, to accommodate counters or chips. Normally one either finds both candlestick stands and counter wells, or else neither, and it is rare to find the one without the other.

The apron is of cross-grained timber and accommodates perhaps the most desirable feature of the table, the concertina action (Plate 33). This allows the piece, when opened, to have a leg at each corner and to appear symmetrical. Below the frieze is a bold moulding of gadrooning (Plate 40) with a small carved motif in the middle. The cabriole legs are well drawn from a large piece of timber, and decorated at the head with carved acanthus leaves spreading from a concave cabochon. It is particularly noteworthy that the decoration is hipped, that is it extends above the cabriole leg and on to the apron. This is a most unusual feature, reserved for finest quality English furniture of this period. The ears are carved with a flame motif spreading from the inside of a 'C' scroll. The feet are of the claw and ball variety, and are vigorously carved, but perhaps one might have liked the ball to be deeper and for more talon to be visible on the end of the claw. Nonetheless there is no meanness in the design, and it is evidently original, for there is no way such a foot could be carved from the end of a pad foot.

Now for the disadvantage! Close examination will reveal that this card table has been restored. The back legs, while original, are joined by a back rail which has been replaced quite recently. Worse still, this rail has an applied gadrooned moulding, and that too has been replaced. A comparison of the crispness of carving and of the surface between these parts and the rail at the front of the piece, will be instructive. Moreover, there is a join some $1\frac{3}{4}$ inches (44 mm) from the back of the top, and this also is a replacement. The top of such card tables is always from one piece of wood and a join immediately arouses suspicion. In other words the piece has been the subject of considerable abuse at some time during its life. The back had obviously become distressed to such a condition that the restorer felt unable to repair the old wood and had to replace it with another piece of timber. The colour and surface are almost what one would expect, as a good old surface has been used, but there are no lines of dirt in the carving on the cabriole legs, or at the junction between the flat surfaces and the carving. The restorer apparently decided to strip the whole piece of furniture and to re-polish it at the same time.

Since the concertina action has not been entirely replaced, we can conclude that the table was originally made in this manner, and looked exactly as it does now. The restoration is not in the nature of an 'improvement', but the fastidious collector may not entertain the idea of acquiring such a piece. Commercially it is worth perhaps half or even less than the same article which has survived intact and unrestored. However, many people who wish to furnish their houses with good-looking furniture are unable to afford the very high prices that such items fetch when they are in an ideal condition. The present example has the same value as an unrestored piece without any carving, with pad feet, and with a plain baize-lined interior, the top supported on a gate-leg action rather than a concertina. It is for the reader to decide which is the better bargain.

In Chapter 2 it was explained that the supply of walnut had dwindled considerably by the 1720s and the vast proportion of fine cabinet-making was then executed in mahogany. The love of walnut, however, did not diminish, and cabinet-makers of quality retained stocks of their finest walnut timbers. The knee-hole desk illustrated in Plate 85 is evidence of this, for it dates from about 1745-50. The top, curiously, is of halved

85 Walnut knee-hole desk. These were made from about 1690, and the handles, bracket feet and mouldings on this example suggest a date of about 1745.

veneers – one might have expected them to be quartered – and is of relatively plain grain. The cross-banding is wide, at nearly an inch (25 mm), but the feather banding is quite narrow, less than $\frac{1}{4}$ inch (6 mm).

The chest of drawers in Plate 69 had a quarter round moulding to the top, and this design was superseded by the cross-banded edge with a small quarter round moulding above it. Usually such a moulding had re-entrant corners (page 172). This in turn gave way to the thumb moulded edge, first done in cross-grained timber and later made long-grain. The present example is a cross-grain thumb moulding veneered on to a triangular section of pine.

The drawers are arranged in a typical layout for a knee-hole desk, three on either side of a recessed cupboard, itself below a flush 'secret' drawer at the top of the knee-hole. The drawers are veneered in the finest burr walnut, outlined with feather banding and cross-banded in a straight grain timber. They are edged with a cock bead of solid walnut and are even veneered on walnut – a truly unusual feature. The drawer linings are in the finest wainscot oak, and the dovetails are of very good quality, ending in a point. The drawer bottoms are rebated into the linings with the grain running from side to side, and the drawer moves on a pair of runners glued to the bottoms. The locks are still made of iron and are almost square.

The handles are perhaps the most obvious dating feature of this piece: they quite clearly show a Rococo influence, although this is not manifest in the backplate. The escutcheons are finely cast in the Rococo style. The carcase is cross-banded throughout in straight grain walnut, but the mouldings are in cross-grain timber. Original, but somewhat archaic, are the 'H' hinges on the knee-hole cupboard, which encloses one shelf. Occasionally, but not on this example, knee-hole cupboards slide forward like a drawer so that the whole cupboard ends up flush with the drawer fronts. If the reader notices wear on the base moulding and on the sides of a knee-hole this would indicate that the cupboard does slide forward. The bracket feet are typical and are held in position with glued blocks.

Had this example been in mahogany, which it could well have been, a date of 1770 might seem more likely. However, the plain back plates to the handles, the use of cross-grained mouldings, and the use of walnut for the whole piece put the date we have given beyond question.

William Kent and Robert Adam drew on classical forms for their inspiration, but their products are never considered reproductions. No doubt occasional copies were made to make up a pair even in the eighteenth century, but the first reproductions as such were made in the nineteenth century. It has been mentioned that in the 1830s the Gothic taste was revived, and that not long after that the elaborate decoration of the Rococo was copied. The chair illustrated in Plate 86 is quite typical of the era, being manufactured around 1840-60. The interlaced, pierced and inverted vase-shaped splat does not appear in Thomas Chippendale's *Director*, written some eighty years previously, but it might easily have done so. The top rail is of the serpentine form typical of Chippendale's designs, and is outlined in 'C' scrolls and terminates in a little acanthus foliage. The stiles are well moulded and shaped, as is the back. The stuff-over seats upholstered in leather are bordered with two rows of brass studs. The legs are not only moulded, but are supported at the ears with carved brackets and sit on diminutive plinths conforming in outline to the mouldings.

How, then, is one to distinguish between a genuine chair and this example? The design is nearly perfect. The first clue lies in the brilliant polish, which is not an accumulation of waxes, but varnish. This appears to be quite original. In the Chippendale period, timber of a uniform quality was freely available, but in

86 Mahogany dining chair (one of a set of eight) of Chippendale style. The lack of stretchers and the lack of chamfering of the back of the splat are easy contrasts to the two period chairs in Plate 3.

the nineteenth century this was no longer the case, and there are members in the present example, noticeably the shoe, where stains had to be applied to match one piece of timber with another. This would not be found on an original. Chippendale-designed chairs have stretchers unless they have cabriole legs. They always have stretchers uniting the front and back legs in an 'H' arrangement, with an additional stretcher uniting the rear legs. The stretchers are not present on this example, nor are there signs where stretchers have once been tenoned into the legs and since removed.

The upholstery is original to the chair, but in eighteenth-century examples the brass studs would have been closer spaced. Still more is revealed when the chair is inverted. The

The underside of the chair in Plate 86. Note the pale edges where stain has worn away on the seat rails, the lack of upholstery marks (indicating the present upholstery is original), the triangular corner braces, serial number, and the unnecessarily chiselled ears to the front legs.

seat rails, quite correctly, are made of beech, but they are covered with stain to simulate age. One would expect $\frac{1}{2}$ inch (12.7 mm) square braces at the front and side rails as in Plate 35, but triangular blocks take their place. The seat rails are marginally thicker than in eighteenth-century chairs, and where the brackets have shrunk and the glue has come away, the original colour of the timber can be seen beneath. That the seat rails are stained is clear not only from the evidence above, but also at the places where hands have rubbed the sides of the rails – they show paler where the stain has been removed, instead of darker where dirt would would have accumulated over many years.

The present example is also stamped with a letter and a four-figure number, a practice very common in the nineteenth century, indicating the serial number of the design from the workshop from which it came. Finally there are small brackets tying the seat rails to the back legs. This, and the proportion of the back seat rail, is again incompatible with construction of eighteenth-century furniture.

On some occasions one is confronted with an object which defies any attempt to establish an obvious date. The oak sideboard illustrated in Plate 88 is a good example of this. It is exactly what it appears to be, namely three drawers below a moulded top and beneath that a pair of cupboards flanking a dummy cupboard. The whole piece has a very good colour and patina, and is supported on diminutive and simple bracket feet. It may well be thought that this sideboard was the lower half of a dresser, but an upper section would have left marks of its fixing, and no such marks exist. One may therefore take it that the piece is an entity.

There are several points worthy of note. The top is cleated, that is it has a strip of wood running along each end with the grain in the opposite direction to the main top planks. It is considered good cabinet-making to edge with long grain timber and this is one method of doing so. On the finest quality pieces, the cleat is mitred at its corners as in the table in Plate 66, but here the easy way out has been taken and the cleat runs to the edge. The moulding round the top gives the first indication that this piece of oak is not seventeenth century; it is ovolo with a further cavetto moulding applied beneath the top. This is repeated on the base moulding. The main carcase is, as one would expect, made with stiles, rails and muntins. What is noticeable, however, is that not all the rails are pegged, although of course they are mortised and tenoned. This also indicates that the piece is later than seventeenth century.

The drawers do not retain their original handles and, although the ones fitted are late seventeenth century, close examination will reveal holes where previous sets of handles have existed. Looking behind the drawer front the observer

88 Oak sideboard dating from the second half of the eighteenth century. The handles pre-date it by some eighty years.

can see three sets of handle holes, and one set is obviously original as the area cut away to accommodate the handle is the same colour as the surrounding wood. Marks where this hole has been can still be traced on the front of the drawer, as can the outline of the handle which went through it. The drawer linings are quite thick, indicating that the piece was made in the provinces, but the dovetails are quite fine which would indicate a later date.

The oval escutcheon plates on the drawers would appear to be original, and are surrounded by a very pleasant patination. The cupboards and dummies are fielded panels. This type of decoration was popular in a shaped form from about 1710-20, after which it became square or rectangular as in the present example, and remained fashionable until about 1780. In the Channel Islands fielded panels continued to be made in mahogany pieces until the end of the century. Still we have not solved the problem of date. Clearly, although the piece is made of oak, it cannot be seventeenth century, and the fielded panels indicate a date after 1720. The case is arguable, but owing to the quality of the dovetails, the type of moulding on the top, and the likely form of handle before the present ones, one suspects that this piece may date from about 1770 and that it was probably made somewhere far away from the centres of fashionable production, perhaps in Somerset or Devonshire. What is strongly borne out by this piece is that one cannot date a piece earlier than its latest original constituent part.

A great deal of eighteenth-century furniture is thought to be important because of its monumental proportions, its gilded enrichments, or the exotic timbers used in its manufacture, but the collector of English furniture does not necessarily regard these features as the sole criteria of desirability. The little cabinet in Plate 94 measures only $18\frac{3}{8}$ inches (467 mm) high, $13\frac{1}{2}$ inches (343 mm) wide, and $7\frac{1}{4}$ inches (184 mm) deep and yet embodies all the fine points that a collector could wish for. To start with, it is rare. It seems that the only diminutive hanging wall cupboards to be found are encountered in the large houses of the wealthy. They were presumably intended to house a pair of works of art of great value and obviously such objects would not be found in a humble household.

In the second place the cupboard illustrated here is quite untouched by a restorer; the wood has never been stripped, cleaned and re-polished and yet there is no open grain. The surface has a deep even and mellow shine. One would hardly expect to see signs of wear on an article such as this, and in fact

89 *Opposite*: Mahogany inlaid corner cabinet. Oval panels and stringing used in this manner often cause such a piece to be called 'Sheraton'. In fact it pre-dates his work and owes little to his design, c. 1780.

133

90 *Below*: Rosewood and satinwood secretaire cabinet with bookshelf superstructure. The quartered veneers are of rosewood and the oval panels West Indian satinwood. *c.* 1790.

91 *Opposite*: Bureau bookcase of typical proportions, made in Jersey *c.* 1800.

92 *Left*: Mahogany bracket clock by Walter Mitchelson with enamelled dials and brass mounts, *c.* 1795.

93 *Below*: An important Regency Coromandel wood centre table supported on gilt wood griffins, *c.* 1815.

94 Small hanging wall cabinet in San Domingo mahogany displaying the influence of the Gothic revival, *c.* 1770.

the mouldings and all the edges are crisp. The mouldings are well designed and somewhat uncommon, and fine quality San Domingo timber has been used in the making throughout.

A particularly interesting point to the collector is the very obvious Gothic influence. One of the great arbiters of taste during the mid-eighteenth century was Horace Walpole, whose house at Strawberry Hill near Twickenham sparked off the first of the Gothic revivals. It had a marked effect upon designers at the time and this cabinet, while being of very ordinary eighteenth-century design in many respects, has the Gothic ogee arch, clearly stamping the Strawberry Hill influence. The ogee has two distinct advantages in being both attractive to look at and useful for the display of small objects.

Thus it is that a rather small, unpretentious cabinet can have a large number of attributes that the collector wants – rarity, academic interest, surface, quality, colour, aesthetic appeal and small size, an advantage that makes its use compatible with living in modern houses.

Early on in the design of bookcases it was realised that a box-like form was aesthetically uninteresting. A solution to this problem was soon found by simply dividing the piece into sections and recessing either end in relation to the centre. This construction also had the advantage of being easily dismantled for transportation, and was called a breakfront bookcase.

The breakfront bookcase illustrated in Plate 77 is a superbly proportioned example, strongly influenced by the designs of Thomas Chippendale. The architectural cornice, with its broken triangular pediment, is delicately moulded with ogee and concave moulds above a dentil section. The broken pediment is filled with diaper lattice work and the whole cornice is closely modelled on Chippendale's 'Chinese frets'. The bookcase section has three doors enclosing adjustable shelves. The central cupboard has a thirteen panel glazed door with astragal mouldings framing the glazing, flanked by delicately fretted pilasters each with an elongated, pierced carved scroll of delightful execution. The side cupboards are not glazed, but instead are fronted with brass wire, producing a honeycomb pattern.

Below the bookcase section is a waist mould above a band of Greek key blind fret, which hides the presence of three drawers (perhaps you can see the key holes). Below this again are three cupboard doors with the centre conforming to the cupboard above, being flanked with a pair of blind frets. The cupboard door itself is a shaped, fielded panel with well-chosen quarter veneers and cross-banded on the bevel. The corners set into the fielded panels are outlined with another 'Chinese fret', and this cupboard is flanked in turn by a pair of similar cupboards decorated in the same fashion. The whole is on a plinth of conforming outline moulded on its upper edge.

Perhaps this piece has everything that a connoisseur of fine furniture could wish for: small size, elegant proportions, (they are anything up to 20 feet (6 m) long – this one is less than 6 feet (2 m), superb craftsmanship, and imaginative use of timbers. The condition is exemplary, with splendid patination and surface – the bookcase has always been well looked-after – yet it still betrays signs of its age: for example, the waist mould is slightly scratched where the door has opened over a piece of grit. There are slight indentations where the occasional foot has marked the plinth. These very minor points in no way detract from its prodigious appeal to the collector.

If the chest of drawers illustrated in Plate 95 were to appear in a catalogue compiled by one of the auction houses, it might well

95 Mahogany chest of drawers of Lancashire origin, with Cuban mahogany matched veneers, and with brass swan neck handles, c. 1770.

be described as follows: 'An early George III mahogany chest of two short and three long graduated drawers, the top well figured and with a moulded edge, the drawers with cock beading and original gilt brass swan-neck handles, resting on a shaped moulding and ogee bracket feet. 45 inches (1143 mm) long, 32 inches (812 mm) high, 22 inches (558 mm) deep. Circa 1770.'

Throughout the eighteenth century a considerable number of chests of drawers were made. The overall configuration remained almost unaltered, but the *minutiae* of construction and points of finishing followed the trends of fashion prevalent at the period in which they were made. Early eighteenth-century chests, for example, had half round mouldings on the carcase (Plates 59 and 69), while mid-eighteenth-century ones had cock beading on the drawer edge (Plates 73, 85). Early bun feet gave way to later bracket feet, and so on. With rare exceptions chests of drawers came in three shapes: the straight, the bow front and the serpentine front (in the same order of difficulty to make and held today in a corresponding degree of

esteem). While the crudest serpentines have straight sides, better ones have canted corners, and it is this feature that lends itself to still further improvement and embellishment. The canting may be fluted or, even better, fluted and reeded like the leg of the Pembroke table (Plate 104) and the corner of the tallboy (Plate 73), and later examples are sometimes inlaid with boxwood to simulate fluting; but the most desirable are those carved or inlaid with foliage, fruit, flowers or other Rococo motifs.

Sometimes the two short drawers were substituted by one long one, and sometimes above that were slides, either for writing or (supposedly) for brushing clothes on. Another variation was the inclusion of fitments in the top drawer to provide the requisites of writing or dressing (considered by some collectors to be a bonus). In such cases the top drawer can be fitted with a ratchetting mirror, powder boxes, compartments and so on, whereas the writing drawer will be fitted with a writing or reading slide and stationery divisions, ink wells and pen trays.

The desirability of chests of drawers depends on several factors. First is the proportion; chests of drawers not more than 32 inches (812 mm) high are considered suitable for reception rooms, whereas if they are higher than this they are thought to be made for bedrooms. The most valuable chests of drawers are very narrow, say 24 inches (609 mm) to 32 inches (812 mm) wide; but anything on the upper limit or larger tends to make a chest less wanted because these too are assumed to be for

Straight

bow

serpentine shapes

bedrooms. However, if the width exceeds 44 inches (1117 mm) and the piece is lower than 34 inches (864 mm) it will suddenly fit into another category and be called a commode. This is merely an adaptation of the French word and has nothing to do with the cupboard containing a chamber pot, called by the same name.

The example illustrated dates from around 1770, and has unusually wide proportions for a straight-front chest of drawers. The drawer linings are of oak and the handles retain their original gilding. The mouldings are good and crisp and, apart from the shrinkage in the sides, it is in an unusually good and unrestored condition. The drawer fronts are veneered with well chosen, matched veneers, as is the top. This is a desirable item as straight fronted chests of drawers go, but had it been 6 inches (152 mm) taller and broader it would be considerably less valuable, worth perhaps 80 per cent less.

The chest of drawers illustrated in Plate 98 is an example of the quaint and amusing in the study of English furniture. It has

98 A quaint mahogany chest of drawers, which, viewed from the top, is rhomboid in shape, *c.* 1770.

some similarities with the chest illustrated in Plate 95: the handles and mouldings are almost identical, and it was made at much the same date. Where the other is classically conventional in its arrangement of drawers and proportions, however, the present example shows the height of individuality. The whole chest is rhomboidal in shape. The top is oak and has a hinged compartment opening only with a key. It is calibrated in inches at its left-hand end – whether this feature is original is impossible to say, but it has certainly been there for most of the chest's life. The compartment revealed when the lid is opened is only 2 inches (51 mm) deep, but it slopes, being deeper at the back than at the front.

The carcase is of pine on the right hand side, and of mahogany on the left, while the drawer fronts are well-figured Cuban mahogany lined in pine and with fairly coarse dovetails. The cock beading is of the simulated scratched type, being merely an incision in the drawer front. To conform with the shape of the piece the drawers have to slide out and up, because of the wedge-shape of the top compartment. The moulding above the shaped bracket feet is typical of the 1770s as is the half round

99 Detail of the top left hand edge of the chest. Note the calibrations, the scratch beading and the detail of the handles. Such precision is not found in reproduction handles.

moulding that edges the top. Had this piece been of fine London production it would have had four drawers instead of three, and perhaps a brushing slide above them. However, it has an enormous charm, with a degree of sophistication which is quite unexpected, and is just the sort of thing many people today seek for their small flats and houses. Its somewhat absurd configuration and mixture of sophistication with rustic crudeness give it a unique appeal.

In the eighteenth century, just as today, one could either buy furniture from stock, or cabinet-makers would construct an object to a client's specific requirements. This chest of drawers obviously falls into the latter category, while the chest in Plate 95 may well have been in the former. It was mentioned earlier that consistency of quality should be sought, but a very fine article is occasionally made with pine sides. These are usually called fitments, and were made for alcoves or recesses, or other places where the owner knew that the pine would not be seen. When removed from its original position, such a piece is difficult to sell, and commercially minded restorers sometimes veneered the sides to enhance the value.

The commode is an important piece of furniture. It was an object of display in a state apartment or grand room, and although it will accommodate goods, it is perfectly apparent that this is not its prime function. For example the object illustrated in Plate 79 only has three drawers in its centre section as it was not necessary to store a great many objects in reception rooms; they were rooms of entertainment and display and were furnished only so as to give a lived-in appearance. With the exception of chairs and card tables etc. furniture did not have a functional role and was intended primarily to complement the architectural design of the room. It is not surprising, therefore, that commodes should be grand in proportions and concept.

The example illustrated here has a most unusual semi-eliptical top. On the edge of the top is a broad cross-banding consisting of nine rows, the principal one being 2 inches (51 mm) wide and of purple-heart inlaid with boxwood with repeating foliage and honeysuckle, referred to in its stylised form as anthemions. This broad band is outlined with boxwood and ebony and repeated again. The main ground of the top is satinwood inlaid with circular paterae, or fan medallions, of shaded boxwood. In the intervening space is a band of draped garrya husks falling in lobes and secured on its apexes with knots of ribbon. From each knot is suspended an oval medallion with a portrait of inlaid wood. At the centre is a large fan outlined with a chevron banding and centred by a curious foliate motif. The edge of the top is inlaid with a running stylised leaf motif. The frieze is of purpleheart inlaid with a most unusual band of motifs of heart-shaped stringing enclosing an anthemoin and tied to the next heart with a circle. The frieze contains one drawer fitted with brass knob handles retaining their original gilding and impressed with a patera. The carcase encloses a single cupboard and is formed from three panels of West Indian satinwood outlined with broad bands of boxwood and ebony. Each panel is centred by an inlaid plaque copiously decorated and depicting scenes from classical antiquity. The stiles, which support the square tapered legs, are also panel-inlaid, and the legs themselves continue this motif, but are inlaid on their bases with etched boxwood foliage simulating the brass sabots which were in vogue with French furniture. The cupboard door encloses two drawers with mahogany fronts, brass swan neck handles and wainscot oak drawer linings.

The chair illustrated in Plate 100 may well be described as a Hepplewhite chair and dates from about 1780. The shield-shape back has a serpentine top rail delicately moulded at the edges and is inlaid at its apex with a small fan patera. The mouldings continue round the remaining shape of the shield and its supports. The radiating splats are decisively modelled with a wheat ear above a husk, carved stylistically, and they radiate from a half sunflower. The side seat rails are distinctly bowed, enabling the front of the seat to be of generous proportions while the back can be delicate. The front seat rail is similarly bowed to complement the shape. The square tapered legs are fluted below and reeded at the top, and finish in diminutive spade feet. One would expect, on looking underneath the chair, that the seat rails would be beechwood – as in fact they are; they are united by braces.

This chair follows very closely the designs of George Hepplewhite, but not closely enough for one to be able to attribute the design directly to him, although there is certainly a very strong influence. On examining the back of the chair the stiles, the top rail and the outline of the shield are well chamfered in order that they may present a slight profile when viewed from an angle. The same has not been done on the splats which are already thin, though this may have been done had the example been twenty years earlier when the splat would have been cut from a piece of timber twice as thick. The surface

100 Mahogany dining chair with shield-shaped back carved and inlaid, and the stuff over seat supported by square tapered legs, carved and ending in spade feet. The design owes much to George Hepplewhite and dates from about 1780.

and patination leave nothing to be desired on the front, and there is a modicum of darkness where the chair would not have been polished in the ordinary course of household cleaning, but the main surfaces glisten with a warm brown mahogany colour. The back of the back shows several shades of a darker grey where, although the chair has been dusted, it has not been polished. As for wear and tear, there is a slight rounding of the back of the back legs and the front of the front legs, but almost none on the side and certainly none on the inside side edges. The chair has been recently upholstered, but the arrangement of brass studs on the lower edge of the seat rail conforms with contemporary practice, and in fact when the author saw the chair before it was upholstered this arrangement of brass studs was quite clear from marks in the seat rails. It was also considered correct to have a second row of studs at the top of the seat rails and sometimes a geometrical pattern at the head of each leg. The Americans who made similar chairs sometimes arranged their studs to simulate drapery.

During the middle years of the eighteenth century, a number of fine corner cupboards were made as well as some of tolerably good quality. They often had fluted pilaster columns on the sides and usually had panelled doors without glass – called in the trade 'dead', or 'blind', doors. Yet for a reason that has eluded everyone, to my knowledge, corner cupboards made in the latter half of the eighteenth century are usually poor quality. Plate 89 is the exception that proves the rule, as it dates from about 1780 and exhibits the finest craftsmanship of its time.

The swan neck pediment terminates in circular paterae. The scroll on the pediment, too, is composed of a convex moulding with a broad band of sevenfold stringing. The finials when viewed individually look abnormally tall, but viewed from below they assume a much more natural proportion. The upper section of the cabinet comprises one large door. The stiles and rails are very narrow considering the width of the piece, and on both edges are outlined with cross-banding flanked on either side by boxwood and ebony stringing. The glass panels are of rectangular outline, except the top three which are lancet-shaped, and all the glazing bars are faced with a cross-banding similar to the stiles. The glazing bars are correctly made in that they run approximately $\frac{1}{8}$ inch (3 mm) into the stiles and rails when seen from the inside (Plate 30). The door is flanked by a chequered stringing, and the same stringing, cut in half, forms oblong and oval panels in the sides.

The door opens to reveal four shelves, the lowest one being the bottom of the cabinet top. The shelves are elaborately shaped and are made of mahogany, as is the back – a most unusual feature. Running round the perimeter of the inside of the cupboard is a dust stop fillet, approximately $\frac{1}{2}$ inch (12.7 mm) wide, again outlined with chequer stringing and finished attractively with moulding. This latter feature is very rare. The waist mould is approximately the reverse of the cornice and is part of the lower section into which the top sits. Just below this is an arrangement of three drawers, faced with veneers and cross-banding to match those of the door. They are lined with

101 Detail of Plate 89. Note the complexity of the cross banding and stringing lines, the crispness of the mouldings, the evidence of former handles, the construction of the cupboard door (one open and one closed in the photograph), the shaping of the shelf and the fillet inside the cupboard door to prevent dust entering.

Honduras mahogany and the bottoms have grain running from back to front – a usual feature for a piece made at this date. The linings of the flanking drawers taper on their outside edge, to conform with the outline of the cabinet itself.

Although the knob handles are contemporary, they are not original and marks can be seen surrounding them where other handles have been. Below the drawers is a pair of cupboards enclosing one more shaped shelf. The doors, while appearing flat on the outside, reveal a panelled construction when opened. They are veneered with quartered timbers outlined like the drawers and the door above, and centring on a figured oval outlined with further chequered stringing. The base moulding is cavetto and the whole piece stands on shaped bracket feet, but it will be noticed that even the base has a small amount of shaping. The cabinet-maker has selected his timbers most carefully throughout, and has veneered them in such a way that maximum advantage is taken of the fine quality woods he used.

Plate 102 illustrates a mahogany table with two flaps. One flap is supported by a gate (or fly) leg, while the other is shown in the

102 An unassuming but quite genuine mahogany dining table, *c.* 1780-90. The utilitarian and pleasant, if not exciting qualities, contrast with some of the greater productions in the other illustrations.

folded position. The top is composed of three planks with a rule joint between each; the edge is unmoulded and quite unadorned, as is the frieze; and the legs are square, unmoulded, and not even chamfered on the inside edge. The fly leg hinges at a knuckle joint (illustrated on page 59), a method used in a great many card and dining tables of the period. The mahogany is fine quality San Domingo timber, of good grain and colour, simple figure and excellent surface, being quite undisturbed. This table measures 42 inches (1067 mm) by $21\frac{1}{2}$ inches (540 mm), and 63 inches (1600 mm) when extended, and provides seating accommodation for six, eight, or even ten people, depending on the proximity of the diners. There are no visible signs of restoration or repair and with all these features one might be excused for feeling that here was a fine and valuable antique – but here the praise must stop. The piece may not be complete.

Superficially this table seems a fairly typical example of those which originally would have had two additional semi-circular tables, each of identical width and standing on four similar legs, which would have been placed at either end producing a surface some 8 feet (2.4 m) long. Each of these ends might have had an additional flap to extend the table to a total of some 11 feet (3.35 m) long, or one flap might have been omitted. A further alternative is that there might be one or more tables identical to this example fitting between the two half-round (or possibly D-shaped ends), producing a table anything up to 25 feet (7.6 m) long. What might have happened to the remainder of such a dining table can only be a matter for speculation, but perhaps the ends were used as side tables or pier tables and, when this part was sold, the owners did not realise there was more to it than met the eye.

The give-away features that this was part of a larger table would be brass clip holders set in the undersides of each flap, and tongues and grooves in the ends, in order that the table may locate with the other sections. However, these brass fittings do not in fact exist and the undersides of the leaves show no signs whatever of having had any clips or catches. Nor have these been removed by shortening the leaves, for the ends (without tongues or grooves) have an original surface. Here, then, is a Georgian mahogany dining table with simple, unpretentious qualities, surprisingly a complete entity in itself, providing utility, originality, and a very pleasant colour and surface. The timber and square tapered legs date it to about 1780-90.

Another item of furniture beyond the means of most collectors is a set of library steps. Large houses usually contained a library of proportionate size and some books would be perhaps as much as 20 feet (6.1 m) from the ground. It was therefore necessary to equip the library with a means of reaching books on the top shelves. Library steps were developed for this purpose, and they took a great many forms. Sometimes they were disguised as other pieces of furniture, say a table, in which case perhaps a drawer would pull out and pivot about its far end to reveal a set of treads; there was also a variety which, when folded, formed a chair. Examples of these can be seen in National Trust collections and other houses open to the public.

In grander houses, library steps were a piece of furniture in their own right, and the example illustrated here is typical, though not the most grand. It is a straightforward flight of four steps and its configuration can be perfectly well seen from the photograph. The whole is made out of well-chosen San Domingo mahogany, and each tread and other members are cross-banded in tulip wood, with boxwood and ebony stringing on every side. The landing is quarter veneered and similarly cross-banded and centred with an oval satinwood panel, again cross-banded. The landing is bounded by a gallery and hand rail of most delicate and diminutive proportions. More grandiose sets of library steps than the example illustrated here were made with two flights of steps meeting on a landing, and were sometimes fitted with a seat and with a

reading desk so that the user could consult a volume without having to descend. Those illustrated here date from about 1785. This date cannot be accurately deduced from the outline or design of the piece, but is suggested by the decorative detail – note the similarity of the inlaid veneer on the landing with the door fronts of the secretaire illustrated in Plate 90, or the door of the corner cupboard in Plate 89. The same could be said of the arrangement of cross-banding and use of boxwood and ebony stringing.

Library steps like this example serve to indicate both the thoroughness with which a room was furnished and also the consideration that was accorded the original owner – note the quality and degree of care which was lavished on these pieces. One would not expect to find a set of library steps of anything other than fine quality as they were only made for houses with rooms of sufficient height to merit their use. One should therefore regard library steps of bad quality with considerable suspicion.

Many tables made in the eighteenth century have a simple top supported on four legs with a frieze below containing one or more drawers. When such a table has flaps on the long side and a drawer on the short side, it is called a Pembroke table, and Plate 104 illustrates such a piece. A few tables of this variety were made in the 1740s although they are most uncommon, but they were made in abundance from about 1770 onwards. The present example dates from shortly after that time, say 1775, and has a top of serpentine outline. Some people call such tables Butterfly tables, because of the shape of the top. The figure in this one is most unusual, hardly a roe figure, but most reminiscent of the pattern left by the tide-washed sand, or perhaps mackerel sky. The frieze contains one real and one dummy drawer, the former being lined with mahogany approximately $\frac{1}{4}$ inch (6 mm) thick and with the finest of dovetails. The edge of the drawer is cockbeaded, again very finely. The drawer front is veneered with the same timber as on the top and is fitted with a pair of handles formed as three interlocking 'C' scrolls. Tables as well made as this have the dummy looking so like the drawer on the other side that it is difficult, and sometimes even impossible, to tell the difference; even the key hole is simulated. As a result of this the unyielding dummy drawer often has its handles lacking where numerous attempts have been made to pull it out. This table

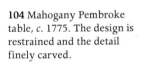

104 Mahogany Pembroke table, *c.* 1775. The design is restrained and the detail finely carved.

105 The top of the Pembroke table in Plate 104, showing the highly figured Cuban mahogany and gentle outline.

has obviously passed through caring hands as the handles are all original. The legs are square and tapered, but like the chair illustrated in Plate 100 they are reeded and fluted. They terminate in spade feet beneath which are brass box casters retaining their original rollers made of leather, and are headed by finely carved floral oval paterae, crisply executed (Plate 36).

One or two things are worth noting here. Firstly, the author finds the restrained outline of the serpentine top delightful although other people will prefer a bolder outline. Usually the top of such a table is moulded, this example however has an unmoulded cross-banded edge – a delightful conformity to the restraint used elsewhere. The top is of a greyish tan and has never been stripped or repolished, and it has one or two minor stains – the result of fair wear and tear. Again the author considers this is acceptable, but this is a matter of personal opinion. It is the tendency amongst experts now to allow such pieces to remain in their present condition, rather than undertake the wholesale cleaning and repolishing which was carried out by dealers earlier this century.

Plate 90 illustrates a lady's secretaire cabinet, and is the epitome of the refined design that is a feature of the last twenty years of the eighteenth century. The upper section consists of three shelves, the lower one being almost integral with the cabinet below. They are of Brazilian rosewood of a rare restrained figure, the edges are cross-banded and outlined with boxwood stringing as is the gallery over the top shelf. The brass supports are gilded and are headed by urn-shaped finials. It is perhaps worth noting that only the finest quality wood could be used to produce bookshelves of such thin proportions. The lower section has a drawer simulating two drawers, which is decorated on the outside with quarter veneered rosewood with oval panels of satinwood outlined, as is the whole drawer, with tulipwood cross-banding and boxwood stringing. Inside is a simple, neat and symmetrical arrangement of drawers and pigeon-holes veneered with satinwood. The front of the drawer lets down on brass quadrants to reveal a leather writing surface. Beneath the drawer is a pair of cupboards enclosing two mahogany shelves, and the cupboard doors are inlaid in precisely the same way as the drawer front above. Both the doors and the drawer are flanked by panels of satinwood of very stripy-figure outlined with a fine stringing. The whole piece sits on diminutive square tapered legs.

A comparison can be made between this piece and the commode in Plate 79, to which it is the ideal complement and which hardly betters it in importance and quality. The workmanship is superb throughout: the stringing lines are very fine, the matching of the timbers perfect, and the use of wood is most imaginative. It has both elegant proportions and utility. In fact it represents a great many of the attributes that a collector may wish for in forming his collection. Unfortunately pieces like this, in this condition, are most uncommon, and because so many people are looking for them their price is very high, if and when they appear on the market.

By 1780 bureau bookcases had been largely superseded by secretaire bookcases. However, the bureau bookcase illustrated in Plate 91 is an exception to this rule, dating from about 1800, and is worthy of note in many other respects. The upper section has a pair of doors with thirteen-panel glazing. The glazing bars are capped with astragal mouldings, which also run round the whole frame and are repeated on the dust mould (the overlapping moulding between the two doors to stop dust entering the shelves). The doors are cross-banded, with mitring at each corner, and they enclose three shelves made of pine, veneered with purple-heart on the front edge and outlined with boxwood stringing lines. The cornice is cross-banded and inlaid with a bee in an oval medallion in the centre, in much the same way as other pieces of furniture are inlaid with shells or symmetrical paterae. The moulding above is of typical outline for a cornice of this date, and also incorporates a band of inlaid zig-zag white lines on a black background.

If one catches the light against the glass in any of the panes, a very irregular reflection is produced indicating that the glass is hand blown and not of modern manufacture. On examining the inside of the doors, the very narrow glazing bars – less than $\frac{1}{8}$ inch (3 mm) – are found not to be flush with the inside of the doors, a most unusual feature (Plate 30). This means that the glazing bars do not show the rebate in the stiles and rails as one would normally expect.

With all bookcases and china cabinets, the left-hand door is normally secured by two bolts. Each bolt is of gilt brass and rebated into the opening edge of the door. The top bolt is normally longer than the bottom bolt because very often the top of a door is as much as 8 feet (2.4 m) above the ground, whereas the bottom bolt can be reached easily. Once the left-hand door is secured, the right-hand door is made fast against it with a lock. Usually the left-hand door is fitted with an escutcheon or key hole to match the right-hand, but this is for decoration only. The present example has a lock of brass and is rectangular; one can see the steel wards showing through the back of the lock which is rebated into the stile and held with steel screws. The key holes are the skeleton outline type and made of ivory.

The middle section has a fall supported on a pair of lopers and when opened reveals a symmetrical arrangement of pigeon-holes and drawers fitted with their original ivory knobs, as are the lopers. There is a recessed area fitted with baize for writing, and the flap has brass hinges set some 4 inches (102 mm) in from the edge.

Below this arrangement are four long graduated drawers, outlined with cock beads and with ivory skeleton key holes. The handles are oval brass with turned pommels and back plates impressed with agricultural trophies of a wheatsheaf, sickle and vine leaves. These retain their original gilding in a bright state, but the bails, while clean, are lacking their gilding for the most part because they experience the most wear. The carcase is cross-banded between the drawers, which in turn matches the decoration on the edge of the fall. The base moulding, a simple step and a cavetto, repeats the moulding on the top, and the whole piece rests on straightforward bracket feet.

I have already said that this piece is remarkable in several ways. First, the top quite obviously belongs to the bottom, which is not true of a great many bureau bookcases. Here the ivory key holes and the timber can be seen to be identical in both sections, and from the matching mouldings on the base and top it is evident that the bureau always accommodated the upper section. Second, the timber has floored many experts, and until scientific aid is forthcoming one would be foolish to attempt any identification beyond 'rosewood-type'. The cross-banding on the carcase poses a similar problem. Finally, by the small details, the ivory key holes, brass plate handles and so on, a dating of 1800 would seem quite reasonable, but as already mentioned bureau bookcases had gone out of fashion by 1780 or thereabouts.

The answer to many of these problems lies in the fact that this example was made in the Channel Islands, more specifically in Jersey. The inlay of the cornice is typical of that area, as is the fact that the drawer linings are made of chestnut wood, although the drawer bottoms are made of pine and covered with a thick pale blue paper, a common practice around 1800. The height of the flap is a good 33 inches (838 mm) and, unless one uses a very high chair, writing is quite uncomfortable. It is amazing, therefore, that the feet have not been reduced in size to allow for this. Although there is one minor restoration to the cross-banding on the right-hand door, and one rear foot has been replaced, the amount of damage and wear is slight, indicating that the piece has never been badly treated throughout its life. Although there are ink stains inside the bureau, they are mostly very small and there are none inside the drawers. Some collectors would dismiss such an article as being out of period, but I leave you to draw your own conclusions as to the validity of this criticism.

Having said that bureau bookcases were not made much after 1780, and having stated that this example dates from around 1800, the reader might well ask how such a date could be set. As I have emphasised, dating can only be done from the latest original feature, and that must set the earliest possible date for the piece. Oval plate handles could date from as early as 1795, and the same could be said for the ivory knobs (perhaps five years later) and also the inlaid medallion in the cornice. But perhaps the latest feature is the shaping of the bracket feet, most reminiscent of the splayed bracket feet one associates with a date of about 1800. All these points, combined with the fact that the piece originates from Jersey (it was recently imported), make it difficult to give a date before 1800. Although this piece is provincial, the quality of the dovetails and the choice of timbers indicate that the craftsman was well aware of the best London standards.

A great many bureau bookcases are 'marriages', in other

words the top half does not belong to the bottom, and the reasons for this are quite straightforward. Many years ago bureau bookcases were considered very saleable objects and there was a large public demand for them. Their price therefore rose out of all proportion to their real worth. At the same time bureaux were relatively cheap, so dealers would buy a bureau and make, or adapt, a bookcase top to fit it. They could then sell the 'marriage' for considerably less than the genuine article to the eager home market as well as supplying a flourishing European demand. When examining a two-part piece, careful comparison of the wood used on either half is essential, and a look at the back will also show if mouldings have been altered to accommodate an alien fitment.

It is quite in order for the back of a bureau bookcase to be planked on the lower half and panelled on the top, but it is quite wrong for the top of the bureau to be polished. This can be seen when the bookcase has been removed. Other features, such as mouldings, handles, the matching of escutcheons (provided they have not been replaced) and other minutiae of detail will make it apparent if the pieces started life together. The present example passes all these tests. Occasionally the top half will overhang the back of the bottom half, as the latter had to stand away from the wall because of the skirting board. Some dealers will say this is not the case, and it has even been known for them to reduce the depth of an original top in order to conform with this mistaken notion.

A piece of furniture which was new at the end of the eighteenth century was the sofa table, a rectangular table with a flap at either end. The earlier and more attractive examples had a standard end support to the top of elegant and simple proportions: see the example illustrated in Plate 106. The top of this very good quality piece measures $36\frac{3}{4}$ inches (933 mm) by 24 inches (609 mm), by $27\frac{1}{2}$ inches (694 mm), and when the flaps are raised and supported by their lopers the top measures 59 inches (1448 mm). The present example is in Brazilian or Rio rosewood, cross-banded with East Indian satinwood and outlined with an arrangement of boxwood and ebony. The frieze contains two real and two dummy drawers so that the table looks identical from either side when the drawers are closed. Because the top is supported on its standard ends, either end of the top must be made of a substantial piece of wood which flanks the drawers, and this often has a decorative inlay.

In the present example there is a lozenge of satinwood

106 Rosewood sofa table on standard supports with a high arched stretcher and paw casters, *c.* 1800.

outlined with boxwood and ebony. Sometimes the central muntin between the drawers gets identical treatment. This example is most unusual in that it has inlay simulating the spine of a book. The standard ends, with their classic outswept legs, are joined in this instance by a high arched stretcher. On later examples this stretcher ran between the lowest point of the standard, while later still, various other complicated arrangements were made to give stability to the design. The legs terminate in brass paw casters. Had the example been slightly earlier it might have had box casters, which are, as the name implies, a simple brass box with the roller wheel beneath. The example illustrated has rounded flaps which are fairly deep, a feature considered desirable, as many flaps are only two-thirds of the depth and present a skimped appearance when they are folded in the vertical position. Sofa tables do exist with square tapered legs at each corner, even with sabre legs, but on early examples the standard end is the classical norm. By the nineteenth century, the standard end had given way to the column or multiple column support in the middle of the table above a platform base.

An essential piece of equipment in any household is a clock, and we have already shown a long-case clock in Plate 7, but a more common method of time-keeping was the bracket clock, an example is illustrated in Plate 92. It is mahogany, and stands 22 inches (559 mm) high. The top is a flattened bell shape and is mounted with brass finials and astragal mould. Below that comes a most delightfully complicated moulding on the main body of the case, which is of carefully chosen mahogany veneers on oak. The front has brass frets backed with red silk, and is flanked by a pair of canted pilasters with brass reeding above an ogee plinth. The base of the clock is brass bound below a cavetto moulding, and the whole sits on ogee brass bracket feet. The sides, as is quite usual, are fitted with shaped apertures with brass grills also backed with red silk.

This clock was, as its name would imply, originally rested on a bracket which hung on the wall. More often than not this bracket is missing, and today most people are happy to let these clocks sit on a piece of furniture.

For the horologically minded, this present example has an eight-day movement with verge escapement, chiming on the quarters. It has a pendulum adjustment dial and a strike/silent dial. The dials are white enamel and signed by 'Walter Mitchelson, London', and the rest of the dial is bright cut and gilded brass; the back plate is similarly decorated and signed inside. It is also fitted with a repeating cord which, when pulled, will strike the previous quarter and hour.

London-made clocks are almost invariably fine quality, and the case-making is, by and large, of a standard superior to that of general cabinet-making. In order to conform with the regulations of the clock-makers' company, it was obligatory for clock-makers to sign their work. As a result of this, one is able to be far more precise about the date than with other furniture. In this instance we know that Walter Mitchelson was working from 1780, and that his address was 3, Helmet Row, London.

The tripod table illustrated in Plate 107 is an example of rustic country-made furniture. The square top is of oak and has four pieces of $\frac{1}{4}$ inch (6 mm) thick oak mould round its edge and mitred at the corners to form a small raised lip. The top is pegged to the frieze which is simply a box opened at one side; the box is held together with hand-made nails and the open side accommodates a drawer with square top edges and thick linings nailed to the front which is fitted with a wooden knob handle. The column is beechwood and of simple tapered form. At the top of the column is a rectangular piece of wood which is chamfered on its end edges and canted so as to show only a small amount at each end. This is pegged to the column. The legs are of ash and slightly cabriole in form; they are of uniform

107 Country-made tripod table, *c.* 1810, fitted with a drawer, made of oak, ash and elm.

thickness and are dovetailed into the base of the column. It is very difficult to assign an accurate date, but an estimate of around 1800 will probably be not far wrong. Certainly the size and overall outline of the base, and the concept of putting a square top of this size on such a piece, is reminiscent of some of the productions of London work of the 1790s. However, the use of pegs for structural security is clearly very archaic, although this has been justified in that this article has remained in fine, sound condition since it was made, there being no signs of the restorer's hand anywhere. The colour and surface are exemplary and there can be no denying that this table has considerable rustic charm. It is also a very useful object.

There are some who may raise their eyebrows at the inclusion of such a piece in this book alongside sophisticated cabinet-made objects. Yet it is just as important to recognise the merits of this table as it is to appreciate, say, the bookcase in Plate 77. They are both unrestored examples of antique English furniture. Whereas one is grand, imposing and of aesthetic and academic interest to the connoisseurs, the other has a delightful warmth and unassuming honesty suitable for the furnishing of a modest house.

The turn of the nineteenth century saw a great revival of interest in the exotic and the East, particularly Egypt, largely as a result of Nelson's victory at the Battle of the Nile.

This preoccupation was so intense that it manifested itself in all art forms, including furniture. The table illustrated in Plate 93 is part of a suite of formal state-room furniture of considerable importance dating from around 1815. The top is of Coromandel wood with finely matched figured veneers. The edge has a broad $4\frac{1}{2}$ inch (114 mm) cross-banding within a broad diagonal banding, but otherwise the top is quite plain. The frieze consists of two cross-banded Coromandel bands underlined by a gilded plain moulding, itself supported by three fabulous griffons carved in the round with scrolled tails and each carrying on its head two counterfacing calyxes – these take the weight of the top. The platform base is of concave triangular outline veneered like the top in segments. The plinth is rounded with a knurled decoration in gilt, which is repeated on the scroll feet.

Such a piece is said to have a platform base and is seldom seen before around 1820, although it was known before then and was perhaps first mooted by Thomas Hope when he produced his book of designs in 1807. The present table is large (5 feet 6 inches, 1.7 m in diameter) and is *en suite* with a set of three console tables, one of which can be seen in the background of the picture. Like the console tables mentioned earlier such an object is very typical of the furniture found in grand state apartments in large houses. The average collector could therefore scarcely expect to acquire such a piece, nor indeed would most houses accommodate it. However examples like this help to put more commonplace furniture into its proper perspective and it can be clearly seen how such a table influenced the design of dining tables in succeeding decades. Such tables continued to be made until the second half of the nineteenth century. Construction follows the standard pattern, and the top is supported round its circumference by an apron or frieze up to 3 inches (76 mm) in depth. Usually the top is of good quality timber, oak, or even mahogany, and is, like this example, veneered with an exotic timber or a fine grain mahogany. Interesting and early examples were supported in the same way as this object, but later on a central column was used which enabled the top to tilt on an arrangement of lopers (see Chapter 4). As the tables developed so the central column became larger and more grand, becoming quite grotesque by the middle of the nineteenth century. Coromandel wood was one of a wide variety of highly decorative timbers imported from around 1800 for the next twenty years. It bears a close resemblance to Zebra wood and Calamander. The reason for the patterns on the top was simply that the tree was very narrow and therefore the pattern repeated itself at regular intervals. It is a very dense timber, taking on a glossy polish.

The box-like object illustrated in Plate 108 is a wine cellaret. The top is plain, but beneath it is an interesting and crisp moulding, and the lid has cock beading on its lower edge. It opens to reveal eight divisions designed for bottles, and one long division. The front is panelled with a double cock bead moulding and below are a pair of cupboards similarly decorated. Each panel and the top is of brilliant flame-figured mahogany, and the base moulding is simply reeded. The whole piece stands on turned feet beneath a little bracket. The quality is particularly good, and it is curious that when a piece of antique English furniture has been fitted with carrying handles, the quality is almost always good. The carrying handles in the present example are a completely typical form of a design which remained unchanged for probably fifty years or more. This fact has been known to dealers for a great many years, and occasionally a piece of furniture is 'enhanced' by the addition of handles. However, the present example has original handles and the condition is exceptional throughout; there appears to be no restoration anywhere, and none necessary. The surface is well polished and has obviously been the subject of lavish attention for a very considerable period of time.

Red wine, brought up from the cellar in a bottle carrier, would be stored in such a cellaret in the dining-room, standing at room temperature for several days. The cupboard beneath was probably intended for the numerous other accessories available at the time this piece was made, for example a punch bowl, ladle, wine taster, bottle labels and so on. A bottle cradle and coasters could also have been kept inside, though these may well have been left on the sideboard with their attendant decanters in them. But most likely the cupboard contained a chamber pot. Such an article was obligatory in any well-equipped dining room, where the gentlemen would have been confined for some time after the ladies left at the end of a meal.

Many people imagine that all antiques must be beautiful, but this piece of furniture surely proves them wrong. In contrast to the concertina card table illustrated in Plate 84, this has all the attributes a collector could wish for – originality of design, superb craftsmanship, exemplary condition – and it is functional. Nonetheless, the reader may feel that this piece is very 'boxy' in appearance and of no particularly aesthetic line.

It should be noted in passing that had the interior of this article been lined with lead, it would have been a wine cooler.

The distinction between a cellaret and cooler is that the latter is designed to contain white wine at a cold temperature. Ice was packed into the lead-lined divisions and, when it melted, the water was let out through a tap fitted below.

It has been my intention, in selecting examples of antique English furniture, to show a wide range of styles, qualities and condition. The set of chairs illustrated in Plate 109 represents the humblest form of English furniture which can be classed as genuine antique. Doubtless I will be shown numerous even more rustic examples of antique furniture, but this set of chairs will serve to make a point. The entire set is made of ash, in itself a cheap substitute for oak, but the style clearly indicates that mahogany was the fashionable ideal. Fruitwoods, particularly cherry, have a reddish hue more closely approximating to mahogany and had this been used the colour would have enhanced this design.

The backs are slightly curved, and in both directions, which is a pleasing feature. The stiles are moulded and the one concession to decoration on the top rail is a roll-over effect created by a chip being taken from the rear edge. The double bar middle rail enclosing three balls is reminiscent of Suffolk-made chairs, often called Mendelsham chairs. The seat is narrow, measuring only $17\frac{1}{2}$ inches (440 mm) wide and $13\frac{1}{4}$ inches (340 mm) deep – compare this with the Chippendale chairs in Plate 3, which are $22\frac{1}{2}$ inches (572 mm) by $17\frac{1}{2}$ inches (445 mm). The wooden seat is fixed to its rails with three nails on each side, and the marks are hidden with putty. The insides of the seat rails clearly betray the marks of the pit-saw, and the undersides are darker where hands have left dirty marks. The front legs are turned and all the legs are joined by stretchers. Two of the chairs slope very considerably and many of the seats are asymmetrical. At first, one might think this was due to the use of unseasoned timber, but in fact it is faulty chair-making. Fortunately there are six chairs rather than a smaller number, but one, while very similar, is not an exact match with the others.

Country-made furniture is usually very difficult to date accurately, but from the design of these chairs, and in particular the overhanging top rail which made its appearance at about the turn of the nineteenth century, it would be impossible to date these before about 1810. However, it is far more likely that they were made fifteen or even thirty years later than this. The chairs retain their original colour and patination, and are typical of the large quantity of genuine, if unimportant, rustic chairs available in the antique market today. While having no grandiose pretentions, they are ideal cottage furniture, and also have the considerable merit of being inexpensive.

109 Matched set of six ash dining chairs, country crafted, and of meagre proportions dating from about 1820-30.

Chapter 7

The market place

There are many people who can give advice on antique furniture and the reader should approach different authorities according to the kind of information required. The commercial aspect is catered for primarily by dealers and auctioneers, while the academic side is looked after by museum staff, lecturers and writers. Then there are other interested people who fall into neither of these categories, who furnish their homes with old English furniture – the collectors and those who have lived with good furniture all their lives and are knowledgeable about what they have. A word of explanation of each of these groups may perhaps be helpful.

The term 'antique dealer' is grossly over-used. A large number of shops which claim to sell antiques have perhaps only two or three items over 100 years old in their stock, the remainder being made up of more recent and second-hand items of varying quality and aesthetic merit. At the other end of the scale are dealers of considerable knowledge and integrity, keeping their stocks of specialised and fine quality items at expensive addresses in London, New York, Paris, or wherever. Very often the dealer discovers things unknown to the academic, and the reverse is also most certainly true. A glass dealer recently pointed out to me that green decanters are rare but green glasses are common, while blue decanters are common and blue glasses are rare. An academic is unlikely to provide such information, but a person who regularly buys and sells will soon make this kind of observation.

In Great Britain there are two organisations of dealers. First, there is the British Antique Dealers' Association (BADA) with a membership numbering approximately 500, of whom more than half are in London. These dealers tend to be specialists in their chosen spheres. Second, there is the more recently formed London and Provincial Antique Dealers' Association (LAPADA). Both these organisations will supply information concerning their membership on request, and among their number are most British dealers of repute.

When owners wish to sell something they may well choose to send it to auction rather than sell it direct to a dealer. The auctioneer merely acts as an agent for the vendors and will hold sales at more or less regular intervals for this purpose. The larger auction houses have regular sales at frequent intervals and may also have specialist sales in particular subjects. Firms with a large turnover have specialist sales as often as once a week. The London market is dominated by two firms, but the remainder are now perhaps catching a larger percentage of the market owing to the fact that these two houses charge a commission to the purchaser as well as to the vendor.

As with the leading dealers, the leading auctioneers have formed themselves into an association called the Society of Fine Art Auctioneers (SOFAA). Most auctioneers charge commission on a sliding scale varying between 10 and 20 per cent to the vendor. Where, however, the commission is charged to the purchaser as well, the vendor's commission is usually a flat 10 per cent. There are some areas in the provinces where auctioneers charge a commission to the purchaser; these include parts of Cornwall, South Devon and Lincolnshire.

Museum staff will often be most helpful in establishing the nature and date of an object, but they are bound to avoid any commercial consideration. The bigger museums have the finest reference libraries available on matters concerning furniture, silver and porcelain, and many books have been written by those who look after our national collections. For example, a considerable amount of research has been done recently by the staff of the Victoria and Albert Museum on the arrangement of furniture – the history and evolution of where furniture was placed in a room. Much work has also been done concerning the correct methods of upholstery, the way a chair is stuffed and how a bed is hung. Few dealers have this kind of information, for the number of eighteenth-century chairs to appear on the market with their original upholstery is negligible. Most such examples are either still in the houses for which they were originally constructed or else in museums. Such objects present problems commercially, since chairs covered in material which is 200 years old cannot be used for their original purpose, namely for sitting on. Nevertheless they do have an enormous value to the academic, and this example highlights the disparity of interest between dealers and museum staff.

Anyone who decided to furnish his house with, say, 'French Hepplewhite' furniture and was able to devote a considerable proportion of his energies to studying this type of furniture would soon know a vast amount about a very limited subject. It is therefore quite feasible that a person who is in no way professionally concerned with the antiques market may be an acknowledged expert in a particular field. A great many collectors have formed themselves into clubs, which operate throughout the country; and the members of these clubs meet at regular intervals to discuss and to hear talks by their colleagues and by visiting speakers. Some of these people are very knowledgeable indeed.

When buying or selling furniture, one has three options. First, one may sell privately, for example to a friend or acquaintance. If this course of action is preferred then it is a good idea to have the article valued first by an independent expert. Second, one may sell at auction. This will generally take a few weeks, or months if it is rare and of special interest and is to be included in a specialist sale, but the price achieved is the highest bid less the commission. Third, one may sell to a dealer, in which case one will normally be paid immediately, unless one sells on a commission basis. Most dealers of good repute are sufficiently jealous of their reputation not to pay too little, but the seller may well feel that more could have been achieved. On the other hand, it must be remembered that by far the largest proportion of goods sold at auction are purchased by dealers and it is unusual to buy something at auction at the top bid one is prepared to pay.

The same arguments apply when buying. Most dealers will maintain a stock of furniture which they bought at auction at prices below those which they were prepared to pay. Purchasing from a reputable dealer is probably the best way of safeguarding oneself against doing the wrong thing, but of course one will be paying a share of the profit and overheads. If the dealer is a member of BADA there is a built-in arbitration system in the very unlikely event of there being any dispute about the object. Buying from a less élite establishment may well be cheaper, but the safeguards are not there. Buying at auctions also has its drawbacks. If one is fully cognisant of the market value of the things one is interested in and knows precisely what one is about, then it may well be less expensive than buying from a dealer. One or two points, however, do emerge. Some dealers make only marginal profits and bidding one more bid than a dealer may not necessarily be cheaper than letting the dealer buy the article first and then sell it to you.

People often wonder how it is that dealers can manage to buy from each other, and the trade is often accused of escalating prices in a heady spiral. Perhaps this criticism has some validity but in practice it should be viewed in another way. There is a kind of pyramidal structure in dealing. At the base of the pyramid are thousands of bric-à-brac shops; above that, shops where the occasional antique is to be found; further up, and correspondingly fewer in number, are dealers who maintain stocks of presentable antiques; while at the apex are the exclusive specialists.

Any object placed on the market will find its own level within this pyramidal structure. Sometimes, of course, the first purchaser sells retail, but if, shall we say, a fine set of twelve Chippendale chairs were to be bought by a bric-à-brac merchant, it is unlikely that intending buyers would be looking for them in such an establishment. More likely, they would peruse the shop windows of the West End. Meanwhile, the West End dealer will not waste time searching countless thousands of bric-à-brac shops, but will call upon a very select number of shops which occasionally have more valuable or specialist objects.

The bric-à-brac merchant will be visited by dealers who buy antiques in a general way and they in turn will be visited by dealers who specialise in furniture. The chairs will therefore quickly pass through these three hands. The furniture dealer may then sell them to a provincial dealer who specialises in antique furniture and it is probably this person upon whom the West End dealer will call. Thus the chairs will find their level within the market, and it is for this very reason that it is possible to buy bargains from a dealer.

To conclude: if one knows exactly what one is about when selling, then one is best advised to go to a dealer and ask for a particular price. If one is uncertain then it may be better to risk perhaps 15 per cent commission and sell at an auction house. When buying, unless one is fully aware of values, it would be much safer to use a dealer.

It must be remembered that auctioneers receive their commission in most instances from the vendor and their allegiance must lie firmly in that quarter. Most auctioneers will proffer opinions as to how much an object is likely to make, but valuation is a most inexact science and that, together with the auctioneer's allegiance, should be taken into careful consideration, particularly with an expensive object.

Glossary

Acanthus Stylised leaf decoration, derived from classical ornament.

Anthemion Stylised honeysuckle motif, commonly used in Neo-classical designs.

Apron A downward extension below what would normally be the bottom edge (e.g. the seat of a chair or the frame of a cabinet).

Arcading A line of ornamental arches, found particularly on oak furniture.

Aumbry Medieval or Gothic cupboard, originally for storing alms, but often used for storing food.

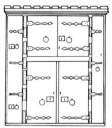

Bail A curved, hanging pull for drawers, etc., usually with a back plate.

Baluster A short pillar, often in the shape of a vase.

Banding A flat, ornamental or veneered border around a door, panel, drawer or table. In cross-banding, the grain runs at right angles to the edge; feather banding and herring-bone bandings are arranged in a continuing chevron pattern, and are normally confined to walnut furniture.

Barley twist Turning in a spiral to give the effect of a twisted column.

Beadwork A decoration on material employing brightly coloured glass beads, which unlike needlework is resistant to fading.

Bevel A slope cut at the edge of a flat surface, most commonly the angled edge of plate glass and mirrors.

Bird-cage A device used in eighteenth-century tripod tables, resembling a cage with vertical bars, which allows the table to revolve as well as tip (page 43).

Bonheur-du-jour A small, writing table of French derivation, with a superstructure containing drawers and cupboards.

Box toilet mirror A mirror mounted on a box-like frame containing small drawers.

Bracket foot A shaped foot used in carcase furniture, projecting slightly from the corner.

Bonheur-du-jour

Canterbury

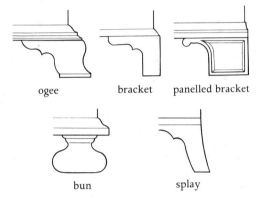

ogee   bracket   panelled bracket

bun   splay

Types of feet

Carlton House desk

Bun foot A flattened ball foot, used on furniture from the mid-seventeenth century.

Bureau A desk with a lid sloping at an angle of about 45° that folds out as a writing table, with drawers beneath.

Cabochon Domed decoration, in particular a raised oval surrounded by a rim.

Cabriole leg A leg curving outwards at the top or knee and tapering in an elongated 'S' towards the foot.

Camel-back A chair of which the top rail is shaped like a Cupid's bow; exaggerated serpentine.

Canted Obliquely faced.

Canterbury A stand with slated partitions, usually with a drawer, for holding sheet music.

Carcase furniture A general term for furniture used for storage, as distinct from chairs or tables.

Carlton House desk A late eighteenth-century writing table in mahogany or satinwood of the type commissioned for the Prince of Wales' residence, with a D-shaped superstructure of small drawers and pigeonholes.

Cartouche A tablet, normally in the form of a curling scroll or shield, to accommodate inscriptions or armorial devices.

Caster A small, swivelling wheel attached to the leg of a piece of furniture.

Channel moulding Term applied to grooved decoration of uniform cross section in early oak furniture. Usually on the inside edge of a panel frame.

Claw-and-ball A carved, ornamental foot in vogue during the eighteenth century.

Cleat A strip of wood fixed to the end of a flat surface to provide additional strength.

Corbel A supporting projection of bracket form

Countersink To cut a bevelled hole to conceal a screw head.

169

Cup-and-cover A bulbous, turned decoration, often elaborately carved and found on the legs of Elizabethan furniture. The top half is frequently gadrooned.

Davenport A small writing desk often with a moving shallow-sloped top.

Dentils A decorative row of small squares.

Distressing A euphemism for superficial damage.

Dovetail A wood joint consisting of a series of interlocking wedge-shaped projections.

Drum table A circular table with drawers, sometimes revolving.

Ear A shaped block of wood applied on either side at the top of a cabriole leg.

Egg-and-dart (egg-and-tongue) A moulding in the form of alternating ovals and wedges.

En suite Matching; part of a series.

Escritoire A cabinet on a chest of drawers or stand, with a drop front writing surface.

Fall front (drop front) The writing surface of a desk or cabinet, which has to be lowered for use.

Figure A general term for the pattern in wood.

Fillet A narrow strip of wood.

Finial A vase, spike or other ornament projecting upwards.

Fluting Ornamentation of close-set, semi-circular, concave grooves.

Fly-leg A leg without stretchers, swivelling to support a table top.

Frieze The horizontal member supporting a cornice, table or bench top, etc.

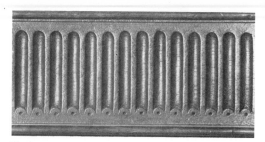

Fluting

Froe See Riving iron.

Gadrooning A decorative moulding of consecutive convex, or alternating concave and convex curves.

Gallery In furniture, a decorative low railing, usually openwork.

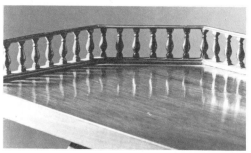

Garya husk (or bell flower) A stylised flower form, like a wheat husk or bluebell, found as carved or inlaid decoration in Neo-classical and 'French Hepplewhite' furniture.

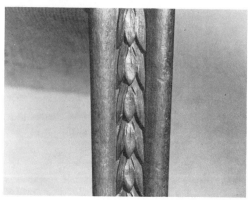

Gate-leg table A circular or oval table, with flaps supported by 'gates' which swing out from the central section.

Gesso A composition material like plaster, usually painted or gilded.

Guilloche Decorative pattern of intertwined circles, usually Neo-classical (opposite top).

Hutch See Aumbry.

Key pattern A geometrical pattern of straight lines and right angles, reminiscent of a maze.

Linenfold A carved ornamentation imitating folded cloth, popular up to about 1570.

Lining The sides and back of a drawer.

Lopers Wooden runners that support a fall front or table top.

Lowboy A table with a symmetrical arrangement of drawers round a knee-hole.

Lozenge A diamond pattern with a horizontal long axis.

Lunette A carved fan-shaped motif.

Marquetry An ornamental pattern on surfaces of furniture made by fitting together pieces of different coloured woods, shell, ivory, metal, etc., into a single sheet which is applied to the surface.

Medallion An oval, circular or square device.

Medullary rays In timber, lines that radiate outwards from the centre crossing the rings. Sometimes visible in oak.

Mitre A corner joint, in which the line of the join appears to besect the angle.

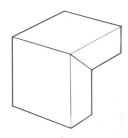

Mortise and tenon A joint in which a rectangular cavity (mortise) in one section receives the projecting tongue (tenon) of the other.

Moulding A shaped strip of uniform cross-section, sometimes carved, applied as decoration or to conceal joints.

Muntin A vertical wooden member between two panels.

Ogee An elongated 'S' shape, as found in bracket feet, arches and mouldings.

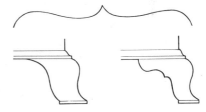

Ormolu Strictly, gilt bronze, but often applied to lacquered or gilt brass.

Pad foot A rounded foot similar to the club foot, the two terms being often interchangeable.

Panel A shaped or rectangular member framed by stiles, rails and often muntins.

Papier-mâché A material consisting of mashed paper combined with a binding agent and various other substances, which hardens when dry.

Patera A Neo-classical design, oval or round, frequently resembling a flower or rosette.

Pediment An architectural or scrolled member on the top of carcase furniture.

Pendant Any form of suspended ornament.

Pie-crust A raised shaped edging resembling a pie-crust.

Pilaster An applied decoration in the form of a flat-sided column.

Plate handle A handle with a protective backing.

Plywood A composition usually of three veneers glued together, the grain of each running at right angles to the others to prevent warping and give extra strength. Used mainly for galleries or tray rims.

Pole screen A firescreen mounted on a pole, usually with a tripod or platform base.

Rail A horizontal member in cabinet-making.

Rebate A groove (also called a rabbet).

Reeding Decoration of consecutive convex curves often seen on legs and as an edging.

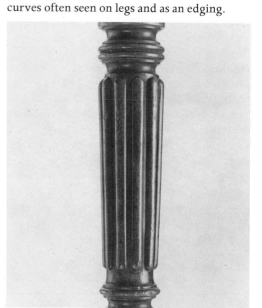

Re-entrant corner A rounded corner incorporating a cusp.

Riving iron (Froe) A medieval tool used for splitting wood into planks.

Rococo A European art style developed from the Baroque, characterised by a profusion of scrolls, shells, foliage, icicles and rockwork.

Roundel Any circular ornament.

Rule joint A stopped and quarter-moulded joint, which allows a table leaf to fold without leaving a gap.

Scribing line Mark inscribed by a cabinet-maker in preparation for cutting joints.

Scroll Curving or spiral decoration.

Secretaire Writing furniture with a drawer the front of which lets down to provide a flat surface.

Scrolling

Shield-back Chair design made fashionable by Hepplewhite in which the rail and stile form the shape of a shield.

Shoe-piece A bar at the base of a chair back into which the central splat was slotted.

Shoulder See Ear.

Slope front See Fall-front.

Splat A vertical member between the seat and top rail of a chair.

Split Baluster A form of decoration used in the seventeenth century where turning is cut in half along its length and applied to a surface.

Stile A vertical member forming the side of a frame.

Strap work Stylised representation of geometrically arranged leather straps.

Straw work A method of decoration employing small slivers of straw, often coloured.

Strap work

Stretcher A member linking and supporting legs of furniture.

Striation Striped imperfection.

Stringing A narrow inlaid strip of light or dark contrasting timber, or of brass.

Stumpwork A seventeenth-century form of embroidery, partly in relief.

Swan-neck An ogee curve applied to handles and pediments.

Tallboy (Chest on chest) A tall chest of drawers in two sections, one above the other.

Teapoy A small piece of furniture with a hinged lid, incorporating tea-caddies, mixing bowls and other accessories.

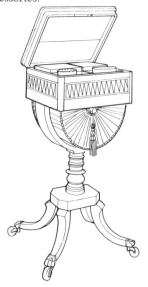

Terminal The end of a chair arm, on which the hand rests.

Tracheid Fibres in timber which produce the grain.

Turning A form of decoration achieved by the use of a lathe.

Veneer A thin sheet of wood, normally of decorative figure, applied to a timber base.

Volute A spiral scroll.

Whatnot A stand of square or rectangular shelves, sometimes incorporating one or two drawers.

Woods

Amboyna A rich, honey-coloured timber used from about 1780. It always has a very pronounced burr figure.

Beech When freshly cut, a pale cream, close-grained wood showing very definite, but very small, medullary rays. Most commonly used for seat rails and in country furniture. On objects older than 200 years, it becomes a dull indistinctive brown. Its ability to take nails and have them removed makes it very suitable for upholstery and this accounts for the many objects for which it is used that appear in this book.

Burrs Undoubtedly the hardest woods to identify are those displaying a burr figure. Most experts have considerable difficulty distinguishing between burr walnut, elm, ash, yew, amboyna and pollard oak. The practised eye will look for a small area of wood where the burr is absent and one will hope to identify the grain at that point to determine what the rest is.

Calamander, Coromandel and Zebra wood These three woods were used from around 1790 as veneers and are all very stripy black to ginger yellow. They are very hard dense grained timbers taking on a brilliant polish. The three woods are frequently confused and for our purposes the easiest distinction is the proportion of light and dark. Zebra wood is predominantly light with dark streaks, Coromandel has an almost even distribution of both, while calamander has light streaks on a black ground.

Fruitwoods (Apple, Cherry and Pear) These are pale brown, medium lightweight close grained woods, and are used in country-made furniture. Pale pear was used as a banding and as a ground for lacquer work in the late seventeenth century. The redder cherry is occasionally used decoratively.

Harewood Green or green/brown stained sycamore (see separate entry).

Holly Pale straw-coloured dense hard wood used as a decorative inlay in the sixteenth and seventeenth centuries and as a substitute for boxwood in the eighteenth. Also used as the ground for inlaid shells, medallions, paterae, etc.

Kingwood In the seventeenth century called Princes Wood, and used as an oyster veneer usually cut on the slant so that the oyster was oval. From 1770 frequently used as cross-banding. Very hard close-grained, brown tending slightly to mauve.

Laburnum Hard, dense wood with sapwood of almost equal density to the heart. The heart is deep chocolate brown, the sap a pale yellow. Used decoratively, often in chevron veneers to emphasise the colour contrast.

Lignum vitae An exceptionally dense hard dark nut-brown wood, frequently used for lathe turning of ornaments and utensils called Treen. Seldom used in cabinet-making.

Padouk (spelt Padauk in America) A very hard and heavy timber. When freshly cut it has a distinct violet hue, but it mellows to a mid nut brown and in sunlight will fade to a rich honey. Has very little figure and a wild grain and is most frequently found on furniture from around 1720-70. Usually employed in the solid.

Purpleheart When freshly cut a brilliant purple colour, but mellowing to chocolate brown, usually displaying slight whitish streaks in the grain. Used as a banding (seldom cross-banding) mainly from around 1770-1800.

Sycamore A soft pale yellow/straw timber often displaying fiddleback figure, used as a decorative inlay when it can closely resemble satinwood in appearance. Stained with iron oxide to a greeny brown, it is called Harewood and used principally on fine quality furniture 1770-1800.

Tulipwood When freshly cut tulipwood is a pale straw colour with magenta streaks. These mellow, leaving the wood a striated deep straw colour used extensively in French furniture as a ground veneer and in England as a cross-banding. Yellower and paler than Kingwood, these two timbers constitute the vast proportion of cross-bandings in furniture between 1770 and 1800.

Yew A dense, closely grained softwood usually of contorted grain and figure with tones ranging from ginger through brown to a slight purple tint. Very seldom used as a decorative veneer, but commonly employed for the decorative members of Windsor chairs. Burr yew used as a decorative inlay from the latter half of the eighteenth century.

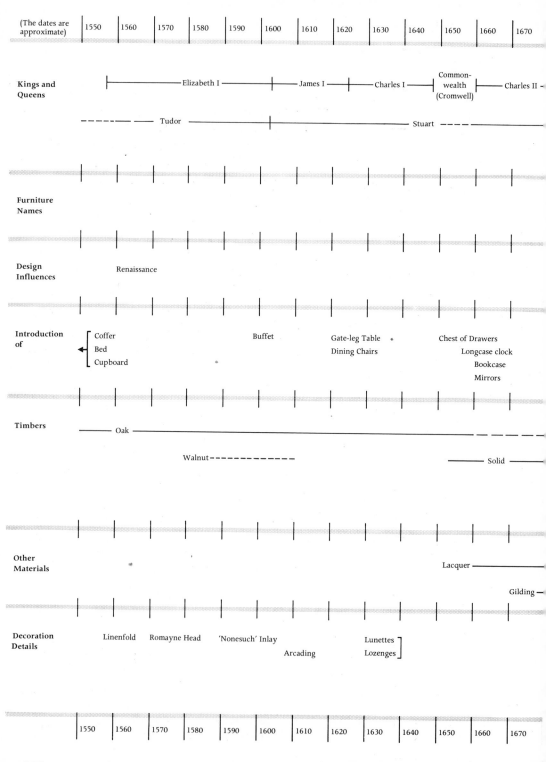

(The dates are approximate)	1550	1560	1570	1580	1590	1600	1610	1620	1630	1640	1650	1660	1670

Kings and Queens

Elizabeth I — James I — Charles I — Common-wealth (Cromwell) — Charles II —

Tudor — Stuart

Furniture Names

Design Influences

Renaissance

Introduction of

Coffer
Bed
Cupboard

Buffet

Gate-leg Table
Dining Chairs

Chest of Drawers
Longcase clock
Bookcase
Mirrors

Timbers

Oak

Walnut

Solid

Other Materials

Lacquer

Gilding

Decoration Details

Linenfold   Romayne Head   'Nonesuch' Inlay

Arcading

Lunettes
Lozenges

	1550	1560	1570	1580	1590	1600	1610	1620	1630	1640	1650	1660	1670

in the history of furniture

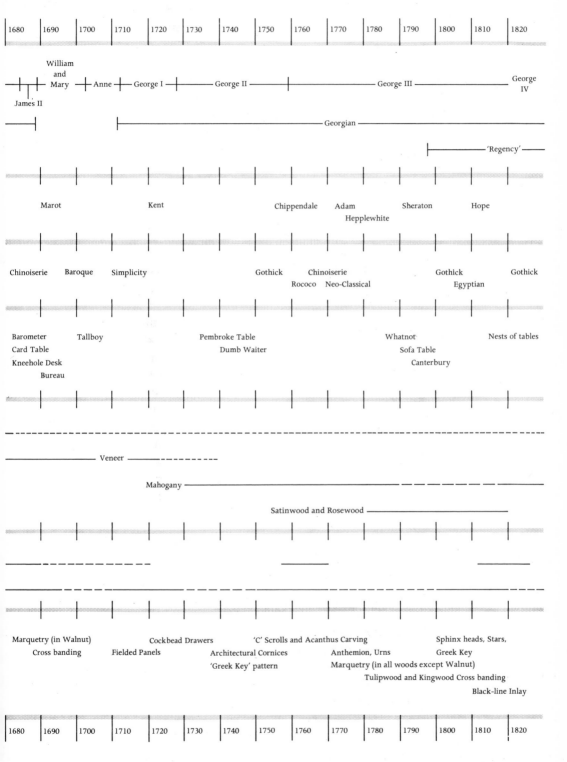

| 1680 | 1690 | 1700 | 1710 | 1720 | 1730 | 1740 | 1750 | 1760 | 1770 | 1780 | 1790 | 1800 | 1810 | 1820 |

James II — William and Mary — Anne — George I — George II — George III — George IV

Georgian

'Regency'

Marot   Kent   Chippendale   Adam   Hepplewhite   Sheraton   Hope

Chinoiserie   Baroque   Simplicity   Gothick   Chinoiserie   Gothick   Gothick
      Rococo   Neo-Classical   Egyptian

Barometer   Tallboy   Pembroke Table   Whatnot   Nests of tables
Card Table   Dumb Waiter   Sofa Table
Kneehole Desk   Canterbury
   Bureau

Veneer

Mahogany

Satinwood and Rosewood

Marquetry (in Walnut)   Cockbead Drawers   'C' Scrolls and Acanthus Carving   Sphinx heads, Stars,
  Cross banding   Fielded Panels   Architectural Cornices   Anthemion, Urns   Greek Key
      'Greek Key' pattern   Marquetry (in all woods except Walnut)
      Tulipwood and Kingwood Cross banding
      Black-line Inlay

| 1680 | 1690 | 1700 | 1710 | 1720 | 1730 | 1740 | 1750 | 1760 | 1770 | 1780 | 1790 | 1800 | 1810 | 1820 |

Bibliography

This is a short selection of the books I have found most useful in the course of both my work and in writing this book. They fall into several categories, as follows.

Early standard reference works containing numerous photographs and mainly published between 1880 and 1925. An enormous amount has been learnt about English furniture since these books were written and, although they make very interesting reading and illustrate some pieces which have long since been lost, they must be read in the context of the limited knowledge available at the time. They are now out of print and are not therefore generally available but may possibly be found in second-hand book shops and established libraries:

English Furniture of the Eighteenth Century H. Cescinsky (3 vols.)
English Decoration and Furniture of the Early Renaissance M. Jourdan
Early English Furniture and Woodwork H. Cescinsky and E. Gribble
History of English Furniture: 1. *The Age of Oak* 2. *The Age of Walnut* 3. *The Age of Mahogany* 4. *The Age of Satinwood* P. Macquoid
The Dictionary of English Furniture P. Macquoid and R. Edwards

More modern general books about English furniture.

The Dictionary of English Furniture, 2nd edition. P. Macquoid and R. Edwards, Country Life 1954
The Shorter Dictionary of English Furniture R. Edwards, Hamlyn 1964
English Furniture Maurice Tomlin, Faber 1972
English Furniture Styles Ralph Fastnedge, Penguin 1969

Most books dealing with a particular period of English cabinet-making can be relied upon to give helpful information. These include:

Furniture in England Samuel W. Wolsey and R. W. P. Luff, Arthur Barker 1968
Chippendale Furniture Anthony Coleridge, Faber 1968
Regency Furniture Clifford Musgrave, Faber 1971
Sheraton Furniture Ralph Fastnedge, Faber 1962
Nineteenth Century English Furniture Elizabeth Aslin, Faber 1962
Victorian Furniture R. W. Symonds and B. B. Whineray, Country Life 1962

Facsimile copies of eighteenth-century master works:

The Gentleman and Cabinet Maker's Director Thomas Chippendale, Dover Publications
The Cabinet Maker's and Upholsterer's Guide George Hepplewhite, Dover Publications 1970
The Cabinet Maker's and Upholsterer's Drawing Book Thomas Sheraton, Dover Publications 1971

Other related works:

Directory of Historic Cabinet Woods F. L. Hinckley, Crown 1960
English Barometers and Their Makers Nicholas Goodson, Antique Collectors' Club 1977
Old Clocks and Watches and their makers F. J. Britten, Eyre Methuen 1973
English Looking glasses Geoffrey Wills, Country Life 1965
Treen and Other Wooden Bygones Edward Pinto, G. Bell 1969
Directory of Tools used in the Woodworking and Allied Trades R. A. Salaman, Allen and Unwin 1975
English Decoration in the Eighteenth Century John Fowler and John Cornforth, Barrie and Jenkins 1974

Museum guides and the journals of appropriate learned societies. For example, The Victoria & Albert Museum guides, i.e. English Chairs, English Desks and Bureaux, etc. The journals of the Furniture History Society for the more advanced student.

POTTERY AND
PORCELAIN

BERNARD PRICE

Chapter 1

An approach to collecting

It is only during the past thirty years that there has been widespread popular interest in antiques. In fact the demand for information concerning the objects made and used in the past appears now to be insatiable. A mystique once enveloped the subject entirely, giving the general impression that certain private individuals and the antique trade in general were apparently born with the requisite insight which the rest of us would find impossible to acquire. There is no doubt that knowledge was jealously guarded, in the belief that if the public knew too much professionals would find it more difficult to buy. Competition does undoubtedly still exist, but at the same time the market for antiques has expanded dramatically even on an international scale.

One reason for the expansion in demand is that it is now no longer only the enthusiasts, the connoisseurs and the true collectors who are interested in antiques and works of art, but also investors. In my experience the latter, not having a clear idea of what to collect, frequently buy on advice and consequently neither acquire good investments nor make good collectors. Yet what is meant by the term 'good collector'? In the second half of the twentieth century, the question of what to buy is one that is most frequently asked, although true collecting depends on instinct as much as on acquired knowledge, and no one person can really say exactly what, and what not, to collect. Yet with this warning in mind, I hope in the following pages to give you some idea of what collecting entails, the paths to follow and the pitfalls to avoid.

Value is always an important consideration for the collector, and the best advice to be given is to always buy the very best pieces you can afford. Do not pay high prices for damaged or heavily restored items unless they are exceptionally rare; always seek out objects in the best condition possible. Avoid the tendency of many people caught in the first flood of their new enthusiasm who frequently try to gather together a collection of their chosen interest overnight: it is far better to purchase one or two really fine pieces a year than fifty commonplace ones in a month. Always remember too that the value of a collection is by no means simply the sum of the prices of each individual object, but rather that each newly acquired item will enhance the value of its companions. Never pay more than you can really afford for any piece, for should you be forced to sell it again shortly afterwards, it is quite possible that you would lose money. Prudent buying depends not only on what you pay on purchase, but also on choosing the right time to sell.

Never collect indiscriminately. To be a magpie may be fun, but it may also be quite meaningless. When you have found an area of collecting that interests you, stay with it: study it carefully and attempt to make the subject your own, but above all enjoy it. Very few bargains are to be purchased today by a collector who is uninformed, but a thorough grasp of your own specialisation will often reveal the wise purchase and also show you what to reject. The collector with knowledge will always reap both pleasure and profit.

There are of course people who on the surface appear to need no advice on collecting. These can usually be recognised by such remarks as 'I don't know anything about it but I do know what I like, and I collect what I like.' This is all very well but if collectors do not understand what they are collecting then the objects they acquire and lovingly cherish may be no more than rubbish. Look long at the objects that interest you, and compare one with another, for it can be alarming to discover how often individual ideas of quality may vary.

Quality, value and interest should therefore be the key words of any collection. A major pitfall to the collector may be fashion. Popular band-wagons should always be avoided, and the publicity given to objects made by some particular modeller or manufacturer treated with scepticism.

The law of supply and demand will always apply and values are therefore created by the intensity of demand coupled with the supply of objects on the open market. Usually, by the time something has become fashionable, the real collections have already been made, and the latecomers pay high prices for what is left. On the other hand it is still possible, surprising though it may seem, to find areas of the applied arts which are relatively unexplored, or even ignored, by the collector, and these are always worth investigating. It takes no courage, only money, to return from an antique dealer or an auction room with a piece whose current value is high; it requires both courage and knowledge to purchase something for which there

appears to be little or no demand. You will need your courage for when you bring your purchase home, or show it to your friends, only to be met with raised eyebrows or even such comments as 'Whatever did you buy that for?'! Take heart, for this happens to all collectors.

It is surprising how rapidly attitudes change towards objects as their value begins to rise. In other words, money invariably brings respectability to items previously regarded as unworthy of serious consideration. A few illustrations will make this point clear. If an antique dealer or an auctioneer had called at your home ten years ago in order to prepare a valuation for insurance, he would undoubtedly have commented approvingly upon your country-made Welsh dresser, and with equal aplomb would have dismissed at a glance the Staffordshire blue-and-white transfer printed earthenware objects that might have been displayed upon its shelves. At that time such pottery could be bought for shillings, and it was this very fact that apparently blinded everyone to the interest and quality that much of it possessed. Yet once recognised, and documentation on it begun, the status of this humble earthenware rose dramatically and continues to do so.

A similar phenomenon can be seen in the rise over the last twenty-five years of the importance of the Victorian Staffordshire pottery portrait figure, originally made to brighten the mantelshelves of the cottager. In 1953, the first book devoted solely to these figures was published by a man named Brian Latham. Previously attention had been given almost entirely to the Staffordshire products of the eighteenth century. Mr

1 Part of a Wedgwood service decorated with the famous water-lily pattern. The decoration here is both painted and transfer printed. First made at Etruria in 1807, the service has been reproduced several times since, particularly in the form of blue-and-white transfer printed earthenware.

2 A pair of Victorian named portrait figures depicting the highwaymen Dick Turpin and Tom King, and with the names visible. Staffordshire.

Latham, however, was the first person to realise that the cheap popular Victorian portrait figure, decorated in very strong colours, offered a vast and highly picturesque panorama of Victorian history. These pieces, although lacking the elegant sophistication of earlier porcelain figures, represented a whole cavalcade of kings and queens, generals, sportsmen, actors and actresses, and even murderers and evangelists. When part of the Latham collection was sold in London the blinkers again fell away from the prejudiced eyes of many buyers, with the result that today not only are a number of lavishly illustrated books devoted to the subject but also some antique dealers now specialise in these wares. The reason why such pieces were overlooked for so long is that they were generally, and quite wrongly, compared unfavourably with earlier fine figure

3 White pottery swans shaped into plant holders were very popular in Victorian homes. The swan, sometimes regarded as a symbol of death, was used to contain evergreen plants, which in turn symbolised eternal life.

groups from English, or even Continental, porcelain factories. Yet such comparisons are invalid and the two products represent two different types of ceramic art destined for two different markets. Victorian Staffordshire portrait figures represent a popular folk art as vigorous as any to be found in the world. It is only in very recent years that we have begun to see the Victorian era in its true perspective, and its products are appreciated for themselves.

It is hoped that these two illustrations will serve as cautionary tales not to follow the prevailing fashion, but to pursue above all whatever captures your imagination. When an object interests you, then if it has quality and historical interest, handle it carefully, and bear the following points in mind. Above all, look for marks, but feel also the glaze and note carefully the colouring. Be aware of the weight: is it heavy for its size or is it surprisingly light? What does the object

4 Parian vase by Samuel Alcock & Co., Burslem, England, *c.* 1850. Victoria and Albert Museum, London.

5 Staffordshire slipware model of a cradle decorated in green and brown on a white slip ground. Late seventeenth or early eighteenth century. City Museum and Art Gallery, Stoke-on-Trent.

represent? Are there any emblems or other motifs to provide you with a clue? Is the mark under or over the glaze? Has the mark been impressed or stamped into the clay? Or has it been incised with a sharp object? (If impressed the mark will have been evenly applied with a stamp, if incised the line of the mark will have cut a furrow like a miniature plough.) All of these details may be of great importance when trying to establish the provenance or date of the object. It will also help if you have a good magnifying glass and a pocket reference book to help you identify marks that apply both to pottery and porcelain (you will find a suggested reading list at the end of this book).

Should you be able to find others with similar collecting interests there is much to be gained from discussing your collections and new purchases together. If you can make friends with an established collector then so much the better; it will also help to get on good terms with as many antique dealers as possible who specialise in the objects which interest you. Many collectors are suspicious of dealers, but they are in fact an essential part of the collecting process. You will find that most good antique dealers are usually prepared to discuss and exchange information with the genuine collector, and a long-term acquaintance with one will invariably prove fruitful. Once a dealer understands the type of collection you hope to form, or knows of its gaps, he can be of great help, for you will find that his network of contacts and coverage of auction sales will almost certainly be wider than your own. All collectors worth their salt will admit to having made mistakes and the new collector must be prepared to make some too.

Having considered the things which a new collector needs to be aware of when choosing objects and building his collection, I shall move on to the question of where to buy. This is an area where great caution must be exercised. There are, for example, many stallholders at the antiques markets which abound today, and it would seem rather foolish to pay a similar price at one of these to that which would be asked in a porcelain gallery in the West End of London. Yet all too often this is precisely what happens.

Markets have changed greatly in character in the last decade, with an influx of amateur dealers. Wherever you buy, in order to safeguard yourself, always obtain a receipt for the money you pay, together with the dealer's full description of the object that you have bought. Read it carefully, for it is this document that you will find essential under any claim you might lodge under the Misrepresentation Act. Until you have the confidence and expertise to buy elsewhere the best advice is to buy from established dealers.

In London many excellent specialist auction sales are held regularly throughout the year, and although attending them may bring pain as well as pleasure, there are few better places than the auction room in which to learn. The new collector may feel somewhat daunted by the suggestion that he should visit the famous London firms, as saleroom reports have now become a regular feature in several national newspapers and it is usually the more expensive objects that are mentioned and which claim the headlines. In fact most sales of pottery and porcelain cover an extremely wide field and you will be surprised at the number of pieces that sell for less than £100. Another difficulty is that many people are diffident about bidding at public auction sales. If you really cannot bring

6 *Far left*: Liverpool Delft puzzle jug with pierced decoration (that is, decoration carried through the walls of the vessel typical of such jugs and painted in blue, *c.* 1750. These jugs were a 'joke' of the period as their contents could only be drunk by covering the side spouts in the rim and sucking the forward spout–the handle and rim being hollow! Royal Scottish Museum, Edinburgh.

7 *Above:* Wedgwood plate with design by Emile Lessor. The work of this French artist is highly distinctive, and he particularly favoured child groups. He worked at the Wedgwood factory between 1858 and 1863 and later continued to produce designs in France.

yourself to bid, then ask someone else to do it for you. The auctioneer's clerk will bid without charge on your behalf, and if you come to know the sales staff well you will certainly find someone ready to oblige. Many antique dealers unable to attend sales frequently make their presence felt by proxy bidding of this kind. If you watch carefully and follow the techniques used you will find the confidence to do it for yourself, and will experience considerable pleasure and satisfaction in the process.

Many of the larger London firms produce catalogues that have been made up with great care and scholarship. Most firms supply these catalogues at an annual subscription rate, and half a day armed with one at the viewing of a sale could not be better spent. You will become fully acquainted with the scope of the subject in which you are interested, and you will also be able to check your own identifications with those of the catalogue. For a fee they will also provide a printed list of the prices obtained following the auction, and again this will help to build up a sense of value and an awareness of what is scarce. Many provincial auctioneers now follow the same practice.

When you check the catalogue descriptions, also check carefully the object that you wish to buy for any tell-tale signs of restoration. It needs to be remembered that enormous advances have been made in restoration techniques in recent years, and such major work as the addition of new limbs to a pottery or porcelain figure may often be achieved in such a way as to be quite invisible to even the experienced eye. Restoration can always be revealed under ultra-violet light and most leading auctioneers and antique dealers are prepared to either guarantee an object as being free from restoration or to define the extent of it. Whenever possible, it is well worth while purchasing damaged objects very cheaply, for there is much to be learned from the examination of such pieces, as we shall discover in the following chapter.

Once you have been to a number of sales, you will come to appreciate more fully the particular fascination of pottery and porcelain. Part of this lies in the unique way in which its story is interwoven with that of man himself: it has existed since prehistoric times as part of human culture and when archaeologists want to find out more about a particular civilisation, it is fragments of its pottery that they seek above all else.

8 Leeds pottery figure of a girl, with an impressed mark on the base. Late eighteenth century. British Museum, London.

Although the terms pottery and porcelain may seem confusing to the new collector, the differences are quite straightforward. Pottery is a simple earthenware made from ordinary clays that are widely obtainable. It is always opaque and needs glazing if it is to contain water. Porcelain, on the other hand, is the product of the much rarer china clay known as kaolin which, when fired, becomes translucent. It is on the whole much more impervious to water than pottery, but needs to be glazed at least on the inside if it is to be made into objects of everyday use such as teapots. Unglazed, it can be used for figure modelling.

The art of making porcelain is therefore much more complex, and was first discovered by the Chinese during the T'ang dynasty (AD 618-906). By the Middle Ages both Chinese pottery and porcelain were known throughout the Middle East and even in Africa. They were carried by sea and by hazardous journeys overland which followed ancient caravan routes. The first European to see porcelain was probably Marco Polo, the great merchant and explorer who travelled across Asia and into China as far as the court of the Great Khan in the late thirteenth century. There is a passage in his famous journal that particularly captures the excitement and adventure to be found in the study of ceramics:

'Let me tell you further that in this province, in a city called Tinju, they make bowls of porcelain, large and small, of incomparable beauty. They are made nowhere else except in this city, and from here they are exported all over the world. In the city itself they are so plentiful and cheap that for a Venetian groat you might buy three bowls of such beauty that nothing lovelier could be imagined. These dishes are made of a crumbly earth or clay which is dug as though from a mine and stacked in huge mounds and left for thirty or forty years exposed to wind, rain, and sun. By this time the earth is so refined that dishes made of it are of an azure tint with a very brilliant sheen. You must understand when a man makes a mound of this earth he does so for his children; the time of maturing is so long that he cannot hope to draw any profit from it himself or to put it to use, but the son who succeeds him will reap the fruit . . .'

The first appearance of porcelain in Europe resulted in attempts to manufacture it that were to continue until the eighteenth century, when the young German apothecary Johann Bottger made his first successful experiments at Meissen on the outskirts of Dresden. It was not until the middle of that century that porcelain was made on a wide scale in England.

Connoisseurs of pottery and porcelain, no matter what their field of specialisation, accept that the finest ceramic achievements in the world are those of the Chinese. The highest price yet achieved at auction by a ceramic object is £420,000, paid for a blue-and-white Ming bottle of the early fifteenth century, although half a million pounds was paid by the Metropolitian Museum of New York when they privately purchased a painted Greek urn of about 530 BC in August, 1972. By comparison, the highest price obtained at auction by a piece of English porcelain is £32,000, for a Chelsea tureen in the form of a boar's head, sold at Sotheby's in 1973. The auction record for a piece of English pottery is £15,015, for an eighteenth-century salt-glaze pew group, sold at Christie's in 1975.

Yet for all the beauty inherent in individual ceramic objects and for all the excitement of the auction, the study of pottery and porcelain must be kept in perspective. Let it be remembered that collecting is also a bug, albeit a delightful one, an acquisitive virus that once caught is unlikely to be cured. Collecting therefore requires the curb of your caution: above all, never let yourself be ruled by your possessions. Antiques have been collected for hundreds of years and many individuals have beggared themselves in the process, and it is for this reason, to prevent us from taking ourselves too seriously, that I recall a passage from Jerome K. Jerome's classic work of humour *Three Men in a Boat*, first published in 1889. 'I wonder if there is real intrinsic beauty in the old soup-plates, beer-mugs, and candle-snuffers that we prize so now, or if it is only the halo of age glowing around them that gives them their charms in our eyes. The "old blue" that we hang about our walls as ornaments were the common every-day household utensils of a few centuries ago; and the pink shepherds, and the yellow shepherdesses that we hand round now for all our friends to gush over, and pretend they understand, were the unvalued mantel-ornaments that the mother of the eighteenth century would have given the baby to suck when he cried.

'Will it be the same in the future? Will the prized treasures of today always be the cheap trifles of the day before? Will rows of our willow-pattern dinner-plates be ranged above the chimneypieces of the great in the year 2000 and odd? Will the white cups with the gold rim and the beautiful gold flower inside (species unknown), that our Sarah Janes now break in sheer light-heartedness of spirit, be carefully mended, and stood upon a bracket, and dusted only by the lady of the house? That china dog ornaments the bedroom of my furnished lodgings. It is a white dog. Its eyes are blue. Its nose is delicate red, with black spots. Its head is painfully erect, and its expression is amiability carried to the verge of imbecility. I do not admire it myself. Considered as a work of art, I may say it irritates me. Thoughtless friends jeer at it, and even my landlady herself has no admiration for it, and excuses its presence by the circumstance that her aunt gave it to her.

'But in 200 years time it is more than probable that the dog will be dug up somewhere or other, minus its legs, and with its tail broken, and will be sold for old china, and put in a glass cabinet. And people will pass it round, and admire it. They will be struck by the wonderful depth of the colour on the nose, and speculate as to how beautiful the bit of the tail that is lost no doubt was.

9 White porcelain figure of a hound. Chelsea, *c.* 1749. Victoria and Albert Museum, London.

'We, in this age, do not see the beauty of that dog. We are too familiar with it. It is like the sunset and the stars: we are not awed by their loveliness because they are common to our eyes. So it is with that china dog. In 2288 people will gush over it. The making of such dogs will have become a lost art. Our descendants will wonder how we did it, and say how clever we were. We shall be referred to lovingly as those grand old artists that flourished in the nineteenth century, and produced those china dogs.

'The sampler that the eldest daughter did at school will be spoken of as tapestry of the Victorian era and be almost priceless. The blue-and-white mugs of the present-day roadside inn will be hunted up, all cracked and chipped, and sold for their weight in gold, and rich people will use them for claret cups; travellers from Japan will buy up all the Presents from Ramsgate and Souvenirs of Margate, that may of escaped destruction, and take them back to Jedo as ancient English curios . . .'

Many a true word is indeed uttered in jest, and I admire his observation that the eyes of his china dog are blue, for such apparently irrelevant detail can be of great help to the porcelain collector when dating objects. Very few English porcelain figure groups of the eighteenth century have so far been found with blue eyes; the majority are brown. Such information forms but a rule of thumb, but what an important one it is to have.

This observation brings us back to the other side of the coin in antique collecting: that it is a fascinating process, full of exciting discovery. It is the intention of this book to encourage you to look at pottery and porcelain with a fresh eye and to help you in the identification and basic understanding of the objects you will come to see and handle.

Chapter 2

Unravelling the mystique

No collector, or antique dealer for that matter, ever stops learning. The new collector in particular will be well advised to look at objects, examine them carefully, and try and absorb new facts all the time. The importance of actually handling pottery and porcelain cannot be over-emphasised. You may read all the relevant books, follow programmes on the radio and television, listen to lectures, but until you handle the pieces themselves none of the information you may have gained from these sources will ever fall properly into place. The following story will serve to illustrate how much can be gained by actually picking an object up and examining it carefully.

Many years ago, just before my sixteenth birthday, I attended an auction sale in a private house in Sussex. I knew nothing about ceramics beyond the fact that a plate was a plate, a vase was a vase, and if an object was called Ming it must therefore be old and valuable. The house had been the home of a porcelain collector, and during the course of that day my eyes were opened. I watched an elderly man lift a plate from a box of miscellaneous items and heard him mutter to a colleague 'Derby, about 1800'. When they had moved on I looked at the plate. It was painted with flowers but, apart from that, there was nothing to indicate who had made it, or where. I was puzzled and at the same time becoming quite desperate to know how anyone should be able to examine an object bearing no mark or label and yet apparently be quite certain of its origins. Later in the day when the sale was in progress I saw another plate, quite dull in appearance, white porcelain with a sketchy decoration in sepia and with slight touches of gold—to my utter astonishment that single plate fetched £30, which was more money than I had in the world. I looked at my catalogue and found the plate was described as 'eighteenth-century Chinese' with the word 'Jesuit' in inverted commas. The triumphant purchaser paid for the plate and carried it off immediately. I soon discovered exactly how this incident confirmed the importance of handling and understanding the porcelain itself: the majority of eighteenth-century pottery and porcelain is unmarked, and it was only during the nineteenth century that factories became more meticulous in marking products. This discovery disclosed to me a more than half hidden and entirely fascinating field of interest.

There are very many small points of observation that reveal so much of importance to the collector of ceramics, and it is difficult for the beginner to know what to look for. Pottery is generally easier than porcelain to understand, but varies in quality from simple earthenwares to formulae including clay, flint and other additives that produce sophisticated stonewares. Some stonewares, like Wedgwood's jasper ware, begin to approach porcelain in quality. However, most pottery is decidedly cheaper and far more simple to produce than porcelain. Early English porcelains, made at such places as Bow, Chelsea, Bristol, Plymouth and Worcester, were largely experimental. Each ceramic formula had methods of production creating various characteristics that are to be observed in shape, decoration, glaze and in the body of the porcelain itself. Coming to understand such characteristics is a long but compulsive process, making it eventually possible to examine an object, diagnose its distinguishing features, and so determine its place of manufacture, date and possibly even its modeller and decorator as well. A few remarks on Worcester porcelain will clarify this comment. It is for example a useful test to hold the object over a powerful electric light bulb—a table lamp without its shade is ideal—and observe the colouring that is transmitted through the porcelain by the light. You might expect the colour to be the whiteness of the porcelain reflected by the bulb, but instead you will find it to be a light green: a distinctive feature of much eighteenth-century Worcester.

Most porcelain items intended to be placed on tables have what is known as a foot-rim, the ridge on which the object stands, and it is this feature that will very often repay careful study. The foot-rim will often clearly indicate the nature of the porcelain used in the object's manufacture, and may also provide information concerning its glaze. Some factories also applied their marks to the inside of foot-rims, which is useful to know as these can sometimes be overlooked. A Worcester foot-rim will reveal, if looked at carefully, something of a 'cheesy' appearance, and the porcelain of which it is made is termed soft paste. This leads us to another interesting feature of Worcester. If you have ever read one of the many old books on

10 'Cistercian' ware vessel in the shape of a trumpet. This together with its glaze makes it typical of monastic wares made during the sixteenth century. Height 8¾ inches (222 mm). Museum of London.

11 Another typical medieval shape with a clear green glaze that was to remain popular throughout the Tudor period. Fifteenth century. Museum of London.

12 An imitation Wedgwood jasper ware teapot made by Neale & Co., 1780. British Museum, London.

13 The base of an eighteenth-century Worcester teapot, showing the irregular spread of the glaze and the narrow unglazed area just inside the foot-rim.

china collecting, you may well have found a statement to the effect that 'Worcester porcelain will usually show a dry edge on the inside of the foot-rim, caused by the retraction of the glaze'. While this dry edge as described is usually present, it is not caused by the reason stated. Glaze can only expand in the kiln, it does not shrink, retract or recoil. The Worcester dry edge was caused by the 'pegger' who, after the object had been dipped in glaze, used a small wooden peg to wipe away the excess within the foot-rim before the object was packed with its companions into saggers and loaded into the kiln for firing. This ensured that the minimum number of porcelain pieces adhered to each other, or to the sagger itself, so reducing the number of expensive breakages. When a Worcester piece is taken out of the kiln the dry edge is revealed as a result of the pegger's work, and the glaze left in the centre of the base will emerge with an irregular line and will in most cases fail to meet the edge of the foot-rim. This technique is an important one as the manufacture of porcelain is far more costly than that of pottery, particularly in the case of figure groups, where modelling, casting, assembling and decorating are all involved in the final result. The same characteristic also appears on objects from Caughley and on some of the Liverpool manufactories.

It is still not infrequent on view days in provincial sale rooms to notice a collector or dealer swiftly allowing the tip of his pencil to slide around the inside of the foot-rim of whatever he is looking at. If the pencil fails to draw a line then it is an immediate indication that the glaze is present across the entire base, whereas if a line is drawn it will show that the graphite in the pencil has crossed a surface of unglazed porcelain and could therefore well indicate an example of eighteenth-century Worcester. Such tests as these, however, valuable as they are, should never be accepted in isolation by the beginner, who should always check as many known characteristics as possible. It is particularly essential to follow this practice when you find objects bearing important eighteenth-century marks, for there are many fakes and copies in existence. Human nature being what it is, the sight of any mark will immediately blind many people to the fact that it might be something other than what it purports to be.

Broadly speaking there are two main categories of porcelain, referred to as hard paste and soft paste respectively. The essential distinction between them is, as their names would imply, one of hardness of substance. A different formula is used for hard paste, which is fired at a much higher temperature than soft paste porcelain. In the nineteenth century collectors carried with them as an aid to identification a file which would cut soft paste easily while making no impression on hard paste. Needless to say this is a practice that is severely frowned upon today, but if you want to see the differences for yourself try obtaining some damaged pieces of porcelain of both types. One thing that you will notice is that the chip in the soft paste has a granular texture not unlike that of a digestive biscuit, whereas hard paste presents a surface that is flint- or glass-like in appearance. Lead glaze is used on most soft paste porcelains, whereas the glaze on hard paste items is sometimes of stone. Lead glaze also tends to gather and pool on a figure, for example, where the bend of an arm or the fold of clothes permits it. This does not occur with glazes made from china stone.

The Chinese, who made the world's first porcelain, did so according to a hard paste formula consisting of china stone (known as petuntse) and china clay (known as kaolin), and produced pieces of outstanding quality. The same formula was discovered in Germany at the beginning of the eighteenth

14 Liverpool transfer printed coffee pot. The shape is typical.

century: the commercial success of the Meissen factory, the popularity of Oriental porcelain imports and consequent decline of interest in earthenware led to intensive experiments into porcelain manufacture. Because of the failure of experimenters to find a harder paste, a number of soft paste porcelains were evolved around this time; English factories in particular, with a few exceptions, used soft paste.

Soft paste has the same attribute of translucency as hard paste but is technically inferior as it is less stable in the kiln. This meant that soft paste figures were difficult to fire; they needed to be propped while in the kiln and lacked the vitality and freedom of the hard paste figures of Meissen. Modelling was therefore restricted. Thus manufacturers were always attempting to produce a harder paste in the knowledge that soft paste was second best. However, generations of collectors will testify that soft paste porcelains have a unique and distinctive charm that will become apparent if the reader perseveres in studying and handling them.

Once the substance of porcelain had been manufactured, it then needed to be shaped into objects of everyday use such as bowls, cups and plates, or into decorative figure models. The next stage was decoration. At first, many pieces of European porcelain were left entirely white, mainly because a tradition of porcelain decoration did not exist in Europe. As we have already noted, Chinese porcelains were well known in Europe long before the method of porcelain manufacture was discovered in the Western world, and it is therefore not surprising that early European porcelains should derive their style of decoration from Oriental sources. In particular, the direct copying or the basing of designs upon known Chinese originals was an obvious step. Most of the English manufacturers of porcelain favoured, particularly in the early stages of their development, the use of blue-and-white decoration. The study and collection of English blue-and-white porcelain of the eighteenth century is a most attractive and stimulating pursuit although, sadly, becoming more costly as each year goes by.

Porcelain decorations in enamel colours (that is, colours which are applied over the glaze) are naturally more striking and have a lustrous appearance. This is particularly so with specimens painted with Oriental figures. In years past many an uninformed country auctioneer sold English porcelain so decorated as Oriental examples, which gives strength to my previous comment that a firm knowledge of the type of porcelain of which the object is made is vital if proper identification is to be achieved. The Oriental style of enamel figure painting, whether carried out at Worcester, Liverpool or New Hall, has a unique quality that is frequently missed by the beginner. Look at, say, a Chinese cup of the late eighteenth century and compare it carefully with its English counterpart. At first glance they both appear to be entirely Oriental, but ignore for a moment the clothing and the background which help to produce the overall effect, and concentrate instead upon the faces. With most of the examples that are examined in this way you will find a subtle difference. The English specimen, while capturing the spirit of the original, usually fails to reflect accurately the Oriental features and the result is more often a face of somewhat Eurasian appearance.

So far in this chapter, we have described the basic materials from which porcelain is made, and the stages it goes through, such as the decoration, before the finished product is achieved, and it is hoped that this will be useful information for the reader to keep in the back of his mind as specific objects and their manufacture are described. It will also be useful to clarify at this point certain confusions arising from the profusion of names used in the study of pottery and porcelain. For a start, the same name can be applied to both the fabric that is used for making an object and the object itself: thus 'porcelain' can mean both the material and the thing or things made out of it. Another difficulty is that during the course of the importation of ceramic objects into this country, many generic terms came to be applied which are inexact and confusing. China, for example, is a word in daily use, but what exactly does it mean? In the next few pages I shall give a brief sketch of the history of the importation of the porcelain objects into this country, in the course of which the different names used will, it is hoped, become clearer.

The main passion for collecting in Britain developed during the reign of William III, and a large collection of Oriental wares and Dutch Delft decorated in the Oriental manner was established by Queen Mary at Kensington Palace; an inventory of this collection was drawn up in 1696. For many people this ceramic enthusiasm became an obsession, and Daniel Defoe writes of finding china '. . . upon the tops of cabinets, scrutores and every chimney piece to the tops of the ceilings . . . till it became a grievance in the expense of it and was injurious to their families and Estates.'

Among the larger decorative porcelains to be imported from the Orient were groups of vases known as *garniture de cheminée*, usually consisting of three covered vases and two beakers. Other imports consisted of items of European design

15 Staffordshire slipware portrait dish depicting William III (1689-1702). The dish is large having a diameter of 16¾ inches (420 mm). Victoria and Albert Museum, London.

16 Delftware plate painted in blue and yellow also depicting William III and Mary II. Probably Lambeth, 1691. Ashmolean Museum, Oxford, Warren Collection.

17 Delftware portrait dish depicting Charles II. Painted mainly in blue with some yellow, brown, orange and purple. Note the blue-dash border, a typical feature of such pieces. Probably Lambeth, 1661. Birmingham Museums and Art Gallery, A. C. J. Wall loan.

manufactured in China, blue-and-white porcelain entirely Oriental in decoration and design, and blue-and-white porcelain brought to Europe for additional decoration. These latter pieces are now referred to as 'clobbered' wares, and although interesting they are usually highly unsatisfactory in appearance. Some examples of Oriental porcelain were brought to Europe 'in the white' for decoration here, but these are not common. Most of the later Chinese porcelains decorated in polychrome (many colour) enamels are described as Canton, for it was in that city on the Pearl River that most of the enamelling was done. Similarly the later blue-and-white Chinese export pieces are termed Nankin, for this was the port from which most were exported. These names, together with the fact that most wares were brought to Europe in the ships of the various nations' East India companies, resulted in India and China being used as generic terms for Far Eastern wares. In due course the word 'china' in England came to describe virtually anything of a ceramic nature, just as the term 'japanned' and 'Indian' were applied to furniture lacquered anywhere in the Far East during the seventeenth and eighteenth centuries.

In the nineteenth century it was firmly believed that large imports of Chinese porcelain in the white had been delivered in the eighteenth century to the Lowestoft porcelain works and decorated there. Hence yet another confusing term: 'Chinese Lowestoft'. In fact products given this name were both made and decorated in China and are true export wares, and yet in many circles, particularly in America, this misnomer still flourishes.

Individuals who imported or sold china were described as chinamen. One such man was Miles Mason, who also established a family manufacturing business renowned for its highly popular Mason's ironstone. His business as a wholesale and retail dealer in Oriental porcelain became impossible to carry on due to the Napoleonic wars, but the following advertisement which he placed in the *London Morning Herald* of 15 October 1804 not only illuminates some of the comments already made in this chapter, but also demonstrates the character and initiative of the man:

'It has hitherto been the opinion, not only of the Public, but also of the Manufacturers of this Country that the Earths of these Kingdoms are unequal to those of Foreign Nations for the fabrication of China. Miles Mason, late of Fenchurch Street, London, having been a principal purchaser of Indian Porcelain, till the prohibition of that article by heavy duties, has established a Manufactory at Lane Delph, near

Newcastle-under-Line [sic], upon the principle of the Indian and Sève [sic] China. The former is now sold at the principal Shops only in the City of London and the Country as British Nankin. His article is warranted from the Manufactory to possess superior qualities to Indian Nankin China, being more beautiful as well as more durable, and not so liable to snip at the edges, more difficult to break, and refusable or unitable by heat, if broken. Being aware that to combat strong prejudices with success, something superior must be produced: he, therefore, through the medium of his Wholesale Friends, proposes to renew or match the impaired or broken services of the Nobility and Gentry, when by fair trial or conjunction with foreign china, he doubts not that these fears will be removed, and, in a short period, the Manufactories of Porcelain, by the patronage of the Nobility of this country, will rival, if not excel, those of foreign Nations.

N.B. The articles are stamped on the bottom of the large pieces to prevent imposition.'

In 1736 a treatise published in France gave enormous encouragement to the endeavours of the European porcelain pioneers. The paper, *A Description of the Empire of China and of*

18 A fine Miles Mason porcelain teapot. The small impressed name mark, 'M. Mason', is just visible on the rim of the base.

Chinese Tartary, included considerable detail of the manufacturing methods and materials used by the Chinese in their production of hard paste porcelain. The information had mainly come from some long, detailed and very charming letters written in 1712 by a Jesuit missionary known as Père d'Entrecolles. The following extracts from these letters are not only interesting for their historic worth, but also help the beginner to understand the nature of porcelain and the various processes which it undergoes during manufacture:

'From time to time I have stayed in Ching-tê-chên to administer to the spiritual necessities of my converts, and so I have interested myself in the manufacture of this beautiful porcelain, which is so highly prized, and is sent to all parts of the world. Nothing but my curiosity could ever have prompted me to such researches, but it appears to me that a minute description of all that concerns this kind of work might, somehow, be useful in Europe.

'Besides what I myself have seen, I have learnt a great many particulars from my neophytes, several of whom work in porcelain, while others do a great trade in it. I also confirmed the truth of the information they had given me by a study of the Chinese books on the subject, so that I believe I have obtained a pretty exact knowledge of all that concerns this beautiful art, so that I can talk about it with some confidence.'

'The material of porcelain is composed of two kinds of clay, one called Pe-tun-tse and the other Kao-lin. The latter is disseminated with corpuscles which have some shimmer, the former is simply white and very fine to the touch. While a large number of big boats come up the river from Jao-chou to Ching-tê-chên to be loaded with porcelain, nearly as many small ones come down from Ki-mên laden with Pe-tun-tse and Kao-lin made up into bricks, for Ching-tê-chên does not produce any of the materials suitable for porcelain. Pe-tun-tse, which is so fine in grain, is simply pulverized rock taken from quarries, and then shaped into bricks. Every kind of stone is not suitable, or it would not be necessary to go for it, twenty or thirty miles away, into the next province. The good stone, the Chinese say, must have a slight tinge of green. The pieces of stone are first broken with iron hammers, and the fragments are reduced to a very fine powder in mortars by means of certain levers which have a stone head shod with iron. These levers are worked incessantly, either by men or by water-power, in the same way as the tilt-hammers in paper-mills. The powder is then put into a great vessel filled with water, and stirred vigorously with an iron shovel. When it has been allowed to stand several minutes, a kind of cream forms at the top four or five fingers thick; this they take off and put into another vessel full of water. The mixture in the first vessel is stirred up several times, and each time they remove the scum that gathers on the top, until nothing is left but the larger particles, the weight of which makes them sink to the bottom; these are finally taken out and again pounded. With regard to the second vessel into which they put all that has been skimmed out of the first, they wait until a kind of paste has formed at the bottom, and when the water above it seems very clear it is poured off so as not to disturb the sediment. This paste is then thrown into moulds which are a kind of large and wide wooden box, the bottom of which is a bed of bricks with an even surface. Over this brick bed a coarse cloth is stretched, up to the sides of the case; this cloth is filled with the paste, and soon afterwards they cover it with another cloth on the top of which they put a layer of bricks laid evenly, one by the side of the other. This helps to squeeze out the water more quickly without losing any of the porcelain material which, as it hardens readily, takes the shape of the bricks. Before it has become quite hard the paste is divided into little bricks, which are sold by the hundred; this colour and the shape have given it the name Pe-tun-tse. There would be nothing to add to this preparation if the Chinese were not in the habit of adulterating their merchandise; but people who roll little grains of paste in pepper dust, and mix them with real peppercorns, are not likely to sell Pe-tun-tse without mixing it with coarser materials, so that it has to be purified afresh before it is used.

'Kao-lin requires a little less labour than Pe-tun-tse; nature has done the greater part. Mines of it are found in the heart of certain mountains, which on the outside are covered with reddish earth. These mines are fairly deep; it is found there in masses, and it is also made up into little squares in the same method as described above for the Pe-tun-tse. I should be inclined to think that the white clay of Malta, known as the clay of St Paul, approaches in its nature to the Kao-lin I am speaking of, although one cannot perceive in it the small silvery particles with which the Kao-lin is sown. Fine porcelain owes its strength to the Kao-lin; it is only the mixture of a soft earth or a soft clay which gives strength to the Pe-tun-tse obtained from the hardest rocks.

'A rich merchant told me that the English or Dutch (the Chinese use the same name for both nations) bought, several years ago, some Pe-tun-tse, which they took to their own country to make porcelain with, but, having taken no Kao-lin, their undertaking failed, as they afterwards owned. The Chinese merchant said to me, laughing, "They wanted to have a body without bones to support its flesh".'

'For the fine porcelains they put as much Kao-lin as Pe-tun-tse; for the inferior ones they use four parts of Kao-lin and six parts of Pe-tun-tse; while the least that they use is one part of Kao-lin and three of Pe-tun-tse.

'The mixture is thrown into a big pit well paved and cemented, where it is trodden and kneaded until it becomes stiff; this is very laborious work; those Christians who are employed at it find it difficult to attend church; they are only allowed to go if they can find substitutes, because as soon as this work is interrupted all other workmen are stopped.

'From the mass thus prepared, lumps are taken and spread on large slates. The workmen knead, beat, and roll them thoroughly, taking care that no hollows are left inside the mass and that no foreign bodies get into it A hair, a grain of sand would spoil the whole work. If this mass is badly worked the porcelain cracks, splits, drops or bends. From these prime materials such beautiful works of porcelain are produced, some by shaping on the wheel, others only in moulds; and they are afterwards finished with a knife. All the plain pieces are made in the first way. A cup, for example, when it leaves the wheel, is very roughly shaped, almost like the top of a hat before it has been blocked. The first workman only gives it the required diameter and height, and it leaves his hands almost as soon as it is commenced, for he receives only three 'deniers' per board, and on each board are twenty-six pieces. The foot of the cup is then nothing but a piece of clay of the necessary width, and it is only hollowed out with a knife when the other operations are finished, and when the cup is dry and firm enough. When the cup leaves the wheel it is taken by a second workman, who puts it straight upon its base. Shortly afterwards it is handed over to a third man, who puts it on its mould and gives it its shape; this mould is mounted on a kind of wheel. A fourth workman trims and polishes the cup, especially the rims, with a knife, and pares it down as much as necessary for its transparency; he scrapes it several times and moistens each time, however little he may have pared it, if it is too dry, for fear he should break it. In taking the cup from the mould they turn it softly on the same mould without pressing it more on one side than the other, otherwise it would develop cavities in the clay or it would go out of shape. It is surprising to see the rapidity with which these vessels pass through so many different hands; and I am told that a piece of fired porcelain has passed through the hands of seventy workmen. I can easily believe this by what I have myself seen, for these great workshops have been for me a kind of Areopagus, where I have preached Him who fashioned the first men out of clay, and from whose hands we depart to become vessels of honour or of shame.'

'It is time to ennoble the porcelain by passing it over into the hands of the painters. These porcelain painters are not less poor and wretched than the other workmen, which is not very surprising when we remember that in Europe they would only pass for apprentices of a few months' standing. All the science of these painters, and of Chinese painters in general, is based on no principles, and only consists in a certain routine helped by a limited turn of imagination. They know nothing of the beautiful rules of this art; though it must be acknowledged that they paint flowers, animals, and landscapes which are much admired, on porcelain as well as on fans and lanterns of the finest gauze. The painting is distributed in the same workshop among a great number of workmen. One workman does nothing but draw the first colour line beneath the rims of the pieces; another traces flowers, which a third one paints; this man is painting water and mountains, and that one either birds or other animals. Human figures are generally treated the worst. Certain landscapes and plans of towns that are brought over from Europe to China will hardly allow us, however, to mock at the Chinese for the manner in which they represent themselves in their paintings.'

'When they wish to apply gold they beat it and grind it in water in a porcelain dish until they see underneath the water a little golden cloud. This they leave to dry, and in use they mix it with a sufficiency of gum-water, and with thirty parts of gold they incorporate three parts of white lead, and put it on the porcelain in the same way as the colours.'

'Great skill is required in putting the glaze on to the

porcelain so that it is not too thick, and that it is evenly spread over the piece. For porcelain pieces that are very thin and light, they apply two slight coats of glaze. If the coats of glaze are too thick the thin sides of the vessel cannot support them, and will instantly sink out of shape. These two layers are equal to one ordinary layer of glaze such as is put on the thicker pieces. The first coating is put on by sprinkling, the other by immersion. The cup is held in the hand from outside, sloping over the vessel that contains the glaze, and with the other hand they pour inside as much glaze as is needed to wet it everywhere. This is done to a great many cups, and when the first ones are dry inside, the glaze is put on the outside as follows: The workman puts one hand into the cup, and, supporting it with a little stick under the middle of its foot, he dips it into the vessel filled with glaze, and quickly draws it out again.'

'I have been surprised to see how a man can balance on his shoulders two long and narrow planks on which the porcelain pieces are carried, and that he goes like that through several well-populated streets without breaking his ware. It is true that the people carefully avoid knocking against him, however slightly, because they would be obliged to pay for the damage they had caused, but it is astonishing that the carrier himself controls his steps and all the movements of his body so well that he does not lose his balance.

'Where the furnaces are we find another scene. In a kind of vestibule before the furnace one sees piles of boxes and cases made of clay prepared for holding the porcelain. Each vase of porcelain, however small it may be, has its case; the pieces that have covers as well as those that have none—these covers are only slightly attached to the bottom part during the firing, so that they easily come apart by a little blow. The small porcelain pieces, like tea- and chocolate-cups, are placed a good many in one case. In this operation the workman imitates Nature, who to ripen the fruit and bring it to perfection, puts it into a case so that the heat of the sun gets at it little by little, and its action inside is not too much interfered with by the air that comes from outside during the fresh nights.

'These cases [saggers] are lined with a kind of sand-down, for they are covered with "kao-lin" dust as this sand does not stick too much to the foot of the piece that is put on it. The bed of sand is first pressed and given the shape of the bottom of the porcelain piece, which does not itself touch the sides of its case. The top of the case has no lid; a second case, after the shape of the first and similarly filled with porcelain, comes on it, so that it covers it completely without touching the porcelain underneath. In this way they fill the kiln with big cases all containing porcelain. Thanks to these thick veils the beauty, and, if I may say so, the complexion of the porcelain piece is not sunburnt by the heat of the fire.'

After reading these descriptions it would be helpful to visit the English potteries and tour some of the modern factories, for it is interesting that the basic philosophy and skills have remained remarkably similar.

In England the man upon whom the letters of Père d'Entre-colles were to have most impact was William Cookworthy (1705-1780), a young Quaker apothecary living in Plymouth. Having read the letters, he spent many years searching the West Country for the materials he saw described as kaolin and petuntse; in fact he had already seen the materials earlier in his life but had been unable then to appreciate their significance. Light finally dawned upon him when he was visited by a man named André Duché. Duché had arrived from North America where his Huguenot parents had settled following the Revoca-tion of the Edict of Nantes in 1685. His experiments with china clay and china stone enabled Cookworthy to see what was required and a letter to his friend Dr Richard Hingstone, a fellow Quaker living at Penryn, demonstrates his enthusiasm. 'I had lately with me (1744) the person who has discovered the China Earth. He had with him several samples of the china ware, which, I think, were equal to the Asiatic. It was found on the back of Virginia, where he was in quest of mines, and having read Du·Halde, he discovered both the Petunse and the Caulin [sic]. He is gone for a cargo of it, having bought from the Indians the whole country where it rises. They can import it for £13 per ton, and by that means afford their China as cheap as common stoneware; but they intend only to go about 30% under the Company.'
Cookworthy then launched into an enterprise to set up a porcelain works in Bristol, but it appears to have failed because Duché was unable to guarantee the regular supply of clay from Virginia, probably due to the flimsy nature of his agreements with the Indians on whose lands he mined.

Cookworthy's efforts successfully to identify and obtain the essential ingredients of porcelain in Cornwall bore rich fruit, but his attempts to manufacture porcelain were beset with difficulties. In a letter to Dr Hingstone he writes:

'I am at a loss to know best how to set about the work of producing porcelain of a fit and proper nature. I have the caulin [sic], which is the best that can be had, and I have the petunse [sic], which I think is equal to the Chinese, and with these two I have both the flesh, the bones and the sinews, but to put flesh on bone to make a whole body, that is what perplexes me. There are times when I think that I shall, God willing, succeed in this enterprise, and other times when I wonder if 'tis destined for me to succeed.'

However, on 17 March 1768 William Cookworthy's Patent for the manufacture of porcelain was issued, part of which reads: 'Now know ye that I, the said William Cookworthy, do by this my deed in writing, declare the nature of my said invention and the quality of the materials and the manner in which the same is performed, which is as followeth:—

"The materials of which the body of the said porcelain is composed are a stone and earth or clay. The stone is known in the counties of Devon & Cornwall by the names of moorstone and growan, which stones are generally composed of grains of stone or gravel of a white or whitish colour, with a mixture of talcy shining particles. This gravel and these particles are cemented together by a petrified clay into very solid rocks, and immense quantities of them are found in both the above mentioned counties. All these stones, exposed to a violent fire, melt without the addition of fluxes into a semi-transparent glass, differing in clearness and beauty according to the purity of the stone. The earth or clay, for the most part, lies in the valleys where the stone forms the hills. This earth is frequently very white, though sometimes of a yellowish or cream colour. It generally arises with a large mixture of talcy mica or spangles and a semi-transparent whitish gravel. Some sorts have little or none of the mica or spangles, but the best clay for making porcelain always abounds in mica or spangles. The stone is prepared by levigation, in a potter's mill in water, in the usual way, to a very fine powder. The clay is prepared by diluting it with water until the mixture is rendered sufficiently thin for the gravel and mica to subside, the white water containing the clay is then poured or left to run off from the subsided mica and gravel into proper vessels or reservoirs, and after it has settled for a day or two, the clear water above it is to be then poured or drawn off, and the clay or earth reduced to a proper consistence by the common methods of exposing it to the sun and air, or laying it on chalk. This earth or clay gives

the ware its whiteness and infusibility as the stone doth its transparence and mellowness; they are therefore to be mixed in different proportions as the ware is intended to be more or less transparent, and the mixture is to be performed in the method used by potters and well known (viz. by diluting the materials in water, passing the mixture through a fine sieve and reducing it to a paste of a proper consistence for working, in the way directed for the preparation of the clay). This paste is to be formed into vessels, and these vessels when biscuited are to be dipped in the glaze, which is prepared of the levigated stone with the addition of lime and fern ashes, or an earth called magnesia alba, in such quantities as may make it properly fusible and transparent when it has received a due degree of fire in the second baking.''
WILLIAM L. S. COOKWORTHY'

Cookworthy later transferred his manufactory from Plymouth to Bristol, and in 1774 he assigned his patent to Richard Champion. When Champion lodged his application for an extension to the original patent in 1775 it was bitterly opposed by Josiah Wedgwood who himself needed to obtain supplies of china clay. After prolonged legal negotiations Champion's patent was severely pruned and this, together with his legal costs, made it almost impossible for him to continue in business. Later, in December 1780, he formed another small company which bought the patent from him and carried on the production of hard paste porcelain similar to the original Cookworthy formula. This company came to be known as the New Hall Co. of Shelton. Further mention of Plymouth, Bristol and New Hall will be found in Chapter 6.

Many variations of formula were used in the production of soft paste. Often it consisted of calcined flint with sand and potash or lead mixed with china clay, which therefore replaced china stone. This type of body, something of a glassy mixture, is termed frit. Other factories substituted soapstone from Cornwall which produced a far more satisfactory soft paste body, enabling very fine potting to be carried out. The soapstone, or steatite body as it is called, was fired in the kiln at a lower temperature than either the hard paste or the frit bodies, and was also commercially attractive in that the products were less subject to cracking or warping.

Even more successful was the bone ash body developed by the addition of calcined ox-bones to soft paste materials. The Bow factory was the first to experiment successfully with calcined bone. When calcined ox-bones were added to the hard paste formula at the end of the eighteenth century, thus creating the now familiar bone china, it was a major break-through in commercial production. Josiah Spode was a pioneer in this respect, and in the early nineteenth century many other factories, including Worcester, Derby, Coalport and Minton, were quick to adopt it. Bone china produced a body of very high translucency that continues to be greatly admired today and is the basic formula for modern porcelain production in England. Felspar china takes its name from the addition of felspar to the bone china formula, at the same time using less china stone. This again resulted in a body that behaved well in the kiln, together with the commercial attributes of trans-lucency and the ability to withstand hard use.

Many confusing names are to be found in the marks of nineteenth-century earthenware, and such terms as semi-porcelain, opaque porcelain, ironstone and stone china are all improved earthenwares and should not be mistaken for por-celain. The majority of porcelain tablewares are easily shown to be translucent and this is, of course, one of the essential qualities of porcelain; the earthenwares always being opaque and usually requiring a glaze to make them impermeable by water.

Once more it is necessary to stress the necessity of handling the products of as many factories as possible in order to be able to recognise the characteristics of the ceramic bodies used. An old friend, a medical practitioner in Wales, once told me how, when caring for an elderly member of a family he had attended for many years, he was surprised to find the family gathered in the hallway one day in order to make a presentation to him before he left. The doctor, having collected porcelain for most of his life, had always noted the cabinets of fine china in this particular house and the family had told him that their greatest treasure was a Chelsea mug on a very high shelf. He had admired the mug frequently, but it was never lifted down for handling. However, the gift they now handed him was nothing less than their treasured Chelsea mug. The doctor described the sense of pleasure and excitement as he reached out to accept it, 'but' he said 'I hope my face did not betray my change of feelings, or my voice my sense of gratitude. As it came into my hands I realised that what I was holding was a French hard paste copy of a Chelsea mug made by Samson of Paris in the nineteenth century.' It is rather a sad story but it does emphas-ise the value of understanding the porcelain itself through a careful handling rather than being merely beguiled by attrac-tive decoration and a false mark, in this case a spurious gold anchor.

Chapter 3

The influences from abroad

English pottery and porcelain in the initial stages of its development was particularly influenced by Oriental shapes and patterns and also to some extent by products from the Continent. The most influential country, so far as the ceramic arts are concerned, is, as will have been apparent from the outset, China.

The Chinese revered porcelain second only to jade. It bore many of the attributes inherent in this hard stone: for example it was hard, pure and translucent and had a musical note when struck. This delight in the material for its own sake has resulted in the finest objects ever made in porcelain coming from China. Nor should our appreciation of this fact be obscured by European misuse of their decorative patterns. It was only in the nineteenth century that the Chinese became increasingly guilty of over-decoration, and much of that was due to the demands of the European market. Traditionally Chinese

19 Delftware dish painted in blue, red, green and yellow. Note the rather elongated female figures, which are known in Dutch as 'Lange Lijzen' and in English as 'Long Elizas'. Bristol, 1733. City Art Gallery, Bristol.

ceramics reflected Chinese religious beliefs and culture, and a whole panorama of their gods and immortals was paraded on their porcelain, which was also decorated with emblems reflecting other aspects of life. To understand the meaning of Chinese decoration it is therefore necessary to have some knowledge of Taoism and Buddhism. The early potters and decorators in England lacked this knowledge and the result is that Oriental emblems are frequently mixed in a most extraordinary manner, attention being paid only to their decorative effect and their cultural implications being ignored.

Thus while some of the Oriental designs were closely followed, the majority suffered badly at the hands of the potters, who seemed to have been most anxious to anglicise them. For example, the Chinese differentiated between ordinary dragons, which were painted with only three claws on each foot, and imperial dragons, which had five: such niceties as these were totally ignored by English painters. Pagodas begin to look more like European follies or outbuildings, seated Chinamen in their broad brimmed hats develop into giant toadstools, and trees and birds become stylised formalities.

One Oriental pattern to become very popular in Britain was the Imari. These porcelains, largely decorated with floral motifs, were made in the Hizen province of Japan, at the Arita kilns celebrated as the home of the Kakiemon family, of whom more later. The Arita kilns had begun production in the early seventeenth century and part of their output was termed Imari simply because it was shipped from the port of that name. They are recognised by the distinctive Imari palette with its dark underglaze blue, its strong red, and its gilding, which is sometimes overdone.

The Dutch were the principal traders with Japan and it was they who encouraged the Japanese decorators to copy designs from brocades and other textiles. Similar brocaded patterns were used by the English factories of Chelsea, Derby, Davenport, Worcester and many others; in fact various Japan patterns after the Imari style remained popular throughout the nineteenth century until the present day, the Derby Japan patterns being an excellent example of this.

The Chinese also manufactured the Imari patterns and technically their porcelain surpasses that of the Japanese. The glaze of the former is thinner and clearer while that of the Japanese often has a pitted muslin-like appearance.

The Kakiemon family worked at Arita. The patterns ascribed to them are highly sophisticated, using a palette that included only a slight gilding, as well as red, light blue, yellow and a distinctive bluish green. Figures, whether human or insect, were executed with a precise charm, as was the floral decoration, and all designs were carefully related to the shape of the vessel being decorated. The use of pattern is restrained and the overall shape and colour of the porcelain speaks for itself.

The Bow factory made great use of the well-known Kakiemon quail pattern around 1750, as did the Worcester factory later in the century. Worcester also used other patterns in the Kakiemon style, such as the Bengal tiger, and Chelsea used the beautiful narrative decoration that we call 'Hob in the Well'. These pieces are rare, and those marked with the Chelsea raised or red anchor dating from around 1752 are most highly prized. The 'Hob in the Well' pattern tells the story of a young boy who saves his even smaller friend from drowning by hurling a stone and smashing the massive fish bowl into which his friend had fallen.

20 Leaf-moulded porcelain dish, with a quail pattern after the Japanese Kakiemon style. Bow, 1755.

A distinguished ceramicist friend of mine noticed recently, in the window of a Surrey antique shop, a plate that appeared to be in the Kakiemon style. On entering the shop and expressing his interest in the plate he was quickly told by the dealer that while he too thought it was most attractive he only regretted that it was Japanese and not Chelsea. The plate was promptly purchased for just over three pounds, the jubilant purchaser leaving the antique shop with a superb specimen of seventeenth-century Japanese ceramic art.

Trade with the Far East had enabled English potters to become well acquainted with the various techniques of decoration available. The colour most widely used among the early English factories was underglaze blue. Derived from cobalt oxide, cobalt blue, the finest underglaze blue, is a colouring agent varying in range of tone from a greyish blue through blackish blue to its ultimate, sapphire. The variation in colour largely depended upon the quality of the cobalt ore used.

21 The underside of a Chelsea dish with a shaped edge, showing the 'stilt marks' where it was separated from its neighbours in the kiln, and, towards the edge, the raised anchor mark.

Cobalt blue was first developed in Persia from where it was rapidly introduced into China some time between the mid-thirteenth and mid-fourteenth centuries. The colour was therefore well established by the Ming dynasty (1368–1644 AD), and full use of it was made by the brilliant potters of that time. Further exports between China and the Middle East later led to several hundred Chinese potters settling in Persia with their families, thus enhancing Middle Eastern pottery.

Cobalt blue was well-suited as a colour for use under the glaze on English soft paste porcelain. The term 'underglaze' simply means that the colour used as decoration develops at the same time as the firing of the glaze. Any colour that is underglazed cannot be touched with the fingers, which means that any underglaze mark immediately indicates that it cannot have been applied to an object later than its manufacture. All overglaze marks should be examined with more care than usual as these will possibly have been added later. Caution should also be exercised whenever an unglazed area is found on the base of any porcelain object where a mark could reasonably be expected. It is not unknown for marks to be removed with acid or an abrasive wheel. This usually indicates that the mark had denoted a lesser manufactory than a previous owner had wished to admit to.

Various marks described as 'pseudo-Oriental' have been used from time to time on English porcelain and due attention has been given to these in the many excellent hand-books and encyclopaedias of marks now available.

Overglaze or 'on-glaze' decoration again means exactly what the name would imply—a decoration painted or printed on to the glazed surface of the object. The colours used in such decoration are enamel and are fixed in an enamelling kiln; and the decoration so formed can usually be felt with the fingers.

Beautifully coloured birds were made in China throughout the seventeenth and eighteenth centuries and there was a very ready market for these in Europe. Some copies of these exotic birds were made in porcelain, but other excellent models were made by Thomas Whieldon and other early eighteenth-century English potters. Later designs of birds painted on porcelain tend to depict either exotic birds copied from the Chinese, or to follow the European tradition of accurate bird and botanical painting.

Many Oriental shapes were taken up in England, most of which were the octagonal, hexagonal and straight-sided vessels introduced by the Far Eastern potters to provide added strength to the objects, usually vases or small bowls. Oriental bottle shapes with their bulbous bodies and tall narrow necks also found favour in England although the delightful double gourd shapes much used by the Japanese were copied far more frequently on the Continent than in England.

Much armorial porcelain, table services decorated with family monograms or coats of arms, was manufactured in China for English customers, and today such pieces are avidly collected, a fact clearly reflected in their value. Although excellent armorial ware was manufactured in England by most of the leading factories from 1750, the bulk of the orders for services and individual pieces went to China. Sketches, paintings, even bookplates, were forwarded to the Far East in order that the

arms might be accurately represented. So meticulous were the Chinese in their ability to copy such things that the waiting list was formidable. An outstanding example of this ware was shown to me some time ago: a Chinese tea service with each piece bearing the arms of the family, although only the outline of the arms and their supporters were visible. A sketch had been despatched to China showing the arms with the words blue, red, and so on, added where appropriate to show the colouring required. Unfortunately for the family concerned, the service arrived in England with no heraldic colours whatever—only the outlines as sketched with the words for the colours written in as on the original sketch. Today, of course, such a service is a great rarity!

The Chinese loved to keep fish in porcelain tanks superbly decorated on the inside. The most colourful of these date from the eighteenth century. The enamel decoration depicts weeds and water insects of all kinds, usually with carp and other fish painted in iron red. When seen through the rippled water in a full tank the fish appear almost alive. Many of these fish bowls and tanks are to be found in England and they clearly became popular from the 1750s. Smaller versions were also produced, sometimes in the form of punch-bowls, and the best of these are to be found in Liverpool Delft, where the fish are painted in blue on a manganese ground.

Delft takes its name from the Dutch town that became such a major centre for these well-known and now highly collectable tin-glazed wares, although it is to the Arab world, which provided another major influence on English and Continental

22 *Far left:* Delftware bottle-shape vase or water bottle, painted in enamel colours. Liverpool, 1750-60. Fitzwilliam Museum, Cambridge.

23 *Above:* Delftware wall pocket in the shape of a cornucopia and decorated in polychrome. Liverpool, *c.*1760. Merseyside County Museum, Liverpool.

ceramics, that we are indebted for the introduction of Delft into Europe. English Delft is discussed in the next chapter, but the background and development of the glaze belongs here.

Oxide of tin (stannic oxide to give it its real name) produces a glaze of opaque white enamel and, as far as is known, it was first used as a coating for building bricks in ancient Babylon and Nineveh. When the Moors conquered much of Spain in the late eleventh century they also introduced tin glazing into Europe. Many of their tiles glazed in this manner are still to be seen *in situ* in the Alhambra in Granada. Tin glazed objects in Spain are termed Hispano-Moresque wares, and their design has been much influenced by Islamic art.

Italian tin glazing is known as Maiolica and was already known in Italy by the fourteenth century. Luca della Robbia, the Florentine sculptor who was born in 1400, used tin glaze many times during his career and it was in his lifetime that enthusiasm for the glaze really developed in Italy. The principal Italian towns producing Maiolica were Urbino, Gubbio, Castel Durante and Faenza, and the products of these towns are now much collected.

The success of the glaze largely stemmed from the fact that it was exceedingly dense and hard, and therefore comparatively poor clays could be used with it. This also provided an ideal background for decoration. As with most materials, however, there were also drawbacks. The soft clay provides little support for its hard tin glazed shell, and for this reason some degree of chipping is inevitable with this type of ware.

Holland undoubtedly became the leading centre in Northern Europe for tin glazed pottery, which reached the peak of its popularity in the late seventeenth century. The commercial success of Delftware led to an increasing demand for it in Britain. This stimulated the establishment of potteries for Delft production in several parts of England, Scotland and Ireland.

In Italy large dishes and wet and dry drug jars comprised much of the Maiolica output. In England the apothecaries were quick to realise the importance of tin glaze, its fine surface being ideal for their purposes. As well as small and humble ointment pots, truly noble drug jars and decorated pill slabs were made, and these are now among the highlights of many private as well as public collections.

English porcelain during the eighteenth century frequently based its enamelled, as well as its blue-and-white, decoration upon Chinese originals. The French language was used to describe a great deal of Oriental porcelain, mainly because much of the early European literature on the subject was in that

language. As a result, many porcelain colours retain their French names: for example, *famille rose, famille verte, famille jaune, famille noire*, to name a few. (These terms are explained in the glossary.)

The Continental porcelain works and potters produced many pieces, particularly vases and figure groups, of outstanding beauty. The English factories were unable to rival such lavish work in the eighteenth century mainly through lack of patronage, whereas the reverse was the case in France and Germany. When we consider that the main English factories were concentrating mainly on table wares rather than figures to ensure the regular sales needed to keep them in business, what they did achieve appears so much the greater. It must be acknowledged that while the soft paste figures may lack the technical brilliance of the German hard paste, the English pieces have a disarming charm.

Yet Continental influence from France and Germany, particularly from the royal manufactories of Meissen and Sèvres, was strongly felt and had a considerable impact on English ceramic art. The style of the Royal Porcelain factory at Sèvres, which removed from Vincennes in 1756, was copied in England with considerable brilliance in the nineteenth century, especially by Minton and Coalport and some fine colours were achieved. Here is a list of some of these colours with their dates of introduction: *bleu de roi* and *gros bleu* in 1749; *bleu turquin* (turquoise) in 1752; *rose Pompadour*, much copied in England and also known as *rose du Barry*, in 1757; and a fine apple green known as *en camaien*, (that is, different shades of the same colour) in 1766. In 1751 the factory introduced *bisque*, that is unglazed and uncoloured, figures. They met with great success, so much so that Derby followed suit, also with highly satisfactory results. The English term for *bisque* is 'biscuit'.

European styles also affected porcelain design, particularly the bases of figures. Attention to style can frequently be of major help in dating porcelain, and a brief mention of the major styles, with which the reader will no doubt already be familiar in other contexts, as they are used in reference to porcelain, will be useful.

The first European style to be seen in porcelain is the BAROQUE. It has good balance, symmetry, and a sense of strength. Figure bases tend to be plain. It was in greatest vogue between the early eighteenth century and 1740. Next came ROCOCO, which is sometimes called 'the spirit of European porcelain'. French in origin, it is full of flourishes and scrolls, rock- and shell-shaped bases, and is usually asymmetrical. At its best it displays a quality of delicate lightness and vigour. The height of its popularity was between 1740 and 1765. A vulgar ROCOCO was also produced in the nineteenth century. A revolt against excessive decoration came in the form of the NEO-CLASSICAL style, which was much influenced by the Roman discoveries at Pompeii and Herculaneum. It lasted from 1760 to the early nineteenth century.

Many Continental potters, decorators and modellers had a direct influence on English pottery and porcelain, for in the nineteenth century many Frenchmen came to work in England. Minton in particular encouraged them to come, although several other factories were also quick to seize upon their skills, a subject dealt with more fully in Chapter 7.

Of all the modellers copied during the eighteenth century, Johann Kändler had most impact. Many English figures are derived from Kändler originals. Kändler, who died in 1775, held the post of Modellmeister at Meissen from 1731. His style was mainly that of the Baroque and his lively versatility made him a leading force in ceramics throughout Europe. Figures from Italian comedy, including the magnificent dancing group of Harlequin and Columbine modelled in 1744, the seasons, the elements and the arts have always been favourites with collectors, and collecting them is a costly pleasure. Kändler also made some fine bird models, many of them observed from nature.

The other name to be remembered with that of Kändler is Johann Bottger (1682-1719). It was Bottger who, while working for the king of Prussia, carried out the successful experiments with porcelain that led to the establishment in 1710 of the Royal Porcelain Manufactory at Meissen and the first hard paste in Europe.

Marks add much to the story of any object, and nineteenth-century marks frequently contain considerable detail for the intelligent interpreter. The extraordinary thing is that so many people, when confronted with a mark, will read its message inaccurately. It is difficult to account for this apart from the fact that surprisingly few individuals are accurate observers and that most people see what they want to see rather than what really confronts them. It is not uncommon for pattern numbers to be mistaken for dates, or for printed dates of a factory's establishment to be considered the date of manufacture. Before listing several important guides to nineteenth-century dating, it is worth reiterating the value of looking closely at earlier specimens of the type being studied. There have been many occasions when well loved objects have been in the possession of families for several generations yet everyone has failed to see the marks. Rare marks on a genuine object are more likely to be discreetly placed than boldly paraded as is the practice with a copy.

Family attributions may also lead to sadly distorted facts and later disappointments. For example, the ownership of a valued object that has been in the possession of several members of a family often results in the lifespans of the people concerned being added together and thereby producing a completely distorted number of years. Thus for example the date believed to be 1750 under these conditions is far more likely to be 1880 in reality. Always regard a generation as being a span of thirty years. Even more difficult to eradicate than the method of family dating mentioned is the attribution of some long dead member of a family who has written an identification of a vase or figure group on a piece of stamp-paper stuck on its base. Firm evidence to the contrary will seldom shake family faith in their stamp-paper heritage. There is of course no harm in this, but it so often leads to great disillusion at a later date.

Here, then, is a list of pointers worth remembering when examining nineteenth-century marks.
1. If the word 'England' forms part of a mark then the date of the object must be after 1891.
2. 'Made in England' or 'Bone China' always indicate twentieth-century manufacture.
3. 'Trade Mark' indicates that the object was produced after the Trade Mark Act of 1862.
4. 'Royal' in a factory mark indicates manufacture since 1850.
5. 'Limited' or 'Ltd.' in a firm's trade name proves a date after 1861.
6. Printed marks that bear the name of a pattern, such as 'Asiatic Pheasant', will always be later than 1810.
7. Printed marks bearing the royal arms are never earlier than the nineteenth century and may well be modern.

27 *Below:* The tiger and bamboo pattern, one of many Oriental patterns popular in England. On the left is the Japanese original and on the right the Chelsea version.

28 *Bottom:* Interesting examples of English hard paste porcelain.

The cream jug and teapot on the left are Bristol, the beaker vase and sauceboat on the right are Plymouth.

29 *Opposite, top:* A two-handled covered pot (right), and a heart-shaped toilet box (left). Chelsea, 1760-65. British Museum, London.

30 *Opposite, bottom:* A very fine early Worcester teapot decorated in the Oriental manner (left), and a Worcester chocolate cup and saucer (right) with paintings of fruit and apple-green borders.

Chapter 4

English pottery

31 *Opposite:* A delightful pair of flat based Chelsea figures, and a milk jug, both from *c.* 1745-50. British Museum, London.

Whenever the term 'The Potteries' is used in England it is immediately associated in peoples' minds with the county of Staffordshire. Staffordshire pottery has become renowned throughout the world and the potteries have developed into one of Britain's major industries. The early years of potting in Staffordshire, however, were primitive to say the very least, and could in no way be described in the late seventeenth or early eighteenth centuries as a major industry. For most of the early Staffordshire potters it was a part-time occupation, for their main livelihood came from such occupations as farming and inn-keeping.

The question often arises as to why it should be that with such major deposits of china clay and china stone situated in the south-west of England the potteries should have taken root so firmly in Staffordshire: the answer of course is coal. The discovery of coal at Stoke-on-Trent changed the landscape and was in due course to produce the distinctive feature of the coal-fired bottle ovens, so that by the end of the last century Stoke-

32 Staffordshire pottery cup with 'feathered' and 'combed' slip decoration (left) and mug with 'combed' slip decoration (right). Late seventeenth century. City Museum and Art Gallery, Stoke-on-Trent.

221

on-Trent had earned the reputation of being one of the dirtiest towns in England. The kilns, with their belching chimneys pouring vast clouds of smoke into the sky, appeared to have placed the potteries under a permanent and unhealthy cloud. Today the bottle ovens still standing may be counted in tens, whereas once they were numbered in thousands.

The advent of gas and electric furnaces again altered the face of Staffordshire and with it the lives of its work-force. Imagine, for example, the great bee-hive shaped brick ovens being laboriously stacked with clay saggers, each packed with ceramic wares of varying kinds. The firing of such an oven was

34 A 'fuddling cup' of the early eighteenth century. Lambeth or Bristol. Such vessels are so called because they intercommunicate, and the only way to drink from one is to drink from them all! Royal Scottish Museum, Edinburgh.

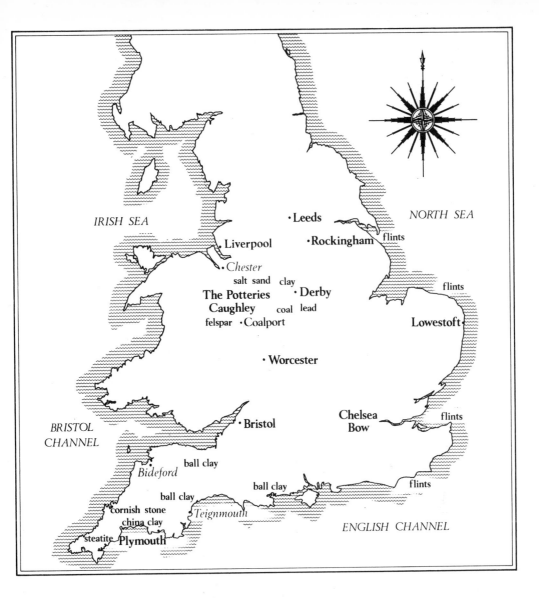

Map showing the main centres of pottery manufacture, sources of raw materials, and harbours used.

supervised by the fireman whose skill was required to create the correct temperatures, temperatures at which the inside of the base of these double-walled structures would become white hot. Large quantities of beer were consumed by the men responsible for the fires and finally, as the oven cooled, came the hazardous task of removing the saggers. In order to save time and money men would enter the kilns while the heat was still very considerable, wearing sacks over their heads and shoulders while others doused them with water. Such, for many, was the way of life in the potteries during the nineteenth century.

One of the earliest potters of whom note must be taken is

223

John Dwight of Fulham. From medieval times a considerable quantity of German salt-glazed stoneware had been imported into England from the Rhineland. Probably the most well-known examples of this ware are the large 'Bellarmine' jugs, sometimes called 'Greybeards', and known as such because of the bearded caricature masks of the unpopular Cardinal Bellarmine that they bear. (Such jugs still exist in considerable numbers but those which bear no mask and are quite plain are usually English, while rare examples are sometimes found with applied Tudor roses or coats of arms.) Dwight obtained his patent for manufacturing his own stoneware from Charles II, producing domestic wares and also figures which tend to be of a pale buff stoneware and are today much admired rarities. Although educated for the Church and appointed registrar to the Bishop of Chester, Dwight very soon turned his thoughts and skills towards becoming a potter. His pottery was established at Fulham in 1671 and he took out several further patents which resulted in legal proceedings during the 1690s when he sued other potters in Fulham and also in Staffordshire because of patent infringements. His main output consisted of hollow wares thrown on the wheel, including such things as jugs, bowls and mugs.

One of Dwight's finest achievements is the Prince Rupert bust now in the British Museum. Once believed to have been modelled by Grinling Gibbons (1648-1721) because of its quality, it is now thought to be the work of John Bushnell (1619-1682) who was also responsible for a terra cotta bust of Charles II to be seen in the Fitzwilliam Museum, Cambridge. Less elaborate examples of Dwight's own work may be seen at the Victoria and Albert Museum in London.

Dwight's family continued with the pottery after his death

35 *Far left:* Brown salt-glazed stoneware bottle with marbled black and white clay patterning and applied moulded reliefs. John Dwight, *c.* 1690. Victoria and Albert Museum, London.

36 *Centre:* 'Malling jug' with a silver mounted rim. Tin glazed jugs of this type, with their mottled decoration, take their name from West Malling in Kent, where the first example was found. London, 1550-75. Birmingham Museums and Art Gallery.

37 *Above:* Bellarmine salt-glazed bottle. John Dwight, *c.* 1680. Victoria and Albert Museum, London.

38 Salt-glazed stoneware mug with a silver mounted rim. John Dwight, 1682. Victoria and Albert Museum, London.

in 1703 but the wares became more coarse and generally rather unsophisticated. Some excellent stonewares were also being manufactured in various other parts of England, most notably at Nottingham and Bristol.

An early form of decorative earthenware which, although rare, has attracted collectors for generations, is known as slipware. The term slip is used to describe a loose clay that has been diluted with water into a creamy mixture. It is usually applied to a brick-coloured clay on which it is trailed, rather in the way that a cake is iced. Wave, trellis and floral designs abound. Particularly valued are items bearing figures, inscriptions, portraits and dates, in other words the documentary piece. Such information always enhances the interest and value of an object.

While slipware was by no means confined to Staffordshire, the most prized examples originated from that county. The most well-known name to be found on slipware is that of Thomas Toft, which occurs on pieces produced between 1680 and 1690. Other members of the Toft family such as James and Ralph, also appear. Further names of note are William Taylor and Ralph Simpson. It is still not known whether the individuals named were themselves potters or whether they were the persons for whom the pottery was made. These slipwares form the first truly English decorative table wares. Important decorations include royal arms and the occasional representation of William III. Most slipware takes the form of plates, chargers and dishes but delightful waisted cups are also found.

Because the decoration on slipware is so simple to apply it was used over a long period, and while slipwares are most highly regarded when they date from the late seventeenth

39 White salt-glazed stoneware figure of Dwight's dead daughter, Lydia. Victoria and Albert Museum, London.

40 Recumbent figure of Lydia Dwight, inscribed 'Lydia Dwight Dyed March 3, 1672'. Possibly modelled by Grinling Gibbons. John Dwight, c. 1672. Victoria and Albert Museum, London.

41 *Right:* Dwight salt-glazed stoneware life-size bust of Prince Rupert, c. 1680. British Museum, London.

42 *Far right:* A smaller Dwight bust of Charles II. Victoria and Albert Museum, London.

century it was also produced during the eighteenth and nineteenth centuries by country potters, and continues to attract many potters today. In 1686 Doctor Plot published his *Natural History of Staffordshire* and in it included a description of the original technique of decorating slipware:

'. . . they slip or paint them, with their severall sorts of slip, according as they designe their work; when the first slip is dry, laying on the others at their leisure, the orange slip making the ground, and the white and red; which two colours they break with a wire brush, much after the manner they doe when they marble paper . . .'

Among the other distinctive slipwares are those from Wrotham in Kent, with their popular tyg shape, that is a pottery vessel of beaker shape with a number of applied handles. Other Wrotham-ware shapes are flagons and dishes.

Yet another type of slipware is known as Jackfield. Jackfield is in Shropshire and red clay products glazed with a glossy black slip have traditionally been associated with that area. Excavations have in recent years provided evidence to suggest that it was also made in other parts of Britain, for example Staffordshire. Once again Jackfield pieces are most distinctive and the ware is most often represented by large teapots, some of which bear documentary inscriptions in gold.

Salt-glaze wares, with their special feel and appearance, have proved attractive to generations of collectors. Although the first commercial examples of salt-glaze were not produced

43 An interesting Nottingham double-walled salt-glazed brown stoneware mug. The outer wall has incised and pierced decoration. Inscribed 'Nottn. 1703'.

44 Slip-decorated dish showing the incident when Charles II took refuge in the Boscabel oak tree, *c.* 1675. British Museum, London.

45 A particularly fine slip-decorated earthenware dish with two shades of brown and white. Staffordshire, *c.* 1675. Victoria and Albert Museum, London.

46 Posset pot with slip-trailed floral decoration. The inscription round the rim reads 'The Best is Not To Good For You 1696'. City Museum and Art Gallery, Stoke-on-Trent.

47 The early use of slip decoration was by no means confined to Staffordshire, and this rare tyg was made of a red earthenware at Wrotham in Kent. Victoria and Albert Museum, London.

48 Salt-glazed brown stoneware two-handled bowl, *c.* 1740. Victoria and Albert Museum, London.

49 *Above:* Large dish depicting 'The Pelican in her Piety', *c.* 1675. Victoria and Albert Museum, London.

50 *Below:* Rare Wrotham dish with incised or 'sgraffito' decoration, 1699. British Museum, London.

227

in England until the last thirty years of the seventeenth century, the original discovery of the glaze was accidental and was made in Germany. It must have been noticed many years earlier that if salt water was allowed to boil over the side of an earthenware pot for any length of time, a glaze of sorts was the result. Simeon Shaw, who knew so many of the later Staffordshire potters, records in his *History of the Staffordshire Potteries*, published at Hanley in 1829, the discovery of salt-glaze:

'About 1680, the method of GLAZING WITH SALT, was suggested by an accident; we give the names of the parties as delivered down by tradition. In this as in many other improvements in Pottery, a close investigation of one subject has frequently reflected fresh light upon another; something altogether unexpected has been presented to notice; and not infrequently from an accident comparatively trivial has resulted a discovery of paramount importance. At Stanley Farm, (a short mile from the small Pottery of Mr. Palmer, at Bagnall, five miles East of Burslem) the servant of Mr. Joseph Yates, was boiling in an earthen vessel, a strong lixivium of common salt, to be used some way in curing pork; but during her temporary absence, the liquor effervesced, and some ran over the sides of the vessel, quickly causing them to become red hot; the muriatic acid decomposed the surface and when cold, the sides were partially glazed. Mr. Palmer availed himself of the hint thus obtained, and commenced making a fresh sort—the common BROWN WARE of our day; and was soon followed by the manufacturers in Holden Lane, Green Head, and Brown Hills; the proximity of their situation to the Salt-Wyches, affording great facility for procuring the quantity of Salt required for their purposes.'

It is a nice story but it really does no more than highlight something that must have been observed long before. It is thought that a highly-skilled Dutch potter named John Phillip Elers was among the first to appreciate the chemical changes that were involved in this kind of glaze. It was used increasingly during the eighteenth century and it may be useful to have a brief description of how such objects were fired. Kilns were made with carefully prepared apertures through which common salt (sodium chloride) could be thrown towards the end of the firing period. In the immense heat the salt would become volatile and rise around the objects in the kiln in a great cloud of white vapour. This would react to the water vapour in the kiln and two chemical changes would then take place. The hydrogen in the water would mingle with the chlorine of the

51 White salt-glazed mug depicting the naval victory of Admiral Vernon at Portobello in 1739. Victoria and Albert Museum, London.

52 Elers unglazed red stoneware mug with applied moulded decoration. Victoria and Albert Museum, London.

salt and become hydrochloric acid. In turn, the oxygen and the sodium would form a silicate. It was this film of silicate that glazed the wares distributed in the kiln. Once handled, salt-glaze is unmistakeable as it has a curious granular texture, rather like orange peel.

It is not only for his work in salt-glaze that John Elers will be remembered, as a very hard and fine red ware was produced by him and is usually referred to as Elersware. He had come to this country from Holland with his brother David around the time of William of Orange, and had settled in Staffordshire a few miles from Burslem where he found a clay which was ideal for the manufacture of red stoneware. It is believed that John Elers was largely responsible for the pottery while David handled the administration of their business. The fine, high-quality clay which formed the body of the red ware allowed it to be lathe-turned before firing and these highly finished pieces became extremely popular. They also used an interesting form of decoration: applying pieces of damp clay to the lathe-turned article and stamping it with a geometrical, floral or sprig pattern. The superfluous clay was then very carefully cut away.

53 Fine red stoneware coffee pot of the type made by Elers. Late seventeenth or early eighteenth century. City Museum and Art Gallery, Stoke-on-Trent.

It is said that the Elers brothers maintained the greatest secrecy over the mixing of their clays. They had established their pottery at Bradwell, north of Newcastle-under-Lyme, in the 1690s, and it was there that they evolved a classic method for the purification of clay. By suspending their clays in water all coarser particles sank to the bottom while the remainder were drawn off into pans where the water would evaporate in the sun. The obvious drawback to this refining method was that it was dependent upon good weather and prevented year-round working. A more commercial process was invented by Ralph Shaw of Burslem in 1732 when he devised the drying of clay on shallow kilns heated by flues beneath.

54 Elers mug clearly showing the outline of a stamped decoration. City Museum and Art Gallery, Stoke-on-Trent.

The variety and shape of the Elers red wares were largely inspired by the increasing demand for tea in England and the importing of red stonewares from Yi-hsing, the Chinese potteries west of the great lake in Kiangsu. These were to be the models for the first European teapots made by Dwight and Elers. During the nineteenth century many copies were made of the early Elersware and care therefore needs to be exercised when confronted with such pieces. The Elers brothers also made a black earthenware known as 'Egyptian black'. This was later to be improved by Josiah Wedgwood into the celebrated black basalt.

John Astbury is another potter of importance in the early

eighteenth century. He worked mainly with earthenware and legend has it that he acquired many of the Elers brothers' manufacturing secrets by obtaining employment with them by posing as a half-wit—the Elers brothers are believed to have employed such men in order to prevent intelligent outside discussion of their work. So industrial espionage has been with us for a very long time!

Astbury became deeply interested in the nature of the clays being used. As we have already seen, while other parts of Britain also had excellent clay deposits, these existed in greater variety in Staffordshire and were supported by the availability of easily mined long-flame bituminous coal. The geological excellence of Staffordshire was further increased by the discovery in 1670 of rock salt near Northwich, in neighbouring Cheshire, and the mining of lead ore in Derbyshire.

Pipe clays, so-called because they were used for the manufacture of clay tobacco pipes, were found in thin seams. From about 1720 similar clays were imported from Devon and Dorset. These became known as ball clays because they were dug out in 35 lb (15·8 kg) balls with a tool not unlike an adze. The clay was then carried by sea from the ports of Bideford, Teignmouth and Wareham to be unloaded at the port of Chester and from there carried by pack-horse into north Staffordshire. John Astbury was delighted with the ball clays and he was also quick to see the importance of adding ground flint into his pottery body to make it harder and smoother. Other potters had also used flint a few years earlier and many

55 Chinese Yi-hsing red stoneware teapot with relief decoration, a kind that probably influenced the work of the Elers brothers and other Staffordshire potters. Victoria and Albert Museum, London.

56 Whieldon coffee pot with crabstock handle. Victoria and Albert Museum, London.

57 Figure of a Turk. Whieldon, *c.* 1750. Victoria and Albert Museum, London.

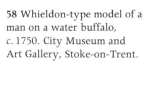

58 Whieldon-type model of a man on a water buffalo, *c.* 1750. City Museum and Art Gallery, Stoke-on-Trent.

workers died of pneumoconiosis when working in the thick dust of the dry stamp mills, where the flint was ground down. In 1726 a patent was taken out for the grinding of flints in water which eliminated many of the earlier problems. The potteries were now beginning to grow and as local skills increased all that remained was the necessity of providing better transport facilities by road and by water, and it was not long before all of these hopes were fulfilled.

The charming Astbury figures of brown and white clays under a transparent lead glaze are easily recognised; their blackcurrant eyes and naive modelling are their hallmarks. Similar figures which are lead-glazed but stained with metallic oxides are referred to as Astbury Whieldon, while earthenware figures with stained or tortoiseshell glazes are known as Whieldon. This classification helps to define the three types of early figures but there must have been many other potters in Staffordshire working in a similar fashion to those already named.

Thomas Whieldon is among the most revered of the early Staffordshire potters, the last of a long line of peasant craftsmen, but while his trade was considerable he firmly belonged to that highly individual period just prior to the new age of industrialisation. He made toys and chimney ornaments of all kinds and his figure models of birds and animals are especially delightful. The birds usually have a variegated glaze, while the small animals, particularly the cats, were made of agate ware which imitated agate stone by the layering of different col-

231

oured clays before cutting and moulding into shape, or by the use of differently coloured slips on the surface of the figure. When made of solid colour clays, such wares are called solid agate and when surface colouring is applied they are known as surface colouring agate. An outline of Whieldon's life and something of an insight into his character is once again given us by Simeon Shaw:

'In 1740 Mr. Thomas Whieldon's manufactory at Little Fenton consisted of a small range of low buildings, all thatched. His early productions were knife hafts, for the Sheffield cutlers; and Snuff Boxes, for the Birmingham Hardwaremen, to finish with hoops, hinges and springs; which he himself usually carried in a basket to the tradesmen; and being much like agate, they were greatly in request. He also made toys and chimney ornaments, coloured in either the clay state or bisquet, by zaffre, manganese, copper, etc., and glazed with black, red, or white lead. He also made black glazed tea and coffee pots. Tortoise-shell and melon table plates, (with ornamented edge, and six scollopes, as in the specimens kept by Andrew Boon, of the Honeywall Stoke) and other useful articles. Mr. A. Wood made models and moulds of these articles also pickle leaves, crab stock handles and cabbage leave spouts, for tea and coffee pots, all which utensils, with candlesticks, chocolate cups, and tea ware, were much improved, and his connections extended subsequently, when Mr. J. Wedgwood became his managing partner. He was a shrewd and careful person. To prevent his productions being imitated in quality or shape, he always buried the broken articles; and a few months ago, we witnessed the unexpected exposure of some of these, by some miners attempting to get marl in the road at Little Fenton. The fortune he acquired by his industry enabled him to erect a very elegant mansion, near Stoke; where he long enjoyed in the bosom of his family, the fruits of his early economy. He was also Sheriff of the County, in the 26th year of the late reign. The benevolence of his disposition, and his integrity, are honourable traits of character, far superior to the boast of ancestry without personal merit. He died in 1798, at a very old age and in 1828 his relict was interred beside him in Stoke Church yard.'

(It has since been proved that Whieldon died in 1795, three years earlier than stated by Shaw.)

The reference to what are known as crab stock handles is particularly interesting for it was a handle in regular use in Staffordshire pottery between 1740 and 1770. Even the finials

to lids of teapots tend to be of this shape, which does indeed bear similarity to that of the body of a crab. Many of the salt-glaze teapots and coffee pots of this period are decorated in enamels and are largely inspired by Chinese originals, particularly the *famille rose* palette. Decoration was also incised or applied and the general care and attention given to both shape and colouring was largely due to the competitive pressures from foreign and British porcelains. While Whieldon's work was not subjected to such commercial pressure, his wares were nonetheless colourful, with their splashes of brown, green, yellow and manganese. Such colours are best shown off in Whieldon's moulded plates with their feathered or trellised borders and frequently milled edges. His output of such wares, together with his animal figures, are among the most collectable of the early Staffordshire pottery.

It is clear from Astbury's work that he favoured the development of figure modelling and his rolled pipe clay figures always

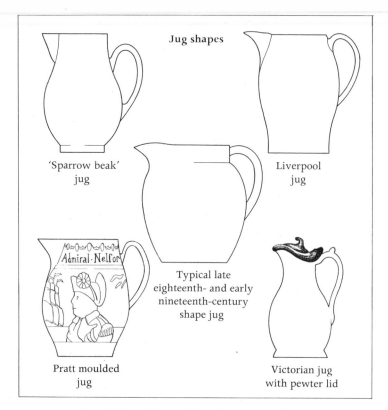

Jug shapes

'Sparrow beak' jug

Liverpool jug

Typical late eighteenth- and early nineteenth-century shape jug

Pratt moulded jug

Victorian jug with pewter lid

possess a cheerful quality and enthusiasm. These were to be surpassed, in both quality and beauty, in the second half of the eighteenth century by the astonishing range of figures modelled by the Wood family of Burslem. In the middle of the eighteenth century the use of plaster of Paris moulds was introduced into Staffordshire from France by Ralph Daniel. Plaster moulds were ideal for ease of use, speed and detailed moulding, but the rival method of pressing 'bats' or cakes of clay into a mould was to continue for a long time, causing moulded decoration to become increasingly poor. Today plaster of Paris moulds are still regarded as the finest method of production available.

Thus the range of English pottery was being extended by potters like Elers, Astbury and Whieldon who experimented with new techniques. They continued to make salt-glaze, however, and it will be useful at this point, before turning to other wares, to give a break-down of the four main stages of its development:

1. *Before 1720.* Engine-turned vessels with impressed or applied ornament.

2. *1720-1740.* The introduction of flint into the clay enabled crisper, finer work to be produced.

3. *1740-1760*. Popular use of coloured enamels in the decoration of salt-glazed wares.

4. *1760-1780*. Increased use of pierced work and a general decline in production.

The market for salt-glaze was being steadily undermined by the development of creamwares with their simple painted or transfer printed decoration. Creamware will be considered in the next chapter, and let us in the meantime return to other forms of English pottery, notably Staffordshire figures and English Delft.

Staffordshire pottery figures

The demand for pottery ornaments at the beginning of the eighteenth century was not large, mainly because social conditions were not yet ready for it. The Staffordshire chimney ornaments came into their own towards the end of the century, and as the nineteenth century progressed so the demand for such ornaments grew. In other words, with the creation of more urban areas and homes with a 'best room' or 'parlour' where furniture and other objects were displayed, pottery became something of a status symbol. Such pieces differed from the earlier cottage ornaments which tended to portray scenes of sport, work and courtship.

The Astbury figures of salt-glazed stoneware, decorated

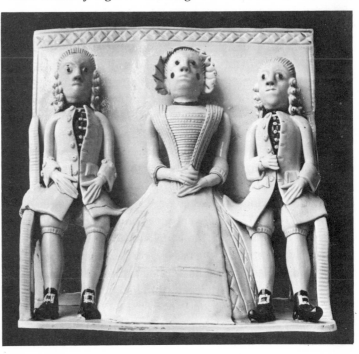

60 White salt-glazed 'pew group', *c.* 1730-45. British Museum, London.

with coloured glazes under a final lead glaze, were produced from moulds, with a great deal of hand finishing. Whieldon's application of coloured glazes is haphazard, and the work of both men may easily be criticised on many counts if precision of detail is regarded as paramount. Yet for many collectors the soldiers, pew groups, musicians and horsemen of this period possess all the charm in the world. Perhaps the attraction is due to the humble materials used and the spontaneous, child-like approach of the modellers. The majority of such figures possess humour and an apparently insatiable concern for such trimmings of dress as buttons, bows, buckles and curled wigs.

The pottery figures that followed were the work of potters who had clearly come of age in the process; something of the earlier imaginative exuberance was lost, but it was replaced with a high level of sophistication. The potters largely responsible for this change were the Wood family of Burslem.

Ralph Wood senior (1715-1772) had worked for John Astbury and Thomas Whieldon before starting to manufacture pottery on his own account in Burslem in about 1754. He was responsible for some superb and justly famous figures, plaques and Toby jugs. Many of the pieces made by this family can be identified with certainty because they impressed many of their figures with mould numbers. Also to be found are the marks of the firm – R. WOOD or *Ra Wood* or *Ra Wood, Burslem* – which are believed to be the marks of father and son. A very rare rebus in the form of a group of trees impressed in the side of a base is also thought to be a mark of Ralph Wood senior.

It would be perhaps better to identify the work of the Woods by their quality. Ralph Wood senior is distinguished by the splendid modelling of his figures and the superbly lustrous transparent glazes that he employed. There was no slipping or dabbing of glazes and trusting to good fortune: care had become the watchword and Ralph Wood applied his coloured glazes with a brush exactly where they were required. To obtain flesh tints he used a highly unusual pale manganese purple.

Similar colouring techniques were also used by Ralph Wood junior (1748-1795) but he went on to adopt the use of enamel colours, as did his cousin Enoch Wood (1759-1840). This new method of decoration by the use of overglaze enamels was very open to misuse and could be applied with a garish brashness like a woman who has failed to understand make-up. Enoch Wood was the son of Aaron Wood (1717-1785), who was the brother of Ralph Wood senior and a brilliant modeller and mould maker. So many of the potters' skills seem inherent in

61 Pottery figure of a young girl decorated in a coloured translucent glaze. The impressed mark reads 'R. Wood' Burslem. *C.* 1770. Victoria and Albert Museum, London.

this family that it is little wonder that the portrait busts by Enoch Wood should be outstanding. Enoch and Ralph Wood junior worked in partnership until Ralph's early death in 1795 when Enoch Wood joined James Caldwell. In 1819 Caldwell was bought out by Enoch Wood and the business then became known as Enoch Wood and Sons. As the father of twelve children 'and Sons' was more than usually appropriate!

The portrait bust of John Wesley is probably the finest work by Enoch Wood but his use of bright enamel colours and his misuse of silver lustre has somewhat undermined his reputation as a potter. As a man he was held in highest esteem in the potteries, and was chief constable of Burslem for two years. Enoch Wood was among the first real collectors of Staffordshire pottery and with his family background and associations he must have owned pieces of the greatest importance. Unfortunately no inventory or catalogue was ever made and when he died in 1840 the collection was dispersed.

Great collections were made in the nineteenth century and the finest private collection of that period which I have seen is that formed by Henry Willett of Brighton, now in the Brighton Museum and Art Gallery. In 1899 it was lent to the Bethnal Green Museum, a branch of the Victoria and Albert Museum, and a most useful catalogue was produced, although unfortunately copies are now difficult to obtain. The catalogue lists 1,715 objects and it is possible to sense the pleasure that Henry Willett must have enjoyed while gathering them together. His brief introduction to the catalogue is well worth quoting for it demonstrates so well the very best of motives for collecting anything:

'This collection has been formed with a view to develop the idea that the history of the country may to a large extent be traced on its homely pottery, and it is not to be regarded as an exhibition of ceramic art.

'On the mantelpieces of many cottage homes may be found representations which the inmates admire and revere, as their ancestors have done before them. They form, in fact, a kind of unconscious survival of the Lares and Penates of the Ancients.

'The classification, whilst confessedly arbitrary, has been made not so much in reference to the maker, the time and place of manufacture, but rather with regard to the greater human interest which each object presents.

'June, 1899.   HENRY WILLETT.'

Willett then goes on to explain his reference to Lares and Penates:

'The Lares and Penates were household gods of the Romans. The former were grouped into various classes, such as: *lares domestici*, departed spirits of the household, only good men being thus honoured; *lares publici*, benefactors to the nation; *lares marini*, victors in naval battles and others. There were also public and private penates, protectors and promoters of happiness and concord. Every meal was a kind of sacrifice to them, often ending in a libation.'

The catalogue's contents list will also help to provide the new collector with an idea of the variety of interest covered in such pottery: Royalty and Loyalty, Military Heroes, Naval Heroes, Soldiers and Sailors, England and France, England and America, Statesmen, Clubs and Societies, Philanthropy, Crime, Professions and Trades, Architecture, Scripture, Religion, Music, Drama, Poetry, Science and Literature, Sporting, Field Sports, Pastimes and Amusements, Agriculture, Conviviality and Teetotalism, Domestic Incidents.

The Wood family modelled a great range of figures of rustic inspiration, from birds nesting to larger animals such as lions and elephants. The seasons were represented, as were many classical figures and a number of literary and scientific personalities such as Milton, Chaucer, Pope and Newton. Some of the Ralph Wood figures were modelled by the Frenchman John Voyez.

An active potter during the early years of the nineteenth century with a considerable output in the field of figures and toys was a man named John Walton (working *c*.1806-1850). He tended to like somewhat sentimental subjects such as allegori-

62 *Far left:* A rare 'Fair Hebe' jug, one of the originals modelled by the Frenchman Jean Voyez, and signed and dated 1788. Voyez worked for numerous Staffordshire potters and some of his jugs have been attributed to the Wood family. Those decorated in enamel colours will be later versions. Hebe was the Greek goddess of youth. Victoria and Albert Museum, London.

63 *Above:* Figure of a gardener. Walton, Burslem, 1825. Victoria and Albert Museum, London.

WALTON

Impressed mark, found on backs of bocage figures, *c*. 1818-35

cal representations of Hope and Charity. His modelling was straightforward and he made great use of the bocage, which is modelled leaves and flowers forming a background, and support for the figures. Soft paste figures needed such support in the kiln and the bocage made a decorative virtue of necessity.

It is thought that the bocage originated on the Continent where figures in stage productions were observed in front of moveable scenery in the form of trees; the idea was then tried out in porcelain and later its use became widespread. Walton's work is often marked on the back of the model in relief-moulded capitals or impressed on a scroll.

Other potters are associated with Walton because of a similarity in style. Most important among these is Ralph Salt (1792-1846): his mark is impressed.

Some very interesting religious figures were manufactured by this school. A famous model is that of the tithe pig. Here we find a man with a pig, a parson, a woman with a child, some piglets, eggs and sheaves of corn. Behind the figures is a bocage. The tithe is due but the wife is offering the parson her baby instead of the expected pig!

James Neale, a London merchant, met the potter, Humphrey Palmer, and took over his business at the Church Works, Hanley, in 1776. His late eighteenth-century wares were well chosen and in the best of taste. His work is recognised not only by the good potting but also by his frequent use of rectangular or square bases around which a red line has often been painted. The business closed soon after 1814 when Neale died. Neale's small figures of the seasons are considered superior to those of Ralph Wood junior.

At the same time, around 1775, a particular type of lead-glazed earthenware was being made at Lane Delph by William Pratt. The ware, primarily jugs and figure models, had a lightweight body, often white but sometimes tinged with blue, and the colours that were used in decoration are browns, greens, yellow, black and orange.

The factory was taken over in 1810 by William Pratt's son Felix and in the nineteenth century it was this factory that produced pot lids. However, it is only the pottery and palette originally used that is termed Prattware.

The work of Obadiah Sherratt (b. 1755), who worked at Hot Lane, Burslem, was continued after his death by his second wife, Martha, until about 1860. While so much of the Staffordshire pottery output was handled in a light and somewhat bucolic manner, the Sherratt figures are bluntly to the point in their vigorous portrayal of life about them and of news stories

SALT
Impressed mark, c. 1820-46

Rare impressed or moulded mark, c. 1776-86

Neale & Wilson
Impressed, c. 1784-95

64 Child figures depicting Winter and Spring. Marked 'Neale & Co.' and impressed on the back. *C.* 1780. Victoria and Albert Museum, London.

of the day. Certainly crude versions of classical figures were attempted, probably copied from Derby originals, but they are not the pieces for which Sherratt is remembered and collected.

Sherratt groups include 'The Death of Monrow' [sic] which depicts the fate of Lieutenant Hector Monroe who was killed and carried off by a tiger near Calcutta. Some rare examples of this group show the tiger as being black rather than striped. Temperance campaigns were assisted by his morality groups, one of which carries the title 'Teetotal Bench'. In this instance accurate dating is assisted by the fact that the word teetotal was not coined until 1833.

Maria Martin and the murder in the Red Barn of 1828 are portrayed, as is bull-baiting. This, his most famous group, is so vigorous that it exudes the cruelty of a sport which Sherratt would certainly have known at first-hand. Bull-baiting was made illegal in 1835, but in Staffordshire it was continued for as long as possible. Suddenly we discover that the English countryside was not all quaint shepherds and shepherdesses, and that life was also riddled with ignorance and barbarity. In an issue of the *Staffordshire Advertiser* in November 1833 is this

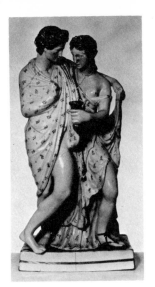

65 Fine lead-glazed Staffordshire figure group depicting 'Bacchus and Ariadni', c. 1790. Fitzwilliam Museum, Cambridge.

dreadful account which enables us to see the pottery of Sherratt as social document:

'At Rowley Regis wake a two-year-old bull was worried in the most brutal manner. Either on the Monday or Tuesday one of the bull's horns was broken off, and the following day the other shared the same fate, and a portion of the tongue was also torn out of its mouth by one of the dogs. On the Thursday he was again dragged to the stake and worried for hours, the whole of his head and face being mangled and covered in blood, in a manner too shocking to describe. Two iron horns had also been riveted on to the stumps, and the bellowings and groans of the wretched beast, while undergoing this barbarous operation, are said to have been truly appaling [sic].'

There are differences to be observed among the bull-baiting groups. Some show the bull with dogs and a man standing at its side, some with a man under the bull and some combine all these features.

Sherratt's large model of 'Polito's Menagerie' is most ambitious, with its human and animal figures. Sherratt also had an eye for marital conflict as a group called 'Battle for the Breeches' well illustrates. In the Willett collection catalogue mentioned earlier, there is an earthenware mug that depicts 'Peggy Plumper proving her man before marriage' or 'Who wears ye breeches'. The mug also bears an inscription in verse that has little to commend it apart from the humour of its times, humour which, no doubt, explains the popularity of such examples with collectors today.

Peggy Plumper, a lass well made tall and pretty,
Was courted by sweet Sammy Spar of ye city:
They jog'd on in courtship, Sam would have gone faster,
But Peg w'd not Wed, till she knew who was Master.

Tho' says She we may live and ne'er quarrel for riches,
Yet it may not be so, about wearing the Breeches.
So saying she squar'd up to Sam very clever,
Thinks he for to gain her the time's now or never.

They had several rounds, who'd the best none did know, Sir,
At last Sam gave Peg a fair knock down blow, Sir;
Then he led her to church as loving as could be,
And the Breeches remain'd in ye place where they should be.

The flat pottery table bases of his groups were usually mounted on four or six short legs. A good general rule of

241

thumb when examining old pottery is to remember that the majority of figures made before 1800 have hollow bases, while those made after this date are solid. Lose no opportunity of handling pottery of all kinds whenever a sale or similar occasion arises.

The most well-known form of Staffordshire pottery must surely be the Toby jug: jugs in human form, with the figure usually holding a foaming tankard and a churchwarden pipe. The Toby's hat or lid, usually missing from old examples, formed the cup to drink from. While the production of Toby jugs was not confined to any one manufacturer, they are most frequently associated with the work of Ralph Wood senior and his son Ralph Wood junior. Again it was the coloured translucent glazes that have made the Wood Toby jugs so desirable. The great collector of Toby jugs, Lord Mackintosh, likened such glazes to the light through stained glass windows.

Uncle Toby in Sterne's *Tristram Shandy* and Sir Toby Belch in *Twelfth Night* have both been claimed as the inspiration for the Toby jug, but it is far more likely that the character originated from a print published in London early in the 1760s from the printshop of Carrington and Bowles. The print was the work of Robert Dighton and it was accompanied by a song called 'The Brown Jug'. In the Copeland Spode Museum there is a relief mould that copies the Dighton print but the jugs themselves bear only a passing likeness. I like to think that the jugs were based on a Yorkshireman named Harry Elwes who is said to have received the nickname of Toby Fillpot for having drunk two thousand gallons of ale from a brown jug. More likely Ralph Wood senior simply copied some local real-life character.

Whatever Toby's identity the jugs have created ample fuel for collectors for they have many variations, including such characters as 'Hearty Good Fellow', 'Toby Fillpot', 'Sir Toby Belch', 'The Squire', 'Drunken Parson', 'The Fiddler', 'Admiral Lord Howe', 'Martha Gunn', 'Admiral Jarvis', 'Nightwatchman', 'American Sailor', and so on. The cult of the Toby jug appears to be very much an on-going tradition, and a fine Toby of Winston Churchill was modelled by Leonard Jarvis and decorated with glazes in the Ralph Wood style just after the Second World War. Churchill also appears as a Toby rather earlier, when he formed one of a series modelled by Carruthers Gould for the Royal Stafford Pottery during the First World War. The characters depicted heroes of the day—King George V, Lord Kitchener, Earl Haig, Admiral Beatty and Sir John French. Most of these Tobys were issued in limited editions of a few hundred and are now very definitely collectors' pieces.

66 Pair of Victorian 'flatback' chimney ornaments depicting the Duke and Duchess of Cambridge.

Victorian Staffordshire figures were mentioned in Chapter 1. They are characterised by their 'flatback' form which, as the name indicates, means that they have no modelling on the back. Flatbacks were made in press moulds and date from shortly before the middle of the nineteenth century. They covered a great variety of subjects and many of them were made by Sampson Smith of Longton after 1855. This style of figure could not have been better suited to the mantelpiece and in recent years there has been a complete renewal of interest in them. Figures bearing the name of the character depicted are particularly valued, and many of them are American. Because of demand there has been an influx of reproductions in recent years that have been made from the old moulds. It is a knowledgeable eye that separates the original from the copy, but copies are most frequently detected by their differences in colouring. For example, bases with a brown and green mottled effect should be regarded with suspicion, as copies were made from moulds discovered just after the Second World War until 1962. It is curious that while this type of pottery has risen considerably in value, Toby jugs have not appreciated to anything like the same extent.

English Delft

A class of English pottery that can still be obtained without too much difficulty is English Delft, manufactured in England from

243

the late sixteenth century until about 1800. This ware and the story of its development has already been mentioned in Chapter 3. The earliest name for tin-glazed wares was 'gally-ware' and the makers were known as 'gally potters'. The tin oxide with its hard white surface provided an ideal basis for decoration and tin was easily obtained in this country from the Cornish mines; in fact the Cornish tin mines supplied the raw materials for much of the production of Dutch Delft and Italian Maiolica. Blue and white decoration is very common on English Delft, the various shades of blue being obtained from cobalt. Other colourings were soon in demand for ornamentation: purple and ranges of that colour were derived from manganese, red from iron, green from copper, yellow from antimony. All these colours vary in tone, and after 1700 greater varieties of green, in particular, were developed.

The first Delftwares made in England were produced by Dutch potters in London and it is difficult to separate the early English products from those made in Holland. From the late 1620s we begin to see Delftware that is definitely English. Some of these pieces bear inscriptions and dates, while blue and white decoration is based on Ming porcelain.

Much of the London output was manufactured at Southwark and in 1969 I obtained a number of fragments of this early Delft from a site between Southwark Cathedral and the Thames. The pottery body is light buff in colour with the tin glaze of eggshell thickness. Foot-rims among the fragments are unglazed and specimens from one kiln site not only showed a variation in the glaze from a pinkish white to a hard whitish blue, but also demonstrated the variance in the blue tones of the painted decoration itself. Unfortunately this merely underlines how difficult it frequently is to attribute particular objects to particular factories. However, fine pieces of English Delft may still be obtained far more cheaply than most English porcelains, and as more excavation and research is carried out in the years to come much more information will become available on both the larger and the lesser known factories. In the following pages, I shall discuss in more detail certain types of these wares which are of special interest to the collector.

Delftware was particularly popular for chargers, a type of large circular dish, of which there are four main types: the blue-dash, the portrait, the Adam and Eve, and the tulip. While most English pottery was made for every-day use, blue-dash chargers were mainly produced as ornaments, to be hung on the wall or displayed on court cupboards. They vary in size,

67 Blue-dash portrait dish painted in blue, green, yellow and red. Note the sponged foliage. Brislington, early eighteenth century. The fragment at the side was excavated in Brislington in 1914. City Art Gallery, Bristol.

68 *Above:* Polychrome dish with a tulip design. All elements in the design appear to spring from a central source – an indication of Islamic influence. Probably Lambeth, *c.* 1690. Nottingham Castle Museum.

69 *Right:* Polychrome Adam and Eve dish. Lambeth, *c.* 1690. Birmingham Museums and Art Gallery.

the largest being about 16 inches (406 mm). They get their name from the blue dashes painted around their borders. Early pieces are clearly inspired in their decoration by Italian Maiolica as well as Chinese patterns. Of special interest are the blue-dash chargers that also carry royal portraits, the very best being the portraits of William and Mary, either standing together or on their own.

A number of fine examples of portrait chargers exist including ones depicting the English kings Charles I and Charles II. My own personal favourite portrait charger depicts General Monk on horseback. The broad border patterns derive their style from the Chinese blue-and-white dishes of the Kang H'si. Foliage that may appear on chargers of this kind is frequently applied with a sponge and the rather crude splodgy appearance, in contrast to the finer, neater decoration applied with a brush, makes it easily identifiable as such.

Adam and Eve chargers are as their name would suggest, with prominence sometimes being given to the apple and sometimes to the snake. The earliest known example is dated 1635. The sponged foliage mentioned above only appears on late seventeenth-century examples.

Tulip chargers are frequently found with blue dash borders

245

and their decoration drew much inspiration from Islamic sources: the leaves and stems spring from one central point to radiate over the whole face of the charger.

The painting of all these subjects is invariably crude, partly due no doubt to the cheapness of the ware, yet at the same time most English Delftware has a sense of spontaneity that is truly refreshing. Often a decorator will capture some current event, such as a balloon ascent, and work of this kind adds further to the interest. There are also many curiosities to be found in the form of ointment pots, jars for wet and dry drugs, tiles, pill slabs, shaving bowls, bleeding bowls, posset pots, fuddling cups, trinket pots, flower bricks, tea caddies, candlesticks and cups of all kinds—to say nothing of the mass of plates, teapots, coffee pots, puzzle jugs, punch bowls and so much else. Many of these pieces bear inscriptions that are well worth noting. An old Bristol punch bowl carries a verse typical of West Country humour:

70 Bowl showing Lunardi's balloon ascent at Lambeth in 1783. Lambeth, *c.* 1783-90. Nottingham Castle Museum.

71 Blue painted barber's bowl, probably Bristol, late seventeenth century. Smaller versions of this bowl (which is 10¼ inches (260 mm) in diameter) were also used occasionally as bleeding bowls. Victoria and Albert Museum, London.

> *John Udy of Luxillion his tin was so fine*
> *It gliddered this punch bowl and made it to shine*
> *Pray fill it with punch*
> *Let the tinners sit round*
> *They never will budge till the*
> *Bottom they sound.*
>
> *1731*

Udy is a Cornish name and Luxillion is a parish a few miles from Lostwithiel. The word gliddered is from an old verb meaning to glaze.

The most celebrated inscribed Delft of all are the plates known as the 'Merry Man' plates made at Lambeth. Several such sets were produced, consisting of six plates each bearing a phrase of a complete poem. Lambeth produced an eight-plate set of octagonal blue-and-white decorated plates and further sets of circular plates were made by them later in the seventeenth century and at various periods during the early eighteenth century. The complete verse is as follows:

> *What is a merry man*
> *Let him do what he can*
> *To entertain his guests*
> *With wine and merry jests*
> *But if his wife doth frown*
> *All merriment goes down.*

246

72 *Above:* Wine bottle with name painted in blue. Height 7¼ inches (184 mm). London, 1651. Royal Scottish Museum, Edinburgh.

73 *Right:* Rare documentary jug painted in blue and purple. Among the many decorative motifs is an applied relief of King David playing his harp. Fitzwilliam Museum, Cambridge.

The spelling used in this verse varies considerably with date and artist; dated examples exist between 1648 and 1742 and only one complete set is at present known.

Lambeth sack bottles, between 6 and 8 inches (152 and 203 mm) high and dating from the middle of the seventeenth century, are also most attractive to collectors, particularly dated examples; while those painted with portraits of Charles II have a special commemorative interest. Many such pieces have a fine white glaze typical of early Lambeth work but there are others with a considerable pinkish tinge giving a somewhat soft appearance.

Successful attributions of eighteenth-century examples are not easy and it is unlikely that the wares of individual potteries in the same area will be separately identified. One of the drawbacks in identification is the fact that many of the potters and decorators frequently moved from pottery to pottery and considerable uniformity was thus brought about in both shape and decoration.

Much Bristol Delftware does incline towards a lavender hue, particularly when decorated with *bianco-sopra-bianco* or white on white. This type of decoration was first used at Faenza in

247

74 Blue painted plate.
Diameter 9 inches
(228·6 mm). Bristol, 1760.
Victoria and Albert Museum,
London.

Italy during the sixteenth century and it was from that town
that the term faience was derived. In their turn the spiral white
enamel designs of *bianco-sopra-bianco* were originally taken
from Chinese border patterns.

Both Bristol and Liverpool favoured the use of ship decoration, as might be expected, but it tends to occur rather more
frequently on Liverpool examples. Liverpool was the only user
of transfer prints taken from copper plates which were then
used on the Delft tiles.

Rectangular Delft bricks with pierced tops appear to be
unique to English Delft. These 'bricks' are usually called flower
bricks but in the opinion of some authorities they may have
been bulb pots or quill and inkpot holders. Many are decorated
in blue and white and were made at Lambeth, Bristol and
Liverpool. Where polychrome decoration is used, however, it
can be observed that the reds and yellows of Bristol tend to
stand proud of the glaze, particularly the reds. Manganese
grounds were also used by the main Delftware centres but most
of them are usually attributed to manufactories in the West
Country.

A polychrome decoration long assumed to have come from
Liverpool is formed from a palette which consists of purple,

248

75 Plate with pale blue glaze. The border is decorated in bianco-sopra-bianco. Probably Bristol, *c.* 1760–70. Merseyside County Museums, Liverpool.

76 *Below:* Fine documentary punch bowl decorated in blue, red and yellow, and showing the 'vessel Whitby'. Liverpool, 1772. Merseyside County Museums, Liverpool.

77 *Far right:* Plate with powdered purple ground. Wincanton or Bristol, 1739. City Art Gallery, Bristol.

blue, green, yellow and red. It is known popularly as 'Fazackerly' since a mug of this decoration is said to have been presented to a Liverpool potter named Thomas Fazackerly. Further pieces decorated in this palette have been excavated in Liverpool, but it would be dangerous to assume that all such examples came from Merseyside.

A decoration that produced rather curious elongated figures of women was the Long Eliza pattern. The name comes from the Dutch Lange Lijzen, the term used for such decorations on Dutch Delftware of the previous century.

Anyone developing a serious interest in Delftware will do well to study the principal literature on the subject and a title is suggested in the bibliography at the end of this volume. He would also be well advised to find out more about the major Delftware centres, and if at all possible, to visit them.

London. Delftware was produced in Aldgate, Lambeth and Southwark, although all London Delftware still tends to be labelled Lambeth. Aldgate began production in the late sixteenth century, while Southwark was once the pottery of Christian Wilhelm who in 1628 was describing himself as 'gallipot maker' to the king.

Bristol. Always a major pottery centre, Bristol contained four Delftware potteries, but Delft was first made just outside the city at Brislington early in the seventeenth century.

In the city itself potteries were established at Temple Back, Limekiln Lane, Avon Street, and in the most celebrated pottery area of the city—Redcliffe Backs.

Wincanton. This Somerset pottery produced Delft during the first half of the eighteenth century. Individual pieces marked Wincanton have been found and manganese borders are also associated with this pottery.

Liverpool. This is another ceramic area of great importance where much else besides Delft was manufactured. In fact several of the Liverpool potters were also making porcelain. The main potteries were:

Richard Holt in Lord Street. Early in the eighteenth century potters came here from Southbank.

Samuel Gilbody in Shaws Brow. Shaws Brow was the main pottery centre of the city, and the Liverpool museums with their fine ceramic collections now stand on the site. Gilbody began early in the eighteenth century. This factory also made porcelain.

Alderman Shaw off Dale Street. Early eighteenth century.

Richard Chaffers on Shaws Brow. Mid eighteenth century. He also made porcelain.

Philip Christian. Mid eighteenth century. He also made porcelain, and took over Chaffers' factory in 1765.

Other Liverpool Delftware potters include George Drinkwater, Zachariah Barnes and James Gibson. Several others can be identified by name if not by their productions.

Lustre

Very little lustre ware is marked and most potteries produced it, so it is often very difficult to attribute to a particular factory.

250

78 Sunderland lustre plaque. Nineteenth century.

Although lustrous effects had been achieved at a much earlier date, the first lustre patent was not granted until 1810, when Peter Walburton of New Hall patented his 'newly invented method of decorating china, porcelain, earthenware and glass, with gold, silver, platinum, or other metals fluxed with lead, which invention leaves the metals, after being burnt in their metallic state'. Lustre may be divided into the following five categories:

1. The total surface of an object is covered with lustre in order to produce a metallic effect.
2. Lustre is used to heighten relief decoration. This is known as relief lustre.
3. Bands or collars (raised circular bands) of lustre are used in conjunction with painted or transfer decoration.
4. Painted or splashed lustre.
5. Resist lustre.

The most common form of lustre is that made by Dixon Austin & Co. at Sunderland between around 1800 and 1850. These products are usually decorated with transfer prints which may depict the famous Iron Bridge over the river Wear, but a mariner's compass is also frequently seen. These transfer prints are surrounded with irregular splashes of pink lustre. It is most likely that such wares were also introduced at other potteries.

All of these lustres have metallic origins, some of which are confusing. Silver lustre for example is in reality created from platinum salts, and the lustre is so called because of the silver colour that emerges during the firing. Copper lustre is the most common and is derived from copper as the name would suggest. The rare lustres are those known as resist, and are the ones where the decoration on the object is the same colour as the body of the object but stand out from a different coloured lustre ground. There were various methods by which this effect was achieved, the most common being the application of a varnish or wax by stencil, which would 'resist' the lustre when dipped and burned out as the original body when fired. The resist lustres frequently depicting birds or sporting subjects are often quite beautiful and for this reason they are much collected and therefore far more costly than the Sunderland or copper lustres.

When handling lustre wares you will notice that the later Victorian products are considerably heavier than the Georgian examples. It should also be remembered that many modern copies have been made of the Sunderland type wares, in particular the large bowls and jugs.

Sussex rustic ware

Regional or country pottery has been manufactured for centuries, although apart from pieces documenting specific occasions few have survived that can be easily attributed to a place of manufacture.

The literature on this subject is not considerable and I was particularly pleased to find a group of nineteenth-century papers published under the title *Sussex Industries* that included an interesting essay on pottery in the county. The anonymous and undated paper was reprinted from the *Sussex Advertiser* and is worthy of a wider audience:

'The name is a good one, for it describes the article faithfully. The ware is "rustic", suggestive of green woods and smiling hop-gardens, rustic in colour, rustic in style, rustic in the object which it represents. Its rusticity is however, attractive–by the combination of colours, by the somewhat roughly artistic moulding, and by its peculiarity of style. Where it is known it is liked. Specimens have been carried long distances to reap their meed of favour, and some pieces have, by Royal command, found their way into Her Majesty's household and Her Majesty's own use. The home of this peculiar product is the ancient cinqueport of Rye, a historic town picturesquely situated on the edge of the flat marshes which once were sea, into which it projects like a promontory of the higher, undulating, and remarkably pretty country which stretches northward into Kent, and westward into the finest part of Sussex. Deserted by the sea, although still in possession of communication with it by the conflux of three rivers, and thus enabled to carry on as of yore–though in attenuated dimensions–its native industry of shipbuilding, Rye, with its interesting and spacious old parish church, its land gate, and its Ypres tower, looks a relic of former ages, a small, self-contained community of last-century type. It is not cut off from contact with the outer world, for the railway carries visitors in on every market day–its markets being noted both for cattle and sheep–and the hopping season enlivens it with the influx of that wild and merry host who help to make out native beverage by reaping, in their own gipsy-like fashion, its most valued–and most frequently adulterated–ingredient. But on days when there is no market, and in seasons when there is no hopping, Rye is quiet enough.

'In its more primitive and more common form, pottery probably has been made at Rye as long as anywhere else. The inventor of the "rustic ware", the late Mr. F. Mitchell, made pots in the ordinary way at his father's works, still existing, until it occurred to him, some fourteen years ago, to strike out a new and original line of his own. He accordingly separated from his father, and set up independently, building up his own kiln, designed by himself. The manufacture of the ware is simple enough, and employs but few hands. The clay is mixed, well beaten, sifted with great care, once, twice, three times, and washed in the clay pan. This is filled every spring. When washed the clay looks like cream. It lies in the pan for months, dries, and then is stored for use—sufficient to last a year. When used it is weighed, so much to each article, and "spun" in the old-fashioned way upon the wheel. The "spinning", of course, gives scope for good workmanship, and such Mrs. Mitchell (whose husband died in 1875) has at her command. Many of the patterns are quaint, but they are all moulded with care and evident skill. The moulded pieces are left to dry until they can bear the weight of ornaments. These are then added, the ware is bis-cuited, glazed, kiln-dried—in saggers—and turned out for sale.

'This is all simple work. The peculiarity lies in the shape, in the combination of colours, and in the peculiar brown which forms the groundwork of the whole. The production of this brown is a trade-secret. It is inherent in the clay, not added by the glaze. It is produced by mixing very thoroughly the native material with Dorsetshire clay. The speckled and streaked appearance of the ware is attributable to the presence of two different materials which cannot wholly blend. It is a pleasant, "taking" sort of colour, setting off the green of the ornaments, the yellow occasionally introduced, to great advantage. But to the outsider, unacquainted with the details of the craft, the distinctive brown will appear less noteworthy than the shape and ornamentation of the articles, which are both exceedingly pleasing, and which represent the successful fruits of persevering study, an artistic mind, and a happy lightness of hand. Less pleasingly moulded, the ware, instead of securing for itself an honoured name in the trade, would presumably have proved a failure. We should here state that every piece turned out is moulded by hand. The wheel, on which the clay is "spun", is the only piece of machinery employed in the manufacture. The knife is used, principally for stippling, a wire for cutting, and moulds are resorted to for producing the ornaments in detail, flowers and leaves, hops and acorns; but all these ornaments, the basketwork—

where used—handles, &c., are put on by hand with very creditable taste and imitation of nature. A writer in the *Art Journal* some years ago bore complimentary witness to this praiseworthy proficiency, stating that "it is obvious that they (*scilicet* the moulder's fingers) have been directed by an artistic spirit." This commendation is deserved. The moulds for ornaments, we may add, are all taken from natural models—leaves from natural leaves, flowers from natural flowers, and so on. Both in respect of ornament, and of the shape of vessels, the late Mr. Mitchell and his surviving widow—who now conducts the works—have studied variety with capital results, but of course some patterns come out with more effect than others. One favourite pattern is the old Sussex "pig", familiar to Sussex potters from time immemorial. The inventive wag who was good-natured enough to assign to the county of Sussex as coat of arms "a pig, *proper*" (the emblem, we suppose, of Plenty coupled with Content), with the expressive motto appended, "Won't be druv", probably had this household ornament in his mind when he dispensed his heraldic honours in this irregular way. The useful office for which the pig was originally designed by our forefathers, and which it still faithfully discharges where ancient custom survives, is to receive the national beverage into its inside. It was usual for it to figure as a bridal present at wedding breakfasts. The head, which is somewhat insecurely fastened by means of a tapering peg inserted in two corresponding holes, made respectively in the head and the neck, takes off, and as the snout is perfectly flat, and capable of serving as a rest for the inverted headpiece, it is qualified to do service as a mug; the idea being that the new couple and their guests should drink "a hogshead of beer". Meanwhile the body serves as a jug or larger receptacle, discharging the liquor out of the neck. The tail is so conveniently curled upward as to assist rather than impede the laridiferous animal in resting—we cannot call it "sitting"—on his haunches, and thus one piece of pottery effectually performs, in its dismembered state, the useful services of two.

'Not a few patterns in use at Rye are faithful imitations of the Mycenae pottery brought to England by Dr. Schliemann, and not long ago exhibited at South Kensington. At the first suggestion it might appear questionable if this is altogether a happy choice, the new patch being made to fit on an old garment. But the result is far from unsatisfactory, indeed some pieces are unusually fine, and have accordingly been much admired, and we are disposed to agree with Mrs. Mitchell, that it is a sound principle to perpetuate the antique forms, and bring home to our living generation the fact that the classic patterns admired in museums were at one time really in every-day use, and intended for every-day purposes. Mrs. Mitchell at present makes "Trojan" pottery in no fewer than eighteen different shapes, every one of them copied from the Mycenae collection. Some, for instance the triangular jugs, present to modern eyes a quaint appearance; most come out remarkably well when moulded in Sussex clay. Other models Mrs. Mitchell has borrowed, with, perhaps, even more satisfactory results, from later times and nearer neighbours. Thus one favourite pattern is in imitation of the French Valérie ware. Another favourite article is the Belgian candlestick, first suggested for imitation by the Rev. J. S. Northcote, the son of the Right Hon. Member for North Devon. A pattern to be met with wherever the ware is seen, is a peculiar kind of bag, evidently moulded on a real bag. This strikes many observers as an odd, if original, shape. The fact is, that it is an imitation of a Russian pattern, brought home by the Duke of Edinburgh, and recommended to Mrs. Mitchell as a model by Mr. J. S. Hardy, the late Member for Rye. There are other candlesticks besides the Belgian pattern, some rather elaborate, many certainly in good taste, and all in frequent practical use. Another species of ware selling well are the Japanese jugs, which are made in different sizes, and prove no less useful than ornamental. One very peculiar shape has been christened "Sussex pails". These are pails resting on a flat bottom or tray, with a hoop handle from the bottom to above the top. Then there are antique lamps, carpenter's bags—most useful as receptacles for flowers—flower-baskets, pilgrim's bottles, Cambridge jugs, and many more. One very peculiar shape goes by the name of "rustic stumps", representing the stump of a tree, stippled with a knife to produce roughness, and used for holding flowers, or else as a jug. Another speciality, original if quaint, is the twisted ware—"folding jugs", as Mrs. Mitchell calls them—having a spiral turn, produced by twisting the jug while soft, and drying it in this condition. A resemblance with the famed Palissy ware has suggested an imitation of Palissy's "reptile" plates. These take a deal of trouble, but they are really works of art.

'As regards pattern, we are, however, inclined to award the palm to those objects which, in shape as well as in make, bear a strong local stamp upon them. Mrs. Mitchell moulds her clay very successfully in imitation of all sorts of leaves and flowers, fuchsias, passion flowers, and what not, but the most telling effect is produced by the rich clusters of flowering hops or the homely sprigs of oak bearing their proper crop of acorns. These are mostly disposed upon appropriate objects, and it is by virtue of these chiefly, we think, that the reputation of the Sussex pottery may be expected to spread. We ought also to mention some really artistic representations of green wheat-ears, which are very effective on a brown ground. They help to preserve the ''rustic'' character of the ware. We have been shown in Mrs. Mitchell's private collection far more elaborate objects, flower-stands, wreaths, and very charming—but laborious—basketwork (which we should like to see, on account of its fine effect, more frequently made)—but it is the jugs and mugs encircled with clusters of hops, and strongly suggestive of the beverage made of that peculiarly indigenous plant, and for which they are intended—the George II jug, in its simple but attractive form, set off by a thick wreath of hops—the very tasteful baskets decorated with the same native green—moreover such objects as cheese-dishes, and simple trays or plates bordered or ornamented with sprigs of green—it is these comparatively homely but particularly appropriate and ''local''-looking objects, which seem to us most deserving of notice, and most calculated to extend the use of the ''ware''. It must be borne in mind that however ''taking'' is the pottery, it is not pottery of artistically the very highest rank, and its models and uses should be selected and assigned accordingly. There is not the same exquisite finish, the plastic imitativeness, the artistic execution about it which distinguishes the best earthenware, say Doulton or Wedgwood. But it has a catching ''local'' look, which grows upon one, and is quite artistic enough to qualify for a prominent place among our native manufacturers. The more it is known the more popular, we are sure, will it become. Greater popularity is not now sought after, because the ware is sold as fast as ever it is made, and the demand is apt, if anything, to outstrip the circumscribed productive power of the existing establishment. But there is no reason why the latter should not be expanded and rendered capable of turning out much larger quantities of ware. It might benefit the neighbourhood in which it is made, if this were done, and it would help to secure to the County of Sussex an honourable place among the industrial counties of England.'

Chapter 5

Josiah Wedgwood

In the last chapter I mentioned the Potteries with their peasant craftsmen, unorganised labour, non-existent sales force and inadequate communications. It was into this setting that Josiah Wedgwood emerged as a giant among European potters. His is now a household name throughout the world, and his ideas regarding production, the management of men and of factories, and division of labour have had a major bearing on mass production today.

The ceramicist William Burton said this of Wedgwood:
'. . . his influence was so powerful, and his personality dominant, that all other English potters worked on the principles that he had laid down, and thus a fresh influence and a new direction was given to the pottery of England and of the civilised world. He is the only potter of whom it may be truly said that the whole subsequent course of pottery manufacture has been influenced by his individuality, skill and taste.'

The foundation stone of the Wedgwood Memorial Institute in Burslem was laid in 1863 by William Gladstone, who was then Chancellor of the Exchequer. Mr Gladstone said of Wedgwood in his address:
'. . . he was the greatest man who ever, in any age or in any country, applied himself to the important work in uniting art and industry.'

During the span of Josiah Wedgwood's life (1730-1795) he brought about a revolution that went even beyond the bounds of pottery. To look at a map of Staffordshire in the early eighteenth century and to note the names of the individual potters with their crude pot-banks scattered across the countryside is like reading the index to a whole volume devoted to ceramic history. The Wedgwood family were already among their number, for several generations of Wedgwoods had earned their living as potters, selling their wares, as did their neighbours, to the casual tinkers who were the principal buyers.

It was at the Churchyard Pottery, Burslem, that Josiah Wedgwood was born in 1730, the youngest of the twelve children of Thomas and Mary Wedgwood. The exact date of his birth is not known, but it would have been very close to the day of his baptism, 12 July, as at that period little time was allowed to elapse between birth and baptism, because of the high infant mortality.

A brief sketch of Wedgwood's career is useful to show the scale of his achievement and also the manner in which his work with ceramics evolved. At the age of six he began a daily walk of three miles to school at Newcastle-under-Lyme, and it was there that the family also attended the Unitarian Meeting House which was always to be an important part of Josiah Wedgwood's life.

Life was certainly not easy for Josiah, but although he had to leave school at the age of nine when his father died, he was able to read, do simple arithmetic and write well. Then, after working at the family pot-bank for five years, he became afflicted, like so many others in eighteenth-century England, with smallpox. It left him with a weakened right knee that was to trouble him for many years and it also meant that it was no longer possible for him to operate a potter's wheel. Perhaps the most bitter blow of all was that his eldest brother refused to take him into partnership. This time of Wedgwood's life must have appeared to him like the end, in fact it was barely the beginning.

For two years he worked with John Harrison at the Cliff-bank Pottery and then, like many another fortunate potter, he met Thomas Whieldon, the most prominent potter of the day. Wedgwood and Whieldon entered into a partnership that lasted five years, years in which Wedgwood discovered all he could of the contemporary wares, the white stonewares, the agates and the tortoiseshells, that largely dominated the output of the partnership. Attractive as these items were, and still are, Wedgwood felt the necessity of improving the body of the clays being used, and of bringing about improvements in glaze, colour and design—what he called 'elegance of form'. As he surveyed the products of the potteries he wrote, 'I saw the field was spacious, and the soil so good as to promise an ample recompense to anyone who should labour diligently'. The words have something of a Churchillian ring and, appropriately, he followed them with action.

In 1759 Wedgwood started his own business at the Ivy House Works at Burslem, renting the premises for £10 a year from his cousins who lived nearby. He invented a new green

79 Queensware teacaddy, with transfer printed decoration. Wedgwood, c. 1770. Victoria and Albert Museum, London.

wedgwood

Probably the first mark, and supposedly used at Burslem, 1759-69

WEDGWOOD

Very rare mark, used at the Bell Works, 1764-69

WEDGWOOD

Wedgwood

Mark used in various sizes, 1759-69

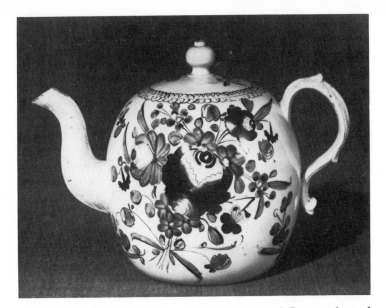

Earliest form of the Wedgwood and Bentley stamp, 1769

Circular stamp, placed around screw of certain bases, but never on jasper ware, 1769-80

Wedgwood
& Bentley
356

Mark used on Wedgwood and Bentley intaglios, 1769-80

glaze which was ideally suited to the cauliflower-shaped teapots and the Rococo style wares of the day. Wedgwood's pottery grew and flourished. In 1762 he moved to the Brick House pot-bank later known as the Bell Works, for the workmen instead of being summoned by the blowing of a horn were called to work by a bell. His experiments with clays led to great improvements on those used by earlier potters such as John Astbury, and the development of a strong, light, elegant creamware began to claim most of his time. It bore fruit in the now celebrated Queensware, so called in honour of Queen Charlotte and her patronage. Creamware was to lay the basis of his fortune and create the finance necessary to carry out his later projects and experiments. It was so successful that within three years Wedgwood was using an agent in London. His creamwares were left plain or either painted by hand or transfer printed by Sadler and Green in Liverpool. With such simple, clean lines these strong and useful wares are as much at home in the twentieth century as they were two hundred years ago.

The Brick House factory not only saw the rise of creamware but also the flourishing of a vital friendship. During one of his visits to Liverpool in 1762, Wedgwood injured his already infirm knee. The pain was crippling, and, unable to ride, he was forced to take to his bed. His doctor, Matthew Turner, then introduced Wedgwood to a man named Thomas Bentley. Although of similar age Bentley was in every way different to Wedgwood: he was a Liverpool merchant of sophisticated tastes, with a wide knowledge and a strong interest in

259

81 Portrait in oils of Thomas Bentley, attributed to the artist Joseph Wright of Derby, and painted in 1775. Bentley was Wedgwood's Partner from 1769 to 1780. His taste, social contacts and knowledge of the arts did much to ensure the success of the firm.

European and classical art. Undoubtedly it was Bentley who opened the eyes of Wedgwood to the classical collections of Sir William Hamilton, British Consul to the Kingdom of Naples. It would have been Bentley who became aware of the beginnings of the Neo-classical movement. In 1766 Wedgwood proposed a partnership, and such was their friendship it was many years before they thought it necessary to sign a formal partnership agreement. It was Bentley who took charge of the London warehouse and showrooms, Wedgwood being among the first to have showrooms in the capital.

The relationship between Wedgwood and Bentley was far more than a mere business association and when apart they corresponded almost daily. Wedgwood once wrote of Bentley's letters that 'the very feel of them even before the seal is broke, cheers my heart and does me good. They inspire me with taste, emulation and everything that is necessary for the production of fine things.' Sadly, few of Bentley's letters to Wedgwood

82 Opposite, above: Wedgwood Queensware group with transfer decoration by Sadler and Green of Liverpool, c. 1770. The print on the teapot depicts the death of General Wolfe.

83 Opposite, below: Part of the famous Wedgwood service made for the Empress Catherine II of Russia, c. 1774.

84 *Opposite, above:* Wedgwood jasper pieces that demonstrate the rich colour range of this fine stoneware. Eighteenth century. Jasper was produced in six basic colours: black, green, blue, dark blue, lilac and yellow.

85 *Opposite, below:* The Wedgwood family in the grounds of Etruria Hall. This portrait painted in oils on a panel by George Stubbs in 1780 depicts the master potter, Josiah Wedgwood, FRS, and his wife Sarah, with seven of their eight children. Josiah and Sarah sit under a tree. The children on horseback are, from left: Thomas (a pioneer of photography); Susannah (who became the mother of Charles Darwin, biologist and author of *The Origin of Species*); Josiah (the second son who inherited the pottery company); and John (the eldest son and a founder of the Royal Horticultural Society). Josiah Wedgwood and Sons Ltd., Barlaston, Stoke-on-Trent.

86 Queensware jelly mould complete with decorated centre-piece. The painted flowers would be visible through the clear translucent jelly. Eighteenth century.

have survived but the Wedgwood correspondence is invaluable to all who are interested in Wedgwood and the potteries. The letters are also interspersed with lines that testify to the good fellowship between them. Once when Bentley moved house Wedgwood wrote to him: 'Do not be in haste to set your second garden. I will come and help you dig and weed, and sow and gather, and we will be joint gardeners as well as joint potters.'

In the spring of 1768 Wedgwood's knee again became inflamed and this time there was no doubt what had to be done. The amputation was successfully carried out (without benefit of anaesthetics) and Wedgwood made a good recovery and in due course an artificial wooden leg was fitted. With his better health, new vistas opened for Wedgwood and Bentley. Thanks to the dowry of his wife Sara, Wedgwood purchased for £3,000 an estate between Hanley and Newcastle-under-Lyme. He built a house for himself and a short distance away he constructed the largest pottery manufactory in the world, which as a factory was second in size only to the Soho works of Matthew Boultin in Birmingham. Wedgwood called the factory Etruria, in honour of that part of Italy where so much ancient pottery was then being unearthed.

The factory opened on 13 June 1769 and to mark the event Wedgwood made six vases with Thomas Bentley turning the potter's wheel and Wedgwood throwing and turning the pots. These vases are known as the 'First day vases' and bear a Latin inscription meaning 'The Arts of Etruria are reborn'. The

263

Etruria of ancient Italy knew nothing like this, with spacious modelling and throwing rooms making it possible to retain quality while large quantities were being produced. The completion of a combined dinner and tea service in creamware for the Empress Catherine II of Russia was a massive advertisement as well as a great achievement for Wedgwood. The service consisted of 952 pieces decorated with 1,244 original paintings of English landscapes; the manufacturing costs were very nearly £3,000. Before the service left for Russia it was exhibited in Wedgwood's London showroom in Greek Street where it proved a great attraction.

For most people the epitome of Wedgwood is jasper ware, which first appeared in 1774. An unglazed vitreous (highly fired, close bodied) stoneware, it was manufactured in various shades of blue, yellow, green, lilac, maroon, black or white. It only emerged after some 10,000 attempts and most of the trial pieces together with Wedgwood's personal notes are still in the Wedgwood archive—no wonder he wrote desperately in his experiment book when success seemed far away 'I am going mad'.

87 The fine black basalt ware shown above and in the opposite column was an achievement of which Josiah Wedgwood was particularly proud, saying that it was 'sterling, and will last forever'.

Wedgwood's search for perfection was unceasing. He invented the pyrometer and so became the first man to devise an instrument that would accurately record the high temperature of a kiln. The man with only three years' formal education was made a Fellow of the Royal Society. He experimented with clays from as far afield as China and North America and gradually the ill-organised Staffordshire potteries were set new standards and transformed into a major industry. George Stubbs painted the Wedgwood family at Etruria Hall and Sir Joshua Reynolds, first President of the Royal Academy, painted his portrait.

Wedgwood's strong Unitarian beliefs led him to oppose the slave trade, as a letter to Benjamin Franklin dated 29 February 1788 clearly shows:

'I embrace the opportunity of a packet making up by my friend Phillip to inclose for the use of yourself and friends a few Cameos on a subject which I am happy to acquaint you is daily more and more taking possession of mens minds on this side of the Atlantic as well as with you.

'It gives me great pleasure to be embarked on this occasion in the same great and good cause with you, and I ardently hope for the final completion of our wishes. This will be an epoch before unknown to the World, and while relief is given to millions of our fellow Creatures immediately the object of it, the subject of freedom will be more canvassed and better understood in the enlightened nations.'

The packet of cameos referred to in the letter was a number of the medallions modelled by Hackwood and designed by Josiah Wedgwood that show a manacled negro slave kneeling with his hands raised while around the edge of the medallion is the inscription 'Am I not a man and a brother?'

Wedgwood had thousands of these cameos or slave medallions as they are called made and distributed them free to anyone who was concerned with the anti-slavery movement. He also supported the Americans during the War of Independence and in a letter to Erasmus Darwin he wrote:
'I know you will rejoice with me in the glorious revolution which has taken place in France. The Politicians tell me that as a manufacturer I shall be ruined if France has her liberty, but I am willing to take my chance in that respect, nor yet do I see that the happiness of one Nation includes in it the misery of its next neighbour.'

At Etruria Wedgwood built houses for his work-force and was the prime mover behind the development of the Trent and Mersey Canal which linked Etruria with the port of Liverpool, a move which cut the factory's road transport costs from $10\frac{1}{2}$d ($4\frac{1}{2}$p) per ton mile to $1\frac{1}{2}$d ($\frac{1}{2}$p) per ton mile by canal.

Deeply involved in the scientific developments of his age, Josiah Wedgwood supplied Joseph Priestley with ceramic tubes and retorts for his scientific experiments, and he installed a James Watt steam engine to drive a special lathe. When he died in 1795 he left not only a personal fortune of over half a million pounds and a large factory, but also a whole tradition both in English pottery and in industrial organisation. He also created a dynasty. His son John was a founder of the Royal Horticultural Society, Josiah junior inherited the pottery, Thomas was a pioneer of photography and his daughter Susannah became the mother of Charles Darwin, the biologist, evolutionist and author of *The Origin of Species*.

Black basalt

The early and crude black pottery named 'Egyptian black' was one of the first wares to which Wedgwood had turned his attention. In 1768 he developed the fine-grained, unglazed, hard black stoneware that is called black basalt. The rich hue of the basalt was created by staining the body with manganese dioxide and cobalt. The basalt wares could be decorated further by being polished on a jeweller's wheel after firing or by the addition of red and white encaustic enamel colours in Greek and Roman styles before a second firing. This basalt is capable of resisting acids and was frequently used as a touch-stone to test the quality of silver and gold. At this period gentlemen were buying books and developing their private libraries, and black basalt life-sized busts of classical and modern authors were popular as decoration as well as cheaper than bronze or marble originals. Some vases were bronzed but these are rare. Fluting and lathe-turning was an easy form of decoration to apply; moulded decorations in low relief took longer as they had first to be moulded and then undercut to make the details precise.

At the same time there arose the taste for collecting ancient and Renaissance cameos, cut from semi-precious stones. Obviously this taste could only be cultivated by the wealthy and many copies were produced in glass, white plaster and red sulphur. Again Wedgwood used contemporary taste to his advantage by reproducing the ancient intaglio designs. Here is an entry from the Wedgwood and Bentley catalogue of 1779: 'The Intaglios in artificial basalts are most excellent seals; being exact impressions from the finest gems; and therefore much truer than any engraved copies can be, with the singular advantage of being little inferior in hardness to the gems themselves.

'In this composition Cameos may be converted into seals without losing the Drawing, the Spirit and Delicacy of the original work; so that gentlemen may have a great variety of seals at small expense, or have an opportunity of making collections of perfect and durable copies of the choicest Gems.'

Between 1800 and 1810, decoration in the Chinese *famille rose* style was applied to black basalt ware and is known as the 'chrysanthemum pattern'. Of black basalt Wedgwood wrote: 'The black is stirling and will last forever'.

Rosso Antico

This red stoneware dates from the early 1760s and is reminiscent of the early Staffordshire red wares. This stoneware was also decorated in much the same way as black basalt.

Variegated wares

These fall into two groups. The earliest was made of cream-coloured earthenware with a marbled surface. The tortoiseshell effect was obtained by dusting metallic oxide on to the surface of the body, and could also be achieved by combing or sponging on splashes of colour. The later type consists of various coloured clays that were kneaded together with the intention of imitating stones such as agate, onyx or marble.

Cane ware

Useful and ornamental wares were made from cane colour earthenware, and frequently a bamboo effect was simulated. Another form of cane ware became known as 'ceramic pastry' because of its use in replacing edible pie-crust. During the Napoleonic wars flour became scarce and costly and one of the immediate results of this was that the game pie served at table in its thick and ornamental cut pie-crust dish became very expensive. Wedgwood's pie dish of 'ceramic pastry' was not only more attractive than most artistic attempts in real pastry, but was also represented as a great saving in time, it was in fact what might be termed the first oven-to-table ware.

Jasper ware

The production of jasper, which is technically a stone ware, was finally perfected in 1774 following years of experiment in the search for the right ingredients. It is a dense white highly vitrified ware that possesses some characteristics of porcelain; that is, when thinly potted it is sometimes translucent. One of the essential ingredients of jasper is barium sulphate. Always unglazed, jasper could be stained lilac, yellow, maroon, green, blue or black to provide the ideal background for applied moulded classical reliefs or portraits. For Josiah Wedgwood it represents his highest achievement as far as colour is concerned, and his uses of it are many and varied.

Portrait medallions, classical panels, jewellery, sword hilts, as well as all manner of vases, were made in jasper. The artists who produced the designs were all highly skilled, among them John Flaxman, William Hackwood, Lady Templeton and George Stubbs. The architect Robert Adam was quick to seize upon Wedgwood's ceramic interpretations of the neo-classic and he frequently used Wedgwood jaspers as features in his designs, especially in fireplaces.

The most celebrated example of jasper is probably Wedgwood's replica of the Portland Vase. This was originally known as the Barberini Vase, and was found enclosed in a sarcophagus of fine workmanship in a burial chamber beneath a mound of earth, 3 miles (4·8 km) from Rome. The sarcophagus was placed in the museum at Rome and the $10\frac{1}{4}$ inch (260 mm) high vase

found its way to the library of the Barberini family in the eighteenth century and was later purchased at considerable expense in Italy by the great connoisseur and collector Sir William Hamilton, who brought it to England in the December of 1784. The fame of the vase had long preceded its arrival and the Dowager Duchess of Portland, a collector on a massive scale, was the first person to visit him at his London hotel. Within a few days she began negotiations for the purchase of the vase through Sir William's niece, who was a Maid of Honour to the Queen. The arrangements were conducted in great secrecy as Mrs Delany, who acted for the Duchess, recorded: '. . . by whispers, signs, confabulations in their parlours and bed chambers, and by notes'. It was Horace Walpole who described the Duchess as: 'A sober Lady but much intoxicated by empty vases'.

Following direct talks between Sir William and the Duchess, the sale of the Barberini Vase was eventually settled. From then until her death the following year, on 17 July 1785, the vase was not seen by anyone apart from a few tried and trusted friends. The Portland family had previously voiced their disapproval of the large sums of money she willingly spent on her personal museum, and it was for this reason that she tried so carefully to keep her latest purchase a secret. When the Duke disposed of the museum he wished to retain at least some of its treasures and although Wedgwood had already tried to buy the vase, the museum was sold at the Duchess's residence in Whitehall. The sale lasted thirty-five days beginning on 24 April and ending on 7 June, 1786. There were 4,155 lots and the vase was the last lot in the sale. It is believed that Wedgwood and the Duke of Portland had come to a previous understanding that the Duke should buy the vase and that Wedgwood should have it on loan to make a copy. The representative of the Duke of Portland bought in the vase for the sum of £1,029, and three days after its sale, it passed into Wedgwood's care upon his receipt of possession and promise of return:
'I do hereby acknowledge to have borrowed and received from His Grace the Duke of Portland, the vase described in the 4155 lot of the catalogue of the Portland Museum, and also the cameo medallion of the head of Augustus Caesar being the lot of the same catalogue and both sold by Messrs. Skinner on the 7th day of the present month of June, 1786 & I do hereby promise to deliver back the said Vase and Cameo in safety into the hands of His Grace upon demand.

Witness my hand this 10th day of June, 1786.
Jos Wedgwood.
(Signed in the presence of)
Thos Byerley.'

The Portland Vase is without doubt one of the great works of art in the world. Once it was in the hands of Wedgwood, and closer examination had enabled him to understand its intricate beauty, his normal self-assurance began to be undermined by doubt. He wrote a letter to Sir William Hamilton setting out the difficulties of the task and sought his advice on a number of points. It seems likely that Sir William advised the pursuit of a copy as close to the original as possible, although correcting the work of damage or decay. Wedgwood's attitude is reflected in this extract from one of his letters:
'. . . now that I can indulge myself with full and repeated examinations of the original work itself, my crest is much

fallen and I should scarcely muster sufficient resolution to proceed if I had not too precipitately perhaps pledged myself to many of my friends to attempt it in the best manner I am able. Being so pledged, I must proceed . . .'

Wedgwood then continues:

'Several gentlemen have urged me to make my copies of the vase by subscription, & have honoured me with their names for that purpose; but I tell them with great truth, that I am extremely diffident of my ability to perform the task they kindly impose upon me; and they shall be perfectly at liberty when they see the copies, to take or refuse them; and on these terms I accept subscriptions, chiefly to regulate the time of delivering out the copies, in rotation, according to the dates on which they honour me with their names.'

Wedgwood's tenacity was to prove equal to the task. He discovered that the original was made of glass rather than hardstone, as had been assumed. The glass itself was of a dark blue, so much so that unless held to a strong light it appeared to be black, while the figures in white bas-relief are also of glass. Even today much inconclusive discussion continues regarding the interpretation of the legends depicted by the figures. The modelling for the copy was carried out by Henry Webber, but it was the task of giving the exact body colouring to the jasper that presented the real problem. After four years of experiment Wedgwood achieved his first copies. Sir Joshua Reynolds, after carefully examining one of them, described it as 'a correct and faithful imitation both in the general effect and the most minute details of the part'. The very first vase was submitted to Wedgwood's great friend, Dr Darwin, for his inspection. He was instructed to show it to no one but his family, but as he later wrote to Wedgwood: 'I have disobeyed you . . . how can I possess a jewel, and not communicate the pleasure to a few Derby philosophers?'

In 1810 the Portland Vase was deposited by the third Duke of Portland in the British Museum on permanent loan and it has remained there ever since, although the Museum purchased the vase from the Portland family in 1945. It is the finest known example of 'cameo glass' and dates from early in the first century AD, and because the figures in white relief depict the marriage of Peleus and Thetis, it was probably originally intended as a wedding gift.

On 7 February 1845 a tragedy of major proportions struck the Antiquities Department of the British Museum. A certain William Lloyd, having picked up a Babylonian stone sculpture, deliberately smashed the glass case containing the Portland Vase, shattering it into over two hundred pieces. The act of this madman appeared to have destroyed the great work of art for ever, but with the help of Josiah Wedgwood's copy the Museum, with infinite patience, was able to repair the vase, and in March 1846 it was again on exhibition. As so often happens good followed disaster, and the smashing of the vase drew massive public attention to it. It was for this reason that after 1845 the Wedgwood company began to make further copies in various sizes. Unlike the original issue, these later copies have the Wedgwood mark and do not include the medallion of the female head on the base which is such a superb feature of the original vase and of the original series of copies. Today the Portland Vase is used as a symbol of Wedgwood and is incorporated in the company's back stamp on fine bone china. The Wedgwood copies still fetch within the region of £20,000 when they appear at auction.

Creamware

The finest creamware of Josiah Wedgwood was superior to anything of its kind already in existence, and firmly established his business. His products were light and white, and could compete with the wares of porcelain manufacturers.

89 Creamware transfer-printed plate by Sadler and Green of Liverpool.

Thus a demand was created for such wares, and other manufacturers became very interested, particularly in Leeds and Liverpool, where they were worked on by the great firm of transfer printers, Sadler and Green, who formed a partnership in 1761 to deal with the mass printing of creamwares that followed the opening of an account with Josiah Wedgwood.

Much creamware, however, was left plain white. Such pieces sold because of good design alone, but white was also an ideal ground on which to have painted personal requests. This was particularly the case with marriage jugs or tankards and christening mugs, but it also applied to jugs commemorating any number of events of family, work, society, or volunteer force. Other jugs were printed or painted with various verses. A great deal of military history is also recorded on creamware, for example the death of General Wolfe at Quebec in 1759, and the victories of Wellington and Nelson. This tradition was carried on through the nineteenth century on jugs and mugs of all kinds of ceramic body; Samuel Alcock & Co. of Hill Pottery, Burslem, produced a fine Crimea jug in 1855. All commemorative creamware is very popular with collectors.

Once Wedgwood's success was seen a host of other manufacturers also launched into creamware production: John Turner, Josiah Spode, William Adams and Sunderland among them. Liverpool potters made good creamware but that of Leeds was at least the equal of Wedgwood. The Leeds pieces were as light and occasionally lighter than Wedgwood, although there is a tendency for the Leeds glaze to appear green where it has run and gathered in crevices.

90 *Far left:* Creamware coffee pot with enamelled decoration. Leeds, *c.* 1765.

91 *Above:* Creamware teapot, Leeds, *c.* 1767.

92 Creamware sparrow-beak milk jug and cover with a crossover handle so typical of both Wedgwood and Leeds. Leeds, *c.* 1780.

93 Creamware centre-piece with detachable nut baskets. Wedgwood.

Tea and coffee ware was made together with baskets and bowls. Some of the larger pieces were decorated by pierced work. Pierced borders were also in favour, although at Leeds dishes and plate rims are often found with feather-moulded edges touched with blue. Cross-over handles are also used.

Messrs. Hartley, Greens & Co., the Leeds potters, issued pattern books from time to time during the late eighteenth and early nineteenth centuries. These books show a surprising range of wares, from spoons to chamber pots, table centres, ink stands and decorative vases. That they were ready to fulfil private orders in respect of decoration is made clear by the wording on the cover of their pattern book:

DESIGNS

of

SUNDRY ARTICLES

of

QUEEN'S OR CREAM-COLOUR'D EARTHEN-WARE

MANUFACTURED BY

HARTLEY, GREENS, AND CO.

at

LEEDS POTTERY

with

A GREAT VARIETY OF OTHER ARTICLES

THE SAME ENAMEL'D, PRINTED OR ORNAMENTED WITH

GOLD TO ANY PATTERN; ALSO WITH COATS OF ARMS,

CYPHERS, LANDSCAPES, &C. &C.

There is no better way of appreciating the rich variety of creamware itself than by quoting some of the verses so often found on it.

On a puzzle jug:

> Within this jug there is good liquor
> T'is fit for Parson or for Vicar;
> But how to drink and not to spill,
> Will try the utmost of your skill.

On a jug dated 1835 and decorated with agricultural implements:

> Let the wealthy and the great
> Roll in splendour and state
> I envy them not I declare it
> I eat my own lamb
> My own chicken and ham
> I shear my own fleece and I wear it

I have lawns I have bowers
I have fruits I have flowers
The lark is my morning alarmer
So you jolly boys now
Here's God speed the plough
Long life and success to the farmer.

On a drinking mug:

Come my old friend and take a Pot
But mark now what I say
While that thou drinkest thy neighbours health
Drink not thine own away
It but too often is the case
While we sit o'er a Pot
We kindly wish our friend good Health
Our own is quite forgot.

On a marriage jug:

In courtship Strephon careful
    hands his lass
Over a stile a child with ease
    might pass
But wedded Strephon now neglects
    his dame
Tumble or not to him tis all the same.

On a lustre wall plaque:

May Peace and Plenty
On our Nation Smile
And Trade with Commerce
Bless the British Isle.

On a Staffordshire frog mug:

Tho' malt and venom
    Seem united
Don't break my pot
    Nor be affrighted.

On a tankard:

Here's to the maid of bashful fifteen
Likewise to the matron of fifty
Here's to the bold and extravagant Queen
And here's to the housewife that's thrifty.

On another tankard:

In Country Village lives a Vicar
Fond as all are of Tithes and Liquor.

On a jug of 1793:

The Martyr of Equality
'Behold the progress of the French System'

> *Here I see the victim bleeding*
> *By a brother doom'd to die*
> *All in vain for pity pleading*
> *Pity dare not lift her eye.*
>
> *May Britain a true*
> *Their rights pursue*
> *And e'er espouse the cause*
> *Of Church and King*
> *And every Thing*
> *That constitutes their Laws.*

Portrait medallions

One of the most collectable areas of eighteenth-century Wedgwood production is in portrait medallions. These include the likenesses of classical figures and also of Wedgwood's contemporaries, and represent a whole gallery of portraits ranging from royalty and republicans, to actors, politicians, scientists and artists. Hundreds of such medallions were made and the tradition has continued until the present day. Wedgwood employed a number of modellers but was particularly pleased with the work of William Hackwood and in 1776 was wishing that 'we had half a dozen more Hackwoods'. Other modellers were John Flaxman, RA, whose services were secured by Bentley, Joachim Smith and John Charles Lochee, who also worked for other concerns. James Tassie was also a source for Wedgwood medallions; this brilliant gem engraver, together with Dr Henry Quin, invented a composition suitable for casting cameos, intaglios and portrait medallions. Although Wedgwood and Tassie were rivals in this field, they remained good friends. George Stubbs designed reliefs of horses, and the work of Lady Templeton and Lady Beauclark are distinctive when employed on sentimental classical reliefs, mainly of women and children.

Wedgwood did not enter the arena of porcelain production, but some excellent bone china was produced by his son Josiah junior between 1812 and 1822; many of the teapots and jugs of tea services were frequently derived from silver shapes of the day. Josiah Wedgwood's grandson revived the production of bone china at the factory in 1878.

Unquestionably there were many important commercial factors that contributed to Josiah Wedgwood's success, and the lessons he learned and put into practice became examples not only for his contemporaries in the Potteries and those who followed them but in many other fields of industry as well.

Etruria was a symbol of change, and the small family potters could no longer cope with demand or the new sophisticated potting techniques. Wedgwood set about solving his problems with strict factory discipline and the division of labour: he kept individual workshops quite separate and believed that the production of what he termed useful works should be kept well apart from that of ornamental works. He trained the men

276

WEDGWOOD

WEDGWOOD

Mark either impressed in the clay or printed in colour on Queensware from 1769, and on ornamental jasper, black basalt, cane, terra cotta, and Queensware from 1780

WEDGWOOD
ETRURIA
WEDGWOOD
ETRURIA
Wedgwood
Etruria

Marks used on very high quality pieces for a brief period from 1840

WEDGWOOD

Mark used for bone china, 1878

to one task, raising the quality of work in the process, and men were paid strictly according to their expertise. The modeller, William Hackwood, might earn forty-two shillings (£2·10) per week, while other painters could earn as little as a shilling (5p). The work force of the potteries had previously enjoyed great freedom, being able to move from one task to another, but under Wedgwood this came to an end. He often needed trained painters and modellers, and he realised that it would be necessary to train workers rather than face the continual problem of trying to find skilled labour on a jobbing basis. He employed artists of renown to produce designs, but he made sure that their contact with his permanent work force was kept to a minimum, for he felt that they were a disrupting influence to his scheme of factory management. He wrote: 'Oh! for a dozen good and humble modellers at Etruria for a couple of months. What creations, renovations and generations should we make! well—fair and softley we must proceed with our own natural forces, for I will have no fine modellers here, though I seem to wish for them they would corrupt and ruin us all.' He took the local semi-skilled potters and made what he called 'mere men' into artists. Five years before his death, nearly a quarter of his work force were apprentices, and he also took on girls.

Wedgwood banned drinking and created a system of fines for transgressors. He insisted upon regular attendance at work, punctuality and the highest standards of cleanliness. He shook off the general belief that a pottery involved waste, dirty conditions and work by unscientific rule-of-thumb. He also invented the first clocking-in system:
'To save the trouble of the porters going round, tickets may perhaps be used, in the following manner—Let some sheets of pasteboard paper be printed with the names of all the work people, and the names cut off, about the size of half a card. Let each person take two of these tickets with him when he leaves work every evening; one of which he is to deliver into a box when he goes through the lodge in the morning, and the other when he returns from dinner. The porter then, instead of going round the works in the morning, looks over these tickets only; & if he finds any deficiency, goes to such places only where the deficiency appears. If the persons have neglected or refused to deliver their tickets on going through, they are to be admonished the first time, the second time to pay a small fine to the poor box. . . . It will be necessary to have divisions for the tickets in alphabetic order, for the greater facility of giving them out.'

It was indeed an industrial revolution. He introduced a clerk of weight and measures who would weigh the correct weight of clay for use for particular wares. When walking through the factory he is said to have smashed any pots that he regarded as being substandard, writing with chalk on the bench of the men responsible: 'This won't do for Josiah Wedgwood'. His attention to cleanliness had a motive not readily appreciated by many of the work force. When going through registers at St John's Church, Burslem, recently, I found the brief comment 'potters rot' against the names of some of the dead. 'Potters rot' was the name given to lead poisoning and it is why Wedgwood did not allow workmen to eat in the dipping room and insisted that 'a pail of water with soap and a towel and a brush for the nails to be always at hand'. The men and boys working in such areas wore smocks as a form of protective clothing, and Wedgwood insisted that floors and other surfaces should be washed or sponged and never brushed when dry, to avoid creating clouds of dust.

Having trained his work force, Wedgwood went to considerable lengths to keep them. It was not merely the competition for skilled men locally that he sought to avoid, but the hiring by agents on behalf of manufacturers in Europe and America. He warned his men that promises made in this country might not be kept when they went abroad and he also appealed to their sense of loyalty:

'You must by this time be fully convinced, how delusive the offers held out to you are, and how contrary it would be to your own interest to accept them. But supposing for a moment, that with regard to your own particular persons there was a real and lasting advantage. Would it have no weight with you to think, that you were ruining a trade, which had taken the united efforts of some thousands of people, for more than an age, to bring to the perfection it has now attained? a perfection no where else to be found – an object exciting at once the envy and emulation of all Europe! but they will both ever be harmless to us whilst we are true to ourselves: for Englishmen, in arts and manufacturers as well as in arms, can only be conquered by Englishmen: the enemy must first gain over some traitors and renegades from among ourselves, before they can attain any decisive advantage. Is there a man among you then who will stand forth, and acknowledge himself to be that traitor to his country and fellow workmen? who will openly avow, that for the sake of a paltry addition to his own wages for few years, he would betray their interests, and wantonly throw

95 *Opposite, above:* Two fine creamware jugs, made in Liverpool and with a typical Liverpool shape, *c.* 1786.

96 *Opposite, below:* Part of a bone china tea service with japan decoration. Wedgwood, early nineteenth century.

97 Creamware portrait plate, Admiral Lord Nelson, Staffordshire, c. 1810. Victoria and Albert Museum, London.

98 *Opposite:* Wedgwood portrait medallions form a unique series of historical portraits, the first of them being offered for sale in 1773. This group includes Captain Cook and William Pitt. The larger portrait medallion is of Erasmus Darwin (1731-1802), the botanist and physician and a lifelong friend of Josiah Wedgwood.

away into the hands of foreigners, perhaps of enemies, the superiority we have thus laboured for and obtained! I wish to entertain a better opinion of my countrymen, than to suspect that there is a single man who could be so base; and am willing to persuade myself it has been owing to want of thought, or of proper information, that any have thus deserted the cause of their country.'

In spite of such strong appeals to his workers Wedgwood seldom objected to other manufacturers attempting the duplication of his own products. Above all, being a man of great energy and having the capacity for long hours of work, he expected similar efforts from his men. It was a discipline that laid the foundations for the industries of the nineteenth century. Having created stable production methods, Wedgwood found it necessary to expand his markets, and employ more salesmen to introduce personally his wares at home and abroad. This sales organisation reaped massive dividends, to such an extent that Wedgwood seriously undermined the business of the Meissen factory. The sale of Wedgwood wares became worldwide in the eighteenth century and with that achievement the whole ceramic industry of Great Britain came of age.

Chapter 6

English porcelain

England was not the first European country to manufacture porcelain, but, unlike many of their Continental counterparts, English porcelain manufacturers worked under highly competitive commercial conditions. The objects they produced were intended to suit the requirements and possibilities of the market in general and were not commissioned by princes and other powerful patrons. This more popular demand resulted in a vigorous commercial life, the growth of great businesses and the encouragement of talent in many fields. British manufacturers had to cater for a largely domestic market, and produced mainly everyday wares, whereas in Europe money was supplied by royal families to produce highly decorated figure models for the luxury market. In the following pages, the distinctively British style in porcelain will emerge through discussion of the main factories.

Bow 1746-1776

The factories of Bow and Chelsea can claim to be the first to have really manufactured porcelain in England in commercial quantities. Bow, however, can also claim the distinction of being the first to introduce 'bone china' to the world. The addition of animal bone ash gave added strength in the kiln during firing. Later after many further experiments with bone made by other factories, bone china became more popular.

The name of Bow is somewhat misleading for the porcelain factory was in fact situated in the parish of West Ham in Essex. In 1744 a patent was granted for the making of porcelain to Thomas Frye of West Ham and to Edward Heylyn of Bow. To date, no trace of porcelain manufactured by them has been found. It would now seem that Chelsea can claim to be the true pioneer, as a few Chelsea items bear the inscribed date 1745. It appears that Bow did not really begin commercial production until the following year. It is most likely that Frye and Heylyn took out their patent after meeting André Duché, a man

Early incised marks

Painted anchor and dagger marks, c. 1760-76

Underglaze blue mark, c. 1760-76

whose contact with William Cookworthy of Plymouth is discussed in Chapter 3.

The early output from Bow consisted entirely of tableware. The first date to be found on Bow porcelain is 1750, and the words 'New Canton' and 'Made at New Canton' also appear, referring to the place where so much Chinese porcelain was enamelled and from where it was exported. This was a period when Chinese motifs were being copied in all aspects of the visual arts.

In the 1760s production at Bow was at its height and the factory was attracting workers from other parts of the country. In the fourth edition of Daniel Defoe's *Tour of Great Britain*, published in 1748, reference is made to

'. . . Bow: where a large Manufactory of Porcelaine is lately set up. They have already made large quantities of tea-cups, saucers, etc. which by some skilful persons are said to be little inferior to those brought from China. If they can work this so as to undersell the Foreign Porcelaine, it may become a very profitable business to the Undertakers, and save great sums to the Public, which are annually sent abroad for this commodity.'

When the sixth edition of Defoe's book appeared in 1761, revised by Samuel Richardson, the entry on Bow testifies to its rapid progress:

'. . . though not as fine as some made at Chelsea, or as that from Dresden, is much stronger than either and therefore better for common use; and, being much cheaper than any other China, there is a great Demand for it. The Proprietors of this Manufactory have also procured some very good Artists in Painting, who are employed in painting some of their finest Sort of Porcelain, and is so well performed, as to equal most of that from Dresden in this Respect.'

Despite this, in 1776, after years of various controlling partnerships, the Bow manufactory was purchased and closed. Although Bow had been in business for less than thirty years its output was astonishing. The early wares were white or blue and white, closely following Oriental examples. Japanese and Chinese styles were copied and plates frequently have the Oriental type foot-rim. One feature of Bow porcelain is its thickness—even if held against a strong light, only the edges will appear translucent on many pieces. This lack of translucency is probably a result of the underfiring of the ware in an attempt to prevent it warping.

The early cream colour porcelain of this factory is subject to firing cracks, some of which may be superficial in appearance,

and may have a wax-like glaze. Later Bow tends to show something of a blue glaze, and a rust-like staining where it is worn or scratched. Many pieces of Bow are very thick and heavy for their size as a result of the paste being pressed into the mould by hand (a process known as press moulding).

Enamel colours are often used in decoration, as are powder-blue grounds. Colouring tends to be bold and puce is much used on the later figures. The first use of transfer printed decoration is found on Bow porcelain before 1760. Figure bases may also be rather tall with four Rococo scroll feet. Look out for a square hole in the back of a Bow figure: it is usually assumed that the purpose of this hole is to support a metal candle bracket if required. Again, pay careful attention to marks: early pieces are unlikely to have these although many examples have been found with several marks associated with the Bow factory (for example a dagger, a longbow, or an anchor) on the one item.

Bristol 1770-1781

William Cookworthy established his hard-paste factory in Bristol in 1770 after its removal from Plymouth. Five

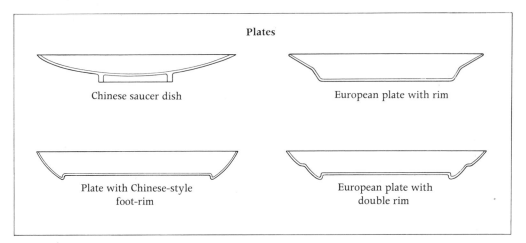

Plates

Chinese saucer dish

European plate with rim

Plate with Chinese-style
foot-rim

European plate with
double rim

Painted 'X' or 'B' mark

Crossed-swords mark,
1770-81

Bristolians had been shareholders in the Plymouth company, including the famous Richard Champion who was to take control at Bristol. Champion, like Cookworthy, was a Quaker; he was also a merchant and a Whig. When Cookworthy retired, Champion became increasingly involved with the production of porcelain. In 1775 he applied to extend the patent that had given Cookworthy 'sole use and exercise of a discovery of materials of the same nature as those of which Asiatic and Dresden porcelain are made'. His plans were frustrated by the Staffordshire potters and in particular by Josiah Wedgwood, who knew that the china clay was the finest available and who also had more money. An expensive case resulted that lasted months and at the end of it the Bristol monopoly no longer existed, and Josiah Wedgwood had access to the Cornish clay he so badly needed for his pottery. This, together with problems of administration and disputes with former colleagues,

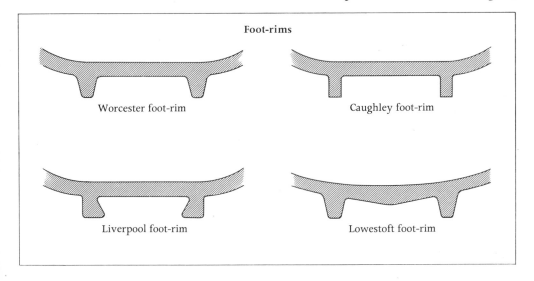

Foot-rims

Worcester foot-rim

Caughley foot-rim

Liverpool foot-rim

Lowestoft foot-rim

meant that costs proved too much and the Bristol factory finished its short life in 1781. Seven years later Champion died at the age of forty-eight.

Bristol porcelain is of very high quality and the domestic porcelains were expensive. It has the finest gilding of all the English factories. Floral garlands are typical and the Rococo style is most favoured. The commissioned wares, however, are in a class of their own. Many good models, most of them human figures, were produced at Bristol. Rarely see now are the biscuit ware plaques, with flowers surrounding a bust, monogram or animal. These originally cost £5 each and were mostly made for presentation.

Caughley 1772-1814

Thomas Turner probably trained at Worcester and after moving to Caughley he went into partnership with Ambrose Gallimore who had a pottery next to a coalmine. After the pottery had been enlarged it was renamed the Salopian Porcelain Manufactory: the name Salopia comes from the Roman name for Shropshire in which Caughley is situated. Porcelain manufacture began by about 1775 although pottery is believed to have been made there from 1754. The fact that so much of Caughley (pronounced 'Calflee') resembles Worcester is no doubt explained by Turner's connection with that factory. The porcelain tends to be slightly more heavily potted (having a thicker, less refined appearance) than Worcester although similar in other ways.

In 1799 the lease of the Caughley factory was sold to John Rose whose factory was at Coalport on the other bank of the

SALOPIAN

Impressed name-mark, c. 1775-99

S So Sx

Painted or printed 'S' marks, c. 1775-c. 1795

Printed and painted 'C' mark, c. 1775-95

river and, for a time, he continued to use the Caughley site for some of his Coalport production.

Most of Caughley products were tea wares and the last factory sale of surplus stock included:

'. . . a great number of beautiful tea and coffee equipages of various much improved patterns, in full and short sets, richly executed in enamel and burnished gold together with a great variety of new and elegant blue and white tea and coffee sets, table and dessert services, muffin plates, butter tubs etc., mugs, jugs, egg-cups and strainers, butter cups, custard cups of different sorts and sizes, pickle-shells, eye baths, asparagus servers, toy table and tea sets and candle-sticks etc . . .'

The output was largely blue-and-white and in the Oriental or 'Nankin' style. 'Nankin' described much blue-and-white, for it was the main centre of the vast export of such wares by the Chinese, just as most Chinese enamelled wares were exported through Canton.

Caughley was regarded by generations of collectors as a poor cousin to the Worcester factory, only 30 miles (48 km) away on the River Severn. Now excavation has proved this attitude to be totally misinformed, as we shall see later. It was Mr Geoffrey Godden who, after investigating the Caughley site, made several major discoveries concerning the wares and their marks, and this table will clarify the differences revealed between Caughley and Worcester as a result.

	Caughley	Worcester
The Fisherman Pattern	The fisherman holds the rod with a taut line.	Fisherman holds rod with very loose fishing line.
	Standing fisherman holds a short fat fish.	Standing fisherman on boat holds a long thin fish.
	The inner border is filled with solid pigment.	The inner border is composed of engraved lines.
Disguised Numeral Marks	No marks of this type revealed by excavation, although formerly attributed to this factory. Thus Caughley is much rarer than originally believed.	Marks (nine) formerly attributed to Caughley now regarded as Worcester.
Moulded Cabbage-Leaf Jugs	The eyes are open but the eyelids are thicker. In other ways the jugs are similar to the Worcester variety.	The eyes are of the Oriental type and appear to be closed.

The porcelain characteristics of both factories are very similar when held under a light bulb: green for early examples, orange for the later ones. This suggests that both factories purchased their raw materials from the same source.

Chelsea

Among the eighteenth-century English porcelains it is only Chelsea that may be ranked with the great wares of the royal factories of France and Germany. English manufacturers did not enjoy patronage on the scale of their Continental counterparts, so the production of luxury items, the marvellous figure models and great vases, was the exception, not the rule. Chelsea, in contrast to other English factories, deliberately catered for the luxury trade.

Remarkably, Chelsea's guiding light was Nicholas Sprimont (1716-1771), a Huguenot silversmith who registered his mark at Goldsmith's Hall in 1742. Several porcelains were experimented with at Chelsea, and numerous differences can be observed among the characteristics of most mixed groups of Chelsea available. In order to clarify its development, Chelsea is usually divided into periods defined by its mark changes:

The Triangle Period. This early period, in the first half of the eighteenth century, is rare. The mark is a triangle incised into

Early triangle marks, occasionally accompanied by the place-name

Underglaze blue crown and trident mark, *c.* 1748-50

288

102 A cream 'goat and bee' jug, relief-moulded and painted. Marked with an incised triangle. Height 4½ inches (114 mm). Chelsea, mid eighteenth century. Victoria and Albert Museum, London.

Raised anchor mark, c. 1749-52

103 *Below:* Leaf-moulded teapot painted with flowers and insects. Chelsea, mid eighteenth century.

104 *Far right:* The same teapot from below, showing the incised triangle.

the paste before glazing, which accounts for its rarity: triangle marks are unusual and some marks have been cut through the glaze at a much later date in the hope that they might be mistaken for an early piece. Some of these pieces are also incised with the date 1745 and 'goat and bee jugs' are good examples of this. These translucent little jugs are a delight with a figure of a bee among the foliage and a goat's head cut into the base. The porcelain has a yellowish tinge and the glaze is often a little cloudy.

In my experience it is the white porcelains that are most often overlooked. During the 1960s a dealer I knew purchased a 'goat and bee jug' as part of an auction lot of miscellaneous white kitchen ware! Most of the output before 1750 was white and designs are often based on contemporary silver shapes.

The Raised-Anchor Period 1749-1752. At this period the now famous Chelsea anchor was moulded in relief on a raised pad. Figure models with this mark are of the highest standard and the white figures of the birds made at this time are outstanding among European porcelains; needless to say they can also be costly. Tin oxide was added to the glaze and can usually be detected wherever the glaze gathers and pools, as it has an opaque milky appearance and is not translucent. Bone ash was also used to help strengthen the porcelain body. When these early pieces are held against a strong light they usually reveal the light patches or pinpoints of extra translucency that are termed 'moons'.

It is at this time that we also see the delightful 'fable painted' wares of J. H. O'Neale. Many octagonal tea wares were decorated by O'Neale, and some of the designs were taken from Aesop.

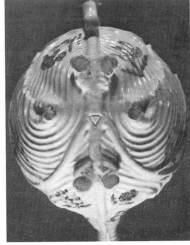

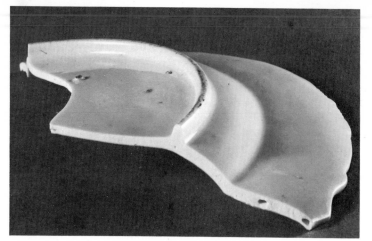

The Red Anchor Period 1752-1756. The red anchor was applied at this period almost as though the manufacturer intended it to be invisible! The anchor is very small and I have seen marked examples that have been in a private collection for many years without the collector ever seeing the marks until they were pointed out to him. It was occasionally applied in brown, though mostly on flat wares.

Red anchor mark, *c.* 1752-56

'Stilt marks', small raised patches, may be found on the reverse of plates and dishes showing where they were supported in the kiln by stilts. Again, small characteristics such as these are most important, for so many of these porcelains bear no factory mark at all. Attention to the marks is all the more important as only they make it possible to separate many of the raised anchor and red anchor pieces, which often have the same milky glaze and crazing.

O'Neale carried out much of his best painting at this period. Vegetable-shaped tureens are distinctive, as too is the use of botanical subjects as decoration. Hans Sloane plates are well-known examples, copied from illustrations in the *Gardener's dictionary* by Philip Miller published under the aegis of Sir Hans Sloane, patron of the Royal Physik Garden, Chelsea, as are drawings from Curtis' botanical works. Figures were sometimes inspired by Kändler's original Meissen models. Classical and emblematic figures were made in quantity. Leaf-shapes were used quite often for sauceboats and dishes. Painted insects or flowers were often used to conceal small faults in the glaze. An object of truly great artistry is the red anchor group of Leda and the Swan painted in enamels.

The Gold Anchor Period 1756-1769. This period is distinguished by the use of a small gold anchor. The porcelain is thick and contains bone ash although there is no longer tin

Gold anchor mark, *c.* 1756-69

oxide in the glaze. The Scotsman John Donaldson, who was influenced by Continental painters, did good figure painting. Some major figure groups, such as 'The Music Lesson', exemplify the overwhelming use of floral bocage decoration at this time. Miniature objects or toys were manufactured, some of them copied from Meissen. Seals and scent bottles proved very popular and have remained so with today's collectors.

Chelsea/Derby Period

Chelsea production came to an end when Nicholas Sprimont sold out to John Cox, who in 1770 promptly sold the Chelsea factory to William Duesbury of Derby. Around this period it becomes very difficult to tell the difference between the products of the two factories.

Double or linked gold anchor marks point to the Chelsea/ Derby period, as do ones crossed or combined with a 'D'. It could well be, however, that many pieces marked in this way were made at Derby rather than Chelsea. As with Derby figures, unglazed patch marks often occur on the base. This is a vital characteristic which the collector should bear in mind when identifying these factories as these rarely occur on work from other factories.

Gold (or occasionally red) mark

Gold mark

Coalport 1796 – present day

The early wares of Coalport are unmarked and often mistaken for Chamberlain Worcester because of the similar decoration. The later Coalport work marked with the date 1750 also gives many a headache to new collectors: the date merely refers to the assumed beginning of the Caughley factory which John Rose purchased in 1799.

Coalport produced porcelain of outstanding quality, and their leadless felspathic glaze (created from ground felspar suspended in water) obtained the Award of the Society of Arts on 30 May 1820. This award was celebrated by Coalport with a handsome special mark.

Coalport marks

1. Impressed mark, 1085-25
2. Early painted mark, c. 1805-15
3. Marks painted in underglaze blue, c. 1810-25
4. Printed mark introduced after Society of Arts Gold Metal award, c. 1820-30
5. Painted or gilt monogram mark, c. 1851-61
6. Mark in enamels or gold, c. 1851-61
7. Painted or gilt 'ampersand' mark, c. 1861-75

291

In terms of translucency and whiteness, Coalport rivalled the products of Swansea and Nantgarw. In 1816 a newspaper went so far as to state:

'The Sèvres China Manufacture has now competitors which bid fair to excel in the Article of China. The Manufactories at Coalbrookdale and at Swansea having just completed some beautiful specimens.'

Rose was a businessman as well as potter, for he signed a seven-year agreement with the brilliant *enfant terrible* of English ceramics, William Billingsley, so stifling the competition from the Welsh factories.

Coalport was, and continues to be, highly regarded for its production of vases and other wares decorated with various flower motifs. As with Caughley, however, there was much upheaval in estimation of the value of Coalport when Geoffrey Godden discovered pattern books at Minton that proved that many pieces always thought to be Coalport or Coalbrookdale were in fact from that factory.

The gilding on Coalport porcelain is rich and thick, the painting is always excellent, and the pieces decorated with Sèvres type coloured grounds are quite beautiful.

106 *Above:* Floral encrusted pastille burner in the form of a cottage. Coalport, 1820.

H. & R. Daniel *c.* 1822-1845

Henry Daniel produced highly competitive porcelain in Stoke-on-Trent, although marked pieces are not easy to find. Daniel had been chief enameller to Spode, and he was joined in the business by his son Richard.

The reputation of this firm's porcelains was held in the highest esteem by the manufacturers, yet it is only during the second half of the 1970s that its products have begun to receive the attention from collectors that they deserve. It is thus yet

DANIEL & SON
Rare mark, *c.* 1822-26

H. & R. DANIEL
Rare written or printed mark, *c.* 1826-29

107 Painted plate, teapot and documentary bowl. Coalport, early nineteenth century.

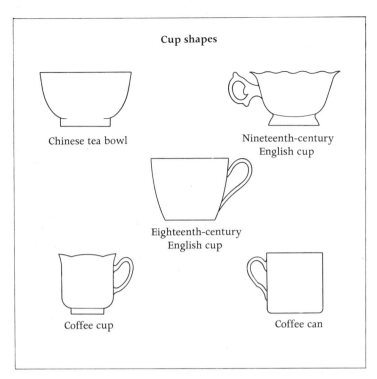

Cup shapes

Chinese tea bowl

Nineteenth-century English cup

Eighteenth-century English cup

Coffee cup

Coffee can

another example of how objects of quality can be completely overlooked until attention is drawn to them.

While Daniel porcelain is subject to cracks during firing and crazing in the glaze is often present in the finished article, the experience their maker gained while decorating for Spode makes these porcelains, with their shaped edges, most desirable.

Standard early impressed mark

Standard printed mark, *c.* 1805-20

Overglaze printed mark, *c.* 1815-30

Davenport *c.* 1793-1887

John Davenport began his family business at Longport, Staffordshire, although at first only earthenware was produced. The quality of the ninteenth-century Davenport pieces was very high, although I am certain that many of their productions, as with Daniel and Coalport, were once classified as 'Rockingham'. Rockingham was a general term for anything Victorian considered to be quality, although as a factory its production is now known to be much smaller than once thought. This arbitrary classification was applied to much nineteenth-century porcelain due to the refusal to believe that so much outstanding work could have emanated from the Victorian era. This firm was also responsible for excellent transfer-printed earthenware, but despite this the business failed in 1887.

293

108 Two nineteenth-century teapot shapes, Davenport (left) and Spode (right). The Spode example bears the pattern number 1968.

The output of the Davenport concern was a large one, particularly in the field of tea and dessert services, and some excellent artists worked for the firm. Many of the Derby porcelains were copied as were those of Spode. As with Coalport, a *rose Pompadour* ground was used. At the same time the cheaper market was catered for with the production of 'opaque semi-porcelain' which simply meant an improved earthenware.

DAVENPORT
LONGPORT
STAFFORDSHRE

Standard printed mark,
c. 1870-87

Derby *c.* 1750-present day

The name Derby is renowned both as a city and as a porcelain manufactory where porcelain of great variety has been produced for more than 200 years. The term is confusing to many because of the changes of ownership, and because many new collectors tend to refer to all Derby wares as Royal Crown Derby no matter what their age. The Royal Crown Derby Porcelain Company Limited takes its name from the time it received a royal warrant in 1889; for objects made before that date other terms need to be used.

Incised or painted mark,
c. 1760-80 (?)

Standard mark, 1782-1818

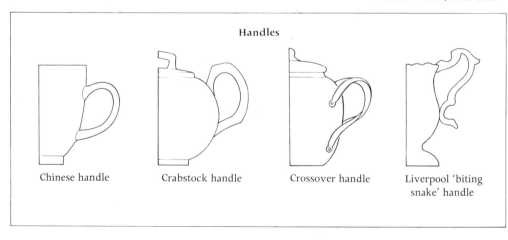

Handles

Chinese handle   Crabstock handle   Crossover handle   Liverpool 'biting snake' handle

109 A charming eighteenth-century Derby figure group.

Later standard mark in red, more carelessly drawn

Transfer-printed mark, 1818-48

King Street Factory mark

Derby came into being largely as a result of the business management and talent for porcelain decoration of William Duesbury. It was Duesbury who agreed at the beginning of 1756 to be co-patron with John Heath, described as a Gentleman, and André Planché, china maker. They set out to work together '. . . in the art of making English china as also in buying and selling of all sorts of wares belonging to the art of making china . . .' Planché was a French refugee who probably began the first porcelain production in Derby some years earlier than 1756. At this time William Duesbury was in London with his own decorating shop, painting wares from Bow, Chelsea, Derbyshire and Staffordshire. In due course Duesbury was left in control of the factory.

Duesbury copied many Chelsea products as well as originals from Meissen. Some of the early figures from Derby have an unglazed edge around the base, known as a 'dry edge', others have a somewhat narrow funnel-shaped hole underneath. The later figures have the 'patch marks' on the base mentioned in the section on Chelsea. Three and sometimes four patch marks, about the size of a thumb print, were created by the small clay pads used to support the figures and these prevented the glaze

295

sticking during firing. Model numbers are also frequently incised in the bases of figures. Gilding is also a feature of Derby, and both honey and mercurial gilding is much admired.

Due to the popularity of the bisque figures being created by Sèvres, Derby began the production of undecorated biscuit figures from about 1770. Only perfect figures were left in the biscuit, or unglazed, state; those having imperfections were sold off cheaply having first been glazed and decorated.

Many famous decorators worked for Derby, but the most celebrated was William Billingsley (1758-1828). After serving his apprenticeship, Billingsley became Derby's principal flower painter in 1790. This complex man was later to move from factory to factory, ever searching for the elusive perfect porcelain formula. Even so, most people take delight in Billingsley for his painting of flowers and roses in particular. He was a naturalistic flower painter, who, having first washed the whole flower with colour, then removed the highlights with a dry brush, before painting in such detail as shading. The 'Billingsley Rose' is unmistakeable.

Billingsley was succeeded at Derby by William Pegg, known more familiarly as 'Quaker' Pegg. Outstanding in the botanical field, Pegg's style was to paint his flowers across the entire width of the piece he was decorating. In 1800 he joined the Society of Friends and developed a form of religious mania. He first rejected his botanical painting in the belief that he was creating idols. After many years he returned to Derby and his painting in 1813, but in 1820 the mania returned and he left for the last time.

A brief chronology of Derby may be given as follows:

1750-1756 First figures made at Derby by André Planché.

1756 William Duesbury senior becomes manager.

1786 Death of Duesbury senior, succeeded by his son William Duesbury junior.

1795 Michael Kean taken into partnership.

1797 Kean becomes manager on the death of Duesbury junior.

1815 Robert Bloor takes over from the Duesbury family.

1848 The old Nottingham Road factory is closed and a small factory started in King Street, Derby, by workmen from the old works.

1878 Formation of the Derby Crown Porcelain Company in Osmeston Road.

1890 Name of factory changed to Royal Crown Derby Porcelain Company.

1935 King Street factory merged with the Royal Crown Derby Porcelain Company.

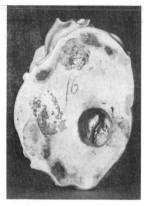

110 The base of the group shown on page 295 revealing such useful points of identification as the hole, unglazed areas usually described as 'pad' or 'patch' marks caused by the pads of clay used to support the figure while in the kiln, and the incised number, another typical feature of later Derby figures.

111 *Opposite:* The so-called 'Maypole Dancers', a rare and exuberant Chelsea group, 1755. Fitzwilliam Museum, Cambridge.

1964 Royal Crown Derby Porcelain Company became part of the Allied English Potteries Group.

Doulton 1882-present day

The porcelains made at Burslem at the Nile Street works in this century are widely known and form a highly collectable series. In particular some beautiful effects have been achieved with rich flambé glazes.

However, it is for the production of stonewares that Doulton is most celebrated, of which more in the following chapter. From the early 1880s some excellent porcelains have been made. From the final years of the Victorian era until the eve of the First World War, pieces of great technical interest and representative of their times were produced. Much interest is now being taken in such pieces for, after some neglect, they were made long enough ago to be seen in their proper perspective. Usually an 'all over' painting technique was employed and the examples of particular note are ones signed by the artist.

Bases

Derby base

Bow base

Obadiah Sherratt table base

Chelsea base

Teapot shapes

Yi-hsing ware teapot

Eighteenth-century globular teapot

Pinxton teapot, late eighteenth century

Caughley teapot, late eighteenth century

New Hall teapots, early nineteenth century

Castleford teapot

Rockingham 'Cadogan' teapot

Coalport teapot, *c.* 1825

'Barge' teapot

Victorian teapot

The reputation of Goss has suffered severely after the great mass of heraldic or crested china that first appeared on the souvenir market during the 1880s. In the first twenty years of this century the collection of such pieces became a craze and their output was very large. Even so, interest in some of these pieces, particularly the figures, houses, cottages, ships and vehicles, has revived among modern collectors. Such items will never rank with those of the great porcelain factories, but they clearly provide pleasure for many.

William Henry Goss (1833-1906) first worked as an artist at a firm known as Copelands (see the section on Spode), and his early parian busts, his 'porcelain jewellery', 'jewelled porcelain' and pastille-burners in the form of cottage models are of real note. Pre-First World War pieces attract most attention: the modelling is often very good and some pieces display a true sense of humour and are genuine curiosities.

Liverpool

In the past collectors have talked of Liverpool porcelain as though it was the product of one factory, although this is in fact not the case.

Eighteenth-century Liverpool was well placed to be a centre of English ceramics. It was an excellent port, and it was also well served by the Trent and Mersey canal which brought cargoes of pottery from Staffordshire. Furthermore, it was the base of Sadler and Green who ran a transfer printing business catering for creamwares and porcelains alike. As we have seen earlier, Liverpool was also the home of a number of potteries producing tin glazed Delftwares.

Various pastes were used by different porcelain manufacturers, but the main decorative output was of Oriental style blue-and-white. Like most of the English porcelains the Liverpool products were made for everyday use rather than pure ornament.

A whole colony of potters grew up at Shaws Brow on Merseyside. The largest among them was probably Richard Chaffers & Co (fl. c. 1754-65). First established as a pottery before 1750, this company began the manufacture of soapstone type porcelain about 1756. The soaprock used was obtained from Cornwall and enamelled decoration was used as well as underglaze blue, but again, it is the Oriental styles that prevail. The body of this porcelain is somewhat grey and the glaze

occasionally gathers within the foot-rims to form a rather dirty discoloration that is frequently termed a 'thunder-cloud effect'.

Many of the Liverpool soapstone porcelains are inferior to those of Worcester but there are frequent exceptions where the potting is thin and crisp, closely resembling Worcester.

The Chaffers factory, like most Liverpool factories, produced jugs with a rather elongated appearance. Philip Christian, who took over after Richard Chaffers's death in 1765, produced pots of rather more elegance including some charming enamelled coffee pots with moulded well placed spouts and lively and well shaped handles. The Philip Christian factory continued until 1776, the year in which he sold his lease of a Cornish soapstone mine to Worcester.

Samuel Gilbody (*fl. c.* 1754-61) was responsible for at least some of the exceedingly rare Liverpool porcelain figures. His modelling and painting has a precise charm about it. There is an enamelled figure of Minerva to be seen in the Victoria and Albert Museum, London.

Soapstone bodied wares are attributed to William Ball (*fl. c.* 1755-69). His blues tend to be bright and the clear, and the soft glaze has a warm feel about it. The painting usually consists of firmly executed chinoiseries.

The porcelain body from the factory of William Reid & Co. (*c.* 1755-1761) is thick and distinctive, rather like the early pipe clays, and the addition of tin oxide to the glaze gives it a dense and bubbled appearance. There is still much to be learned about these porcelains from excavation, however, and there

114 *Far left:* A very fine example of a moulded and blue painted porcelain mug. Liverpool, eighteenth century.

115 *Above:* Herculaneum plate, part of a service decorated with the arms of the City of Liverpool. Early nineteenth century.

may be yet more re-attribution of Liverpool porcelains.

The Penningtons were an important family of Liverpool potters and formed a company known as Pennington & Part (*c.* 1770-1799). The bone-ash bodies believed to be by this factory are often decorated with prints in underglaze blue but they are poor in comparison with Worcester or Caughley.

The body used at the factory of Thomas Wolfe & Co. (*c.* 1795-1800) is of a harder paste and some of its products are not unlike those of New Hall. The translucency shows a greenish tinge. A number of the Liverpool porcelains have printed decoration, and those used at the Ball factory were frequently overpainted in enamels. Finials on Liverpool teapot lids often seem unusually high and handles in the form of a biting snake — where the snake appears to be biting the rim of the pot — are a firm help in identification.

The name of the Herculaneum factory (*c.* 1793-1841) was chosen out of the same motives that led Wedgwood to call his great factory Etruria. Herculaneum was one of the first factories in England to produce a non-frit bone china, although its first wares were entirely earthenware. The creamwares and stonewares frequently carry the impressed mark 'Herculaneum' and are of a fine standard. Blue transfer-printed earthenware was also produced but the porcelain is of great interest and was much overlooked in the past. Particularly important are vase decorations in the French Empire style but with very English enamelled reserves.

Longton Hall 1749-1760

This was the first porcelain factory to appear in the Potteries and is situated near Stoke-on-Trent. It was founded by William Jenkinson, and the first products show the influence of salt-glaze pottery.

Jenkinson was followed by a number of partners, one of whom was William Littler who gave his name to the bright blue used at Longton, called 'Littler's Blue'. Littler is said to have been the first potter to introduce cobalt blue into the Potteries.

The porcelain body is heavy and often clumsy, a soft paste glassy frit, but it is much admired by many collectors. Many soft pastes have more charm than the technically perfect hard pastes, but this is very much a matter of personal opinion.

The surface of many examples is uneven and the thick glaze has a candle-wax appearance. Most characteristic of the Longton wares are the leaf-shaped examples with the veins of the leaves often outlined in pink.

Some good painting was done at Longton, and a series of white porcelain figures, representing animals, characters from classical mythology and models based on Meissen originals, are known as 'the snowmen group'. The glaze of these pieces is thick, bubbly and glassy while the paste is subject to fire cracks.

116 Longton Hall two-handled sauceboat and two dishes. They show the leaf-moulding so characteristic of this factory and the heaviness of the porcelain. Mid eighteenth century.

Lowestoft 1757-1799

A fishing port on the coast of Suffolk, Lowestoft has long been a celebrated name among porcelain collectors. With no more than thirty workers, it was probably the smallest porcelain factory in England; it was also the best example of a soft paste one. It catered mainly for local needs and even after twenty years of production the business was still being described as "China Manufacturers and Herring Curers". It sold well to the middle-class population of East Anglia, as well as supplying a stream of souvenirs for the eighteenth-century tourist.

135

Rare painter's numbers, in underglaze blue, *c.* 1760-75

Copies of blue Worcester crescent and Dresden crossed-swords, *c.* 1775-90

One visitor, a man named Thomas Wale, made the following entry in his diary in 1777: 'Drove down with Mr. Smith and two sons to Lowestoft where we saw the china ware fabric, etc. and all of us bought some of it. Saw ye hanging gardens and ye fine prospect of ye sea. Excellent bathing machines etc.'

Views of Lowestoft and portraits of ships formed ready subjects for the Lowestoft decorators, who also copied the Oriental wares that had such popularity.

The factory closed by 1800, and although production was

considerable, examples of Lowestoft are not easy to find. They attract the collector for two reasons: their simple charm that results from the Chinese designs and the fact that such products as eye-baths, ink pots, and birth tablets recording the name and date of birth of local children, are appealing in their homeliness.

Flat bases are glazed over, and on wares with foot-rims, painters' numbers are to be found on the inside of the rim. The most famous products of this factory are those marked 'A Trifle From Lowestoft'.

Lowestoft wares are thick and have a thick bubbled glaze. Enamel colours were used after 1770, sometimes in conjunction with underglaze blue borders. Early specimens often have relief moulded decoration with reserve panels in underglaze blue. Of the enamel patterns, the bold floral sprays applied to tea and coffee wares, with a prominent tulip, are very fine. A few rare figures were also made at Lowestoft.

Minton c. 1793-present day

Thomas Minton was born in 1765 and began his career as a potter when he was apprenticed to Thomas Turner at Caughley. In Shropshire he learned the skills of engraving copper plates for the production of blue printed ware, and he would also have met Robert Hancock, the leading exponent of ceramic engraving. It proved an ideal environment for such an intelligent young man. When his apprenticeship was over Minton stayed briefly at Caughley before going up to London where he is said to have engraved work for Josiah Spode.

Following his marriage in London, Minton moved to Stoke-on-Trent and established himself in business as a designer and engraver. He then decided that he must have his own pottery

117 *Below:* Two Lowestoft mugs of the late eighteenth century.

118 *Far right:* Floral encrusted two-handled porcelain bowl and cover. Minton, nineteenth century. Crossed-swords mark on the base in underglaze blue. Such pieces were in the past frequently thought to be either Meissen or Coalport.

and, as Simeon Shaw in his *History of the Staffordshire Potteries* describes:

'About 1793 Mr. Thomas Minton connected himself with a Mr. Pownall and Joseph Poulson, and at Stoke commenced the manufacture of Blue Printed Pottery, of much excellence of quality and with additional elegance of Pattern, which speedily secured considerable celebrity. A few years afterwards, the manufacture of porcelain was connected with the other and has been attended with success. The manufactory is now the property of Mr. Minton alone. The Porcelain there fabricated possesses great excellence for fine texture and elegant ornaments . . .'

It appears that the years of Minton's production of porcelain are 1797 to 1816 and after 1824. It was during the latter period that a large number of decorative wares were made by Minton which in later years, as records were overlooked, became attributed to many other factories such as Derby, Rockingham, Spode, Swansea, Worcester and Coalport. This designation was corrected by a discovery made in the late 1960s by Geoffrey Godden, author and china expert. Researching the Minton archives he found design books that proved Minton's production of wares previously unsuspected. 'It was', he wrote, 'as if a new factory had been discovered.' Mr Godden tells the story in full in his book *Minton Pottery and Porcelain of the First Period 1793-1850.*

Minton travelled to Cornwall in 1798 and 1799 with other major potters in an attempt to stabilise the cost of china clay. When he died in 1836 he was succeeded by his son Herbert, an outstanding figure in the history of the Potteries in the nineteenth century. He attracted the finest decorators in Britain and some of the most notable from the Continent. Herbert Minton gained an international reputation for his company as well as royal patronage, and at the Great Exhibition in 1851 his ceramic innovations and displays won wide acclaim. We shall examine some of the nineteenth-century productions of Minton in more detail in the next chapter.

New Hall 1782-*c.* 1835

The patents of the Bristol factory were sold by Richard Champion in 1781 to a new company in the Potteries. The factory was first at Tunstall before moving to Shelton Hall, later known as New Hall. Production consisted chiefly of utility wares, particularly tea wares of all kinds. The decoration consists largely of small floral sprays, and larger bunches

1. Painted mark in overglaze blue enamel, *c.* 1805-16
2. Dresden crossed-swords mark, 1820s

3. Incised mark, *c.* 1845-60
4. Painted or printed ermine device, *c.* 1850-70

MINTON   MINTONS

Impressed name-mark, 1862+

L. Solon
or
M. L. Solon

Artist's signature

1. Painted pattern number, *c.* 1781-1812
2. Printed mark, *c.* 1812-35

119 Shapes and decoration typical of the New Hall factory. Note the coffee pot with its unusual stand, and the teapot with its floreat-like feet shown in the top left of the photograph, a feature only found on early examples.

and baskets of flowers, and at times a distinctive yellow shell. Gilding is often of good quality and Oriental mandarin patterns were also produced. After 1810 the porcelain body changed from the Bristol formula to bone ash. Tablewares are often banded round the base and printed outlines are sometimes enamelled. The early hard paste pieces are seldom marked with more than a pattern number, and those bearing the factory name are usually from the bone china period.

Pinxton 1796-1813

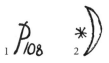

Rare painted or gilt name-mark, c. 1796-1805

1 P_{108} 2 $*)$

1. Rare painted initial, with pattern number
2. Painted crescent and star mark

John Coke (1776-1841), having become interested in the porcelain factory at Meissen on a tour of France, returned to his estate at Pinxton, on the borders of Nottinghamshire and Derbyshire; there he noticed some interesting clays and wrote to William Duesbury about them.

Duesbury was apparently not interested, but the news reached the ears of William Billingsley and he was immediately enthusiastic. He persuaded Coke to build a factory and told him that he would like to become works manager. The first porcelain was fired in April 1796 and Billingsley moved from Derby to Pinxton late in the autumn of that year.

Unfortunately there were no profits to pay Billingsley and he left Pinxton to go to Mansfield. His place was taken by William Caffee, also from Derby. In 1806 John Coke leased the factory to John Cutts but when Cutts moved to Wedgwood in 1813, the factory at Pinxton was closed.

The main Pinxton decoration consists of landscapes and flowers. The early Pinxton resembled the Derby body and has a green translucency when held in front of a bulb. Billingsley no doubt saw Pinxton as a heaven-sent opportunity to attempt to perfect his own porcelain body. At this time Pinxton closely resembles the bodies used by Billingsley in Wales at Swansea and Nantgarw. It is thinly potted and highly translucent. Under John Cutts the body thickened again and the translucency becomes yellowish.

120 Sugar box (centre), tea cup and saucer (right) and coffee can and saucer (left), all showing the fine painting and high quality porcelain associated with Pinxton.

Plymouth 1768-1773

This was the first English factory to use hard paste and it is curious to note how closely the Plymouth figures resemble the soft paste productions of Bow and Longton Hall.

It was William Cookworthy who opened the factory, and although supported by Lord Camelford it became clear even after two years' production and considerable expenditure on the part of both men that the factory was unlikely to become a financial success. The real difficulty arose in achieving a consistent paste, as Lord Camelford was to write in 1790: 'The difficulties found in proportioning properly the ingredients so as to give exactly the necessary degree of vitrification and no more, and the niceties with regard to this manipulation discouraged us from proceeding with the concern after we had procured the patent for the material

Painted marks in underglaze blue or enamels, *c.* 1768-70

Impressed mark

and expended on it between two and three thousand pounds.'

Some of the early figures were left undecorated, which made the flaws in the porcelain after firing very visible. Tall, hexagonal, broad-shouldered vases are typical but glazes were often discoloured during the firing. Resemblance to Bow and Longton Hall is found in the shell pieces, which consist of either a simple scallop shape or more than one shell joined together, and in the fact that some Longton Hall moulds were bought by Cookworthy in 1760. There are fine bell-shape mugs, sometimes showing 'wreathing' or faint spiral markings in the paste that can be felt with the fingers. Some of the later Plymouth vases are often beautifully painted.

Ridgway c. 1808-1855

The Ridgway family were all considerable potters but in the field of porcelain it is John Ridgway who particularly interests us. His father, Job Ridgway, had returned to Hanley in 1781 after working in Swansea and Leeds, and five years later his son John was born. The Cauldon Place Works at Shelton was built in 1802 and it was here that John, together with his younger brother William, joined their father in partnership in 1808. The same year they began the manufacture of porcelain. The best period, however, is regarded as being from 1813 until 1830 when the bone china body is heavy, with a clear paste and a clear glaze.

John Ridgway's main output was of tea and dessert wares, often richly decorated.

Rockingham c. 1826-1842

Printed griffin mark, c. 1826-30

This short-lived but much attributed factory takes its name from Earl Fitzwilliam, Marquis of Rockingham, on whose Yorkshire estate the factory was built. The potters here were the Brameld family, and the sons, Frederick, George and Thomas, managed the factory during the years of porcelain production.

The Rockingham bone china type body appears softer than other bone china of the time, which perhaps explains the tendency of the glaze to craze. Shapes used by Rockingham are very characteristic and a feel for them is easily obtained after a little study, and the same can be said of the colours (green, puce, grey). There is also some excellent landscape painting in the reserves (the areas left free of background decoration).

Some figures were made as were models of cottages and castles. Dessert services are of high quality, such as the one made for William IV in 1830, but it is a fortunate collector who finds one complete. The decorative style favoured at Rockingham was the Rococo, with plenty of scrolls and applied flowers.

Spode 1770-present day

Spode was not producing porcelain until the 1790s in the time of Josiah Spode junior, who was responsible for an excellent body. Under his brilliant direction the Spode factory and its products became known throughout the world.

The first Josiah Spode (born in 1739) had, when he was sixteen years old, worked with Whieldon and once again we see how this great potter was able to fire the enthusiasm of his young workers and stimulate their work.

In 1970 one of the most remarkable exhibitions of the ceramics of one manufactory was held in London, at the Royal

Spode marks

1. Impressed mark, *c.* 1770
2. Painted mark, *c.* 1800
3. Impressed mark, *c.* 1800
4. Painted mark, *c.* 1812
5. Printed mark, *c.* 1833
6. Impressed mark, *c.* 1833
7. Printed mark, *c.* 1850
8. Printed mark, *c.* 1855
9. Printed mark, *c.* 1894
10. Printed mark, *c.* 1970

Academy of Arts at Burlington House: it celebrated '200 years of Spode'. The catalogue of that exhibition, which was remarkable in its range and quality, is itself an excellent introduction to Spode.

In 1813 Spode introduced a stone-china body so that replacements could be made to china trade porcelain. It was a time of many innovations and improvements. The rich decoration of the porcelain was carried out in a separate decorating establishment in the Spode factory that was owned and managed by Daniel. This unique arrangement was terminated in the summer of 1822, Daniel establishing his own factory in Stoke.

A felspar porcelain was introduced in 1821, and this fact is commemorated in the factory mark.

The Copeland family had long been associated with Spode, and in March 1833 a partnership of Copeland and Garrett succeeded him. They began to market their new statuary porcelain, or 'parian', in the early 1840s.

Copeland and Garrett were succeeded by Messrs W. T. Copeland. A considerable number of marks were used by the factory incorporating the names of Spode and of Copeland, but far from creating confusion the mark changes are most helpful in providing accurate dating. The factory is now owned by the Royal Worcester Porcelain Company.

Worcester (and Lund's Bristol)

The story of this factory began in Bristol with the establishment there about 1748 of a soft paste porcelain manufactory owned by Benjamin Lund. It was here that Cornish soapstone was first used in a porcelain formula, known as 'soapy rock' because of its slippery feel, producing the distinctive porcelain that so many collectors have come to admire. It is often impossible to separate early Lund blue-and-white and early Worcester blue-and-white. The Lund factory had a short life of some three years but the quality of production achieved in that short time was to have great influence on the subsequent success of Worcester.

Where pieces are known to be the products of the Bristol soft paste factory they are termed Lund's Bristol. The factory is believed to have been first established at Redcliffe Backs in the Bristol dock area, by someone involved in the failed London Manufactory of Limehouse. The porcelain characteristics of this early Bristol include a green translucency, which is continued in the Worcester porcelain, and the glaze may be considerably blued or at times rather grey in appearance with a certain amount of sanding. There is also a tendency for the porcelain to warp and the majority of wares are moulded. As might be expected the Lund designs were largely influenced by Chinese and Japanese patterns. Marks of BRISTOL and BRISTOLL have been found on bases.

In 1752 Lund's Bristol was purchased in its entirety by the Worcester company and when the manufactory was removed to that city, some of the Bristol decorators moved with it. A partnership deed dated 4 June 1751 is in the archives of the Worcester Royal Porcelain Company, and it tells of how fourteen local men and Edmund Cave of London, the editor of *The Gentleman's Magazine*, founded the Worcester Tonquin Manufactury, later known as the Worcester Porcelain Company. Worcester remains today the only English porcelain company with an unbroken line of tradition.

It was Dr John Wall, M.D., and the apothecary William Davis who are named as having invented the Worcester formula. The years between 1751 and 1786, when Dr Wall died, are known as the Dr Wall period and, for many, it contains some of the most attractive porcelain of the eighteenth century.

A feature of the Worcester wares is the precise quality of its potting. The early decoration of Worcester is carried out in underglaze blue to be followed by Oriental overglaze in enamel. Excellent transfer printed pieces were done by Robert Hancock, and some of the finest of these are the portraits, usually found on mugs, of Frederick the Great, King of Prussia, and an ally of England in the Seven Years War.

Porcelain was also sent out of the factory for decoration. James Giles of Camden Town was a prominent decorator of this kind and was in demand by most of the leading factories. He

First standard blue crescent mark, *c.* 1755-83

Blue painted or printed mark, *c.* 1760-80

Painted 'square' or 'seal' mark in underglaze blue, *c.* 1755-75

Worcester version of the Dresden crossed-swords mark

Printed numeral marks, *c.* 1770-83

Impressed or incised marks, *c.* 1807-13

123 Two examples of
moulded Worcester
sauce-boats, *c*. 1755-60.

also bought porcelain in the white from factories for resale in
his own retail premises in Soho after he had decorated them.

The similarity of decoration of a high standard has been
noticed many times between factories and this has led to the
identification of painters by style where their real names are
unknown to us. Hence such descriptions as 'the cut fruit'
painter, and 'the dishevelled bird' painter. Even the hand of
individual painters can be identified from among the early
blue-and-white porcelains. Workmen's marks appear on the
wares of several factories and a large number have been
recorded on Worcester pieces. More famous painters are less of
a problem to identify: Fidelle Duvivier, the French-born
Chelsea painter, may have worked for Worcester at the factory,
and he is credited with painting Sèvres-style exotic birds on
some pieces. The Irishman Jeffreys Hamet O'Neale and the
Scotsman John Donaldson have signed their work for Worcester, a privilege given to very few ceramic artists in the
eighteenth century.

The late Dorothy Doughty remains outstanding among a
long list of superb modellers who have worked for Royal
Worcester. Probably no other modeller in the history of
ceramics has received such public acclaim in their own lifetime. All her models were made in limited editions, mostly
between 255 and 500, after which the moulds were destroyed.
Dorothy Doughty, who died in 1962, delighted in modelling
birds and flowers; indeed her bird models are usually associated with flowers and plants, for this remarkable woman
believed that the two were inseparable. She began by making a
series of American birds of which the first pair was issued in
1935, and their success was phenomenal. Wherever possible
she observed her subjects from life and the timeless quality of
her work is such that she succeeded in creating a likeness close
to life itself. She bequeathed three of her models to the Victoria
and Albert Museum, London. All her designs of birds and
flowers may also be viewed at the Dyson Perrins Museum in
Worcester.

124 Model of a meadow pippit on silverweed. Dorothy Doughty, Worcester.

125 *Opposite:* Coalport pot-pourri vase and cover of typical high quality and with floral decoration. It was described as a 'new poperee vase' in the Coalport *Traveller's Design Book* and sold originally for three guineas, then a considerable sum of money. Height $11\frac{1}{2}$ inches (292 mm), *c.* 1830-35. Victoria and Albert Museum, London.

It may be useful to explain the changes in partnership that followed the death of Dr Wall, for Worcester porcelains are most often referred to by the title of the company in control at the time. Wall's successor was William Davis, who continued until his own death in 1783. The factory was then purchased by Thomas Flight, Worcester's London agent. In 1793 Martin Barr was taken into partnership, and from then on the changes in organisation became a little confusing, for example: Flight & Barr 1793-1807, Barr, Flight & Barr 1807-1813, and Flight, Barr & Barr 1813-1840.

The sale of the factory in 1783 had caused Robert Chamberlain, a decorator, to leave and set up a studio of his own in King Street, Worcester. He began by painting porcelain in the white from Caughley, and he started his own factory for porcelain manufacture in 1792 on the site of the present Worcester factory. The Chamberlain factory introduced a porcelain of quite exceptional quality in 1811 and called it 'Regent'. It was in honour of the Prince of Wales who had become Regent in that year. Perhaps the greatest commission they ever received had come a few years earlier, a service for Lord Nelson in 1802.

FBB

Standard impressed mark, *c.* 1813-40

126 *Right:* White porcelain
figure of a goat. Plymouth,
*c.*1768. British Museum,
London.

127 *Below:* A Rockingham
porcelain basket painted
with a view of Brighton. It
shows Brighton's first pier
with its chain construction.
There is a griffin mark on the
base.

128 *Right:* 'King of Prussia' mug. Worcester, 1757. Observe the fine potting, the reeded handle, and the superb transfer decoration based on engravings by Robert Hancock. Frederick the Great of Prussia was England's ally during the Seven Years War (1756-63).

129 *Far right:* Compote dish from the 'Shakespeare' service made by the Worcester factory of Kerr & Binns. The parian figures are of Quince and Flute from *A Midsummer Night's Dream*, and are modelled by W. B. Kirk. Dyson Perrins Museum of Worcester Porcelain, Worcester.

Standard printed or impressed mark, *c.* 1862-75

Difficult trading conditions and the fierce competition from the improved earthenware and stoneware of the Potteries caused the amalgamation of Chamberlain's factory with the original one. In 1840 Flight, Barr & Barr moved to the Chamberlain factory. From 1840 until 1851 the factory was called Chamberlain & Co., and even the Great Exhibition did little to raise the company's standing.

After the Exhibition the factory was taken over by W. G. Kerr, a partner in the Chamberlain Co., and R. W. Binns. This partnership restored Worcester porcelain to its proper place in English ceramics. From 1852 to 1862 new products appeared and new highly talented decorators emerged. In 1862 when Kerr retired, his partner formed a joint stock company and the firm became the Worcester Royal Porcelain Company.

130 An example of the remarkable 'Limoges' style of decoration perfected by Thomas Bott at the Kerr and Binns factory, 1859. The cup and saucer with its two handles is inspired by the Greek kylix shape, and is painted in white enamel on a deep blue ground. Victoria and Albert Museum, London.

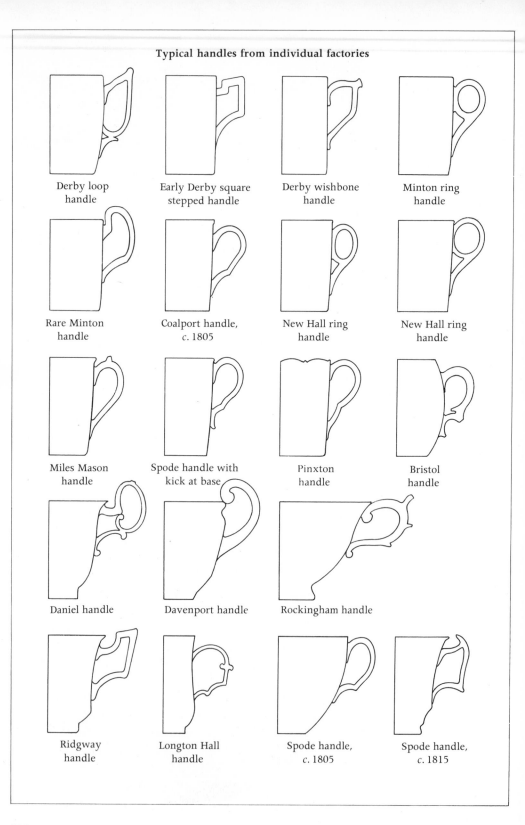

Typical handles from individual factories

Derby loop handle

Early Derby square stepped handle

Derby wishbone handle

Minton ring handle

Rare Minton handle

Coalport handle, c. 1805

New Hall ring handle

New Hall ring handle

Miles Mason handle

Spode handle with kick at base

Pinxton handle

Bristol handle

Daniel handle

Davenport handle

Rockingham handle

Ridgway handle

Longton Hall handle

Spode handle, c. 1805

Spode handle, c. 1815

Chapter 7

The nineteenth century

Whereas the eighteenth century had been one of the ceramic entrepreneurs, so the nineteenth century was quick to follow in the wake of the pioneers and their valuable discoveries, and to build upon them. Development and innovation followed one upon the other; more factories, new forms of ceramic bodies, and advances in decorative techniques. Markets were expanding rapidly, although all were to suffer in varying degrees during the 'hungry forties'. Above all, the earlier sense of adventure was maintained. There was much cross-fertilization of ideas between Britain and the Continent, and there was an increasing awareness of design. As the nineteenth century progressed so did the recognition of machine methods of production and the need to balance such advances with something of the old craft skills of hand and eye. It was such thought that led to the establishment of the art potteries whose work is now increasingly sought by collectors.

A man who bridged the two centuries well was Miles Mason (1752-1822), who described himself so accurately and delightfully as a chinaman. Born at Dent, Yorkshire, he eventually left the wool town to work for an uncle in London. He then joined Richard Farrar, a glass merchant and chinaman; later he married Farrar's daughter.

When the Napoleonic war seriously affected his trade as an importer of Oriental porcelain, he gave up the business and began the manufacture of porcelain in partnership at Liverpool and then, in the year before Trafalgar, he set up his own manufactory at Lane Delph, near Newcastle-under-Lyme. Here he produced good quality porcelain and continued doing so until 1813. Some pieces carry a tiny impressed mark, sometimes on the edge of the base, which can be difficult to find.

M. MASON

Standard impressed mark, c. 1800-13

MILES

MASON

Blue printed mark, found on willow-pattern porcelain, c. 1800-13

Mason's ironstone

For most people the mention of the name Mason means 'ironstone': it is a trade-name that indicates strength, an attribute

319

that should have made it commercially attractive. Ironstone was not, however, the invention of Miles Mason, but of his son Charles James Mason, who took out a patent in 1813. In the words of the patent the formula consisted of '. . . slag of ironstone, pounded and ground in water in certain proportions with flint, Cornwall stone and clay, and blue oxide of cobalt'.

Most of the patterns used to decorate the ironstone were in the Japan style and the ware was produced in large quantity. Although it was both attractive and cheap to produce, commercial success eluded ironstone and the enterprise of Charles James Mason failed. The moulds, patterns and plates were bought by Francis Morley of Shelton who had purchased the business of Hicks, Meigh and Johnson, also ironstone manufacturers. Morley gave ironstone new impetus, producing a greater variety of wares, and he turned ironstone into a flourishing business. He gained a medal at the French Exhibition of 1855, but four years later he retired and the new purchaser was the wealthy Ashworth family from Lancashire. In 1881 it was bought by the Goddards, who in 1973 sold the company to Wedgwood, who have considerably revived the output of ironstone yet again.

The Ashworths introduced a great variety into their production and ironstone became highly popular. Fine gilding, Indian patterns, floral studies, mazarine blue, relief moulded jugs, and some rare painted pieces joined the ubiquitous Imari patterns. It would have pleased Miles Mason, who had originally sought to provide a substitute for the massive imports of Chinese porcelain into England.

PATENT IRONSTONE CHINA

Impressed mark, *c.* 1813 +

Standard printed mark, *c.* 1815 +

131 *Left:* Three examples of Mason's work. In the foreground is a porcelain sugar box; the two dishes are both of ironstone, the one on the right being landscape-painted and rare, while that on the left bears the more common 'japan' decoration.

Transfer printed wares

Transfer printed earthenware in underglaze blue also became a massive commercial success in the nineteenth century. The process was introduced by Thomas Turner at Caughley in 1780. Among the most popular designs were various forms of chinoiserie, although the most celebrated of these, the willow pattern, did not appear in its true form until 1819.

There are a few rare and early examples of hand-painted willow pattern, but these are obviously the exception. Before 1800 the transfer decoration was line engraved, but after that date stipple engravings are most common.

Thomas Minton had worked on the early Caughley plates when he was with Turner. After leaving him he engraved the pattern for other manufacturers, in each case with slight differences. It will be noticed that the number of figures on the bridge may vary, or there may be no figures at all. The pagoda

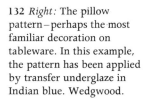

132 *Right:* The pillow pattern – perhaps the most familiar decoration on tableware. In this example, the pattern has been applied by transfer underglaze in Indian blue. Wedgwood.

may be seen in different positions, apples on the tree may vary vary in number; the fence design changes from maker to maker. Manufacturers who were swift to see the interest of the pattern were Adams, Spode, Davenport and Wedgwood, and they continued the pattern over long periods; but it should be remembered that there were nearly two hundred manufacturers of willow pattern before 1865.

The story that the willow pattern represents must surely be well known, although it is a modern one. Briefly, it is that of a Chinese mandarin who lived in a pagoda, by an apple tree, near a bridge, over which a willow tree throws its shade. The mandarin's daughter had been promised in marriage to an old but wealthy merchant, but she was secretly meeting a young man with whom she was in love. When their meetings were discovered the girl was locked in a room overlooking a river, but on the day of her marriage with the merchant she and the young man eloped. The pursuit by her father is usually shown by the figures on the bridge, the two young people having endeavoured to make their escape by boat. But when they were caught they escaped the mandarin's anger by being transformed into doves, or, as the old Staffordshire rhyme has it:

> *Two pigeons flying high;*
> *Chinese vessels sailing by;*
> *Weeping willows hanging o'er;*
> *Bridge with three men—if not four—*
> *Chinese temple there it stands*
> *Seems to take up all the land;*
> *Apple trees with apples on;*
> *A pretty fence to end my song.*

It is very difficult to attribute unmarked specimens of transfer printed earthenware in underglaze blue, although attention to detail may well identify the manufacturer. Attention to the base of the plate or dish is particularly important, noting foot-rims and of course any marks. Most of the old pieces tend to have glazes that produce a rippled effect and the colour range of the blue printing may vary from a dark, strong blue down to an extremely light blue; also look for signs of wear on bases—this can at least indicate some degree of age. Printed earthenware of this type has risen considerably in value since the 1960s; even so, fine examples of this process may still be found without too much difficulty, and in the author's view are still considerably undervalued. Although the early transfer prints are based on Chinese designs, it was not long before engravings were being made of typical English rural scenes, including country houses, castles and other celebrated landmarks and buildings. A large trade was also maintained with North America and those pieces bearing scenes of American interest are much in demand on that continent.

The success of a print, apart from meeting the interests and requirements of the general public, depended on a good engraver, an artist able to cut his design into a copper plate by means of either lines or dots. The closer the lines or dots the darker the colour became. The printing ink was usually cobalt blue, mixed with flint into an oily pigment. After first warming the copper plate, ink was spread on with a palette knife in order to work the pigment into the etched detail. The surface of the plate was then wiped clean and the transfer paper was applied, enabling it to pick up the impression which was to be transferred ink-side down on the ware to be decorated. Printed borders were applied separately and the joins can often be seen, particularly when the transfer was applied in several sections. After the paper was removed the pattern on the ware was fixed by heating in a muffle oven, which remains at a low temperature. This was followed by dipping the object in glaze which was in turn fixed in a glost oven. Such a process produced bright, attractive, hard wearing products to which so many collections now testify. Examples printed in this manner are at their best between 1800 and 1825. As well as the subjects already mentioned animal and sporting subjects also became popular, as did Italian and Indian scenes. John and William Ridgway of Caldon Place made a superb series of views of Oxford and Cambridge colleges.

Other outstanding examples came from the Spode works at Stoke-on-Trent. Spode were among the first potters to manufacture blue printed wares, and the story of Spode transfer printing is better charted than that of any other Staffordshire pottery. Of quite extraordinary interest are the early nineteenth-century services with scenes of Indian sport. It includes such titles as 'Hog Hunter Meeting by surprise a Tiger', 'Syces or Grooms leading out Horses', and 'Dooreans, or Dog Keepers leading out Dogs'. It is a series that seems to reflect Britain's continuing interest in India, but the scenes themselves were taken from a book published in London in 1805 under the title *Oriental Field Sports*, *Wild Sports of the East*, written by Captain Williamson, with aquatints by Thomas Howitt. Illustrated books of a sporting or topographical nature were to have increasing influence upon ceramic artists.

Pot lids

The colour-printed pot lid of the nineteenth century is something that most people easily recognise. Pot lids were the work
of F. and R. Pratt of Fenton in Staffordshire and were made
between 1846 and 1880. From 1846 to 1849 the lids were decorated in only two colours but improved mechanical processes were to change all that. The earlier pottery of the firm
known as Pratt ware has already been mentioned in Chapter 4,
but the nineteenth-century wares, decorated with polychrome
transfer prints, must not be confused with the earlier products.
Jesse Austin of Longton (1806-1879) was the major figure in
colour printing during the nineteenth century and it was he
who developed the process for decorating the pot lids. He had
much in common with George Baxter, inventor of Baxter
prints. Baxter's technique was to apply the engraving first and
subsequently use a number of other plates to apply the separate colours; it called for exact methods of working in order
to ensure the correct registration of each colour to prevent
overlap. Jesse Austin applied the same principle but the other
way about. He used up to five plates in each work, but applied
the colours first and the engraving last. Some of his pot lids are
signed, either with his name in full or with his initials. The
interest in these is very understandable for the illustrations
portray a great deal of the life, events, and topography of that
period as well as earlier historical occasions and characters.
There are a host of pod lids covering such diverse subjects as
the Australian gold strike, the Crimean war, and the plays of
Shakespeare.

During the 1840s small earthenware pots were in demand.
The new industries of fish paste and potted shrimps demanded
containers. At the same time powdered wigs were now only
occasionally to be seen and men displayed their natural hair
although heavily greased. The containers of this grease were
known as pomade pots, and frequently have bear designs – the
pomade inside was in fact bear's grease. As the highly commercial paste and pomade pots became widely popular a
number of other Staffordshire potters began to make them.
The great shrimping company Tantell and Son, used some
fifteen different designs connected with Pegwell Bay for their
product. These are among the more common pot lids.

The majority of pot lids found have rather convex surfaces,
and the earliest lids have a tendency towards unevenness but are
basically flat and smaller in diameter than the later ones. Many
reproduction pot lids have been made, but most of the early

135 *Right:* The 'Hop Jug', an impressive example of Victorian Majolica ware. Minton, *c.* 1860. Victoria and Albert Museum, London.

136 *Below:* Ruskin Pottery with flambé glazes by William Howson Taylor.

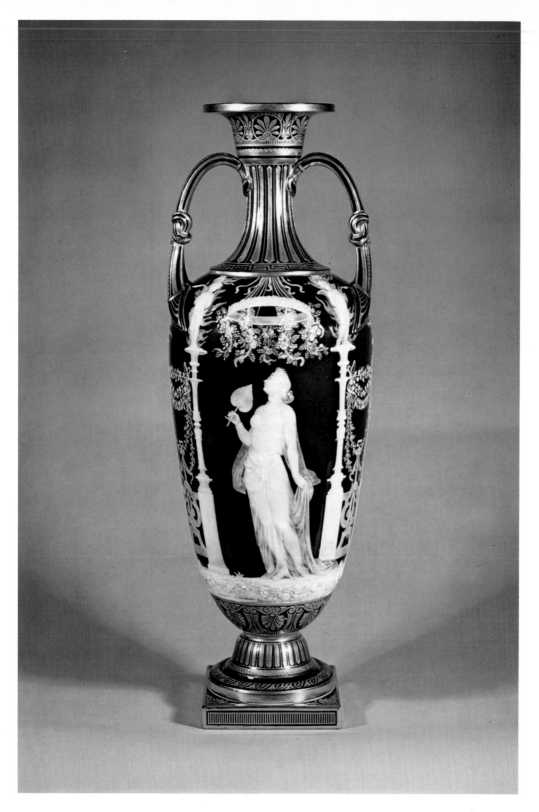

lids show signs of crazing. If you suspended an early lid from your finger and tapped it with a pencil the resultant sound should be completely dull, whereas a reproduction may produce a ringing sound. Another point is that the old colours are invariably brilliant, particularly the reds and the blues.

Parian

During the nineteenth century outstanding works of ceramic art were achieved by the firms of Copeland and Minton respectively. Here we will deal with the discovery that first belongs to Copeland, that is the successful production of an unglazed biscuit porcelain that in appearance resembles marble; hence its name, inspired by the marble from the island of Paros. By far the majority of parian is white but some examples are tinted. While 1846 is generally regarded as the date when parian was first launched upon the world, one account declares that it was first introduced in 1842. This is contained in Hunt's *Handbook to the Official Catalogues of the Great Exhibition* published in 1851.

' The first idea of imitating marble in ceramic manufacture originated by Mr. Thomas Battan, the artist directing the extensive porcelain manufactory of Mr. Alderman Copeland at Stoke-upon-Trent, in the commencement in 1842. After a series of experiments he succeeded in producing a very perfect imitation of marble, both in surface and tint. One of the earliest specimens was submitted to His Grace the Bishop of Sutherland who expressed his unqualified admiration of the purposes to which it was applied, and became its first patron by purchasing the example submitted. This was on the 3rd August 1842 . . .'

Hunt is not regarded as a particularly reliable writer although it is obvious from reports in the Art Union magazine that Messrs Copeland and Garrett were producing fine parian wares well before 1846. The Art Union of London were intensely concerned about the relationship between mass manufacture and art, and they decided to issue a fine statue, in a limited edition, made of stone china as manufactured by Messrs Copeland and Garrett. The interest of the sculptor John Gibson, RA, proved readily forthcoming, and the first figure to be commissioned by the Art Union of London was his 'The Narcissus' in parian. Other similar societies were also important in providing a stimulus to artistic manufacture. Prince Albert was ready to give these Unions his blessing 'feeling assured that these Institutions will exercise a most beneficial

329

influence on the Arts'. Fifty parian copies were made of 'The Narcissus' when it was completed in 1846. The copies were given as prizes and had cost the Art Union £3 each–for which sum, ten years ago, they might well have been purchased at auction. Parian figures are of outstanding quality and it can only be that their lack of colour was the reason for the twentieth-century buying public's cool attitude towards them. Once again we have the situation of quality being overlooked for a long period and the result is that the best parian figures

138 Two parian figures. In the foreground is Narcissus by John Gibson made by Copeland and the first such model to be commissioned by the Art Union of London in 1846. In the background is a Minton parian figure of a dancer.

139 'Innocence', a parian porcelain figure. Copeland, 1847. Victoria and Albert Museum, London.

are now climbing considerably in value, and are unlikely ever again to fall.

'The Narcissus' proved highly popular with the members of the Art Union, with the result that many more such figures were commissioned by them. Parian examples that were used for prizes will always be found to be marked, either printed or impressed to that effect. In some ways the Art Unions were similar to the book clubs and record clubs of the twentieth century.

The Art Union of London was established in 1836, each member paying an annual subscription entitling him to take part in an annual draw or raffle. The main prizes were all works of art, usually paintings from Royal Academy Exhibitions. It was immediately clear that the new statuary porcelain or parian was the perfect medium for filling the role of the lesser prizes. As they grew in popularity more prizes of a ceramic nature were introduced and while the Art Unions succeeded in their endeavours to raise the standard of design, they also engendered a similar awareness among their prize winners who may never otherwise have purchased the objects concerned.

Even though Copelands were undoubtedly the first to produce parian on a commercial basis, and certainly, in the production of figure groups, there are earlier claims for its invention, e.g. Thomas Boote of Burslem who claimed its manufacture in 1841, and Messrs Minton were also pioneers in the field and produced some excellent figure models.

Majolica

The word Majolica is frequently used to indicate tin glazed wares in the Italian Maiolica style, but it should really be applied only to English earthenware decorated in coloured lead glazes; in particular those of Minton for which Majolica was a trade name.

In 1850 Majolica joined the many other art products of Minton and although it became a fashionable ware of the period, and most other factories made wares of a similar type, Minton reigned supreme. It was part of the factory's policy of re-introducing many of the Renaissance styles which they did with great aplomb – but none achieved such popular success as Majolica. The vigorous character of the wares they made and the purity of colour and glaze created several minor works of art. Most remarkable among the Majolica was a life-sized model of a peacock by the French sculptor Paul Comolera from Limoges. Comolera undertook the modelling and decoration

140 *Far left:* Moulded white stoneware 'Minster' jug with figures in Gothic niches, by Charles Meigh of Hanley, *c.* 1840. Victoria and Albert Museum, London.

141 *Below:* Minton vase in the Sèvres style with rose Pompadour ground and painted panels. Minton, *c.* 1905.

142 Victorian Majolica group showing a cupid figure riding a sea-horse. Minton, 1859. Victoria and Albert Museum, London.

using hand painted soft colour glazes. After three years Comolera returned to France and only five such peacocks were made. Majolica glazed cockerels by John Henk, standing 13½ inches (340 mm) high, are also of immense quality, but it was such satisfying wares as the covered 'hop' jug that found popular appeal on the mass market and were produced over several years.

Pâte-sur-pâte

In the second half of the nineteenth century a series of porcelains of great richness emerged from Minton. Artists and designers of international repute came from the Continent to work at Stoke-on-Trent. The reason they came was the success in international exhibitions that Minton achieved after their large scale display at the Great Exhibition of 1851.

A French influence began to pervade the Minton factory. Not only the Sèvres ground colours were copied but the Sèvres shapes too. The results were hand-decorated, richly gilded

vases and other porcelains so lavish that it is unlikely that any English manufactory will ever make such wares again. The painters of these pieces were Sèvres-trained artists of the calibre of Anton Boullemier. As well as realising that Minton were making some of the richest porcelains in Europe, there was also the knowledge that Minton's Art Director was a Frenchman, Léon Arnoux (1816-1902) who arrived at Minton towards the end of the 1840s. This was the man the *Art Journal* described as '. . . among the most talented and accomplished Frenchmen who ever honoured our shores and aided us in the development of our art industries'.

The Franco-Prussian War in 1870 proved an added incentive for French artists to come to England, and one in particular has become known to connoisseurs all over the world; his name was Marc Louis Solon. In fact Minton, Marc Louis Solon, and the technique known as pâte-sur-pâte (paste on paste) have become synonymous.

Solon's offer to work for Minton was accepted by Arnoux and he remained with them until his retirement in 1904. What is more he was given encouragement to perfect his beloved pâte-sur-pâte. The process had evolved at Sèvres but Solon's work in England gave it an entirely new dimension.

The basic shape to be decorated in this manner was made in tinted parian ware but it was not fired. Then came the application by hand of 'slip' or liquid porcelain that was built up day by day until it reached the required thickness. It was a process that always took weeks and often months to achieve. Then the slip was cut in cameo fashion and fired. The diaphanous translucency achieved by this method is astonishing, but until the firing and the moment when the piece of pâte-sur-pâte emerged from the kiln it was never known whether the work of months would end in triumph or disaster. The most complex piece that Solon ever attempted took seven months to complete. Pâte-sur-pâte could only be tolerated if it were perfect, and this, coupled with the expense and time involved, dissuaded other factories from following suit although attempts were made.

Solon trained apprentices from 1873 and their names are Alboine Birks, Lawrence Birks, H. Hollins, T. Mellor, A. Morgan, Frederick Read, T. H. Rice, H. Saunders and C. Toft.

Of these students it was Alboine Birks who proved second only to Solon himself. Birks continued working on pâte-sur-pâte until his death in 1940. Very little signed work by the pupils mentioned above is found. The reason is that Solon disliked the idea.

Doulton of Lambeth

DOULTON & WATTS
LAMBETH POTTERY
LONDON

Standard impressed mark,
c. 1820-54

DOULTON
LAMBETH

Standard impressed mark,
c. 1854+

The Lambeth pottery has a long history which, as far as collectors are concerned, begins with the partnership of Doulton and Watts at the beginning of the nineteenth century. The main figure, however, in the rise of Doulton as a major pottery was Henry Doulton, who began his apprenticeship in 1835. Later in the century he was to receive a knighthood as one of the leading figures in the ceramic industry and one of the most respected luminaries of Victorian art. Henry Doulton was a man of great foresight who was quick to see talent wherever it lay and to give it every encouragement and practical help. The basic output of the Lambeth pottery was sanitary stonewares, drain pipes etc. In a century when cholera was still rife in England, the supply of Doulton stoneware water filters played a vital role in maintaining health when so many local water supplies were suspect. Today these water filters, either the large domestic model or the smaller versions for use at table, are

335

Vase shapes

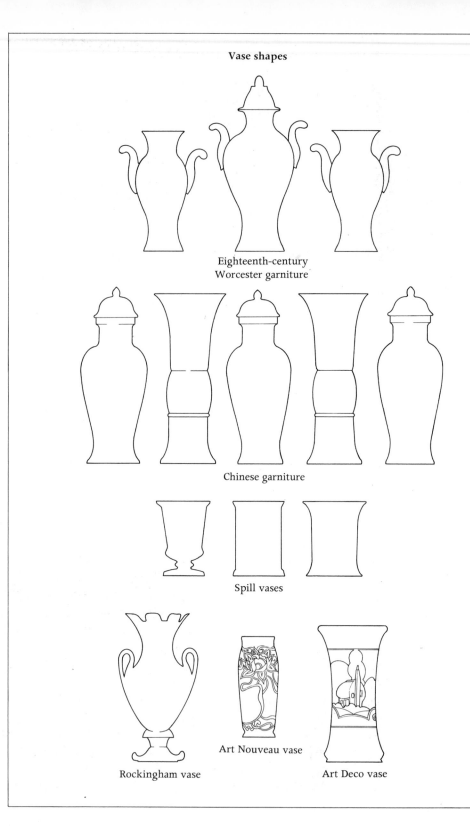

Eighteenth-century
Worcester garniture

Chinese garniture

Spill vases

Rockingham vase

Art Nouveau vase

Art Deco vase

144 Nineteenth-century Doulton stoneware vessels decorated by Hannah Barlow.

Impressed mark, *c.* 1877-80

Impressed or printed mark, *c.* 1872+

Standard impressed mark, *c.* 1902-22 and *c.* 1927-36

Standard impressed mark, *c.* 1922-56

often collected as 'by-gones' or to provide a decorative feature in a room.

At the 1862 Exhibition, Doulton exhibited wares with simple incised designs. They were far from satisfactory but it was to sow the seed of Doulton art pottery and it soon began to flourish under Henry Doulton's enthusiastic guidance.

The Doulton decorated stonewares manufactured over the following thirty years provide a rich field for the collector. Part of Henry Doulton's philosophy of encouragement was that his artists should be permitted to sign their work; this is of course particularly attractive to the collector for such full documentary information is rarely available to him. The signatures take the form of initials or monograms incised into the clay. While the identification of such pieces is therefore a comparatively simple matter in comparison with the experience required to identify eighteenth-century unmarked wares, the artists themselves are nonetheless entirely worthy of attention and high regard.

The most celebrated decorative artists at Doulton are undoubtedly the Barlow family, in particular Hannah B. Barlow (working 1872-1906), Florence Barlow (working 1873-1909), and Arthur Barlow (died in 1879).

Hannah Barlow, like so many other of the artists of her day, created her designs with incised outlines into which colour was applied and burnt in. The proper name for this type of decoration is called *sgraffito*. Her work is unique in that none of her pieces are alike. In particular her designs depict animals, ranging from lions and horses to less exotic but equally beautiful cows.

337

Florence Barlow's work was similar to that of her sister but again no two pieces are alike. Her principal decoration was birds, usually raised in low relief. Arthur Barlow was the brother of Hannah and Florence, and his work differs from theirs in that he concentrated his efforts upon foliage rather than animal life. He worked at Doultons for only eight years, therefore his work is rare.

Another artist whose work has attracted collectors for many years is George Tinworth (working 1866-1913). Much of it is in the form of miniature sculpture, he produced plaques and models of children and small animals. This, however, was only part of Tinworth's career. John Ruskin regarded him as an artist of the utmost importance and encouraged him in the production of large terracotta sculpted panels. In 1883 a massive exhibition of his work was held in London, and a book superbly illustrated in photogravure, *The Critical Essay of the Life and Works of George Tinworth*, appeared the same year. Unfortunately most of the edition was destroyed in a fire at the Fine Arts Society, and this book is now of great rarity.

Eliza Simmance was also a highly productive artist who, like Arthur Barlow, was intensely interested in foliage decoration. Collectors of Art Nouveau find her particularly interesting because of the influence of the movement in her designs, some of which were by Charles Rennie Mackintosh.

The Doulton collector will find a host of other artists well worth collecting and in this respect further research is recommended.

In the early years of the Barlows' work there were no studios for them in the pottery and they worked in the Lambeth showroom at a table, with a screen between them and the public. Hannah Barlow has recorded how the artists looked forward to the daily visits of Henry Doulton, which were always courteous, enthusiastic and encouraging. She later wrote:

'When first I came to the Potteries, few people knew what reverses I had in my home, and what a dreadful undertaking it was to me to meet strangers. I shall never forget the first time I encountered Sir Henry Doulton, how great my alarm was, and how kindly and considerately he received me. He was always encouraging. He made it impossible for me not to enjoy my work, and his great love of animals made his visits to my studio most helpful. He would rarely come without telling me of some trait of the life of horses or cattle which he had observed, or some grouping of them in the fields which he believed would aid my imagination.

Hannak Barlow, *c.* 1872-1906

George Tinworth,
c. 1867-1913

Florence Barlow,
c. 1873-1909

Arthur Barlow, *c.* 1872-79

'I always noticed that Sir Henry Doulton never forgot a promise . . . In all the years I have worked at Lambeth, I never once had the sensation that money was the ultimate object of my art. Sir Henry and his family have always shown an extraordinary tact in preventing such a feeling. I hold this to have been one of the great charms of my work at Lambeth. Sir Henry always seemed to urge me to do my best, without respect to its commercial value to him, and his enthusiastic interest in my designs had the effect of constantly rousing me to try to do still better things.

'Of late years, it was not possible for him to be such a constant visitor to the Studios. Since he has ceased to come, we have missed him very much. My sister Florence agrees with me that some of the pleasantest memories of our life are of the days when we began the decoration work upon the stoneware, and with them the eager and generous sympathy of Sir Henry Doulton is indissolubly connected.'

The following extracts from the writings of Sir Henry Doulton will give some insight into his attitude to his art. 'The progress of the art of pottery affords many striking instances of the laws of growth, perfection and decay. As schools of philosophy, poetry and painting are subject to rise, culmination, decay and fall, so is the potter's art. Except in the East, where tradition operates so powerfully, and where tribes, castes and families carry on their trade for ages, these industries rarely maintain their highest development through more than two or three generations.

'In our own country we have several examples of schools of pottery which have existed but are now extinct. Chelsea, Bow, Lowestoft, Liverpool, Bristol and Swansea have all become names of the past, notwithstanding their high excellence and the extensive patronage which they once received. Most of these have succumbed before the introduction of cheaper methods of decoration and more economical modes of manufacture. Indeed, it is a striking fact that, with scarcely an exception, only those potteries have been able to maintain a long-lived career which have relied for their staple manufacture on utilitarian rather than decorative wares. This principle is true even of artistic pottery. A proportion of the useful seems to be an essential condition of any degree of permanence. A school of decorative pottery only is short-lived – firstly, because it is dependent on individual taste and culture and, secondly, because it is not by itself remunerative.

'Wedgwood, Worcester and Minton have, undoubtedly,

maintained their continuous production through so long a period by careful attention to domestic requirements as well as original art wares.'

'There is with the public of the present time a morbid craving after novelties, irrespective of their intrinsic excellence, which leaves neither designer nor manufacturer time to develop full capabilities of his productions before the passing day of their public appreciation has gone by.

'Of course, public taste cannot altogether be disregarded; and if a master is to provide for the dependent army of workers the demand must to some extent regulate the supply – although the intelligent and enterprising manufacturer will always endeavour to lead the public taste; certainly, if he leaves it at too great a distance it is at a great cost.

'It is needful that beauty of design should go hand in hand with economy of technique; it is still more necessary that those who have this matter in hand should realise that their true mission is not accomplished until they have rendered art "a language understood of the people".

'Then, and then only, will designers find ready outlet for their conceptions; then and then only, will manufacturers realise that their interest is to produce good art rather than bad, and strive after excellence rather than novelty, after grave rather than cheapness.'

'The artists of England cannot all be Royal Academicians of the great luminary in Picaddilly [sic]! Some may also be

145 Ruskin Pottery vase, 1922 (left), and a Martin brothers jug decorated with grotesques.

altogether outside the planetary system which it can weigh or measure. Yet it is possible that these neglected lights may be radiances of another and even larger system only discoverable by powers more catholic, comprehensive and accurate than Burlington House commands.'

Martin Ware

R W Martin -84
Fulham

c. 1873-74

R W Martin 9
London

c. 1874-78

R W Martin 21
Southall

OR R W MARTIN
SOUTHALL.

c. 1878

R W Martin
London & Southall

c. 1879-82

R W Martin & Brothers
London & Southall

1882+

This is the name given to the remarkable stonewares made by the Martin brothers at Fulham and at Southall between 1873 and the First World War. The idea of the individual craftsman as opposed to the mass produced item had already begun to emerge at Doultons of Lambeth, but the Martin brothers are generally regarded as being the first craftsman potters of the modern school. The four brothers are as follows:

Robert Wallace Martin (1843-1923)
Charles Douglas Martin (1846-1910)
Walter Frazer Martin (1859-1912)
Edwin Bruce Martin (1860-1915)

Edwin Martin had once worked at Doultons, where he learned the art of incising pottery. Charles carried out some decoration but mainly dealt with administration. Walter dealt with clays, glazes and firing, while Wallace was the main sculpture and modeller.

Their work is astonishing in its diversity and in the range of models and decorations described as grotesques. Although their products today are much collected and therefore valuable, they were never so prosperous during their own lifetime.

Their work is normally stamped or incised with signature marks, date and address, e.g.:

R. W. Martin. Fulham 1873-1874.
R. W. Martin, London 1874-1878.
Signature marks with address Southall 1878-1879.
Signature marks with the address London and Southall date from 1879.

'Brothers' or 'Bros' was added to the signature mark in 1882, although it will be found that most examples include the incised date of manufacture.

One of the most interesting accounts of the work involved during the firing of a kiln is to be found in the *Pall Mall Gazette* of January 1890, which contains a description of a visit made to the Martin brothers at their Southall Pottery:

'Their kiln, which stands about a hundred yards from the Grand Junction Canal, is built within an irregular-looking building of stone, cement, brick, iron and wood; the shaft, which juts out from the centre of the roof for several feet, and the vaporous smoke, which rolls away before the wind to join the scudding clouds, being the only outward and visible signs of its inward fiery presence. On the threshold I met Mr. R. W. Martin, who at once led the way into the kiln. The heat was so terrific that the atmosphere appeared to be glassy and wavy. Two men stripped to the shirt, and with bared arms and throats, were leaning against the wall, the one resting on a long iron rod and the other on a coalheaver's shovel. They were grimed with smoke, and dust and clay, perspiration trickled down their arms and faces like rain on the panes of a window, black beads of perspiration clung to their swarthy throats, their hair was matted and their voices were as the voices of men in the Sahara Desert. The elder of the two, who had entire charge of the kiln, was Walter Martin and the younger, who was assisting him, was his brother Edwin. They had both been at work in that building, turn and turn about, since Thursday midday, and for the last twenty hours Edwin Martin had never left the fires. "How can you stand this fearful heat?" I asked. They said that it was "nothing", and Walter Martin, after having cautioned me to "stand by", opened the door of one of the fires directly opposite to where I was standing, and said, "Now that *is* heat". It was indeed: he closed the door again in an instant, but not before I felt as though I had been done through and through. Then they began to coal up for the last time before salting off. Each of the five doors at the base of the kiln was opened in quick succession and large logs of wood and shovels of coal thrown in to feed the fire. Each time a door was opened the heat became well-nigh unbearable—the wooden beams and rafters became so hot that I could scarcely bear to touch them, and iron girders and binders warped like warm sealing-wax. Next they mounted a narrow flight of stairs leading to the floor above, from whence they stoked the kiln in five more places, but there the heat was not so fierce. At the base of the kiln it was impossible to get more than about four feet distant from the fires; neither was it possible to stand upright, because the beams and rafters of the floor above were not more than about five feet from the ground, while upstairs there was plenty of breathing space. As Walter Martin went from firehole to firehole I noticed that he limped painfully; an iron lean-to had fallen overnight, he told me, and struck his foot a crushing blow, and what with the heat and the continual exertion it had gradually become extremely painful. As time wore on the heat grew more intense. The beams and rafters scorched and blackened and had to be drenched with salt and water to prevent them from bursting into flames. I looked into the kiln from above, while the salt was being put in to glaze the pottery, and saw the raging fury of the flames in all their gorgeous splendour . . . And there, within that living hell, splendid examples of the potter's skill were being fired without protection of any kind. While others protect their wares with "saggers" or "slugs" these potters are content to trust theirs to the most terrible of the elements in *puris naturalibus.* How they can have the courage to run the risk is almost inconceivable. Meantime Walter Martin's foot became worse, and he had to be provided with a stick to lean on while he worked with his right hand; and, finally, a pair of crutches were procured for him from a neighbouring cottage. He grew anxious. He had packed the kiln, and only he could fire it off. If an accident happened, or if an error of judgment were committed, four months' work might, and probably would, be either destroyed or rendered valueless. But he stuck to his post like a man, and, although occasionally he groaned aloud with agony, he resolutely went round and round the fires, up stairs and down again, shovelled the salt in, tried his proofs, had the fires once more renewed and superintended the plugging of the fireholes to exclude the draught. Then, his labours having for the time being come to an end—for it takes five days for the kiln to cool—he was carried by his brothers in to the cottage, his foot was dressed, and he was wheeled home on a tricycle to sleep the sleep of the brave and the just.'

Other art potters and potteries whose work will repay further study and will no doubt be increasingly collected in future years, are as follows:

William De Morgan, born 1836. After early experiments in tile decoration he set up a kiln in Cheyne Walk, Chelsea, between 1872 and 1881. From 1882 to 1888 he worked at a kiln at Merton Abbey, Wimbledon, moving to Fulham in 1888. Among his partners were the artists Charles and Fred Passenger.

The Compton Pottery, Guildford. Started by Mary Watts, wife of the celebrated Victorian painter. The pottery closed in 1956.

The Della Robbia Pottery, Birkenhead, began in 1894 and produced some fine vases decorated in enamels and coloured glazes.

146 'Tree of Life' bowl by Bernard Leach, *c.* 1923. Victoria and Albert Museum, London.

The Watcombe Pottery, south Devon, established in 1869. Wide range of products including terracottas.

William Moorcroft of Burslem, Staffordshire. Moorcroft began his design career in 1897 and died in 1945. Produced a wide range of shapes and decoration, and has particularly come into prominence during the last ten years.

Pilkington's Lancastrian Pottery, near Manchester. Established 1891.

Ruskin Pottery, Smethwick, established by W. Howson-Taylor in 1898. The pottery takes its name from Howson-Taylor's regard for Ruskin. Just before his death in 1935 he destroyed all his materials and papers, and wrote in a letter to a friend: 'Why let another firm make rubbish and call it Ruskin?'

Clarice Cliff. This remarkable lady designed for the industrial factory rather than the small studio concern. Her designs bear her facsimile signature. While intense interest is now being given to her work the author believes that the collector should concentrate upon acquiring major examples of her designs.

Charles Vyse. Charles Vyse and his wife, had, like William De Morgan, a kiln at Cheyne Walk, Chelsea. He was responsible for some very interesting figure groups that were decorated by his wife. Their studio was established in 1919.

There are a large number of art potteries to be considered by the collector and there is an increasingly large amount of information and literature published on the subject. The doyen of English art potters is Bernard Leach, who was born in 1887. His knowledge and understanding of Oriental pottery and his intensive studies under Japanese master potters has greatly influenced not only his own work, but also the work of other distinguished potters and countless aspiring students.

Glossary

Acid gilding Method of gilding using acid to create a pattern on the body of an article, leaving areas untouched by it in relief. The surface is then gilded and the parts untouched by acid are polished with an agate, leaving the remainder matt.

Applied flowers Term used when flowers are modelled or moulded separately before being affixed to a vase or figure.

Ball clay Pipe-clay from Dorset and Devon so called because it was originally transported to the potters in large balls.

Basalt A black, hard unglazed body able to take a polish, introduced by Wedgwood in the 1760s.

Bat printing A design first created on a copper plate but transferred to the object being decorated by a 'bat' or slab of gelatine. The result is more delicate than the usual line engraving.

Biscuit Term used for objects of unglazed and undecorated porcelain after the first firing.

Body (paste) Material or materials that form the basic substance of any ceramic object.

Bone ash Ox-bones reduced to ash, today usually obtained from the Argentine and India.

Café-au-lait A soft brown, used either as a ground colour or plain, banded or decorated.

Ceramics Name given to all types of fired clays, whether pottery or porcelain.

Chinoiserie European version of an Oriental scene or style.

Cottages Name given to the many models of cottages and houses made in Staffordshire as pastille burners.

Crazing The minute mesh or tracing of lines that appears in the glaze of some factories' products e.g. eighteenth-century Derby.

Delft Soft clay body with a hard opaque white tin glaze.

Famille jaune Term used to describe a whole range of yellow enamels. It is particularly used as a ground colour, often with decoration from the green palette.

Famille noire A so-called black enamel used by the Chinese. It is decorated from the green palette.

Famille rose A beautiful pink enamel first made in Europe and introduced into China during the late seventeenth century. The Chinese developed it and used it extensively, particularly on their export wares.

Famille verte Green enamel, among the earliest of enamels used by the Chinese.

Foot-rim The turned foot upon which most plates, cups and dishes stand.

Glost kiln Kiln in which objects receive their second firing in order to mature the glaze.

Hollow ware Literally, items that are hollow, such as cups, bowls and teapots, in contrast to flatware like plates and dishes.

Ironstone Strong, heavy earthenware patented by Charles Mason in 1813.

Lithophane Thin porcelain plaques with an intaglio moulded decoration that shows up best when viewed under strong light. Originally made on the Continent, they were produced in England during the nineteenth century, but marked specimens are rare.

Mocha ware Banded mugs and jugs with a curious tree-like decoration. These often bear an excise mark, as many of them were used in taverns.

Pot bank Very early, primitive form of kiln, used by individual potters. The name remained in use long after the introduction of more sophisticated technology in eighteenth-century industrial potteries.

Sagger Container in which ware is fired in the kiln.

Sang de boeuf The term used for the ox-blood glaze used for its brilliant and lustrous effects.

Slip Finely ground clay mixed with water for glazing or decorating earthenware.

Soufflé Name given to an attractive powder blue ground. The colour was used under the glaze and was applied in powder form, the decorator blowing it onto the porcelain through a bamboo tube. In English porcelain the term *soufflé* is substituted for 'powder blue' which does not indicate the shade of blue used but the method of applying it.

Throwing The process of actually forming pots on a potter's wheel.

Tyg Drinking vessel with several handles.

345

Bibliography

Jewitt's Ceramic Art Of Great Britain 1800-1900, revised by G. A. Godden, Barrie & Jenkins, 1972.

English Pottery And Porcelain, W. B. Honey, A. & C. Black, 1962.

Wedgwood Ware, A. Kelly, Ward Lock, 1970.

English Delftware, F. H. Garner, Faber & Faber, 1972.

Royal Doulton 1815-1965, D. Eycles, Hutchinson, 1965.

Spode, A History Of The Family Factory And Wares From 1733-1833, L. Whiter, Barrie & Jenkins, 1970.

Blue And White Transfer Ware, 1780-1840, A. W. Coysh, David and Charles, 1970.

English Blue And White Porcelain, B. Watney, Faber & Faber, 1963.

The Handbook Of British Pottery And Porcelain Marks, G. M. Godden, Herbert Jenkins, 1968.

British Porcelain, An Illustrated Guide, G. A. Godden, Barrie & Jenkins, 1974.

British Pottery, An Illustrated Guide, G. A. Godden, Barrie & Jenkins, 1974.

USEFUL ADDRESSES

Wedgwood:

Josiah Wedgwood and Sons Limited, Barlaston, Stoke-on-Trent, ST12 9ES

The factory has a special 'Visitor Centre', with a museum and a demonstration hall where the traditional manufacturing processes can be seen. At the museum the Assistant Curator will answer queries and supply a guide to the various year-marks (indicating year of manufacture) on nineteenth-century Wedgwood pieces.

Worcester:

Worcester Royal Porcelain Company, Merrivale House, Deansway, Worcester, WR1 2JH

The Group Public Relations Officer will supply a guide to the year-marks on nineteenth-century Worcester items, as well as more general information. The *Dyson Perrins Museum* (Severn Street, Worcester) has the finest collection of Worcester in England and will also supply information on the history of the firm and its wares, on the composition of the porcelain, and on marks.

Spode:

Spode Limited, Stoke-on-Trent, ST4 1BX

The Historical Adviser will give information on the history of the firm and its wares, and will supply a guide to marks. It is also possible to tour the factory by special arrangement.

Royal Crown Derby, Doulton and Minton:

Royal Doulton Tablewares Limited, PO Box 100, London Road, Stoke-on-Trent, ST4 7QD

It is possible to visit each of these three factories now owned by Royal Doulton. Royal Crown Derby and Minton have museums, and monthly open days for the public to bring in pieces to be identified. A Doulton museum is due to open in the near future. The Historical Adviser for the Doulton Group will send booklets on the background and development of the factories, as well as on marks and other details of identification.

The *Gladstone Pottery Museum, Longton, Staffordshire* is an industrial museum in the form of a nineteenth-century Pottery where the original kilns and methods of production can still be seen.

GLASS

JOHN BROOKS

Author's note

The story of the development of the glass industry falls into two distinct periods, the first up to 1700, before which time so few examples of glassware survive that one's interest must be largely academic. It is, however, necessary to have some knowledge of the development of the trade to set the scene for the period after 1700 when the manufacture of domestic glass increased to such an extent that many thousands of examples survive today in museums and private collections. This is the period of interest to collectors, and what I have to say is based upon proven fact and commonly accepted opinion. But twenty years of interest in the subject has led me to a number of opinions and conclusions of my own which I find other authors have not discussed. In addition, after years of talking to collectors of all degrees of experience, I have found that there are certain questions or problems which arise time and time again. I have tried to deal with these in a way which I hope will be of value to anyone to whom this is a new interest.

I have given a reading list at the end of the text and tried to point out what I feel to be the particular value of each book. Where my narrative is brief and lacks detail these books will compensate for my shortcomings.

This book, then, is intended to appeal to several groups of readers. To the person who was unaware that there was any history in the development of glassmaking in the British Isles in the hope that it will reveal in some degree what an ordinary domestic article can tell us about our past. To the budding collector whose enthusiasm has been recently acquired, in the hope that it will both inform and stimulate him or her to further interest and reading on the subject. To the experienced and knowledgeable collector, in the hope that my own opinions will either confirm your own conclusions, give you cause for further reflection, or where you disagree strongly, to stimulate further research and discussion on the subject.

Chapter 1

Glass: Its nature and early history

For many centuries glass has been an important material to developing societies, to such an extent that I doubt whether our modern technological world could function without it. In our own domestic lives I am sure that we all take the many uses of glass entirely for granted, but pause to reflect how different our lives would be without it. No windows, no television, no light bulbs, and although one can drink from a variety of other vessels I imagine there are very few homes which don't boast a set of good drinking glasses to grace the dinner table. It is a material which satisfies both functional and aesthetic needs.

To appreciate the true romance of the development of the glass industry which the following pages catalogue, I would like you to try and forget that it is the commonplace material of today and imagine instead that glass is a rarity and glassmaking is an art surrounded in mystery and practised for the benefit of a privileged few; to provide windows for the larger churches and drinking vessels for the rich and powerful.

Glass does occur naturally in some parts of the world, as a result of volcanic action to form a material usually called obsidian, and as rock crystal, a particularly clear form of quartz. Both these materials have been used to produce decorative and ritual objects, but there has never been enough for widespread use, and they can only be worked upon by laborious methods such as carving and grinding. Imagine, therefore, the impact of a process which can produce from the most unlikely materials (sand and wood ash) an endless supply of a substitute for these rare and desirable natural minerals that can be wrought easily into shapes which previously took endless time and trouble to produce from a solid lump of material.

Today the concept of a solid material which is completely transparent does not trouble us at all, but when clear glass was first produced long before the beginning of the Christian era the whole idea of being able to see something which one could not reach because of a near invisible barrier would have seemed akin to magic. One has only to watch a fly buzzing at a window, able to see daylight but unable to understand the impediment to its progress, to see what I mean. The whole history of glassmaking until recent times has been surrounded by this air of mystery and secrecy which I am sure the glassmakers did their best to promote, since it enabled them to keep firm control over the industry and limit the spread of knowledge of the art to those whom they chose.

For instance, Assyrian clay tablets of the seventh century B.C. bear inscriptions giving recipes for glass which stress the necessity to placate the spirits and observe the true ceremony required to produce a satisfactory product.

When Venice was at the height of its importance as a glassmaking centre (the fifteenth to seventeenth centuries A.D.) laws were passed to prohibit any Venetian glassmaker practising his craft anywhere other than Murano. In an article of the Statutes of 1454 it was ordered that if any workman of any kind should transport his craft into a foreign country and refuse to return an emissary should be commissioned to slay him. There is evidence that this threat was carried out several times. In letters patent of September 1567 John le Carré was given a licence to make glass in England for a period of twenty-one years. One of the conditions was that the French glass makers he proposed to import to carry out the work should teach and train Englishmen. In the event his Lorraine glass makers, rather than do this, quit their jobs and returned to France. These recorded instances indicate how closely the glassmakers guarded their art and how mysterious a process it must have seemed to the general public.

How glass is made

I have already mentioned the materials used to make glass and before starting on the history of the development of glass making in England and Ireland it may be appropriate to consider both the material itself and the basic techniques used to fashion it.

Basically glass is made from one of the various forms of silica: sand, quartz, flint. The temperatures required to melt these on their own are so high as to be uneconomical and the resultant glass is too viscous for practical use. However, with the addition of a flux this temperature is reduced by about half and glassmaking becomes possible. How this technique was first discovered no-one knows, although evidence of glassmaking goes back some 3500 years. The two principal fluxes which have traditionally been used are carbonate of potash and

351

carbonate of soda. The former was generally obtained from the ashes of burnt vegetation, i.e. brushwood, branches and leaves, while the latter came from natural mineral deposits (Pliny refers to deposits imported from Lower Egypt) or the ashes of a marine plant called Barrilla obtained from Spain. As a general rule potash-based glass was a product of Northern Europe where forests were abundant, the glass produced having a marked green tint. Soda-based glass was a Mediterranean product which in the hands of the Venetian glass makers became a fine clear glass they termed 'cristallo'.

The other important additions to glass were lime, which helped to produce a harder and whiter metal, and lead oxide which produced the English 'lead crystal' glass with which much of our story will be concerned. In more recent times other elements such as barium, strontium and titanium, have been added to produce glass for special purposes.

In spite of the secrecy surrounding the art of glassmaking, written records trace its history as far back as the Assyrian tablets already noted. Pictorial evidence certainly goes back as far as an eleventh century manuscript which shows the various basic operations of glassmaking in progress. Remarkably, the method of making glass by hand has changed little since the discovery of glass blowing in the first century B.C. Indeed,

1 An engraving from an eighteenth century encyclopedia showing the several stages in the manufacture of a drinking glass.

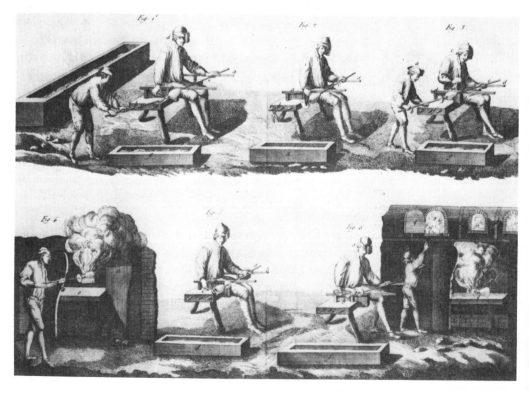

practically all the basic manufacturing and decorating techniques known today have been in existence for at least 2000 years; they include cutting, engraving, gilding, carved overlaid colours and the use of colour. The only important form of decoration to be developed since the beginning of the Christian era was the white lacy pattern invented by the Venetians in the sixteenth century and which English glassmakers revived as the opaque twist stem of wine glasses in the eighteenth century.

It is clear, then, that only the simplest tools are necessary – a metal tube on which to gather and blow the molten glass, pincers to stretch and draw it, shears to cut it and a holder to carry it when it is completed.

Hand made vessel glass is traditionally made by a team of three or four men called a chair. This takes its name from the chair or bench on which the leader of the team sits, and which has long arms extending in front of him. In the case of a drinking glass the leader, or gaffer, blows the glass bubble which will become the bowl, other members of the team apply the stem and foot to this bubble and then an iron bar termed the pontil iron, heated at one end, is applied to the under side of the foot. The bubble is then cut away from the blowing iron leaving the glass, with a bowl of irregular shape, supported on the pontil iron. The gaffer supports this across the arms of his chair and whilst rolling it back and forth with one hand, manipulates the bowl to the desired shape with a small forming tool of wood or metal held in the other. Since the glass only remains plastic within a particular temperature range it may be necessary to offer the glass up to the mouth of the furnace to reheat it several times during the course of manufacture. (People often comment on the fact that so many eighteenth century glasses have stems which are neither straight nor at right angles to the foot. With the foregoing in mind it will be obvious that with a hot, plastic glass held parallel to the floor there will be a tendency for it to droop, which is neutralised by the rolling along the arms of the chair. But at whatever point the gaffer stops it spinning, if it is still soft enough it will show some small tendency to bend out of square to the foot which is at right angles to the floor.)

The glass is then separated from the pontil iron and because the reheating process induces internal stresses in the glass it is transferred to a section of the oven where it can be annealed by reducing the temperature gradually.

I have yet to meet anyone who is not fascinated by the sight of a skilled glass blower at work, and even when one can see a

glass vessel taking shape before one's eyes there is still that hint of magic and mystery about it that has always made glass a desirable material right down the centuries.

There is one other fact about glass which I may mention at this time and that is that it does not deteriorate with age. I have seen glassware made in Roman times looking as clear and as pristine as if it were made today. Indeed, this is one aspect of the material that concerns would-be collectors because if it doesn't change how can one tell the difference in two pieces of glass made several centuries apart. This is one of the things I hope to explain in this book.

Wealden glass

The earliest glass to have been discovered in Britain dates from Roman times. It is unclear whether this was made here or was imported; the majority of it is tied in style to the glass known to have been made in Northern Europe, particularly Germany. My own feeling is that with the difficulties of transport it could have been easier and more economical to set up furnaces in places where there was a demand. However, no proven glasshouse sites of this period have yet come to light and the problem cannot be resolved on the basis of style, since under Roman influence the same styles were made throughout the Roman Empire.

After the decline of Roman influence, regional styles did start to emerge but glassware of the post-Roman years found in this country still displays this general Northern European fashion.

It is not until the advent of written records that we have any further knowledge of the history of glassmaking. The Venerable Bede in his *Ecclesiastical History*, wrote that in A.D. 675, for his church and monastery in Wearmouth, Benedict Biscop 'sent messengers to Gaul to fetch makers of Glass who were unknown in Britain at this time, that they might glaze the windows of his church'. Again in 758 Cuthbert, Bishop of Jarrow, wrote to Lullus, Bishop of Mayence, 'If there be any man in your diocese who can make vessels of glass well, pray send him to me, I beg your fraternity that you will persuade him to come to us, for we are ignorant and helpless in that art.' These suggest that in the north of England, at least, the knowledge of glassmaking had disappeared.

I think that there is more likelihood that, whatever glass-making was undertaken in this country was done in the south of England in that area of Sussex and Surrey known as the Weald. The earliest records and evidence of an established and continuous glass industry all point to it having settled around the area of Chiddingfold in Surrey. From work carried out by the Reverend T. S. Cooper and S. E. Winbolt in the early years of this century, and more recently by G. H. Kenyon and Mrs. E. S. Godfrey we have built up a picture of an industry which operated somewhat precariously from the early years of the thirteenth century to the mid-sixteenth century and after the arrival of le Carré an expanding industry given a new lease of life as a result of a vastly improved product.

The first certain records of glassmaking establishing itself is with the grant of twenty acres of land in Chiddingfold to Laurence Vitrearius in 1226. He was probably a Norman glassmaker and after establishing himself he received contracts for the glazing of Westminster Abbey. Records point to his descendants continuing as glassmakers into the fourteenth century when another family, the Schurterres, make their appearance. Then in the fifteenth century the Peytowes make an appearance. Although all these families settled on the Weald and ultimately became good yeoman stock I feel that they were all originally immigrant craftsmen working in the French Lorraine and Norman traditions. At that time French glass-making was much more highly developed than ours. Most of their business was in window glass, which the French supplied for the glazing of all the great churches and abbeys which were being built during the thirteenth to fifteenth centuries.

Why they settled at Chiddingfold is uncertain because of the three essentials for glassmaking—fuel, sand and clay for pots—only fuel was present in abundance. This was the bulkiest of the three, and was needed in considerable quantities, both as fuel for the furnaces and to provide wood ash as the source of potash. If one had to transport anything into the area, clay in relatively small quantities and sand were the easiest to manage.

3 A beaker found at Kempston, Bedfordshire, dating from the late fifth century A.D. It is green with both horizontal and vertical trails. British Museum, London.

The glass furnaces themselves were generally small structures of about 12 ft. long by 6 ft. wide and 4 ft 6 in. high. There were openings along each side giving access to the glass pots which sat, probably two or four to a side, on shelves either side of the central furnace, which was fed from either end. The glass pots varied, but a typical size was about 12 inches diameter by 12 inches high, holding some two to three gallons of molten glass. These small furnaces could be built fairly quickly and, when sources of fuel in the immediate vicinity were exhausted, abandoned and new ones established close to fresh woodlands.

4, 5 *Above and opposite:* Two stages in the manufacture of glass at an eighteenth century English glass furnace. *Above:* Glass is blown. *Opposite:* The glass is cast. These are engravings by Henri Gravelot, a French artist working in England 1733-45.

The product was principally window glass, made by both the crown and broad sheet methods, and the number of men employed at each furnace being from two to four. As the great period of ecclesiastical building continued the demand for stained glass increased, and all authorities are agreed that as this was an art not practised in this country, France became the new source of window glass, and demand for clear window glass diminished. Since few private owners could afford glazed windows the market was then only for replacements. The glassmakers of the Weald obviously didn't supply glass for the windows of all the great abbeys around the country. There is evidence of glasshouses at Salisbury and Rugeley in Staffordshire, but nowhere else has such a concentration of glasshouse sites been discovered as at Chiddingfold and nowhere else has evidence survived of continuous glassmaking over such a long period.

Vessel glass had always been a minor part of the business. The quality of the glass and the skill of the operatives did not lend itself to elaborate or sophisticated vessel glass. Most of the vessels they turned out appear to have been for medical or chemical uses. From earliest times the manufacture of urinals is recorded.

By the middle of the sixteenth century glassmaking in England seems almost to have disappeared. At the same time the Venetian glass trade based on Murano was becoming famous for the quality and style of its 'cristallo' wares and there was undoubtedly a growing market amongst the European nobility for these fine glass wares. As early as 1398 Venetian ships had been allowed into the port of London to sell glass and earthenware vessels. Henry VIII had his glassware mounted in gold.

Thus the arrival of John le Carré in London in 1567 signalled a new lease of life for the English glass trade.

Le Carré was a native of Arras in Northern France, which at that time was part of the Low Countries. A merchant with

connections in the glass trade, he probably came to England, where Queen Elizabeth was on the throne, to escape religious persecution, since he was a Calvinist and Protestant, and also because he had a daughter who had married and settled in London.

Presumably he soon discovered the opportunities that existed to develop glassmaking, and in conjunction with several others, including his son-in-law, applied for and got licences to open a window glasshouse on the Weald and a furnace to make the Venetian style of glass in London. After further negotiations he was finally granted a monopoly for a term of twenty-one years. The actual terms of le Carré's patent were that:

1. Anyone infringing the patent was liable to have his tools, work and supplies confiscated and be required to pay £100.
2. The patentees had to produce sufficient glass to satisfy the home market.
3. The glass was to be as cheap or cheaper than imported glass.
4. They were to teach Englishmen the art of glassmaking so that at the expiry of the patent the trade would be in the hands of natives.
5. The patentees to pay the Crown at least as much as would have been raised by taxing imported glass, although the import of glass was not abandoned.
6. The patent was to lapse at Christmas 1568 if the licensees were not producing enough glass to satisfy domestic requirements.

With the granting of his monopoly le Carré contracted with Thomas and Balthazar Hennezell to come to England and bring four other 'gentlemen glass makers' with them. These included members of the Thisac and Thietry families, later to become famous in the history of English glassmaking as Tyzack and Tittery. These were glassmakers in the Lorraine tradition but le Carré also attracted Norman glassmakers named de Bangard (later Bungar) to make crown glass in the Weald glasshouse.

Trouble eventually arose over item four in the monopoly quoted above, when the Lorrainers refused point-blank to pass on their knowledge to English operatives. Rather than do this they returned to France. The Bungars also refused to fulfil this condition. This led to a Court enquiry which decided that there was no hope that the glassmakers would honour that part of the licence and that it should not be enforced, for it was in the best interests of the country that glassmaking should continue.

In 1570 le Carré introduced Venetian craftsmen into his London 'cristallo' glasshouse, and decided to concentrate his efforts on improving the Wealden vessel glass. However, he died in 1572 before making any great progress in that direction.

Glassmaking continued after the death of le Carré, but his partners were divided among themselves. Lawsuits were undertaken, taxes due under the monopoly were not paid, and other French glassmakers entered the country and set up in competition. By 1576 the patent had fallen into abeyance. This state of affairs brought to the fore the next important figure in our story, and the last man of any importance to make his mark on the history of glassmaking in this country before the advent of coal fired furnaces. The man was Jacob Verzelini, who was a Venetian glassmaker originally brought to London in 1570 by le Carré to make crystal glass in the Venetian style. He was born in Venice in 1522, moved to Antwerp in 1549 (presumably in defiance of the laws controlling glassmakers) and married there in 1556. After the death of le Carré, he appears to have taken over the glasshouse at the Crutched Friars.

By 1575 Verzelini was sufficiently well established to apply for, and obtain, a licence for a monopoly of fine crystal glassmaking in England. This was, strictly speaking, before the expiry of le Carré's patent, but as we have shown this was inoperative anyway. The one important condition he procured, which le Carré had not been able to do, was the ban on imports of foreign glass which might compete with his own product, and there are records showing that he took action when necessary to protect his patent.

Glasses have survived which are attributed to Verzelini's glasshouse, or to his period. In this country they may be seen at the Victoria and Albert Museum, the British Museum and the Fitzwilliam Museum in Cambridge. These glasses are mostly engraved, and where dates appear they coincide with the period when Verzelini's glasshouse was working in Broad Street. The style is basically Venetian, but show variations which must be attributed to local requirements and preferences. Against all the odds another glass in this group turned up in a private house in England as recently as 1978. It was dated 1584, which meant it had led a charmed life for nearly 400 years. Are there any more to be found?

Verzelini became a respected and established figure in England and died in 1606 at the age of 84. He is buried with his wife at Downes Church in Kent, where they are commemorated by a pair of brasses.

After the death of Verzelini and the expiry of his patent in 1596 the whole glass trade was heading for a complete change of direction. The trade was about to become organised under

6 An English glass goblet, dated 1578, from the glasshouse of Jacob Verzelini. Fitzwilliam Museum, Cambridge.

the influence of Englishmen for the first time. The introduction of coal fired furnaces was instrumental in this change.

During the latter half of the sixteenth century glassmaking in the Wealden tradition had continued around Chiddingfold with a marked improvement in the quality of the wares they produced. This was undoubtedly due to the influx of new craftsmen brought into the country by le Carré. As these new glassmaking families increased they spread their influence westwards and northwards, opening up new sites in Staffordshire and Shropshire. Landowners encouraged them, since glassmaking created revenue by the sale of wood and Staffordshire produced a supply of clay ideally suited for glass pots.

Coal and Sir Robert Mansell

More and more industries were becoming the subject of monopolies during the reign of Elizabeth I, the monopolies being granted to courtiers and favourites as rewards for service. For the crown it was a cheap way of rewarding the recipients, since it cost the exchequer nothing. Indeed the crown profited from the levies which the monopolists had to pay for their privileges.

One man who obtained such a monopoly was Sir Jerome Bowes. With Verzelini's patent due to expire at the end of 1595 he was awarded a twelve-year monopoly in 1592 to take over when the other was ended, for a fixed levy of 100 marks per year. Bowes appears to have had some trouble in maintaining a supply of glass to the market, since Verzelini's sons continued in production at Broad Street. Eventually Bowes made an arrangement with two London businessmen, Turner and Robson, that they should take over glassmaking under the term of his monopoly in return for £500 per annum. After his payment to the Crown this left him with a profit without having to do anything for it himself. Turner and Robson, by dubious means, put the Verzelinis out of business, took over their staff and went into production at Blackfriars. Bowes had various problems over illegal imports and others trying to set up in competition, but armed with a new patent to run for a further twenty-one years, and as a result of actions through the courts, by 1610 he was in sole command of all crystal glassmaking in England, and the trade for the first time was in the hands of Englishmen, even though most of the work was still being carried out by Venetian craftsmen.

The increase in the glassmaking industry began to have serious repercussions on the woodlands of Britain. The Wealden glasshouses were consuming ever-increasing quantities of timber and numerous accounts record the denuding of large areas of woodland on the Sussex/Surrey borders. The landowners often had more concern for the income from their timber than the preservation of their woodlands. By 1580 the demands of the glass and iron smelting industries made the situation critical and laws were passed controlling the erection of new iron furnaces, and in 1584 a Bill was introduced to limit the operation of glasshouses, requesting that all foreign craftsmen be prevented from operating at all, and that native Englishmen should not operate within thirty miles of London. These terms were somewhat modified in the event, but we may gather from this the concern that the problem was causing.

Transport, over such roads as existed at that time, was expensive and laborious. The glasshouses being small it was easier to move them when supplies of fuel close to hand were exhausted. This was not the case with the iron smelters. Their works, being bigger, were static and fuel had to be brought from as far as was necessary. This did not endear the glassmakers to the iron smelters, whose operation suggests to me that of locusts. The practice of coppicing, or the planned regeneration of the woodlands, either did not appear to have been known or was not widely developed.

The big problem, however, was that the further afield the glassmakers had to travel to establish themselves, the more problems they created regarding access to markets. Waterways were the favourite routes of communication for most manufactured products, and various Bills introduced into Parliament were aimed at pushing the consumers of wood further and further from these lines of communication.

With these pressures upon the industry, the advent of coal fired furnaces was in the long term to prove the salvation of the trade. But such was the conservatism of the glassmakers that the transition was not achieved easily or willingly.

The first record of a patent taken out to cover the use of coal in furnaces was in 1610. This was worded to cover all industrial processes requiring the use of a furnace, but in the following year another patent was granted which was aimed specifically at glassmaking. This patent was sought by Sir Edward Zouch, Bevis Thelwell and Thomas Percival with others. Percival is the person actually credited with the invention of the coal-fired furnace. Zouch then came into conflict with Robson (who had bought out the patent of Sir J. Bowes) over who should make what; and how, but the former, after successful lobbying of the Court, managed to obtain, in 1614, a new patent for twenty-one years, to cover the use of coal in glassmaking, which revoked all other patents, forbade the use of wood and banned importation of foreign-made products. Whereas the original patent regarding the use of coal was of the type we know today, protecting the method only, this last one was a monopoly patent which gave the most wide-ranging protection to its holders of any patent so far issued. They proceeded to bring pressure to bear on Robson, and eventually forced him out of business. They pursued similar courses with the forest glassmakers, and in 1615 secured themselves with yet another patent which included, for the first time, the name of Sir Robert Mansell.

This is the first we hear of Sir Robert, but for the next forty years, until his death in 1656, the glass trade was to revolve around him.

Before pursuing the thread of our story, let us pause to consider the question of coal fired furnaces. Although the declared aim of the patents regarding the use of coal was to relieve the pressure on the forests and woodlands of England, its protagonists must also have been aware that a new technology was required to make effective use of it.

Wood-burning furnaces used open-topped crucibles with the flames circulating freely around and over them. The fumes from coal used in the same manner contained carbon and sulphur, which discoloured the glass. This problem was solved by enclosing the tops of the glass pots, but then it was found that higher temperatures were required to melt the raw materials. This led to modifications in furnace design to increase the draught and the head generated.

Although the introduction of coal was resisted (in fact it would seem that nearly two hundred years were to pass before it was accepted in Europe) this patent was to prove to be one of the great turning points in the development of the English glass trade. Not only was it a step forward in the technology of glassmaking, but because it was protected by patent, the holders of the patent had the opportunity to dominate and control the progress and direction of glassmaking in this country.

The arrival of le Carré some sixty years earlier had revived what was an ailing and declining industry. The new impetus provided by the coal burning process allowed it to be organised in a manner which was to lead to the dominance of English glassmaking in the eighteenth century.

Since the new patent had such a fundamental effect on the operation of glassmaking, whoever controlled the patent was in a position to control the whole industry. The patents had been granted in several names: Zouch, Thelwell, Percival. While they undoubtedly perfected the process they were also involved in litigation over several years with Robson and the Wealden glassmakers over patent infringements. It was not until the appearance of one strong directing influence that the financial and economic opportunities offered by the patent could be exploited. This influence appeared in the person of Sir Robert Mansell.

Mansell was born in 1573, the eighth son of Sir Edward Mansell of Margam in Glamorgan. At the age of fifteen he served under Lord Howard against the Armada: he earned a knighthood at Cadiz in 1596, was promoted Vice-Admiral in 1603, and in 1604 became Treasurer to the Navy. He was one of the patentees named in the patent of 1615 and in 1618 sold the office of Treasurer to concentrate on the glass trade. His first wife, who was somewhat older than himself, had died some time before 1617, for in that year he married Elizabeth Roper, a lady-in-waiting to Queen Anne, wife of James I. Elizabeth proved to be a capable businesswoman, looking after his interests whenever he had to be absent. At first sight it might seem strange that an officer in the Navy should become involved in business matters. It is recorded that even James I was moved to wonder that Robert Mansell 'should fall from water to tamper with fire'. However, I feel that there were not such sharp distinctions in those days between serving the crown, one's country, or one's own interests. The idea of naval vessels plundering foreign ships for material gain was still commonplace and the navy would have been closely involved in setting up and maintaining business interests in newly discovered parts of the world. With this in mind it is not so unlikely that Mansell's naval service had developed his business instinct and that he would avail himself of an opportunity to make a business investment with a view to financial gain.

After the granting of the patent of 1615 he apparently found difficulty in getting his partners to agree to a concerted plan of action, so he bought them all out on the promise of paying each of them an annuity of £200. At this time the two glasshouses operating under his patent were still suffering competition from wood-burning glasshouses, he had liabilities of £2800 per annum incurred by the partners of the earlier monopolies to settle earlier litigation, and in addition he had to deal with his glassmaking craftsmen while knowing nothing of the practical side of the industry himself. Starting from this unlikely beginning it is a measure of his determination and tenacity that he managed to control the glass industry in Britain for the next twenty-seven years.

With the introduction of coal firing, it became advantageous to set up the glasshouses near the sources of coal, or at sites to which coal could easily be transported. This led initially to the establishment of glasshouses in Dorset where there was shale coal, the West Midlands, in Staffordshire, Shropshire, Notts and Newcastle. Problems arose over the cost of transporting the finished product to the principal markets, and eventually production settled in places where transport of either coal to the glasshouses or the finished product to the markets was cheapest. Since transport by sea was cheapest, this effectively meant that glassmaking settled near large ports such as Bristol, London (where it had been practised since le Carré) and Newcastle. It is recorded that the cost of shipping window glass to London from Newcastle was half that of carrying it from Nottingham to London.

Mansell's method was to licence independent glassmakers to set up glasshouses to manufacture window glass or vessel glass on payment of royalties, and usually with restrictions as to where their products could be sold. Most of his licensees were the descendants of the same Norman and Lorraine glassmakers who had settled around Chiddingfold in the mid-sixteenth century. The Hennezells, the Tyzacks and Titterys had spread slowly westwards and northwards to find security of operation and supplies of fuel. Under Mansell's monopoly most of them seemed to be amenable to adopting the new method and thus they became the founders of the new trade in Stourbridge and Newcastle. Not all of them gave in so easily, and the whole period of Mansell's efforts to control the industry was punctuated by lawsuits against those who wanted freedom to continue the use of wood-fired furnaces or unrestricted opportunities to trade. Isaac Bungar was probably the most persistent of these, and he continued the fight against Mansell until his death in 1643. He lived just long enough to see Mansell's monopoly revoked by Parliament in 1642, the year in which the Civil War began.

The changing mood of the country, when the Commons became independent of the Crown, was against the idea of monopolies based on privilege and personal advantage. The Civil War finally put an end to the system of monopolies, Mansell applied unsucessfully for an extension of his patent in 1652, but continued in production at the glasshouses he had set up in London and Newcastle until his death.

We have seen how the manufacturing side of the industry

had become organised throughout the country under one hand. It consisted, though, of two distinct sections, those for window glass and for vessel glass. In due course the retailers of both these commodities also considered it advantageous to organise themselves into Guilds. Window glass manufacture went back to the earliest days of recorded glassmaking in this country, so it is not surprising that the retailers of window glass had formed themselves into the Glaziers Company in the early fourteenth century.

With the rise of Venetian glass in the sixteenth century and the growth of fine glassmaking in London, the retailers of drinking glass and mirrors also felt the need to organise themselves. They felt that in speaking with one voice they could better contest the ever-increasing taxes being levied on them and the harm which they felt travelling hawkers of glass were doing to their business and reputation. In 1635 they petitioned the King and were granted a charter for the incorporation of the Glass Sellers Company, but the Court of Aldermen of the City of London, for some reason, refused to enrol them as a Guild. It was not until after the restoration of Charles II in 1664 that they were finally enrolled. Their charter gave members of the Company exclusive rights to sell vessel glass and mirrors and the powers to prosecute the travelling hawkers. Their main complaint against these being that they sold poor quality glass and thus brought the trade into disrepute, although it is more likely that having few overheads they sold glass very much more cheaply than the Glass Sellers. The Glass Sellers Company grew steadily in influence and ultimately succeeded the monopolists in the power they exercised over the glass trade. I mention this at some length because, as we shall see, the Glass Sellers Company has an important part to play in the next stage of our story.

It finally remains to consider what sort of glassware was made during the period of Mansell's monopoly. Our attribution to Verzelini of the glasses referred to earlier depends on the fact that they are engraved with dates and names which are obviously English, and Verzelini's monopoly meant that no-one else in England should have been making glass of this type. Unfortunately, no glasses survive of the Mansell period with the same identifying decoration. In Mansell's crystal glass-houses the styles produced, and most of the workmen, were Venetian, so although complete specimens may survive, they are what would generally be termed 'façon de Venise', i.e. a style derived from Venice but adapted to the taste of Northern Europe, and made widely throughout that area. However, we know something of the types of glasses which Mansell made, because of a document he presented to the House of Lords in about 1635. This lists certain types of drinking glasses, giving the prices he charged, to show how he had kept prices down. They include:

Ordinary drinking glasses for beer	4 shillings per dozen.
Ditto for wine	2/6d. per dozen.
Cristall beer glasses—formerly bought from Venice to sell at 20/- and 24/- per dozen	Now sold for 10/- and 11/- per dozen.
Ditto wine glasses brought from Venice and sold at 18/- per dozen	Now sold at 7/- and 8/- per dozen.

The 'cristall' glasses would be those made in London in the 'façon de Venise' using soda derived from barilla which had been imported into the country since the days when John le Carré set up his first glasshouse to produce 'cristallo'. 'Ordinary glasses' were obviously of an inferior quality because of the great discrepancy in price, but they were still presumably some form of 'cristall', since he states later in the same document that he had let the rights for making 'green' glasses to a 'gentleman of known experience'. Glasses made from a potash glass similar to that produced by the Wealden glassmakers were commonly referred to as green glass.

1660-1700

During the period of the Commonwealth up to the restoration of the monarchy in 1660 the Puritan outlook of the administration was against any form of frivolity and display. Glassmaking retreated to a purely utilitarian craft and the market for the elaborate 'façon de Venise' glasses disappeared.

With the restoration of Charles II the social climate soon altered, and, encouraged by the court, style, fashion and novelty were soon evident. Following the tradition of James I and Charles I monopoly patents were still to be obtained by members of the court, and the first to obtain such a licence was the second Duke of Buckingham. The Duke appears to have acted as a middleman, putting up capital and taking his cut as a percentage of the profits. He acted in this way first in 1660 for John de la Cam, a Frenchman, for Martin Clifford and Thomas Powlden in 1661 and for Thomas Tilson in 1662. The Duke then obtained a licence to make mirror glass in 1663 and set up a glasshouse at Vauxhall which was managed by an Englishman, John Bellingham. In this way he nominally had a controlling interest in the industry, but not the complete domination achieved by Mansell. His patents expired in 1674, which date coincides with the appearance of the man who effected the third and greatest turning point in our story, George Ravenscroft. I suspect that his importance has as much to do with the changing times and the new spirit of enquiry as with any actual demand for a new material.

Along with the resurgence of style under Charles II came an awakening interest in scientific matters. The Royal Society had been founded in 1662 and its members, of many different disciplines, met to promote scientific research and enquiry. Among its members was Doctor Christopher Merrett who translated from the Italian what was probably the most important book on glassmaking *L'Arte Vitrearia*, written by Antonio Neri and published in 1612. That it had to wait fifty years for an English edition is strange, since it would surely have helped to educate English glassmakers to the trade during those years when such an objective had been so important to the English industry. Whether the publication of this book played any part or not, there seems to have been developed between 1660 and 1674 a better quality of glass which was generally described as English crystal.

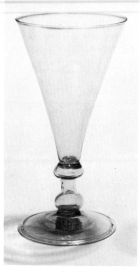

There appears in a series of bills for glass supplied to the Duke of Bedford between 1650 and 1690 several types of glass which are referred to specifically by name, i.e. Venice glass, crystal, English crystal, flint, single flint and double flint. These bills cover the period during which Ravenscroft's new glass of lead was introduced. I shall have more to say about the 'flint' glasses later, but the crystal glasses are very much of the Restoration period.

Much of the glass described as Venice glass was supplied by London glass seller John Greene, who was initially in business with Michael Measey at Cary House, Strand, and later on his own at No. 10 Poultry. His invoices cover the period 1669 to 1675. Venice glasses continued to be supplied by another glass seller, Thomas Apthorpe, until 1686.

There is a further connection between John Greene, the Bedford bills and Venetian glass in a series of letters which have survived written by Greene to his glass supplier in Venice, one Alessio Morelli. In this correspondence Greene gives exact specifications for the glasses he orders, complains generally about the quality and that the goods he receives bear no relation to his orders, and on several occasions is not above giving instructions as to the method of packing his goods and the falsification of invoices with the obvious intention of evading customs duty on their arrival in London. There also survive several sheets of drawings of the glasses which Greene ordered from Venice. It is noticeable that these patterns are practically all for plain glasses of generous capacity, avoiding the excesses of decoration which Venetian glass was prone to; the serpentine stems, pincered trails and elaborate moulding. These are sometimes referred to as 'Greene's glasses', not to be confused with the term 'green glass' which refers to the cheap potash glass made generally throughout England up to that period.

In a letter of 3 May 1671 Greene writes to Morelli:
'Sir, I pray you once again to take such care that I may have good, and be used very kindly in the price, else it will not be in my interest to send to Venice for neither drinking glasses nor looking glasses, for we make now very good drinking glasses in England and better looking glasses than any that comes from Venice'.

This would seem to imply that the prices Greene was paying for glass shipped from Venice were sufficiently below the prices of London-made glass that he was prepared to put up with the inconveniences of doubtful quality, breakage *en route* and the disregarding of his specifications.

The use of the word 'crystal' on the invoices undoubtedly refers to the 'façon de Venise' glasses made in London since the time of le Carré. These glasses, made by craftsmen reared in the Venetian tradition and from materials used in the Venetian product, were the domestic equivalent of the glasses which Greene and others were importing from Venice.

The description 'English Crystal' appears in the invoices for a short period between 1669 and 1672, while the term 'crystal' appears on the earliest in 1652 and continues until 1691. Since an invoice of 1674 bears the words 'Flint christalline' and 'flint' comes into common usage on the invoices from 1675 onwards, it seems as if 'flint' replaces 'English crystal'. We know that 'flint' is a term used to describe Ravenscroft's newly developed lead glass. If 'English crystal' was different from 'crystal' and bearing in mind the sequence of dates, is it possible that 'English crystal' was a transitional development which was either created by Ravenscroft in his bid for a new metal, or used by him as a stepping stone for his own researches? One of his workmen named Da Costa had apparently introduced him to the use, as his source of silica, white quartz pebbles imported from the region of the River Po in Italy. With this thought in mind let us have a closer look at what is known about Ravenscroft and his contribution to English glassmaking.

George Ravenscroft For many years it had been assumed that George Ravenscroft was born the second son of George Ravenscroft in 1618 at Sholton in the parish of Hawarden in Flintshire, dying in 1681. However, in an interesting paper presented to the Glass Circle in 1974 Rosemary Rendel suggests that he was in fact the second son of James Ravenscroft of Huntingdonshire, born in 1632, dying in 1683. This George is known to have been a merchant, to have had trading links with Venice and to have been involved in dealing in glass. He sounds a much more likely candidate to be the owner of a glasshouse at the Savoy in 1663. Nothing is known of how he got into the operative business of glassmaking, but by April 1674 he had made sufficient progress to approach the Glass Sellers Company with examples of 'a particular sort of chrystal-line Glass resembling rock crystall, not formerly exercised or used in our Kingdome'. He had also taken the precaution of applying for a patent in March 1674 before approaching the Glass Sellers. This was granted in May of that year for a period of seven years, and the Glass Sellers Company was sufficiently interested to offer him the use of a glasshouse at Henley-on-Thames. There is evidence that he experienced problems with his new metal, since there are references to crizzling and decay by Dr. Robert Plot, a Fellow of the Royal Society, who visited him at Henley, and by the Glass Sellers when they issued their Certificate of Merit in June 1676. Crizzling, which is a fine crazing and deterioration of the surface of glass, had to do with the porportions of his ingredients, and it can be assumed that it was during the resolution of these problems that he introduced lead oxide into the mixture. The use of lead in glass was known to the Venetians and since it is referred to in Neri's book—and remember that because this was only translated in 1662 it would have recently become available to English glassmakers. Very probably it was read by Ravenscroft.

By 1676 he had managed to produce a sufficiently stable metal in a manner consistent enough to encourage the Glass Sellers Company to issue a certificate of merit, which I give with the spelling modernised:

'We underwritten, do certify and attest that the defect of the flint glasses (which were formerly observed to crizzle and decay) have been redressed several months ago and the glass since made have all proved durable and lasting as any glasses whatsoever. Moreover that the usual trials wherewith the assay of glasses are made have been often reiterated on these new flint glasses with entire success and easy to be done again by anybody, which proofs the former glass would not

9 A bowl, diameter 11¾ inches, that shows signs of crizzling. This piece dates from 1675-80. The Museum of London.

undergo, besides the distinction of sound discernible by any person whatsoever. London 3 June 1676.'

This document is signed by the Clerk to the Glass Sellers Company, Samuel Moore, who had been instructed by the Company to liaise with Ravenscroft, and by Hawley Bishop. Hawley Bishop was a member of the Glass Sellers Company and had for some time before the date of the above certificate been working with Ravenscroft at Henley, so was in a position to be sure that the problem of crizzling had been cured.

The certificate enables us to draw several conclusions about Ravenscroft's progress towards his lead glass. If we can assume that he had been satisfied with his new glass to such an extent that he took out his patent and approached the Glass Sellers in 1674 it is likely that the crizzling problem occurred only after his removal to Henley. So his experiments continued while he was there. Since the Glass Sellers were interested in his progress (they undertook to sell his whole output), if the problems started at Henley they would surely have been aware of them, and it is reasonable to assume that they would be sufficiently concerned to put one of their own members (Hawley Bishop) into the glasshouse to supervise progress. Since this certificate was published several times in the London Gazette, and its general tone appears to be to reassure customers who may have had trouble with glasses they had bought, it would appear that the Glass Sellers had already been selling Ravenscroft's glass before 1676. Since the certificate says (in June 1676) that the trouble had been corrected 'several months ago' and Ravenscroft had not started in business at Henley until some time after April 1674, the problem of crizzling must have been one which made itself apparent fairly quickly in finished glasses. It is unlikely that the problem lasted more than one year. In fact, Dr. Plot, visiting Ravenscroft at Henley in April 1676, commented on the quality of the glass he was then producing.

In October and November of 1676 the London Gazette carried notices stating that Ravenscroft was permitted to mark his glassware with a seal bearing the mark of a raven's head. This must have been some form of guarantee of quality since the Glass Sellers (in an effort to restore confidence among their customers?) offered raven's head items with the offer 'no crizzling or money returned'.

In 1677 Ravenscroft agreed a price list and a further three-year contract with the Glass Sellers for the items he was supplying to them from Henley, and also by this time his Savoy glasshouse. It includes glasses for beer, claret, sacks and brandy at prices from 6d. to 1/8d.

For some reason unknown, Ravenscroft gave six months notice to terminate this contract in August 1678. Rosemary Rendel suggests that this was linked with the fact that Ravenscroft was a Catholic and the political climate at that time was unfavourable towards Catholics. His patent still had nearly three years to run, however, and although he no longer had any legal tie with the Glass Sellers, as long as he was in business making glass he would have had to deal with them. He appears to have given up work at the Savoy in 1681 or early in 1682 since in February 1682 the Glass Sellers signed a fresh agreement with Hawley Bishop for twenty-one years to continue work at the Savoy glasshouse, the property then being referred to as 'late in the occupation of George Ravens-croft Gent'n.'

That Ravenscroft was the first glassmaker to use lead in some form, although it is not mentioned specifically in either the patent or any surviving correspondence with the Glass Sellers Company, is supported by the fact that the sealed pieces which have survived are of lead glass and must have been produced between 1677 and 1679. The term which is generally used when referring to this lead glass is 'flint', qualified by 'single flint' or 'double flint'. (See the Duke of Bedford invoices and the 'Certificate of Merit' already referred to.) Houghton, in one of his *Letters for the Improvement of Commerce & Trade* in 1696 states, 'I remember the time when ... Mr. Ravenscroft first made the flint glasses'.

I feel this use of the word flint for lead glass deserves some explanation. In an effort to improve the quality of the crystal glassware made in London from the mid-sixteenth century onwards, various methods and materials had been used to improve the quality of the product. From le Carré onwards the

10 An English glass decanter jug from the seventeenth century. Fitzwilliam Museum, Cambridge.

soda derived from Spanish barilla had been imported into London. Various forms and sources of silica had been tried. One of these was calcined flint; that is, it was first burned in a furnace and crushed to a white powder. This had produced some improvement, and according to Dr. Plot this is the material which Ravenscroft was using before he was introduced to the white Italian quartz by Da Costa. There is little doubt that the public was aware of and accustomed to good quality glassware based on flint, and that the term flint would be associated with a high standard. Merrett, on p.261 of *The Art of Glass* (a translation of Neri), 'Flints indeed have all the properties, and when calcined, powdered and ferced (sieved) into a most impalpable powder, make incomparable pure and white crystal metal.' The addition of lead to the glass was initially a commercial secret, so the product containing it could easily be represented as being a better type of flint glass. We see from the Duke of Bedford invoices that 'flint glass' was being supplied from March 1676 onwards, when invoices refer to 'new flint wine glasses'. The term also seems to have been adopted by the glasshouses. From this time on, glasshouses are defined as being 'flint glasshouses' making vessel glass for domestic use, or 'bottle glasshouses'.

The term flint glass survived right to the end of the nineteenth century when firms such as Sowerbys in Gateshead, mass-producing pressed glass, still used the word to denote any of their products in clear glass as opposed to coloured glass, although by this time there was no lead in the glass at all.

The terms 'single' and 'double' flint were used to denote glasses of differing weight. In fact before these terms became popular, glasses were described as being thin or thick. This, I think, gives us the clue to their true meaning. Since glass was commonly sold by weight, a hangover from the days when window glass was the principal product of the glass industry, the thickness of the glass determined the price. Among the Woburn Abbey invoices there are many recording both single flint glasses and double flint glasses, the prices for the latter being exactly twice the prices for the former.

All the evidence so far discovered points, I think, to the conclusion that lead was first introduced into glassmaking in this country to act as a stabilising agent and to solve the problems of crizzling in glass. It is not clear how much lead Ravenscroft introduced initially, but over the years following his discovery the lead content increased until as much as 37% by volume was being used.

The great benefit of the use of lead was to produce a glass of greater transparency, whiter colour and with greater refractive properties than the Venetian 'cristallo' which rendered it highly suitable for articles of cut glass. It was also a softer material, which was to make it attractive to the glass decorators, particularly the great Dutch engravers of the mid-eighteenth century. For the first time glass of considerable thickness could be made which retained the transparency of the very thinly blown Venetian 'cristallo'. This new material was prized as much abroad as at home, and considerable quantities were exported to Europe and later to North America. In view of its popularity and its rapid adoption among the glasshouses of the British Isles it surprises me that it was not equally rapidly taken up in Europe. There are one or two references to attempts to produce the English crystal in Europe. In Spain as early as 1720 and in Germany a little later, but they were apparently unsuccessful, and it is not until 1784 that there is a reliable record of lead crystal being produced in France. I think this is probably tied in with the fact that Continental glasshouses stuck to their wood-fired furnaces for so long after coal was generally used in this country.

Ravenscroft imported Italian glassmakers to run his glasshouses and the earliest lead glass shows strong evidence of this Venetian influence. Surviving articles in glass dating to about 1685 have blown quatrefoil knops, pincered wings, applied trailing and other features typical of Venice. But this new glass of lead had noticeably different handling qualities from the light Venetian soda glass, and did not really lend itself to the elaborate decorative techniques of that tradition. By 1690 lead glass was being widely used in Britain and the rapid increase in production began which was to bring the use of glass table ware to an ever-increasing market. This increase must have demanded a corresponding increase in the number of glassmakers, and more and more English men undoubtedly entered the trade. Thus the transfer of the glass industry from foreign craftsmen, who guarded their secrets jealously, through the English monopolists and the Glass Sellers Company was finally completed when the craftsmen themselves were predominantly English. The combination of these three factors, a new metal, a new breed of glassmakers and a wider public, all tended to turn fashion away from the effusiveness of Venice and to create a truly English style which was to make English glass the most important in the world for the next hundred years. The next chapters deal with the development of this style.

Chapter 2
Styles
of eighteenth century
drinking glasses

As far as the collector of English glass is concerned, the narrative so far can only be of academic interest. So little glass made prior to 1690 survives today that there is hardly sufficient to form a worthwhile collection, and prices of early pieces are beyond the means of almost all private collectors. Before the advent of Ravenscroft, good quality glassware was made in a very few glasshouses for a wealthy but limited clientele. From 1690 onwards the quantity that has survived is relatively plentiful and varied, two essentials to any form of collecting. This, then, is the period which is of most interest to collectors, and it is fortunate that the progression of styles throughout the eighteenth century was both orderly and well documented. Briefly, the knopping of the baluster stemmed glasses of the early eighteenth century gave way to the plain stems of the middle of the century. These were followed by the air and opaque twist stemmed glasses of the third quarter of the

11, 12 Thomas Pelham-Holles, 1st Duke of Newcastle, with his nephew Henry Clinton, Earl of Lincoln and later the 2nd Duke of Newcastle. The glasses are drawn trumpet bowls on baluster stems (see enlargement). The painting is by Godfrey Kneller, *c.* 1721, and was painted for the Kit Kat Club. National Portrait Gallery, London.

century, which in turn were succeeded by the facet stems of the late eighteenth century. Before considering these styles in detail it would be appropriate, I think, to explain a number of the terms used in describing old glass which will occur in the ensuing chapters and some of the hallmarks of old glass which will help to identify it.

Explanation of terms

One of the most difficult things for the novice in old glassware to do is to describe satisfactorily the style, shape and character of a piece of glass to anyone else. This generally seems to be accomplished with much hand waving and vague references to the owner's ancestors. There are, however, a number of descriptive terms and expressions which are generally used between knowledgeable people.

Until the last few years of the eighteenth century, drinking glasses were composed of three elements: the bowl, the stem and the foot. Each of these elements could be in a variety of shapes, each of which has its own name. The two diagrams show all the important shapes of bowls. Knops are shaped sections decorating the stem, and where they are sufficiently well defined they may be referred to by name. The later glasses generally have knops which are nothing more than swellings in the stem, so they may be referred to as base, shoulder or centre knops. Air twist and opaque glasses are known with up to five knops, and the more knops there are, the rarer is the glass. Where there are one or two knops these are usually in the middle of the stem or at the top, i.e. centre or shoulder knops. Glasses with base knops only are uncommon. Another line drawing on page 389 shows all the major knop shapes.

Although I have said that glasses have three elements, most drinking glasses are described as being two- or three-piece glasses. A two-piece glass is one in which the bowl and stem are made from one piece or 'gather' (see below) of glass, with the foot made separately. A three-piece glass is made from three separate pieces of glass. As a general rule all glasses with drawn trumpet or bell bowls on plain or air twist stems are two-piece glasses, while glasses with any other bowl shape, and all opaque twist glasses are three-piece glasses. Three-piece air and opaque twist glasses can usually be detected because the pattern ends abruptly where the stem meets the bowl. Three-piece plain stem glasses can usually be detected by holding the glass at an angle to the light and by looking up the stem towards the bowl a slight change in the reflection of the light across the joint may be seen.

13 A goblet c. 1690-1700, 12 inches in height. British Museum, London.

374

Heavy baluster, light baluster and Newcastle baluster stems are often made in several sections, according to how many knops there are. Such glasses may be four, five or even six-piece glasses.

The 'gather' is the amount of glass taken from the glass pot, and from which the vessel is to be made. The glass is commonly referred to as 'metal'. This has always been the trade term for it and probably takes its origin from the similarity of molten glass in the glass pot to any molten metal in its crucible.

The foot

The foot is generally the most informative part of the glass when age and authenticity are in question. It is my belief that whenever a glassmaker has copied an earlier style, no matter how accurate the bowl and stem may be, the foot is always made in a manner appropriate to the period in which he is working. Briefly, the feet of glasses made in the first half of the eighteenth century have fairly highly conical feet, well defined pontil marks and the majority have folded rims. Later in the century the feet tended to be thicker, flatter and folded rims virtually disappear. By 1800 more and more feet have ground pontil marks. The feet of these eighteenth century glasses usually show distinct circumferential flow lines and have a very slight irregular under surface. By the mid-nineteenth century the feet are once again fairly thin, have a very smooth under surface and many good quality glasses are star cut underneath. The pontil is almost invariably ground out. By the late nineteenth century and into the twentieth century the pontil mark disappears entirely, the under surface is very smooth and free from flow lines. Frequently there is a shaped profile so that the edge of the foot is not in contact with whatever surface the glass stands on.

14 A wine glass c. 1730. It is 7 inches in height and has a moulded trumpet bowl on a domed and folded foot. Pilkington Glass Museum, St Helens.

During the early years of the nineteenth century many small wine glasses, up to about 4 inches in height, were made with folded feet. It is commonly thought that any glass with a folded foot must be eighteenth century, but this is not so. The style of the glass must be taken into account when assessing age.

There is one other characteristic mark to be found on the underside of the feet of glasses. This is a capital T or Y mark impressed into a flat foot with no sign of a pontil mark. This was caused by a springloaded instrument, called a 'gadget', that succeeded the pontil iron as a means of holding the glass while it was finished off. It was much easier to use, since the glass was not firmly fixed to it as it was to the pontil iron. Occasionally one may see two parallel lines on the upper

15 The typical Y mark left by the 'gadget' which was used as an alternative to the pontil iron during the nineteenth century.

375

surface of the foot, either side of the stem, where the arms of the gadget pressed into the still soft glass.

The folded foot was inherited from Venetian glassmaking. The fine 'cristallo' of the Venetians was generally very thinly blown, and as the foot was also blown, extra strength was required at its edge to prevent it being damaged. This was achieved by turning the rim to produce what was, in effect, a hem. English glassmakers continued this practice for a long time until the thicker foot became popular, when the extra strength that was inherent in this type of foot obviated the need for a folded edge. The wisdom of all this is apparent if you stand several eighteenth century glasses side by side. When touching each other it will be seen that the edges of the feet come into contact first, the bowls not touching at all. Now try the same thing with modern glasses. This time the sides of the bowls will touch first. Although this fact gives modern glasses that difference of balance which is one of the main contrasts between the twentieth and eighteenth centuries, to have bowls in contact is more practical since these glasses are less likely to get damaged. The edges of the feet of antique glasses coming into contact with each other must have been the major cause of damage to them.

16 A toasting glass c. 1760. It consists of a drawn trumpet bowl on a tall slender plain stem and a plain foot.

The pontil mark

This, I find, is another very common factor in the mis-dating of drinking glasses. The pontil mark, a circular rough mark in the centre of the underside of the foot, is only a sign of the method by which the glass was made. If a glass is made in that fashion today, and most handmade glasses are, then it will have a pontil mark. It is the practice nowadays to remove it by grinding and polishing, but that does not alter the principle. Since practically all glass in the eighteenth century was finished on a pontil iron I expect such glass to show signs of this. Therefore eighteenth century glass should show evidence of the use of a pontil iron, but signs of the use of a pontil iron does not of itself guarantee that a glass is antique.

The ground pontil became necessary as the eighteenth century gave way to the nineteenth, and the feet of glasses were made progressively flatter. Unground, the mark could protrude and prevent the glass sitting properly on a flat surface. In glasses of high quality it would also be normal to give a glass that extra finish by polishing out the pontil mark. The earliest evidence I have come across of this practice dates from about 1760.

17 Three fragments of late sixteenth or early seventeenth century drinking glasses. (Left) The foot and knopped stem of a wine glass. (Centre) The foot rim and high kick-in base of a tall beaker which probably had tapering straight sides. This style was also made in Germany, and some reconstructions were produced in the 1920's by Powell's Whitefriars Glassworks from fragments found in Surrey. (Right) A wine glass base with a flat knop. This illustration and **18** overleaf demonstrate the varying shades of the coarse, common glassware known as 'green' glass. Ashmolean Museum, Oxford.

18 *Above:* Three fragments of
late sixteenth or early
seventeenth century glass.
(Left) A wrythen bottle.
(Centre) The neck of a larger
wrythen bottle. (Right) The
base and part of the body of
a barrel-shaped beaker.
Ashmolean Museum, Oxford.

19 *Opposite:* A small cream
jug in amethyst glass with an
applied handle. This is
probably from Bristol,
c. 1790. L. M. Bickerton Esq.,
Worthing.

380

20 *Opposite:* A Richardson's
jug in white glass with a
trailing handle gilded to
imitate a snake, *c.* 1860. The
original drawing for this
pattern survives. Miss A.
Carwardine.

The bowl

Most modern glasses are blown into moulds, even those made
by hand on a blowing iron. This produces the desired shape
consistently without the need for hand finishing. The interior
of the mould will have an almost mirror finish so that the
finished product will have a similar surface. Antique glasses
which were free blown and then shaped by hand exhibit
several characteristics which are different from modern ones.
Since the glass did not take its smoothness from a mould there
are usually striations and flow lines visible in the glass. These
are usually more or less at right angles to the vertical axis.
When the bubble forming the bowl was cut from the blowing
iron with a pair of shears it nearly always left a mark which can
be detected by either a slight step in the rim or a slight
thickening of the edge at the point of separation. However
slight these may be they can usually be detected by turning the
glass around against the light. The other sign of a handmade
glass is the presence of marks in the bowl which are generally
parallel to the vertical axis and were caused by the tool with
which the glassmaker produced the finished shape of the bowl.
Again, these can generally only be seen by looking through the
glass from the inside of the bowl, whilst turning it against the
light. These marks tend to be more noticeable in thinly blown

21 Three plain stem wine
glasses all with folded feet
c. 1750. (Left) An engraved
ogee bowl. (Centre) A drawn
trumpet bowl with a plain
air stem containing an air
tear. (Right) A bell bowl.

glasses of the first half of the eighteenth century and are less often seen as the century progresses.

Some glasses with elaborately moulded patterns on the bowl have poor definition at either the rim or the base. This is because as the glass is inflated into the mould the temperature drops and the glass becomes less plastic. Since the rate of expansion was limited by the power of human lungs, the glass blower would not always have enough strength to produce a clear impression over the whole surface of the mould. The first part to come into contact with the pattern while it is still hot picks up a good impression; the last part making contact may be indistinct. It depends so much on the skill of the blower.

Colour and impurities

Another topic we need to examine, and one which is open to much discussion and different interpretations amongst collectors, is the relevance and importance of colour in old glass.

Although Ravenscroft's glass was noted by Dr. Plot as being 'hard, durable and whiter than any from Venice' it would not compare in clarity with modern crystal glass. The state of chemical knowledge in the late seventeenth and early eighteenth centuries was such that the impurities in silica which produce the tints could not be properly controlled or accurately removed. I am sure that every glassmaker's ambition was to produce a glass which was white and clear and every so often a batch would be melted that produced such a glass. In the great majority of cases, however, a wide variety of black, green, yellow and blue tints occurs in old glassware. The tint in

22 *Above:* Three dram glasses. (Left) An ovoid bowl on a plain stem and oversewn foot, *c.* 1750. (Centre) An engraved round bowl on a plain stem and foot, *c.* 1750. (Right) A ribbed ovoid bowl and stem on a plain foot, *c.* 1770.

Opposite: **Bowl shapes of drinking glasses** (Part one).
1, 2 The narrowest and widest variations of round funnel bowls.
3 The round funnel bowl of an ale glass.
4 The round funnel bowl of a Continental glass. Its sides are more parallel than 3 and has a fuller base.
5, 6 The narrowest and widest variations in wine glasses of ogee bowls.
7 Ogee bowl of an ale glass.
8 A double ogee or pan-type bowl.
9 A double ogee or saucer-topped bowl.
10 A double ogee or cup-topped bowl. This occurs rarely on baluster stem glasses.
11 A shallow-lipped double ogee bowl. This is most commonly found on sweetmeat glasses.

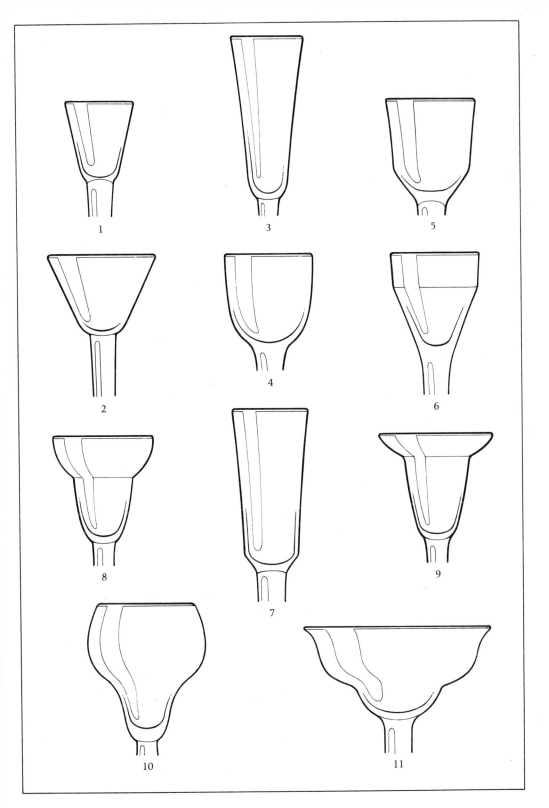

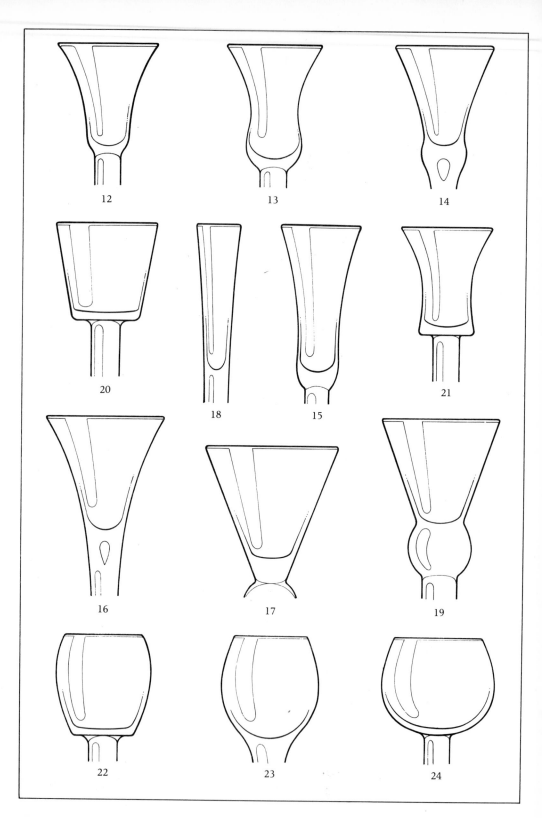

Opposite: **Bowl shapes of drinking glasses** (Part two).
12 A bell bowl.
13 A waisted bell bowl.
14 An intermediate form of bell bowl midway between the drawn trumpet bowl and the true bell bowl. It is solid at its base and usually has an air tear.
15 A bell bowl of an ale glass.
16 One of the most common forms of drawn trumpet bowl.
17 A straight-sided funnel bowl.
18 A narrow drawn trumpet bowl. This rare shape usually occurs on ratafia glasses.
19 A thistle bowl, usually solid at the base.
20 A bucket bowl.
21 A waisted bucket bowl.
22 A barrel bowl. This is most commonly found in the nineteenth century.
23 An ovoid bowl.
24 A cup bowl, most often found on mead glasses.

any particular glass, viewed in isolation, is not always easy to see, but if several are stood side by side the differences are much more apparent.

Some people consider that green or yellow tints are an indication that a glass is made of soda glass rather than lead glass. While soda glasses are frequently of these colours, it is not necessarily true. I have seen English soda glasses of as clear a colour as any lead glass, and lead glass of a distinct green hue. While these undesirable colours could be corrected with the use of neutralising agents (manganese was the commonest of these), the problem was minimised by using sand of the highest known purity. Kings Lynn in Norfolk was one of the best sources, and sand from this region was shipped to most glassmaking areas. Many collectors consider a black or blue tint in antique glass to be desirable, and quite a lot of early baluster stem glasses are of a dark metal. All of this means that the newcomer to glass collecting faces a problem when attempting to tell lead glass from soda glass. The surest way is to apply ultra-violet light to the glass, when soda glass will give off a strong yellowish green reflection, while lead glass shines with a purple light. Until recently ultra-violet lights were bulky and expensive, but there are now several lightweight battery powered lamps on the market so that such a test may be conveniently be carried out anywhere.

By the latter part of the eighteenth century technical and chemical improvements ensured that the metal used was of a high quality and glass from that time onwards became consistently whiter and clearer.

In many glasses of the eighteenth century one can see small lumps of foreign matter which are usually referred to as seeds. These are either pieces of undissolved raw materials or impurities from the furnace finding their way into the glass pot.

In assessing the genuineness of early glass, any or all of these faults or signs may be present. The presence or absence of any one is not sufficient to prove the glass genuine or otherwise, but an examination taking account of all the factors I have mentioned is essential to arrive at a correct appraisal.

Proportion, weight and sound

Proportion and balance are other factors to be considered in assessing old glass, but this is difficult to explain. I am sure it is a skill acquired by looking at many glasses over a long period. I will have more to say about this when discussing fakes and reproductions. I occasionally see a glass which I know instinctively is not true to its apparent period, but am not able to say why without detailed examination. Another dilemma facing the newcomer to glass collecting is how to tell lead glass from soda glass. In the previous section I discussed how to do this by using ultra-violet light, but as an alternative one can resort to more elementary tests. Given two glasses of about the same size, the lead glass example will generally be noticeably heavier than its soda glass counterpart. With some experience one develops an idea of what the weight of a glass will be on picking it up. Soda glass invariably feels lighter than one expects. It is for this reason that the novice should handle as many pieces of glassware as possible, since it is by this means that one comes to judge weight, texture and balance; all factors that enable a correct assessment to be made of antique glassware.

As I have already mentioned, soda glass is often of a noticeable yellowish green tint, but this should never be taken as proof one way or the other on its own. The other factor one may wish to distinguish lead from soda is that of the ring or sound of a glass. Lead glass vessels usually give off a clear ringing sound when lightly struck. This sound depends very much on the size and thickness of the glass, but with large, thinly blown items the sound can be like that of a bell, continuing for a minute or more. Soda glass, on the other hand, produces either a dull thud or a sharp sound which dies away almost instantly when struck in the same way. This, like the other points mentioned, is not infallible since a short, thick lead glass is inflexible and will not produce the characteristic ring. It is rather a combination of all these points which will enable one to differentiate lead from soda; weight, colour, sound. One final comment; be circumspect when striking glass which is not yet yours, it is quite fragile.

Returning to our examination of eighteenth century styles in glass we begin with the period of plain baluster stemmed glasses.

Baluster stems

The expression 'baluster stem' applies to a wide variety of drinking glasses which have in common the fact that the stems are composed of one or more shaped sections which are commonly called knops. These knops are identified by different names, some of which specifically include the word baluster. Thus the word baluster is both a generic noun to cover all glasses with these knop formations and a specific word when applied to knops termed 'true' or 'inverted' balusters, the word baluster being an architectural term for the vertical section of a balustrade, which has a gradually changing section leading to a swelling at either the top or the base.

This group of glasses merits consideration in some detail, since they endured for about fifty years, changing their character considerably over this period. For the sake of simplicity most authorities group these as heavy baluster, light baluster and balustroid, but not everyone groups the same glasses under the same heading. Thus, what is heavy baluster in one book is light baluster in another, while different writers illustrate similar glasses under the titles light baluster and balustroid.

My own experience indicates that there is considerable overlapping of the styles and many transitional glasses which fit precisely into none of the accepted categories.

The baluster stems generally are the last demonstration of the Venetian tradition in English glassmaking. Although the glasses we are talking about—those from 1690 onwards—are very different in character from their Venetian forebears, the more or less elaborate stem formulations derive directly from that Venetian tradition. The decorative aspect of the glass is created in the making rather than in any subsequent operation. The knops of the stems take their inspiration from the elaborate blown and moulded knopped stems of Venetian glasses. Initially, however, they had a much more puritanical aspect. The earliest of the truly English baluster stems were the inverted baluster. In these we find round funnel or funnel bowls set on heavy, squat inverted baluster stems. These glasses have a proportion that marks them out from similar glasses of only ten or fifteen years later. Most of these can truly be termed 'double flint'. Some of the 'single' flint examples show even more sympathy with the Venetian style. These latter have wide, thinly blown round funnel bowls and folded feet, which have the narrowest of turning at the edge, a feature seen in most Venetian made glasses. Although the physical size and weight of these glasses can vary considerably, from 12 inches to 13 inches tall and 10 lbs. or so in weight to 5 inches and 4 to 5 ozs. or so in weight, there is a character which runs through the whole group, putting them all firmly in the category called 'heavy baluster'.

Glasses in the heavy baluster style continued in production until about 1725, and during that period a number of different knop shapes made their appearance. Most of them are self-descriptive: thus we get acorn knops, egg knops, mushroom knops and so on. Generally the stems of the heavy baluster

group consist of one knop only, with the knop forming the major part of the stem. Where there is more than one knop it is usually no more than a plain round knop at the base of the stem. The majority of glasses of this period have bowls which are solid at the base, while most feet are of the folded conical variety. Domed feet and plain feet are in the minority.

The heavy proportions of these glasses gave way to another group of baluster stemmed glasses which date generally from about 1720 to 1735. These are generally called light baluster, and again this is not so much a comment on their weight as their general proportions and character. From about 1720 drinking glasses tended to become more slender relative to their height. Where before the knop took up practically all the stem when there was only one knop involved, it now took up only part of the stem and parallel plain sections make up the rest. More importantly, stems now appear which consist of more than one knop, usually one of the types mentioned above in conjunction with an inverted or true baluster section. A popular one was the annulated knop, which consists of a series of layers

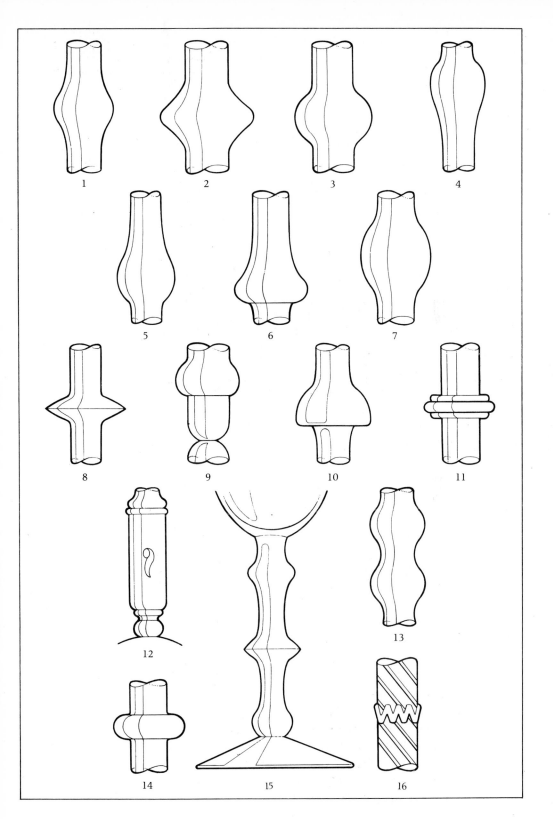

diminishing in size above and below the central one. This type, although rare in heavy baluster glasses, had as many as seven layers, but on light baluster stems it was almost always limited to three rings. While the bell bowl was occasionally met with on heavy baluster glasses, it became one of the most popular types on light balusters. The curved and flared sides of this type of bowl always seem to me to add to the lightness of the style.

These were not quite the last glasses to depend on the well defined knop formation for their decoration; that was reserved for the Newcastle light balusters which will be discussed later. For general use the light balusters gave way to the balustroid group of glasses. The name derives from the fact that although they incorporate knops in the stems the knops themselves are debased in style and usually appear as interruptions in a plain stem rather than the most important part of the stem.

Balustroids fall into three sub-divisions, and cover the period from about 1730 to 1750. The first of these is a group of glasses which still have fairly elaborately shaped stems, generally incorporating an angular knop, an inverted baluster and a base knop. However, they differ markedly from the light baluster in that the stems are usually almost hollow since they contain large and elongated air tears, the general outline is not so well defined, they lack the elegance of the true light baluster

24 *Left:* An ale glass, *c.* 1710. It consists of a tall bowl on a collar above a small spherical knop, true baluster stem and folded conical foot.

25 *Centre:* A light baluster wine glass, *c.* 1720. A bell bowl on a double drop knop stem and a folded foot.

26 *Above:* A light baluster wine glass, *c.* 1725. A bell bowl, the stem having a dumb-bell knop between two ball drop knops. There is a folded foot.

27 *Above:* A wine glass, c. 1740. A drawn trumpet bowl with a plain stem section over a rudimentary ball knop and a large ball knop containing air beads. There is a domed plain foot.

28 *Centre:* A light baluster wine glass, c. 1730. The bell bowl surmounts a collar and a true baluster stem and a base knop. There is a domed and folded foot.

29 *Right:* A sweetmeat glass, c. 1730. The folded rim of the double ogee bowl is decorated with loops which end in prunts. The baluster stem has an annulated knop over a plain section and a base knop. There is a domed and folded foot.

and, most noticeable, they are generally not so well made. This last characteristic is even more true of the next sub-division in the group. The glass is usually of a distinct yellow or greenish tint. It has noticeable striations or flow lines in the metal, and often contains small lumps of impurities or raw material which has not properly melted. It was as if these glasses originated in glasshouses where the operatives were not experienced, or they were quickly made for a cheap market. I am sure they all date from a relatively short period, but too many have survived for us to believe that they all came from one source. They are basically plain stemmed glasses which have one, two or three very simple or rudimentary round knops. The plain sections are often irregular and tapering. It is in this group, however, that the ogee bowl makes its appearance in any quantity. This is a straight-sided bowl with a sharp incurve at the base.

It is debatable whether the third division of this group should be related to the balustroids or the plain stems. Basically they are glasses which have similarly knopped stems to the group above, but they differ in two respects. The knops are more usually angular knops rather than round ones and the glasses are very much better made and of a better colour. This last aspect has a much closer affinity with the truly plain stem glasses which followed them. In any case this was, for all

practical purposes the last expression of knopped stem glasses as a general manufacture.

I mentioned earlier that there seem to be some transitional types, and the most noticeable of these are glasses that occasionally turn up which display the most obvious characteristics of both light baluster and balustroid glasses. They have well-defined knops, solid stems and good metal, but their general weight, balance and style seems to tie them in with the balustroid group. Whether they represent a step forward or the last expression of a passing style is hard to say.

Although glassmaking had firmly established itself in several provincial centres by the early eighteenth century, London was still the centre of influence and the source of taste and style. Given the conservatism of the provinces and the slowness of communication, the overlap of changing styles is understandable. What London did today would take several years before being generally adopted throughout the country. One startling exception to this, however, was a group of glasses I have already referred to in passing, the Newcastle light balusters.

By 1740 glasses with knopped stems had all but gone out of fashion, but about this time a new style of glass appeared in

30 *Above:* Three balustroid wine glasses, all with folded feet, *c.* 1740. (Left) A round funnel bowl, a stem with shoulder and centre knops. (Centre) A bell bowl, a stem with a plain section over an inverted baluster. (Right) A bell bowl with two knops.

31 *Opposite above:* A wine glass, *c.* 1740. A bell bowl surmounting an angular knop over a rudimentary inverted baluster stem.

32 *Opposite below:* Three Newcastle baluster wine glasses, all with plain feet, *c.* 1750. (Left) A round funnel bowl. Its stem has a ball knop over an inverted baluster. (Centre) A bell bowl engraved with a foliate border. The stem has four knops. (Right) A drawn trumpet bowl on a plain section over an inverted baluster stem with air beads.

which elaborately knopped stems were the most important feature. These are commonly associated with Newcastle-on-Tyne, although I can find no positive evidence for this association. In fact, books published early in this century make no connection between these glasses and Newcastle. W. A. Thorpe in his *History of English and Irish Glass* published in 1929, appears to be the first author to make the attribution, but he gives no firm evidence to support the idea. Other authors subsequently made the same connection, but again I can find no firm evidence to support the idea. There are, however, certain inferences that may be drawn as to their origin, but let us first consider what makes these glasses so distinctive. (See illustrations **32-35**.)

Whereas the average height of light baluster glasses is $6\frac{1}{2}$ inches to $6\frac{3}{4}$ inches, the 'Newcastle' type averages $7\frac{1}{2}$ inches. While the light balusters have all the standard bowl types, the Newcastle glasses have predominantly wide round funnel bowls, the remainder being mostly trumpet bowls. The metal is of a uniform whiteness and of high quality, but it is the stems which are most distinctive. They are tall and slender incorporating as many as five different knops. Air beads in the knops are a frequent feature. The quality and style are

consistent throughout the whole group. So why should they be attributed to Newcastle?

As we have shown, Newcastle was one of the important glassmaking centres of the country. It undoubtedly made all the other styles of glass as they became popular throughout the eighteenth century and there is generally nothing to distinguish the Newcastle product from that made anywhere else. The two important factors about the glasses under discussion are their uniform quality and the fact that they date from a period when baluster stems had generally gone out of fashion. By 1740 the knops of baluster stems had generally declined to become vague swellings in otherwise plain stems, but the Newcastle glasses were just making their appearance and were to continue for another twenty-five years. This suggests to me glasses made in a provincial centre rather than London, and made for a particular reason or market. It is an interesting fact that most of these glasses are engraved, and there is little doubt that most of the engraving was carried out in Holland. Inscriptions are usually in Dutch and a number of signed pieces have survived, the signatures being of well-known Dutch engravers. On closer examination it will be discovered that although these glasses are undoubtedly English, using well-

33 *Left:* A Newcastle light baluster wine glass, *c.* 1750. The round funnel bowl is engraved with Baroque foliage. The unusual composite stem has a knopped air twist section over an inverted baluster stem containing air beads. There is a small base knop and a plain foot.

34 *Above:* A Newcastle glass goblet, wheel-engraved in Holland. The inscription wishes happiness to the newly married Christina and Ysbrant Cardinaal, 18 April 1741. Pilkington Glass Museum, St Helens.

35 A Newcastle wine glass, wheel-engraved in Holland. It bears the arms of William IV of Orange, who married Anne, daughter of George II, in 1734.

known English shapes, the overall effect is more closely allied to the Nuremberg goblets (in silver and glass) made in Germany in the fifteenth to seventeenth centuries, and 'façon de Venise' goblets made in the Netherlands during the seventeenth century. That there was a well-established trade between Newcastle and Holland in the eighteenth century is on record.

We can now build up a picture of a product being deliberately developed to satisfy a specific demand from an overseas market. All these factors would certainly tend to make Newcastle a very likely source of these glasses. One final point: there are several glasses of this group enamelled in colours by the Beilby family, who were working in Newcastle in the 1760's and 1770's. It is surely most likely that they used locally made glass.

Plain stems

Much significance has been placed by other writers on the effect of the Excise Duty imposed on glassmaking by an Act of 1745. This was introduced to raise revenue to pay for the wars being waged in Europe by George II. It consisted of a sum of 9/4d (47p) on each hundredweight of metal for making crown plate and flint glass, i.e. window glass and vessel glass, while bottle glass attracted a duty of 2/4d (12p) per hundredweight. The tax was thus levied on the metal coming from the glass pot, not the finished article, so that the specific gravity of the metal became an important consideration.

Specific gravity affects volume in relation to weight, the higher the specific gravity the lower the volume. Since lead has a high specific gravity it follows that the more lead there was in glass the smaller the volume per pound weight. As the tax was levied on weight, the glassmakers could mitigate slightly its effect by decreasing the lead content, thereby increasing the volume. This would give them more material per pound weight to turn into finished vessels. However, I do not think that this had quite so much effect on design as has been represented. The tendency towards smaller, lighter and less elaborate glasses was already well advanced before the duty was introduced. Fashion is a pendulum which swings between extremes of elaboration and plainness. It affects most things, particularly those for domestic use, and glassware was only following the trend that can be seen, for example, in furniture and silver of the same period. The excise may well have accelerated that trend, but was not, by itself, entirely responsible for it.

A type of glass occasionally turns up which has a hollow

stem, virtually a tube between bowl and foot. These are sometimes claimed to be glasses specifically designed to defeat the excise by reducing weight to a minimum. If this was the case they should be much more common than they are in relation to other glasses of the period which have survived. In any case the practice of incorporating air into the stems of glasses had been used since the days of the heavy balusters. When a distinctive feature such as these tubular stems occurs on glasses only occasionally I am more inclined to think that it is the product of one particular glasshouse rather than something which was in widespread use by the glass trade.

By the middle of the eighteenth century plain stemmed glasses had become the most commonly produced, and the classic patterns of the period are the drawn trumpet bowl on a plain stem containing an air tear, and the bell bowl on plain stem which often contains an air tear where the bowl joins the stem. The former are widely known as 'tear glasses' although, as I have said, the idea of using air as a decorative feature in glass was by no means confined to this particular style.

By this time the capacity of stemmed drinking glasses averaged between 2 and 3 fluid ounces, and many people, on first becoming interested in eighteenth-century glass, comment on this, assuming that the contents would be much stronger than the equivalent beverages today, and that their owners therefore drank less. This is not so. Most of the glasses we collect today were made as wine glasses, and the alcoholic strength of wine was the same then as now, since it is achieved naturally. Size was dictated rather by what was considered socially correct than by the strength of the drink to be consumed. After all, it is not the amount which a glass holds which makes one drunk, but rather the number of times it is filled up. Our attitude to these small capacity glasses is influenced, I am sure, by the glasses we accept as normal today. In mid-Victorian times, by contrast, large wine glasses were made which would be considered gross today. Having said this, one does occasionally come across very large glasses all through the eighteenth century but they do not appear to have been in general use.

Silesian stems

Before we go on to examine the styles of the second half of the eighteenth century there is one group of glasses that we have not yet considered. They have tapering moulded stems and take their name from Silesia, an important glassmaking region of Germany which became Czechoslovakia after the First

36 *Opposite above left:* A wine glass, *c.* 1720. It comprises a round funnel bowl on a ball knop over a hollow six-sided Silesian stem and a plain foot.

37 *Opposite above centre:* A Silesian-stem wine glass. This is an example of the continental origin from which the preceding illustration derives; compare the relative proportions of the stem to the bowl.

38 *Opposite above right:* A wine glass, *c.* 1725. The bell bowl is on a six-sided Silesian stem and folded foot.

39 *Opposite below left:* A sweetmeat glass, *c.* 1740. The ribbed pan-topped bowl is on an eight-sided Silesian stem and a domed and ribbed foot.

40 *Opposite below right:* A candlestick, *c.* 1720. The semi-solid Silesian stem has eight sides; there are large studs on the shoulder above it, and below this are knops containing rows of tears. There are larger studs on the domed foot. Pilkington Museum of Glass, St Helens.

World War. They don't fit into the natural progression of English styles but were introduced as a compliment, to mark the accession of George I who came from Germany. They derive from a style which was common in Germany but the English glassmakers soon managed to endow it with a native character that immediately distinguishes it from its Continental original. The earliest ones had four-sided square stems and a very small number have survived which bear, in embossed letters round the shoulder the words 'God Save the King' or 'God Bless the King' and sometimes a crown as well. These commemorate the accession of George I and must therefore date from about 1714. Soon afterwards the English glassmakers modified these stems to six and eight sides. They fall into two groups. One consists of glasses of very light weight, usually having a funnel bowl on a six-sided stem, and not particularly well made. The other group is generally of very high quality, heavy, and of good colour, with several bowl shapes on both six- and eight-sided stems. They often have diamonds or stars clearly moulded at the top of each corner of the stem.

The main distinction between the English and Continental versions is that the latter are of soda metal and the bowls usually dominate the stems, which are rarely well-defined. The English glasses, even the lightweight ones, are lead glass, the

41 Three air twist glasses, all c. 1760. (Left) A drawn trumpet bowl on a multi-ply spiral air twist stem on a folded foot. (Centre) A bell bowl on a mixed-twist air stem with central air gauze surrounded by a two-strand opaque-twist spiral. There is a plain foot. (Right) A round funnel bowl on an air twist stem with shoulder and centre knops. There is a plain foot.

42 *Below:* A wine glass, *c.* 1760. The bell bowl is on an air twist stem with an applied vermicular collar. There is a plain foot. Notice how some of the air threads peter out before reaching the base of the stem and that the air threads start in the solid base of the bowl. This latter feature shows it to be a two-piece glass.

43 *Centre:* An ale glass, *c.* 1760. The deep round funnel bowl is engraved with hops and (unusually) four ears of barley. There is a double-series air twist stem and a plain foot.

44 *Right:* A wine glass, *c.* 1760. It has an engraved drawn trumpet bowl, 'mercury' twist stem and a plain foot. This is in fact an air twist pattern, but its highly reflective nature explains the name of the stem.

stems are nearly always crisply moulded and the bowls are more in balance with the stems. On drinking glasses the style appears to have been in production for about twenty years before going out of fashion in the 1740's. Silesian stems did survive, however, on sweetmeat glasses, candlesticks and tazzas until the 1760's. I think that this was probably because these items had their counterparts in silver which continued to be made with Silesian style stems until late into the century.

Air twist stems

The idea of incorporating air into the stems of drinking glasses was not a new one. Glassmakers had long been aware of the fact that a bubble of air trapped in glass could be drawn out and elongated as the glass was manipulated. What was novel was the idea of arranging a series of air bubbles so that the elongation produced a definite pattern. When this technique was first developed is uncertain, but it was certainly being practised during the first half of the eighteenth century. F. Buckley recorded a glass bearing the date 1737 and another glass which went through one of the London sale rooms in 1979 was dated 1742. This latter was of the conventional drawn trumpet bowl type, but it had a domed foot, which is unusual.

Although this method of decoration was known before 1750

it was not until after that date that changing fashion and a demand for something more decorative created a climate which led to its general adoption. The third quarter of the eighteenth century produced the highest standards of aesthetic taste and an increasingly affluent society was in a mood to patronise artists, designers and craftsmen. A reaction set in against the plainness of the 1740's and paved the way for rococo and chinoiserie. There was no going back to the elaborately knopped and heavy glasses of the early eighteenth century. The Excise Act with its inhibiting effect on size, and the new elegance, demanded something different. It was in this context that the air twist and opaque twist styles of glassmaking became universally popular and cut glass found a market in spite of its price.

The commonest pattern of air twist stem is that known as a multi-ply spiral, which is a circle of air threads drawn out and twisted so that it fills the stem. Less common are the double series patterns that usually consist of a central twisted column of air threads surrounded by two opposed spiral threads. The other type of air pattern is that generally called 'mercury' twist. This is invariably composed of two thick strands of air, having a rectangular cross-section, twisted into a tight cork-screw. This pattern has a highly reflective quality which gives the air threads a silvery metallic appearance, and hence their name.

Because the air bubbles from which air twist stems were produced had a finite volume, there was a limit to how far they could be drawn out without breaking up or disappearing. It is not uncommon to come across air twist wine glasses where one or more of the individual strands terminate before it reaches the foot of the glass. Most air twist glasses are two-piece glasses, so that the stem of each one is individually made. For three-piece glasses the stems were made in lengths and then cut to size. Because of the limitations already described these lengths were short compared to the lengths produced for the opaque twist glasses discussed in the next section.

Having referred to dated glasses in this section, it would be convenient at this point to discuss the dating of glass generally. Most collectable antiques are fairly accurately identifiable and dateable. Silver has its hallmarks, pottery and porcelain their factory marks and pattern numbers, clock makers are well researched, and so on. Glass, however, is anonymous stuff and although the periods covering the principal styles have been identified, the actual maker and date of manufacture can only rarely be determined. This is why dated pieces, or glasses carrying inscriptions relating to known events are so important. They give us reference points to which we can relate other similar glasses. For the same reason, registration marks are also useful (see p. 495).

Opaque twist stems

I use this term out of personal preference, although 'enamel twist' and 'cotton twist' are other terms that are equally popular. All these terms describe that large quantity of eighteenth-century glasses which have a pattern of twisted white threads running through the stem. In a sense this could be described as a reversion to Venetian glassmaking, since this method of glass decoration was a peculiarly Venetian invention of the sixteenth century. They incorporated these lacy white patterns into glass vessels of all types under the names 'latticinio' or 'vetro di trina'. The fact that opaque twist and air twist complemented each other so well brought the style to prominence.

Although the general effect was the same as air twist, the method of producing it was quite different. In this case a series of white glass rods (called enamel) are set into a mould which is then filled with molten clear glass. When this is set the resultant block is removed from the mould and coated in clear

45 Three opaque-twist wine glasses, all with plain feet, *c*. 1760. (Left) A 'Lynn' wine glass which has a round funnel bowl with the distinctive horizontal rings associated with its Kings Lynn origin. (Centre) A drawn trumpet bowl. (Right) A round funnel bowl with moulded flutes.

glass. It is this mass which is re-heated, drawn and twisted to produce the rods from which the stems of glasses will be cut. Apsley Pellatt in his book *Curiosities of Glassmaking* gives a detailed account of this process, stating that lengths of up to sixty or seventy feet could be drawn.

Since the process was one of assembly rather than manipulation it meant that much more elaborate patterns could be achieved than was the case with air twist stems; limited only by the ingenuity of the glassmaker. Some collectors spend their time searching for as many variations of these stems as possible.

In addition to the white rods used to create these patterns coloured rods were sometimes used. These produced what are usually referred to as 'colour twist' glasses. The usual colours were red, blue, green and yellow, in descending order of frequency. Occasionally glasses appear with several colours in the stem, and these are called 'tartan' twist. Technically I can see no reason why it should be more difficult to include coloured threads among the white ones, but the fact remains that colour twist wine glasses account for a very small percentage of those that have survived. Perhaps they were not popular with the customer.

Opaque twist glasses are usually classified as having single, double or triple series twists. Where there is only one strand of enamel running through the stem this is clearly single series, but it is also possible to have a pattern consisting of a number of threads which is still single series. The criterion is that all the threads should form part of one distinct pattern. When a central pattern of one style, say a straight multi-strand tube, is surrounded by a spiral consisting of a series of threads in parallel, this is clearly double series. Three separate and distinct patterns gives a triple series twist, but this is extremely rare.

The English style of opaque twist and colour twist glasses was much copied on the Continent towards the end of the eighteenth century but they are fairly easy to distinguish, since they are made of soda glass, the bowl shapes are slightly different and the threads of colour are translucent. Bell bowls are narrower and flare more at the rim. Round funnel bowls have more parallel sides and are fuller in the base than English ones.

Although F. Buckley reported an opaque twist glass with a date as early as 1747 the bulk of these date from after 1750 and were contemporary with the air twist types. In 1777 another Excise Act doubled the duty on flint glass and introduced a new tax of 18/8d (93p) per cwt. on enamel glass. This must

46, 47 Two wine glasses, c. 1760. (Top) This bucket bowl, opaque-twist air stem with two spiral gauzes and plain foot is an unusual combination. (Above) A double ogee, or pan-top, bowl with faint vertical moulded flutes, a centre-knopped opaque-twist stem and a plain foot.

48 *Top:* A close-up view of an incised-twist air stem.

49 *Above:* A wine glass, *c.* 1750. The round funnel bowl is dimpled at the base; there is an incised-twist stem and a plain foot.

have had a harmful effect on the trade in opaque twist glasses anyway, but it also coincided with another major change of style which put them quite out of favour. This was the introduction of cut or facet stem glasses.

Before going on to look at these in detail, there are three variations of the opaque twist/air twist period to consider.

Incised twist stems

For a short period in the middle of the eighteenth century, about 1750 to 1765, glasses were made with finely ribbed and twisted stems, and these are called incised twist. There are amongst them some well-made lead glass examples, but the majority are of indifferent quality, many of them being made of soda glass. They were fairly easy to make and it is likely that they were made as a cheap imitation of air twist glasses, as from a distance the appearance is similar. Many of the lead metal incised twist glasses have tapering, round funnel bowls which are distinctly dimple moulded at the base. This suggests to me a common origin and that they all originated from one glasshouse.

Mixed twist stems

As the name suggests, these are glasses which contain both air and opaque threads. Mostly these are white threads, but a few have survived with air threads in conjunction with colour or white and colour threads. The distinguishing characteristic of a mixed twist glass is that the two elements of the pattern should be distinctly separate. Either a central air pattern surrounded by a different pattern of opaque threads, or the reverse of this is a true mixed twist. I make this point because I occasionally have glasses represented to me as mixed twist when a single insubstantial thread of air follows closely the line of one of the strands of the opaque twist pattern. This, I am sure, was unintentional and was an accident of manufacture.

Churchill's Glass Notes published annually between 1946 and 1956, gave comprehensive check lists of different types of glass and the rarity of mixed twists is demonstrated by the fact that of all the glasses in the air/opaque categories which are recorded, the mixed twist ones account for only 3·2%.

Composite stems

A composite stem glass may be described as one which has a stem containing sections of more than one recognisable style. The majority have stems consisting of an air twist section and a plain section, but opaque and plain sections are known. One

403

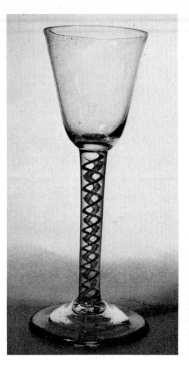

very rare glass has air and opaque sections separated by a central knop. When the air twist section is uppermost it usually runs into a large knop containing a ring of air beads before changing to a plain stem. They are usually quite striking glasses, but again from Churchill's check lists, account for only 6·5% of glasses with twist stems. It is not easy to determine whether they were made throughout the period of popularity of twist stem glasses or were confined to a few years during that period.

Facet stems

The last quarter of the eighteenth century saw the introduction of a totally new style of decoration, the cut or facet stem. For the whole of the eighteenth century the decorative aspect of drinking glasses had been incorporated during manufacture, either the external decoration produced by knops or the internal decoration of the air and opaque twist stems. Now, for the first time, the essential character of the glass was achieved by an applied technique.

Applied decorations such as engraving, gilding and enamelling had been practised at various times throughout the century, but they could be applied to any style of glass. With this last group, the decoration is the style.

Throughout the century cut glass had been made to serve a

50 *Left:* A mixed twist wine glass, *c.* 1760: round funnel bowl, stem with intertwined spiral gauze and a single opaque spiral thread, and plain foot.

51 *Centre:* A composite-stem wine glass, *c.* 1760: a thistle bowl with a solid base over a 'mercury' twist ending in a ball knop, a short air-beaded inverted baluster stem, a plain foot.

52 *Above:* A wine glass, *c.* 1790: a round bowl with everted rim and geometric cutting to the base, a stem cut with vertical flutes and a centre knop cut into diamonds, a plain foot cut into facets and with a scalloped edge.

53 A set of six wine glasses, c. 1790. The round bowls are engraved with an 'egg and dart' border and fine floral sprays. There are diamond-facet cut stems and plain feet.

luxury market. During the early years before a native tradition for glass cutting had grown, craftsmen were imported from Germany. With the imposition of the Excise in 1745 the market for cut glass was limited to an area where price was of no consequence. Cutting meant thick glass, thick glass meant weight, and weight cost money. This is why such articles as were cut for most of the period were luxury articles such as might grace a rich man's house. Chandeliers, candelabra, sweetmeats, dessert services and so on.

Cut stems first make their appearance in any quantity during the 1770's. As we have shown with the air and opaque twists, the techniques were known long before they became universally popular, and I am sure that the same was true of facet stems. How much the Excise of 1777 destroyed the market for opaque twist stems and left the market open for the introduction of facet stems, or how much they were a reflection of changing taste we shall probably never know. Whatever the reason, facet stems became the most popular glasses of the late eighteenth century because with them everybody could afford to have cut glass on their tables at a reasonable price. Reasonable, because the item to be cut (a plain stemmed wine glass) was easy to produce, because it did not have to be made especially thick and heavy to take the decoration, because the cutting was repetitive and did not require very skilled labour,

405

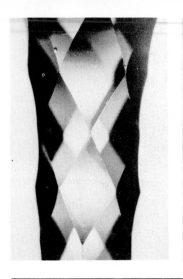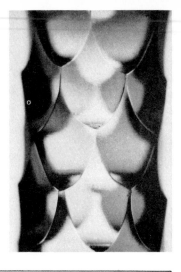

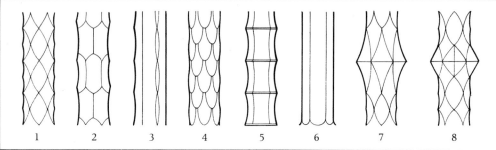

| 1 | 2 | 3 | 4 | 5 | 6 | 7 | 8 |

and because once mastered I am sure the operation was quickly carried out.

I have explained elsewhere in the book how the feet of drinking glasses developed during the century, and I sometimes come across plain stemmed wine glasses of a good clear metal with typically late eighteenth century feet that I am sure were meant to have cut stems but for some reason or another the operation was never carried out.

So much for the background; what of the cutting itself? There are two main types of facet cutting: diamonds and hexagons. Together they account for 80% of all cut stems. The pattern is achieved by first cutting the stem into a number of vertical flutes (six is the usual number) and then cutting a series of slices along each resulting edge, gradually cutting in deeper. The slices meet and the intersecting edges produce either diamonds or hexagons according to the length of the slice.

The remaining glasses in this group have a variety of patterns (see the diagram above) and it often surprises me that collectors do not show the interest in these variations that they show to unusual glasses of other styles. Apart from the

54, 55, 56 *Top:* Close-up views of: (Left) A diamond-facet stem. (Centre) A hexagon-facet stem. (Right) A scale, or shield, cut stem.

Above: **Facet cut stems.**
1 Diamond facets.
2 Hexagon facets.
3 Cut vertical flutes with alternate edges notched.
4 Scale or shield cutting.
5 Cut vertical flutes with band reliefs to produce narrow flat rings.
6 Cut plain vertical flutes.
7 Diamond facets with a central knop cut to plain straight edges.
8 Diamond facets with a swelling knop cut into pointed diamonds.

variations in cutting, the number of sides to the stem can also vary from four to eight. The greater the number of vertical flutes into which the stem is cut, the smaller are the resultant facets.

These glasses also occur with knops in the stems, and this feature also gives rise to variations in cutting. The cutting on the stem is usually carried over onto the base of the bowl and this is called bridge fluting or cutting. A further decorative feature commonly found on cut stem glasses is a band of small round polished circles alternating with crossed lines around the rim of the bowl. This is generally referred to as an 'egg and dart' or OXO border.

One final point of interest about this group is that one occasionally comes across an example with features that are out of character with the period; a folded foot, a domed foot or a drawn trumpet bowl are examples. All these features are more typical of glasses of the mid-eighteenth century and that, I am sure, is what they are. Remember that a facet cut stem starts out as a plain round stem. I think that when these cut stems became popular, people with glasses which were already thirty or forty years old sent them to be 'modernised'. The alternative to this is that these glasses were made with faceted stems in the mid-eighteenth century. If this were the case I would expect to come across far more of them than the two or three which I have seen over a period of many years. If one accepts that they were altered some years after they were made, and given the average collector's reluctance to buy pieces which have had later alterations made to them, should they be considered as desirable as facet cut glasses which are true to their period? I do not consider these as copies meant to deceive, but rather an expression of a domestic custom of the period and they are therefore worthy of attention now.

These glasses constitute the last group of typically eighteenth-century glasses; small bowls on tall stems and wide feet. By 1800 a totally new approach to style was making itself felt.

The glasshouses and glassmakers of the eighteenth century

So far this chapter has dealt only with the product of the eighteenth century and not with the industry itself. This is in contrast to the first chapter which dealt mainly with the developing glass industry. The reason, of course, is that little of the product of those early years has survived but the changing nature and the development of the industry is interesting

57 An example of what I am sure is an earlier glass cut later. A domed foot in conjunction with a drawn trumpet bowl and plain stem would have been uncommon in 1750 but non-existent in 1780, when I think the cutting was done. Had the cutting taken place in 1750 I should expect to find more glasses of that period with cut stems.

because it laid the foundations for the explosion in production during the eighteenth century. That explosion was due to the fact that the glass trade settled down into an orderly and well regulated industry lacking in the drama and excitement of earlier years. In a sense it had got over its growing pains, had settled down and become respectable.

In 1696 Houghton listed eighty-eight glasshouses in England and Wales, of which forty were making bottles and twenty-seven were making flint glass. Of the eighty-eight there were twenty-four in London, nine in the Bristol area, seventeen at Stourbridge and eleven in Newcastle-on-Tyne. Thus these four areas then accounted for 70% of glasshouses known to be working just before the start of the eighteenth century.

During the eighteenth century there are records of twenty-five glasshouses working in London, fifteen in Bristol, fourteen in Stourbridge and sixteen in Newcastle. By the time of the Excise Commission investigation in 1833 these figures had altered to four in London, four in Bristol, seventeen in Stourbridge and thirty-eight in Newcastle. It can be seen from these figures that by the end of the Georgian period glass-making had centred on Newcastle and Stourbridge. Today glassmaking has entirely disappeared from London and Bristol. Some industrial and utilitarian glassmaking survives in the Newcastle area and Stourbridge is the last of the great glassmaking districts still producing good quality domestic flint glass.

I am sometimes asked what antique glassware cost when it was new. This is an interesting question because if one knows what an article costs in relation to earnings when it was made, it is possible to draw conclusions as to what sort of market the object was made for and what class of people were likely to own it.

There are more records surviving today of glass prices during the late seventeenth century and early nineteenth century than there are for the collectable items of the eighteenth century. The main problem, though, is to know exactly what glasses are being referred to. Catalogues giving descriptions and prices before 1800 are virtually non-existent. Our main source of information is from surviving bills and invoices. These seldom list anything other than the mere shape or use of the glass.

The two most complete sources for seventeenth century glass are the list of prices agreed between Ravenscroft and the Glass Sellers Company and the Woburn Abbey invoices for glass supplied to the Duke of Bedford. From these it is possible to show that glassware was generally a rich man's luxury.

In the Ravenscroft/Glass Sellers price list of 29 May 1677 the prices were fixed by the weight of the glasses. Beer glasses, ribbed and plain, weighed 7 oz. and were 1/6d each, white beer glasses, nipped diamone waies, weighed 8 oz. and were 1/8d each. Claret glasses of the same two types weighed 5 oz. and $5\frac{1}{2}$ oz. and were 1/- and 1/3d each. These, of course, were prices to the Glass Sellers. The retail prices were higher, and it is interesting to see if any relationship can be made between these prices and those invoiced by the Glass Sellers to Woburn Abbey.

On 23 June 1676 we find twelve new flint wine glasses marked at 16/- but by August 1690 one dozen 'double flint' wine glasses were only 6/-. It is impossible to tell whether these were different types of glasses or similar but at much lower prices. It is perhaps reasonable to assume that during the life of Ravenscroft's patent his was the only source of supply of lead glass, so prices could be controlled. By 1690, however, the use of lead glass was widespread, competition was fierce and prices could have fallen considerably. So many of the Woburn invoices just refer to glasses without specifying exactly what they were. As a guideline, here are some typical examples of contemporary wages: In 1736 craftsmen such as carpenters and stone masons earned 7/- to 8/- per week. An estate bailiff living in earned £4.10.0 a year and a labourer 8 pence a day. In 1770 a weaver earned 8 shillings a week and miners fifteen shillings a week. By contrast professional men earned from £500 upwards. When we compare these figures against the cost of glass in the eighteenth century we can gain some idea of the market which the glassmakers catered for.

Examples of prices charged during the eighteenth century come from a number of surviving invoices. For example, according to the accounts of Thomas Betts, a glass seller, in 1747 a dozen air twist wine glasses cost 6/- (30p) and in 1755 a dozen air twist champagne glasses with moulded bowls cost 10/6d ($52\frac{1}{2}$p) and six opaque twist wine glasses cost 6/- (30p). In 1773 Coleburn Hancock of Cockspur Street, Charing Cross supplied to Edward Gibbon: three pairs of quart decanters without stoppers at 12/-; two dozen wine glasses at 10/-; a dozen champagne flutes at 8/-; six half pint goblets at 4/6d. In 1791 tumblers sold at 6/- a dozen, and Rodney decanters at 6/- each. Some prices for Irish glass quoted by Westropp include two decanters for 5/8d in 1816, three pairs of salt cellars for 15/- in 1827 and best rummers at 8/6d a dozen in 1835.

If one can translate these sums into today's prices at current wage rates, wine glasses in the 1750's at 6d each (2½p) equals half to three-quarters of a day's wage for a working man, that is, about £8 to £12 today. A tumbler in 1790 at 8d equals £12 to £16 today. A Rodney decanter at 6/- would be £80 to £90 today, a figure which agrees very closely with the price of good quality modern cut lead crystal decanters these days.

For domestic use glass was undoubtedly confined to the middle and upper classes. What is less certain is how far it was in common use in inns and taverns. Then, as now, I imagine that when glass was used in such public places the quality would generally be inferior to that used domestically and the wastage rate was almost certainly much higher.

While lead glass reigned supreme, glass vessels were still being made from soda glass. These were generally more crudely made and were undoubtedly for a cheaper market. Given the wastage rate and the fact that soda was more brittle than lead glass, comparatively few have survived.

58 A goblet on a cut glass stem, c. 1740. It has been wheel-engraved with the motto of the Walpole family: 'Fari quae Sentio Prosperity to Houghton'. Museum of London.

Cut glass

There is a fairly widespread popular belief which equates all cut glass with Ireland and then, by association, with Waterford. While Irish glassmaking undoubtedly became famous for its cut glass, the art was exported there from England, where it had been developed throughout the eighteenth century. Before going on to examine the Irish glass trade in more detail, let us consider the development of glass cutting in England.

As we have already seen, glassmaking in England derived from the Venetian tradition which was built around elaborate, thinly blown glass. This was not a product which was suitable for cutting, indeed even engraving on Venetian glass is unusual. This meant that when lead glass was developed there existed no native tradition of cutting except the bevelling and polishing of mirror plates, to exploit the possibilities of this new material. The softness of the metal, the increasing thickness of the sections it was possible to produce while preserving its clarity, and the lustre with which it reflected light were all qualities which made it ideal for cutting, and it is to the credit of the English glass trade that it realised the possibilities of this new method of decoration.

In Northern Europe, on the other hand, the Bohemian glassmakers had developed, during the seventeenth century, a hard white soda lime glass, which also lent itself to engraving and cutting, so by the time lead glass was making an impact on the English market the German cutters and decorators were already highly skilled in the art. It was to these craftsmen that

410

the English glass trade turned, and the first cutters we hear of by name were Germans, and the earliest datable examples of English cut glass are very much in the German manner— baluster stem glasses with faceted knops. Before we learn of anyone cutting glass in this country the *London Gazette* in 1709 advertised a parcel of 'German cut and carved glass'. Then John Akerman, who was most probably German, comes to our notice in 1719 with an advertisement in the *Whitehall Evening Post* which said that he 'continues to sell . . . plain and diamond cut flint glasses'. He became a member of the Glass Sellers Company and was Master of that company in 1741. This illustrates the fact that the decoration of glass—engraving, cutting, enamelling, etc.—was related to the retail side of the trade rather than the manufacturing side. The work was done either in independent decorating workshops or by craftsmen employed by the Glass Sellers.

After this, Thomas Betts, whose trade card survives, had a shop in Pall Mall in about 1738 and Jerome Johnson, who advertised from 1739 to 1752, were only two of the many retailers selling all manner of objects in cut glass. Lustres, bowls, plates, dishes, mugs, bottles, cruets, decanters, salts, globes for lamps, salvers, even hookah bases for export.

During this period, from the introduction of German craftsmen up to the time of the 1745 Excise duty, the trade in cut glass expanded so that native English craftsmen were introduced to the art in the same way that they had been

59 A sweetmeat glass, *c.* 1780. The ogee bowl has a cut everted rim and geometric cutting; the knopped stem is scale cut; the domed and cut foot has a scalloped rim.

60 A cut glass water jug, *c.* 1835. The shoulders are cut with short vertical panels between bands of prismatic cutting. The body is cut with alternate panels of fine diamonds and printies and gothic arches cut with larger pointed diamonds. The base is star cut.

411

61 *Above:* A canoe-shape bowl, *c.* 1820: scalloped rim with fan-and-husk cutting to the bowl, plain stem on a large square moulded foot ('lemon squeezer' foot).

62 *Left:* An unusual pair of cut candlesticks in the Adam style of 1780, but I believe these were made in the early nineteenth century.

63 A cut glass covered butter dish with stand, *c.* 1830.

brought into the glassmaking business during the years of Mansell's monopoly over a hundred years earlier. In the same way also this infusion of new blood and the requirements of English taste produced new styles of cutting which were distinctively different from their German origins.

With the imposition of the excise duty in 1745 and the consequent increase in the cost of raw material for cut glass wares, the market was severely inhibited, as explained on page 405. This led to a period of stagnation in design when the only part of the cut glass trade which flourished was that which supplied a market where price was no object. It is interesting to note that during the period from 1745 to the rise of the Irish Trade in the 1780's many of the surviving advertisements for sales of cut glass are those of retailers going bankrupt.

It was not until 1835 when the Glass Excise Tax was finally lifted that the cut glass trade really began to flourish in England, but as if it was a reaction against the restraints which had been imposed upon them for so many years, cutting was then practised to excess, with patterns becoming deeper and increasingly florid. Some of the examples of cut glass shown at the Great Exhibition of 1851, while demonstrating the highest degree of skill, exhibited a taste that was vulgar in the extreme. It was also incidentally the swan song of the Waterford Glass Company.

Because the styles of cutting, once developed, tended to change but little throughout the eighteenth century it is difficult to differentiate between early and late examples, and equally between English and Irish work. Generally, however, eighteenth century cutting tends to be shallow, or flat as it is sometimes described, which enables the glassmakers to keep the uncut weight to a minimum.

413

Chapter 3

Irish glass

There is a widespread popular belief that Irish glass has some quality not shared by glass made elsewhere in the British Isles. It is as if it arose complete and perfect like Venus from the waves to create a new standard of excellence. While this may seem a somewhat sweeping generalisation, I am intrigued by the considerable number of pieces of glass which are represented to me as being Irish and the frequency with which I am asked if pieces in my possession are Irish. The one thing they all have in common is that the pieces referred to are always cut glass. This highlights, perhaps, the most popular misconception of all. I hope during the course of this chapter to demonstrate that: *a* the widest variety of glassware was made in Ireland; and *b* that it was made there over a long period, usually by English glassmakers trying to escape political or economic restrictions in England but always working in the tradition in which they were raised.

The earliest records concerning the glass trade in Ireland go back to the middle of the thirteenth century, but until the late sixteenth century these more probably refer to glaziers rather than glassmakers, and if this is the case they would have imported their window glass from England. Both le Carré and Verzelini, when they obtained their licences, included the right to set up glasshouses in Ireland, but no evidence has come to light that they did so. It was more likely that they did this to protect themselves from unlicensed glassmakers setting up businesses in Ireland and evading the terms of their monopolies.

The first real evidence of a glasshouse working in Ireland dates to some time immediately prior to 1589. In that year the State papers of Ireland record the granting of a licence to run for eight years to Captain Thomas Woodhouse. The Patent Rolls of 1588 record that he had 'lately erected certain glass houses for making glass for glazing and drinking'. Woodhouse sold this licence to an Englishman, George Longe who in an effort to establish glassmaking in Ireland, introduced a Bill into

64 A peculiarly Irish vessel called a 'piggin', distinguished by its single handle. It is cut with alternate plain and diamond panels. The piggin derives from a wooden dairy vessel of the same name which was made of short barrel staves with one stave longer than the others to act as a handle. Glass copies such as this piece, *c.* 1830, were used as receptacles for milk or cream at table.

Parliament asking for the suppression of glasshouses in England and the transfer of the industry to Ireland, his argument being that such a course would preserve English woodland, exploit the abundance of wood in Ireland and provide employment for Irish workmen. Needless to say, such a grandiose scheme was contrary to the interests of both the English landowners and the glassmakers in England and so it failed, but there is evidence that a glasshouse existed for some years at this period near Curryglen in County Cork.

Subsequently several more patents were obtained for glass-making in Ireland, including one by Sir Robert Aston in 1606, but none of these schemes resulted in any progress being made towards developing an Irish industry. However, in 1611 William Robson, who had bought Sir Jerome Bowes' patent in England, also bought Aston's patent. These two patents gave him effective control over all glassmaking in Ireland, and in anticipation of the introduction of the coal fired furnace he set up a window glass factory in Ireland which, until it closed in 1618, sent considerable quantities of window glass to England.

It is possible that there were other glasshouses working in Ireland in 1613 because a letter from the Privy Council to the Lord Deputy for Ireland reminds him that there are patents in force covering glassmaking in Ireland and that all glasshouses not covered by these patents should be destroyed.

65 A large bucket-bowl rummer cut with the pillar-and-arch decoration found on a number of marked Waterford decanters, c. 1830.

The closure of William Robson's glasshouse appears to have resulted from the action taken by Sir Robert Mansell in 1616 to prevent the import of foreign glass (including Irish) into England in order to protect his own patents. Without this export market the glasshouse was uneconomic. This suggests that there was not sufficient demand in Ireland at that time to maintain a domestic source of supply.

There are subsequent records of glasshouses in 1618 at Ballynegery, County Waterford, and in 1623 at Birr in King's County. This latter was run by a member of the Bigo family, a descendant of the Lorraine De Bigaults who had settled on the Weald in the sixteenth century. The Bigo's were still operating glasshouses there in 1660. Boak's *Ireland's Natural History* records that this glasshouse made drinking glasses as well as window glass and that it imported sand from England. In 1670 Ananias Henzy, a descendant of the de Hennezells who had also helped to create the Wealden glass industry, started up a glasshouse at Portarlington in Queen's County.

In 1641 a Bill was passed prohibiting the use of wood in glasshouse furnaces, some twenty-five years after a similar one had been passed in England. Prior to this all the Irish glasshouses had been away from large-towns, close to the woodlands, their source of fuel, but thereafter they moved into the coastal towns which gave easy access for the supply of fuel and raw materials: Dublin, Belfast, Waterford and Cork.

It can be seen from the foregoing that during the sixteenth and seventeenth centuries there was never sufficient domestic demand to support anything but the most meagre glass industry in Ireland; it was a poor country with very few people able to afford glazing for their windows or drinking glasses for their tables, and attempts to increase output by supplying the English market were at the mercy of the English monopolists.

From the end of the seventeenth century and during the first half of the eighteenth century glasshouses operated at Waterford and Dublin, but the Excise Act of 1745 not only created a burden for English glassmakers but dealt a death blow to the infant Irish industry. It provided that no glass could be exported from Ireland except on payment of ten shillings per pound duty and no glass could be imported into Ireland except that which was made in Great Britain. As a result of this, glassmaking was severely discouraged in Ireland, with glassmaking disappearing from Waterford and surviving only precariously in Dublin.

The glasshouse at Waterford had been established at a place called Gurteens just outside the town in about 1729, and advertised that it could supply 'all sorts of flint glass, double and single'. It also appears to have made all other types of glass, including bottles and window glass. It was advertised to let in 1740 but no other evidence suggests that it continued in operation.

Glassmaking in Dublin met with a little more success. There is evidence of glassmaking in the city from about 1677, but the most detailed evidence concerns a glasshouse set up in St. Mary's Lane about 1690 by a Captain Philip Roche. This survived as an operative glasshouse until about 1760 and it appears on Dublin maps subsequent to this date, but it was finally demolished in about 1787.

A number of advertisements in *Faulkner's Dublin Journal* spread over thirty-nine years from 1713 to 1752 give an insight into the enormous variety of glassware made in this glasshouse. There are only two references to cut glass: 'fine salts ground and polished' in 1729, but in 1752 they advertise 'all sorts of cut and flowered glass may be had of any kind to any pattern'. It is also interesting to note that in this last advertisement 'no pains or expense have been spared by the proprietor to secure the best workmen and newest patterns from London'. This

66 An early eighteenth-century goblet commemorating the Battle of the Boyne, 1690. It shows William III with cavalry and infantry crossing the River Boyne.

suggests that the wealthier members of Irish society looked to London as the source of fashion and quality.

Another Dublin flint glasshouse opened about 1734 in Fleet Street, which advertised of its wares 'workmanship equal to those made in London'. It appears to have burned down in 1741. A further bottle and window glasshouse operated in Batchelors Walk from 1725 to the 1740's. Other bottle glasshouses operated from about 1750 onwards, and again in 1754 the Dublin Journal stated that 'Mr. William Gordon (had) just brought over from England a complete set of as good workmen as any in the country, for the new glasshouse at the Ship Buildings'.

In 1759, three Englishmen, Jeudwin, Landon and Lunn, took over the Abbey Street glasshouse to make window glass, and stated before the Dublin Society in 1762 that they employed sixty workmen, of whom fifty were Englishmen. In 1768 they gave evidence before the Irish Parliament that they had instructed Irish hands and trained Irish apprentices but that the foreign artists (English) refused to work with the Irish. (Shades of le Carré's problems with the Lorraine glassmakers in the 1560's.)

The third important flint glasshouse to operate in Dublin was that of Richard Williams & Company. There were several members: Richard William, Thomas and Isaac. They came from England and appear to have taken over an existing bottle glass factory in Marlborough Green in 1764. From 1770 their advertisements offered a wide range of glassware 'equal to any imported in quality of metal and workmanship', and in 1774 they offered glass lustres, girandoles and chandeliers. These are essentially cut glass items for a luxury market. This firm, then, was well established by the time the export restrictions were lifted in 1780 and in a good position to take advantage of the new opportunities about to be offered.

There were several window and bottle glasshouses working during this period, but it is clear that English workmen and English taste played an important role in the manufacture of glass during those years.

We now come to the period which allowed Irish glassmaking to expand and develop a product that has impressed itself on our consciousness down to the present day. The events which triggered off this dramatic change were the doubling of the duty in 1777 on glass made in England and, more importantly, the Act of 1780 which exempted the Irish glass trade from the duty and removed the restrictions on exporting glass. Another Act of 1781 lifting the duty on imported coal used in

67 *Far left:* Irish decanter, *c.* 1800, marked on the base 'B. Edwards'. There are three feathered neck rings and moulded flutes to the base. This latter feature is common among Irish decanters.

68 *Left:* Although this decanter is similar in style, it is marked on the underside 'Cork Glass Co.', *c.* 1800.

glassmaking also contributed to the economic advantages of making glass in Ireland. Within three or four years glasshouses were operating in Dublin, Belfast, Cork, Waterford and Newry. The many surviving records and advertisements for these glasshouses show that they made all types of glassware, but cut glass accounted for an ever-increasing amount of the output. The glassmakers must have realised that the prohibitive duty on cut glass in England gave them a greater advantage in that field than in the plainer glass. This price advantage probably meant that much more cut glass was exported than the other types and thus, outside Ireland, Irish glass would have become synonymous with cut glass. Before going on to examine the product and the styles, let us have a look at these glasshouses in the years following the 1780 Act.

Dublin

The Williams family business appears to have been variously under the direction of its several members until 1827 when it closed, but during its life it was the most important glasshouse in Dublin. Other firms who operated there were Charles Mulvaney from 1785-1846 and Thomas and John Chebsey from 1786-98. Another business started as J. D. Ayckbown & Co. about 1799 and closed as J. Jynn Rogers & Co. about 1808. Ayckbown came from England where he had been a member of a glassmaking family who had probably originally come from Germany as glass cutters in the early years of the eighteenth century. The only other important glasshouse to operate in

Dublin was that of Thomas & John Pugh, which started in 1852 and ran until 1895 when Westropp says that the manufacture of flint glass ceased in Ireland.

One of the problems in tracing the history of glasshouses is the frequent changes of ownership they seemed to enjoy. Partners came and went and bankruptcies were not uncommon.

Belfast

Glassmaking in Belfast centres around Benjamin Edwards, an English glassmaker from Bristol. In 1771 the owners of the Tyrone Collieries decided to set up a glasshouse since there were readily available supplies of the necessary raw materials: coal, sand and clay. Edwards went to Ireland to initiate this enterprise at Drumrea near Dungannon, but it seems to have survived for only a very few years, since in 1776 he set up a glasshouse in Belfast where he advertised all kinds of glassware for sale. One of the advertisements states that he had brought a glass cutter from England. Edwards had three sons, and until Benjamin Snr. died in 1812 the management of the business changed frequently amongst them. After this the company was run by Benjamin Jnr. until 1827.

One of the sons, John, set up his own glasshouse in 1803 but was not successful, and sold out in 1804. Various interests ran this as the Belfast Glass Works until 1840.

Cork

It was the practice of the Dublin Society to offer premiums, or subsidies, to encourage the setting up of business enterprises in Ireland in an effort to encourage trade. Cork, because of its good natural harbour and trade links with the rest of the world, was an ideal centre for this, and the Dublin Society had offered premiums for the erection of a glasshouse there in 1753. It was not until 1783, however, after the granting of free trade, that Hayes, Barnett and Rowe petitioned Parliament for aid in introducing the glass trade to Cork. They had sent to England to obtain the best equipment, materials and workmen available and had established two glasshouses, one for bottle glass, the other for flint.

This was the origin of the Cork Glass Company which ran until 1818. During that period there was a succession of partners and changes of ownership but, after Waterford, the Cork glasshouses are the best known and remembered. In 1815, towards the end of the life of the Cork Glass Company, Daniel Foley set up a new glasshouse on Wandesford Quay. This was the Waterloo Glass Company and again it survived various bankruptcies and changes of ownership until 1835. Its demise was largely due to the effects of the Excise Duty imposed on Irish glass in 1825. (We know this from notices in Cork newspapers advertising the auction sale of equipment of the glasshouse at Wandesford Quay to recover unpaid excise duty.) In competition with it for most of its life was the Terrace Glass Works, started by brothers Edward and Richard Ronayne in 1818 and surviving until 1841.

I think that the reason the Cork Glass Company and the Waterloo Glass Company are so much better known than the last mentioned is that glassware marked with the names of both these companies has survived, while I know of no marked piece of Terrace Glass Works glass.

Waterford

As mentioned earlier, there was no glassmaking in Waterford after 1740 until 1783. In that year brothers George and William Penrose, merchants in Waterford, realising the advantages offered to them by the Act of 1780, established the Waterford Glass Company. This was to become the most famous of all the Irish glasshouses, and is even today credited with most of the cut glass made during the nineteenth century.

The Penrose brothers were not glassmakers themselves, so they had to import the expertise they required. Thus the Waterford glasshouse was started up by John Hill of Stourbridge, who took with him a sufficient number of glassmakers to carry out all the functions of a glasshouse.

After three years in charge of the glasshouse, Hill was accused (we don't know whether justly or unjustly) of some indiscretion by the wife of one of the Penroses. This resulted in him leaving Waterford for France, but before leaving he entrusted his glassmaking recipes to Jonathan Gatchell, a clerk at the glasshouse, with whom he had become friendly. The mixing of the batches of the raw materials was most important, for on this rested the quality of the glass. Presumably it was also fairly secret because it made Gatchell a most important man in the glasshouse. He went on to learn the whole glassmaking business, and some time after William Penrose's death in 1796 he bought out the remaining brother in 1799, going into partnership with James Ramsey and Ambrose Bancroft, these two putting up the capital while Gatchell supplied the expertise. However, Ramsey died in about 1811 and Gatchell then bought out Bancroft and became the sole owner. The Waterford Glass Co. remained with descendants of the Gatchell family until it finally closed in 1851 after having exhibited at the Great Exhibition. No glass was then made in Waterford until a new company started up in business as Waterford Glass Ltd. in 1951.

The vogue for cut glass carried on well into the second half of the nineteenth century and much of the glass I see represented as Waterford falls into that period when there was no glasshouse working there.

One other point I must emphasise, although many writers have already dealt with the subject, is the question of colour in Waterford glass. Hartshorne in his book *Antique Drinking Glasses* of 1896, attributed a blue colour to Waterford glass, and although so many writers have since tried to dispel this mistake I find that it is still a widespread belief. Westropp in 1920 wrote that none of the examples of Waterford glass in his possession showed a blue tint, and in a catalogue to accompany an exhibition of Waterford glass at Waterford in 1952, it is stated that 'Waterford glass has many . . . qualities, but a bluish colour is not amongst them'. The colour in old glass is accidental, depending on the presence of impurities in the silica. Old records show that much of the sand used at Waterford was shipped from the Isle of Wight and Kings Lynn, with the Lynn sand being considered the better.

During the years from 1780 to 1825 the Irish glass trade flourished. England had always been looked to as the source of style and fashion, and during much of the eighteenth century Englishmen had set up glasshouses in Ireland and English glass craftsmen had found employment there. This trend accelerated after the granting of free trade, and there are many reports of English operatives working in Ireland. There are those who argue that a distinctive Irish style arose out of this upsurge in trade, and from marked pieces of Irish glass it is possible to identify recurring patterns which can sometimes lead to a reasonable attribution to a particular glasshouse, but these spring from the preference of the management or the cutters and were not exhibitions of a uniquely Irish style. The English craftsmen must have taken with them the tradition in which they were trained, and would continue to make styles which were equally popular in England at the same time.

Much has been made of the pages of designs left by Samuel Miller, foreman cutter of Waterford, of patterns used in the 1830's and 1840's. There is no evidence to suggest that they all originated in Waterford, and many decanters turn up in England today which conform to some of these patterns. Numerous records have survived of Irish glass exports covering the years 1781 to 1822 and the only town which appears to have exported to England was Cork, otherwise the principal markets for these Irish exports were the West Indies and North America, with some being sent to Italy, Spain and Denmark.

In the Waterford records there are several references of attempts to export to England. About one such venture in 1832 Jonathan Wright and George Saunders took a consignment to Southampton to sell by auction. Many people looked at the goods but would not buy and some, on learning they were Irish said they could not be any good. The reputation of Waterford was apparently not as strong then as now! But in Exeter in 1832 Elizabeth Walpole, another partner in the firm, persuaded a local retailer to stock Waterford glass, which he apparently found acceptable.

In 1825 the Irish glass trade was subjected to Excise Duty. This was calculated on a complicated basis relative to the weight of glass metal in the glass pots and the finished weight of goods manufactured. Some relief was granted for exported glassware. The collection of this duty was strictly supervised with Excise Officers being stationed in each glasshouse and having absolute control over the mixing, loading and firing of the raw materials. They controlled access to the glass pots and the amount of metal taken from them. In fact the whole operation of the glasshouse was at the mercy of these Excise Officers. During the first year of its operation the Waterford Glass Company paid £3910.7s.5d. in duty.

It is not surprising that from this time Irish glassmaking started to decline. It had lost its competitive advantage over English glass and the liberty of the glassmakers was inhibited by bureaucracy. From a high point in 1825, when there were eleven glasshouses working in Ireland, by 1852 there were only three. What finally put paid to the industry in Ireland was the lifting of all Excise Duty on the industry throughout the United Kingdom in 1845. Ireland could not then hope to compete with glass made in England and Scotland, and had to be content with satisfying the small domestic market.

Products and identifying characteristics

After this review of the Irish glassmaking industry, what of the products it made? The following is a list of some of the articles named in advertisements appearing in Irish journals from 1729 onwards.

1729 Salvers, baskets with handles and feet for desserts, salts, decanters, lamps.

1749 Fine large globe lamps for one to four candles. Bells and shades, sweetmeat and jelly glasses, glasses for apothecaries, water glasses, jugs, orange glasses, covers for tarts.

1752 Claret and Burgundy bottles, saucers, sillabub glasses, sucking bottles, cupping glasses, funnels. All sorts of glass for electrical experiments. Wine glasses with a vine border, toasts or any flourish whatever, beer ditto; tea canisters, mustard pots.

1816 Goblets, tumblers, ladles, salad bowls.

1823 Ringed decanters, footed salts.

1842 Chandeliers, lustres, hall bells, candelabra.

1849 Liqueur bottles, carafes, pickle urns, claret jugs, celery vases, sugar bowls, butter coolers, cream ewers.

Many of these appear in more than one advertisement, of course, but it does give some idea of the tremendous variety of glassware available during the eighteenth and nineteenth centuries.

It has never been easy to discriminate between English and Irish glass made prior to 1780. There are a number of glasses which bear engraving relating to Irish organisations or events. These are identical with English glasses of the period, and if they were in fact made in Ireland, they emphasise the similarity between the two manufactures. There is one type of glass, however, which is normally given an Irish attribution and this is a cordial glass with a small bowl, an unusually thick, tall plain stem and usually a domed foot.

We then enter a period, from 1780, when it is easier to relate pieces to particular factories. The bulk of attributed or proven glass was made after that date, and most of it is cut to some degree. Fortunately, several of the Irish glasshouses adopted a method of making certain items which, when taken in conjunction with the styles of decoration, enables us to make reasonable attribution of unmarked items. The method used was to blow flat-bottomed pieces such as decanters and finger bowls into open moulds, which had the glass company's name incorporated into them. Pieces marked with the names Cork Glass Co., Waterloo Co., Cork, Penrose, Waterford, and B. Edwards may be found. There are other names marked on pieces of Irish glass, but they are for retailers rather than manufacturers. Among these are Francis Collins, Dublin; J. D. Ayckbown, Dublin; Armstrong, Ormond Quay (Dublin); C. M. & Co. (for Charles Mulvaney).

Associated with the name moulded into the base is usually a ring of fine vertical moulded flutes around the lower half of the vessel. On decanters particular types and numbers of neck rings are associated with particular factories. These are the distinguishing marks which are incorporated at the time of manufacture. The cutting is applied afterwards and can, of course, vary enormously, but particular patterns turn up frequently enough to allow reasonable attributions to be made on unmarked pieces. Thus, the pillar and arch cutting and single rows of strawberry diamonds occur on Waterford pieces.

Engraved bows between cross-hatched loops and circles are typical of marked Waterloo pieces.

Looped vesica pattern with cross-hatching alternating with stars is a typical Cork Glass Company feature.

All Edward decanters have only two neck rings (but so does at least one Armstrong decanter).

Amongst table glass, the canoe bowl on moulded pedestal foot, the kettledrum bowl and bowl with turn-over rim are all shapes associated with Irish glassmaking.

These associations provide sufficient evidence, I think, to make reasonable attributions in unmarked pieces, but other than this I am sure there is much wishful thinking in adding the word Irish to examples of cut glass. That is not to say that there are not many examples of glassware made in Ireland surviving today. My point is that it is unwise to accept as Irish any piece of glass for which reasonable evidence is not forthcoming. If the item is attractive and well made in its own right, does the label Irish suddenly make it more desirable?

One last point which, if not realised, can only lead to more confusion is that skilled glassmakers and decorators were always in demand, and they often moved from one glasshouse to another, so very similar styles and patterns were executed in several glasshouses.

Before leaving the subject of Irish glass I must refer to that most Irish of all styles the Williamite glass. This is a style of engraved decoration which appears on a number of different types of drinking glass and takes its inspiration from the victory of William of Orange at the Battle of the Boyne, 1 July 1690. The earliest glass I know of with this engraving dates from about twenty-five years after the event and it then appears regularly on glasses made during the next 200 years. Many people refer to these as copies or fakes, but we have here an instance where a particular historical event became adopted as the symbol of a political idea. So when the inscription 'To the Glorious Memory of King William' or 'Battle of the Boyne, 1 July 1690' appears on a glass made in late Victorian times it is not a copy in the normal sense of the word, but the continuing expression of the political ideals of the Orange Order.

Types of cutting found on decanters.

1 Vertical panels. Used for base and shoulders.
2 Strawberry diamonds.
3 Crosscut relief diamonds.
4 Fine relief diamonds.
5 Pillar flutes.
6 Swags or drapery.
7 Bulls eye or lunar slices.
8 Flat hobnail diamonds.
9 Prismatic cutting.
10 Comb flutes.
11 Slanting blazes.

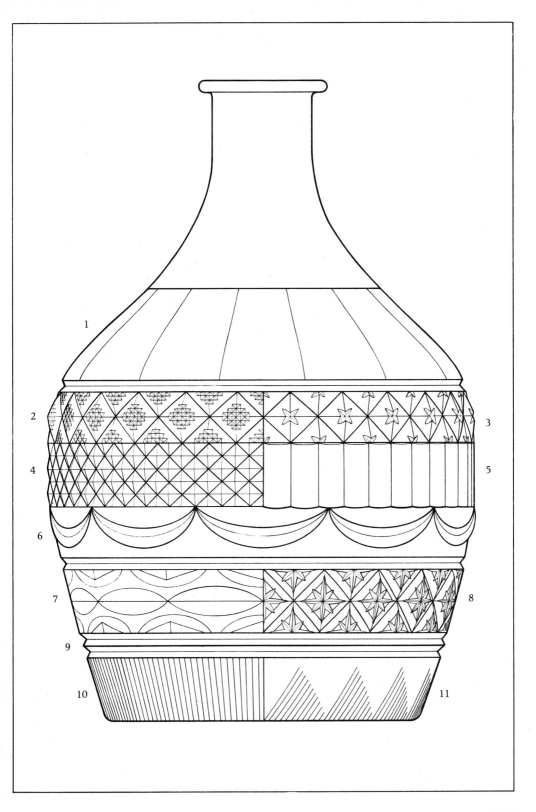

Late Georgian glass

The published literature on glass deals exhaustively with the history and development of the glass trade up to about 1800. After that date most writers have concerned themselves either with late Georgian cut glass or Victorian coloured and decorative glass. Nineteenth century drinking glasses have not generally merited the attention which their increasing interest to collectors demands.

The last decade of the eighteenth century saw a change in taste away from the long-stemmed glasses which had dominated the market for so long, towards glasses on short or rudimentary stems. For the first time for over a century drinking glasses came into general use which had a capacity conforming more nearly to modern ideas. In contrast to these, an endless variety of small glasses was made for a market which had apparently tired of the stemmed glasses of the previous years.

It might be argued that this was a period of decline leading to a new departure in glassmaking, but this would belie the many variations that may still be found on a limited number of themes. They represent a rich source of material for the collector of modest means. They are generally very reasonably priced in comparison with the better-known glasses of the eighteenth century. They satisfy that widespread preference for collecting things which are 'Georgian' and they are sufficiently varied to enable an interesting collection to be built up. I have met many enthusiastic collectors who made their first acquaintance with antique glass through examples of this period and who, as their knowledge and confidence grew, graduated to collecting earlier specimens.

Rummers

Drinking glasses of the early 1800's fall generally into three categories: rummers, ale glasses and small glasses for wines or spirits. Rummers were the largest of these and their bowls, holding eight to ten fluid ounces, contrast sharply with the

69 A roemer not a rummer, c. 1820. It has a cup bowl surmounting a hollow stem decorated with an applied collar and prunts. The foot is conical with a trail of glass applied to the upper surface. In the continental originals the foot was made of a thread of glass wound around a cone.

two- to three-ounce capacity of the earlier glasses. The origin of the title 'rummer' to describe these glasses is obscure, but there are two main schools of thought. The first suggests that the word is a corruption of the German 'roemer'. This was a wine glass, popular in Northern Europe from the sixteenth century, which was used for Rhenish white wine. Its principal characteristics were that it had a large capacity round bowl on a wide hollow stem and a small conical foot made of a single thread of glass wound round a wooden cone. It may be seen represented in many Dutch and German still-life paintings of the seventeenth century. Rhenish wine has been drunk in Britain for centuries and this style of glass was well known. There is a design for such a glass among the patterns which Greene ordered from Morelli in Venice and a large example bearing the raven's head seal of Ravenscroft is in the Victoria and Albert Museum. Although the name and style does not appear to have been used during the eighteenth century there was a revival of interest in them in the early nineteenth century when an anglicised version was made in coloured glass in Britain. A pattern book of the Edinburgh & Leith Glass Company illustrates these glasses, calling them 'Romers' but they are of much smaller capacity than their Continental originals. The only connection I can make between these roemers and the British rummer is that they both have large bowls on short stems and feet smaller than the diameter of the bowl.

The other derivation of the name is linked to the increasing popularity of rum-based drinks during the later eighteenth century. Whereas neat spirits would only require small glasses,

70 Three rummers. (Left and right) A pair of round bowl rummers with square 'lemon squeezer' feet, c. 1820. (Centre) A rummer with a round bowl engraved with bows and festoons, c. 1800. There is a short plain stem and a folded foot, the latter is rare on rummers.

rum-based toddies, to which hot water was added, presumably required larger ones.

Whatever the reason, rummers made their appearance late in the eighteenth century and by the early years of the nineteenth century had become one of the most popular styles of drinking glass. As they came into more general use I am sure they were used for a wider variety of drinks; there are many engraved with hops and barley, denoting their use as ale glasses, and occasionally one may find one engraved with grapes and vine leaves, which suggests its use as a wine glass.

The earliest rummers had thinly blown round bowls with moulded panel decoration to the lower half, a short rather thin stem and a plain foot much smaller than the diameter of the bowl. A little later a collar or merese was introduced between the bowl and the stem, which then tended to be made somewhat thicker. As time went on new bowl shapes were introduced. It is hard to be precise about the order in which these were developed, but based on slight changes in quality and detail amongst those I have examined, my own opinion is that the sequence was probably: round bowl, ogee bowl, bucket bowl, double ogee bowl, barrel bowl. Whatever the order, all these shapes appeared during the first quarter of the nineteenth century. One feature which is noticeable is that as the century progressed the glass tended to get thicker, the quality of the metal improved, and more decoration was achieved by cutting. Ogee bowl rummers usually have thick plain stems while the others frequently have short stems with somewhat rudimentary knops, the earlier ones having blade knops while later on the ball knop was popular.

71 A bucket-bowl rummer engraved with a crest and monogram and the year 1826. There is a short knopped stem and a plain foot.

Ale glasses

Although many rummers were used as beer glasses, the ale glass proper had been a staple product of the glass trade from pre-Ravenscroft days. True ale glasses were distinguished by their narrow, deep bowls which are generally referred to as flutes. Greene ordered ale flutes from Morelli, but these were almost certainly much taller than those made by the English glassmakers. Ravenscroft supplied beer glasses to the Glass Sellers Company but it is not clear just what shape these were. By 1700, however, the style of ale glass which is familiar to all collectors of English glass had evolved. These typically had a narrow funnel bowl with wrythen or gadrooned decoration and often a flammiform fringe on a short stem. This was sometimes pincered into four or five wings beneath the bowl, to create the so-called propeller stem, and the folded foot. As

72 A panel-moulded rummer with an ovoid bowl engraved with festoons and stars. There is a short plain stem and plain foot, c. 1800.

73 Four ale glasses: (Left to right) Gadrooned wrythen bowl, plain stem, folded foot, *c*. 1690; Wrythen funnel bowl, propeller knopped stem, folded foot, *c*. 1700; Gadrooned wrythen bowl with a flammiform fringe, short plain stem, folded foot, *c*. 1720; Wrythen funnel bowl, short knopped stem, folded foot, *c*. 1730.

this style of ale glass continued to the 1730's it changed its character slightly. The gadrooning was not so heavy, the wrythen pattern became more precise and the stem was reduced to little more than one or two rudimentary knops between bowl and bowl and folded foot. I emphasise this because some authorities credit this type of ale glass to the late eighteenth century, but my own experience suggests that gadrooning on these glasses went out of fashion by the 1730's, never to return.

The standard bowl shape survived the decline of gadrooning, and it appears on all the different stem types of the eighteenth century from baluster stems to facet stems. Several of the well-known bowl shapes were elongated and modified to produce the typical ale glass style; round funnel, ogee and bell bowls among them. At the end of the century, as the short stemmed glasses found favour, the ale glass reverted to the proportions it had had at the beginning of the century but this time it had an entirely different character. The wrythen pattern was achieved by blowing the bowl into a conical mould which had vertical grooves. This produced a ribbed effect on the glass. If the bowl was twisted while the metal was still plastic the ribs were twisted and produced the typical wrythen pattern. The plasticity of the glass affected the amount of twist that could be imparted to it and so one rarely sees two wrythen ales of this period with exactly the same amount of twist. The stem is usually reduced to one or two ribbed knops with no

more than a token plain section, and the foot is a thick, plain, flat foot which is common around 1800. A variation on this is an ale having a short incised twist stem with the pattern running up into the lower part of the funnel bowl.

Other than these wrythen patterns there are many other patterns of ale glass covering the period 1800-40, plain bowls and stems, panel moulded bowls, knopped stems, plain and folded feet. Many of them are engraved with hops and barley denoting their use.

I have already mentioned that rummers became both thicker and heavier by the middle of the nineteenth century, and this is equally true of ale glasses. The dwarf ale flute of the early nineteenth century, which was about $5\frac{1}{2}$ inches high, gradually gave way to ale glasses which were about 7 inches high with parallel-sided, round-bottomed bowls on short, thick plain stems and wide feet. When these were decorated the most popular pattern was a series of round polished depressions called printies. These were in rows around the bowl and for most of its height.

Small glasses

As I mentioned at the beginning of this chapter, the wide variety of small glasses made during the late eighteenth and

74 Five ale glasses spanning the period 1720-1820: (Left to right) Knopped facet-stem ale glass, *c.* 1780; Dwarf ale glass engraved with hops and barley, *c.* 1820; Funnel bowl baluster-stemmed ale glass with an annulated knop, *c.* 1720; Facet-stemmed ale glass engraved with Masonic symbols, *c.* 1790; Plain-stemmed ale glass engraved with hops and barley, *c.* 1750.

early nineteenth centuries have been neglected by earlier writers. Such was the variety of period glassware available before the last war that none of the standard works on the subject considered them worthy of any attention. Since then they have slowly received more recognition but I still meet many collectors who complain of a lack of information regarding the dating of these glasses.

First let us define them. What sets them apart from other small glasses of the eighteenth century? Until about 1780 small glasses which are generally referred to as spirit or dram glasses were scaled down versions of the standard wine glasses of the day. Thus we find the standard bowl shapes and sizes on short, thick, opaque twist and plain stems, usually in conjunction with a thick foot. From 1780 we find that they have been replaced by glasses which generally have funnel bowls on thin plain stems with plain or folded feet. They are seldom more than $4\frac{1}{2}$ inches high. The change, then, is not only one of style but also of weight and I think this is the key to their appearance. The doubling of the Excise Duty in 1777 with further increases in 1781 and 1787 put an enormous burden on the glassmakers. Much of the business must have been with innkeepers where spirits, mainly gin, were an important part of their trade. To satisfy this market, cheaper and therefore lighter glasses were necessary. Many of these glasses are engraved with decorated borders. The poor quality of this engraving also suggests they were made for a cheap market.

Slowly the use of these glasses became established and as it did so the variety of patterns increased. As new shapes of rummer made their appearance, so they were copied in smaller versions. Also, as their use extended they lost their connection with spirits and became accepted as wine glasses. By 1830 they had become standard domestic drinking glasses and continued so for about another twenty years. Those that follow the rummer shapes are easy to date, but by the 1830's they were beginning to develop a style that owed nothing to larger glasses. They have relatively deep, straight-sided bowls, rounded at the bottom. Panel moulding was common and many of them have an out-turned lip. The stems are decorated with small ball knops at the centre and the base or both and the feet are flat, somewhat roughly made and relatively thick.

One thing about glasses of this period which troubles many people is that they have folded feet. Popular opinion has it that a folded foot is a guarantee of an eighteenth century glass, but this is not so. There was a period between 1800 and 1830 when the folded foot was commonly used on many small glasses. I

75 *Above left:* Two small wine glasses, both with folded feet, *c.* 1820. (Left) An engraved bucket-bowl with a short knopped stem. (Right) An engraved and panel-moulded ogee bowl on a stem with ribbed knops.

76 *Above:* Two small wine glasses, *c.* 1850. Both have panel cutting to the bowl, knopped stems and plain feet.

77 *Left:* Two small wine glasses. (Left) Cut bucket-bowl, *c.* 1830. (Right) Plain bucket-bowl and a folded foot, *c.* 1820.

think this was partly weight-saving and partly because the lighter character of the folded foot was more in keeping with the glasses themselves. The thing to bear in mind is the style of the whole glass, particularly the bowl. Where rummer shapes are copied, that should establish the date with certainty.

The most popular of these rummer shapes translated to small glasses was the bucket bowl. It occurs on glasses of every quality from the plainest to the most elaborately cut versions which suggests that the popularity of these little glasses reached every level of society. The years between 1820 and 1830 saw the introduction of plain stems but with vertical flutes and it became more and more normal for the pontil mark to be polished out.

432

Extending into early Victorian times these glasses became even more sophisticated with cut panels replacing the moulded panels, and the simple knopping giving way to miniature versions of the early baluster stems, inverted and true balusters, blade, angular and dumbbell knops may all be found on these glasses. They survived as general purpose glasses until the later Victorian glassmakers introduced the idea of having suites of glasses with a different shape being made for each type of drink.

There is one very distinctive feature of this period which was so widely used on glass of all types that I feel it best to discuss it separately. This was the moulded pedestal base or foot. It is popularly known as the lemon squeezer foot, since most examples are ridged inside in the manner of old-fashioned lemon squeezers.

This type of base first made its appearance in the late eighteenth century but enjoyed its greatest success in the period up to 1830. Glassware incorporating this feature is made by two techniques: moulding and blowing. The method is ideal where short stems are used, since the foot and stem can be moulded as one unit and then fixed to the bowl. The technique was to squeeze the glass into a shaped mould using a punch which produced the plain or patterned recess in the base. The process could not have been exact since there was usually a surplus of glass which emerged to leave a ragged edge around the foot, and this had to be removed by grinding and polishing. While the majority of these feet are square, many other shapes were produced, diamonds and ovals for salt cellars, hexagons and octagons for ale glasses, and indented quatrefoil shapes for condiment bottles. Massive versions were produced for the canoe-shaped bowls associated with Irish glassmaking, and recently several salt cellars have come to my notice which have raised letters moulded on the upper surface. The letters are *P* and *H,* or *P, T* and *H*. The exact sequence is unknown, since nobody knows the starting point. Presumably these refer to the maker, but I have so far been unable to find the name of any glassmaking company whose name starts with these letters.

From dated examples I believe that the earliest square moulded feet had only a plain depression in the underside, the ribbed pattern making its appearance a little later. It was widely used on rummers, and some of the most pleasing ones have a straight-sided bucket bowl on a tall moulded base with the ribbed pattern deeply indented into the underside so that it shows through. The bowls are generally thinly blown and invariably of good quality. One feature like this can become the theme for an interesting collection. I am sure it would be difficult to exhaust all the possibilities of foot pattern and the vessels on which they are found.

Decanters

Although the majority of Georgian decanters which survive today date from the years after 1800, their history goes back to the late seventeenth century. Their original purpose was to replace wine bottles on the table, and some of the very earliest examples are no more than clear glass versions of contemporary green glass wine bottles. At that time wine bottles were of a squat onion shape with tapering necks. The clear or flint glass versions of these usually had longer, somewhat narrower, necks and are generally referred to as shaft and globe decanters. That some decoration was added to these is shown from a surviving price list of Ravenscroft which refers to quart, pint and half pint ribbed bottles and similar sizes 'nipt diamond waies', i.e. with a trailed diamond pattern all over them, which is referred to on p. 409.

By the early years of the eighteenth century the body of these serving bottles had been developed into hexagonal or octagonal shapes and they often had a loop handle added. However, it was not the practice to have fitted glass stoppers; the old practice of adding a string ring to the neck still survived. Before the advent of accurately cut corks and corking machines bottles were stopped with plugs of oiled hemp or tapering corks. These were held in place by a thread passed over the top and anchored to the string ring.

From about 1730 to 1750 a new shape appeared. This was the cruciform decanter, which in plan view looked like a very short-armed cross. These still retained the string ring, but it often consisted of a thread wound two or three times round the neck. Although it would not be normal practice to stopper these bottles, this multiple string ring provided a useful grip when using the bottle.

The essential thing about all these early styles was that they were purely serving bottles rather than storage bottles. The contents would be decanted from wine bottles or barrels and what was not drunk at table could presumably be returned to the storage vessel.

It is not until about 1760 that the first bottles appear which we would term decanters today. These were more elegant containers with slightly tapering cylindrical bodies with shoulders which curved inward to a short parallel neck. These dispensed with the string or neck ring, and for the first time

78-82 These decanters were all made between 1790 and 1860.
Above: A mallet-shape decanter with facet-cut neck and stars to the body, *c.* 1790. *Opposite above left:* An elaborately cut decanter, *c.* 1820. *Opposite above right:* A decanter cut with diamond columns and gothic arches, *c.* 1840. *Opposite below left:* A Prussian-style decanter which has three triple neck rings, *c.* 1830. *Opposite below right:* A straight-sided decanter with its body divided into vertical panels, *c.* 1860.

435

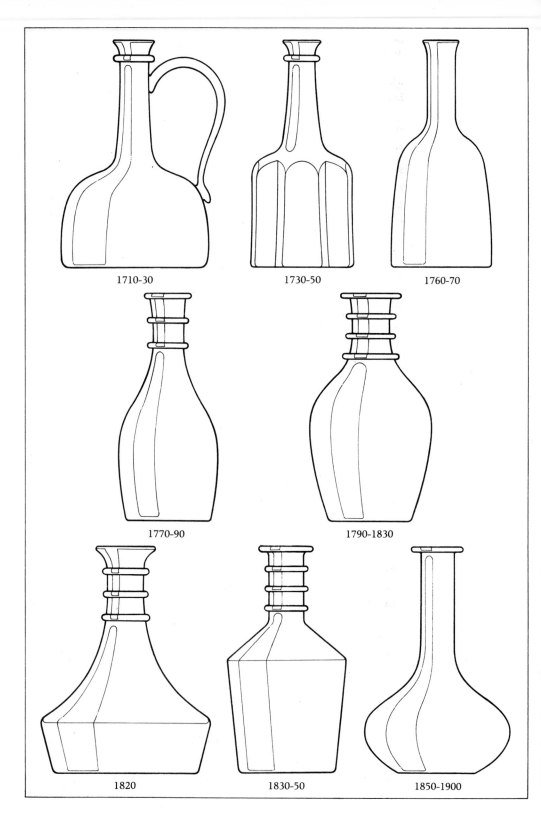

1710-30

1730-50

1760-70

1770-90

1790-1830

1820

1830-50

1850-1900

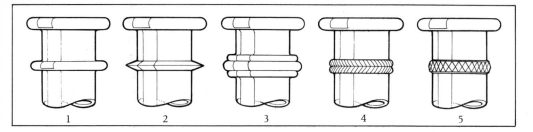

Above: **Decanter neck rings.**
1 Plain ring.
2 Triangular or knife-edge ring.
3 Triple or annulated ring.
4 Milled ring.
5 Cut or faceted ring.

Opposite: **The development of decanters**

had stoppers of glass. These were usually uncut ball or spire stoppers which were not always ground to fit the neck. The custom arose of having the name of the intended contents engraved in a cartouche upon the body, and these names include white wine, Madeira, Mountain (a Spanish wine from near Malaga) Port, Lisbon, Ale, and so on.

This tapering 'mallet' shape gave way to a similar style in which the body was wider at the shoulder than at the base, and cutting makes its appearance for the first time. This is usually in the form of diamond facet cutting on the body and neck, or neck only. The stoppers were cut to match.

From about 1800 onwards decanters evolved into the styles which are well known to collectors today. These are variations on a bulbous shape which has tapering shoulders leading to a short neck with a flange at the mouth, and anything from two to four equally spaced applied neck rings. They vary considerably in quality from the Irish ones which were thinly blown into shallow moulds, producing a flute moulded base to the richly ornate and heavily cut versions produced both in Ireland and England in the 1830's. During this period the two most popular stopper shapes were the flat round target or bulls eye and the mushroom. The former generally being used with the plainer decanters.

During the early years of the 1800's many coloured decanters were made which were usually sold in sets of three and were often gilded with imitation wine labels. The names used are generally those of spirits, usually Brandy, Rum and Hollands (gin). Whisky does not occur, since it was not generally drunk in England until the 1880's. These nineteenth century decanters are usually of two sizes. The small ones are not so popular today because it is claimed they do not take a whole bottle at one filling. This is because at the time they were popular, bottle sizes were based on the imperial pint and imperial quart. Our modern 26-ounce bottles fall between these two sizes.

As fashion has a habit of repeating itself, during the second half of the nineteenth century the globe and shaft decanter

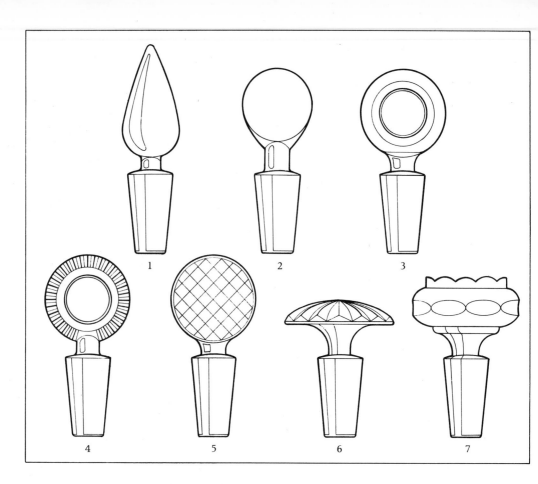

made its reappearance and, in a wide range of qualities, became the most popular decanter style of Victorian times.

The late Georgian era presents several other opportunities for exploring and collecting the wide variety present in a single type of vessel. Condiments and jelly glasses are two of them. Both of these were, of course, also made during the eighteenth century but there was a greater variety of them produced during the first half of the nineteenth century than either earlier or subsequently.

Condiments

The practice of seasoning food with made sauces and seasonings is a very old one. Not only did one add flavour to the food, but from the strength of some of them they undoubtedly also served the purpose of masking the flavour of food which may not have been very fresh. We know what some of these sauces were from the names engraved on silver labels or engraved or gilded on glass bottles. Kyan or cayenne, anchovy, lemon pickle and ketchup or catsup are just a few examples. The use

Decanter stoppers.
1 Spire stopper, plain or facet cut, 1760-80.
2 Lozenge stopper, 1760-1820.
3 Target or bull's eye stopper, 1780-1820.
4 Target stopper with radial grooves, cut or moulded, 1780-1820.
5 Flat round stopper with moulded cross-hatching, 1780-1820. This is often found on Irish decanters.
6 Mushroom stopper, cut or moulded, 1790-1840.
7 Hollow faceted stopper with a raised platform cut with radial grooves, 1830-50.

83 *Top left:* An unusual condiment set of five thinly blown wrythen bottles in a wooden stand, *c.* 1790.

84 *Top right:* Three salt cellars, all on 'lemon squeezer' feet, *c.* 1820.

85 *Above:* Three condiment bottles: (Left to right) Dry mustard bottle, *c.* 1800; Pepper bottle, *c.* 1830; Pepper bottle, *c.* 1820.

of these seasonings was not limited to any particular social class. Condiment sets were made to suit all pockets from the elegant cut glass sets on silver stands of the 1780's to the humble bottles that could be bought individually and knew no container. While complete sets are rare today and command good prices, individual bottles exhibiting all the well-known forms of cutting can be found at quite reasonable prices. Those cut with vertical panels, diamond facet cut bottles, bullseye cutting and various types of diamond cutting are only some of those which have survived.

At a more plebeian level there are many bottles on moulded pedestal feet which can be found individually to make up sets. These generally have bulbous bodies decorated with moulded vertical ribs. It was commonplace to cut small notches in these ribs, either on each or alternate ones. To match the bottles, which usually have pouring spouts, there are mustard pots which are shorter than the bottles. These have short wide necks with a flanged rim, and without their lids (which is usual) look like small Grecian urns. Mustard was generally used as dry, crushed seed, rather as we use black pepper today, and these pots are usually referred to as dry mustards. To match these there were salt cellars, usually with round oval bodies, with the same ribbed patterning as the bottles. Since oil and vinegar were also commonly used it would not be too difficult to assemble a reasonably matching set in this pattern, consisting of salt, mustard and several bottles.

I have mentioned the canoe-shaped salt cellars in connection with the diamond-shaped moulded pedestal feet, but there is one other type of salt cellar which is still fairly common: the monteith or bonnet glass. This consists of a small double ogee bowl of thick glass on a round foot. Some are decorated with cutting to the body and rim, but most have moulded patterns of diamonds or vertical ribs. The feet of these are sometimes roughly lobed to produce what is known as a petal foot.

When electroplating and mould-blown bottles became commonplace later in the nineteenth century, no home, however modest, need be without its cruet stand. However, the commercial sauce bottle seems to have put paid to the use of condiment bottles in recent years.

Jelly glasses

In these little glasses we have another example of domestic glassware which was widely used in the British Isles for two hundred years, but has now gone out of fashion. They fall into two distinct types: tall narrow bell-shaped bowls without stems but with plain or folded feet, and shallow cup-shaped bowls, invariably fitted with handles. Catalogues of the late nineteenth century differentiate between these two styles, calling the tall ones jelly glasses, while the cup-shaped ones are custard glasses.

During the eighteenth century the deep narrow bowl, decorated with various moulded patterns, was universally used, and these were sometimes fitted with one or two plain loop handles, and much more rarely, with double loop or *B*-handles. Although these glasses are generally referred to as

86 *Above:* An early jelly glass with double loop, or *B*, handles. There is a ball knop and a domed foot, *c*. 1740.

87 *Opposite top:* Three jelly glasses. (Left) Funnel bowl with a band of husk engraving, *c*. 1820. (Centre) A heavily cut bell bowl with an everted rim on a star cut foot, *c*. 1830. (Right) A bell bowl with a gadrooned base on a rudimentary stem and a plain foot, *c*. 1860. There was a brief revival in Venetian gadrooned decoration in this period.

88 *Opposite centre:* Two custard glasses, both *c*. 1850. (Left) A waisted bowl and ribbed base. (Right) A waisted gadrooned bowl.

89 *Opposite bottom:* Three custard glasses. The first has a bucket bowl and dates from 1840. The others both have cut bowls and date from 1870.

jelly or custard glasses I can find no reference to them under these names in contemporary lists. However, syllabub, or sillibub, glasses are mentioned quite commonly. A few of these glasses have spreading tops similar to the double ogee type of bowl, and I have had these represented to me as syllabub glasses, but my own opinion is that all these glasses were used as dessert glasses for any of these sweets. Syllabub is made of whipped cream flavoured with white wine and lemon. A whole range of creams or custards were made using egg yolks, milk or cream and flavourings. Jelly was made using calves feet, isinglass or hartshorn (obtained from the antlers of deer) and flavoured sweet or savoury according to its use. Sets of glasses containing these sweets were presented at table on glass stands or tazzas.

By the early nineteenth century the cup-shaped bowl, with no stem or foot, had become popular and these can usually be identified by the elaborate cutting, in the style of the period, which decorates them. During much of the century plain, tapering bowled custards with flared rim were in vogue and towards the end of the century the cup-shaped bowl on a short stem and plain foot makes its appearance. During the latter half of the nineteenth century there was a change in the way handles were applied to glass vessels. This is discussed on pp.

90 *Above:* An eighteenth century tazza, or comporte, showing how the custard and jelly glasses were served to the table. Victoria and Albert Museum, London.

91 An early eighteenth century tazza with a baluster stem consisting of an annulated knop over an inverted baluster and a domed and folded foot, c. 1725.

488 and 492 but it is interesting to note that alone of all the glass of the late Victorian period the fashion persisted of applying the handles to custard glasses in the older manner.

Toddy lifters and stirrup cups

Two small novelty items are associated with this period. They are the toddy lifter and the stirrup cup. Toddy lifters, which usually look like small, long-necked decanters with a hole in the middle of the base, work on the same principle as a pipette. The thick end is immersed in the punch or toddy, it fills under atmospheric pressure, the thumb is placed over the hole in the neck, which prevents the liquid immediately running out again, and then it can be transferred to the glass. When the thumb is removed from the neck the liquid then falls into the intended receptacle. These curiosities were made in a variety of patterns and according to Percy Bate in his book on glass published in 1913, they were peculiarly Scottish. I had never seen any corroborative evidence for this until reading *Notes on a Cellar Book* by G. Saintbury. In a footnote on page 116, relating to toddy made in Scotland, he says 'you do not swig it brutally from the rummer or tumbler, but ladle it genteelly, as required, with a special instrument made and provided for the purpose, into a wine glass . . .' That sounds to me remarkably like a toddy lifter.

Stirrup glasses or cups are usually funnel-bowled wine glasses with a stem but no foot. This leads to suspicions that

they are glasses which have had the feet broken off. There is a good general test to discover whether this is likely. Stand the glass on the end of its stem and try to imagine it with a foot. Would it then conform to the general size and proportion of conventional wine glasses of the period? With true stirrup glasses the answer to this is always 'No', since the bowl is always large in relation to the stem. In other words, it would look top heavy as an ordinary drinking glass. In addition, the stem often terminates in a large facet cut knop which again would be out of character if it were followed immediately by a plain foot. Stirrup glasses were used from the 1830's onwards and are difficult things to date, since they vary little over the years. Their use at hunt meets accounts for their 'gimmicky' nature, since riders on horseback presumably had nowhere they could stand a wine glass with a foot. They are also sometimes called coaching glasses, suggesting that passengers on the outside of the coach could have something warming before starting their journey.

Coloured glass

'Coloured glass' tends to mean slightly different things to different people. To the collector whose interest is centred on drinking glasses of the eighteenth and early nineteenth centuries it is strictly as a term for coloured utilitarian wares. The collector whose interest lies in the late nineteenth century sees it as relating to colour used purely as a decorative

92 *Left:* Two funnel-bowled stirrup cups, *c.* 1840.

93 *Above:* Three toddy lifters, *c.* 1830. The first one has been made to resemble a wine glass but notice the hole running through the stem.

94 *Opposite, above left:* A glass tankard with its body divided by two horizontal applied collars. This style of decoration was used widely in Germany in the seventeenth century on a type of glass called a 'Pasglas'.

95 *Opposite, above right:* A tankard with a gadrooned base and a strap handle, *c.* 1850.

96 *Above:* An oil lamp,
c. 1860. The globular
reservoir held the oil with
the wick showing through a
metal plate on top. The
handle has a thumb grip; the
stem is fixed to a base which
has an upturned rim,
presumably to catch any
drips.

expression of the wealth of ornamental glass produced during
that period. It could be said that the subject is particularly
relevant to the years covered in this chapter, since it was
during the early 1800's that colour became a dominant feature
in glassware. Let us consider, then, the history of the use of
colour in British glass and treat it as a bridge from the
utilitarian to the purely decorative.

The knowledge of, and the ability to produce, colours in
glass is as old as the art of glassmaking itself. In ancient Egypt,
yellow, blue, green and purple, as well as white, were all
colours employed to decorate the small bottles and jars which
have been found by modern excavators. The Portland Vase,
dating from the first century A.D. is an example of blue glass
covered or cased with a layer of white glass. The Venetian
glassmakers of the sixteenth and seventeenth centuries produced glass of every hue, including multi-coloured glass in
perfect imitation of agate and chalcedony. Neri's *L'Arte
Vitrearia* of 1612 gives the recipes for producing every possible
shade of colour in glass. The other important use for coloured
glass had been for windows, principally in churches. This was
an art which had continued in Britain since earliest times.

Although this knowledge was readily available, it was left to
European glassmakers to exploit the use of colour in domestic
glass, and even during the eighteenth century when British
glassmaking reigned supreme, it was largely disregarded in this
country. Could it be that the English Glass Sellers and their

445

customers were so obsessed with the clarity and brilliance of their lead crystal that there was no demand for coloured glass?

Some coloured glass was made, however. One or two globe and shaft decanters made of lead glass and coloured a rich amethyst are attributed to the Ravenscroft period, and one or two early eighteenth century green wine glasses are typical of the baluster and Silesian stem period. However, coloured glasses datable before 1750 are rare. From that date all the principal styles are represented by coloured examples: plain stems, opaque and air twist stems and facet stems, but they remain rare. There are variations among the opaque twist stems, some having clear stems with a white twist, but coloured bowls and feet that are either blue or green. It is interesting to note that while blue, green and purple glasses were made, no yellow or red ones from before 1845 have been identified. The use of threads of colour in opaque twist glasses has already been discussed (see page 401).

From about 1800, and for the next forty years, coloured drinking glasses and decanters were very popular, and most of the coloured glassware to be found today was made during that period. The two most popular styles for coloured drinking glasses were the funnel bowl on a short stem having a central blade knop, and the tulip shape bowl on a plain stem. These survived until about 1830 when styles changed, and in the same way that light baluster glasses had developed from the heavy balusters a century earlier, the coloured wine glasses became lighter, taller and the stems had either ball knops or baluster shapes. These were followed by slender plain stems. In addition to the blue, green and amethyst glasses of this period, brown was also used. It produced glasses ranging from pale amber to a rich caramel brown.

Coloured decanters have already been referred to but a curiosity is that while green wine glasses are common and blue ones are rare, the reverse is true of decanters with the blue ones considerably outnumbering the green ones.

The other colour which was produced during the eighteenth century was opaque white. We have noted its use as the white twisted decoration in the stems of wine glasses, but it was also used in the 1760's to produce glass in imitation of porcelain. At that time porcelain was beginning to be made in England, but it was expensive. By colouring their glass with arsenic or tin oxide the glassmakers could produce a dense opaque white glass which bore a striking resemblance to porcelain. The similarity was enhanced by employing porcelain decorators to paint it. Among these opaque white pieces are some of the earliest glass articles which were more decorative than useful: hanging wall baskets shaped like cornucopiae and small baluster vases to stand on sideboards or mantels.

I have no doubt that many of my readers will be wondering why I have discussed coloured glass at such length without mentioning the name of Bristol. Glass is generally such anonymous stuff and its place of origin unknown that collectors love to have a name to use as a peg on which to hang their acquisitions, and Bristol is the name which is constantly pressed into use as the origin of all coloured glass. I have seen glass of every colour and period represented as Bristol glass, but the facts don't really bear out these sweeping attributions. Coloured glass was undoubtedly made in Bristol, but the Bristol glassmakers had no monopoly. Coloured glass was also made in London, the Midlands and Newcastle, and references to coloured glass made in these areas pre-date the first reference to blue glass made in Bristol, which occurs in the ledgers of Michael Edkins, a decorator of ceramics and glass. In 1763 he recorded 'To gilding four blue jars and beakers for 2/-'. He also recorded work carried out for Lazarus Jacobs, who by 1793 was listed in the Bristol Directory as a 'glass merchant in Avon St.'.

In 1805 Isaac Jacobs (son of Lazarus) opened the Non-Such Flint Glass Manufactory and advertised that he manufactured 'every article in the glass line'. In the following year he again advertised glass, adding 'Coats of Arms, Crests and Cyphers done upon the same in the greatest style, by some of the first artists in the Kingdom . . .' Jacobs is important since a number

97 A perfume bottle, c. 1770. It has fired gilt decoration on faceted blue glass and was made in Bristol. Pilkington Glass Museum, St Helens.

447

of pieces of coloured glass survive, decorated with gilding and marked underneath I. Jacobs, Bristol. These are usually plates or finger bowls bearing a gilded Greek key pattern. It is generally thought that Jacobs was the decorator, but from the above advertisements it is clear that he employed decorators and had his name marked on the product in the same way that Absolom was doing in Yarmouth at the same period.

The only other coloured glass which can be definitely attributed to Bristol are several items marked Wadham Ricketts & Co., who were owners of the Phoenix Glass Works from 1785.

These definite attributions have been largely responsible for linking the name of Bristol so strongly with coloured glass, but there is one other reason which I think has had even more influence, for I am certain that this association is not a recent one, developed in recent years with the enormous increase in interest in old glass. Many people talk of the distinctive purplish tinge in blue glass which proves a Bristol origin. This colour was achieved by using, as a colouring agent, cobalt oxide imported from Saxony. Cobalt had been mixed there from the sixteenth century when it was found that a treated oxide of cobalt called smalt was ideal for producing a blue dye for decorating pottery and for producing a rich blue tint in glass. During the eighteenth century this was imported into England through the port of Bristol, and differing authorities say that it was sold by auction there, or that the supply was controlled by William Cookson, a wholesale druggist in Bristol. There were periods when supplies were interrupted and the glassmakers had to turn to alternative supplies which did not produce such satisfactory results. The quality of the Saxon smalt, then, was such that it was in demand wherever glass was made, and since the sole source of supply in Britain was through Bristol it is quite reasonable to assume that 'Bristol blue' became a widespread hallmark of quality in coloured glass. Link this with marked pieces known to have originated in Bristol and a myth is born.

Glassmaking in Bristol was at its height during the eighteenth century when up to fifteen glasshouses were working, but by 1833 this had declined to four, and by 1900 they had virtually disappeared. If Bristol can claim any special distinction in coloured glassmaking it is for the dense white opaque glass for which it acquired a reputation, rather than the blue and green glass which was made everywhere. The Bristol flint glasshouses also produced the full range of clear and cut glass in all the styles of the eighteenth century and also had a

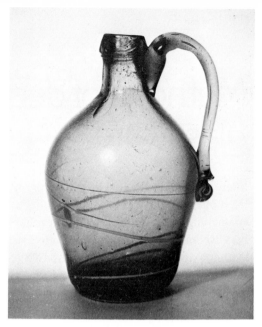

98 *Above:* A striped jug of the Nailsea type, *c.* 1800. The glass made at the Nailsea factory became so popular that it was widely imitated, making a definite identification of the place of manufacture almost impossible. Victoria and Albert Museum, London.

99 *Above right:* Nailsea bottle of green bottle glass with white trailed threads and an applied loop handle, *c.* 1830.

flourishing bottle glass industry which exported vast quantities of bottles to the West Indies and North America.

The mention of bottles brings us onto the other famous glasshouse of the Bristol area which has captured a place in the popular mythology of glass collectors, the Nailsea Glass Company. This was started at Nailsea, a village some miles south-west of Bristol, in 1788 by John Robert Lucas, who came of a Bristol glassmaking family. It was essentially a bottle glasshouse which established a high reputation in that art. It is better known, however, for a variety of domestic articles made of bottle glass but enlivened with flecks or threads of coloured glass. Among these are rolling pins, carafes and jugs. One or two sealed bottles are also known, one of which is dated 1837. These wares are also attributed to a glasshouse at Wrockwardine in Shropshire.

By extension, all decorative glass objects with threads or flecks of colour have become associated with the name, so that now any flask, pipe, rolling pin, hat or other purely ornamental piece of coloured glass is labelled Nailsea. The glasshouse was controlled for many years by the Chance family who were famous glassmakers in the Bristol area and later in Birmingham. A descendant of that family, Sir Hugh Chance, has effectively proved the fallacy of this idea, and it is now accepted that such articles were more generally made in the north of England. The Nailsea glasshouse continued in production until 1869 when it finally closed down.

449

Chapter 5

Methods of decorating glassware

Many different methods of decorating glass have been practised over the centuries. Several of them, such as gilding and enamelling, are also carried out on other materials, but glass, because of its transparency, lends itself uniquely to two methods, those of cutting and engraving.

It is perhaps an indication of the sophistication which glassmaking achieved in the past that almost every important technique for decorating glass was already known 2000 years ago. Many of these died out with the decline of the Roman Empire, and were only rediscovered during the eighteenth and nineteenth centuries.

There are basically two methods of decorating glass—that which is incorporated during its manufacture and is therefore an integral part of the glass, and that which is applied subsequently.

The former was in the control of the glassmaker and included the use of such devices as the knops of baluster stems and the twisted patterns in opaque and air twist stems. Drawing on the inventiveness of the Venetian glassmakers of the sixteenth and seventeenth centuries the English glassmakers also applied threads of glass to their products to embellish them. These were either simply wound round the body of the glass, or were drawn into patterns resembling chains or diamonds. This latter was the 'nipt diamond waies' pattern of Ravenscroft's price list. Thicker threads of glass were added, and then shaped with patterned pincers. The bowls of glasses were blown into moulds to produce particular patterns such as hexagons or ribs, or to receive indented moulding around the base: flutes, dimples, diamonds, etc. All these were to improve the aesthetic appeal of the article, and can therefore be termed decorative techniques.

All other methods of decorating were added by craftsmen working outside the glasshouse, and usually in the employ of the glass sellers. Let us consider these techniques and see how they differ from the same methods used in Europe.

450

Gilding

This was a decorating method which never achieved the same degree of popularity in Britain that it did in Europe. In fact, what popularity it commanded seems to have been prompted by gilded glassware imported from Germany in about 1750. Robert Dossie in his *Handmaid to the Arts* published in 1758 describes at length methods of gilding employed both in Britain and Germany. There were two principal methods: oil gilding and fired gilding. In the former gold powder or leaf was applied over an oil or varnish-based size, which was then burnished. This was applied either to plain surfaces or to heighten engraved decoration. In either case the fixing medium tended to be water soluble, so the gilding was easily removed during normal use. Where it was applied over engraving usually the only evidence of it now is a discoloration caused by the fixing medium rather than the gold.

Fired gilding, on the other hand, was always applied to plain surfaces and heated in the annealing furnaces to produce, when burnished, a firm, durable film of gold. This lasted very well and the small amount of gilding which survives today was executed in this method. Dossie complained that many glasses were gilded in Britain by the oil process in imitation of the German ones, but the poor durability of the gold gave this method of decoration a bad name.

Only one or two names have come down to us as exponents of the art of gilding. James Giles, who had a workshop in London, and is probably better known as a decorator on porcelain, is credited with many fine examples of gilding on scent bottles, decanters and vases. His use of gilded insects has a parallel on early porcelain plates, where they were used to cover blemishes in the firing or glazing. Sprays of flowers and chinoiserie decoration are also motifs attributed to Giles.

I have already referred to Isaac Jacobs in the section on coloured glass, and although it is his name which appears on several gilded pieces it is unlikely that he carried out the work personally. It is more probable that he had a decorating workshop employing both enamellers and gilders.

Michael Edkins, who is better known as an enameller, also carried out gilding, as shown by the ledger entry (page 447).

William Absolom of Great Yarmouth was a retailer of pottery, porcelain and glass from the 1780's to about 1815. A number of glasses have survived, mostly square based rummers and barrel shaped tumblers which carry gilt inscriptions and pictures relating to Great Yarmouth. These frequently have views of Yarmouth Church or a particular type of two-wheeled carriage known as a Yarmouth cart. Other subjects refer to specific persons, associations or regiments. Very rarely these are marked underneath 'Absolom, Yarm 25' referring to his address at No. 25 Market Row. Many of these gilded subjects also appear as engravings on other glasses, but these will be dealt with later.

This flat gilding, practised in Britain, takes its influence from the German style. Gilding in France was of a somewhat different nature since it was more thickly applied and during the nineteenth century when French glassmaking started to achieve some distinction it developed almost to an encrusted technique, with the gilding standing proud of the surface.

Enamelling

Painting in coloured enamels on glass had been practised in Venice and Germany from the late sixteenth century onwards, and in Germany had been brought to a very high standard. As with gilding, it was not until the middle of the eighteenth century, however, that it seems to have made any impact as a decorative technique in Britain. Thorpe suggests that applied decorative techniques in this country were in response to the Excise Act of 1745 which inhibited the glassmakers from expressing themselves in glass. My own feeling is that the demand was as much the result of changing taste which expressed itself in all domestic articles during the reign of George III.

Enamelling, like gilding, was applied by two different methods. Cold enamelling was simply painted on glass. This was a quick and cheap method, but suffered from the fact that it was easily rubbed off. It was used mostly on cheaper goods and it is unusual, these days, to find examples which have survived in good condition. This technique was used on jug and basin sets which were popular in the early 1800's. The decoration was generally floral or consisted of mottoes like 'Be canny with the cream' or 'Remember the Giver'. Much cold enamelling was also applied to the decorative rolling pins which the sailors on the coastal ships reputedly bought in the north of England and decorated during their voyages to sell at their ports of call. The decoration on these was often a combination of freehand enamelling and applied transfers which were over-painted.

The other, more important, method of enamelling, dates back to the mid-eighteenth century when several decorators used a vitreous enamel which became permanent when the

100 *Opposite above:* Four 19th century green wine glasses showing typical styles covering the period 1810-80. Note how the shade of green varied considerably. Miss A. Cawardine.

101 *Opposite below:* An elaborately gilded set of decanters for Madeira, Burgundy and Champaigne with cut spire stoppers gilded to match. These names are unusual to find on the mock inscribed wine-labels applied to decanters from 1760 to 1830.

102 *Above:* A selection of opaque white glass enamelled with floral and chinoiserie subjects, all 1760-70. This type of glass was made in both Stourbridge and Bristol, and the floral decoration is often associated with Michael Edkins, who worked in both places (pages 447 and 455). This type of ware was made in imitation of porcelain and the small vases are some of the earliest examples of glassware made for decorative rather than utilitarian purposes.

103 *Left:* A dark-blue cut butter dish with a domed lid, *c.* 1800. The style of cutting suggests this could have been made in Ireland, and to many people the colour would suggest a Bristol origin. My comments in the text on these areas of glassmaking will show the difficulty of making a definite attribution. Miss A. Cawardine.

104 A typical Jacobite pair of wine glasses of the mid-eighteenth century, bearing the portrait of Charles Edward Stuart. Victoria and Albert Museum, London.

glass was reheated. The two artists whose names are known to us, Michael Edkins and William Beilby, both worked at some time in the Birmingham area where Bilston was renowned for its enamelling trade. They both learned the art there; Edkins then going to Bristol in about 1762 and Beilby setting up his enamelling workshop in Newcastle-on-Tyne in 1760. As they were both of a similar age I wonder if they knew each other before going their separate ways?

Quite a lot is known about Edkins. Some of his ledgers and notebooks have survived and family history was passed on to succeeding generations. At various times he worked as a decorator of Bristol pottery and as a coach and carriage painter before turning his hand to decorating on glass. He painted and gilded for several of the Bristol glass manufacturers including Lazarus Jacobs (father of Isaac) in the mid-1780's. It is difficult to connect his name with any particular item, but by association with articles of pottery he is known to have decorated several pieces of glass painted with sprays of flowers, and birds have also been attributed to him. The finest painting of this period occurs on the opaque white tea caddies and vases for

455

which Bristol is well known. Another favourite subject was chinoiserie decoration showing figures in Chinese dress; the colours are always brilliant and reminiscent of porcelain decoration of the period.

By contrast, William Beilby seems to have confined himself to decorating on glass right from the beginning of his independent career. It is interesting that as late as 1925 the major books dealing with glass made no reference to Beilby and generally attributes his glasses to a Bristol origin. Since then, however, several glasses signed by him have come to light and modern research has given him due credit for his work.

Beilby's work falls into two main categories: commercial work which consists mainly of standard wine glasses of the period decorated in white enamel with a variety of motifs which were repeated many times, and his commissioned work. Among the former are pieces with the grape and vine leaf border, the classical ruins and architectural studies, the sporting and rural pursuits series. Very rarely the rural scenes are executed in a limited colour palette of green, yellow and aubergine. The grape and vine leaf glasses are repetitious, although occasionally the grapes are executed in a pale purple colour. The pictorial glasses are always charming, with the rural scenes showing some affinity with the later wood-engraved vignettes of country life executed by Thomas Bewick, who was apprenticed to William's brother Ralph Beilby. These scenes show huntsmen, anglers, rowers and shepherds.

Beilby's sister Mary is also known to have executed some of the decoration on these little glasses, and much effort has been devoted to trying to distinguish which hand was at work on particular glasses. It is probable, however, that there were other people at work enamelling on glass in Newcastle at this period. Thomas Bewick wrote a memoir of his life which was published in 1862, some years after his death, after careful editing by his daughters. On page 56 of this book there is the following reference:
'. . . and the latter (William) taught his brother Thomas and sister Mary enamelling and painting and, in this way, this most respectable and industrious family lived together and maintained themselves'.
Later:
'He (brother Ralph, an engraver) had also assisted his brother and sister in their constant employment of enamel painting on glass'.

More interesting is the text as Bewick originally wrote it,

456

which was not published until 1975. In this is a reference which does not appear in the 'official' memoir of 1862:
'In my attendance at the work shop of Gilbert (Gilbert Gray, a book binder) I got acquainted with several young men who like myself, admired him – but one of the most singular of these was Anthony Taylor, a glass maker – he was a keen admirer of drawings and paintings but had no opportunity of shewing his talents in the Arts, otherwise than in his paintings and his enamellings on glass, in which way, considering his situation he was proficient'.

Although most of the 'Beilby' glasses are in a closely similar style, and cover the range of subjects I have mentioned, there occasionally appears an enamelled glass in an obviously different hand, and sometimes with enamel of a different quality. With these three names given by Bewick, the question of attribution becomes more difficult.

The commission work that Beilby carried out was usually more elaborate than his commercial work, and often applied in coloured enamels. Among these are glasses inscribed with references to particular groups or individuals, such as 'Success to the Swordmakers' dated 1767, and 'Thos Brown, Nenthead, 1769'. Many of the commissions were for armourial decoration on large goblets which required the use of a wide variety of colours. The Beilby colours are much more subtle than those found in the Bristol enamelling, with a delicate gradation of shade to give the decoration some modelling. The best known of these are the bucket bowled opaque twist goblets with the Royal coat of arms, the Prince of Wales feathers and Beilby's signature, thought to have been produced in 1762 to commemorate the birth of the future George IV.

The Beilbys pursued their profession until about 1770 when they seem to have left Newcastle.

One other small group of glasses is known which has enamelled decoration, and those have a portrait of Bonnie Prince Charlie in Highland dress, executed in coloured enamels. The draughtsmanship is crude when compared with any other enamelling on glass, and may be the work of an amateur.

Cutting

The decoration of glass by cutting is a process that produces highly polished, deeply indented geometric patterns. This process is unique to glass because the refractive property of light passing through it enhances what might otherwise seem a dull, mechanical form of decoration. Glass has been cut from earliest times, and during the seventeenth and eighteenth centuries German decorators developed it to a very high standard, using as their medium the hard, white soda/lime glass which the glassmakers of that country had developed.

When Ravenscroft's lead glass became popular and generally made in Britain it was not long before its advantages as a material for cutting became apparent. Its softness made it easy to cut, and its clarity meant that thicker sections, to carry deep cutting, could be produced. Also, the addition of lead altered the refractive property of the glass so that the cut surfaces produced brilliant prismatic effects. There was little or no experience of cutting in this country because the Venetian tradition on which our industry had grown up depended on a thinly blown product unsuitable for the cutter's wheel. The earliest cutters were German craftsmen imported to work for the glass sellers here. Several early baluster stem glasses have survived decorated with cutting in the German manner; the bowls cut with vertical panels and the knops covered with diamond facets.

The *London Gazette* of 18 October 1709 carried an advertisement which stated, 'There is lately brought over a great parcel of very fine German cut and carved glasses . . .'. Thereafter advertisements for cut glass appear regularly indicating that there was always a market for it. With the imposition of the Excise Duty in 1745 cut glass became an expensive luxury and most of the articles from that period onwards are in the luxury class: chandeliers, girandoles, sweetmeat glasses and salvers.

After the granting of free trade to Ireland in 1780 it is noticeable that the Irish glasshouses which sprang up in response to the opportunity did not have to 'invent' cut glass but imported their equipment and labour from England, which shows that it was a continuing, if exclusive, tradition.

The cutting process consists of marking out a piece of plain blown glass, known as a 'blank' and then roughing out the pattern on a coarse wheel of sandstone or iron on to which was directed a stream of sand and water. This rough pattern was finished to the desired limits and rough polished with a finer wheel, and the resulting design polished with a buffing wheel coated with putty powder or jeweller's rouge. In the early twentieth century a method of polishing called acid polishing was developed whereby the entire surface of the vessel was lightly etched by an acid which produced a bright surface finish. Since this acid attacked the whole surface evenly it is possible to distinguish between this treatment and the earlier hand polishing. Polishing by hand produces sharp crisp edges and it is usually possible to see the 'flow line' produced by the uniform direction of the polishing wheel. Acid polishing removes the sharp edges of the design and leaves a uniform finish over the whole surface.

In the later 1800's it was quite normal for cut glass to be press-moulded to bypass the roughing process so that only a light cut and the polishing processes were required, thus saving time and money.

Various cutting patterns were discussed in the chapter on Irish glass, and the diagram on page 425 illustrates the principal ones used in both countries.

Engraving

Engraving, although it is a form of cutting carried out on a wheel, is a quite different technique from cutting. Engraving is the abrasion of the surface of the glass to produce a roughened area which forms an inscription or a pictorial design. In other words, engraving is a form of writing or drawing on glass which can be carried out in one of two ways—either on a small copper wheel with a shaped profile which is fed with an abrasive compound, or freehand with a sharp pointed tool such as a diamond.

Engraving with a point also can be carried out by two methods, a straightforward line technique as if drawing with a pencil, and another technique known as stipple engraving in which the artist lightly taps the surface of the glass with a point

105 *Below:* A large bucket-bowl rummer engraved to commemorate the establishment of the Steam Engine Makers Society in November 1824. It bears engravings of a steam railway engine, a steam sailing ship and a beam engine.

106 *Below right:* A pressed tankard commemorating the iron bridge over the River Wear at Sunderland, *c.* 1825.

459

to produce a series of minute dots. The density of these dots gives effects of light and shade so that the areas with least dots seem darkest while a close pattern of dots produces the light areas. This is an extremely difficult method of engraving and has only ever had a very few good practitioners.

The earliest English glasses which carry engraving are all examples of diamond point work. Nearly all the surviving examples from the Verzelini glasshouse are decorated with inscriptions and designs using this technique. Wheel engraving, as with other methods of decoration, seems to have been imported here during the eighteenth century from Germany where it had been in common use for a hundred years or more. Engraving never reached a particularly high standard in the British Isles during the eighteenth century, although a distinct improvement can be seen in nineteenth century glasses such as the Sunderland Bridge rummers and various sporting goblets. It is interesting that the best engraving on glass ever produced in this country is being done today by a number of very fine artist engravers. During the eighteenth century the only engraving which could compare with this modern art was carried out by Dutch engravers who achieved most of their best work on English glass. The wheel-engraved work of Jacob Sang is so detailed and delicate that it hardly seems possible that it could have been done freehand by human agency. The stipple engraving of Wolff and Greenwood is so delicate as to be invisible from some angles but brilliant and full of subtle gradation when looked at from the right point of view.

One of the important contributions of engraved decoration is that so much of it was commemorative. Apart from the aesthetic qualities of the engraving such a great deal refers to particular people, places and events. These often serve to define the period when the object was made and thereby give us a reference point to date similar vessels. Collecting commemorative glass is a most worthwhile hobby since one not only learns something of military, political and economic history but at the same time one has reliable evidence for dating the glass.

While many inscriptions refer to known persons or events many others were engraved for private individuals about whose lives we can learn little. But many are dated, and this is the important thing. The following is a list of some of the main subjects commemorated.

Royalty Every monarch from Charles II onwards is referred to on glass. A tall seventeenth century ale flute bears a portrait of Charles II and the inscription 'God Bless King Charles the

Second'. George I is remembered on the four-sided Silesian stem glasses moulded with the words 'God Save the King G.R.'. Queen Victoria's Golden and Diamond Jubilees are remembered on innumerable pressed plates.

Historical events William III's victory in Ireland is found on glasses bearing the words 'To The Immortal Memory' and 'Battle of the Boyne 1 July 1690.'. Every one of Nelson's naval battles may be found mentioned on glass.

Personalities Nelson and Wellington are remembered on many glasses. Admiral Byng, who lost Minorca to the French and was executed in 1757, Admiral Keppel, the Duke of Leinster, Edmund Burke and William Pitt are among many famous people to be found illustrated on drinking glasses.

Political There are many electioneering glasses commemorating candidates for Parliament. Jacobite glasses cover several groups. Many recall the Jacobite cause, some carry portraits of Charles Edward Stuart (Bonnie Prince Charlie) while others were engraved for clubs or societies with Jacobite sympathies; the Society of Sea Serjeants and the Beefeaters Club.

'Wilkes and Liberty' on a glass remembers John Wilkes who attacked the Government in his newspaper *The North Briton* in the 1760's and who, in spite of being gaoled, was elected to Parliament. Other glasses rail against particular taxes and are inscribed 'No Excise'.

On pressed glass can be found references to Gladstone, Disraeli and the Congress of Vienna in 1882.

Industrial One glass has a whaling scene on it; others wish success to 'The Coal Trade', 'The Wool Trade', 'Agriculture' and so on. Several glasses refer to canals, and another which I possessed several years ago was engraved to mark the founding of the 'Steam Engine Makers Society' in 1824.

Bridges were a favourite subject. Everyone has heard of the Sunderland Bridge rummers. This bridge was the largest single-span, vast-iron bridge built in this country. It spanned the Wear at Sunderland and was opened in 1796. Other bridges commemorated are the Scarborough high level bridge and the Newcastle high level bridge which is featured on a press-moulded tankard. Several small glasses recall pit and colliery disasters in which varying numbers of miners lost their lives. These are always cheap glasses coarsely engraved. They were presumably owned by the families of the victims. I wonder how this tradition arose?

Sporting Several hunts and huntsmen are mentioned on glass. Boxers, racehorses and jockeys also feature. Henry Greener of Sunderland produced a pressed glass tankard to honour

107 A pressed tankard commemorating the opening of the high level railway bridge over the Tyne in 1850.

Edward Hanlon, an oarsman who was World Champion sculler in 1880, when he beat Edward Trickett of Australia. This same tankard was re-issued two years later with a slightly altered inscription when he beat Boyd of England.

General Under this heading we may group all those glasses which bear names or initials of ordinary people. Some also have the name of a public house and one may imagine a regular customer insisting on using his own named glass. Sometimes a pair of glasses carries the names of a man and woman and the same date, surely to commemorate their wedding. One mid-eighteenth century glass which passed through my hands was roughly engraved in diamond point 'D. G. died 1826 aged 93 years'. Had D. G. owned that glass since it was new some seventy years earlier?

The practice of commemorating people and events is not dead. A number of modern glasses have been decorated to celebrate Churchill, the Royal Silver Wedding Anniversary, Prince Charles on being made Prince of Wales, the first American space capsule and various boroughs and cathedrals. While many of these may be of doubtful value as investments currently, two hundred years from now I am sure that those which survive will be highly prized. To handle a piece of glass decorated with a reference to some well-known person or event of the past, knowing that it was made and decorated when the subject was alive, or the event topical, gives me a stronger feeling of history and a closer relationship with the past than anything else I know. This must also be the fascination for many people, and account for the high prices which such pieces command when they appear in the sale rooms.

One of the reasons why so many people, places and events are remembered on engraved glass is that it was such an ideal medium for decoration. It was widely and readily available at all price levels, it was a durable material, it didn't require much equipment to carry out the decoration which could be applied anywhere at any time, and it required no subsequent finishing treatments. By contrast, decoration on pottery and porcelain required the availability of glazing equipment and kilns for firing. The potting process did not lend itself so well to the production of 'one-off' pieces. Commemorative scenes and inscriptions engraved on silver and gold were only for the wealthier classes, and in any case would not display as well as decorated glassware.

There is much confusion between wheel engraving and the acid process described next. Although the general apperance

108 *Top:* Electioneering glass. Its ogee bowl is inscribed 'Sir Francis Knollys and Liberty 1761'. In that year Knollys was returned to Parliament as MP for Reading.

109 *Above:* A privateer glass. The bucket bowl reads 'Success to the Defiance privateer'. The glass has an opaque-twist stem and a plain foot. The Defiance sailed from Bristol.

110 *Top:* A sporting goblet. The round funnel bowl is engraved with a fox hunting scene and the words 'Prosperity to Fox Hunting'. The unusual air twist stem has knops at shoulder and base, *c.* 1760.

111 *Above:* An opaque-twist wine glass engraved in the manner of David Wolff. Two mannikins clasp hands and drink a toast.

is often similar, there are distinct differences. Close inspection with a magnifying glass will show the individual strokes of the engraver's wheel quite clearly. Acid etching produces an even finish on the decorated area free from the variations of depth associated with wheel engraving. The outline of acid etched areas is also much more sharply defined than on engraved glasses.

Acid etching

This is another process which originated in Europe and was only taken up generally in this country very much later. The earliest known piece of glass decorated with acid was made in Germany, and dated 1686. It is not known exactly what sort of acid was used, but with the discovery of hydrofluoric acid in Sweden around 1770 a most effective medium for etching glass came into being.

The method generally used was to cover the vessel in an acid resistant varnish, the desired decoration was inscribed through this coating to expose the glass, which was then subjected to attack by acid. After the correct depth of pattern was achieved the acid was washed off and the varnish dissolved. An English example dated 1783 survives using this technique. This method proved nearly as laborious as engraving, but eventually two faster methods were developed for producing the decoration. One was in effect a transfer on paper which could be produced in quantity from an engraved plate. Instead of printing ink the transfer was coated with the masking varnish which could be applied in one go to the glass. This was then dipped in acid, and after the removal of the varnish the subject of the transfer appeared on the glass. This method had some currency from about 1840 to 1860. In about 1860 John Northwood of Stourbridge introduced a semi-mechanical process for acid etching. This was a form of copying machine in which a pointer traced round a master pattern transferred the design to a needle in contact with a varnish-covered glass. This meant that quite elaborate patterns could be copied exactly many times with little skill required from the operator. Patterns produced in this way are distinctive because the outline, when viewed through a magnifying glass, is of an even width and depth.

Northwood subsequently developed a machine for producing geometric patterns directly onto the vessels covered with protective varnish, and these were produced in large quantities well into this century. The Greek key pattern was one of the most popular achieved by this method.

463

Chapter 6

Victorian glassmaking

In 1833 a Commission on Glass Industries had investigated the state of the trade. Although it had reported its parlous condition, it took until 1845 before declining revenues from the punitive Excise Duty made the Government feel that the return did not justify the cost of collection and withdraw it. While the Excise Duty was in force no glassmaker could call his business his own. Every step in the process was under the control and supervision of the Exciseman resident in the glassworks. The withdrawal of the Excise Duty, followed by the Great Exhibition of 1851, signalled both an ending and a beginning.

What ended was the orderly progression from one style of glassmaking or decorative fashion to another, which had endured for a hundred and fifty years, during which time the glass sellers had largely dictated the direction in which domestic glassware had developed, and the manufacturers had claimed that the Excise Duty had inhibited experimentation.

The new beginning was initially a reaction which set in when the relief from Excise Duty encouraged the glassmakers into a new exuberance because the amount of metal in any article they made was no longer limited by financial considerations. This led to deeper and more elaborate cutting which found its culmination in the Exhibition of 1851. Some of the glassware shown there was technically marvellous but totally impractical. At the same time English glassmakers began experimenting with the decorative techniques then popular in Europe; the use of coloured glass, coloured overlays, opaline glass and so on. The Great Exhibition brought many manufacturers of these wares to England, and the public was introduced to a diversity of decorative glassware that it had not seen before. Some of these caught the public imagination, and the English glassmakers, realising the potential business to be done, and looking for outlets for their new-found freedom of expression, seized upon these foreign styles and started to diversify as they had never done before. When new techniques were required such as the overlaying of one colour upon another, or the very individual styles of decoration which made these foreign wares attractive, they did not hesitate to import foreign craftsmen from whom they could learn these new skills.

The results of all this were an infusion of new blood into the industry, a widening of the variety of glass being made, a new approach to glassmaking which placed the emphasis on decorative effect for its own sake and, most far-reaching, a strong tendency of the glass companies to be the originators of ideas and new styles, so that production, decoration and distribution were all controlled by one source. Arising from these circumstances the British glass industry of the second half of the nineteenth century became a major manufacturing industry which exercised an important influence on domestic style and taste. It is this movement and these companies that we shall look at during this chapter.

The Great Exhibition of 1851 was held in a building specially built for the purpose. The glassmakers played an important part in its construction and decoration, as well as featuring among the exhibitors. The exhibition hall, which became known as the Crystal Palace, was covered entirely in glass. The building covered about nineteen acres, and Chance Bros. of Birmingham supplied nearly 900,000 square feet of glazing which weighed about 400 tons. One of the principal features in the centre of the edifice was a large fountain standing twenty-seven feet high, constructed of glass and supported on an iron frame hidden within it which was made by F. & C. Osler of Birmingham. In addition, Thorpe states that there were as many as seventy-nine glass companies exhibiting their products, but that presumably included non-flint glass firms, decorating companies and foreign exhibitors since Powell records only seventeen British glass manufacturers. The list of these included names of companies who became the major innovators and leaders of the industry throughout the next fifty years: Bacchus & Co. of Birmingham; Lloyd & Summerfield, Birmingham; Pellatt & Co., London; Richardson, Stourbridge; Molineaux & Webb, Manchester; James Powell & Co., London.

Among the foreign exhibitors were Harrach of Bohemia showing overlay and coloured glass, Hoffman of Prague showing opaline glass and Neffen of Austria, similar to Hoffman. All these products were subsequently copied in the British Isles.

Because of the great diversity of glass which was made during the second half of the nineteenth century and the

112 The glass fountain built for the Great Exhibition of 1851 by F. & C. Osler.

copying and overlapping between one company and another it is not easy to plot the progress of glassmaking during this period in an orderly and coherent manner. In an effort to provide the interested collector with a framework on which to hang this bewildering variety I have arranged the opposite chart showing the principal and best-known firms with the bare facts of what is known about them. (The entries are grouped by town of operation, and the firms appear alphabetically within each sub-group.) This chart is followed by notes on each one, elaborating the chart. Finally I will review the principal types of glass which they made.

113 A glass plate with sulphide encrustation marked on the back, c. 1840. This piece was manufactured by Pellatt & Green, who formerly had been Apsley Pellatt & Co.

Apsley Pellatt & Co., Falcon Works, Southwark, London Apsley Pellatt Senior took over the Falcon Glassworks in Southwark about 1790 and was succeeded in about 1820 by his son Apsley Pellatt Junior. For a while the firm operated as Pellatt & Green but subsequently became Apsley Pellatt & Co., Pellatt Junior retired in 1852 on becoming a Member of Parliament, and the firm continued variously under the control of other members of the family until 1895. Apsley Pellatt Junior was of an enquiring turn of mind, published several books, of which *The Curiosities of Glassmaking*, 1849, is the best known, and patented several new glassmaking techniques. He was best known for the incorporation of small relief-moulded plaques into crystal glass vessels which are commonly called sulphides. I have seen one of these set in a glass plate marked 'Pellatt & Green, Falcon Works, London': the only other mark I know of is on an engraved goblet made for the 1862 Exhibition marked 'Pellatt'. The cut glass which this company produced at the time of the Great Exhibition was of a brilliant whiteness and clarity, with cutting of a very high standard, but generally over-elaborate.

James Powell, Whitefriars Glassworks, London The glasshouse at Whitefriars in London had existed from about 1700 and, as was the case with many glasshouses, had had a succession of owners over the years until it was acquired by James Powell & Sons in 1835. The Powells had come from Bristol where glassmaking was on the decline and they continued in London until 1923 when they moved to Wealdstone so that they could claim to be the last of the London flint glasshouses, which had numbered about fifteen in 1760.

They also showed cut and engraved glass in 1851, but later in the century worked closely with members of the Arts and Crafts Movement.

Powells also made many copies of earlier styles, particularly Venetian and English baluster types. In the 1920's they made

466

Name	Town	Operating period	Trademark	Principal products
Apsley Pellatt & Co.	London	1820-95	Pellat & Green, Falcon Works, London	Fine cut glass, sulphide encrustation
James Powell	London	1835-1980		Cut glass, copies of antique styles, Arts & Crafts Movement styles
George Bacchus	Birmingham	1818-97	George Bacchus & Son	Coloured glass, transfer prints
Lloyd & Summerfield	Birmingham	1780-?		Glass busts, coloured glass for church windows
F. & C. Osler	Birmingham	1807-?		Cut glass, glass busts, monumental and large glass
Rice Harris & Co.	Birmingham	1830?-60+	I.G.W.	Paperweight, pressed glass
Boulton & Mills	Stourbridge	1876-1925		Coloured, applied foliage, epergnes
W. H., B. & J. Richardson	Stourbridge	1837-1937	Richardson Vitrified	Cut glass, coloured glass, overlay, Etruscan style, painted, transfer
Thomas Webb	Stourbridge	1856-today	Thos. Webb & Sons	Satin glass, Burmese, cameo, coloured, engraved, gilded
Stevens & Williams	Stourbridge	1847-today		Rock crystal engraving, threading, coloured, overlay
Birtles Tate & Co.	Manchester	1858-1922+		Pressed glass, coloured glass
J. Derbyshire & Co.	Manchester	1873-?	JD superimposed on an anchor	Pressed glass, translucent colours, cast animal figures
Molineaux Webb & Co.	Manchester	1825?-1900+		Cut table glass, pressed glass
Percival Vickers	Manchester			Pressed glass
G. Davidson	Gateshead	1867-today	Lion from mural crown	Pressed glass (slag) coloured
Sowerby	Gateshead	1850-today	Peacock head	Pressed glass (slag) coloured
H. Greener & Co.	Sunderland	1869-today	Lion with star or axe	Pressed glass (slag)
W. H. Heppell	Newcastle	1850+-84		Pressed glass (slag)
J. Ford	Edinburgh	1815-1904	Thistle?	Cut glass, pressed glass, engraved glass
J. Couper & Co.	Glasgow	1853-1913	Clutha	Decorative bubbly glass

some reconstructions of fifteenth century glasses based on fragments found in the Chiddingfold area.

George Bacchus, Birmingham This firm exhibited cut overlay glass in the style of Bohemian glass at the 1851 Exhibition. They also produced delicate black transfer prints in the Etruscan style on white opaline glass. They later went on to make pressed glass.

Lloyd & Summerfield, Birmingham Heath This firm exhibited in London both in 1851 and in 1862. At the former exhibition their display included very ornate jugs in coloured overlay glass with applied bunches of grapes in glass, also elaborately engraved wine glasses with serpentine stems in the Venetian style. They are probably best known to collectors, however, for the busts they produced in cast glass with a frosted finish of notable people of the day. Among these were Queen Victoria, Prince Albert and John Wesley.

F. & C. Osler, Broad Street, Birmingham The main claim to fame of this firm seems to have been the outsize examples of cut glass fabrications they produced for the 1851 Exhibition. These included a twenty-foot chandelier as well as the fountain already referred to, which weighed nearly four tons. It is illustrated on p. 465. They also produced glass busts similar to those of Lloyd & Summerfield.

Rice Harris & Co., Islington Glassworks, Birmingham The Art Journal catalogue of the Great Exhibition devoted two pages to the display of Rice Harris, which consisted of extremely elaborate and over-decorated examples of decorative glassware, most of which has a pseudo Bohemian Moorish appearance. Such was the love of ornament at that time that the writer in the Art Journal says: 'The space we have devoted to illustrating a portion of them is not greater than their excellence demands'. The display consisted of 'Ornamental glass of various colours, gilt and enamelled, cut and engraved, consisting of tazzas, compotiers, liqueur services, toilet bottles, claret jugs, vases, specimens of colour combined by casing or coating, specimens of threaded or Venetian glass.'

At the same time they were showing pressed and moulded tumblers, goblets and wine glasses. This was a fairly new art at that time, and Rice Harris must have been among the pioneers of the technique in the Midlands, since they were the only firm recorded as exhibiting these products.

The mark I.G.W. appears in one or two millefiori paperweights and is always taken to refer to the Islington Glass Works.

Boulton & Mills, Audnam Glassworks, Wordsley, Stourbridge This firm made coloured decorative glass, much of it decorated with applied pincered trails of foliage and fruit in coloured glass. They were also leaders in the design and manufacture of épergnes and table centrepieces, without which no Victorian home was complete. These were composed of branches forming flower holders, and arms for hanging baskets.

W. H., B. and J. Richardson, Wordsley, Stourbridge The initials refer to three brothers, William Hayden, Benjamin and Jonathan. The first two worked at the Wordsley Glass Works, which had been in operation since about 1720. In 1829, in conjunction with Thomas Webb, they acquired these works and set up as Webb & Richardson. In 1836 Webb left them, whereupon they were joined by their brother Jonathan to form the company of W. H., B and J. Richardson. This proved to be one of the most adventurous and innovative of all the Midlands glassworks. Benjamin was the most renowned of the three, and under his leadership the firm developed many new styles of colouring and decorating. At the Great Exhibition they showed some of the most florid and heavily cut glass that anyone had ever seen, but by the 1860's they had turned to coloured glass decorated with transfers or coloured enamels in a much more natural style.

They also favoured the Etruscan style which George Bacchus produced, although their wares were more colourful. Another motif they used was the application of handles or ropes of glass to the outside of opaline vessels, which were gilded to look like snakes.

My own personal favourite among their products is a series of water sets which were very realistically painted with water plants—marsh marigolds and yellow irises among them. These patterns were also engraved upon jug and tumbler sets. Their mark is usually Richardson on a banner, with the word 'Vitrified' underneath. The firm survived under the name of Richardson until 1937.

Thomas Webb, Stourbridge This is probably the best known of all the Midlands glass companies, surviving down to the present day under various names, but currently operating as Dema Glass Ltd.

Thomas Webb (1802-69) inherited the White House Glass Works at Wordsley from his father in 1836, which was the reason for his leaving the firm of Webb & Richardson already referred to. After one year he acquired the Platts Glasshouse at Amblecote which had then been making glass for over a hundred years. He continued there until 1855 when he built the new Dennis Glass Works at Amblecote. This became the Webb's Crystal Glass Company in 1919 and in 1964 became part of the Dema Group which includes the old Edinburgh & Leith Flint Glass Company.

At the 1851 Exhibition Thomas Webb & Co. showed table glass, but the Art Journal did not think it important enough to illustrate. However, during the later years of the century they employed some fine engravers, including Fritsche and Kny, and made Burmese glass under licence from the Mount Washington Glass Co. in Boston, U.S.A. They produced cameo glass, which has become so desirable today, satin glass and several other attractive styles with names like 'coraline', 'Peachbloom', 'Alexandrite'. In 1882 they persuaded Jules Barbe, a French gilder, to set up a workshop on their premises and he was responsible for some superb gilding for Webb.

Stevens & Williams, Brierley Hill, Stourbridge This glasshouse arose from the marriage of William Stevens and Samuel Williams to the two daughters of Joseph Silvers, who operated the Moor Lane Glass House in Brierley Hill, the glasshouse having started in about 1779. They changed the name to Stevens & Williams in 1847 and it continues in production at the present time.

They do not appear to have exhibited at the major exhibitions of the period, but were responsible for some good quality and imaginative coloured decorative wares. One of their more striking products was called 'Silveria'; glass vessels of double thickness enclosing a layer of silver leaf and with random threads of coloured glass trailed on the outside. They also manufactured a pinkish-red glass coloured with gold, which contained pockets of air which shine golden as the article is turned. The outside is entirely covered with a fine thread of trailed glass. They had German engravers working for them producing glass engraved in the 'rock crystal' style. Probably the most famous glassmaker and designer to work for them was Frederick Carder who went to America in 1903 where he founded the Steuben Glass Works. He was a prolific designer of both cut glass and coloured decorative glass.

Birtles Tate & Co., Oldham Road, Manchester This wellknown Manchester firm made a whole range of glassware, including pressed glass, a number of designs for which were registered. They produced one of the many versions of shaded glass which were popular in the 1880's which they called 'Sunrise'. They also made épergnes. The company was working well into this century.

114 *Opposite, above:* Three examples of George Davidson's *Pearline* glass. The white areas are achieved by partial reheating. *Pearline* glass was made from 1889 onwards. Miss A. Cawardine.

115 *Opposite, below:* Four wine glasses having colour twist stems, all *c.* 1760. The green and blue pattern of the extreme left example is rare. These English glasses should not be confused with the Continental colour twist glasses which are much more common.

116 *Left:* Two examples of the revival of the Venetian style. Both were made by James Powell's Whitefriars Glassworks in the 1880's. (Left) A tall ale flute with a hollow quatrefoil knop. (Right) A small beaker decorated with applied threads of glass.

117 *Below:* An overlay vase by Thomas Webb & Sons in a pseudo-cameo technique *c.* 1926. The relief is achieved by acid etching (page 463). Miss A. Cawardine.

118 *Bottom:* A pair of white vases transfer-printed with Greek classical scenes, a style much in vogue in the 1860's and 1870's. This pair is marked 'Geo. Bacchus and Son'. Miss A. Cawardine.

119 A typical mark of a glassmaker, in this case that of J. Derbyshire & Co.

120 A pressed glass sugar basin and cream jug by Molineaux Webb & Co. of Manchester. They carry the registration mark for 1865.

J. Derbyshire & Co., Manchester There were two firms operating under this name. It would seem as if John and James worked together initially in the 1860's as James Derbyshire & Bros. After changing to J. J. & T. Derbyshire they finally separated, James to set up in Hulme as James Derbyshire & Sons, and John Derbyshire to set up the Regent Flint Glass Works in Salford.

The products of John Derbyshire are better known because he used a trade mark and registered some of his designs. His mark consisted of JD superimposed on an anchor. This is a little confusing, since John Davenport of Longport also used the anchor mark on his pottery. In Davenport's case the anchor was used only until 1830; Derbyshire didn't introduce his until the 1870's.

He appears to have been exclusively a pressed glass manufacturer, and amongst his best-known wares are a series of moulded figures, Punch and Judy, Britannia, Queen Victoria. These are distinctive because of the very oily looking shades of translucent green and yellow glass from which they were sometimes made. His copies of the Landseer lions made for the foot of Nelson's Column are also well known.

In 1877 the company changed its name to the Regent Flint Glass Co., so it is possible that John Derbyshire severed his connection with it. This firm continued into this century but little more is known of it or Derbyshire.

Molineaux Webb & Co., Ancoats, Manchester At the 1851

Exhibition this company displayed a variety of cut and coloured glass which compares favourably with the other products of other, perhaps better known, glasshouses. They are much better known to collectors, however, for their pressed glass and it would seem that later in the century these wares accounted for the bulk of their production. Their work can be identified from the many patterns which they registered. These have such a distinctive quality that with a little practice even their unmarked wares can be identified. Crispness of moulding, the weight and liberal use of frosted areas are typical characteristics of Molineaux Webb. Interestingly these qualities are also apparent in the cut wares they made, which seems to indicate that they translated their attitude towards cut glass into their pressed products.

Percival Vickers, Manchester Although this company made a range of glassware by all the normal methods they were among the first to register designs for pressed glass as early as 1847. The firm began life as Percival Yates; Vickers joined them around 1860, and Yates disappeared about 1870 to leave them with the name they are best known by. They were still registering designs in 1883, the last year of the diamond registration mark.

121 A pressed comporte by Percival Vickers of Manchester. It has the registration mark for 1878.

474

G. Davidson, Team Glassworks, Gateshead This was one of the two great northern glassmaking firms standing equal in importance with Sowerbys. It was founded by George Davidson, a local businessman, in 1867 when one of its principal products was glass chimneys for oil lamps. In 1881 they acquired the stock, moulds and patterns of the Neville Glass Works (the same Samuel Neville who had left Sowerbys in 1874). Then in 1884 they also acquired the moulds and stock of W. H. Heppell & Co. of Newcastle and also those of Thomas Gray & Co. of Gateshead. This gave them a large and varied range of patterns which appeared subsequently in their own pattern books.

It was to prove of great benefit when George's son Thomas Davidson joined the company in the 1870's. He was a man of great imagination and artistic ability, and became responsible for the great majority of the designs produced by the company. There is some similarity between the Davidson 'slag glass' patterns and colours and those of Sowerby, but each firm had its own distinctive style, so that with a little practice it is usually possible to identify unmarked pieces. Davidsons used the mark of a lion emerging from a mural crown, but rarely registered any of their patterns. From looking at surviving catalogues it appears to me that G. Davidson & Co. produced a wider range of patterns and designs, but many of them were for purely utilitarian domestic use. They also continue in production up to the present time making industrial glassware.

Sowerby's Ellison Glassworks, Gateshead Like so many glassworks, this one had a long and varied history before it became known by the name above, and produced the glass for which it is best known.

George Sowerby set up a glasshouse in Pipewellgate, Gateshead in about 1765. It continued in the control of the family, moving to new premises in Ellison Street in 1850. This must have been large by the standards of the day, since it had six 8-pot furnaces.

It was from this time that pressed glass manufacture was started, and Sowerbys went on to become one of the most inventive and innovative in this field in the United Kingdom.

In 1855 John Sowerby took into partnership Samuel Neville, who had learned his craft in Stourbridge, and the firm became Sowerby & Neville. Neville left in 1874 to start his own glasshouse, and for the next eight years the firm was Sowerby & Co. In 1882 another John Sowerby changed the name to Sowerby's Ellison Glass Co. Ltd.

By 1887 the company had offices in the major capitals of

Europe, much of their production was exported, and they were employing up to 1000 men.

When the registration of trade marks was introduced, Sowerbys were among the first to register, using a peacock's head mark which was the family crest of a branch of the Sowerby family. Much of their production bore this mark and the registration mark, thus making it attractive to collectors today since it can be readily identified.

They are best known for that type of pressed glass which is commonly called slag glass today, but which they called vitro-porcelain. It was opaque coloured glass pressed into a wide variety of attractive shapes and patterns. At the height of its popularity Sowerbys were producing 150 tons per week of finished products. The company survives today making industrial glassware.

H. Greener & Co., Wear Flint Glassworks, Sunderland
Glassmaking in Sunderland goes back to the eighteenth century, and Henry Greener was born into a glassmaking family in 1820. He was apprenticed in Newcastle, and for a time worked for Sowerbys.

In 1858 he formed a partnership with James Angus and operated the Wear Flint Glass Works as Angus & Greener. In 1869 Angus died, and Greener then built a new glasshouse at Millfield. When Henry Greener died in 1882 he instructed his executors, members of the family, to continue the business in the same way under the same name. Apparently this was not a good idea, since in 1885 the business was taken over by James Jobling, a Newcastle chemical merchant. The name was changed to Greener & Co., and the company took on a new lease of life, extending its range of domestic and industrial wares. In the 1920's it introduced the first heat-resistant domestic glassware under the name of Pyrex.

H. Greener & Co. was another of the few firms to use a trade mark. Initially this was a demi-lion rampant bearing in its right paw a star. After the business was taken over by Jobling the star was changed for a halberd. Neither Greener mark is common, but the latter mark is much more infrequent than the former. There is sometimes confusion between the Davidson and Greener marks, but the thing to remember is that the Davidson mark is distinguished by the mural crown, which looks like a crenellated turret.

Although Greener used most of the same opaque colours as the other 'slag glass' manufacturers, they have their own style. One popular feature on their jugs and tankards was a handle made with a rustic or wood finish. They also seem to have been quick to issue commemorative items.

W. H. Heppell, Newcastle Flint Glassworks, Newcastle
Although this company did not have a very long life it deserves notice because it registered some twelve designs, and its authorship of these can be traced from the registration marks.

William Henry Heppell took over an existing glasshouse in about 1869 and produced some interesting pressed glass until George Davidson acquired the moulds and patterns in 1884. Best known, perhaps, are a series of jugs formed like fish standing upright, the tails folded round to provide the handle and the mouths open to form the rim and pouring lip.

J. Ford, Holyrood Glassworks, Edinburgh This company was started in 1810 by William Ford, who acquired a glasshouse which had been in operation since the late eighteenth century. He died in 1819 and the company was taken over by Bailey & Co. of the Midlothian Glass Works, with his nephew, John Ford, being one of the directors. In 1835 the company was dissolved and John Ford took it over on his own account. This was when it became the Holyrood Flint Glass Works. The business expanded and produced a wide range of good quality domestic glassware.

John Ford died in 1865 and the name was changed to John Ford & Co. under the management of William Ford, John's son, and Francis Ranken, a member of another local family of glassmakers. The manufacturing side of the business ended in 1904, although the retail side continued under the Rankens until 1959.

Much of the product was engraved, and the fern leaf decoration, so popular in Victorian times, was one of their most popular subjects. In the 1860's, a Bohemian engraver named Müller came to work in Edinburgh, and over the following years he and his son carried out some excellent work on the glass made by J. Ford & Co. They produced pressed glass in quantity and a thistle mark which very rarely appears on these wares is sometimes attributed to them, but there is no proof of this so far.

J. Couper & Son, City Glassworks, Glasgow This firm is interesting because William Haden Richardson of the Stourbridge glass family worked for them for a period from 1853. In the 1890's they produced a style of greenish glass inset with bubbles of air which gave it a distinctly antique appearance. This was called 'Clutha', and was designed for them by, among others, Christopher Dresser, well-known in the 'Arts and Crafts' Movement. Some of the patterns drew on Roman and Persian styles for their inspiration.

477

Chapter 7

Victorian decorative glass

I have already remarked on the difficulty of dating Victorian glass or putting it into any coherent sequence. This is because some styles became popular and enjoyed a long period of popularity (e.g. some styles of decanters) whereas others came and went in a short space of time to be replaced by other styles totally dissimilar. One good generalisation which can be made, however, is that cut glass fell out of favour by the 1860's and did not become popular again until the 1880's. The reaction that set in during the intervening period led to the popularity of thinly blown glassware either made in a free flowing style or decorated in a naturalistic manner.

Because of these extremes of taste it will be easier to discuss Victorian glass under the headings of decoration.

Cut glass

Although I have dealt largely with this subject in chapters two and especially five, there are one or two further points to make with regard to the cut glass of the late Victorian era. As cut glass began to regain its popularity in the 1880's the old shallow cutting of the Georgian period and the deep mitre cutting of the early Victorian era gave way to very elaborate and ornate styles which covered the surface with a multitude of straight lines which produced patterns of stars and diamonds. This can be seen on many of the square decanters of the period which were made in sets of two or three to fill a lockable stand known as a tantalus. In America this type of cutting was known as brilliant cutting, which describes it exactly. In the twentieth century this over-effusive style gave way to patterns of a few deep cuts crossing one another at angles and leaving most of the surface untouched.

Engraved glass

The standard of engraving on glass improved dramatically during the nineteenth century. Some of the finest exponents were artists from Germany and Bohemia who settled in Britain;

Frederick Kny and William Fritsche are probably the best known because they left signed pieces and well documented items which were exhibited at all the major exhibitions. As well as these two, who worked in the Birmingham/Stourbridge area, other Continental names which are recorded include F. Scheibner, J. Schiller and J. Keller. In London Paul Oppitz was a freelance engraver who worked for, among others, Copeland. In Scotland Miller, another Keller, Lerche and Tieze were all European craftsmen who engraved for Edinburgh and Glasgow glasshouses. The last named, Tieze, also worked in Dublin where Joseph Eisert is recorded as an engraver. There was nothing new about this influx, of course. When the demand for cut glass arose in the early eighteenth century, German cutters were introduced into Britain, so the story was repeating itself.

This influx of foreign talent encouraged a rise in the art generally, and a number of native-born engravers rose to great prominence during the second half of the century. W. J. Muckley engraved for Richardsons and exhibited at the Great Exhibition, as did Thomas Wood of Stourbridge. Probably the most important amongst the English decorators was John Northwood. Born in 1836, he learned the art of decorating glass with W. H., B. & J. Richardson, to whom he was apprenticed in 1848. He was a fine artist and studied at the Stourbridge School of Art. In 1859 he set up his own design and decorating workshops, where he was responsible for a number of advances in decorating technique. Among these were 'intaglio' cutting—a method which combined the freedom of engraving with the depth of cutting; the pattern copying machine for acid etching, and most important of all, the art of cameo engraving on glass. In 1882 he joined Stevens & Williams as artistic director, where he remained until his death in 1902. During his life he was at the hub of the glass industry in Stourbridge and was associated with all the leading members of it.

Wheel engraving achieves its effect by the abrasion of the surface over the whole area of the design. Intaglio engraving is more deeply cut into the surface, so that elements of the pattern may be said to be in reverse relief, with the highest points of the pattern being the surface of the glass. The Germans called this 'Tiefschnitt' (deep cutting).

A development of this technique led to one of the most distinctive forms of Victorian engraving, the style known as 'rock crystal'. In this the whole surface of the vessel was worked on to produce intaglio designs, usually in panels, which were surrounded by ornamentation. The surface was then highly polished to produce the effect which the Chinese carvers had achieved on blocks of natural crystal, hence its name. Leading exponents of this technique were Kny, Fritsche and an Englishman, John Orchard, who worked for Stevens & Williams. This highly ornate and elaborate style is sometimes mistaken for moulded work, but its very high polish distinguishes it.

Cameo

In its purest form this style is carried out by carving rather than engraving, but over the years the method was modified to include wheel engraving and acid etching.

It owes its development in England to a desire to produce a copy of the famous Portland, or Barberini, vase which Sir William Hamilton brought back from Italy in the eighteenth century. It is a first century Roman vase, about 9 inches high, of dark blue glass overlaid with carved classical scenes in white glass. John Northwood was encouraged to attempt a copy by Benjamin Richardson and Phillip Pargetter, whose glassworks produced the blank which had a layer of white glass over a base of dark blue glass. With carving tools of his own design and manufacture Northwood spent three years from 1873 to 1876 in producing this copy. Unfortunately, when nearing completion it cracked, and Northwood attributed this to stresses induced by the differences in the two layers of glass. After several more years of experimentation he solved this problem and evolved a technique for producing cameo glass with as many as four different layers of colour. As the technique of cutting through these layers developed it became common to remove the surplus metal by grinding or by acid etching, while only the finishing was carried out by carving.

There developed some very able exponents of this method, George and Thomas Woodall being perhaps the most famous after Northwood. The modelling of the designs is achieved by the degree to which the base colour shows through the superimposed layers.

As with so many Victorian styles, the mass demand for expensive objects was met by reproducing them in the crudest and coarsest manner. This was true of cameo glass, and one often finds vases in the typical colours of blue, dark red and amber overlaid with painted white enamel decoration which gives it a superficial impression of cameo work.

Silver coating

The foregoing comments apply equally to a type of glass patented in 1849 by F. Hale Thompson and Edward Varnish.

480

123 A pair of 'Queen's Ware Burmese glass' vases by Thomas Webb & Co, *c.* 1886, made under licence from the Mount Washington Glass Co. of America. The colouring was obtained by the inclusion of gold and uranium among the ingredients.

124 *Right:* A small vase that combines the revival of the Venetian taste with the fashion for iridescent glass. The iridescent bronze-green body has applied shell prunts studded with coloured glass jewels. It was possibly manufactured by Stevens & Williams, *c.* 1880. Miss A. Cawardine.

125 *Below:* A vase by Thomas Webb & Son. The enamel and gilt decoration is signed by Jules Barbe, a French decorator who had a studio at the Webb factory from 1882 to 1920.

126 *Above:* A pair of small white jugs with hand-painted floral decoration in the manner of Thomas Bott, who worked for Richardson's of Stourbridge, *c.* 1860.

127 *Left:* As with **124**, another example of the Venetian revival, but with a strong English flavour to it. The red body has an applied trailed thread overlaid with prunts and vertical lines of clear glass, *c.* 1880.

This was made in a manner similar to the silvered container in a vacuum flask today, in that a solution of silver was deposited on the interior of a double walled vessel, which was then sealed to protect the coating. This was then often covered with a layer of transparent coloured glass, and through this a pattern was cut to expose the bright silver finish beneath. Genuine pieces are of noticeably good quality and set into the base is a disc bearing the words 'Hale Thompson's Patent, London', 'E. Varnish & Co. Patent, London' or, much more rarely 'W. Lund, Patent, London'. These wares were obviously very popular since one sees, even today, many badly made copies of extremely light weight, with no seal in the bottom and usually with crudely applied enamel decoration.

Enamelled wares

I have already referred to the beautiful enamelled wares of Richardsons, which they produced in the 1860's, but the enamelled decoration with which most people are more familiar is that known as 'Mary Gregory'. It takes its name from a lady who worked as a decorator for the Boston & Sandwich Glass Co. in America during the 1870's and 1880's. There has been some controversy over the years as to whether she actually existed, but in a book on the subject by R. W. Miller published in the U.S.A. in 1972 there are two photographs of her. She lived from 1856-1908.

The subjects she is most associated with are the figures of boys and girls, usually in some form of floral landscape. These are mostly in white enamel, but in the last years of the nineteenth century coloured enamels were used for the hands and feet.

These pieces achieved considerable popularity in Britain, but it is difficult to establish which examples may have been imported from America and which, if any, were decorated here. The style was extensively copied in Bohemia and Austria and from the very varying quality of the examples I see, I think most of what appears on the British market came from Europe. Collectors of this type of ware should be wary, as they are being copied today, both in America and in England. In the same style are many coloured jugs with floral decoration on them, usually lily of the valley. These certainly came from Europe.

Venetian and 'aesthetic' glass

The reaction against cut glass and heavy white crystal that set in during the decade from 1850 was encouraged both by the

485

leaders of fashion and by several exhibitions of old Venetian glass which caught the public imagination. John Ruskin in *The Stones of Venice* declared that 'all cut glass is barbarous' and made a plea for glass that was an expression of artistic freedom rather than mechanical formality. This trend coincided with a revival of glassmaking in Venice itself and from 1862 onwards modern Venetian made reproductions of antique patterns were exhibited at all the major European exhibitions.

This revival of interest in Venetian glass meant that the wheel of fashion had gone round full circle, and the art from which English glassmaking of the eighteenth century had sprung once again found favour. The Venetian style was expressed in two ways by British glassmakers; some of them including James Powell & Son at the Whitefriars Glassworks and Jenkinson in Edinburgh produced faithful copies of the originals, while others used the patterns of Venice as a springboard from which to develop their own ideas. This revival gradually evolved in two directions; the first leading to the glassware of the Arts and Crafts Movement during the 1860's and 1870's, the second to the multitude of decorative coloured patterns of the last twenty-five years of the century. The former may be seen as the intellectual expression in glassmaking, while the latter, catering for a mass market, was its popular demonstration.

Venetian glass, with its thinly blown elaborate shapes, was a glassblower's art rather than a decorator's art. So in returning to this style the glassmakers were once again given an opportunity to express themselves as they had not done for many years. All the decorative devices of the Venetians were rediscovered. The diamond pattern produced by drawing together trailed threads of glass which Ravenscroft referred to as 'nipt diamond waies' they recreated as a diamond moulded pattern. This in turn led to a method of trapping pockets of air between two layers of glass which became popular as satin glass. The serpentine stems of Venetian wine glasses were copied; hollow blown knopped stems and pincered trails found favour and for a few years Venice became the most important single influence. The use of colour became widespread, not only as plain colours but also as mixtures of colours on the same object. The Venetians applied blobs of different coloured glass to the outside of a vessel, but the Victorians incorporated reds, yellows, greens and blues into the body of the vessel. This type of ware is often called 'end of day' glass, suggesting that these colours were the scraps left over which were casually incorporated into glass vessels. This is not true, since there are so many of them, even today, that they must have been in regular production.

Alexander Jenkinson in Edinburgh produced some very good copies in the 1870's, particularly those with 'latticinio' decoration. This was the pattern of fine white threads sometimes straight, sometimes twisted, which spread through the whole article. It was from this technique that the opaque twist stems of the eighteenth century had derived.

One of the leaders of the Arts and Crafts Movement was William Morris, and he was instrumental in encouraging a new aesthetic approach to design amongst the leading artists and craftsmen of his day. Although, with Ruskin and others, he was an advocate of the idea of freedom of expression for creative minds, the glassware that was produced under his patronage was much plainer than the Venetian glass of the day. The first designs he commissioned were those by Phillip Webb in about 1860, and Webb then went on to produce a series of designs which were made by James Powell & Sons and sold by Morris & Co. These were thinly blown glasses on slender stems almost free of adornment. They depended on outline and proportion rather than decoration for their appeal.

Powells also commissioned designs from T. G. Jackson, an architect and designer who was also a member of the Arts Movement. They continued to be associated with the artistic movements of the last part of the century, including Art Nouveau and under the direction of H. J. Powell (1853-1922) experimented with ideas drawn from the past as well as the present so that much of Powell's work remained distinctively different from the mainstream of later Victorian glassmaking.

The 'aesthetic' designers were not afraid to draw their inspiration from any period that they considered acceptable, and their products sometimes showed the effect of a mixture of sources. At the end of the nineteenth century Powells produced wine glasses which captured the spirit of English baluster glasses, but in combinations which never occurred in the eighteenth century. Another source of inspiration was Roman glass and James Couper of Glasgow produced a range of designs in the 1890's created for them by Christopher Dresser and George Walton, which they called 'Clutha'. These were made in a greenish glass shot through with air bubbles in vaguely antique shapes to imitate Roman glass both in texture and shape. This name should not be confused with 'Cluthra', another name found occasionally on glass, but which was made by Frederick Carder at the Steuben Glass Works in America in about 1930.

In the late 1880's cut glass started to regain its popularity and the Arts and Crafts Movement declined. However, the general taste for coloured decorative glass was well established, and this side of the industry continued to flourish.

The major manufacturers vied with each other to produce new colours, and articles in which colours changed gradually with no visible line of separation were popular. This effect was achieved by including some chemical in the composition of the glass which caused a change of colour when part of the vessel was reheated. The best known of these is Burmese glass. First introduced in 1885 by the Mount Washington Glass Co. in America it was made here by Thomas Webb as Queens Ware Burmese. This glass contained uranium which produced, in the first instance, an opaque yellow colour and when this was partly reheated the glass shaded to a bright pink. Other versions produced by other companies went under the names of 'Amberina' (amber to ruby), 'Alexandrite' (purplish red to blue) and 'Sunrise' (similar to Burmese).

Glassware decorated with iridescent colours became popular in the last years of the century. The idea originated on the Continent, and examples appeared at several international exhibitions. The firms of Lobmeyr and Loetz in Austria were specialists in this type of decoration, and Thomas Webb & Sons appear to have been the first company to produce it in England, having taken out a patent for it in 1878. The effect was achieved by coating the glass with a film of metallic salts which, when heated, became iridescent.

The Venetian aspects which survived, usually in an exaggerated form, included frilled edges to vases and bowls, which were produced with crimping tongs, and ribbed handles and prunts. The handles had fine ribs running along their length which produced a multi-pointed star effect where they joined the body of the vessel. When the ribbed pattern was used on prunts it produced an effect like a scallop shell.

A useful way to judge the period of any glass vessel with a handle is from the way in which the handle is applied. As a general rule, up to 1860 handles were added by applying a lump of glass to the rim of the vessel, which was then drawn out and the end crimped on to the body. After this date the general practice was reversed, with the glass being applied to the body, drawn up, and the end turned in before it was applied to the rim. The result is that the handle generally tapers from the point at which it is applied to the point where the free end is attached. Exceptions to this rule are the small round-bodied custard glasses of the late nineteenth century which

128 *Above:* A heavy bowl engraved with alternate panels of dragons and flowers in the 'rock crystal' style. It is signed on the shoulder FRITCHIE, which is probably a corruption of (William) Fritsche. Fritsche was a famous exponent of this style of engraving, and in the Stourbridge area his name was commonly used in the manner found on this bowl. Miss A. Carwardine.

129 *Right:* A wheel-engraved water jug showing a cottage scene, dated 1860. Pilkington Glass Museum, St Helens.

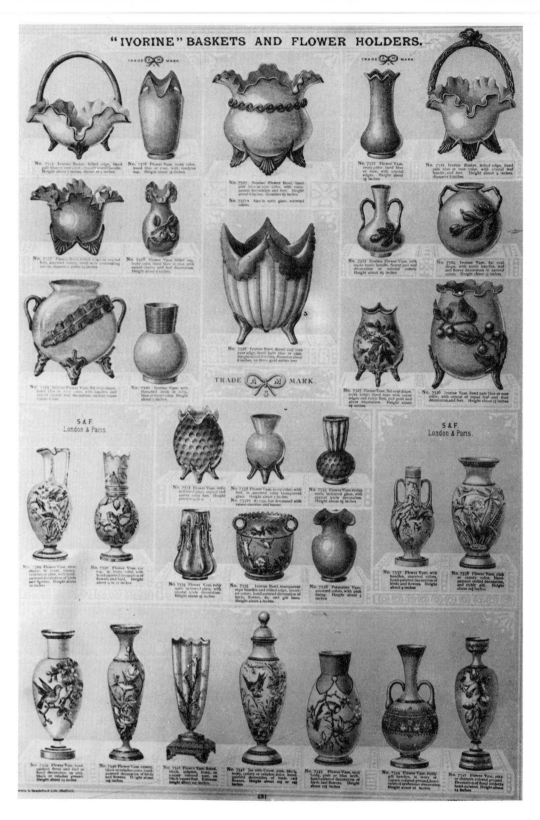

"IVORINE" BASKETS AND FLOWER HOLDERS.

usually have handles applied in the earlier method.

Satin glass which I mentioned earlier, was made by several firms. The usual method was to blow opaque white glass into a mould to produce a diamond pattern. When this was cased with a layer of coloured glass, usually red or blue, a series of air pockets were formed between the two layers. The satin finish was achieved by etching the finished vessel in acid. The practice of coating a base layer of opaque glass with various colours of translucent glass was widespread and popular.

The coloured decorative glass of the last quarter of the nineteenth century was produced in such profusion that it inevitably varies widely in quality. Unfortunately it is generally judged by the standard of the worst, but there is much that is worth a closer look, for the best is very good, and it will

132 *Left:* Girandole candle lustres in ruby and clear glass. Private Collection.

133, 134 The two ways handles were fixed in the nineteenth century.
(Top) This method was used mainly before 1860.
(Bottom) This method was used mainly after 1860.

certainly attract more attention as time passes. Remember that popular taste changes, and one should try to judge this type of glass as our forefathers did. It may be largely out of favour at the moment, but it has a vitality and exuberance that will surely make it collectable in the future.

Pressed glass

The production of glass objects by the moulding method is as old as the material itself, but during the nineteenth century the process was improved by the development of a technique whereby the glass was forced into a mould under pressure. This meant that the shapes produced and the decorative effects achieved were limited only by the imagination of the designer and the ability of the mould makers. The equipment consisted of a mould and a punch. The mould, which was normally made in two, three or four sections, carried the pattern for the outside of the article, while the punch was shaped to the profile of the interior. When the punch was lowered into the mould the two met to form an enclosed space of a fixed volume. The process required a measured amount of molten glass of this volume to be placed in the mould, and when the punch was brought down the glass was forced out into the shape of the

135 *Opposite:* A page of pressed glass patterns from a catalogue of 1885. It includes items by George Davidson and Sowerby.

SUPERIOR PRESSED, ENGRAVED AND CUT GLASS.

No. 7806 Oval Dish, pressed glass, made in five sizes; length, 6 inches, 7½ inches, 9 inches, 10½ inches, and 12 inches. Round Dish, to match, in five sizes; diameter, 5 inches, 6 inches, 7½ inches, 9 inches, 10½ inches, and 12 inches

No. 7805 Butter Dish and Cover, pressed glass, diameter about 6 inches

No. 7807 Butter Dish and Cover, pressed glass, diameter about 6½ inches

No. 7809 Oval Dish, plain, clear glass, notched edge, star bottom, made in seven sizes; length, 5 inches, 6 inches, 7 inches, 8 inches, 9 inches, 10 inches, and 11 inches. Round Dish, to match, in seven sizes; diameter, 5 inches, 6 inches, 7 inches, 8 inches, 9 inches, 10 inches, and 11 inches

No. 7808 Butter Dish and Cover, cut one row hollows, diameter about 6¼ inches

No. 7810 Butter Dish and Cover, engraved, diameter about 6¼ inches

No. 7812 Oval Dish, pressed glass, made in five sizes; length, 6 inches, 7½ inches, 9 inches, 10½ inches, and 12 inches

No. 7811 Butter Dish and Cover, pressed iced glass, extreme width about 8 inches

No. 7813 Butter Dish and Cover, pressed glass, diameter about 7½ inches

S&F London.

S&F London.

No. 7815 Oval Dish, pressed glass, made in four sizes; length, 6½ inches, 7½ inches, 9 inches, and 10½ inches. Round Dish, to match, made in five sizes; diameter, 5 inches, 6½ inches, 8½ inches, 9½ inches, and 10½ inches

No. 7814 Butter Dish and Cover, frosted ground, cut stars, diameter about 7 inches

No. 7816 Butter Dish and Cover, oval, perforated edge, pressed glass, length about 7 in

No. 7818 Oval Dish, pressed glass, made in seven sizes; length, 6 inches, 7 inches, 8 inches, 9 inches, 10 inches, 11 inches, and 12 inches. Round Dish, to match, made in eight sizes; 5 inches, 6 inches, 7 inches, 8 inches, 9 inches, 10 inches, 11 inches, and 12 inches

No. 7817 Butter Dish and Cover, pressed glass, diameter about 6½ inches

No. 7819 Butter Dish and Cover, pressed glass, diameter about 7 inches

TRADE MARK

MANUFACTURERS, IMPORTERS, WAREHOUSEMEN AND AGENTS

451

CAUTION. Any person infringing the Copyright of this Book will be prosecuted under the Act

493

mould. If the quantity of glass was less than the space between punch and mould there would be holes or gaps in the finished article. If there was too much glass the excess would overflow the mould and prevent the punch making contact with it. Since the punch has to be withdrawn from the glass vessel when it is formed it must be tapered so that the end which forms the bottom of the interior is narrower than the root which coincides with the mouth of the vessel. With flat objects such as plates this problem does not arise.

The introduction of press moulding produced a number of advantages for the glassmaker. It obviated the need for skilled glass blowers (which was not well received); it enabled cheap versions of expensive items like cut glass to be mass produced; the mass production enabled the manufacturers to reach a wider market, and the decorative possibilities offered by this method of manufacture were far greater than could be achieved by any other method.

I often meet people who talk of pressed glass in disparaging terms, and I think this arises from their experience of the mass produced copies of cut glass patterns. The difference in quality is generally so noticeable that it can only compare unfavourably with the real thing. When the technique was used to exploit the full potential of press moulding the products were

136 Two pressed tankards. The first is an unusual pictorial piece by George Davidson; the second is an imitation cut glass tankard marked on the base with a thistle.

137 An unusual pressed celery vase. It appears that the decoration on the body has been highlighted by polishing the pattern and that the obscured surface finish has been achieved manually. There is a registration mark for 1868.

distinctive, owed nothing to any other method, and were often very attractive.

Press moulding, as a mechanical method of glass production, was first developed in the United States. The first patents were taken out in about 1830 and during the succeeding years the American manufacturers were quick to develop and exploit the process until it became an entirely mechanical one.

It found its way across the Atlantic during the 1830's and Apsley Pellatt in *The Curiosities of Glass Making* illustrates an early hand-operated press for making moulded glass. It is not easy to identify early examples of press moulded glass, but there are examples which commemorate the coronation of Queen Victoria in 1837 and her marriage to Prince Albert in 1840. For the most part they were probably used for utilitarian wares such as tumblers. The first patterns to be registered were those of Rice Harris in 1840; from then on patterns were registered regularly, mostly by firms in Stourbridge and Manchester. The first of the northern glassmakers to register a design seems to have been Angus & Greener of Sunderland in 1858. This firm registered their designs regularly from then on, but it is not until 1872 that Sowerbys first registered any designs for pressed glass. Sowerbys gradually increased the number of patterns they registered until by 1877 they were registering more than all other firms put together.

If a registration mark is found on a piece of glass, it is a useful guide to the age of the piece. From 1842 it was possible to protect new patterns and designs by registering them at the registry office. These patterns may be identified by the diamond registration marks which, in the case of pressed glass, were incorporated in the mould and appear somewhere on the surface of the finished article. The registration mark consisted of a diamond divided into five parts with a partially hidden circle at its apex. The Roman numeral in the circle referred to the class of manufacture (III meant glass), the internal segments of the diamond showed the date the patent was registered and by which manufacturer. The following chart gives the sequence of code letters for the months and years, which will enable the exact date of registration to be identified. The presence of a registration mark on any object does not guarantee that it was made at that date. The design protection lasted four years and after that the mark no longer had any significance but would continue to appear as long as the mould bearing it remained in use.

The letters of the alphabet were used in a random sequence for the first twenty-six years after which the order was

1842-1867	Years		Months	
	1842 – X	1855 – E	January	– C
	1843 – H	1856 – L	February	– G
	1844 – C	1857 – K	March	– W
	1845 – A	1858 – B	April	– H
	1846 – I	1859 – M	May	– E
	1847 – F	1860 – Z	June	– M
	1848 – U	1861 – R	July	– I
	1849 – S	1862 – O	August	– R
	1850 – V	1863 – G	September	– D
	1851 – P	1864 – N	October	– B
	1852 – D	1865 – W	November	– K
	1853 – Y	1866 – Q	December	– A
	1854 – J	1867 – T		

(R may be found as the month mark for 1-19 September 1857, and K for December 1860.)

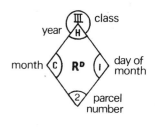

year — class

month — RᴰD — day of month

parcel number

1 January 1843

1868-1883	Years		Months	
	1868 – X	1876 – V	January	– C
	1869 – H	1877 – P	February	– G
	1870 – C	1878 – D	March	– W
	1871 – A	1879 – Y	April	– H
	1872 – I	1880 – J	May	– E
	1873 – F	1881 – E	June	– M
	1874 – U	1882 – L	July	– I
	1875 – S	1883 – K	August	– R
			September	– D
			October	– B
			November	– K
			December	– A

(For 1-6 March 1878, G was used for the month and W for the year.)

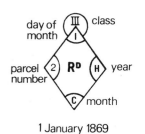

day of month — class

parcel number — Rᴰ — year

month

1 January 1869

repeated, but in a different division of the diamond. In 1884 these marks were abandoned and replaced by the more familiar registered numbers.

Surviving catalogues of pressed glass issued by George Davidson, John Ford and some of the Stourbridge manufacturers show pages of designs for utilitarian tableware in clear glass. It was the firms of the north-east who developed the decorative or fancy side of the trade by introducing ornamental wares in a variety of opaque colours. Sowerby's catalogues for 1879 and 1882 have survived, and these are entirely devoted to ornamental and decorative wares in such colours as white, black, turquoise, malachite, green, a cream colour they called Ivory Queens Ware, in imitation of creamware pottery, and an opalescent colour called 'blanc de lait'. The colours they are best known for today, however, is a marbled purple and white. There were other marbled colours, blue and white and green and white, but none of these were exclusive to Sowerby. Davidson, Greener and Heppell all

138 *Opposite:* A page from the Art Journal catalogue of the Great Exhibition of 1851, showing some of the display of Richardsons' of Stourbridge. Note the elaborate and heavy cutting on many of the pieces.

novel in style and rich in colour; of these we shall

engrave specimens. The two DECANTERS with which we commence our illustrations, are of the purest crystal; the lozenge-shape cuttings bring out the prismatic colours with exceeding brilliancy: the GOBLET at the head of the second column is elegant in form, and the introduction of the vine upon the cup,

of the cutting, while it retains all its boldness. The next subject is a BUTTER DISH of crystal.

designed after the style of the antique. The VASE that follows is very elegant; it is manu-

enamel colours. The DECANTER completing

that page is most lustrous, and the lozenge-shaped cutting exceedingly bold. All the objects introduced in this page are of crystal of the purest kind; the beauty and variety of the cutting in the

though not a novelty, is appropriate. The FRUIT DISH and STAND that follows is of ruby glass covered on flint, and then cut through, showing the two colours to great advantage. The WINE GLASS is very elaborately ornamented, and the stem, which looks a little heavy in the engraving, loses this appearance in the original object, by the style

factured in opal; the scroll and band at top and bottom are gilt; the flowers and fruit painted with vitrified

whole of these works cannot fail to secure to them unqualified admiration. The large group at the bottom consists of one of each articles in a set of glass for dessert purposes, consequently they are all of a similar pattern, except the CLARET JUG, which is cut in a similar style, but is somewhat varied in its decoration.

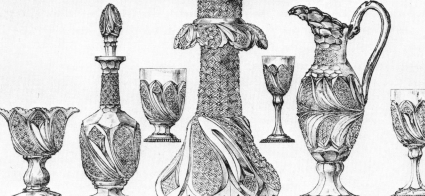

139 *Left:* A moulded celery vase bearing the mark of George Davidson, *c.* 1885. Miss A. Carwardine.

produced articles in these combinations. One useful point of identification, when trade marks are absent, is that George Davidson frequently used a series of concentric moulded rings on the underside of their products.

The peacock's head was Sowerby's trade mark, and they also used the peacock motif on a number of their products in the form of a decorative border. They also produced a whole series of posy vases of different shapes, each bearing a pattern derived from a nursery rhyme. The commonest of these are Old King Cole and Oranges and Lemons, but others such as Mary Mary Quite Contrary and Little Jack Horner are quite rare. Some examples are embellished with gilding over the figures, while some of the jug and basin sets have the floral patterns

140 *Above:* A collection of Victorian drinking glasses. Private Collection.

141 *Right:* Three pressed jugs. The outer ones are by George Davidson. The central one is unmarked but probably dates from about 1850 since the handle has been applied by hand.

hand painted in coloured enamels. Sowerby also introduced a series of translucent colours which included red, lime green and ice blue.

Although the Sowerby pattern books are concerned principally with press moulded articles, they contain a few patterns which could only be achieved by blow moulding. In this technique the shape is produced by air pressure, usually from the glass blower's lungs, and they are easily recognised because the narrowest part of the body is at the neck, and the pattern is never as distinct as on press moulded items.

The popularity of these coloured pressed wares lasted for about fifteen years from 1875, but gradually the taste for cut glass reasserted itself and the geometric pattern took over from the naturalistic design.

As explained earlier, G. Davidson acquired the patterns of several other firms, but of their own designs some of the most distinctive and attractive are a range of wares covered in a marine design consisting of coral and shells. Davidson's most distinctive product, however, was their 'Pearline' glass. This was translucent blue or yellow fading to opaque white at the rim or edge, which they introduced in 1889. This shading was achieved by reheating the object after it was pressed, whereupon the high spots or edges turned opaque.

The only colours used by the Manchester pressed glass makers seem to have been translucent shades of green, yellow and a dark purple which appears black until a strong light is shone through it. Otherwise they confined themselves to domestic articles like jugs, basins, celery vases, comports, plates, tumblers and so on. Colin Lattimore's book on pressed glass gives a list of registration marks for pressed glass and the firms who registered them. By reference to this, and with a little practice the individual style of each firm becomes recognisable so that even unmarked pieces may be attributed to their manufacturer.

Occasionally one may find marked pieces of pressed glass which bear marks that do not relate to any of those I have mentioned. It is most likely that these are of American origin, and the marks that I see most frequently are a capital $\dot{C}$ within a triangle for the Cambridge (Ohio) Glass Company; *I. G.* for the Imperial Glass Company and *W. G.* for the Westmorland Glass Company. These last two marks are usually on modern reproductions of old patterns.

As a collectable commodity pressed glass is just beginning to attract the attention it deserves and I am sure that during the next few years we are going to see a rapidly increasing interest in what was, after all, one of the major nineteenth century contributions to glassmaking.

142 *Opposite, above:* A group of items from the Sowerby's Ellison Glassworks at Gateshead, all *c.* 1880. The back four pieces are press moulded and carry the Sowerby peacock head trademark. The pattern was occasionally picked out in colour as in the example on the extreme right. The piece in the foreground is an example of their hand-blown Venetian style, and is similar to one of their pressed patterns. Miss A. Cawardine.

143 *Opposite, below:* A vase composed of a type of glass popular from the 1860s onward. The translucent yellow body has a raised moulded pattern which shades to an opalescent white. This type of glass was widely used for lamp and light fittings. Miss A. Cawardine.

144 A double-walled and silvered inkwell marked 'W. Lund, London', *c.* 1850.

145 *Overleaf, page 502:* A pair of vases shading from pale to dark blue and with gilded decoration. This is Stourbridge work of very high quality.

146 *Overleaf, page 503:* A Richardson's water jug and goblet in white glass with enamelled decoration of reedmace, *c.* 1880. The firm produced other fine sets decorated with water plants such as marsh marigold and yellow iris. These patterns may also be sometimes found engraved on clear glass.

503

Chapter 8

Copies and fakes

I regularly meet people who are totally unaware of the diversity and quality of antique glassware. After the initial reaction of surprise the next question is invariably 'How can one tell that it is genuine and not a later copy?'. This is undoubtedly prompted by the fact that they see a strong similarity in the metal of two hundred and fifty years ago with that of the glassware which graces our tables today. This problem is made more difficult to resolve since glass, given reasonable care, does not deteriorate with age. I have seen pieces of Roman glass of such clarity that they look as if they had just come from the glasshouse. Most other materials that man uses to manufacture his domestic and utilitarian objects show the effects of use and wear. Wood discolours with age, or acquires a patina with constant polishing, fabrics fray and become threadbare, metals also acquire a patina or wear at the edges. Glass, on the other hand, retains its lustre and its clarity unimpaired by age. It was either broken and disposed of, or it survives to stand comparison with the best that modern glassmakers can produce.

As much for its enduring appeal as for probably any other reason, glassware has been copied down the ages, and the ability to distinguish these copies from the originals is to some extent a matter of experience. After looking for long enough at any type of object I am sure that one acquires an instinctive feel for what is right or wrong. Sometimes this is apparent even before a close examination reveals the tell-tale signs of the copy. It is a question of proportion, balance, style and character. These are the things that are almost impossible to put into words, but there are a number of more specific details that one may look for to decide whether a glass is genuine or not.

The words copy, reproduction and fake are commonly used indiscriminately to signify anything meant to deceive, but this is not necessarily so. Copies are usually limited numbers of an article individually made, and not always exact imitations. Modern limited edition paperweights are an example of this.

505

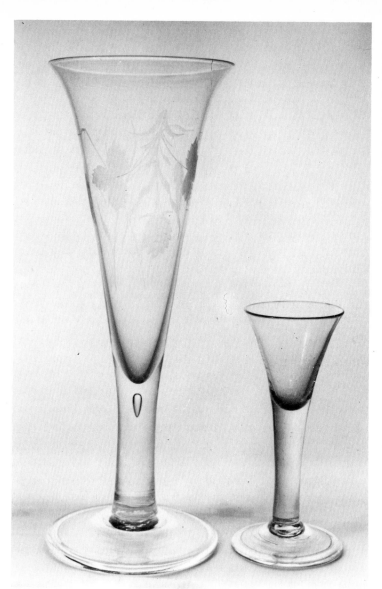

148 *Left:* A Victorian copy of an ale glass. The eighteenth century original is beside it for comparison. The copy is 12 inches high, the original is 6 inches high.

149 *Opposite:* A copy of an 18th century ale flute. Although it has an air twist stem and a domed foot, the bowl lacks striations and the foot is much too smooth and regular. It is difficult to date but is probably *c.* 1900.

The styles of the much sought after French weights of the 1850's are copied, but the modern ones usually contain a date cane to show that they have merit in their own right. A common sight in some art galleries is the person copying a famous painting. These are either intended to be an exact replica or use the original as an inspiration for the copyist's own talent; these will be dissimilar, but both are copies.

Reproductions are those articles made in imitation of an original pattern but on a commercial scale. Many people invest in reproduction furniture, feeling that the originals are too expensive or are unavailable. The paradox of this is that

150 *Opposite:* A copy of an 18th century incised-twist glass with Jacobite decoration. A period Jacobite bowl on a stem like this would be rare, but I have in fact seen several similar pieces; its foot is the most obvious give-away, *c.* 1920.

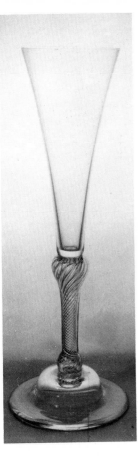

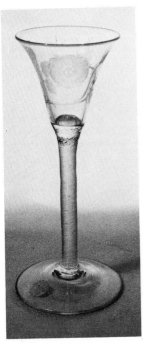

modern good quality, handmade reproduction furniture can be almost as expensive as the antique original. Such furniture is not made with intent to mislead. Most modern reproductions are marked with the maker's name. Recently a firm in America was reproducing the Burmese glass invented at the Mount Washington Glass Co. in the 1880's. It comes complete with an explanatory leaflet and is marked with its maker's name.

Fakes, on the other hand, are made with the express intention of being passed off as the originals, or rather to be sold at the prices which the originals will command. The examples of this kind of trickery are legion and hardly any class of goods which commands a high price has not been subject to this form of misrepresentation.

Having said all this, marks can be removed or altered, objects can appear in places which may lead one to suppose they are older than they are, and the unwary or unknowledge-able can let their enthusiasms get the better of them. It is these considerations which make it necessary to try and explain the pitfalls that beset the glass collector. For the sake of convenience I shall refer to them all as copies.

The copies I have come across fall into several well-defined groups:

a Nineteenth century copies having a good similarity to the originals.

b Nineteenth century copies based on eighteenth century styles but noticeably different in character.

c Later nineteenth and early twentieth century copies of early baluster styles.

d Modern copies of eighteenth century styles.

e Modern copies of nineteenth century styles.

I have already referred to *The Curiosities of Glassmaking* by Apsley Pellatt. This book, published in 1849, gave detailed descriptions of making the opaque twist rod from which the opaque twist stems were produced. At that time most glass was still being made by hand in the same manner that it had been made for centuries. It seems reasonable to assume, therefore, that there was nothing to prevent the glassmakers of the 1850's producing glasses identical to those of the 1750's. Bear in mind, though, that by the middle of the nineteenth century public taste had changed, and drinking glasses were then being made with larger bowls and more slender stems. Anyone producing styles a century out of date was obviously going against current practice. This consideration has led me to the con-clusion that anyone copying an earlier style does it as an act of conscious effort. The glassmakers of 1750 were working in a tradition which was current, in which they had been raised through years of apprenticeship and which thus became an entirely instinctive and natural process. The glassmaker of 1850 setting out to achieve the same end had to refer to his model and think of what he was doing every step of the way. This inevitably produces a more contrived and self-conscious end result. It is possible, therefore, to detect a degree of regularity and a degree of stiffness in the good Victorian copy which the original lacks. As I said, this is not easy to convey in words but is an instinct acquired with experience.

As well as these very good copies of earlier glass, nineteenth century glassmakers produced opaque twist glasses with a twist which was in complete contrast to those I have just mentioned. They are composed of finer strands, more open in arrangement and generally with a much more gradual and irregular twist. They lack the substance and vigour of the earlier ones. These stems give themselves away when seen in conjunction with bowl sizes and shapes which are Victorian in character.

That leads me to the second group. These are glasses, usually engraved, which take their inspiration from eighteenth cen-

151 An oval cut glass bowl with the cutting typical of the late eighteenth century, but this was made in Bohemia/Czechoslovakia c. 1920.

152 A small Victorian sherry glass with Jacobite engraving. This is interesting since as the glass is so obviously of its period it would seem that the decoration was not added to deceive in any way. Perhaps there were Jacobite Societies as late as the 1880's.

tury originals but are expressed in a nineteenth century idiom. Among these are privateer glasses, Jacobite glasses and others bearing engraved commemorative sentiments. They differ from the originals in being larger and having coarser engraving. Eighteenth century privateer glasses are nearly all opaque twist glasses, about six inches high and with bucket bowls. The nineteenth century copy is about eight inches high with a bucket bowl which is wide in comparison to the height. The Jacobite glasses, while having the conventional emblems engraved on them (p. 461, illus. **104**) are up to 12 or 13 inches tall, a size of glass never made in the eighteenth century. I have recently seen a plain stemmed bucket bowl wine glass engraved with ships and 'Success to the British Fleet. 1759'. This compares to a glass in the Higgins Museum in Bedford engraved with the same sentiment, but the date 1749. In the eighteenth century, wheel engraved letters were generally produced by a series of straight strokes. The lettering on the former glass conforms to this method, but the date 1759 is carried out in the free-flowing continuous style of wheel engraving used for inscriptions in the late nineteenth century.

Other styles of the eighteenth century were copied, but given the proportions of the second half of the nineteenth century; bowls overpowering the stems and feet.

The third category produced some very good copies, and some flights of fancy. Before one has acquired the feeling for the style appropriate to any particular period it is not uncommon to encounter a glass which exhibits typical stylistic detail of a period, but in a combination which further experience would immediately make suspect. Two glasses which come to mind are a baluster stem glass with tall drawn trumpet bowl on a ball knop stem and folded foot. The other is a glass having a round funnel bowl on a multi-knopped stem, some of which contain air beads, the foot being domed and folded. The individual parts of these glasses are correct for period, but the combinations are wrong.

In contrast to these pseudo glasses, there are some very good copies which I am sure would mislead many people. These are harder to explain, but generally the clarity and brilliance of the metal is against them, and that sure give-away, a foot which is not quite true to period. Amongst these I have seen Silesian stemmed sweetmeats and baluster stemmed glasses. One firm which is known to have made these was Powell's Whitefriars Glassworks, where they copied glasses of many earlier periods. In the 1920's they even produced reconstructions of the glasses found as fragments on the Wealden glasshouse sites.

The next group of glass copies is probably the one which gives modern collectors the most trouble, if only because there are so many of them. These are copies of most of the eighteenth century styles and which were circulating freely some twenty years ago. No-one seems too sure where they originated, but I have heard both Italy and Norway suggested as their source.

Since they have many characteristics which proclaim their common origin and which can be compared to similar details of genuine glasses, I am sure that once these are appreciated the aspiring collector need not be caught out more than once.

1 They are invariably of soda metal (see page 385).

2 The metal of the bowl is usually slightly thicker than one would find in a genuine glass, and the bowl has a gathered, thickened rim which is much more irregular than one would expect in a genuine glass.

3 Twisted stems have three distinct characteristics.

a Opaque twist stems are composed of threads of a greyish white colour in contrast to the dense opaque white of genuine ones, and on close inspection it will be seen that the texture of these threads is of a chalky, granular quality rather than the smooth surface of the true opaque twist.

b Air twist stems have a close pattern of threads which give a congested and ravelled appearance instead of the well-defined and separated threads of earlier glasses. In addition, some of them contain air threads of a sharply rectangular appearance.

c Mixed twist examples contain alternate strands of air and opaque enamel twisted into one pattern. I have not yet seen a genuine glass which did not have the two elements, air and enamel, clearly separated (see page 403).

4 Plain stem varieties, of which the drawn trumpet with air tear is most common, reveal themselves by the swelling at the base of the stem where it joins the foot. This is not like a base knop but more in the nature of a platform or step. This device became quite common in the later nineteenth century and is one of the significant details in Victorian glasses.

5 Some of them have plain feet which compare reasonably with original ones, but many have what appears to be a folded foot. On closer examination it may be seen that this is not a true fold, since there is not in fact a double layer of glass but a thickening of the rim with a step down which looks at first glance like a fold. The point to bear in mind here is that the fold was originally necessary to reinforce the thinness of the glass in the foot so that in an early glass the folded rim is still quite thin. In these later copies the 'folded' section at the rim will be twice as thick as in any genuine glass, the thickness of the remaining part of the foot being at least as thick as in any plain footed glass of an earlier period.

6 While there is always the appearance of a pontil mark close examination will reveal that this is an impressed mark giving a roughened appearance to the metal. Most genuine glasses have a pontil mark showing a clean break.

Such is the varied nature of old hand-made glass that if any one of these points is taken in isolation (except 3c) I am sure that sooner or later an example will turn up which contradicts what I have said. However, when several of these failings appear together on one glass then I am sure that the glass will prove to be a copy. The following technique is a useful one for assessing any piece of glass. Do a mental balance sheet covering all the details and points one has learned to look for in old glass. If there are one or two points against and the rest in favour then the odds are that it is genuine; three or four points against and then it must be considered doubtful, to say the least.

The final group to consider are the modern copies of nineteenth century styles of both glass and decoration. These are being produced today both in this country and abroad. English-made copies include 'Bristol' blue glass and 'cranberry' glass. I have also seen modern copies of 'Mary Gregory' style decoration advertised recently. From abroad many imitations of the multi-coloured baskets and vases popular in Victorian times are being made in China, and the air-bubble filled lumps of pale green glass, generally called door dumps, are being made in Italy. All these are distinguishable by their strident colours and shiny surface finish and usually their lack of any wear marks, although these can be faked. The English makers of copies mark these articles with their name, but unfortunately these can be removed without too much difficulty. The best protection against being misled by these is to find the manufacturers' leaflets illustrating the patterns they make, and learn to recognise them. Finally, now that the interest in pressed glass is growing, I am beginning to find copies of the opaque glass commonly known as 'slag' glass. These are detectable by the shiny, oily appearance of the surface and the poor definition of the moulding. This leads me to believe that whoever is producing them is doing so by making a mould from an actual example, rather than from an original, or copy of, a metal mould. These copies carry the original factory marks and registration marks. These must surely come under the heading of fakes.

Chapter 9

About collecting

In years gone by collecting was usually the preserve of the wealthy intellectual, and many of our museums owe their finest exhibits, and sometimes their existence, to the scholarship of such people. Since the last war the picture has changed dramatically. The dissemination of knowledge, through books and television, about our domestic and cultural heritage has encouraged people to an appreciation of our past that has created a new generation of collectors which includes people from every walk of life.

Most collectable items carry distinguishing marks which help to make identification and attribution easy, but the glass collector is not so fortunate with his chosen subject as most other collectors. How then is one to get this experience? Little antique glass is marked, and the qualities and characteristics such as weight, colour and striation which the aspiring collector must familiarise himself with are just those qualities which do not lend themselves to illustration. So what opportunities are there for practical experience to supplement the textbooks? The problem is to find opportunities to handle a sufficient variety of glass objects that the appraisal of these factors become second nature.

It is my experience that there is a limited amount of old glass almost everywhere one looks, antique shops, stately homes, museums, but the places where one may find large quantities or fellow collectors are much fewer. It is important to find and visit these places, since there is much to be learned from the comparisons it is possible to draw when looking at a lot of glass assembled together, as well as from individual items. The two principal sources for large collections are museums and the auction rooms.

There are a number of museums with very good collections of glass which are permanently on display. Among these are:

The Victoria and Albert Museum   London
The Ashmolean Museum   Oxford

The Fitzwilliam Museum	Cambridge
The Higgins Museum	Bedford
The Pilkington Glass Museum	St. Helens, Lancashire
Broadfield House Glass Museum	Kingswinford, W. Midlands
The Huntley House Museum	Edinburgh
Mompesson House	Salisbury
The London Museum	Barbican, London
The City Art Gallery	Bristol
Laing Art Gallery	Newcastle-on-Tyne

These are by no means all the museums with collections of glass, but between them they cover the whole history of glassmaking in the British Isles. In addition to what is on display there are often reserve collections which are available to the serious student if reasonable and proper notice is given. Many smaller museums also have collections of glass which may not be on display, but are worth enquiring after. Remember that museums are not only repositories of the nation's heritage but are also there for the benefit of us, the public, and it is up to us to make use of them. Another service that museums offer is the identification and dating of objects which members of the public take to them. Bear in mind, though, that not every museum has experts in every subject. If you have something of specialist interest then it is better to approach a museum which, itself, has a specialist collection of that type of article.

The museum collections are static in that they don't readily dispose of their exhibits, so that a collection can be visited more than once and its contents used for reference purposes. Equally interesting, and more challenging, I think, are those auction houses which hold regular sales devoted entirely to glass. Sotheby's and Christie's are the principal ones, each holding four or five sales per year with from 200 to 300 items of glass in each sale. The glass in their sales is generally on display for several days beforehand, but one usually has to apply for a pass, in advance, to gain unrestricted access to view the contents. However, the porters in charge will usually hand over individual items for examination. The advantage of sales like this is that each one contains a wide variety of glass which changes with each sale. The catalogue provides useful descriptive material for the novice and, in due course, the list of prices realised, which one may order, acts as an indication of current prices. As a word of caution, don't read too much into prices realised unless you have viewed a sale, since condition and quality have a considerable bearing on price.

Most other sale rooms which feature glass regularly usually sell it in conjunction with their ceramics sales, and occasionally complete collections are offered at specialist sales in one or another of the provincial auction rooms. Sales where quantities of glass are offered usually attract all the specialist dealers and collectors, so prices are generally in line with current values. The best opportunities for buying bargains in sales are those where the glass is not well catalogued and the sale is not widely enough advertised to attract much attention. But that brings us back to the point of this chapter. How does one acquire the knowledge necessary to take advantage of these situations?

The other source of knowledge is that possessed by other collectors. Unfortunately, glass collecting being a somewhat specialist interest, there are never very many glass collectors in any particular area. Contact with other collectors can usually be made through local antique circles or societies, and for anyone who has reasonable access to London, The Glass Circle is a society which specialises in the study of glass of all periods and which draws its members from all over the country. It has published three books of its transactions which are all of interest to any serious student. They may be obtained from the publishers, Gresham Books, Old Woking, Surrey, GU22 9LH.

To sum up then. The best way to cultivate one's own judgement is to handle as much as possible. Don't be afraid to ask questions and be prepared to make mistakes. As long as it is not bought too dearly one should always learn something from one's excess of enthusiasm and write the cost off to experience. If there is one further point to be learned from this, it is that nobody has a monopoly of knowledge, and in the study of glassware particularly I am sure there is as much opportunity for the beginner as for the long time student to discover new information or come up with a fresh conclusion. By making the most of opportunities to handle glass, by discussing the subject with other people sharing the same interest and by reference to the wealth of published material one may eventually lay claim to that much overworked title of 'expert'.

With regard to the collection itself, I strongly recommend that a suitable glass fronted cabinet or display case be acquired. If it can be fitted with lights so much the better. Left exposed, glass quickly gathers dust and the more often it is handled to clean it the greater the risk of some mishap. Behind glass doors it may be seen to advantage, it is protected and will not become dirty so quickly. This applies equally to the modest collection of Victoriana as to a collection of rare, baluster stem glasses.

Glossary

Acid etching A pattern produced on glass by the action of acid, usually working through the gaps in an acid resistant film applied to the glass.

Air twist A pattern inside the stem of a glass produced by a series of elongated threads of air.

Annealing Relief of stresses in glass that have been caused by the blowing process. The glass is reheated to a little below melting point and allowed to cool slowly.

Composite stem A stem of a wine glass that comprises two or more different styles, such as air twist and plain stem or opaque twist and air twist.

Crizzling A fine crazing and cloudiness occasionally found in glass with incorrect proportions of raw ingredients. It is much associated with early Ravenscroft glass.

Cullet Broken glass formerly added to the glass pots to be remelted with the raw materials. There was once an active trade in cullet which explains why so few pieces of glass are found on glasshouse sites.

Facet stem A pattern of facets cut on to a plain stem from the late eighteenth century. Also known as a cut stem.

Flashed glass A thin layer of coloured glass laid over a thicker layer so that patterns of colour are produced when the outer layer is cut.

Flint glass Glass using calcined flint as a source of silica. In general, lead glass from the 1680's onward and any clear glass in the late nineteenth century.

Folded foot The rim of the foot of a drinking glass which has a double thickness to give extra strength. Most frequently seen up to 1750 but rare thereafter.

Gaffer The man in charge of a team of three or four glassmakers, and who does the blowing.

Gather The molten glass collected on the end of the blowing iron and from which the glass vessel is produced.

Incised twist A twisted spiral produced by a series of fine grooves on the outside of a drinking glass stem.

Knop A swelling on the stem of a drinking glass. Knops were most elaborate in the early eighteenth century; by the 1740's they were reduced to simple swellings in the stem.

Lead glass A type of glass developed by George Ravenscroft in the 1670's which contains a high proportion of lead oxide. Although common in the British Isles from that date onward, it was not generally adopted on the Continent until the late eighteenth century.

Merese A thin collar found between the bowl and stem of glasses, particularly rummers, c. 1800.

Metal A glassmaker's term for glass. It is probably explained by the similarity of molten glass and molten metal.

Moulding Shaping glass by pouring or blowing it into a mould.

Opaque twist A pattern of twisted opaque white or coloured threads of glass found on drinking glass stems. Also known as cotton or enamel twist.

Overlay A technique similar to that used for flashed glass, but the outer layer is thicker so that some relief-work can be obtained when the decoration is cut into it. Overlay was used in producing cameo glass.

Pontil The iron rod on which a glass object is supported after it has been removed from the blowing iron so that further work can be carried out on it. The mark left when the pontil has been removed is the pontil mark, which is characteristic of hand-made glass.

Pressed glass Glass made by a mechanised process of moulding that does not require a skilled glassblower. Developed in the USA and widely used in the British Isles in the late nineteenth century.

Prunt A blob or button of glass applied to the outer surface of a glass vessel for decorative effect. It was often impressed with a pattern.

Rummer A large capacity short-stemmed drinking glass of the late eighteenth and the nineteenth centuries. The name may either be a corruption of the German word Roemer (a sixteenth century European drinking glass) or be derived from its use as a glass for rum-based toddy. Take your pick!

Seed A small particle of unmelted raw material or foreign matter found embedded in old glassware. One of the characteristics of old glass.

Soda glass Glass that does not contain lead. The standard type of glass before Ravenscroft.

Tear A bubble of air contained in the stem or in the base of the bowl of many eighteenth century glasses.

Trailing A fine thread of glass applied to the outside of a glass vessel for decorative effect. Its use dates back over 2000 years; in the nineteenth century a method of applying it mechanically was invented.

Wrythen A twisted pattern of ribs or lines incorporated in the body of a glass vessel.

Bibliography

There are many titles on the history of British glass, and each one offers some new knowledge or opinion which should stimulate the serious collector. Those I have listed, however, seem to me to offer the widest possible range of information for the least amount of reading.

To 1700

The Development of English Glassmaking 1560-1640, Eleanor S. Godfrey, Clarendon Press, 1975. A scholarly and readable account of the most formative years of the English glass industry. Well researched, and deserves to be more widely known.

The Glass Industry of the Weald, G. H. Kenyon, Leicester University Press, 1967. This covers all the work done by S. E. Winholt in his *Wealden Glass* of 1933 with further useful additions.

Ravenscroft to Victoria

Antique Drinking Glasses, A. Hartshorne, Brussel and Brussel, 1968. This is a reprint of *Old English Glasses*, first published in 1897. The first important book on glass from the collector's point of view. The text is dated but appendices giving original documents are most important.

Collecting Glass, Norman W. Webber, David and Charles. Good readable account of the subject.

English, Scottish and Irish Table Glass, G. Bernard Hughes, 1956. Contains a good number of illustrations showing glass depicted in paintings. Also has chapters dealing with minor articles of glassware like finger bowls, sweetmeats and candlesticks.

History of Old English Glass, Francis Buckley, 1925. Well researched, like all Buckley's books. Useful for original documents quoted. Good illustrations.

How to Identify English Drinking Glasses and Decanters 1680-1830, Douglas Ash, Bell, 1962. Still the best book describing the development of decanters.

An Illustrated Guide to 18th Century English Drinking Glasses, L. M. Bickerton, Barrie and Jenkins, 1971. Probably the widest range of illustrations of any book on English glass. Excellent reference work which also contains one of the very few comprehensive bibliographies on the subject. Already hard to obtain.

Old English Drinking Glasses, Grant R. Francis, Herbert Jenkins, 1926. Never reprinted, so it is hard to find and is expensive. Best for its illustrations, many of which appear nowhere else, and the section on Jacobite glass.

19th Century

English 19th Century Press Moulded Glass, C. Lattimore, Barrie and Jenkins, 1979. The first book to deal comprehensively with one of the most important aspects of Victorian glassmaking. Well researched and illustrated.

19th Century British Glass, H. Wakefield, Faber, 1961. A short text with good illustrations of, mainly, documented pieces.

Victorian Table Glass and Ornaments, Barbara Morris, Barrie and Jenkins, 1978. Most informative book yet on this wide subject.

Irish Glass

Irish Glass, D. Westropp, Herbert Jenkins, 1920. Recently re-published by Allen Figgis and Co., Dublin. A good account quoting many original documents.

Irish Glass, Phelps Warren, Faber, 1970. Covers the period 1780-1830. The best illustrations of a wide range of cut glass in any book yet.

General

Coloured Glass, Middlemas and Davis, Herbert Jenkins, 1968. Not to be confused with *Antique Coloured Glass*, which is currently in print. This is the only book aimed at this aspect of collecting.

Curiosities of Glass Making, Apsley Pellatt, David Boyne, 1849. Facsimile Reprint 1968 by The Ceramic Book Co., Newport. An excellent first-hand account of glassmaking by a working master craftsman.

A History of English and Irish Glass, 2 vols, W. A. Thorpe, Medici Society, 1929. Reprinted in one volume by Holland Press, 1969. I have included this book here because it is still the definitive work on the whole history of the subject from Roman times to the 20th Century. Rather academic in tone, but a must for the serious student. Has a tendency to date things earlier than current knowledge suggests.

An Illustrated Dictionary of Glass, H. Newman, Thames and Hudson, 1977. A useful reference work which updates Elville's *Dictionary* of 1961, but still has omissions.

PEWTER, COPPER AND BRASS

PETER HORNSBY

Chapter 1

Collecting base metal

Interest in base metal, as the alloys of copper and tin, are termed, has grown considerably in recent years. Attractive displays of brass and pewter especially are to be seen in many antique shops and most sale rooms regularly offer base-metal objects at auction.

Almost everything that has at one time or another been made in metal has been worked in copper, brass and bronze and there are a very substantial range of objects in pewter. Copper alloys have played their part in industry, science and agriculture and pewter was to be found in church and tavern.

For several hundred years base metal was to be the main material used in the home where wood could not serve. Our forefathers relied on bronze and brass for cooking, ate and drank from pewter, lit their homes with base-metal candlesticks and came to rely on these alloys for a great range of household duties.

This book looks at British domestic metalware in the alloys of copper and tin. In order to deal adequately with this considerable area the focus has to be narrow. Thus iron work is not included, because of its different technology, use and development, and though Europe has been the birthplace of many of the styles most used in the home, things made on the Continent are outside the scope of the book.

Whilst it is necessary to separate these alloys from other metals used by man in the home we must never forget the debt that is owed to the people who worked in other materials. Base metal is only infrequently innovative of changes in style. Most movements have been ushered in by the inventiveness of other craftsmen; especially the silversmith.

Likewise although we are considering only British domestic metalware, the links with Europe have been strong. In the Middle Ages ours was a universal Christian world. The creations of the nation state, the diversive pull of language and religious schisms have obscured this universality. But many of our designs find their origins in Europe and it is important that we recall our debt to the European masters.

What is the appeal of base metal?

It is never easy to answer such questions. Just why do people collect? Our motivations are always complex and deeply buried. I can only hazard an explanation of its appeal.

Domestic metalware is mostly simple in style and made for use. This is in contrast to most things worked in other materials where a utilitarian purpose is often combined with a decorative theme. Most silver, gold and glass objects, for instance, though they were made to be used were also designed to give aesthetic pleasure to the user.

The virtue of domestic metalware is in its simplicity. In this troubled and changing world this seems to offer, to some people, something stable and timeless. Moreover, whereas most fine-art objects were made for the few to enjoy, base metal was made by ordinary men and women for everyone. It thus has a universality.

Twenty years ago I would never have thought it possible that I would be writing a book on antique metalware. I was a political scientist and economist by training and was then working in and out of Africa. Had it not been for a chance visit to our local sale room in Kent I might still have been so engaged. But on the spur of the moment my wife and I went to the auction and bought a pair of plated egg warmers for 2/6d. We enjoyed ourselves so much that we went back to the sale room two weeks later.

Within two years we had both become deeply involved in the world of antiques and later we opened our first shop. For the last ten years we have been operating from Oxfordshire where we specialise in antique metalware.

Looking back I am not sure just why it was that we gradually directed our interests in that direction. Perhaps it was that I sensed a good commercial opening – or again, perhaps it was the gift of a glass-bottomed pewter tankard!

Dating hypothesis

The story that came with it caught my fancy. It was glass bottomed, I was told, so that in the turbulent seventeenth century anyone drinking from it would still be able to see an attack coming through the glass bottom. My researches show-ed that it was actually nineteenth century. So were the pair of fine, cross-stretchered Glastonbury oak chairs which I bought as seventeenth century on my third visit to the sale room! We all make mistakes and would that all mine dated back to those early days!

520

There is no exact answer in matters of authenticity. Of course, an item is either period or not, but in most cases there is not yet a scientific way to prove this beyond doubt. It is knowledge and experience allied with flair that provides the weapons by which we have to make our judgements as to authenticity.

Inevitably, a book such as this has to offer some precision in its judgements, particularly as to period because people want to know when things were first made and when they went out of fashion. But really all such judgements are only working hypotheses for we were not there to see for ourselves. We postulate dates, we categorise objects, we note changes of style and we build up certain helpful rules. Yet never forget that it is we who do these things. The original maker was not bound by our rules. He made what he did because he wanted to or because people asked for it. Old-fashioned objects remained on sale long after the trend-setters had changed to a new style. And somewhere there may well have been a man ten or twenty years ahead of his time making things long before we believe they were first designed.

The danger with all these helpful rules therefore is that by repetition they become entrenched into final judgements. Early writers on pewter suggested, for example, that the broad-rimmed plate did not appear until the 1640s yet now we know, through research, that they were in use eighty years before. Likewise most writers on base metal suggest that medieval objects were made from either latten (an alloy of copper, zinc, lead and tin) or bronze whereas we know that many are mixed alloys or with a very high copper content and that what to us is a clear distinction between brass and bronze was not one recognised in the language of the times.

So treat my judgements with caution. They will be as fallible as those of the next man. Test them with your own experience. Be sceptical; that is the way progress lies.

Starting a collection

What can be done to learn more about base metal and how ought someone to go about starting a collection?

There is no doubt that wide reading, not just of the books in the areas in which you are interested, but on the social history of the times and of other forms of antiques can be most helpful. A great deal of background knowledge can be gleaned from books and the illustrations will help to familiarise you with the different styles and periods.

Yet in the end things must be handled and examined. For this, attendance at specialised sales in the major London sale rooms is one very good way of learning. View the sale, note condition, look at estimates, mark the items you like in the catalogue and those you don't. Then either sit through the sale or get the prices from the auction house afterwards. Then see what prices things made. How much did condition influence the price? Were you right or wrong in your choices as far as prices went? Why did some pieces expected to do well sell for less than expected and on the other hand, why did other pieces do much better than expected?

Six months in and out of sale rooms would be one of the best ways of learning.

Get out and talk to dealers. Most antique dealers like meeting people and talking about antiques. If you find one that doesn't you do not need to go back. Handle pieces in stock, listen to what you are told and measure it up against what you have learnt so far.

Ask around the antiques trade as to who they would suggest as a reliable dealer in your chosen area of collecting. Don't ask a specialist in that area himself as the advice might not be too reliable! Ask about generally and I suspect that sooner or later one or two names will begin to emerge.

Go and see them. Chat to them. Look at their stock. So far you will note that I have not suggested buying anything. Because until you know what you want and have some knowledge to back up this judgement it's best to keep your cheque book in your pocket.

Some people do their buying at auction. Most auction rooms will give advice, but remember that, as with the dealer, this cannot be entirely altruistic as their commission is based on the amount the items make. They are in the business of selling. Remember that they all exclude in their conditions any liability for the descriptions that they give in their catalogues. Though they are bound by the Trade Descriptions Act, I know of no prosecutions of auction rooms yet mistakes are regularly made. Certainly, while the major rooms employ experts in most fields the small provincial auction houses have one or two trained staff who, however well trained they may be, can not cover every field equally well. This is why dealers do occasionally come up with bargains bought at auctions.

Many collectors find in the end it is best to establish a relationship with one or two specialist dealers on whose knowledge and judgement they can gradually come to rely. It is in your favour, however distrustful a view you take of dealers, that they will hope to do business with you, not just once, but over several years. They will know that you may one day plan to sell back to them what you are now buying. But don't expect bargains from specialists. They may or may not be more costly than a general dealer, but they are not likely to sell something for very much less than its market value; not if they know their stuff!

Bargain hunting takes people to the corners and byways of the antiques world. Sometimes the hunter is blessed by success, but usually if a piece is cheap there will be a reason!

Whichever route you choose to collecting get to know the people with whom you are doing business. Many worthwhile friendships have been made this way.

Chapter 2

The metals
and processes

Copper, brass and bronze

Copper was the first metal to be worked by man and its discovery lies deep in antiquity. With its low melting point even the primitive furnaces could extract the metal from the ore.

Copper has two disadvantages. It is soft and when in contact with acids or salts it gives off poisonous oxides. Although some kettles were made in copper they were used to heat water for household purposes not for cooking or drinking, and the use of copper in the home was limited until sometime in the seventeenth century when a system was invented for coating the copper with a thin coat of tin. This, whilst it lasted, made the copper safe. Spoons are marked double-whited as an indication that two coats of tin were applied, and I think that it is likely that this system was derived from Holland.

The first disadvantage, softness, was overcome, probably by chance, by the discovery that if copper is mixed with other metals a strong alloy is obtained.

You may from time to time see references to other alloys of copper not discussed in detail in this book. You will see that people speak of 'Bell metal', 'Gun metal', 'Princes metal' and 'Tutania' for example.

In each case this is the name given to a particular alloy. In some cases, as with Tutania, basically an alloy of antimony (a metal not extensively used) with brass and tin, this is a precise description; but in others, as with Gun metal and Bell metal, it is a term which tells us more about the purpose of the alloy than its content, which will have varied from maker to maker.

There are almost no limits to the variations that can be worked with copper as the basic metal. By allocating a particular combination a name we imply a precision which is usually actually not present. In any case even if we call a certain combination by a special name, there is no way of knowing whether a piece of metal is or is not what we are calling it unless it is analysed. We are probably safer to stick to a general term for copper alloys with some zinc – 'brass' – and accept that other unexpected metals may also be present. If we really need to know what an object is made of there are the techniques available to have it analysed, but for most general purposes all that is important is to establish its content in relation to its main constituent.

Tin was the first hardener used in a copper alloy and the resulting metal that we know as 'bronze' was to give its name to the civilisation that developed two thousand years before Christ.

Calamine zinc was the other hardener used from the Middle Ages to make brass.

Each metal or alloy had its advantages. Copper could be easily beaten into shape, but was soft; bronze cast well, but could not be hammered whilst brass could be both cast and worked into sheets of what was to be called 'latten'. Brass was thus the more versatile of the alloys.

The process for making brass was at first an arduous one. Calamine zinc had to be chemically absorbed into the copper in a complicated process which was costly and not very efficient. There was a natural limit to the amount of zinc that could be incorporated into the copper. It was technically possible to reach about 30 per cent of zinc by this method, but early makers seldom achieved anything like this level and many alloys contained both zinc and tin.

With the discovery in the eighteenth century of a way to extract mineral zinc from the calamine deposits brass of a higher, more even quality could be obtained and if required could contain much larger proportions of zinc.

In addition to tin and zinc other metals such as lead have been added to copper. Many mortars of the seventeenth century are of a lead bronze and some early objects with a high copper content actually have both tin and zinc added.

From the late Middle Ages to the early nineteenth century there were difficulties extracting the trace elements from copper ore and these small proportions of other minerals tended to be left within the refined copper. Their complete absence in an alloy is a definite indication that the metal is nineteenth century or more recent.

As already mentioned in Chapter 1 the divisions between copper, bronze and brass which appear to us to be so clear are very much less defined historically.

In English, for example, there was no word for bronze until the eighteenth century; brass and bronze were both termed 'brazen'. Brass and copper products were sometimes called 'battery' after a name derived from the method by which many were raised; by hammering. Cast brass was 'brazen' whereas hammered sheet metal brass was known as latten.

The same confusion between alloys existed in Europe. In Dutch 'copper' or 'copperwerk' applied to both alloys, in France the same was true, 'Laiton or cuivre'; in German the word for brass, 'messing', does not appear until the eighteenth century.

To our forebears all these products were copper based and they did not feel the need to distinguish so clearly between any one alloy and another. It is only after the discovery of mineral zinc that the sharp distinction between brass and bronze arose, when it became possible to make an alloy containing over 30 per cent of zinc.

There were several ways in which brass and bronze could be cast. The most famous, the 'cire et perdue' method involved making a model of the object to be made, covering this with a thin layer of wax and then creating an outer mould in clay by covering the core and wax with a clay coating. By baking the complete mould the wax would run out leaving the space into which the metal could then be cast. There would have been a small wire join between the inner core and the outer clay case to keep the two in position. The disadvantage of this method was that only one object could be cast before the mould was broken up and it was slow. It was especially useful for fine work as great detail could be modelled onto the wax. Many early bronze figures were cast in this way.

For larger objects or things which were more robust and did not need such fine detail another method was employed.

A clay model was made of the object, baked, and then covered with an even coating of clay. Next an outer coating of clay was applied and then removed by cutting the model in half and lifting out the core and its (first) unbaked clay cover. This unbaked clay cover was then taken off the core. The outer mould was now baked and the two moulds put together, using wire or sticks to keep the core in the right position, viz à viz the casing. The metal could now be cast into the mould which was then broken up.

The use of a different technique made it possible to cast more than one object. By the seventeenth century sand casting, as it is called, was widespread.

The moulds consisted of two boxes filled with a mixture of silica, clay, horse hair and other ingredients. It had to be soft enough to take an impression, but firm enough for this to last after the model had been removed.

A wood model was then made and impressed into the bottom half of the mould encased in one of the boxes. The process was reversed in the other box and the two halves if now put together would contain the shape of the piece to be reproduced. If this was a plate or flat object that is all that needed to be done.

If however, the object to be made was hollow, an inner core had to be constructed. There are several ways in which this might have been accomplished. A clay core slightly smaller than the original wood or pottery pattern could have been used. Another possibility is that the pattern was not modelled in the solid, but was itself made in two halves and was hollow. Then the core of clay could be cast into the pattern. By keeping the core in the correct position in the outer sand mould with wire the object could be cast. The excess wire could then be cut away and on some early cooking pots a small plug of this copper can actually be seen.

For open-mouthed hollow objects the inner core could be composed of the sand mixture provided it was firm enough not to collapse when in use.

Where a two-part mould had been used it is often possible to see the lines on the object where the mould came together. If there was much excess metal this was taken off by scraping, but mould lines are an indication of these early casting methods.

In the seventeenth century bronze moulds became popular especially for small objects such as spoons and candlesticks. More costly to make, they lasted well and made possible a much faster rate of casting. There was a trade in both moulds and patterns. Cooke White, a Derby brazier was offering moulds for sale in 1780 for example, and another maker in the same year had on offer a 'neat assortment of brass founders patterns'.

After the casting was complete the excess metal had to be removed with files or shears and the surface rubbed smooth and then polished. Polishing was accomplished on a wheel.

Copper and brass were also used in sheet form. Sheets of latten were hammered out from ingots by hammermen or under trip hammers, often water powered. This sheet latten was by its nature uneven in thickness. It was used by people making battery. They took the sheets and formed them into the objects required by hammering.

In the eighteenth century rolling-mills, at first also water powered but in the nineteenth century driven by steam engines, took over the manufacture of sheet metal. These mills were capable of making a much thinner and more even sheet.

Prior to 1600 although brazen objects were being made in this country much was also imported from the great workshops of Europe; in Germany and Flanders.

The Founders' Guild, responsible for casting and the Braziers' for hammerwork, were involved from the early Middle Ages, but never had the influence of the more powerful Pewterers' Company. The Founders' Guild would have worked with imported copper and Cornish tin or foreign brass ingot. Likewise the hammermen of the Braziers' would have had to use imported materials. In the late sixteenth century under the expansionist policies of Elizabeth the British copper mining industry was founded and subsequently brass was made here for the first time. It is from these beginnings that the British brass industry developed.

Throughout its history casting and hammerwork in Britain were on a small scale until the eighteenth century. The individual master worked with one or two journeymen or apprentices, each piece being carefully made by hand using a series of technically difficult processes.

Whereas the British manufacture of 'battery' was on a small scale prior to the eighteenth century the pewter industry was long established and reached its peak in the seventeenth century.

Pewter, the alloy of tin

Pewter is an alloy of tin with a number of other ingredients which have varied from time to time and with the purpose of the items being made. Copper and lead were the most frequently used ingredients.

Because tin by itself is brittle, it is liable to crack under heat and fracture under the strains of daily use. So though domestic articles were made in tin from the seventeenth century to the nineteenth, their importance was limited. Tin was also difficult to cast and thus had a limited application in the home.

By the addition of one or more other elements, it was found that tin could be made to cast easily, hammered to gain strength and was strong and reasonably durable.

The principal additional metals employed were copper and lead. Copper gave the tin additional strength and lead made it cast more easily. In some pewter 'tin glass' or bismuth as we would know it, was added, but proportions were small, usually less than 0·3 per cent. Analysis of antique pewter can tell us what was put in the furnaces, but we quickly learn that there was enormous diversity. The idea that pewterers of the seventeenth and eighteenth centuries worked to a fixed formula is disproved. They varied the amounts of tin according to its cost and in accordance with the purpose of the object they were about to make. Plates needed a high tin content to make them durable. Flagons and measures which had to be cast were more easily made with a greater proportion of lead. Even given a standard set of formulae the addition of old damaged pewter traded in by buyers and added to the new metal will have distorted the contents of the melting pot.

Analysis confirms that nearly all plates contain more than 90 per cent of tin and indeed most of them have a tin content in excess of 94 per cent. The remaining elements are copper and lead. Copper seldom rose above 1·5 per cent nor lead above 3·5 per cent.

By and large this pattern is true for flagons and tankards. Only when it comes to baluster measures does the proportion of tin fall to below 70 per cent and the amount of lead rise to above 25 per cent. Tavern mugs and regional measures fall some way in the middle between these two extremes.

Traditionally there were three basic standards for pewter. 'Fine metal' with a high proportion of copper; 'Lay' with around 20 per cent lead, and 'Trifle' used for making small items made up of 50 per cent lay and 50 per cent 'new metal'. But in practice few objects analysed conform to any of these standards. There are, of course, exceptional items with a higher copper or lead content, but in general we find that most objects in pewter are predominantly of tin.

Perhaps this ought not to surprise us for in Europe they do not have a special name for the alloy as we do. In France it is 'étain', in Germany 'zinn', in Holland 'tenn'; all translate as 'tin'.

In the late eighteenth century it was found that by cutting down the proportion of lead and copper and including antimony, a harder alloy could be easily obtained. Subsequently it was discovered that this metal could be worked in different ways, more in keeping with the new industrial methods then sweeping through British industry. But most items in pewter are still fundamentally tin with other elements to give strength or malleability.

Traditionally pewter was made by casting in a mould. The furnaces were fired by wood until, from the seventeenth century onwards, coal was increasingly used. The tin and lead would have been melted together; the copper separately and then added later. The moulds needed to be coated with a substance to help the tin to run; pumice, carbon; egg and ochre

529

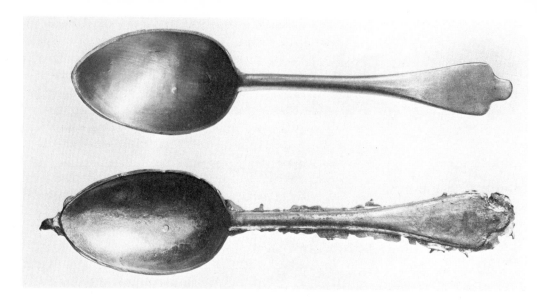

were amongst the materials used. The moment for pouring was crucial, but was measured by the eye rather than scientifically. When the casting came out of the mould it was still rough and had to be scraped or cut to remove the surplus metal. Then, if it was flat ware, it was given to the hammerman for beating. This hammering gave the plate or dish stability and strength. There is evidence that some pewterers tried to save money by not beating their flat ware in the booge (the part of plate that comes between the rim and the bowl, i.e. the rounded sides – these traditionally had to be hammered to give the plate extra strength) and eventually the guilds did permit the sale, for export only, of unhammered plates. These were known as 'Spanish trenchers' – an early case of dumping of inferior products!

For hollow ware the various parts had to be soldered together once they had all been cast. For a simple tankard there were several moulds, one for the body, another for the handle, one for the lid, another for the thumbpiece and hinge. For shaped flagons several additional moulds were necessary. Each part had to be cleaned and then soldered together. When the piece was completed it had to be burnished to an even polished surface. This was accomplished by using burnishers or planishers of steel, agate or bloodstone with a wheel.

To the amateur, pewter is not easy to cast. The temperature of the alloy must be right and the mould must also be at the correct temperature for the metal to flow freely. Yet an experienced caster can, at a glance, know exactly when to pour.

The apprenticeship for pewterers lasted seven years. During

1 Both these spoons have been cast in the same mould. That below is as it came out from the mould, whilst the example above has begun to be cleaned off and finished. The first task of the pewterer was to cut off the surplus metal from where it was poured into the mould and where it spread. Then it is cleaned off using a plannisher and finally polished by further plannishers and then buffed. These spoons were cast by Mr William Kayhoe of Richmond, Virginia, from an old mould. Private collection.

that time the apprentices lived with their master who stood 'in loco Parentis' over them. John Payne of Oxford, for example, had two apprentices Cullis and Mathews living with him in All Saints in 1667.

The moulds used for pewter were generally bronze, but there is some evidence that clay or plaster was used in the more remote areas. For smaller objects stone moulds were also used and Coventry museum has a fragment of a seventeenth-century stone spoon-mould. Many masters worked alone and undertook all the tasks. In larger workshops there was a basic division of labour between the caster, melter, and turner on the one hand and the more skilled hammerman and plannisher on the other. The power for all the work was provided by apprentices; muscle power!

As the number of pewterers grew in the late Middle Ages they tended in England, to organise themselves together into guilds, of which the London Guild was the most powerful and important. In some remote areas, in Scotland and Ireland there were insufficient pewterers so they joined up with other trades to form hammermen's guilds.

The history of pewter in the seventeenth century includes many episodes in which the London Guild, The Worshipful Company of Pewterers, tried to control the activities of the rural pewterers, often without much success. Although they continued their claims into the eighteenth century, the increasingly parlous state of the craft made them less able to enforce their will on provincial workers.

Pewter was never a large-scale industry. Its Masters, journeymen and apprentices worked in small workshops right up to the nineteenth century. It never employed as many people, for example, as pottery. It also never successfully made the transfer from the craft-based trade into factory organised industries that brass was to accomplish in the mid nineteenth century.

Chapter 3

Pewter: the historical background

The earliest British pewter dates back to the last days of the Roman occupation around AD 250, but with the departure of the Roman legions most industrial activity, such as tin mining, declined rapidly. There is no direct evidence of the production of pewter in Britain in the period after the departure of the Romans.

It is not until the ninth century that there is sound archaeological evidence of a revival of tin mining in England, a necessary pre-requisite for the production of pewter.

From the ninth century in Europe there is documentary evidence of the use of pewter. The Council of Rheims (808-13), for example, permitted the use of pewter in church services, but it was not until the 'Council of Westminster' in 1076 that pewter was allowed in churches in England and then only subject to subsequent periods of prohibition.

Thus the first resurgence of pewter in both England and Europe was for ecclesiastical purposes whereas the Romans had put pewter to work in the home.

A number of early chalices and pattens have been found in the graves of prelates and bishops. By 1400 most parish churches had several items of pewter; unconsecrated chalices, cruets (small communion flagons), candlesticks, pyxes (for the host), and christmatories (for the oils).

From the fourteenth century onwards there is fragmentary evidence of the use of pewter in the home, but it was limited to the houses of the nobility and of wealthy institutions.

Gradually the demand for pewter grew helped by a thriving export trade. London was dominant in the late Middle Ages, but other pewter centres were established in such cities as York, Norwich and Coventry. By 1500 most towns possessed their working pewterer some of whom would have been members of the London Guild.

This Guild evolved slowly from the Merchants' Guild during the Middle Ages. The first legal recognition that can be traced was the granting of ordinance in 1348. The Guild received its

2 A fifteenth-century drawing of a pewterer at work. He is casting the body of a flagon.

Royal Charter in 1473.

During the fifteenth century other Guilds were established in York (by 1419), Bristol (1456) and Norwich (1490). In a few smaller towns the hammermen came together with other similar craftsmen like silversmiths, braziers and pewterers to form hammermen's guilds. This was done in Ludlow by 1511. In Scotland and Ireland this was the pattern of development too, with the Edinburgh Hammermen's Guild incorporated by 1496.

It was not until the sixteenth century that pewter began to appear more widely in the homes of the middle classes.

The Tudor period was one of great economic expansion. The growing wealth of the merchants and traders allied with the drive and enterprise of the nobility led to many social changes. Tudor man spent his new found wealth rebuilding his home and refurnishing it; silk hangings for the walls, carpets for the floors, new 'joynt' furniture in the rooms and plate in silver or pewter for the table.

John Harrison, a contemporary observer wrote at the end of the sixteenth century of three things 'marvellously altered'. One was the 'exchange of vessel as of treen platters into pewter' and he spoke of even a farmer having a 'fair garnish of pewter on his dresser'. The thesis that pewter was steadily finding its way into the homes of the less well-to-do is supported by the evidence of sixteenth- and seventeenth-century wills and inventories. Two studies of inventories of the period 1550-1600 have shown that at least 83 per cent of them listed pewter amongst the possessions of the deceased. It is true that such inventories were only required by law from those with estates of some substance, but many poorer people also completed the procedure and the inventories show that amongst people of very modest means (owning less than £11 of goods at death), most owned items of pewter.

A good example would be Richard Symmons of Banbury who died in about 1572-3 leaving goods worth £1.9.8d which included '5 pieces of pewter' worth 3/4d.

On the other hand men of wealth often had considerable quantities of pewter. To take an example, from my own home town of Witney in Oxfordshire, Thomas Taylor who died in 1583 had over 200 items of pewter including 'twoo dyssen of plate trenchers' and 'Twoo Flagynn peowter pottes'.

Most frequently found were plates, dishes, chargers and saucers. Including spoons more than 80 per cent of all items listed were used for eating. The only other significant group of articles listed were candlesticks and drinking 'pottes' and cups.

London dominated the pewter trade, but the major cities like York, Bristol, Norwich and Edinburgh all had well-established pewter industries. Most smaller towns would have had one or more working pewterers. Estimating the numbers involved in the craft is very difficult, but it appears that at its peak around 3,500 people were engaged in making pewter. Important as the craft was, it was never a major source of employment.

Even the most successful pewterers worked on what we would consider a small scale, employing one or two journeymen with a few apprentices learning the trade. Most pewterers, especially those in smaller towns, would have worked on an even more modest scale. The workshops were situated in the back of the shop, the pewter being sold from the front. Most pewterers will have made the standard items such as plates, dishes and spoons, but there was also a thriving wholesale trade in the more elaborate articles requiring costly moulds. Most pewterers were likely to have had other craftsmen's work

to sell in their shop. The stock of Rogers, of Malmesbury in 1677 is probably typical. He had the work of three other masters in his shop at that time. It was common practice to buy what you could not easily or economically make yourself.

In the towns the potential buyer would have had no difficulty, but as late as 1700 most people would have had to make a journey to the nearest large town or the local fair to buy pewter.

Pewter was never cheap. In the seventeenth century it cost around 1/- to 1/2d a pound and its second hand value was about 10d a pound. So a set of twelve plates would have cost perhaps 12/3d when an average unskilled man earned 10d a day. Part of the costs could be defrayed by handing in old damaged pewter.

The working pewterer needed considerable capital to start up. He required a furnace for melting the tin, multi-part moulds for casting for each object, many tools for working the pewter including a wheel and also substantial quantities of tin. The will of an Alcester pewterer who died in 1684 tells us something about the value of all this equipment. His furnace was worth over £2, his wheel and tools £4, his moulds £10 and the metal in stock for use £45. A total of over £60 plus his stock for sale which with some brass was valued at £18.

It was possible to set up as a pewterer by buying an existing business or else to start from scratch. Fryer set up in London in 1683 at a cost of £300 and he was in need of more capital quite quickly. In the eighteenth century it appears that between £500 and £1,000 was required to establish an adequately capitalised pewter business, no small sum for those days.

Although the craftsmen were proficient and speedy in their work, the lack of power and the essentially craft orientated methods of working meant that the level of production was low and profit margins easily eroded.

During the seventeenth century the demand for pewter rose steeply and it should have been a time of high profits. But at the same moment that demand was moving steeply upwards so were both the price of tin and the wages that had to be paid.

Pewterers must have faced the early years of the eighteenth century with some confidence. The growth of their trade over the last two decades of the seventeenth century and the universal use of pewter in the home surely promised prosperity. However, although the first twenty years or so of the new century probably saw few changes within the craft the seeds of future decline were already sown.

In theory the eighteenth century ought once again to have been a century of expansion for the population was to double and every new home meant a potential buyer of pewter. It has been suggested that the success in developing the market in the last years of the seventeenth century created some of the difficulties that were faced later. Pewter was not an everyday purchase and it had a useful life of about twenty years if it was well treated. So that the achievement of bringing pewter into almost every home by 1700 left little room for expansion. The success of the last century may have made some impact in the first decades of the next, but by 1730 the rise in the population ought to have brought increased demands for pewter. This would probably have occurred but for the manufacture, and greatly increased popularity of, new cheap substitutes.

These problems had already been recognised as early as 1696 when to protect the pewter industry and ensure fair measure in taverns the House of Commons voted that ale should be served 'but in sealed measures made of pewter' rather than the 'mugs of earth'. The competition of pottery was thus already being felt in 1700.

In the eighteenth century the pottery industry was to expand rapidly. In 1730 there were approximately 1,700 workers making pottery, but by 1770 there were over 5,000; more people involved than there had ever been engaged in pewter. Pottery was cheap, more easily produced in quantity and could be gaily decorated to appeal to the current taste.

Indeed had it not been for the demand from the colonies and other overseas markets the pewter trade might have been in even more serious trouble.

The average level of exports 1700-25 was 4,833 cwt, but this rose steeply between 1726 and 1750 to over 10,398 cwt per annum. The next quarter-century saw further progress as the demands of the American and West Indian colonies increased. Exports reached a peak at an average of 16,799 cwt in 1751-75, and though the War of Independence held back growth over the next twenty-five years by the turn of the century more than 34,000 cwt were going overseas, some eight times the level of export of one hundred years earlier.

The eighteenth century saw some new demand from the growing population, but fierce competition from pottery and later in the century, porcelain and brass jeopardised the stability of the craft, and only the demand for exports saved the trade. Even so, by 1800 the industry was in serious disarray. Techniques had altered very little in over one hundred years. Workshops were still basically small; a master, one or two journeymen and apprentices. Machinery was still manually operated and primitive. The changes brought about by the use of steam engines, machine tools and the other developments of the industrial revolution which were to have an effect on the rest of industry had little impact on the pewter trade. Smaller margins, restricted demand and rising costs all discouraged development. Fundamentally the industry simply did not offer much scope for the new methods.

It is true that the eighteenth-century improvements in communication, the better roads following the turn pike acts and the building of canals did encourage a few enterprising pewterers to develop on a semi-factory basis. Perhaps the most prolific of eighteenth-century pewterers were the Duncombe family who worked near Bewdley. Little is known about their operations and it may be that they were the first to introduce factory methods to their craft. I suspect however, that their large production was partly due to the use of out-workers or to the sub-contracting of work to smaller pewterers, but nevertheless the Duncombe workshops must have been substantial by about 1760.

The dramatic movement of people from the countryside into the towns brought about major shifts in population.

Pewter remained an expensive commodity to transport so that although it was moved by sea, canal and wagon the traditions of the industry had been for local production to supply much of the local needs. In the new cities there was no established pewter industry so that the eighteenth century saw the expansion of the trade to many new centres to supply local demand and Liverpool, Birmingham, Manchester and Glasgow gradually developed into pewtering centres.

With many traditional industries in decline and with the shift in population to the new towns many of the well-established cities were themselves to suffer a considerable decline in the eighteenth century. Norwich and York, two of the leading centres both saw the virtual death of the craft. After 1750 the number of pewterers started to decline and even London was affected. This retraction in London can be illustrated by the number of apprentices admitted to the 'Mystery' as the craft had been called in medieval times. Down from 165 in 1700-1709 to only 35 by 1790-99.

The start of the eighteenth century saw Bristol the leading provincial centre with about 75 masters, journeymen and apprentices engaged at any one time. York came next with an average of about 50. By 1740 the industry in Bristol had hardly changed, but at York it had shrunk to about half. By 1780 whilst Bristol was even more important with about 80 people working, York had sunk to a handful and new cities like Liverpool, Manchester and Birmingham were much on a par. In Scotland the story was the same. The craft remained strong throughout the century in Edinburgh, but grew considerably in Glasgow, a new industrial city, whilst it declined in the older cities.

It thus seems likely that during the eighteenth century the number of people actually working in pewter probably remained unchanged, but that there was a considerable shift within the industry in favour of the new cities at the expense of the older centres.

The crude figures probably disguise a gradual shift away from Master, journeyman and apprentices working in small shops to a fewer number of larger undertakings, with semi-skilled employees, in the new cities able to compete successfully with the smaller traditional pewterers attempting to survive in the increasingly adverse and difficult conditions of the day.

If the second half of the eighteenth century had been bad for the pewter industry the nineteenth century was disastrous. The competition offered by pottery, porcelain and brass became even more severe and the craft was further damaged by the popularity of the new medium: silver plate.

As if these pressures were not enough, the heavy inflation of the late eighteenth century forced up prices and this, together with the demand for skilled men in the new industries led to a heavy increase in the wage rates. The movement towards larger-scale production was aided by rapid improvement in communications following the growth of the canal system and then after 1830, by the success of the railways. Goods made in Manchester or Birmingham could find their way economically to most parts of the country and the smaller old-fashioned rural based industries were to suffer increasingly. This is still basically what the pewter industry was, small scale and local, and suffer it did.

The dramatic decline in home demand was matched by the interruption of exports during the Napoleonic wars and the pewter trade never recovered the lost ground, as their principal market, North America, was quickly developing its own pewter industry.

By 1800, outside of London, only Bristol could still boast of a well-established pewter industry, though towns like Birmingham, Bewdley and Manchester in England, Edinburgh and Glasgow in Scotland and Cork and Dublin in Ireland still had a number of pewter establishments at work.

The introduction of the Imperial Standard in 1826 gave a fillip to the dying craft as nearly all the existing tavern mugs and tankards had to be replaced over a few years. Not only did the introduction of the standard help the trade, but the vast increase in beer drinking which was to follow in the 1870s provided another impetus for those firms which had survived. Beer consumption rose fourfold in the third quarter of the nineteenth century and the demand for tavern mugs, brewery equipment, pumps, washing stands and other items for the tavern trade kept alive a dying industry for a few more years.

After 1800 the bulk of pewter made in the traditional way was made for taverns, except for a few domestic items like candlesticks and tobacco boxes. Apart from this the industry faced an almost complete loss of its traditional markets due to competition from other material.

There was another major change within the industry. Around 1770 several makers found that by including antimony in their pewter and excluding lead they could make a thinner, harder alloy. This was at first used in traditional ways to make

539

cast pewter. Some of the pieces marked 'Hard Metal' and 'Superfine Hard Metal' are made of this tin and antimony alloy.

In the nineteenth century this new alloy began to be used in a different fashion. Pewter was spun from sheets rather than cast. A wooden model, of the object to be made, was constructed. This was fastened by a chock to the lathe. A sheet of the pewter alloy was gripped against the form or master and the wheel spun. Pressure was then placed by the operator, with a brass or steel spinning tool, against the sheet so that it gradually changed shape to take the form of the master beneath it. Naturally this technique could only be used for flat ware or for those hollow objects where the widest part was at the top thus making it possible for it to be removed from the form when spinning was complete. Thus items could be raised from the sheet without any casting being involved and with less metal needed. With items of a complex design they were made in separate parts and then soldered together. Tea pots and coffee pots had cast handles, spouts, lids and feet soldered onto the spun and seamed body. In early hard metal, spouts are often made of cast pewter when the body is of the hard metal.

This hard metal is widely known today as 'Britannia metal' although correctly this is the trade name for an English patent metal, which was granted to Richard Forge Sturges in 1842 for the name and composition of the metal. The use of Britannia metal meant that the old long drawn out apprenticeship could be done away with and less skilled and cheaper more easily available labour employed. It also had the great advantage that such techniques were much more fitted to large scale enterprise and steam and water power could be used to drive the spinning machinery.

The new centre for Britannia metal was Sheffield, though work was also done in Birmingham, London and Glasgow. Many domestic objects were made in this metal, perhaps the best known being the multitude of tea and coffee pots made right up to the 1900s by famous makers like James Dixon and Ashberry; who produced scores of designs. To begin with they chose simple neo-Georgian shapes, but with the changes in taste later in the century, pieces became much more elaborate. It was found that designs could be added to the basic form by using metal stamps to create relief designs. Terminals, handles and knops were made in the representation of flowers, leaves and fruit.

Side by side with many tea and coffee pots in Britannia metal are found sugar bowls and cream jugs and also made in great quantities are salts, peppers and mustards, the latter often with blue glass liners as well as countless other small household objects.

One of the mistakes most often made by beginners is to think that the stock or pattern number beneath a piece is its date. These stock numbers are a sure sign that the object is Victorian even if the number suggests a twelfth century origin!

Britannia metal provided a cheap substitute for silver plate and a new alternative to pottery.

It was bought by the less well-to-do, whereas pewter in its hey-day was found at all levels of society. Britannia metal was definitely 'lower' class; hence perhaps the antagonism that most pre-war collectors had for its 'pretentions'.

London and a few provincial makers still continued to make traditional cast pewter, but the day of the traditional pewterer was really over by 1840. From then on there were only a few firms making a limited range of pewter for the Public House trade and the new industrial companies turning out in quantity cheap thin Britannia metal objects, many of which were subsequently plated. The initial letters E.P.B.M. stand for Electro-plated Britannia metal just as E.P.N.S. stands for Electro-plated nickel silver.

The 1841 census listed only 300 persons in London claiming to be pewterers and outside the capital only 72 persons listed this as their occupation. These figures will not include those who thought of themselves as factory workers rather than as skilled pewterers. Many more people will have been working on pewter, but the figures nevertheless give an indication of how fast the decline in the industry had accelerated.

The spectacular rise in the brass industry, the dramatic growth of demand for pottery and porcelain, the demand for silver plate and the inability of pewterers to respond to technical change meant that by 1840 the craft was almost extinct. It was to linger on producing Britannia metal and a few individual pewterers continued to eke out a living in the big cities. But its day had passed.

Chapter 4

What to look for in pewter

Condition and colour

Many collectors at the start buy damaged pewter because it is cheap. It's not easy to put out good money when you are not yet confident in your judgements or fully aware of values. Yet there is little doubt that in the long run this is a mistaken policy for eventually the imperfections will come to grate on you. As you get more experience your standards will certainly rise. Frequently I have heard the lament, when looking at a damaged piece, 'I bought it when I first started'.

The other reason why buying damaged pewter is not a good policy relates to its long-term value. Top-quality undamaged pewter appreciates far faster than the damaged. No collector ought to buy only with investment or profit in mind. Such a person is really an investor who should apply financial rather than aesthetic judgements to his buying. Yet it is still only natural to hope to see a collection, bought with care and effort over the years, increase in value. Should one ever wish to sell, damaged pewter never shows the increase in value which attend good-conditioned purchases. This is true with all forms of antiques and the first rule of collecting, in my view, ought to be to buy the best-quality pieces that you can afford.

It's true that there are exceptions to the rule. I would, for instance, never turn down a Tudor flagon just because it was damaged, but on the other hand I would never look at another plate with a hole.

Damaged pewter is not easy to repair. Pewter has a low melting point and its only too easy to do further damage if too much heat is applied. Many old repairs are unsightly. The work was often given to a passing tinker or the local plumber who used a heavy lead solder. These repairs are not easy to remove.

Even a good professional repair can be obvious. If you have to make good a split in a piece with a good colour or patina, the new metal that is added will be bright and stand out like a sore thumb. The solution is to clean the whole surface which will make the repair less easily seen, but may make the piece look over-cleaned. So the best advice is to steer clear of damaged pewter. My own rule is only to buy items that are exceptionally rare if they need repair. Then one has a duty to see that the damage is stabilised for if it is not made good it will surely worsen in the fifty years to come.

Colour is very much a matter of taste. There are two schools of thought. The first says that when new and while it was in use in the home pewter was kept clean and polished. This approach holds that what is called 'patina' is actually dirt or unsightly oxide and that all dirty pewter ought to be cleaned. This is the general attitude of collectors in the USA and Belgium. In England and in most of Europe the patina developed on pewter through the passage of time is highly appreciated. This second view prizes that soft gleaming grey colour which is actually given the name of 'pewter' in the colour charts.

Very heavily oxided pewter can be unsightly particularly if it has patches of rough oxide lifting off the surface. But equally, a newly buffed surface can be too bright. In the end it is a matter of individual taste and judgement. A heavily oxided tulip tankard is shown on plate 43.

If you do want your pewter clean it may not respond if the oxide is at all thick, to rubbing with a cloth. A standard wadding, spirit-based polish will usually remove a light film of oxide and this type of polish is to be preferred to a creamy liquid as the latter tends to dry in the cracks and scratches and leave deposits.

Should the film of oxide be too thick to remove by polishing with a commercial polish you will have to abrade the surface by using either sandpaper or a caustic solution. It is very easy to damage the pewter by either method. Too rough a sandpaper will leave scratches that cannot be taken out and caustic soda or hydrochloric acid can eat away the pewter to say nothing of your fingers.

So unless you are used to handling dangerous chemicals it is best to leave the cleaning of pewter to someone experienced in the task.

Where you do have pieces cleaned by caustic treatment the oxide will be lifted off but you will be left with a new unpolished surface. This will have to be re-finished by buffing on a wheel.

If you do have pewter cleaned try and leave some part of the original surface untouched. If the whole surface is removed then there is little left other than the style to give a confirmation of age. I have seen what may have been rare and genuine pieces of pewter cleaned in acid all over and then so buffed that not one inch of the original surface has been left.

The best way to have your pewter cleaned is to have it done by hand using very fine emery paper and rubbing away the oxide, but this is slow and costly though in the end more easily controlled and less liable to damage the article.

Fakes and reproductions

In Europe pewter has been prized since the nineteenth century and there has thus been an economic motive for the faking of pewter for over 100 years. In this country pewter was not appreciated or valued until after the first Exhibition at Clifford's Inn in 1904. This was the start of British collecting but few pieces had any great value during the first ten years or so of interest so that it was not until after the First World War that any real incentive to fakers existed. Most British fakes are thus less than sixty years old.

This is long enough for some of them to have acquired a genuine coat of oxide. The most valuable in the inter-war years were, as now, Stuart candlesticks and flat-lidded tankards, and these were the items of pewter most often faked in the early days of collecting.

How do you tell a fake from a genuine article? It is certainly not easy with the handful of good early fakes. An analysis of the metal would probably confirm any doubts, but in spite of new methods of analysis this is still not easy to arrange.

Probably the best advice is to seek help if you come across an exceptionally interesting item in pewter. If you decide to buy first and seek confirmation afterwards make sure that you get a clear and detailed statement from the dealer. He is bound to stand by any description that he offers, but in the sale rooms you are less well protected for most salerooms have clauses in their conditions expressly denying any responsibility for the attributions. In practice, though, most sale rooms will discuss any problems that you may have in regard to a piece bought in their rooms.

If you have bought first and intend to ask afterwards you had best contact another collector if you know one, or go and see one of the few specialised dealers and seek his help.

But the best bet is to try and get help first from someone with more knowledge than yourself. In any case approach a really rare item with some natural caution. Ask yourself why it is so cheap (if it is!) Ask why you were able to find it while other more experienced collectors or dealers were not fortunate before you. Perhaps it has already been seen by others with

4 *Opposite and overleaf:* Two pages from a Catalogue of Reproduction pewter *c.* 1926. Note that the Normandy flagon (nos. 17804 & 17803) are wrongly called tappit hens. The maker used his imagination with nos. 17223, 17339 & 17368, the like of which will not be found in antique pewter.

No. 17804.
Tappit Hen.
6in. high. 7in. high
26 –   31 –
$13.00 $15.50

No. 17809.
Complete as illustrated, 55/- $27.50
Oval Dish only, 11/- $5.50
Jug only - 22 – $11.00

No. 17803.
Tappit Hen.
5¾in. 6½in. 7in. 8¼in. 10½in. high.
26 –   31 –   45 –   55 –   75 –
$13.00 $15.50 $22.50 $27.50 $37.50

No. 17223.
Tappit Hen.
9¾in. high.
50/- $25.00

No. 17333.
African Jug.
11in. high.
70/- $35.00

No. 17339.
African Jug.
11in. high.
84/- $42.00

No. 17368.
Tappit Hen.
8in. high.
38/- $19.00

No. 17222.
Jug.
8¾in. high.
36/- $18.00

No. 17338.
Measure.
½   1   2   4 pint.
4½in. 6½in. 7⅜in. 9¼in. high.
28 – 45/- 68/- 105/-
$14.00 $22.50 $34.00 $52.50

No. 17224.
Tappit Hen.
10in. high.
50/- $25.00

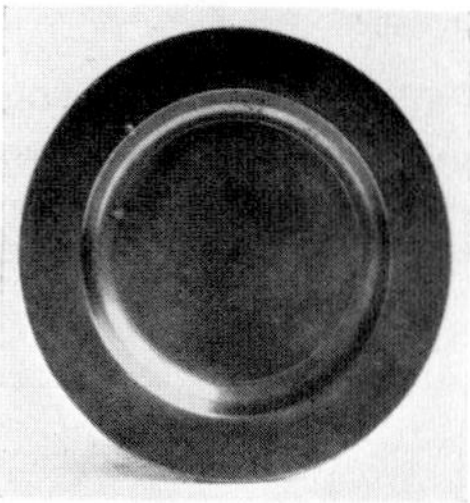

No. 17210.
Plain Round Plate.

6	7	8	9	9½	10	12	14	16	18in.
6/6	8/6	11/-	12/-	13/6	15/-	20/6	36/-	45/-	54/-
$3.25	4.25	5.50	6.00	6.75	7.50	10.25	18.00	22.50	27.00

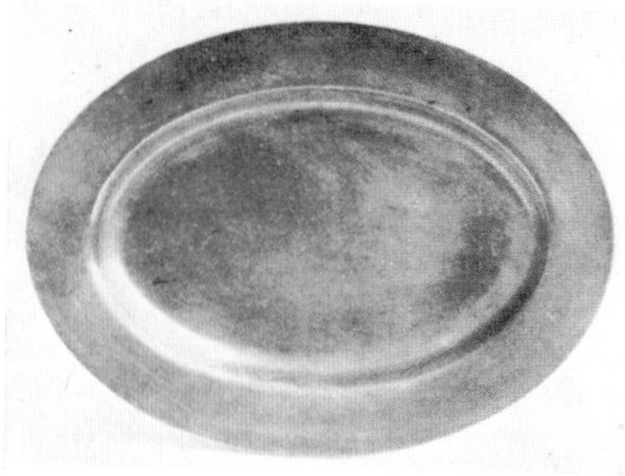

No. 17211.
Plain Oval Dish.

14in. × 9 in.	...	34/-	$17.00
16in. × 11¼in.	...	40/6	$20.25
18in. × 13¼in	...	50/-	$25.00
20in. × 15 in.	...	60/-	$30.00

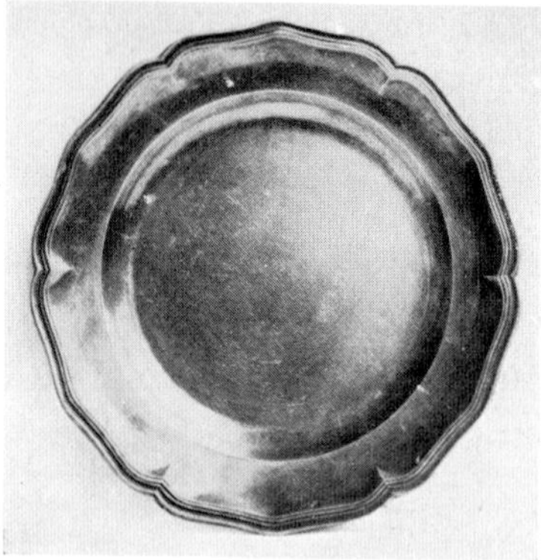

No. 17800.
Fancy Edge Plate.

7½	9	10½	12½	14½in.
13/-	15/-	23/-	40/-	55/-
$6.50	7.50	11.50	20.00	27.50

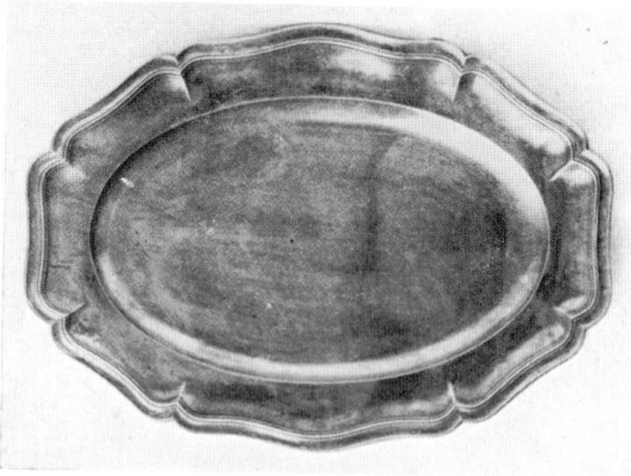

No. 17801.
Fancy Edge Oval Dish.

8½in. × 6 in.	11/-	$5.50	14¼in. × 10 in.	42/-	$21.00
11 in. × 7¾in.	21/-	$10.50	16½in. × 11½in.	50/-	$25.00
12½in. × 8¾in.	25/-	$12.50	19½in. × 12½in.	70/-	$35.00

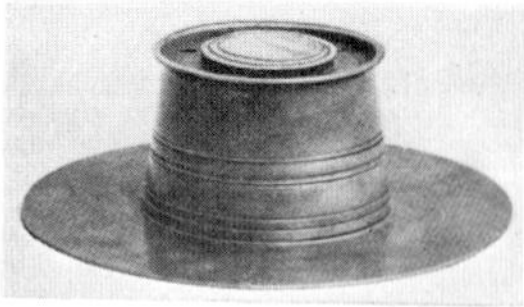

No. 17334.
Inkstand.

5 in. base	× 1⅝in.	high	12/-	$6.00
6 in. ,,	× 1⅞in.	,,	15/6	$7.75
7 in. ,,	× 2⅜in.	,,	21/-	$10.50
7½in. ,,	× 3 in.	,,	26/-	$13.00
9 in. ,,	× 3¾in.	,,	38/-	$19.00

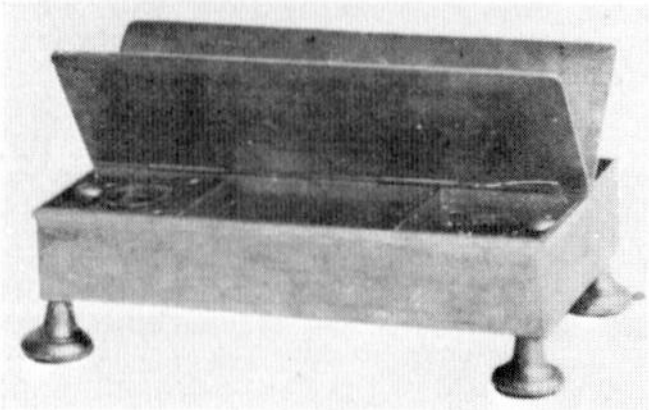

No. 17337.
Inkstand.
8in. × 4in. × 2⅜in. high.
60/- $30.00

more knowledge? You can have beginner's luck, but usually there is another explanation! It is greed that most often blinds a potential buyer and depresses that natural caution that ought to be at work.

Post-World War II fakes, that is items deliberately made to deceive a buyer into thinking that they are old when they are not, are generally of poor quality. Recently there have been a batch of heavy poorly-cast high-lead-content pieces with an acid colouring in sale rooms, but an application of common-sense to these pieces ought to lead to their being discounted before a second glance.

More difficult are the reproductions made before and after the war. These were made for sale in gift shops and the like and there was no intention to deceive. There has always been and probably always will be a market for copies of fine things. Indeed, large quantities of reproductions were made between the wars and since, and many of these are now old enough to have attained a film of oxide and some wear.

Some of these pieces are copies of early styles, others were the invention of the makers and bear no resemblance to period pieces. They are mostly well made, but because they are basically lead free are likely to feel harder than most antique pewter and they are usually of a thinner material. They have seldom been turned off as they would have been in earlier times and plates are not hammered in the booge. Look too for signs of genuine wear.

The problem of these reproductions is made worse by the fact that before the war there was no trade descriptions act to prevent makers putting the names of genuine historic makers on their reproductions! So that you can find pre-war pewter with the mark of genuine seventeenth and eighteenth century makers. These false marks include, 'S. Duncombe', 'Bush and Perkins', 'William Eddon' and 'John Trout'. There is also a small group of pewter with the mark 'N.R.' which is sometimes mistaken for a period maker, but which is the 1930s mark, of one of the men making reproductions at the time.

In addition to genuine earlier marks used on reproductions, a number of other marks in the period style were invented. They can sometimes confuse less experienced collectors. Such reproduction marks include 'P & D', 'JA with an anchor', and a group of marks with an Irish harp.

Things are complicated still further by the fact that some greedy people have taken reproduction items and have set out to age them and to give them a false degree of wear in order to pass them off as antique.

If all this frightens the life out of you perhaps I should add that much the same could be written about every branch of antiques. Where things are valuable there are people who will try and make a dishonest living by making and selling fakes.

With some experience it is at least a little easier to tell new pewter from old than it is to distinguish many other reproductions from the genuine article.

It takes time to obtain this experience and few collectors or dealers acquire their knowledge without making some expensive errors. Try to find some other local collector and learn from him and his mistakes.

The dating of pewter

As you will appreciate the dating of any article is not an exact science. Much must be left to individual judgement based on knowledge and experience.

Within ten years our judgements will be reinforced by a scientific analysis of the alloys used. It is already possible to have a small sample of pewter analysed which can tell you something about its manufacture, but at present there is insufficient comparative material for this to have much value and in any case it is not easy to get it done.

How then are we to make our judgements? The areas that must be examined are style, purpose, marks, wear and methods of manufacture.

Let us start with the purpose of the object. What can this tell us about its possible period? For example, you will not find Tudor coffee pots a hundred years or so before coffee was in use in this country, nor are you likely to find a Victorian porringer as these were out of fashion by that time. Sometimes, but by no means on every occasion, a consideration of the original purpose of a piece will tell you something about its period.

Examine it for style. Does it conform to any particular period? Look through illustrations of similar articles. This should suggest a possible date based on style.

Next any marks should be examined. If there is a makers' mark can you read it? Consult *Old Pewter, its Makers and Marks* by H. H. Cotterell and *More Pewter Marks* by C. A. Peal, both maybe available in your local public library. If you can identify a maker you are further on your way to dating the piece. Are there any other marks? Such as capacity marks, engraved coats-of-arms or stamped initials? All of these can add something to one's understanding of the period in which the example was in use.

By now the purpose, style and marks ought all to have suggested a possible date to you. If they all say the same thing then you have made some progress. If they suggest several different periods, then leave a question mark hanging over it and move on.

The next stage is to examine the condition of the item. Look at it carefully. Handle it. Run your fingers over leading edges, open and shut the lid to check the degree of wear on the hinge. If a piece of pewter has been in use for a hundred years or more there must be plenty of signs of this use. It might be possible to find an unused seventeenth-century piece of pewter, but I would not bank on it. Because by and large pewter items and those spun in Britannia metal differ in period and method of manufacture, there ought to be no difficulty in telling them apart. In practice whilst the Britannia metal tea pot is not likely to be confused with the Stuart flagon, there are difficulties with pewter and the spun productions both made around 1800-30 where styles are very similar.

The first thing to look for is the thinness of the metal. If it is rather thicker than with tea pots and the like it may be a sign that sheet metal was not used. Look also for evidence of casting and whether or not the object has been hammered. Another tip is to look at the edges of the object. How are they formed? Has the metal been bent back over itself to form a thicker edge? If so, then it's been spun. For example, a cast plate has a reeding beneath the rim in pewter formed in the mould. In Britannia metal the rim has been turned over and shaped down and with a glass it is often possible to see that this has happened.

To take another example, a bowl, if it has been cast, even if it has not been hammered will show signs of having been turned off. Whereas the Britannia metal bowl will have been made by spreading the sheet of metal over the form and, though this is difficult to see with the naked eye, there will be small ridges across the surface which can sometimes be discerned by running the hands over the piece.

Oxide can sometimes help to tell a piece with lead from another with a high antimony content. Pewter oxides faster because of the lead in the alloy and the oxide tends to be uneven, often erupting in bubbles or patches of what used to be called 'tin pest'. Hard metal with antimony has an even, usually rather darker, colour oxide which is very hard and difficult to chip away and which is much less likely to erupt.

But in attempting to make these judgements do not forget that around 1770-1800 many items were cast in hard metal which had they been spun we would have called Britannia

metal. It's the method of construction that separates these spun items from cast pewter.

If all the tests each indicate the same general period then you can say with some confidence that you have been able to date it. If there is conflict between the suggested dates then it needs further study or someone with more experience.

Let us take a practical example of this method of dating pewter. Look at the wavy-edged plate (Plate 15). A plate is a plate so we can learn little about its date from its purpose, but the style clearly indicates an eighteenth century origin. We will see later that, wavy-edged plates were mostly made between 1730 and 1780.

This plate is made by John Home and by consulting Cotterell we see that he worked after 1749. So far, so good. Now let us imagine you can handle the plate. Has it been cast? Are there clear hammermarks on the booge? Does it show signs of wear? The answer is affirmative in all cases. If you could handle it you would see knife marks on the surface. There are no casting faults or pock marks to suggest a later manufacture and it has been hammered and turned. All of these tests thus confirm that it is probably from around 1750-80.

Take another example; the small saucer illustrated here (Plates 6–7) was out of fashion by the early eighteenth century so it is likely from our knowledge of its purpose that it is before 1700. Yet it has a triple-reeded rim; a style going out of fashion at that date. A small seed of doubt ought to have been sown.

Is the plate hammered in the booge? The answer is no. This reinforces our growing uncertainty. Is it well worn? Are there knife marks? Again the answer is in the negative. Does it have any makers' mark? The back carries a crude London mark in a cartouche but no makers' mark, unusual for an early piece.

Purpose, style, method of manufacture, wear and mark, tell conflicting stories and you can safely say that it is not period.

Not all examples are so straightforward, but most genuine

5 *Far left:* Pewter was well finished. This is the base of an eighteenth-century tappit hen showing the excellent turning used to tidy the base.

6 *Centre:* Triple-reeded saucer with broadish rim. Made in the 1930s as a reproduction.

7 *Above:* The back of the same saucer illustrating its lack of finish and crude London mark.

pieces will tell a consistent story; it's the inconsistencies that ought to raise doubts.

Marks on pewter

Most pewterers marked their wares, but in spite of guild regulations to this effect by no means all the genuine items are so identified.

Marks were in use in the Middle Ages, but though the guilds will have encouraged the marking of pewter it was not obligatory until 1503. London pewterers placed their marks on a touch-plate, but these plates were destroyed in the Great Fire of London in 1666, thus depriving us of valuable evidence of the earlier pewterers.

All those pewterers still at work in London re-struck their marks after the Great Fire and from then on until the end of the craft all London makers admitted to the Guild struck their marks on a touch-plate. The last pewterer recorded his touch in 1875. There are five touch-plates and they contain 1090 makers marks, a good start to identifying makers as London was dominant throughout the history of the craft.

It is probable that other centres used similar touch-plates. It is known that this was so in York, but only the Edinburgh touch-plates still survive. The Edinburgh plates were started about 1600. There are 143 touches, the last struck in 1764.

1 John Jolly, c. 1720, Edinburgh
2-4 Seventeenth-century marks of William Eddon, Roger Willoughby and Thomas Cowley
5 Scottish seventeenth-century mark of Alexander Ferguson
6 Compton of London, c. 1800
7 John Duncombe, early eighteenth century
8 Burgum & Catcott, late eighteenth century
9 Joseph Morgan, c. 1810
10 Typical hallmarks of Thomas Mundy, c. 1760
11 J. Moyes, c. 1860
12 James Yates, nineteenth century
13 John Home, c. 1750
14 James Hitchman, c. 1720
15 Pitt & Dadley, late eighteenth century

Top row: typical Continental marks
1 A Dutch crowned rose
2 A German angel mark
3 A French hammer mark
Bottom row: Quality marks; German and Swiss

Howard Cotterell in his monumental work recorded the names or initials of some 6,000 pewterers and assigned marks to many of them. Recently the late C. Peal has issued two further lists of makers, and marks. There are certainly many other makers to be discovered from local records and many more marks to be recorded. Makers' marks take many forms. The earliest tended to be small and simple with a device and initials; later marks became larger and in the eighteenth century often included the full name of the maker as well as some device. Some typical marks are illustrated here.

From around 1630-40 another form of makers' mark was gradually adopted. These took the form of false 'hall marks' similar in design to the silver and goldsmiths' marks which still remain in use. These false hallmarks did not include either a date letter nor town mark and were selected not by the guild, but by the individual maker. There can be little doubt that their use was dictated by a desire to ape silver marks and to bring to pewter some of the glamour and value of the silversmiths' products. No one will have been fooled into believing pewter was silver, but similar marks may have made people believe that they were comparable in importance. A typical hallmark is shown here. These marks continued in use into the early nineteenth century, but appear less frequently after about 1750.

Pewter had an active life and marks are often rubbed and difficult to read. The use of the index in Cotterell often enables a maker to be identified on the strength of part of the mark alone.

Where a mark is worn or rubbed there are several ways of making it more clear. The use of a lens may help, but it is a strange fact that with very worn marks more can often be seen with the naked eye than with a glass. Photography can sometimes bring out a mark and a tracing on paper or a rubbing made on foil can also help. Perhaps the most effective and simple way of enhancing a mark is to use a lighted candle and allow the carbon from the candle to be deposited over the mark. Then take a piece of translucent sellotape and press onto the mark. Remove and put on white paper and the mark will be clearly highlighted. But keep the flame well away from the pewter; you don't want holes in your plate!

Just as silver had its Britannia standard for higher quality work so pewter had its mark for the best quality. This was a crowned X. At first it was indeed a sign of above average quality metal, but soon its use became widespread and appeared on almost everything wholly devaluing the mark.

Other marks found on pewter include origin marks such as 'MADE IN LONDON', or 'LONDON'. Provincial makers were not above claiming London origin for their work! Other marks on British pewter indicate the type of metal being used; 'HARD METAL' or 'SUPERFINE HARD METAL'.

Owners often marked their pewter and Housemarks were often stamped on pewter. Where an owner had the right to bear arms, that is carry an armorial coat of arms, these were sometimes engraved on to the surface. Colleges and other institutions often marked their pewter in this way and it is sometimes possible therefore to identify the former owner of a piece by the arms engraved upon it.

People also used to stamp their initials on their possessions. Where the initials are two in number, set side by side they are the Christian and surnames of the owner. Where they appear as a triangle normally the top initial stands for the surname and the bottom two for the forenames of the husband and wife involved. So

H

P   I

would stand for Peter and Jennifer Hornsby; remember that the J does not appear until the eighteenth century. Where the initials are two pairs they again usually refer to a husband and wife.

Pewter of standard capacity designed for use in the market-

1

2

3

4

5

6

7

8

9

1 William IV capacity mark
2 William III standard
3 George IV capacity check
4 Victorian capacity mark after 1879
5 Many items carried a mark to indicate the nature of the pewter used
6 Capacity marks of George V & VI
7 Crowned 'X' mark, once the quality mark but much devalued by over use in the eighteenth century
8 Typical London mark
9 Edwardian mark

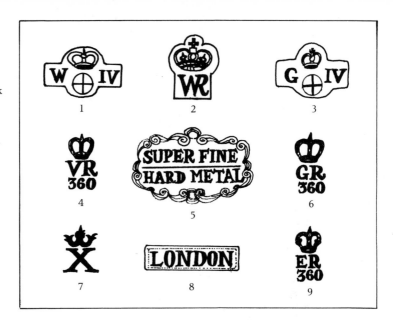

Coats of arms
1 1635-1655
2 1650-1670
3 1650-1685
4 1685-1705
5 1720-1740
6 1730-1770
7 1770-1785
8 1780-1805
9 1790-1810

place also often has marks stamped on it by the Weights and Measures authorities. These marks indicate that the measure conforms to the standard of the day.

The earliest mark found is 'HR' or 'hR' for Henry VIII and there are rare occasions when 'CR' is used for Charles I or II. All three marks are very uncommon. The standard adopted under William III continued in use until 1826 and such pieces conforming to those standards are marked with 'WR'. There are a few 'AR' and 'GR' marks indicating Queen Anne and the Georges, but they are not common. Just why it was that the WR mark continued in use is not certain unless it was to confirm the actual standard involved.

On the death of George III a new mark was introduced, 'GRIV' and this was linked with the introduction in 1826 of the new imperial standard. Both William IV and Victoria used the same basic design of capacity marks, with different royal initials.

Victorian capacity marks at first often included a country or town mark, but after 1878 a new style of marking was adopted with a simple 'VR' and a number to indicate the origin and confirming authority. From these numbers it is sometimes possible to identify where a pot was in use, but as numbers were re-allocated from time to time this is not always so. Major cities often had several numbers; Birmingham included 6, Liverpool 147, Manchester 5, Bristol 490, Glasgow 34-36, 59-62, etc. while London had many allocated including 4, 13, 21 and 28.

Edward VII and George V and VI all used this same system. It is possible though unlikely, that tavern pots in use before 1878 were re-stamped with the new system. If this 1878 style of mark is combined with an earlier then the first indicates the date of manufacture, but if only the post-1878 mark is present it is asking a lot to accept that the item was in use in a tavern for many years before being capacity marked. Whilst this is just possible with the 1878 VR marks once the only marks are ER and GR then the piece is definitely after 1902.

In Scotland capacity marking was the duty of the dean of Guild who marked the piece if it conformed to the standard measure with his initials. For example, the mark $\frac{RW}{DG}$ refers to Robert Whyte, an Edinburgh Dean of the Guild in the early nineteenth century. In addition, until 1878 a town mark was also added; in the case of Glasgow for example, a tree. After that the same numbering system that was used in England was adopted.

Decoration on pewter

Most British pewter is plain in contrast to much early European ware. In spite of the general preference for unadorned pewter there have been periods in which British pewter was decorated and some of these pieces are especially prized.

Some European cast decorated pewter is of the finest order. In this country cast decoration is much less common. It is found only on a few pieces before 1620 or so, such as some rare drinking cups with the Prince of Wales feathers cast upon them.

Pewter was also decorated by punching elaborate designs on to the rims of dishes. These punch-decorated pieces first appeared around 1580 and were being made up to the 1680s. Some we know were made in the West of England, but only a dozen or so of these dishes still exist. Sometimes three, more rarely up to five, different punches were used to make the design and they always included a fleur-de-lys.

About the middle of the seventeenth century another form of decoration became popular. It is known as 'wrigglework'. The maker of the piece took a hammer and nail and punched a series of small marks to form shapes or patterns. The effect is similar to engraving, but the lines are not continuous. Most wrigglework pieces are crudely done, for the guilds did not permit the employment of artists and the task had to be completed within the pewterer's own workshop. Many Stuart tankards have this 'wriggled' decoration. There is also a series

8 A group of finely decorated plates *c.* 1700-15. The wrigglework decoration was applied with a hammer and nail by the craftsmen who made the plates. Animals, birds and flowers are popular motifs.

of fine dishes decorated to commemorate the marriage or restoration of King Charles II. There are a number of wrigglework plates which continued to be made up to about 1720. Hitchman was a prolific maker of wriggleworked flat ware. Designs included flowers (the Tulip and Rose being popular), birds (the Dove and Peacock occurring frequently), as well as Royal portraits and other more intricate patterns.

Later in the eighteenth century dishes with line engraving appear briefly though they are very uncommon and most of this type that you will see are Continental.

There are also a few dishes made in this country that are reminiscent of the Nuremberg Latten Alms dishes with their embossed centres and wrythen swirls round the centre of the dish. These appear to have only been made by a few makers around 1730, probably apeing Continental designs.

Continental pewter

In spite of the fact that for long periods the importation of European pewter was discouraged there is much Continental pewter in this country.

Much of this was brought back by Georgian or Victorian gentlemen on the grand tour or by troops after two World Wars.

European pewter is more prized in the country of its origin than it is in Britain. Lead by the Dutch, Continental dealers have been combing British shops since the war. Yet in spite of all their efforts much still remains and every so often a piece of exceptional quality will appear.

Whether out of chauvinism or ignorance, European pewter was traditionally denigrated by British collectors, but much of it is of very high quality indeed, well made and with fine lines. The best of European pewter is equal to or better than our own. If you are attracted by it and can learn to identify it, European pewter can be a rewarding field for collectors. It is however, important for anyone wishing to collect only British pewter to be able to tell the difference.

There are a number of foreign-language studies, but only a few works in English to guide collectors. Perhaps the best is Vanessa Brett's *Pewter* published by Phaidon.

Considerable help comes from the system of marking adopted in most European countries. Much pewter is marked 'tenn', 'zinn', 'étain' or 'Englishe zinn', 'engles tenn', etc. and such marks are obviously of Continental origin.

The crowned rose mark is used in several European countries and where the maker's initials are incorporated within the crown it is a sure sign of European origin. Most eagle marks are German or Austro-Hungarian, marks with a hammer possibly French or Swiss. All marks incorporating three maker's initials and almost all marks with angels are Continental. Likewise small sets of three marks, one incorporating a coat of arms or a town mark are from Europe.

Some of the more familiar themes in Continental marks are shown here.

The principal differences in style between English and European pewter come out when one looks at flagons and tankards. There is a great variety of styles in Europe. Clearly Continental are those pieces with pronounced parrot-like pouring lips, large ball-thumbpieces or with shield or ball feet. Acorn thumbpieces are frequent in Europe and only found on Channel Island pewter in the British Isles. Most cast decorated pewter is European.

Some of the leading shapes of Continental flagons, measures and tankards are illustrated here.

Collecting pewter

What should the collector look for in pewter?

It would cost a small fortune to build up a collection representative of all periods and of all types of objects. It is probably wise to select an area that attracts you, because of the style or shape involved or perhaps the purpose of the goods or their origin.

For example, some people collect just spoons, salts, tavern mugs or plates. Others concentrate on Scottish, West of England, Channel Islands or Irish pewter. Some people collect certain periods, others even try and build up representative collections of one pewterer.

There are a multitude of possibilities open to the would-be collector. I would suggest that two rules ought to be applied.

Continental pewter flagon shapes
1 Flemish
2 German
3 French
4 Swiss
5 German
6 Swiss
7 Dutch
8 French
9 Swiss
10 Normandy
11 French/Belgian
12 French/Belgian

1

2

3

4

5

6

7

8

9

10

11

12

Buy items which are in the best condition that you can find and concentrate on the rarest within whatever field you have selected. This probably means that the items will be more costly than buying more broadly, but you are much less likely to come to regret your purchases later if you buy quality items. I am sure it is better to buy less often, but better items than spread your resources over easily found pewter.

It's a costly pastime so make sure you like what you have chosen to collect. Seventeenth-century pewter for example, will naturally be expensive, whereas Britannia metal is still very much undervalued. Many collectors become very knowledgeable about their field and some devote considerable energies to researching the objects they buy. You may not be of this frame of mind, but do remember that buying takes but a few minutes and there is more to ownership than mere possession.

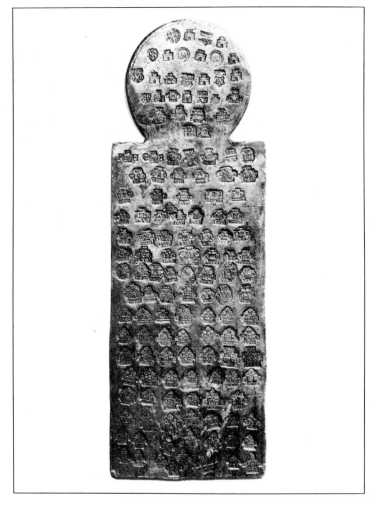

9 The Edinburgh touch-plate which contains the marks struck by Edinburgh pewterers from around 1600 to 1760. National Museum of Antiquities, Edinburgh.

Chapter 5

Pewter for kitchen and dining room

At some point in his history, man stopped tearing at raw meat with his hands and sat down to a lightly grilled fillet steak! Just when the transition took place is lost in the mists of the past, but for the whole of the last six hundred years, and indeed for many centuries before, man has made a ceremony out of eating. That is not to say that the serf in his hovel ate his gruel from a silver bowl, but even in the direst surroundings he used a wooden bowl and spoon to sup his evening meal. The Lord and Lady, in Manor House or Palace took part in more elaborate ceremonies; sharing a bread plate or later a wood, silver or pewter dish throughout a meal of many courses.

We take time off work to eat and in the Western world at least, we eat not just to survive, but as a pleasure. So man has developed utensils and rituals or patterns of behaviour and the kitchens and dining rooms of yesterday and today reflect this.

For the mass of people the diet remained unchanged over centuries. Bread, cheese, ale and less frequently meat or fish were the daily repast. Great quantities of bread and ale were eaten and drunk and these provided the bulk of the calories taken. In winter salted or smoked meat was all that was available and by March this was often a little high; hence the highly spiced dishes so popular to medieval man.

It would be wrong to think that all food eaten before the modern era was plain and simple. Even for the poor, whatever the regularity and paucity of their day to day food, there were feast and saints days to be enjoyed; the roast goose stuffed with apples for Michaelmas. For the rich and powerful, vast meals were served in which the appearance was almost as important as the taste. Twenty courses was in no way unusual, washed down with spiced wine; perhaps the popular 'bastard piment'.

From the sixteenth to the nineteenth century pewter was dominant at the table. It was never used for cooking as it is too soft and has too low a melting point. It appears at the table during the fourteenth century in a few great houses, but it was not until the Tudor economic expansion that it was to appear in

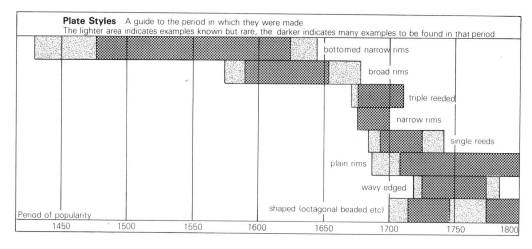

Plate Styles A guide to the period in which they were made
The lighter area indicates examples known but rare, the darker indicates many examples to be found in that period

bottomed narrow rims

broad rims

triple reeded

narrow rims

single reeds

plain rims

wavy edged

shaped (octagonal beaded etc)

Period of popularity

1450   1500   1550   1600   1650   1700   1750   1800

more ordinary homes. The new wealth stimulated a demand for new forms of furnishing and pewter plates and dishes were amongst the first things bought.

Had you been able to glance into a Tudor farmhouse you would perhaps have been surprised at the starkness of the rooms, the simplicity of the furniture, the rushes on the floor and the poor light offered by the rush lights or guttering candles, but your eye would have been caught by the light gleaming off the pewter plates and dishes used by the family and servants alike, stacked upon the Buffet or Court Cupboard in the hall.

It is highly likely that more pewter plates and dishes were made than there are all other items in pewter put together. There are certainly more plates and dishes to be seen than any other forms of pewter.

All medieval pewter is rare and plates are no exception. There were probably several popular styles of plates, but only those with narrow rims and a central boss have survived in any numbers. This central boss, known as a 'bumpy bottom' in the rather prosaic language of collectors, is a distinctive feature of nearly all early plates and dishes until the 1630s. The slope of the bowls does change, becoming more sloping by the sixteenth century and the boss is less pronounced by that time, but it is broadly true that the 'bumpy bottom' plate was in popular use for several hundred years even hanging on in the home until 1670 or so.

Yet the next century, the Stuart era, was to see many rapid changes in taste. In the late sixteenth century a new style of plate made its appearance. This still possessed the central boss, but in place of the narrow rim there was a much broader rim.

In contemporary documents they are referred to as 'new

562

10 A sixteenth-century pewter plate with narrow rim and central boss. The mark is of a rowel and spur, an unknown maker's mark. The initials belong to a former owner. Private collection.

fashioned broad brymmed plates' and are known to collectors as 'broad rims'. By the middle of the seventeenth century the central boss is now starting to be replaced by a flat-bottomed plate. The width of the rim varies according to the size of the plate or dish, but on a nine-inch plate it would be perhaps $2\frac{1}{4}$ inches wide or more and many broad rims had a total rim diameter amounting to over 50 per cent of the total width of the plate. These broad rims are very rare and are amongst the most attractive pieces of British pewter.

Around the time Charles II was restored to the throne, perhaps reflecting a desire for more vivacity after the starkness of the Puritan period, the rims of plates were engraved with lines. At first these reeds were cut into the plate, but later they are cast in relief on the surface. These 'triple-reeded' plates as they are termed embraced both broad-rimmed examples and by 1670 onwards plates with a more conventional width of rim. This style was going out of fashion by 1710.

Another style to appear in the reign of Charles II were the narrow-rimmed plates. These had rims below half an inch, usually with cast reeds upon them and were popular for about thirty years.

Towards the last decade of the seventeenth century another fashion began to gain in popularity. These are the single-

11 On the left a narrow-rimmed plate, on the right a plate with triple-reeded rim. Late seventeenth century. Both show typical traces of oxide which has built up since the plates were in daily use. Signs of genuine wear, the knife marks, are also clear.

12 *Far left:* A typical single-reeded plate.

13 *Left:* The plain rim; the most frequently found form in plates and dishes. This is an eighteenth century dish 18 inches in diameter.

reeded plates, with what we would consider a normal width of rim between the extremes of the broad and narrow rims, but with a single cast reed upon the upper edge. The single-reeded type was manufactured up until the 1730s, but was slowly replaced in favour by plates with a plain rim.

These plain-rimmed plates were to dominate the market from the 1720s until 1830 when pewter plates went out of fashion. The earliest plain-rimmed plates can be dated to around 1695 but they were not numerous until the reign of George I. Plain-rimmed plates are sometimes confused with broad-rim plates because neither has any reeding upon the rim, but the sizes are very different and the width of a plain rim would seldom exceed $1\frac{3}{4}$ inches.

Several other styles of plates were made in the eighteenth century. Plates with six or eight sides were briefly popular in the first decades of the century and a style imported from the Continent, the wavy-edged plates were very fashionable from the 1730s for about fifty years.

Towards the 1770s a revolutionary style was developed. The strangely shaped 'Hot water plates', as they are known, had a plain rim and the plate was mounted on a round hollow base.

14 *Right:* An octagonal plate. Eighteenth century.

15 *Far right:* A wavy-edged plate from the mid eighteenth century. The beading was at first cast with the plate but by 1800 it was often applied later in strips.

The rim had a small hinged flap through which hot water could be poured so that they became table pewter hot water containers, the heat designed to keep the food palatable. They are not very attractive and as they are rather bulky and more costly to make their popularity was limited although they were made into the nineteenth century.

There is no way of knowing just how many plates of any one style were made but it is possible to obtain some idea of the frequency with which they can now be found by analysing the style of plates offered for sale in London in recent years.

Perhaps not surprisingly, plain-rimmed pewter plates which were in fashion for the last 120 years of pewter's popularity are by far the most numerous as the diagram shows. This underlines just how rare the broad, narrow and triple-reeded styles are. It is not possible to incorporate sixteenth-century bumpy bottomed plates as they occur too infrequently to be treated statistically.

Most plates of whatever period are between 8 and 10 inches

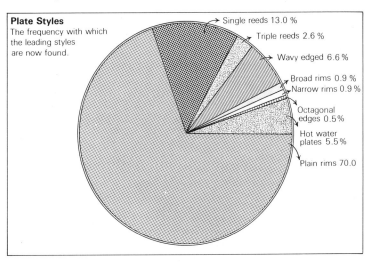

Plate Styles
The frequency with which the leading styles are now found.

Single reeds 13.0 %
Triple reeds 2.6 %
Wavy edged 6.6 %
Broad rims 0.9 %
Narrow rims 0.9 %
Octagonal edges 0.5 %
Hot water plates 5.5 %
Plain rims 70.0

and the general pattern is that plates before 1700 are under 9 inches whilst those that are eighteenth century are usually above $9\frac{1}{4}$ inches in diameter.

Saucers are very much smaller at between 5 and 6 inches. These were not connected with tea, but were as the name implies, small plates for holding sauces. Saucers follow the styles then popular in plates and were widely used up to the 1700s when they seem to go out of fashion.

An unusual plate is the tazza or footed plate of the late seventeenth and early eighteenth centuries. Some of these tazza were used for the host in communion, but most were domestic, used perhaps to serve the popular sweetmeats or sugar confections. They are usually between 8 and 10 inches in diameter and have narrow-reeded rims. They stand on a widening foot.

Few dishes or chargers before 1580 survive. There are a few

17 *Below left:* Broad-rimmed dish *c.* 1650 with less pronounced central boss. 16 inches diameter.

18 *Bottom:* A small serving dish with hollow base for hot water. The spout through which the hot water was poured is in the front. On hot water plates the lid of the aperture fits flush with the plate.

19 *Below:* A pewter tureen by Compton of London *c.* 1800.

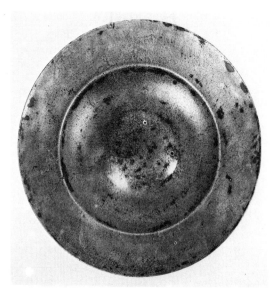

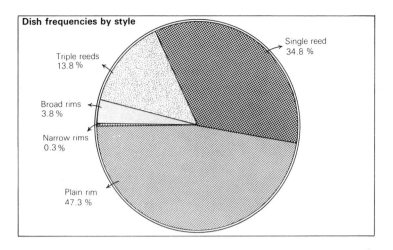

Dish frequencies by style

Single reed 34.8 %

Triple reeds 13.8 %

Broad rims 3.8 %

Narrow rims 0.3 %

Plain rim 47.3 %

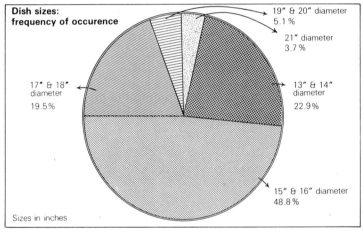

Dish sizes: frequency of occurence

19" & 20" diameter 5.1 %

21" diameter 3.7 %

17" & 18" diameter 19.5 %

13" & 14" diameter 22.9 %

15" & 16" diameter 48.8 %

Sizes in inches

bumpy bottomed dishes, but the earliest style likely to be met in any quantities are the broad rims.

Early records give a range of names for the various sizes and purposes to which dishes were put. The actual purpose of many of these are now unknown and modern collectors have simplified the division by calling all dishes below 20 inches dishes and those above chargers. Chargers greater than 22 inches are very uncommon, but there are a few monsters up to 36 inches in diameter.

Dishes and chargers follow the styles described for plates. The sizes and the relative frequency in which they are found are illustrated.

Broad-rimmed and triple-reeded dishes are slightly less rare than plates of the same style, but narrow-rimmed dishes are most uncommon. Far more single-reeded dishes have survived than with plates so that the plain-rimmed dishes or chargers are less common than one might have expected.

Large rectangular hot water dishes up to 30 inches or more in length were used for the serving of food. They stand on applied feet and have a well for the meat juices. Most are around 1800 and Britannia metal examples appear in the 1820s. These dishes are sometimes called 'venison' dishes even if they were more likely to carry boiled beef and carrots!

One type of dish not matched by a similar style in plates are the oval dishes and chargers so popular in the eighteenth century. These range from 12 inches in length to over 30 inches. Some have plain rims, others are reeded or with wavy cast edges. These may have been made as dishes to go with wavy-edged plates or plain-rimmed plates.

Sets of plates and dishes are not found very often. Originally plates and dishes were sold as garnishes, full services for a dozen or more people. Over the years they have been broken up. Complete garnishes are occasionally offered for sale, but in most cases all that survive of large sets of plates or dishes are the odd sixes or twelves that have managed to remain together throughout an active life. Any number above six are now called 'sets'. A set of plates is more valuable than the same number of individual examples. Plain-rimmed sets are about ten to twelve times more common than single-reeded sets and broad-rimmed, narrow-rimmed and triple-reeded sets are seldom seen.

Pewter bowls are frequently found from the eighteenth century. The average bowl is round, between 8 and 10 inches wide with a small reeded rim and they rest on a flat base. They were used for all domestic purposes. Smaller bowls, on a short stem with a round foot were broth bowls. Many were used in military and naval messes or in other institutions, such as

21 *Opposite:* Fine Charles I pewter flagon with its bun lid and elegant form. *c.* 1625-35.

568

569

22 *Left:* Fine broad-rimmed pewter saucer, *c.* 1570-90. It has been excavated and bears traces of 'natures' gilding; the effect of trace elements in the soil on the pewter. Private collection

23 *Opposite:* Rare flagon from Wigan with wide base, double-eagle thumbpiece and spout. By Baldwin *c.* 1770.

24 *Below:* Cast decorated tea pot after the Portland Vase. Made around 1800-20.

571

25 A rare pewter dish with wrythen bossed centre and punch decorated rim. The punch decoration is similar to that found on dishes of the late sixteenth and seventeenth centuries. This dish is probably early eighteenth century. The 'jelly mould' design is taken from Nuremberg dishes in brass. Private collection.

26 An attractive wrigglework plate. Although it has a single-reeded rim it dates from the last years of the seventeenth century, being made by Edward Gregory of Bristol who died in 1696. The naive Lion is typical of the designs on these decorated plates. Below the plate is a fifteenth-century pewter spoon with a diamond point knop. Private collection.

27 Pewter was often bought as a 'garnish' or set, plates and dishes sufficient to fill the needs of the family. Part of an eighteenth-century garnish, here the round plates are matched with wavy-edged oval shaped dishes.

prisons, poor law almshouses and schools as well as in ordinary homes. Beware of bowls with Naval inscriptions as some are later engraved. The broth bowl appears in the late seventeenth century and remained popular into the 1880s.

Porringers, a form of eating bowl, were very popular until the early eighteenth century. Porringers have small round bowls with either one or two handles known as 'ears'. They were ideal for the soups, potages, gruels or stews of the times.

Sixteenth-century porringers, have either one or two ears, whereas most seventeenth-century examples have but a single ear. The ears on early porringers were solid, but on most seventeenth-century examples the ears are fretted or cut and shaped into various designs. Porringers' ears in the shape of dolphins and crowns were popular. Porringers up to 1630 tended to be flat bottomed with straight sides, but later in the seventeenth century porringers with rounded sides, and a central boss were introduced. Around 1690-1700 this boss is disposed with and the sides straighten.

Between 1680 and 1710 a series of fine two-eared porringers appear with cast royal portraits in the base, often with elaborately decorated lids. By 1720 the porringer appears to have gone out of popularity in this country though they continued to be made and exported in large quantities to the USA throughout the eighteenth century.

There are some small rare cups, with either one or two handles used for drinking caudle or punch. These mostly date from the 1680-1710 period and many have a gadrooned body. Loving cups, larger in size, were passed from hand to hand on a convivial occasion. A few loving cups with straight sides and two handles are to be found from the late seventeenth century,

but most are rounded in form and are Georgian. They are bucket shaped with a small stem opening out to a wider foot and many have ball terminals to the handles.

Until the eighteenth century most people would have carried their own knife to the table. Forks were seldom used until after 1700 and were seldom made or mounted in pewter. Pewter spoons, however, were very popular. In relative terms a large number of early pewter spoons have survived. Many were lost in wells, sewers or rivers to be found generations later by archaeologists, or mislaid under the floor boards to be rediscovered when alterations were made.

Several specialist studies have been made of early base metal and silver spoons. There are many varieties of bowl shape, handle style and knops.

Before 1600 bowls tended to be fig-shaped or like leaves, but in the seventeenth century they become more rounded. There are many interesting knops to be found on early spoons. Knops in the shape of a melon, lion sejant, ball, hexagonal, apostle, maidenhead or seal top were dominant before 1600 together with a group of spoons without a knop, termed 'slipped in the stork', or 'sliptops' for short. There were disputes within the Pewterers' Guild over the use of latten knops on pewter spoons. There are a few such spoons dating either from the early fifteenth century or again in the mid to late sixteenth. These are very rare, but if you are to come across one it will probably be a pewter spoon with a latten seal-top.

In the seventeenth century the slip tops and apostles continue to be popular and are joined by other shapes such as the pineapple or strawberry knops. By 1640 a plainer style, the puritan spoon arrives, with a flattened handle and a straight

Pewter knops
1 slip top
2 acorn
3 apostle
4 baluster
5 diamond
6 hexagonal
7 lion sejant
8 horned head-dress
9 maidenhead
10 tryfid
11 seal top (simple bell)
12 stump end

Pewter bowl shapes
1 pointed round bowl *c.* 1300
2 round bowl *c.* 1400
3 fig bowl *c.* 1500
4 oval bowl, fifteenth century
5 oval bowl, sixteenth century
6 round, seventeenth century
7 late Stuart bowl

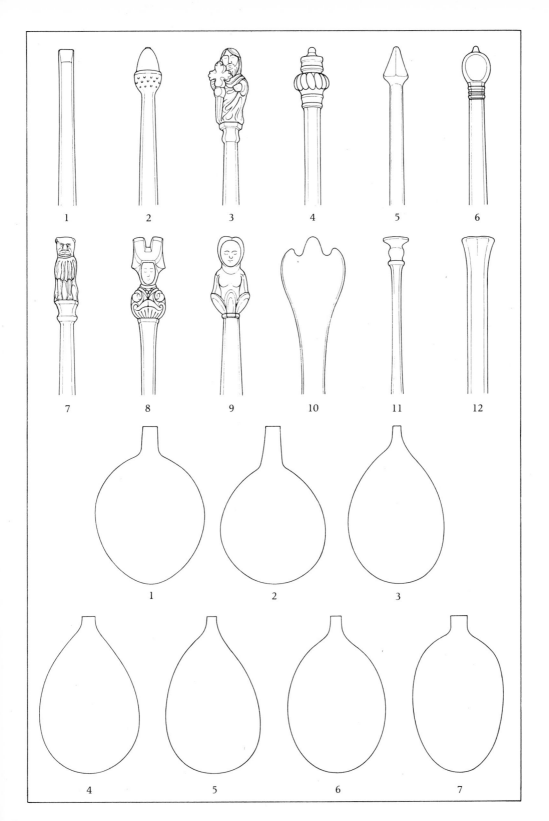

end and after the restoration the handles of spoons become even wider and the plain ends of the puritan are shaped and divided to give us the tryfid.

In turn the tryfid developed into the dog nose and from thence the transition was the same as for silver spoons, gradually leading into the Georgian styles largely still with us. Around the period 1680-1710 there are some fine spoons with cast royal portraits, perhaps matching the excellent cast portrait porringers.

During the eighteenth century pewter spoons become rare, driven out perhaps by silver plate or even brass spoons, but in the nineteenth century pewter spoons grow more numerous again and there was a considerable industry in Birmingham, for example, making spoons. Many nineteenth-century spoons are in hard metal.

An analysis of several hundred spoons over the last ten years has shown that only the slip top and tryfid re-occur with any frequency. Together they account for around 70 per cent of all pewter spoons with slip tops being slightly more common than tryfids, probably because of their longer popularity.

All other knops occur less frequently than four times in 100. Such knops are the hexagonals, seal tops, acorns, balusters and puritans. Knops which appear less frequently than twice per

29 A group of salts *c*. 1680-1720. Note the small recess or container.

30 On the left a spice pot. The taller piece is a sugar sifter, the rest peppers. The sifter is 6 inches tall. All except the second piece, a slim waisted pepper which is in Britannia metal, are eighteenth century.

100 include the beehive, horned head dress, lion sejant, maidenhead and stump ends as well as others either unique or known in only two or three instances.

Salt is essential to life. Today, because of its cheapness and easy availability we tend to take it for granted, but to our predecessors it had great importance. The bulk of animals had to be killed each winter as there was insufficient forage to maintain the whole stock. Smoking and salting were the only two ways of preserving the meat during the hard winter months, and salt was needed too, to help make the diet more palatable.

In silver, gold and bronze some wonderful medieval master salts still survive, but salts before 1600 in pewter are virtually unknown. Even in the seventeenth century, salts are rare and never match the magnificence of their more august predecessors.

Salts before about 1720 tend to be made with an inner and outer skin so that the salt does not rest on the outer walls, but sits in a small separate container. Most salts of this period are small for it was a costly commodity. The small bowl was made up into many varieties of shapes; and amongst the more important and attractive are the spools, capstan or octagonal salts. Examples from the 1690s are often gadrooned, that is with raised curved decoration worked onto the surface, or with cast beading on the base. As the eighteenth century developed, salts became larger and the cup salt dominated the last fifty or so years of the century. The nineteenth century saw the appearance of Britannia metal salts, usually with small, round or oval-shaped bowls often with applied feet. Salts in pewter were made into the late nineteenth century alongside their Britannia metal counterparts.

Peppers before 1700 are very rare indeed, but during the eighteenth century they became popular. The baluster shape is the most common style, but during the late eighteenth and nineteenth centuries other shapes such as the 'urn' or 'waisted' styles became popular. Britannia metal peppers are often similar in style to those in pewter, but have thinner bodies and usually a harder oxide; more elaborate shapes of peppers are all nineteenth century and most probably from the second half of the century.

Sifters are sometimes mistaken for large peppers. These were used for sugar or spice or for sprinkling flour. Sifters are less common than peppers and are up to 6 inches or more high. A small group of 'blind' peppers, that is with lids without any apertures are spice canisters for ginger, cinnamon or other

spices, used to flavour food at the table, just as we now use salt and pepper.

Tea and coffee, both introduced in the mid seventeenth century were costly and only drunk by the well-to-do.

Pewter tea pots are rare before the nineteenth century. A few round or bullet shaped tea pots are found from the 1750s but as this style was much copied in the 1920s care must be taken.

Gradually, as the price fell, tea took the place of ale and beer in the nation's diet. From 1800 onwards tea pots were made in Britannia metal. The simple Georgian forms of 1800-20 were replaced by the elaborately shaped and decorated tea pots of the Victorian era. Many hundreds of designs were made; many in Sheffield and Birmingham. The bodies, shaped with floral or patterned decoration, with applied knops and feet in a variety of styles. Pewter tea cups do not appear until the 1890s.

Coffee never attained the importance of tea and was initially drunk in coffee houses. In Europe pewter coffee pots are common, but few are found in Britain until in the nineteenth century when they were made in quantity in Britannia metal. As with tea pots the earlier simple shapes were gradually replaced by the highly decorated Victorian coffee pot.

Many other items were made in pewter for use in the kitchen or in the dining room, but few are of great significance or are found in any quantity.

31 *Above left:* A bulbous tea pot of the late eighteenth century with wooden ebonised handle and knop.

32 *Left:* An early nineteenth century oval tea pot. The body decorated with bright cut engraving, a form often found on silver.

33 *Above:* A spouted coffee pot from the first quarter of the nineteenth century. The lid and spout in cast pewter, the body spun in Britannia metal.

Chapter 6

Pewter for drinking

For several hundred years ale and beer were a staple part of the national diet. Wine, though imported in considerable quantities since the Middle Ages was, because of its cost, only drunk by the wealthy. Spirits were rarely taken until the gin craze of Hogarth's time.

Most ale was brewed at home until the eighteenth century. It was made from malt, yeast and water and was a thick, heavy and nutritious drink. As with most things Shakespeare had something to say about Ale; 'A quart of Ale is a dish for a King!' and a sixteenth-century writer speaks of it as 'thick and fulsome'. Often drunk warmed and spiced as well as cold, it did not store well and would last only up to two weeks. Beer, made with the addition of hops, was lighter and longer lasting. Until the reign of George II most country houses would have had their 'Yeling' house or brew room and their brasen 'woort' pans for ale making.

Only in towns and villages was ale or beer brewed for sale in any quantities. We are inclined to think of beer in the early days being made in and sold from casks, but even in the seventeenth century beer was being exported in bottles to the Americas.

Considering the importance of ale, beer, wine and other drinks it is not surprising that most households had several utensils, many in pewter, for serving drink. One of the problems that customers for most commodities faced was the danger of receiving short measure. Traders, stall holders, shop keepers or tavern owners were only too ready to give less than the legal standard.

There were frequent attempts to establish national standards. Perhaps the most effective were the standards introduced by William III at the end of the seventeenth century. Standards for wet and dry measure, including different standards for ale and for wine were universally enforced in England, and continued in use until the adoption of the Imperial Measures in 1826. The capacity of pieces can help to date

34 *Far left:* The strong erect thumbpiece and knopped lid are typical of this most stately of flagons. Made in the reign of James the first.

35 *Left:* The 'beefeater' flagon with its flat lid and usually twin-cusp thumbpiece came into popularity in the middle of the seventeenth century and were still being made around 1700.

pewter measures. Although measures made to a capacity standard were mostly intended for use in the market place, many were to be found in homes; often used for bringing goods, or drink, back from the market or inn.

A whole range of items were made in pewter for the serving of ale, wine and other drinks.

Flagons, large vessels for bringing drink to the table were in use until the late eighteenth century. Ale and cider measures were popular in the eighteenth century and for the serving of wine the baluster measure remained in service for many hundreds of years. Tankards, both lidded and unlidded, cups, beakers and mugs were used for drinking although the role of pewter was challenged by vessels in leather, horn, wood, pottery or brass.

Although there were flagons in Tudor homes almost no examples now survive. The earliest domestic flagons that can be seen outside specialised museums are those known as James I flagons. These stately and robust flagons were also used in considerable numbers as Communion flagons after the use of pewter in the communion was formally sanctioned in 1602. Many James I flagons are thus ecclesiastical, but Church examples are usually dated or inscribed whilst domestic flagons tend to bear no identification. James I flagons vary in height from perhaps 9 inches to 14 inches. They have slightly tapering sides, rounded lids with a pronounced knop and heavy 'erect' thumbpieces. Early examples have a rounded base, when looked at from below, and stand upon an applied skirt. By 1630 flagons with flat bases appear and flagons without knobs and with different thumbpieces became fashionable during the reigns of Charles I and II.

Few seventeenth-century flagons have lips or spouts and pouring would not have been easy. They were not made to any standard of capacity.

Around 1650 a new style became popular. Known as a 'beefeater' from a supposed resemblance of the lid to a Yeoman warder's hat, a considerable number of these fine flagons have survived. They have wide and on a few exceptional examples very wide bases. Most beefeaters have the twin cusp thumbpiece, but there are several variations and there are some examples with knobs to the lid.

The next major change in flagon styles to be made nationally was the 'Spire' flagon of the eighteenth century. The Spire is so named because its tall knob is superficially like a church spire. These flagons have stepped lids and their handles are more elaborate than those of earlier flagons. Early Spire flagons are usually tall and tapering, but by the mid eighteenth century the bodies have become broader. The thumbpieces most commonly found on Spires are the chair or scroll. From around 1770, the open chair is almost universal. Spire flagons were made into the nineteenth century.

There are several regional styles of flagons of which the York, 'Acorn' flagon is perhaps the rarest and most attractive. These were made between 1680 and 1740 and have a most unusual acorn body shape. A straight-sided flagon with domed lid was made on both sides of the Pennines during the early eighteenth century and there is also a distinctive 'Wigan' flagon with a very broad base and domed lid. Around 1700 a number of flagons were made similar in style to the flat-lidded

36 *Below:* Spire flagons from the early eighteenth century usually have a slimmer form. This example was made by Christopher Bankes of Bewdley and given to his local church in 1780 when he was its churchwarden. Note the unusual wide base and common 'open chair' thumbpiece.

37 *Centre:* A development from the flat-lidded tankard, these tapering flagons with flat stepped lids were made either side of the Pennines from 1690 to about 1720.

38 *Right:* The tapering form of ale jug. This is a half gallon by Henry Joseph of London *c.* 1780. Note the scroll thumbpiece.

39 *Far left:* The Oxford ale or cider jug in use from the late eighteenth century up until about 1900. This example is a half gallon. The handle is bound with split cane to act as an insulator. A sign of nineteenth-century construction.

40 *Left:* A rare west of England measure. The even rarer style is much more tapering. A half pint made in Bristol *c.* 1800.

tankards which are discussed later, but much larger than could have been used for drinking.

Measures, unlike flagons, are made to a standard measurement of capacity. That many measures were in private ownership is certain. It was also the practice for publicans to supply mugs and measures for those wishing to buy ale or wine to drink at home. An American commented in 1796 that he often sent to the tap house for his ale and the 'tap house man ... sends his servant with it to your house and also provides mugs for the purpose'.

There are several regional styles made in Scotland and the Channel Islands, but in England, two shapes dominated the eighteenth century. These are the tall straight-sided measure and the squat bulbous lidded jugs, sometimes called an 'Oxford' ale jug.

The eighteenth century ale measure is similar in size to earlier flagons. It has a domed lid and usually a pouring spout. Gallon and half-gallon measures are the most commonly found sizes; the unlidded examples tend to be in smaller capacities. The ale measure was at its peak from about 1750 until the early nineteenth century.

The bulbous-lidded jugs for ale or cider had stepped lids and were also made in ale standard sizes. The half-gallon and quart are the most common. Later in the eighteenth century lidless examples of these measures appear. Most lidded bulbous ale jugs have the open chair thumbpiece whilst a shell thumbpiece appears on many late-nineteenth-century examples. These jugs continued to be produced up to 1900, many by Gaskell and Chambers. Many of the earlier examples have a grid or grating behind the spout to keep out the hops from the glass, but this is no certain guide as to period.

An interesting style of measure is a rare group associated

Pewter thumbpieces: flagons

Erect (1580s-1640s)

James I flagons. Later on tappit hens and pot belly Scottish measures.

Erect with opening (1630-60)

Charles I and II flagons.

Twin cusp (1640s-1710)

Beefeater flagons, flat-lidded tankards, Stuart flagons, and Scottish lavers.

Rams horn (1650-1710)

Beefeaters, flat-lids, Georgian tankards and Lancaster flagons.

Scroll (splayed) (1690-1760)

Lancaster flagons, York flagons, Spire flagons.

Scroll (1700-70)

Double-domed and tulip tankards.

Chair (1730-80)

All tankards. Spire flagons.

Pierced chair (1740-80)

tankards

Shell (1800-90)

Ale and cider measures, Scottish balusters.

Open chair (1760-1820)

All tankards and measures of the period.

Acorn (1700-1820)

Channel Islands and European.

with the west of England. These have narrow mouths, broad bodies and are always lidless. There are two styles, one being more bulbous than the other. The narrower style is associated with the Fothergill workshop in Bristol. They appear to have been made as spirit measures, but many must also have been used in homes in the late eighteenth and early nineteenth centuries.

The principal thumbpieces used on flagons, measures and tankards are illustrated on p. 583. For every rule there is an exception, but if this is borne in mind these illustrations may help in the identifying and dating of lidded British pewter.

The story of the measure and flagon is thus one of continual change. The baluster, the standard measure for the serving of wine, shows a very different development. With few alterations it continued in service for more than 400 years. Unlike most other forms of pewter it owes nothing to silver or other materials, for the baluster is a design unique to pewter.

Balusters have flat round lids and usually simple strap handles, although in later examples this often ends in a ball terminal. The sixteenth-century balusters tend to be slimmer than the eighteenth-century examples. Over the centuries the thumbpiece, that was used to open and shut the lid, and also the strengthening across the lid where it joins the thumbpiece, varied in design several times. The earliest thumbpiece incorporates a wedge, a heavy bar of pewter running from the middle of the lid to the top of the hinge. In some cases they may never have had a thumbpiece on top, but in others there is evidence of a missing thumbpiece. It is not certain how many genuine wedge balusters there are without a purchase. In the sixteenth century the wedge appears with a ball thumbpiece and from the end of that century until the end of the seventeenth century they often had a 'hammerhead' like thumbpiece.

Because of their rarity it would be well to seek expert advice if faced with any of these early thumbpieces for not only are there modern copies, but genuine early balusters of the seventeenth century with the more common bud thumbpiece have been altered.

The dominant baluster of the seventeenth century, which was also made into the eighteenth, is the bud baluster. The Bud is named after its resemblance to a spring bud. The wedge on the lid is replaced by a small V-shaped attachment. From the second quarter of the eighteenth century another style change takes place and the double-volute baluster with its fleur-de-lys support replaces the bud.

The lidded baluster was on its way out of fashion by 1800 though for a brief time lidless examples were made. These lidless balusters in turn developed into the bulbous measures so common in Victorian times.

The rarest sizes in all balusters are the gallon, half-gallon and the small half-gill. Regard with some caution any half-gills of the bud period or earlier. Our ancestors had little use for such small quantities of wine and spirits were seldom drunk. More commonly found in all balusters are the pints, quarts, half-pints and gills.

The thumbpieces and lid supports of the baluster are illustrated together with the leading Scottish types which are discussed further in Chapter 8. There are, of course, a number of small variations particularly to the later Scottish thumbpieces.

585

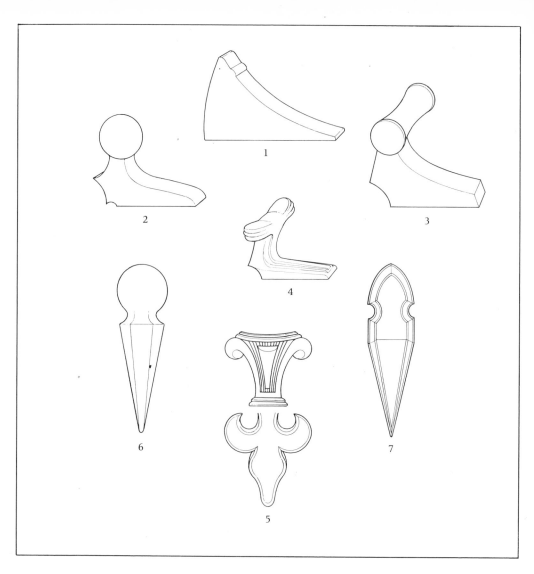

Flagons, measures and balusters were used to bring drink to the table. To actually drink from a smaller more easily held container was needed. Drinking tankards were made in many materials; leather, wood, silver, brass and pottery, as well as pewter.

Tankards before 1650 are very rare. The first group of lidded tankards to survive in any quantity are the Stuart flat-lidded tankards of the 1650-1710 period. They follow the silver style, and are amongst the most attractive and prized objects in pewter.

The Stuart tankard has a flat lid and plain slightly tapering drum. Most have a rams horn thumbpiece although other decorative thumbpieces are found. They were not made to any

Pewter thumbpieces: balusters
1 Wedge – prior to 1600
2 Ball – Sixteenth-century and on Scottish balusters of the late eighteenth century
3 Hammer head – Sixteenth- and seventeenth-century balusters
4 Bud – Seventeenth- and eighteenth-century balusters
5 Double volute – Eighteenth-century balusters
6 Modified shell – Scottish, 1800-70
7 Spade – Scottish, 1780-1840s

42 A group of tankards. On the left and right are double-domed tankards, both with rams horn thumbpieces from around 1700-20. In the centre is the famous flat-lidded Stuart tankard so prized amongst collectors. The serrated edge is on the front of the lid.

capacity, but exist in several sizes. Some of the most interesting have been engraved with 'wrigglework'.

The earliest flat lids have fretted protuberances at the front of the lid, but by about 1700 this had disappeared. The handles of flat lids are simple, straps, and usually end with a spade like terminal.

By the early eighteenth century the flat-lidded style gradually gave way to what we know as the Georgian double-domed tankard. This style first appeared about 1680 and stayed popular until the end of the eighteenth century. On the earliest double-domed tankards the fretted lip can still be found together with the 'rams horn' thumbpiece. By 1715 or so, the commonest thumbpieces are the 'scroll', the 'chair' or the 'pierced scroll'. The plain body of the earliest tankards gives way to a single fillet cast around the body and the spade or flat ended terminal to the handle is replaced by a ball terminal. By 1770 the 'open chair' thumbpiece is most frequently found and by this time the bodies have become taller, and without the fillet.

The next major change in style appeared in the 1730s with the tulip shaped tankard. These had the same thumbpieces found on straight-sided tankards; they also retained the double-domed lid. The open chair thumbpiece became almost universal on tulip shaped tankards after 1760-70. Although not marked to a capacity most appear to have been made in a quart size, though smaller tankards are known.

By 1800 lidded tankards were going out of fashion. A few 'U'-

shaped domed examples were made in the early nineteenth century, but from 1840 the lidded tankard is out of style and only appears again briefly as the sporting trophy of the later part of the nineteenth century.

Lidless tankards were in use from the sixteenth century onwards, but those before 1700 are very rare indeed. A few tall graceful tankards with two or three filets round the body date from about 1660 until about 1720. Most were made to ale standard and were probably for use in taverns.

In the eighteenth century lidless mugs were squatter and spouted examples occur. As the century moves on, the straight-sided mug is replaced with a variety of body styles and handle shapes; the equivalent of the tulip being popular. Most were made to the ale standard. Mugs are rare until the nineteenth century. Many hundreds of thousands of mugs were been made in the decades after the new standards were adopted in 1826, mostly for the inns and taverns though some will have been bought for domestic use. A group of the more popular styles of the nineteenth century are illustrated here. Glass-bottomed tankards are known from about 1800, but most with this feature, sometimes in plain glass, sometimes coloured, are mid-Victorian. Around 1850 a series of tavern mugs, both straight-sided and bellied, were produced with thick, applied brass rims. These must have been difficult to drink from, but gave added strength. Examples are also known with the thick rim applied in pewter and these date from 1880 to 1900.

Ale and wine were also drunk from footed cups and beak-

43 *Left:* A tulip shaped Georgian tankard with double-domed lid and with scroll thumbpiece and ball terminal to handle. The body is heavily oxided.

44 *Above:* A rare late seventeenth century lidless drinking tankard. The twin bands round the body are found on most of the Stuart lidless tankards. The William III capacity mark indicates that it is *c.* 1690-1700. The mark is just below the rim.

Tavern mugs
1 1800-1830 barrel
2 1800-1840 tulip
3 1820-1860 U-shaped
4 1820-1900 pot belly
5 1826-1880 concave
6 1830-1870 cone or straight sided
7 1830-1900 flared
8 1850-1900 round handled
9 1850-1900 brass rimmed
10 1860-1900 cone

1

2

3

4

5

6

7

8

9

10

ers—two styles which developed in the eighteenth century. The earliest cups to survive are a few cast decorated wine goblets from around 1600. Most of the footed cups we find with a short stem, are nineteenth century. The beaker, a straight or tapering sided vessel without a handle first appears about 1690 when it is tall and thin, but later beakers were more squat.

There are more tavern mugs of the Victorian era to be seen in shops than any other item in pewter.

45 Two typical post-imperial pewter beakers with their former owner's initials engraved on the front.

46 A late-nineteenth-century tavern mug with its tamper or wooden form used to remove small dents created by the heavy daily use such mugs faced.

Chapter 7

Pewter in general use

Most of the items in pewter to be found in our forefathers' homes were linked with cooking, eating and drinking, yet pewter filled many other roles in the home.

Before the nineteenth century the candle was the principal source of light. Pewter candlesticks, although nothing like as common as examples in brass or bronze, were made in considerable quantities and most homes prior to 1700 would have had one or more examples. However, only a handful of candlesticks made before 1600 have survived and seventeenth-century patterns are also very rare.

The sixteenth-century candlesticks which have escaped the pressures of daily use and subsequent neglect are nearly all bell-based with a mid drip pan (a round sheet to catch the melting wax and situated at the middle of the stem), much in the style of latten or bronze examples.

In the seventeenth century there were certainly several different varieties, but few of each have endured. The shape most frequently found has an octagonal base, a low drip pan and straight stem. A variation of this form has a scalloped base and drip pan and some examples of each style have heavily reeded stems.

These shapes appeared around 1650, but as few candlesticks bear makers' marks the exact time-span of the shape is obscured.

Less frequently seen are a group of candlesticks with a similar shaped base and mid drip pan, but with a large turned knop in the stem and a candleholder similar in style to the latten candlesticks of around 1600, so this form probably predates the examples with straight stems.

To match the trumpet based brass candlesticks examples were made in pewter both with and without the mid drip pan and these candlesticks were popular in the last forty years of the century.

Towards the end of Charles II's reign candlesticks became generally smaller, the mid drip pan is replaced in position, if

not in purpose, with a large ball knop and whilst most candle-sticks of this shape have the octagonal base there are some with a round base.

The final transition in the late seventeenth century is to a form made familiar in brass; the octagonal based, multi-knopped stemmed sticks. Pewter examples appear to predate their brass compatriots by a few years.

The growth of the population in the eighteenth century and the rising standard of living must have meant a considerable increase in the demand for candlesticks and yet only a very small number of authenticated eighteenth century British pewter candlesticks exist. Such rarity is in marked contrast to the relative frequency with which eighteenth century brass sticks are found. It is very difficult to explain the almost total absence of pewter examples made after 1720. It must be that brass drove out pewter, perhaps because brass was cheaper and new. But whatever the reasons very few British pewter candlesticks of the eighteenth century are known. Those that do exist are similar in form to the brass sticks of the time, usually with octagonal or round bases and knopped stems.

In Europe pewter candlesticks have survived in greater quantities and some of the French and Dutch candlesticks are often mistaken for British.

Towards the end of the eighteenth century pewter candle-sticks began to re-appear. Most have round bases and baluster knopped stems. These continued to be made in substantial quantities into Victorian times. Perhaps the ubiquitous brass

47 *Far left:* There are only a handful of pewter candlesticks made before 1600. This example has a bell base and mid drip pan. Late sixteenth century. Private collection.

48 *Centre:* A fine mid-seventeenth-century octagonal-based candlestick with drip pan. Note the ribbed stem and stepped base and drip pan.

49 *Above:* A ball knop candlestick from around 1690. These are to be found in pewter but are very rare in brass. Private collection.

Pewter candlesticks
1 mid-drip-pan trumpet base c. 1650
2 ball knop, late Stuart
3 octagonal-based, Charles II
4 fluted octagonal with low drip-pan c. 1670
5 knopped octagonal, Stuart
6 eighteenth-century knopped
7 late Tudor bell
8 stepped round base, nineteenth century
9 Victorian round base with tulip sconce
10 straight sided, nineteenth century
11 rectangular-knopped, late nineteenth century
12 Victorian round base

1

2

3

4

5

6

7

8

9

10

11

12

candlestick was losing its novelty or maybe pewterers, by now in real difficulty, lowered their prices.

It is not easy to distinguish between late-eighteenth and nineteenth-century sticks. The hard-metal examples are certainly nineteenth century, those with a pusher in the stem are probably after 1820. Most oval sticks date from 1820-30 and rectangular-based sticks in pewter are generally mid-nineteenth century. Pewter candlesticks in these Georgian styles were still being made as late as 1880-1900.

Pewter chandeliers and wall sconces are known to have been in use, but though a number of Continental examples still exist few English examples have been found. Brass chambersticks were made in great quantities, but pewter examples are rare and it is likely that the only ones that you will see are late nineteenth century or made more recently.

Before the invention of the fountain pen the only source of ink in the classroom, office or home was from a bottle. Pewter ink stands or 'standishes' with inkwell are often to be seen. Naturally, early examples are rare, but two main styles, made in the eighteenth century, are still to be seen. One form consists of a small square box-stand with one or two drawers in the base. The ink being reached by lifting a small domed lid on top. The other eighteenth-century type is the 'treasury' ink stand, a rectangular box with the lid divided down the middle and lifting in two flaps. On one side the pens or nibs were stored and the other side held the ink pot, paunce pot (which held the sand for drying the paper) and sometimes a small box.

In the middle of the nineteenth century another pattern of ink stand developed. This is a simple round, unlidded pot on a wide round flat base. This type of ink stand often had a pottery

50 *Left:* A small square ink stand with two drawers to hold wafers and nibs. The ink is in a well beneath the domed lid on top. Eighteenth century.

51 *Above:* The two most common forms of tobacco boxes. Both are early nineteenth century.

container for the ink which had small holes set round it to take the pens and quills. Such ink pots were still in use in schools, the civil service and offices as late as 1900.

Many items of pewter are found associated with smoking or snuff taking. There are two main forms of pewter tobacco boxes. Oval boxes are mostly late eighteenth century whilst round boxes are generally from the nineteenth century. Both patterns have concave knopped lids and, like other table tobacco boxes, pewter examples would all have had an inner lead press made to hold down the tobacco.

Pewter pipe stands, tampers and small personal tobacco boxes are still to be found generally dating from the middle of the nineteenth century.

Pewter snuff boxes come in all shapes and sizes, some round, others oval or square, some boxes are engraved or embossed. Boxes can be discovered in the shape of a high-heeled shoe, a woman's leg, books or other curious shapes. Some interesting Scottish snuff mulls are discussed in Chapter 8. Pipe tampers and pipe stands were mostly made in brass, but pewter ones can be found.

One object in pewter whose purpose might, at first glance, be rather obscure is the 'Welsh hat', so-called for its similarity in form to the national headgear of Wales. Whilst they are now often bought to hold flowers they were originally commode pots.

This form of 'potty' was used inside a piece of furniture. The user lifted the lid and 'sat down'. Welsh hats were first made in the seventeenth century and were made for the next hundred years. The more traditional form of pot, easily recognised by its familiar shape, rounded with a handle, is more often found in pottery or china, but pewter ones were in use from 1600 onwards though few still exist. Whichever form was used in the home their methods of handling the waste product left much to be desired!

The standard advice to servants was never to risk carrying the full pot through the house, but to make use of the windows! hence the Scottish cry of *Gardes lou*. Not all potties sat beneath the bed for as a French visitor commented it was common practice for gentlemen, when dinner was over and the ladies had retired to the drawing room, to use a pot, stored in the sideboard.

For the sick, bedpans were also made in pewter, mostly in the early nineteenth century. They were very similar to those still in use today with round bodies and a short wooden handle.

Medical items made in pewter were in extensive use in the nineteenth century. Syringes of dramatic size and unmentionable purposes were perhaps seldom used by the untrained hand, but small pap boats or invalid feeding cups would have been found in most family medicine cupboards, shaped rather like small boats with a pouring lip on one end. They appear first in the nineteenth century and those made by Dent or Maw are late in the century. There are also many reproductions of these pap boats.

Castor-oil spoons, cunning devices, were in frequent use in Victorian nurseries. They are small spoons with hinged covered tops into which the medicine was poured. The spoon had a hollow handle and when tilted the oil or medicine could be kept in place by putting the thumb over the hole at the end of the handle. When the spoon was in place at the back of the child's mouth the thumb was lifted and down went the medicine!

Most homes would have had a pewter funnel. Funnels were used as we still do today, for transferring liquid from one container to another. They were first made in pewter in the eighteenth century and were made for the next century. They are found in several sizes, some with, some without, straining grids, but all fitting into the end of a standard bottle.

A diligent search of attics, junk shops or cellars will probably reveal other objects in pewter used in home in the nineteenth century for a vast range of items were made in pewter. Few played any more than a transitory role in the domestic life of our forebears, but the hunt may yet produce something of great rarity and importance. The pleasures of the chase remain with us whenever we enter sale room or shop for the unique can be just round the next corner.

Chapter 8

Scottish, Channel Islands and Irish pewter

The pewter industry in Scotland developed quite independently from the English trade. Scotland was a poor and very under-populated nation and the demand for pewter was limited by these factors as well as by the fact that all tin used had to be imported; Scotland mined no tin.

In England the gradual breakdown of the Merchant Guild based on all crafts and trades led to the formation of individual craft guilds, but in Scotland few trades were powerful enough or numerous enough to sustain such craft guilds. As a consequence groups of tradesmen with some common feature linked themselves into united guilds. The pewterers were no exception and formed with other tradesmen Guilds of Hammermen. Such 'Incorporations' as they were called were formed in Edinburgh, Canongate, Stirling, Dundee, Perth, Aberdeen, Glasgow and St Andrews. All these incorporations admitted pewterers, smiths and founders. Many other crafts were permitted membership, some a little surprising to our eyes. Amongst crafts generally admitted were sadlers, silver and goldsmiths, armourers, cutlers, glovers and tinkers.

Often only a small proportion of the guild members would have been pewterers. For example, in Dundee in 1587 only one member out of 35 was a pewterer whilst in St Andrews in 1720 there was not one pewterer amongst the 22 members. Membership of the guilds was obtained only after seven years apprenticeship. As a consequence of the low demand for pewter, few centres attracted more than a handful of pewterers, only Edinburgh, before the late eighteenth century, could boast of a substantial industry. The eighteenth century saw the virtual elimination of the craft in the traditional centres like Dundee, Aberdeen, and Perth, where the last pewterers to be admitted to the guilds were in 1746, 1765 and 1771 respectively.

At the time that these older centres were in decline Glasgow was on its way to becoming a rival to Edinburgh.

Pewter continued to be in use in taverns rather later in

Scotland than in England and for this and other reasons the craft took longer to die.

The last Scottish pewterer, James Moyes, did not give up his shop in West Bow, Edinburgh until the 1870s.

As in England, there were frequent attempts to legislate for and enforce standards on those selling liquid and dry goods. Scotland had its own independent standards up to the Act of Union. Even after the Act special Scottish standards remained in use into the nineteenth century.

The traditional Scottish liquid standard was the Scottish pint, based on the Stirling stoup and roughly equivalent to three pints of the English Ale Standard, (actually 60 fl. ozs., exactly three Imperial pints). The chopin, a name derived from the French, was half a Scottish pint and the mutchkin was a quarter-pint (30 and 15 fl. ozs. respectively). The Scottish pint became known as the 'tappit hen', a confusing name as this is also the term given to the most famous of Scottish measures.

Although the Act of Union officially imposed English measures, the Scottish standards continued in use into the nineteenth century and remained legal even after the introduction of the Imperial Standards in 1826. It was not until 1855 that Scottish measures were finally outlawed. Between 1826 and 1855 they were allowed, if marked in their equivalent imperial measure, and you can find a few measures bearing such odd identifications as '3/5th IP' (meaning three-fifths of an imperial pint), or the like. In addition there were various local standards such as the Glasgow and Hawick two and four glass measures and the muckle gill.

Although the story of Scottish standards is a complicated one, measurement of capacity can sometimes confirm the Scottish origin for unmarked pieces and it may also help in dating.

The French influence was strong in Scotland and French styles influenced Scottish pewter. The most famous of all Scottish pewter measures, the tappit hen, is directly derived from the French *pichet* of the sixteenth century. The Scottish *quaich* or porringer comes from the French *equelle* and the pot belly flagons have their derivation in Flanders.

The Scottish pot belly measures are very rare, robust pieces of pewter from between 1680 and 1730. They have an erect thumbpiece, rounded body and a flat-domed lid. The Scottish pint, chopin and mutchkin sizes are the most frequently found, but half and quart mutchkins also exist. Some pot belly measures were made without lids, but make sure, first, that any you come across have not lost their lids during a busy life.

53 *Above:* A lidless Scottish pot belly flagon. The lidded examples are flat domed with solid, erect thumbpieces. Private collection.

54 *Right:* A set of three Scottish tappit hens: pint, chopin and mutchkin. Eighteenth century.

55 The tappit hen on the left has a knop and is called a 'crested' tappit hen. On the right is a Scottish 'Laver' or flagon *c.* 1800. Earlier examples are usually without spouts.

It seems likely that the first tappit hens were made in Scotland in the sixteenth century, but the first examples to have survived are from the late seventeenth century. The tappit hen has changed its shape very little from when it was first made until it ceased to be produced towards the end of the nineteenth century. Few tappit hens have makers' marks and they were never made by English pewterers. 'Made in London' on a tappit hen is a sure sign that it is modern. The tappit hen has a similar lid and thumbpiece to the pot belly, but has a waisted neck and straight body. As tappit hens were made both before and after the Imperial Standards were introduced they can be found in up to nineteen different sizes. The Scottish pint is the most common. Some tappit hens have a small knop on the lid and these are known as 'Crested' tappit hens. The crested examples were only made in the three principal sizes and only the pint is found with any regularity. Tappit hens and pot belly measures often have a small plouk inside the neck. This marked the level to which the vessels should be filled to conform to their capacity. The existence of a plouk does seem to indicate an eighteenth century date for the item.

There are some tappit hens that were made without a lid and there is also a variant made in Aberdeen, but this type is rare and only found in small sizes.

The third style of Scottish measure is called the 'Laver'. This is a flat-lidded measure with a straight-sided body and twin cusp thumbpieces. It takes its shape from a rare English flagon of the 1700s.

Eighteenth-century examples are robust whilst those made in the nineteenth century are more attenuated, often with pouring lip and knopped lid. The term 'Laver' (derived from the French word laver, to wash) is a misnomer for many are to be found amongst church pewter. Others were used in the home, so it may not be a wholly inappropriate name.

The baluster also found its way to Scotland though no Scottish seventeenth-century examples are known. The earliest Scottish balusters, with ball thumbpieces appear about 1770. Later Scottish balusters had first a spade then embryo shell and finally shell thumbpieces. Scottish balusters have an unusual feature, also found on some north of England measures. There is an anti-wobble rim, a small applied circle of pewter, under the lid which helps to keep it in place. The inner rim limited the give of the lid and its presence is a sure sign that the piece is northern.

Whilst the early Scottish balusters have much the same body shape as those made in England, after the baluster was out of fashion further south in the 1820s, they developed a more rounded form. Three varieties of nineteenth-century balusters exist. One group comes from Edinburgh and has a small flat top to a concave sided lid. There are two Glasgow styles, both with a flat capacity seal on the top of the lid. In the more common style there is a single dome whilst the rarer examples have double-domed lids. Most of these Scottish balusters were made for tavern use, but some will have found their way into homes.

During the nineteenth century several styles of lidless tankards were made in Scotland. Most will have been made for tavern use. There are also local beakers, some of them made to fit into the neck of a tappit hen.

Scottish flat ware is far less common than English plates and dishes, In general, styles and their periods are the same as in the south. The only unusual Scottish flat ware is the single-reeded deep dish, many of which were used in church as well as domestically.

The Scottish quaich or porringer is very rare indeed. Nearly all examples that you might see are Continental for the solid ear continued to be applied to porringers in Europe long after it had died away in Britain.

There are several very interesting types of snuff mulls of Scottish origin: some made for the pocket out of deers feet; others for the table, made from rams horn; each mounted in pewter. Durie of Inverness was a prolific maker of these around 1800.

The variety of pewter in England is not matched in Scotland. There are for example no marked Scottish lidded tankards, spoons or salts though it may be that some unmarked examples are from Scotland.

56 A group of three Scottish baluster measures: the rare double dome Glasgow form (top); the slightly concave Edinburgh lid form (centre); the more common Glasgow style (bottom). Private collection.

57 A typical Scottish pear-shaped tavern mug of around 1830.

58 A full size Jersey flagon of pottle capacity. Eighteenth century.

There are some very fine pieces of Scottish pewter to be seen in museums including, for example the Stirling Town Measures, a set of straight-sided measures with the Stirling arms on the front with two plain strap handles and the Pirley Pig, the name given to a unique box in the shape of a pig for receiving the fines of members of the Dundee corporation who failed to attend meetings, but the variety of items is generally much smaller than in England or Europe.

Although the Channel Islands owed loyalty to the British Crown, through the Dukedom of Normandy, the history of their pewter owes much to the links with France.

In spite of their small size it is likely that pewter was being made in Jersey and Guernsey, the two principal islands, during the seventeenth century and there is evidence that some pewter was exported to Britain.

From the eighteenth century onwards, two distinct types of measures were to be found in use in the Channel Islands, both derived in form from the Normandy *pichet* in use just across the water.

The Jersey measure, usually made to the local Jersey standard, has the same heart-shaped lid, double-acorn thumbpiece and body style of the Normandy *pichet*, but the overall form is more rounded. Measures in Jersey are to be found in six sizes from the pot down to the half-noggin. There have been a number of different standards in force in Jersey, but the eighteenth-century pot was roughly equivalent to 92 per cent of an English ale half-gallon and thus gave a pint of roughly 18 fluid ounces compared with the ale standard pint of 19·7 fluid ounces. The Jersey seal for their standard is a GR crowned, which, with variations, was used from 1727 to 1901. Measures were also made in the same capacities in the lidless style.

Guernsey measures have the same lid and thumbpiece and the body form is again rounded, but it is rather more pear-shaped and often has engraved bands of reeding. The Guernsey measures also have a more inverted foot and are not always made to the local standard. They are only found in four different sizes from the pot down to the half-pint. The capacity seals in Guernsey are the rose or the fleur-de-lys. The Guernsey pot was slightly larger than the one in Jersey and was equal to about 96 per cent of the English half-gallon giving a pint of 19 fluid ounces.

Some of the prolific eighteenth-century makers of Channel Island pewter are known to have worked, for part of their lives at least, in England. There is no direct proof that any measures were made on the Islands, although in their study, Arkwright and Woolmer advanced considerable evidence that makes this likely.

Carter and Wingod, makers of Guernsey and John de St Croix of Jersey all worked in London at one time and struck their marks there. William de Jersey and Hellier Perchard who mostly made flat ware and who came from the Islands also worked in Britain, but there were also local pewterers on the Islands in the eighteenth century. Whether or not the Guernsey and Jersey measures were made in England or on the Islands is, in the end, academic for without doubt the style is unique and their capacity confirms that they were made for use on the Islands.

The development of the pewter trade in Ireland is similar to that of Scotland, although there was no direct Continental influence at work.

Ireland was also a poor nation and the demand for pewter was never strong enough to sustain sufficient pewterers to support separate pewter guilds. The Hammermen came together in multi-craft guilds, in Dublin, Cork and Youghal. The Incorporation is known to have been working in Dublin as early as 1556 and the guilds in Cork and Youghal were both active in the seventeenth century.

The general pattern of development in Ireland is similar to that of England and Scotland: the industry grew rapidly in the early part of the eighteenth century, but after 1800 fell away.

Most of the pewter made in Ireland follows the same style as English pewter, but there are a small group of pieces unique to Irish pewter.

The earliest is a type of flagon which was made in the first half of the eighteenth century. These have domed lids, sturdy, straight bodies and elaborately curved handles, and stand on very wide bases. Many of the Irish flagons are lipped and there is a small blip to be found placed just beneath the spout. Some will have been church flagons, but others will have been used in the home. They were also made without lids and all are very rare.

The two other Irish pewter forms are more common. One is a baluster-shaped measure without a handle. Slightly more angular in form than their English cousins, they were used as Spirit measures and were made from the pint size down. The smallest of the set, the quarter-gill is convex in shape rather than of the baluster form. They are mostly nineteenth century and rarely have a makers mark. They have been much repro-

59 A Guernsey pottle flagon or measure. Eighteenth century.

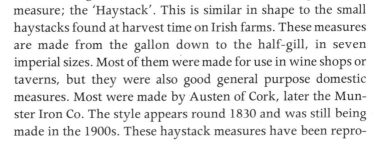

60 A set of Irish 'haystack' measures by Austen of Cork c. 1820-40 from quart to gill.

duced so care should be taken when buying.

The same goes for the third and best known shape of Irish measure; the 'Haystack'. This is similar in shape to the small haystacks found at harvest time on Irish farms. These measures are made from the gallon down to the half-gill, in seven imperial sizes. Most of them were made for use in wine shops or taverns, but they were also good general purpose domestic measures. Most were made by Austen of Cork, later the Munster Iron Co. The style appears round 1830 and was still being made in the 1900s. These haystack measures have been reproduced and the problem has been made even more difficult in recent years as someone has marked these copies with false Victorian capacity marks.

There is little to say about Welsh pewter as no pewter is known that was made in Wales and there are no uniquely Welsh forms. On occasions flagons are found with Welsh church inscriptions and in St Asaph Cathedral there is a fine example, probably made in Wigan, with an unusual thumbpiece. But Welsh pewter is conspicuous for its absence.

Though pewter made in England was far more prolific than in the rest of Britain the contribution of these other areas has been considerable. In particular the Channel Island measures and the Scottish tappit hens are world famous.

61 Half pint Irish baluster measure without handle c. 1800.

603

Chapter 9

The history of the copper brass and bronze industry

Copper was not mined in this country on any commercial scale until well towards the end of the sixteenth century. Yet we know that there was a steady production of cast and hammered metalware from the Middle Ages.

The absence of local copper implies that the ore was imported and we know that this is what happened. The only local source of supply of brass or copper came from scrap metal. There is no doubt that this restricted the development of our local metalware industries and that much of the demand in this country was filled by exports from the great European centres right into the early eighteenth century.

It seems likely that most of the early work carried out in this country was in bronze, whilst when brass was worked it would have been imported in sheet or ingot form to be worked here.

Because of the links between this country and Europe in taste, style and even the alloys, it is not easy to state with certainty which items were cast over here or which were imported.

In any case the level of production must have been very low and few pieces from these periods are ever to be seen outside of museums. British manufacture would have been on a small scale, individual craftsmen, often itinerant workers, moving from church to church to cast bells, and then perhaps making a few mortars or pots for the manor house.

The position in Europe was very different. From the tenth century onwards Germany was dominant in the production of copper though the ore was also mined in Sweden, Hungary and Russia.

The largest most productive mines were near Mansfeld in Germany and copper was taken from there to the centres of production, often where the calamine was itself available. From the tenth century brass was worked at Huy and Dinant in the Meuse basin and later Augsburg and Aachen became centres of production. In the fifteenth century Nuremberg became the

62 A copperworker
hammering a container into
shape. An eighteenth-
century print.

most important area of brass and bronze production.

The trade was controlled by the Hanseatic League and the products were sold at fairs throughout the Continent or shipped from ports like Antwerp to the rest of Europe including Britain.

Most early brazen products were, as we saw with pewter, made for church rather than for secular use. The use of brazen products in churches was widespread; for candlesticks, crucifixes, portals, grills, reliquaries, christmatories, pyxes, chandeliers and chalices.

There are some magnificent early pieces, many beautifully decorated with enamels and inlaid with precious stones, or gilded. The workmanship was superb and the whole area worthy of further study, although basically outside the scope of this book.

Brazen objects were also made for home use including candlesticks, cooking pots, aquamaniles, mortars, dishes and objects of adornment like rings, buttons, buckles and seals.

Most of these earlier pieces are scarce and valuable and few are to be seen outside the museums. One category of object that can still be found is the alms dish. Made in Nuremberg or perhaps Flemish in origin they have decorated centres and some have finely worked designs such as Adam and Eve, St George and the dragon and similar scenes. Others a little later, are worked in swirls and fluteings with great dished centres. Some of these may have been used for rinsing the hands before a meal, but most of them were purely decorative.

Up to the third quarter of the sixteenth century this would have been the general pattern in this country. Limited local production and a larger scale import of brazen objects from Europe via Antwerp. The 'Merctores de Dinant in Alemania' had their headquarters in London near the German steel yards and were in control of this import trade.

For military and economic reasons Queen Elizabeth decided to encourage the birth of a British copper mining and copper working industry. She needed ordinance for the re-armament of her ships and armies in the face of the threat from Spain. At that time all cannons were cast in Flanders! Beyond the military needs she was motivated by a general policy of encouraging self-sufficiency at home.

In 1564 discussions took place between the Queen's representatives and those of Haug and Co., a subsidiary of Fugger, a firm which was already heavily involved in British trade. Daniel Hochstetter from Augsburg led the company in these negotiations, which culminated in the incorporation of the 'Mynes Royal Societie' in 1568 and later in the sinking of a mine in what Hochstetter had decided would be the most likely area, near Keswick in Cumberland. Hochstetter was resident in Keswick from 1571 and was even permitted to bring in up to four hundred skilled German miners.

At roughly the same time William Humphrey, the Assay master of the Mint, in conjunction with Schultz of Saxony successfully petitioned Lord Burghley to obtain the right to mine calamine zinc. In 1565 they were granted the rights to mine the mineral, work battery and draw wire and in 1568 the 'Society of the Mineral and Battery Works' was incorporated. Calamine zinc was found in the Mendips in Somerset and soon afterwards Humphrey set up their headquarters near Tintern Abbey on the banks of the River Wye.

The efforts of both societies were not initially rewarded. Both went through periods of great tribulation. The Mines Royal found that there was not the market that they had envisaged for their copper; many merchants preferring to maintain their contacts with Europe for commercial reasons and their efforts to open up the Cornish Mines were not successful. The Mineral and Battery Society also faced many problems as they lacked the skills for making brass. Their products tended to be of lower quality and though they brought in new blood in 1596 neither mining or processing was properly established by the end of the first quarter of the seventeenth century.

Ingot and sheet metal was being worked at Tintern and in Rotherhithe from whence it was being sent out to be worked by outworkers. British copper was being mined and sold in this country, but the progress being made was very limited. All was to be destroyed in the Civil War, both physically in the case of Keswick, sacked by Scottish troops, and economically elsewhere, with political divisions of Britain separating the mines from the brass-making areas.

The initial effort to establish a British copper and copper working industry was not very successful, yet the need was clearly there. There was a growing demand for brass goods, especially in the domestic area and it was not economic sense to allow this to be filled by European imports.

That there was a very considerable demand for domestic metalware is confirmed by the evidence of wills and inventories of the sixteenth and seventeenth centuries. By 1600 most homes contained several objects in worked copper, the bulk of these being associated with the cooking of food. Sixteenth century inventories examined show that 70 per cent of all homes had brazen objects listed. In the seventeenth century the proportion was even higher. The following table shows the types of pieces most frequently recorded.

Sixteenth and seventeenth century inventories

Classification	*% of total objects listed made in copper, brass or bronze*
Cooking pottes, cauldrons etc	74·1
Skillets, posnets etc	6·2
Mortars	1·6
Skimmers and ladles	2·9
Chaffing dishes	2·9
Candlesticks	9·4
Basins and ewers	2·0
All others	2·3

Thus more than 86 per cent of all brazen objects in the home were involved in the preparation or cooking of food. Only candlesticks also appear in significant numbers in the average household.

Even quite poor men usually had a few pieces of brassware in their homes. John Mason of Banbury for example, who died in 1574 in possession of only £2.11.2d worth of goods nevertheless had 'a bras pane three kettles one bras pot' worth 5/-. Men of substance could have considerable quantities of brassware in their homes. John Clifton of Hook Norton who died in 1683 worth £50 had thirty-two pieces of copper ware including 'three latten basons' all valued at £2.14.4d.

That British production was not yet significant is confirmed by John Harrison who wrote at the time ' . . . of brass bell metal and such as are brought over for merchandise from other countries; and yet I cannot say but there is some brass found also in England but so small is the quantity that it is not greatly to be esteemed or accounted for.'

Throughout the seventeenth century, at the very time when the British industry was trying to get off the ground great quantities of copper alloys were being imported into England. To illustrate this traffic into the Port of London, the cargoes for the month of May 1680 were examined. Sixteen cargoes of battery ware amounting to 149 cwt were imported, shipped either from Hamburg or from Rotterdam. In addition there was 21 cwt of wrought copper, $\frac{3}{4}$ cwt of latten wyre and $5\frac{1}{2}$ cwt of copper ingot all in that month alone. Sometimes shipments could be considerable. In January 1680 Matthew Jasen received 17 cwt of battery from Rotterdam whilst the same port sent John Landfewer $19\frac{1}{2}$ cwt in July of that year.

After 1660 the incipient copper mining and brass manufacturing industry was revived. In 1668 the two Societies were combined into a United Society. Initially their products remained low quality and imports as we have seen continued apace. The United Society never reopened the Keswick mines as the cost was thought to be too high. With little copper being mined in the country the supplies for the United Societies and other works had to be imported, yet at this time the Society was trying to ban the import of copper to speed up the development of mining here. When eventually, for a brief time, they were successful, the effect was the reverse of what they planned for the absence of alloys to work killed off the incipient brass making industry. For a short time all finished products on the market were imported.

In spite of the monopoly of the United Society other enterprises were started. In Wandsworth in 1671 a Flemish family set out successfully to make brass plate for kettles and frying pans and works were soon to be found in Newcastle-under-Lyme, Coalbrookdale, Studley and Birmingham.

It is important to remember that even though the number of specialised brass works was limited in the late seventeenth century there were many individual masters working in the towns. In Chipping Norton for example, there were five braziers at work in the late seventeenth century. In many cases these men also worked pewter. Such a well-known pewterer as John Payne of Oxford, Mayor of the City in 1687 sometimes listed his occupation as brazier.

The exclusive right to mine held by the Crown was surrendered in 1689 and this stimulated the hunt for calamine zinc and for exploitable copper. The last decades of the seventeenth century saw steady improvements in techniques and a gradual expansion of production though imports remained high.

One of the main reasons why the British industry was less than successful in its first hundred years was the difficulty in bringing together the copper and calamine to make a brass of even quality. Though these skills had been known in Europe from the thirteenth century or even earlier they were not part of the British traditions.

Brass was made at this time by the cementation process, it was undertaken in circular domed furnaces lined with fire bricks. The furnace was filled with pots each holding 40 lb of charcoal mixed and riddled with 100 lb of calamine; then two gallons of water were added. To this mixture they added 66 lb of copper shot. The firing of this mixture would last 10 to 12 hours and involve the use of $3\frac{1}{2}$ cwt of coal. The weakness of this method was that fusion between the two metals was erratic and often uneven as it could not be stirred. There was no access until the process was complete, so very variable brass resulted.

It can be seen that substantial amounts of both calamine and coal were needed to make 1 cwt of brass. In the eighteenth century calamine was being extracted in Derbyshire, Flintshire and in Somerset. The demand for calamine grew apace with the increasing production of brass. From Derby for example, 40 tons was taken out around 1746 but by 1796 the quantity had grown to over 1,500 tons per annum.

The eighteenth century saw rapid progress. In 1704 Abraham Darby opened the Baptist Mills near Bristol and set in train the great period of growth in the British brass industry. However he found the process of casting in brass too slow and tried to find a way of casting iron more efficiently. From his researches the coke smelting process for iron was born, and he moved to Coalbrookdale. Baptist Mills were renamed the

Bristol Brass Company and they continued to operate successfully.

Other works were opened at Keynsham, Chew Hill, Siston and Redbrook in Monmouth. In 1711 a copper refinery works was started near Bristol to supply the ore for the new processing works, though much imported ore was still used.

In 1719 a new works was opened in Cheadle which made sheet metal and ingots to be turned into the finished products elsewhere. Bristol in contrast was primarily a producer of drawn wire or finished battery.

Some of Cheadle's sheet metal or brass ore went to Birmingham, but the growth of this city's brass industry was handicapped by the distance both the ore and coals had to be brought. In 1740 a brass works was opened at Coleshill and from then on Birmingham had its own local supply of brass. This local supply stimulated the growth of the Birmingham manufacture of battery and with the opening of the canal to the Staffordshire coal fields in 1769 the growth of Birmingham received another major boost.

Over the next thirty years Birmingham became not only the centre of the brass industry in this country, but the largest in the world.

Throughout the eighteenth century the production process remained small scale. Most workshops employed only a few employees. The largest undertakings were naturally the mines and the workshops where the copper was turned into brass; the smallest were operated by craftsmen who made this brass into the finished products.

In spite of the vast expansion of the industry many were to find the going tough. The newspapers in the middle of the century were full of bankruptcies of brass and copper workers. But for every failure there was another man ready to try his luck. Most of them were under-capitalised and if they possessed the necessary technical skills, were often without business experience.

The expansion in brass and copper manufacturing can be illustrated by two sets of statistics. British copper mined rose from around 400 tons per annum in 1725 to over 2,000 tons per annum in 1760 and reached a peak around 1780 with over 5,000 tons. This peak was due to the great productivity of the new Anglesey mines. This massive production flooded the market and briefly drove copper prices down. Production was limited to about 3,000 tons per annum by the 1800s.

The second indicator of the growth of domestic production are the levels of finished goods imported into this country.

63 An eighteenth-century print showing brass and copper workers engaged in several tasks. The power is provided by a man turning a wheel (fig 3). A vessel is being turned to finish it (fig 2) and hammermen are at work (figs 1 & 6).

Between 1700-1704 an average of 227 tons of finished battery were brought in yet by the 1720s this had shrunk to 64·7 tons. After 1725 exports of battery began to exceed imports, and by 1770 only 7 tons of worked battery were disembarked, whereas exports amounted to 2,725 tons in an average year.

The growing standard of living and the expanding population led to a great increase in demand and the brass industry was also able to develop substantial markets overseas, especially in the North American Colonies and as barter for the slave trade to West Africa.

The following table shows the average level of exports for copper- and brass-worked products during the eighteenth century.

EXPORTS
WROUGHT COPPER AND BRASSWARE
10 year averages

Years	*Tons*
1700-09	92
1710-19	160
1720-29	230
1730-39	485
1740-49	846
1750-59	1243
1760-69	2251
1770-79	2725
1780-89	3131
1790-99	7228

Thus exports rose 79-fold in the eighteenth century. During the same period pewter exports only increased by $5\frac{1}{2}$-fold which illustrates dramatically the speed with which brass and copper products created a world market for themselves and led to the decline in pewter. The export figures do include all forms of production and are not exclusively domestic in purpose.

During the first half of the eighteenth century the methods used to make brass remained unchanged in this country and in Europe. Once the brass was made it was either turned into sheet metal using heavy trip hammers or sold as brass ingots to be cast. The two-part sand mould was universally used for larger objects by now. The use of patterns meant that an object could be cast several times and a degree of mass production was now possible. The making of these patterns was a very skilled task and there was a considerable trade in finished patterns. For example Horton and Jarvis of Birmingham were in 1775 offering for sale 'a sett of the neatest and newest patterns'.

When the casting was complete the item had to be cleaned off to remove excess metal. It was then burnished whilst held in a vice. Then the piece was finally polished by hand. Lathes were used in the second half of the eighteenth century for the speeding up of the finishing process. A polishing lathe was offered for sale in Birmingham in 1756, an engine lathe in 1763 for example. Such machinery was costly; a new engine lathe was worth up to 80 guineas.

After polishing was complete the piece was dipped in an acid bath and then it was often lacquered to prevent oxidisation.

In 1769, a process patented for stamping small objects out of sheet metal was taken up by Richard Forde of Birmingham who later used the process for larger products like warming pans, saucepans, ladles, basins and kettles. However, there is evidence that ten years earlier stamping had been in use for small objects. In 1757 stamps were offered for sale, one big enough 'to stamp buckles'.

A major change that was to revolutionise the brass making industry was ushered in in 1738 when William Chapman of Bristol took out a patent for the distillation of pure zinc. From this time on it was possible to use pure zinc ore rather than the crushed calamine zinc with all its impurities and complications. Chapman built the first zinc manufacturing plant in Bristol in 1743. Once the method of refining metallic zinc had been discovered it ought to have been possible to make brass by direct fusion, but the final step was not taken until 1781. Makers continued to use the old cementation process but replaced the calamine zinc with the metallic zinc. In the cementation method the temperature did not need to rise above 1000°F for the copper did not have to melt. The calamine was absorbed into the copper, fused to it while the copper was solid. It was a wasteful process with much loss of zinc. As the zinc was gradually absorbed into the copper the melting point of the copper-zinc alloy fell and at that state the copper may have melted. In the direct fusion process the copper was heated to above 1150°F and the zinc added to it. If just placed on the surface much would boil off at once, but by pushing the zinc below the liquid copper this loss could be contained and much higher proportions of zinc incorporated with the copper which, as it could be stirred, was more evenly mixed. The new process led to the abandonment of the old ways of brass making and eliminated the cause of the uneven quality of the brass. Without such a move the mass production which was to follow this and other changes would have been held back.

Though the role of Birmingham was very important brass was made in several other parts of the country throughout the eighteenth century. Bristol retained its secondary role and there was casting in Bridgewater, Chester, London and St Albans as well as in many small country towns where one or two craftsmen would have made things for the local populace.

Many of these local braziers also worked in other metals; it was also true that even in the major centres like Birmingham many men worked in more than one area of metal production. John Pidgeon of Digbeth Street and Edward Durnell of Bull Street (who in 1778 claimed to have the oldest established braziers shop in town) both made pewter as well as brass and copper ware.

Though most firms making brass objects did so on a small scale there was one exception. This was the great Birmingham Brass Company formed by Matthew Boulton and James Watt. From 1781 it was far and away ahead of all its rivals both in size and techniques.

The growth of brass manufacture, though spectacular, was not without its setbacks. The war of 1793 had a considerable impact on the export trade, holding back the natural growth of trade.

The industrial revolution had already taken much of Britain in its grip by 1800. Factories using steam or water power were engaged in the production of textiles. Iron was being smelted in iron foundries in great quantities. There was a dramatic movement from the land to the factory, from the small villages and towns to the cities. Whereas in 1700 eight out of ten lived in the country, by 1900 four out of five were city or town dwellers. Development and change were everywhere, bringing with them abject poverty and appalling slum conditions as well as, for many, another chance in life as an alternative to nearly equally awful rural poverty.

The movement to the towns is highlighted when one finds that cities such as Manchester and Glasgow saw their population rise by two and a half times in the same period and Birmingham, Liverpool and Leeds by over twofold. Manchester with a population around 75,000-80,000 in 1800 had over 400,000 people by 1850. Over the same period the total population grew one and a half times.

Industrial production doubled between 1801 and 1831. Indeed the growth of the population, the drift to the cities and the vast growth of industrial production transformed the whole face of Britain within forty years. Yet if this phenomena of change was rapid in the first three decades it was nothing to the vast increases in production, the startling changes in techniques and the improvements in transport the next fifty years were to bring. In statistical terms a new scale for comparison is needed to appreciate the magnitude of the development within the economy. Industrial production, for example, which had risen twofold in the first thirty years of the century was to rise by nearly another sevenfold by 1913. Between 1800 and 1870 the production of coal rose twelvefold and in place of canals and their barges and roads and the cart, by 1870 more than 15,000 miles of railways were linking the industrial cities to the ports and the great cities with their insatiable demand for the products of the steam-powered factories.

Birmingham saw its share of this prosperity. In 1800 the total British production of copper was some 3,000 tons per annum, yet by 1865 Birmingham alone used 20,000 tons a year, some imported, some from the new Cornish mines.

Even as early as 1802-3 Birmingham was rightly described as the most important brass producer in the world. A Scandinavian writer in 1802-3 wrote about the city 'which is famed on account of its factories and on account of its vast quantity of ornamental and metalwares which for thirty years have been directed from there all over the world'.

In spite of the vast changes in industry as a whole and not denying the substantial increase in production that occurred in brass making, the amazing feature of this period of great technological change is that in the brass industry the change was so small and so slow.

It would have been natural to assume that in brass making as

Firms engaged in various sections of brass industry in Birmingham
Some firms appear more than once if they worked in more than a single area

1830:
- rest 9%
- lamps and tubes 16%
- wire and milling 6%
- candlesticks 6%
- plumbing 12%
- foundary and stamping 51%

1865:
- plumbing 12%
- lamps and tubes 25%
- wire and milling 7%
- candlesticks 2%
- rest 12%
- foundary and stamping 42%

with other industries such as iron, textiles and engineering, the workers would have been brought together in large factories, operating steam-powered machinery and adopting as their brothers in other crafts were, all the latest skills. The picture of what occurred in the brass industry in Birmingham is very different. Progress was slow. In the 1850s and '60s, for example, local commentators were still writing about the failure to adopt steam power as a means of improving production. Steam did not become really widespread in the brass industry until after 1865. Whereas in the eighteenth century most small Birmingham factories employed a handful of men and only a few as many as twenty or more, there was some increase in workshop size but nothing like the scale found in other industries. The numbers of people employed in Birmingham in the brass industry did rise from around 1700 in 1831 to over 8,000 by 1861, but it was not to reach its peak of 45,000 until 1913. The bulk of these men and women were still employed as late as 1870 in small units.

Just why brass makers in Birmingham were so slow to adopt steam power, the principles of the division of labour and factory methods is not clear.

The very success which attended the craft may have blinded masters to the advantages of the changes open to them. With production and demand rising fast they may not have felt any economic impulse for technological change. It may be that with individual skill so vital in the craft the great traditions of individuality helped to discourage change.

Linked with this increase both in employment and production was a steady increase in the number of firms working in brass or its allied trades. In 1800 it is estimated that perhaps fifty firms worked in the brass industry in Birmingham. By 1830 this had risen to 160 and by 1865 to 216.

The nature of the products worked also showed a considerable shift. More than half of the fifty or so firms operating in 1800 were founders or stamped out metal and the remaining number of firms were more or less equally divided amongst those operating in the plumbing area, candlestick makers, rolled brass or wire makers and other smaller trades. The pattern changed by 1830 with the appearance of many firms working in gas fittings, lamps and tubes and by 1865 the greatly expanded number of firms now included 25 per cent devoted basically to these new areas and the traditional field of candlestick making had slightly contracted in real numbers and relatively had lost considerably in importance. The changing pattern between 1830 and 1865 is illustrated in the diagrams on p. 615.

There were of course, those firms who did adopt new technology sooner than the majority and there were many important innovations during the nineteenth century. For example, in 1838 the making of seamless tubes was made possible following the work of Charles Green and this opened up the market for the manufacture of gas fittings more cheaply. Shortly after William Grice found a way to ornament these tubes using dies and thus led the way to the many decorated gas, electric and candle fittings based on arms made of tubes that were to be found in Victorian Britain.

All this production placed strains on the availability of copper from the Cornish mines and considerable quantities had to be imported. Old metal was still re-used and in 1865 it has been calculated that it accounted for 30 per cent of the copper ore.

A brass founder wrote in the eighteenth century that the practice of the Birmingham manufacturer '. . . was to keep within the warmth of his own forge'. Traditionally the makers made their goods, placed them in their own shops and sat back and waited for orders. This may have worked in the early years of the eighteenth century, but a more efficient way of bringing products to the attention of potential customers was needed. One way adopted by manufacturers was to produce pattern books. These pattern books throw a fascinating light on the kind of brassware being produced in Britain in the late eighteenth century. They show a great range of goods being marketed of which only a small proportion are household objects. They show too that though the manufacture of household items was still important in the nineteenth century the great advances in production were mostly in the industrial field. What in 1700-1750 was basically a domestic market had become, by 1900, industrial.

Chapter 10

What to look for in brass copper and bronze

Marks, makers and decoration

Very few brass, copper and bronze pieces carry any makers mark. As a consequence one of the most effective ways of dating is denied to students of base metals.

However, there are exceptions. A few early cooking pots or cauldrons have a merchants' mark, usually a simple device originally cut into the clay mould. Time has hidden where these makers worked, or who they were. Fine mortars were also often signed. Here we are more fortunate and we have been able to identify some of the makers.

In the north of England there are several mortars signed 'SS' and 'Ebor', the Latin for York. The Sellars family, including a Samuel, worked in York around 1680, and there was also another founder Samuel Smith at about this time.

In London, the famous Whitechapel foundry was run by Joseph Carter at the start of the seventeenth century and then by his son William *circa* 1615. Mortars are found with both their signatures. Thomas Bartlett who took over the Carters' works also marked mortars. There are many other makers of the seventeenth century whose names have been found on mortars and these include Henry Knight of Reading, *circa* 1618, John Martin of Worcester, *circa* 1681, Henry Bagley of Banbury, *circa* 1680, the Ashtons, Ralf and Luke of Wigan from 1700, Thomas Cheese of Bury St Edmunds, *circa* 1603-33 and John Palmer of Canterbury, the skillet maker, made several mortars around 1630. Near to where I live, the Neale family, father and son, worked throughout the 1630-85 period in Burford and there are several mortars signed Edward Neale either by father or son.

With skillets we will see later that the Palmers and John Fathers signed many of their products in the seventeenth century. In the eighteenth century Robert Bayley of Birmingham and Street of Bridgewater were prolific makers. Street was

64 A maker's signature on a skillet handle. This is by Thomas Palmer of Canterbury, a skillet maker, brazier and general merchant *c.* 1670.

for a time in partnership with another Bayley. The Street family appear to have been active between 1730 and 1810. Street in partnership with a Pike for example, advertised in the Exeter *Flying Post* in 1775 to sell 10,000 sets of money weights. Another active eighteenth-century maker was Rice of Bristol and Warner, also probably a west of England maker who was busy around 1800.

Many skillets are found signed Washborough and these are often erroneously attributed to the seventeenth century. Washborough worked on his own in Bristol between 1793 and 1826 and both before and after these dates in partnership with other makers. Most Washborough skillets are nineteenth century.

Surprisingly, few candlesticks have been marked by their makers. The following is a list of those I have found and where I have been able to trace their origins or period this is indicated:

I. Bayley	Birmingham	*circa* 1760
Barlow		*circa* 1800-20
'D' possibly Durley	Birmingham	*circa* 1770
George Grove	Birmingham	dead 1768
G.M.		mid-eighteenth century
E.K.		1780-1820
Joseph Wood		1735-60
Turner & Co.		*circa* 1750
William Lee	Birmingham	retired 1780
Lakin		*circa* 1740
Smith Carlisle		1760
W.S. with Crown		*circa* 1800-20

A substantial number of other firms are known to have made domestic brass in general and specialised lines as well, but it was not the general practice to mark their products until the late nineteenth century.

In spite of the absence of makers' marks there are words or phrases on metalware which can be of help in dating.

For example the word 'Patent' is an indication that the piece is no earlier than the mid eighteenth century. The use of a

Victorian registered number indicates an item made after 1884. The appearance of the words 'Trade Mark' means that the piece was made after 1862 and probably some time later. The origin of the object indicated by the word 'England' shows that it is after 1891 whilst the phrase 'Made in England' is twentieth century. The words 'Limited' or the letters 'Ltd' do not appear until after the Companies Act in 1862.

It became the practice for major stores and some larger makers to stamp on the base of their stocklines the pattern number of the object. The existence of such a stock number is an indication that the object was made in the last half of the nineteenth century or later.

Standard markings, that is those marks placed on objects by the weights and measures inspectors can help on occasions in dating things made for public use in the tavern or market place. Few pieces of brassware or bronze carry marks before the 1826 Imperial Standards. Thereafter the GRIV, WRIV, VR marks etc are all indicators of age. The chances are that anything with an ER or GR stamp being made prior to 1902 are not high, but it is possible that some Victorian items may have escaped marking in the early part of their working life.

Brass and copper did not receive the stamps of the authorities as easily as did pewter, and it was often the practice to add a small lead seal to a vessel and then place the capacity stamp upon that seal. The presence of such a seal, which has been defaced, is a strong indicator that someone wanted you to think that it was earlier than it is.

We will see that many items in copper, brass or bronze are decorated.

This can take many forms. Cast decoration is not uncommon and many patterns have also been raised on objects by either embossing on a form or under a machine while some patterns have been raised by hand. Punched designs are frequently found and fretted brassware was especially popular. There are many examples too, of the work of engravers both to decorate or to identify the owner of a piece.

Many early pieces of copperware were gilded and it was common too in Europe for some early copper to be treated similarly with silver. Some such work may have been undertaken over here, but most pieces with gilding or silvering are European.

The whole field of ormulu, the form of eighteenth-century gilding created in France and adopted in this country is outside the scope of this book. It is always necessary to look carefully at pieces which might at one time have been silver-plated whether in the traditional Sheffield form or more recently through electro-plate. Items once silver-plated have a diminished value and appeal to pieces made to stand in their own right unadorned.

Condition, cleaning and restoration

There is no doubt that the same rules ought to be applied to buying copper, brass and bronze as I have suggested for pewter. Look for the best-quality items that you can find and avoid as far as possible damaged or repaired pieces.

If you do have a piece that you want repaired the task is less difficult to get done than with pewter for there are more metalsmiths about than pewterers these days. Most towns have someone capable of brazing brass and the problem of the low melting point so important with pewter is less likely to appear with copper alloys.

Simple repairs can be made with a silver or lead solder which if well done can almost be invisible. More professional repairs, actually brazing the piece, are a little more dangerous as the temperature has to be lifted to a point close to the melting point of the original materials. It must be realised too that heating brass or bronze changes the colour of the metal and that it will normally have to be repolished.

Should there be a piece to be replaced it is necessary to make a judgement as to the nature of the alloy originally used for otherwise the repair will stand out from the original only too clearly.

The colour of a piece may give you some idea of its contents. Under about 30 per cent of zinc, the colour will be golden, getting stronger or more red as the proportion of zinc falls. Over 50 per cent zinc gives a whitish colour while naturally, pieces with little zinc at all will be highly copper coloured.

Copper, brass and bronze do all oxidise slowly, but this rarely forms the same thick coat as is found with pewter. The eruptions found in pewter, once called tin pest, are also not matched in these copper alloys.

The debate regarding favoured colour as a consequence hardly exists. Most people prefer their brass or copper cleaned and polished. There are a few connoisseurs, especially in Europe who look for a dark even patina of oxide, but most collectors accept pieces far more polished than they would in pewter. Bronze by contrast, is often sought in its original dark condition and pieces which have been cleaned and buffed are less prized.

There is a danger too in cleaning bronze that has been used

in the fire over long periods. The original imperfect mixture of the alloys may have allowed some of the trace elements and hardeners to be burnt out of the metal and if this pocked surface is now cleaned small pits and indentations may appear.

One of the objections that some people have to brass and copper is that it does need regular cleaning. It very quickly shows signs of oxiding, especially if handled. The use of any spirit-based cleaner will quickly restore the piece to its original colour unless the oxide is very old and deep when it may have to be dipped in a caustic substance and rebuffed. But this should always be done professionally and most carefully so as not to damage the piece or take away any signs of age and wear.

How to date copper, brass and bronze

In Europe there was considerable interest in brass and bronze and copies abound. There were copies of Roman and Greek bronzes being made in the sixteenth century. In the nineteenth century the interest in the Gothic style was considerable. Amongst the items most copied are Dutch dated mortars, Italian cooking pots, many of them dated about 1610 and German alms dishes. In this country the interest in brass is very recent and until the last fifteen years or so few items had much value. Hence, whilst they have been extensively reproduced the number of deliberate fakes is very small indeed.

You are up against therefore, not the skilled faker trying to fool you with his skill, but a modern copy. The enemy is ignorance and gullibility fathered by greed. The task is basic-ally to separate modern copies from the original not to try and distinguish a finely crafted fake. But do remember that your grandparents were buying brass objects for use from some of the major stores as late as 1910, similar in style to many of the Georgian pieces that we will examine. Throughout the 1920s and '30s there were several firms who specialised in casting and making up direct copies of earlier pieces and also pieces which ape the style of the old, but which were never actually made historically. Extracts from some of these catalogues are illustra-ted to show the kinds of things that were being reproduced. Not all dealers can tell the old from the new; and as someone once suggested to me some will never be able to do so whilst there is a financial advantage in ignorance. A few shady characters may be actively ageing modern reproductions, acid etching the surface, putting on artificial wear with knife and hammer, turning a rough casting off to resemble the old finish, etc.

But if you remember that up to the middle of the nineteenth

century all copper and brass was made by hand, each piece individually finished to a high quality, and that domestic objects were made to be used, then many of the problems will fall away.

The first thing to look at, I would suggest, is purpose; what was the object made to do. This will often tell us something about the period in which it may have been made. This is not always so as something may have remained in use over very long periods, but it is surprising how often the reason why a piece was made can help to date it for us.

We know for example that flat-bottomed cooking vessels were seldom used before the late seventeenth century. And at the most obvious level you are not likely to find a Tudor gas light nor a Victorian acquamanile!

The style in which a thing is made may also help to date it. Compare the piece with illustrations in general and specialised studies. Identify if you can the kind of style that is closest to that of the piece you wish to identify. This will probably give you a further indication of its possible age, though it is always necessary to remember that some styles lasted over many years.

The alloys of which it is made would, if you could have the article analysed, add some further information, but this is normally not possible. If you think, however, that the proportion of zinc is likely to be above 30 per cent then you have a watershed (around 1770 when the use of mineral zinc became more widespread) after which it is likely to have been made. The whiter the colour the less golden the brass, the higher the zinc. The existence of trace elements would also be a sign that the piece was made prior to the ability to refine copper effectively for pure copper was seldom used prior to the mid nineteenth century.

Much more can be learnt by looking carefully at how the thing was made. Has it been cast or was it raised from sheet metal by hammering?

If cast, does it appear to have been a one off production of sand or clay moulds, often a little crude and irregular, or does it clearly bear the signs of a very even highly accurate mould? If it is made from sheet metal, how thick is the sheet? Is it rather thicker than most modern brass and is it a little uneven? If so it may have been hammered out by trip hammers or by a hammer-man rather than rolled out in a rolling mill.

Look at any joins in the piece. Are there seams and what form do they take? Dovetailing was the traditional way of making joins. The dovetails were carefully cut, the two pieces

65 Not only were many objects raised from sheets of metal by hammering but nearly all were finished by this technique. Here is an illustration of an eighteenth-century bowl, showing the hammermarks where the bowl was shaped. The turning on the body can also be clearly seen.

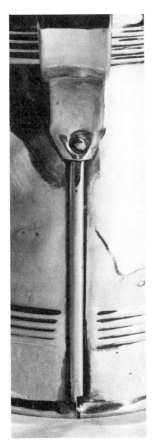

66 The overlap seam, a sign of nineteenth-century manufacture. The sheets of metal are bent over each other and hammered or pressed into position.

67 *Opposite:* A dovetailed seam. The most frequently used method before the advent, in the nineteenth century, of machinery to make overlap seams.

put together and hammered to complete the waterproof joint. Dovetailing was in use up to 1900 but was generally out of fashion by the mid nineteenth century.

The other popular seam was the overlap. That is a small piece of the metal was bent back to form a narrow flange and this was locked into a similar flange on the other piece to be joined, the two interlocking flanges then being hammered out to make the joint permanent. Such a form of seaming indicates a nineteenth century date.

Another method used was to solder the joint and this method was used in the seventeenth century, but not where any great pressure was to be brought to bear or where the temperatures involved in the life of the piece were going to be high. A simple soldered seam is an indicator of a modern finish.

Other indicators are the thickness of the metal in castings. The use of patterns, sand moulds or metal moulds produce a thinner casting than the earlier clay mould would have done.

Handles too can give further help. If they are hollow cast are they seamed on one side? If so they can be of any age, but if seamless they must be nineteenth century. Solid handles are an indication that a piece is prior to 1700.

Look at the way the piece has been finished off after manufacture.

The bases of flagons, tankards and the like were all carefully cleaned off and then turned on a wheel to give a fine even finish. An eighteenth-century maker would in no way have thought of sending out something with the marks of the sand casting still upon it than the modern maker of a Rolls Royce car would countenance selling it unpainted. The presence of a surface still rough from the casting is almost without exception a sign that the piece is not old.

Where it was possible, for example on all round based objects, the bases were carefully polished on a lathe and there will be signs of this fine turning. Years of use and care will have smoothed out the ridges. If the turning is still rough to touch and consists of deep ridges well spaced out it may well be of recent origin.

The three main techniques for joining parts together where seaming was not appropriate are casting in the mould, soldering and riveting.

The term cast joints is misleading for there is no joint at all, the pieces being cast as one within the original mould. This technique was mostly used in bronze pieces where the stresses would be very heavy such as skillets, cooking pots and mortars. The soldering of parts is a sign of nineteenth-century

Scale ⅑ Size

1302

1303

1297

1308

1305

1299
LARGE

1307

1306

1309

1311

1310

1312

1286
LARGE

1299
MEDIUM

1313

68 A page from a 1920s catalogue of reproduction brass. Most jardinières that you will see are from this period.

construction and should be suspect if found on a piece de-signed to carry considerable stresses. The most effective way of joining two parts is to rivet them together; early rivets were thick and hammered on both sides to complete the joint. Thin rivets, often only visible from one side, are a sign of later construction, perhaps post-1860.

Screw threads are another way of dating metalware. When they are present they should be examined to see whether they have been hand cut or machine made. Hand cut threads are always further apart, more uneven and the ridges are usually

1082 28/-

1076 26/-

1079 24/-

1080 30/-

1072 14/-

1894 26/-

1073 3½in. 2 -

1070 4½in. 13/6

1085 5½in. 14 -

1896 26/

672   11 6
672ʙ 9 6

1077 6in. 24/-

69 A group of reproduction candlesticks from the same catalogue.

deeper. The presence of modern screws is a sure sign of recent manufacture, unless they are clearly replacements. In eighteenth-century and some earlier candlesticks there were threads cut onto the stems. The use of a separate screw to join the two parts of the candlestick is a sign of nineteenth-century origin.

The last criteria for judging age to be examined is 'wear'. Does the item show sufficient evidence of age to support the kind of date that the other tests have suggested? Is the wear in those parts which naturally carry the most stress? Basically this is a matter of common sense; plates should have knife scratches, bowls, dents and so on. The eye can tell a lot, but let the fingers do the talking as well. Run your hands over the piece; are there sharp edges? If there are these should either have been taken off when made or worn down by use. In the end it's a simple question that you have to ask yourself? Is there the kind of evidence of hard uncaring use that you would expect to see. Loving care came with the first collector to own the item and if you doubt that and have romantic ideas of how your forefather's looked after their possessions look at some of the baking tins and other kitchen utensils in your own kitchen and you will see what I mean!

One area which can present difficulties is where an original part has been married to an original part of another object. Good period metalware is sometimes found with a recently made replacement. Charles II trumpet-based candlesticks seem particularly vulnerable to this treatment because of their value. There are also marriages to alter the purpose of a piece. Some fine Stuart warming pan lids have, for example, recently been converted into wall sconces by adding candle-holders to them. Always check that the colours of a piece made in more than one part are the same, that they carry the same basic degree of wear and that they fit properly together.

The technique for dating all these objects, therefore, involves looking at their purpose, construction, style and wear. Where all tell the same story a clear date will probably emerge; where there is conflict then there are grounds for further examination and consideration.

A couple of examples may help to illustrate how this can work out in practice.

Take the curfew illustrated on plate 129. From the section on keeping warm (Chapter 13) we have learnt that curfews gradually went out of popularity in the eighteenth century. In style you would find if you were able to examine others in museums and reference books, that it is similar to examples from around 1680-1720. It was made by carefully riveting hand raised sheets of latten to each other and as you can see the surface shows plenty of evidence of wear including the tops of the slight embossing being polished out. All of the factors therefore tell the same basic story that the curfew is probably around 1700.

Let us now look at a Georgian style candlestick. We can learn nothing much from its purpose, but style will tell us a little more.

From its square base you would suppose that it must date from after 1760 and the Corinthian stem suggests also a date of about 1780.

The method of construction confirms that it has been cast and that as there is a pusher in the base it is likely to have been hollow cast. This strengthens our hypothesis that it is around 1760.

We now look at the way it has been finished, its wear and general appearance. By turning up the candlestick we find that it has not been turned off, that there are, under a glass, some remnants of the metal deposited in the mould and not completely cleaned off. Compare the base with that of the other candlestick shown here.

By running our fingers over the edges of the base and candle holder we may be able to feel a certain sharpness. The surface is smoothly buffed with few signs of wear and tear. There is very little damage at any point. So whilst the method of construction and style suggested an eighteenth-century date this we must now revise as it does not have sufficient wear nor is it well enough finished for that period. It may be nineteenth century or more recent, but it is not likely to be Georgian.

Where the bases are square they could be well finished off with chisels, and whatever roughness was left will probably have been worn away by rubbing and cleaning over the candlesticks' life.

In addition to re-turning the bases of candlesticks some sticks were also aged on the base by hammering to add a false impression of wear.

627

72 Sixteenth-century brass alms dish. The scene is of St George and the Dragon. From either Dinant or Nuremberg such dishes were on display in wealthy homes. None were made in this country but many were imported for use here.

73 A fine medieval jug. Its bronze-like colour disguises its high copper content. *c.* 1450. Private collection.

Continental forms: brass and copper
  1 Dutch kettle
  2 German kettle
  3 Dutch tankard
  4 North European ewer
  5 German/Dutch jug
  6 German coffee pot
  7 Dutch coffee pot
  8 Dutch/German coffee pot
  9 German ewer
10 German coffee pot

74 *Left:* Decorated seventeenth-century lead –bronze mortar. Private collection.

75 *Below:* A set of three brass tavern mugs from the late nineteenth century. Mostly used in public houses some will have been domestic.

76 *Opposite:* Fine late Victorian tea urn with gadrooned body. Earlier examples are mostly somewhat plainer in style.

77 *Pages 632-3:* An array of copper and brass pans such as would have been used in a great house, *c.* 1800-20. Royal Pavilion, Brighton.

631

78 *Above:* Brass and copper ladles, skimmers and serving spoons. All eighteenth century. Some with iron handles, others in brass.

79 *Left:* Copper kettles, saucepans and a food warmer from the Prince Regent's Kitchen. Royal Pavilion, Brighton.

80 *Opposite:* An eighteenth-century fireplace. The saucepans and kettle are probably nineteenth century but give an excellent impression of how a working kitchen's fireplace might have looked *c.*1800. Cambridge and County Folk Museum.

81 *Opposite:* A display of copper jelly moulds from the Royal Pavilion.

82 *Opposite below:* A pair of 'Irish Peat' bellows. These were used with all types of fires and many were made in Great Britain as well as Ireland. Collection of the Curator of Horsham Museum.

European metalware

There is no easy way to tell British from European base metalware. So few pieces are marked that it is necessary to learn the styles involved before the differences are apparent.

This becomes more and more possible in the seventeenth century and easier thereafter as the similarities in style gradually disappear. Judgements are made by experts about the origin of most medieval objects, but few readers will be faced by these problems. With the establishment of the British brass industry the styles popular in Europe and Britain did begin to take different routes.

On the whole, European brass ware and copper work is rather more elaborate. Spouts are more common and are larger, embossing is more pronounced, knops larger and lids bigger, handles are more decorative, feet more often seen.

But all these hints may just serve to confuse as there are elaborate, highly decorative British products! You will probably need to consult specialist books on those aspects of the industry that appeal to you most to learn about the Continental forms. Illustrated on p. 628 are some of the more important Continental shapes.

83 A typical coffee pot in copper, a form seldom found in this country but popular in Europe during the early nineteenth century.

637

Chapter 11

Copper brass and bronze in cooking

Because of their comparatively high melting points these alloys were ideal for cooking. Their only rivals until modern times were pottery, which was easy to break, and iron, which was difficult to cast before the early eighteenth century and liable to fracture.

Until the eighteenth century cooking was done over an open fire and this method survived in rural areas into the last century. Two principal forms of cooking utensils were used. The larger, used suspended over the flames or stood in the fire, the smaller with a handle and feet placed only in the flames.

These early pots were basically of a bronze alloy, but by the late seventeenth century brass was increasingly used for cooking utensils.

Except for the low temperature bread ovens, most cooking was done over the open fire. When there was meat to roast it was suspended on a spit before the fire and to help it to roast evenly the spits were turned either by hand, clockwork or even by animals.

The growing use of coal, especially in the towns, whose nearby countryside was denuded of timber by the late seventeenth century, led to grates replacing the andirons (these were metal stands used for supporting burning wood on the hearth). Gradually hobs were positioned by the fire and used for cooking. Out of these hobs in turn ovens were created so that by the late eighteenth century most town dwellers will have had a hob and oven. By the middle of the nineteenth century kitchen ranges were popular in large houses. Thereafter gas and then electricity were adopted for cooking though this development had less significance on cooking-pot design than the first great change from the open fire to the hob.

Every family needed hot water and the fire was the only means to provide this. A large pot was kept on the fire throughout the day and often overnight. These vessels were called 'kettles'. Many early kettles were flat-bottomed containers made of copper beaten into shape and riveted together.

84 *Right:* Fifteenth century bronze cooking pot with small mouth and tall feet. Victoria & Albert Museum, London.

85 *Far right:* A cooking pot from around 1600 with wide mouth and iron handle.

Other kettles had the more common rounded base and were made from bronze.

The cooking pot was used for cooking most food, especially the potages, porridge, gruels and stews. Roast meat would have been uncommon except in the great houses, and the bulk of a family's food was prepared in the rounded crock or cauldron suspended over the fire.

These cooking vessels were in use up to the seventeenth century and changed little in form. They were made all over Europe as well as this country and many pots were imported.

The earliest cooking pots were very rounded with small openings, but gradually the mouth became larger and the form less rounded. There are many local variations. By the sixteenth century the rims of cooking pots are larger than before and more flared.

Most, but not all of these cauldrons had three feet so that in addition to being suspended by their small handles, they could be stood directly in the fire. The regular contact with heat has meant that in most pots the feet are partly burnt away. In a few cases the pots will not stand on their legs, but wobble about in a most unseemly manner on their bottoms.

These pots came in many sizes, from the largest for hot water to small pots for sauces. In great houses many cooking pots will have been available for use; while in the poorest homes perhaps just one would have fulfilled all the family's needs. Very large quantities of these cauldrons must have been made and they have survived in some quantity. It is not easy to say with confidence whether any particular vessel was made in this country or in Europe as so many were imported and styles are very similar.

The other main group of early cooking utensils are the skillets or posnets. These smaller cooking vessels have three feet and a long handle at one side. Early posnets had the same rounded form as the cauldrons or crocks, but by the early seventeenth century the body is being made with straight sides slightly tapering outwards. About this time makers began to cast their names or to add suitable inscriptions on the handles. Most of these inscriptions had a political or religious basis; 'C you be Loyall to his Magister', 'Honour thy King', 'Pity the Poore', 'Love thy God' and the like are amongst the more popular exhortations.

There are a number of makers who signed their skillets, including the father and son partnership of John and Thomas Palmer of Canterbury (John *circa* 1635, Thomas 1660-80), and John Fathers/Feathers, presumed to be a west of England maker from around 1680. In the eighteenth century the Street family of Bridgewater were prolific makers. Skillets were still being made as late as 1830.

Some of the early skillets had finely cast feet on the bottom of the legs in the shape of an animal's hoof. As with cauldrons many of these feet and legs have been partly burnt away through use. You will find that skillets often lean slightly forwards having one foot, that most frequently in the fire, shorter than the other two.

Early skillets had a strap-like support beneath the handle reinforcing the joint. This strap is rather like the handles on cauldrons. By the eighteenth century this has been replaced by a solid stepped support. Skillets marked 1, 2 or 3 are usually post-imperial and the numbering indicated the capacity in pints.

Few cooking pots have a makers' mark other than a symbol scratched into the outer clay mould and it is not possible therefore, to identify cauldron makers. Dated cauldrons are also uncommon and even with skillets few bear dates prior to

1660. A dated pot before 1600 will be rare.

The move from cooking over the fire to using a hob which started in the seventeenth century, saw the greater use of flat-bottomed cooking vessels. The first to be popular was the frying pan. These were in service in the late seventeenth century. Frying pans up to perhaps 1800 had long handles, often in iron. They were slightly deeper than the pans we use today and considerably larger. The handle is joined to the body by heavy rivets, the pans raised from latten sheet by hammering.

During the eighteenth century saucepans with flat bottoms, deeper bowls and long handles began to be used. Gradually the handles of both frying pans and saucepans became shorter as the significance of the change from open cooking to using a hob became clear.

It is important to remember that all saucepans of this period were hand made, each individually raised from sheets of copper or latten. Joints when they existed were dovetailed. These sheet metal cooking utensils were heavy and thick. To our eyes they are crude and only in basic outline similar to what we now use.

Few of these saucepans or frying pans have lasted. They were heavily used and then traded in for new ones when no longer serviceable.

In the nineteenth century the sides of the saucepans become straighter and the handles are now always short. Later in the century a more rounded style again appears. A glance at the Army and Navy Stores catalogue for 1909 will show that many such saucepans were still being made and marketed. The basic difference between the products of the Regency days and those of the last decades of the nineteenth century is that the vessels

87 A mid-nineteenth-century saucepan and flat lid, both with iron handles.

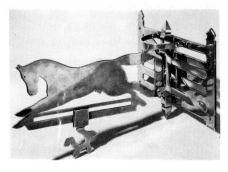 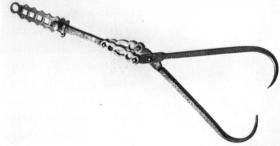

are now no longer made by hand, but either cast or stamped out from sheet. The unevenness of manufacture has given way to a conformity. Many Victorian and Edwardian saucepans had lids. The early form was a flattish disk which rested on top, the lid having its own separate iron or copper alloy handle. Later the lids were rounded and had a small strap handle on the top. After the 1870s many utensils were stamped either with a makers' mark or a patent number, but sometimes these have been filed off to give the pot an earlier appearance.

When you start looking about you at frying pans and saucepans on the market you will naturally see many more from the Edwardian days than you will genuine Georgian examples. A fine display of Regency cooking equipment is shown in the kitchen of the Royal Pavilion in Brighton.

One variety of cooking pan found in the nineteenth century was used mainly for jams or preserves. These jam pans have a flat base, usually dovetailed into the sides, and are well made of a heavy metal. Mostly made in brass the earlier examples have swing handles, but after the 1850s the handles are usually fixed in place.

Whilst most cooking was done over the open fire the pots had to be suspended above the flames by some device. Cranes or pot hooks were generally used. Cranes were much as their name implies. An arm set at right angles to the back of the chimney which could be raised or lowered by using ratchets. Most cranes are made in iron. There are however, a number of variations including some with a hook, moved up and down a straight bar on ratchets. There were also hooks, usually used in sets made of different sizes so that by selecting which to use the height of the pot above the flames could be correctly judged. Many of these were made in brass or copper.

Prior to the use of ovens, roasting was done on a spit. There were many varieties mostly made in iron, but a few decorated in brass or copper were made. The simplest form would have been a large iron spit, stood before the fire, which was turned

88 *Left:* A nineteenth-century brass crane for suspending pots and pans over the fire.

89 *Above:* A steel and brass meat hook *c.* 1700. The weight of the meat in the pincers kept them closed and the height could be adjusted by regulating the ratchets at the top.

90 A bottle Jack or clockwork spit. Nineteenth century. Brighton Museum.

by a handle. The most complicated were the clockwork spits of the eighteenth century. The earliest made by clockmakers were large and heavy. Later simple 'bottle' shaped spits were popular with a clockwork mechanism inside. These are usually made in brass and are called 'bottle jacks'.

Many other metal tools were to be found in use in the kitchen. Cutting tools were normally made in steel or iron, but spoons, ladles and skimmers were also in frequent use and many were in brass and occasionally copper. Prior to 1700 most were raised from sheet metal. Some handles are riveted onto the bowl; others are integral with it. In the eighteenth century iron handles were frequently used, but after 1850 'all brass' spoons were again produced. These have been extensively copied. There are some very decorative brass skimmers. These were called 'scummers' in the seventeenth century and were used to separate the butter from the butter milk, cream from the skimmed milk, fats from stews, etc. Early skimmers were simply flattened ladles with crude holes driven through the bowl. Most are made in brass. Later, iron handles were favoured and the holes in the brass more evenly punched. Very decorative shaped skimmers, made all in brass, are nineteenth century. The likelihood is that the more decorative they are the later they will be.

Colanders and straining dishes were to be found in many eighteenth-century homes; some in slipware or salt glazed pottery, a few in sheet or cast brass.

Pies have always been a popular form of food, hence 'simple Simon and the Pie man' and other nursery rhymes. From the late eighteenth century through the nineteenth, pastry wheels were used to add decoration to the pie crust. Early wheels or 'jiggers' sometimes have a spoon at one end. All the eighteenth-century examples appear to have been made wholly in brass. Wooden or bone handles were sometimes used in the nineteenth century and some of the later jiggers have three or even four different wheels or cutters.

The housewife of yesterday had no recourse to a mincer or blender. These tasks were performed with a pestle and mortar. The meat for the stew would have been pounded, herbs and spices ground and even medicines prepared, using the family mortar. Most seventeenth-century English mortars are made of a lead-bronze though for some of the specially commissioned mortars a lead-free alloy was used.

Most of the mortars made before the second half of the seventeenth century have either two or four lugs or handles. These lugs made it easier to hold and use the mortar.

643

During the seventeenth century many mortars were made without lugs. Though many sizes are found, the average size for a mortar was about four inches high.

Most seventeenth-century mortars are decorated. The principal emblems used have a political or religious meaning. There are mortars in honour of King Charles I with his portrait, death mask or coat of arms. There are a few of the Commonwealth period with the arms of Scotland, England and Ireland. Religious symbols used include the fleur-de-lys, symbolising both the holy trinity and purity, the griffin with a key for the keys to the kingdom of heaven, the deer representing the hart in the field or Christ, etc.

Some mortars have a temporal decoration for example, those bearing City Arms or decorated with swags of flowers or owners' or makers' names or initials. During the seventeenth century mortar shapes started to become less rounded. Mortars were still widely used into the nineteenth century, but after about 1750 they became plain and many were made in iron.

Pounded meats and grains were popular foods for our forefathers and in the Middle Ages they were known as 'mortrews'; an indication of the importance of the mortar and pestle to the cook of those times.

With the popularity of the 'cook book' in the late seventeenth and eighteenth century and more formal cooking, the need for measured quantities increased. Most early weights had been made for the market or fair. By Victorian times sets of weights were being made for domestic use. Several styles were made; the most popular of these are in the earlier waisted form. An average set would run from a seven-pound weight down to a weight of a quarter of an ounce. Nearly all of them had their weight engraved upon them or carried a lead stamp with a

91 *Left:* A fine lead bronze mortar by William Carter of the Whitechapel Foundry in London dated 1615. Later seventeenth-century mortars are usually straighter and more flared. Victoria & Albert Museum, London.

92 *Above:* A set of brass weights from the 7 lb down, for use in kitchen or shop. Victorian and therefore post-imperial measures.

confirmation of weight from the weights and measures officer. These check marks often help to date a set. Later sets of weights in the disc form are still often found, but not yet much collected.

To most people in the early days getting enough food to sustain life was a problem, especially in winter, but for the favoured few, food could be a pleasure as well as a necessity. Elaborate medieval banquets are recorded with much emphasis placed on display. A feature of these banquets was the sugared confections made in the shapes of birds and beasts.

In the eighteenth century the table was decorated with castles, boats, swans and elaborate designs made from spun sugar or cast in moulds. The making of desserts like jellies and custards in different shapes developed from these early decorations and were very popular in the nineteenth century.

Most jelly-moulds are made in copper, tinned inside. Moulds of the Regency period are likely to be larger than the later ones. They are made in a heavier metal and many are seamed. By the late Victorian times moulds were smaller, often stamped out of sheet and with a stock or pattern number on the base or side, a clear indicator on a piece of late construction. They were made in many hundreds of shapes and sizes mostly in the shapes of birds, flowers or fruit. The first Duke of Wellington possessed over 500 in his kitchen and many of them are now on display in the Royal Pavilion in Brighton.

In the medieval times, water was brought to the table in fine bronze containers known as aquamaniles. Many of them cast in elaborate shapes. Few if any of them are likely to have been made in this country. The simpler water or wine jug however was also used. The earliest were cast in clay moulds with heavy mould lines. Those with a high copper content probably date back to the 1400s. During the following 200 years pewter largely replaced bronze at the table, but in the eighteenth century copper and brass jugs were again widespread.

The most popular form is bulbous, usually spouted. They were made of sheet metal, seamed with dovetails, up the body behind the handle. The eighteenth-century jugs are made in heavy metal; in the nineteenth century thinner sheet metal was used. The straight-sided jug was probably first made around 1780-1800. Both of these types normally have hollow cast handles.

In Scotland two other shapes were popular in the nineteenth century. One of baluster form, mostly made in copper, occasionally in brass, is found in the imperial measure from the gill upwards and many will have been used in public

93 A quart copper jug with hollow handle *c.* 1800. The body was raised by hammering and the marks can still be seen.

94 Copper harvester measure. These measures were made in both brass and copper throughout the nineteenth century. Mostly for use in markets and shops a few will have been used in the home. Check the lead capacity seal as it may help to date the measure.

95 Two Scottish measures. The baluster style on the left is often in copper. That on the right the rarer thistle style usually in brass. Both are post-imperial.

houses. The smaller sizes are lidless, but from the quart upwards they have slightly domed lids.

The other Scottish type is thistle-shaped, again made in both copper and brass. Examples have hollow handles and the bases underneath are slightly concave and have been soldered into position; another indicator of their nineteenth century origin. Brass tappit hens are occasionally offered for sale, but I have yet to see an example which I have thought to have been made before the end of the nineteenth century.

The importance of ale, beer and wine gradually declined with the introduction of tea and coffee to the national diet.

Coffee which first appeared in Europe around 1580 reached these shores in 1650. It never attained the importance of tea over here and at first was mostly drunk by gentlemen in coffee shops. The first to be opened, it is claimed, was in Oxford.

The earliest coffee pots are tapering in form with a tall rounded domed lid which has a small knop. They have a long pouring spout set at right angles to a straight wooden handle. Later a strap handle replaces the wooden grip and the handle is placed opposite the spout. The tapering body then gives way to a more rounded pear-shape and later in the eighteenth century the body takes on a concave form and the straight wooden handle opposite the spout reappears. Most coffee pots made after the 1840s are in copper and have been tinned.

Chocolate pots are often very similar in shape to the coffee pot, but have a small hole in the lid through which the sticky liquid could be stirred. In the mid to late nineteenth century

646

the handles of both coffee and chocolate pots were often bound with raffia or cane to make them heat resistant. The concave form of pot was still being made in the 1900s.

Tea reached Europe, via Portugal and Holland, in the seventeenth century. The first public tea sale was held in 1657 and at the start it was a very costly commodity and limited to the homes of the rich. In the 1660s tea cost £3.50p a pound, a year's wages for a maid. By 1700 it was still over £1 a pound and though its price was to fall in the next half-century, in the 1760s you would have had to pay 50p a pound when meat was under 1½p per pound.

In spite of this high price the demand for tea rose dramatically and it had adherents at all levels of society. Boswell wrote of it, 'I am so fond of tea that I could write a whole dissertation on its virtues'.

In the well-to-do home it was drunk with lemon or sugar and a high-quality tea could be afforded. In the working-man's home it was taken with brown sugar and was a weak brew from inferior leaf. Whatever its cost or quality it had replaced beer as the national drink by 1800.

At first tea was drunk from porcelain tea bowls and poured from tea pots made in the Chinese style. Around 1700 silver was used to make tea pots and there were also a few pots made in pewter. Tea pots in brass or copper are rare from all periods as silver, plate, pottery and porcelain seem to have been preferred.

Of the few made in brass or copper the earliest form is bullet-shaped and later they were made in the typically Georgian and Victorian styles. But look out for coffee or tea pots that were at one time silver-plated.

96 Two coffee pots; both forms found in copper and brass. That on the left is *c.* 1800; the example on the right from the early nineteenth century.

Tea urns were made in both copper and brass. The straight-sided and baluster-shaped urns of the eighteenth century are mostly Dutch imports but from 1800 onwards many urns were made here.

Some stand on a pedestal base and have round knopped lids. A few have spirit lamps beneath for heating the water. They all have small taps in the base. Many tea urns or 'samovars' as they are called were made in silver plate. Urns with pottery finials or taps are likely to be Edwardian in period.

Tea kettles developed parallel with the habit of tea drinking. There are many hundreds of designs in copper or brass. Kettles were made in a number of sizes from a pint up to a monster of two gallons or more. They come square, round or oval. As with all domestic metalware the early kettles are made from heavy duty sheet dovetailed together; later kettles from thin sheet evenly rolled. Kettles with rounded movable handles tend to be early nineteenth century, those with fixed handles later. Handles made of other materials indicate a late-nineteenth-century origin.

Kettles in copper and brass were made in vast quantities for export as well as for the home market. Recently copper kettles sent to North Africa in the late nineteenth century have been brought back here and at the same time modern copper kettles from the Middle East have been imported in quantity to fill the demand for these attractive pieces, so pleasing when placed by the fireside.

Kettles were made to withstand plenty of hard wear and if they have been around they should show signs of heavy use, especially on the base.

97 A group of kettles. Usually in copper but brass examples do occur and are much valued. The two kettles on the left have straight rounded handles and are mid nineteenth century. The example on the right is slightly earlier.

98 A seventeenth-century apostle spoon in brass; the round bowl dates it to be about 1650.

Brass and copper were also used at table. A few brass-handled steel knives are known, but forks were seldom made in brass or bronze and those that do appear are French or Italian. Spoons in latten or brass, on the other hand, were numerous and spoons with an interesting variety of knops can be found. Examples from as early as the 1300s can still be bought; many of the early examples will have been made in Europe and imported, but their use in Britain is authenticated.

Most of the knops found in pewter are duplicated in latten. The later-eighteenth-century examples are not common and in the nineteenth century whilst copper spoons were made they were mostly plated though by now this plate may have worn away.

Latten spoons are not found quite as frequently as pewter spoons, perhaps in the ratio of 6 to 5. About 40 per cent of all latten spoons have seal-top finials. Apostle spoons make up about another 20 per cent, although many of these are Continental. The trifid, slip top, horse's hoof and puritan knopped spoons account in total for about 15 per cent. None of the other knops appear on more than one spoon in a hundred.

Salts in brass are not common even in the eighteenth century. The few that there are are mostly in cup salt form or on a short stem.

Peppers, sanders, sugar and spice sifters are less rare though seventeenth-century examples are hard to find. Most of those that are still around are in the baluster or urn shape. The straight-sided sifter with strap handle was used for spices or for flour.

There are far fewer brass or copper plates and dishes than are found made in pewter. Those plates that do exist are mostly in copper, made with a single-reeded rim. Dishes are even rarer though there are a few examples. Be careful when buying oval or round copper dishes to ensure that they were not once silver-plated.

A very few brass or copper porringers from the 1700s have survived, they are similar in shape to those in pewter, but beware of small two-eared brass porringers with a cast Tudor rose in the base; these are modern and made in Holland.

Plate warmers, stands on which pewter or china plates would be kept warm for use at the table, are often found in brass. The most popular form is the four-legged 'cat' in which the plates rest on the four arms which cross to form the feet beneath. Less common is the style with round base and uprights into which the plates are put one on top of the other.

Brass or copper tankards and flagons are rare. There are a

few fine early-eighteenth-century examples, in most Georgian styles. Concave-sided copper tankards were common in the second half of the nineteenth century. Again often plated, most were for use in taverns which is also where most of the brass and bell-metal bellied and straight-sided tankards were used. These styles are all similar to the pewter mugs from which they are derived.

There were also some goblets made in brass in the late nineteenth century, with deep bowls and short stems they were made of good heavy cast metal.

There are very few antique brass or copper pails or buckets, those pails that can be seen on the market are mostly of recent origin and probably imported from Turkey and the East.

Wine cisterns in copper or brass were used in many middle class homes in the eighteenth century for chilling the wine. Most of them were imported from Holland and are repoussé (i.e. raised in relief by hammering from behind or inside) decorated. There are many smaller round or oval containers in both brass and copper. These are jardinières or large vessels for flowers. Most of them are late nineteenth century or modern; the true wine cooler is large, over 24 inches wide, whilst the jardinières are only 12 to 18 inches wide. Period wine coolers had their decoration hammered into the sheet metal whilst the more recent jardinières are made of stamped out metal.

To open their wine bottles some brass corkscrews were made in the eighteenth century, but they are fairly rare.

Another small decorative piece of brass is the chestnut roaster. These are small shaped boxes on long handles and were used to roast the nuts in the fire. There are a few genuine nineteenth-century roasters about, but the bulk of those available were made for decoration not use, and date from the end of the nineteenth century or during the first quarter of the twentieth century when many reproductions were made.

Chapter 12

Lighting and candlesticks

From the earliest times to the nineteenth century the only means of illumination was provided by the candle, oil lamp or rush light. We are accustomed to instant light at the touch of a switch, but there was no such luxury available to our forefathers.

Nor were any of the methods very effective and people had to make do with a limited smoky and short-lived light. Early to bed and early to rise was more than a prescription for good health, wisdom and riches. There was not much alternative unless you were rich enough to afford costly light into the night.

In our temperate climate, vegetables for oils did not grow so these had to be imported and were therefore expensive. Animal fats could be burnt in lamps, but they were very smoky and gave off little light. Lamps were thus a rather ineffective source of light and for many the alternative was to use rushes.

'Rushlight holders' are stands which hold the rush as it burns away. These rushes were cheap and plentiful. They were picked usually in mid-summer. The outer cover was then stripped off just leaving two thin bands to slow down the burning and to help keep the rush from bending. The peeled rushes were then diped in animal fat or tallow which was quickly absorbed into the porous structure. Such rushes would then burn well and gave a good clear light.

Great dexterity was achieved by people stripping rushes and even a blind woman could work at a great speed. Gilbert White calculated in 1789 that each rush burnt for about 30 minutes and that 1 lb of rushes, perhaps 600 or more, could be bought for 3/-; providing $5\frac{1}{2}$ hours of light for a farthing.

But even if they lasted this long it meant changing the rushes regularly and they were inclined to smoke heavily.

Candles were the best, but most costly, form of light. Provided they were regularly trimmed they gave off less smoke and they would each last several hours. For most people a single candle would have lit the parlour and would have guided them to bed. For the halls of the wealthy many dozens of candles gave a fine light.

Country folk used candles made from mutton fat or tallow and they made their own. The rich used beeswax and in the towns, candles would have been bought from the local chandler.

Candles could be made in several ways. They were cast in moulds, often of wood or tin, rolled from sheets of wax or hand dipped. This last method involved immersing the wick in the hot wax or fat, removing and allowing it to cool off a little, then repeating the process until a thick layer had been built up round the wick.

The candles were held in candlesticks and throughout the last two thousand years these have been made in most materials including brass and bronze.

Apart from their other advantages candles could be made more portable than rush lights. No one in his senses would carry a lighted lamp rush about the wooden house of the past whilst outside the first gust of wind would blow them out.

Lamps were used to protect the candle from the wind. Most lamps were made in iron or later, tin, but brass and copper examples are to be found. The light from the candle shone through a thin sheet of mica, horn, oiled paper or even glass.

Until the eighteenth century there were no real alternatives to lamps fuelled by animal or vegetable fats, rushes or candles ... Around 1780-1800 whale oil was imported and there were improvements in lamp design and in the 1840s slate oil was refined which with colza oil derived from rape seeds circa 1870, widened the choice of fuels for lamps. Then after the discovery of mineral oil in the USA, paraffin and other oils were increasingly used and soon drove out all other alternatives for fuelling lamps.

Although coal gas was first put to work in around 1805 it was neither safe nor serviceable until the 1860s as a form of domestic lighting. Electricity, first used in the 1840s was, after the invention of the filament bulb, an alternative in the 1870s, but its use in Britain was very limited until after the First World War.

After centuries of limited choice and poor light the use of mineral oils, gas and electricity revolutionised lighting and led to substantial changes in the way we live.

Apart from electricity all forms of lighting have to be lit by a flame. There were no lighters to respond to a flick of a finger! Setting aside the use of wood and bow, the only way of getting a light before the invention of matches was by flint, steel and tinder, a slow and cumbersome method.

Few lamps have survived other than those of the crusie form which hung on small backplates. Crusie lamps were particularly used in Scotland and the north of England. Care should, however, be taken as many have recently been imported from Spain. Most crusie lamps are in iron though a few may occur in bronze or even brass.

Rush light holders are also mostly in iron though a few have brass decoration. Rushlights now to be seen may date from the late seventeenth century into the early nineteenth. There may be some in brass, but I suspect these to be few and far between.

Candlesticks, however were made in great quantities over many hundreds of years and there are many forms still to be seen.

Prior to the establishment of the British brass industry, many brazen candlesticks were imported and as a consequence the early European and British styles have become inextricably mixed. The founders were casting bronze candlesticks from the Middle Ages, but it is not easy to tell these from their Continental brothers made at the same time.

Until the late Middle Ages the ruling class were French-speaking and owed much to French culture. As these were the people able to buy expensive bronze, most pieces were made to their Continental taste.

There were a few sixteenth century candlesticks either made in or used in this country, but all are rare and costly.

The first style of candlesticks to be made in this country independently of Europe are probably the trumpet-based candlesticks of the 1640s. These are so-called because of the obvious resemblance of the base to that musical instrument. Most trumpet-based candlesticks have a mid drip pan, called according to contemporary evidence, rather delightfully, the 'flower'. They have round bases and straight stems which are cast separately, turned and either riveted to the bases or fastened with a hand-cut screw thread. Trumpet-based candlesticks without the drip pan are also known.

All trumpet-based candlesticks are well made from good solid metal well-finished and are highly attractive.

In pewter, the dominant style of the late seventeenth century was the octagonal candlestick with a low drip pan and there is no equivalent in brass or bronze. But pewter, brass and bronze come together again with the knopped stems of the late seventeenth century.

Most brazen candlesticks of the period 1680-1710 have

100 A fine brass or latten trumpet-based candlestick with mid drip pan c. 1650. These candlesticks usually vary from 5 inches high to about 9 inches.

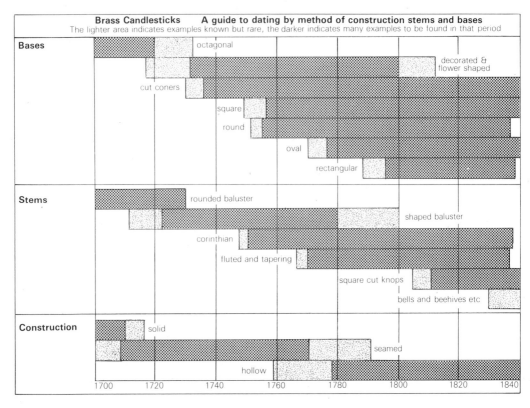

Brass Candlesticks   A guide to dating by method of construction stems and bases
The lighter area indicates examples known but rare, the darker indicates many examples to be found in that period

Bases
- octagonal
- decorated & flower shaped
- cut coners
- square
- round
- oval
- rectangular

Stems
- rounded baluster
- shaped baluster
- corinthian
- fluted and tapering
- square cut knops
- bells and beehives etc

Construction
- solid
- seamed
- hollow

1700   1720   1740   1760   1780   1800   1820   1840

octagonal bases, but to say this is to disguise many varieties, based on this general form. There are examples with more or fewer sides, bases made with prisms, fluted or with cut corners as well as other variations on the main theme.

The eighteenth century saw brass candlesticks drive out pewter and many hundreds of thousands of candlesticks were made in countless designs. Indeed the eighteenth century has been termed the 'age of candlelight'.

When we look at the products of the past it is natural that we should attempt to categorise them in order to understand better how they changed and developed. It is of course, we who make the categorisation and it is subjective. No craftsman at work in the early eighteenth century was bound by the rules that we try and establish.

Thus for every hypothesis that is advanced there is sure to be an exception, but if this is firmly borne in mind it is possible to divide the candlesticks of the eighteenth century into several distinct patterns and thus help to date many examples.

The criteria we shall examine are therefore:
1. Method of stem construction
2. Shape of the bases
3. Stem or column style

654

101 Three eighteenth-century brass candlesticks. Each is seamed. That on the left has an octagonal base, the other two have fluted or petal bases.

Each has its own contribution to make in dating candlesticks.

Before about 1700 all stems were cast solid and then turned off on a lathe. Although knops could be made, there was a technical difficulty in making them too elaborate. After 1700 the stems were cast in two separate parts and carefully seamed together. The stems could now be hollow or solid though solid stems are more frequently found. It was also easier to make more complex decorative knops in this fashion.

The final transition which occurred in the 1760-80 period was for hollow cast stems to be made in one piece. This speeded up production as the stems no longer had to be carefully seamed together. The change also made it possible to place a central rod up the inside of the stem so that the used candle could be pushed out. While the invention of the hollow cast stem is known to have been in use by 1760 most such candlesticks were probably made rather later in the century.

The shape of the bases which from 1700 to around 1730 were still basically octagonal underwent several subsequent changes all of which help us to date examples.

Gradually the octagonal base became more decorative and the straight lines are superseded with curves so that around 1730 the first of what we term the flower-based candlesticks appear. By 1750 these petal or flower bases are found with fluting or swirls rising to the stem and ape the very fine styles then being made in silver.

Square-based candlesticks make their appearance around 1760 but are probably uncommon for another twenty years and oval bases first appear about 1780.

Round-based candlesticks, though they appear very briefly *circa* 1700, do not reappear until the 1770s. Sometime in the early nineteenth century the octagonal base re-surfaces and

rectangular shaped bases are likewise from the first part of the nineteenth century onwards.

Taking the last criteria next, the stems which were decorated with simple rounded knops in the period 1680-1710 are gradually made more decorative with shaped knops, smaller and larger balusters, knops with flutes and even 'wrythen' or twisted knops appear around 1750. In general the longer the eighteenth century lasted the more decorative the knops became until about 1760 when the first of the plain stem candlesticks re-appear. This was the Corinthian column candlestick and around 1780 stems with flutes, or which rise to a single knop—often an urn, appear. Square knops make their début around 1780, but those with cut corners or facets are after 1820. Knops in the form of a beehive or a bell are probably after 1850 whilst candlesticks with two twisted stems are from the late nineteenth century.

Within these general patterns there are naturally many dozens of variations and there are other features that change: the nature of the actual candle holder, the sconce or bobeche for example which was originally part of the stem and was then made separately for a period in the mid eighteenth century, only once more to be re-incorporated with the stem in the early nineteenth.

Using these 'watersheds' it is often possible to pinpoint the earliest date that a candlestick is likely to have been made.

To take an example. If you find a seamed Corinthian column candlestick, the method of manufacture suggests a date before 1780 and the column itself suggests a date after 1760. So the chances are that it is about 1760-80.

102 *Above:* A group of brass round-based candlesticks from the period 1760-1820.

To take a further example; a petal-based candlestick with a hollow stem. The petal base suggests that it is likely to be mid-eighteenth century whereas the hollow stem proposes a date after 1760-80. It may therefore, be either a rather late example or perhaps made more recently and an examination for wear, turning etc. may well tell which it is.

There are of course, many other candlesticks whose form is not described within these hypotheses. There are for example in the early nineteenth century a group of candlesticks with telescopic stems, usually with round or square bases.

It is always possible that an item may have gone on being made in a particular style long after it has been assumed that this style went out of fashion. On the other hand it is not easy to sell yesterday's style in a market demanding the new fashions.

104 *Opposite bottom:* Late-eighteenth-century Corinthian column brass candlestick.

105 *Right:* Pair of early-nineteenth-century telescopic brass candlesticks. The example on the left has been extended to its maximum height.

106 *Far right:* Eighteenth-century brass candlestick with extractor operated from the side.

657

Such a fashion-conscious market existed in the eighteenth and nineteenth centuries so that some of the items in a style out of period may be genuine but many will be later copies.

As we have seen the hollow cast stem made possible the use of a centrally placed pusher to extract the used candle. In very early candlesticks this was done with the point of a knife using a hole filed away on the candle holder or later still drilled into it with a bit. Both methods did damage to knife and candleholder and were out of fashion in the seventeenth century.

With the arrival of seamed candlesticks that could be made hollow a pusher could be employed, but as the candlesticks were still riveted or threaded to their bases this had to be accomplished by cutting a rectangular hole in the side of the stem and fastening the pusher onto a small knop which could then be raised or lowered from outside. At the same time some straight-stemmed candlesticks with pushers were more simply made by bending a sheet of metal to form a circle and then seaming it together up one side.

In addition to the central pushers of the late eighteenth century onwards other more elaborate schemes were invented to get rid of the dead candle. Barlow was one of the many makers who obtained patents for extractors. His method was to have a small group of claws positioned within the candle holder turned by a knop outside. If the knops were turned in one way it gripped the candle more tightly; if turned in the opposite direction the grip was loosened and the candle pushed upwards. There are other variations on this theme.

The main styles of candlestick of the eighteenth century are illustrated on pp. 655-7.

A recent survey that I made of candlesticks on offer in the market place is given opposite. It shows that as you might expect, the vast majority of examples on sale are nineteenth

107 When candlesticks could be hollow cast it was more effective to put the pusher or extractor at the base of the candlestick.

108 Brass chamber candlestick, early nineteenth century.

century, but it also underlines just how rare early-eighteenth-century examples now are, so that when you come across them approach with caution. In undertaking this survey into candlesticks thought to be made after 1700 no attempt was made to date each example. The survey was into the method of construction, stem form and base shape. A sample of 400 candlesticks offered for sale in antique shops or sale rooms over a three-months period was examined.

Construction	%
Solid	1
Seamed	5
Hollow	89
Others	5
Stems	
Multi-knops	50
Round knops	15
Beehives	9
Fluted/tapering	8
Baluster	7
Straight/pushers	6
Corinthian	4
Spiral	1
Bases	
Square	42
Octagonal	30
Round	17
Oval rectangular	9
Petal/flower	2

As would be expected the method of construction, and the forms of knop, stem or bases most frequently found confirm that most candlesticks on the market are likely to have been made after 1760 and most will be nineteenth century.

Remember too that candlesticks in the Stuart and Georgian styles were being made in the twentieth century as reproductions. Whilst these may not fool an experienced collector the task of differentiating the good from the bad is complicated by the fact that recently some of the reproduction sticks have been returned to the workshop to have their rough cast bases neatly filed away and turned on a lathe so that they gain more of the appearance of old candlesticks. So look at the bases carefully. The turning of early sticks is very fine and now is usually worn smooth. Recent turning is usually wider apart and the ridges are plain to see.

Chamber-sticks, small round pans with a short stem and a

carrying ring handle were used when travelling from room to room. In eighteenth-century examples the stem is riveted to the base and later in the nineteenth century, screws are employed. Examples before the 1840s are made from heavy sheets of metal hammered into shape, those of more recent manufacture stamped out from sheets of thin brass or even soldered together.

Chamber-sticks with punched out fretted walls set at right angles to a flat base are also late Victorian or Edwardian. They are most attractive if well made.

In some cases the base incorporates a small box which was used to store the flint steel and tinder. Most of these candle-holders and flint boxes are eighteenth century.

Most people had to be content with the light from their rushes or a candle, but a few could afford to use several candles at once to light their drawing rooms. Chandeliers were in use from the medieval period onwards though few before the seventeenth century have endured.

Until the eighteenth century the bulk of chandeliers used in this country were imported from Flanders. Even when we did make them they were constructed in the Dutch 'taste'. Seventeenth-century chandeliers have wide-spread arms with the candle holders at the end, usually in two banks spread about a round central knop. In the next century the arms are made closer to the core and this is often oval or pear-shaped. Chandeliers with more than two banks of arms are also found more frequently in late rather than in earlier times.

The earliest wall fittings for candles were simple holders driven into the stone walls of the castle or the beams of the house. By the seventeenth century they are backed with a reflector. They are now called 'wall sconces' and they usually have rounded, fretted and engraved backplates with a polished central panel to reflect the light back into the room. The candles are held in two holders at the end of a pair of arms.

Brass wall sconces are rare, but many fine examples do exist. In the eighteenth century the candle holders are sometimes placed on a small tray at the base of the reflector and the backplate becomes rectangular, the top often tilted forwards to help reflect the light. Some examples were imported from Holland but others were made locally.

The large wall sconces with octagonal backplates, decorated with embossing, flowers and fruit with a second separate reflector added above, tilting down, are mostly from the Baltic area and were imported from the seventeenth to the nineteenth centuries.

109 Edwardian brass fretted chamber light with glass flue and snuffers. Brighton Museum.

110 An interesting brass wall sconce which has a scratch date of 1695.

111 A late Stuart pair of oak bellows with fine brass spout and applied brass decoration. Private collection.

112 *Left:* An Edwardian brass jardinière of typical wrythen form.

113 *Below:* A group of brass lighting implements. On the left a wall sconce and in the centre a tinder box with candle holder, both late seventeenth century. On the right a pair of early-eighteenth-century brass candlesticks.

114 *Opposite top:* A small collection of brass snuffers and doubters. Collection of the Curator of Horsham Museum.

115 *Opposite bottom:* Two mid-seventeenth-century candlesticks with trumpet bases. That on the left is in latten or brass. The example on the right, with a less pronounced base and heavier turning is in pewter.

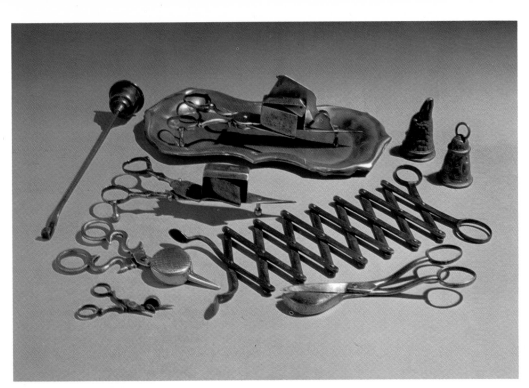

116 A student's lamp in brass, the reflector helped to concentrate the light of the single candle. Nineteenth century. Collection of the Curator of Horsham Museum.

117 A mid nineteenth century oil lamp of classical form. The glass flue and shade are missing.

In the Victorian period large embossed wall sconces were made with tubular arms, often with embossed historic figures.

Collectors also ought to be warned that some fine early warming pan fronts, now separated from their pans, have been married with arms to produce decorative wall sconces, but whilst they are often attractive they are marriages and their purpose has been altered and they have only a decorative not an antique value.

Lamps burning vegetable oil or animal fats gave a poor smoky light. The invention of Argand, a Swiss inventor of an improved lamp with a shade did much to improve the quality of the light and cut down on pollution. The Argand lamp was gradually adopted in this country and offered a twelve-fold improvement in brightness. The oils used were thick and did not flow from the reservoir easily, which was at first situated in the base. Other lamps were made with reservoirs just below the burner to reduce the distance the oil had to move and after Carcel had invented a clockwork powered pump, increasingly the oil was driven upwards rather than relying upon a gravity feed.

After 1800 whale oil was also available and from the 1840s slate oil was refined and gradually made available. After the discovery of mineral oil in the United States the next three decades saw the rapid expansion of oil lamps fuelled by kerosene or paraffin.

The speed of change is illustrated by the number of patents for new or improved lamps which were taken out and which averaged over eighty per year after the 1870s.

The next improvement was the use of the incandescent mantle for both gas and oil lamps.

There were many hundreds of lamps manufactured. A few mainly in brass, but many more combining pottery, glass or other materials with copper or brass. Many of the lamps and shades used in oil lamps were later to be matched on gas and electric fittings.

Oil lamps reached their peak in the 1880s though they continued in use for several decades, even after gas and electricity had reached most homes, as a stand-by system.

Although gas was first used for street lighting as early as 1805 it was not until after the incandescent mantle was available after 1884, that it became popular for lighting the home. The invention in 1838 of a process for making seamless brass tubes made possible the widespread use of gas and these tubes were also used for holding electric cables when electricity reached the home. Many wall or ceiling fittings are made with

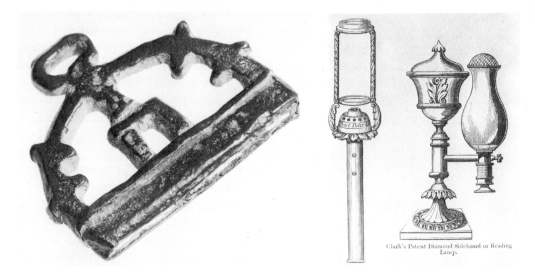

Clark's Patent Diamond Sideboard or Reading Lamp.

this brass tube often decorated at the time of manufacture.

So many different lamps were produced in such a short period that the task of codifying them is complex.

By 1900, in spite of gas and the appearance of electricity most homes would have been lit with oil lamps. But with another ten years the pattern was to change again.

A London store catalogue in the early years of this century devoted 6 pages to gas lamps, 10 to electricity, 19 to oil and $1\frac{1}{2}$ to candlesticks; giving an idea of the relative importance of the various forms of lighting on offer in Edwardian days. Twenty years before only oil lamps and candlesticks would have been significant.

For many household purposes the easy availability of a light was essential. Short of rubbing two sticks together most people had to make do with a flint, steel and tinder. By striking the steel against a flint sparks could be obtained and with skill and care a flame created by blowing on the smouldering cotton waste often used. It was common for 'strike, flint and floss' to be kept in a small box and some of these were made in copper or brass though tin and iron boxes were also popular. Few tinder boxes still contain their original equipment. Some of the tinder boxes were rounded and had a small candle on top and occasionally one finds quite large brass or copper candle holders with a box beneath, now usually empty.

A more efficient but costly mechanism was the mechanical pistol known as the 'Tinder pistol' or 'strike a light'. The mechanism used for this is the same as for a weapon, but instead of exploding the powder the spark is applied to the tinder. Many strikes have a small candleholder fixed to the end

118 *Left:* A bronze 'strike a light'; the flint was sandwiched between the two straight edges. Sixteenth century. Private collection.

119 *Above:* A brass lamp from the Great Exhibition of 1851. One of very many designs patented in the last half of the century.

666

so that when the flame has been coaxed it can be used to light a small candle. 'Strike a Lights' were at their most popular in the eighteenth century, and had wooden grips like the pistols of the period. In the late seventeenth century they mostly had metal ball and stem grips. Many 'pistol tinders' were made or decorated in brass and in fully working condition they are well worth seeking.

By the end of the eighteenth century there were experiments with matches; the earliest sulphur tipped and self-igniting were very dangerous. Later other types of inflammable material were employed but all were risky. The invention of the safety match was a great boon and by 1900 these provided the means of a light in most homes. Many different boxes and containers were in use during the nineteenth century for holding matches and many of these are in brass or decorated with copper or brass. By 1900 vesta stands were popular and these can be found in many forms.

120 Two early pistol strikes, both eighteenth century.

When lit, candles needed trimming regularly if they were not to gutter, give off smoke and eventually die. Special instruments were used for this trimming called doubters or snuffers. Made in the form of a pair of scissors with a small box on one side for the trimmed wick and a sharp-edged blade to cut with on the other. Seventeenth-century brass examples are often beautifully engraved or embossed. Rather more eighteenth and nineteenth century examples will be seen, most in steel. Most snuffers after 1700 are plain.

121 A group of late-nineteenth-century matchboxes or vesta boxes.

Early-eighteenth-century snuffers were also made with a small stand with a candlestick-like base and an aperture for fitting the snuffers where the candle would have been placed. Sets of candlesticks and snuffers were made, but most have long been parted.

Eighteenth-century snuffers with trays for them to stand upon were also popular. These trays had separate handles for carrying and rarely appear with their original snuffers. In the nineteenth century the trays no longer had a separate handle. Care must be taken with copper trays that they have not been plated at one time.

'Doubters' or 'extinguishers' were used for putting out the candle and thus avoiding the smoke that follows if the candle is blown out. Early doubters consisted of two small circular metal discs on a scissor-like device, similar in form to snuffers, but without a box to take the wick, or the blade. Later little conical devices were used to put over the top of lighted candles to extinguish them. These were often fitted to candlesticks, chamber sticks or supplied with snuffers and trays.

Copper and its alloys have played a significant role particularly in the centuries before the industrial revolution, in lighting our homes. They played their part too, in the constant struggle to help us keep warm as we will see in the next chapter.

122 Early-eighteenth-century snuffers and stand. These were often made ensuite with candlesticks of a similar design.

668

Chapter 13

Keeping warm

Cold was always an enemy. For centuries the harsh winters of Northern Europe were a constant challenge to survival.

Not only were there times when the winters were more severe than we face now, but the homes did little to keep out the pervasive cold. The wind drove in through the cracks and crannies of the lath and plaster houses or through the open windows, mostly only protected by wooden shutters. The damp rose up from the earthen floors or the chilly stone flags. Long woollen gowns or furs were some protection, but the key to survival was the open fire.

While the fire was centred in the middle of the room the family could all gather round, though the smoke, making its way slowly up to a hole in the roof, must have been a hazard. With the gradual adoption of the chimney the fire moved to the walls of the house and this discomfort must at least have been reduced.

Whilst wood was the principal fuel, the logs rested upon andirons, or fire dogs as they are usually known today. Later as the use of coal became more widespread, grates were used to hold the coals.

Iron was the material most used in the hearth though from the late seventeenth century onwards, brass and copper were used to brighten up the fireplace.

Even the provision of coal-burning grates in most eighteenth-century homes did not banish the cold. A Swedish observer in 1784 complained that rooms never rose above 50°F in winter and that during his visit he was always cold.

Whilst the fire was in the centre of the room the andirons were made to face in two directions, but with the adoption of the chimney the andirons faced outwards only. By the seventeenth century they started to be decorated with copper or brass, usually with cut and fretted sheet applied to the iron frame. As Fuller wrote in 1662 'brazen Andirons stand only for state'.

In the eighteenth century andirons were often made with

cast brass pillars. These are found in most styles with baluster knops, urn knops and columns being popular. Many andirons also had brass feet and the ball, ball and claw and the slipper shape are the most frequently found styles.

In the USA where the use of timber as a fuel continued right into the nineteenth century, andirons were still needed and many fine brass pairs were made up to the 1900s. In this country the use of coal drove out wood, already scarce by 1600 and the use of fire dogs went out of fashion during the eighteenth century, only to be revived this century with the reproduction of many fine pairs.

The fire backs, necessary to protect the back of the chimney and to reflect the heat of the fire into the room, were always made of iron.

The steady increase in the use of coal as a fuel led to the invention of the basket to hold the coals and provide sufficient draught to keep them burning brightly. At first the basket was probably suspended from the andirons, but later purpose built grates were made, combining andirons, firebacks and basket. The first grates gave the impression of being made up of several independent parts, but by the eighteenth century more harmonious grates were being constructed. Up to 1730 the grates had flat fronts, but later serpentine- and round-fronted grates became fashionable. Hardly any baskets or grates are wholly in copper or brass, but both materials are used to decorate the basically iron constructions.

By putting a plate of iron at the side of the grate or fire a hob was formed on which a kettle could be boiled or a stew cooked.

As with grates, the earliest stoves tend to look as if they are

123, 124 *Far left and centre:* A magnificent pair of seventeenth-century andirons with applied brass and enamel decoration. Victoria & Albert Museum, London.

125 *Above:* Pair of early-eighteenth-century brass andirons. A style much copied in the 1930s. Victoria & Albert Museum, London.

126 An interesting group of grates designed by Chippendale.

made up of several parts, but by the late eighteenth century designs begin to have a stylistic unity. Most stoves are in iron though again copper and brass were used as decoration.

Kitchen ranges were the next major development, incorporating ovens round the central fire with plates above for cooking on. These were popular in large kitchens by the 1850s though in the country cottage or industrial slum the grate and hob continued in use into this century.

Fenders were first used in the late seventeenth century, for preventing the logs from falling into the room, the earliest forms are large and straight, usually made of punch decorated or fretted sheet copper or brass applied to an iron frame. By the second quarter of the eighteenth century fenders with corners to hold them in place appear and the shapes become more fluid reflecting popular taste of the day. Many of the well-known furniture designers also worked designs for fenders. By the middle of the eighteenth century examples predominantly in copper or brass were made. Although a few early fenders have applied feet to give them greater stability it was not until the nineteenth century that this became common practice. Early fenders which were used with open fires or grates are usually large, often 4 or 5 feet long. Coal brought smaller grates and most nineteenth century fenders are small, by as much as one or two feet. Fenders range from 4 inches high to 10 inches or more and the taller examples are usually later.

127 Pierced eighteenth-century brass fender. Victoria & Albert Museum, London.

Large fire-guards with copper or brass wire mesh fronts, to prevent sparks flying into the room, appear around 1800 and were at the peak of popularity in the 1850-1900s.

The earliest fire tool was probably the two-pronged fork, needed as an alternative to singeing one's boots kicking the logs back into the fireplace! With coal grates other tools were needed; tongs or shovel for putting fuel onto the fire, a poker to stir and revitalise the fire and sometimes too, a brush was needed to sweep up the ash into the ember bucket to take away. The tongs and shovel were the earliest additions and later in the eighteenth century came the poker. Tongs usually had a disc terminal for gripping, those with claws are mostly Victorian or even later.

Most fire tools were basically of iron or steel, but there are a few fine brass pairs. Many examples have copper or brass handles. Eighteenth century tools are usually 24 to 28 inches long, made for the larger fireplaces of the day. The smaller Victorian fireplace brought shorter tools, but there were larger sets made even as late as the 1930s.

Early fire-irons had baluster or acorn knopped handles, but later perhaps reflecting the changing styles of candlesticks, more elaborate shaped knops became popular.

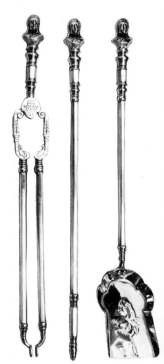

128 A fine set of brass fire tools with cast portraits of Queen Victoria c. 1870-90.

Sometimes you may find small pairs of brass tongs, 9 to 12 inches long. These were ember tongs, used for taking a small coal from the fire to light either a pipe or another fire. These were usually made with knopped handles. Beware of recent reproductions. Antique ember tongs should show considerable signs of wear and tear.

Bellows have been in use since medieval times; in the blacksmiths shops, in the brass workers forge and in the home. The increase in the supply of oxygen that a pair of bellows can provide makes a fire burn fiercely. Industrial bellows are often very large, but domestic bellows operated by hand mostly take the form that is still made today. Bellows are normally found in wood with leather used to make them air tight. Many have brass or copper nozzles, less frequently bellows are decorated with sheet copper or brass, fretted, engraved or embossed to add colour to the hearth. Early bellows have heavy large cast metal nozzles, but by the middle of the eighteenth century they become smaller and simpler. Another form of bellows which were used from 1750 onwards are mechanically operated by a wheel turned by hand which turns paddles to expel the air. These peat bellows, as they are now known, were popular in Ireland, but many were made in this country for use with coal fires. Like ordinary bellows these are mostly made of wood,

129 A late-seventeenth-century brass curfew.

130 Fine brass trivet dated 1668. Victoria & Albert Museum, London.

iron and leather with the brass or copper applied as decoration.

In the seventeenth century a device known to us today as a 'Curfew', a term derived from the French 'couvre feu' was used to place over the embers of a fire at night. There are fanciful stories of a curfew being applied to the fire at the curfew hour. This idea was the production of the nineteenth century romantic imagination. The curfew was one way of preventing sparks from flying into the room; remember how vulnerable the wooden homes of yesterday were to fire, or helping to keep the fire alive through the night. Most seventeenth or early-eighteenth-century curfews are Dutch in origin and are made in a rounded form embossed with patterns. They usually have a single handle made of the same metal. Later iron-handled curfews appear. They are also found with iron feet and with an iron grid across the back, presumably used in cooking. From this design came the better-known Dutch oven or Hastener with its sheet of metal reflecting back the heat of the fire to speed up the cooking of a joint or other food. Dutch ovens were imported into this country in the eighteenth century and many

673

of them were also made in this country. They were mostly made of tin or iron, but some have copper or brass decoration.

Just as the Dutch oven was placed before the open fire to cook on so the footman or trivet was used as a stand on which a kettle or pan could be placed in front of the fire. Trivets were first used in the middle of the seventeenth century. There is a fine example in the Victoria and Albert Museum dated 1668. Most early trivets had three legs as on an uneven surface three legs are more stable than four. Their legs were normally made of iron to withstand the heat of the fire. The top is usually made of brass or copper or at least decorated with these metals. Trivets are decorated in a number of ways, fretted, with punch decoration or engraved. Most early trivets are small, only big enough to take a single pot or kettle. Later trivets tend to be larger.

The use of coal in the house meant that it had to be brought into the house and stored near the fire. At first, buckets were used and coal stored in baskets or copper vats. In the eighteenth century special coal buckets were designed and by the start of the nineteenth century these had evolved into the helmet style coal bucket we are all familiar with. Most of these were made in brass or copper.

131 Design for a coal bucket introduced in 1851.

From the 1850s gas was used increasingly in the home. The kitchens of the Reform Club in London had gas cookers as early as 1841 and water heating by gas appeared only a few years later, but was limited in use to the homes of the well-to-do until the twentieth century. The Great Exhibition of 1851 had several gas-fired stoves on view and in the 1870s their use increased. But even in 1900 it would still be true that most domestic heat was provided by a traditional fire burning a coal or wood fuel.

Electricity was not used for heating until this century.

Whereas much brass, copper and bronze is highly utilitarian, most used in the fireplace is decorative. It's not surprising that this is so for the gleam of the flames reflected on the brass or copper around the fire will cheer up even the bleakest winter evening.

Chapter 14

General household uses

Although they were especially important in the kitchen and dining room, things in brass, bronze and copper were to be found in profusion everywhere in the home.

We probably prize the warming pan above all other objects. For us they are highly decorative, but in the past they had a more serious purpose. No electric blanket, centrally heated room or rubber hot water bottle for our great-grandparents! They will not have found the task of defeating icy toes too easy, but the warming pan was reasonably effective. A round-lidded box on a long handle, it was filled with burning coals or charcoal and put into the bed to take off the chill. To our minds this sounds a lethal way of keeping warm, both dirty and risky, but until the stoneware bottle of the mid nineteenth century it was the only way of having a warm bed short of sending your spouse in first, to warm it up!

Sizes do vary, but as a rough guide most seventeenth century pans are above 12 inches in diameter and many up to 15 inches or so. Whereas pans from 1750 tend to be below 12 inches. The bowls on early pans are deeper than those used later.

Originally, the lid fitted close to the base, clipping neatly over it. In later examples, after about 1750, the lid rests on a step within the body of the pan. Where the lid is very much larger than the body, suspect a marriage.

A very few fine pans have turned and knopped brass handles and Dutch pans, imported in the eighteenth century in considerable numbers, often have steel handles. Most eighteenth century and later pans have turned wood handles.

Early warming pans have finely fretted fronts, often engraved with coats of arms or religious scenes. The frets were not just for decoration, but allowed the smoke to escape. During the eighteenth century fretting and engraving were replaced by punch decoration. By the nineteenth century pans are plainer, often with rows of punched holes on the lid. In Victorian times whilst warming pans were still in use in rural

132 Two fine brass warming pans. On the left a brass handled pan inscribed 'The Earle of Essex his arms'. On the right with a steel and brass handle a pan engraved and fretted with flowers and birds. Both seventeenth century. Victoria & Albert Museum, London.

133 An eighteenth-century copper pan, the lid fitting into the body.

areas they began to be made simply for decoration. A warming pan, frequently filled with hot coals, is going to show substantial signs of wear: the base holed, the lid cracked by heat and the hinge given way. Pristine pans are decorative and thus of more recent origin.

Bedrooms were not the only cold and draughty places in the house. As we have seen in the large rooms of the seventeenth and eighteenth century temperatures seldom rose to what we would now consider satisfactory levels and anyone working in a library, reading or doing embroidery in the living room was likely to get cold feet. Churches too, although heated were cold places in winter and sermons were longer than they are today. The gentleman would have to stamp his feet, but the lady could take advantage of a foot-warmer; a box filled with hot coals or charcoal, placed beneath her voluminous skirts. Most foot-warmers were made in wood with a tin liner and perhaps not surprisingly few wooden footwarmers have survived undamaged. There are, however, some fine Dutch copper and brass ones, usually octagonal or square with fretted sides and decorated lid. Later examples are round with iron sides and plain copper or brass lids. Some of these may have been made in this country. The earliest ones that we can see date from around 1700 and by about 1820 they had gone out of fashion.

Before the nineteenth century metal beds were unknown, but by the 1850s servants were often provided with iron bedsteads and brass examples were becoming popular. A fine brass bed is very attractive and they command high prices today. Many of the Victorian patterns for brass bedsteads are being copied at the present time.

The night over, the task of preparing for the day also involved brass and copper utensils. Until this century most families would have had their morning wash in a hand basin of pottery, copper or brass and the hot water for washing and shaving came in a jug, often brass or copper.

Soap, an expensive commodity, was kept in small soap boxes frequently of copper or brass. Not until its cost dropped did we become more cavalier with it and let it melt away.

Bowls in bronze, copper and brass were in use from the earliest times, but few examples before the last decades of the seventeenth century will now be found. Bowls before 1700 or so have slightly rounded sides, rims parallel with the ground and pronounced central bosses similar to those seen on early pewter plates and dishes.

From about 1700 the sides become straighter and the rim tilts slightly upwards. The central boss remains till about 1730 when the base becomes flat.

Very similar styles of bowls were in use in Europe; indeed it is likely that most seventeenth century examples found in this country were made in Germany or Holland. Normandy bowls take a similar flat-bottomed form to our eighteenth century bowls but usually have decorated rims.

In recent years a number of Russian nineteenth-century bowls have been imported into this country; these have slightly concave sides and wide rims. Bowls are also to be

134 *Below:* Fine brass footwarmer. This is a Dutch piece but many similar footwarmers were made or used in this country, *c.* 1700-20.

135 *Right:* Domestic brass bowl with central boss. The boss which was out of fashion in pewter by 1660 continued in brass until about 1720, the date of this bowl. Used for most domestic purposes.

found which have been recently imported from the Middle East.

Nineteenth-century brass and copper bowls are less easily found than ones made in pottery. Pottery was cheaper. Bowls of this period are usually stamped out of sheet metal or shaped under pressure over a form, seldom cast.

Occasionally brass and copper bowls are found still with their nineteenth century jugs. There are a number of hot water jugs, some with lids, dating from 1870 onwards, still about. These take many forms, but are nearly all made of thin sheet metal with overlap or rolled seams. Few early soap boxes are English; most of the fine-fretted or plain-topped round boxes, with hinge and clip, are French. Later oval and round boxes, in thin sheet metal do still exist, some made for holding soap and the others for general domestic purposes.

Buckles were made in bronze from medieval times and from the mid eighteenth century buttons in brass, stamped out from sheets and decorated under the dies were made, in Birmingham particularly, in great quantities.

Drip-dry shirts are a blessing denied the housewife of the seventeenth century. For her smoothing she used a wooden board. By the 1700s irons were used. These had to be heated and therefore needed a small rest or stand to sit upon when not in use. Most early irons are of ferrous metal though occasionally you might find one decorated with brass. Many of the small stands, usually the shape of the iron, are made partly of brass. Another form of iron, the 'goffering' iron was used for shaping ruffles and flounces. The iron itself was ferrous, but the stand is usually made of brass. Goffering irons were in use from the eighteenth century but most that you will now see are nineteenth.

The next area to be examined is that of snuff-taking and tobacco smoking. Taking snuff, a mixture of tobacco and spices, inhaled up the nostril was a popular habit, especially amongst the more well-to-do. Cigarette smoking finally drove it out of fashion in the late nineteenth century. Gentlemen would carry their snuff in small decorated boxes and fine examples in silver, gold, agate and the like are much prized. There are also many brass and copper boxes, mostly nineteenth century. They come in all shapes, oval, round, square, rectangular, some plain, some decorated. Beware of boxes with early-eighteenth-century dates inscribed upon them for several factories were making such reproductions in the 1930s. The number of genuine eighteenth-century dated boxes is probably very small though fine examples are found in a

136 Sixteenth-century brass ring. Private collection.

number of collections.

The smoker used many different pieces of equipment; pipes for smoking, holders for storing the tobacco, cases for cigarettes, cutters for cigars, rests for pipes and pipe tampers.

Most pipes were made in clay up to the mid nineteenth century though a very few base metal pipes were around. Pipes made before the 1800s were all long-stemmed and are known as 'churchwarden's' pipes.

Most men had their own tobacco boxes. They are larger than we would now be likely to use; but were nevertheless easily fitted into the voluminous pockets of the eighteenth-century coat. Most of the boxes made before the 1750s are Dutch or German in origin. They are mostly rectangular in shape though there are a few oval boxes. Most are in brass, but you can also find them with copper sides and a brass lid, as well as all in copper. Many early boxes are decorated with embossed scenes. After about 1720 engraved boxes became popular. By the 1750s, boxes were being made in this country and the oval form became as popular as the older rectangular style. Boxes after 1750 tend to be plain, perhaps only inscribed with the owners name. In the 1800s personal tobacco boxes became smaller and much more common. They were still in use in the 1880s and plenty of genuine dated examples from the later Victorian period exist, some of the small personal boxes were also made in unusual shapes including the heart, some were fitted with combination locks to prevent the theft of the costly tobacco.

Table tobacco boxes were bulky objects. Found in most basic shapes they were made in a number of materials including lead, iron, pewter, copper and brass. Most of these boxes are nineteenth century. Many have finials representing human figures or animals on the lids and originally they all had lead or heavy metal pressers inside which rested on the tobacco to keep it moist and compact.

Some of the brass boxes of the 1850-1900 period are very elaborate, shaped in the form of medieval caskets, the sphinx or other unusual designs.

Pipe tampers were made in the nineteenth century, small objects, they were used to push the tobacco down into the bowl of the pipe. Many are in brass.

The cigarette was first smoked towards the end of the nineteenth century. The earliest cigarette boxes are thus late Victorian or Edwardian. Most are made in silver or plate, but a few brass or copper examples were made around the turn of the century. Cigar cutters are another piece of smoking equipment and some were made in or decorated with copper or brass.

Pipe rests, small sloping stands which were made to hold the pipe when lit but not being smoked, also occur from the late Victorian period and some of these were made in brass in the shape of boats or birds.

We are used to the fountain pen, the felt tip or the ball point; all with their own ink supply. Until the late nineteenth century the pen had to be dipped into the ink. Most people wrote with a quill until steel nibs came into fashion.

Ink stands, known as standishes were extensively used. They were basically small trays on which stood pots or containers. Most standishes have either square, rectangular, round or oval trays holding from three to five objects. One pot was for ink and another for sand used for drying the ink. This was called the 'paunce pot'. Additional containers, a bell, a stand for the quills and a holder for the taper might also be provided.

Some fine eighteenth-century standishes can be seen. Most from this period have three containers. The more elaborate sets with finely polished thinner containers and where screws have been used to fasten the pots to the stand are Victorian or later. The bulk of those seen today are less than 100 years old and with experience it will soon be possible to sort out those made by hand from the machine-made later examples.

137 Brass wax Jack. The thin wax wick was curled round the base on the narrow stem and fed up through the small candleholder which was opened and shut via the pincers on the right. This is from about 1830. Cambridge and County Folk Museum.

For travelling scribes, pen cases holding a small pot for the ink, have been made from medieval times. Two very fine seventeenth-century dated examples made in Sheffield can be seen in the Victoria and Albert Museum. Later plainer examples were made but care should be taken with these as many pen cases were also made in the Middle East and these are very similar in style to those made in Europe.

Many other items for the house were made in brass and copper. Watch cases to fit the half-hunter watches, clock faces for the popular long case clocks, watch stands for placing the watch in at night, for example. The ladies used brass and copper thimbles, fed their birds in brass cages, kept their keys and scissors on brass chatelaines and rang brass bells for service. They kept their jewellery and face creams in brass and copper pots and boxes, put their plants and flowers in copper vases or pots, held back their curtains, which ran on brass poles, with brass curtain grips and kept the doors of the rooms open with brass 'porters'. The multiplicity of objects made in brass and copper is enormous. It is natural that most of these are nineteenth century and probably most from the last half of the century, for it was only when the demand for the essential equipment for the home had been filled by the brass and

138 Hanging brass wall box. Larger examples were for candles or salt, smaller boxes for spices and various household objects. This is a nineteenth-century example.

139 Fifteenth century bronze personal seal. The engraving is especially interesting as it portrays two common metalworkers' tools; the hammer and pincers. Private collection.

copper smiths that the peripheral areas could be catered for.

In the eighteenth and nineteenth centuries there were several styles of hanging wall-boxes to be found about the home, most were in wood, but some were in copper and brass. Some were large enough to hold candles, others perhaps used for salt, spices, flour or other household materials.

In those rooms most frequently used, several candles will have been lit at any one time. After an hour or so these will have had to be replaced so there was a need for a ready supply of candles. Two principal forms of metal candle boxes were used. One basically rectangular with a hinged flat lid and a backplate for hanging on the wall, the other a round type also with a small backplate, but with a rounded hinged lid. Similar boxes were also used for other household purposes and it is not always easy to see at once the purpose of such a box. Very thin rolled sheet metal boxes with soldered or overlap seams are probably of recent origin for there were many reproductions being made in the 1920s.

Several pieces of brass would have been found in the study or library. For the sealing of letters and documents, and remember that envelopes are a recent invention, sealing wax was used. The flame needed to melt this wax was provided by a wax jack or taper candlestick. Most taper sticks are made like a very small candlestick and in the eighteenth century were made in all the popular styles. These are much rarer in the nineteenth century. Some of the Victorian small candlesticks are not taper sticks at all but made as toys for the nursery. Wax jacks are special devices which held not a small candle as with the taper stick, but a very much thinner and longer waxed thread. This was curled round the base of the stand and led up to the grip at the top, operated with finger and thumb. The heat of the flame would soften the waxed thread and allow it to be pulled through into position from time to time.

Jacks of a different form were in use in the 1700s, but most of those we now see from the late eighteenth or nineteenth century, take this form. Where the round bases are solid the jack is probably eighteenth century, where fretted from the nineteenth century.

Hand-cut seals in bronze have been made for ecclesiastical and personal use since the fourteenth century; occasionally these may be seen for sale. From the seventeenth century seals in wood, silver and brass were popular, but the majority of seals now available date from the nineteenth century. They carry crests from coats of arms or the owners initials and brass examples are not very common.

Appendix:
the level of survival

What are the chances that the candlestick on your mantlepiece is from the seventeenth century or that the warming pan on your great-aunt's wall is a genuine antique?

I have preached a certain scepticism throughout this book. Let me now try and show why this is necessary.

Anything made for use in the home will have a limited life. Some things will last for years, others will cease to be useful after a short period. We all know this only too well.

There is a natural life cycle for all things and domestic metalware is no exception. This will vary for individual objects within a class according to use and other factors.

Most brass and bronze objects will (probably) last a good many years before they break and have to be replaced. Pewter has a lower life expectancy.

Generally once the average life of an object has been reached there will be a steadily faster rate of depreciation until finally a plateau of what survives is achieved. Then it is kept apart, treated with a new respect as a survivor and its future more or less assured.

The speed of change can also be affected by dramatic changes in taste. A large proportion of gas and oil lamps will have been discarded in the 1920s with the widespread adoption of electricity. The two World Wars, with their calls for scrap for armaments must have speeded up the loss of many metal objects.

A series of theoretical life expectancy graphs are illustrated here. I think that you will accept that there is a natural life expectancy for most objects though it is not easy to quantify this.

For pewter we might expect a plate to last some twenty years on average, whereas brass and bronze cooking pots might survive for sixty or seventy years.

Now let us make an assumption. Let us assume that there is some domestic metal object which has been made over the last two hundred years at an even rate of production. That is each

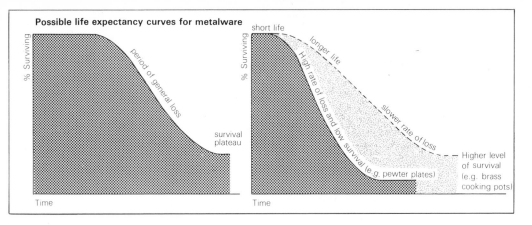

Possible life expectancy curves for metalware

% Surviving · period of general loss · survival plateau · Time

% Surviving · short life · longer life · High rate of loss and low survival (e.g. pewter plates) · slower rate of loss · Higher level of survival (e.g. brass cooking pots) · Time

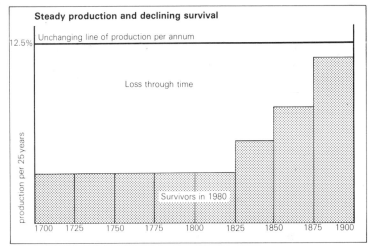

Steady production and declining survival

12.5% Unchanging line of production per annum

Loss through time

production per 25 years

Survivors in 1980

1700 1725 1750 1775 1800 1825 1850 1875 1900

year the same number of items are made. Annually therefore, $\frac{1}{2}$ per cent of all those made will have been produced. So that for every 25-year period since 1700 to 1900 $12\frac{1}{2}$ per cent of all those items made will have been produced. But all will not have survived.

Let us next impose on this pattern of production a survival curve. Let us assume that the objects will all last 50 years and that thereafter they will be thrown away at a steady rate until a plateau of survival is reached which leaves us 20 per cent of the objects.

You will appreciate that this will change the proportion of the total we can expect to have lasted from each period. The chances of survival of those made in 1700-25 will be less than those made in 1875-1900.

The effect of this assumed rate of loss on the age of those that will have lasted is illustrated in a graph. Whereas $12\frac{1}{2}$ per cent were, we assumed, made between 1700-25 only one-fifth will

683

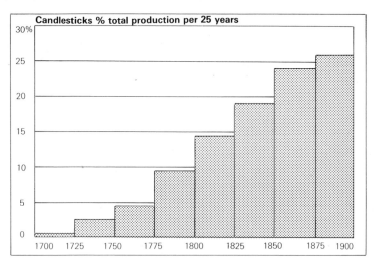

Candlesticks % total production per 25 years

have survived whereas of the similar amount made in the last quarter of the nineteenth century all will have lasted according to our theoretical analysis. This will considerably affect the age pattern of those that have endured. Only 7 per cent will now be over 175 years old; a very much smaller proportion than we started with.

Now let us turn nearer the real world; nothing has been made in equal proportions over 200 years. The population has risen eight-fold in this time. The amounts of copper used in industry rose ten times in the eighteenth century and at least eight times in the nineteenth. Not all of this will have been used in domestic metalware, but there will have been a very great increase in total production of brass objects for the house.

I have made an attempt to quantify the production of brass candlesticks in relative terms over the last 200 years. These theoretical production figures are illustrated.

You will see that I propose that less than $\frac{1}{2}$ per cent of all the candlesticks made will have been produced before 1725 whilst over half will come from after 1850.

These production figures do not yet take into account the natural losses that time brings. I assume here a life of some 75 years with a steady decline thereafter for another 85 years until a plateau of survival is reached at 15 per cent.

If these figures are applied to the production figures the picture will change considerably. The proportion of candlesticks made before 1725 will fall to around 0·14 per cent while candlesticks made after 1850 will now represent over 68 per cent of the total that survive.

It is possible to argue with the levels of production and the rate of decline and the final survival level, but the basic theory

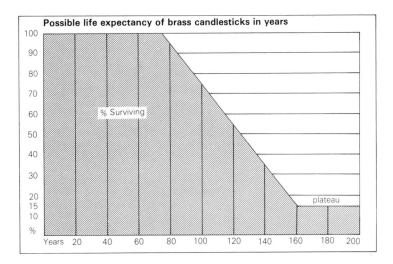

Possible life expectancy of brass candlesticks in years

% Surviving

plateau

Years 20 40 60 80 100 120 140 160 180 200

is I think clear.

If anything I think it is possible that I have underestimated the amount that is lost, leaving the plateau of survival still too high and again probably overestimated the levels of production in the eighteenth century.

Let us now take a single practical example. The exact figures must of course be taken with a degree of caution, as they are based on statistical assumptions as to the population, family size and ownership patterns of the population long before any reliable figures are available. We know from the study of inventories already mentioned in this book that where homes had pewter *circa* 1650-1700 there was on average $1\frac{1}{2}$ pewter candlesticks per house. Take the population at that date and eliminate half as being too poor to own such a possession, calculate the number of households and you will find that there were around 700,000 candlesticks in pewter in Britain, about 1700. Yet we know that less than 500 have survived; a level of survival of 0·07 per cent.

Brass and bronze will have had a longer active life and may endure in larger proportions than pewter.

The overall message is clear. Antiques more than 150 years old are uncommon and objects that have lasted from the 1700s are rare – the few who have managed to survive the tribulations of a long and active life.

Given this basic theoretical analysis it would be possible to count the numbers that have survived of certain objects and work backwards to the kind of levels that such a survival would imply. I suggest that in some fields, this might engender a certain anxiety! The numbers of 'seventeenth'-century coffers about imply a rather larger population than existed!

Glossary

Alloy A mixture of metals; an amalgam.

Andirons Fire dogs, bars of metal on feet used to rest logs on in the fireplace.

Antimony Bluish-white metallic element used in several alloys in small quantities.

Battery The term for copper and brass products that have been hammered by hand or under presses; 'battered' into sheet. Sometimes also used in the past as a general term for copper-alloy products.

Bismuth A reddish-white metallic element used in pewter and in other alloys.

Bobeché The loose fitting candleholder. In early candlesticks the holder or sconce was part of the candlestick, later it was made as a separate part and fitted loosely into the candlestick and was known as a bobeché (from the French).

Booge or Bouge The part of a plate or dish between the rim and the bottom or base; the side of the plate. The bouge traditionally had to be hammered in flatware manufacture in the pewter industry to give it additional strength.

Brass An alloy of copper and zinc; pure brass is mostly late eighteenth century or more modern. The earlier alloys of copper, sometimes called brass, usually contained other additional elements.

Brazen A description applied to copper alloys that have been cast; sometimes brass sometimes bronze or similar alloys.

Britannia metal A term used to describe the products of the last period of the pewter industry's eminence. Sometimes used to denote an alloy without lead (but with antimony) but as this was also strictly pewter, more exactly a method of manufacture of pewter using forms or patterns and shaping the material rather than by casting.

Bronze An alloy of copper and tin. Often also contained other materials.

Chock An item used to hold a piece of wood or metalware so that it can be turned on a lathe or formed round a pattern; the wedge or support used to prevent an object slipping off a machine.

Chopin A Scottish term (from the French) for a half Scottish pint or tappit hen (roughly 30 fl. ounces). Also used to describe the second size of tappit hen measure; of chopin capacity.

Copper The basic material used for making brass and bronze as well as an additional element in pewter.

Drip pan A rim or circle of metal sometimes placed half way up the candlestick (hence mid drip pan); sometimes nearer the base to catch the melted wax and prevent it from spreading onto the furniture.

Fine metal A term used in the pewter craft to denote the top quality tin alloy; usually a mixture of tin and copper with some other materials.

Flange The bent back edge of a plate or other item; a method of strengthening the construction of an item of pewter or copper alloy by turning the rim back on itself.

Gadrooned A form of decoration, usually cast, where the edges are shaped in scallops or fashioned into a series of convex curves.

Hollow ware A term used for items made in pewter and other materials which are not made in the flat; flagons, tankards etc.

Journeyman A fully qualified craftsman working as an employee for a master.

Latten A term used to describe copper alloys such as brass which have been hammered into sheet. Also loosely used to describe copper-alloy products that have been cast.

Lay Another pewterers' term denoting a lower quality material with lead as an addition to tin.

Mutchkin The quarter Scottish pint, similarly used as a name for the mutchkin, or half chopin (15 fl. ounces).

Ormolu A form of gilding; also an alloy for jewellery.

Pewter An alloy of tin with other elements such as lead, copper and later antimony.

Reeding A descriptive term used for the form of decoration mostly found on pewter plates and dishes. Sometimes incised into the rim, later cast with it. Brass and copper alloy items are also often reeded in this way.

Repoussé A form of decoration. The sheet metal is either cast or hammered so that the pattern is lifted on the front and hollow on the back of the object.

Sad ware A term for flat ware, or plates and dishes.

Sconce A reflecting back plate for a candleholder. Also a socket used to hold candles.

Trifle An expression identifying smaller less important items of pewter such as spoons and small boxes. Trifle metal was an alloy made of old pewter and tin suitable for such purposes. All three terms, *Fine metal*, *Lay metal* and *Trifle* had precise meanings, historically, in theory but in practice few alloys conform to any one description exactly.

Wrigglework The most famous form of decoration in British pewter, undertaken with a hammer and nail by a member of the work shop which made the object rather than by a professional.

Wrythen Another method of decoration where the shape of the body is formed, usually by casting, by twisting or distorting the line.

SILVER

BRAND INGLIS

Chapter 1

The goldsmith's trade

The extraordinary qualities of silver, a metal which is at once beautiful to look at, easy to work, useful and hard-wearing, were recognised in prehistoric times. The ancient civilisations of the Near East used it (there are many references to silver in the Old Testament), Homer's heroes drank from silver goblets, and the Celts fashioned objects of mysterious splendour from silver. It is the most malleable of metals after gold and can be worked by skilful craftsmen into remarkably delicate forms, while its lustrous grey colour can be polished to a brilliant finish.

During the early Middle Ages silver virtually disappeared in Europe, probably because the local mines had been worked out. Around the end of the ninth century, large deposits of gold and silver were discovered in the Rhineland, and medieval European goldsmiths (a more common term than 'silversmith' which means the same, since no smith worked exclusively in gold) were supplied from this German source. However, not every article was made from new metal; on the contrary, silver articles which had become worn, broken or old-fashioned were frequently melted to be used for a new piece. In the sixteenth century, when German silver was becoming scarce, the Spanish empire builders in the New World discovered the immensely rich silver mines of Mexico, Peru and Bolivia. Much silver is still supplied by Mexico today, though larger quantities now come from North America and Australia.

Pure silver is too soft for normal use, and it must therefore be alloyed, i.e. combined with another metal, to make it harder. Though other base metals were used in the distant past, copper has long been established as the most useful for this purpose. In the sterling standard, to which for the most part all English silver has adhered for seven centuries or more, the proportions are 11 ounces 2 pennyweights of silver to 18 pennyweights of copper, which is equivalent to 925 parts per thousand pure silver.

The craft of the goldsmith is an ancient one which has changed remarkably little over the course of many centuries.

1 One of a fine pair of silver-gilt covered cups made by Nathaniel Underwood in 1699. They were made for John, 3rd Duke of Newcastle, K.G., and show his arms engraved within the Garter motto.

The tools and techniques used in a goldsmith's workshop in—for example—the eighteenth century would be largely familiar to a modern craftsman or a medieval one.

The typical goldsmith's shop was run by a master goldsmith, a man who had served his seven-years apprenticeship in the trade and been accepted as a freeman of the Goldsmiths' Company. To assist him he usually had at least one journeyman who received a regular wage. The journeyman was, like his master, a qualified craftsman, but he chose to work for a master, perhaps because he did not have the capital to set up shop on his own. Very often his employer was the man under whom he had served his apprenticeship. There were also one or two apprentices, boys contracted to the trade at an early age who learned the craft while assisting the goldsmith and lived as members of his family. In spite of many stories of mistreatment, apprentices were protected by their articles of apprenticeship, and unless they had the bad luck to serve under a particularly brutal or unpleasant man their existence was reasonably comfortable by the standards of the time.

One way to understand the daily work of a goldsmith's shop is to follow the progress of a single article—a coffee pot for example—from start to finish.

The master goldsmith first makes a drawing of the coffee pot he intends to fashion, which he discusses with his patron, for in those days there was often a direct relationship between craftsman and customer, and the manufacturer was, as a rule, also the retailer. One important question to be discussed is the amount of silver that will go into the article, as this will obviously affect the price to be charged. The customer himself may hand over some old, unwanted silver, which is weighed and credited against the final bill.

The old silver is melted down together with sufficient new metal to make up the total amount required. The silver ingot that results is hammered into a thickish pancake shape by the master and journeyman, using a heavy, two-handed sledge hammer. With lighter hammers, the metal is gradually beaten out into a thinner sheet, as evenly as the experienced eye of the goldsmith can measure. The long and tiresome procedure of turning a chunky ingot into a thin sheet was gradually taken over by the rolling machine in the late eighteenth century.

When the metal has been hammered to the correct gauge, the goldsmith marks a circle on it with a pair of heavy dividers, and the metal beyond the circular outline is trimmed off with shears. The next step is to 'sink' the body of the pot. The circular sheet is held over a hollowed-out section of tree trunk,

2 *Far left:* The apprentice holds the silver ingot as the goldsmith slowly hammers it into a flat sheet. These photographs are stills from an excellent film made at the James Geddy shop in Colonial Williamsburg, in the United States.

3 *Left:* A circular piece of silver is then cut out and the fashioning process begins.

4 *Above:* The circular disc has been sunk and the goldsmith begins to raise the body of the coffee pot on his raising stake.

and with a round-faced 'blocking' hammer, the flat sheet is slowly and patiently hammered into the hollow. The smith begins at the edge of the sheet, turning it fractionally after each blow and making a pattern of concentric circles of steadily diminishing diameter, until every part of the metal has been struck and the rows of concentric circles have reached the centre.

When the sheet is removed from the block, it has acquired a strongly dished shape. The practised eye of the goldsmith tells him whether or not he has managed to sink it evenly all round.

The constant hammering and stretching of the metal distorts its crystal structure, making it brittle and liable to crack. To overcome this it must be annealed. In a dark corner of the workshop one of the apprentices has prepared a fire. The silver is placed in a pan called a 'hearth' and turned around in the heat until it glows a dull cherry red. This requires fine judgment and a practised eye; the dim light makes it easier to tell when the right stage has been reached, whereupon the silver is quenched in a tub of water standing nearby. The reheating or annealing process allows the crystal structure to adjust to the new shape of the metal, making it soft and workable again. It must be repeated many times in the course of working.

The 'sinking' of the circle of silver is followed by 'raising'. The dish-shaped circle is worked over a cast-iron anvil called a raising stake. Turning the silver all the time, the goldsmith begins hammering it, starting at the centre of the base and making a series of concentric circles of steadily increasing diameter, until the edge is reached. The edge, which will become the rim of the pot, is hammered down all round to thicken it. The silver is then annealed again and the process is repeated over a slightly narrower raising stake. With each working, the body of the pot advances further towards its final form, becoming elongated and vase-shaped. Finally the goldsmith lays down his raising hammers, judging that he has achieved the final shape of the pot. To aid his expert eye, he places it on a lathe, which reveals any slight deviations. Depending on the size and shape of the coffee pot, the process of raising the body takes about one working day.

Although the body of the pot is now in its final form, the raising hammers have left it in a comparatively rough state, a mass of circular hammer marks which must be painstakingly removed by planishing. The body is placed over a rounded stake and struck all over with a heavy, flat-faced hammer. It is here that the ability of a true master is most evident, as he carefully flattens out irregularities, gradually creating by eye and hammer alone a final texture smooth enough for polishing. At this exacting stage of the work, the young apprentices will be watching closely, while the hammer rises and falls and the silver is turned constantly on the stake so that no hammer blow falls in exactly the same spot as another.

While the master has been raising the body, the journeyman has been preparing the various other pieces which have to be cast and fixed to the pot—the spout, the handle sockets, the

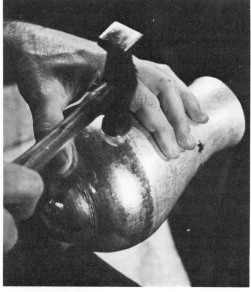

5 *Far left:* The body is turned on a lathe to check that it is absolutely true.

6 *Above:* The body is carefully planished until all the uneven areas are flattened out.

7 *Left:* The spout is first fashioned in modelling clay to make sure the proportions are correct.

8 The journeyman prepares the sand casting-blocks; the spout is cast in two halves.

foot and the finial for the lid. The master may have casting patterns, but if not he must model the spout and other parts in wood, plaster or modelling wax. The spout is the most difficult, and while carving it, the master frequently holds it against the pot to ensure that the proportions are right. The model of the piece to be cast is pressed into a type of sand held in an iron box which is made in two parts. When the model has been pressed halfway into the sand in the lower half, the whole is dusted over with charcoal or some similar substance to ensure that the two halves of the sand-filled box will separate easily. The top half of the model is pressed into the sand in the upper part of the box. The two parts are pressed together, then separated and the model removed, leaving a perfect mould in the sand, which dries hard. The mould is then held firmly together while the molten silver is poured in and time is allowed for it to cool and set.

The cast pieces are finally fixed to the pot with solder, a tricky operation that demands meticulous neatness. Probably the foot is soldered first. It is clamped to the body with silver wire, then small pieces of silver alloyed with brass (nowadays zinc, which gives a harder solder) are placed around the join. The goldsmith takes a long thin pipe which he uses to blow a flame from a charcoal lamp directly at the solder, which melts and flows around the join. After it has cooled and hardened, the two parts of the pot should be firmly attached. Any superfluous pieces of solder beneath the foot are polished off on a lathe.

The spout is made in two halves which must first be soldered together. A hole is then cut in the body of the pot where the spout is to be soldered in place or, if a strainer is required, a

9 Soldering, with a charcoal brazier and blowpipe.

group of small holes are made with a bow drill. The lid will be attached to the body by a hinge, made from tubular silver, which is soldered on along with the sockets for the handle. The handle itself is not, of course, made of silver, which would be too hot to hold, but usually of wood. The goldsmith probably buys a ready-made fruitwood handle from a turner or a handle-maker. It is held in the sockets by two silver pins.

Assuming that the pot is a plain one, with no extra ornamental work to be done, it is now complete, though in a rough unpolished state, and ready to be assayed, or tested, to ensure that it is of sterling standard. The goldsmith first puts his maker's punch mark on it. The fineness of the silver content is strictly his responsibility, and he would place his mark on the piece even if it were some small item made entirely by his journeyman.

At the assay office, minute scrapings of silver are taken from each part of the pot, and analysed to ensure that the entire pot is made of sterling standard silver; there are several, comparatively simple ways of making a chemical test. If the silver comes up to standard, it is 'touched' with the hall marks of the assay office and returned to the goldsmith. All silver was and is supposed to be assayed but occasionally, perhaps for no more important reason than the customer's eagerness to have the article quickly, this legal obligation was neglected. The absence of hall marks does not necessarily mean that silver is not of sterling standard.

The coffee pot was sent to the assay office unpolished, and the finishing touches are made after its return to the workshop. Probably the apprentices undertake the job, as for the most part it does not demand special skill, unless, for instance, there is some chasing to be done on the spout, to smooth out possible irregularities in casting. There are three stages in polishing, using successively finer abrasives. To get rid of substantial scratches, file marks or 'firestains' (caused by oxidisation of the copper alloy during annealing) and to remove the marks of planishing, ground pumice mixed with oil is used, probably on a wheel. This first stage may be unnecessary if the planishing has been done very expertly, and in that case Tripoli powder or Trent sand, less abrasive than pumice, will be sufficient, followed by the third stage, jeweller's rouge rubbed in by hand (some goldsmiths use the inside of their forearm). The coffee pot is at last finished and ready to be delivered to the person who commissioned it.

There are other ways of making a vessel similar to that described above. Seaming, for example, is an easier and more rapid way. In this method, a sheet of silver is bent around to form an open-ended cylinder, and the two edges are soldered together. The cylinder is then hammered into the required shape over the raising stake, and a disc of silver is soldered to the bottom end.

Another method quite common today, though it was also used in ancient Egypt, is spinning. A flat sheet of silver is rotated on a lathe and worked into shape on a pre-formed chuck made of hard wood. The spinner applies pressure with a steel-headed tool with a long handle which he steadies under his arm.

A very important tool in the goldsmith's shop is the wire drawer. This is a long wooden rack-like device to draw silver wire into various thicknesses, which has been in use in England since the sixteenth century at least. A rod of silver, tapered at one end so that it can be drawn more easily, is drawn through holes of diminishing size, making it progressively thinner. Silver wire can be drawn so fine that it can be manipulated like thread for decorative work and for strengthening the rims of vessels. The wire must be annealed several times in the course of the work as drawing, like hammering, makes the silver hard and brittle.

The process of making a coffee pot outlined above does not include any ornamental work. Some people prefer their silver plain, relying for its effect on shape and surface, but in most periods silver has received some form of decoration. There are a variety of different ways in which silver can be decorated, but basically they all fall into one of three groups: applied decoration, made separately; embossed decoration, in which the metal is hammered, punched or otherwise manipulated; and engraved decoration, in which it is cut or incised. The main types and techniques involved in the decoration of English silver are best described in an alphabetical list.

10 Acanthus

Acanthus A classical motif representing the prickly leaves of the acanthus plant, used in a formalised way in the capitals of Corinthian columns in Greek architecture, and common in silver, both embossed and applied.

Amorini Putti or cherubs, a common decorative motif in the Baroque period.

11 Anthemion

Anthemion A stylised classical motif based on the honeysuckle flower; found on silver of the Adam period usually as part of a decorative band. A single anthemion is sometimes to be seen under the spouts of jugs.

695

Applied Ornamental wire, mouldings or cast pieces which were made separately from the main body of the article and soldered on are said to be 'applied'. Applied ornament is sometimes purely decorative but may also serve to strengthen the body of the piece.

Arabesque Engraved ornament of intertwined foliage, found most frequently in the late sixteenth and early seventeenth centuries, and in pierced work of the eighteenth century.

Baluster An elongated pear shape of varying breadth, like a banister (baluster) in a staircase, sometimes incorporating an inverted acorn. Wine cups frequently had baluster stems in the late sixteenth century, and most eighteenth-century candlesticks are in one of many possible baluster forms. This type of stem was generally made by soldering two castings together, thus ensuring perfect symmetry. It is generally possible to see the solder line running along either side of the stem.

Beading A cast wire shaped like a string of small beads, usually found as a decorative addition on the borders of salvers, tea sets and sauceboats from about 1760 to about 1820, though also occurring in the late nineteenth century.

12 *Above:* Arabesque

13 *Left:* Beading

14 Bright-cut engraving

696

15 Chasing

Bombé A swelling, bulbous, kettle-like form in a vessel such as a soup tureen.

Bright-cut engraving A visually striking form of engraving used in the late eighteenth and early nineteenth centuries. Instead of incising lines in the silver, the engraving tool gouges out cleanly and flicks away tiny particles, leaving a jewel-like faceted line which catches the light brilliantly.

Burnishing Polishing with a hard smooth stone or, nowadays, steel.

Cartouche A device containing the owner's initials, coat of arms, etc., engraved, chased or cast; it often formed an important part of the overall design in the early eighteenth century, incorporating shells, masks and foliage.

Caryatid A female figure used as a column in classical architecture, sometimes adopted for the handles of porringers.

Castwork Decorative or functional elements made in a mould and soldered on to the vessel.

Chasing Decoration in relief made with a hammer and a multitude of punches of different shapes. The metal is raised or pushed in to form patterns of, chiefly, flowers, foliage or figures. Chasing has been done through the centuries, enjoying periods of great popularity and periods of almost complete disuse. The sixteenth and early seventeenth centuries used it extensively, but from about 1610 to 1640 or 1650 it was much less popular and though still done it was far less robust and exuberant. In the second half of the seventeenth century embossed chasing became again very fashionable, but from 1690 to 1740 it was scarcely used at all. In vogue during the Rococo period, it was used in a more limited way in the Adam style, though the Rococo revival of the nineteenth century adopted it once more. See also *Flat chasing.*

Chinoiserie Pseudo-Chinese designs, fashionable in flat-chased form in the 1680s, chased form in the mid-eighteenth century and applied form in the early nineteenth century.

Coats of arms Heraldic engraving on plate is a study of which anyone who is seriously interested in collecting English silver should have at least rudimentary knowledge. From the type of shield and the style of its surrounding cartouche, the date of an engraving can be determined to within a few years, which is a great help in dating a piece of silver that has no marks, or a maker's mark only, and a greater knowledge may reveal the

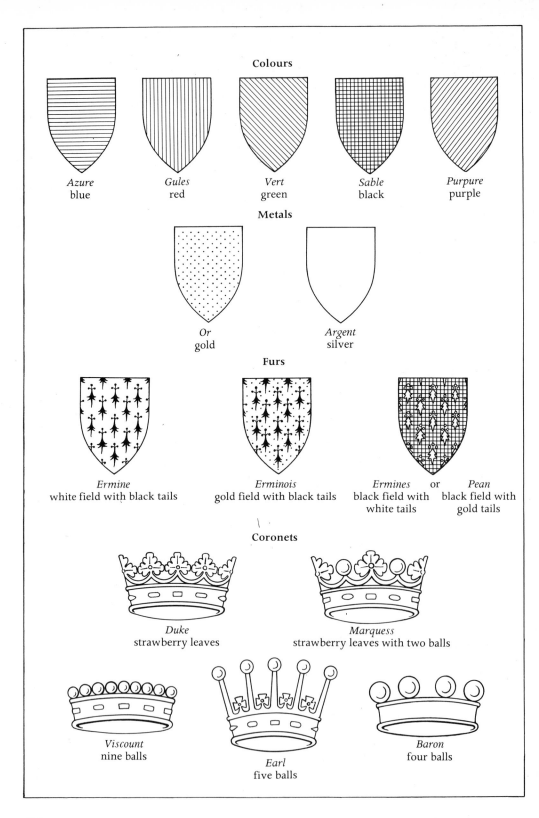

Colours

Azure
blue

Gules
red

Vert
green

Sable
black

Purpure
purple

Metals

Or
gold

Argent
silver

Furs

Ermine
white field with black tails

Erminois
gold field with black tails

Ermines or **Pean**
black field with   black field with
white tails   gold tails

Coronets

Duke
strawberry leaves

Marquess
strawberry leaves with two balls

Viscount
nine balls

Earl
five balls

Baron
four balls

16 Heraldry: c. 1680

17 Heraldry: c. 1730

18 Cut-card work

Opposite: The system of engravings conventionally used on silver to indicate heraldic colours, metals, furs and coronets.

original owner of the piece. Altogether, a genuine interest in heraldry will be found to add a fascinating new dimension to the collecting of English silver. This is not the place to attempt even the briefest explanation of the highly complex subject of heraldry, which has a language all its own, but one common mistake should be pointed out. A coat or shield of arms is not the same as a family crest, in spite of the belief of numerous people to the contrary. The crest, originally worn on the helmet, can belong to many unrelated families. A coat of arms may do so also, but much less frequently, while a full achievement of arms – crest, coat, supporters, motto and so on – ought, in theory anyway, to be attributable to one family alone.

C-scroll A term chiefly applied to the handles of cups and other vessels formed roughly in the shape of a C.

Cut-card work A simple but very attractive form of applied decoration found in very basic form as early as 1640 but more characteristic of the period from 1660 to 1710. It consists of sheet silver cut in foliate, trefoil or fleur-de-lys designs and soldered on to the main body of the piece. It occurs most often as a calyx for a bowl or as a border. It was also used, mainly in the first decade of the eighteenth century, as a decorative feature around joints, such as the emerging handles of coffee pots, and in that position served the additional purpose of strengthening the joint.

Diaperwork Engraved or flat-chased patterns resembling a trellis or lozenge-shaped network.

Egg and dart Ornament used for mouldings, usually stamped, found in the sixteenth century. It consists of a series of ovolos (eggs) alternating with spear-like forms (darts).

Egg and tongue Similar to egg and dart, and found in the same period; the ovolos are interspersed with a small tongue-like motif.

Embossing Strictly speaking, the form of chasing in which the metal is hammered and worked from the inside surface, pushing it outward, but frequently used in a more general sense. See *Chasing; Repoussé.*

Engraving A form of decoration which consists of lines cut in the surface of the metal, in reality a whole art form in itself. The engraver of silver cuts into the surface and actually removes the metal with a graver, or burrin, in a series of lines, some deep

699

19 Flat chasing

20 Gadrooning

and some shallow to form shading and give a three-dimensional effect. Engraving was the method for inscribing names and coats of arms, but was also used for purely decorative work, particularly in the staggering pictorial engraving found on a small group of sixteenth-century silver and that done in the late seventeenth and early eighteenth centuries by Gribelin or Hogarth. Engraving is probably the most important aspect of silver which was not done by the goldsmith himself. It was a separate skill, and the work would be sent out to an artist-engraver. See also *Bright-cut engraving*; *Coats of arms*.

21 Greek key

Etching A technique similar to engraving except that the metal is bitten out by acid instead of being cut with a graver; very rare in English silver, though used occasionally in the sixteenth century.

Feather edge Chased slanting lines, as seen on the edges of some spoon handles.

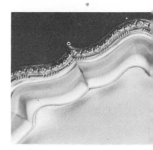

22 Guilloche

Festoon A garland of fruit or flowers suspended at either end, which is found engraved or, more often, chased or stamped. It was used as a decorative device in the sixteenth century and the second half of the eighteenth century.

Flat chasing Decoration in low relief which, like chasing, *moves* the silver rather than *removing* it. When done extremely finely it can look like engraving. A quick test is to look at the back: if the imprint of the decoration is visible, the piece has been flat chased; if not, it is engraved.

Fluting A pattern of concave chased channels running parallel, adopted from the fluted column of classical architecture.

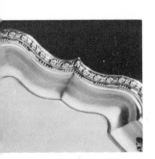

Gadrooning Similar to beading except the 'beads' are roughly oval in form rather than circular; frequently found after about 1690 on the borders of plates and dishes, salt cellars and sauceboats.

Greek key An ornamental band of geometric, repetitive pattern made up of a series of right angles, popular chiefly from about 1780 to 1810.

Guilloche Moulded border ornament of two interlacing bands enclosing a quatrefoil or rosette at tightly spaced intervals; found throughout the eighteenth century but perhaps more used by the Huguenots before about 1750.

Knop A bulb-shaped projection in the stem of a candlestick, goblet, etc.; also, the finial of a cup or spoon.

Matting A form of ornament made by striking the silver many times with a hollow tubular punch, to give a dull, rough surface; it was frequently used as a background for some ornamental motif, giving it more of a three-dimensional effect, but in the seventeenth century it was often used as a decorative element on its own.

Ogee An S-shaped curve made by alternate concave and convex surfaces.

Ovolo A convex oval or egg-shaped ornament, chiefly used repetitively in a border in the sixteenth century and occasionally in later periods.

Parcel-gilt Partly gilded.

Patera A circular ribbed motif usually encircling a flower head.

Piercing Fretwork decoration, the silver being cut out by saw (since the eighteenth century) or by chisel in a pattern of some kind. On the top of a caster it served a practical purpose; in a cake basket, for example, it is purely decorative. Pierced work is sometimes found as applied decoration.

Pricking Engraving made with a needle point, used mainly for inscriptions, coats of arms, etc.

Pouncing A stippled effect made by lightly pricking the metal, a decorative detail used mainly in the late seventeenth century.

Punched A term sometimes given to the rather primitive embossed decoration, usually of simple floral designs, on some seventeenth-century silver.

701

Reeding Engraved or moulded ornament usually found on the rims or edges of objects, consisting of parallel lines dividing convex forms.

Repoussé Decoration in high relief made by beating out the metal from the back, the richest form of ornament, especially fashionable in the mid-seventeenth century. It was often combined with surface chasing.

Ropework Ornamental borders or girdles suggesting a rope, frequently found both embossed and applied.

Scalework A pattern of fish scales, engraved or flat chased, found on silver between about 1735 and 1765.

Silver-gilt Silver with a thin surface coating of gold. The traditional method, most injurious to health, was to paint the surface with a gold-mercury amalgam, then apply heat to drive off the mercury and fuse the gold.

23 Reeding

Stamping or die stamping Relief ornament made by hammering the metal into an intaglio-cut die, used in the sixteenth century for borders and, very extensively, in Sheffield in the late eighteenth century for making candlesticks and other items. Die-struck candlesticks, if unworn, can look fine, though they sometimes have a stiff and mechanical appearance.

Strapwork A pattern of interlacing strap-like bands which, as used by the Huguenots in the early eighteenth century, was cast and applied; it occurred in earlier times engraved or repoussé.

Volute A scroll form as seen on an Ionic capital.

Wrigglework Engraved wavy lines.

24 Ropework

25 Wrigglework

702

Chapter 2

Hall marks

As a general rule, most silver and gold objects bear four small, punched symbols or marks. They are often called hall marks – though, strictly speaking, the maker's mark is not a 'hall' mark, the marks struck by the assay office which confirm where the silver was assayed. They include, besides the maker's mark made by the goldsmith before the ware was submitted to the assay office, a date letter, made by the assay office signifying the year in which the article was made and the sterling mark, the familiar lion passant. There are, naturally, various exceptions (some of the main ones are described below), and occasionally pieces of English silver may be found with no marks at all.

Hall marking in England was instituted by statute as long ago as 1300 and has continued to this day, a remarkable and invaluable record and not the least of the reasons why English silver is of such great interest to collectors worldwide. All gold and silver articles were to be assayed to ensure that people were not defrauded through buying metal of lower quality than the sterling standard, which was fixed at 11 ounces 2 pennyweights of silver to 18 pennyweights of alloy in Troy weight. The origin of the word sterling is a mystery, but the most likely explanation is that it derives from the 'Easterlings', German coin makers brought to England by Henry II (1154-89) to improve the quality of the coinage. At the same time as the sterling standard for silver, a standard for gold was introduced at $19\frac{1}{5}$ parts gold to $4\frac{4}{5}$ parts alloy. The 'parts' are usually expressed in carats: a carat, in reference to gold, is not a strict expression of weight as it is when referring to diamonds, but simply a unit representing one twenty-fourth of the whole. In 1477 the standard for gold was reduced to 18 carats (i.e. 18 parts gold to 6 parts alloy), but in 1575 it was raised to 22 carats. In 1798 two standards were permitted, 22 carats and 18 carats, and in 1854 three lower categories were added, 15 carats, 12 carats and 9 carats. Thus, when buying a gold ring for example, there will be a considerable difference in price between 9-carat gold and 22-carat gold.

The first hall mark to be used in England was a leopard's head, which became associated with London though it was used elsewhere as a standard mark. In the most unlikely event of finding a piece of silver made in England in the early fourteenth century, the leopard's head will be the only mark, but from 1363 the maker of the piece was required to stamp it with his own mark, which had to be first registered at Goldsmiths' Hall. A third mark was instituted in 1478, a letter of the alphabet which was changed annually and thus revealed the year in which the article was made. The purpose of the date letter was obviously not to make life easier for twentieth-century silver dealers and collectors. It was simply a means of checking on the identity of the assay master. Thus, if a piece of silver which had been correctly hall-marked was later found to be sub-standard, the warden of the Goldsmiths' Company would know by the date letter who had been assay master when it was assayed. The date letter was changed on St Dunstan's Day, 19 May, every year (St Dunstan is the patron saint of the Goldsmiths' Company). After 1660 the day was changed to 29 May, to commemorate Charles II's Restoration.

The fourth mark, the sterling mark of a lion passant, was added in 1544. There is some uncertainty over exactly why or even when the sterling mark was introduced, but the generally accepted explanation is that it was meant to reassure the public . that, at a time when the coinage had been seriously debased in order to replenish the depleted treasury of Henry VIII, assayed silver still adhered to the sterling standard.

Coins nowadays are merely symbols, but in those days their value depended on the precious-metal content, and this fact had repercussions for the goldsmiths on more than one occasion. In the Civil War period, much silver was melted to be turned into bullion, or cash, and after the Restoration, when plate became so fashionable and the demand for silver far outstripped supply, the reverse process occurred. Coins were melted, or their edges were clipped, to be made into plate, with the result that they became desperately scarce. To combat the destruction of existing coins, the government in 1697 introduced a new, higher standard for plate of 11 ounces 10 pennyweights, or 958 parts per thousand. At the same time, a new system of marks was created.

The maker's mark had previously been some kind of symbol or device or, more recently, the initials of the goldsmith – the first letter of his first name and the first letter of his surname. The act of 1697 compelled him to make a new punch with the first two letters of his surname. For example, had there been a goldsmith called Brand Inglis active at the time, his old mark would have been BI and his new mark IN.

A new cycle of date letters was begun in 1697, beginning with the letter A. It came into effect on 27 March, so the A mark lasted only about two months, being changed on 29 May to B, which ran for a year to be followed by C, and so on. Thus, for those who wish to memorise London date letters – different systems prevailed in provincial centres – the cycles of twenty letters (A to U omitting J) begin in '58, '78, etc. until 1678, and thereafter in '96, '16, etc., with the exception of the short-lived A of 1697. The complete series, until 1896-7, is illustrated in the tables at the end of this chapter.

The other two new-standard marks were a lion's head erased for the London mark and a figure of Britannia instead of the old sterling mark of a lion passant. The new standard is generally called the Britannia standard, after the Britannia mark.

In 1720 the obligatory use of Britannia-standard silver was abolished, though some articles continued to be made in the higher standard and still are today. Their marks remained the same, while sterling-standard silver, to which most goldsmiths returned with relief, reassumed the old marks of a leopard's head crowned (London) and a lion passant.

A great deal of antique silver is found with an additional mark – the head of the reigning sovereign at the time the piece was made, shown in profile. The purpose of the sovereign's-head mark was to show that the duty on silver had been paid. The duty was first imposed in 1719, though the sovereign's-head mark was not adopted until 1784. When the duty on silver was lifted in 1890, the sovereign's head disappeared, though it has occasionally been used since for special occasions such as the coronation of Elizabeth II.

Thanks to the records which have been kept safely by the Goldsmiths' Company – there are remarkably few gaps, all things considered – the history of hall marks in London is very well established. The situation is rather different in the provinces. Many towns had authorised assay offices at one time or another, some for a comparatively short period, and most of them used their own town marks. But some marks are found from towns which appear to have been unauthorised, and there is altogether more inconsistency and confusion outside the capital. Today, the only authorised assay offices outside London are Edinburgh, Birmingham and Sheffield; the latter two achieved their status as recently as 1773. The following tables, necessarily incomplete, should provide some guidance to provincial silver centres.

		TOWN MARK	STANDARD	DATE LETTER	DUTY HEAD	COMMENTS
London 20-letter cycle, A-U, exc. J	1558-9	(crowned leopard)	(lion)	a		
	1578-9	,,	,,	a		
	1598-9	,,	,,	a		
	1618-9	,,	,,	a		
	1638-9	,,	,,	a		
	1658-9	,,	,,	a		
	1678-9	,,	,,	a		cycle ends with T
	1697-8	(lion head)	(Britannia)	a		lion head erased replaces crowned leopard Britannia standard replaces sterling
	1716-7	,,	,,	A	(leopard & lion)	former town mark and sterling standard reinstated 1719-20
	1736-7	(crowned leopard)	(lion)	a	(D)	date-shield style alters for D onwards, although straight-sided D also appears
	1756-7	,,	,,	A		
	1776-7	,,	,,	a	(heads)	duty mark of George III introduced 1784-5 new duty mark of George III appears 1786-7
	1796-7	,,	,,	A	,,	
	1816-7	,,	,,	a	(heads)	leopard uncrowned from 1821-2 duty mark of George IV appears 1820-1 duty mark William IV appears 1831-2
	1836-7	(leopard head)	,,	A	(head)	duty mark of Victoria appears 1837-8
	1856-7	,,	,,	a	,,	
	1876-7	,,	,,	A	,,	(B) data-shield style alters for B onwards duty mark dropped 1890-1
	1896-7	,,	,,	a		
York 24- or 25- letter cycle, exc. J and (1787-1837) U	1559-60	(town mark)		A		
	1583-4	,,		B		
	1607-8	,,		C		
	1631-2	,,		D		
	1655-6	,,		A		
	1679-80	,,		A		date-shield style varies assay office closed 1696
	1700-1	(cross)	(Britannia & lion)	A		new town mark introduced on re-opening Britannia standard in operation date-shield and letter style varies office closed 1716
	1776-7	(shield)	(lion & leopard)		(head)	(D) sterling standard in operation no date letter before D known duty mark of George III introduced 1784-5

		TOWN MARK	STANDARD	DATE LETTER	DUTY HEAD	COMMENTS
continued	1787-8			A		date-shield style varies new duty mark of George III appears 1787-8
	1812-3	,,	,,	a	,,	
	1837-8	,,	,,	A		date-shield style varies duty mark of Victoria appears 1840-1 office closed 1856
Norwich 20-letter cycle, A-V exc. J and U	1565-6			A		date-letter system breaks down c. 1574-5
	1624-5			A		
	1688	,, ,,		a		dissolution of provincial offices 1696-7
Exeter 24-letter cycle, exc. J and U, until 1797-8; thereafter 20-letter cycle, A-U, exc. J	1571-1698					various crowned X's in use several possible early attempts at date-letter system
	1701-2			A		Britannia standard in operation sterling standard reinstated 1721-2 date-shield style varies
	1725-6	,,		a		
	1749-50	,,	,,	A		
	1773-4	,,	,,	A		leopard head dropped 1788-9 I used for two years duty mark of George III introduced 1784-5 new duty mark of George III appears 1786-7
	1797-8	,,		A	,,	
	1817-8	,,	,,	a		duty mark of George IV appears 1822-3 duty mark of William IV appears 1834-5
	1837-8	,,	,,	A		duty mark of Victoria appears 1838-9
	1857-8	,,	,,	A	,,	
	1877-8	,,	,,	A	,,	office closed 1883
Newcastle 19-letter cycle, A-T, exc. J, until 1740-1; thereafter 24-letter cycle, exc. J and U	1658-1701					new town mark appears 1680 no standardised date-letter system
	1702-3			A		Britannia standard in operation irregular use of date-letter system
	1721-2	,,		a		shield of town mark alters 1722-3 sterling standard reinstated 1721-2
	1740-1		,,	A		date-shield style varies
	1759-60	,,	,,	A		B used for 8 years date-letter style alters 1773-4 duty mark of George III introduced 1784-5 new duty mark of George III appears 1786-7
	1791-2	,,	,,	A	,,	
	1815-6	,,	,,	A		duty mark of George IV appears 1820-1 duty mark of William IV appears 1832-3

		TOWN MARK	STANDARD	DATE LETTER	DUTY HEAD	COMMENTS
continued	1839-40			A		25-letter cycle, J being excluded
	1864-5	,,	,,	a	,,	office closed 1884
Birmingham alternative 26- and 25-letter cycles, exc. J	1773-4	⚓		A		duty mark of George III introduced 1784-5 new duty mark of George III appears 1786-7
	1798-9	,,	,,	a	,,	
	1824-5	,,	,,	A		duty mark of Victoria appears 1838-9
	1849-50	,,	,,	A	,,	S date-shield style alters for S onwards
	1875-6	,,	,,	a	,,	U date-shield style alters for U onwards duty mark dropped 1890-1
Chester 25-letter cycle, exc. J, until 1751-2, thereafter 20- or 21-letter cycle, A-U/V, exc. J	1668-1700					occasional use of town mark some abortive attempts at date-letter system
	1701-2			A		sterling standard reinstated 1719-20
	1726-7	,,		A		
	1751-2	,,	,,	a		date-shield style varies
	1776-7	,,	,,	a		new town mark 1779-80 duty mark of George III introduced 1784-5 new duty mark of George III appears 1786-7
	1797-8		,,	A	,,	
	1818-9	,,	,,	A		duty mark of George IV appears 1823-4 duty mark of William IV appears 1835-6 leopard head dropped 1839-40 25-letter cycle, excluding J duty mark of Victoria appears 1839-40
	1839-40	,,		A		
	1864-5	,,	,,	A	,,	
	1884-5	,,	,,	A	,,	duty mark dropped 1890-1 cycle ends with R in 1900-1
Sheffield 25-letter cycle, exc. J	1773-4					date letters used in no regular order duty mark of George III introduced 1784-5 new duty mark of George III appears 1786-7
	1799-1800	,,	,,		,,	irregular order of date letters
	1824-5	,,	,,	a		some date-letters accompanied by crown I, J, N, O, W, Y not used duty mark of George IV in operation duty mark of William IV appears 1831-2 duty mark of Victoria appears 1840-1
	1844-5	,,	,,	A	,,	
	1868-9	,,	,,	A	,,	duty mark dropped 1890-1
	1893-4	,,	,,	a		
Edinburgh 25-letter cycle, exc. J	1552-1613					appropriate deacon's mark also used

708

		TOWN MARK	STAN-DARD	DATE LETTER	DUTY HEAD	COMMENTS
continued	1617-77	🏰				appropriate deacon's mark also used
	1681-2	,,				assay masters' marks appear after town mark date-shield style varies no U in cycle
	1705-6	,,				assay masters' marks date-shield style varies
	1730-1	,,				assay masters' marks
	1755-6	,,				thistle replaces assay master's mark 1759-60
	1780-1	,,				G used for two years date-shield style alters for I/J onwards duty mark of George III introduced 1784-5 new duty mark of George III appears 1786-7
	1806-7	,,	,,			26-letter cycle duty mark of George IV appears 1823-4
	1832-3	,,	,,			duty mark of William IV appears 1832-3 duty mark of Victoria appears 1841-2
	1857-8	,,	,,		,,	date-shield style alters for I onwards
	1882-3	,,	,,		,,	duty mark dropped 1890-1
Glasgow 25-letter cycle, exc. J; 26-letter cycle from 1819-20	1706-1800					town mark varies in detail, though generally within an oval S or O possibly represent 'sterling' or 'old standard' date-letter system breaks down
	1819-20					town mark on rectangular shield duty mark of George III in operation duty mark of William IV appears 1832-3
	1845-6	,,	,,			duty mark of Victoria appears 1845-6
	1871-2	,,	,,		,,	duty mark dropped 1890-1
	1897-8	,,	,,			
Dublin 19- or 20-letter cycle, A-U, exc. I/I and J; from 1678-9, 24-letter cycle, exc. J and V; from 1821, 25-letter cycle, exc. I/J	1638-9					date-shield style varies
	1658-9	,,				
	1678-9	,,				certain letters used for 2-4 years
	1717-8	,,				date-shield style varies
	1720-1	,,				figure of Hibernia appears 1731-2 L used for 2 years
	1747	,,				
	1773	,,	,,			pellet at base of D to M
	1797	,,	,,			date-shield style alters from N onwards, although straight sided N also appears duty mark of George III introduced 1807
	1821	,,	,,			date-shield style varies duty mark of George IV appears 1822 duty mark of William IV appears 1831-2 duty mark of Victoria appears 1838-9
	1846-7	,,	,,		,,	date-shield style varies
	1871-2	,,	,,		,,	date-shield style alters from K onwards duty mark dropped 1890-1
	1896-7	,,	,,			

709

Chapter 3

Changing styles in British silver 1500-1900

Decorative art in the West has always tended to follow current styles in architecture and the fine arts, and style in silver therefore reflects the rules and conventions of the period in which a particular article was made. Other forces, economic pressures for example, may also have some influence in determining style. The present age is a good example, for the plain forms and straight lines of contemporary design probably owe something to the high cost of labour as well as to purely aesthetic ideas. However, styles change as surely as the seasons, and over the centuries style in the decorative arts appears to swing like a pendulum from the plain and austere on one hand to the rich and fanciful on the other. The simple and severe forms of the present have been with us for half a century, but sooner or later the pendulum will begin to swing back (if it has not already started), and designs more ornate or more fanciful will return.

Besides the changes in style which are more or less common to all the decorative arts, and the effects of economic circumstances, such as high labour costs in our period or a scarcity of raw material in an earlier one, social customs also have some effect. This is not so much a matter of style as of the *type* of object made in a particular period. One generation regards as unnecessary what a previous generation found utterly indispensable, while habits that are perfectly tolerable in one period appear vulgar and tasteless in another. In the early eighteenth century, for example, it was quite normal to keep a chamber pot in the dining room in case anyone wished to relieve himself during the meal, but by the end of the century such behaviour had ceased to be respectable and the chamber pot was banished. That is why silver chamber pots dating from the early eighteenth century are far from rare today although there is hardly a single example of one made later than about 1750. Similarly, the new custom of tea and coffee drinking dramatically increased the repertoire of the goldsmith in the eighteenth century, more than compensating for the earlier loss of the rosewater ewer and dish, a common item of plate in the sixteenth century which all but disappeared when it ceased to be necessary to wash one's hands at frequent intervals during the course of a meal.

Historically, goldsmiths in general and English goldsmiths in particular have not been great innovators in design. As a rule they copied the creations of artists, most of whom were interested in design exclusively and never actually made any of the objects which they designed and published in books of engravings. Such designs were made for all manner of objects, besides silver and gold, and the pattern books were bought or borrowed by the craftsmen who executed the designs.

Tudor and Jacobean silver

English goldsmiths usually looked across the Channel for inspiration. During the sixteenth century they were almost totally under the influence of Germany, so much so that it is sometimes difficult to tell whether a particular piece was made in England or imported from Augsburg or Nuremberg and subsequently marked in London at Goldsmiths' Hall (so that it could be legally sold). A clue may sometimes be provided by the quality of the piece, for undeniably the goldsmith of the south German cities was a finer exponent of his craft than his English contemporary. The general standard of workmanship, especially repoussé work and flat chasing, was much higher in Germany, and although English engraving was frequently of the very finest quality, the English goldsmiths, unfortunately,

26 *Below:* Font cup and cover, made in London, 1503. A particularly fine and simple form of cup, it has a finial enamelled with the arms of John Cressener of Hinckford Hundred, in Essex. Height 6½ in. The Worshipful Company of Goldsmiths, London.

27 *Right:* Rosewater basin, made in London, 1556. Incorporating extremely delicate engraving as well as bold chased work, the piece is parcel-gilt and has very great strength. The raised central boss is enamelled with the arms of Legh of Lyme in Cheshire. Diameter 17½ in. The Worshipful Company of Goldsmiths, London.

cannot take the credit, because what seems to have happened as a rule when engraving was required was that the unfinished article was given to an artist-engraver to complete. It is often difficult in any period to decide how much of a finely engraved silver object is actually the work of the goldsmith who fashioned it, and in the sixteenth century this problem is particularly acute.

The sixteenth century, as everyone knows, was a time of great upheaval and readjustment, both spiritual and temporal. The dissolution of the monasteries under Henry VIII had a catastrophic effect on goldsmiths because the monks had been among their greatest patrons, but the rising affluence of the gentry – due partly to their acquisition of monastic property – and to some extent of the merchant classes also, brought reasonably swift compensation. There is no point in being rich if one cannot demonstrate the fact, and affluence, especially when recently acquired, creates a natural desire for ostentation. In Tudor England it was expressed in fine houses and furnishings, in which the family plate figured large. For in spite of religious and political upheavals, the England of the sixteenth century was strong, bold (not to say brash) and assertive. Fortunes and reputations could be made in a generation or less, and there were no guilt-ridden protestations of egalitarianism to spoil the enjoyment of earthly riches. Renaissance optimism was reflected in architecture, from the brilliant and daring fan vaulting of Henry VII's chapel in Westminster Abbey at the beginning of the century to the proud magnificence of a country house like Hardwick Hall, in Derbyshire, at the end. On a smaller scale, the silver of the period equally proclaims the prosperity and ambition of its original owners. Some of it, judged by absolute standards, is perhaps not very distinguished either in general form or in its decoration, but that does not detract from its general vitality. Moreover, we should be wary of judging the whole output of the century by what happens to survive till today. A glance through an inventory of the jewels and plate of Queen Elizabeth I demonstrates with breathtaking impact how little we know at first hand of the true magnificence of the finest gold and silver of that time.

The Renaissance sprang largely from the reading and dissemination of the works of classical authors and, consequently, classical influences were predominant in art and design. English silver of the sixteenth century is to a large extent neo-classical in conception. Its frequent allusions to the classics and classical mythology, breaking away from the more

28 *Opposite:* Rhodian jug, Isnik ware, with silver mounts, about 1580. Height 10$\frac{1}{4}$ in. Victoria and Albert Museum, London.

712

713

714

29 *Opposite:* Tazza and cover, silver gilt, maker's mark IG in a shield, 1584. Height 13½ in. Diameter 7⅛ in. The Worshipful Company of Goldsmiths, London.

30 *Left:* The Methuen Cup, silver gilt and rock crystal, maker's mark VH, made in Scotland, mid-sixteenth century. Height 7 in. Foreground, a perfume burner, maker's mark TI, 1628. Height 8¾ in. Both pieces are in the Los Angeles County Museum of Art, California. Gift of William Randolph Hearst.

31 *Below:* A magnificent pair of silver-gilt Elizabethan tankards, maker's mark IB, 1602. Height 8¼ in.

716

32 Standing salt and cover, silver-gilt, made in London, 1542. The cover is surmounted with a figure of the boy Hercules. Height 10 in. The Worshipful Company of Goldsmiths, London.

33 *Opposite:* Silver-gilt cup of the type known as a grace cup, maker's mark RP, 1616. Height 7½ in. The Worshipful Company of Goldsmiths, London.

constraining hierarchical configuration of the Middle Ages, are another manifestation of contemporary feelings of prosperity and optimism.

Flatware – that is cutlery, spoons especially – is described in the following chapter. What else remains of the variety of objects made in silver in sixteenth-century England?

Perhaps the most distinctive articles of the period are the rosewater ewer and dish. These were essential adjuncts to the dining table in medieval and Tudor times to wash off the sticky traces of food that clung to the fingers. The fork was not unknown in Elizabethan England – the Queen herself was presented with some fine gold ones – but it was generally regarded as an article fit only for effete foreigners. In fact the prejudice against forks lasted a remarkably long time; not until the end of the seventeenth century did they become at all common. Attendants therefore circulated among the diners with a water jug, or ewer, a dish and a towel. The dish is invariably circular, the rim engraved with arabesques or flat chased with a formal pattern of interlacing strapwork enclosing paterae, sea creatures or classical heads. Surviving examples of these dishes of early date have comparatively plain bowls, with a central boss on which the ewer rested when not in use. As the century went on, there was a tendency towards more elaborate embossing of the bowl, frequently with a bravura design of tritons and sea monsters, or quasi-classical triumphant processions. In general ewers followed the same decorative pattern; early sixteenth-century examples are of a somewhat ill-formed beaker shape, while later ones take on a more elegant vase form. Decoration relies chiefly on flat chasing, embossing and engraving, and there is little use of cast ornament.

In the sixteenth century, the standing salt was still as important a piece of plate as it had been in the Middle Ages, and examples from the early years of the century remain distinctly Gothic in appearance. They are generally shaped like an hour glass and frequently display the spiral fluting that was so favoured a form of decoration in the late fifteenth century. There is usually a central band or girdle ornamented with applied crockets, a device taken directly from Gothic architecture. Indeed, the total effect of these early sixteenth-century salts is decidedly architectural.

In the Elizabethan salt, neo-classicism takes over. The repoussé ornament is of swags of fruit, lion masks, classical heads and sometimes whole scenes from classical mythology. There is an excellent example of a salt of this type which

34 *Left:* The Gibbon Salt, 1576. Height 11¾ in. The Worshipful Company of Goldsmiths, London.

35 *Above:* The Rogers Salt, rock crystal mounted in silver-gilt, made in London, 1601. Inside the rock crystal is a vellum scroll painted with the arms of the Goldsmiths' Company. The Worshipful Company of Goldsmiths, London.

belongs to the Vintners' Company of London. It is square and straight-sided in outline and rests on four mask feet, with a typical guilloche border at the base. Each side is embossed in low relief with the cardinal virtues in neo-classical style, the virtues being personified by female figures in Roman dress with classical coiffure. The lid supports an urn with a finial in the form of a male warrior. The piece was made in 1569 and may be regarded as a typical salt of the period. Others are circular, rather than square, in section but otherwise similar.

One of the most beautiful Elizabethan salts is the Gibbon Salt which was presented to the Worshipful Company of Goldsmiths in 1632 and has remained in their possession to this day. This exquisite object stands almost twelve inches high and is architectural in concept, representing in perfect proportions a little classical temple, with four Ionic columns enclosing a figure encased in rock crystal. The lid supports a delicately proportioned classical urn finial. Made in London in 1576, the Gibbon Salt is highly unusual both in the advanced understanding of technique that it displays and in the flair and ingenuity of its original design (Plate 34).

A new type of salt appeared in the 1580s. Its general shape is not unlike a bell and such a piece is therefore called a bell salt. As there appears to be no continental equivalent, perhaps it can be claimed as a truly native, English design. Bell salts are usually flat chased with interlacing strapwork on a matt ground, but some are quite plain. They were made in three sections. The lid on top, in which a small caster is incorporated, removes to reveal a depression for salt, and this in turn acts as a lid covering a second, slightly larger depression below. Bell salts are seldom very beautiful; the craftsmanship is usually routine and the decoration coarse and repetitive. But the occasional example stands out because its maker devoted a little extra care and attention to his creation. Bell salts became less popular after the turn of the century and by 1620 the type was extinct.

A common drinking vessel in the sixteenth century was the tankard, and there are a fair number of them still to be seen today. One early example, made in 1556, is a pear-shaped vessel with a band of arabesque design engraved around the rim and simple bands on the lid and the handle, which is of plain S-scroll form. It bears the London maker's mark of a stag's head, by which it can be attributed to Robert Tallboys. A finer example, with more sophisticated engraving, is the tankard made in 1567 by Richard Danbe which is now in the possession of the Armourers' and Braziers' Company in London. This too

36 Silver-gilt tankard of typical Elizabethan design, made in London, 1591. As is often the case, the barrel is engraved but the foot and lid are chased. Height 7 in.

is pear-shaped, a form no doubt derived from stoneware and earthenware models which at this time was already being superceded by a straight-sided form. Elizabethan tankards are either engraved or embossed in much the same way as the salts of the period. One curious characteristic of the embossed decoration on the tankards is that it is always in noticeably lower relief on the barrel of the tankard than it is on the foot or the lid. On the whole, the tankards with engraved barrels are rather more attractive than those with the somewhat coarse flat chasing of the inevitable interlaced strapwork, paterae and lions' heads.

One of the most beautiful objects of the Elizabethan period is the wine cup, not to be confused with the communion cup or chalice which is usually accompanied by a paten forming a lid for the cup. Elizabethan wine cups occur with two basic shapes of bowl. The first, with a tulip-shaped bowl, is altogether taller than the second, shallow-bowled type. Some have bowls so shallow that it is doubtful if they were wine cups at all; more likely, they were used for holding sweetmeats of some kind. A cup of this type with a wide, shallow bowl is called a tazza, though it is arguable that this is a modern term only. To add further confusion, almost any shallow dish on a central foot is liable to be called a tazza nowadays.

While the taller type of wine cup was sometimes engraved, or left plain, the very shallow cups—the so-called *tazze*—were often quite highly embossed, with classical, mythological or sometimes biblical scenes (Plate 29). This tends. to support the view that their purpose was different and that they were food servers rather than wine cups.

Towards the end of the century, a new type of wine cup appeared. This had a cover surmounted by a tall pyramidal steeple and is accordingly known as a steeple cup. For some reason steeple cups appear disproportionately tall even with the cover removed. Most of them have flat-chased and matted bowls, but a few of them are engraved. This type of wine cup remained popular up to the reign of Charles I.

During the sixteenth and early seventeenth centuries a wide variety of objects in various different materials were mounted in silver or, more frequently, silver gilt. Probably the best-known objects of this kind are the Rhenish stoneware jugs with foot rim, neckband and hinged lid of silver. They were made in Exeter, York, Norwich, Barnstaple and no doubt other places, as well as London, and judging from the number that have survived to the present they must have been made in their thousands. Some are very beautiful, although others are more

37 *Opposite, top:* Standing cup, silver-gilt and rock crystal, made in London, 1545. Height 11½ in. The Worshipful Company of Goldsmiths, London.

38 *Opposite, bottom:* Steeple cup, 1611. This is a peculiarly English form of cup and cover. The Company of Armourers and Brasiers, London.

39 *Above:* Pomander, particularly beautiful late Elizabethan piece, about 1600. The top unscrews and the six hinged segments fall outwards. Each segment would have contained different herbs and aromatics.

40 *Centre:* Late Elizabethan wine cup, parcel-gilt, made in London, 1592. This simple but beautiful cup illustrates the freedom of movement found in the engraving of this period. Height 5½ in.

41 *Far right:* Jug of white unglazed Rhenish pottery, silver-mounted, with die-stamped neck band, the lid chased with typical masks and strapwork, and beautifully engraved birds on the box hinge, made in London about 1585 (it bears the maker's mark only). Height 9 in.

perfunctory and slightly coarse in treatment. Chinese blue-and-white ware was also mounted in this way, and so were a great many more unlikely objects, such as coconuts, ostrich eggs and rhinoceros horns, as well as glass, turned wood and hard stones such as agate and onyx. The contrast of such disparate materials often results in a highly successful 'marriage' and the great majority of these items are strikingly attractive.

Styles do not change neatly at convenient dates such as the end of a century or the death of a sovereign, but at the end of the sixteenth century, or at the death of Elizabeth I soon afterwards, the beginnings of a basic change in fashion can be discerned. The queen's death brought not only a new monarch to the throne but also a new dynasty, and although fashion is not governed by monarchs or dynasties, general trends are, or were, often dictated by what is fashionable at court.

For a time there was no evident break, but what is apparent in the decorative arts of the reign of James I (1603-25) is, as so often when the pendulum of fashion is beginning to swing back, a loss of character and meaning, a symptom that the old fashion is dying and that it is time for new developments. There is a faintly lifeless look about the silver and other art objects of the early seventeenth century, a certain coarseness of form and decoration. Of course, to condemn outright all silver objects wrought between about 1600 and 1625 would be absurd, yet their general lack of spontaneity is undeniable.

One new and notably attractive object of the period is a shallow pierced or openwork dish on a central foot. These dishes probably evolved from the sixteenth-century tazza, but they also owe something to Portuguese design; they usually have elaborately scalloped or crenellated borders. Tankards and ewers and dishes are not markedly different in design from earlier examples, and wine cups show little change either in form or ornament, although they seem to be on the whole rather taller than their sixteenth-century counterparts.

The seventeenth century

Insofar as it is possible to date a fundamental change in design, the change from the highly decorative, flamboyant era of the Elizabethans to the simpler, plainer style of the mid-seventeenth century occurred about the beginning of the second quarter of the century, or at the accession of Charles I.

The reasons behind the change to a simpler style have been often debated. It used to be said that it was all due to the influence of Puritanism, but this is an unsatisfactory explanation. Not everyone in England was a Puritan, and not all Puritans took a special interest in artistic affairs. Moreover, the simple, plain designs characteristic of England and of most other European countries never prevailed in Holland, where contemporary silver was highly elaborate. Yet Holland was the most rigorously Protestant country in Europe! The austere style common elsewhere was due in part to the inevitable though unpredictable swing of the pendulum of taste, but there is no doubt that it was also largely due to economic causes. 'The years around 1625', wrote Charles Oman, 'were in fact unfortunate for the goldsmiths in Western Europe – Germany was well launched into the Thirty Years' War, France had her

Salts

c. 1500

c. 1570

c. 1600

c. 1635

c. 1670

c. 1690

c. 1700

c. 1710

c. 1720

c. 1735

c. 1745

c. 1760

c. 1770

c. 1790

c. 1810

c. 1825

Huguenot troubles, whilst Spain was faced by the facts that the attempt to reduce the Duke [Olivares] had failed and that troubles were building up within the Peninsula. . . . The only part of Western Europe where there appeared to be no limit to the prosperity of the goldsmiths was Holland.' (*Caroline Silver*, Faber, 1970).

One obvious sign of the shift to plainer styles is the decline in silver gilt. By far the majority of pieces surviving from the sixteenth century and the first quarter of the seventeenth are gilt or parcel gilt (partly gilded), but in the reign of Charles I people turned away from the richness of gilding. In general, the preference was to leave surfaces entirely plain, but one comparatively new and extremely effective form of decoration became popular in this period. It is an effect called matting, produced by hitting the metal lightly with a small round-headed punch (Plate 44). On wine cups matting was usually made between two engraved lines around the bowl, leaving two small plain bands at the rim and the base of the cup. This very simple, almost naive form of decoration was to prove lastingly popular; it was still common well after the Restoration, when sober decoration was no longer in vogue.

A complete change in style is evident even in important pieces of ceremonial plate. The old rosewater dish and ewer with their heavily embossed strapwork, sea creatures and so on, their monster spouts and elaborately cast handles have gone. In the new version, the dish is a simple, circular plate with perhaps two or three bands of reeding at the rim and no other decoration apart from the occasional coat of arms engraved on the boss. The ewer is usually beaker-shaped, with straight sides and a slightly everted rim, a long beak-shaped spout and simple S-scroll handle; it stands on a plain trumpet-shaped foot.

The standing salt underwent a similarly dramatic change. By this time the salt was fast losing the social significance it had formerly commanded, when the importance of a guest at the dinner table could be gauged by whether he sat 'above' or 'below' the salt, and a less ostentatious design .was therefore natural. The salts of the 1630s are generally plain drum-shaped objects with three simple scrolls set vertically on top. The purpose of these scrolls is somewhat enigmatic: some writers have suggested that they were intended to support a dish, but it would have been a precarious perch and a more likely explanation is that a napkin was draped over them to protect the salt in the bowl beneath, taking the place of the fitted silver cover that was almost invariably provided with earlier salts.

44 *Above:* Charles 1 tankard, made in London, 1639. An example of the prevalent use of matted ornament, it stands on a wide skirt foot – a very early use of this device. Height 7½ in. Boston Museum of Fine Arts, Mass..

45 *Below:* Silver wine cup of the reign of Charles 1 (the pricked initials and date were added in 1667), a fine example of this austere style. Height 6½ in.

724

46 *Above:* Bible, with finely fashioned silver-gilt mounts, about 1640. This beautiful piece was made for Colonel Sir George Strode, who was wounded at the Battle of Edgehill. Height 7 in.

47 *Far right:* Oval box with hinged lid, 1651. As is often the case, it is difficult to know what this very plain Cromwellian box was for – perhaps nothing in particular. From a modern collector's point of view it would be very exciting to own, but the actual quality of the work leaves much to be desired. The Worshipful Company of Goldsmiths, London.

Another type of standing salt, also with vertical scrolls, was made in plain capstan form. It seems to have superseded the drum-shaped variety and continued to be made throughout the century, until the standing salt ceased to exist as a standard item in the goldsmith's repertoire.

A single large standing salt was, anyway, rather inconvenient, and the reign of Charles I provided the first extant examples of the trencher salt (though some were certainly made as early as the sixteenth century). The trencher salt is a much smaller receptacle, which stood beside the diner's plate, or 'trencher' (from which we get the expression 'a good trencherman'). Usually round, sometimes triangular, and normally made in sets, the little trencher salt in silver was probably intended to provide a more refined alternative to the custom of placing a little pile of salt on the side of one's plate. (Many old wooden platters probably had a small circular depression in the rim for this purpose, and the same device can be seen in some English earthenware plates of the early eighteenth century.)

The tankard in the reign of Charles I was reduced virtually to the most elemental form possible. As a rule, the body was raised from a single sheet of metal. Straight-sided and tapering gently inwards towards the top, the typical Charles I tankard was not even provided with an applied rim foot. The lid is quite flat, with a simple rolled billet as a thumb-piece, and the handle is an unadorned S-scroll. It is hard to imagine a more striking contrast with the elaborately chased and engraved tankard of fifty years earlier.

When all, or almost all ornament is eschewed, shape and line become so much the more vital, and on the whole this challenge was met successfully by the goldsmiths of the period. Like

725

Tankards

c. 1550

c. 1570

c. 1630

c. 1655

c. 1670

c. 1680

c. 1690

c. 1700

c. 1730

c. 1760

c. 1790

c. 1830

tankards, wine cups are beautifully proportioned, with V-shaped bowls on cast baluster stems, a type which had first appeared towards the end of the sixteenth century. Signs of the general aversion to ostentation are the scarcity of large standing cups with covers, the relative profusion of pleasant, simple goblets, and the appearance of plain beakers, an ancient form of drinking vessel certainly, but uncommon before this period. Beakers are usually straight-sided, with everted rim and turned, reeded rim base. Sometimes they have arabesque ornament engraved below the rim in a style that was slightly archaic.

During the reign of Charles I, an object which in a multitude of guises was to retain its popularity to the present day made an embryonic appearance. This was the two-handled cup. These cups are of simple pear-shaped outline with strikingly small circular ring handles at opposite sides just below the rim. They represent, in fact, the basic form of the porringer and cover, of which there are innumerable examples from the middle of the century onwards. This early form, of which the first known example is dated 1616, is generally called an ox-eye cup, for reasons that become obvious when it is viewed from the side with the handles at right angles to the line of vision. Another name for it is college cup, which presumably derives from the coincidental fact that a large proportion of extant examples are owned by the colleges of Oxford and Cambridge.

The question of nomenclature in silver, as in other decorative arts, is often a vexed one. It is worth repeating that the names used to describe objects of a certain type today are not necessarily the names used at the time, and many of the names that *were* used are either unknown or obscure to us today. It is

48 Two-handled sweetmeat dish, 1642. These dishes are almost invariably quite small and tend to be exactly the same size, about 6 in. wide. The Worshipful Company of Goldsmiths, London.

not clear, for example, what distinction was implied in the seventeenth century between 'bowls' and 'cups', or even if there was any distinction at all. What we call a tankard seems to have been generally known as a 'pot', while the name 'porringer' is nowadays likely to be applied to almost any cup or bowl with two handles, with or without cover. Another much-argued term is 'strawberry dish'. This is the name given to a type of shallow fluted dish with two shell handles which was very popular in the seventeenth century (Plate 48) and plain, fluted shallow bowls without handles of the early eighteenth century. There seems to be no contemporary evidence that these dishes were intended for strawberries, and it has been pointed out that, owing to their great variety in size, you would have received either a gigantic portion or a rather mean one, as some 'strawberry' dishes are considerably smaller than the average saucer – hardly generous even for red currants. At about the same time there appeared another type of small, shallow dish, about three inches in diameter, with two plain scroll handles (Plate 49). These dishes, which retained popularity in a form almost unchanged well into the 1680s, are today often known as wine tasters, but it is extremely unlikely that this description is correct. There are a few somewhat similar vessels surviving which are definitely known to be wine tasters – they often have a raised dome in the bowl to show off the colour of the wine. The authenticated wine tasters are normally engraved with the name of a vintner, but in no single case that I know does a vintner's name appear on the former variety. Moreover, these exist in such quantity today that, if they were wine tasters, then every vintner in England must have owned dozens of them. It seems odd, to say the least, that none carries a name, and odd too that the Worshipful Company of Vintners does not possess a single one. Surely some member

51 *Above:* Tobacco box of the Commonwealth period, made in London, about 1652. It is engraved with the arms of John Burwell of Woodbridge in Suffolk and his name appears as an anagram. Length 5 in.

52 *Far right:* A Cromwellian porringer and cover made in London, 1656. Though a remarkably fine example of its type, it is made in a rather slap-dash manner, typical of its period. Height about 5 in.

would have presented his favourite wine taster to his company? The exact purpose of these doubtful 'wine tasters' must remain uncertain, but probably they were for small sweetmeats; alternatively, they were 'saucers' in the original meaning of the term – containers for sauce.

The Restoration of the monarchy in 1660 represents an important milestone in the history of English silver in that the surviving pieces from about 1660 onwards are far more numerous and more diverse than those of any earlier period. Before this time, a man's plate was his capital – he had no stocks and shares or bank account – and in time of need the family silver was melted down to be turned into ready cash. The hard times of the 1630s, followed by the Civil War, placed a heavy call on this form of capital. The needs of King and Parliament to pay their soldiers caused the reduction of plate to bullion on a massive scale, larger even than the melting down of monastic plate during the Dissolution of the Monasteries a century before. It is therefore not surprising that English silver surviving from a period earlier than the mid-seventeenth century is rare, and often not found outside museums and institutions. Moreover, the survivals, however beautiful, rare or interesting they may appear to us, tend on the whole to be the smaller, less important pieces. Owners who had to raise money by sacrificing their plate would naturally select the large, ceremonial pieces first, hoping to retain the smaller and more personal articles, which were probably more useful in the house and were anyway less valuable in terms of weight.

Since the Restoration, there have been no more great assaults on silver. With the rising prosperity of the late seventeenth century and the growing use of banks both for storing capital and for business speculation, silver became more of a luxury item and less of a capital investment. After 1660, far fewer

53 Salver on a foot, engraved with the arms of Fettiplace, 1677. It makes a striking contrast with the salver of 1672 in Plate 54. The chased decoration and pie-crust edge strengthen the middle, allowing a much thinner gauge of silver to be used. This salver, though considerably larger than the silver-gilt example, is noticeably lighter in weight. Diameter 14 in.

pieces were melted merely for cash, and the main threat to survival became nothing more formidable than natural wastage – wear and tear, theft, or occasionally the desire of an owner to have a piece melted and reworked into something more fashionable. At the same time, production increased dramatically. The destruction of silver in the Civil War period still had to be made good, which, combined with the general increase in consumer spending, especially on luxuries, meant that the goldsmiths were busier than ever before. No one had greater reason than they for cheering King Charles II when he rode into London in 1660.

The Restoration of the monarchy, the renewal of a spirit of expansive optimism, and the general increase in prosperity combined to revive a delight in luxury. The decorative arts became more obviously 'decorative', and silver more ornamental.

Of course, this did not happen suddenly in 1660. As mentioned earlier, during the period of Carolean austerity in English silver, the Dutch silversmiths were producing plate in designs of almost riotous splendour, extravagantly chased with scenes from domestic life, allegorical and mythological subjects, classical motifs, sea monsters and other grotesques.

England was not entirely cut off from this influence. During the 1630s Christian van Vianen, a member of a famous family of silversmiths, came from his native Utrecht to work for Charles I, a great patron of artists and craftsmen. His major commission was a service of plate for St George's Chapel, Windsor, but unfortunately it was looted in 1642 and never seen again – no doubt it was melted down for its value as bullion. Nevertheless, several pieces in the voluptuous, perhaps over-ripe Dutch decorative style (known as the auricular style), which were made by van Vianen in England, have survived.

It was this style, though seldom exercised by craftsmen as talented as van Vianen, which dominated English silver in the period from 1660 to 1680. The first signs of it were evident earlier, under the Commonwealth, with objects such as dishes, porringers and wine cups given more ornament than they would have received ten or twenty years before.

In the Restoration period the porringer, both with and without a cover, became a standard piece of plate. Some collectors make a distinction between the 'porringer' and the 'caudle cup', on the basis of the shape of the bowl or some other subtlety, but contemporaries were probably less pedantic. It is unlikely that a 'porringer' was exclusively for porridge or a 'caudle cup' for caudle (gruel spiked with wine or beer).

Commonwealth and Restoration porringers are usually pear-shaped, with the lower part heavily embossed with flowers and foliage, sometimes interspersed with a lion and unicorn, a hound and stag, or, on one rather eccentric example, an elephant. Handles were often in the form of caryatids (female half-figures) and for the most part they are poorly cast and finished. The covered porringer of the last quarter of the seventeenth century is more often straight-sided than pear-shaped, and the decoration on the lower part is a more formal design of vertical acanthus leaves; the caryatid handles are often replaced by simpler S-scrolls.

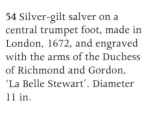

54 Silver-gilt salver on a central trumpet foot, made in London, 1672, and engraved with the arms of the Duchess of Richmond and Gordon, 'La Belle Stewart'. Diameter 11 in.

Two-handled cups

c. 1620

c. 1655

c. 1680

c. 1670

c. 1670

c. 1700

c. 1705

c. 1720

c. 1735

c. 1770

c. 1805

c. 1840

55 The Seymour Salt, silver gilt, unmarked, about 1662. Height $10\frac{1}{2}$ in. Diameter $9\frac{1}{4}$ in. The Worshipful Company of Goldsmiths, London.

56 Silver porringer and cover, maker's mark GS with two dots above and a crozier between in a shaped shield, 1658. Height 4 in. Diameter $4\frac{1}{2}$ in. The Worshipful Company of Goldsmiths, London.

57 Toilet service of seventeen silver-gilt pieces, made by Daniel Garnier, about 1680 (maker's mark only). Height of mirror 31¼ in. Birmingham City Museums and Art Gallery.

58 *Left:* A pair of Queen Anne silver-gilt tapersticks, made by Thomas Merry, London, 1713. Height 5 in.

59 *Below:* Silver oval dish, with the initials of Catherine, wife of the 6th Earl of Thanet, maker's mark IC conjoined, made in London, 1683. Length 19 in.

One innovation dating roughly from the Restoration was 'a newe fashioned peece of plate, broad and flat, with foot underneath ... used in giving beer, or other liquid thing to save the Carpit or Cloathes from drops'. This useful piece, described by Thomas Blount in his *Glossographia* (1661), was the salver. First made, as Blount says, as a tray for a porringer or other container for liquids, it soon gained an independent existence. Early salvers generally have a broad, highly embossed rim, with the shallow central depression left plain, to be engraved, if desired, with a coat of arms; they stand on a central, trumpet-shaped foot. As the century drew to a close, the broad rim disappeared, leaving a flat surface with a reeded or 'rope-edge' rim, and the salver, apart from its central foot, took on more of the appearance of the typical eighteenth-century piece.

During the second half of the seventeenth century the English goldsmiths' main sources of design were the Netherlands and, in the later years especially, France. Both these foreign influences encouraged extensive ornament on silver,

60 Parcel-gilt tankard made by Jacob Bodendick, about 1665-70 (maker's mark only). Bodendick was a German goldsmith who came to England shortly after the Restoration and made some silver of the greatest virtuosity. Height 7½ in.

but some articles nevertheless remained comparatively plain. Perhaps the most notable example is the tankard. Apart from a group of tankards dating mainly from the 1680s which have a broad band of stiff, vertical acanthus leaves around the base (like the decoration on some porringers of the same period), the general pattern was plain and straight-sided. A spreading 'skirt' foot which was popular for a time in the 1640s and 1650s was soon abandoned in favour of a low, moulded rim foot; handles are of plain S-scroll form while the hinged lid, no longer completely flat, is stepped – a single step on earlier examples, two steps later. It should be emphasised that this is the general pattern only; there are numerous examples which do not exactly fit this description.

Among the exceptions is a notable group of tankards from York and, to a smaller extent, Newcastle, which were derived from Scandinavian design. The barrel rests on three pomegranate feet, and the rimless, rounded cover has a double-pomegranate thumb-piece. Many of them have two other features in common: a handle in double C-scroll form rather than the plain flowing S-scroll of London-made examples, and a 'bullet' hinge – much more common in Europe than in England. The barrel is sometimes plain or engraved with a coat of arms, but some are embossed with flowers and foliage all around. Perhaps the most beautiful – arguably the most beautiful of all English tankards – are those made in York from the late 1650s to the early 1670s by John Plummer (Plate 62). They are engraved with flowers and foliage, from which spring half-figures or monsters. The quality of the engraving is exceptional, and it is a great pity that the name of the engraver

61 *Far left:* Tankard, made in London by Thomas Jenkins, 1675. Compared with the Bodendick example, this tankard appears superbly austere, relying on simplicity of line and decorated only with a bold lion thumbpiece and beautiful plumed mantling around the coat of arms – typical of the period. Jenkins was one of the finest English goldsmiths of the latter half of the seventeenth century. Height 5½ in.

62 *Above:* Tankard, made in York by John Plummer, 1662. A beautiful example of Plummer's work, it is engraved with flowers and rests on pomegranate feet. Huntingdon Library and Art Gallery, San Marino, Calif..

63 Counter box, probably made in London, about 1680 (it has no marks). Counter boxes are not usually the most exciting objects, but this is a charming example, engraved with roses and thistles and containing thirty-six gaming counters. Height 2 in.

is unknown. Of course it may have been John Plummer himself, though the only evidence for that conclusion is that nearly all the tankards bearing this superb engraving were made by him.

An interesting example of the diversity of surviving silver is the candlestick. Both wall sconces and hanging chandeliers were made in considerable quantity, sconces especially. These things were certainly made in the previous century, but we have little idea of what they looked like at any time before about the middle of the seventeenth century because not one has survived from the earlier period.

A mark of the demand for luxury in the home was the greater use made, certainly by the aristocracy, of plate in the bed chambers and dressing rooms. Typically, the mantelpiece

64 A Charles II pin cushion, unmarked, about 1675, originally no doubt part of a toilet service. It is extremely well chased but its main distinction is the form of its four extraordinary little feet, apparently demi-phoenix rising from flames. Length 7 in.

supported a pair of silver ginger jars with covers, tall and embossed flower vases and silver mirrors. There was even a vogue for silver furniture. A silver bed was made for Nell Gwyn in 1674 and another of the royal mistresses, the Duchess of Portsmouth, had tables and fireplaces made in silver. But few people could afford to indulge in such expensive tastes, and it is difficult to know how far the fashion spread. (Today, a remarkable display of silver furniture can be seen in the throne room of Rosenborg Castle, Copenhagen.)

The silver or silver-gilt toilet service became the traditional wedding present from husband to wife. John Evelyn described it in verse:

> *A New Scene to us next presents*
> *The Dressing Room and Implements*
> *Of Toilet Plate Gilt, and Embossed*
> *And several other things of Cost,*
> *The Table Mirror, one Glue Pot,*
> *One for Pomatum, and what not?*
> *Of Washes, Unguents and Cosmeticks,*
> *A pair of Silver Candlesticks,*
> *Snuffers and Snuff Dish, Boxes more*
> *For Powders, Patches, Waters Store,*
> *In silver Flasks or Bottles, Cups*
> *Covered or open to wash chaps.*

These services were frequently as large and elaborate as Evelyn's description suggests, consisting generally of a mirror, a pair of candlesticks, a large oblong box, two medium-sized boxes and two small ones, a pair of scent flasks, a pair of covered two-handled bowls, a pin cushion, sometimes a snuffer and tray, and various brushes, combs and whisks. Altogether they present an impressive array (Plate 57), but unfortunately many have been broken up recently and the items sold individually. However, something of the feeling of exciting, perhaps slightly cloying, opulence of this era can be seen in the state bedroom at Knole, or at Ham House near Richmond.

It is possible to see this whole period as one of gentle evolution, with gradual change but no dramatic breaks, with the single important exception of an extraordinary style of decoration, more notable in silver than in the other decorative arts, known as Chinoiserie. The interest of Europeans travelling to the Far East was primarily economic, but inevitably they brought back travellers' tales, wrote accounts of the sights they had seen, and published drawings of the Chinese style in architecture or dress. For a short time, roughly between 1675 and 1690, these were copied, in a naive way, in flat chasing on silver articles ranging from whole toilet services to individual tankards, bowls and other small everyday items.

The designs, fantastic in conception but realistic in execution, are of such marked similarity on all surviving examples that it is tempting to assume that one workshop was responsible for almost the entire output – the various goldsmiths all sending their work there to be chased in this new fashion. It was almost entirely confined to London, though there is one

66 Porringer and cover, 1680. This example is decorated with flat chasing in the Chinoiserie manner with birds, trees and a fountain and, unlike many porringers of this period, relatively well constructed. Height 7 in. The Worshipful Company of Goldsmiths, London.

67, 68 Silver-gilt bowl and cover, made by Pierre Harache, about 1695 (it bears his maker's mark only). This superbly made small bowl was given by the Bishop of Salisbury to his godson, John Warner, in 1697. Length 5½ in.

striking exception, which is a small group of pieces made in Newcastle around 1690 in which the decoration, though similar, lacks the versatility of London and is altogether so dissimilar that it can be confidently classed as local work. There are also some Chinoiserie pieces bearing Dublin hall marks, but the decoration is so like that of London as to suggest that they were sent to London to be chased and finished. The only other exception of which I am aware is a pair of bulbous mugs made in Barnstaple about 1685, in which the design is similar but executed with such crude naiveté that it seems safe to conclude that it was done locally. The mugs were probably made to the order of a local patron who had a London-made example for the Barnstaple craftsman to copy, a task he completed with indifferent success.

It is dangerous to generalise about silver in the latter half of the seventeenth century, but very broadly, and with a number of striking exceptions, it could be said that it looks rather better from a distance than it does when examined closely. The English goldsmith seems to have been less concerned with the

742

finest quality and detail and more concerned with making a grand general display. The heavy repoussé style which had originated with van Vianen and the Dutch in the Carolean period had become so diluted as to be almost unrecognisable, while the French taste had as yet made comparatively little impact, probably because it required exceptional ability in the goldsmith which, with one or two exceptions, was simply not available. By about 1690 the pendulum of style had once more swung to its limit, and the time was ripe for a new style and new techniques. The impetus for change was partly provided by emigré craftsmen from France.

Queen Anne and early Georgian silver

In 1685 Louis XIV revoked the Edict of Nantes, which had given a measure of toleration to the minority of French Protestants, or Huguenots. Already, some Huguenots had come to England, and the revocation of the Edict of Nantes forced

69 A cup and cover, made by Matthew Lofthouse, 1695. This is a typical English piece of the period. Note how weak the handles look compared with the remarkable cut-card cup and cover of the unknown Huguenot goldsmith in Plate 70. Height about 7 in.

70 A cup and cover by an unknown Huguenot goldsmith, 1697. The superb craftsmanship of this piece provides a startling contrast with the somewhat coarse work of an English counterpart in the 1690s in Plate **69**. Height about 7 in.

71 *Opposite, top:* A George II soup tureen with dolphin handles, shell feet and a crab finial (for fish soup, clearly), made by John Edwards, 1737. Width 16¼ in.

72 *Opposite, bottom:* Three early eighteenth-century snuff boxes, illustrating the very fine quality of engraving prevalent at this period, about 1720.

them to leave France in much greater numbers. Though more went to the Netherlands or to North America, some came to England, especially after the Glorious Revolution of 1688 had rid the country of the Catholic, pro-French James II and introduced the solidly Protestant William III. A quite extraordinary proportion of the Huguenot emigrés proved to be craftsmen – including goldsmiths – of exceptional talent. William III appointed as his own court architect and designer a Huguenot named Daniel Marot, whose designs helped to cause a swift and dramatic change in England.

The grand, Baroque style of Louis XIV's France demanded higher technical skill, particularly in the use of cast ornament, than the average late seventeenth-century English goldsmith possessed, and it was perhaps this fact that enabled the Huguenots to achieve such prominence in the craft. They arrived as oppressed emigrés, and although their presence was eventually to prove an inestimable boon to the English silver trade, it did not seem so at the time. Many attempts were made to prevent the 'strangers' practising their craft. It was necessary for a goldsmith to have his wares assayed before he could legally sell them, but he could only get them assayed if he were a freeman of the Goldsmiths' Company. The Company refused to admit the Huguenots unless they first served the full seven-years apprenticeship, an absurd provision since most of them had already completed a far more rigorous apprenticeship

73 *Right:* A George II silver-gilt cup and cover, by William Kidney, London, 1740. Height 14¼ in. The Worshipful Company of Goldsmiths, London.

74 *Below:* 'The Tea Party', an oil painting by an unknown artist, about 1720. The Worshipful Company of Goldsmiths, London.

75 A small single-handled wine taster (I think this really *is* a wine taster), made in London by Samuel Wastell, 1701. It is an unusual, rather French-looking object, though made by an Englishman.

in France. Meanwhile, many gifted French goldsmiths were compelled to work as employees of established English freemen of the Company. However, thanks largely to English patrons who appreciated their worth, the barriers were soon broken down, and by the end of the century a substantial sprinkling of French names appears in the records of the Goldsmiths' Company. Simultaneously, those English goldsmiths who would not or could not cope with the new demands upon their competence gradually disappeared, leaving only those who could compete on equal terms with the 'strangers', frequently by learning from them.

From about 1700 it is possible to distinguish two emergent styles, different but complementary. On one hand there is the true French, Baroque style with its bold use of cast forms, a heavy style of restraining grandeur, displaying the utmost finesse in technique and design and relying mainly for decorative effects on bold, applied strapwork (in the cut-card technique), heavy cast handles and tightly drawn cast gad-rooning (Plate 78). Embossing was rejected, and a heavier gauge metal helps to impart the effect of magnificence. On the other hand, from the new generation of English goldsmiths, there is a simple purity of form, relying more on elegant lines than ornamental technique to achieve a satisfying balance (Plate 80). But it would be wrong to imply that these two groups are mutually exclusive. On the contrary, many coffee pots, teapots and salvers in remarkably austere style were made by Huguenots, and equally, English goldsmiths turned out many a two-handled cup and cover adorned with rich strapwork mouldings. Both styles relied on simplicity of form, though their marked difference in ornament signifies their origin in different camps.

747

The two-handled cup, which had evolved from its simple origin in the ox-eye cup through the porringer, now began to be made in more massive proportions. The basic outline is bell-shaped; it stands on a shortish, spreading, turned foot, and is topped by a stepped-dome lid with a bold baluster or acorn finial. In earlier examples the handles are harp-shaped, but from about 1700 they generally have S-scroll handles with an acanthus leaf overlaid at the top. The strapwork calyx around the lower part of the cup is usually of simple lobate forms around the turn of the century, but after about 1715 it is much more elaborate, frequently pierced and incorporating classical heads, and often alternately matted and plain.

In tankards it is possible, if not perhaps wise, to distinguish between an 'English' form—straight-sided with a moulded girdle and domed lid—and a 'Huguenot' variety—slightly bellied with cut-card work around the base and possibly a baluster finial to the lid. Pear-shaped jugs with covers for wine or beer made their appearance, while other, once-common vessels declined—the old ewer and dish had become a rarity

79 *Right:* A Queen Anne chocolate pot, perfectly plain and simple, made by Gabriel Sleath in London, 1709. The second hinged lid, which was used for stirring the chocolate, can be clearly seen. Height 10 in.

80 *Below:* George I octagonal sugar caster, 1719. Though extremely competent and very pretty, it does show the difference between the simple lines of the English goldsmith and the luxuriant genius of the Huguenot craftsman.

and silver wine cups had been largely displaced by glass since the improvements in making flint glass associated with the name of George Ravenscroft (1618-81).

While the English had more or less ceased to drink their wine from a silver cup, they had adopted new drinking habits which offered greater scope to goldsmiths. The drinking of tea, coffee and hot chocolate became customary in the late seventeenth century and grew increasingly popular in the eighteenth. Silver provided the most suitable containers for

749

Teapots

c. 1710

c. 1710

c. 1715

Scottish
c. 1725

c. 1735

c. 1755

c. 1790

c. 1770

c. 1800

c. 1815

c. 1825

c. 1875

81 Queen Anne pear-shaped teapot, made by John Fawdery, 1713. The shape is particularly attractive and this is a favourite teapot of mine. Some tend to be a little elongated and therefore not quite so pretty. Height 5 in.

these very expensive beverages. The first coffee pots and teapots were made as individual items; the idea of a matching set was not taken up until later. Coffee and chocolate pots are generally tall and straight-sided, with either a swan-necked or straight – sometimes faceted – spout. Lids are tall and domed up to about 1720, thereafter lower and more rounded. The handle, of wood or other material, is mounted either in the conventional position opposite the spout or at right angles to it; the latter form is always less common in England and tends to disappear after 1720. Probably, the same pot was used interchangeably for coffee or chocolate, but some pots were made especially for chocolate. Unlike coffee, chocolate does not actually flavour the water; what one tastes is the particles of chocolate suspended in water. To ensure that the first cup is not pale and flavourless and the last strong and sludgy, it is best to stir it briskly before pouring. For this reason, chocolate pots were provided with a small, extra lid, set into the normal cover, through which a rod could be lowered to whisk up the chocolate without too much heat being lost (Plate 79).

A different form was adopted for teapots. Tea came from China, and the shape of the English teapot was also adapted from the Chinese (though the vessel concerned was actually used in China for wine rather than tea). Up to about 1715 teapots tend to be pear-shaped, after that a slightly squashed sphere. In Scotland the globular or bullet-shaped teapot was popular longer than in the south; it tends to be more nearly

751

spherical and stands on a somewhat higher foot. It would be hard to find a 'bullet' teapot made in London much later than 1740, but Scottish examples can be found as late as 1760.

Other accoutrements of the tea table were sugar bowls, almost exact copies of the Chinese covered tea bowls of the period, more or less hemispherical and standing on a low rim foot, with a shallow cover. Cream jugs are usually pear-shaped, with simple S-scroll handles. Kettles conform in outline to the teapot, but are obviously considerably larger. They stood on a four-legged stand which supported a spirit burner. The purpose of the burner was to keep the water hot, not to boil it. The truth of this I once proved to my own satisfaction when trying to make a cup of tea during a power cut: the eventual result was not a success.

The tea- or coffee pot sometimes sat on a tray which, at this period, is either square or rectangular with in-curving corners, or occasionally octagonal. The number of trays that have survived, however, is small compared with the number of teapots and coffee pots, which suggests that many people did without a tray. Last but not least, the tea itself was kept in a tea caddy, rectangular or square and taller than its length. They often have cut corners. The tea was poured through a smallish aperture with a removable domed cover. This was less convenient when it came to filling the caddy, which was therefore made with a sliding base or top.

Between about 1710 and 1725 a delightful new pattern was popular, in tea equipage especially, in which the circular form was modified into an octagonal, occasionally hexagonal outline (Plate 82). This attractive variation is also evident in the candlesticks which were made during the period.

82 A pair of Queen Anne tea caddies made by Louis Cuny, 1709, over-struck by Pierre Platel. The arms, Aylmer impaling Ellis, are those of a famous admiral, Lord Aylmer. Commander-in-Chief of the Fleet, 1709-11 and 1714-20. One caddy has a letter B and the other a letter G engraved above the arms and on the lid; these stand for Bothea and Green, two kinds of tea.

83 *Right:* A set of coffee pot, teapot and kettle by Joseph Ward, 1719, a truly superb example of the octagonal form. The Worshipful Company of Goldsmiths, London.

84 *Below:* George I octagonal sugar caster with heavy lobate straps, made by David Tanqueray in London, about 1720. It is engraved with the arms and cypher of George I and once belonged to Sir Robert Walpole. Height 7½ in.

85 *Below right:* Silver-gilt toilet box, originally from a large toilet service, made by John Edwards, 1725. The arms, which are superbly engraved, are those of Joseph Gascoigne Nightingale and his wife Elizabeth, eldest daughter of the 2nd Earl Ferrers. Length 9¾ in.

There is a startling difference between the candlesticks of the Restoration period, up to about 1685 or 1690, and those made subsequently. In the earlier period they are almost invariably fashioned from thin sheet silver, the earliest ones with a plain trumpet outline roughly bisected by a large drip pan. Then there are various forms of the cluster column. Most of these are of rather poor quality, but some really exceptional examples were made by Jacob Bodendick, a German immigrant goldsmith of astonishing ability and versatility; there is a magnificent pair of candlesticks by him belonging to Harthill Church in Yorkshire. The early Huguenot candlesticks are invariably cast and are fairly plain, with either a circular or, more commonly, a square base with cut corners, and a baluster

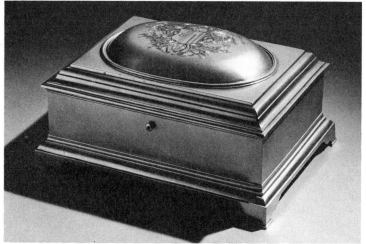

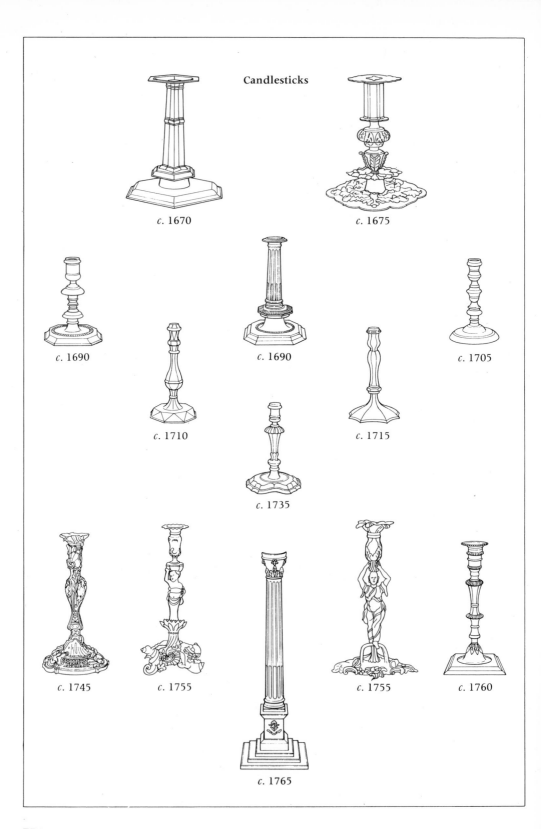

Candlesticks

c. 1670

c. 1675

c. 1690

c. 1690

c. 1705

c. 1710

c. 1715

c. 1735

c. 1745

c. 1755

c. 1755

c. 1760

c. 1765

c. 1770

c. 1780

c. 1780

c. 1800

c. 1810

86 *Left:* Hand candlestick, unmarked but probably made by Paul Crespin, one of the great Huguenot makers, about 1730. This remarkable little candlestick illustrates the transition between Baroque and Rococo. The flat-chased ornamental band on the border still harks backwards in spirit but the cast rim looks towards the Rococo.

87 *Above:* A little pear-shaped pepper caster, made by Jonah Clifton in London, 1719. This is an unusually heavy example; as a rule they tend to be disappointingly light and tinny.

stem incorporating an inverted acorn motif. They are much superior to the general run of rather inferior Restoration candlesticks, but in this instance the Huguenot goldsmiths did not dominate the trade because the English goldsmiths changed over to the new cast type almost overnight. Possibly the finest candlestick maker of the first two decades of the eighteenth century was Thomas Merry, who appears to have specialised solely in candlesticks and snuffer stands.

Up to about 1730 the square base with cut corners remained popular, though octagonal and hexagonal examples were also made in large quantities. There is also a rare form with a base like an open umbrella. Virtually every known form of candlestick in this period was also made in miniature, and these are known as taper sticks. Their purpose is not known for certain, but the usual explanation is that they were used at a desk for melting the sealing wax necessary for sealing letters. The fact that taper sticks are nearly always found as single articles, rather than pairs (like candlesticks), is evidence in support of this explanation.

Apart from the majestic Baroque style of France, the Huguenots also brought to England towards the end of the seventeenth century a number of new objects. The soup tureen, the sauceboat and the hand candlestick all seem likely to have had a French rather than an English origin, and so does

that long-popular article, the helmet-shaped jug. Other comparatively new objects, such as those associated with tea and coffee, of course developed from changing social customs rather than the background or imagination of silversmiths, while the greater use of cut-card work, for example, was partly the result of the invention of a metal-rolling machine, which greatly reduced the time and effort needed to convert an ingot into a thin sheet.

Like most small foreign communities, the Huguenot craftsmen tended to stick together, often marrying among their own people and, judging by the large number of objects which have one maker's mark overstruck by another, often helping each other in fulfilling a large order. They also remained in closer touch with developments in their native France than did their English contemporaries. By 1726 the French goldsmith Just Aurèle Meissonnier had been appointed court designer to Louis XV, and he was experimenting with a new style which came to be known as Rococo.

Rococo

The Rococo style is easy to recognise visually though not simple to describe in words. It was in part a reaction against the calm monumentality of Baroque, abandoning strict symmetry in favour of flamboyant and whimsical forms and vigorous, even frantic movement. The architectural element in Baroque was totally abandoned and line disappeared under lavish ornament, with decorative motifs drawn from naturalistic forms—the asymmetry of rocks (the original meaning of 'rococo' was 'rockwork'), sea creatures and shells. Ornament was cast, chased and engraved with riotous abandon, so that

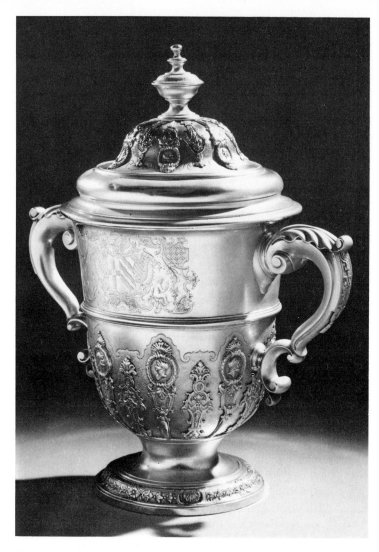

the eye finds no place to rest and even something as solid as a
piece of silver seems to be in constant writhing movement.

In England the Huguenots were the leaders in the new style.
Paul de Lamerie (1688-1751), arguably England's greatest
goldsmith in this period, was beginning to break away from the
conventional production of his time, and in certain of his pieces
in the late 1720s and early 1730s the awakening of Rococo can
be detected (Plate 88). In England, however, Rococo never
reached quite the heights of extravagance it achieved in
France, even in the hands of the Huguenot craftsmen who led
the way. There are probably two main reasons for this. It is
possible that even the finest English goldsmiths, de Lamerie,
Paul Crespin, Nicholas Sprimont and others, were not quite
capable of fully realising the Meissonnier designs, which began

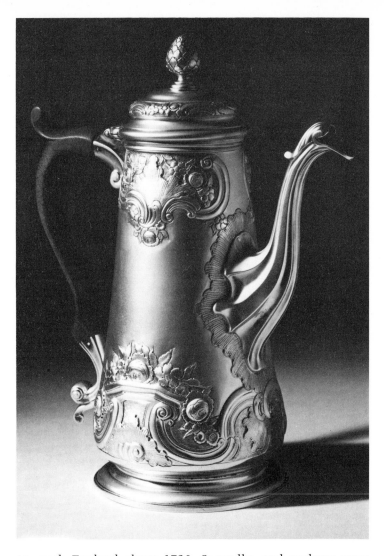

90 George II coffee pot with elegant and refined Rococo decoration, made by John Carman, 1749. Height 9½ in.

to reach England about 1736. Secondly, and perhaps more significantly, it was not the goldsmith but his customer who had the last word on the object being made. English taste has often tended to be more restrained than French, and the Rococo at its most lavish never had quite the same popular appeal on the English side of the Channel. Even when the style was at its height, large numbers of objects were being made which are essentially plain and simple, perhaps paying faint-hearted lip service to the Rococo in an asymmetrical cartouche for a coat of arms or some other inconsequential feature.

It was not only the customer's taste which decided whether his plate should be plain and simple or elaborately ornamental. The depth of his purse was an equally important factor. The goldsmith charged his customer so much an ounce for the silver

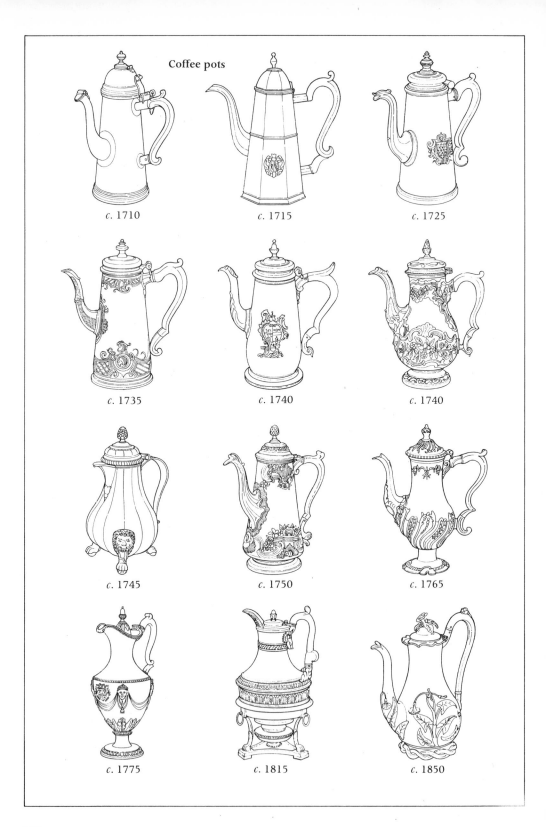

Coffee pots

c. 1710   *c.* 1715   *c.* 1725

c. 1735   *c.* 1740   *c.* 1740

c. 1745   *c.* 1750   *c.* 1765

c. 1775   *c.* 1815   *c.* 1850

he used and so much an ounce for the actual fashioning. Obviously, the latter sum depended on the amount of work the goldsmith put into the piece, and possibly the comparative paucity of decoration on many pieces of English silver in the Rococo period was the result of necessary economy rather than a distaste for the current high-flown style.

The two-handled cup and cover, which had come to form such an important part of the goldsmith's oeuvre, retains the bell-shaped outline that was characteristic of it in the early years of the century. The decorative strapwork, however, becomes increasingly naturalistic: gone are the baluster-shaped straps enclosing classical busts; instead, the strapwork bands are formed of shells and flowers winding around the lower half of the body. Handles become more elaborate, consisting of double S-scrolls overlaid with shells and acanthus leaves, while the lids rise to grotesque leaf and rock finials. One unusual series of covered cups, made by Paul de Lamerie, has a snake writhing in and out of the bowl to form the handles, which are richly decorated all over with scalework and grotesque masks.

By and large, teapots and coffee pots escaped the more extreme forms of the new style, especially in the early years of Rococo. However, the plain, straight-sided shape which had characterised the coffee pot for such a long time was gradually abandoned in favour of a taller, baluster form on a moulded foot. In the 1760s they were sometimes given exotic decoration in the Chinese manner. This second period of Chinoiserie is more evident in tea- and coffee pots and their accompanying pieces than in other types of plate. It seems to have been largely inspired by the paintings of Boucher and his school, who were fascinated by the vision of 'Cathay' (China), though of course they knew little of its reality.

Of all the pieces of plate associated with the drinking of tea and coffee, the kettle was most attractive to the Rococo goldsmith, offering plenty of scope for him to exercise his imagination and talent. Some astonishingly elaborate and exquisitely made examples have survived. The tea tray and the salver also offered a generous surface for ingenious and extravagant engraving, though cast work, for obvious practical reasons, was confined to the borders. There are some remarkable Rococo salvers with fine cast openwork borders, but in general it is the engraving that is most striking.

A new piece of plate appeared in the centre of the dining table, the épergne. Essentially, it was a stand for sweetmeats or fruit, consisting of one large basket and a group of smaller ones

hanging from or fitted to the ends of scrolling branches. It was ideally adapted to the lush ornament of the period, and to Rococo goldsmiths like de Lamerie it offered an opportunity to indulge in thrilling flights of fancy.

Candlesticks wrought in the ornate style of high Rococo are not very common, and those that exist were almost all made by Huguenot goldsmiths (though by this time, of course, the majority of 'Huguenots' were English-born). The most common candlesticks of the period were made by specialist candlestick makers like the Goulds, the Cafes and Ebenezer Coker. They are taller – about ten inches from the 1740s onward compared with an average height of six or seven inches in the first twenty years of the century. The basic pattern is a shaped square base with a shell at each corner, rising to a baluster stem, with a drip pan at the top in the same style as the base. Among other contemporary patterns are hexafoil bases and square, gadrooned bases, often with a swirling lower stem. There are many others.

The branches of candelabra are usually of plain double S-scroll form, the nozzles and drip pans following the form of the candlestick itself. The general run are less than inspired; they

91 *Above:* Silver tray, a real tour-de-force of engraving with its bold border of intertwining foliate scrolls and swags and a brilliant piece of design work for the central cartouche. Length 30 in. Weight approximately 266 ounces. Colonial Williamsburg Foundation, Williamsburg, Virginia.

92 *Opposite, top:* Silver-gilt inkstand and bell, the former by Paul de Lamerie, 1741. It was ordered by the Goldsmiths' Company to accommodate the bell, which has a maker's mark WW and is dated 1666.

93 *Opposite, bottom:* Gilt cup and cover, or tea caddy, in the Adam style by J. Arnell, 1772, with a black basalt ware vase and cover made by Josiah Wedgwood. Victoria and Albert Museum, London.

764

94 *Opposite, top:* A pair of George III bottle coasters by William Plummer, London, 1773.

95 *Opposite, bottom:* A pair of George III silver-gilt candelabra, made by John Scofield, London, 1783. Height 16½ in.

96 *Right:* A pair of the highest quality candlesticks in the best early Rococo taste, with applied masks, shells and foliage, made by Peter Archambo, 1738. Height 8 in.

must have been turned out in thousands for everyday use in the home, although there are some fine flights of fancy by Huguenot makers. Since the late seventeenth century at least, candlesticks had occasionally been made with a human figure forming the stem, and under the influence of the renewed taste for Chinoiserie, some makers, including Aymé Videau and – rather unexpectedly – John Cafe, produced the slightly zany conceit of a Chinese male figure standing on a boldly Rococo, triangular base and holding the actual candleholder and drip pan with both hands above his head.

Like kettles, tea urns, punch bowls and soup tureens were large enough for the goldsmith to display the full exuberance of the Rococo style. An outstandingly elaborate tureen was made by Paul Crespin. It is covered with a cascade of fruit and the bowl is supported by two reclining goats – altogether an ingenious and exceptional piece. Another, by John Edwards, has dolphin handles and swags of crustacea and seaweed, while the finial is a most alarmingly realistic crab. No doubt this was intended for fish soup (Plate 71).

Sauceboats underwent a transformation of form as well as decoration. As we have seen, the early sauceboats are oval, with a lip at either end. By about 1725, they have a lip at one

97 A pair of candlesticks, made by John le Sage, one of the Goldsmiths in Ordinary to the King, 1759. The amusing conceit of caryatid candlesticks was quite popular in the late 1740s and 1750s. These examples are engraved with the arms of George II and are considerably better made than most similar candlesticks. Height $11\frac{1}{2}$ in.

98 Sauceboat, made by William Woodward in London, 1744. The plain body of this fine piece is augmented by a bold Rococo handle, though in general the Rococo feeling is restrained. Length 7 in.

end only, with a single scroll handle at the other, though the oval form, with an oval collet lip, remains. In general these early Georgian sauceboats were left plain or engraved with a band of trelliswork. A more elaborate form began to appear in the 1730s, standing on four lion-mask feet and sometimes with heavy cast festoons, and by 1740 the true shell form of boat had evolved. The sheer exuberance of some of these Rococo sauceboats—a mass of swags and shellfish with handles made as herons or eagles—is a joy. In a particularly beautiful set in the royal collection at Windsor, the shell bodies of the boats rest on dolphins among shells and rocks, while the handles are fashioned as young tritons, scantily clad, seated on the rim. They were made in 1743 by Nicholas Sprimont, who had recently come to England from Liège. He worked as a silversmith for only about seven years before taking charge of the Chelsea porcelain factory in 1748, and as a result his work is unfortunately rare today. What there is of it confirms his astonishing inventiveness and technical virtuosity.

Salt cellars evolved similarly to sauceboats. The salt cellar of the 1720s and early 1730s is usually circular and stands on a collet foot which, as in the sauceboat, eventually gives way to three or four lion-mask feet interspersed with foliage, while a slightly undulating gadrooned rim becomes common. Casters adopt a more pronounced baluster shape. The more expensive ones received extensive applied decoration of swags, masks,

99 A salt, in strong Rococo form, made in 1749. To acquire a superb example of something, it is not always necessary to buy pairs or sets of four. This little single salt probably belonged to a set of four.

shells and scrolls, while those made for the cheaper end of the market are naturally much plainer, with the piercing of the lid alone reflecting the Rococo. Casters were frequently made in sets of three, one larger than the others. The larger one was for sugar, the others for pepper and mustard (which was then taken dry) or other spice. The mustard caster is often engraved in the same pattern as the other two but not actually pierced. Occasionally, the three casters are found in a stand or frame together with two glass bottles for oil and vinegar.

That very delightful object, the silver basket, though made in the sixteenth century, did not become a common article until the 1730s. They are generally oval, and some of the early ones are fashioned in rough imitation of actual basketwork. More typically, the sides are pierced in an elaborate pattern of scrolls, with a wavy or scalloped edge and a central swing handle. There is often an engraved coat of arms on the base,

100 A George II oil and vinegar set, made in London by George Wickes, 1742. The sides are pierced in elaborate intertwined scrolls and foliage.

with a border of shells and trelliswork, sometimes flat chased, sometimes engraved. After about 1750 they are lighter in weight and the decoration tends to be less rich, with the luxuriant Rococo ornament giving way to Chinese fretwork and simpler borders, sometimes incorporating a wheat-ear motif. Although these objects are usually called cake baskets, their exact use is not certain. Probably they held cake, bread, fruit, or anything else their owners chose to put in them.

The great quantity of plate produced during the Rococo period without much sign of Rococo ornament should not be forgotten. Plates are a good example. A great many, probably the majority, are relatively plain. At the beginning of the century they were given a simple moulded rim, but later the edges were shaped, with a gadrooned wire border. With some exceptions, they have continued to be made in more or less the same way until the present. Mugs (generally smaller than

101 Silver basket by Paul de Lamerie, 1739. It has cast and applied work, engraving and flat chasing, and is altogether a beautifully composed piece. The detail of the inside of the basket shows how it is still possible today to find silver of this period in mint condition.

770

102 *Opposite:* Silver-gilt cup and cover, showing the quite extraordinary elaborations that the High Rococo goldsmiths employed, unmarked but almost certainly made by Thomas Hemming, about 1745-50. The tambourine held aloft is engraved with the arms of Tatton. Height 14 in.

103 *Above:* A pair of tea caddies and a sugar box, displaying good Rococo flat chasing, made by Elizabeth Godfrey in London, 1742. They fit into a sharkskin case.

tankards, and lidless) and tankards were similarly little influenced by the Rococo. The tapering straight-sided form current at the beginning of the century gave way about 1730 to a baluster form, but there is little sign of Baroque grandeur or, later, of Rococo extravagance. Of course there are exceptions. Some very splendid ornamental tankards were fashioned for very wealthy patrons, but most people made do with tankards in a much-diluted version of the prevailing fashion.

The Adam style

Every style eventually provokes a reaction against itself: the pendulum can swing only so far before it reverses direction, and the end of the Rococo came rather swiftly. In little more than the single decade of the 1760s, the pendulum swung sharply away from the whirling extravagance of Rococo: in 1760 the style was still in full bloom, but ten years later it was virtually dead. Hardly a single Rococo object was made after 1770.

The new style was a relatively austere and refined neo-classicism. It is usually known as the 'Adam' style because of the overwhelming influence of the Adam family, especially the great Robert Adam (1728-92). But while Robert Adam did make many designs for silver, they were only a small and insignificant part of his total influence, which embraced everything

from the architecture of a house, the colour of the ceilings, walls, carpets and curtains, down to the smallest details of interior decoration, even including the view from the windows. Hundreds of his designs are kept today in the Sir John Soane Museum in London, and to see them is a fascinating and rewarding experience.

By the middle of the eighteenth century the Grand Tour was an essential part of an English gentleman's education, and thus many people (Robert Adam among them) went to Italy and other parts where they could see—and sometimes purchase—for themselves the works of the ancient Greeks and Romans, especially the extraordinary discoveries of classical antiquities that had been made recently at Pompeii and Herculaneum. Public interest in antiquity was further stimulated by the writings of art historians like J. J. Winckelmann. With remarkable speed—and remarkable thoroughness—popular taste em-

104 *Above, left:* Adam-style tea urn, typical of the extreme elegance of the period.

105 *Above:* Hot-water or coffee jug, 1796. The urn-shaped outline typifies the Adam period. Height *c.* 13 in.

106 *Opposite, top:* Silver-gilt inkstand, by Digby Scott and Benjamin Smith, London, 1803. The Worshipful Company of Goldsmiths, London.

107 *Opposite, bottom:* Silver-gilt cup, based on a cup found at Herculaneum, by Edward Barnard and Sons, London, 1840.

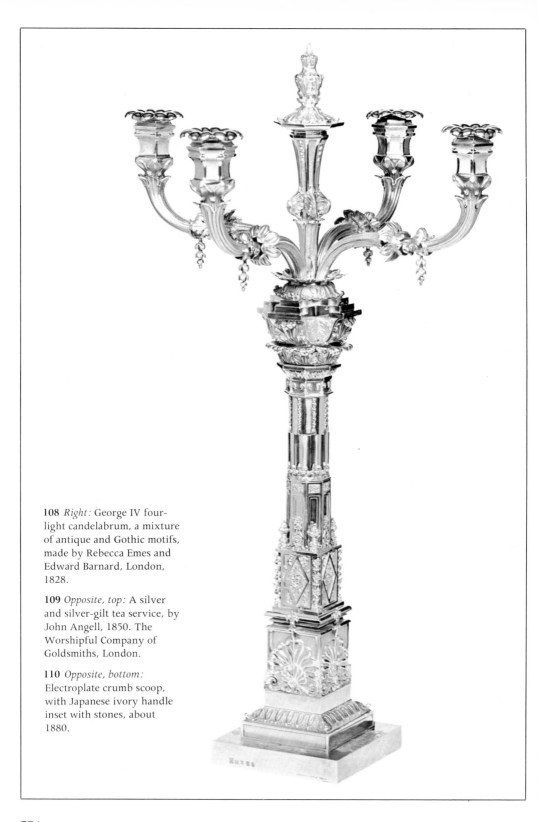

108 *Right:* George IV four-light candelabrum, a mixture of antique and Gothic motifs, made by Rebecca Emes and Edward Barnard, London, 1828.

109 *Opposite, top:* A silver and silver-gilt tea service, by John Angell, 1850. The Worshipful Company of Goldsmiths, London.

110 *Opposite, bottom:* Electroplate crumb scoop, with Japanese ivory handle inset with stones, about 1880.

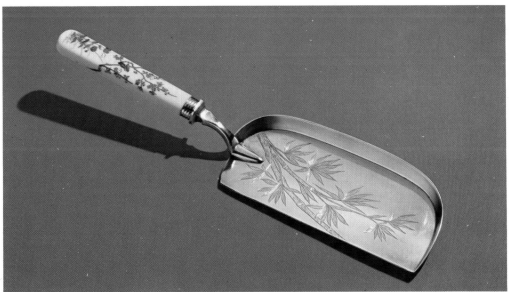

braced the classical. Customers demanded only 'the most refined Grecian articles', although in fact many of the patterns adopted were Roman rather than Greek, and many were not strictly either. The use that Adam and others made of the classical was essentially adaptative rather than slavishly imitative. The Adam style has never really gone completely out of fashion, and it is therefore familiar to most people at least through later copies. Much of the decoration is in relief, usually applied on grander pieces, but engraving was also revived, often in the new form of 'bright-cut' engraving – clean and sparkling lines made with a special graver. The forms of silver vessels are frequently based on the urn or the vase, and classical decorative motifs – paterae, ram's heads, anthemion scrolls, laurel festoons and acanthus leaves – are everywhere.

The sauceboats on Georgian dining tables were joined by sauce tureens. These generally look like miniature soup tureens, the favourite shape being oval. They have two elegant C-scroll handles and domed lids with baluster finials. Salt cellars were made to match, with the same elegant handles but no lids. It was now, too, that full tea or coffee services came into fashion. Tea urns are large and gracious (Plate 104); they frequently come in matching pairs of two sizes. Jugs for hot water or coffee follow a similar urn shape, while the teapot and the sugar basin are usually oval, with straight sides and perhaps shaped corners. The milk jug, tall and helmet-shaped, stands on a square or circular collet foot with an elongated C-scroll handle. The commonest form of decoration for the tea and coffee services is bright-cut engraving which, on pieces that

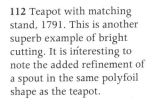

111 *Opposite:* Two Victorian candlesticks, from a set of four designed by G.A. Carter for Hunt and Roskell, London, about 1880.

112 Teapot with matching stand, 1791. This is another superb example of bright cutting. It is interesting to note the added refinement of a spout in the same polyfoil shape as the teapot.

have been protected from much wear, creates a beautiful and sparkling effect. Unfortunately, however, much old silver is not in pristine condition, and this form of decoration loses its original diamond sharpness rather easily.

The appearance of the Adam style roughly coincided with the introduction of new, industrial methods of production. The long-established predominance of London in the silver trade was threatened by the rise of Sheffield and Birmingham, where factory production made silver articles much more easily available. Birmingham goldsmiths had always been regarded as trinket makers and little more, but Matthew Boulton and others employed the methods which the Industrial Revolution spawned to create a genuine art industry in the city. The die-stamping process allowed candlesticks, baskets and similar items to be turned out in thousands. Mass production, plus the thin gauge of metal used (the hollow candlestick was filled with pitch and the base weighted), made them inexpensive. The best work was still done in London, but the cheap filled candle-sticks that poured out of Birmingham must have taken some of the trade away from London, although they also found a new market among people who were not able to afford traditionally hand-wrought silver. Birmingham production, moreover, should not be dismissed as worthless. Some very beautiful candlesticks were made there and in Sheffield, and the rising new middle class, while they required inexpensive articles, also had an eye for general quality and workmanship.

Another development which had enormous effect on the silver trade was the production of what is known as 'Sheffield plate'. Strictly, 'plate' is the term for all silver and gold articles, but it is commonly used for plated silver, i.e. a layer of silver on base metal. The process of fusing a thin layer of silver on to a copper core had been discovered more or less by chance by Thomas Boulsover in 1742, though it was not employed on a commercial scale until the 1760s. A copper ingot is married to a sheet of silver about one-eighth of an inch thick, hammered firmly and placed in a furnace. Heating fuses the two inseparably together, and after cooling the ingot can be rolled into a workable sheet, then hammered or punched in the same way as solid silver without separating the silver coating from the copper. Any object which can be made in silver can be made in fused plate, and it is obviously much cheaper because of the small quantity of silver used.

During the 1770s and 1780s the commonest object made in Sheffield plate was the candlestick, though some coffee pots and tea urns were also made. From about 1785 a huge variety of objects—épergnes, baskets, teapots, wine coolers, even such small things as wine labels and coasters—were produced in Sheffield. During the last twenty years or so of the eighteenth century Sheffield plate was at its height, and the care lavished on its finishing was equal to that of solid silver. About 1830 a decline is evident. The industry was no longer engaged in making fine objects in the latest manner, and its general

114 A striking pair of silver candelabra made in London, 1807, and presented to Admiral Sir John Duckworth by the Island of Jamaica after he had defeated the French fleet off Santo Domingo. They are of massive proportions and an interesting feature is Duckworth's crest fashioned as a finial in the centre of the three branches. Height 24 in.

115 A pair of George III
sauceboats, covers and
stands, made in the Egyptian
taste by Digby Scott and
Benjamin Smith, London,
1806.

production became old-fashioned and rather dull. Finally, the
successful commercial exploitation of electrolytic techniques
made Sheffield plate obsolete. Today, however, as long as the
piece has not been over-cleaned so that large areas of copper
show through, Sheffield plate forms a delightful and highly
collectable part of the silver of the Adam period.

Before the end of the eighteenth century the light and pure
classical elegance of the 1770s and 1780s was being dissipated,
and a tendency towards a grander style, more Roman than
Greek, was appearing. It is generally in this new movement
towards more massive styles, which remained characteristic of
the early nineteenth century also, that high-quality work is
most obvious. At the lower end of the scale, mass production
resulted inevitably in dilution of the Adam style, and the
vitality of the early years diminished. As the end of the century
drew near, writes John Culme, 'the charm of the Adam style
became less apparent, until even the King complained that the
Adam brothers had "introduced too much of neatness and
prettiness . . ." ' (*Nineteenth-Century Silver*, Country Life, 1977).

About 1800-10, the neo-classical was briefly and partially
diverted to themes inspired by Ancient Egypt. Sphinx-like feet
and masks made a brief appearance, though the Egyptian style
never had as much influence on silver as it did on, for instance,

116 *Above:* A pair of outstanding sauce tureens, by Digby Scott and Benjamin Smith, 1803, good examples of the new fashion for massiveness. They have certain characteristics that could almost make them French. Length about 8 in. each.

117 *Right:* A silver-gilt cast bottle-label for sherry, 1830. Many bottle-labels are dreary, but others were made with great care and effort: this example is unusually well made.

furniture. One characteristic of the late Rococo period had been the increasing diversity of styles (even Gothic enjoyed a brief vogue), and the later years of the Adam period show a similar tendency. This time, however, there was to be no sudden and overwhelming changeover in fashion. What is here discernible is the beginnings of nineteenth-century eclecticism.

Nineteenth-century silver

For a number of reasons it is very difficult to describe the silver of the nineteenth century briefly without creating some misleading impressions. One problem is the vast amount of silver made, the prevalence of several different styles, and the mingling of disparate styles in individual pieces. At the same time there was much mere copying, not only of eighteenth-century designs but also of Renaissance or 'Neo-Renaissance' designs. Then there is the enormous quantity of silver of no particular form or merit which was manufactured by the ever-increasing use of mechanised processes. All this creates a good deal of confusion – and distrust – in discussions of nineteenth-century work.

At the beginning of the nineteenth century, the most influential firm of retail jewellers and goldsmiths was the remarkable house of Rundell and Bridge. It began in 1772 when Philip Rundell went into partnership with William Pickett. In 1785 he bought Pickett out and took on John Bridge as a partner. They were men of very different but complementary temperaments, and it was their successful working partnership that raised the firm to the top of the trade. In the earlier period, however, although Rundell and Bridge were already employing the foremost goldsmiths of the time, their silver was not, in general, outstanding. The ambitious and lavish plate for which the firm became famous was mostly made after the time when Rundell's nephew joined it, in 1805 (thereafter it became Rundell, Bridge and Rundell).

The goldsmiths who worked for Rundell and Bridge and dominated English silver for the first thirty years of the nineteenth century included Digby Scott and Benjamin Smith, a partnership which produced some of the most splendid and massive silver ever made, as well as Paul Storr, probably the most famous silversmith of the nineteenth century though arguably no greater than Scott and Smith. The mixture of styles and themes which in the hands of less gifted craftsmen often led to rather curious-looking objects was carried out by these men with striking success. There is, for instance, a dinner service by Paul Storr which combines elements of the classical

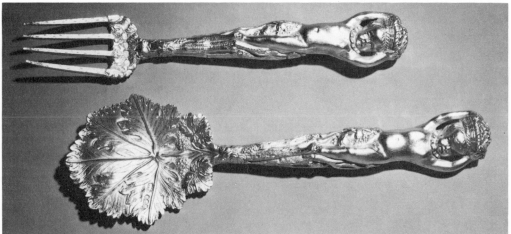

118 *Top:* A pair of typical
Regency silver-gilt salvers or
dessert stands on a central
foot, superbly made and
engraved with the arms of
the Duke of Richmond and
Gordon, 1807. Diameter 12 in.

119 *Above:* A delightful pair
of silver-gilt fruit servers of
outstanding quality, made
by Edward Farrell, 1816.

with Egyptian and Rococo motifs – a very surprising mixture
which nevertheless 'works'. The extravagant naturalism that
marked the Rococo was not lost but modified by Romanticism.
Edward Farrell produced a wide range of pieces employing
flower forms in the most naturalistic way, combined with cast
cherubs and foliage. Edward Barnard and Sons, another
eminent firm which is still in business today, made many
articles of similar feeling. One example is a perfect pair of salts
in the form of an idealised peasant boy and girl each holding a
basket for the salt receptacle. However, a tendency towards

the sentimental is often evident, as it is in a pair of silver-gilt candelabra in the form of flower sellers standing on a grassy knoll with a tree whose branches support the candle holders (Plate 120). Designs of this kind, while possessing less appeal for modern eyes than they did for contemporaries, nevertheless represent some of the loveliest Victorian silver.

Not so long ago, writers often dismissed the last seventy years of the nineteenth century as unworthy of serious consideration. There is certainly much to criticise, both in design and workmanship, but it would be easy to find many examples of faulty design and poor craftsmanship in any other period. Even the most devoted collector should be prepared to admit this fact. Age is not necessarily synonymous with good quality.

The liking for naturalistic decoration gave rise to a rather unfortunate habit among the Victorians which is perhaps largely responsible for posterity's accusations of poor taste and philistinism. A large quantity of eighteenth-century silver was sent by its Victorian owners to be ornamentally embossed. To

120 *Left:* A pair of silver-gilt Victorian candelabra, 1861. These beautiful examples of Victorian goldsmithing take the form of fruit and flower sellers leaning against a tree, each of which branches into a two-light candelabrum.

Georgian bowls and cups they added scrolls and foliage, hunting scenes or industrial scenes, or sometimes simply a foliate cartouche in which the name and accomplishments of some civic worthy might be engraved. Much as we may deplore this habit, it should be looked at rationally. Old silver is not necessarily sacred, and for the Victorians Georgian silver was no older than Victorian silver is today. Conservation of old things was not—and, to be fair to the Victorians, did not have to be—so much a matter for concern. Moreover, Victorian design was not always bad. An objective judge would have to say that many 'doctored' articles were at least not spoiled by Victorian additions.

Such an extraordinary multiplicity of designs, such ingenious new methods of manufacture, such creative inventiveness on a scale unrivalled in any other century is displayed by the silver of the Victorian period that it would be absurd for us to treat its aspirations and achievements with scorn or indifference. Not many years ago some of the best work of Victorian goldsmiths used to be melted down without compunction. Let us hope that the work of our best goldsmiths today is treated with greater vision by our descendants a hundred years hence.

In the area of design, there is only space here to pick out some of the main developments. In the Victorian period there was, as everyone knows, a great revival of the Gothic, much more wide-ranging and more authentic than the brief and less serious 'Gothick' revival of the eighteenth century. Silver designed in this Gothic style was, in my opinion, generally

121 *Below:* An inkwell in the form of a lily, made by Walter Jordan, 1834. This is an early example of the charming nineteenth-century naturalistic form.

rather unsuccessful. True, some very remarkable pieces were made, and some church plate in particular is thoroughly satisfactory. Secular objects, however, have to my eyes rather an uneasy feeling.

During the latter part of the century there was enormous interest in a style in art and decoration that could hardly have been more of a contrast—the style of Japan. Some of the most delightful examples are the tea sets of about 1870-90, which have parcel-gilt decoration of engraved birds, flowers and butterflies, with handles looking like bamboo and fan-shaped trays (Plate 122). Highly imaginative card cases were also made in the delicate Japanese style, and altogether this is a delightful and (except by a few discerning people) little-known area of Victorian silver. A firm like Elkington and Company made great use not only of Japanese designs but also Japanese techniques, for instance in their employment of cloisonné enamelling on silver or, more often, electrotype wares.

Elkington's of Birmingham achieved their prominence largely as a result of their virtual monopoly of electroplate. Experiments in gilding by electrolysis had begun very soon

122 *Above:* Parcel-gilt tea set and tray in the Japanese taste, by Edward Charles Brown, 1879. Scarcely recognised as something worth considering by collectors until quite recently, the work and craftsmanship of this set is, in fact, simply marvellous.

123 *Opposite:* Wine or water ewer made in Sheffield by James Dixon, 1884. Though known as the 'Cellini pattern', this is not a pure copy of a Renaissance ewer and it should certainly not be dismissed as merely derivative. Height 12¼ in.

787

124 *Above:* An electroplated tea service, by Christopher Dresser, 1880. Even today, this tea service seems reasonably contemporary and it is a striking example of the power of Dresser as a pioneer of modern design. Victoria and Albert Museum, London.

125 *Left:* One of a pair of electrogilt (gilding on base metal) dishes, made about 1855. Although beautifully made and to my mind extremely attractive, Victorian electroplate like this would have been thrown out a few years ago.

126 *Opposite:* Glass wine jug overlaid with silver, made by Elkington and Company, 1897. An example of the 'aesthetic' taste of the 1890s, the glass is the colour of crushed blackberries. Height about 14 in. Boston Museum of Fine Arts, Mass..

after the invention of the electric battery, and in 1814 Paul Storr had made his famous electrogilded 'Galvanic Goblet' from a design by John Flaxman. The method used then was not practical, but improvements followed, while Elkington's, with great foresight, managed to secure patents for all the most commercially useful techniques. By about 1855 electroplate had driven Sheffield plate into oblivion. Elkington's also produced electrotypes, precise copies of objects (usually in copper) made by electrodeposition, which were then electroplated in silver. Any object could be faithfully reproduced by this method, including natural objects like flowers or sentimental objects like a baby's outgrown shoe. At the same time new alloys like Britannia metal and nickel silver were employed in mass production, using steam-driven machinery. Art schools were established to encourage design, though the new ability to reproduce exactly the articles of earlier times inhibited the development of style.

At the very end of the century, however, a revolution in taste occurred with the flowering of Art Nouveau, a genuinely new and universal style (arguably the last example of such a phenomenon), though it did not supercede all other styles. Owing a good deal to the 'Japanese taste', Art Nouveau's sinuous lines might seem, superficially, not ideally suited to metalwork. The contrary proved true, and some of the most beautiful of all Art Nouveau objects were made in silver. Less than twenty years ago, Art Nouveau silver could be purchased in the most unpretentious antique shop for a song, but since then the style has been engulfed by a wave of renewed popular enthusiasm and prices have risen to what may perhaps turn out to be a somewhat over-inflated level.

127 Carving knife and fork rests in the form of a soldier and sailor having a tug of war, made in electroplate, about 1880. They are characteristic examples of Victorian inventiveness. Length about 3 in.

128 *Right:* A dramatic Art Nouveau cup and cover depicting a triton rising from swirling waves and grasping a cup in his outstretched hands, made by Aldwinkle and Slater, 1902. Height 14 in.

129 *Below:* A charming little butter spade engraved with flowers and a butterfly, made towards the end of the nineteenth century. This is a perfect little piece for a discerning collector without too much money.

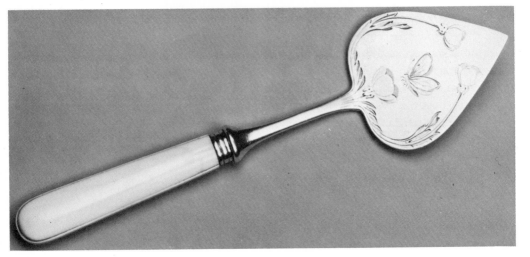

Chapter 4

Cutlery 1500-1900

Cutlery or 'flatware'—the rather curious term used by gold-smiths for sets of cutlery—requires a chapter to itself. Apart from the engraving or other ornamental details, it can best be categorised by features of design that are often not directly connected with the changing fashions in silver generally. Moreover cutlery, or spoons at least, provides the best opportunity for a collector today who is interested in early English silver—made before about 1600. Larger pieces of silver from the Tudor period do occasionally come up for sale, but being so rare they are naturally very expensive. No one can reasonably contemplate making a collection of English silver earlier than the eighteenth century unless he or she is either very rich or is prepared to confine his or her interest to that fascinating subject, the silver spoon.

Early spoons

The sheer variety—and to some extent perhaps the survival rate—of early spoons owes something to the fact they were often given as presents on special occasions such as christenings. Apart from the many different patterns, the early spoon also offers the collector a greater chance to investigate provincial silver—objects made outside London which sometimes manage to escape the powerful influence of the capital on the silver trade throughout the centuries. It is only quite recently that collectors have become aware of the vast number of goldsmiths who were at work, before 1700, in places as far apart as Inverness and Falmouth, or Carlisle and Beccles (Suffolk). It is not always possible even now to ascribe every provincially made spoon to a particular maker or even to a particular town, but research goes on continuously and new discoveries are constantly made—often by spoon collectors—so that our knowledge of the craftsmen of the past is expanding all the time.

Most early spoons are hall-marked, and can therefore be dated accurately, but provincially made examples may well have no marks associated with the town of manufacture.

London-made spoons up to 1660 are marked with a leopard's head in the bowl with the maker's mark, date letter and hall mark at the base of the stem. (The only exceptions to this rule are early spoons without a finial, such as 'slip-end' spoons, on which the date letter is placed at the top of the stem.) Provincial spoons tend to follow the London practice inasmuch as they have the maker's mark on the base of the stem and something in the nature of a town mark in the bowl. However, in the smaller centres the marking was rather slap-dash: there is sometimes only a single mark, either in the bowl or at the base of the stem, and it is frequently impossible to say whether it is a town mark or a maker's mark.

Such spoons cannot be dated accurately by their marks, and it is therefore necessary to adopt other means. One clue may be provided by the finial or 'knope', as medieval goldsmiths called it, at the end of the handle, which was usually cast and soldered on to the spoon. Some of the main types of early spoon finial are shown in the drawing, with a rough indication of the period in which they were made, but these dates must be treated with caution as the finial is a far from foolproof indication of date. A sounder guide, at least to the approximate date, is the shape of the bowl, which gradually changed over the period from about 1400 to 1650. There are three general rules, which were described in the definitive work on this subject by G. E. P. and J. P. How, *English and Scottish Silver Spoons* (3 vols, 1952). These are the points to watch: (1) the later the spoon, the greater the angle made by the sides of the bowl as they leave the stem; (2) the later the spoon, the smaller the angle of the drop between the stem and the base of the bowl; (3) the curve of the bowl away from the stem, viewed from above, is a concave curve in early examples and changes gradually into a convex curve in later ones.

The great majority of early spoons have an ornamental finial of some kind. As a rule, the finial was cast and then soldered on to the handle. There were two methods of doing this, one characteristic of London and the other of provincial goldsmiths. The London goldsmith or spoon-maker (there were some specialists), having fashioned his spoon, cut a V-shaped notch from front to back in the stem and fitted the finial into the notch before soldering. The provincial spoon-maker preferred a lap joint. This difference continued as long as spoons were made with separate finials. No one has ever explained why, and it seems very remarkable that, over so long a period, all London goldsmiths should use the one method and all provincial goldsmiths the other. But the fact remains that

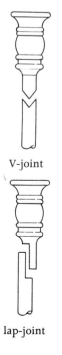

V-joint

lap-joint

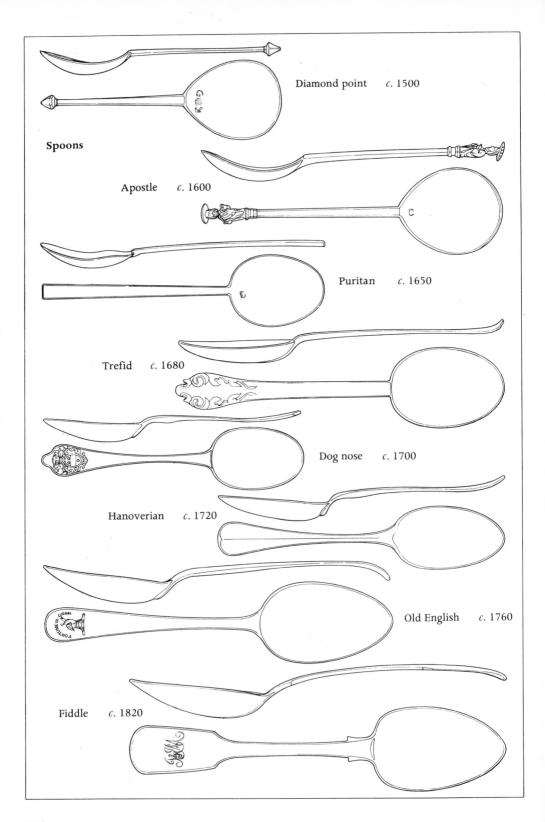

Diamond point   *c.* 1500

Spoons

Apostle   *c.* 1600

Puritan   *c.* 1650

Trefid   *c.* 1680

Dog nose   *c.* 1700

Hanoverian   *c.* 1720

Old English   *c.* 1760

Fiddle   *c.* 1820

lap-jointed London spoons are extremely rare, while V-jointed provincial spoons are practically non-existent (I have seen just one example). Of course, goldsmiths, like all craftsmen, tend to be professionally conservative, but that is hardly sufficient explanation.

The spoon was hammered from a single small ingot. First, the stem was roughly fashioned, then the chunk of metal left at one end – the future bowl of the spoon – was hammered out into a rough, flat oval. The bowl shape was obtained by hammering it into a lead die, and the whole spoon was filed and planished, ready for the finial to be soldered on. The stem was hexagonal, but as time went on the top and bottom facets became steadily broader, possibly to make more room for the marks, and eventually the two facets at each side of the stem disappeared altogether, making a rounded, more 'modern' shape. By the end of the seventeenth century a strengthening rib or 'rat tail' was made from the junction of bowl and stem, extending about half-way along the underside of the bowl.

In these early spoons, the finial was invariably gilt, though the spoon itself was usually left white, i.e. ungilded. All-gilt spoons do exist, but they are comparatively rare, especially if the gilding is original. The inexperienced collector should try to make himself familiar with the appearance of genuine old gilding, which to the practised eye is not difficult to spot; a dealer who specialises in spoons will probably be the best person to guide him in the detection of the small but important variations in gilding. Then he can at least be sure that the gilding on a spoon is old, even if it is difficult to tell whether it is as old as the spoon.

Apart from the gradual changes in the shape of the bowl and stem, early English spoons are categorised by their finials. Some types which the collector is most likely to come across are listed below.

Acorn knop A small finial in the form of an acorn appears to have been popular in the Middle Ages. The majority of those surviving were made before 1500, and therefore hardly belong in this chapter. The acorn is usually little wider than the stem, and with one or two exceptions it was fashioned from the same piece of metal as the rest of the spoon.

Diamond point This is also a rare early type, made during the fourteenth and fifteenth centuries. The finial which, like the acorn knop, was generally fashioned in one piece with the spoon, comes to a faceted point like a diamond or a small pyramid.

Acorn knop

Diamond point

Apostle spoon This is without doubt the best-known and most keenly collected of all early spoons, gaining its name from the figure of an apostle forming the finial. Apostle spoons, which were being made in the mid-fifteenth century and probably earlier, were no doubt made singly to be given as christening presents, but they were also made in sets of thirteen – the twelve apostles (St Matthias replacing Judas Iscariot) and Christ himself, the Master spoon. Each figure can be identified by the emblem he holds, frequently the symbol of his martyrdom.

The Master always carries an orb and cross in the left hand, with the right hand upheld in blessing. St Peter holds a key. St John, who is the only apostle not holding a book in one hand, raises his right hand in blessing and holds the cup of sorrow in his left. Sometimes the cup has been broken off and it is difficult to distinguish St John from Christ; however, St John is generally (there are some later exceptions) depicted clean-shaven, while all the other figures are bearded. St James the Great carries a pilgrim's staff and occasionally a shell on his back or hat: he is the patron saint of pilgrims and the shell was the sign of the pilgrim in the Middle Ages. St Andrew carries a saltire (X-shaped) cross; St Simon the Zealot a saw; St James the Less a fuller's bat, a slightly curved club-like object; St Thomas a spear. St Matthew sometimes carries a carpenter's square, symbolic of the church he is supposed to have built for the king of Ethiopia, but after about the mid-sixteenth century he is generally shown with the money bags of a tax collector. St Bartholomew carries a flaying knife; St Philip three loaves commemorating the feeding of the five thousand or, from about 1570, the short Latin cross; St Jude a long cross; and St Matthias a halberd or pole-axe.

Occasionally other saints appear. St Paul, for example, although not one of the twelve apostles, frequently crops up singly and is sometimes found in sets, usually taking the place of St Matthew; he is identifiable by the sword he carries. His appearance is largely due to the fact that he was (and is) the patron saint of London. All the figures generally, though not always, have a nimbus or halo, which in earlier examples is pierced but, towards the end of the sixteenth century, becomes solid, with the Holy Spirit as a dove impressed upon it. In London, Apostle spoons ceased to be made in the 1630s or early 1640s, but in the West Country, notably in Exeter and Taunton, they were still being made in the 1660s and 1670s, although by that date spoons with ornamental cast finials of any type were something of an anachronism.

130 A magnificent set of twelve silver-gilt Apostle spoons, the most keenly collected of all early English spoons.

The Master | St Peter | St John | St James The Greater | St Andrew | St Simon | St James The Lesser

St Thomas | St Matthew | St Bartholomew | St Philip | St Jude | St Matthias | St Paul

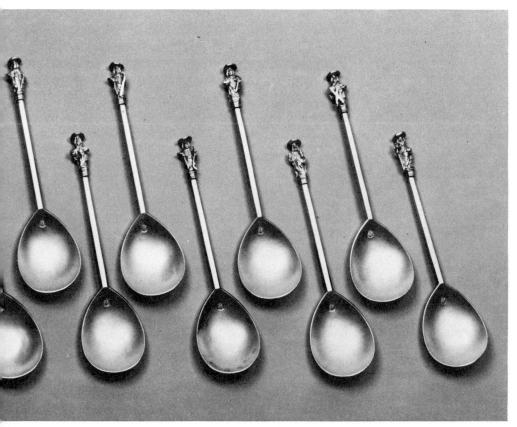

Wrythen knop An extremely attractive finial in the shape of a ball with spiralling lines, it was invariably cast as a separate piece. Surviving examples, which are rare, date mainly from the late fifteenth or early sixteenth centuries. The same form, incidentally, can sometimes be seen on casters made in about the third quarter of the eighteenth century.

Wrythen knop

Seal top A fairly common finial varying in form according to place and date of manufacture, the seal top is something like a shortened baluster top sliced off halfway up. Examples are known from the early fifteenth century up to about 1660; earlier seal tops are small, and the finial tends to grow larger and more elaborate with the passage of time.

Maidenhead finial It was once assumed that this finial of a female head and bust emerging from foliage or set on a plinth was intended to represent the Virgin Mary. However, there is no halo, as one would expect, and the woman's hair is done up, though maidens, or virgins, in the Middle Ages were accustomed to wear their hair hanging down. It is therefore unlikely that the figure is intended to represent a virgin, still less the Virgin Mary. There are some other spoons which do have the lady's hair down and, since she is holding the Sacred Heart, they can be taken as representing the Virgin. Maidenhead spoons were made in the fifteenth century and only disappeared about 1650.

Maidenhead

Lion sejant A finial in the form of a seated lion was certainly made in the fifteenth century and continued until the early seventeenth century. On early examples, the lion sometimes sits sideways (sejant guardant), but more commonly it faces forwards. It sometimes holds a shield before it, on which, presumably, the owner might have engraved his arms or initials.

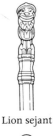

Lion sejant

Baluster top This occurs in a variety of forms, often bearing some resemblance to the shape of a pawn in a traditional chess set. Examples are known from the late fifteenth century or earlier, but there are a greater number from the late sixteenth and early seventeenth centuries.

Slip top Slip-top spoons have no finial: the top of the stem is cut upwards from the front at a sharp angle. There are French spoons of this type from the fourteenth century, and though the earliest English example found so far is hall-marked 1487, they were almost certainly made earlier. The slip top was a very popular type: they were still being made in the reign of

Baluster top

Slip top

798

Puritan

Trefid

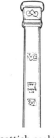

Scottish seal top

Scottish disc end

Charles I, and there were even a few made after the Restoration.

Stump top They are similar to the slip top, except that instead of the angled cut, the top is rounded off. They usually have heavy, octagonal stems and the rounded terminal, when new, would sometimes have been pyramidal in form.

'Puritan' spoon The name is rather unhelpful except that it provides an indication of date, which is from the mid-1630s to the Restoration, or to about 1670 in the provinces. A development of the slip and stump tops, with the end cut at a right angle, they were the first spoons to be made with flat rather than faceted stems, and although their period of popularity was short, they led the way to future developments.

Trefid spoon The 'Puritan' spoon was superceded by the trefid spoon: the end was flattened out and two small notches cut in it. In its pure form, the trefid spoon lasted from about 1660 to about 1700, although it was still being made in Exeter in about 1720 and in the Channel Islands thereafter. Later varieties are sometimes called 'dog-nose' and 'wavy-ended' finials: the notches were omitted and the finial was broadened and shaped. The 'rat tail' made its first appearance on the underside of the bowl of the trefid spoon, which is the true ancestor of the modern spoon.

The early spoons described above were made both in London and, to a greater or lesser extent, in the provinces too. There are, however, some types of spoon which appear to have been made in the provinces only and betray marked regional idiosyncrasies.

Scottish spoons, which are generally rare, have a definite character of their own. The Scottish seal top, for example, is markedly different from its English equivalent. The stem is thin and flat, unlike any English spoon of the late sixteenth century, and the finials are small and oblong.

Disc end The most familiar of early Scottish spoons is probably the disc-end spoon, which seems to have been the most widely used silver spoon in Scotland in the late sixteenth and seventeenth centuries, though few have survived nonetheless. The Scottish disc end appears to be the only spoon of its type made anywhere in the British Isles at that time, though there are somewhat similar ones from the North of England. The shape of the bowl is very nearly circular, the stem is flat and the finial consists of a disc at the top with a smaller, secondary disc below it. Initials are usually engraved on the top disc, with stylised acanthus leaves below.

799

A small number of Scottish 'Puritan' spoons exist. They have the same nearly circular bowl, a characteristic not found in southern England at that time, while the stem is broader and more splayed at the top. There is often some stylised acanthus decoration on the front of the stem, as in the disc-end spoon from which they evolved. Dating from the mid-seventeenth century, they form a link between the disc end and the trefid spoon.

South of the border, there are fewer exceptions to the general types of spoon being made in London. In York some *memento mori* spoons similar in type to the Scottish disc end were made in the reign of Charles II. The bowl is generally shaped like a trefid spoon of the period and at least one example has a standard trefid top instead of the Scottish disc. There is either a coat of arms or a death's head engraved on the top disc, and the stem is engraved with the words 'Die to live' on one side and 'Live to die' on the other. While normal spoon forms sometimes have birth dates engraved (e.g. 'Eliz: Nubery, born a Tuesday nite Sept^re 17th'), these memorial spoons appear to have been made exclusively in York and for a period of not more than about twenty years.

To the observant and experienced spoon collector there are differences to be detected in the majority of spoons made in different parts of the country, but for the most part the variations are so small that to attempt to describe them would be more confusing than helpful, especially as there are always so many exceptions to every rule. However, there are two varieties of early spoons from the West Country which should be mentioned, as they appear to have no parallel with spoons made in London or any other part of England.

Female-figure top Also called a mermaid spoon, this bears no relation to the maidenhead finial described earlier. The figure, or rather half-figure, is semi-nude, with hair worn long and arms akimbo below very prominent breasts and above an equally prominent belly. All known spoons with this finial are of good quality, some exceptionally good, and are often finely engraved with intertwining foliage as seen on the best London-made tankards and wine cups. So it is safe to assume that they were held in high regard. They were made towards the end of the sixteenth century and nearly all of them seem to have come from Barnstaple, though one or two may have been made in Plymouth. The caryatid form of the finial on these spoons can also be seen in the carved woodwork and plaster of the period and as part of the strapwork decoration on some London-made

Scottish Puritan

York death's head

Female figure

silver-mounted jugs. This makes it all the more surprising that spoons with this finial should apparently have been made exclusively in Devon.

Buddha knop

Buddha knop This also comes from Devon, chiefly Barnstaple, and dates from about 1630. No one really knows what the figure represents: it may be no more than a crude and debased version of the female-figure top, it may be an oriental deity (Krishna has also been suggested), and some authorities have even suggested an African origin. The one thing that can be said of these finials with complete conviction is that they are excessively ugly.

Knives and forks

Though knives are as old, or older than spoons, silver does not make a good cutting edge and blades were therefore usually made of steel. Silver-handled knives were made at an early date, though examples from before the mid-seventeenth century are so rare as to be virtually non-existent today. The earliest knives found in sets were made about 1690, with tapering, rounded or polygonal handles. A curved handle like a pistol grip prevailed in the early eighteenth century; a few specimens from the Rococo period are highly ornamented. The curve of the handle gradually shrank and in the Adam period became straight again, and sometimes reeded.

Although some heavy cast handles have survived reasonably well, after about 1760 the high price of silver encouraged the use of very thin stamped silver sheet on a resin core. With only a few exceptions these knives are in a sorry state today, full of holes and apparently on the point of disintegration. They are hardly worth the attention of the collector.

The history of the fork in England before 1700 is almost entirely conjectural. To the disgust of more sophisticated foreigners, the English in general continued to use the point of their knives to convey food from plate to mouth, though in the houses of the nobility forks were probably in common use at a date earlier than 1632, the year in which the oldest known example was made. Now in the Victoria and Albert Museum, this is a two-pronged fork in the 'Puritan' style, made in London. However, a set of twelve forks was recorded in the inventory of the royal jewels as early as 1550, and there is other documentary evidence of table forks not much later, though it appears from contemporary descriptions that forks were more often used by boisterous guests to poke their neighbours in the posterior than to eat their meat. Forks followed the pattern of spoons, and trefid forks from the late seventeenth century can be found, though there is virtually no chance of acquiring more than single specimens.

Eighteenth- and nineteenth-century cutlery

At the beginning of the eighteenth century the prevailing pattern in flatware was the dog-nose pattern, a development of the trefid spoon and fork. The bowl of the spoon is long and oval with a 'rat tail' on the back, the stem is more rounded than the earlier trefid type and terminates in a scalloped or shield-shaped top. Fork stems conform in design and usually have three tines or prongs, rounded in section, though they are sometimes found with two tines.

The dog-nose pattern lasted from about 1690 to about 1710, when the plain and elegant Hanoverian pattern became dominant. On early spoons of this type, the 'rat tail' is still in evidence, but by about 1730 it tended to be replaced with a shorter tongue-shaped support. The rounded tops of spoon and fork turn up at the end, and for that reason they were always engraved on the back of the stem. Forks are still usually three-pronged, though examples with both two and four prongs exist.

About 1760, the spoon stem acquired a downward turn and the bowl became more egg-shaped; at the same time all forks were made with four tines. This is known as the Old English pattern, and it lasted with a number of minor variations until about 1820. During the 1770s the Old English pattern was sometimes feather-edged, and when that was done the spoons and forks were sometimes given a small shoulder just above the base of the stem. Since spoons now turned downwards, the engraving was done on the top of the stem. In the 1780s fashion dictated a still lighter and more delicate version of the Old English pattern, and that resulted in the hall marks being moved from their usual situation near the bowl to a point near the top of the stem. Bright-cut engraving became common at this time, and although it was quite short-lived in England, in Ireland it remained popular much longer. In Ireland, and in Scotland too, the spoon and fork in the Old English pattern tended to be slightly elongated by comparison with English-made equivalents, and normally had terminals which were slightly pointed.

A totally different pattern, standing apart from the general evolution of Hanoverian and Old English, appeared in about 1745. It is called the Onslow pattern, allegedly named after a well-known speaker of the House of Commons, and had deeply

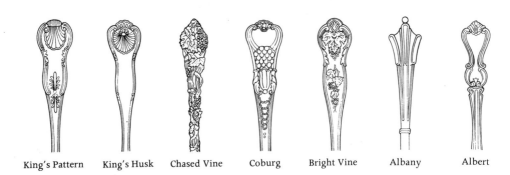

| King's Pattern | King's Husk | Chased Vine | Coburg | Bright Vine | Albany | Albert |

fluted stems and scrolled terminals. Though attractive, it was never very popular and disappeared again about 1770, the reason no doubt being that its visual appeal did not compensate for the fact that it was inconvenient in use; significantly, surviving examples are often gravy spoons or ladles rather than ordinary table cutlery.

About 1820 the Old English pattern gave way to the fiddle pattern, which had gained its name from the superficial resemblance of the outline of the stem to a fiddle or violin. The bowl of the spoon is egg-shaped – the standard form since the third quarter of the eighteenth century – while the shoulder above the bowl and the matching spatulate top of the stem create the impression of the 'fiddle'. There are three main variants of this pattern: (1) fiddle thread, in which a single line is deeply incised around the stem about one-sixteenth of an inch from the edge; (2) fiddle shell, in which a shell, made by sinking into a die, appears in relief at the top of the stem; (3) fiddle thread and shell, combining the two former elements.

After about 1820 there was an insatiable demand for more and more elaborate die-struck patterns, such as King's Pattern, King's Husk, Queen's, Chased Vine, Coburg, Albert and many others. Most of them, like the fiddle pattern, are still being made today and a visit to a large cutlery shop is the simplest way to become acquainted with them.

Victorian flatware is not, perhaps, of very great interest to most serious collectors, but it does have the advantage of being much more readily available than earlier cutlery. There is little point in a collector seeking sets of spoons and forks of even the Hanoverian period: they exist certainly, but not only are they expensive and hard to find, they almost invariably consist of 'made-up' sets – individual matching pieces collected from different sources. One tip worth remembering, for anyone who is considering collecting a set, is that, whatever pattern strikes his or her fancy, it is advisable to look for dessert forks first. They are invariably the most difficult pieces to locate.

Chapter 5

Collecting silver

Collecting things seems to be a common human preoccupation; but not everyone starts a collection, whether of antique silver or postage stamps or even football programmes, for the same reason. Someone who is contemplating a collection of silver, and therefore preparing to spend quite large sums of money, should consider carefully his or her reasons for doing so before making a start. Some collectors are not really interested in art objects as such but feel that in an age when the value of money is declining so swiftly their capital would be more profitably invested in English watercolours or Chinese jade than it would be in banks or building societies. This is not a good reason for becoming a collector. People who are governed by purely commercial motives seldom accumulate a collection of silver or anything else that is really valuable. Because they tend to think only in terms of relative values, graphs and statistics, they are wary of high prices and unwilling to spend what seems to be above the norm. Therefore they never acquire the finest examples in whatever field they happen to be operating. They may well end up, sadder if not wiser, as financial losers. Objects of any aesthetic merit cannot and should not be treated as mere commodities. In the words of John Culme and J. G. Strang, 'Anyone . . . who collects silver for its investment value alone misses much. To feel a piece of Queen Anne silver, for example, with its cool blue lustre, to study the proportions thoughtfully and to consider its details and artistry elevates us above the mischief of finance and the snobbery of taste. In its finest forms silver almost lives. Like velvet, or polished wood, it invites touch, sight and thought' (*Antique Silver and Silver Collecting*, Hamlyn, 1973). In any case, and on a more mundane level, the price or value of silver is affected by other factors besides the money supply or the state of the capital market. They are affected, for example, by changing taste: what seems particularly attractive and desirable now may have lost its popularity in a few years' time and its real value in cash terms will decline accordingly. Not since the seventeenth century have people generally put their money into plate. They found

131 Water jug in the Adam style, made in London by John Schofield, 1781. An attractive and useful piece, it would be a fine addition to late eighteenth-century dining-room furniture. Height about 12 in.

better methods of investment, and it is strange to think of
modern collectors reverting to such primitive behaviour.

Of course, it is unlikely that a collection of silver will decline
in actual cash value over a period of time. Inflation alone will
prevent that, and a collection purchased with reasonable care
and common sense will most likely appreciate. Even so, the rate
of inflation in recent years has outstripped the rise in price of
many art objects, and this, plus the unforseeable vagaries of
fashion, makes collecting silver for commercial reasons alone a
very doubtful activity.

Although silver has been made for many centuries, the
collecting of old silver is comparatively recent. Art collecting
on a large scale – pictures, sculpture, porcelain and other

objects – was well established in the eighteenth century, but silver, except for the odd old and spectacular piece, was not generally collected until Victorian times. Silver objects were made for use or display, or both. At the same time they represented, especially in the days before banks, a convenient and attractive way of storing cash. Large or sudden expenditure was met by melting down the family plate; similarly, a surplus of cash was invested in silver. But it would be wrong to suppose that this was ever the sole reason for owning silver; otherwise, it would have been better to invest in silver ingots rather than hand-wrought vessels. No doubt the delight that

135 *Far left:* Tea caddy with wooden box, 1776. Not very useful today, but a pretty thing to place on a table nevertheless. It is unusual to find single caddies in a box; more often they were boxed in pairs or sets of three.

136 *Above:* Small inkstand, made in London by Edward Feline, 1749. A perfect piece for an early eighteenth-century desk or bachelor's chest. Length about 6 in.

137 An unusual pair of old Sheffield-plate tea caddies, about 1785.

138 *Above:* A pair of George II candlesticks, made by John Alleine, 1757. Height 10 in.

139 *Far right:* A pair of caddies in somewhat restrained Rococo style, made in London, 1744. They fit into a carved ivory, silver-mounted casket. Such ornamental pieces need careful placing on the right piece of furniture, where they will not be overpowering.

people take in displaying their wealth to impress their neighbours encouraged the conversion of cash into the visually striking form of cups and goblets rather than dull chunks of metal, but silver, nevertheless, was always meant to be useful and decorative besides.

Collections of silver today may take many different forms, according to the interests (not to mention the wealth) of the individual collector. Broadly speaking, there are two types of collector. There is the specialist, who manages to accumulate an astonishing collection of – for example – early spoons or snuff-boxes or vinaigrettes. These may be called study collections; they do not necessarily have any connection with the collector's general style of living (everyone has read of people living in the humblest conditions who nevertheless own a priceless collection of this kind), but merely express the meticulous character of someone who has made a certain aspect of the goldsmith's art his lifelong interest. A larger proportion may be called general collectors, those who accumulate certain objects which for one reason or another have a special appeal for them. They probably collect other kinds of antiques also, maybe concentrating on a particular period – for a neo-classical, Adam-style gilt race cup is not ideally situated on top of a Jacobean oak cupboard!

Most collectors do concentrate on a certain period in silver, and the period they choose naturally depends on individual taste – the type of furniture they like generally. Someone whose house is furnished with plain and simple country furniture is unlikely to choose Rococo candlesticks for the mantelpiece, while someone who regards a Louis XV commode, all boullework and ormolu, as the finest expression of the cabinetmakers's art will presumably not be afflicted by an overwhelming passion for Queen Anne coffee pots. However, it is not easy for the tyro to be certain of what exactly he does like, and before embarking on any purchases he should make himself thoroughly acquainted with the whole range of English antique silver. That is something that cannot be done from books alone. The beautiful lustre that old silver acquires, or the lovely pale lemon colour of old gilt, are not easily conveyed by photographs, however good, nor can a flat page adequately illustrate a three-dimensional object. Therefore, the new collector should visit one or more of the good public collections in museums. This may not always be easy (by far the best collection of English Elizabethan silver is in Moscow), but most people in the British Isles will find that there is a good display to be seen not very far away. A guide to the main collections of British silver open to the public will be found on page 829.

Some people think of silver primarily in terms of what is placed on the dining-room table before dinner and returned afterwards to the shelter of the sideboard. Having acquired their service of cutlery, a couple of salt cellars and pepper casters, a mustard pot, a pair of entrée dishes and perhaps two or four candlesticks, they feel their silver collection is complete. This is a rather dull and unimaginative approach. Silver is surely better used to enhance the whole house: not too much of it, since all excess is vulgar, but the odd piece here and there in the way that, rather more frequently, porcelain is displayed. If one is lucky enough to own a few fine pieces of porcelain, or fine old furniture, they may be splendidly enhanced by the thoughtful and imaginative addition of silver pieces.

140 An elegant silver-mounted glass claret jug in late eighteenth-century style, but made in Sheffield, 1879.

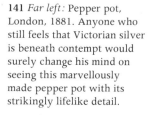

141 *Far left:* Pepper pot, London, 1881. Anyone who still feels that Victorian silver is beneath contempt would surely change his mind on seeing this marvellously made pepper pot with its strikingly lifelike detail.

142 *Left:* Pepper mill, made by Louis Dee, London, 1880. This enchanting mill might go with the canine caster (Plate 141). To my mind, it could be placed on a table of almost any period without creating a jarring note.

Silver and glass are also mutually enhancing, and a mixture of the two in the dining room can be most effective—wine glasses with silver cutlery, glass salt cellars and silver pepper pots, glass candlesticks and a silver centrepiece, with perhaps a pair of Chinese blue-and-white porcelain sauceboats instead of silver ones. Tastes vary, but on the whole such an assembly looks more attractively balanced than a table groaning under a mighty accumulation of glittering plate.

Antique silver can be bought either from a dealer or at an auction. By and large, the inexperienced collector will find that silver dealers, or indeed dealers in any other kind of antiques, are ready and willing to discuss his particular interests. Dealers, of course, make a living from selling, but a good dealer should never attempt to persuade a customer to buy anything until a mutual rapport has been established and the customer's interest and knowledge of the subject are well understood. There is a saying in the jewellery business, 'If you do not know about jewellery, at least know your jeweller', and it is a good

143 Silver-gilt bowl, by Andrew Fogelberg and Stephen Gilbert, 1789. This remarkable bowl, which looks fresh from the workshop, is one of my favourite pieces of pure Adam neo-classical silver. Diameter of bowl about 14 in. Victoria and Albert Museum, London.

rule for silver also. Most dealers are enthusiasts, as are most collectors, and there should be no difficulty in establishing friendly communication and understanding. When I started to take an interest in silver as a schoolboy, two dealers in the neighbourhood showed me great kindness, giving me a large amount of their time, trouble and experience. Regardless of the fact that I was obviously not in a position to do business with them, I was always made welcome and allowed to look at and discuss at length anything I wanted. Not all dealers are so agreeable, but many are and all should be.

It is also possible to pick up a good deal of knowledge about silver in the sale rooms of auctioneers. Unfortunately, silver of good quality does not often appear these days in any great quantity outside London, but if London is too far away, the major auction rooms up and down the country which hold regular weekly or monthly sales of silver and other antiques— good, bad and indifferent—are well worth visiting. The rapid turnover of silver, pictures, furniture and so on can be highly informative.

At auctions, however, one must always be prepared to some extent to take pot luck, and on balance it is probably better to get to know one or two thoroughly reputable dealers and listen to their advice. The auctioneer, after all, is merely the agent for the seller; he does not take the same responsibility for what he sells as a good dealer should, and he has neither the time nor, possibly, the capacity, to discuss his wares fully with potential buyers.

The amazingly orderly history of English hall marks has been mentioned in Chapter 2, and it is not surprising that, for some people, the hall marks on silver have become a fascinating subject in themselves. However, this is an interest that can

144 *Far left:* Sugar box (probably) hall-marked 1734. It is often difficult to know the exact purpose of objects made 250 years ago, but, whatever its original function, this is a piece of fine quality.

145 *Above:* An unusual pair of soap boxes, made by Peter Archambo in London, about 1725-30 (they bear the maker's mark only). These boxes were made both in France and England; some are very prettily pierced on top. Height about 3 in.

146 *Above:* A pair of Victorian silver-mounted glass wine jugs, the mounts very beautifully formed as lotus leaves, made in London by E.H. Stockwell, 1881. Each holds about one bottle of wine.

147 *Far right:* A beautiful, very small salver engraved with the royal coat of arms, made by Paul Crespin in London, 1723. This was probably ambassadorial plate – part of a large service given to an ambassador when he went abroad to take up his post. Diameter about 5 in.

perhaps be carried too far, and some collectors, especially young people who acquired their interest in silver in their magpie age, are so gripped by this aspect of the subject that they neglect the silver itself. Hand them some beautiful piece and they will immediately turn it over, looking for the marks, like Beachcomber's character who never bothered to read his letters and kept only the envelopes bearing his favourite twopenny stamps. The fact that a piece of silver was made in Chester in 1763, or even in London in 1902, can – absurdly – assume greater interest than the article itself. The experienced collector, however, will look at the piece as a whole, observing its condition and calculating its date from the general style, form of decoration, heraldic engraving if any, and so on. Only then will he look at the hall marks to see if there is a date on the piece which verifies his conclusions.

In fact, some of the most attractive pieces of silver bear no hall marks at all, and the collector should never be put off by their absence. It does not mean that the article is a fake, or that it is in some way inferior, or, as some people assume, that it was not made in England at all. A fine piece of silver with no marks at all is, or ought to be, far preferable to a second-rate piece with full hall marks. It is the silver that matters, not the marks.

There are a number of reasons why a piece of silver should have no hall marks, or a maker's mark only. It may have been made in the sixteenth or seventeenth century in some fairly remote town which was far from the assay office and had no marks of its own. However, London-made pieces may also occur without marks. In theory, of course, they should always be present, but some people will try to circumvent the law whenever possible, especially if compliance involves them in extra expense, and it cost money to have a piece of silver assayed. It might be held up at the assay office for a week or two, and during that time the goldsmith naturally could not sell it. To send it to Goldsmiths' Hall and to get it back again meant losing the services of an apprentice for several hours. All these may have been minor irritations, but when a goldsmith felt confident that he could sell the piece safely without hall marks, he probably did so.

The law stated that goods made for sale to the public had to be hall-marked, but goldsmiths, clearly infringing the spirit of the law if not its letter, interpreted this as applying only to articles made speculatively and offered for general sale. In a private transaction between a goldsmith and a patron for whom he executed a specifically commissioned article, they reasoned, the law did not apply, as the article was never offered for public sale. When the goldsmith had completed it, he simply stamped it with his own maker's mark—perhaps not even that—and delivered it to the customer. Of course the customer himself may have had something to say about such a procedure. Many people obviously preferred their commissioned silver articles hall-marked, to prove that they conformed to the sterling standard. Others, however, enjoyed a sufficiently trustful relationship with their goldsmith to make such precautions unnecessary.

In general, then, it is unwise for collectors to allow themselves to become obsessed by hall marks. No one would deny that the study of them can be fascinating, and for someone who wishes to make a serious collection of provincial English, or Scottish or Irish silver, then the marks indicating the place of manufacture are vital. But whatever the interest and importance of hall marks, they cannot compare with the fierce, atavistic excitement that the collector feels when he comes, perhaps unexpectedly, upon a piece of silver which by the sheer beauty of its fashioning stands out from its run-of-the-mill counterparts like a beautiful woman in a crowd. When that happens the hall marks, present or absent, are of definitely secondary importance.

Hall marks were introduced to protect the public from fraud, but their very existence has tempted dishonest people to forge them. On the whole, forgeries and fakes are not very common in English silver, although a few turn up every year, but really skilfully executed forgeries are fortunately quite rare. Forged hall marks usually assume one of two possible forms. Either the punches themselves, which make the marks, are forged, or genuine old hall marks are introduced to the piece—it would be worth removing the hall marks from something small like a

148 A set of salt cellars, made in London by David Tanqueray, about 1725 (maker's mark only). These spool-shaped examples are among the most pleasing of small salt cellars.

spoon, for example, in order to use them in a much larger and accordingly more costly piece. Very often the forgery is so poorly executed that even the novice, perhaps without quite knowing why, senses something wrong. Sometimes, however, it is done very expertly, and the collector would do well to consult a reputable dealer whenever he feels an element of doubt.

Forged marks may be more easily spotted by a dealer, who is accustomed to looking at silver hall marks every day and is therefore familiar with all their characteristics. He will know not only what the marks should look like but also whereabouts on the article they should appear, knowledge that can only come from long observation. Besides the placing of the marks, there is usually some slight difference between a modern, forged punch and a genuine old one. The tiny details that give the game away are not easy to describe, but are learned slowly from constant observation.

The transposing of hall marks from one piece to another was sometimes done in the past, especially between 1719 and 1758, to avoid the duty payable on silver. Such pieces are known as 'duty dodgers'. In more recent times it was done to convince the unsuspecting buyer that the piece – possibly made the week before – was an antique. A suspicious eye, however, should be able to detect this type of forgery with a good

149 *Left:* Tea caddy, with a very attractive type of latticework engraving that is found on a number of caddies dating from the 1760s and 1770s. The severity of outline indicates that not everybody wanted all his silver in the current Rococo style.

150 *Below:* Shaving bowl, 1712. The recess in the rim was made to fit around the neck of a customer being shaved by the barber. These are rare objects, seldom found after the middle of the eighteenth century, and usually pleasantly simple in design. Diameter about 14 in.

magnifying glass: the little oblong piece bearing the genuine hall marks has to be let into the bogus article, and close examination will usually reveal the thin tell-tale line of solder around it.

Another type of forgery, most often found in spoons, is to make a cast of a genuine old piece. This is not, as a rule, hard to detect. The marks usually appear rather fuzzy, and the stem of the spoon is softer than in a genuine hammered article. Moreover, if a set of spoons is in question, the hall marks will appear in precisely the same place on each one—impossible if they had been individually stamped by hand.

It is always difficult to draw a line between honest restoration or 'improvement' and intent to deceive. Engraved and chased decoration can be sharpened up, and if done well the evidence is not obvious. However, under a powerful lens, the line of the engraving tool can be detected *inside* the line of the original engraving. A good engraver can put an elaborate and stylistically accurate coat of arms on a plain and otherwise not particularly interesting article in order to enhance its appeal to a collector. This too may be very hard to detect, but frequently the general condition of the piece reveals the fraud. Old silver inevitably becomes somewhat worn by time and usage. If the engraved coat of arms is brilliantly sharp while other parts, notably the hall marks, show signs of wear, then it would be wise to regard the piece with a certain scepticism.

As we have seen in Chapter 3, it was the occasional, rather deplorable custom in the nineteenth century to have old silver chased or embossed with decorative details that appealed to its owners more than its original plain appearance. This was not done with intent to deceive anyone, and it was not illegal. In fact, decoration more recent than the original article is in most cases quite obvious.

Collecting silver can be in every way a rewarding pursuit, and the silver dealer, who is, of course, normally a collector also, usually feels that he is making a living in the most exciting and delightful way imaginable. He is often asked how he can bear to sell pieces of silver which clearly arouse his warmest enthusiasm. His answer is, 'Ah, wait until you see what I might find next week!'

Chapter 6

Provincial goldsmiths

From the time of the Norman Conquest, and no doubt earlier, down to quite recent times, hundreds of goldsmiths were at work in large towns and small throughout the British Isles. They made new articles in silver and occasionally perhaps in gold also, though it is important to remember that many references to 'gold' articles in old records actually refer to silver-gilt. They also made jewellery, for the jeweller's trade, as distinct from that of the goldsmith and enameller, did not become established in its own right until the Renaissance, and no doubt a good part of their time was spent in repairing and renovating worn or broken wares. Many of the goldsmiths active in provincial centres – large places like Dublin, Edinburgh, Norwich and York, as well as smaller ones like Barnstaple, Carlisle, Limerick and Wick – are recorded in the monumental work of Sir Charles James Jackson, *English Goldsmiths and their Marks* (2nd ed. 1921), which despite its title also includes Scotland and Ireland. Many new discoveries have been made since the publication of Jackson, but a great deal of work still remains to be done. The keen amateur collector, no less than the academic researcher, can be of great help in tracking down makers who have not yet been identified and deciphering town marks that have not yet been located. Detective work is needed especially for the period before 1697, the year of the reform of the hall-marking laws and the introduction of the Britannia standard.

Part of the interest of provincial silver lies in its variations from contemporary styles in London. Some examples, like the engraved pomegranate tankards made by John Plummer in York in the 1650s and 1660s, or the disc-end spoons of Scotland, have already been mentioned in Chapters 3 and 4. From Scotland also came that notable vessel, the quaich, which was never made anywhere else. A shallow, two-handled bowl, it derived its form from a wooden prototype, and early examples (from the late seventeenth and early eighteenth centuries) are engraved in a manner resembling the staves and bindings of the wooden originals. Tumblers made in the north-

151 *Above:* Coffee pot, made by Samuel Blatchford in Plymouth, about 1725. Despite its provincial origin, this is one of the most elegant coffee pots that I have ever owned.

152 *Top right:* A sauceboat, made in Edinburgh, about 1740. The flat chasing around the rim proclaims its Scottish origin, although the dolphin handle is something I have not seen before on Edinburgh silver. It is an ideal piece for a collector who wants an article that is both out of the ordinary and eminently usable.

153 *Bottom right:* Quaich, a typically Scottish object, made by James Anderson in Edinburgh, 1729. Width (including handles) 9 in.

east and in Chester display marked differences from London tumblers, those from York, Hull, Leeds and Newcastle having a lower profile and a more flattened base, while the typical Chester tumbler is closer to the London type, taller and more rounded at the base. Then there is a very pleasing form of cream jug which we owe to the goldsmiths of Plymouth around the 1730s. It is really a shallow bowl with a slightly everted rim, small lip, and scroll handle at right angles to the lip-handle line. There are three examples, two of them forming a matching pair, which were made in London, but in this instance it seems certain that the London ones are copies and, for a change, the London makers imitated a Plymouth design.

Some articles were never made at all in the provinces, or at least only in certain places. If one were to amass a collection of one hundred vinaigrettes, for example, one would probably find that ninety of them were made in Birmingham and ten in London, with not one from any other place.

The medieval goldsmiths in the provinces were regulated, in theory at any rate, by the Company of Goldsmiths in London,

until 1423 when seven provincial centres—York, Newcastle upon Tyne, Lincoln, Norwich, Bristol, Salisbury and Coventry —were permitted by statute to adopt their own 'touches' or town marks and to regulate their own affairs. Elsewhere, the London Company retained responsibility. From time to time the wardens of the Goldsmiths' Company would make searches throughout the kingdom, calling on every goldsmith in a

154 *Far left:* A beautiful tankard made by Gabriel Felling in Bruton, Somerset, dated 1683. Felling was a most accomplished goldsmith who was probably apprenticed in London.

155 *Above:* Card case, made in Birmingham by Nathaniel Mills, 1845. It is typical of the work done in Birmingham during the nineteenth century, and cases like this are eagerly collected today.

156 *Left:* Gold box, made by Edward Smith in Birmingham, 1850-60. It was probably bought for stock and the scene inside the lid engraved specially for a customer. Length about $3\frac{1}{2}$ in.

157 *Above:* Beaker, made in Newcastle, about 1660, though the style suggests it might be earlier. Its main interest lies in the contemporary inscription, which proclaims that it was a gift from King Charles II.

158 *Far right:* Tumbler cup, about 1715. It shows all the signs of a North Countryman, with a flatter base and slightly lower sides than London counterparts.

certain area and assaying all the pieces in his shop on the spot. If any were found to fall below the sterling standard, they were broken up; the goldsmith was fined and made to swear not to commit the offence again.

Very little is known of activities in the seven towns named in the act of 1423 in the fifteenth century. York began an annual date letter cycle in 1559 which continued, with a long gap from 1713 to 1778, until the final closure of the York assay office in 1856. Norwich maintained a date-letter system sporadically from 1565 until 1697, when the licence of the assay office was not renewed. Newcastle used a variety of town marks, usually in the form of a castle, in the seventeenth century, but the punches seem to have been made by individual makers, not by the official assay office.

The act of 1697, reactionary in many ways, once more removed the privilege of marking plate from the seven provincial centres and confined it to London alone. Obviously this caused great hardship to goldsmiths a long way from the capital, who now had to send their work to London for assay, and the chorus of complaint led to a new act in 1700 permitting the establishment of assay offices in Bristol, Chester, Exeter, Norwich and York. Newcastle was particularly incensed at being left out. However, two years later it succeeded in regaining permission to operate its own assay office.

159 Irish tray, engraved by Thomas Bewick of Newcastle, 1806. The tray is not particularly Irish in character, but the superbly executed engraving is unmistakably Bewick.

This was the situation for most of the eighteenth century. As things turned out, neither Bristol nor Norwich ever became major centres of silver, and for practical purposes the centres of the trade outside London were York, Newcastle, Chester and Exeter, as well as Edinburgh, Glasgow and Dublin.

In 1773 Sheffield and Birmingham petitioned the House of Commons for assay offices to be established there because of the vast amount of silver they produced, which at that time had to be taken to London or Chester for assay and marking, a very troublesome and expensive business. The London assay office was understandably unwilling to lose the lucrative rewards it gained from marking the silver articles being turned out in such numbers by the new industrial giants, and cross-petitioned vigorously against independence for Birmingham and Sheffield. Common sense prevailed, however, and both cities received their assay offices later in the same year. Today, the only British assay offices outside London are Birmingham, with its mark of an anchor, Sheffield, a crown (the lobbyists from Sheffield and Birmingham in 1773 are said to have held meetings at an inn called the Crown and Anchor), and Edinburgh, a castle.

Provincial silver offers an endless field of fascinating study for the local historian. There are large piles of manuscript, as well as printed sources, to be gleaned for information on

820

160 *Above:* Teapot of the so-called 'bullet' type, London-made, 1730.

161 *Above right:* Scottish teapot and stand, made in Aberdeen by George Cooper, about 1725.

162 *Below:* An Edinburgh 'bullet' teapot, 1724.

163 *Below right:* A small sweetmeat basket, made by George Hodder, one of Cork's leading goldsmiths, about 1745, a very rare piece. Length 4 in.

provincial goldsmiths over the centuries. The Public Record Office in London of course contains a vast, in a way rather too vast, repository of information for the painstaking researcher. Then there are the county archive offices, which can frequently provide such source material as rate books, church wardens' accounts and so forth. From such material one can gradually compile a list, albeit an incomplete one, of the goldsmiths resident in a particular town, and having discovered their names, try to find out the marks they used.

Hitherto unidentified provincial marks are found in the greatest number on two types of silver. There are hundreds, if not thousands of spoons which were made before the end of the seventeenth century by local goldsmiths. On some, the marks can be identified without doubt, and others have been tentatively attributed to a particular maker. But there are still many different marks that remain more or less a mystery, though it is reasonable to hope that the majority will one day be identified, providing the present level of interest in provincial silver is maintained. Spoons, however, are easily portable,

and when they are discovered in a particular place it is only rarely that there is any sound reason for assuming that they have been there ever since they were made, and that they were therefore probably made in the vicinity. For this reason, spoons are rather less useful as a primary source for the investigation of provincial goldsmiths than the other main category, church plate.

Church plate was often fashioned locally because it was less expensive than having it done in London or one of the grander provincial centres. Communion plate of local make is a fruitful source of information, particularly for the post-Reformation period, when there was a massive changeover from the old chalice of the mass to the new, simpler form of communion cup.

Communion plate was sometimes presented as a gift, but if not, its purchase is almost invariably recorded in the church wardens' accounts. Providing these accounts are still available, as they are in a surprisingly large number of parishes, it is nearly always possible to find the record of the purchase. Unfortunately, however, the relevant entry probably says only 'Payed ye goldsmythe for new makinge ye cuppe', or some such phrase. Only very seldom does it mention the actual name of the goldsmith. When his name does appear, the diligent researcher feels a sense of profound satisfaction, but he (or she) should not congratulate himself just yet. He has the name of the goldsmith, and he has only to compare it with the cup mentioned in the accounts to discover the goldsmith's mark. But what does he find? Only too often the original communion cup has gone, and he is confronted by a Victorian replacement. It can be very frustrating work.

Nevertheless much can be accomplished by searching local records, and as an appendix to this chapter I reprint some of the results of my work undertaken a few years ago in an effort to classify local goldsmiths' work in King's Lynn, an important town and port in the Middle Ages.

164 Communion cup, made in Coventry, about 1570. The maker, whose mark is IF, is so far unidentified, but there seems to be no doubt where it was made as all cups with this maker's mark are to be found in churches within a 25-mile radius of the city.

The King's Lynn goldsmiths

The following account is a shortened version of a paper which appeared in the *Journal of the Society of Silver Collectors* and is reprinted here by kind permission of the editor.

Towards the end of the eleventh century the town of Lynn was founded by the bishop of Norwich, Herbert de Losinga, at the request of a group of traders who were perhaps already established on the western shores of the Manor of Gaywood. The bishop founded the church of St Margaret and a priory in fulfilment of a promise to Pope Pashal II, as penance for the various acts of simony which had marked his ascent of the ecclesiastical ladder, and he laid the foundations of an economic and commercial community by establishing a grant of a market and a fair.

The town was in a good position to develop trade both by road into the hinterland and also by sea to places farther afield, and these advantages were successfully exploited by the townspeople: until the advent of the Black Death the population was constantly expanding, and in the early fourteenth century reached an estimated 5,700 inhabitants. An interesting book called *The Making of King's Lynn* by Vanessa Parker includes a table of the various occupations of the freemen of Lynn which she has culled from the freemen's register. She lists the occupations under the following headings: merchants; food and drink; clothing; local industries; building; miscellaneous and unspecified. Goldsmiths appear under 'miscellaneous', which comprises freemen of the following occupations: apothecary, barber, clerk, customer, chapman, goldsmith, jeweller, mariner, organ-maker, musician, shipmaster, surgeon, tobacco seller, waterman, and gentleman. If one adds up the freemen in each period into which the table is divided, it is interesting to compare that total with the goldsmiths who were present and working in Lynn according to my own researches.

Time	Total freemen	Miscellaneous	Goldsmiths
1300-05	94	2	2
1342-70	266	1	10 (sic)
1371-1400	255	8	1
1401-30	206	3	3
1431-60	455	7	3
1461-90	274	22	2
1491-1520	388	21	0
1521-50	364	10	1
1551-80	504	20	6
1581-1610	438	26	6
1611-40	452	21	3
1641-70	605	150	1
1671-1710	635	220	4

We see here a fairly typical picture, at least when compared with other places where I have investigated local goldsmiths: first a steady number during the Middle Ages, with usually a downward turn around the late fourteenth and early fifteenth centuries owing to successive and economically disastrous outbreaks of plague; a rise into the mid-sixteenth century, and then a steady lessening of numbers throughout the seventeenth century. This is, of course, a general picture, but it does hold true in a surprisingly large number of cases.

It is really impossible to decide how much work the medieval goldsmiths did, as there is virtually no work left now for us to estimate the quantity – or quality – of their output, but it seems reasonable to suppose that they fulfilled a need similar to the goldsmiths of the second half of the sixteenth century, as suppliers of fair-to-mediocre plate for the churches and monasteries in their area and as repairers and small-workers.

In Norfolk particularly there are large numbers of pre-Reformation patens still in existence, mostly unmarked, which seem almost certain to have been made in one or other of the various towns in that county which supported goldsmiths. Take for instance the list of plate of St Nicholas in Lynn, which was sold in 1543:

1 little Crosse of silver	xvi [ounces]
1 little Crosslet of silver	
1 little cruett of silver gilt	x
1 cruett of silver gilt	viii
1 Pair Censors Gilt	xxxvii
1 Crucifix of silver gilt	xv
1 Scrip of silver	x
1 Pyxe of silver gilt	xxx
1 Broken Cross of silver pt gilt	xxiii
1 picture of Christ crucified	iii
2 knoppes of silver gilt	xvi
1 pyxe gilt	xxi
4 pyxes gilt	xvi
1 Chalice cover gilt	x
4 pattens silver gilt ⎫	
4 chalices of silver gilt ⎭	LXXViii
1 Scepter part plate	ii
1 Chalice silver Patten gilt	xiii
1 Holy water stoop with a sprinkler	LXXXX
1 Chalice silver with Paten gilt	XLiii

It seems unreasonable to suppose that this large amount of plate was all made in London. There can be no proof, but assuming the plate was accumulated over many years, it is significant that between 1415 and the date of the sale, 1543, no less than eight goldsmiths were working in Lynn. Surely there would not have been so many as this if they had not relied on getting a fair proportion of local church work. So little survives from the period that conclusions are impossible.

The period of religious disruption in the 1540s and 1550s must have been very bad for the local goldsmith, who relied to a large extent upon church patronage not only for new commissions but for a constant stream of the repairs that are so frequently noted in church wardens' accounts in almost any period. In the period of the Dissolution of the Monasteries and, later on, the commissioners' reports on church goods, nervous churchmen were clearly unlikely to give large orders to the smiths. This is born out by the list of Lynn freemen, which in the sixty years from 1491 to 1550 contains only one goldsmith. It seems clear that in King's Lynn changing economic and ecclesiastical conditions had an important effect on the number of working goldsmiths.

New cups for old

The accession of Elizabeth I marked the beginning of a long period of full employment for the local goldsmiths, and there is no doubt that the Lynn men were there in force to take what they could of the new orders forthcoming after the Queen's proclamation restoring the cup to the laity, on 22 March 1559. It has been shown by Charles Oman that there must have been some staging system for implementing Archbishop Parker's order to change mass chalices into communion cups, as it would have caused endless confusion if every church in the realm had been compelled to make the change in the same year. The plan that appears to have been adopted was that each year one or two dioceses were instructed to start their conversion. In 1564 the London Company of Goldsmiths had warned their colleagues of the Norwich Goldsmiths' Company that their turn was imminent and that they should regularise their system of hall marking, as the sudden influx of orders could lead to a number of abuses. Presumably, the goldsmiths in outlying areas of Norfolk and Suffolk were similarly informed, and in consequence were ready for the rush of work that must have followed this order. It would appear that the turn of the Norwich diocese came in 1566-67, and in that year Lynn had four goldsmiths available to take as many orders as they could from their Norwich and London competitors. I have so far found seven cups by one maker, some of which bear engraved dates corresponding to the year of the great changeover, but unfortunately I have been unable to trace which of the four goldsmiths it could have been.

The cups bearing this mark, which looks like a leaf over a circle enclosing the letter I, are not very beautiful nor particularly well executed, but they are fairly representative of Elizabethan communion cups as a whole. Their real interest lies in the inscriptions to be found encircling the bowls, all of which are similar but not identical. On the seven cups by this maker there are five different inscriptions:

> *All glory be vnto the O Lord*
> *All honor and glory be vnto the O Lord*
> *O Lord all glory be vnto the *Amen**
> *All honor *and glory = be — vnto B God Amen*
> *All honor and glory be vnto God*

The source is probably the last prayer in the communion service, which reads 'all honour and glory be unto thee O Father Almighty, world without end'. This small group of Elizabethan communion cups seems to be the only one of that period bearing such inscriptions. In fact the presence of the inscriptions originally led me to ascribe them to about 1640 when they would not have been unusual, but I now feel that there is no doubt of their sixteenth-century date; they represent, therefore, an extremely rare and interesting item in the history of church plate. The inscription must have been the goldsmith's own idea, not what the parish wanted, as it exists on all his cups, made for several different churches.

825

A second group of pieces, also Elizabethan but slightly later in date, bears a single mark which I have taken to be TC conjoined and fairly confidently ascribe to Thomas Cooke. Cooke gained his freedom by purchase in 1579 but was sworn in by a visiting party from the Goldsmiths' Company in 1578. Perhaps they felt he was practically ready to become a goldsmith in 1578 and the purchasing of his freedom was simply a matter of time. Although I have been unable to find any document linking the TC conjoined with Thomas Cooke, I believe it can belong to no other person. There was, however, another possible candidate: some years ago I found a note in the goldsmiths' minute book of one Thomas Christian of Cambridge. Against his name is drawn a copy of his mark which does look rather like the one that I ascribe to Thomas Cooke. The date of 1566 against Thomas Christian's name would also roughly correspond with the mark in question, but I have found no mention of Thomas Christian ever having lived or worked in Lynn, nor does it seem likely that a man from Cambridge, nearly 50 miles away, managed to secure so many orders from churches all within fifteen miles of King's Lynn.

The communion cup at Fring, about twelve miles north-east of Lynn, is obviously Elizabethan though altered later. It has a rather strange mark which I take to be a battle-axe. Since no other piece has come to my notice bearing this mark, the suggestion that it was made in Lynn can only be speculative, but there was a man working in Lynn called Thomas Bolden who seems a possible candidate. Could this mark be a rebus or a pun on his last name?

Another sixteenth-century goldsmith to whom I have been able to ascribe a mark with more certainty is James Wilcocke. He was made a freeman in 1593 and was still working in 1635. Wilcocke may have been a prolific goldsmith, but so far only two cups and one large gilt paten cover that were without question made by him have come to   light. He was the first to use the town mark of Lynn (three dragons' heads erect, each piered with a cross crosslet) along with his own maker's mark, IW, mullet above and below. The communion cup and cover at Congham, although it does not bear Wilcocke's personal mark, is struck with the Lynn mark that he used and I believe is almost certainly made by him. There is also a small paten and three spoons that can possibly be ascribed to him. His work shows him as a sensitive, even sophisticated maker, and one who was well aware of contemporary London styles. It is a great pity that no more of his work has been identified.

It must be assumed that some of the church wardens in the Lynn area had been rather dilatory in the process of converting their old chalices into communion cups in 1567 because there are a fair number of cups made by William Howlett in the 1630s, following Bishop White's visitation of 1629. Howlett was a competent craftsman, as the diversity of his work shows, but what is puzzling is the even greater diversity of quality, which runs from excellent to rubbishy. Another slightly puzzling feature of his work is that he appears to have 'cannibalised' older pieces of silver in making some of his works. A few pieces made by William Howlett have been recorded bearing the full London hall-marks of 1638 but what made him suddenly decide to take or send his silver to London to be marked remains a mystery. It is possible that owing to some misdeed discovered by the Goldsmiths' Company, he was ordered to bring one parcel of silver to London for trial. Howlett gained his freedom by purchase in 1629. He was certainly the most prolific of all the Lynn makers judging by the amount of his work still extant. He used as a maker's mark H over W,

and a Lynn mark similar to that used by James Wilcocke. On certain pieces he used a third mark formed of the letters ST in monogram, the S being reversed. This mark has been the subject of much controversy, but the almost certain explanation is that ST stands for sterling and affirms the standard of the silver. The fourth mark Howlett occasionally used is in fact a unicorn's head incuse.

Robert Howlett, who was possibly the grandson of William Howlett, was made free as a goldsmith in 1661. The only pieces of silver which might be by his hand are unfortunately unmarked. Superbly made and now belonging to the Corporation of King's Lynn, they are a pair of heavy plain beakers, both pricked just below the rim, 'Lenne Reges', the larger one also pricked '1664'. They are engraved with a scratch weight of 38½ ounces, and as they weigh 7 ounces each it is possible that they were originally a set of six. In September 1663 it was ordered that three silver cups, each weighing over 13 ounces, should be 'taken out of ye treasury and delivered to Mr Thomas Robinson, one of ye Chamberlains to be sold and three cups to be bought instead thereof at the discretion of Mr Howlett and the said Chamberlain'. The scratch weight coincides with the amount of silver to be used for the three beakers mentioned, and it seems likely that Robert Howlett persuaded Mr Robinson, the chamberlain, to let him make these six attractive little cups instead of the three originally ordered. If the missing beakers could be found, perhaps just one might be marked. In their absence, a definite attribution is impossible, but they are obviously not London-made and since Robert Howlett was the only goldsmith known to be working in Lynn in 1664 it seems a reasonable supposition that they represent the only examples from his workshop known so far.

A final mark which I have tentatively identified appears on three silver alms dishes, all in churches within five miles of Lynn. They bear the mark RM and were probably made in the workshop of a goldsmith known to us simply as Mr Marsh, who was active around the end of the seventeenth and beginning of the eighteenth century. They are all rather crude in execution and were surely not made in London. When the first name of Mr Marsh is finally discovered, it seems likely that it will begin with an R. One rather remote possibility is that this is the same man as a Richard Marsh who was working in Ipswich in 1683.

The total surviving output of the Lynn goldsmiths over a period of about 140 years that I have so far discovered is fewer than fifty pieces.

Cleaning silver

In the days when people who owned large quantities of silver also employed large numbers of servants, cleaning silver was no problem. Nowadays, some people feel that the need to keep silver polished is a slight deterrent to its display on their shelves and sideboards. But in fact silver takes very little polishing, and many people tend to polish it too much rather than too little.

Silver that is corroded or completely blackened as a result of generations of neglect is perhaps best cleaned by a silversmith. Otherwise, jeweller's rouge–a pink powder worked into a paste with a few drops of water–will do the job adequately. Cutlery or other silver in fairly frequent use will seldom need polishing if it is washed in soap (or washing-up detergent) and water, carefully dried (silver should never be left wet), and stored in acid-free tissue paper or baize, or in a plastic bag. Proprietary brands of silver cleaner, such as Goddard's Silver Foam, may be used, or alternatively a soft, sludgy paste made up of powdered chalk and equal quantities of ammonia and methylated spirits.

The cleaner should be rubbed on with a damp sponge; an old, soft, natural-bristle toothbrush may be used to get into awkward corners. All traces of polish should be washed off in hot soapy water, again using the sponge and, if necessary, the toothbrush. The silver should then be rinsed, dried with a linen cloth, and polished gently with chamois leather. At no time should great pressure be exerted: continual hard buffing of silver does not polish it so much as wear it out. Extra care should be taken with silver gilt; in particular, brushes and any abrasive material should be avoided.

Collections of British silver

Museums and galleries in Britain and Eire

London   *Apsley House*, 149 Piccadilly.
Marvellous collection of massive Regency silver-gilt belonging to the 1st Duke of Wellington.

British Museum, Great Russell Street.
Not a large collection, but the Waddesdon Bequest has some fine sixteenth-century German and English pieces and there is a good collection of Huguenot silver.

Victoria and Albert Museum, South Kensington.
Wonderful study collection on the first floor from all periods and on the ground floor in the period rooms.

Abingdon   *Abingdon County Hall Museum*, Market Place.
Good small collection of seventeenth- and eighteenth-century plate given by different aldermen to the borough.

Belfast   *Ulster Museum*, The Botanic Gardens.
Good general collection but particularly strong on Irish silver.

Birmingham   *Birmingham City Art Gallery*, Chamberlain Square.
A well-displayed and carefully balanced general collection of English silver covering most periods.

Brighton   *The Royal Pavilion.*
Examples of George IV's exotic taste in silver.

Cambridge   *Fitzwilliam Museum*, Trumpington Street.
Not very much English silver but a fair collection of early continental work.

Cardiff   *National Museum of Wales*, Cathay Park.
This houses the Jackson Collection, a good general collection for the student.

Dublin   *National Museum of Ireland*, Kildare Street.
Fine collection of Irish silver. A must for any collector of Dublin or Irish provincial silver.

Edinburgh	*National Museum of Antiquities of Scotland*, Queen Street. A small but very interesting collection, notable are the Scottish standing mazers, highland jewellery, and quaiches.
	Royal Scottish Museum, Chambers Street. A larger, less specialised collection of Scottish silver, possibly more useful to the collector, with a wider range of Scottish pieces and also some English silver.
Exeter	*Royal Albert Memorial Museum and Art Gallery*, Queen Street. A truly remarkable collection of Devonshire-made silver–thoroughly worthwhile.
Leeds	*Temple Newsam House.* Superb collection of mainly eighteenth-century silver.
Manchester	*Manchester City Art Gallery*, Mosley Street. The Assheton–Bennett Collection of silver, ranging from Elizabethan to the mid-eighteenth century. An excellent and well-formed collection including good examples of early spoons.
Newcastle	*The Laing Art Gallery*, Higham Place. Small collection of mostly Newcastle-made silver, including the city church plate.
Norwich	*Castle Museum* Beautifully displayed collection of mostly Norwich-made silver, ranging from early Elizabethan to about 1700; also some London pieces. Well worthwhile.
Oxford	*Ashmolean Museum*, Beaumont Street. Arguably the most important silver collection outside the Victoria and Albert Museum. Particularly strong on Elizabethan silver and mounted wares; also highly important collection of Paul de Lamerie silver. A must for any serious collector or student.
	Town Hall, St Algate's. The city plate and regalia.
Southampton	*Southampton Art Gallery*, Civic Centre. Good, small general collection.

Houses, etc, open to the public

Bury St Edmunds	*Ickworth* (National Trust) Fine collection of silver by Paul de Lamerie and other Huguenots made for the Marquess of Bristol.
Cambridge	*Anglesey Abbey* (National Trust) Good silver and gold boxes.

Dorking	*Polesden Lacey* (National Trust)
	Mostly late seventeenth-century silver in the chinoiserie style.
Manchester	*Dunham Massey* (National Trust)
	Fine silver made for George Booth, 2nd Earl of Warrington, mostly from the first half of the eighteenth century.
Sevenoaks	*Knole House* (National Trust)
	A remarkable small collection of late seventeenth-century silver, notably in the State Bedroom, with silver furniture, wall sconces, mirrors and so on.
Woburn	*Woburn Abbey*
	Fine collection of silver including a pair of baskets by Paul de Lamerie of outstanding quality.
Woodstock	*Blenheim Palace*
	Silver made for the 1st Duke of Marlborough.

Church treasuries

Certain English cathedrals hold interesting collections of church plate from the surrounding diocese. Particularly worthy of note are the cathedrals at Canterbury, Chichester, Durham, Gloucester, Lincoln, Norwich, Ripon, and Winchester. Other recommended sites: Bristol's St Nicholas Church Museum, the Minster at York, and Oxford's Christ Church Cathedral.

Museums in the United States of America and Canada

Boston	*Boston Museum of Fine Arts*, 465 Huntingdon Avenue.
	Highly important museum containing a really fine collection of English silver from the sixteenth to the nineteenth centuries. Also one of the great collections of American silver.
Chicago	*Art Institute of Chicago*, Michigan Avenue at Adams Street.
	Smallish general collection including some important Art Nouveau pieces.
Cleveland	*Cleveland Museum of Art*, 1150 East Boulevard.
	Some important pieces of silver and an excellent general study collection.
Hartford, Conn.	*Wadsworth Atheneum*
	A fine collection of sixteenth-, seventeenth- and eighteenth-century silver, collected by Mrs Eugene Miles and presented by her to the museum. Good catalogue.

Los Angeles	*Los Angeles County Museum*, Exposition Park.
	Some remarkable pieces, including part of the William Randolph Hearst Collection; mostly early silver.
New York	*Metropolitan Museum of Art*, Fifth Avenue and 82nd Street.
	The famous Untermeyer Collection of English silver was recently left to the museum. This is a highly important collection, and there is an excellent book devoted to it (see Bibliography).
San Marino	*Huntingdon Art Gallery*
	The Munro Collection is housed here, including a fine set of Apostle spoons of 1524 and some startling sixteenth- and seventeenth-century silver.
Portland, Oregon	*Portland Art Museum*, S.W. Park and Madison Street.
	Small collection devoted mostly to London makers of the early eighteenth century.
San Francisco	*M. H. de Young Memorial Museum*, Golden Gate Park.
	A small general collection.
Toledo	*Toledo Museum of Art*, Monroe Street at Scottwood Avenue.
	A startling collection of great quality though smallish quantity, it should not be missed, being beautifully organised and displayed.
Toronto	*Royal Ontario Museum*, 100 Queen's Park.
	The Lord Lee of Fareham collection. A remarkable collection of silver and silver-mounted pieces, mostly of the fifteenth and sixteenth centuries, both English and continental.
Williamsburg	*Colonial Williamsburg Foundation*, Goodwin Building.
	An altogether remarkable place, this restored town was once the capital of British Virginia. It has a wonderful collection of silver of the seventeenth and eighteenth centuries. Unfortunately not all of it is on view but there is an excellent catalogue devoted to the silver collection.

Glossary of articles

This list excludes techniques and types of decoration (described in Chapter 1) and patterns in flatware (Chapter 4).

Andirons or **firedogs** Metal brackets for supporting logs in an open hearth. They are uncommon in English silver, but were made occasionally from the late seventeenth century, sometimes cast, sometimes on an iron core.

Argyll or **Argyle** A gravy warmer, resembling a coffee pot but incorporating a heating element, sometimes a central tube or surrounding jacket containing hot water. First made about the third quarter of the eighteenth century, they gained their name from one of the dukes of Argyll who is alleged to have invented the idea.

Asparagus tongs Early examples, from the eighteenth century, are scissor-like, with claws instead of blades. In the nineteenth century they were made in bow form, like sugar tongs, often to match a table service.

Basket For cakes, etc., some of the prettiest products of the silversmith, made in various forms but typically oval in plan with pierced sides and a swing handle.

Beaker A cup with no stem, handle or cover, usually cylindrical in form. They were made in every period but became less common in silver in the eighteenth century.

Bell Silver hand bells for summoning a servant were made at least as early as the sixteenth century. They are sometimes found as an adjunct to an inkstand.

Biggin A small coffee pot, probably named after a type of child's night cap.

Billet In silver, either a metal ingot or a thumb-piece.

Bleeding bowl A shallow circular bowl with a single flat pierced handle. In the United States it is called a porringer, and that – not a bowl used by barber-surgeons – is probably what it is.

Butter dish Made in silver with a glass lining since the eighteenth century. Early examples are oval and pierced, later ones are circular or oblong.

Can or **cann** A mug. The term is more common in the United States.

Candelabrum A standing candlestick with several branches. In style candelabra generally follow contemporary candlesticks.

Caudle cup A porringer.

Candlestick Normally a single candleholder on a stem of columnar or baluster form, with numberless variations. Almost none has survived from before the late seventeenth century, but thereafter they become steadily more common. Chamber candlesticks – candleholders on a wide base with a handle and no stem – were also made in silver.

Canister A box-like container for tea, made in a great variety of forms, often in pairs for two varieties of tea.

Canteen A travelling set of knife, fork and spoon and perhaps beaker and small box, made in the late seventeenth and eighteenth centuries.

Caster A shaker or sprinkler for sugar, pepper, etc., usually in vase or similar form and often made in sets of three.

Centrepiece A very large and elaborate ornament for the centre of the dining table. Rococo and Regency goldsmiths really let themselves go when making these non-functional objects, often incorporating spectacular decoration.

Items from a canteen

Centrepiece

Chafing dish Any dish which is provided with some means for keeping the food warm, such as a bowl for burning charcoal or a small lamp.

Chalice The large standing cup for the wine in the Roman Catholic mass, usually silver gilt if not gold. English examples are of course mainly medieval and rare. Protestants, denying the doctrine of transubstantiation, preferred a more modest vessel usually called a communion cup.

Chandelier A multi-branched candleholder suspended from the ceiling, as distinct from a candelabrum which stands on a surface.

Charger A large plate, circular or shield-shaped, which stood on the sideboard. The decoration of some chargers makes it obvious that they were intended for display only, and they were sometimes presentation pieces.

Cheese scoop Silver scoops with ivory or wooden handles were sometimes made in the Regency period and later to match a table service.

Chocolate pot Similar to coffee pots but with a little lid in the cover for stirring the chocolate.

Coaster A small circular stand with silver sides, often pierced, and a silver or wooden base, on which a bottle stood. It is frequently found in old Sheffield plate.

Coffee pot A tall covered jug, made from the late seventeenth century onwards. See page 760.

Cream jug A small jug made in many forms in the eighteenth and nineteenth centuries, when cream was drunk with tea and coffee.

Cruet The original cruets were the vessels used in the mass, but the name was later applied to sets of casters, etc., which were often made accompanied by a frame or stand.

Dish cross An eighteenth-century device for keeping dishes warm, consisting of a central lamp with adjustable arms capable of holding dishes of various sizes.

Dish ring A low circular ring, or bowl with flat base and, often, concave sides, on which dishes were placed. They come from Ireland and date from the mid-eighteenth century.

Douter A rare scissor-like device with flat blades for extinguishing candles.

Dredger A pierced box or caster for pepper or other spice.

Egg frame Egg cups were sometimes made in pairs in a frame in the late eighteenth and early nineteenth centuries, with a spoon and sometimes a salt cellar.

Entrée dish A dish, circular, oval, rectangular, etc., with a cover, sometimes made with a stand for a lamp.

Épergne A centrepiece, usually highly ornamental, with a central bowl and little dishes for sweetmeats, often hanging from branches, as well as candleholders, casters, and all manner of decorative conceits.

Étui A small slim case containing articles like scissors and needles, for ladies.

Ewer A type of jug standing on a foot, usually accompanied by a basin, used for carrying water at the dinner table.

Flagon A tall type of tankard, uncommon after the mid-eighteenth century, for beer or other liquor. They usually follow contemporary tankards in style.

Goblet A large wine cup.

Inkstand They are often elaborate pieces, including pots for ink and sand, a bell, taperstick, etc., on some kind of tray, usually rectangular. Some were given as presentation pieces, suitably engraved, and some were made in wood and/or glass with silver mounts.

Kettle They usually conform to contemporary teapots in style but were often made with a stand containing a lamp.

Ladle Made for various purposes—cream, soup, sauce, etc. They often matched table services.

Mace The instrument of civic authority, deriving from the type of club used by medieval knights, usually with a crown finial. Some towns proudly own a mace as old as the fifteenth century.

Mazarine A flat pierced plate for straining food. The name no doubt derives from Cardinal Mazarin, who is dubiously credited with so many innovations in the decorative arts.

Mazer A silver-mounted wooden bowl on a foot. They were used for drink in the Middle Ages.

Monteith Similar to a punch bowl in appearance but characterised by a scalloped rim, in which wine glasses were slotted to cool in iced water. The rim is often detachable. Tradition states that the monteith, which first appeared in the late seventeenth century, is named after a Scotsman whose cloak had a serrated edge.

Mounts At every period vessels and objects of disparate materials were fitted with rims, lids, spouts, handles, feet, decorative bands, etc. of silver or silver gilt. A well-known example is the coconut cup, in which a coconut makes the bowl of the cup while the rim, stem and foot are of silver.

Muffineer Another name for a caster, usually a small one.

Mug A drinking vessel with a handle, normally smaller than a tankard and without a lid.

Mustard pot Until the mid-eighteenth century mustard was served dry in a caster with an unpierced top. The more familiar pot for ready-mixed mustard appeared about 1760, usually with a blue glass liner.

Nef A medieval vessel in the form, beautifully worked, of a ship, carrying a napkin, knife, spoon, etc. The masterpieces of the south German goldsmiths, they were not made in England until the form was revived in the eighteenth and nineteenth centuries as a container for bottles or decanters.

Pap boat The eighteenth-century alternative to a baby's bottle – a small oval bowl with a narrow lip. They are sometimes found converted to cream jugs or sauceboats.

Paten The plate used for the bread at the communion service.

Peg tankard Though rare in England, some tankards are found with little pegs or markers at regular intervals inside. The tankard was passed from hand to hand, and the pegs marked how much each person was supposed to drink.

Pipkin A small saucepan with a spout and a wooden handle for warming brandy.

Plateau A large mirrored base, sometimes over twelve feet long, on which candlesticks and a centrepiece were placed, usually of basically oval form and with a low silver-gilt gallery. They were popular in the early nineteenth century.

Pomander A small pierced spherical box for sweet-smelling herbs, etc. A useful object in less hygienic days, it became obsolete in the seventeenth century.

Porringer A small two-handled bowl or cup, with or without cover. See Plate 56.

Pouncebox Often part of an inkstand, for sprinkling a fine powder called pounce on writing paper. Pounce is usually thought of as the equivalent of blotting paper, but it was probably more often sprinkled on the paper to prepare the surface before writing.

Punch bowl A large circular bowl, often with two drop-ring handles. They were an important part of the goldsmiths' production from the late seventeenth century, and continued to be made as presentation pieces after drinking punch had fallen out of fashion.

Quaich A drinking cup with two handles, unique to Scotland. See Plate 153.

Salt A large ceremonial container for salt which took pride of place on the dining table before the centrepiece or épergne. It was gradually replaced in the seventeenth century by smaller, more convenient trencher salts or salt cellars.

Salver A flat, usually circular plate, placed underneath another plate or bowl. Salvers became, and still are, largely ornamental presentation pieces.

Sandbox Indistinguishable from a pouncebox.

Sauceboat A container for sauce. As Judith Banister remarks, although Voltaire may have complained that the English had only one sauce, they had many types of sauceboat. Early eighteenth-century examples have a lip at each end, later ones are more like a low, elongated jug.

Sconce A wall-mounted candle holder, typically in the form of a cartouche with two or more projecting branches. The name was sometimes applied to ordinary candlesticks or candelabra.

Skillet A saucepan, in particular a pan on three feet with a flat cover, made in the seventeenth century and later.

Snuffer For trimming candles. They look like scissors with a little box mounted on the blade for the trimmed wick, and were often made with a tray or frame.

Spice box There are a number of smallish silver boxes, frequently in the form of a shell, made in the seventeenth century, some of which were no doubt intended for spices. The name is applied generally to any box or casket with no very obvious purpose.

Standish An old name for an inkstand.

Strawberry dish The arguments over these pretty little saucer-like dishes are summarised on page 728.

Tankard A vessel for drinking beer, with a capacity of over half a pint and usually one pint or more. Tankards normally have a single handle and a hinged cover. They were made in large numbers from the Middle Ages, but became less popular in the late eighteenth century. They were mostly made with hard use rather than decorative effect in mind and, with some notable exceptions, they tend to be comparatively plain in style.

Taperstick A small candlestick.

Tazza A wide shallow bowl on a central foot.

Teapot Common from the eighteenth century, deviating early from the cylindrical form adopted by the coffee pot. See page 750.

Tea urn A large vase-shaped alternative to the kettle. They had some popularity in the late eighteenth and nineteenth centuries.

Toast rack The earliest silver toast racks date from the second half of the eighteenth century. They were generally formed of wire on an oval base. Later ones went through the whole gamut of Victorian styles.

Trencher salt A small salt cellar, usually made in sets, one for each place setting, from the seventeenth century onwards.

Tumbler Similar to a beaker but usually with a rounded base.

Tureen A large bowl for soup, usually with cover. Some early eighteenth-century examples exist with matching ladles.

Vinaigrette A smallish box with pierced lid, made in a great many decorative forms from the seventeenth century. A sponge with scented vinegar was kept inside for the use of ladies feeling faint.

Warming pan These pleasant devices, looking like a vast frying pan with a hinged lid (burning charcoal therein), were very occasionally made in silver for sybaritic customers.

Whistles Silver whistles or rattles were made for babies in the eighteenth and nineteenth centuries. They had bells and corals (for teething) attached.

Wine cooler or **ice pail** A bucket for a single bottle, common since the late eighteenth century. Larger vessels, often urn-shaped, were made for several bottles as early as the second half of the seventeenth century. Similar pieces were later incorporated in sideboards.

Wine label Small silver plaques, engraved with the name of a drink and suspended on a chain, to be hung on a bottle or decanter. They have been made since the early eighteenth century.

Wine taster A small flattish bowl or cup, usually with a raised dome in the base. See page 728.

Bibliography

These are the books I have found most useful in the course of my work and in the writing of this book.

Ash, Douglas, *How to Identify English Silver Drinking Vessels, 600-1830*, G. Bell and Sons, London, 1964.

Bailey, C. T. P., *Knives and Forks*, Medici Society, London, 1927.

Banister, Judith, *Introduction to Old English Silver*, Evans Brothers, London, 1965.

Banister, Judith, *English Silver*, Hamlyn, London, 1969.

Bennett, Douglas, *Irish Georgian Silver*, Cassell, London, 1972.

Bradbury, Frederick, *History of Old Sheffield Plate* (reprint), J. W. Northend, Sheffield, 1968.

Burns, Thomas, *Old Scottish Communion Plate*, R. and R. Clark, Edinburgh, 1892.

Carrington and Hughes, *Plate of the Worshipful Company of Goldsmiths*, Oxford University Press, Oxford, 1926.

Clayton, Michael, *Collector's Dictionary of the Silver and Gold of Great Britain and North America*, Country Life, London, 1971.

Collins, A. J., *Inventory of Jewels and Plate of Queen Elizabeth I*, British Museum, London, 1955.

Cripps, Wilfred J., *Old English Plate: Ecclesiastical, Decorative and Domestic–Its Makers and Marks*, E. P. Publishing, East Ardsley, West Yorkshire, 1977.

Dauterman, C. C., *English Silver Coffee Pots–The Folger Coffee Company Collection*, Portland Art Museum, Portland, Oregon, USA, 1961.

Davis, John D., *English Silver at Williamsburg*, Colonial Williamsburg Foundation, USA, 1979.

Ellis, H. D., *Silver Belonging to the Worshipful Company of Armourers and Brasiers* (2 vols), Waterlow and Sons, London, 1892 and 1910.

Ellis, H. D., *Silver Plate, Worshipful Company of Cloth Workers*, privately printed, London, 1891.

Ellis, H. D., *Collection of Sixteenth and Seventeenth Century Provincial Spoons*, Sotheby, London, 1935.

Evans, Joan, *Huguenot Goldsmiths of London*, Proceedings of the Huguenot Society, 1936.

Finlay, Ian, *Scottish Gold and Silver Work*, Chatto and Windus, London, 1956.

Gardner, J. S., *Exhibition of Silversmiths' Work of European Origin*, Burlington Fine Arts Club, 1901.

Gardner, J. S., *Old Silver Work, Chiefly English*, Burlington Fine Arts Club, 1903.

Gilchrist, James, *Anglican Church Plate*, Michael Joseph, London, 1967.

Grimwade, Arthur, G., *Rococo Silver*, Faber and Faber, London, 1974.

Grimwade, Arthur G., *London Goldsmiths, 1697-1837: Their Marks and Lives from the Original Registers at Goldsmith's Hall and Other Sources*, Faber and Faber, London, 1976.

Hackenbroch, Yvonne, *English and Other Silver in the Irwin Untermeyer Collection*, Metropolitan Museum of Art, New York, 1974.

Hayward, John F., *Virtuoso Goldsmiths and the Triumph of Mannerism, 1540-1620*, Sotheby Parke Bernet Publications, London, 1976.

Hayward, John F., *Huguenot Silver in England, 1688-1727*, Faber and Faber, London, 1959.

Heal, Ambrose, *The London Goldsmiths, 1200-1800: A Record of the Names and Addresses of the Craftsmen, Their Shop Signs and Trade Cards*, David and Charles, Newton Abbot, 1972.

Holland, Margaret, *The Phaidon Guide to Silver*, Phaidon, London, 1978.

How, George Evelyn Paget and How, J. P., *English and Scottish Silver Spoons: Medieval to Late Stuart and Pre-Elizabethan Hall-marks on English Plate* (3 vols), How (of Edinburgh), London, 1952.

Jackson, Sir Charles J., *English Goldsmiths and Their Marks* (reprint), Dover Publications, New York, 1965.

Jackson, Sir Charles J., *An Illustrated History of English Plate* (reprint, 2 vols), Dover Publications, New York, 1977.

Jewitt and Hope, *Corporation Plate of England and Wales* (2 vols), Bemrose and Sons, London, 1895.

Jones, E. Alfred, *Old Plate of the Cambridge Colleges*, Cambridge University Press, Cambridge, 1910.

Jones, E. Alfred, *Old English Gold Plate*, Bemrose and Sons, London, 1907.

Jones, E. Alfred, The Old Royal Plate in the Tower of London, Fox Jones, Oxford, 1908.

Jones, E. Alfred, *Catalogue of the William Francis Farrer Collection*, St Catherine Press, London, 1924.

Jones, E. Alfred, *The Gold and Silver of Windsor Castle*, Arden Press, Letchworth, 1911.

Jones, E. Alfred, *Old English Plate of the Emperor of Russia*, privately printed, 1909.

Lee, Georgina E. and Lee, Ronald A., *British Silver Monteith Bowls: Including American and European Examples*, Manor House Press, Byfleet, Surrey, 1978.

Mahaffy, J. P., *The Plate in Trinity College, Dublin*, Macmillan, London, 1918.

Mayne, Richard, *Old Channel Islands Silver: Its Makers and Marks*, Société Jersiaise, St Helier, 1969.

Mercers Company, *Plate of the Worshipful Company of Mercers*, privately printed, London, 1940.

Milbourne, Thomas, *Plate of the Worshipful Company of Vintners*, privately printed, London, 1888.

Moffatt, H. C., *Old Oxford Plate*, Archibald Constable, London, 1906.

Oman, Charles C., *English Silver in the Kremlin, 1557-1663*, Methuen, London, 1961.

Oman, Charles C., *English Engraved Silver, 1150-1900*, Faber and Faber, London, 1978.

Oman, Charles C., *English Church Plate, 597-1830*, Oxford University Press, Oxford, 1957.

Oman, Charles C., *Caroline Silver*, Faber and Faber, London, 1971.

Oman, Charles C., *English Domestic Silver*, A. & C. Black, London, 1968.

Oman, Charles C., *The Winchester College Plate* (reprinted from *The Connoisseur*), London, 1962.

Parrish and Bowen, *Antique English Silver in the Lipton Collection*, Dayton Art Institute in collaboration with Thomas J. Lipton Inc., Dayton, Ohio, 1958.

Phillips, P. A. S., *Paul de Lamerie, His Life and Works*, privately printed, London, 1935.

Preston, Arthur and Baker, A.C., *The Abingdon Corporation Plate*, Abbey Press, Abingdon, Berkshire.

Reddaway & Walker, *Early History of the Goldsmiths' Company 1327-1509*, Arnold, London, 1975.

Ridgeway, Maurice H., *Chester Goldsmiths: From Early Times to 1726*, John Sherratt & Son, Timperley, Cheshire, 1968.

Rowe, Robert, *Adam Silver*, Faber and Faber, London, 1965.

Taylor, Gerald, *Silver*, Penguin, London, 1956.

Ticher, Kurt, *Irish Silver in the Rococo Period*, Irish University Press, 1972.

Watts, W. W., *Old English Silver*, Ernest Benn, London, 1924.

CLOCKS

DAVID BARKER

Introduction

In recent years old English clocks have become very popular. Like other antiques, high-quality examples command a premium price; even modest clocks are in great demand. In effect, the last few years have seen a sudden emergence of clocks as an area of interest to collectors. Where for years they had been regarded as unimportant machines simply for telling the time, today more and more people are learning to appreciate the artistic and industrial skill that went in to making even the most common English clocks; others are trying to document this forgotten chapter of English industrial and trade history; and yet others are turning to clocks as a profitable field of investment and a hedge against inflation. Families who have had a few clocks for generations are discovering that their old clocks may represent a wealth of fascination and of potential value; worn but original clocks are being lovingly restored.

In some ways the sudden fascination for old clocks has allowed scope for unscrupulous dealers to exploit the public. Sometimes too, dealers with little or no knowledge of the subject have helped to create a demand and push up prices. It is not uncommon to find – though without any shady intentions on the part of the dealer – examples of a clock and casework of very poor quality, perhaps wrongly married, shabby or with pieces missing, offered at a high price in a local antique shop. On the other hand the revival in interest in old clocks means that there is far more knowledge available for the would-be collector to study his subject before committing himself to a purchase. Whereas 25 years ago ignorance was rife and very few restorers even knew how to reproduce the materials and the movement of old clocks, today it is far easier to find someone to advise you on what is worth buying, what is overpriced, what needs expensive repairs and what is beyond hope. The intention of the present book is to provide the reader with an introduction to the history of the clockmaking industry in England, to describe the various different types of clock that have been made and can still be found for sale, and to help the reader to understand the intricacies of the movements, to explain the qualities of individual clocks and to appreciate how and why a clock is worth restoring.

The English clockmaking industry was, in its heyday in the 17th and 18th centuries, equal to any in the world; it produced large numbers of high-quality clocks, both for specialist precision purposes and for domestic use. Based on the prosperity of the middle classes in the years preceding the industrial revolution, the industry flourished both in London, where the finest and most expensive examples were made, and also in many country towns, the products of which occasionally equal the quality of the London-made clocks, and are full of fascination and imagination in their own right.

Clockmaking in England goes back as far as the Middle Ages, when timepieces were made for installation in the towers of some of the cathedrals, such as in Salisbury. But the domestic clockmaking industry, with which we are principally concerned here, did not properly emerge until the 17th century. At this time clocks were still rare and expensive treasures, and many exquisite examples were produced. In the mid-17th century there was considerable scientific interest in producing extremely accurate clocks, and many notable scientists contributed to the development of new devices. The most important of these developments, claimed to be the invention of Galileo, was the pendulum escapement, which meant that a much higher degree of accuracy could be attained.

The incorporation of these devices in clocks of extremely high-quality craftsmanship brought about a flowering of English clockmaking around the end of the 17th century and the beginning of the 18th; this period has been known ever since as the Golden Age of English clockmaking. The clocks of this date, especially the long-case clocks and bracket clocks, featured fine and delicate movements with long durations between windings, performing complicated striking and chiming feats and even carried astronomical or automated functions.

The long-case clocks, which became in a sense the epitome of the English industry, developed in style until the mid-18th century, when demand fell off in London. The most fashionable clockmakers turned their attention to portable clocks such as bracket clocks, and in the most elegant households the long-case was demoted from the place of honour it had once held. In the provinces, however, a reverse trend took place, and the long-case was taken up by many country makers to cater for the growing market among the prosperous middle classes, who seem to have had little interest in the bracket clock.

In the 19th century, the specialist clockmakers in London

introduced yet more features for better timekeeping in all forms of clock. The distinctive class and provincial tastes of the previous century continued throughout the Victorian period, although, as the long-case became something of a status symbol in the lower-middle and working-class home as the century wore on, it tended to increase in size and decline in quality. Nevertheless, the 19th century witnessed the decline, and indeed the virtual demise of the English industry: large numbers of mass-produced clocks of inferior quality and low price were imported from Germany and the United States. The English clockmakers, who had always organised their industry on a system of craftsman's workshops and apprenticeships, were unable to compete. Many firms went to the wall and many of the traditional skills were lost as clockmakers were forced to diversify their product in order to stay in business at all.

In the 20th century, old clocks were only rarely considered as important items of workmanship or design until the 1960s, when the present revival of interest began. A few people, even so, saw the importance of the field, and built up fine collections of their own. The early years of the century saw the accumulation of the famous Wetherfield Collection which was described by F. J. Britten in 1907, and much of which was sold after Mr Wetherfield's death in 1928. In the 1920s W. Iden began collecting clocks and watches; most of this collection is now in the British Museum

Generally, though, the early and mid-20th century saw remarkably little interest in old clocks. Now it seems almost unbelievable, and very tantalising, that shortly after World War II it was possible to buy rare and beautiful clocks of the 17th century in London for next to nothing.

Today, the situation has changed. It is no longer possible to buy a good clock – and particularly one by a maker of repute – without paying a high price. This no longer only applies to the work of Tompion, Knibb and their like, whose work is anyway mostly in museums, but even to the work of provincial makers who have been recognised widely as producing top-quality work. However, the would-be collector should not despair. There *are* still bargains to be had; enough to make collecting a real possibility. Care is needed in choosing your clocks, and there are many pitfalls for the unwary and those who do not understand the workings of clocks. But the fact remains that thousands of old clocks still survive, and many of them have intrinsic interest and value. I have often been struck by the idea of collecting the clocks of a particular town or region; preferably a local town which had reasonably good clock-

843

1 Long-case clock by John Farrer of Pontefract, belonging to the author and from which he learned to tell the time.

makers at several different dates. Over the years – patience is a valuable quality for any collector – it should be possible to come across clocks at bargain prices, and you would end up with a probably unique collection of clocks of that town at a fairly modest outlay. It is still not too late for such an enterprise.

This book is intended for the average collector, and I have therefore concentrated on the sort of clocks you are likely to come across in antique dealers' showrooms and salerooms, rather than on the clocks at the top end of the market. Like so many other type of antique, these have become a form of international currency over the last few years, and are collected for their monetary value, not for their worth. The only consolation in this state of affairs is that we can presumably rest assured that they will be kept safe, and will never again be damaged or altered by the ignorant or the unscrupulous.

Personally, I was first drawn towards clocks by my grandfather's love of his old long-case clock, which was a modest but pleasant eight-day clock made by John Farrer of Pontefract in about 1830. For as long as I can remember it stood in the corner of his front room. My family lived next door and it was from the dial of this clock that I learnt to tell the time. I never saw another clock like this one; none of the neighbours had one and my grandfather considered it very rare. He was of course quite wrong, but it was a mistake that was understandable in the period of extraordinary ignorance about clocks, after World War II. But that his pride was misplaced is not important; my fascination with clocks was born from it, and I have been absorbed by clocks ever since. The clock is still with me and I treasure it as much as ever he did (Plate 1).

My reasons for mentioning this clock are twofold. Firstly it illustrates well how a love of clocks can grow up; I am sure that there are thousands of people who remember a vague interest in clocks from their childhood and who would welcome having this interest rekindled by an introduction to the mechanical mysteries of clock design. For these people I have tried to express my own technical interest in the workings of old clocks and show how satisfactory it is, once the basic principles of clock movement design have been grasped, to see the individual and original qualities of each clock that you come across.

The second point to be made about my grandfather's clock concerns the importance of maintenance. A large number of clocks have been looked after very badly over the years; they may have had no maintenance at all, or they may have suffered from the attentions of an unskilled bodger armed with a soft soldering iron and an oily feather. My grandfather, I regret to say, was one of the second sort. He boasted that the clock had never stopped in sixty years, and this was more or less true; but when I inherited it from him in 1972, I found that it was very worn and it had never been properly cleaned. Dust and oil had formed a grinding paste on the pivots and other moving parts; the gut lines were pieced together with bits of nylon fishing line, and the brass hands had been repaired with ugly lumps of soft solder. This clock is by no means untypical. Many long-case clocks, for instance, are driven by weights that are far too heavy, and suffer stress on that account so that, although they may run well for years, they will eventually become worn out and break down entirely. Very few clocks, even today, enjoy the weekly attention of a clockmaker with his clean rag, clock-oiler and pocket chronometer.

As we become conscious of the need for conservation, and as clocks rise in value, it becomes clear that professional restoration is an essential task, to maintain our old clocks in working order. If the parts are replaced as they become worn, and if the intentions of the original clockmaker are respected, there is no reason why a good-quality clock should not last almost indefinitely. Admittedly many of the tasks required to look after an old clock are beyond the amateur, but it is well worth anyone's time to understand how a clock works, how it is liable to become worn and what needs to be done to restore it to a reasonable state.

I hope therefore that this guide will enable its readers to identify styles and periods; to appreciate the quality of a clock, both in appearance and in its mechanics; to understand how to spend their money on clocks wisely; and perhaps, to find themselves drawn into the fascinating subject of the history of clockmaking. Essentially, though, I hope that this book will help its readers to gain as much pleasure from their clocks as I myself have done, for surely with their unique blend of mathematical accuracy, fine metal-working and beautiful wooden cases, they rank among the finest works of craftsmanship, even among the finest works of art.

Chapter 1

Clocks and horological terms

A clock is fundamentally a device that transfers a potential force, whether contained in a lifted weight or in a wound-up spring, into the regular motions of a hand around a dial at a constant and adjustable rate. The clockwork is simply a gearbox which transfers this force into the correct speed and controls it to ensure that it is not used up at an ever-increasing speed. The works also contain similar movements to drive the striking system of the clock, and any other features that may be fitted, such as a date dial, or a second hand. Anyone interested in collecting or owning antique clocks will need to understand the basic principles involved in how a clock works; and the more knowledge that can be built up in this area, the greater will be your enjoyment of looking at clocks. To this end, I have attempted to explain as simply as possible the elements of a clock in the following paragraphs; and then to cover in more detail the meaning of the (inevitably) many technical terms that will crop up, in the form of a glossary for easy reference. Rather than explain the basic terms several times over, those which are defined elsewhere in the glossary are in *italic type.*

The lifted weight or wound spring (whichever is used to drive the clock) applies power directly to the first wheel of the *train*. For a spring-driven clock a device called a *fusée* is introduced at this stage to ensure that the pull of the spring is even, whether or not the clock is fully wound. The train is simply a gearbox which is made up of a series of *wheels* and *pinions*. Its function is to transmit the power to the *motion work* – another set of wheels which divide the power into two, and pass it to the pipes on which the hour and minute hands are fixed. The train (or trains, since extra trains may be added for strikework and other special features) and the motion work together form the *movement*, which is effectively the entire 'works' of the clock. This movement is fixed between two solid metal *plates* held together by *pillars*; the dial is attached to the front plate of the clock, or to a *false plate*, itself fastened to the movement.

The essential element in a clock's design is the *escapement*, which ensures that the movement works at a regular and even pace, rather than at great speed until fully unwound. The escapement is a device by which a catch oscillates at a regular rate, alternately holding back and releasing the last wheel in the train, which is known as the escape wheel. Many forms of escapement have been contrived to regulate the speed of the clock. The earliest clocks used a simple oscillating *foliot balance* or *balance wheel* system; but these were not capable of fine timekeeping. A revolution in clock design was effected by the introduction of the *pendulum* to the escapement. Since a pendulum swings with an absolutely regular beat, it proved an ideal means of ensuring that the escapement worked smoothly and evenly. All that was required was some form of feedback whereby the movement of the escapement also gave an impulse to keep the pendulum in motion. At first a short *bob-pendulum* was used with a verge escapement, but better results were soon achieved with a *seconds pendulum* (which had the convenient beat of exactly one second), connected with an *anchor* or *recoil escapement.*

This is the essence of the English clock. There are plainly many complications – the device whereby the spring or weight is wound up; the striking mechanism; the means of regulating the clock or driving special features and so on. These have all been described both in the glossary which follows, and in the relevant chapter where each device has had the greatest impact on a particular type of clock.

Anchor escapement The most popular and widely used *escapement* for domestic clocks, from its introduction in about 1675 until today. So-called because of its shape in the form of inverted anchor flukes, the pallets of which act on the escape wheel placed vertically beneath it. In long-case clocks this escapement was commonly used in association with the *seconds pendulum.*

Arbor The arbors in a movement are shafts, pivoted through the plates, on which wheels are fixed. Arbors may also pivot *lifting-pieces* for strike-work. The shaft on which an *anchor escapement* is mounted is known as the pallet arbor.

Balance wheel An oscillating control in the shape of a single spoked wheel, used in early domestic clocks. The original balance wheel was mounted outside the top plate of the clock and connected directly to the vertically arranged *pallet*-staff.

Barrel A barrel is used for storing and transmitting power to the train of a clock. If the clock is weight-driven, the barrel is directly connected to the winding *arbor*, making key-winding possible. An eight-day clock barrel revolves with its great wheel once in twelve hours; it may be cut with 16 shallow

Anchor escapement

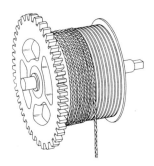

Barrel

grooves. The barrel of an English spring-driven clock has no winding facility; it is simply a round brass box which contains a strong spring. The spring barrel revolves on a fixed arbor and is connected to the *train* by a line which winds from *fusée* to barrel while the clock is running down and the reverse direction when the clock is being wound.

Bell staff The curved steel or iron rod by which the bell is fixed to a striking-clock movement. This is normally fixed to the backplate.

Birdcage Also known as posted movement; used in chamber, lantern and some long-case clocks. It has four vertical posts, one at each corner of the movement, and plates top and bottom.

Blade spring Blade springs give impetus to a hammer in the strike train. They are of a straight shape, diminishing in thickness towards the top to a right angle where they engage with the projection on the hammer *arbor*. They are fixed to the inside of the clock backplate or baseplate.

Bob pendulum The short pendulum usually associated with the *verge escapement* and lantern clock. It terminates at its lower end in a small pear-shaped brass bob threaded on to its rod.

Boss Name given to a plate or applied tablet on a dial on which the maker's name, a legend, motto or similar may be engraved.

Bridge A bracket having two fixing points, held by screws. This holds the back pivot of an escape arbor at the back of the clock, or, if used in the motion work, it is to support the hour wheels. In the position when it is also supporting the pendulum it is known as a back cock.

Centre seconds Seconds indicated by a large counter-balanced hand radiating from the centre of the dial. Counter-balancing the hand was necessary as the hand was otherwise heavy enough to stop the clock, since it worked directly from the delicately-poised escape wheel. Centre-seconds work is found on long-case clocks, tavern clocks, etc.

Chamber clock The earliest domestic clocks, made from Tudor times until the establishment of the lantern clock in its traditional English form. These clocks were large and of posted-frame construction. They were controlled at first by a *foliot* and then *balance-wheel escapement.*

Chapter ring The detachable ring or circle, on which the chapters or hours are engraved. It is usually made of brass and silvered, but silver chapter-rings are known on some high-quality bracket clocks.

Click So-called because of its actions and the noise it makes; a small piece of steel or iron held loosely by a screw and a spring to retain its tension, and used with a ratchet wheel.

Cock A bracket usually having only one fixing point on the clock plates, used for fixing the reverse minute wheel and occasionally other parts of the motion work including the strike-rack, which is sometimes pivoted. See also *Bridge*.

2 Cock

Collet A collet is a piece of brass driven, brazed or soldered on to an *arbor* and then turned to provide a true running seat with a shoulder on which a *wheel* is mounted. Collets can be plain or decorative and are useful in estimating a clock's age: the older ones are generally large and domed or cheese-shaped behind the shoulder.

Contrate wheel A wheel with teeth on its edge, to transmit the power of the train to the next pinion through 90°, usually to a *crown-wheel* of the *verge* or *balance-wheel escapement*.

Count-wheel The method of regulating strike work used in clocks before about 1675, and sometimes used later for regulating hour-striking and in quarter-chime mechanisms. Sometimes mistakenly referred to as a locking wheel. It is a flat disc with irregular but progressively wider spread slots around its edge. A *lifting-piece* runs along the edge of this wheel during striking, until it reaches a slot, and causes the strike train to be locked up on a separate wheel (the locking wheel). The strike order will only coincide with the time shown on the dial if arranged to do so.

3 Contrate wheel

Crown-wheel The escape wheel of a *verge escapement*, so-called because of its resemblance to a medieval crown, with teeth cut on its edge. The crown-wheel is usually placed at the top of the movement and arranged in a horizontal plane with the points of its teeth uppermost.

Crutch In movements where the pendulum is supported by a flat steel spring from a back-cock, the pendulum is connected to the escapement by the crutch. The crutch is usually riveted into the *pallet arbor* at the arbor's rear end. The connection between the crutch and the pendulum is a sliding fit, sufficient to give impulse to the pendulum and yet keep it as free of the action of the escapement as possible.

Day of the month Date or day of the month indicators are shown on most English clocks. They are worked from an extra wheel or wheels, or a pin arranged in the motion work of the movement.

Dead beat escapement A refined version of the *anchor escapement*. Its *pallets* are shaped to give a positive locking action between beats of the pendulum and no recoil is caused to the escape wheel. The dead beat is more suited to accurate timekeeping than the anchor escapement, and was used on fine regulator types of clock.

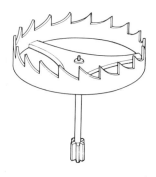

Crown wheel

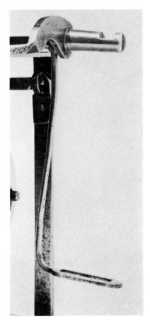

4 Crutch

5 Fly

6 Foliot balance

Detent Generally a detent is a part of the movement which detains; such as a lever which drops against a pin to cause the strike to lock up. The term is used for any lever work positioned in a downward plane, particularly if connected with locking or unlocking the strike work.

Dial foot Brass pillar riveted into the dial, by which the dial is pinned to the front plate or false plate. Four dial feet are normal in eight-day long-case work and three in 30-hour clocks. Some later eight-day clocks however use only three.

Dial plate The basic brass plate on which the various rings and decorations of a dial are fixed. Holes for mounting the hands and winding the clock are drilled into the dial plate.

Escapement The escapement imposes measured time upon a clock and keeps it to a regular rate of timekeeping. It usually takes the form of a pair of oscillating *pallets* whose faces intercept the teeth of the escape wheel.

False plate Backing plate to a white or painted dial, fixed close to the dial by four short dial feet, and enabling the clockmaker to drill holes and attach to his movements at any convenient place on the false plate's surface.

Finial Ornament forming the topmost terminal of a clock case, made of turned and gilt wood or more usually in brass.

Fly A vane or fan in the shape of a wide flat piece of brass mounted centrally on an *arbor* and arranged to be at the top of the striking train. This regulates the speed of the train by resistance to the air when revolving, giving a measure of rhythm to the strike, when otherwise it would gain speed on a long run such as in striking twelve. It also removes impetus from the strike train and allows smooth locking up on termination of the strike.

Foliot balance A medieval escapement control involving an oscillating bar moving to and fro while attached to a vertical pallet staff working against a *crown wheel*. It could be adjusted by lead weights hung on the foliot arms and moved outwards to slow down the period of oscillation.

Fret Decorative pierced work cut with a fretwork saw or piercing saw in either wood or metal. This may be used on cases, either backed by silk or similar material to let out the sound of the bells, or as decoration only, mounted on a solid wooden ground. This is known as blind fret work.

Fusée A device developed to regulate the uneven pull of a mainspring, which is strong when fully wound and not so strong just before rewinding. The fusée is a cone-shaped drum mounted on the winding *arbor* of the movement and is connected to the *barrel* or drum containing the mainspring by a

851

small chain or length of gut line. Winding the train coils all the line on to the fusée and puts the mainspring in tension. During the running of the clock the spring-barrel revolves and coils the line back around itself. When fully wound the line is pulling on the narrow end of the fusée and therefore requiring a spring's full energy to turn the train.

Gongs The alternative to bells in a striking or chiming clock. These may be either of straight or coiled wire spring. Gongs were not a feature of English work until the 19th century and are never original features on good antique clockwork.

Hood The top part of a long-case clock, which is removable to facilitate access to the movement. Some 17th-century clocks were arranged with a hood, mounted by grooves to the tongued edges of the backboard of the case: they were not removed but slid upwards and held by a catch for access – the so-called rising hood. These hoods had a fixed front with no door. Most clocks however have a hood which has an opening front and which also slide forward for complete removal from the case.

Latch Small flat catch which is pivoted on a screw or loosely riveted to the clock plate, adjacent to a pillar hole. When the plates are put together the latch is turned down to engage in a slot cut in the end of the protruding pillar. Dial feet are sometimes also fastened on in this way.

Leaf Leaves are the teeth of the pinion. A *pinion* proper has fewer than 20 leaves. If it has more then it is technically called a wheel. Usually pinion leaves are of steel.

Lenticle The small circular or oval window in the trunk door of a long-case clock, put in for decorative effect and so that one can see at a glance that the clock is going.

Lifting-piece Lifting-pieces can be found in any part of the movement, but usually in the striking train; they are lifted by a pin to fulfil part of the train's function. Unlocking the strike train is carried out by a lifting-piece situated in front of the reverse minute wheel in the motion work of a movement.

Lunette A lunette on a clock dial is a semi-circular aperture in the lower half of a dial plate centre through which the revolving disc date indicator is viewed.

7 Lifting piece

Maintaining power On most clocks power is removed from the train while winding. In precise regulator clocks, and those with delicate escapements, some form of maintaining power is necessary. One device was Huygens' endless rope principle involving only one weight to drive both going and striking trains. The winding click or ratchet work operating only on the strike side of the clock, causing no interruption in power to the going train when winding.

Moon work The indication of the age and the phases of the moon incorporated into a clock's dial. Four main types of moon work were used: 1) a revolving disc showing the moon's phases pictorially and numerically through a small circular aperture situated just below the XII. Known in London work at the end of the 17th century, it was more frequently used by clockmakers in the area of Halifax, Yorks, in the 18th century and was known as a half-penny or a Halifax moon; 2) a spherical ball moon, divided vertically, half being silvered and half coated with black wax, situated usually in dished portion of an arched dial. This revolves on a vertical shaft, geared from the motion work; 3) the more common moon work in the arch of a clock is a large flat disc with two painted or engraved moons revolving two-monthly. Humps at the sides of the aperture are usually decorated with hemisphere decorations and are supposed to give the correct silhouette to the representation of the waxing and waning moon; 4) on some square dial clocks, white dials and clocks from makers in the north, the moon's aperture is turned upside down and placed in the dial centre underneath the chapter XII.

8 Motion work

Motion work Motion work is the arrangement of wheels and pinions placed on the face of the front movement plate immediately beneath the dial. Their purpose is to transmit the drive to the hands and provide the 12 to 1 reduction necessary for minute and hour indications on the dial. Coupled with this is usually an arrangement for unlocking the strike train.

Movement The total mechanical part of the clock as made by the clockmaker. Horologists refer to this as the movement, others may call it the mechanism or works.

Music barrel A revolving barrel driven from a musical train by a fixed wheel at one end. Pins are arranged in its surface in order to activate the hammers and play the tune on a scale of bells, as the barrel revolves.

Pallets The tips or extremities of an escapement which momentarily stop and check the revolution of an escape wheel. In a *verge escapement* the pallets are sometimes known as flags.

Pillars Pillars may be made in metal or wood and found in a movement or a clock case. They are slender columns and generally shaped like and named after the architectural pillar. Movement pillars of brass hold together the plates of a clock and are found on clocks of both birdcage and plate frame construction. Wooden case pillars are generally seen in the hood, flanking the dial; they may be plain, twisted, or reeded.

9 Pinion

Pinion A pinion is a toothed gear which has less than 20 teeth or *leaves*. Often driven by a brass wheel, the pinion leaves are formed on the arbors of a movement and the name pinion is sometimes wrongly given to the whole pinion and arbor.

Pivot At either end of an *arbor* is found a reduced portion which forms the pivot on which the arbor revolves through holes in the plates. The pivot is made absolutely parallel and then hardened and polished.

10 Pivot

Plate A sheet of brass used in clockwork. Those most commonly referred to are movement plates between which the wheels and pinions are pivoted to form the movement. The large sheet which forms the basis of a dial is called the dial plate.

Pull repeater A clock which is arranged to repeat the last hour or hours and quarters, on the pulling of a cord. The hours being struck on one bell and the quarters on a smaller one. Thus three blows on the large bell and three on the smaller would indicate quarter to four.

Rack striking The most commonly found strike work on domestic clocks from its introduction about 1675. The action takes place on the front plate of the clock, and the strike is counted by a toothed rack dropping against a cam or *snail*, connected to the hour wheel. The further the drop permitted by the snail the greater the strike. The rack is gathered back to its locked position by a small single toothed pallet and each tooth gathered represents a single blow on the hammer.

11 Pull repeater

Rating nut The threaded nut at the base of the pendulum rod by which the bob may be raised or lowered, thus altering the rate or timekeeping of a clock.

Recoil The recoil is the momentary backward motion made by the escape wheel of an anchor escapement. It is pushed by the action of the pendulum after an escapement pallet has contacted the wheel. At the end of the pendulum's swing in one direction, the wheel exerts pressure on the escapement and gives impulse to the pendulum to maintain its swing.

Repeating work See *Pull repeater*

Seat board The wooden board with appropriate holes and cutaway section, which is fixed in the case to support the clock movement.

Seconds pendulum The pendulum generally associated with a long-cased clock which is 39.14″ and beats one second. It was found to be a convenient size for long-case clocks and its duration meant that the arbor of a 30-toothed escape wheel could be extended forward to provide the drive for a seconds hands.

Signatures The name of the clockmaker and sometimes town or place of business engraved on the dial. Bracket clocks quite often had the name engraved on the decorated backplate also.

12 Snail

Painted dials also carried the maker's name but later in the white-dial period the man whose signature was painted on the dial would most likely be the retailer only.

Silvering The depositing of a silver coating to certain brass parts of a clock dial, prinicpally chapter rings, name-bosses, calendar discs, etc.

Snail A disc cam with twelve levels around its circumference, used in conjunction with a rack whose tail falls against the snail to determine the amount of blows to be struck by the striking train. Since the snail is normally advanced by the hour pipe the number struck always corresponds to the hour shown by the hands. (See *Rack striking*).

Spandrel The spandrel is the triangular space created at the dial plate corners by the rim of the chapter ring. The spandrel may be decorated with engraving, punched decoration or a legend, usually relating to the passage of time. More commonly however a cast brass decoration, loosely known as a spandrel, is applied and held from the back by a single screw.

Throw A hand-cranked lathe on which work is mounted and turned using a hand-held tool.

Train A group of wheels and pinions running in series and with a specified purpose such as telling the time (the going train) or striking the hours (the strike train). These are commonly found side by side in any key wound movement. Another name given to the going train is watch train; W is often found scratched on the winding barrel of an eight-day long-case clock. The strike train maybe referred to as bell train.

Verge escapement An early type of escapement used on domestic clocks. This was developed from the *foliot balance* and *balance wheel escapement*. Both these escapements used a *crown-wheel* in a vertical plane. The verge escapement involved the use of a crown-wheel in the horizontal plan. The pallets on the verge *pallet staff* were controlled by the first *bob-pendulums.*

Weight Usually a lump of lead or iron with a ring or hook at the top to provide motive power for the driving of clock trains. Weights never break down or alter, providing a cheap and constant source of energy, but space is needed in the case or below a wall clock to allow for their descent.

Wheel Brass disc with teeth cut in its periphery, designed to transmit motion, and one of the most basic components of a clock movement.

Winding squares The extended ends of *fusée* or of barrel arbors, shaped to a tapered square section in order to accommodate the winding key, and transmit its circular motion to the spring or lines which are to be wound.

Chapter 2

The clock movement

The clock movement is the most confusing part of a clock for the amateur. It is also, however, the heart of the clock, the part that must be understood to see whether a clock is worth buying, and the area of the clock that most clearly reveals the quality of the whole. It is also, though the novice may not immediately realise this, the part of the clock that was actually made in the workshop of the man whose name appears on the dial, whereas other work, such as the design and construction of the case, may have been put out to a specialist cabinetmaker or a joiner. The clockmaker, his helpers, apprentices and outworkers, on the other hand, will certainly have been responsible for the design of the movement, and for making it up from scratch.

Most successful English clocks were made in metal (although a few have been known in wood), and any study of the history of the clock movement must involve a discussion of the metals used and the engineering principles involved. Although this discussion may seem forbidding at first sight, it is an essential background to any understanding of the qualities of a clock, and the issues at stake in restoring it. In this chapter, I have therefore begun with the basic material, the metals used by the clockmakers. Since most old clockmakers' workshops included the actual making up of most if not all the individual parts, the wheels, arbors, pinions and so on, I have next described the methods used in actually producing these pieces. This aspect of the subject is not only of special fascination to many people, who tend to marvel that old clockmakers could produce such precise movements without the advantage of modern methods, but it is also very necessary to appreciate the quality of the clockmaker's art. The third part of this chapter discusses the various ways in which clockmakers have approached the structural problems of making a movement that will hold together, run smoothly and reliably for many years. I hope that the result is to produce an introduction to the clockmakers' craft as seen from the very practical point of view.

The metals primarily used in the construction of old English clocks are brass and steel. Generally speaking, moving parts, such as the pivots of a clock, need to revolve on a dissimilar metal to prevent rapid wear. This principle is found in modern engineering in the steel and bronze bush; in clocks it means that the plates are usually made of brass, and the arbors or shafts which turn on them are of steel. The way in which brass and steel act on one another is a matter of prime importance. In some cases, the harder metal may, strangely at first sight, be worn away by the softer: for instance, a brass wheel turned by a small steel pinion will tend eventually to wear away the leaves of the pinion while leaving the brass unmarked. The reason for this phenomenon is that grit and dirt tend to become embedded in the soft brass and then grind away at the harder steel. This is accentuated by the quicker motion of the pinion relative to the wheel. From this example it will be seen that the way in which the metals are used in a clock movement is itself a matter of considerable expertise on the part of the clockmaker.

The yellow brass used in the 17th and 18th century was quite unlike the brass that we have today. Its delicate yellow colour is immediately obvious in contrast to repairs or replacements made in new brass, which looks quite orange in comparison. Specialist restorers have castings made in yellow brass of the old recipe to repair old and valuable clocks more convincingly. Judging by its colour and its nature, the old brass contained tin and possibly more zinc than today's brass. One of the earliest things I learned about restoration of old clocks was not to try and heat up a cracked or broken dial plate in old brass; unlike most brass available today, which is normally softened by heat, this old brass was sure to crack and completely de-nature. Possibly this is due to its method of preparation and age changing its properties. When buying brass today, it is possible to obtain a polished and uniformly thick sheet or round bar of the required gauge. This was not so in the old clockmaker's workshop. The molten brass had to be poured into a flat mould for sheet and when cold was laboriously beaten, scraped and filed in order to obtain a flat sheet for plates, and discs for wheel blanks, dials and so on. Its surface then was irregular, bearing all the marks of its preparation. More solid parts, such as pillars, cocks and lantern clock finials, and pendulum bobs were rough-cast in sand; round parts were then turned up in a hand-cranked lathe using hand-held cutting tools, and flat parts filed to shape. The high standard of tools and materials is something that we expect today, but their preparation and making was a major time-consuming factor in early workshops. Hours must have been spent in keeping a good edge on cutting tools.

Steel is a word used very loosely when talking about old movements, and just as I have qualified the word brass I must also say something about the nature of steel available to the old clockmakers. In fact it would be more honest to describe it as hardened iron. Various methods were used to harden iron for tools used in cutting and for the working parts of the clock. These methods were developed empirically through experience and were by no means dependable. Each man had his own preference. One clockmaker hardened his pinions by cooling them in a bar of soap, another chose to do it in bacon fat, but generally the iron would be heated to a cherry red and then quenched in cold water. Many 17th-century clocks are found to have very soft pinions and if they have been run regularly and are original, these will be very worn indeed today. Plate 17 shows a set of worn pinions that I replaced from a lantern clock made by Edward Norris of London in about 1670.

In order for a metal to become hard through the process of heating and rapid cooling, carbon must be present. Much of the early iron used was low in carbon content and it was discovered, though not by scientific methods, that if iron was put with charcoal or bone in a simple furnace and subjected to intense heat for a few days, a carbonisation of sorts would occur, though leaving a blistered and scaly finish to the shallow, hardened steel surface. The process was tedious, long

13 *Left:* The back of a lantern clock dial plate, showing its variable thickness and other marks of its preparation. Temple Newsam House, Leeds.

14 *Right:* A selection of clockmakers' screwplates, used to fashion the screws used in various parts of the clock.

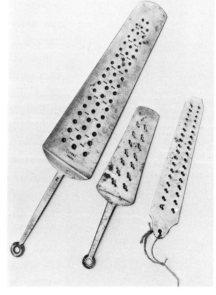

and frequently unsatisfactory in the final analysis.

Crucible steel, the next stage in the development of hardening iron, was unknown in Europe until 1746 when it was developed by the clockmaker, Benjamin Huntsman of Doncaster. Clearly he must have experienced the frustrations just described and, desirous of something better, embarked upon a series of experiments by which he carbonised and made crucible steel by heating small quantities of molten metal in a clay crucible together with wood. The whole was contained in a small conical furnace and blown with bellows for several hours. The improved steel and shorter preparation time was such a success that Huntsman gave up clockmaking, moved to Attercliffe, Sheffield, and became a crucible steel manufacturer on a larger scale.

After discussing the limitations in the materials available and marvelling at the skill of the old clockmaker, we ought to consider how they actually carried out the day-to-day business of clockmaking and what tools were used for what purposes. Round brass parts such as pillars, pipes and small finials were made or bought in as castings and turned up on the throw or clockmaker's lathe. Screws have been made from the earliest times but even at the end of the 18th century tended to be shallow-threaded and highly individual in their form. No deep- or blind-threaded holes were attempted in clockwork and the female threads were usually restricted to the thickness of a clock plate, cock or detent, and these hold surprisingly well. To make a screw, the clockmaker had the use of a screwplate which had a variety of threaded holes cut in it. The screwplate, usually with a small handle at one end, was made by hand-shaping the threaded holes with a hardened male screw matrix. The screws are almost always iron although brass screws, particularly in dial spandrel castings or holding a spring behind a moon dial, are not unknown. Cheese-headed screws and round domed-headed screws are also common and are found on work from every period. Decorative screws are found in high-quality work and in such cases are restricted to features on the backplate which was the area most commonly seen when the case was opened, or in the case of a long-case clock, when the movement was lifted down. These are illustrated in a long-case clock movement of a high quality by Thomas Ogden of Halifax (Plate 15), in which backplate screws resemble the open mouth of a serpent or similar decorative creature.

One of the questions frequently asked about clockwork is how the clockmaker made such accurate and evenly spaced wheels. How did they cut them and how did they decide on the shape of the teeth? We know today that the shapes of the teeth of clock wheels are important, but the old clockmaker did not consider this to be a major problem as it had been overcome successfully by trial and error and the shapes found to be a success were used unchanged in many workshops for decades. A variety of tooth forms are found in old English clocks and early work does not necessarily mean crude work, though early work from a country district frequently was. Crude work might involve flat-topped teeth, irregular depth at the bottoms or roots of the teeth and even leaning teeth, caused by applying the cutter to the blank off-centre. Regular but oddly-shaped tooth forms are also found in later clocks, particularly white-dial 30-hour clocks whose movements were frequently handwrought by country makers well into the 19th century. The well-formed tooth most commonly seen on English work settled into a style resembling an early English or Gothic arch. This shape proved to work very well and was close to the tooth form that we now know to be the ideal shape for clock wheels based on the epicycloid curve. This allows wheels to engage smoothly with their pinions and move freely, provided the correct depth or spacing is observed when laying out the trains.

Dividing the wheels, or providing a means of cutting any

15 *Left:* Movement of a revolving-ball moon-clock by Thomas Ogden of Halifax circa 1740, showing the fine turning and exquisite details in this exceptional clock. Its dial is shown in the frontispiece. Temple Newsam House, Leeds.

16 *Right:* Old Town Clock of York, 1658, formerly in St Williams Chapel, Ouse Bridge. The vertical straps of the frame are held in position by wedges. Museum and Art Gallery, Scunthorpe.

given number of teeth with even spacing, was a little more difficult and in medieval times this probably had to be done by measuring with a tape around the circumference of the wheel blank, then cutting and filing by hand. By the 16th century a mechanical means was devised of mounting a wheel blank rigidly above a plate which had been punched and drilled with a variety of numbers of holes arranged in concentric circles around the diameter; the greater numbers at the rim and the lesser towards the centre. By the end of the 17th century such dividing engines, or wheel cutting engines as they came to be known, were regularly used in the better workshops. These machines served successive generations with little development or alteration, and in common with other valuable machines and tools were passed down from father to son and master to journeyman. With the problem of holding and dividing a wheel solved, another problem yet remained. The cutter, and the method of mounting and revolving it formed the next problem. It was necessary to divide the pitch circle of the wheel blank by the number of teeth required. The pitch circle lies just within the outside diameter of the blank and forms the actual point at which the finished teeth engage with the pinion leaves or teeth of a wheel. Once this division had been made it was halved again to calculate the space to be cut away; the tooth and the space were generally of equal width. At first the teeth cut by the dividing engines were rectangular in shape and square at the tips. The tips were afterwards filed up by hand to the arched shape. Later in the 18th century a special engine called a rounding-up tool was designed to do this separate job. The cutter for the dividing engine was itself shaped and formed from a round piece of hard metal bar, turned or filed to the desired shape and then ground to half its thickness. The tip was then ground back to enable the cutter to cut through brass with the minimum of effort on the hand-cranked machine.

Pinions were difficult to make and their slender shape made them fragile and tricky to hold during the making. At first they were filed up and turned from the solid, being rather more coarse on early chamber and lantern clocks than they were in later clocks. By the late 17th century, however, a method was devised by which pinions were reliably made for over a hundred years. Pinion wire, which was in effect a continuous grooved pinion, was drawn while still hot through a hard draw-plate. Bought from a material dealer or manufacturer, the wire was parted off to the length required. The leafed portion of the pinion was marked round in the throw and unwanted portions removed to form the arbor. More recently pinions have again been worked from a solid round bar, with the leaves cut in specialist machines and the arbor turned smooth in the lathe. This is a more accurate way of forming true leaves since pinion wire was frequently distorted in its manufacture or by the breaking off of the unnecessary leaves along the arbor.

Early clocks had a high proportion of iron in their construction, and medieval, ecclesiastical and similar clocks were almost exclusively made that way, with only occasional brass bushes. Even these may have been the result of later repair, for many iron clocks had pivots driven and then broached into the iron frame in their original construction. Early lantern clocks in iron are not unknown, but by the 17th century it was increasingly unusual to find wheels and plate made in anything but yellow brass. Iron persisted as a material for pillars in some lantern and country long-case clock work. Count-wheels and some cocks were also occasionally made of iron. The items generally made of iron and steel are hammers, locking levers, lifting pieces, and the staff on which the bell sits. These iron parts were filed up from the solid or cast into required shapes pivoted in the lathe where necessary and fabricated by brazing when this was needed. This latter process gave way to silver-soldering, although it is difficult to state when this change occurred.

Unlike engineers and motor mechanics, clockmakers do not secure their clocks together with nuts and bolts, although screws are used for some jobs. These jobs are quite few in number and nothing so ambitious as long blind holes were attempted. In the normal clock of the 17th, 18th and 19th centuries the bell staff is generally secured through the backplate by a steady pin and a single screw. The back cock which provides a pivot or a knife-edge for the escapement arbor as well as the suspension point for the pendulum is also screwed to the backplate in two places. Blade springs and bridges of various types are also held to the plates by screws.

The framework of a clock is usually formed by pillars and plates. It is held together in three main ways; sometimes two of these methods are found on the same clock and they all occurred throughout the period under discussion. Fastening a clock by wedges appears to have been the earliest method used – allowing one bar to pass through a hole in another, cross-drilling the protruding part and fastening the joint with a wedge. This was a blacksmiths' method of fastening together a cage or framework of bars before the era of welding, and it was usual on the earliest clocks, especially iron turret clocks, which can loosely be described as of birdcage construction. The method was strong and had the advantage of being capable of being dismantled again. It was also an easy way in which to build an early iron clock frame and fasten in its upright plates. The smaller chamber clock and the lantern clock continued to use this method of fastening, with subtle variations introduced as the clock became more delicate. Country 30-hour long-case clocks which retained the birdcage layout for their trains also retained the wedge as a means of fastening until as late as the last quarter of the 18th century. When clockmakers started to put the strike and going mechanisms, known as trains, side by side, the clock plates were placed fore and aft and held together with pillars in a horizontal plane. These were riveted to the backplate; the fronts of the pillars protruded through a hole in the front plate and were cross-pinned by a taper pin pressed into a hole. This method of fastening accounts for 95 per cent of all clocks in period English work. Contemporary with the introduction of this method of fastening, and just as common in later 17th century London work, was the latched pillar in which the protruding end of the pillar was slotted at one side instead of being drilled. The slot was then fastened by a latch or flat hook, which was pivoted by a rivet from the plate. These latches were sometimes decorative and punched with eyes which made them further resemble a bird or a fanciful creature. Latching was the method used almost exclusively by the famous Tompion for all his complicated long-case and bracket clocks and not only for fastening plate pillars, but was also used to attach pillars between dial and front plate.

Occasionally one comes across a clock on which the middle plate pillar, of a five-pillar eight-day movement, is latched, while the four pillars at the corners of the plates are conventionally pinned. The explanation for this is that when a clock is being assembled in the clockmaker's workshop it is usual to pin, loosely, two of the pillars, possibly diagonally at top and bottom, before checking all is in order. Also to check that the trains have the correct free movement and that the strike train has the correct relationship of its wheels, hammer pins and lifting pieces and so on to achieve a smooth strike. Once this is found to be in order, the pins can be pressed home firmly. If, as is often the case, the plates have to be parted again momentarily to effect an adjustment, it is much easier to slip aside a single latch in the centre than to push out two pins, which may need the aid of a pair of pliers or other tool.

The method of fastening wheels to their arbors changed

subtly throughout the development of the English clock, and the way in which this was done can help to date the work. If the style is not consistent within a single clock, it can also tell us that there have been repairs or alterations; but more of that in a later chapter. Generally speaking, the stubbier the arbor and collet the earlier the work, though in much early work the collet was not used at all. Early- and mid-17th-century lantern clocks frequently had their wheels squared on to thick arbors. The wheels at this period were thick enough to make this method possible, but accuracy was not guaranteed. Sometimes a shallow seat shape was turned integral with the iron arbor and when drilled the wheel could be mounted direct. This is also found on some early long-case work but it is not common. Brass collets used on lantern clocks and some early case clocks were driven or brazed on to the arbor to form a broad seating for the wheel. This seat was reduced to size and trued after the collet was brazed firm.

The first English clocks took the form of an iron cage with arbors supported by vertical bars; this arrangement was favoured by the maker of smaller domestic chamber clocks and continued into the 17th century in the lantern clock. The fact that in such clocks the strike train was arranged behind the going train was of no importance, as winding was done by pulling on a rope, and clock weights at this time were rarely enclosed so that one had a visual reminder that the clock needed winding every twelve hours or so. However, with the development of the anchor escapement and the seconds pendulum in about 1675, clocks with increased accuracy and a more delicate construction were feasible. Something more delicate than a rope was required to hold the weights of the clocks that were designed to go for increased periods of time. Long lengths of gut needed to be wound on to barrels, turned with a key, and, since the key had to pass through the dial plate, it was necessary to place the going and strike trains side by side. This departure from the medieval birdcage design caused the plates to be arranged vertically and, where they had previously been merely top and bottom plates, they now became integral to the design of the movement, carrying pivots, motion wheels and lever work. Although lantern clocks were still made for many years in London, mainly as travelling alarms, and also in some country regions, most clocks were now made in the new plate form rather than the birdcage form.

The development of ideas was rapid. The golden period of English clockmaking was now begun and clocks were made that would go for periods of one month, three months and even

17 Worn-out pinions removed from the lantern clock by Edward Norris, London, shown in Plate 68.

18 *Opposite left:* Anonymous country long-case clock with one hand, dated 1672. Towneley Hall Art Gallery and Museum, Burnley.

19 *Opposite right:* Sophisticated marquetry long-case clock of about 1680, by Matt Crockford, London. Towneley Hall Art Gallery and Museum, Burnley.

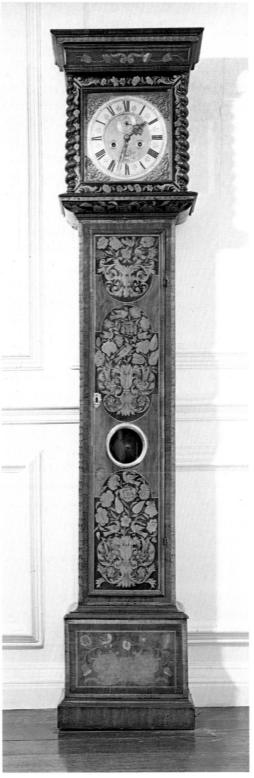

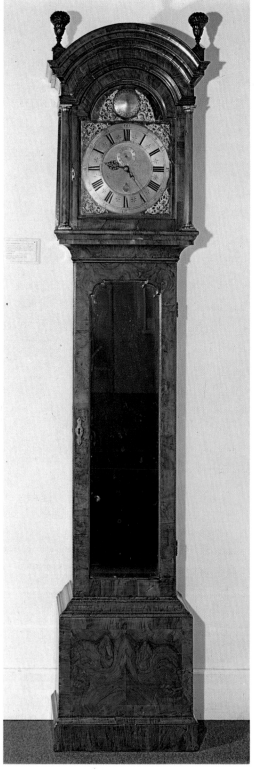

866

a year between windings. Complicated clocks were made which would tell the mechanical time as well as solar time, spring-driven bracket clocks and clocks which struck on great numbers of bells and played tunes. London makers developed horological skills at a rapid rate. Many of them at this time were inventive and capable men, able to work out wheel patterns and the numbering of trains to achieve a specific result. The best craftsmen continued to do so and through the 18th century the work of a good maker was individual and original in execution and concept. As a result dates alone can give a misleading impression of the development of the craft. Contemporary with the fine and sophisticated marquetry-cased London clocks of the 1680s, country styles of clockmaking flourished in the more remote centres, in which the work bears no resemblance to the London clocks. Country clockmakers up to the mid-19th century would probably make only two types of clock: the 30-hour long-case clock and occasionally the eight-day long-case clock for a special order. Bracket clocks, which were driven by springs, had particular problems associated with the type of steel needed for the springs, which was unreliable and difficult to make at this early date. The movements used in country clocks tended to be of a similar pattern and type, probably from a pattern book started by father or master and followed with little inventiveness except perhaps in decoration. It is also likely that country clockmakers would have facilities for cutting only limited tooth numbers on wheels, and so arranged the movements to suit the teeth they could produce.

It is impossible to be dogmatic about the type, shape and materials used for clock weights. More than all other parts, these were lost, sold for scrap, or have been exchanged freely in recent years. Enough clocks remain in their original state, however, to determine some patterns to look for, though this is not always an infallible guide. The earliest chamber clocks had lead weights and counter-weights were used at the reverse end of the rope, particularly in an alarm, to keep it taut. Various shapes from a bell shape to a dumpy pear drop were used, though a parallel weight was the norm. High-quality hooded wall clocks and the sophisticated long-case clock in the period immediately before and after 1700 used lead weights cased in thin brass. Tops to these weights were carefully turned and screwed on to a threaded bar protruding from the lead. From early to mid-18th century long-case clocks generally had plain uncased lead weights, though high-quality clocks and some precision clocks continued with brass casing until the early 19th century. The white-dial clock period, after 1770, marked the almost universal change from lead to iron for clock weights. Occasionally, especially on later products, the weight of the iron used was lettered and cast at the bottom of the weight. The average weight of a 30-hour long-case weight was 7 lbs, and an eight-day weight 12 lbs. Very rarely the maker's or ironfounder's name would be cast into the weight also.

The monastery bell was an established way of marking the routine of services and dividing the working day long before clocks were introduced to this country. The Venerable Bede mentions the use of bells in this way at the end of the 7th century. It was natural therefore that a bell should be used to sound the hours on early mechanical clocks. Since nothing better or more pleasing was discovered, this idea was carried over into domestic clock production. Clock bells are almost invariably cast in 'bell metal', a variable alloy composition which usually contained a large part of copper with antimony and tin. It is almost certain that bells were bought in by the clockmaker, not made in his workshop, and bell founding existed as a separate craft from an early period. Travelling bell founders cast church bells on site in the middle ages. This is known to have gone on into the 18th century and since the setting up of clay moulds and pouring the metal was a specialised skill it seems likely that such craftsmen would also make bells for the clockmaker. Bells used in clockwork were never significantly 'bell'-shaped, with rare exceptions, but were instead a flatish domed shape of a circular plan, rather like a deep, inverted saucer. Clocks playing tunes or providing a quarter-chime and so on had a number of bells; often eight bells making a scale, fastened on a bell staff and dished closely inside each other at the top of the movement where they could be struck by the hammers with the smaller bells playing the higher notes. These are referred to in clockwork as a nest of bells. Clock bells can be tuned to achieve the desired note by turning away the metal at various points. From the beginning of the 19th century, spiral wire gongs struck by leather-tipped hammers were used as an alternative on some bracket or table clocks. Sometimes a clock can be found with the tune or quarter-hour chime on bells, and the hours sounded on a gong. These are not generally well regarded and while they were almost always very well made at this period they do not give as pleasing and subtle a sound as an early bell delicately struck by a light hammer. Anything other than a bell in long-case clockwork should be regarded with suspicion. These were sometimes altered to arrange the strike on wire gongs screwed into the back of the case and I have even seen a chrome chime tube hanging in the case of an altered clock.

It will be apparent that the skills and methods of making parts of a clock movement are many and various. Few clockmakers possessed all the skills necessary to make a complete clock and even those that did rarely worked alone. Factory methods of splitting up the work into different parts were adopted early on, for we can tell from engravings of early clockmakers' workshops that even chamber clocks were made by division of labour. Thomas Tompion had many helpers at his workshop in Water Lane and from the rate book of 16th July 1695, we see recorded 19 people, two of whom were Tompion and his sister, and the rest were servants, journeymen and apprentices. After buying in of bells and castings such as dial spandrel decorations or finials in rough-cast metal, all the rest would be fashioned and wrought by the men, working long hours under the direction of the master clockmaker. It is often stated that apprentices started their apprenticeship by making clock hands. I have even heard it suggested that they travelled the country taking orders for clocks. There is no factual evidence of this being true, and it would seem to me that both arguments are unlikely. Finely wrought hands are of great importance to a good clock and required skilful sawing and filing up if they were to do justice to a handsome dial. The job of representing the workshop to customers would be done by the master and the important business of discussing a new clock and costing the same would not be entrusted to a mere beginner. Clocks did of course sell on the reputation of a clockmaker and in such cases the orders were dealt with by the master or by a member of the clockmaker's family.

Apprentices would sample all of the skills throughout their seven years of training. Perhaps they would start with base tasks such as preparing brass by hammering and scraping to obtain a surface. They would also make their first observations of the wheel-cutting process by turning the crank to provide power for the cutter. Crossing out wheels (that is, cutting away the unwanted portions in the wheel to provide the crossing or spokes in the wheel centre) would also occupy them. Turning at the lathe, marking out and making of hands would require lots of patience to master the necessary required skills. All of these tasks would have to be learned before specialisation could take place, when obviously a man would have preferences and likely do one job better than another.

Since clock manufacture in the 17th and 18th century was truly laborious and all power was supplied by hand, fitness for purpose was one of the yardsticks in manufacturing, although delicate, decorative touches here and there and beautiful turning have always been a part of English clockmaking. Engraving too has always been used to beautiful effect. The engraved backplate of an English bracket clock is usually a delight to see. Nevertheless the design of the movement of a clock is one of the most important things to those who understand horology. An expert can date a clock and sometimes make an accurate guess at its maker by examination of the movement alone. Within the general framework of craft practices, each maker had his own little way of doing things, whether it be finishing off the head of a screw or engraving a bird's head on the tail of a hammer spring. The good makers had a sense of design and aesthetics which rarely failed them, and it is this along with their mechanical skills which we have come to admire in their work.

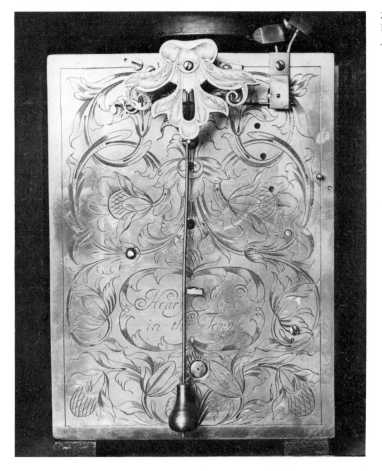

22 Engraved backplate of a bracket clock by Henry Jones, London, about 1680.

Chapter 3

Dials and hands

The Man is yet unborn that duly Weighs an Hour

From the dial of an eight day clock
by Thos. Radford of Leeds about 1775

Much as we recognise the character of a person by looking at
his face, we are immediately able to gain an impression of a
clock by looking at the dial. The quality of the clock is largely
reflected in the dial, and if this is of good quality – well-
designed, of good proportions and skilfully engraved – then
the movement is likely to be so too. At any rate, the legibility
and design of the dial is important for obvious reasons and
much care was spent, throughout the history of domestic
clockmaking, in making them as fine and clear as possible, even
though sometimes legibility was sacrificed for the sake of
decoration.

Early church clocks, such as the one erected at Salisbury
Cathedral in 1386, had no dial at all but struck the passing
hours on one of the church bells. This was not unusual in the
few public clocks erected and what was not an expected
feature in those early days was not missed. The bell recording
the hours was quite accurate enough to regulate the ecclesiastical orders and the rural community in the surrounding fields.
To people working by sunlight, divisions of less than an hour
were hardly relevant at all. The continental idea of using Jacks,
carved and jointed figures which struck bells, spread to
England in the 16th century and was used on clocks with and
without dials. The idea of Jacks in clockwork kept its appeal.
Special public clocks incorporating them as a decorative
feature have always been built. The modern Jacks clock at
Fortnum and Masons in Piccadilly, London, is known
throughout the world. Dials of these large public and church
clocks, if they existed at all, were made of various materials,
sometimes of carved stone if not too large, but mainly of wood.
These were built out in an architectural style, not unlike the
interior church woodwork decorated with carved mouldings
and finials. The whole was finished in bright painted colours
and gilt work.

The first domestic clocks in England were scaled-down iron

clocks, and dials were either set to revolve and were marked by a fixed hand in the Continental manner, or were fixed and marked by a revolving hand. This second, later idea has come to be the accepted pattern. Sheet-iron and sheet-brass dials were at first oblong front covers pinned between vertical plates into the front of the clock, the dial markings swept by a single hand for a twelve-hour period being crudely engraved or punched between concentric circles scribed on to this plate. Some early 16th-century spring-driven clocks appear to have had cast brass and gilt cases incorporating their cast and chased dials among the architectural and astronomical pattern work. These were largely of German design, and in many cases executed by Continental craftsmen or their apprentices. By 1600 English characteristics began to appear in clocks whose design had previously been dominated by the Continental influence and craftsmen. It had become usual to make dials with a dial plate and a separate engraved ring with numerals for the hours or chapters (hence the name chapter ring) pinned on to the front. For about 170 years this design became the norm for all dials and later any sub-dials were applied to the dial plate in the same way. Early lantern clocks, which were the first English clocks to be made this way, had a very narrow chapter ring, allowing only about $\frac{3}{4}''$ for the height of the numerals. Its spread was restricted by the distance between the front clock pillars. Since these clocks were not particularly accurate anyway, one hand only was usual. Engraving was therefore simple; Roman numerals with designs such as a crow's foot pattern or a simple star between them, for decorative effect as much as to mark the half-hour. Sometimes only the numbers XII, III, VI and IX were engraved and plus marks sufficed for the other hours. The main decorative area on these very early balance-wheel clocks was within the chapter ring and the engraving continued to be astrological or geometrical, often radial in general arrangement.

By the mid-17th century chapter rings had become slightly wider and covered a greater area of the front of the clock, stretching to outside the width of the clock and a little beyond. Still marked for one hand only, the engraving was more sure and quarter-hour divisions appeared within the ring at the inner edge. The dial centre had now become an engraver's showpiece, with overall foliage and scrolls. Floral bouquets, frequently of tulips or roses, were used. The corners of the dial plate outside the chapter ring were also engraved with simple sprays or leaves to match. Often the clockmaker's name was incorporated in a cartouche at the centre of the dial, usually

23 *Left:* Lantern clock by William Selwood at Ye Mermayd in Lothbury (1635) showing early dial features. A disc for setting the alarm should cover the plain dial centre, but is missing.

24 *Right:* An East Anglian lantern clock with broader chapter ring than its earlier London counterparts. Jeremy Spurgin, the maker, died in 1699.

above the mounting of the hand. No fixed place was used to engrave the maker's name and three places were normal at this time: in a cartouche above the mounting of the hand on the dial plate beneath the chapter ring, or at the base of the front fret which fastened to the horizontal top plate of the clock.

Consideration must now be given to the dials of the three main types of clock which became common after the invention and rapid spread of the pendulum. These were the lantern clock, the long-case clock and the bracket clock. Chapter rings on all these types were similar in style though different in size and preparation. Lantern clocks were perhaps a little more crude in some country districts, although very sophisticated lantern clocks do exist with dials and movements made to the highest London standards. The first long-case clocks had square dials with very narrow chapter rings and, because the introduction of the pendulum offered increased accuracy, they had the addition of a minute hand and the resultant marking of the outside edge of the hour circle. It had now become realistic to divide an hour into portions of 60 seconds each and to mark them in the minute circle. Some high-quality clocks towards the end of the 17th century had each minute numerically engraved in full, though this fashion was rare and did not persist. Most dials were engraved in the spandrel corners and the centres could be a riot of beautiful engraving of flowers and foliage. The clockmaker's name was often incorporated among the engraving in the dial centre or even at the base of the dial plate underneath the VI on the chapter ring.

The seconds indicator with its separate ring was not introduced to the dial until after 1672 when the long pendulum beating the seconds became the norm. After this date many features became accepted which remained in the dial's make-up until the demise of the brass-dialed clock. The box calendar with a peep number changing every 24 hours was a feature dating from the last two decades of the 17th century. So too was the matted- or punched-dial centre and the applied cast decorations for the spandrel corners. By 1680 the dial plate of a long-case clock was likely to be 10″ square with a chapter ring of slightly broader proportions than before and simple cast cherub spandrel decorations in the corners, a slim but large seconds ring pinned on to the dial plate in the same way as the chapter ring and engraved with 60 divisions, each five being numbered in Arabic numerals, matt-dial centre and the clockmaker's name at the base of the dial plate. The box calendar was cut in the dial plate just above the VI position. Arabic numerals were commonly used on the calendar engraving. Roman numerals were used for marking the hours on the chapter rings of almost all clocks, and a little error has traditionally been accepted in the numbering for the sake of balance in design of the dial. The figure four in Roman numerals ought to be written as IV but is always engraved with four wide strokes. This creates a visual balance as the figure eight in the opposite lower position has also four wide strokes in its engraved form. Winding-holes on these late 17th-century dials were plain and sometimes had shutters covering them from behind. Mounted on a pivot, these were moved aside when a maintaining power device was applied, prior to the winding of weight-driven clocks. Shortly before 1700, however, it became fashionable for the winding-rings, the seconds indicator aperture and the calendar box, if circular, to

25 *Above:* A 10″ square dial showing cherub spandrel decorations, an applied seconds ring and well-proportioned chapter ring, by John Williamson of Leeds, circa 1690.

26 *Above right:* An 11″ dial from a long-case clock by Edward Speakman, London, made in about 1710. The chapter ring shows quarter-hour markings and fine half-hour decorations.

27 *Right:* Detail of a dial from a clock by Henry Hindley of Wigan (about 1730), with shutters covering plain winding holes. This feature indicates a clock with bolt-and-shutter maintaining power.

be heavily ringed with turned and polished circles. These formed a pleasing contrast to the matt centre which was textured and rough though bright gilt in finish. The cherub spandrel decorations had additional foliage scrolls added to the tops and sides, and in consequence filled the corners to give a busier look to the whole dial. On the chapter ring half-hour decorations were delightfully engraved, often based on the *fleur de lys* and sometimes a decorative cross pattern. Quarter-hour markings, which occupied the circle at the inner side of the chapter ring and had served to mark the progress of the now-obsolete single hand, persisted and added to the charm of the dial at this particularly beautiful period. Signatures were now engraved between the V and VII and often gave the town or city of origin as well as the name. From this period it is less common to find the name at the base of the dial plate.

Though similar in most respects to those of long-case clocks, the dials of spring-driven bracket clocks frequently had a mock pendulum aperture in the dial centre, beneath the figure twelve. A concave curved slit was cut away from the dial plate and a small patterned disc of brass which was wired to the verge escapement arbor, showed from behind, thus simulating the action of a bob pendulum and showing at a glance that the clock was working. This explanation always seems to me to be curious, as the characteristic busy click of a verge escapement clearly indicates to all but the very deaf that the clock is in working order. Possibly its decorative appeal was important too. Lantern clock dials too changed subtly and the tall slim lines of the early models began to thicken with age. The chapter ring grew broader and became wider than the body of the clock. In some country districts where the lantern clock retained its popularity well into the 18th century, the chapter ring grew extremely wide, out of all proportion to the clock. These were given the name sheep's head clocks – possibly for their bland, numb look when hung on the farm kitchen wall. One hand was usual until the end of the lantern clock period although lantern clocks with minute indications and even a third, musical train are not unknown. These are, however, very rare.

The next major development in dials occurred about 1715-20 when the arched top was added to the dial plate. At first this varied in size. Occasionally an arch was quite deep and wide but more generally the early arches were shallower than later examples. Common on both bracket and long-case clocks from this period, the arch began as a decorative feature and was fully engraved all over, though sometimes containing the clock-maker's name in an engraved cartouche at its centre. This was sometimes supported by a specially cast brass decoration or, instead of the name, a corner spandrel was used with its corner upright in the arch centre. Possibly the first use to be made of the arch was to provide a lever or single hand with which the strike of the clock could be silenced. This is known as strike/silent indicator, from the words with which the backing ring was engraved. Calendar hands or, more rarely, very early moon phase indicators were incorporated into the early arched dial. Subsequent to its introduction makers of most quality clocks began to use the arched dial form, and by now the long-case clock dial had grown to 12″ square plus the arch. Some early clocks were modernised at this date to acknowledge the new fashion and had an arch added to their square dial plates. These added arches were riveted on by means of brass

28 *Above:* A dial of a late London lantern clock by Henry Webster, made in about 1700. The chapter ring extends beyond the width of the dial plate. Temple Newsam House, Leeds.

29 *Above right:* Detail of a cherub spandrel decoration.

30 *Below right:* Detail of spandrel decoration of two cherubs holding a crown. This design dates the decoration to some time after 1705.

reinforcing straps at the back and were used for a variety of purposes, though mainly decorative as an existing clock would already carry its maker's name. It also happened that a maker had some square plates in stock when fashions changed, and these too would have been modernised in the same way. Clocks with early alterations can be found, but they should not be confused with spurious examples altered recently to fit odd clock components into an arch dial case. After a few years the arch settled into a more regular shape and from then until the end of the long-case clock period it was usually about a half-circle in shape. Bracket clocks of the first quarter of the 18th century particularly were likely to differ from the square dial with an arch at the top. Some had tall oblong dials and others had tall oblong dials with an arch. The extra spaces were filled with sub-dials for such purposes as regulating the length of the pendulum, strike/silent calendars and moon phases. If the clock was a musical one, the tune could be chosen by rotating a pointer in the sub-dial. The titles of the tunes were frequently fully engraved around the edges of the ring.

From 1700 some variety is to be expected in the design of the cast spandrel decoration, although there were never a great number of spandrel decorations throughout the entire clock period – possibly about 30 including those used in the arch as well. It is rare to find a new or unique design. Makers and regions appear to have had their favourite designs and stuck to them with infrequent deviations. Like bells and other castings, spandrels were bought in from foundry representatives. Following the enlarged cherub spandrel decoration and becoming popular about 1705, was a design featuring two cherubs holding a crown and flanked by foliate scrolls. This is thought to celebrate symbolically the Protestant ascendancy. Similar designs were carved into the front rails and crestings of chairs during the William-and-Mary period. Many Dutch craftsmen were working in the London furniture and clockmaking crafts at this time and their influence on decoration was considerable. Later versions had a larger crown, and generally this design persisted for a long time.

Satyrs and also female heads flanked by foliage scrolls were used at this time as spandrel ornaments. The satyr head was particularly used by good London makers of the beginning of the 18th century. Later into the century, patterns became more numerous and the degree of finish in the casting diminished.

From about 1730, an urn provided a central feature for some spandrel decorations. Many others were produced with foliage only and the rococo period influenced the design by introducing C- and D-scrolls, common in all decorative features of the period about 1770. Three or four variations of this type are known. The later northern brass-dial clocks, particularly the Lancashire type, are typified by their use of a large openwork rococo spandrel decoration with an apex scroll resembling a question mark. A late version of the cherub spandrel decoration also occurred in the north from about 1750. A large cherub head with heavy scroll and scallop work characterises this type, which was used until the end of the brass-dial period. A decoration during the mid- and late-18th century, which is not very highly regarded by most horologists, is the set of four corners showing figures symbolising the seasons. This idea was also common on Dutch clocks and carried over into the painted-and white-dial period, when figures representing the seasons were painted into dial corners. Also during the painted-dial period the 'set of four' as a decoration extended to figures in the corners representative of four known continents: normally a Red Indian, a Negro African, a Chinese woman, and a European.

Before describing further developments, it is as well to look at the skills involved in making a brass dial. We expect to see the delightful variety of surface on cast and hand finished brass plate until the late 18th century. After this time, when machine-rolled brass plate became a possibility, it was occasionally used. Even then its use was very limited in clockwork. The reverse of a dial plate or chapter ring gives a clear indication of this method of production. It may also render a

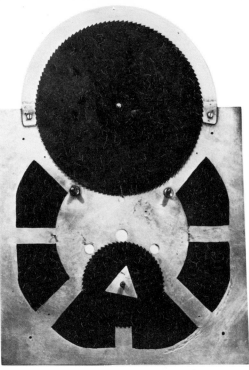

31 *Left*: Large open-work rococo spandrel decorations, on which the apex scroll resembles a question mark. The engraving of the dial centre has a similar rococo quality. Long-case clock by Dollif Rollisson, Halton, Leeds, circa 1770. Temple Newsam House, Leeds.

32 *Right*: A north-country dial plate from the rear, showing the gaps left behind the chapter ring.

few clues to the clock's history with inscriptions scratched by repairers, or may show the engraver's trial strokes as he practised the forming of a letter. This is more common in country work. Sometimes too a date or a journeyman's name is engraved in places not normally seen by anyone other than the restorer. A feature found in the dials of clocks made north of the Midlands is the cut-away or, more precisely, cast-away section left in the area of the dial plate covered by the chapter ring. This practice, very likely done for reasons of economy, was the norm in the mid- and later-18th century but was not always carried out on northern clocks of the very early 18th century.

It is often obvious that country makers in isolated places did their own engraving, and on some of those country 30-hour clocks one can see the greatest departures from the normal way of doing things in this highly conservative craft. Imperfections in brass castings leaving pit gaps and sandmarks, thin scratchy engraving, punched decorations, crudely engraved patterns and naively lettered legends and verse often relating to the passage of time and Man's mortality, all add up to the charm of some country 30-hour clocks. Finely engraved dials were clearly the work of a master engraver and when we consider the division of labour that went on in the clockmaker's workshops of any size, it is plain that the clocks were engraved

by one who was a specialist in that field. He may have been an employee of the clockmaker, but most dials were sent out. Throughout the 18th century the engraver was an important and busy craftsman engaged upon engraving printing plates, book illustrations, maps, silver plate and many other items including clock dials which would form his everyday business. It is sometimes suggested that mistakes, for example in the spelling of a clockmaker's name, indicate that the engraving was sent out. However, variety in spelling, even of a name, was not uncommon in those days and an obvious mistake can be made, even of one's own name, when concentrating on the letter form and making a good job of the engraving. From time to time, one also sees a mistake in the numbering. Recently I saw a clock with two 25s engraved in the minute band when the correct figures should have read 20 and 25. Over-concentration probably led to this charming error.

After the introduction of the applied brass chapter ring and sub-dials, it became the norm to provide contrasts of finish by the use of gold, silver and black wax in differing parts.

The dial plate and spandrel decoration of early clocks were nearly always mercurially gilt to give a bright glow, richer looking than polished brass. This was particularly so in the 'golden period' at the end of the 17th century and the beginning of the 18th. The chapter rings and any sub-dial rings pinned on to the dial plate and the calendar ring which revolved on rollers behind the dial plate were given a silvered finish by applying an amalgam of silver chloride paste, salt and

33 Detail of a dial by John Ismay, Oulton, Cumberland, circa 1710. Imperfections in the casting of the metal can be seen on the chapter ring between the hours nine and ten. Simple decoration and scratchy engraving make this a typical early country clock. The hands are a replacement. The movement of this clock is shown in Plate 85.

tartaric acid. Although this produced a silver deposit it did not resemble polished silver, but when correctly done gave a good white finish to the rings. The engraved numerals, which had previously been filled with black wax, showed through and gave a clear and beautiful contrast.

It is very rare to find evidence of the original dial surface on a clock, for this has often been destroyed by active cleaning and polishing of the dial, or has perished by neglect or even age. If exposed to atmosphere silvering, like the solid metal, quickly blackens. When the hands are moved on manually, or catch the ring, or even when the dial is rubbed with a duster, the protective lacquer wears through and the silver coating on the rings deteriorates.

Before moving on to the new fashion for the white- or painted-dial it should be said that for a brief period around 1770-80 dials were made for long-case and bracket clocks which were engraved from a full and plain sheet of brass. These are referred to as a single-sheet dial. Their outline was the same as the conventional dial with applied rings and can be seen in round, arched or square dial form. Corners and sub-dials, as well as hour and minute numerals were all fully engraved. The engraving was filled with black wax and the dial fully silvered, giving a clear black-and-white quality to the finished dial. Many of these dials are admired for their tasteful and restrained style of engraving, and the clarity of the hands when viewed across a room.

By 1772 a startling new departure was made in dial production which led to mass-produced dials to help cater for increased demand for clocks from the growing middle and merchant classes. This was the painted face or white-dial, painted on an iron base or dial plate. Cheapness and speed of manufacture cannot have been an important factor in its introduction for the painting- and number-writing would have taken almost as much time as engraving, and when it was first produced, the white dial was more expensive to produce than the brass dial. It seems possible to account for introduction of the white dial for fashionable reasons alone, for new products were avidly admired then as now. Contemporary advertising lists its advantages, and it is not difficult to imagine that the new white dial was much admired and in great demand. Like the brass dial, the new product went through various stages of development. Contemporary with its introduction came the single-sheet brass dial mentioned above, whose silvered appearance is very similar at first glance; so much so that some authorities feel that the simple style of decoration used on the first white-dials was derived directly from the engraved dial. Others feel that the single-sheet brass dial was introduced by the engraved-dial makers to combat the commercial success of the white-dial. However, which came first is not at issue here. It is enough to say that their design features were both products of the same taste and on the surface they appear very similar indeed. A feature of the earliest white-dials was the simplicity of decoration and the amount of clear white ground which was shown. Decoration was mainly restricted to the spandrels and the edges of the arch, if there was one. This was usually gold rococo work on a raised gesso ground. The black number-writing was delicately done and copied precisely the quality and proportion of the late engraved-brass dial. The maker's name too was written precisely by brush, but in the flowing style of the engraver.

Gradually the dial painters introduced more and more into their dials and areas, such as the dial centre and spandrel corners which had formerly been delicately decorated with swags and scrolls now supported exotic birds, floral bouquets, shells and fans. Less of the white background was left. The trend continued until corners, arches, and sometimes a large part of the dial centre were fully painted. Many dials of about 1830 could even be said to be rather vulgar, and their gaudy colours and brash renderings of such subjects as country cottages, sailing ships, hunting scenes, battle scenes, and pastoral scenes with figures owe more to folk art than the fine craftsmanship shown in earlier white dials.

There had to be some provision for attaching the movement to these new white dials. It had been customary to rivet dial

34 *Opposite above left:* An 11″ dial of a long-case clock by William Tipling of Leeds, circa 1705. The particularly beautiful hands are its finest feature.

35 *Opposite right:* Fine marquetry month-going long-case clock by William Honeychurch of Rotherhithe, London, circa 1710, with added arch.

36 *Opposite below left:* Painted arched dial signed Booth, Pontefract. It is signed on the back by the dial painter Schwanfelder. The arch of the dial features a rocking ship, while the lower dial centre shows Britannia pointing upwards to indicate the fate of the dying Nelson.

37 *Left:* A 14″ square white-dial clock signed Barrow, Stockport, about 1790. The false plate fixing is marked Osborne Birmingham; the same firm was also the true dial makers.

38 *Right:* Rear view of the same dial, showing the cast-iron false plate supplied with the dial to enable it to be fixed to the movement.

882

feet into the old brass dial at any point underneath the chapter ring, once it had been established that the dial feet would not foul the strike work or any other of the motion work of the clock. Carried out in the same workshop that the clock was made, this was an easy job. The new white-dial was factory-made (most of them were made in Birmingham) and also the painted surface could be damaged by later riveting on dial feet, so that a means was introduced to overcome this problem. This was the 'false plate'. Attached to the back of the dial by four very short dial feet, the false plate was an intermediary plate of ample proportion to allow further brass feet which would fasten the false plate to the movement at a convenient point. This meant that the dial's surface was not damaged and all riveting could take place on the removable false plate. Once this problem was removed the only remaining consideration was to see that the movement was designed to match up with the winding holes, seconds-hand hole and date hole or lunette aperture if fitted. Makers using Birmingham dials must therefore have had to buy in a dial and use it to lay out the final placing of clock train before drilling the plates. In eight-day white-dial clocks after 1800 the absence of a false plate can indicate that the clock movement as well as the dial was bought complete by the man whose name appears on the dial. In these cases three dial feet are often used in preference to the more usual four. Thirty-hour clocks, which are wound by pulling on a rope or chain, never had the complication of aligning winding holes with winding squares or the seconds indicator with its hole in the dial. Much of their strike work was placed between and behind the plates of the clock. The false plate was therefore not necessary and in fact they are rarely if ever fitted to an unaltered 30-hour clock, even though Birmingham white-dials were commonly used in their making. Made of cast iron, the false plate adds an additional interest to the clock for nearly all examples were cast with their maker's name. Thus the dial-maker's period of working can be established as well as the clockmaker whose name is on the dial, giving a further guide to dating the clock accurately.

Few artists ever signed the dials they painted. Indeed, of the hundreds of dials that I have handled, only one has been signed by its painter. Since the clock in question is a white-dial, long-case clock by Booth of Pontefract, Yorkshire, made about 1830, and has three dial feet and no false plate, it is quite likely to have been bought in by Mr. Booth from a Birmingham factory. No markings are evident on the dial plate or movement, but the artist has signed the back of the dial plate in such a way that suggests that he always did this, but no others as far as I know have yet come to light. It says clearly and simply:

Schwanfelder

Painter and Clock Dial Enameller

Bottom of Wade Lane, Woodhouse Bar

Leeds.

There is nothing written about the actual painting of clock dials, who did what, and at what stage. It seems to me, from handling and restoring many of them, that the colour-work and the black numerals and signature were often done at different times. It could be that in some cases the coloured pictures or decorations were painted on in the factory, and the black work added later by the clockmaker's local artist, dial writer or, as in the case of the Schwanfelder dial, the whole thing painted by arrangement after the dial left the factory. I make those points as no-one else has recorded that many worn and rubbed dials have lost their black work, when the colour-work still retains much of its original surface. The oil-painted coloured areas are quite heavily protected by varnish, whereas the numerals and signature in black have been carried out in what appears to have been a water-based paint or ink and left unprotected. Over the years washing has removed many of the numbers and frequently the maker's name and town of origin as well.

Bracket clock dials during the late Georgian period changed in the same way as on the long-case clock; the single-sheet silvered brass dial was used by some makers for a time. However, variations never regularly used in long-case work were introduced. French clocks commonly have enamelled dials. That is a true enamel, kiln fired on a copper base, giving a ceramic like hard surface which should not be confused with the painted surface of a white-dial. Never a typical feature of English work, enamelled centre parts such as a chapter ring and dial centre all in one were very occasionally used on an arched brass dial plate and flanked by the traditional cast spandrel decoration. As early as 1760 a bracket clock was made by John Ellicot of London with a simple circular convex enamelled dial. This must have looked particularly plain at this period but we know it to have been a forebear of the circular painted dial style which was almost exclusively used on bracket clocks in the Regency period. The full-coloured pictorial dial was never a feature of bracket-clock work, and during the period 1810-40 it was almost exclusively used on the long-case clock. The painted dial applied to the bracket clock was usually a plain circular product whose main claim to

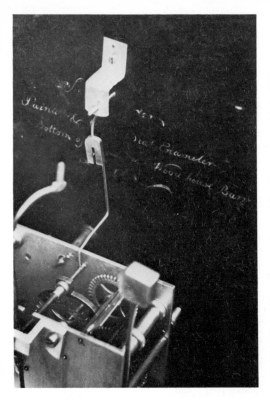

40 *Left:* Rear of the dial of Plate 36 painted by Schwanfelder and showing the painter's signature and address. The lead-off from the escapement working the rocking ship can be seen.

41 *Right:* A bell-topped bracket clock with a circular enamel dial. Anonymous, circa 1770.

popularity must have been its legibility. These dials too were made by the Birmingham dial-makers and also had a false plate for affixing to the movement. This plate was a full circular sheet, usually of thin tin- or zinc-plate pinned directly to the back of the convex circular dial.

Nothing can spoil the appearance and balance of a clock dial more than ill-considered replacement hands. Rarely was the original clockmaker's choice a poor one when making or fitting hands. Sufficient original examples exist on the correct dials for us to know what is right for any particular period. While the detail and finish varied from clock to clock and workshop to workshop, the design of hands was, like dials and corner pieces, a fairly conservative area and certain shapes, scrolls and loops were expected at certain times. Occasionally a spectacular pair of hands appeared on a dial of a special clock. Such a pair are illustrated in Plate 34 and were made in about 1705 by William Tipling of Leeds for an 11″ square-dial eight-day clock. To appreciate such hands fully it is necessary to know how they were made. A number of skills were necessary and to cover the whole process it is generally said that steel hands were 'wrought'. Viewed from the side the hand generally has a variable thickness, as the first part of the making was to

hammer a hot piece of iron so that it was thinned at the tip or decorative part of the hand whilst remaining about $\frac{1}{8}''$ thick at the boss, or part which was attached to the clock. The later the clock and the plainer the hand, the more regular its thickness will usually be. In late 18th-century clocks and some bracket clocks of the 19th century hands were made from a very uniform sheet of metal, shaped only in two dimensions. The shapes and scrolls of the outline would next be drawn or scribed on to the surface of the metal and then cut and pierced into the general shape required. Finishing would be carried out with fine files and the front surface sculptured and engraved at points where scrolls flowed together or met the rounded edge of the hand. This important and skilled work would not be entirely the job of an apprentice, though it is often quoted as an apprentice's job by writers on the subject. Great care is required in the finishing of a hand and this very obvious part of the clock needed a steady and skilled craftsman's touch.

The early domestic clock featured only a single hand. At the beginning of the 17th century and before even lantern clocks

42 A lantern clock by John Ball of Newport Pagnell, featuring a single hand with oval boss, and a tail to aid setting.

became plentiful, a feature of these hands was their thickness and simplicity of construction. They often had a flattened oval shaped boss. The tail, a feature of single hands, aided the owner in setting the clock to time, and was plain and about a third of the length of the main part of of the hand. The tip of the hand terminated in a plain arrow-head shape. Slightly later but still seen in very early clocks was the variation terminating in a blunt fork-shaped hand as illustrated on page 890 (B). These styles were developed and followed by a simple loop pattern with drilled ears at either side of a short blunt point. By this time it had become customary to use a heavy circular boss on all hands; infrequently, but on some high-quality clocks, this was ring turned just inside its outer edge. During the last quarter of the 17th century when verge lantern clocks were made in increasing numbers, the decorative loop-ended hand was made in some variety, although it never became complicated in the same way that long-case clock hands were to become in the early years of the 18th century.

From 1660 or thereabouts two hands were introduced into clockwork, as a result of the development of the pendulum and increased accuracy in timekeeping. At first these were a decorative hour-hand and a much longer and simpler minute pointer. This arrangement persisted for more than a hundred years until matching steel hands became fashionable on early painted dials. The hour-hand which was thus paired up with a minute pointer was at first little more than an elongated lantern clock hand without the tail while the minute-hand was a plain pointer for the final three-quarters of its length, mounted on a base shaped like a small looped S and then the circular boss. A section through the top of this pointer would show that it was filed up to a triangular section, the base of which was nearer to the dial surface.

During the golden period of English clockmaking after about 1680 hour-hands became extremely elaborate and finely detailed. London clockmakers in particular needed to make fine hands in order to match the engraved surfaces of their beautiful dials. Hour-hands developed into a multiplicity of loops and scrolls and as a result of this became larger. The decorative portion of some was cone-shaped and rather slim, whereas others were broad with ear-like projections, depending on the preference of the clockmaker. Minute pointers, while becoming a little broader at the base remained similar, using the same S shape with some individual variations. Seconds pointers used on eight-day long-case clocks from this time were always perfectly plain, being small parallel pointers

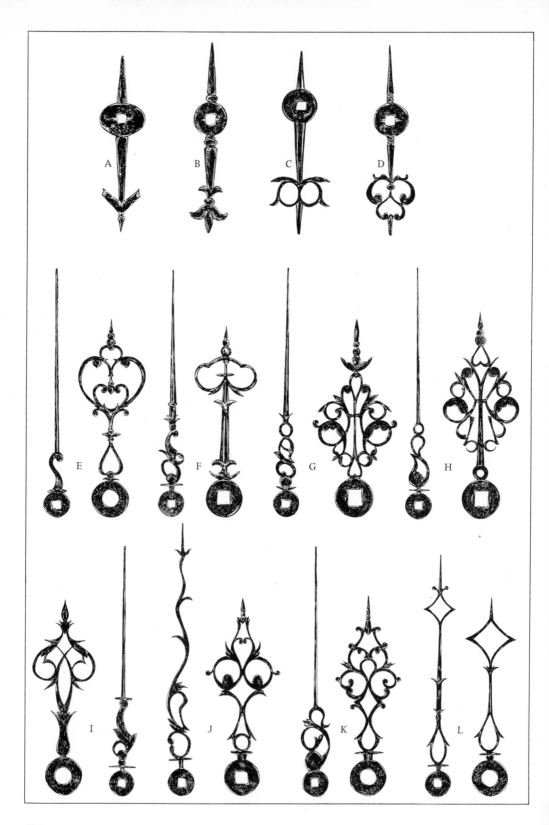

A,B,C,D Lantern clock hands showing their development.

E,F Clock hands from the period 1660-70.

G,H Two pairs of fine clock hands from the 'Golden Period' 1680-1710.

I Cross-over loop pattern found on hour hands after 1750.

J A pair of hands from about 1760-70. The minute hand shows the wavy Dutch pattern.

K A pair of steel hands of a pattern commonly found on provincial dials of 1770-80.

L A pair of matching steel hands of diamond pattern, often used on early white-dial clocks.

M,N Two pairs of brass hands of the type used on the 19th-century white-dial clock, with punched decoration.

O A seconds hand of a plain early type.

P A date pointer of 1760.

Q A seconds hand from a clock by Thomas Ogden of Halifax, circa 1740.

R A date pointer with an unusual curving tail from a white-dial clock of about 1800.

S,T Brass seconds pointers from 19th-century long-case clocks.

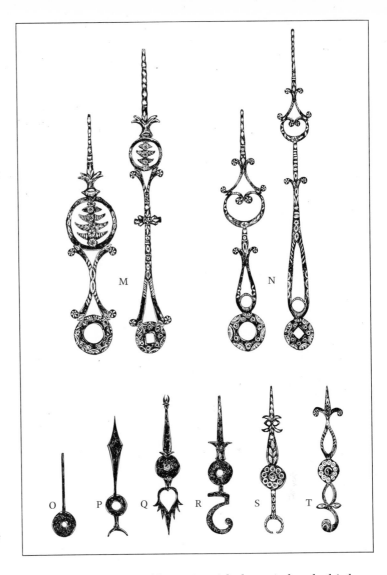

emanating from a round boss. As with the main hands this boss was sometimes ring-turned to add to its decorative quality. In the first three decades of the 18th century hand shape and quality remained very fine. The hour-hand continued with variations of pierced scrolls and loops interspersed with fine straights and strapwork holding together the elaborate design. From the turn of the century, however, a change came about in the design of the minute hand; the base section which had previously been a form of solid S shape was now frequently pierced and scrolled, with a large scroll towards the boss and a smaller one, eccentrically curved towards the plain pointer. Less popular but nevertheless a type of this period was the minute pointer with an S-shaped base, solidly cut with leaf-like projections at either side. Bracket clock hands were exactly the same at these times, but of course on a reduced scale to suit the smaller dials.

A gradual decline in quality and style is noticeable from the middle of the 18th century, although many fine hands were produced on clocks from provincial and country districts as well as London-made clocks. Less detail was generally put into the hour-hands decorative spade and many of them were of a crossover loop pattern, similar in style to the splat of a country Chippendale chair. From this period too the wavy-style minute-hand, which is said to have been a Dutch idea, became increasingly popular. With certain designs repeated and with quality depending more on the individual maker rather than the date or place, these styles carried on into the white-dial period. Later brass or single-sheet engraved dials often had hands that could be interchanged with the first white-dial examples.

Shortly after the introduction of the white-dial, the fashion for matching steel hands came about. These matched in style but were of course proportionally different to suit their differing roles. A well-made hour-hand should just reach the hour circle at the base of the hour numerals and a minute-hand should reach exactly the divisions in the minute band. By 1800 brass clock hands were extremely popular on the Birmingham dials, although special clocks and some fine regulators continued to have simple and functional hands made in steel. As well as an obvious change in material the manner of making the brass hand was also very different. These were almost always pressed or sheared out of sheet brass. The surface decoration which was closely filled with punched patterns was probably also impressed at the same time. It seems likely that these hands were mass-produced in Birmingham and other centres. Many matching patterns were available, from a diamond-shape with crossover loop corners, a crown design, to a Scottish thistle pattern. Many were fine and delicate in their execution, although, as in each preceding style, time broadened their proportions, and towards the end of the long-case clock period they had become quite heavy and ugly in appearance. While seconds-hands with simple tails were not uncommon in the period of steel hands, those made to use with the matching brass hands had heavy curved decorative tails. Few bracket clocks had brass hands and they were in any case never decorated to quite the extent found in long-case work. With the coming of the circular white and enamelled dial, simple hands were preferred, many of them in the French style

892

43 Unusual use of brass hands on a clock by William Lister of Keighley, circa 1760. The Lister family of clockmakers almost always used heavy brass hands of this type on their brass dials.

made popular by the watchmaking family Breuget.

Special and unusual indications were added to the clock's function by clockmakers at the end of the 17th century in order to impress. Skills were developed to such an extent that clocks could be made to go for twelve months at one winding and to play music, complicated chimes and strike the hours. Astronomical and zodiacal indications were sometimes added and at least one workshop, that of Fromanteel and Clarke of London, showed the moon's phases on their clocks at this early date. All these functions influenced the design of the clock, for selector hands, chime/silent or strike/silent hands, moon and astronomical indications had to be shown on the dial. The first function of the arch in early arched-dial clocks from about 1720 was almost always to house a strike/silent hand. It must have been considered necessary in those days to switch off the strike when going up to bed. It seems then that customer require-ments in clocks must have been taken into account. From time to time we see a clock with a very specialised function such as tidal dials or day-of-the-week indicators. One day-of-the-week indicator disc on a rather special year-going long-case clock by Morgan Lowry of Leeds in about 1740 has, under the name of the day, an engraving of the mythical character after whom the

day is named. A date disc showing the year and the Dominical letter for use by a clergyman in planning his services is sometimes seen. By far the most important addition to the clock, however, and regularly seen was a dial indicating the phases of the moon. It may seem a pleasing novelty to us but it was vital in the 18th century. An evening journey would be made at or near a full moon, as highwaymen in the country and footpads in the city were a serious hazard. Plates 44 and 45 show two types of moon dials used through the whole period of long-case clockmaking. They were rarely if ever used in bracket clocks. A solar disc is very rare and usually placed in the arch of the dial, showing the position of the sun in the heavens. It can sometimes be mistaken at first glance for a moon dial, as its arrangement and position are the same. The solar dial is, however, driven directly by gears from the 24-hour wheel in the motion work behind the dial and, unlike the moon dial which revolves every two months, the solar dial revolves every 24 hours, the sun rising to a visible position at 6 a.m. and setting or revolving out of view at 6 p.m. The painted sun is therefore at its highest position at 12 o'clock and at night a dark blue sky is visible on the painted disc. Engraved above on a fixed semicircular rim plate is the position of mid-day in various parts of the world.

Tidal indications were marked in conjunction with a moon

44 *Left:* The most common type of moon dial in the arch of a clock.

45 *Right:* A revolving-ball moon. The moon's age is shown by a hand pointing to the calibrations at the ball moon's centre. This is from a clock by Thomas Ogden of Halifax and is the best and rarest type of moon indicator.

Detail of the dial of the
eight-day clock by William
Bothamley about 1780,
showing the tidal indicator
carrying information used by
cattle drovers in the region
of the Wash. The Spalding
Gentlemen's Society
Museum.

dial and, when this was done, a separate scale showing the local
tides was engraved on a ring next to the moon's age. A pointer
for each indication was used for whereas the moon's phases are
fairly constant, the tides are later by so many minutes each day.
The tidal pointer could be set to this difference once it was
known. An eight-day clock in the Museum of the Gentlemen's
Society, Spalding, Lincolnshire, made by William Bothamley of
Kirton in about 1790 shows not only time of day, day of the
month and phases of the moon in the arch of the dial, but also
points, on a special dial marked with a hand, to the safe and
proper time for guides and drovers to start crossing the Wash
with their cattle. It is said that the clock was kept in an old inn
at Fosdyke and was anxiously consulted by travellers before
venturing on to the two miles of shifting sand and the varying
channels of the of the estuary. Tidal dial clocks were naturally
popular and useful in coastal areas.

Animated or rocking figures are sometimes seen in weight-
driven long-case clocks, particularly those made in provincial
centres. These occur on both brass and painted dials and are a
very attractive novelty, although if badly balanced they play
havoc with the timekeeping qualities of the clock. Subject
matter for these figures was very varied and among the most
popular was a fully rigged sailing ship. Father Time rocking
away the seconds with his scythe and hour glass was another

great favourite. Others noted less frequently are a musician whose arm moves to bow his cello, a man sawing wood, a rocking swan, two figures on a see-saw and so on. Very infrequently two figures or moving parts of figures are seen pivoted from the dial and coupled at the back, then worked by the same wire from the escapement arbor. Early examples of these on brass dials, seen from about 1770, were engraved on thin brass plate and appeared in cut-away section of the arch, often backed by a darkened backplate and surrounded by an applied engraved ring bearing a legend *Tempus Fugit*. Later examples used on brass dials were frequently painted. The painted style naturally carried through on to the painted dial and was usually rocked against a painted background on the dial's surface plane, supported on a pivot which passed through a small hole in the dial's arch. Later still a large irregular space was cut into the dial arch and this was backed by a fully painted second arch, held with dial feet. The rocking figure, usually a swan or a ship, appeared between these two, supported from below by a wire from the escapement. This is a dramatic and effective way of presenting the feature as it resembles a proscenium arch.

47 Animated figures on the dial of the musical organ clock by George Pyke, circa 1765, featured on Plates 108 and 123. Temple Newsam House, Leeds.

Chapter 4

Clock cases

48 Simple hollow base with a door made for the support of a lantern clock. This may date from the late 17th century. Towneley Hall Art Gallery and Museum, Burnley.

In books written until fairly recently, much is said about early cases and indeed of all London clocks before 1700. Later clocks, particularly those made in provincial centres after 1750, have been given very little regard and are often dismissed as being ill-proportioned and of inferior quality. Recent work has shown that many fine clocks were made by craftsmen working all over the country, and beautiful, well-proportioned cases made from fine woods can be found at all periods.

Opinions differ, but the truth is that no-one knows how the first wooden cases for clocks came about. Their arrival in the true and recognised long-case form occurred at the same time as the introduction of the pendulum control from Holland, about the year 1658. Other wooden items such as shelves, hood and tubes on which lantern clocks stood, had existed for many years before this time. It seems likely that the long wooden case was developed simultaneously in various centres, perhaps sometime during the 16th or early 17th century, in an effort to protect the hanging weights from interference by domestic animals, children or others who might otherwise stop the clock. Hollow oak topless cases exist, on which lantern clocks stood, their weights descending into the trunk and out of view. These were a step in the direction of the totally enclosed wooden case. Naive and primitive oak cases which fully enclosed lantern clocks and single-handed country 30-hour clocks are known from the late 17th century. They were also made by country craftsmen until the late 18th century and so give no guide as to the main development in clock-case making.

Plates 18 and 19 show two clocks made about 1680 and illustrate the fine London-made clock case and the simple, honest country product in solid oak.

From the outset the first London long-cases were complete and sophisticated products, made from the finest woods and embellished with gilt metal mounts. They were architectural in style, usually made from oak and veneered in ebony. The very narrow trunk allowed only for the fall of weights, for the pendulum was about 9″ long. Case doors and sides were

897

A Ebony veneered case made 1660-70.

B Parquetry case of 1670-80.

C Bird-and-flower marquetry case of the Dutch type, 1680-90.

D All-over marquetry case sometimes known as seaweed marquetry, about 1710-15. From 1700 a concave moulding under the hood was usual.

E Walnut case of the London type, circa 1725-40.

F Provincial oak case, mid-18th century.

G Provincial case displaying elements of the Sheraton and Adam styles, using mahogany as the principal wood, circa 1790.

H Mahogany case with a brickwork base of the type favoured in the Liverpool area, circa 1780-90.

I A London mahogany case. The corner columns are reeded with brass at their lower ends, circa 1780-90.

J North-country white-dial clock case. Its principal wood is oak but it is strung and cross-banded with various woods; circa 1800-20.

K Scottish mahogany case with shaped trunk and carved top to the door.

L Yorkshire clock case with diminutive door and wider proportions, but made in exquisite woods, circa 1840-50.

panelled or the veneers were beaded round to give the appearance of panel construction. The hood was made to rise in order to give access to the movement, and was attached to the back board of the case by tongues and grooves which allowed for upward movement. Once raised, a metal catch stopped the hood from falling down. A latch which, because of its shape, was known as a spoon, held the hood secure when closed. To open this one only had to open the case door and as this would normally be kept locked no unauthorised person could interfere with any part of the clock. Hoods did not have doors yet.

At either side of the dial aperture and closely attached were plain pillars with brass bases and capitals. The capitals, of Corinthian style, were castings finely finished, gilt and built up from various pieces. Side glasses in the hood gave a view of the movement and became a regular feature of good London casework, certainly until 1740-50. The cases were small compared with later products. A plain base was usually supported on turned bun feet, but many have been damaged and restored since feet of all types of old furniture have been damaged by hard use and damp floors. Only reaching 6 ft or so from the ground, the portico tops of these clocks often had a metal mount in the triangular space of the pediment. This was

E   F   G   H

I   J   K   L

usually a draped swag with a central garland or something similar. A convex moulding in the shape of a quarter-circle under the hood is an indication of a clock of the 17th century. This is a reliable pointer when dating a case, for the practice seems to have stopped after about 1700, when a concave moulding was introduced and became popular. From their design and excellence in construction it is obvious that from the earliest times London cases were the work of men who specialised, within the cabinet-making trade, as clock case-makers. Since they did not sign their work and few records exist, they are unfortunately an anonymous group. One man did, however, leave his mark, in the shape of a token which remained in a specially-made cavity in the base of the case. This has been discovered during restoration and so Joseph Clifton became the earliest recorded English casemaker. The case was made for a clock by Ahasuerus Fromonteel and other cases made for the most important clockmaker of this period have also been seen to bear the same casemaker's style.

The 'architectural' style was brief, for with developments in clockwork and the introduction of the long pendulum changes in case design were necessary. The ebonised case had previously housed a dial of 8″ to 9″ square and was only slightly wider in the trunk. The larger pendulum needed a larger space in which to complete its arc and so cases became wider, and possibly to retain good proportions the size of the dial also increased to 10″ square. Walnut was the wood favoured, used as a veneer on the oak carcase though the very earliest long-pendulum clocks still came within the ebonised, portico-topped period of casemaking. It is worth noting that in some examples the term ebonising refers not only to veneering with ebony, which is a very rare and expensive wood, but also to the application of pearwood or similar fruitwood veneers stained black and making a very good copy of the real thing. Three important changes also took place in the detailing and by 1680 these had become standard features in the design of the walnut case. The hood became flat-topped, surmounted by a frieze of pierced fretwork, backed by silk or similar material and a simple moulding. Barley-sugar-twist columns were used. These were cut from the solid and ebonised to contrast with the rich colour of the walnut hood. A glass lenticle or window was provided in the case door opposite the pendulum bob. This made an attractive feature in the long door and was also useful for it showed at a glance whether the clock was going. These lenticles were large at first and could be circular or oval; eight-sides ones are rare but not unknown. The glass was usually

49 Bird-and-flower marquetry on a month-going long-case clock by Peter East, London, circa 1690. The hood pillars and the plinth to the base are not original. Temple Newsam House, Leeds.

50 *Left:* Superb walnut year-going long-case clock by Morgan Lowry, Leeds, circa 1740. Abbey House Museum, Kirkstall, Leeds.

51 *Above:* Large red lacquer musical bracket clock by John Hodges, circa 1735. Temple Newsam House, Leeds.

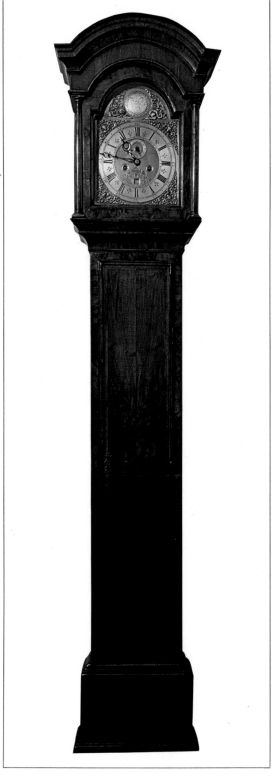

52 *Opposite left:* Country long-case clock by William Noke, Bridgnorth, about 1740.

53 *Opposite right:* Walnut long-case clock by William Troutbeck, Leeds, about 1725. The trunk and door are unusually long and the base is shallow, though showing no signs of having been cut down. The clock hands are not original.

54 Detail of the base moulding of a walnut long-case clock showing the character of cross-grain moulding.

plain, but bulls-eye glass with its green tint was also used. Undoubtedly this provided the most pleasing and decorative look as it distorted and obscured the view of lines and the case backboard, while at the same time the pendulum's glint makes an attractive kaleidoscope. A brass or wooden bezel was used to edge this feature. The wooden ones were polished or gilded; some were ebonised. A few cases from the brief experimental period in the 1670s when pendulums were not a standard length can be seen with a glass lenticle in the base of the case. This indicates that the clock was equipped with a $1\frac{1}{4}$-seconds pendulum, some 61″ long; but these are very rare.

Case doors were large, and in fact took up the whole frontal area of the trunk. They were plain and straight-topped, surrounded with a beaded edge that overhung the dimensions of the door.

In line with other items of furniture at this time, veneered walnut clock cases showed a distinct progression in style. In Restoration times many Dutch craftsmen were employed in England and their massive influence can be seen in the use of parquetry designs in the 1670s and later bird and flower marquetry in the 1680s in panels on the main parts of the case such as the trunk and base. Borders were cross-banded in walnut veneer, and the whole laid on a purpose-built oak carcase. Various woods were used to make veneers for marquetry work and some were stained to give unexpected colours such as green. The edges of a piece in the marquetry design might be burnt in hot sand to give a contrasting dark-shaded edge, and so enhance the sense of drawing in the designs. Mouldings which could not be veneered were made in walnut pieces with the grain laid across the width of the mould. These were glued on to an oak backing piece before being shaped by the moulding plane. This characteristic style is known as cross-grained moulding and is a distinct feature of the walnut period.

By the 1690s marquetry work on clock cases had reached a high level and all-over designs of the so-called seaweed marquetry covered the cases in delicate arabesque designs. This was considered to be a truly English style and was far more delicately executed than the relatively crude Dutch-inspired work of the previous decade. Marquetry was cut from sheets of differently coloured veneers while cramped together, and identical work has been found on two cases which indicates the marquetry was cut at the same time.

While these developments were taking place, clock cases also grew taller to suit the higher plaster-ceilinged interiors of

903

the town houses of the day. With this, dial sizes increased to 11″ and case trunk width also increased in proportion, but generally no more than an inch wider than the dial. Also from this time it became usual for the clock hood to slide forward, and a door was made in the hood for winding and setting the hands. A cushion top was added above the moulding of the hood, often flanked by two or three plinths surmounted by brass ball, or ball-and-spire finials. Some clocks had turned wooden ball finials which were finished with gesso and gilded. This also added to the clock's height. If a marquetry case was not required then the wood used would be well-figured walnut, veneered and crossbanded in just the same way, but with choice burr veneers used on trunk, door and base. Thomas Tompion was known to favour a plain veneered walnut case throughout the marquetry period. On some of these cases the veneers were arranged in the method known as 'oyster shell' parquetry, after their similarity in appearance to that species. The veneers were cut as a section across a small branch, its annular rings giving the irregular circular design. Both olive wood and walnut were used to make the oyster pieces.

55 *Left:* A bird-and-flower marquetry panel, from the case door of the month-going clock illustrated in Plate 35.

Provincial makers in cities throughout the country must have ordered cases from London makers, for occasionally one comes across a high quality walnut- or marquetry-cased clock in original and unaltered condition by such a clockmaker. There are also lesser cases with marquetry more sparsely arranged and not so well carried out which are presumably the work of provincial cabinet makers. From 1720 there was an increasing number of country clocks with solid oak cases. These were of both the 30-hour and eight-day duration; many of these were nicely made and echo the proportions and style of more sophisticated London clocks.

Lacquer cases decorated in the oriental manner began to appear in England in the last 20 years of the 17th century. Oriental furniture had been imported in small quantities since the reign of Elizabeth I but the flamboyant tastes of the Restoration provided for its popularity. Opinions differ about whether cases were made in England and sent on the long sea voyage to the East for lacquering or whether they were lacquered in England in imitation of the oriental style. Early in this period of popularity some cases were undoubtedly sent to the East but most were made and decorated in London to oriental recipes and designs. The pictorial parts of the design were raised up in a gum-based gesso and then gilt with details drawn in by brush. This was backed by an overall coloured lacquer ground. Colours were mainly dark; blues, greens and black and more rarely red, yellow and a paler turquoise blue were used. In bracket clocks lacquering did not enjoy the same popular appeal as on the long-cases. At the same time the lacquer artists were well known for their imitation of tortoise-shell and marble effects used successfully on bracket clock cases. The carcase wood for cases was more usually oak but occasional high-quality lacquer clocks were made from pine. This taste for lacquer spanned the period from the square dial to the beginning of the arched dial clock about 1720. The art was taken up by amateurs who were said to lacquer many unsuitable pieces of furniture of all types; the style flourished and then by 1730 lost its appeal.

Later in the 18th century lacquering again became popular for long-case clocks. The carcase wood at this time was invariably oak and the shape of the cases was generally that typical of the pagoda-style hood or round-topped mahogany clock of this period. The fashion lasted for about ten years and died out finally in about 1780.

In their *Treatise of Japaning and Varnishing* (1688) J. Stalker and G. Parker claimed that 'no damp air, no moulding worm or corroding time, can possibly deface the work'. Many cases which survive are distinctly shabby now and unlike polished wood they are difficult to renovate successfully. Consequently they have been less than popular with collectors in recent years.

Towards the middle years of the 18th century London clockmakers were not called upon to make so many long-case clocks. Portable or bracket clocks and clocks fulfilling a special need, such as precision regulators for observatory or similar work, continued to be made, with some fine domestic long-case clocks later on in the mahogany period around 1760-90. The emphasis of case development from this period onwards therefore shifts from London to provincial centres and from specialist clock-case makers to cabinetmakers and country joiners who made all manner of things from breakfront bookcases to coffins. The factor in deciding its style depended not entirely on when it was made as where it was made and by whom. Geographical differences made quite a number of variations in the interpretation of a nationally used style, and an expert can begin to say what part of the country a piece was made by looking at the case alone.

By far the most common wood used for provincial cases was oak. From the early 18th century this was used on its own, relying on the decorative rays of its grain in quarter-cut form for case doors, base panels and so on. From about 1740 cross-banding was popular and, in common with other country-made pieces of furniture, this was applied to the edges of doors and base panels in bands varying in width from $\frac{1}{2}''$ to $2''$. The veneer used in banding was usually mahogany although walnut is not unknown. Cases made in this later style might have had a backboard in oak, but deal was equally common. Mahogany is not generally thought to have been used in furniture-making until after the mid-18th century; 1760 is the date usually given. Robert Gillow, a joiner and cabinetmaker and founder of the important firm of Gillows of Lancaster, is recorded as making 'a clockcase of mahogany' in 1743. The firm went on to produce many more fine clockcases in mahogany, oak and pine during the 18th century, and has left us a unique record of their work in ledgers, estimate books and drawings. Plate 57 shows the handwritten estimate for a mahogany long-case and Plate 58 the design and measurements for the case.

The better-quality mahogany cases were those using choice mahogany veneers glued on to an oak carcase. Mouldings and cornices were made from the solid and occasionally

56 *Above:* Country oak case of a one-handed clock by Jeremy Spurgin, Colchester, of about 1695.

57 *Opposite:* Estimate for a mahogany long-case from one of Gillows' handwritten estimate books.

2¾ ft of 1 Inch Mah:y and Birch: Vin: the door at 1/10¾ — 5 0½

2½ ft of 1 Inch Oak and Birch: Vin: and Kingwood do.
the Pedistall ffront _____ at 1/6 P ft — 3 9

10½ ft of ½ Inch Mah:y Sides of Body Head and
Pedistall _____ at 7d P ft — 6 1½

9½ ft of 1 Inch Mah:y Mouldings Pillers Columns
and Part of ffront and Glassframe &c — at 1/2 P ft — 11 1

2 ft of 1 Inch deal. Mah:y and Kingwood Vin:
a Part of the Head _____ at 1 P ft — 2 0

1¼ of ½ Inch Part of the Glass frame _____ 7½

1¾ ft of ¼ Inch Mah:y _____ at 4d P ft — 7

9¾ ft of ½ Inch Oak the Back of do. at 2¾ P ft — 2 2½

3½ ft of ½ Inch and ¼ Inch deal _____ at 1¼ P ft — 4¼

1 Lock Escutchion and Hinges _____ 1 10

1 Pair of Swan Neck Hinges and Ring for Glass door — 3

2 Pair of Corinthian Caps and Bases _____ 5 4

Turning the Columns Caps and Bases and Moulds — 2 4

1 Sheild and 2 Roses for do. _____ 2 6

Glew Oil wax Nails and incidents. _____ 2. 10

Makeing do. Christn. Procter _____ £.v.

Glass for the door in the Head. _____ ..4.
_____ £ 0. 00. 10½

June y:e 19th 1788   a Bracket for a Bust or Vase

2 ft of 5/8 Inch Mah:y _____ at 7d P ft _____ 1 2

1 ft of ½ Inch Mah:y _____ at 6 P ft _____ 6

Mah:y Vin: for the Rim glew'd up in three _____ 4

a Piece of Mah:y for a Block on the top of do. _____ 2

3 Brass Holdfasts and Shrews for do _____ 3

Makeing do. Thos. Romney _____ 2 days _____ u.v

Glew Oil and incidents _____ u.d

_____ m ∠

a Case to Pack do. 8½ ft of ½ Inch deal at 1¼ P ft — 10½
Sprigg Nails _____ 1½
Makeing do and Packing 1 Stone _____ 190

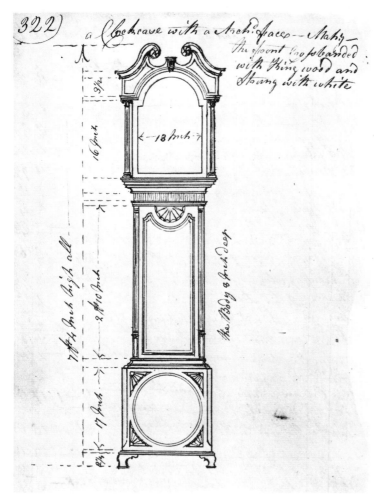

322) a Clockcave with a Arch'd faces — Mahy —
the spront Cropsbanded
with King wood and
Strung with white

<-- 13 inch -->

58 *Left:* Drawing with measurements relating to the estimate shown in Plate 57.

59 *Below:* Cuban mahogany long-case clock by John Hawthorn, Newcastle, circa 1780.

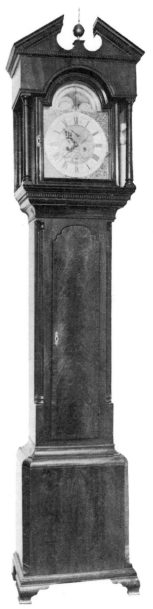

used the cross-grained style for effect, but straight-grained mouldings were more usual. Flame or feathered designs could be achieved by matching veneers cut from the same piece of wood and arranging them symmetrically side by side. Mahogany cases of this type tend to be in the dark rich wood known as Cuban mahogany, as much of it was imported from there. Probably one reason for its early use by Gillows is that it would have been imported into Liverpool, an important port trading with the Caribbean at that time. When used in the solid, mahogany never seemed to have been worked with the same kind of flair, and most used wood with unexciting grain and paler colour known as bay-wood or Honduras mahogany. Late 18th-century cases made for both the brass and enamelled dial frequently displayed features common to the designs of Hepplewhite and Sheraton, particularly boxwood stringing, design of cornices, circular and oval outlines to veneered

60 A mahogany veneered white-dial clock by William Jackson of Workington. Boxwood stringing is used as decoration and the pediment of the hood is faced with blue glass with gilt decoration.

panels and the delicate splayed feet (known as French feet) of certain heavy white-dial clocks. Many mahogany cases at this period used a combination of thinly cut solid mahogany planks and mahogany veneers backed with pine in their carcase construction.

Many country-made clocks particularly of the 30-hours winding type with both brass and painted dials were originally housed in pine cases. These were almost always of a plain construction and shape. Flat tops were most usual but a simple version of any regional style of top can be expected.

It is currently fashionable for some antique dealers to strip and polish pine cases, leaving the wood with an exposed grain and its pale natural colour. This was never the original intention of the casemaker, who would have variously had them painted or scumbled and grained to resemble a darker and more expensive wood. Fittings used with pine cases and occasionally on less expensive country oak cases were commensurately cheaper. Instead of a small lock and key for the trunk door, a simple turn-buckle fastening was used. This was turned from the outside of the door by a simple brass ring.

The feature which most characterises the difference in case shapes is generally the hood and its decorative treatment above the dial. The hood A on page 910 is the most common shape for country work with square dials, and with minor differences was made in all regions. Side pillars to the hood could be either attached to the glazed door or separately fixed, as they were in most northern examples. Fixed pillars were most likely to have wooden turned capitals and bases finished in gesso and gilt. Separate pillars were attached to the hood by brass caps and bases. These were fastened with small brass nails to the horizontal parts of the hood. Drawing B is a development of this style with a built-up cushion or caddy top. In the example shown here this has been further heightened with another phase surmounted by a spire finial, from an eight-day clock of some quality with a solid oak case of about 1740 by James Woolley of Codnor in Derbyshire.

The swan-necked or horned pediment was another style to enjoy inter-regional popularity, but it was in the north that it was used most. Many inexpensive square-dial clocks were made in this manner, but with the popularity of the arched white-dial clock the style came into its own and 90 per cent of these clocks were housed in cases with hoods like drawing D. Another elaboration of this basic style is seen on high-quality mahogany cases by some clockmakers in the north-west of England and a type which is generally thought to be

909

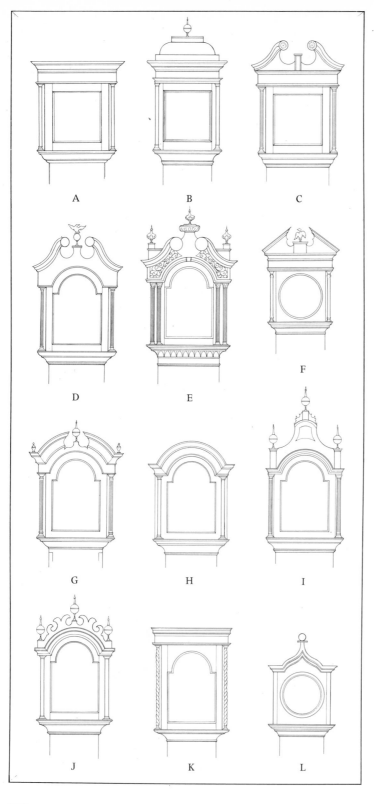

A Square-topped hood with simple moulding. This is the most common shape for country work.

B A more sophisticated variation of A, with a cushion top.

C Hood with square aperture and horned pediment.

D Hood with arched aperture and horned pediment. This was a common style for north-country white-dial clocks.

E Over-elaborate hood of the type used on mahogany clocks in the late 18th century made in the north-west of England.

F Hood with a broken-arch pediment. Although fairly rare, this type is often associated with a round dial.

G Hood with broken-arch top.

H Arched-top hood. This type had a few variations.

I Pagoda-topped hood. This example shows the more sophisticated type; less well-proportioned examples are also to be found.

J Arched-top hood with whale's tail cresting.

K Scottish hood, usually found with an arched white-dial.

L Mahogany hood of a Scottish clock, with round dial.

made by Gillows of Lancaster because of the occurrence of certain features. These include the built-up box section behind the swan neck pediment, an exaggerated cushion mould or a heavy central plinth surmounted by decorative finials. Underneath the curving forms and forming the pediment proper are glass panels, usually a rich blue decorated with gold painted scrolls and foliage. The supporting pillars, usually reeded, may come in pairs either side of the hood but more usually they are single separate pillars with high-quality brass capitals and bases. This style is illustrated by drawing E. Circular decorations or paterae decorated the terminal scroll of the horns and these could be made in various ways.

Early clocks of the brass dial era were likely to have cast brass paterae finished in gilt. Later clocks, forming the majority under consideration, had stamped out brass paterae which were finished in gilt or simply polished and lacquered. Simple ring-turned wooden paterae were occasionally used, while on high-quality clocks various innovations have been seen. Thomas Ogden of Halifax on a clock similar to drawing E used a pair of lion's-mask paterae, which when cleaned proved to be a gilt finish on solid lead. Cases by Gillows of Lancaster are frequently seen with paterae carved in high relief from mahogany in the shape of roses. One of the styles of hood least often seen in later work is the architectural, broken-pediment style; although a similar top has been used in some fine work by Justin Vulliamy, the London clockmaker, at the end of the 18th century. It is seen also from time to time in northern clocks. The mouldings which form the top of the broken pediment being decorated in true architectural style with a dentil course. The broken pediment is also used in conjunction with round dials. Although unusual in long-case work they are sometimes found on clocks made in the Sheffield and Derbyshire area. Very similar but with a rounded profile is the broken-arched style shown in drawing G. On some simple renderings this can also look like an ill-formed and incomplete horned top but the better versions with deep-cut top moulding can be very pleasing. It is one style used nationally but seen infrequently, which suggests that it was not popular in its day. Two Leeds-made clocks known to me have hoods in this manner and their styles of construction and choice of oak suggest that they are both by the same casemaker. One of them illustrated here (Plate 61) in a plain unstrung oak case is by Henry Gamble of Bramley, Leeds, and dates from about 1770. The domed or arch-shaped top generally denotes a brass dial clock, since white dials are rarely found in a case of this style. The broken arch was used from an early date and occasionally for high-quality cases in the era of walnut about 1730. In these examples, and London ones made in the later mahogany period of 1760-80, the moulded arch surmounts a delicately fretted frieze. The style was also used early in the 18th century on well-made provincial eight-day clocks. The curved top mould in these examples was either built up in blocks and then veneered in the cross-grained manner or shaped and carved from the solid in the case wood, usually oak. Drawing H on page 910 is a hood made up in exactly this manner. Other hoods of the same design were made in southern counties, East Anglia and northern England – a particularly fine example with a walnut-veneered top-moulding is recorded by John Burgess of Wigan in about 1730. A delicate version of this style was also used on high-class London regulator clocks by makers such as Thomas Mudge and Thomas Dutton. These clock cases were made in fine well-figured mahogany and were austere in their general outlines, relying on the simplicity of line and the figure of the wood for decorative effect. In the view of many people these are among the most pleasing cases ever made.

The whale's tail cresting added to an arch-topped hood gives a completely different character to the clock and is also an interesting regional characteristic (drawing J). It was popularly used by makers in the west country. The Somerset clockmaker, Isaac Nichols, made some fine clocks using cases decorated in this way.

In the same way that long-case clocks of north-western England were typified by the swan-necked top and the majestic mahogany case in the late 18th century, the east coast of England was similarly seen to have a style of its own. The styles were not entirely exclusive to each region, for while it is common to see a pagoda-topped case on a clock made on the Yorkshire coast, it is equally common to find one made in Ipswich or even Kent. This was also a style favoured by some London makers for mahogany- and lacquer-cased clocks at the close of the 18th century. The better mahogany case of this type was likely to have brass inserts to the reeding, half way up from the base of the hood pillars. The pagoda top has, in common with all styles, many variations and interpretations. The better clocks resemble closely the tall shape illustrated by drawing I, but shallower, less-understood versions were used in some country districts.

In the pediment at the top of the hood two main types of treatment are found. A cut-away portion echoing the outline of

61 Broken-arch topped eight-day clock by Henry Gamble, Bramley, circa 1770.

62 Shallow pagoda-topped hood on a black and gold lacquered long-case clock by Robert Cutbush of Maidstone, Kent, circa 1740.

the hood would be fitted with a decorative fret cut in a curving loop pattern or occasionally with a geometric fret in the Chinese taste. This backed with silk or something similar, would serve to let out the sound of the bell, but its true purpose was decoration. Marquetry inlay was frequently used in small pointed oval panels at this point on the hood, and also on the trunk door, beneath the hood moulding on the trunk and in the hood frieze, on particularly fine mahogany examples. The subject of these inlays varied but the main ones are the cornucopia and the star-shape fan typified by the work of Robert Adam in his interiors of this time. Oak examples of this style exist in some numbers, and when well chosen and nicely shaped they look well in an undecorated form.

In a book of English clocks it may be inappropriate to mention Scottish cases, but they are so frequently seen south of the Border that all must be dealt with if only for purposes of identification. Nearly all Scottish cases are in the later phase of mahogany, using solid wood with no distinct figure; but exceptions are occasionally seen. I know of no Scottish white-dial clock case made with oak as its principal wood. The hood may look unusually top-heavy. Many hoods such as that in drawing K have a great deal of plain wood above the dial top. The pillars do not always just flank the glassed door but sometimes rise almost to the top mould, giving a distinctly odd appearance to the clock which is at first glance often hard to identify. These pillars may be plain, reeded, or even twisted in style and this can add to the unsuitability of their proportion and presentation. I hope that I may be forgiven for describing the style as distinctly numb in appearance. From time to time one sees a much more delicate style of Scottish long-case. Dating from 1780 onwards, these are usually quite delicate and whimsical in silhouette, and are made from good, well-figured mahogany. Hoods are generally variations on the style shown in drawing L; trunk doors may be shaped or decorated with carved wooden relief towards the top. On occasions the trunk sides may even be tapered or have an entasis which fits in with the whimsical and interesting appearance.

With the increased number of clock cases made by local craftsmen in town and country areas as the 18th century progressed, the frequency of maker's labels also increased, although to find one is an unusual experience. Information about the maker may also be found recorded in pen on the carcase wood of the case. I have seen two examples of this, one written underneath the seatboard of the movement and another recording the clockmaker and the first owner, written

63 A case-maker's label pasted inside on the backboard of the clock by Thomas Wilson of Spalding (Plate 64).

in ink on the edge of the hood door. The label illustrated on Plate 63 is from the backboard of the eight-day clock by Thomas Wilson of Spalding (Plate 64) dated to about 1830 by its style. It is a pleasing later case, finished with well-figured mahogany veneers; the following facts are recorded about the two makers involved. Charles Oliver, the casemaker, disappeared from local trade directories by 1842. A press notice announcing the sale of the jewellery business of Thomas Wilson 'before leaving England' appears in 1849. These contemporary records show that both men were in a position to have done this work in 1830 and so confirm our dating, which was initially made on stylistic grounds.

The spreading outlines of the north country long-case clock in the 19th century have been responsible for the criticism levelled at them by clock connoisseurs over the years. However, it must be said that the workmanship and woods used in their construction were never better. On their surfaces can be seen the choicest mahogany veneers, inlays of rosewood, boxwood and sections of marquetry in satinwood, while stringing in boxwood is a common feature. Gilded patterns were sometimes used on the surface of the veneers in places such as the frieze under the hood moulding of the trunk and also on the hood frieze above the dial. Pillars in the hood were sometimes built up of a sandwich of different coloured

914

64 Mahogany veneered case, circa 1830, made by Charles Oliver of Spalding, for a clock by Thomas Wilson. Museum of Lincolnshire Life, Lincoln.

woods before turning. These would be bobbin-turned, balister-turned or even cut with a heavy spiral twist. Usually quarter-pillars adorned the front corners of the trunk flanking the door, which over the years became smaller and smaller until it was a disproportionate vestige of its former self. Its diminished size also hindered its function, as you will know if you have ever tried reaching inside to put on a weight. The trunk corner pillars are a typical but not exclusive feature of north-country work. This style is also found on other country-made pieces of furniture such as dressers, cupboards, chests and drawers from the mid-18th century. Capitals and bases were turned in the same wood, usually mahogany, for this wood was often used even when the pillars were to go on a basically oak piece. On occasions a better case might have brass capitals and bases. When cases originated from the Birmingham area, where foundry work was one of the local trades and castings were more plentiful, the capitals would generally be of the Corinthian type, elaborate and well finished.

Brick-work bases, arranged in mahogany veneer so that the front corners of the base looked like the corner construction of a house, were a common feature on some cases made in the north-west. The style is thought to be a feature of some of Gillow's work. The feature is generally called a Liverpool base since clockmakers in that region favoured cases in this style.

Bracket clocks were never produced in great numbers in country districts or indeed in any centres outside London. A number were made in the south, and some examples were made in East Anglia and the west country. In the north, however, bracket clocks are a distinct rarity. Personally I cannot recall seing one example made in Lancashire. As a result, a discussion of bracket clocks must centre upon London-made cases. The standard was almost always high. Country versions generally adhered to the prevailing style in London and indeed many cases may have been bought in from London casemakers.

Few bracket clocks did actually stand on wall brackets. Those that did are usually of a very late date and few original brackets survive. In fact these clocks were designed for occasional carrying and intended for use on the side table of the drawing room or at night in the bedroom, where the repeating mechanism could be used to indicate the hours and the quarters in the dark. Consideration was also given to their use on the mantelpiece, standing in front of a glass overmantel or mirror; the glass backdoor of the clock allowed a view of the elaborately engraved backplate to be reflected into the room. Bracket or mantel clock cases were at first so similar in style to

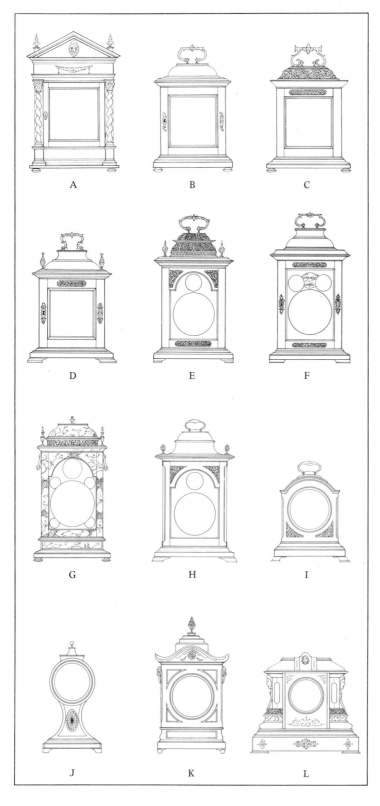

A Architectural-topped bracket clock case with elaborate metal mounts, circa 1665.
B A cushion-topped case with carrying handle, circa 1675.
C Square-dialled case with metal basket-top and elaborate carrying handle, circa 1680.
D Inverted bell-topped case, circa 1710.
E Early arch-dial case with elaborate metal basket-top, circa 1715.
F Case for clock with oblong dial. This also has an inverted bell top and carrying handle.
G Lacquer case with arch-dial aperture and side handles, circa 1740.
H Bell-topped case with plain carrying handle and brass bracket feet.
I Mahogany case for a clock with round dial, circa 1780.
J Balloon-shaped case with circular dial aperture and parquetry medallion, circa 1790-1800.
K Regency case with an oriental flavour but featuring more typically a pineapple top finial and lion's-mask carrying handles at either side.
L Black marble case of the Victorian period.

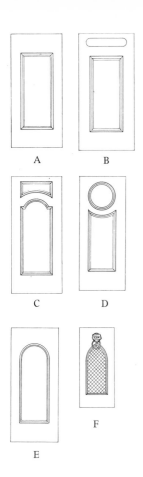

Progression of side glasses of bracket clocks:
A Simple oblong glazed aperture, circa 1670.
B Oblong-glazed aperture with round-ended fret above, circa 1680-1710.
C With the introduction of the arch-dial, side glasses echoed the arch shape, and the fret was given a concave base line; 1715-70.
D A side glass with a concave top and a circular fret. This style is associated with the bell-topped case, 1760-80.
E The shape of the side glass and fret were now combined. It might be filled with either glass or a wooden fret; circa 1780-1800.
F Gothic side fret. This was usually made in fretted brass and backed with silk.

the long-case that they looked exactly like the hoods of the tall clocks. Both portico and flat tops were used and the cases at these dates did not have the top carrying handle. From the 1670s a shallow cushion top was used on cases and the carrying handle was introduced. Ebony and ebonised pearwood veneers on bracket clock cases persisted long after they had become unfashionable on long-cases, and in fact they are not unusual on bracket clocks as late as 1770 when mahogany was the most popular wood for clock cases. Some exotic features were used on the better table clocks which never found their way on to long-case work. Metal basket tops in the shape of a bell were finely cast and chased. In some rare examples these were made of silver, but generally they were finished, along with finials and other brass mounts, in mercury gilt. The dramatic red and black veneers of tortoiseshell were sometimes used. Marquetry, kingwood and walnut were used as an alternative to the usual ebonised surface. Side glasses as well as glass doors, back and front, give an all-round view of the beautiful movements. Escutcheon plates on the front doors were balanced at either side, one for the key hole and one remaining blank. Small pierced frets were let into the tops of the doors and above the case side glasses. About 1″ deep and round-ended they were cut from a thin piece of ebony veneer and backed with silk in the usual way. Pierced basket tops were lined with silk to give a pleasing look and to keep out the dust. Areas of fretwork increased as the time went on. With the introduction of the arched dial in about 1715, the spandrel areas at the top of the door were usually filled with a suitable fretted design. From this period too, the fretwork above the side glasses tended to be shaped in sympathy with the arched side glass, and later on, with the bell-topped style of case, became circular above a concave top to the glass. This is clearly shown by the diagrams on this page. After 1780 it was fashionable to run the two shapes together and fill the total area with either fretwork or glass. Regency and Victorian bracket clocks are typified by brass side frets in a fish-scale design.

As the tops of the cases became higher and more decorative, the carrying handle was magnificently scrolled and finished, until about 1700 it slowly became more simple in its outline. Sometimes a heavy, elaborate clock such as drawing G, in the illustrations of bracket clock cases on p. 916, had no top handle at all. A departure from the basic shape, which had lasted for some 65 years, occurred with the introduction of the circular enamel and painted dial. By 1780 the style shown in drawing I was found alongside more traditional examples. Instead of

917

having a wooden door, only the brass bezel which held the glass opened for winding and setting the hands. This idea persisted throughout the remaining years of craftsman-made cases. The most delicate and pleasing of all circular dial styles, the balloon-shaped case, is illustrated in drawing J. This style of about 1790 is almost always built up in mahogany and pine carcase woods and veneered in satinwood. It was often cross-banded in tulipwood or similar and strung with box and ebony. A shell or oval fan medallion in sand-shaded marquetry usually decorated the lower stages of the front. Cast brass ogee bracket feet complete this most elegant of designs. The topmost stage, forming a support for the finial, was not always included in this design.

Gillows of Lancaster list one of the balloon-shaped cases in their estimate book for 1800 which was made for a 'Mr Bell Lancaster'. This was likely to have been Henry Bell, Watch and Clockmaker, who was known to be working in 1800, but died in 1801. The example shown in Plate 67 was veneered in mahogany and cross-banded in canary wood, with double stringing in 'Black and White'. This was their way of saying ebony and box, which would give a black-and-white effect. Unusually the case is shown with a 'large brass lifting handle' and no medallion in the base, and while costs are shown for parts and labour, no mention is made of the brass bracket feet shown in the drawing:

A mahogany bracket clock case, crossband mahoy vinear all round the sides, birchin mahoy vinear in the front, banded with canary wood, & a dble string on each side of the band say black & white cross band mahoy O.G. & small hollow, rim, round the glass.

		£	s	d
6 ft 6 of 1 in mahoy in the head, sides and top vineard with mahoy	@ 2s/3d		14	7½
2 ft 6 of ⅝ in mahogany in the back	@ 14d		2	11
4¼ ft of 1 in oak and mahogany birchin vinear in the case & canary wood banding	@ 20d		7	1
Turning—compute				9
Large brass lifting handle				7
Brass lock 6d, one escution 1d. 2½ in brass hinge 4d				11
An ivory knob 2½d, 1 pair small brass but hinges 3d				5½
One brass turnbuckle				3
Glue screws, & incidents			1	6
Making by Simon Bryham 1 week			18	0
Glass for the door, by I Herbert			2	0
Varnishing by Thos Romney			1	6
Setting out the above at large			1	0
		2	11	7

65 Marble-cased mantle
clock with French movement
and side ornaments. Clocks
of this type were popular in
England after the death of
Prince Albert. This is a
presentation clock set, and is
dated 1883.

66 Verge lantern clock by Thomas Creed, London, circa 1670. The pendulum, in the shape of an anchor, is placed between the trains. This clock should have decorated side boxes to the doors, and the holes for fixing them can be seen behind the slot in the door.

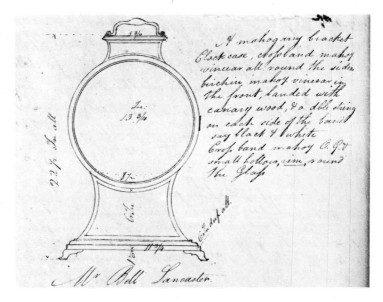

67 A Gillows' sketch for a balloon-shaped bracket clock case of 1800.

Perhaps the last wooden bracket-clock cases made in case-makers' quality and style were those produced in the Regency period. Quality was present in the materials used and, if a trifle heavy in appearance, many of them were very fine. Styles varied from the plain arch-topped case to the quasi-oriental and the woods used were various, including some mahogany but rosewood in veneered form was a firm favourite. Stringing and inlay work was frequently done in brass. Metal mounts were also common, and lion's-mask side handles and pineapple finials were a distinct feature of the time.

Much could be written about the Victorian mantle-clock case, for they were made in wood, porcelain, marble, iron and brass. Many novelty clocks were made and some fantastic styles made as 'show stoppers' around the time of the large international exhibitions of 1851, 1867 and 1889. No particular style existed in the direct line which we have traced back to the mid-17th century. One case does, however, perhaps typify the period more than most: the black Belgian marble clock, which is found in great numbers. These cases had a lasting appeal, for their black architectural cases with incised classical revival decorations and castings conveyed the mood of sorrow felt at the death of Prince Albert, and fitting perfectly with the over-furnished velvet draped interiors of the mid-Victorian period. Although typifying the English middle-class taste these cases were largely made in Belgium and usually imported with a French movement. From this point imported work from many countries caused a decline in the English craft and a general deterioration of standard followed.

Chapter 5

Lantern clocks

Soon as ever the clock struck one I kissed my wife in the kitchen by the fireside, wishing her a merry new yeare, observing that I believe I was the first proper wisher of it this yeare, for I did it as soon as ever the clock struck one.

The Diary of Samuel Pepys.
Entry for the 31st December 1664

The lantern clock, which is the name given to the fully-developed clock of its type, is essentially a weight-driven, brass, wall-mounted striking clock, without wooden case, but generally protected from dust by a back plate of iron and side-doors of brass. It reached its fully-developed and significantly English form in the third quarter of the 17th century, when it incorporated the verge pendulum control. From this date it declined in importance to the mainstream of development in English clock design, although it was produced in country districts well into the 18th century, and as a curious anachronistic Turkish export model as late as 1820.

The immediate precursor of the lantern clock, the somewhat rare (even in its own day) chamber clock of the 16th century, was a larger and more varied type. Chamber clocks were likely to have had foliot balance escapements and possibly were the work of foreign craftsmen in a style similar to German iron wall-clocks of around this time, although their rectangular metal cases were chased and decorated in flowing Renaissance forms. A chamber clock can be seen in various pictures by Hans Holbein at the home of Sir Thomas More, Henry VIII's Chancellor. In common with other chamber clocks and the twelve-hour lantern clocks, More's clock is hung near the ceiling in order to obtain a long period of running before the weights reached the floor.

The lantern clock was the common clock, indeed the only clock, in general use during the early and middle part of the 17th century. Spring clocks were never common or reliable at this early date, although rare table-clocks did exist from the 16th century, such as Nicholas Vallin's drum table-clock. The chamber clock of the 16th century and its natural heir the

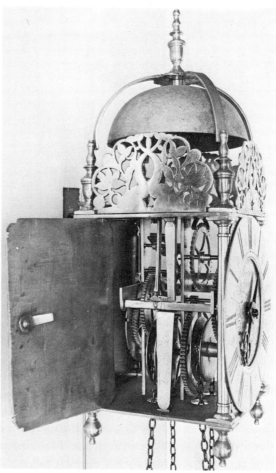

68 *Left:* Lantern clock by Edward Norris, London, circa 1670. Temple Newsam House, Leeds.

69 *Right:* Lantern clock by Jeremy Spurgin showing the original anchor escapement. The general construction of the clock can be clearly seen.

lantern clock derived their layout from the upright iron bar form of frame used in medieval horology. In this design, wheels and pinions were pivoted into the upright members of the iron frame which were then wedged into position. In the same way brass or iron chamber clocks, and later lantern clocks made with brass posted-frames, all had their pinions supported in three narrow plates. The two outer plates had cruciform arms to support lever work for the strike, and all three were wedged in the top and bottom plates of the main frame. One sometimes hears these clocks referred to as bedpost clocks, probably because the frames resemble a fourposter bed, with its turned feet and top finials. It could even be that these clocks had been hung on the bedpost when used as travelling alarms. However, I think this an unlikely explanation, as they would have been very noisy companions when hung so close to the sleeper. The term lantern clock is most favoured and appears to be the one now accepted for general use, although latten clock (latten is

an early brass alloy) and Cromwellian clocks are names heard from time to time. There is little wrong with the description Cromwellian clock, for this reflects the time when the clock was at the height of its popularity and manufacture, even though it was also made before and after the Commonwealth period (1649-60). Perhaps an argument against the name Cromwellian is similar to one against calling any flowering floral pattern Jacobean: it is generally used loosely by those who do not know really what they are talking about. I like to think that the lantern clock was so-called because, in its position on the wall, with polished side doors and a rounded bell on top, the clock resembled a simple candle lantern.

Lantern clocks were arranged with their trains one behind the other and the striking work at the back. At first they were driven by two weights, one for each train hung directly from a hook at the end of the rope; the large, somewhat coarsely-pitched nature of their gearing meant that they would only run for twelve hours or so between windings. Control or time-keeping was imposed upon the clock by a balance-wheel es-capement; this was rather insensitive and could be overcome by the pull of the weight if this became too great. The weight was increased or decreased to gain some degree of accuracy, and on some examples a dished top was included on the weight, where lead shot could be added or subtracted, to give a means of adjustment. The balance-wheel at the top of the clock was connected to the vertically-placed verge by a single spoke. As the balance-wheel oscillated to and fro the two pallets shaped like flags on the verge engaged with teeth of the escaping crown-wheel in turn, thus making it necessary to check on the escape-wheel and imposing timekeeping on the clock. The escape-wheel was arranged as the third wheel in the train, and in a vertical plane. Underneath the escape-wheel and protruding from the centre plate, a cock supported the lower pivot of the pallet arbor. Developed from the much earlier foliot balance, the principal governing the action of the balance-wheel was rather like that of swinging a large farmyard gate backwards and forwards: a natural rhythm developed, quicker than which it was impossible to go. A pin was provided to stop the balance-wheel from turning too far in either direction.

Two click springs for pull-winding and two weights were necessary to obtain going and striking in the clock. An additional small weight, and a counter-weight, was also needed to equip the clock with an alarm. These hung down at the back of the clock. The two main lead weights, each about 4 lbs to 5 lbs of lead, hung directly from the rope looped over the spiked pulley in the clock. The going-weight generally fell to the left and the strike-weight to the right. This arrangement meant that the weights would look balanced and not foul each other as they descended. Since the strike-weight fell to the right, and the rope was looped directly to the main pin-wheel, the hammer clearly needed to be situated on the right side of the clock. The hammer was later moved to the other side of the clock, and this became its accepted position in all but the later 30-hour plate-framed long-case clock. A firm indicator in identifying an early balance-wheel lantern clock, even if it has been subsequently altered, is therefore the placing of the hammer to the right of the clock when viewed from the front.

These clocks were about $15\frac{1}{2}''$ high to the top of the bell finial and $5\frac{3}{4}''$ at their widest point. Narrow chapter rings, a single simple hand and stubby finials and feet characterised them. Makers of these early lantern clocks were relatively few in number and all known examples bear the names of a fairly small group of no more than a dozen men all working in London. These included Ahasuerus Fromanteel and his family, in business with a variety of family members at Mosses Alley, Southwark; his son-in-law Thomas Loomes later at the Mermaid in Lothbury; this had previously been the home and workshop of William Selwood, who was another early maker of balance wheel lantern clocks. William Bowyer too made fine clocks at this time, and his clocks were generally shorter and rather stubby in general outline. Thomas Knifton at the Cross Keys in Lothbury too was a balance-wheel lantern clock maker of good reputation. Clocks made by all these makers and others frequently had an alarm mechanism situated out of the way on the iron backplate of the clock. This was a convenient placing as the back of the clock was always clear of the wall while still being sheltered because of its method of hanging. Only very occasionally were these clocks placed on a bracket; they were generally hung by a stout iron hoop riveted into the top plate of the frame, and protruding backward and horizontally. The clock was kept level by a pair of spurs fixed into the back feet or the backplate at its lowest point. Similar in appearance to the escapement of the clock, the alarm work meant that pallets had to be placed on the alarm hammer staff which was oscillated by the teeth of the crown-wheel when the weight, which was hung from a pulley behind the alarm crown-wheel, was released. The double-headed hammer extended upwards and struck the main bell from inside. The alarm continued to sound until the weight was fully run down. The alarm was set on a special disc, on the top front dial-plate and behind the single hour-hand. When set, the pipe which carried the alarm-disc progressed with the hour-wheel and hand. A pin on this mechanism released the alarm at the appointed hour. The necessary lever work was pivoted from behind the dial-plate and carried through to the backplate of the clock, where the alarm work is situated. A clock which originally had an alarm, subsequently removed, can be identified by the plain, undecorated circular area, consisting of 2″ of the dial surrounding the hand boss, and also the existence of the pivot hole for the alarm arbor pivot above the chapter XI on the dial-plate corner. On pendulum lantern clocks with the hammer placed to the left-hand side of the clock, the alarm arbor could be on the right-hand side and consequently pivoted through the dial-plate. The example shown by Thomas Creed illustrates this (Plate 66).

Two important developments in horological thinking changed the lantern clock. One of them, the introduction of the pendulum control from Holland in 1658, changed the whole course of clockmaking in England. The debate as to who was the first to introduce control of an escapement by a pendulum as applied to the clock, has gone on for centuries. Many have been claimed as its inventor, including Leonardo da Vinci and Galileo Galilei. However, its first successful application, in a design that subsequently spread to general use, was by the Dutch clockmaker Salomon Coster of The Hague, working to the ideas of the physicist Christiaan Huygens of Zulichem in 1657. Huygens published these ideas and others in a work entitled *Horologium* in 1658.

Working with Salomon Coster in Holland was John Fromanteel, the son of the London clockmaker Ahasuerus. John was a young man probably gaining experience in Holland, but it seems unlikely that his father knew nothing of the important developments there. Shortly after John's return to London in May 1658, Ahasuerus Fromanteel was able to advertise rather grandly, and somewhat mysteriously, what we now know to have been the first pendulum clocks in England. This advertisement was placed in the *Mercurius Politicus* of 28th October 1658. I quote the part dealing with clocks.

'There is lately a way found out for making of clocks that go exact and keep equaller time than any now made without this Regulator examined and proved before his Highness the Lord Protector, by such Doctors whose knowledge and learning is without exception and are not subject to alter by change of weather, as others are, and may be made to go a week, or a month, or a year, with once winding up, as well as those that are wound up every day, and keep time as well; and is very excellent for all House clocks that go either with Springs or Waights: And also Steeple Clocks that are most subject to differ by change of weather. Made by Ahasuerus Fromanteel, who made the first that were in England: You may have them at his house on the Bankside in Mosses Alley, Southwark, and at the sign of the Maremaid in Loathbury, near Bartholomew lane end, London'.

From 1658 therefore, clocks made in London and certainly those by the Fromanteels and their associates, had the short bob pendulum and verge escapement referred to by Fromanteel in his advertising.

The other important change, which was also described by Huygens in his *Horologium*, is the system of looping the clock rope or chain around both going- and strike-train pulleys, in such a way that one endless rope or chain could be used. Pull-up winding, made possible by a single click on the strike-train only, did not interrupt the power to the going train while winding. This provided a means of maintaining power while using only one weight of about 7 lbs. (The drawing of a clock in Huygen's book does not have a strike-train, but a separate pulley and click for the specific purpose of winding while maintaining power to the going-train is shown). The diagram on the left shows how this simple system was applied to the English lantern clock and subsequently to 30-hour clocks through to the end of the long-case clock period in about 1850.

In order that the loops of the rope would not hang crossed

Huygens' endless rope principle for winding and maintaining power:
A Going-side pulley riveted to the first wheel.
B Strike-side pulley with click spring to facilitate winding.
C Endless rope.
D Weight pulley.
E Weight.
F Lead ring to keep rope taut.

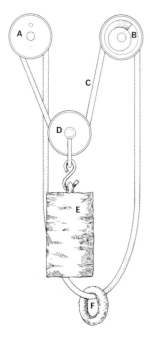

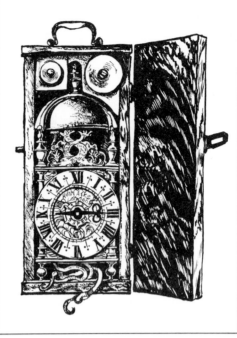

and foul each other in action, the weight-pulley suspended in the driving-loop from both going- and strike-trains was hung at the left of the clock. The left side was not chosen arbitrarily. To impart a clockwise motion to the hour-wheel (and hence the hand), the immediate driving member on to which the rope pulley was fixed needs to revolve in anti-clockwise direction, or be pulled downwards from the left. Pairing this action to the action of the strike meant that the strike pin-wheel, also the main drive-wheel, fixed via the winding click to the rope pulley, was also driven to the left. The hammer-placing also needed to be moved to the left so that its tail could be activated by the downward sweep of the hammer-pins to strike the bell from the inside. The incorporation of this endless rope principle coincided with the adoption of finer gearing and larger numbers of wheel teeth. As a result clocks could be made to run for approximately 30 hours at one winding.

The crown-shaped escape-wheel still played a central role after the change from balance-wheel to verge-pendulum. Instead of being the third wheel in the train it now became the fourth, and was moved into a horizontal plane above the top plate of the clock. The third wheel is the contrate wheel, cut with teeth on its flank and so able to transfer the motion to the vertically placed arbor and pinion of the crown-wheel. The 9"-long bob-pendulum was rigidly fastened to the pallet arbor and

71 *Left:* Lantern clock, showing the arrangement of the crown wheel, verge, and bob-pendulum, as well as hoop and spurs for fixing the clock to the wall.

72 *Right:* Travelling alarm by Henry Aske of London, circa 1680, in its original oak carrying box.

made its short, fussy journeys to and fro between the spurs at the back of the clock. The pallet-arbor or verge position just above the crown-wheel is pivoted into a cock behind the front fret and comes backwards across the centre of the crown-wheel; its back support was of a knife-edge design and worked in a V-slot in the back cock. Two flag pallets hang down from the verge. Set at 45°, these intercept the crown-wheel at each swing of the pendulum and impose measured time on the progress of the hand with an accuracy that had never been possible before. The pendulum was placed in precisely the area normally occupied by the alarm work, and older balance-wheel clocks which were improved by altering to the new verge pendulum control invariably lost their alarm work as a result. Pendulum lantern clocks, newly-made for those customers needing alarm-work, needed re-thinking and various answers to this problem were devised. Perhaps the most successful idea for the sleepy traveller was to remove the hour strike-train completely and put the alarm work in its place. Unable to strike the hours, the clock was lighter and often much smaller. Some as small as 6″ or 7″ high were made, and some still retain their oak carrying-boxes with partitions and fittings for the secure packing of clock and weights. Lantern clocks of this type are known as bedchamber alarms and were made by the most eminent of makers including Tompion and Knibb. The verge-pendulum escapement was very convenient for travelling clocks or clocks which might be hastily set up. Its design is such that it is not too sensitive and will still go even when not quite level. For this reason these little clocks remained in use well into the second half of the 18th century, long after the normal lantern clock had gone out of vogue for regular domestic use. Very occasionally the sides of the lantern clock were used for mounting an alarm, which meant that the pendulum could be fitted in the conventional rear position. This was not a convenient arrangement as it made side access to the movement difficult. It is frequently necessary to open both side doors of a rope-driven lantern clock and blow out all the dust and fluff which has been accumulated by the action of the rope. If this is not done it picks up on the oil, wraps round pivots and fills the teeth of wheels and pinions. Since the verge-arbor could cross the centre of the crown-wheel at any point the pendulum could be made to work equally well at the side of the clock. This is very rarely seen but is recorded and examples are known. These examples, however, are converted from balance-wheel clocks, and it is my view that this arrangement was to save a backplate-mounted alarm.

929

A most picturesque and interesting variation enabled the alarm-work to remain on the backplate and the pendulum was moved to the centre of the clock, swinging between the two trains. This simply meant that the strike- and going-arbors were made a little shorter and an additional upright plate was needed in the middle. The space left between the two centre plates, generally about $\frac{3}{4}''$, was ample room in which to swing a pendulum. The novelty value of this arrangement did not pass unnoticed; the conventional idea of a pear-shaped brass bob was replaced by an anchor-shaped elongated bob with flukes protruding out of the case at each side with every swing of the pendulum. Slots were cut into the clock side doors to allow for this and were further elaborated with open-fronted triangular boxes decorated on the top surface by a specially-made brass fret. This greatly increased the width of the clock, and what had begun as a necessary alternative became a decorative feature as well. These winged clocks were extremely popular between 1660 and 1675 and quite a number of them survive. Because of the pendulum side boxes they are known as winged lantern clocks. Even when they have later been converted to the long-pendulum and anchor-escapement, as many were, the clues that tell of the clock's original centre pendulum are un-mistakeable unless major alterations to the trains have also been carried out: the existence of four vertical plates instead of three with a $\frac{3}{4}''$ gap between the middle two. The hammer arbor is shortened and pivoted only between the two rear plates so as not to foul the pendulum with its arbor and associated blade-spring. At the left-hand side the lifting arbor, which is needed to trigger off the hour strike, must travel from front to back and so is curved upwards in an inverted 'U' for the same reasons.

The period immediately after 1672 and the introduction of the anchor-escapement and the long-pendulum saw the rapid development and increasing popularity of the long-case clock. Strictly speaking, this rendered the lantern clock out of date. Some were still made however, for the style must have been pleasing to many traditionalists who would consider the long-case to be cumbersome and unnecessary. A lantern clock made at this time by Henry Webster of London (Plate 75) remains unaltered. It was made without an alarm but with an anchor escapement and long pendulum. Another feature of this clock which illustrates a departure from the normal is the mounting of the bell by an internal bell-cage arrangement, while still retaining the traditional top finial with a nut inside the bell for fastening. Towards the end of the 17th century – a period of

930

experiment and innovation – the lantern clock was developed in the hands of a few clever makers to include novel and untypical features. Minute-markings on the chapter-ring and two hands sometimes accompany the use of the long pendulum and in rare cases this was used on verge pendulum clocks. Among others recorded are quarter-chiming clocks, musical clocks incorporating a rotary barrel to activate the hammers, and key-wind lantern clocks with weights suspended on gut-line and running for eight days. Seen in the light of mainstream development these are highly untypical. A clock of this sort offered for sale today should be viewed with suspicion for few were made originally and there will be many others sub-sequently 'improved'.

Care is necessary in dating a lantern clock, for individual features seen in isolation cannot give a firm indication of its age. Fortunately clues do exist in altered specimens so that detective work, if undertaken carefully, will often reveal all. Spare holes were rarely filled in, for alterations made in years gone by were not done to deceive. Holes in the top plate usually indicate where a cock has been positioned to hold the top pivot of a balance-wheel staff, or of a crown-wheel in the case of a later verge. Similarly holes, usually square, will exist in the centre plate if the bridge, used to bypass the verge

73 *Left:* Verge lantern clock showing the alarm on the iron backplate and a gap between the two trains in which the anchor-shaped pendulum is placed.

74 *Right:* Spring-driven movement with rear-facing winding squares, 'lantern clock hands' and hammer for striking the inside of a bell. This movement was specially made for 'modernising' lantern clocks.

and pivot the vertical crown-wheel, on a balance-wheel clock, has been removed. This bridge may have been retained and altered to accommodate the back-pivot of the contrate-wheel arbor if the clock had been altered to a verge-pendulum after 1658. These old clocks were converted to anchor escapement throughout the 19th century and in this century until very recently. Other features were improved and replaced with very little regard to aesthetic considerations or authenticity. Spring-driven movements were at one time made with fusée arbors extended backwards to provide rear-winding especially for use in 'modernising' lantern clocks. One such, with a pair of 'lantern-clock' hands is illustrated in Plate 74. A balance-wheel lantern clock by William Selwood, which had been converted to anchor-escapement some time ago, is illustrated in Plate 23, on page 873. The anchor is clearly more sophisticated in style than the rest of the clock, but what really gives it away is that it is attached to its arbor not by brazing or by being driven on, but to a collet by two delicate 19th-century screws. Such clues are there if you take the trouble to look. As so often, authentic technical details have been ignored in the interests of 'improving' a fine old clock.

The method of fixing of the large bell in lantern clocks changed little. It was suspended from a bell cage or from straps of four arms radiating from a central point. These were curved round outside the bell and pegged into holes cross-drilled into the very tops of the four corner finials flanking the frets and surmounting the main clock frame. The pegs or pins are a fixture in the ends of the bell-cage arms and are sprung into position. Small pierced, decorative features occur between the arms around the central boss. These are usually more pronounced on examples of London origin and by good makers. Bell-cages are usually made of brass, although iron is used in the case of the Henry Webster clock where the bell-cage fits inside the bell. Very rare indeed, but not unknown, is the bell fixed by a single bell-staff. In all cases the bell is surmounted by a matching finial which gives poise and finish to the clock. In early examples, frets, screwed to the top plate of the frame on three sides of the clock, fill in the awkward area between the top plate and the underside of the bell, and hide the workings of the hammer and the escapement. Frets are a characteristic and highly decorative part of the clock but they can never be regarded as firm indicators of age, particularly when considered in isolation. Some observation can however be made. From the earliest times the base of the front fret, like the central or lower part of the dial plate, occasionally carried

75 Lantern clock by Henry Webster, London, showing the unusual iron bell-cage, which supports the bell from the inside. Temple Newsam House, Leeds.

the maker's name, place of trading, city and so on. When signed in this way on the fret, it must be remembered that frets are only held by two screws and may not be original to the clock. The front fret is always engraved and usually well finished. On better clocks the side frets may also be engraved. Drawing A shows an heraldic fret, so-called because of the central shield. This could be used to record the date of making, maker's initials or even those of the first owner. However, they were often left blank, the maker choosing to sign his work across the fret-base or elsewhere. In this example the supports to the shield are of a foliage design but animals such as unicorns are known. Drawing B shows another early style with a curving design of leaves terminating in blunt-ended scrolls. This design was known to have been used by William Bowyer and William Selwood on their balance-wheel clocks. By far the most common of any design seen is the dolphin fret. Various versions are seen but perhaps the one shown here in drawing C is most typical. This is seen on the very earliest and the very latest lantern clocks and so it must have had an enduring appeal. Drawings A and C are also used in a type, raised up on an arcaded base as shown in drawing D, used here on yet another foliate example. A symmetrical leaf design as shown in drawing E is used occasionally on some London work. This was equally as popular as the dolphin fret with the East Anglian makers of lantern clocks. The next fret, shown in F, shows non-European influence, coming from an out-of-period lantern clock destined for the Turkish market.

Regional versions of the lantern clock were found mainly in

Lantern clock frets:
A Heraldic fret, pre-1650.
B Early fret with blunt-ended scrolls.
C Dolphin fret. The most common type, used throughout the lantern-clock period.
D Foliate fret on an arcaded base. The arcaded section was occasionally applied to all types of frets.
E Fret using a leaf design favoured by some East Anglian clockmakers.
F Fret from a lantern clock for the Turkish market. Islamic features are apparent and include the crescent moon.

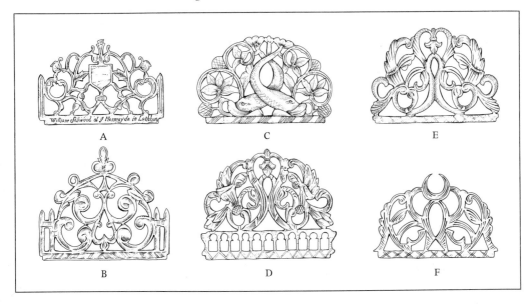

the south. Since lantern clocks were the first domestic clocks, these regional forms can provide an indication of the areas in which clockmaking began earliest. Isolated examples are sometimes found in an area where a maker was trained in London and then moved to a provincial centre to carry on his work. Thomas Cruttenden of York, by whom a few lantern clocks are known, is an example of this. He had been an apprentice in London but set up a workshop in York after 1679, where he died in 1698. Perhaps it is understandable that no lantern clocks are recorded from far-flung northern areas such as Westmorland and Cumberland, although I am not so sure about Cornwall. A lantern clock or two might be known in an area such as Lancashire with a long clockmaking tradition, but I have seen no mention in any records or books. A number were made in the Midlands however, and in the area which extends towards Bristol in the west. *Somerset Clockmakers* by J. K. Bellchambers illustrates a fine balance-wheel lantern clock by Samuel Stetch of Bristol, and good examples by three other local makers are shown. This suggests quite a colony of makers there in the mid-17th century. William Holloway of Stroud, Gloucestershire, was an early provincial maker of lantern clocks but judging by the appearance of his work and also the Bristol work previously mentioned, there is nothing provincial about the quality.

Most lantern clocks made outside London were made in East Anglia, where the taste for the style lasted well into the 18th century. At this time they were obviously preferred to the oak-cased 30-hour clock, with one or two hands, which was the normal product of many other regions such as Westmoreland, Lancashire, Cheshire and Yorkshire. It is not difficult to see the reason for this preference of the lantern clock: East Anglia is the nearest part of the British Isles to Holland, and many Dutch merchants and craftsmen had settled in East Anglia during the 16th and 17th century. Ahaseurus Fromanteel himself, the London clockmaker, was born in Norwich in 1607 of a Dutch emigré family. His father was a wood-turner, probably employed in the furniture trade. Many ideas which helped develop the English clockmaking industry had come from Holland and a clock in the shape of a lantern which had grown up along with these developments was naturally one which would be revered for many years. The frequency of brick-built Flemish gables in the architecture of this region can be attributed to the import of ideas by Flemish workmen in the same way. The manner of putting brick together in a certain way is still known as Flemish Bond. Even in East Anglia,

76 Early 18th-century long case made to house a lantern clock.

934

however, the production of clocks did not get underway as early as it did in London and most East Anglian lantern clocks were made after 1700. Some, though, were made in the second half of the 17th century and original verge-pendulum lantern clocks by a number of makers have been recorded. East Anglian lantern clock is a phrase used to describe that group of clocks from the area originally made using the anchor escapement and long pendulum. These clocks were generally typified by their broader chapter-rings and absence of alarm work; otherwise their general appearance and size is very much the same as others from a different time and area. Later in the period the broader chapter-ring occasionally became quite wide in relation to the frame and these clocks, and the provincial travelling-alarms with untypical square dials, with arched tops, became known as sheeps' heads.

In discussing the sheeps' head lantern clock, later travelling-alarms and others, we come to the group of lantern clocks that were clearly made unusually late. Obviously the travelling-alarm might be kept in its box for many years and used only infrequently. Those ordered and newly-made in the late 18th century were still probably the best thing for the job and, unlike the owner of the very first balance-wheel lantern clock, the 18th-century owners of these small portable clocks would be likely also to have a grand long-case clock and maybe a bracket clock for use at home. The fact that small lantern-shaped alarms retained the verge escapement and short bob pendulum provides a clue to its continued popularity. Setting up the clock, perhaps hurriedly, on a makeshift nail in the bedroom of an inn required a stable temperament in the clock if it was to be reliable. The crown-wheel escapement was and still is the least sensitive pendulum escapement, and will go reliably when not absolutely level.

By far the most interesting group of lantern clocks of the ones that persisted 'out of period' are those made for the Turkish market. The Muslim Ottomans had a delight in English clocks and watches and they imported them in great numbers over a long period of time. The brassy lantern clock was a firm favourite and, perhaps because it came nearest to their ideal, they caused it to be made until the early 19th century.

The crescent was a favourite Turkish symbol, and suggests the Islamic religious preoccupation with the moon. We have previously seen this depicted on the drawing of the typical Turkish-market fret on page 933 (F). The photograph of the clock by Isaac Rogers clearly illustrates this influence in the engraving of its side doors (a very untypical practice for

935

England). Isaac Rogers was Master of the Clockmakers' Company in 1813 and we may assume that it could be as late or even later than this.

Although this book divides styles and types of clocks into separate chapters, the reality is never as clearly defined as that. Some lantern clocks which had originally been given a square arched-dial and a wooden hood became hanging wall-clocks. This type of clock was seen, albeit rarely, in non-lantern clock areas during the early 18th century. These are not to be confused with the more sophisticated hanging wall-clocks which had plate frames, key-wound movements and were made in the early long-case clock period; these can be

78 Small hooded alarm with posted movement by James Field, Dunstable; after 1758.

described as identical in most respects to the long-cased clock but without a trunk.

Sometimes a lantern clock was cased up in a country-style long-case of oak or pine. It is likely that some were made up in this way during the early 18th century but it equally seems possible that some customers chose the case when the clock was new. It is obvious that the cases are made specially for lantern clocks as their upright elongated hood-doors are sometimes arch-topped, showing the top fret, and sometimes square-cut when the front fret of the clock has been removed. Their simple style and manner of construction usually underlines their age and purpose.

Chapter 6

Long-case clocks

1724 July 10th Bought at Derby Market from Wolley of Codnor, square oak clock Paid £4. 10s. 00d. He wanted £5.

From the diary of a Lincolnshire farmer

Long wooden cases were used to house certain lantern clocks fairly late on in the lantern-clock period. However, this is not a real pointer to the development of the long case, as it took place. Lantern clocks cased in this way were not usual until the early 18th century and the first true long-case clocks in England were made, in quite a different way, soon after the introduction of the pendulum in 1658. From the clocks which survive and the evidence we have already discussed about the pendulum, it would seem likely that Ahasuerus Fromanteel was the first to make long-case clocks in Britain.

A new method of winding the clock was devised at the very outset of long-case clock manufacture. It would be too easy to forget to pull up a weight hidden behind a closed door and the clock would stop, possibly causing great disruption in the household. It was no easy matter in those days to set the clock to time, for reference had to be made to the sundial, and its reading converted to equal time as shown on the clock dial, by referring to tables specially provided for this purpose. It was understood that running a clock with rope was a crude and dusty business. The spikes in the clock pulleys shredded the rope and quickly made it unserviceable. Chains too had their disadvantages. If a chain twists slightly and the link does not quite fit over the spike in the movement pulley, then a sudden judder is likely to occur in the clock. Greater time between windings and smoother running could be achieved by using thinner lines and winding them many times round a grooved drum or barrel. This drum was mounted on the same arbor as the main wheel in each train. When provided with a click-and-ratchet arrangement, which freed the barrel in one direction, the clock could be wound by key. This was easily arranged by making the front of the barrel-arbor terminate in a winding square on to which a cranked key could be placed through a

79 Early architectural long-case clock by Fromanteel, London. British Museum, London.

938

hole in the dial. Until this date it had been customary to place the strike-train behind the going- or watch-train in the movement, but now this was no longer convenient if key winding and greater duration was to be achieved. A change came about in the layout of the clock movement which was both fundamental and very simple. It provided many advantages and facilitated the rapid development of clockmaking skills towards the many refinements and innovationary features which followed.

The plate movement was made up of almost exactly the same units as the lantern type of movement, in different proportion. Instead of the brass plates being used top and bottom as in the lantern clock, they were now arranged back and front and held together by somewhat shorter pillars at each corner. The wheel arbors could now be pivoted directly into these plates with trains side-by-side, giving front access for winding at any point convenient to the clockmaker. Decorative finials and the brass feet were left out of this arrangement. Usually the plate-pillars were riveted into the backplate and protruded only a little way through in order to be secured with pins or latches. The movement stood firmly on the lower edges of the upright plates. More complicated movements, involving the use of heavy weights, had more than the usual four pillars in their movement construction; five or six pillars were common in these examples. Later London-made examples, and some of the best country work, used five pillars as the normal arrangement. The extra pillar comes between the two winding barrels, giving extra support and stopping the plates from flexing where the stress is greatest.

Pillars in the 17th century were seen by makers as an area for decorative turning. Different workshops showed characteristic variations in this treatment. Baluster shapes were usual and these are either symmetrically turned to give equal weight to both ends or, less frequently turned to emphasise the part nearer the backplate. Towards the year 1700, however, these too took on a more general character and most work done in London and the provinces at this time had delicately turned and finned pillars as shown by Plates 81 and 92.

The development of the long pendulum and the associated anchor-escapement allowed great strides to be made towards the good timekeeping which still typifies long-case clocks. They were first recorded as used, not on a domestic clock, but on a tower clock made for a Cambridge College, by William Clements about 1672. This clock can now be seen in the Science Museum, London. There is still debate as to who invented the anchor escapement; some authorities credit it to William Clements himself. What is certain is that there was much experimentation, discussion and correspondence in the late 1660s between people interested in horological development. Dr. Robert Hooke, the eminent physicist and member of the newly-formed Royal Society, was at the centre of these developments and caused Thomas Tompion to make him clocks with experimental anchor escapements of the long-pendulum type. At one stage, when he was impatiently awaiting the making of a clock to test one of his theories, he flew into a rage and 'Fel out with Thompian' calling him 'a clownish churlish Dog'. During his work on escapements, Hooke demonstrated to the Royal Society a small watch controlled by a very long pendulum. Hooke claimed to have invented the anchor-escapement in 1665 but although this is quite possible, no proof exists to substantiate the claim. John Flamsteed, the first Astronomer Royal, also joined in the development of the anchor escapement and Tompion made two precision clocks using the anchor-escapement and long pendulum which were set up in the new Royal Observatory at Greenwich for Flamsteed's use in experiments on the equation of time. Letters exist from Flamsteed to Richard Towneley of Towneley Hall, near Burnley, Lancs, explaining the intricacies of the new

80 *Left:* Eight-day long-case movement seen from below. Three of the five plate pillars can be seen. Holes in the two outer pillars are for screws fixing the clock to the seatboard.

81 *Right:* Finned pillars typical of London and good provincial work at this time. The clock movement is by John Williamson of Leeds, circa 1690.

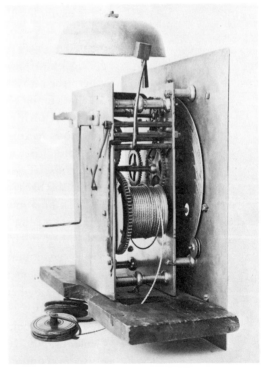

escapement and Towneley, himself a scientist and experimenter in horological matters, also made suggestions for its refinement. People tried pendulums as long as 61″, almost reaching the bottom of the case for a brief period, as was previously mentioned in the chapter on cases. Eventually the seconds pendulum, which was some 39″ long, was found to be most convenient and this, coupled with an anchor-recoil escapement, was used subsequently on almost all long-case clocks made for household use. Another advantage of the seconds pendulum was that the escape-arbor, extended forwards and, provided with a hand, gave a seconds indicator to the clock. The pendulum was so central to thinking in clockmaking circles at this time that the word 'pendulum' was often used in place of the word 'clock'. I am not sure whether it was because of its regal dominance over the motions of the clock or to honour King Charles II, but the seconds pendulum came to be known as the Royal Pendulum.

Equipped with these developments and their undoubted skills, the best clockmakers in London developed the craft to an exceptionally high standard and the period from about 1670 to 1700 became known as the golden period of English clockmaking. Long-case clocks were made to go for a month, three months, or even a year at one winding. In fact year-clocks were more common at this period than ever since. The addition of extra wheels to the train made year-clocks possible, but the weights needed to keep the clock going and to strike for a year were very heavy indeed. An eight-day clock, intended for weekly winding with a day in reserve in case you forgot, had four wheels in its going-train and generally needed a weight of between 10 lbs and 16 lbs to drive it. The strike-train was geared in a similar way and used a similar weight. A month-going clock usually had five wheels in its train and weights of about 24 lbs each. There were various ways in which a maker might 'gear up' a year-clock, but one way was by using six wheels and a vast differential of gearing and pitch between the main wheel which bore the winding-barrel and weight, and the escape-wheel. The main-wheel was massively constructed whilst the escape-wheel was more delicately made than even the ones on the eight-day clock. The weight needed to drive such a train would be in the region of 50 lbs. Some year-clocks are timepieces only, as the amount of weight needed for a striking-train as well was excessive indeed. During a year some 60,000 blows would be struck on the bell to record every hour. Joseph Knibb invented a method of striking which reduced this considerably and, because it related to the hours engraved

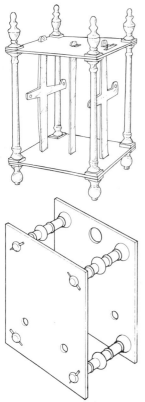

Below: A posted-frame construction as used in lantern clocks. *Bottom:* A plate-frame movement in which trains were placed side by side.

82 A 12″ square dial of an eight-day clock by Henry Hindley of Wigan.

on the chapter-ring, it was known as Roman-striking. Two bells and two hammers were provided in the movement, a blow on the deep bell indicating the Roman figure V and a blow on the lighter bell the figure I; X was indicated by two blows on the deeper bell. Thus XII would sound with two blows on the deep bell and two blows on the light bell—a saving of eight blows. Though this was a good idea it did not last and its use was restricted largely to Knibb himself.

The application of a long pendulum, an improved escapement and the constant force of a lead weight, gave such good timekeeping results, that the difference between meantime (the division of a day into 24 equal hours as shown by the clock) and solar time (as measured from the motions of the sun) became very obvious. The difference at its extreme periods is $16\frac{1}{2}$ minutes fast on 4th November and $14\frac{1}{2}$ minutes slow on 12 February. Since clocks at this period could be accurate to within one minute per week, great frustrations would be experienced in trying to set them to time with a sundial alone. Only on four days a year does equal time and solar time coincide exactly. Many makers were aware of this problem and issued a printed table of the differences enabling the sundial reading to be modified to equal time. Other makers made ingenious clocks which showed solar and equal time on separate rings. Often these were highly involved and consisted of full-sized chapter-rings side by side, worked by two movements in the same large case. Daniel Quare made a clock of this type in about 1710. Joseph Williamson made a clock with a dial at each side of the clock and placed back-to-back each side

942

83 The Morgan Lowry year clock, showing the massive weights for going- and strike-trains. The key is in place on the winding square of the going-train. Abbey House Museum, Kirkstall, Leeds.

84 Winding key of the Morgan Lowry year clock (Plate 83; left) showing its long cranked handle for winding the huge weights. A more conventional eight-day clock key is shown to the right. Abbey House Museum, Kirkstall, Leeds.

of a common, but complicated, movement. One dial showed equal time and the other meantime. However, these were very rare and special clocks. They were never intended to be used in a domestic situation, but were made as showpieces and found in palaces and country houses where they were no doubt a good advertisement and a talking-point for all who saw them. Less flamboyant equation-clocks doubtless did have a scientific use in observatories and some fine ones of this type were made by Thomas Tompion using the more conventional long-case form without any exaggerated variations. Some high-quality clocks became so accurate that even the amount of time it took to wind the weight was thought to be important. Ingenious makers took this into consideration and devised a system of maintaining power for key-wound clocks. The most usual method employed at the end of the 17th century involved the use of discs or shutters held in place behind the winding-holes by a strong blade-spring. Pulling these aside by a cord or lever to place a key on the winding-square also lifted a bolt or lever into engagement with a wheel in the going-train. This exerted enough pressure on the wheel to keep the train in motion during the few moments of winding. Restoration of power and the advance of the wheel gradually dislodged the bolt, allowing it to return to its normal position. The shutters sprang back into position at the same time. The clock shown here by Hindley de Wigan (Plate 82) has this feature, and the little catch which pushes the shutters aside can just be seen above the mouth of the face of the spandrel decoration in the bottom-right.

Strike-work in clocks was also changed and improved. Clockmakers put most of their energies into developing the escapement, and changes in strike-work came slightly later. The rack-and-snail method of striking was introduced by the avant-garde makers in 1675-80. To explain the advantages of this method over the previous count-wheel strike which had been used since medieval times, it is first necessary to explain how the older method worked. Like the going-train, the strike-train, is made up of a number of wheels and pinions: three wheels in the lantern and 30-hour long-case clocks and four in the more usual eight-day clock. Three main factors have to be considered in order that the train can perform its basic function of reliably recording the passing hours on a bell (bells were always used on traditional English clocks until the 19th century). A wheel low down in the train needs to be pinned in order to pick up, or push aside, the tail of the hammer. As the hammer falls off the revolving pins, a blade-spring, also

943

bearing on the hammer-arbor, causes the hammer to make a swift light blow to the bell. The speed of the train is also important if an even, measured rhythm is to be given to the strike. A hurried and erratically struck bell would be very unpleasant to hear and, if the train ran too quickly, locking-up at the end of the strike would be a hazardous business causing rapid wear and even breakage. To give this even strike and smooth locking an additional feature is put into the bell train. Made in the shape of a flat rotating vane, it is known as the fly. It is made with a friction fit to its arbor. The fly's resistance to the air slows down the train and its friction fit allows it to travel on briefly after the hours have been struck and absorb the power of the train and give smooth locking. The train is unlocked by the lifting-piece, positioned by the motion work between the dial and the front plate of the clock. This is raised by a pin on the motion work itself about five minutes before the hour; the pin unlocks the strike work by lifting the locking detent from the locking pin or slot, and allows it to proceed a short way before being held temporarily by a pin especially placed to catch the warning-piece. When the hour is reached, the lifting-piece falls from the lifting-pin and in turn allows the warning-piece to fall and set the strike train in motion. These features are common to all striking methods and it is the way in which the hours are counted that is different and gives the two main types of strike train their names.

85 *Left:* Posted-frame movement of a clock by John Ismay of Oulton, Cumberland. The count-wheel for the strike can be seen to the left of the picture.

86 *Right:* Rack-striking, plate-framed 30-hour clock by Thomas Lister, Halifax, circa 1760.

944

The first method was known as count-wheel strike and consisted of a brass count-wheel or disc, slotted irregularly around the circumference. The distance between the slots represented the duration of strike and the lever (or detent) which falls into the slots causes the locking at the end of the strike; thus the area for twelve blows is the greatest and the distances get progressively shorter towards the lower numbers. There is no distance at all for striking one and the detent falls back into the same slot. Usually count-wheels revolved every twelve hours and their layout was based on 78 divisions – the number of blows struck by the clock in that period. This is clearly visible in the left of Plate 85 which I hope will clarify this rather complicated explanation. The wrong name of locking-plate strike is sometimes used when describing this method. This suggests that the progression of the strike-train is halted by the detent holding in the count-wheel slots. This is not so. A separate wheel on which is mounted a stop-pin or a slotted-hoop is provided for the actual locking-up. The detent which drops into the count-wheel slots is directly connected to a further detent which falls against this stop at the appropriate time. The count-wheel is, as its correct name implies, a device for counting or measuring the blows.

On lantern clocks and during the verge-pendulum period of long-case clocks, the count-wheel was mounted externally at the back of the movement. Later it was situated within the plates and usually mounted on the side of the strike main-wheel, which also makes one revolution every twelve hours. At first it was mounted behind the wheel nearest the backplate but later it was moved and placed between the wheel and the winding barrel.

The count-wheel system can easily get out of step with the clock. Care has to be taken, when setting the hands, to let each hour strike out, as it is passed. Once out of step the clock has to be struck round to the correct hour by lifting the detent out of the count-wheel until the correct hour is reached. When very worn, as many old clocks are today, this mechanism is prone to get out of step. A common problem is that it will fail to lock-up after a strike, running two or more numbers into one and getting the sequence mixed up. Even when well-adjusted this system had its disadvantages and one of them was that it could not be made to repeat the hours struck; once past the count-wheel could only measure the next hour. In the days of the candle, before the invention of the safety match, obtaining an instant light to check the time at night would have been very inconvenient, and a strike-repeating clock was obviously useful. This feature was used principally in portable clocks, but more long-case clocks than are generally realised were also equipped with repeating facilities. This was particularly true for clocks made in provincial centres after about 1750. Passing the clock in an unlit hall, one only had to pull the repeat cord to make the clock sound the last hour. The newly developed rack-strike could repeat naturally if provided with a simple blade-spring and cord extending from the strike lifting-piece to the outside of the case. The snail – which is the part that determines the number of blows struck – is principally connected to the hour-wheel of the motion work and so is advanced at the same time as the hands. In this way the strike cannot get out of step and when in good repair it monitors accurately the hours shown on the dial, however many times the repeat may be used. There is a further advantage, in that if a fault arises in the striking of one particular hour it does not necessarily throw the whole sequence out of step, and the hands can be set without waiting for the hours to strike out, although it is advisable to allow the twelve to do so for fear of breaking the rack-tail. The reason for this can be seen in the drawing on this page. The rack-strike technique was more reliable but more expensive to make. Using the same methods of unlocking, warning and lifting of the hammer-tail as the count-strike did, the difference was in the way that the hours were counted. The diagram shows the front of a rack-strike movement as it would appear with the dial removed.

The count-wheel strike continued in use, even on some quite sophisticated eight-day clocks made in London well into the 18th century. Country makers, particularly in the Lancashire region, favoured this type of strike for their eight-day clocks through into the 19th century; and the 30-hour long-case clock, whether made in birdcage or in plate form, used it almost exclusively. The count-wheel was rear-mounted in both cases. Just occasionally a plate-framed 30-hour clock will be found with a rack-strike, but this is highly untypical and quite rare. Plate 86 shows the movement of one such clock made about 1760 by Thomas Lister of Halifax.

·Refinements of the anchor-escapement were discussed and experimented with almost immediately after its introduction. The first anchor was so-called because it resembled the downturned flukes of a ship's anchor. The shape of the teeth of the escape-wheel gave a recoil action to the train, causing it to halt and make a momentary backward gesture before dropping forward on to the opposite pallet. This can be seen if you look at the seconds hand of a normal eight-day long-case clock. It

Diagram showing the working parts of a rack-striking eight-day clock as it would appear with the dial removed. The snail (A) can be seen attached to the hour-pipe, immediately in front of the hour-wheel. The snail revolves with the hour hand; the highest point on its circumference represents one o'clock and the lowest twelve o'clock. The rack (B) has teeth set on its top surface, each one representing a single blow on the bell. A pin on the tail of the rack (C) drops against the snail's edge just before the hour. The whole of this unit is mounted on a pin (D), and the spring (E) helps to throw the rack-tail on to the surface of the snail. Shortly before the hour the warning lever (F) falls from a lifting pin on wheel (G) to free the train and allow the rack to be gathered up by a small gathering pallet (H). The number of teeth gathered (and consequently the number of blows struck on the bell) depends on the distance the rack tail falls to the surface of the snail. While gathering is taking place the rack is prevented from falling back by the rack hook (I). At the end of the strike the train is usually locked by the extension at the side of the gathering-pallet engaging with a pin on the left side of the rack-top (J). A repeat-cord, when fitted, was usually fastened to the point (K) on the lifting piece; when pulled, it caused the clock to repeat its last strike.

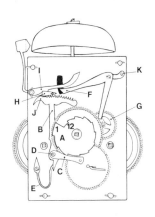

may seem a strange arrangement but it was partly the shape of the teeth of the wheel, and the pallets, which caused this recoil that gave impulse to the pendulum to keep it going. As early as 1675 Tompion developed a style of escapement which was described as dead-beat, because of its precise and accurate action involving no recoil and consequent better timekeeping qualities. But the credit for inventing a true dead-beat escapement is given to Tompion's nephew-in-law and successor George Graham. Graham had been born in Cumberland and travelled to London as a boy. He became an apprentice to Henry Aske, and trained to be a clockmaker for seven years. On the completion of his training he joined Tompion as a journeyman and was possibly responsible for many clocks made in Tompion's name. Precision timekeeping was Graham's special interest and he must have had ample opportunity to see all the latest developments as they occurred in Tompion's workshop. A proven dead-beat escapement whose pallets caused no recoil but worked with a positive sliding action was made by him about 1720, and its principal uses were for observatory and fine regulator clocks, where timekeeping with a high degree of accuracy was essential. His clocks were so accurate that a normal pendulum hung on a simple iron rod was not considered good enough for precise timekeeping because the rod varied with changes of temperature. Graham was a great believer in the use of mercury in his work. As well as making many fine mercury barometers he adopted its properties of expanding when warmed to make a mercurially-compensated pendulum. This worked very well. He described it to the Royal Society, of which he was a very active member, and made examples for his dead-beat regulators in the early 1720s. The length of a pendulum (from the point of suspension to the centre of oscillation, generally considered to be the centre of the pendulum bob) regulates the speed at which it swings. The iron rod of a pendulum naturally expands when warmed and contracts when cooled, sufficiently for the seasons to upset the timekeeping of a fine clock. A glass jar partially filled with mercury was suspended in a stirrup at the base of an iron pendulum and expanded upwards on warming, thus counteracting the downward expansion of the iron rod. This principle was highly successful in its day and was used for many years in precision clocks.

John Harrison, best-known for his work on the marine chronometer, also developed a complicated pendulum which was highly regarded and used more regularly on precise clocks than any other. Harrison too developed his pendulum in the

1720s, working in Lincolnshire before coming to London in order to promote his life's work on the marine chronometer. His pendulum was known as the grid-iron pendulum and was constructed of nine rods, some of brass, some of iron. The differing expansion rates of the two metals and the way in which they were held together to suspend the heavy brass bob gave extremely good results in timekeeping throughout the seasons.

After the mid-18th century London makers did not make as many long-case clocks as before. Nevertheless the quality of the ones that were made was extremely high. Cases of mahogany were made on simple lines but movements were of the highest order and, with some exceptions in clocks for the domestic market, this was the time of the precision-regulator long-case clock. The precision-regulator almost certainly incorporated a dead-beat escapement, one of the temperature-compensated pendulums mentioned, and some kind of maintaining power for use while winding. A month duration was thought to be a good period of going for regulator clocks although, in common with domestic clocks, eight days was most common. Dial layout could be unconventional to do away with extra motion work which was detrimental to timekeeping properties. Hours might be shown through a lunette aperture in the centre of the dial. Seconds were normally shown, while minutes would be shown around a minute ring in conventional plan. Strike-work and other indications were absent in a true regulator-clock. John Ellicot, Thomas Mudge and William Dutton were all highly skilled makers of clocks of this type. John Ellicot, who worked at a slightly later date than Graham and Harrison, designed his own compensated pendulum. It looks less complicated than the other two described but it used the differing expansion rates of brass and iron just as Harrison's grid iron does. Ellicot's pendulum is known as a compensated pendulum. There was a fourth way in which the expansion rate of a pendulum could be minimised and this method was cheap enough to make it popular for some types of long-case pendulum clocks during the late-18th century. This was to use a piece of wood to make the pendulum rod. While not perfect this gave a far more stable rate than the ordinary iron rod.

London clockmakers in the early long-case clock period devoted their energies to making the clock go for a longer duration than had previously been possible, and very few 30-hour long-case clocks were made. Even so, some are known, including top makers. These generally had the conventional posted movement, count-wheel strike and of course retained the pull-wind. Provincial makers had not yet begun production of the 30-hour clock on a large scale. At this time they were divided into two groups, those who had London connections or training, and made quite sophisticated eight-day or even the odd month-clock in the London tradition, and a much smaller body of makers working in country places who made unsophisticated pull-wind clocks based on lantern form and copied from clocks they had seen by other more capable makers. This was more common in the south of England for in the north before 1720 very few 30-hour clocks of any type are known. Traditional lantern-clock areas can therefore be considered to be leaders in 30-hour clockmaking. Care is needed, however, in defining the age of a long-case clock with birdcage or posted frame construction. This need not necessarily be an early design. Some makers from traditional areas used the arrangement on all their 30-hour clocks until the end of the brass-dial clock period and white-dial clocks featuring this type of movement are sometimes seen. Simplification of the framework of the movement is a pointer in identifying clocks made after this first quarter of the 18th century. The pleasing turned posts gave way to plain iron strips riveted into both top and bottom plates of the movement and on some the plates too are made from thin iron sheet. The reverse may equally apply, and brass could have been used throughout for either material that came easiest to hand would be used, but of course in either case brass was still used for the upright strips into which the arbors were pivoted. The posted movement on the country 30-hour clocks was generally used in traditional lantern-clock areas, but exceptions are found from time to time and so should be borne in mind when identifying a discovery. Plate 85 shows a posted movement and a large square dial of a clock by John Ismay of Oulton, near Wigton in Cumberland. It seems unlikely that this clock would have been made after 1720, but this is an early date and the clock has an unusually large dial for that time. Unfortunately the original case does not exist, but it must have been a fairly simple oak example, compatible with the crude but pleasing style of this movement. I know of one other posted-framed movement and square brass-dialled clock made in a non-traditional area, by Anthony Demaine of Skipton, Yorkshire. This is a clock with two hands, dating from 1770 and housed in its original pine case.

A country maker may often have asked his customers whether they wanted one hand or two, when ordering a 30-hour long-case clock. It could be argued that the persistence of the style of using only one hand on such a clock along with the posted-frame movement was just another lingering lantern-clock feature. Its use was, however, just as common on plate-framed clocks made in various areas until the middle of the 18th century. While 30-hour clocks with one hand only do not form a massive proportion of the total output, there were many made. This tells us that they were a distinct favourite in some country districts. The simplicity would also help to keep down the cost of making the clock and this is probably why, of the few anonymous clocks which exist, a good portion of these are single-handed. Unfortunately many of these humble creations have been altered over the years and given a different movement, usually an eight-day one with two hands. Drilling of the dial-plate to gain access to the winding squares frequently spoilt the engraving on the dial plate centre or even fouled the edge of the chapter-ring on smaller examples. A chapter-ring engraved with divisions for quarter-hours only and no minute-circle clearly gives away this alteration. Often the two substituted hands were of an unsuitable type and too large for the dial. matching brass hands made for larger white dials were commonly used for these 'improvements'. We may feel shocked that these acts of vandalism took place at all, but even 70 years ago a clock was only considered a machine for telling

88 Country long-case 30-hour clock with one hand by Elizabeth Hunt, Overton, near Basingstoke; mid-18th century.

the time, and it would be cheaper to modernise than to replace. Even so it is harder to accept that this sort of thing went on, than it is to accept an escapement modernisation which at least did not spoil the appearance of the dial. Still more difficult to accept is that these and similar alterations are carried out today by people who should know better. Only last year I was approached by a very reputable gentleman in the antique trade who wanted to substitute an eight-day movement for a 30-hour one in a long-case clock. The reason was that his customers did not like winding their clocks every day. It seems however that they don't mind their old clocks being butchered and consequently reduced in interest and value.

So far I have talked a great deal about the nature and make-up of posted movements and not so much about the variations that can be seen in the plate-movement from different work-shops. While the movement of the eight-day clock tended to be a fairly conservative area with no more recent innovation than the rack-strike of 1675, the country-made 30-hour clock tended to be more of an individual product, displaying un-expected and odd features from differing workshops up and down the country. Odd ways of doing things enable us to identify a maker by his movement alone. Generally plates were oblong, slightly taller than wide and held by a pillar at each corner. Thomas Ogden of Halifax almost always made his clock plates with a shallow arched top, while Christopher Johnson of Knaresborough frequently cut away a large semi-circular area at the base of his plates, leaving the appearance of plates with French feet. Perhaps the most curious plates can be seen on 30-hour clocks made by Will Snow of Padside, Yorkshire, for his were completely skeletonised in the interests of economy. The last two makers mentioned also incorporated the escapement-arbor between the plates with a riveted-in steel back-cock for pendulum suspension only. In Will Snow's movements steel was also used for the pillars and these were made parallel and completely undecorated. The customer who could only afford a 30-hour clock and as a result felt some shame in having it in his house, was catered for with a little deceit. Dummy winding-squares were put behind an eight-day type of dial to give the appearance of a key-wound clock. This was done on both brass- and white-dial examples in the 18th century. To com-plete the illusion, a seconds indicator was sometimes provided, even if it meant putting an idler wheel into the movement to reverse the direction of the escape wheel, for on a normal 30-hour, three-wheel train the escape-wheel runs in an anti-clockwise direction. Various methods of fitting dummy squares were adopted but generally they were simply screwed into the front plate of the clock or fixed behind the dial holes on a sheet-metal bridge. On some white-dial examples the deception was really cheapened for the squares were merely painted on to the surface of the dial—a decoration that would fool nobody.

Ninety-nine per cent of all 30-hour clocks have count-wheel strike. Very few have rack-and-snail striking because in some ways it defeats the object of making a cheaper clock. However, it did add to the reliability of the strike-work and give a repeating facility if this was desired, while still not reaching the cost of making an eight-day clock. One such is illustrated by Thomas Lister of Halifax (Plate 86) and is a good example of work by this fine provincial maker. A very odd variation in strike-work is that used by Sam Deacon of Barton in the movement of a square-drilled 30-hour clock dated December 1773 and numbered 44. The count-wheel is unconventionally placed inside the movement and pivoted over the main wheel-arbor towards the backplate. The outer rim of this wheel is not slotted but toothed like a normal wheel. The wheel is advanced by a pin mounted in the second wheel of the train which engages these teeth. This doubles as the warning- and locking-wheel. Counting the strike is done by pins along the front side of the

90 Plain posted frame movement with anchor escapement and count-wheel strike by Jeremy Spurgin.

count-wheel and the detent is lifted by these pins to cause the locking. A simple hammer blade-spring is screwed to the bottom-right pillar and the pillars themselves are completely parallel except for the enlarged area at each end. These oddities, along with other unexpected and charming features, make the collecting of country 30-hour clocks an area which still has exciting possibilities.

After the middle of the 18th century provincial clockmaking really got under way and most towns and some villages could boast a clockmaker in the community. Some towns had many clockmakers, which probably indicates the increasing market for clocks at this time. Yorkshire and Lancashire makers thrived particularly well and considering the number of clocks made and the undoubted quality of many of them, they can almost be said to have taken over where London makers left off. To qualify this statement, the changes tended to be merely stylistic, for the movement continued to be made in plate form with anchor-recoil escapement and rack-strike on eight-day clocks with little variation until the end of the long-case period. Things were not, however, as dull as this may sound. Individual makers had methods of making even the most everyday features exciting and fresh. Screw heads were sometimes shaped to look like serpents, tails of springs and other steel parts were delicately chamfered and filed, and in the days before the Birmingham movement, the front plate was nearly always interestingly scribed for the layout of the trains.

In provincial work, fancy striking is extremely rare. The usual form of strike expected in a long-case clock was for hour-striking only on a bell. The Dutch fashion of sounding the half-hours on a smaller bell never caught on in England. Similarly I have only seen, or heard of, ting-tang quarters or elaborate quarter-chiming on early London clocks. Musical long-case clocks exist and the idea of adding a third train to play music appealed to a number of makers throughout the country. These usually occur in the second half of the 18th century and most seem to be from the period of the final phase of the brass dial clock. Like a musical box, the musical train of a clock makes use of a revolving barrel, which is often pinned for a number of tunes. The pins push against and activate the hammers when the train is set in motion and the music is played on a nest of bells. The usual number in the nest is eight bells which form a complete scale. Arranged in order of size, these are usually fixed to a common staff, spaced by leather washers, and look like a stack of saucers on their sides. The number of hammers vary. Some bells may be struck by two hammers and the least-used bells by only one. Barrels which are pinned for more than one tune are made to slide horizontally so that a different set of pins are in line with the hammer tails. Tunes can usually be selected manually by moving a pointer set against a ring on the dial. The titles of the tunes are often engraved round this ring and very occasionally the clock may have a built-in facility to select a tune for each day. Some years ago I made notes about a musical clock that passed through my workshop, by John Hall of Beverley circa 1785. This clock played four tunes, and a Psalm for Sundays, on eight bells, struck by thirteen hammers. Tunes could be set manually but the clock was made to do this automatically by an arrangement of levers and stepped cams. Days and tunes are engraved round the selector ring:

Sunday – Psalm 149
Monday – Britain Strike Home
Tuesday – Lady Coventry's Minuet
Wednesday – Foot's Minuet
Thursday – Britain Strike Home
Friday – Lady Coventry's Minuet
Saturday – Foot's Minuet

The tune was played and then the hour followed, struck on the hour-bell.

The general arrangement of trains, which relates to most clocks of this type, is to have the hour strike-train on the left, the going-train in the centre of the movement and the musical-train on the right. The Hall clock which was made in this way has many features including a painted moon-dial in the arch, a chime/silent lever and the usual seconds pointer and a date-ring at the base of the dial centre. Winding of the going-train

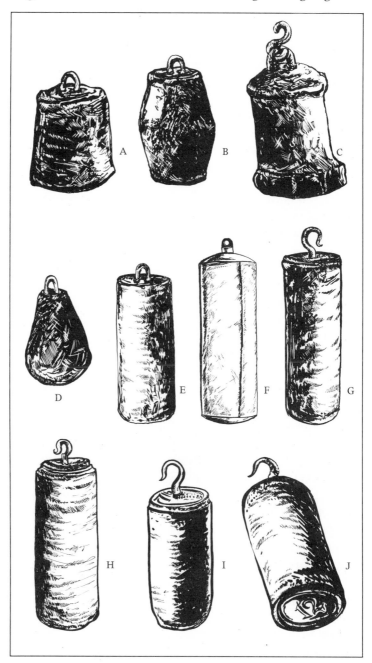

A,B,C Lantern clock weights of lead, of various shapes.
D Pear-shaped lead weight from a lantern clock alarm train.
E Lead weight used on early types of long-case clock.
F Brass-cased weight of the type used on early clocks of high-quality, particularly London-made ones.
G,H Two iron weights generally associated with white-dial clocks.
I Cast-iron weight showing the weight cast into its upper surface. This would be intended for a 30-hour clock.
J Cast-iron weight, one of a pair intended for eight-day clock use. Its weight, 12 lbs, is cast into the bottom surface.

is done through the centre of the calendar-hand, whose mounting-pipe, or cannon, had been made especially large to allow this facility on a crowded dial.

One of the most neglected areas in writing of old clocks is that of the weights, whose constant and unaltered pull help to give the long-case clock its reputation as a timekeeper. We have dealt with the expected weight on clocks going for various durations except to say that 7 lb is the normal weight for a going and striking 30-hour clock. The very first weights used on domestic clocks were made of lead. Like most things of this period, individual shapes are met with and weights were often round chubby lumps of lead, or they could be eight-sided or sometimes pear-shaped. The very first long-case clocks were equipped with cylindrically-shaped lead weights, and the higher quality clocks, which meant many of them towards the end of the 17th century, were encased in brass. These were carefully made with domed tops incorporating a cross-drilled boss at the top of fixing the suspension hook. Generally these tops are screwed on to an iron centre-rod in the weight by a female thread in the previously mentioned boss. Lantern clocks and 30-hour clocks almost always retained the basic lead weight. Provincial clocks are rarely seen with brass-encased weights as an original feature. The high-quality, eight-day and longer duration clocks usually have rather long cylindrical weights. With the increased production of clocks, and the manufacture of parts in factories, the clock weight received its share of attention. We therefore expect a white-dial clock to be driven by cast-iron weights, though I have no doubt that some did begin life with lead weights and some late brass-dialled clocks with iron weights. Large flat hooks were generally cast into the iron variety whereas lead weights often had an unbroken iron staple cast into their tops for suspension by a wire hook attached to the weight-pulley. Some iron weights are seen with their weight cast into the surface. This is found on the top rim or sometimes on the bottom, where it is more likely to be large and in the centre, protruding rather than in inverted form. On an eight-day clock, where a pair of weights were involved, one is often seen to be larger than the other although matching in other details. The larger weight goes to the strike train. Many clocks are over-weighted and a well-adjusted eight-day clock in good order may be found to run perfectly well on a 4 lb weight. The 12 lbs to 16 lbs which is normally found, will keep the clock running long after it should have stopped for attention. This is one of the reasons why so many clocks that have been used regularly are considerably worn.

Chapter 7

Bracket clocks

Portability was one of the most attractive features of the bracket clock. It could be carried from room to room and used on a side-table or stood on the mantle-piece, as its less commonly used alternative name of mantle-clock implies. In many examples the bracket clock was more of a jewel than the long-case clock. This was not just because of its size but its decoration was frequently more elaborate and the extra work involved in the making of reliable springs to drive it was extremely costly. It was partly these two factors of expense and the very considerable difficulty in drawing out reliable steel springs which made the bracket clock a rarity in provincial centres at an early date. The spring would not give an even pull to the clock. It was particularly strong when newly-wound but not so vigorous when running down. As a result a special feature was developed to overcome this problem of unevenness in the spring-action. This device is known as the fusée, found in all good English spring-driven clock and watch work. The principle involved in this mechanism is one of ratios, as in a variable gearbox; but the spring barrel and the fusée are not directly linked except by the line which is wound from the spring barrel to the fusée in winding and in the opposite direction as the clock runs. The spring inside the barrel is arranged to remain partially wound even when all the line is back onto the barrel and the clock is wound down. This is necessary to keep the line in tension or it will fall off the barrel and onto the arbor, causing great problems at each winding time. In 19th-century bracket-clock work a finely pitched roller-chain or a twisted wire line replaces the more traditional gut-line used in the 17th and 18th century work. Even with this sophisticated device, rates of timekeeping never equalled those obtained with the constant weights and the long pendulum of the long-case clock.

It was for portability and reliability that the bracket clock retained its use of the verge escapement long after it became obsolete for good timekeeping. The reasons are similar to those given in the chapter on lantern alarm clocks: a clock which

might be stood on a rickety tripod table or an uneven mantle-shelf needs to be fairly insensitive to levels. Clocks were made by sophisticated London makers and others with the verge escapement and bob-pendulum as late as 1780. The short bob-pendulum directly linked to the pallet-arbor did not have to be used with the verge escapement. Early high-quality examples are found with provision on the dial for making the clock go slower or faster. This is done by turning a hand which is set in a sub-dial. The pendulum could be raised or lowered from its point of suspension by leverage controlled by this adjustable hand. The pendulum therefore had to be suspended from this lever by a flat spring, and control the escapement via a crutch, just as the long pendulum does in long-case work. An elaborate and heavy clock, perhaps situated permanently on the mantle-piece, could therefore have its pendulum adjusted for time-keeping from the front. Otherwise there would be the incon-venience of lifting the clock down to open the back door. From about 1690 until approximately 1740 the mock pendulum was used as a decorative feature on the dial's centre. This showed

91 *Left:* An ebony chiming bracket clock by Tompion and Banger, London, clock no 92. The dial plate is an upright oblong shape, to accommodate the two sub-dials at the top; circa 1710.

92 *Right:* Movement of a bracket clock by Henry Jones, circa 1680. The verge escapement and bob pendulum, as well as the pull-repeat mechanism can clearly be seen.

through a lunette-shaped slot of about $2\frac{1}{2}''$ cut in the dial-plate, immediately beneath the figure twelve. This small disc, often engraved with a sunburst design, was directly connected to the pallet-arbor by a wire and monitored the action of the pendulum. It is sometimes stated that this device allowed one to see at a glance if the clock was going. This is hardly necessary, for its characteristic noisy click is unmistakeable.

As in other types, the earliest striking bracket clocks used the method of count-wheel strike. Mounted externally on the backplate these count-wheels tended to be rather small and placed high, to the right of the plate. Many bracket clocks did not have a strike-train but were made with a pull repeating facility for bedroom use. Others had both an hour-strike and the repeat-work, which was usually the type known as quarter-repeat, making use of two bells. The deeper-pitched bell struck the hours and on the higher, one blow indicated each quarter passed. The principle of a snail and a gathered rack was first used in bracket clocks to facilitate this pull quarter-repeat and later it was used for the conventional hour-strike-train as well. When used in pull-repeat work the rack was made without a tail. An extension on the end of the toothed rack butted against the snail and was gathered up not by a single-toothed pallet but by a pinion with six or more leaves. The action of pulling the repeat-cord both wound the spring which gave the power and forced the rack-extension against the edge of the snail. When the cord was released the rack was wound back by the pinion to strike the approp-riate hour and quarter. Since the amount of the rack's movement towards the snail depended upon the hour, it can be seen that the cord could not be pulled quite so far at one o'clock as it could at twelve o'clock. In later bracket clocks, using the conventional rack-and-snail method of strike, the snail was mounted independently of the hour-wheel and changed by a star-wheel in one positive action just before the warning for the next hour. This provided accuracy when using the strike rack to repeat the previous hours. The example shown in Plate 94 works as an hour-repeater in this way. This example on a long-case clock dated about 1740 is extremely unusual for the feature is rarely found outside bracket-clock work.

The repeat facility does not seem to have been used quite so much during the last quarter of the 18th century, when the anchor escapement became a regular feature in bracket clock movements. The elaborate repeat and strike work which was found early in the century was abandoned. Most bracket clocks were now made with a simple hour-strike.

959

Musical-trains were found in bracket clocks more regularly than in long-case work and also had their more popular period earlier. Most were made in the second quarter of the 18th century. These worked in just the same way as described in the chapter on long-case clocks but were driven by a strong spring and not a weight. Occasionally musical-trains also operated automated figures in the dial-arch. These were frequently musicians or dancers for the tunes played were often marches, jigs or minuets.

Since it was an achievement to operate the clock at all with the springs available, bracket clocks which go for longer than eight days are extremely rare. One magnificent year clock was made by Thomas Tompion for William III. This clock struck the hours and also incorporated a repeating facility. The spring barrels and fusées needed to run the clock are so large that they took up three-quarters of the total space of the movement, and the wheels and pinions of the rest of the trains are extremely delicately constructed.

The fully-blown bracket clock was a showpiece of superb craftsmanship, and above all it provided a focus for the engraver's skills. Backplates came to be highly decorated in

93 *Left:* Another view of the movement by Henry Jones (Plate 92), showing the rack-and-snail arrangement, used as a pull quarter-repeater.

94 *Right:* Long-case clock movement (eight-day) by James Woolley of Codnor. The strike snail is mounted on a twelve-toothed star-wheel. This is advanced by a pin (hidden) in twelve distinct movements, to give increased accuracy in striking of the last hour in repeat work. This feature is unusual in a long-case clock, but was frequently used in bracket clocks.

96 *Opposite:* Satinwood bracket clock, by James Stewart, Glasgow, circa 1795. The case is inlaid with tulip wood and holly. Temple Newsam House, Leeds.

97 English cartel wall-clock in carved and gilded wooden case. Movement by James Gibbs, London, around 1760. Lady Lever Art Gallery, Port Sunlight.

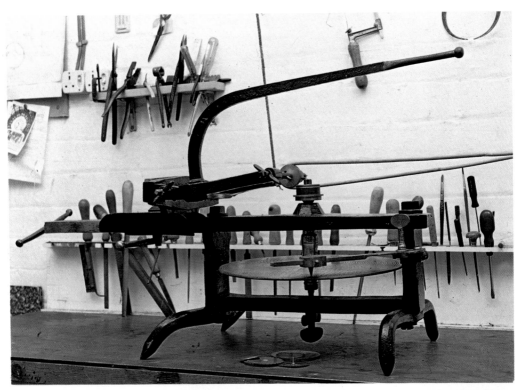

98 Anonymous bracket clock backplate, with fine rococo engraving. The bob-pendulum is seen hooked to one side for carrying.

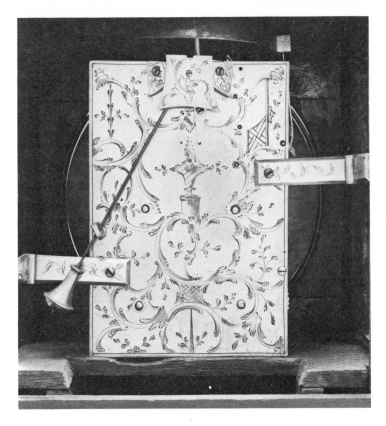

99 *Opposite above:* 18th-century wheel-cutting engine by Thomas Green of Liverpool. The concentric rings of holes for dividing the teeth and the peg used to measure out the number of teeth required on the wheel, are clearly shown. Craven Museum, Skipton, on loan from the Rector and Church Wardens of Carlton Parish Church.

100 *Opposite:* A modern method of wheel cutting using a small lathe fitted with a dividing attachment (left); fly cutter on the vertical slide (right).

this way. At first, in the late 1660s and 1670s, the engraving was restricted to the count-wheel whose centre was usually engraved with a Tudor Rose. On some fine examples each hour was numerically engraved beneath the appropriate slot. The backplate was decorated only with the maker's name. By the 1680s floral and foliate engraving spread over the backplate and was enclosed by an engraved line close to the plate's edge. The maker's name continued to appear in an engraved cartouche in the lower central area and, on some clocks, not on the dial at all. The overall decoration continued on most examples and styles developed with the taste in vogue. Examples with foliage arabesques from 1700 will often be found enclosed by a wheat ear or herringbone border while in Rococo examples in the mid-18th century, the shapes are free and unbounded except by the limits of the plate. Highly decorated and exaggeratedly shaped back-cock covers were fitted in clocks between 1680 and 1700. The practical purpose of these was to hold the rear of the pallet-arbor into its V-slot, but they were developed into intricately engraved and pierced decoration. An example of work of this period is shown by Plate 92 on a clock by Henry Jones. Circular clock plates are

965

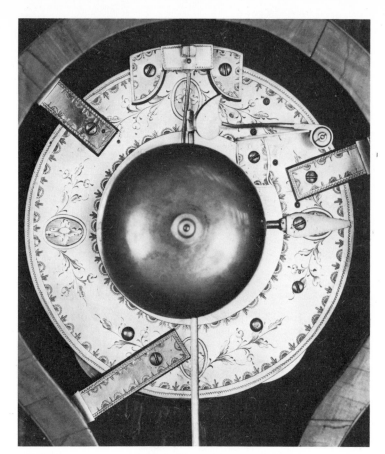

101 *Left:* Circular bracket clock plates engraved in the neo-classical taste, from the clock by Stewart of Glasgow, circa 1795, shown in Plate 98. This clock is controlled by an anchor escapement. Temple Newsam House, Leeds.

highly unusual on English clocks, but are clearly an obvious choice when the movement is fitted into the upper part of a narrow-waisted, balloon-shaped clock such as the one shown from Gillows' estimate books (Plate 67) and the example shown on page 962 by Stewart of Glasgow (Plate 96). This clock dates from about 1795 and has an anchor-escapement and hour-strike of the rack variety. While the layout is conventional enough, the design and finish are superb, a great deal of thought having been given to the engraved backplate and positioning of the bell, even though the back door is not glazed. The engraving is seen to be in the neo-classical taste which was popular with decorators at this time.

The movement and case of these clocks can be seen to have very little contact when viewed from the back and sides, though firm fixing is essential if the clock is to be reliable. The clock by Henry Jones shows how the oblong movement-plates sit on strips of oak in the case bottom. Two square-headed screws pass upwards from underneath the case and into threaded holes cross-drilled into the bottom two movement

Right: Methods of fixing a bracket clock into its case:
A Right-angled metal straps screwed to backplate and case sides.
B Circular discs with one flat side. These are fixed to the back of the dial and are shown in the locked position with the round edge turned into a slot in the case. To remove, the flat side is turned toward these slots thus releasing the dial from the case. These are principally used on early clocks, in association with C.
C Large screws which come from beneath the case and fix into threaded holes in the bottom two movement pillars.

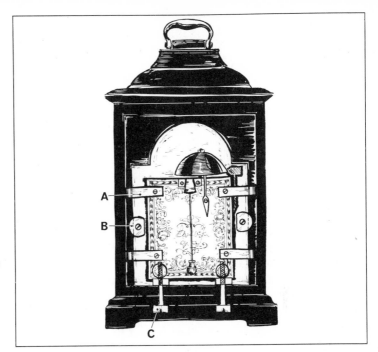

pillars. This fixing is very firm but occasionally augmented by a rotary latch at each side of the back of the dial-plate. This is an ingenious little device which will be better understood by means of the drawing above. Slightly later and possibly introduced initially for heavier and more complicated movements was the right-angled or elbowed bracket; this was screwed to the backplate and also the inside of the case. The screws passed from the outside of the case to a threaded hole in the elbowed bracket. At first these were used in conjunction with pillar-screws through the base. On later clocks these were used as the sole means of fixing the movement to the case, and were engraved to match the backplate.

In order to stabilise the bob-pendulum while carrying the clock, a hooked device was normally fitted to the backplate of the movement. Since the wire pendulum rod is usually somewhat flexible, the pendulum could be sprung into this hook, where it would safely stay. Later clocks with pendulums hung from a suspension spring needed an even more rigid fastening and this was achieved by fixing a block to the backplate which was slotted to the width of the pendulum rod. A broad-headed screw could be screwed into the block next to the pendulum rod which trapped the rod firmly while travelling. When the clock was in action, the screw could be placed safely out of the way by screwing it into a specially provided hole in one of the movement fixing brackets.

Chapter 8

Wall clocks

This chapter deals with clocks made to hang on the wall. It was never really a very popular area once the lantern-clock period had passed. Possibly this was something to do with the difficulty of suspending heavy movements and weights when a long-case clock could be had that would easily stand on the floor and take up very little extra room. Early examples were weight-driven and from the mid-18th century clocks driven by springs were introduced.

Mention has already been made in the chapter on lantern clocks of the hooded wall clocks made at the end of the 17th century. Constructed like a long-case clock in most respects but with no trunk, these cases were mainly in walnut, with or without marquetry inlay. A decorative carved under-structure on the bracket supported what was virtually a smaller version of the long-case clock hood. The weights—one or two depending on whether it was an eight-day or 30-hour clock—were always on view, generally cased in brass to enhance their appearance. These clocks may have had one or two hands, or be of plate or posted construction, and long-pendulum or verge-pendulum control. Few were made in comparison to other types and they are now so rare that today's collector may almost disregard them.

During the early years of the 18th century a large wall-hung, weight-driven clock was developed for use in public buildings. This is known as an Act of Parliament clock, after an Act of 1797 which imposed a stiff tax on ownership of clocks and watches. Clocks were charged with an annual tax of five shillings. This tax, similar to the one imposed on house windows, was soon seen to be unwise and was repealed after only nine months. During its period of enforcement however, people were said to have hidden, or in some way disposed of, their clocks and pocket watches, relying on the large Act of Parliament clocks provided in inns. We know that clocks of this type had been made for at least 80 years before the Act and so, although providing a horological reminiscence of an unpopular parliamentary decision, the name is not very accurate.

102 Tavern clock by William Scafe, London, circa 1760. This is a large clock and should have a sweeping centre seconds hand, which has been temporarily removed. The principal hands are not original; the movement is shown in Plate 106. Temple Newsam House, Leeds.

These clocks were used in a variety of public places. They are recorded in churches, chapels and in the corridors and kitchens of country houses, but their main use seems to have been as tavern clocks and I think we should favour this name for historical accuracy.

Some coaching inns did have lofty rooms even at the end of the 17th century and tavern clocks would have been hung high up in a prominent place. The earliest known clock of this type has a japanned case and eight-sided dial surround, with inscribed on a curious carved medallion below the clock: 'The Gift of Sir Frances Forbes 1714'. Unfortunately it is not known for what purpose the clock was made.

The predominant feature of the tavern clock is its large dial compared to its short case body, which is just long enough to accommodate a seconds pendulum. Since visibility was the important factor this is to be expected. Dials were as large as 30″ in diameter and were virtually made as part of the case. To start with they were made of wood. Oak was frequently used for the dials, which were constructed of two or three pieces or planks placed vertically side-by-side, butt-jointed and reinforced with cross-members at the back. Case bodies and decorative features were usually made in pine. The finish of the majority of the clocks up to about 1780 was black japan work. The lettering and dial work were in gold on the black ground, and decorative detail frequently was inspired by the oriental, although always japanned in this country. The door of the trunk was usually treated pictorially and these pictures often give a clue to the original use of the clock. The clock by William Scafe illustrated in Plate 102 shows three men in European dress, seated at a table drinking. Above this scene and providing a japanned border to the arched door are bunches of grapes. Carved ornaments at top and bottom of this case also have the grape as their subject, indicating that this clock was made for a tavern. A late tavern clock by Moore of Ipswich makes use of a montage of figures made up of coloured engravings on its door. Paper prints were cut out and stuck on to make a picture depicting an English tavern scene. That this is original work seems to be in no doubt since it is bordered by gold lines and varnished in, taking on the same patination and age as the rest of the case.

Most of us can recognise tavern clocks from their large dials and small bodies but their silhouettes can vary radically. The first examples had octagonal edges to their dial frames but had round painted rings, indicating the minute and other markings. A half-round wooden bead formed decoration along this octagonal edge. This shape of dial proved a favourite and

969

occurred on tavern clocks throughout the period of popularity (drawing A). Another early style was a straight-sided dial with an arched top, with the bottom corners of the dial area cut away to provide a smooth flow between the line of the dial and the case (as in B). Some kept the base of their dials square and had fretted ear-pieces or brackets to provide the same visual flow into the line of the trunk (drawing C). A re-occurrence of the octagonal dial is shown in D, this time with a plain parallel trunk to the case and the whole of the case front taken up by the arch-topped door. The style using a round dial and parallel case trunk shown in drawing E dates from about 1770-80 and was of the later type. Occasionally, these were made in pine and veneered in mahogany.

In many ways the dials of tavern clocks are reminiscent of the dials of church-tower clocks, with their plank construction and gold-leaf number work. Also the way in which the dial is presented, with its surface unprotected by glass or a cover of any sort. As a result the clock needed to be hung high out of

A Early tavern clock with octagonal dial, circa 1714.
B Straight-sided dial with arched top, circa 1755.
C Elaborate case with carved decoration and brackets under the lower squared edge of the dial, circa 1760.
D A simple octagonal-dial tavern clock, circa 1770.
E Round-dialled tavern clock with decorative brackets, circa 1770-80.
F Early English dial with well-proportioned case. Late 18th early 19th century.
G Later English dial with less pleasing lines. Mid-late 19th century.
H English drop dial. Late 19th century.

reach of interfering hands. Early dials were usually written in gold on a black ground and after about 1770 a white ground was used for the dial, lettered in black. This, however, is not a firm rule, for on the previously-mentioned clock inscribed 'the gift of Sir Francis Forbes' the lettering was written in black on white, and it has more finely detailed brass hands than later clocks do. Polished brass hands were used throughout and these were fairly simple and frequently matching in the same way as on a long-case clock, the minute-hand being an elongated form of the hour-hand. A favourite device for terminating the counter-balanced end of the minute-hand was a crescent moon.

The clockmaker's name or signature was a prominent feature of the tavern clock's design and was written in large flowing gilt script, sometimes as much as 4″ high. On the earlier and middle period clocks this is to be found in the area of the dial, underneath the 30-minute marker. Usually the name of the town was written in the same flowing script. Later tavern clocks are generally found to have the signature painted on the trunk, just below the rim of the dial. When this is the case the trunk door top is convex, to afford the space, and the letters are similarly placed to echo this convex arrangement. The maker's name continues to be written in script but the town is often found in capital letters of a less flowing type. To call these timekeepers' clocks is not strictly accurate as they were invariably without a striking-train. The reason for this is not hard to find. We have already mentioned the difficulty of fixing a heavy clock and large lead weights to the wall. The weight needed to drive these clocks for eight days (the normal duration) was heavier than that in a long-case clock because the cases only allow the weight a very short fall. To compensate for this, an extra wheel was needed, making five in the train; and this required additional weight to drive it. The hands too were larger than usual. So large, in fact, that a counter-balanced design of minute-hand was always used, to reduce the drag imposed on the movement in lifting the hands. Sometimes the hour-hand was decoratively counterbalanced too and very occasionally one also sees a centre seconds hand. The high-quality movement shown in Plate 106 is from the tavern clock by Wm. Scafe, London, in about 1760 and shows that it has its escape-wheel placed in line with the hand pipes, with the escape arbor extended through the centre of these to provide a drive for centre seconds work. The minute work is geared from the second wheel of the unusual hour-wheel train, between the plates, while the hour pipe is driven from the same arbor but

103 Unusual anonymous tavern clock dated 1776. This clock has a single counterbalanced hand. The case has been altered, and made longer in order to increase the duration between windings. The clock was designed as a pull-wind 30-hour clock.

971

104 English dial with single train, shown from behind with the case backbox removed.

via a gear squared on to it, outside the main plates. The movement is fixed to the back of the dial by four wooden screws from the brass fixing plate attached to the front of the movement. While this fixing plate is laid in a horizontal plane to the vertical arrangement of the movement plates, its front surface is partially scribed and laid out with the same unusual wheel arrangement as the clock. This was obviously intended as the front plate, before being discarded, turned on its side and then used as an earlier form of the later iron false plate used to connect some white dials to their movements. The wheel work and design for the pillars is London work of high quality. The weight needed to drive this sturdy train is 18 lbs. Because of this centre seconds feature and the larger number of teeth in the wheels, the movement of this clock is unusually large, having plates measuring $6\frac{1}{2}'' \times 4\frac{3}{4}''$, more like the plates found on an eight-day striking clock. The single train of a tavern clock could easily be incorporated in plates much smaller than this and usually were. A reduction was made in their width, leaving the plates parallel, though long and thin in shape.

The usual way of mounting a movement in these cases was to sit it on a wooden seatboard built at a suitable height inside the case. The dial, which was detachable, was not directly connected to the movement but to the sides of the case trunk. Holes for the hand pipes and winding arbor were made to coincide.

105 *Opposite:* Black Forest novelty clock, surmounted by a carved and painted wooden figure which eats plums. P. Dickinson of Preston would be merely the retailer. Late 19th century or possible even 20th century.

50 *Left:* Superb walnut year-going long-case clock by Morgan Lowry, Leeds, circa 1740. Abbey House Museum, Kirkstall, Leeds.

51 *Above:* Large red lacquer musical bracket clock by John Hodges, circa 1735. Temple Newsam House, Leeds.

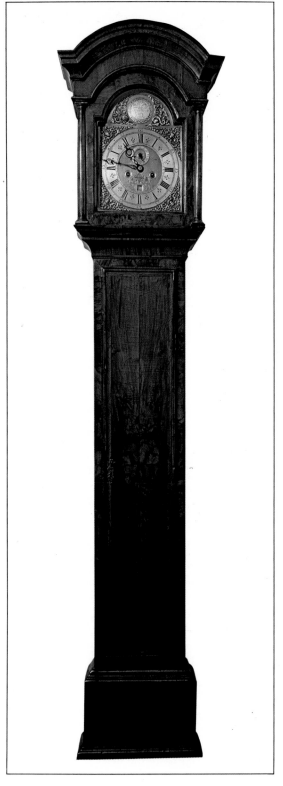

902

52 *Opposite left:* Country long-case clock by William Noke, Bridgnorth, about 1740.

53 *Opposite right:* Walnut long-case clock by William Troutbeck, Leeds, about 1725. The trunk and door are unusually long and the base is shallow, though showing no signs of having been cut down. The clock hands are not original.

plain, but bulls-eye glass with its green tint was also used. Undoubtedly this provided the most pleasing and decorative look as it distorted and obscured the view of lines and the case backboard, while at the same time the pendulum's glint makes an attractive kaleidoscope. A brass or wooden bezel was used to edge this feature. The wooden ones were polished or gilded; some were ebonised. A few cases from the brief experimental period in the 1670s when pendulums were not a standard length can be seen with a glass lenticle in the base of the case. This indicates that the clock was equipped with a $1\frac{1}{4}$-seconds pendulum, some 61″ long; but these are very rare.

Case doors were large, and in fact took up the whole frontal area of the trunk. They were plain and straight-topped, surrounded with a beaded edge that overhung the dimensions of the door.

In line with other items of furniture at this time, veneered walnut clock cases showed a distinct progression in style. In Restoration times many Dutch craftsmen were employed in England and their massive influence can be seen in the use of parquetry designs in the 1670s and later bird and flower marquetry in the 1680s in panels on the main parts of the case such as the trunk and base. Borders were cross-banded in walnut veneer, and the whole laid on a purpose-built oak carcase. Various woods were used to make veneers for marquetry work and some were stained to give unexpected colours such as green. The edges of a piece in the marquetry design might be burnt in hot sand to give a contrasting dark-shaded edge, and so enhance the sense of drawing in the designs. Mouldings which could not be veneered were made in walnut pieces with the grain laid across the width of the mould. These were glued on to an oak backing piece before being shaped by the moulding plane. This characteristic style is known as cross-grained moulding and is a distinct feature of the walnut period.

By the 1690s marquetry work on clock cases had reached a high level and all-over designs of the so-called seaweed marquetry covered the cases in delicate arabesque designs. This was considered to be a truly English style and was far more delicately executed than the relatively crude Dutch-inspired work of the previous decade. Marquetry was cut from sheets of differently coloured veneers while cramped together, and identical work has been found on two cases which indicates the marquetry was cut at the same time.

While these developments were taking place, clock cases also grew taller to suit the higher plaster-ceilinged interiors of

54 Detail of the base moulding of a walnut long-case clock showing the character of cross-grain moulding.

903

the town houses of the day. With this, dial sizes increased to 11″ and case trunk width also increased in proportion, but generally no more than an inch wider than the dial. Also from this time it became usual for the clock hood to slide forward, and a door was made in the hood for winding and setting the hands. A cushion top was added above the moulding of the hood, often flanked by two or three plinths surmounted by brass ball, or ball-and-spire finials. Some clocks had turned wooden ball finials which were finished with gesso and gilded. This also added to the clock's height. If a marquetry case was not required then the wood used would be well-figured walnut, veneered and crossbanded in just the same way, but with choice burr veneers used on trunk, door and base. Thomas Tompion was known to favour a plain veneered walnut case throughout the marquetry period. On some of these cases the veneers were arranged in the method known as 'oyster shell' parquetry, after their similarity in appearance to that species. The veneers were cut as a section across a small branch, its annular rings giving the irregular circular design. Both olive wood and walnut were used to make the oyster pieces.

55 *Left:* A bird-and-flower marquetry panel, from the case door of the month-going clock illustrated in Plate 35.

Provincial makers in cities throughout the country must have ordered cases from London makers, for occasionally one comes across a high quality walnut- or marquetry-cased clock in original and unaltered condition by such a clockmaker. There are also lesser cases with marquetry more sparsely arranged and not so well carried out which are presumably the work of provincial cabinet makers. From 1720 there was an increasing number of country clocks with solid oak cases. These were of both the 30-hour and eight-day duration; many of these were nicely made and echo the proportions and style of more sophisticated London clocks.

Lacquer cases decorated in the oriental manner began to appear in England in the last 20 years of the 17th century. Oriental furniture had been imported in small quantities since the reign of Elizabeth I but the flamboyant tastes of the Restoration provided for its popularity. Opinions differ about whether cases were made in England and sent on the long sea voyage to the East for lacquering or whether they were lacquered in England in imitation of the oriental style. Early in this period of popularity some cases were undoubtedly sent to the East but most were made and decorated in London to oriental recipes and designs. The pictorial parts of the design were raised up in a gum-based gesso and then gilt with details drawn in by brush. This was backed by an overall coloured lacquer ground. Colours were mainly dark; blues, greens and black and more rarely red, yellow and a paler turquoise blue were used. In bracket clocks lacquering did not enjoy the same popular appeal as on the long-cases. At the same time the lacquer artists were well known for their imitation of tortoise-shell and marble effects used successfully on bracket clock cases. The carcase wood for cases was more usually oak but occasional high-quality lacquer clocks were made from pine. This taste for lacquer spanned the period from the square dial to the beginning of the arched dial clock about 1720. The art was taken up by amateurs who were said to lacquer many unsuitable pieces of furniture of all types; the style flourished and then by 1730 lost its appeal.

Later in the 18th century lacquering again became popular for long-case clocks. The carcase wood at this time was invariably oak and the shape of the cases was generally that typical of the pagoda-style hood or round-topped mahogany clock of this period. The fashion lasted for about ten years and died out finally in about 1780.

In their *Treatise of Japaning and Varnishing* (1688) J. Stalker and G. Parker claimed that 'no damp air, no moulding worm or corroding time, can possibly deface the work'. Many cases which survive are distinctly shabby now and unlike polished wood they are difficult to renovate successfully. Consequently they have been less than popular with collectors in recent years.

Towards the middle years of the 18th century London clockmakers were not called upon to make so many long-case clocks. Portable or bracket clocks and clocks fulfilling a special need, such as precision regulators for observatory or similar work, continued to be made, with some fine domestic long-case clocks later on in the mahogany period around 1760-90. The emphasis of case development from this period onwards therefore shifts from London to provincial centres and from specialist clock-case makers to cabinetmakers and country joiners who made all manner of things from breakfront bookcases to coffins. The factor in deciding its style depended not entirely on when it was made as where it was made and by whom. Geographical differences made quite a number of variations in the interpretation of a nationally used style, and an expert can begin to say what part of the country a piece was made by looking at the case alone.

By far the most common wood used for provincial cases was oak. From the early 18th century this was used on its own, relying on the decorative rays of its grain in quarter-cut form for case doors, base panels and so on. From about 1740 cross-banding was popular and, in common with other country-made pieces of furniture, this was applied to the edges of doors and base panels in bands varying in width from $\frac{1}{2}''$ to $2''$. The veneer used in banding was usually mahogany although walnut is not unknown. Cases made in this later style might have had a backboard in oak, but deal was equally common. Mahogany is not generally thought to have been used in furniture-making until after the mid-18th century; 1760 is the date usually given. Robert Gillow, a joiner and cabinetmaker and founder of the important firm of Gillows of Lancaster, is recorded as making 'a clockcase of mahogany' in 1743. The firm went on to produce many more fine clockcases in mahogany, oak and pine during the 18th century, and has left us a unique record of their work in ledgers, estimate books and drawings. Plate 57 shows the handwritten estimate for a mahogany long-case and Plate 58 the design and measurements for the case.

The better-quality mahogany cases were those using choice mahogany veneers glued on to an oak carcase. Mouldings and cornices were made from the solid and occasionally

56 *Above:* Country oak case of a one-handed clock by Jeremy Spurgin, Colchester, of about 1695.

57 *Opposite:* Estimate for a mahogany long-case from one of Gillows' handwritten estimate books.

June y 19th 1788 — a Clockcave with arch'd Face, Mah'y (323)

- 2¾ ft of 1 Inch Mah'y and Birch'r Vin'. the door at 1/10 p ft — 5 0½
- 2½ ft of 1 Inch Oak and Birch'r Vin'. and Kingwood d° the Pedistall front — at 1/6 p ft] 3 9
- 10½ ft of ½ Inch Mah'y Sides of Body Head and Pedistall — at 7 p ft] — 6 1½
- 9½ ft of 1 Inch Mah'y Mouldings Pillers Columns and Part of front and Glass frame &c — at 1/2 p ft] — 11 1
- 2 ft of 1 Inch deal, Mah'y and Kingwood Vin'. a Part of the Head — at 1/— p ft] 2 0
- 1¼ of ½ Inch Part of the Glass frame — 7½
- 1¾ ft of ¼ Inch Mah'y — at 4 p ft — 7
- 9¾ ft of ½ Inch Oak the Back &c d° — at 2¾ p ft — 2 2½
- 3½ ft of ½ Inch and ¼ Inch deal — at 1½ p ft — 4 ¼
- 1 Lock Escutchion and Hinges — 1 10
- 1 Pair of Swan Neck Hinges and Ring for Glass door — 3
- 2 Pair of Corinthian Caps and Bases — 5 4
- Turning the Columns Caps and Bases and Mould's — 2 4
- 1 Shuld and 2 Roses for d° — 2 6
- Glew Oil wax Nails and Incidents — 2 10
- Makeing d° Christ'n Procter — Compute as per c. v.
- Glass for the door in the Head — — 4
                                        £ 0 00 10½

June y 19th 1788   a Bracket for a Bust or Vase

- 2 ft of 5/8 Inch Mah'y — at 7 p ft — 1 2
- 1 ft of ½ Inch Mah'y — at 6 p ft — 6
- Mah'y Vin'. for the Rim glew'd up in three — 4
- a Piece of Mah'y for a Block on the top of d° — 2
- 3 Brass Holdfasts and Skrews for d° — 3
- Makeing d° Tho' Romney — 2 days — u v
- Glew Oil and Incidents — d d
                                        m ∠

- a Case to Pack d° 8½ ft of ½ Inch deal at 1½ p ft — 10½
- Trunk Nails — 1½
- Makeing d° and Packing 1 Hour — 1 9 0

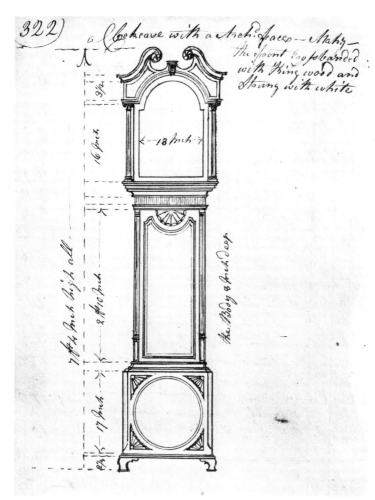

322)

a Clockcase with a Arch'd faces — Mahy
the front Crossbanded
with King wood and
Strung with white

58 *Left:* Drawing with measurements relating to the estimate shown in Plate 57.

59 *Below:* Cuban mahogany long-case clock by John Hawthorn, Newcastle, circa 1780.

used the cross-grained style for effect, but straight-grained mouldings were more usual. Flame or feathered designs could be achieved by matching veneers cut from the same piece of wood and arranging them symmetrically side by side. Mahogany cases of this type tend to be in the dark rich wood known as Cuban mahogany, as much of it was imported from there. Probably one reason for its early use by Gillows is that it would have been imported into Liverpool, an important port trading with the Caribbean at that time. When used in the solid, mahogany never seemed to have been worked with the same kind of flair, and most used wood with unexciting grain and paler colour known as bay-wood or Honduras mahogany. Late 18th-century cases made for both the brass and enamelled dial frequently displayed features common to the designs of Hepplewhite and Sheraton, particularly boxwood stringing, design of cornices, circular and oval outlines to veneered

908

60 A mahogany veneered white-dial clock by William Jackson of Workington. Boxwood stringing is used as decoration and the pediment of the hood is faced with blue glass with gilt decoration.

panels and the delicate splayed feet (known as French feet) of certain heavy white-dial clocks. Many mahogany cases at this period used a combination of thinly cut solid mahogany planks and mahogany veneers backed with pine in their carcase construction.

Many country-made clocks particularly of the 30-hours winding type with both brass and painted dials were originally housed in pine cases. These were almost always of a plain construction and shape. Flat tops were most usual but a simple version of any regional style of top can be expected.

It is currently fashionable for some antique dealers to strip and polish pine cases, leaving the wood with an exposed grain and its pale natural colour. This was never the original intention of the casemaker, who would have variously had them painted or scumbled and grained to resemble a darker and more expensive wood. Fittings used with pine cases and occasionally on less expensive country oak cases were commensurately cheaper. Instead of a small lock and key for the trunk door, a simple turn-buckle fastening was used. This was turned from the outside of the door by a simple brass ring.

The feature which most characterises the difference in case shapes is generally the hood and its decorative treatment above the dial. The hood A on page 910 is the most common shape for country work with square dials, and with minor differences was made in all regions. Side pillars to the hood could be either attached to the glazed door or separately fixed, as they were in most northern examples. Fixed pillars were most likely to have wooden turned capitals and bases finished in gesso and gilt. Separate pillars were attached to the hood by brass caps and bases. These were fastened with small brass nails to the horizontal parts of the hood. Drawing B is a development of this style with a built-up cushion or caddy top. In the example shown here this has been further heightened with another phase surmounted by a spire finial, from an eight-day clock of some quality with a solid oak case of about 1740 by James Woolley of Codnor in Derbyshire.

The swan-necked or horned pediment was another style to enjoy inter-regional popularity, but it was in the north that it was used most. Many inexpensive square-dial clocks were made in this manner, but with the popularity of the arched white-dial clock the style came into its own and 90 per cent of these clocks were housed in cases with hoods like drawing D. Another elaboration of this basic style is seen on high-quality mahogany cases by some clockmakers in the north-west of England and a type which is generally thought to be

A Square-topped hood with simple moulding. This is the most common shape for country work.

B A more sophisticated variation of A, with a cushion top.

C Hood with square aperture and horned pediment.

D Hood with arched aperture and horned pediment. This was a common style for north-country white-dial clocks.

E Over-elaborate hood of the type used on mahogany clocks in the late 18th century made in the north-west of England.

F Hood with a broken-arch pediment. Although fairly rare, this type is often associated with a round dial.

G Hood with broken-arch top.

H Arched-top hood. This type had a few variations.

I Pagoda-topped hood. This example shows the more sophisticated type; less well-proportioned examples are also to be found.

J Arched-top hood with whale's tail cresting.

K Scottish hood, usually found with an arched white-dial.

L Mahogany hood of a Scottish clock, with round dial.

made by Gillows of Lancaster because of the occurrence of certain features. These include the built-up box section behind the swan neck pediment, an exaggerated cushion mould or a heavy central plinth surmounted by decorative finials. Underneath the curving forms and forming the pediment proper are glass panels, usually a rich blue decorated with gold painted scrolls and foliage. The supporting pillars, usually reeded, may come in pairs either side of the hood but more usually they are single separate pillars with high-quality brass capitals and bases. This style is illustrated by drawing E. Circular decorations or paterae decorated the terminal scroll of the horns and these could be made in various ways.

Early clocks of the brass dial era were likely to have cast brass paterae finished in gilt. Later clocks, forming the majority under consideration, had stamped out brass paterae which were finished in gilt or simply polished and lacquered. Simple ring-turned wooden paterae were occasionally used, while on high-quality clocks various innovations have been seen. Thomas Ogden of Halifax on a clock similar to drawing E used a pair of lion's-mask paterae, which when cleaned proved to be a gilt finish on solid lead. Cases by Gillows of Lancaster are frequently seen with paterae carved in high relief from mahogany in the shape of roses. One of the styles of hood least often seen in later work is the architectural, broken-pediment style; although a similar top has been used in some fine work by Justin Vulliamy, the London clockmaker, at the end of the 18th century. It is seen also from time to time in northern clocks. The mouldings which form the top of the broken pediment being decorated in true architectural style with a dentil course. The broken pediment is also used in conjunction with round dials. Although unusual in long-case work they are sometimes found on clocks made in the Sheffield and Derbyshire area. Very similar but with a rounded profile is the broken-arched style shown in drawing G. On some simple renderings this can also look like an ill-formed and incomplete horned top but the better versions with deep-cut top moulding can be very pleasing. It is one style used nationally but seen infrequently, which suggests that it was not popular in its day. Two Leeds-made clocks known to me have hoods in this manner and their styles of construction and choice of oak suggest that they are both by the same casemaker. One of them illustrated here (Plate 61) in a plain unstrung oak case is by Henry Gamble of Bramley, Leeds, and dates from about 1770. The domed or arch-shaped top generally denotes a brass dial clock, since white dials are rarely found in a case of this style. The broken arch was used from an early date and occasionally for high-quality cases in the era of walnut about 1730. In these examples, and London ones made in the later mahogany period of 1760-80, the moulded arch surmounts a delicately fretted frieze. The style was also used early in the 18th century on well-made provincial eight-day clocks. The curved top mould in these examples was either built up in blocks and then veneered in the cross-grained manner or shaped and carved from the solid in the case wood, usually oak. Drawing H on page 910 is a hood made up in exactly this manner. Other hoods of the same design were made in southern counties, East Anglia and northern England – a particularly fine example with a walnut-veneered top-moulding is recorded by John Burgess of Wigan in about 1730. A delicate version of this style was also used on high-class London regulator clocks by makers such as Thomas Mudge and Thomas Dutton. These clock cases were made in fine well-figured mahogany and were austere in their general outlines, relying on the simplicity of line and the figure of the wood for decorative effect. In the view of many people these are among the most pleasing cases ever made.

The whale's tail cresting added to an arch-topped hood gives a completely different character to the clock and is also an interesting regional characteristic (drawing J). It was popularly used by makers in the west country. The Somerset clockmaker, Isaac Nichols, made some fine clocks using cases decorated in this way.

In the same way that long-case clocks of north-western England were typified by the swan-necked top and the majestic mahogany case in the late 18th century, the east coast of England was similarly seen to have a style of its own. The styles were not entirely exclusive to each region, for while it is common to see a pagoda-topped case on a clock made on the Yorkshire coast, it is equally common to find one made in Ipswich or even Kent. This was also a style favoured by some London makers for mahogany- and lacquer-cased clocks at the close of the 18th century. The better mahogany case of this type was likely to have brass inserts to the reeding, half way up from the base of the hood pillars. The pagoda top has, in common with all styles, many variations and interpretations. The better clocks resemble closely the tall shape illustrated by drawing I, but shallower, less-understood versions were used in some country districts.

In the pediment at the top of the hood two main types of treatment are found. A cut-away portion echoing the outline of

61 Broken-arch topped eight-day clock by Henry Gamble, Bramley, circa 1770.

62 Shallow pagoda-topped hood on a black and gold lacquered long-case clock by Robert Cutbush of Maidstone, Kent, circa 1740.

the hood would be fitted with a decorative fret cut in a curving loop pattern or occasionally with a geometric fret in the Chinese taste. This backed with silk or something similar, would serve to let out the sound of the bell, but its true purpose was decoration. Marquetry inlay was frequently used in small pointed oval panels at this point on the hood, and also on the trunk door, beneath the hood moulding on the trunk and in the hood frieze, on particularly fine mahogany examples. The subject of these inlays varied but the main ones are the cornucopia and the star-shape fan typified by the work of Robert Adam in his interiors of this time. Oak examples of this style exist in some numbers, and when well chosen and nicely shaped they look well in an undecorated form.

In a book of English clocks it may be inappropriate to mention Scottish cases, but they are so frequently seen south of the Border that all must be dealt with if only for purposes of identification. Nearly all Scottish cases are in the later phase of mahogany, using solid wood with no distinct figure; but exceptions are occasionally seen. I know of no Scottish white-dial clock case made with oak as its principal wood. The hood may look unusually top-heavy. Many hoods such as that in drawing K have a great deal of plain wood above the dial top. The pillars do not always just flank the glassed door but sometimes rise almost to the top mould, giving a distinctly odd appearance to the clock which is at first glance often hard to identify. These pillars may be plain, reeded, or even twisted in style and this can add to the unsuitability of their proportion and presentation. I hope that I may be forgiven for describing the style as distinctly numb in appearance. From time to time one sees a much more delicate style of Scottish long-case. Dating from 1780 onwards, these are usually quite delicate and whimsical in silhouette, and are made from good, well-figured mahogany. Hoods are generally variations on the style shown in drawing L; trunk doors may be shaped or decorated with carved wooden relief towards the top. On occasions the trunk sides may even be tapered or have an entasis which fits in with the whimsical and interesting appearance.

With the increased number of clock cases made by local craftsmen in town and country areas as the 18th century progressed, the frequency of maker's labels also increased, although to find one is an unusual experience. Information about the maker may also be found recorded in pen on the carcase wood of the case. I have seen two examples of this, one written underneath the seatboard of the movement and another recording the clockmaker and the first owner, written

913

OLIVER,
Clock-Case Maker,
SPALDING.

63 A case-maker's label
pasted inside on the
backboard of the clock by
Thomas Wilson of Spalding
(Plate 64).

in ink on the edge of the hood door. The label illustrated on Plate 63 is from the backboard of the eight-day clock by Thomas Wilson of Spalding (Plate 64) dated to about 1830 by its style. It is a pleasing later case, finished with well-figured mahogany veneers; the following facts are recorded about the two makers involved. Charles Oliver, the casemaker, disappeared from local trade directories by 1842. A press notice announcing the sale of the jewellery business of Thomas Wilson 'before leaving England' appears in 1849. These contemporary records show that both men were in a position to have done this work in 1830 and so confirm our dating, which was initially made on stylistic grounds.

The spreading outlines of the north country long-case clock in the 19th century have been responsible for the criticism levelled at them by clock connoisseurs over the years. However, it must be said that the workmanship and woods used in their construction were never better. On their surfaces can be seen the choicest mahogany veneers, inlays of rosewood, boxwood and sections of marquetry in satinwood, while stringing in boxwood is a common feature. Gilded patterns were sometimes used on the surface of the veneers in places such as the frieze under the hood moulding of the trunk and also on the hood frieze above the dial. Pillars in the hood were sometimes built up of a sandwich of different coloured

64 Mahogany veneered case, circa 1830, made by Charles Oliver of Spalding, for a clock by Thomas Wilson. Museum of Lincolnshire Life, Lincoln.

woods before turning. These would be bobbin-turned, balister-turned or even cut with a heavy spiral twist. Usually quarter-pillars adorned the front corners of the trunk flanking the door, which over the years became smaller and smaller until it was a disproportionate vestige of its former self. Its diminished size also hindered its function, as you will know if you have ever tried reaching inside to put on a weight. The trunk corner pillars are a typical but not exclusive feature of north-country work. This style is also found on other country-made pieces of furniture such as dressers, cupboards, chests and drawers from the mid-18th century. Capitals and bases were turned in the same wood, usually mahogany, for this wood was often used even when the pillars were to go on a basically oak piece. On occasions a better case might have brass capitals and bases. When cases originated from the Birmingham area, where foundry work was one of the local trades and castings were more plentiful, the capitals would generally be of the Corinthian type, elaborate and well finished.

Brick-work bases, arranged in mahogany veneer so that the front corners of the base looked like the corner construction of a house, were a common feature on some cases made in the north-west. The style is thought to be a feature of some of Gillow's work. The feature is generally called a Liverpool base since clockmakers in that region favoured cases in this style.

Bracket clocks were never produced in great numbers in country districts or indeed in any centres outside London. A number were made in the south, and some examples were made in East Anglia and the west country. In the north, however, bracket clocks are a distinct rarity. Personally I cannot recall seing one example made in Lancashire. As a result, a discussion of bracket clocks must centre upon London-made cases. The standard was almost always high. Country versions generally adhered to the prevailing style in London and indeed many cases may have been bought in from London casemakers.

Few bracket clocks did actually stand on wall brackets. Those that did are usually of a very late date and few original brackets survive. In fact these clocks were designed for occasional carrying and intended for use on the side table of the drawing room or at night in the bedroom, where the repeating mechanism could be used to indicate the hours and the quarters in the dark. Consideration was also given to their use on the mantelpiece, standing in front of a glass overmantel or mirror; the glass backdoor of the clock allowed a view of the elaborately engraved backplate to be reflected into the room. Bracket or mantel clock cases were at first so similar in style to

A Architectural-topped bracket clock case with elaborate metal mounts, circa 1665.

B A cushion-topped case with carrying handle, circa 1675.

C Square-dialled case with metal basket-top and elaborate carrying handle, circa 1680.

D Inverted bell-topped case, circa 1710.

E Early arch-dial case with elaborate metal basket-top, circa 1715.

F Case for clock with oblong dial. This also has an inverted bell top and carrying handle.

G Lacquer case with arch-dial aperture and side handles, circa 1740.

H Bell-topped case with plain carrying handle and brass bracket feet.

I Mahogany case for a clock with round dial, circa 1780.

J Balloon-shaped case with circular dial aperture and parquetry medallion, circa 1790-1800.

K Regency case with an oriental flavour but featuring more typically a pineapple top finial and lion's-mask carrying handles at either side.

L Black marble case of the Victorian period.

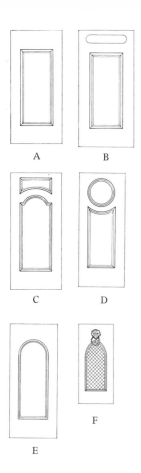

Progression of side glasses of bracket clocks:
A Simple oblong glazed aperture, circa 1670.
B Oblong-glazed aperture with round-ended fret above, circa 1680-1710.
C With the introduction of the arch-dial, side glasses echoed the arch shape, and the fret was given a concave base line; 1715-70.
D A side glass with a concave top and a circular fret. This style is associated with the bell-topped case, 1760-80.
E The shape of the side glass and fret were now combined. It might be filled with either glass or a wooden fret; circa 1780-1800.
F Gothic side fret. This was usually made in fretted brass and backed with silk.

the long-case that they looked exactly like the hoods of the tall clocks. Both portico and flat tops were used and the cases at these dates did not have the top carrying handle. From the 1670s a shallow cushion top was used on cases and the carrying handle was introduced. Ebony and ebonised pearwood veneers on bracket clock cases persisted long after they had become unfashionable on long-cases, and in fact they are not unusual on bracket clocks as late as 1770 when mahogany was the most popular wood for clock cases. Some exotic features were used on the better table clocks which never found their way on to long-case work. Metal basket tops in the shape of a bell were finely cast and chased. In some rare examples these were made of silver, but generally they were finished, along with finials and other brass mounts, in mercury gilt. The dramatic red and black veneers of tortoiseshell were sometimes used. Marquetry, kingwood and walnut were used as an alternative to the usual ebonised surface. Side glasses as well as glass doors, back and front, give an all-round view of the beautiful movements. Escutcheon plates on the front doors were balanced at either side, one for the key hole and one remaining blank. Small pierced frets were let into the tops of the doors and above the case side glasses. About 1″ deep and round-ended they were cut from a thin piece of ebony veneer and backed with silk in the usual way. Pierced basket tops were lined with silk to give a pleasing look and to keep out the dust. Areas of fretwork increased as the time went on. With the introduction of the arched dial in about 1715, the spandrel areas at the top of the door were usually filled with a suitable fretted design. From this period too, the fretwork above the side glasses tended to be shaped in sympathy with the arched side glass, and later on, with the bell-topped style of case, became circular above a concave top to the glass. This is clearly shown by the diagrams on this page. After 1780 it was fashionable to run the two shapes together and fill the total area with either fretwork or glass. Regency and Victorian bracket clocks are typified by brass side frets in a fish-scale design.

As the tops of the cases became higher and more decorative, the carrying handle was magnificently scrolled and finished, until about 1700 it slowly became more simple in its outline. Sometimes a heavy, elaborate clock such as drawing G, in the illustrations of bracket clock cases on p. 916, had no top handle at all. A departure from the basic shape, which had lasted for some 65 years, occurred with the introduction of the circular enamel and painted dial. By 1780 the style shown in drawing I was found alongside more traditional examples. Instead of having a wooden door, only the brass bezel which held the glass opened for winding and setting the hands. This idea persisted throughout the remaining years of craftsman-made cases. The most delicate and pleasing of all circular dial styles, the balloon-shaped case, is illustrated in drawing J. This style of about 1790 is almost always built up in mahogany and pine carcase woods and veneered in satinwood. It was often cross-banded in tulipwood or similar and strung with box and ebony. A shell or oval fan medallion in sand-shaded marquetry usually decorated the lower stages of the front. Cast brass ogee bracket feet complete this most elegant of designs. The topmost stage, forming a support for the finial, was not always included in this design.

Gillows of Lancaster list one of the balloon-shaped cases in their estimate book for 1800 which was made for a 'Mr Bell Lancaster'. This was likely to have been Henry Bell, Watch and Clockmaker, who was known to be working in 1800, but died in 1801. The example shown in Plate 67 was veneered in mahogany and cross-banded in canary wood, with double stringing in 'Black and White'. This was their way of saying ebony and box, which would give a black-and-white effect. Unusually the case is shown with a 'large brass lifting handle' and no medallion in the base, and while costs are shown for parts and labour, no mention is made of the brass bracket feet shown in the drawing:

A mahogany bracket clock case, crossband mahoy vinear all round the sides, birchin mahoy vinear in the front, banded with canary wood, & a dble string on each side of the band say black & white cross band mahoy O.G. & small hollow, rim, round the glass.	£	s	d
6 ft 6 of 1 in mahoy in the head, sides and top vineard with mahoy @ 2s/3d		14	7½
2 ft 6 of ⅝ in mahogany in the back @ 14d		2	11
4¼ ft of 1 in oak and mahogany birchin vinear in the case & canary wood banding @ 20d		7	1
Turning—compute			9
Large brass lifting handle			7
Brass lock 6d, one escution 1d. 2½ in brass hinge 4d			11
An ivory knob 2½d, 1 pair small brass but hinges 3d			5½
One brass turnbuckle			3
Glue screws, & incidents		1	6
Making by Simon Bryham 1 week		18	0
Glass for the door, by I Herbert		2	0
Varnishing by Thos Romney		1	6
Setting out the above at large		1	0
	2	11	7

65 Marble-cased mantle
clock with French movement
and side ornaments. Clocks
of this type were popular in
England after the death of
Prince Albert. This is a
presentation clock set, and is
dated 1883.

66 Verge lantern clock by Thomas Creed, London, circa 1670. The pendulum, in the shape of an anchor, is placed between the trains. This clock should have decorated side boxes to the doors, and the holes for fixing them can be seen behind the slot in the door.

120 *Opposite:* Hooded wall-clock of about 1680, with an eight-day striking movement. British Museum, London.

provincial centre (Leeds) at the end of the 17th century and the beginning of the 18th century, and bears all the hallmarks of an original and highly skilled workshop. Williamson's name occurs on a year clock, two-month clocks and two eight-day clocks, all of which are known to me. He was not a run-of-the-mill maker of provincial 30-hour clocks. All those mentioned are cased in walnut, parquetry, and marquetry cases. All their known clocks are long-case clocks, although other types may remain undiscovered. Both men signed their dials similarly at the base of the dial plate and used the forms 'John Williamson at Leeds Fecit' and 'William Tipling in Leeds Fecit' or very similar variations. The engraving on each dial appears to be by the same hand. Certainly their dials were inspired by the same man and were almost certainly from the same workshop.

The layout of the movements too appear to derive from the same workshop design book. Dates available suggest that Tipling, the younger man, may have been apprenticed to John Williamson, although I have no proof of this. In 1682 a John Williamson was recorded as being a member of the London Clockmakers' Company, which would account for the quality of his training. A man of this name is recorded as marrying Rebecca Whalley in Leeds, on 5th December 1683, and it seems probable that this is the clockmaker for the Leeds clocks by John Williamson date from about this time. A young man, newly married and setting up business as a clockmaker in a northern city would require an apprentice. William Tipling married Ruth Norton at St John's Chapel on 10th April 1692; in 1683 he could have been a boy of the right age to be apprenticed to Williamson. From 1692 onwards it seems likely that Tipling set up his own business, continuing to make quality clocks in the manner of his training. At this period Tipling lived at Bridgegate (Briggate) and Williamson lived at Hillhouse Bank. Williamson lived a long and productive life, having made some superb clocks; he also married three times and had fourteen children. Pre-deceased by his third wife, he died in the work-house in 1748 a very old man. Tipling on the other hand died young. He seems to have had a maintenance contract for the clock and bells at St. John's Church in Leeds, where he worked from 1694. In 1701 he received a payment of 10 shillings as his annual salary, and he died in 1712.

Henry Hindley of York (1701-71) was a clockmaker whose contribution to horology and engineering has recently been re-evaluated. After recognition in his lifetime, and shortly afterwards, his importance seems to have gone unnoticed until fairly recently. Though Henry Hindley's name is associated with

993

York where he spent most of his working life, his birth and apprenticeship were in Lancashire, possibly Manchester. Little, however, is known about this period of his life, but at least one clock signed Hindley de Wigan and made during the period 1725-30 is known. This clock bears many of the features associated with his style, along with bolt-and-shutter maintaining power and a $1\frac{1}{4}$-seconds pendulum. He moved to York as a fully trained young man in 1730 or 1731 where he set up in business as a clockmaker. As well as possessing horological skills, he was a clever engineer making many of his own tools, engines and scientific instruments for others. His renowned wheel-cutting engine made before 1741 was considered to be the best ever made and appears to have been an instrument of precision and refinement involving some very fine gear-cutting. He also developed a device for accurate cutting of fusées, used in spring-driven clockwork. He made a large tower clock for York Minster in 1750 at a cost of £300. Bracket clocks of a unique type and involving many advance features were also made. The making of bracket clocks in itself was fairly unusual, for they are extremely rare from Yorkshire makers in the 18th century. Hindley thought out every part of his work for himself and there is no doubt that he was a brilliant and inventive man. Recognisable Hindley features in a clock movement include fine gear-cutting and high numbering of his wheels and pinions, crossed-out ends to the weight clock winding barrels and knee or L-shaped blade springs to the hammers. He developed an early type of dead-beat escapement and made year-going and revolving ball moon clocks.

George Pyke (apprenticed 1739). The inspiration for including this note on George Pyke, who was active in London during the mid-18th century, is his imposing pedestal organ clock at Temple Newsam House, Yorkshire, illustrated by Plate 108.

John Pyke, his father, was a clockmaker of some eminence, but George was perhaps less so and is now remembered particularly for his automated organ clocks, a number of which survive. Both father and son were interested in making clocks with automated features and musical work, and it is thought that this interest stems from work that the elder Pyke did to complete a musical pedestal clock after the death of Charles Clay in 1740. Clay had made a number of similar clocks throughout his career and can be said to be the originator of the style, although it seems that most of Clay's musical clocks played on bells. One made in 1736, exhibited before the Queen and ultimately sold by a raffle, incorporated bells which were played by a weight-driven mechanism. The George Pyke organ clock and others known can be said to represent the mature culmination of the same style. It is detailed both in its outward appearance and the complication of its working parts. The peninsular cornered base, veneered in ebony, is hollow and gives space for the descent of the massive weight, needed to drive the organ pin-barrel and provide wind for its pipes. Plate 47 shows the dial proper and the large dial plate which is in various phases to allow for the animated figures articulated by complicated motion work via a gear-drive from the organ mechanism. These are activated three-hourly when the organ plays.

The clock mechanism is a conventional English bracket fusée movement with anchor escapement and hour striking independent of the organ. The organ consists of three registers, two of pine and one of tin, each of twenty pipes tuned at 8, 4 and 2 ft pitch governed by three manual stops (flute, principal and piccolo). There are eight tunes, selected on a numbered dial at the side. There is also an 'off/play' pointer. Two sheepskin leather bellows are pumped by a connecting rod attached to an extended 8″ flywheel, the whole being driven by a massive lead weight descending into the pedestal. The music is discharged every three hours:

Pretty Polly Hopkins
Drops of Brandy
Unidentified
Life Let us Cherish
Mrs. Whitmore
Why ever don't you come
Bergère Légère (Manimet)
Sicilian Mariner's Hymn

The tune selection dial is engraved by the maker George Pyke, Bedford Row, London, and the sound board is inscribed March 1765.

James Woolley, Codnor, Derbyshire (c. 1700-86). That James Woolley made superb high-quality long-case clocks there is no doubt. Most of the stories of him, however, refer to his miserly attitude and to his eccentric behaviour. It is said that he was caught poaching on a nearby estate when quite young and having paid the penalty vowed to work non-stop until he had acquired his own estate on which to shoot 'without dreading the frowns of his haughty neighbours'. By work and thrift he seems to have achieved this and more and when he died in 1786 he had amassed a considerable fortune.

James Woolley is thought to have been apprenticed to the Nottingham clockmaker John Wild. A clause in Woolley's will substantiates this idea to some degree for he left to 'the two children of John Wyld Watchmaker, Deceased and grandchildren of the late John Wyld clockmaker of Nottingham the sum of five pounds each'. Baillie's *Watch and Clockmakers of the World* lists John Wild of Nottingham as about 1780 but by this time he must have been long dead.

The first mention of a clock by James Woolley is from the diary of a Lincolnshire farmer giving the date 1724 and recording the purchase of a square, oak clock from Woolley of Codnor at Derby Market for £4.10s.0d. although Woolley had asked £5 for it. Shortly afterwards Woolley gave a clock for use in the New Exchange Hall at Nottingham. This hall was almost built in 1724 and from all accounts the clock appears to have been a turret clock with a dial on the front of the building. The account from *Hanes Every Day Book*, Vol. II, of 1827 reads as follows: 'Once in his life Woolley was convicted of liberality. He had at great labour and expense of time made what he considered, a clock of considerable value, and as it was probably too large for common purposes, he presented it to the Corporation of Nottingham, for the Exchange. In return he was made a freeman of the town 1728. They could not have con-

122 Dial from a long-case clock by James Woolley of Codnor, Derbyshire, circa 1740. It has especially fine hands and an unusual calendar. Its movement is shown in Plate 94.

123 *Left:* Musical organ clock by George Pyke with hood removed. The clock movement cannot be seen, but wheels which activate figures on the dial are visible on the left. The large toothed wheel behind the tune-selector disc is fixed on the end of the pin barrel; the fly wheel and linkage to the bellows are in front and beneath this. Organ pipes are ranged at the back of the clock to the right. Temple Newsam House, Leeds.

124 *Right:* Thirty-hour movement of Will Snow's 473. The hammer tail and the pins which lift it can be clearly seen bottom right.

ferred on him a greater favour; the honour mattered not–but election dinners were things which powerfully appealed through his stomach to his heart. The first he attended was productive of a ludicrous incident. His shabby and vagrant appearance nearly excluded him from the scene of good eating, and even when the burgesses sat down to table, no-one seemed disposed to accommodate the miserly old gentlemen with a seat. The chairs were quickly filled; having no time to lose, he crept under the table and thrusting up his head forced himself violently into one, but not before he had received some heavy blows on the skull.' The clock was in regular use until 1881.

At first it may be difficult identifying authorship of a clock by James Woolley for he frequently signed his dials 'Wolley Codnor', giving the impression that this was a complete name. No explanation is offered for this oddity in dropping one of the Os from his surname; Codnor is the name of the village where he lived. Some of his clocks were occasionally signed James Wolley of Codnor Fecit. It seems he was something of a specialist in repeating strike work, for of the three clocks by him that I noted, all have pull-repeat work and two have a precise quarter-repeating facility on two bells. In each case the gearing of the strike-train has been given extra duration to account for this. The clock illustrated in

997

Plate 94 is an hour-repeater only but uses a star-wheel method of advancing the rack, for greater accuracy and a more precise change. The steel work is well detailed in all his movements and the terminals of various features are filed and carved in the manner of a gunsmith. He is also known to have used as a decorative feature a rocking dove, with olive branch, before an engraved ark, in the arch of a long-case clock. It is not known who made his clock cases but a firm quality and a sophisticated line is evident in their construction. An early 10″ square-dialled long-case clock is recorded in an ebonised case. The one illustrated in Plate 94 is in a heavy solid oak case and another is recorded in oak with walnut crossbanding. The dial shown in Plate 122 can be dated about 1740 and is of good classic line though unusual in one or two respects. The use of a hand and an engraved applied ring for calendar work is early; generally this feature is found on white-dial clocks of the late-18th century. The curious cast satyr head decorations at either side of the seconds dial are unusual but pleasing. I have seen them on clocks by other makers but only rarely. The hands, in common with all other steel work, are of the finest quality.

125 Thirty-hour clock by Thomas Ogden, circa 1750, with a Halifax moon. The hour hand is not original.

James Woolley died, a very old man, in November 1786, and in his will left a considerable portion of his large estate including farms and houses to John Woolley his nephew. John Woolley was also a clockmaker but perhaps due to his inherited wealth and consequent lack of drive did not make as many or as good-quality clocks as his uncle had done. His works are signed, variously Jno Wooley Codnor, John Wooley Codnor, or Woolley Codnor, and they are often clearly from a later period than James Woolley's clocks. John Woolley died in March 1795 aged 57 years.

Thomas Ogden of Halifax (1693-1769) was a second-generation clockmaker of an ardently Quaker family. Branches of this family spread north and made clocks in Alnwick and Newcastle, but Thomas Ogden stayed in Halifax and became its finest clockmaker. His speciality was in moon-dial clocks and he was a successful exponent of the revolving-ball moon dial type of work, making many fine examples. This uncommon feature is often mistakenly called a Halifax moon. The true Halifax moon which is illustrated by Plate 125 was often used by the town's many clockmakers in the 18th century, but was in fact originated much earlier and was seen on some of the work of the Fromanteel family at the end of the 17th century. From contemporary writings, Thomas Ogden comes down to us as a rather straight and somewhat patriarchal Old Testament character. His obituary notice in the Leeds Mercury 1769 confirms

126 *Left:* Octagonal dial of an extremely fine eight-day clock by Thomas Ogden of Halifax, circa 1750.

127 *Right:* Thirty-hour long-case clock dial, Sam Deacon's No 44.

this estimate of his character. 'On Thursday last October 3rd died in his 77 year of his age, Mr. Thomas Ogden of Halifax, clock and watchmaker. His superior abilities in his profession are sufficiently well known in this and some neighbouring counties. A great many gentleman's houses being furnished with the productions of his labours. He was one of the people called Quakers. His moderation and charity to all other religious sects was truely exemplary. His peculiar diction in the Epistolatory Style made his correspondence greatly desirable by everyone who had any connection with, many of his epistles, being preserved on the closets of the learned and curious. He was a steady friend and a facetious companion compassionate and indulgent, a great promoter of industrious merit, but a severe scourge to the slothful and indolent. He died without issue, and he left his fortune to a numerous train of relations.'

A man with firm views, he was fond of legends about the passage of time and Man's mortality. The following are typical of those found engraved on his dials. *Tempus edox rerum* (Time devourer of all things) and *Memor brevis esto aevi* (Be mindful of thy short life).

On a long-case timepiece made early in his career for the Northgate End Unitarian Chapel, Halifax, he used the following Latin phrase to decorate the four spandrel corners instead of cast decorations. *Fugit hora ora labora* (The hour flies pray labour). A fine eight-day long-case clock with an arched dial recently seen, surprised me by having no moon work. Engraved on a tablet in the dial arch was the instruction 'Wind me on Monday'. Thomas Ogden was also a maker of watches;

but these are rarely come across these days. It seems unlikely that he made many. The frontispiece illustrates what must be his finest ball-moon clock known to exist. It is signed 'Thos Ogden de Halifax'. I have seen three others but the movements, though on the same lines, are not so fine. Plate 119 shows a perfect specimen of his work in its original mahogany case which has Lancashire and possible Gillows characteristics.

Samuel Deacon of Barton in the Beans, Leicestershire (1746-1816). Sam Deacon, clockmaker of Barton, has come to prominence recently not for his outstanding skills (and he was a capable and comprehensive maker of clocks and watches) but for the discovery in 1951 of his virtually intact workshop by John Daniells of the Leicestershire Museum. Samuel's son John Deacon was also a clockmaker and, when his father died, carried on working in the family workshop though he concentrated on making up movements for Birmingham dials and later using both dials and movements, bought in from Birmingham factors. John's son, also Samuel, succeeded his father but was principally engaged in repairing and not making clocks. It is thought that the workshop was idle from the mid-19th century but the property and adjoining house were retained by members of the Deacon family until 1951. When the family moved away, Mr Daniells was allowed to look round the outbuildings and found the amazingly complete 18th-century workshop as set up by Sam Deacon in 1771. The tools and equipment gave an insight into the scope of Samuel's work and the working life of a country clockmaker at this time. On the ground floor was the forge complete with large bellows, and upstairs in the workshop proper were found the old wooden benches, vices, a lathe and a wheel-cutting engine. There was also a testing frame of wood on which the movements were tried out before fitting to their long cases. A separate area was partitioned off for making watches and barometers. The most important find, however, was the account books and workshop records, which begin in 1771 and end in 1860, long after Samuel's death. The books tell us much about the work, the costs and the selling price of the clocks as well as domestic accounts and information relating to Deacon's interest in the Baptist Church of which he was a deacon and an active local preacher.

Deacon's 30-hour clocks appear to have been cheaply made, with small movement plates and plain parallel turned pillars. They frequently incorporate a curious form of internal countwheel, pinned instead of slotted for its division. Plate 127 shows a clock of this type, No. 44, dated 1773. Some of his eight-day clocks, however, including No. 338 of 1789, have much fine

128 Front plate showing the marking out of the trains. Sam Deacon's No 44, made in December 1773. It can be seen from this plate that the escape-wheel pivot hole is worn oval and is badly in need of bushing.

decorative work including eccentric baluster-turned pillars and a steel rack-hook, shaped and engraved to look like a bird. It seems that Samuel Deacon's work could vary to suit the requirements of his market and he could do work as good as most. **William Snow of Padside, near Pateley Bridge, Yorks** (1736-95). Clocks by William Snow will not be known nationwide, but a few will almost certainly have removed to other parts of the country with their owners. As far as is known Will Snow was a first-generation clockmaker and no information exists about his training, although he was followed in the clockmaking trade by three sons, William, Richard and Thomas. Will Snow was probably foremost a hill farmer and used clockmaking to occupy the winter months and supplement his income. Generally clocks by him are of the 30-hour country variety and I have never heard of an eight-day clock or any other type. The movements of these clocks are very unusual because of their simplicity. Plates are cut away in rectangular skeleton form in order to save material. Pillars are normally a piece of parallel round steel bar with no decorative turning. The normal bridge or back cock to retain the escapement arbor is dispensed with, the arbor being assembled in with the plates. The cock for suspending the pendulum is simply a length of steel rod riveted into the backplate. Both one and two hands were used and following the normal pattern the single-hand variety tend to be earliest. Dials of 11″ square vary little, but are tastefully laid out and nicely engraved, the centre with lunette calendar and scrolling leaf engraving. This area was usually silvered along with the chapter-ring. Hands were nicely made and conform to the style of the period. In fact all the visible and dial parts of his clocks suggest a delicacy not expected from a country maker working in relative isolation. A pleasing touch occurs in the signature, as a result of Will Snow's fortunate habit of numbering his work. Engraved on to the chapter ring, the number usually follows the name and often leads to him including an 'S' after Snow. Thus we see Will Snow's 660. I like to think that the possessive S is a proud touch, and indeed the man had much to be proud of for if his numbering system is accurate he produced up to 900 clocks in a busy life. From the clocks that are dated, and the general distribution of the numbers seen and recorded, we are able to assume that Will Snow aided by his family made an average of 25 clocks a year. After Will's death his three sons continued making clocks separately in nearby market towns. These are of the white-dial variety. The last son died towards the middle of the 19th century.

Chapter 11

Buying and restoring clocks

The Clock may be sett up by any carefull Carpenter if he attends to the following directions: having taken off the lid of the packing case, let him then take out the weights, ball and keys which are in the corners at the Case Head, also take out the bars of wood which go across the Clock Case and which are fastened by screws on the outside of the packing Case: he will then take out the Clock Case, and set it carefully in the place it is to stand in: this being done, he may open the Clock Case door, and set the body of the Clock case as perpendicular as he can, by a plumb line both in front and at the side (in this part of the business he should be very attentive, as the well going of the Clock depends upon it) he should then fix the case by screwing it fast with two screws screwed thro' the back as high as he can get them for the door, as also two below, as low as he can get for the door also: perhaps it may so turn out that he cannot find a place in the wall to hold the screws mentioned if so should prepare two pieces of wood and fix them to the Wall and then screw the case to them. All this done he will find a piece of wood unscrewed . . . pendulum ball with two screws this he must take off by unscrewing . . . he will then find a piece of wood screwed behind the pendulum ball, these screws he will also take out, and by drawing the pendulum ball gently and carefully forward, he may take the piece of wood from behind it: he may then hang on the weights and set the clock a going. The smaller weight hangs under three o'clock and the larger under nine o'clock.

The Clock is at present very near time, but perhaps some little derangement may take place by the Carriage and if it should be found to go too fast or too slow it may be brought to time by screwing up the small ball of the pendulum which is below the large ball to make it go faster, or down to make it go slower and one turn will alter the rate of the clock one second per day—below the regulating ball is a small nut which should always be kept close to the ball to keep it in its situation.

Left: Notes for setting up the long-case clock by John Holmes, bought by Godfrey Wentworth of Woolley Hall, Wakefield in 1794.

If you have bought a clock or have spent any time looking round antique shops checking on the prices and condition of those offered for sale you will already have formed some opinions and maybe gained a little knowledge. Not all will be about clocks. Very few dealers have a thorough knowledge of clocks and many of them make no secret of the fact, simply offering the clock for sale at a fair profit and in much the same condition that they bought it in. Others, sadly, will spin you a yarn about its pedigree, its restoration and often accompany these half-truths with a story or two. In either case you will need to have the knowledge yourself or be able to take someone along who really does understand old clocks. An illustration of this latter breed of dealer is shown by my experiences some years ago when a friend approached me to look at a small pretty mahogany long-case clock that he wished to buy. The price was fairly high, but the clock certainly looked attractive in its well-polished case, standing beneath a spotlight in the shop window. I removed the hood and looked at the clock thoroughly, taking in features such as a hardboard surround to the dial and nuts and bolts soldered to the dial to hold it to the movement. What we were looking at was a clock made from various pieces, all of about the same age but put together unskilfully, exposing the deceit. Its condition suggested that this clock had recently been 'got up' for sale. Wishing to advise my friend of this fact and not wanting to cause offence to the attentive and pushing salesman, I awaited an opportunity that never came. Instead I was trapped in conversation and was forced to either go along with his inaccurate appraisal of the clock or call his bluff. I tried to do this politely and suggested that hardboard was not a natural material for the 18th century cabinet-maker, nor were dials normally held on with nuts and bolts. The conversation became more and more heated, and when he realised the sale was no longer possible, the salesman informed me in no uncertain manner that I was no longer welcome and that he did not care for people who knew everything, showing us both the door as he did so. Salerooms can also be a problem area for people with little knowledge. It is not easy to be sure about a clock on a crowded view day and the clock need not even be a good one to make it attractive to people who are prepared to pay a high price. The atmosphere of the sale will possibly be infectious, causing the unwary to go too far and pay a ridiculous price.

The best way to acquire an old clock is to inherit it, for at least one does not feel cheated if it turns out to be not quite right and sentiment can often make up for any deficiency in its originality or condition. Unfortunately this method of acquisition can be ordered by few of us; undoubtedly the next best method is to visit a specialist dealer. Anyone who specialises in clocks has usually a good selection on display in restored and working condition, and is likely to know something about what he sells and be prepared to back his descriptions, as well as the clock's condition with a guarantee. Talk to the dealer, tell him what you are looking for and get him to show one or two examples of his stock and tell you about their age, the maker and even the restoration that has been necessary to present the clock in good condition. A dealer who is truly interested in his stock and know about it will be pleased to do these things, providing he recognises that you are not wasting his time. In buying a clock from such a man there will be no bargains, but at least you will know that you have got what you have paid for. The dealer's profit will usually take account of the amount the clock's value will probably rise in about twelve months, but after this period the clock should be worth more than you paid for it. A further safeguard, in addition to dealing with a reputable and experienced man, would be to have a second opinion; so if you can, take along with you a restorer or person with a good knowledge of the subject. Book knowledge can also be gained, for there are many excellent books on the market today. This does, however, need to be supplemented by actually seeing clocks for there are certain areas which are not always clear to those with knowledge, and even experts disagree.

The word 'fake' is one not commonly associated with clocks. At least it is not a word that I have heard used recently. The tone of intentional deceit conjured up by this word does not often apply to the clock market today. Few if any clocks are made from the outset to imitate a valuable old clock in the hope of gaining a massive sale-room price. It would in most cases cost as much to do this as the genuine clock would be worth. In the past, names were altered on chapter-rings and dials but it was often done unskilfully and in a way which fools no-one with a reasonable knowledge. Faking of this sort went on when less well-known makers had the names of the famous (such as Tompion) put on their work in order to obtain a better price for it. There is a story of person bringing to the Tompion workshop of The Dial and Three Crowns a watch engraved with Tompion's name as its maker to be repaired. Tompion, recognising the watch as a forgery, smashed it to pieces with a hammer and handed the customer a genuine watch saying, 'Sir, here is a watch of my making'. One of the functions of the Clockmakers' Company, formed in 1631, was to stamp out this

129 Long-case clock with the hood removed to show the seat board sitting on the side of the case in an unaltered example.

sort of practice and generally to encourage high standards within the trade. A fortunate result of this was that most clocks and watches bear their maker's name, making it easier and more enjoyable for collectors to trace the origins and provenance of their old clocks.

The most usual problem area in authenticating a clock is in establishing whether or not the movement and dial are housed in their original case. In the past it was common for some antique dealers to take a handsome case from a 30-hour clock and fit it up with a well-made eight-day movement with a brass dial, probably putting the 30-hour movement and dial into the plainer case. Fortunately now most people know better, but for many clocks it is too late. The movements and dials were not often interchangeable without alteration to the case. While the dial size may have fitted the case aperture perfectly, the board on which the movement sits may have been too high or too low—and in these cases it will seem that the side cheek, on which the seat board sits, may have been cut down or built up. If the alteration has been done recently a new seat board, or one altered with newly-sawn edges or holes for the line, may give it away. Arched-dial clocks and cases are difficult to 'marry' since few arches are of exactly the same portion of a circle and the difference often shows. More glaringly obvious still are examples whose period of making have not been carefully matched or ones which have had strips of wood crudely placed inside the hood door to reduce the aperture for a smaller dial. I saw recently a clock illustrating both these examples of a bad marriage. It was a delightfully small and early eight-day clock with a 10″ square dial by Thomas Cruttenden of York, 1680, cased in a rather large mahogany and oak example from Lancashire or Yorkshire, and made about 1820. Examples such as these should be observed for they form an ideal testing ground for one's knowledge.

If a movement is wrongly cased and a pleasing clock results, then no great harm has been done, for the two parts were anyway made by different craftsmen. I am not suggesting that this is a desirable practice but suggest that the results are preferable to live with than a marriage between a movement and a dial. This latter practice has already been mentioned in the chapter dealing with 30-hour clocks but the practice was by no means restricted to long-case clocks. I have seen all kinds of clocks where this practice, usually badly done, has spoiled a good clock. The signs to look for are spare holes left in the front plate of a movement, where dial feet from a previous dial have been planted. These are rarely filled-in by a clock bodger.

Occasionally bent dial-feet are seen. This is done to get them to clear an obstruction in the motion work of a movement or even to fit them into a crude and inaccurately drilled new hole. It is quite possible to find a clock made not only with components from two clocks, but three or maybe four lots of parts may have been put together to make one saleable clock. But the signs are there if you are able to read them.

One area of faking which is fully recognised by horological scholars, but cheerfully dismissed as nonsense by many present-day owners of these clocks, is the quasi-17th-century water-clock consisting of an oak frame, a crude brass dial with a large counter-balanced hand controlled by a chain and a float, which presumably was intended to descend as water siphoned from one cistern to the other. Examination will often show a cast, not engraved, dial-plate and modern methods of construction of some parts. The top of the float cistern is often rolled over a steel wire to form the edge. An engraved plate, often on the lower cistern or in that area of the clock, proclaims an early origin and a fictitious maker. The example (Plate 130) shown informs us that 'Night Cometh' and that Edward Larkins of Winchester made it in 1621. A more likely explanation is that the clock was made in Birmingham in the early 20th century, when at least one firm of ornamental brassware manufacturers included them in their catalogues.

The shape of the lantern clock has had an enduring appeal and forms the basis of many clocks made today – though these are not fakes, merely borrowing a quaint and nostalgic shape for commercial reasons. Most of them are small and vary from those with French carriage-clock movements to the cheaply-produced battery-driven mantle-shelf perennial at the other end of the scale. During the last few years, however, a number of lantern clocks have come into the country from a Continental source, bearing the name of Thomas Moore of Ipswich, a reputable maker from the early 18th century. These clocks of the correct size and layout are mass-produced and will not bear a detailed examination, but were carefully prepared by some people in this country to attract the unwary. One that I saw had purposely been weathered and the steelwork rusted, giving it a venerable quality that one might have expected of an original; another example of 'buyer beware' for a little knowledge can be a dangerous thing.

It is often said that an old English clock never wears out; within that saying there is a lot of truth, but it needs clarifying. What can be done and what should be done are two different things,

130 Spurious water clock, signed Edward Larkins of Winchester.

and techniques employed must be suitable to avoid expensive damage to a movement or dial. The definition is often quite subtle and based on feeling and experience for old clocks more than on engineering skill. Old English clocks, like any other machines with moving parts, do of course eventually wear, but the way in which the majority are made, with generous use of good materials and incorporating sensible design, means that most parts can be repaired or compensated for wear by a variety of techniques. It is perfectly possible to restore most clocks to full working condition without affecting their value or originality if the restorer has the correct degree of feeling and knowledge. Many jobs that he will have to do will involve undoing the damage done by generations of unskilled bodgers who seemed particularly prevalent in the field of clockwork. This kind of restoring is particularly taxing and will in some cases need skills equal to, if not more than, those required in making a new clock from raw materials. Chapter-rings that have been chrome-plated, escapements that have been savagely mutilated and plates that have been distorted by punch-marks and hammer blows are the sort of damage that I have in mind – and are extremely hard to deal with successfully. If you are fortunate enough to have acquired a clock which is substantially as made, then wear and neglect may have taken a toll of its appearance and functions, making some restoration work necessary on movement dial and case. It is not by any means desirable to keep old clocks in a grubby and worn condition for while this is an undoubted indication of their age it is misguided to keep them that way. When made they were presented bright and fresh, their metal parts silvered, polished or gilt, with the cases newly polished to show off the grain or inlays of their wood. When carefully done, restoration can return them to this state in which their makers intended them, and substantially increase their value and visual appeal.

First we shall deal with the wooden case, for this is an important area in most clocks. Naturally I shall not go into the finer points of cabinet-making, as I have neither the knowledge or the experience, but will concentrate on those areas which can be easily understood and which I hope will make good sense to the clock owner. In long cases stability is all important, and rickety fittings such as the seat board and its union with cheeks at the top of the trunk sides need to be made stable so that they will support the heavy weights and allow the movement a firm enough base to run correctly. If a seat board is thin and seen to bend or has been damaged by splitting or woodworm, then it will need to be replaced with a piece of old oak, which is the most suitable wood. A copy of the old shape will need to be made carefully, for as well as needing two square holes for the gut lines to run from the barrels it will need to be relieved at the back to clear the pendulum rod. It may also be similarly relieved at the front if calendar work or other functions are present in the bottom half of the dial. Small areas could need to be scooped out on the front edge where various pieces project from behind the dial plate. The bottom movement pillars usually accommodate a pair of fasteners which hook over the pillars, and are tightened up by a nut from below, thus making the movement firm with the seat board. This makes handling much easier since the looped ends of the weight pulley-lines have also to be fastened in to the board. If the movement and its supporting board were not firmly connected a tangle could easily ensue.

The seat board may just sit on top of the trunk cheeks but is held in some cases by wood screws, which are usually a later addition. Thirty-hour clocks' seat boards are often a fixture in the case, being nailed to the cheeks with square hand-made nails. Since there is no need to fasten the loop end of the gut line into the seat board on these examples, the board is not usually lifted off with the movement as in eight-day work. In the case of a 30-hour clock the holes in the seat board are quite different since we are only concerned with the descent of a single weight. Although the source of the rope or chain is from two pulleys in the clock, this hangs through a single slot, cut on a shallow curve rather like a dog's hind leg. This allows for the offset of the driving pulleys in the clock and also means that the weight pulley and ropes can be lifted through the slot while allowing the seat board to remain in the case. If seat-board alterations are made it is as well to check, before making the final fixing, that the dial fits nicely up to the aperture in the hood door and fits equally at either side. This is also an important check to make when setting up a clock for often there is sufficient sideways movement to leave an unsightly gap at one side of the dial.

The condition of the mouldings and the state of the glue should also be looked at carefully. The mouldings under the hood form a surface on which the hood slides on to the case. Slots of wood, glued just above these and on the rising checks of the case side boards prevent the hood from toppling forward as it is being slid on and off. Check that they are firmly fixed. One of the most important areas in which the glued joints between mouldings and carcase wood need to be secure is in the region of the waist of the case, at the point where trunk joins base. Very often the thinly-cut moulding and the backboard which may no longer be firm, are all that keep the case upright at this

131 Glue blocks used to strengthen the joint between backboard and side of a long-case clock, circa 1830. These are part of the original construction.

132 Replacement frets for the hoods of long-case clocks. Paper on the surface of the upper one has not yet been sanded away.

point. If there is much looseness here it is as well to take the case to an experienced cabinet-maker, as very often the backboard will have to be strengthened and the inside of the case braced with a number of glue blocks and at the same time the mouldings will need to be refixed in a way which will not spoil the appearance of the wood's old surface. Split panels, missing veneers, and marquetry work will likewise need to be dealt with by an expert. Where an old wooden fret, such as those fitted above the dial in the frieze of the hood, is damaged or missing, a suitable replacement can usually be fretted out by a clockmaker who is capable of making clock hands, for the same kind of skills apply. Since the wood used will need to be little more than a thick veneer, a method has to be devised to stop it splitting along the grain during the fretting operation. Two methods are used to overcome this problem and one of them is to paste paper back and front of the wood to help hold the grain. The other is to cut two frets at once and back these with a strip of thin wood or hardboard during the cutting. The paper on the front piece of wood will need to be a drawing of the design. This is put together to make a sandwich with glue carefully placed only at the edges, so that the final cut when the strips of wood are cut to width, will remove the glued portions and allow the frets to separate. It only remains to sand off the paper on the surface which will be seen. Old frets and some wooden inlays were similarly prepared in manufacture. I have frequently seen such scraps of printed paper when taking old work to pieces.

At the top of the hood, holes which have formed a base for finials are frequently widened or broken away at the edges, particularly if they were mounted on short square plinths or drilled in an applied block behind the centre of a broken arch or swan neck pediment. Glue blocks can easily be replaced and holes can be filled with a piece of shaped soft wood before re-drilling a hole the correct size. If finials were orginally fitted and are now missing, look round for a suitable set as they improve the appearance of a clock enormously. Good reproduction finials are now made in a number of patterns and these do not look out of place if old replacements are unobtainable. There are various views on the polishing of brassware on clock cases. Fortunately there is not very much brass visible, but the average long-case usually has an escutcheon or lock-plate and acorn hinges to the trunk door. The hood may have brass capitals and bases to its columns and brass paterae may decorate the terminals of a swan-necked pediment. In my view these should be bright and clean and once this has been achieved they should be lacquered over. Repeated cleaning of brassware with metal polish tends to fill in the lower portions of the design with a milky deposit of metal polish and polishing also affects the surrounding wood in a similar unfortunate way. To avoid this, care needs to be taken in cleaning the brasswork; however, you may prefer to leave it in a dull unpolished condition whose appearance merges it into the surrounding wood.

One of the most common breakages that can occur in dealing with cases is of the glass in a hood door. A hood removed from the case should always be placed with its face to the wall. Since it is face- or front-heavy it will always fall that way if knocked over and broken glass will be the result. Many clocks will be found to have had the glass replaced, some with the wood of the door badly damaged as a result. Patience is required in removing the old hard putty and an extremely sharp wood chisel is the best tool for this job. This putty is then cut away. On later clocks where a strip of crossbanding or a mahogany veneer is found to form the front of the glass rebate, even more care is required. A hidden danger in this operation is present if you allow the door frame to slide about on the bench while removing the old putty—particles of grit and glass will badly scratch the polished surface. For this reason I keep a grip on the door frame with a wood-carver's vice whose jaws are covered with cork. I then turn the door as each side is carefully cleaned up. Any good glass merchant can cut even the most complicated arched dial shape, but take the door with you so that it is his responsibility to fit the glass. This is one area where measurements are not enough. Putty, normally grey, can easily be coloured by the addition of pigment such as oil paint or powder paints. A middle-brown shade looks good with the wood of most cases.

133 Original reinforcing blocks, shown in the construction of a hood with swan neck pediment.

Old glass can be identified by its imperfections and the lack of uniformity in its thickness. Occasionally it may not be flat and pulls away as much as $\frac{1}{4}''$ from the corners of the hood door. If the lenticle glass in the trunk door gets broken, it can be replaced in the same way. A bull's-eye glass is a much more difficult proposition. It would be wrong to use a modern bull's-eye of the type commercially available; an old piece of glass will need to be found. I recently discovered and obtained two of these from a workman's cottage built about 1800 and due for demolition, but this was a very lucky find. Fortunately the thin edges of the glass did not break when the glass cutter was applied, and I was able to make the first one into a suitable oval with no breakage.

A frieze of blue glass is often found on the hoods of long-cases from the north-west. This occurs on both square and arched cases and on an arched hood is made in two panels. The glass is usually decorated in patterns of scrolling rococo arabesques, usually accompanied by a centrally placed urn or similar classical feature. The gold-painted pattern is frequently rubbed and needs retouching, which may be quite easily done with a high-quality paint or gold leaf and requires the same skills as those possessed by a dial painter, namely a steady hand and a knowledge of the type of decoration used in old work.

While the basic reason behind cleaning a clock movement is to remove the dirt, old oil and grit to reduce wear on the moving parts, it is gratifying to polish the metal and make a complete and thorough job of the restoration, repairing all broken parts and replacing those which are missing. This way it should be a long time before the plates will need to come apart again. The following paragraphs give some indication of the kind of problems that might be encountered in a movement and what can be done to improve them.

By far the most common ill is wear to the pivot holes in the plates. Any wear that goes uncorrected will allow the wheels and pinions to have the wrong engagement or depth and wear will in turn occur on the pinion leaves and eventually on the teeth of the brass wheels. In correcting this wear, it is essential that the new bushes installed in the plates are not left too tight, as it takes very little friction to stop a clock, particularly in the higher-geared wheels at the top of the train. Perceptible horizontal movement (end shake) must also be retained between the plates and the shoulders of the pinion. The worn pivot holes are enlarged with a five-sided cutting broach or reamer, sufficient to admit a brass bush whose central hole is fractionally tighter than the hole required. The bush is riveted home, filed level with the plate, and polished before the hole is correctly sized to give a snug fit to the pivot. Before this is done the pivot should be examined carefully, for a worn hole is always accompanied by a worn pivot. Most wear will have occurred at the point where the pivot bears on the plate and the end of the pivot which pokes through the plate will not have worn at all. This gives a dumb-bell look to a worn pivot. The pivot will need to be mounted in a lathe and filed up until it is reduced to an overall parallel shape. The pivot is polished and is then ready to be tried in the new bush. It is necessary to fit the arbor between the plates and try it for a free running fit before trying it in relation to the other wheels, when the question of depth of engagement between the wheel and pinion is another factor

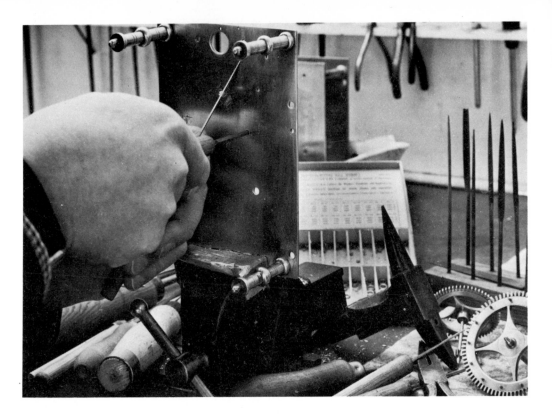

which needs to be checked. Both these tests are necessary before final re-assembly of the movement. It is easy to identify a tight pivot this way and almost impossible to do it once the clock has been assembled.

If the clock has been neglected for a long time many bushes may require attention. I recently restored an eight-day striking clock which needed twelve in both its trains. Two of the pinions were worn so thin that they had to be broken off and replaced. This is not an easy job and in order to do it one needs a lathe and an accurate chuck, for the area to be drilled is small and needs to be drilled in the very centre. The depth of the hole will need to be at least that of the length of the pinion to be formed. A piece of pinion steel or silver steel will then be prepared to be a tight fit and driven home.

Escapement faults are also common on worn house-clocks and are particularly tricky to correct if they have previously been repaired by an unskilled hand. It is essential that the pallet arbor does not have worn pivots and it will be necessary to ensure that there is no up and down movement here if an anchor escapement is to be correctly impulsed by the escapement teeth, thus retaining its momentum. Ruts worn in the faces of the pallets will need to be ground or stoned out and the

134 A clock backplate in the process of rebushing. Cutting broaches of all sizes may be seen. The bush to be inserted in the new hole is held on the second broach also in the clockmaker's hands. The small anvil is fixed in the vice when riveting the bushes firm.

pallets re-polished. A file will not touch the extremely hard surfaces that are needed at these points. Once this is done it will be found that the pallets do not have sufficient engagement with the escape wheel and will require closing slightly in order to overcome the excessive drop. This requires great care if breakage is not to occur. The arms of the escapement need to be softened with heat and they can then be closed slightly by squeezing them in a vice. A little distance will be all that is required and, so that one can see what progress has been made, it will be a help if a measurement is taken beforehand with a pair of dividers. The pallets have to be measured outside the vice, for the steel is springy and opening of the vice will mean that the pallets return some way towards their previous gaps. It may be found that unskilled repairers have achieved this repair by lowering the back of the escapement arbor, often by removing the steady pins from the back cock and cutting the screw holes into slots. The pallet arbor can then be roughly dropped into depth, but it will be out of line and out of square with the escape wheel. This type of repair should be corrected as it spoils the appearance of the movement and causes more wear to occur in the escapement. Another common escapement pallet repair is done to save grinding out the ruts caused by the action of the pallets on the escape wheel. This is to cover the faces with a piece of thin steel, such as a portion of pendulum-suspension spring. These are fixed by tinning the pallets with soft solder before applying the cleaned and fluxed pieces of spring. When cool this can be tidied up with a file, and if well done can make a very acceptable repair. Although not as hard as the original face, the repair will withstand many years of wear.

A verge escapement will need its pallet arbor pivots to be in good order. The rear suspension, usually a knife-edge or V-shaped extension to the arbor runs in a brass V-slot and is particularly susceptible to wear. This can, however, easily be built up and refiled to shape. Depth can be adjusted on these escapements by raising or lowering the crown-wheel arbor. Placed vertically in the clock, the bottom pivot revolves on an adjusting screw placed in the underside of the bottom cock. Screwing this in further raises the escape wheel and unscrewing it allows the wheel to drop.

The moon dial is a feature which adds to the value and interest in many old clocks, but frequently they are disconnected or in a bad state of repair. When old clocks were not so well thought-of as they are today these 'unnecessary details' were considered clock-stoppers and many of the connecting links and wheels for calendar- and moon-work were committed to the repairer's scrap box. Dials in the arch of the dial are remote from the hour pipe from which the drive is provided. As a result, repair of this type of moon dial involves the most work. Various methods are used to give the disc its impetus, moving it on one tooth every twelve hours; it is often difficult to see which method was used if all the old work has been removed. Most moon discs have escapement or saw-like inclined teeth; this indicates that they are advanced by a pin or a peg revolving on a twelve-hour wheel or pushed by a slotted or jointed lever pivoted on to the back of the dial. Very rarely, however, the teeth are conventional wheel-teeth and are in constant mesh with the motion wheels, driven by the hour wheel. Whatever method was used it can be tricky to reproduce, but a good restorer should be able to take this sort of work in his stride. If wheels are missing for moon- or calendar-work, they can easily be cut after working out the number of teeth required and the pitch of gearing needed to work with the existing wheels. Date-work of the open lunette type with a fan-shaped portion of the date disc visible through this aperture is only rarely removed. Such an action spoils the appearance of the clock by leaving a large hole in the dial. It was far easier simply to remove the pin which pushed on the teeth. Calendar indications by a hand needs two wheels behind the dial to make them work; they are often found to have one of their intermediary wheels, the 24-hour wheel, removed. The wheel immediately behind the dial will generally be in place, for the calendar hand is screwed into it, and each holds the other in place. The most usual type of calendar is the box type, with a large internally toothed ring running behind the dial's surface and showing the date through a box in the lower part of the dial plate. This also needs a 24-hour wheel and pin to advance it. This 24-hour wheel is very often missing and replacing this is a regular task in a restorer's workshop.

135 Side view of a 30-hour movement and dial. The toothed discs behind the dial, both advanced by the same pin, can be clearly seen. The top one moves a halfpenny moon and the bottom a lunette calendar.

A leaf broken from a steel pinion almost certainly means that a replacement has to be made for this is impossible to repair. Teeth are frequently found to be broken from a brass wheel. This is a problem which occurs when the mainspring of a clock breaks or comes adrift from its anchorage in the spring barrel. The shock imposed on the train often does much damage, especially to pivots, wheels and pinions. If the number of teeth broken is not too great – perhaps up to three – repair is feasible. More than this and it is usually easier to replace the whole wheel. To replace teeth, the wheel rim is cut with a wedge-shaped gap of the required length; a piece of brass scrap of the same thickness as the wheel is shaped into a tightly-fitting

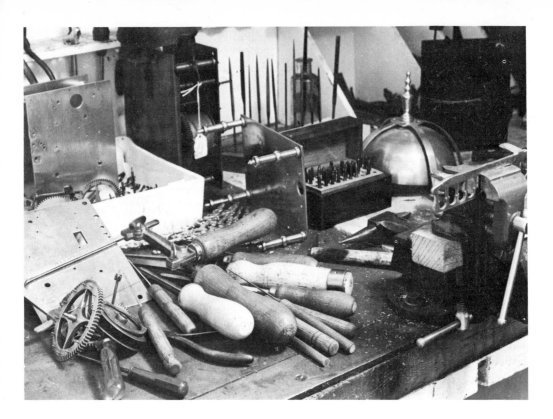

136 A clockmaker's bench showing various tools and movement parts. At the left can be seen a piercing saw used for cutting out clock hands, brass frets and so on. The small open box in the centre contains a variety of fine punches. The hand tools in the foreground are reamers and cutting broaches. In the background centre, standing in a block, can be seen a selection of needle files.

wedge of the same size as the gap and let in with soft solder. The teeth can be fretted and filed up with a piercing saw and needle files. Care and a steady hand will usually give first-class results. After polishing a good repair should be barely perceptible. Often wheel-teeth have been pushed over by a sudden force such as that caused by a breaking spring. Straightening them is not often successful as they tend to be brittle. This should only be done by leverage applied from the root at the next good tooth, otherwise further damage may result. The teeth will usually break off as they are straightened or be weakened enough to crumble later. It is usually best to replace them right away.

Faults in strike work are extremely common and wear in these parts will usually result in the strike being run together and unable to stop after striking the appropriate number, or not being able to strike at all. Most faults are as a result of breakage or wear, and often an unskilled repair means that the work has to be done again. In rack-striking examples the small pallet which gathers up the rack during striking may have dropped off its square, causing continual striking until the weight is removed. The rack-tail is often found to be badly bent or in-expertly soldered together. Both these parts can be easily remade. Wear in lifting-pieces, hammer-tails, locking-pieces and count-wheels can all be overcome, but experience is necessary otherwise the correct sequence of strike action will not be understood. Repairs of this type are therefore best left to an expert restorer.

Eight-day clock-lines and thirty-hour clock ropes are still relatively cheap and should be replaced each time the clock is cleaned, or sooner if they show signs of wear. This point applies even more to clocks with a greater duration than eight days for a clock going a longer period will have heavier weights. A broken line will result in a falling weight and possibly damage to the base of the case or even floor-boards. Gut is the traditional material for clock lines, made from the twisted lining of a sheep's stomach. It is perfectly adequate for most weight clocks and looks correct on old clocks. However, for a clock with very heavy weights, it may be safer to consider a modern brass wire line coated with plastic. These lines are soft and pliable in use, will not damage the clock and will last longer than gut lines. They can also be used with considerable success in connecting a spring barrel and fusée, in bracket and English-dial-clock restoration.

Whether or not a 30-hour pull-wind clock is equipped with rope or chain to support the weight, problems are bound to occur. To find out which was original to the clock, the spiked pulleys inside the movement will need to be examined. A rope pulley has an even surface in its valley, interrupted only by five or six spikes arranged to stop the rope slipping as it drives the trains. A pulley intended for use with a chain will have cutaway sections or depressions between the spikes, intended to accommodate the obverse link of the chain. The chain will need to be of a measured pitch in order to lie smoothly over the pins as the pulley revolves. A chain of incorrect pitch will jump, causing possible damage and irritating and unexpected noise. It is possible to run a chain clock with a rope but not the other way round as the obverse link would stop the other from settling firmly over the spikes, even if these were of the correct pitch.

Specially-made ropes are available from material dealers. These have a loose weave in order to give grip on the pulley spikes. I managed to have some good hemp rope made up by a specialist rope-maker. This works out rather expensive but makes a long-lasting job, and does not shred as much as the more usual cotton rope. Worn spikes or an unsuitable 'hard' rope will allow the rope to slip, usually during the strike and particularly when fully wound. This greatly reduces the duration of 30-hours (which is all too short anyway) and may in extreme cases cause the weight to drop to the floor in one massive slide. Spikes are replaceable by taking the pulley to pieces and screwing or pulling out the worn ones. New ones can be made from silver steel and put back before riveting the pulley back together. The disc type of click-spring for the pull-wind may be checked at the same time. These are often worn and loose on their rivets. At this stage this spring can be re-riveted or remade depending on its state of repair. In fitting a new rope a decision needs to be made about the way in which the ends are joined together. This needs to slide over pulleys and cause no obstruction. I find it best to butt-joint the rope after first binding round the two separate ends. The two are placed end to end and sewn together by stitches coming from behind and among the binding. This in turn is wrapped round and stitched through carefully. This is done with a fine but strong bookbinder's thread, which I have found to be excellent and lasts for years. When correctly spiked and equipped with a new rope the problems of dust and fluff in the movement caused by the rope passing through the pulleys remain. It is a problem we can do little about. The movement will need to be dismantled and cleaned more regularly than others.

Pendulums are fragile and very easily broken. It is fortunate therefore that they are also easily repaired. At the top the suspension spring will snap suddenly if knocked or bent too far. It is easy to do this while transporting a clock and while fitting the pendulum into the clock case. New springs are readily available from the material dealers and come complete with the top brass by which the pendulum will hang from the movement back cock. The suspension is held into the brass block by a single rivet which is easily punched out and later replaced. If the block is worn or, as is often the case, mis-shapen because of repeated spring replacements this too should be replaced. A replacement can easily be filed up in the workshop, or it is possible to buy a suspension with top brass and brass block complete and ready to screw on to the pendulum rod. Adjustment will have to be made in individual cases but this usually only involves filing a little off the thickness of the block to achieve a sliding fit in the escapement crutch—essential to good running of the clock—or reducing the length of the suspension spring which naturally needs to vary from clock to clock. This is done by punching out the lower rivet and shearing a portion from the suspension spring before returning it to the slot and tapping back in the securing rivet. A smooth finish is essential on the flanks of the block and its point of contact with the crutch should be as near the centre of the block's length as possible. A badly damaged or roughly repaired pendulum rod can easily be replaced with a length of $\frac{1}{8}''$ wire. A 4BA thread at the top and bottom of the rod will usually secure it into the block and the tapered iron blade at the bottom on which the bob slides. If the hole is too large at this point then the rod may be silver-soldered neatly into position. It is essential to check that the pendulum bob is a free sliding fit up and down over this blade, as easy adjustment of timekeeping depends on it. A pendulum which has fallen or been dropped may have broken or damaged the rating thread and nut at the very bottom of the pendulum. It is not unknown for this portion to spear the floorboards when suspension breakage unexpectedly occurs. The rating nut and its threaded stud are also easily replaced. The pendulum should be arranged by the length of its rod, to have good adjustment both up and down, when the clock is keeping good time. This way the clock may be brought to time with ease, should a change in the rate occur. Most people find that house clocks with a long pendulum need attention twice a year. When the weather cools in the autumn, clocks tend to gain and the pendulum will need lengthening, and with the return of milder weather in the spring the pendulum will need to be marginally shorter.

The last job in setting up a movement in the workshop is to oil its pivots, levers and other parts which move against each other. However, the wheels and pinions should never be oiled as brass and steel will work together quite easily in a dry state. To coat them with oil would simply encourage the adhesion of dust and dirt and cause increased wear in the pinions. A special clock oil made with qualities suited to a slow moving mechanism should be used. A good clock oil will stay where it is placed and not run down the plates or move along the arbors and on to the pinions. It will also stay liquid and remain in a non-sticky state for a long time. If a clock has been thoroughly cleaned and degreased during restoration, the initial oiling will probably last only a few months, particularly if the clock is housed in a warm dry centrally-heated atmosphere. Afterwards annual oiling should be quite sufficient. Since the oil needs to be carefully placed, a precise method of doing so involves using a clock oiler. This need be no more than length of 20-gauge wire bent at one end into a loop holder and at the other flattened by a hammer blow into a spade which will pick up a drop of oil from the bottle. This can then be accurately placed where it is needed in the movement.

There are many occasions when attention to clock hands is

necessary. Very often old repairs have been carried out by plating from behind. This makes a strong but unsightly job. The plating and soft solder has to be warmed and cleaned off before a more delicate repair is carried out with silver solder, butt-jointing the parts and afterwards removing all excess solder with needle files. Steel hands can then be blued by heat in the traditional manner. Only a small yellowish line of solder will then be seen and this is easily touched over with a spot of matt black paint before oiling the surface of the warm hand. When repaired carefully with silver solder brass hands can be polished so that the repair is almost impossible to detect. The hands should be protected with a transparent lacquer before returning to the clock. Hand collets are often overlooked in restoration. These too should be brightly polished and fastened with a neatly fitting pin, to give the perfect finish to a handsome pair of hands.

There are no hard and fast rules for the making up of a woman's face. Dial restoration needs to be approached in the same manner, bearing in mind that each will require a different degree of attention. Brass dials tend to lose their gleam over the years, and when breaks in the lacquered finish occur they allow the surface underneath to deteriorate fairly quickly. These can be caused by a careless scratch with the winding key or by a finger while pushing on the hands. The silver deposit on chapter rings blackens and the brass dial plate will turn dirty with green markings that will eventually eat into the plate, causing pitting and deterioration of the surface. For this reason alone it is essential that a brass dial is kept in good clean order and lacquered against the corrosive tendencies of the atmosphere. As a rule chapter rings, calendar and seconds circle were silvered to contrast with the gilt or polished brass of the dial plate corners and its matted centre. On later brass-dialled clocks, particularly those produced in the north, an engraved centre may also have been filled with black wax and silvered. Spandrel casting and dial plates may still exhibit signs of their original gilt surface. Since it is almost impossible to have this restored today, preservation of this surface is essential. First of all it should be washed in domestic washing-up liquid and very hot water, perhaps aided by a nail brush to remove the dirt. If this is not successful in restoring the surface, a very weak solution of ammonia should be tried, which should be washed off almost immediately and the part washed in clean warm water afterwards. It will be impossible to achieve the brilliance of a newly gilt surface, but a surface which looks clean and retains a good measure of the warm glow associated with a gilded surface could be considered a success. Silvered surfaces may be restored but the secret lies in preparation of the parts. These are usually rings which require rubbing-down with a circular motion to obtain a good matt brass surface, free from scratching, grease or any other imperfections which will spoil the surface. The wax-filled engraving will usually be intact and rubbing-down of the plate surface will not affect this. After silvering the wax will be unaffected and continue to show as a good black. I rub down with a variety of materials but usually finish with a fine pumice powder worked with a cloth pad. Some restorers use an electric wheel, rather like a potter' wheel. This spins the rings, which are finished by holding an emery cloth against them; this gives a uniform and mechanical appearance to the chapter-ring, rather like the surface of a gramophone record. This is not generally considered to be good practice as it is too mechanical and uniform a way to restore an antique finish. It may also be harmful to the engraved surface if done too vigorously. The silver surface is imparted to the brass by the chemical action of silver chloride paste and tartaric acid. This is applied evenly on a piece of cotton wool and rubbed into the surface. The ring is then polished, or at least rubbed to a good white, by the application of a creamy paste of tartaric acid in water. The ring needs to be dried quickly by dabbing with a clean linen or cotton cloth and then left in a dry atmosphere for a while before lacquering. Like the solid metal, silvering will rapidly tarnish if unprotected. The old craftsmen used a lacquer made by dissolving shellac in alcohol but a more expedient and lasting method is available today. A transparent cellulose lacquer may be brushed on. Care will have to be taken in the application, however, for the lacquer may tend to melt the engraver's wax and if these areas are lingered upon or the brush is rubbed over them several times then the black may be picked up and spoil the silvering. The same lacquer will usually be suitable for finishing all surfaces on the dial, including the polished brass and the cast spandrel decorations.

There is no short-cut to the skills required in restoration of a painted dial. One is either capable of the brushwork and lettering needed or not. If not then the work should be entrusted to an expert restorer. Many dials have been badly re-painted and the beauty of the original lost. Removal of the unskilled paint job is sometimes possible and then often the signs 'photographed on the dial plate' enable a good dial restorer to put back the original character of the dial's black work. As stated earlier the polychrome sections were usually painted in oil-bound colours and are generally well preserved. Exceptions to

137 A newly-silvered chapter ring giving a good black-and-white effect, on a lantern clock by Richard Fennel of Kensington.

1020

1021

this come in various ways. A dial whose surface has been chipped or burnt (with a candle) is occasionally seen; these have to be patched. Colour-work on a brass ground such as found in a moon disc or rocking-figure backing sheet does not hold quite so well as it does on iron, and frequently needs touching up around its edges. A dial which has suffered a blow or a fall will have sections where the paint and background has come away from the metal. Dial feet which have worked loose will also have caused the ground to chip and crumble. Most of these repairs can be dealt with successfully by filling and matching the colours. Artist's oil colours should be used mixing with a quick-drying medium such as Winton retouching varnish for the pictorial work. Care must be taken to use the colours in the same way as the original and not put thick blobs of paint where the original was built up in thin delicate layers. Mixing the correct colour for the dial ground is often the trickiest job of all, and most will be found to be a delicate green or brown tint and not white as we might suppose. Most dials are restorable with the right amount of expertise except perhaps those on which a good part of the ground has perished or started to lift away from the metal. The hard fine surface achieved by the old dial-making firms is difficult if not impossible to copy. It was probably done by a stoving type of process and to do this on large sections of the dial while attempting to preserve the original section is a tall order. Once the dial's surface has been restored, cleaned and degreased the painting of the chapters, moon indication's name and so on, in black can take place. The various concentric circles – and there are often quite a few – can best be put on with a ruling pen and black ink, the lettering and numberwork with a variety of fine brushes and signwriter's black paint. Any retouching of the coloured areas should come next as it is essential for the black line to be done first when the surface is free of grease, enabling the ink to flow freely from the pen. After the artwork is complete it will need to dry in a warm atmosphere for a few days before the dial is given a final surface. What should be done next is a matter of some debate, but to cover all the surface with a shiny varnish is definitely wrong. Although it gives a lasting finish it will destroy the correct period look that is necessary in such a dial. In the old workshops, only the colour work was varnished over and the black work left unprotected. This accounts for the eventual loss by washing of so many dial features and names. An improvement on this method is one I use, which goes a long way towards preserving an authentic appearance and also adds a little to the preservation factor. Colour-work is varnished over in panels using a light thin artist's varnish such as Winton picture varnish. This is quick-drying and colourless. Once this is dry the rest is given a coat of wax polish. When polished up with a soft clean cloth this gives a good protective finish and a sheen which is very acceptable.

By virtue of their tall thin shape long-case clocks are precarious and require very careful placing, if stability and safety are to be achieved. Stability is of course essential if the clock is to run properly and if the safety of the clock is ignored it may mean total destruction. I was once called upon to restore what was left of a clock after it had fallen on its face and then down a flight of stairs. Setting up the clock should start with the choice of position. This should be away from a busy or precarious part of the house. A quiet corner of the hall or landing has traditionally been a favourite place, although I do not actually advise that a case should be placed across a corner: an additional wooden support will be needed to make the clock adequately secure and stable. It is not necessary to go to the length of securing a case to a flat wall with screws. The many holes in the backboards of old clock cases indicate to us how common this practice was in the past. The following procedure will give excellent results and make the clock secure by use of its own weight. First of all obtain a piece of wood slightly less wide than the case but equal in thickness to any skirting board that may be in the room. Fix this wood to the outside of the backboard at about the height of the top of the hood door. Two $1\frac{1}{4}''$ panel pins are usually enough to stop this piece of wood falling. Place the case back in contact with the wall an cut two more small pieces of wood each about $\frac{3}{4}''$ thick. These should then be placed under the two front corners of the case at a point where base moulding or feet reaches the floor. The case should now stand level from all angles, and because the front corners are lifted clear of the floor, all weight of movement, weights and so on, will cause the clock to be pushed firmly against the wall, and be held securely. An uneven floor should be compensated for in a block placed under the front feet to make the case vertical. Appearances are all-important here and it is unnecessary actually to check a clock's setting with a spirit level at any stage. Next the seat board and movement should be lifted into place and held secure until the weights are hung on the pulleys ensuring that it cannot fall forwards. While doing this, check that the lines are gathered on to the winding barrels and have not slipped round arbors or into the ratchet click and spring wheel which make winding possible. The movement should now run on vigorously until the pendulum is lifted into the case, slipped upwards through the crutch and hung on its supporting cock. The final part of the setting-up now needs to be done. This is an adjustment common to most clocks using a pendulum and is not restricted to the long-case variety alone. First however, temporarily place the hood on to the case and check that the movement is centrally placed; if too far back or to one side, it will leave an unsightly gap between case and dial. Adjust this before finally setting-up the escapement. Remove the hood and set the clock in motion by giving the pendulum a gentle swing. The clock should tick and then tock when the pendulum is equally positioned either side of its centre (or the position at which it will hang when the clock is stopped). If this is taking place to one side the clock will 'limp'. It is then said to be 'out of beat' and the clock will stop after a short while. This problem can be seen by looking into the case when the pendulum is working. Some people prefer to make the adjustment while listening to the beat of the escapement. To adjust, you will have to place both hands behind the movement and feel for the escapement crutch through which the pendulum slides. An escapement action which is exaggerated to the left-hand side of the pendulum swing will mean that a small bend to the right will be needed in the crutch, and vice-versa. The crutch arm is made of bendable iron wire for this purpose. Bending should take place, pushing gently with the thumb of one hand against the wire arm while the other thumb is placed at the top of the wire near its junction with the pallet arbor and take the strain in order that no damage to the escapement occurs. One or two little bends may be necessary but it will be seen that the clock will readily come to beat this way. When done, let the clock settle down and you will soon hear if you have been fully successful. Move the hands to time, allowing the strike to sound out if you are dealing with a count-wheel clock, and similarly the twelve must be allowed to gather in a clock with rack-striking. Check that the moon is correctly phased, and that the date is correctly shown. Finally replace the hood or close the case, check that any finials on the hood are correctly standing to attention. Then put the winding key in a safe place. If everything is carefully done, you may now sit down and admire your handiwork, knowing that the clock will run for many years.

INDEX
AND
ACKNOWLEDGEMENTS

INDEX

*Numbers in italics refer to the pages on which
illustrations appear.*

Absolom, William 448, 451-2
accuracy in clocks 942, 943, 947, 957
Aberdeen 821
acid etching 463, 491, *501*
acid polishing 458-9
Act of Parliament clock *see* tavern clock
Adam, James 31
Adam period style *763*, 771, 772, *772*, 777-80,
782, *804*, *809*
 decoration 695, 697, 772, 777
 knives 801
 Sheffield plate 778-80
Adam, Robert 31, 128, 267, 771-2, 777
Adams, William 272, 322
'aesthetic' taste *788*
air beads *391*, *392*, 393, *393*, 404, *404*
air bubbles 399-400
air tears *381*, 390, 396, *397*
air twist stems *398*, *399*, 399-401, 403-4, 510
Akerman, John 411
alarm mechanisms *873*, 926, 929, 930, *931*, *937*,
955
Aldgate 250
Aldwinkle and Slater *791*
ale glasses *390*, *399*, 428-30, *429*, *430*, *506*
ale muller *650*
Alleine, John 317
Allied English Potteries Group 299
lloys 524, 525, 539, 549, 608, 620, 622, *633*,
688, 693, 790
American clocks 978, 979, *979*, 985
amethyst colour *378*, 446
anchor escapement 848, 864, *923*, 930, 932,
939, 941, 946, 959, *966*
Anderson, James *817*
andirons 669-70, *670*
Angell, John 774, *805*
Angus and Greener 476, 495
annealing 691, 695
antique dealers' associations 164-7
antimony 529, 539, 549
anti wobble rim 600
apostle spoons
 (copper, brass and bronze) 649, *649*
 (pewter) 574
 see also under spoons, early
apprenticeship 530-1, 540, 597, 689, 744, 869
Apsley Pellatt & Co. 465-7, *466*
aquamanile 645
arbor 848, 857, 862
Archambo, Peter 758, 765, 810
arched dial clock 876, 893, 909, *916*, 917
architectural-topped case 911, *916*, 939
arch-topped hood *910*, 911
Arita kilns *816*
armchairs 67, *110*
arms 553, *554*
Arnell, J. *763*
Arnoux, Léon 334
Art Nouveau 790, *791*, 831
Art Union of London 329-32
ash wood *26*, 38
 ssay offices, centres 703, 704, 705, 816-20
assaying procedure 694
Astbury, John 229-31, 233
Astbury Whieldon 231, *233*
Aston, Sir Robert 415
auction houses 165, 167
Audnam Glass Works 469
aumbries 18

auricular style 731
Austen of Cork 603, *603*
Austin, Jesse 324
Austrian clocks 980, 981
Avon Street, Bristol 250
Ayckbown, J. D. 418, 423

Bacchus, George & Son 467, 468, 469, *472*
balance-wheel escapement 848, 849, 872, 924-5,
932
Ball, William 302
ball baluster *584*, 585, 600
ball moon 853, *860*, *894*, *991*
balloon-shaped case *916*, 918, *921*
baluster measure 529, 580, 584-5, *584*, 600, 602
baluster stems *367*, 386, 387-95, *388*, *390*, *391*,
392, *394*
balustroid stems 390-1, *392*, *392*
Bancroft, Ambrose 420
Bankes of Bewdley, Christopher *581*
Barbe, Jules 470, *483*
Barberini Vase *see* Portland Vase
Barlow, Arthur 337-8
Barlow, Florence 337-8
Barlow, Hannah B. 337-8, *337*
Barnard and Sons, Edward 773, 783
Barnard, Edward 774
Barnstaple 720, 742, 800, 801, 816
Baroque style 23, 215
Barr, Flight & Barr 314
Barr, Martin 314
barrel 848, 849
Barry, Sir Charles 90
basins and ewers 607, *628*
baskets 768-9, *769*, 779, 831
basket-topped clock *916*, 917
'battery' 525-6, 528
Baxter, George 324
beading *565*, *566*
beakers *355*, *377*, *472*, 588, 590, *590*, 600, 727,
819, 827
Beccles (Suffolk) 792
Bedford, Duke of (invoices) 366, 370, 371,
408-9
bedpan 596
bedpost clock 923
beds 18, 19, 96
Beilby, William 455, 456-7
Belfast 416, 418, 419
Belfast Glass Works 419
bell *763*
'Bellarmine' jugs ('Greybeards') 224, *224*
Bellingham, John 365
bell metal 524, 608, 650, 868
bellows *636*, *661*, 672-3, 740
bells 868, 871, 932, *932*, 943, 944, 954
bell staff 849, 862, 932
bell-topped case 887, *916*, 917, *917*
benches 18, 93, *93*, 94, 95
Bengal tiger patterns 210, *218*
Bentley, Thomas 259-60, *260*, 263
Betts, Thomas 409, 411
Bewick, Thomas 456-7, *820*
Bible, silver mounted 725
Billingsley, William 296, 307
Binns, R. W. 317
bird-and-flower marquetry *900*, *904*
birdcage construction 849, 863, 864, 949, 950
Birks, Alboine 335
Birmingham *449*, 455, 467, 468, 479, 778, 817,
818
 assay office 705, 820
Birtles Tate & Co. 467, 470

Bishop, Hawley 369, 370
bismuth 528
bisque ('biscuit') 214
black basalt *264*, 265-6
Black Forest clock *973*, 979, *979*, 980, 985
blade spring 849
Blatchford, Samuel *817*
Bloor, Robert 296
Blount, Thomas, *Glossographia* 737
blue glass 445-8, *447*, *454*, 511
bob pendulum 849
Bodendick, Jacob 737, 753
Bohemia 410, 465, 478, 479, 485, *508*
Bolden, Thomas 826
bone china 282
booge 530, 547, 550
bookcases 56-7, 107, *115*, 138, 153-5
Boote, Thomas 332
Booth of Pontefract 883, 885
boss 562, 563, *563*, 566, 572, 573, 677,
 (clocks) 849
Bothamley, William 925, 933
Bott, Thomas 317
Bottger, Johann 188, 215
bottle glass 395, 449, *449*
bottle jack 643, *643*
bottle label, wine label 779, *781*
bottles
 condiment 438-40, *439*
 Nailsea 449, *449*
 perfume *447*
 Roman 354
 sauce 438, 440
 stoppers 434
 wine 434
 wrythen *378*, *439*
Boulle, André Charles *32*
Boullemier, Anton 334
Boulsover, Thomas 779
Boulton & Mills 467, 469
Boulton, Matthew 778
Bow 192, 206, 210, *210*, 282-4, *284*, 298
Bowes, Sir Jerome 359, 360, 415
bowls
 (copper, brass and bronze) 622, 677-8, *677*
 (glass) 369, *412*, 440, 442, 489, *508*
 (pewter) 549, 568, 573, *575*
 (silver) 740, 742, 765, *805*, *809*
bowls (drinking glasses) 374, 381-2, *382*, *383*,
384, 509-10
 bell *367*, *381*, *384*, 390, *390*, *392*, 396, 402
 bucket *384*, 402, 432, *432*
 funnel *383*, *384*, 387, *392*, *393*, *394*, *397*,
398, *399*, 401, 402, 403, *403*, 404
 ogee *381*, *383*, 391, *391*, *402*, 411, 428
 ovoid *382*, *384*, 428
 thistle *384*, *404*
 trumpet *373*, *375*, *376*, *381*, *384*, *391*, *393*,
396, *398*, 399, 407, *407*
boxes 725, 739, 740, 830
boxwood 40
bracket clocks 842, 876, 877, 886, 887, 888,
892, *902*, 905, 915, *916*, 917, *917*, 921,
921, 957-67, *989*
Bradwell 229
Brameld family 309
brass 525-8, 604-16, *611*, 620, 627, 857, 858,
862, 878, 892, 948, *955*, 1009, 1010
brass-dial clock 878, 911
brazen 525, 526
Braziers' Guild 528
Brick House pot-bank (Bell Works) 259
brick-work base *898*, 915

bridge 849
Bridge, John 782
Brighton Pavilion 66
Bristol 192, 206, *218*, 247, 248, *248*, *249*, 250, 284-6, 818, 819, 820
  glass decorating 455-6, 457
  glassmaking 363, 408, 419, 466
Bristol glass *378*, 447-9, *447*, *454*, 511
Britannia metal 540-1, 549, 560, *576*, 577, 578, *578*, 790
Britannia standard 705, 816
British Museum 224, 270
broken-arch topped hood *910*, 911, 912, *912*
bronze 525, 526, 527, 604-16, 620
broth bowl 568, 573
Brown, Edward Charles *786*
Bruton (Somerset) *818*
buckles 678
Buckley, F. 399, 402
bud baluster *584*, 585
buffets 81-4, *82*, 97
bumpy bottom 562, 567
Bungar, Isaac 363
bureau bookcases *108*, *135*, 153-6
bureaux 18
Burgum & Catcott *551*
Burmese glass 467, 470, *482*, 488, 507
burnishing 612
Burslem 229, 236, 257, 258
Burton, William 257
Bushnell, John 224
butter dishes *413*, *454*
butter spade *791*
buttons 678
buying a clock 1002-06

Cabinet Maker's and Upholsterer's Drawing Book, The 31
Cabinet Maker's and Upholsterer's Guide, The 31
Cabinet Maker's London Book of Prices, The 31
cabinets 18, 19, *22*, *23*, *25*, *132*, *133*, *134*, 137, *137*, 146-7; *see also* cupboards
cabriole legs 31, 62, 67-8, 112, 119, 122, 125, *125*
Cafes 762
Caffee, William 308
calamine zinc 525, 604, 606, 609, 612, 613
Caldwell, James 237
calendar 874, *884*, 1014, *1014*
Cambridge (Ohio) Glass Co. 500
cameo technique 470, 480
candelabra 762, *765*, *774*, *779*, 784, *784*
candle boxes 90, 681
candlesticks *397*, 412, *491*, 740, 752, 753-6, *756*, *765*, *766*, *776*, *807*
  copper, brass and bronze 605, 607, 608, 618, 625, 626, 627, 651-9, *653*, *654*, *655*, *656*, *657*, *658*, *662*, *684*, *685*
  Corinthian column *654*, 656, *656*, 659
  evolution of *754-5*
  flower based 655, 659
  octagonal *654*, 655, *655*, 659
  of thin sheet, filled 778
  oval based 655, 659
  petal based 655, *655*, 657, 659
  pewter 591-4, *592*, *593*, 653, 685
  rectangular based 655, 659
  Rococo 762, *765*, *765*
  round based 655, *656*, 657, 659
  Sheffield plate 779
  square based 626-7, *627*, 655, 657, 659
  trumpet based 626, 653, *653*, *663*
  wall sconces 739
  see also candelabra; chandeliers
Cane ware 267
  ceramic paste 267
canoe bowls 413, 424, 433
canteen *834*
Canton ware 197
capacity seal or mark 553, 555, *555*, 588, 600, *601*, 603, 619, 640, *645*
card cases 706, *818*
Carder, Frederick 470, 487
Carlisle 792, 816

Carman, John *759*
cartel clock *963*, 976, 977
Carter, G. A. 776
Carter & Wingod 602
carving knife and fork rests *790*
cases 897-921, *935*, 937, 938, *962*, *963*, 968-9, *970*, 971, 976, 977, 978, 981, 1007-09
casters 62, 63, *63*, 767-8, *798*; *see also* sugar casters
casting
  copper, brass and bronze 526, 527, 528, 609-10, 612-16
  pewter 529, 530, 531, *533*
castor-oil spoon 596
Catherine II of Russia:
  Wedgwood service 261, 264
Caughley (Salopian Porcelain Manufactory) 194, 286-8, *286*, *288*, 305, 314, 321
Cauldon Place Works, Shelton 309
cauldrons 607, 617, 639, 640
Cave, Edmund 312
celery vases *495*, 498
'Cellini pattern' *787*
centrepiece *834*
centre seconds 849
Chaffers, Richard 250, 302; *see also* Richard Chaffers & Co.
chafing dishes 607, *834*
chairs *19*, *118*, 119
  arm 67
  construction of 60-3
  design of 66-8
  dining 18, 31, 32, 60, *64*, *65*, 111, *111*, 112, *112*, 117, *117*, *129*, 130, 144-6, *145*, 163
  Gothic style in 128, 130
  Hepplewhite 144-6
  lacquered 106-7, *114*, 117
  Mendelsham 163
  Queen Anne 117, 119
  rustic *118*, 162-3
  spoonback 117
  trap seat 60, 73
chamber clock 849, 861, 863, 864, 922, 923
Chamberlain & Co. 317
Chamberlain, Robert 314
Chamber pot 710
chambersticks 594, *658*, 659-60
Champion, Richard 206, 285-6, 306
chandeliers 594, 605, 660, 739
Channel Islands 799
Channel Islands measures 601-2, 603
Channel Islands pewter 597, 601-2
Chapter ring 849, 872, 873, *873*, 874, 875, *877*, 880, *880*, 1020
chargers 567; *see also* English Delft
Charles I period *724*, 725, 727, 731
Charles II 33, 66
Charles II bust (John Bushnell) 224, *225*
Charles II period 739-41, *739*, *740*, 800; *see also* Restoration
Chebsey, Thomas and John 418
Chelsea 190, 192, 209, 210, *210*, *218*, 219, 282, 288-91, 289, 290
  Gold Anchor Period 290-1
  'Maypole Dancers' 297
  Raised-Anchor Period 289
  Red Anchor Period 290, *298*
  Triangle Period 288-9
Chelsea/Derby Period 291
Chester 817, 819, 820
chestnut roasters 650
chests 19, 80-1
chests of drawers 18, 46, 77, 104-6, *105*, 119, 127, 138-43, *139*, *140*, *141*, *142*
chests on chests *see* tallboys
Chiddingfold 355-6, 359
china 197
China 188, 194, 199, 208
china clay (kaolin) 194, 199, 201, 204
china stone (petuntse) 194, 199, 201, 204
'Chinese Lowestoft' 197
Chinese manner, Chinoiserie 697, 751, 752, 831
  early period 741-2, *741*

fretwork 769
  Rococo period 761, 765
Chinese porcelain 188, 189, 196-9, 208-12
  hard paste formula 194-5
  manufacture of 199-204
  stoneware *230*
Chinese ware, silver mounted 721, *722*
Chippendale, Thomas 12, 14, 15, 29, 31, 115, 128-9, 138
  Chinese influence on 30
chocolate pots 646-7, *749*, 751
chopin 597, 598
Christian, Philip 250, 302
Christian, Thomas 826
Christie's, London 189
church clock 871, 970
church copper, brass and bronze 605
church pewter 532, 580, 600
Church plate 786, 822, 830, 831
  alms dishes and marks 825
  chalices, communion cups 822, 825, 826
  font cup and cover 711
  of St Nicholas Church, King's Lynn 824
  patens, paten cover 824, 826
Church Works, Hanley 239
Churchyard Pottery, Burslem 258
cigar case *805*
cigar cutters 679-80
cigarette boxes 679
'Cistercian' ware 192
civic regalia 830
clay 188, 225, 230-1
  ball 230
  kaolin 188
  pipe 230
  red 226, 229
cleaning
  copper, brass and bronze 620-1
  pewter 543-4
  silver 828
Clements, William 939, 940
click 849
Cliff, Clarice 344
Cliffbank Pottery 258
Clifford, Martin 365
Clifton, Jonah 756, *756*
Clinton, Henry, Earl of Lincoln 373
'clobbered' wares 197
clocks 157
  bracket *136*, 157-8
  long-case (grandfather) 13, *21*
C.M. & Co. (Charles Mulvaney) 418, 423
coaching glasses 444
Coalbrookdale 291, 292
Coalport 207, 214, 286, 291-2, *291*, *292*, 315
coasters 765, 779
coats of arms 697-9, *698*, *699*, 815; *see also* heraldry
cock 850, *850*, 862
coffee jug 772
coffee pots 747, 753, 759, 761, 779, 817
  copper, brass and bronze *628*, *637*, 646, 647
  early 751
  evolution of *760*
  manufacture 689-94, *690*, 692, *693*
  pewter 540, 548, 578, *578*
coffee service 777
coffers 18, 19, 45, 77, 80, 80-1, *87*, 89
coins 704
Coke, John 307-8
Coker, Ebenezer 762
colanders 643
collars 389, 390, 391, 399, 426, 428, 445
collecting 520-3, 542-8, 558, 560, 620-7, 665
collecting silver 804-15
  and dealers, sale rooms 809-10
  and hall marks 810-13, 815
  spoons and forks 792, 796, 803, 815
collections of British silver 829-32
collet 850, 864
Collins, Francis 423
coloured glass
  late Georgian 444-9, *447*, *449*, *454*

Victorian *481, 482, 483, 484,* 486-8, *490,*
491-2, 496, 497, 498, 499-500, *501, 502*
colours (pewter, copper and brass) 543, 549,
620, *629*
colours (pottery and porcelain) 233
bianco-sopra-bianco 247-8
bleu de roi 214
bleu turquin (turquoise) 214
cobalt blue 210
enamel 236
en camaien 214
English blue-and-white 195
gros bleu 214
'Littler's Blue' 303
rose Pompadour (rose du Barry) 214, 294
see also decoration of pottery and
porcelain
colour twist stems 402, *471*
commemorative articles 800, *805*
commemorative glass *394, 395, 416, 455,* 457,
459, 460, 461-2, *461, 462, 463,* 495, *506,*
509, *509*
commodes *15, 116,* 141, *143,* 153
Commonwealth period 20, *729,* 731; *see also*
Cromwellian silver
Communion plate *see under* Church plate
Comolera, Paul 332-3
compensated pendulum *948*
comportes *442, 474*
composite furniture 13, 17, 74, 85
composite stems *394,* 403-4, *404*
Compton of London *551, 566*
Compton Pottery, Guildford 343
condiment bottles and sets 438-40, *439*
Congham Church (Norfolk) *826*
contrate wheel 850, *850*
Cooke, Thomas *826*
cooking pots 607, 617, 621, 622, 623, *634,* 638-
42, *639*
Cookson, William 448
Cookworthy, William 204-6, 284-5, 308
patent (for porcelain manufacture) 205-6, 285
Cooper, George *821*
Copeland and Garrett 311
Copeland, Messrs W. T. 311
Copeland Spode Museum 242
copies 385-6, 407, 505-11, *506, 509*
copper 524-8, 604-16, *605, 611, 627*
cordial glasses 423
Cork *821*
Cork Glass Co. *418,* 419, 420, 423, 424
corkscrews 650
Corsham Court 30
Coster, Salomon *926, 927*
Cotterell, H. H. 548, 550, 552
counter box 739
country clocks *865, 867,* 876, 879, *880, 901,*
905, *906,* 909, *910,* 913, 946, 949, *950,*
950, 951, 953
count-wheel striking 850, *944,* 945, 946, 949,
950, 951, 953
Couper, James & Son 467, 477, 487
Coventry 818, *822*
Cowley, Thomas *551*
Cox, John 291
cradles 96, *96,* 97, *97*
cranes *642, 642*
cream jugs *752, 817*
creamware 271-5, *271, 272, 273, 279, 281;*
see also Wedgwood
credenza 32
Creed, Thomas *920,* 926
Crespin, Paul *756, 758, 765, 811*
crested tappit hen *598, 599*
'cristallo' glass 352, 356, 357, 365, 372, 376
Cromwellian clocks 924
Cromwellian silver *725, 728, 729; see also*
Commonwealth period
crown wheel 850
crumb scoop 775
crutch 850
Cruttenden, Thomas *934,* 1005
Crystal Palace, The *465, 465; see also* Great
Exhibition

Cuny, Louis *752*
cupboards 84-6, *85, 87, 91,* 91-2, 119
corner 146-7
see also cabinets
cups 556, 573, 588, 590, *746, 748, 758, 770,*
791
'caudle' *731*
dram *728*
grace *716*
Methuen Cup *715*
of King's Lynn Corporation *827*
ox-eye, college *727*
silver-gilt and rock crystal *720*
two-handled *727, 727, 743, 744,* 747-8, 761
evolution of *732*
see also wine cups
curfew *626, 673, 673*
cushion-topped clock *909, 910, 916*
custard glasses 440-2, *441,* 443, 488, 491
cut glass 410-13, *410-13, 454,* 478, *497, 508*
decanters *434-7,* 437-8
facet stems 404-7, *404-7*
Irish 414, *414, 415,* 416-24, *454*
cutlery 792-803, *828; see also* forks; knives;
spoons
Cutts, John 308

damage to furniture 68-74
Danbe, Richard 719
Daniel, H. & R. 292-3
Daniel, Ralph 234
date letters *703, 704, 705, 706-9, 793,* 819
dating a clock 850, *877,* 931, 949, 976, *1005,*
1006
dating copper, brass and bronze 621, 682-5
bowls 677-8
candlesticks *618, 626,* 654-9, *655*
chambersticks 660
coffee pots 646
cooking pots 639-42
fenders 671
handles 623
jelly moulds 645
joints 622, 624
marks 617-19, *645*
mortars 644
porringers 649
screw threads 624, 625
skillets 617-18
tea kettles 648
warming pans 675
weights 645
dating pewter 548-56
analysis 585
bowls 549
bud baluster 585
candlesticks 591-4
capacity *555,* 598
cups 573, 574
dealers 544
decoration 556-7
flagons 580-2
marks 547, 548, 551-6, *551, 552*
measures 579-80
plates 521, 549, 550, 562, *562,* 565-6
porringers 573
salts 577
saucers 550
spoons 574-6
tankards 556
tappit hens 599
thumbpieces 584
tobacco boxes 595
touch-plates 551-2
dating silver 697
spoons by shape 793
Davenport 209, 293-4, *294,* 322
Davenport, John 293
Davidson, George (G. Davidson & Co.) 467,
471, 475, 477, *494,* 496, 498, *498, 499,*
499-500
Davidson, Thomas 475

Davis, William 312, 314
day-of-the-month indicator 850
Deacon, Samuel *952, 999,* 1000-01, *1000*
dead-beat escapement 850, *947,* 948
dealers 809-10, 813, 815
decanters 434-8, *434-5,* 478, *453*
globe and shaft 434, 437-8, 446
Irish *418,* 423-4, 437, *438*
neck rings *418,* 423-4, 437, *437*
stoppers 434, 437, *438, 453*
decoration added at later period, touched up
784-5, 815
decoration of copper, brass and bronze 604,
619-20
alms dishes 606
andirons *669, 670*
bellows *661, 672*
cast 619
church 605
engraving 619, *676*
fenders 671
gilding 619
mortars *630,* 644, *644*
punch decoration 619, 671, 674, 675
repoussé 650
stamping 612, 650
trivets 674
'wall sconces' 660
warming pans 675, *676*
wine cisterns 650
decoration of furniture 18-31, *20, 21,* 66, *83,*
90, 91
decoration of pewter 556-7
beading *565, 566*
cast *570*
engraving 557
plates *568, 560*
punch decoration 556, *572*
tea pots *570, 578, 578*
wrigglework 556-7, *557, 572,* 587
decoration of pottery and porcelain 195, 233
enamel 195-6, 236
Long Eliza pattern 249
transfer-printed *195, 276, 284,* 312, 321-3,
321
decoration: types and techniques 695-702
bright-cut engraving 696, *697,* 772, 777-8,
777, 802
caryatid, human figure *697, 731, 765, 766,*
784, 784, 800
classical *717, 719,* 772, *773, 774*
cloisonné enamelling 786
cut-card work 699, *699, 743,* 747, 748, *748,*
757
embossing 695, *699, 717, 720, 731,* 738
engraving 695, 699-700, 711-12, 738-9, *762,*
814
flat chasing *700, 700,* 711, *720,* 741, *741*
gadrooning *700,* 701, 747, 769
guilloche *701, 719*
matting *701, 720, 724, 724*
naturalistic *757, 761,* 783-4, *784, 785,* 790
pierced openwork *701, 722, 722*
sea creatures *717, 745, 757, 761, 765, 767*
strapwork 702, *717, 719,* 747, 748, *748, 758*
Dee, Louis *808*
Defoe, Daniel (*Tour of Great Britain*) 283
Delftware *196, 208, 212, 212,* 213, *214; see also*
Dutch Delft; English Delft; Liverpool Delft
Della Robbia Pottery, Birkenhead 343
De Morgan, William 343
Derby 207, 209, 214, 294-9, *295, 296*
Derby Crown Porcelain Company 296
Derbyshire 230
Derbyshire, John and James 467, 473, *473*
*Description of the Empire of China and of
Chinese Tartary* 198-9
desks
knee-hole 74, 105, 122-3, *123*
portable writing 18
see also escritoires
dessert stands *783*
detent 851
dial foot 851

dial plate 851, *858, 879, 883, 958*
dials 871-96, *915, 916, 942,* 969, 970, *970,* 983, *999,* 1019-23
diamond point engraving 459-60
dimple mouldings 403, *403*
dinner service 782-3
dishes 566, 567-8, *567,* 568, *572, 573,* 600, *629,* 649, 722, *722, 736, 788*
dish ring *695*
Dixon Austin & Co. 251
Dixon, James *787*
dolphin fret 933, *933*
Donaldson, John 291, 313
Dossie, Robert 451
double whited 525
doubters *662,* 668
Doughty, Dorothy 313, *314*
Doulton and Watts 335
Doulton of Lambeth 299, 335-41, *337*
Doulton, Sir Henry 335, 337, 338-41
dovetailing 622, *622,* 641, 642, 645, 648
dovetail joints 46-50, *47, 48, 49*
dram glasses *382,* 431
drawers 47-56, *48, 49,* 101-2
    cushion 102, *102*
    handles 51-4, *52, 54, 55*
    linings 47-51, *48, 49,* 105, 127
    mouldings 50-1, *104*
    runners *48,* 71, *71*
    secret *103*
drawer stop *71*
Dresser, Christopher 477, 487, *788*
dressers 106
drinking glasses
    coloured 446
    copies and fakes 507-11
    hand-made 381-2
    shapes *433*
    size and capacity 396
    two- or three-piece 374-5, *399*
    weight 385-6
    see also bowls; feet; stems
drinking glasses: 16th/17th centuries 358, *358,* 364-7, *366,* 370-2, *374, 377, 378*
drinking glasses: 18th century 373-407, *373, 375, 376, 381, 382, 388, 390-1, 398-9, 401-5*
drinking glasses: 19th century *415,* 426-34, *426-8, 432, 453, 495*
drinking glasses: types: *see* ale glasses; beakers; cordial glasses; dram glasses; flute glasses; goblets; roemers; rummers; small glasses; tankards; wine glasses
drip pan 591, *592, 593,* 653, *653*
drop dial *970,* 975, *975,* 976
Dublin 742, 816, 820
Duché, André 204, 282
Duesbury, William 291, 295, 307
dummy winding squares 951, *952*
Duncombe family of Bewdley 537, *551*
Durnell, Edward, of Bull Street 613
Dutch Delft 196, 244, 249
Dutch silver 722, 730-1, *740*
Dutton, William 912, 949
duty on silver 705, 813
Duvivier, Fidelle 313
Dwight, John 224, *224, 225*
Dyson Perrins Museum, Worcester 313

'ears' 573, 600, 649
earthenware 207, 225
    'Egyptian black' 229, 265
    slipware *185, 196,* 221, 225-6, *226, 227*
East Anglian lantern clock *873,* 935
ebony 40-1, *897, 898,* 900, 903, 917, 918, *958*
Eddon, William *551*
Edinburgh 467, 477, 479, 486, 487, 816, *817, 821*
    assay office 705, 820
Edinburgh & Leith Glass Co. 427, 470
Edkins, Michael 447, 451, *454,* 455-6
Edwards, Benjamin 419, 423, 424
Edwards, John (glassware) 419

Edwards, John (silverware) 745, 753, 765
Egyptian style 32, 780, *780,* 783
Eisert, Joseph 479
electrolytic techniques 780, 786, 790
electroplate 786, 790
Elers, David 229
Elers, John Phillip 228
Elersware 228-9, *228, 229*
Elizabethan silver 712, *715,* 717-21, *719, 721,* 808, 830
    church plate 825-6
Elizabethan style 20, 32
Elkington and Company 786, *788,* 790
Ellicot, John 886, 949
Elliott, John 886, 949
elm 38
Emes, Rebecca *774*
enamel 886, *887*
enamelling 395, 452-7, *454,* 483, *485*
enamel twist stems 401-2
'end of day' glass 486-7
English blue-and-white porcelain 195, 213
English Delft 243-50, *246, 247*
    chargers 244-5, *244, 245*
engraving *393, 394, 394, 395,* 410-11, 478, 479-80, *557, 578, 587,* 619, *676, 681*
    commemorative *see* commemorative glass
    technique 459-63
    wheel *410,* 459, 460, 462-3, 479, *489,* 509
Enoch Wood and Sons 237
Entrecolles, Père d' 199
épergnes 761-2, 779
equation clocks 942, 943
escapement 851
escritoires *88, 99,* 102, *103,* 105
escutcheons *see* handles and escutcheons
Etruria factory *see* Wedgwood
Etruria Hall 262
European copper, brass and bronze 619, *629, 637, 637,* 676, 677, *677, 678*
European pewter 552, 557-8, 564
Evelyn, John 740
ewer *786; see also* rosewater ewer and dish
Exeter 720, 796, 799, 819, 820
export 530, 537, 539, 610-12

facet stems 404-7, *404-7*
façon de Venise 364-7, *367, 388,* 395
Faenza 213
'Fair Hebe' jug *238*
fakes 13, 17, 1003-06; *see also* reproductions
Falcon Glass Works 466-7
Falmouth 792
false plates *851,* 885, *887, 975, 976*
fan-and-husk cutting 412
Farrar, Richard 319
Farrell, Edward 783, *783*
Farrer, John *844,* 845
Fazackerly, Thomas 249
feet (clocks) 898, 909, 918, 932
feet (glassware) 374, 375-6, 388, 431-2, 510
    domed *375, 388, 391, 397,* 407
    folded *367, 375, 381,* 390-2, *427, 429,* 431-2, 510
    moulded pedestal ('lemon squeezer') *412, 424, 427,* 433, *439*
    oversewn 382
    plain *376, 382,* 388, *397, 398*
    ribbed *397*
feet (pewter, copper and brass)
    andirons 670
    cooking pots 639-40, *639*
    fenders 671
    salts 577
    tazzas 566, *566*
Feline, Edward *806*
Felling, Gabriel *818*
fenders 671, *671*
Ferguson, Alexander *551*
fine metal 529
finial 851
fire-irons 672, *672*
fireplaces *635,* 669-74
fireplaces, silver 740

flagons 529, 530, *533,* 562, *580,* 581, *581,* 585, 599, *599*
    acorn 581, *583*
    beefeater 580, *580*
    casting 530
    Charles I *569*
    communion 580
    Continental 558, *559*
    copper, brass and bronze 649
    Guernsey 601, *602*
    Irish 602
    James I 580, *580*
    Jersey 601, *601*
    Normandy *545*
    pot belly 598, *599*
    Scottish 598, *599*
    spire 581, *581*
    Wigan *571*
flammiform fringe 428, *429*
Flamsteed, John 940
Flaxman, John 267, 275, 790
Flight & Barr 314
Flight, Barr & Barr 314, 317
Flight, Thomas 314
flint glass 366, 367, 368, 370-1, 387, *388*
    single or double flint 366, 370-1, 387, *388*
floral decoration *394, 405,* 451, *454,* 455, *484*
flower vases 740
flute glasses 428, *430, 472, 506*
flutes *402,* 406, *407, 418,* 423
fly 851, *851,* 944
Fogelberg, Andrew *809*
Foley, Daniel 419-20
foliate fret 933, *933*
foliot balance 849, 851, *851*
food warmer *634*
foot-rims 192, *285*
footwarmer 676, 677, *677*
Ford, John 467, 477, *496*
Ford, William 477
forgeries 812-13, 815
forks 717, 801-3
Fortnum and Mason's clock 871
Fothergill workshop 584
France 722, 724, 737, 743-4
French Baroque style 695, 744, 747
French clocks *982,* 985
French feet 909
French polishing 77-9
fret *851, 917,* 932, 933, *933, 1009*
Fring church (Norfolk) 826
Fritsche, William 470, 479, 480, *489*
Fromanteel, Ahasuerus 893, 900, 923, 925, 934, 938, *939,* 986-7, 998
fruit servers *783*
Frye, Thomas 282
frying pan 641-2
'fuddling cup' *222*
Fulham 224, 341
funnel 596
furnaces 356, *356-7,* 359-61, 362, 363, 372
Furniture History Society 12
furniture, silver 740, 831
fusée 851, 957, 960

gadrooned decoration 428, 429, *429,* 441, 445
gadrooning 577, *631*
Galileo 842, 926
Gallimore, Ambrose 286
'galleyware' 244
Gamble, Henry 911, *912*
Garnier, Daniel 734-5
garnishes 568, *573*
garniture de cheminée 196
Gaskell & Chambers 582
Gatchell, Jonathan 420-1
Gentleman and Cabinet Maker's Director, The 14, *14, 15,* 30, 128
George I style 117
George III style 15
Georgian glass, late *412, 413,* 426-49, *426-8,*

430, 432, 434, 435, 439–42, 444–5, 447, 449, 453, 454
Georgian silver 767, 777
    additions by Victorians 784–5
    George I *748, 753*
    George II *744, 746, 758, 759, 768, 807*
    George III *765, 780*
    George IV *774, 829*
    see also Regency period
German clocks 979, 980, 985
Germany *377, 395, 410–11, 413, 427, 444, 451, 452, 458, 460, 463, 478, 479, 711, 722*
    Silesian stems 396–9, *397*
Gilbert, Stephen 809
Gilbody, Samuel 250, 302
gilding 447, *447*, 448, 451–2, *453*, *483*, 570, 619
ginger jars 740
Giles, James 312, 451
Gillows of Lancaster 906, *907*, 908, *908*, 911, 915, 918, *921*, 966
girandoles *492*
Glasgow 467, 477, 479, 487, 820
glass 56, 57, 107, 154, *909*, 911, 1010, 1011
Glass Circle, The 514
Glass Sellers Company 364, 368–70, 372, 408–9, 411, 428
glazes 188, 193
    felspathic 291, 311
    lead 194, 231, *241*
    overglaze ('on-glaze') 211
    salt 224, *224*, 225, 226, *226*, 227, 228–9, *228*, 234–5, *235*
    stone 194, *228*, *229*, 299
    tin 213, *224*, 244
    underglaze 210–11
    see also Hispano-Moresque ware; Maiolica
Glaziers Company 364
glazing bars 56, *56*, 57
glue 57–8
'Goatherd, The' *217*
goblets *358, 374, 394*, 395, *410, 416, 463*, 650, 727
Godfrey, Elizabeth *771*
goffering iron 678
gold boxes *818*, 830
Goldsmith's Hall 288
Goldsmiths, The Worshipful Company of 689, 704, 705, 719
    and Huguenots 744, 747
    and provincial goldsmiths 817, 818–9, 825, 826, 827
gold, standard for 703
gongs 852
Goss 301
Goss, William Henry 301
Gothic style 90–1, 978, *979*, *982*
Gothic style, motifs 717, 774, 782, 785–6
Goulds 762
Graham, George *21*, 947, 989
grasshopper escapement 989
grates 670, *671*
gravy spoons, ladles 803
Great Exhibition (1851) 413, 421, 464–5, *465*, 466, 468–74, 479, 497
Great Yarmouth 448, 451–2
Greene, John 366, *366*, 367, 427, 428
Greener, Henry (Henry Greener & Co) 467, 476–7, 496
'green' glass 365, 367, *377*, *378*
green glass (coloured) 446, 448, *453*
Gregory, Edward, of Bristol *572*
grid-iron pendulum 948, 989
guilds 528, 530, 531, 532, 533, 551, 556, 574, 597, 602
gun metal 524

Hackwood, William 267, 275
Hale Thompson, F. 485
Halifax moon 998, *998*
hall marks 552, 694, 703–5, *706–9*, 812, 825
    absence of 694, 703, 811–12
    and collecting 810–11
    forged, transposed 812–13, 815
    of spoons 792–3, 802

Ham House: toilet service 741
Hamilton, Sir William 260, 268
hammerhead *584*, 585, 586
hammering 527, 528, 530, *605, 611*, 622, *622*, 641, *645*, 650
hammermen's guilds 531, 533, 597, 602
Hancock, Robert 312
handles (glassware) *445, 449*, 488, 491, *492*, *499*
handles (pottery and porcelain) 573, 581, *582*, *618, 623, 634*, 639, *639*, 640, 641–2, *641*, 643, 647, 648, 672
handles (silver) 761
    manufacture 691, 694
    side 749, 751
handles and escutcheons 28, 51–6, *52, 54, 55*, 71, 86, *88*, 98, 106, 120, 122, 128, 131–2, *131*, 139, 144, 147, *147*, 154–5
hand-made glass 352–4, 376, 381–2
hands 871–96, 950, *969, 970*, 971, *971, 975*, 976, 1018, 1019
Hanley 309
Harache, Pierre *742*, *748*
hard metal 539, 540, 549, 576, 594
hard paste 194–5, 199, 206, 307, 308–9
    English *218*
Harewood House 30
Harrison, John (clocks) 947, 948, 988–90, *89?*
Harrison, John (pottery and porcelain) 2?*
Harthill church (Yorkshire) 753
Hartley, Greens & Co 273
haystack measure 603, *603*
Heath, John 295
Hemming, Thomas *770*
Henk, John 333
Hennezell, Thomas and Balthazar 35?, 363
Henzy, Ananias 415
Heppell, William Henry (W. H. Heppell & Co.) 467, 475, 477, 496
Hepplewhite, George 31, 32, 66, 67, *67*, 144, 165
heraldic fret 933, *933*
heraldry, heraldic engraving 697–9, *698*, *699*
Herculaneum *302*, 303
Heylyn, Edward *282*
Hicks, Meigh and Johnson 320
Higgins Museum 509, 513
highboys see tallboys
Hill, John, of Stourbridge 420
Hindley, Henry *875*, *942*, 943, 993–4, *994*
hinges 45, 45, 84
hinges, manufacture of 694
Hingstone, Dr Richard 204
Hispano-Moresque ware 213
History of the Staffordshire Potteries (Simeon Shaw) 228, 232, 306
'Hob in the Well' pattern 210
Hodder, George *821*
Holland 209, 213, 722, 724; see also Dutch silver
Holland: engravers from 394–5, *394, 395*, 460, *463*
hollow stems 395–6
holly 41
Holt, Richard 250
Holyrood Glassworks 477
hood 852, 898, 900, 904, 909–13, 968, 1009, *1009, 1010, 1010*
Hope, Thomas 32, 160
hops and barley design *399*, 428, 430, *430*
horned pediment see swan-necked pediment
hot water plate 564, 565, *565, 566*
house mark 553
Howlett, Robert 827
Howlett, William 826–7
Howson-Taylor, W. *327*, 344
Huguenots 15, 21, 102, 724, 743–4, *744, 748, 756*, 757, 829, 830
    and Goldsmiths' Company 744, 747
    articles introduced by 756–7
    candlesticks 753, 756, 762, 765
    style and decoration used 701, 702, 747, 748, 758

Hull 817
Hunt and Roskell 776
Huntsman, Benjamin 859
hutch 18
Huygens, Christiaan 926, 927

Imari porcelain 209
Imperial Glass Co. 500
Imperial standards 598, 599, 619
incised twisted stems 403, *403*
ingots 604, 607, 608, 610, 612
initials 553, *563*, *590, 640*
ink stands 594–5, *594, 763, 773, 806*
inkwell 785
inlay 19–20
inscriptions *805, 819*, 825
'intaglio' cutting 479
Inverness 792
Ireland 414–24, 458
    Irish glass *414–16, 418, 434*, 437
    iridescent glass *483*
Irish copper, brass and bronze *636*
Irish pewter 597, 602–3, *603*
Irish silver 802, *820, 829*
iron 862, 868, 872, 947, 948, *955*
ironstone 319–20; *320*; see also Mason's ironstone
iron turret clock 862
Islington Glass Works (I.G.W.), Birmingham 467, 468
Ismay, John *880, 944*, 950
Ivory Queens Ware 496
    ? House Works, Burslem 258

Jackfield 226
Jacks 871
Jackson, T. G. 487
Jacobean period 721–2
Jacobite glasses 455, 457, 461, 507, 509, *509*
Jacobs, Isaac 447–8, 451
Jaco?s, Lazarus 447, 455
ja? ?an 642
Jap? ? 209
    tiger pattern *218*
Japanese style 774, 786, *786*, 790
Japan work 969
jardinière *624*, 650, *662*
Jasper ware see Wedgwood
jelly glasses 440, *440, 441*, 442
jelly mould *636*, 645
Jenkinson, Alexander 486, 487
Jenkinson, William 303
Jenkins, Thomas *738*
Jersey, William de 602
jiggers 643
Jobling, James 476
Johnson, Christopher 951
Johnson, Jerome 411
joints (furniture) 44–50, *44, 45, 47*, 72, *72*, 90
    dovetail 46–50, *47, 48, 49*
    mortise and tenon 44–6, *45*
joints (pewter, copper and brass) 622–4
    casting 623
    dovetail 622, 641, 642, 645, 648
    rivet 624
    solder 620, 623
Jolly, John *551*
Jones, Henry *958, 960*, 965
Jordan, Walter 785
jugs (pewter, copper and brass) 540, 581, *582*, *582*, 629, 645, *645*
jugs (pottery and porcelain) *380*, 449, *484, 499*
    cream *379, 473*
    decanter *371*
    water *411*, 489
jugs (silver) 748, 772, *804*
    helmet-shaped 757, 777
    pottery, silver-mounted *713, 720, 721, 728*
    see also cream jugs

Kakiemon 209–10, *210*
    Bengal tiger *210*
    'Hob in the Well' *210*

Kändler, Johann 215, 290
kaolin *see* china clay
Kean, Michael 296
Keller, J. 479
Kensington Palace 196
Kent, William *123*, 124, 128
Kerr and Binns *317*
Kerr, W.G. 317
kettles 525, 608, *628*, *634*, *635*, 638-9, 648, *648*, 752, *753*, 761
kettle stands 70, 76
kick-in base 377
Kidney, William 71, *746*
'King of Prussia' mug *317*
Kings Lynn 385, *401*, 421
King's Lynn, goldsmiths in 822-7
kists 80-1; *see also under* coffers
Kneller, Sir Godfrey 373
Knibb, Joseph 929, 941, 942
knives 801
knobs 51, 53
Knole: toilet service 741, 831
Knollys, Sir Francis 462
Knops (glass) 373-5, *377*, 386, 387-94, *389-94*
knops (pewter, copper and brass) 540, 574, *575*, 576-7, 578, *578*, 580, *580*, 581, 591, 598, 599, 655, 659
acorn *575*, 576, 672
apostle 574, *575*
ball 574, 592, *593*
baluster *575*, 576, 592, 659, 670, 672
beehive 577, 656, 659
bell *593*, 656
diamond *575*
dog nose 576
fluted/tapering 659
hexagonal 574, *575*, 576
horned headdress *575*, 577
horse's hoof 649
lion sejant 574, *575*, 577
maidenhead 574, *575*, 577
melon 574
pineapple 574
puritan 574, 576, 649
round 659
seal top 574, *575*, 576
slip top 574, *575*, 576, 649
spiral 659
square 656
strawberry 574
stump end *575*, 577
urn 670
wrythen (twisted) 656
Kny, Frederick 470, 479, 480

lacquer *902*, *905*, *913*, *916*, 1020
ladles 607, *634*, 643
ladles, gravy spoons 803
Lambeth *214*, 246-7, 248, 250; *see also* Doulton
Lamerie, Paul de 757, 758, 761, 762, *763*, 769
silver in collections 830, 831
lamps 652-3, *660*, 664, 665-6, *666*
Lane Delph 239, 319
lantern clocks *858*, 861, 862, 864, 872, 873, *873*, 876, 877, *888*, 922-37, *941*, 945, 1011
Larkins, Edward 1006, *1006*
latch 852
latten 521, 525, 526, 527, 574, 606, 641, *653*
latten clocks *see* lantern clocks
'latticinio' 401, 487
Laver 599-600, *599*
lay 529
Leach, Bernard 344, *344*
lead 525, 528, 529, 549
lead bronze 525, *630*, *644*
lead glass 366-72, 409, 458
how to tell from soda glass 385, 386
leaf 852
le Carré, John 351, 356-9, 365, 367, 371, 414
Leeds 817
Leeds Pottery *187*, 272-3, *272*
lemon squeezer *see* feet, moulded pedestal
lenticle 852, 900, 903

Le Sage, John *766*
Lessor, Emile *186*
levelling a clock 1023
library steps 149-50, *150*
lifting-piece 852, *852*, 862, 946
lighting 651-68, *662*, *664*
Limekiln Lane, Bristol 250
limerick 815
Lincoln 818
lion's-mask side handles *916*, 921
Lister, Thomas *893*, *944*, 946, 952
Littler, William 303
Liverpool *278*, 301-3, 793
Liverpool base *see* brickwork base
Liverpool Delft *186*, 248, 249, 250
Lloyd & Summerfield 467, 468
Lloyd, William 270-1
locks *48*, *49*, 55, *55*, 56, 103, 109, 154
Bramah 55, 56
Lofthouse, Matthew *743*
London 720, 741-2, 778, 800-1, 817, 827
hall marks 704, 705, 793
spoons and forks 793, 795, 796, 799, 801
London Delftware 250
London Delftware 250
long-case clocks 13, *21*, 842, 843, *844*, 845, *865*, *866*, 875, *883*, *884*, 901, *902*, 908, *913*, 938-46, *955*, *961*, *991*, 1005, 1023-4
Longe, George 414-15
Longton Hall 303-4, *304*, 308, 309
looking-glasses 24, 30, 107, 109, 122
Loomes, Thomas 925, 987
loop handles *449*
loving cup 573
lowboys 69, 121-2, *121*
Lowestoft 304-5, *305*
Lowry, Morgan *893*, *902*, *943*
Lucas, John Robert 449
Lund, Benjamin 311
Lund's Bristol 312
Lund, W. 485, *500*
lunette 852
lustres 492
lustre (ware) 250-1, *251*
'Lynn' wine glasses *401*

Mackintosh, Charles Rennie 338
mahogany 23, *23*, *25*, *26*, 39-40, 76, *899*, 906, *907*, 908, *908*, 909, *909*, 910, 911-15, *915*, *916*, 917, 918, 921, 976, 978
maintaining power 852
maintenance 929, 1007-24
Maiolica 213, 244, 245
Majolica 332-3, *333*
makers' marks 694, 703, 704-5, *706-9*, 793, 821
and Huguenots 757
King's Lynn goldsmiths 825-7, *826*, *827*
makers of copper, brass and bronze 617-18, *618*, 640
'Malling jug' 244
Mansell, Sir Robert 361-6, 415
mantle clocks *919*, 921
manufacture
hand-wrought 689-94, *690*, *692*, *693*, 795
industrial processes 778-9, 782
spoons 795
wire drawing 695
Marco Polo 188
marine chronometers 947, 948, 988-90, *989*
marks 184-5, 192, 194, 215-16, 239, 284, *310*
Chelsea 288-91, *290*, *291*
Coalport 291, *291*
Daniel 292
Davenport *293*, 294
Derby 294, *295*
Doulton *337*, *338*
Goss 201
Herculaneum 303
Liverpool 301
Longton Hall 303
Lowestoft 304
Martin Ware 341
Mason 319, *319*
Minton 305, 306

New Hall 306
Pinxton 307
Plymouth 308
Rockingham 309
Spode 310
Worcester *312*, 313, *314*, 317
marks on copper, brass and bronze 617, 618, 640
marks on pewter 547, 548, *550*, 551-6, *551*, 552, 555, 563, 588, 591
European pewter 558
Irish pewter 602-3
Scottish pewter 551, 598, 599
marks on silver 703-5, *706-9*
applied to imported articles 711
on spoons 792-3
see also date letters; hall marks; makers' marks; sterling standard and marks; town marks
Marot, Daniel 21, 744
marquetry 88, 99, 102, 104, *865*, *883*, *898*, 903, 904, *904*, 905, *913*, 914, 917, 918, *991*
Marsh, Richard 827
Martin brothers 341-2
Martin Ware *340*, 341-3
'Mary Gregory' 485, 511
Mason, Charles James 320
Mason, Miles 197, *198*, 319-20, *319*, *320*
Mason's ironstone 319, *320*
match boxes 667, *667*
mazers 830
mean time 942
Measey, Michael 366
measures 529, 579-80, 582, *582*, 584-5
baluster *see* baluster measure
Channel Islands 601-2, *602*
harvester *645*
haystack 603, *603*
Irish 602-3, *603*
pot belly 598
regional 529
Scottish 598, 601, *646*
meat hook *642*
medieval copper, brass and bronze *629*
medieval period 717
provincial goldsmiths 817-18, 823
spoons 793, 795, 796-7, 798
medieval pewter 562
Meigh, Charles
'Minster' jug 332
Meissen 188, 195, 214
Royal Porcelain Manufactory 215
Meissonnier, Just Aurèle 757, 758-9
melting down, re-working 689, 729-30, 785, *805*, 806, 825, 826
Merchants' Guild 532, 597
merchants' marks 617
'mercury' twist 399, 400, *404*
Merrett, Dr Christopher 366, 371
'Merry Man' plates 246
Merry, Thomas *736*, 756
metal-rolling machines 689, 757
milk jug 777
Miller, R.W. 485
Miller, Samuel 421
Mills, Nathaniel 818
Ming 189, 210
Minton 207, 214, 305-6, *305*, 327, *328*
Majolica 332, *333*
parian 329, 332
pâte-sur-pâte *328*, 333-5, *334*
Minton, Herbert 306
Minton, Thomas 305-6, 321
mirrors 740
Mitchell, F. 253
mixed twist stems 403, *404*
modernisation 876, 877, *931*, 950, 951
Molineaux Webb & Co. 467, 473-4, *473*
monasteries, dissolution of 712, 824
Monteith 835
month clock *883*, *900*, *941*, 948
moon dial 853, 859, *860*, 894, *894*, 895, 998, 1000, 1013, 1014

Moorcroft, William 344
Moore, Thomas 969, 1006
Morelli, Alessio 366, 367, *367*, 427, 428
Morgan, Joseph 551
Morley, Francis 320
mortar 525, 604, 607, 617, 621, 623, *630*, 643, 644, *644*
mortise and tenon joints 44-6, *45*
Moscow, Elizabethan silver in 808
motion work 853
moulded flutes 402, *418*, 423
moulding, press 492, 494-5
mould lines 527, 645
Mount Washington Glass Co. 470, *482*, 488, 507
movement 853, 856, 857
Moyes, James 551, 598
muckle gill 598
Muckley, W.J. 479
Mudge, Thomas 912, 949
mugs 742, 749, 769, 771
Mulvaney, Charles 418, 423
Mundy, Thomas 551
musical clocks 896, *902*, 954, 960, 995, *997*
music barrel 853
mustard caster 768
mustard pots and bottles *439*, 440
mutchkin 598, *599*
mysterieuse clock *982*, 985

nails 37, 44, 47
Nailsea glass 449, *449*
Nankin ware 197
'Narcissus, The' (John Gibson) 329-31, *330*
Natural History of Staffordshire (Dr Plot) 226
Neale, James 239, 240
Nelson, Admiral Lord 32, 53, 159
Neo-classical style 31, 32, 215, 717, 719, 780, 809
Neri, Antonio 366, 368, 371, 445
Netherlands 737; *see also* Holland
Neville, Samuel 475
Newcastle glasses 390, 392-5, *393*, *394*, *395*
Newcastle upon Tyne 363, 408, 447, 455-7, 467, 477, 738, 742, 817, *819*, 820
    assay office, town mark 818, 819-20
New Hall Co., Shelton 206, 251, 306-7
new metal 529
nickel silver 790
'nipt diamond waies' 434, 450, 486
nomenclature for silver articles 727-9
Norris, Edward 858, *923*
Northwood, John 463, 479, 480
Norwich 720, 816, 818, 819, 820
    Norwich Goldsmith's Company 825
Nostell Priory 30
numerals 872, 874, *936*
Nuremberg dishes 557, *572*, 606, *629*
nuts and bolts 53, 54

oak 15, *26*, 37-8, 109, 897, *898*, 905, 906, *906*, 911, 913, 937, 969, 976
octagonal and hexagonal form 752, 756
Ogden, Thomas 859, *860*, 891, 894, 911, 951, *991*, 998-1000, *999*
ogee bowls 381, *383*, 391, *411*, 428, 462
    double ogee *391*, *402*, 428
oil and vinegar set *768*
oiling a clock 1018
oil lamps 445
Oliver, Charles 914, *915*
O'Neale, J.H. 289, 290, 313
opaque twist stems 389, *398*, 401-4, *401*, *402*, *462*, *463*, 507-10
opaque white glass 446-7, 448, *454*, 455-6, 491
Oppitz, Paul 479
Orchard, John 480
Oriental influence 196-7, 208-12
oriental style 905, 913, *916*, 969, 977
origin marks 553
Osler, F. & C. 465, *465*, 467, 468
Osterley Park House 31
overlap *622*, 623, *623*

Oxford ale jug 70, *70*
oxide 549, *564*, 588, 620
'OXO' border (egg and dart) *405*, 407
oyster shell parquetry 904

pagoda-style hood 905, *910*, 912, *913*
pails 650
paint 1022, 1023
painted dials *883*, *884*, 886, 1020, 1022; *see also* white dial
pallets 853
Palmer, Humphrey 239
panelling, linenfold 19, *19*
panel moulding *428*, 431, *432*
pan-topped bowls *397*, 402
pap boats 596
paperweights 505-6
Pargetter, Phillip 480
parian *184*, 329-32, *330*, *331*; *see also* 'Narcissus, The'
parquetry 903, *916*
'Pasglas' 445
pastry wheels 643
pâte-sur-pâte *328*, 333-5, *334*
patina 543, 620
pattern books 616, 711
patterns 612, 623
Payne, John, of Oxford 530-1, 609
Peale, C.A. 548, 552
'Pearline' glass *471*, 500
pedestal feet, moulded *412*, 424, 427, 433, *439*
'peggers' 193
Pegg, William ('Quaker') 296
Pellatt, Apsley 402, 495, 507
pen cases 680
pendulum 940-1; *see also* bob pendulum; seconds pendulum
Pennington & Part 303
Penrose, George and William 420, 423
pepper bottles *439*
pepper casters, pots 756, 768, *808*
pepper mill 808
Perchard, Hellier 602
Percival, Thomas 360, 362
Percival Vickers 467, 474, *474*
perfume burner *715*
Persia 210
petuntse *see* china stone
pewter 528-31, *570*
    cleaning 543
    collecting 542-8
    colour 543
    Continental *552*
    dating 548-56
    decoration 556-7
    drinking 579-80
    fakes and reproductions 544-8
    general use 591-7
    history 531-41
    kitchen and dining room 561-78
    marks *see* marks on pewter
    medieval 562
    Scottish, Channel Islands and Irish 597-603, *598*, *599*
    Stuart 562-3
    Tudor 561-2
    Welsh 603
Peytowe family 355
Phoenix Glass Works 448
pichet 598, 601
Pickett, William 782
Pidgeon, John, of Digbeth Street 613
piggins *414*
Pilkington's Lancastrian Pottery 344
pillar and arch cutting *415*, 424
pillars 853, 862, 913, 914, 915, 939, *940*
pincered wings 372
pin cushions *739*, 740
pineapple finials *916*, 921
pinion 853, 857, 858, 860, 861, 862
Pinxton 307-8, *307*, *308*
pipe stands 595, 680

pipe tampers 595, 679
Pirley Pig 601
pistol strikes 666-7, *667*
Pitt & Dadley 551
pivot 854, *854*
plain stems *381*, *382*, 395-6, 510
Planché, André 295, 296
plated silver 778-9; *see also* electroplate
plate frame movement 939, *941*, 944
Platel, Pierre 752
plates 529, 530, 549, 557, 562-6, *562*, 565, *572*, *573*, 649, 769, 854, 857, 862, 966
    broad rimmed 521, 562-3, *562*, 565, *565*
    flat bottomed 563
    medieval 562
    narrow rimmed *562*, 563, *563*, *564*, 565, *565*
    octagonal *562*, 565
    plain rimmed *562*, 563, 564, *564*, 565, *565*
    single reeded *562*, 564, *564*, 565, *572*, 649
    triple reeded *562*, 563, *564*, 565, *565*
    wavy edged 550, *562*, 564, *565*
plate warmers 649
Platts Glasshouse 469-70
Plot, Dr Robert 368, 369-70, 371, 382
plouk 599
Plummer, John 738-9, *738*, 816
Plummer, William 764
Plymouth 192, *218*, 308-9, *316*, 800, 817, *817*
polescreens 75-6, *75*
polishes 77-9
polishing 527, 530, *530*, 612, 623
polishing silver 694, 828
pomade pots 324
pomander *721*
pontil marks 375, 376, 432, 511
porcelain, manufacture of 192-5, 199-204, 205-6
porringers 548, 573, *574*, 598, 600, 649, 727, *729*, 731, *733*, 741
    and nomenclature 728
Portland, Dowager Duchess of 268
Portland, Duke of 269
Portland Vase (Barberini Vase) 267-71, *268*, 445, 480
Portuguese influence 722, *722*
posnets 607, 640, *640*
posted frame movement 944; *see also* birdcage construction
pot hooks 642
pot lids 324, *325*, *326*, 329
'Potteries, The' 221
pottery, manufacture of 192-3
Powell, James & Son 377, 465-8, 472, 486, 487, 509
Powlden, Thomas 365
Pratt, F. and R. 324
Pratt, Felix 239, *325*, *326*
Pratt, William 239
Prattware 239
precision regulator 946, 948, 949
pressed glass 459, 461, 467, 473, 474-7, *474*, 492-500, *493-5*, *499*, *501*
Prince Rupert bust (John Dwight) 224, *225*
Prince's metal 524
printies *411*, 430
privateer glasses *462*, 509
propeller stems 428, *429*
provincial goldsmiths 816-22
    King's Lynn 822-7
prunts *391*, *426*, *484*, 488
Pugin, Augustus 90
punch bowls 765
punch decoration 556, *572*, 619, 671, 674, 675
pushers 115, 655, 658, *658*, 659
Pyke, George 896, *974*, 994, 995, *997*

quaiches 598, 600, 816, *817*, 830
quartz 350, 351, 367, 371
Queen Anne period *736*, 748, 749, 751, *752*
Queen Anne style 15, 21, 33, 107, 109, 119
Queensware *see* Wedgwood
Queens Ware Burmese *482*, 488
Quinn, Dr Henry 275

rack-striking 854, *944*, 946, *947*, 952, 959, *960*
Ramsey, James 420
Ranken, Francis 477
rating nut 854
Ravenscroft, George 366-72, 382, 427, 428, 446, 458, 486
  price list 408-9, 434, 450
recoil 854
Redcliffe Backs 250, 312
Regency period *783*, 829
Regency style 15, 32, 66, *916*, 917, 921
'Regent porcelain' 314
registration marks 473, 474, *474*, 476, 495-6, 500; *see also* trade marks
Renaissance and design *712*, 713
repairing a clock 1007-24
repair of copper, brass and bronze 620
repair of pewter 542-3
repeat striking facility 854, 945, 946, 958, 959, 960, *960*
repoussé 650
reproductions (copies) 13, 17, 385-6, 407, 505-11, *506-9*
reproductions and fakes 544-8, *545*, 550, 573, 602-3, 624, 625, 627
Restoration 724, 729-31, 737, 753, 756; *see also* Charles II period
Restoration style 20-1, 32
Reynolds, Sir Joshua 270
Rhenish stoneware, mount... *720*, *721*
Rice Harris & Co. 467, 468, 495
Richard Chaffers & Co. 301-2
Richardson, W. H., B. and J. *380*, 467, 468, 479, *484*, 497
Ridgway 309
Ridgway, John and William 323
rings 678
Robbia, Luca della 213
Robson, William 359, 360, 361, *362*, 415
'rock crystal' style 479-80, *489*
rocking figures 895, 896, *896*
Rockingham 293, 309-10, *310*, 316
Rococo style, period 25, 29, 31, 32, 66, 215, 284, 286, 310, 697, 757-71, *757*, 759, *771*, *807*, 878, *879*, *965*, 977
  and Huguenots 758, 762, 765
  candlesticks 762, 765, *765*
  decoration 757-8, 761, 767
  diversity of styles 759, 769, 771, 782, *783*
  knives 801
  salt cellars 767, *767*
  sauceboats 765, 766, 767
roemers *426*, 427
Rogers, Isaac 935, 936, *936*
Rogers, of Malmesbury 534, 535
Roman glass 354, *354*, 487
Roman-striking 942
Romanticism 783
'Romers' 427
Ronayne, Edward and Richard 420
ropes 927, 1016, 1017
Rose, John 286, 292
Rosenberg Castle, Copenhagen: silver furniture 740
rosewater ewer and dish 710-11, *711*, 717, 722, 724
rosewood 27, 41
Rosso Antico 266
Royal Academy of Arts, Burlington House 310-11
Royal Crown Derby Porcelain Company Limited 294, 296; *see also* Derby
royal pendulum 941
Rugeley, Staffordshire 356
rummers *415*, 426-8, *427*, 428, 430, 431, *459*
Rundell, Bridge and Rundell 782
Rundell, Philip 782
Ruskin, James 338
Ruskin Pottery, Smethwick *327*, *340*, 344
Rye 252

Sadler and Green *271*, 272
saggers 193

St George's Chapel, Windsor 731
St Nicholas Church, King's Lynn 824
sale rooms and collecting 810
Salisbury 818
Salisbury Cathedral clock 871
Salopian Porcelain Manufactory (Caughley) 286
Salt, Ralph 239
salts, peppers and mustards 540, *576*, 577, 649
salts, salt cellars 433, *439*, 440, 777, 783-4, *813*
  bell 719
  development of *723*
  Gibbon Salt *718*, 719
  Rococo 767, 767
  Rogers Salt 718
  Seymour Salt *733*
  standing 717, *717*, 719, 724-5
  trencher 725
salt-glaze *see* glazes
salvers 730, *731*, 747, *805*, 811
  introduction of 737
  Regency *783*
  Rococo 757, 761
samovars 648
Samuel Alcock & Co. *184*, 272
sand casting 526-7
Sang, Jacob 460
satin glass 467, 470, 486, 491
satinwood 27, 41, 76
sauceboats 756, 765, *766*, 767, 780, *817*
sauce containers, 'saucers' 729
saucepans *632-3*, 634, 641-2, *641*
saucers 550, *550*, 566
sauce tureens 777, *778*, *781*
Saunders, George 422
Savoy glasshouses 368, 370
Scafe, William *969*, 971, *975*
Scandinavian design 738
scent flasks 740
Scheibner, F. 479
Schiller, J. 479
Schwanfelder *883*, 886, *887*
Scofield, John 764, 804
Scott, Digby *773*, *780*, *781*, 782
Scottish cases 898, *910*, 913
Scottish copper, brass and bronze 645-6, *646*
Scottish pewter 597-601, *599*, *600*, *601*
Scottish pint 598, *599*
Scottish silver *817*, *821*, 830
  'bullet' teapot 751-2, *821*
  Methuen Cup *715*
  quaich 816, *817*, 830
  spoons and forks 799-800, 802, 816
screws 858, 859, 862, 932, 953, 954
scriptors *see under* escritoires
seals 681, *681*
seat board 854
seaweed marquetry *898*, *903*
seconds hand 874, *891*, 892, 941, *969*
seconds pendulum 848, 854, 864, 941
secretaires 113, 121, *134*, *150*, 152-3
'seeds': in glass 385
Selwood, William *873*, 925, 932, 933, 987
sets (of plates, etc) 568, *573*, *630*
setting a clock 938, 942, 1018, 1024
Sèvres 214, 333
  Royal Porcelain Factory 214
sgraffito decoration 227, 337
shaded glass 470, 488, 500, *502*
shaft and globe decanters 434, 437-8, 446
shaving bowl *814*
Shaw, Alderman 250
Shaw, Ralph 229
Shaws Brow 250, 301
Shearer, Thomas 31
sheep's head clock 876, 935
sheet metal 527, 540, 604, 607, 610, 612, 641
Sheffield 702, 778, *778*, *808*
  assay office 705, 724
Sheffield plate 778-80, *778*, 790, *806*
shelf clock 978, 979, *979*
Sheraton, Thomas *28*, 31, 76
Sherratt, Martha 239

Sherratt, Obadiah 239-41
sideboards 109-11, *110*, 130-1, *131*
side glasses 917, *917*
sifters *576*, 577, 649
Silesian stems 396-9, *397*
silver coating 480, 485
silver-gilt 702, 720, 724
silvering 855, 1011
silver-mines 688
silver-mounted articles 725, *740*, *807*
  glass, rock crystal *715*, *718*, 720, *808*, 811
  natural objects 721
  pottery *713*, 720-1, *721*, *722*, 801
Silvers, Joseph 470
Simmance, Eliza 338
Sir John Soane Museum 772
skeleton clock 982-5, *982*
skillets 607, 617, 618, *618*, 623, 640, *640*
skimmers 607, *634*, 643
'slag glass' 467, 475, 476, 511
Sleath, Gabriel 749
slip tops 574, *575*, 576
Sloane, Sir Hans 290
small glasses 430-3, *432*
Smith, Benjamin 773, *780*, *781*, 782
Smith, Edward *818*
Smith, George 32
Smith, Sampson 243
snail 855
Snow, William 951, *952*, 997, 1001
snuff boxes 595, 678, *745*
snuffers, snuffer stands *660*, *663*, 668, *668*, 741, 756
snuff mulls 595, 600
soap boxes 677, 678, *810*
soapstone 311
soda glass 372, 385, 386, 398, 402, 403, 410, 510
  how to tell from lead glass 385, 386
soda: in glass making 352, 371
soft paste 194-5, 206, 303, 311
solar dial 894
solar time 942
Solon, Marc Louis 334-5, *334*
Sotheby's 189
soup tureens *745*, 756, 765
Southall 341
Southwark 244, 250
sovereign's head mark 705
Sowerby's of Gateshead 371, 467, 475-6, 495, 496, 498, 499, *501*
Spain 724
spandrel 855, 874-8, 880, 882
Spanish trenchers 530
spiral air twist stems *398*, 400
spiral gauzes 402, *404*
spirit (dram) glasses *382*, 431
spits 642-3, *643*
Spode *294*, 310-11, *310*, *311*, 322, 323
Spode, Daniel 311
Spode, Josiah 207, 272
Spode Jr., Josiah 310
spoons 524, *530*, 574, 576, 577, 596, *634*, 643, 649, *649*
  and identification of goldsmiths 821-2
  forgeries 815
  see also spoons, early; spoons and forks from 1700
spoons and forks from 1700 802-3
  finials 794, 799, *799*, 802-3, *803*
  'rat tail' 802
spoons, early 792-800, 826, 830
  dating by shape 793
  finials 793-801, *793*, *794*, 796-7, *798*, 799, 800, *801*, 832
  manufacturing method 795
  marks 792-3
  'rat tail' 799
spouts 691, *692*, 693-4, 751
Sprimont, Nicholas 288, 291, 758, 767
spring-driven clocks 922, *931*, 957
Spurgin, Jeremy *873*, *906*, *923*
Staffordshire (county) 222, 230, 257

Staffordshire (pottery) 184, *185*, 221-3, *221*, *226*
  creamware 281
  figure pottery 235-43, *236*, *238*, *241*
  see also Victorian Staffordshire
stamping 612, 650
standards 579, 580, 582, 584, 598, 599, 601
standishes 594, 680
star wheel 960, 998
steel 852, 857-9, 862, 892, 957
steeple cup 720, *720*
stems 373-5, 386-407, 446, 508-10
  baluster 367, 386, 387-95, *388-95*
  balustroid 390-2, *392*, *393*
  composite 399, 403-4, *404*
  facet 404-7, *404-7*
  plain *381-2*, 395-6, 510
  Silesian 396-9, *396*
  twist 398, 399-404, *399*, *401-4*, 471
sterling, standard and marks 688, 703, 704, 705, *706-9*, 819
  and assaying 694, 703
  for solder 693
  see also Britannia standard
Steuben Glass Works 470, 487
Stevens & Williams 467, 470, 479, 480, *483*
Stewart, James *962*, 966, *966*
stipple engraving 459-60
Stirling stoup 598
Stirling town measures 599
stirrup cups 443-4, *444*
Stockwell, E. H. *811*
Stoke-on-Trent 221-2, 305
stoneware 229, *229*, 230, 266, *332*, *337*, 341
  Rosso Antico 266
stoneware silver-mounted jugs 720, *721*
stools 18, *69*, *93*, *94*, 95
Storr, Paul 782
  'Galvanic Goblet' 790
Stourbridge 363, 408, 420, *454*, 463, 467, 469-70, 479, 495, 496, *502*, *505*
strap handles *444*
'strawberry dish' 728
Strawberry Hill 137
strike a lights 666-7, *666*
strike/silent indicator 876, 893
striking mechanism *see* count-wheel striking; rack-striking
Stubbs, George 267, 275
  portrait of the Wedgwood family *262*
style, factors influencing 710-11
sugar basins, bowls 473, 540, 752, 777
sugar boxes 771, *810*
sugar casters 748, *749*, 753, 768
sulphide encrustations 126, *126*
Sunderland *251*, 272
Sunderland Bridge rummers *459*, 461
'Sunrise' glass 470, 488
superfine hard metal 540
survival of pewter and copper, brass and bronze *615*, 682-5, *683*, *684*, *685*
Sussex rustic ware 252-6
  'pig' *254*
swan-necked pediment 909, *910*, 911, 912, *1010*
sweetmeat dish, basket 727, *821*
sweetmeat glasses *383*, 391, *396*, *411*
sycamore 41
syringes 596

'T' (or 'Y') mark 375-6, *375*
tables
  butterfly 151
  card 59-60, *59*, 124-6, *125*, 148, 157
  centre *136*
  console *123*, *124*, 160
  construction of 57-60
  dining 93-4, 99-102, *101*, 147-9, *148*
  gate-leg *37*, *37*, 59, 99-102, *100*, *101*, 147
  Pembroke *27*, 151-2, *151*, *152*
  pier 122-3
  pre-seventeenth century 18
  side *97*, *98*
  sofa 153

state-room 160
tea 59
three-quarter side *see under* lowboys
tripod 74, 75, *159*
wine 76
tallboys *113*, 120-1, 140
Tallboys, Robert 719
T'ang dynasty 188
tankards (glass) 444, *459*, *461*, *494*
tankards (pewter, copper and brass) 529, 530, 539, 544, 580, 586-8, 649-50
  casting 530
  Continental 558, *628*
  flat lidded 544, 581, *581*, 586-7, *587*
  Georgian 587, *588*
  glass bottomed 520, 588
  lidless 588, *588*, 598, 599, *599*, 600
  Scottish 600
  Stuart 556, 586, *587*, *588*
  tulip shaped 587-8, *588*, *589*
tankards (silver) 722, *737*, 738, *738*, 748, 771, *818*
  Charles I *724*, 725
  evolution of *726*
  nomenclature 728
  Tudor, Elizabethan *715*, 719-20, *719*
  with pomegranate motif *738*, *738*, 816
Tanqueray, David *753*, *813*
taper sticks 681, *736*, 756
tappit hens 545, 550, 598, 599, *599*, 600, 603, 646
'tartan' twist stems 402
Tassie, James 275
Taunton 796
tavern clock 968-75
tavern mugs 536, 539, 588, *588*, 601, *630*
Taylor, Anthony 457
tazzas 399, 442, *442*, *443*, 566, *566*, *714*, 720
tea caddies *763*, *771*, 806, 807, *814*
  Queen Anne *752*, *752*
teapots 540, *570*, 578, *578*, 647, 747, *753*, 761, 777, *777*, 779, *821*
  'bullet' 751-2, *821*
  evolution of *750*
  Queen Anne 751-2, *751*
'tear glasses' 396
tea services *774*, 777, *788*
  depicted in 'The Tea Party' *746*
  Japanese taste *786*, *786*
tea trays 761, *786*
tea urns *631*, 648, 765, 772, 777, 779
teeth 860, 861, *964*, *1014*, *1014*, 1015
Temple Back, Bristol 250
Temple Newsam House, Leeds 16, *22*
Templeton, Lady 267, 275
Thelwell, Bevis 360, 362
thimbles 680
Thomas Wolfe & Co. 303
Thorpe, W. A. 393, 452
throw 855
thumbpieces 571, 580-1, *580*, *581*, 582-7, *582*, *583*, *586*, *587*, *588*, 599, *599*, 600
'Tiefschnitt' (deep cutting) 479
Tilson, Thomas 365
tin 524, 525, 528, 529, 597
tin glazing *see* 'gally-ware'; glazes; Hispano-Moresque ware; Maiolica
tin glass 528
'tin pest' 549, 620
tints: in old glass 382, 385, 421
Tinworth, George 338
Tipling, William *883*, 887, 990, 991
toasting glass 376
tobacco boxes 594, 595, 679, *729*
Toby jugs 236, 242
toddy lifters 443, *444*
Toft family 225
toilet service, toilet articles 734-5, 740-1, *753*, 831
Tompion, Thomas 863, *866*, 869, 904, 929, 940, 947, *958*, 960, 987-8, *989*, 1004
torchères 75, 99

touch-plates 551, 552, *560*
tower clocks 970
Towneley, Richard 940, 941
town marks 705, 793, 816
  of named towns 704, 705, *706-9*, 818, 819, 820, 826
trade marks 467, *473*, 475-7, 498; *see also* registration marks
trailing threads 372, 450, *472*
train 855
transfer-printed wares *182*, *195*, 321-3; *see also* decoration
transfer printing 468, 469, *472*
trays 58, *58*, 75, 76, *76*, 752, 762, 826; *see also* tea trays
'treasury' ink stand 594
Trent and Mersey Canal 265
'trifle' 529
trivets 673-4, *673*
Tudor period 711, 712, 719-21
tumblers, tumbler cup 816-17, *819*
tureen 566
Turner, John 272
Turner, Thomas 286, 305
Tutania 524
twist stems 398, 399-404, *399*, *401-4*, 471

Underwood, Nathaniel *688*
upholstery 66-7, 72-3, 130, 145-6, 165

Vallin, Nicholas 922
van Vianen, Christian 731, 743
Varnish, Edward 485
vases 451, 455, 468, *472*, 481, *482*, *483*, 488, *501*, 502, *504*
  celery *495*, 498
  Portland 445, 480
veneers *27*, 46, 50, 102, 104, 105, 122, 126-7
Venetian style 357-9, 364-7, *366*, 372, 376, 387, *388*, 395, 401, 410, 450, 458
  'façon de Venise' 364-7, *367*, *388*, 395
  Victorian revival *472*, *483*, 484, 485-8, *491*, *501*
Venice 351, 352, 353, 356, 445, 452, 486
  glass supplied by Morelli 366, *366*, 367, 427, 428
venison dish 568
verge escapement 849, 855, *920*, 922, 928, 929, 931, 932, 935, 945, 957, 958, *958*
vermicular collar *389*, 399
Verzelini, Jacob 358-9, *358*, 364, 414, 460
Victoria and Albert Museum 16, 117, 165
Victorian furniture 15, 16, *32*, 90-2
Victorian glass
  decorative *471*, 478-500, *481*, *482*, *483*, 499, *501*, *504*
  manufacturers 464-77
Victorian marble clock *916*, *919*, 921
Victorian silver *784*, *785*, *788*, *790*, *805*, *808*
  additions to older articles 784-5
  characteristics 783-4
  copying of designs 782
  flatware, and collecting 803
  glassware, silver-mounted *808*, *811*
  Gothic style 785-6
  Japanese style *786*, 790
Videau, Aymé 765
Vienna regulator 980, 981, *981*
vinaigrettes 817
Vintners' Company of London 719
Vitrearius, Laurence 355
'Vitrified' (Richardsons) 467, 469
Walburton, Peter 251
wall boxes 681, *681*
wall clocks 936, *963*, 968-77, *992*
Wall, Dr John 312, 314
wall sconces 594, 626, 660, *660*, 662, 665, 739
walnut 21, 23, *37*, 38-9, *898*, 900, *901*, *902*, *903*, 904, 905, 906, 912, 917
Walpole, Horace 137
Walton, John 238-9, *238*
Ward, Joseph 753
wardrobes *29*, 84-5, *85*

warming pans 626, 665, 675-6, *676*
Wastell, Samuel 747
watch cases and stands 680
watches 988, 989, 990
Watcombe Pottery, Devon 344
water clock 1006, *1006*
Waterford 415, *415*, 416, 418, 420-2, 424
Waterford Glass Co. 413, 420-1, 422, 423, 424
water jug *804*
Watts, Mary 343
wax jacks *680*, 681
Wealden glass 354-9, 415, 509
Webb & Richardson 469
Webber, Henry 270
Webb, Thomas (Thomas Webb & Sons) 467,
  469-70, *482*, *483*, 488
Webster, Henry *877*, 930, 932, *932*
wedges 585, *860*, 862, 863
Wedgwood *182*, *186*, 257-65, *279*, 320, 322
  black basalt *264*, *265*, 265-6
  bone china 275
  cameos 266
  'ceramic pastry' 267
  'chrysanthemum pattern' 266
  creamware 259, 271-2, *273*
  'Egyptian black' 265
  Etruria factory 263, 265
  Etruria Hall *262*
  jasper ware 192, *193*, *262*, 264
  Portland vase (replica) 267-71, *268*
  portrait medallions 275, *280*
  Queensware *258*, *259*, *261*, *263*
  service for Empress Catherine II *261*, 264
  willow pattern *321*
Wedgwood, John *262*, 265
Wedgwood, Josiah 206, 229, 257-65, *262*, 269-
  71, 276-81, 285
Wedgwood Jr, Josiah *262*, 265, 275
Wedgwood Memorial Institute 257
Wedgwood, Susannah *262*, 265
Wedgwood, Thomas *262*, 265
weights 644-5, *644*
weights (clocks) 855, 867, 868, 925, *927*, *943*,
  956, 975
Welsh hat 595-6
Welsh pewter 603

Westropp, M. S. D. 409, 419, 421
Wetherfield collection 843
whale's tail cresting *910*, 912
whatnots *58*
wheel 855, 860, 861, 862
wheel engraving *410*, 459, 460, 462-3, 479,
  489, 509
Whieldon *230*, 231, *231*
Whieldon, Thomas 231-2, 258, 310
Whitechapel foundry 617
White, Cooke 527
white-dial 855, 860, 881-2, 885-6, *891*, *898*,
  909, *910*, 913, 949, 955
Whitefriars Glassworks *377*, 466-8, *472*, 486,
  509
white glass *380*, 445
white glass, opaque 446-7, 448, *454*, 455-6, 491
White House Glass Works 469
Whyte, Robert 556
Wick 136
Wickes, George *768*
Wilcocke, James 146
Willaume, David *748*
Willett, Henry 237
William III 21
William III period 744, *748*
William Reid & Co. 302
Williams, Richard & Co. 417, 418
Williamson, John *875*, *940*, 990, *991*, 993
Willoughby, Roger 551
willow pattern 321-2, *321*
Wilson, Thomas 914, *914*, 915
Wincanton 250
Winckelmann, J. J. 772
winding *927*, 938, 939, 941, 943, *943*
winding holes 874, *875*, 943
winding squares 855
wine cellarets 161-2, *162*
wine cisterns 650
wine coolers *31*, 161-2, 799
wine cups 722, 724, *724*, *728*
  Charles I 720, 724, 727
  Elizabethan 720, *721*
  steeple cup 720, *720*
wine glasses
  coloured 446, *453*

copies 507-11
  prices 365, 370, 371, 408-10
  size and capacity 396
  small glasses 430-3, *432*
  see also drinking glasses
wine jug, silver on glass *788*
wine label, bottle label 779, *781*
wine tasters 728, *728*, 747
  and nomenclature 728-9
winged lantern clock 930
wire drawing 695
Woburn Abbey: invoices 366, 370, 371, 408-9
Wolff, David 460, *463*
wood 897-921, *898*, *899*, *962*, *963*, 1007-10
Wood, Aaron 236
Wood, Enoch 236-7
Wood, Ralph 236, *236*, 242
Wood, Thomas 479
Woodall, George and Thomas 480
woods used in furniture making 26, 27, 33-41,
  34, *35*, *36*, 37
Woodward, William *766*
woodworm 60-1, 76
Woolley, James 909, *960*, 996-8
Woolley, John 998
Worcester 192, 207, 209, 210, *219*, 287, 311-17,
  314
Worcester Royal Porcelain Company 311, 312,
  317
Worcester Tonquin Manufactory (Worcester
  Porcelain Company) 312
workmanship, quality of 65-6
wrigglework 556-7, *557*, *572*, 587
Wright, Jonathan 422
Wrotham 226, *227*
wrythen decoration *378*, 428, 429, *429*, *439*

'Y' (or 'T') mark 375, *375*, 376
Yates, James 551
year clock *866*, 941, *943*
Yi-hsing *230*
York 720, 738-9, *738*, 800, 816, 817
  assay office 818, 819, 820

zinc 525, 526, 611, 612, 620
Zouch, Sir Edward 360, 362

Acknowledgements

FURNITURE

The photographs were taken by Robert Du Pontet for the Hamlyn Group with the exception of those on the pages listed below:
A. C. Cooper, London 70; Hamlyn Group Picture Library 14, 32, 140 right, 169 centre right; Hotspur, London 22, 23, 24, 25, 28, 29; Victoria and Albert Museum, London 15, 21 top, 31.

The line drawings are by The Hayward Art Group.

POTTERY AND PORCELAIN

The author and publishers are particularly grateful to Mr Geoffrey Godden for allowing the following illustrations which are of items in the Godden Reference Collection to be included in this book: 13, 14, 18, 20, 21, 28, 30, 99, 100, 101, 103, 104, 105, 106, 108, 109, 110, 111, 112, 113, 114, 115, 116, 117, 118, 119, 120, 123, 127, 128, 131, 137, 138, 141, 144, 145.

Illustration numbers 17, 25, 36 and 69 are reproduced by courtesy of the Birmingham Museums and Art Gallery and number 129 by courtesy of the Trustees of the Dyson Perrins Museum, Worcester.

Photographs
Ashmolean Museum, Oxford 16; Birmingham Museums and Art Gallery 17, 25, 36, 69; British Museum, London 8, 12, 24, 41, 44, 50, 60; City Museum and Art Gallery, Stoke-on-Trent 58; Dyson Perrins Museum, Worcester 129; G. W. Elliott, Stoke-on-Trent 5, 32, 33, 46, 53, 54; Fitzwilliam Museum, Cambridge 22, 65, 73, 107; Hamlyn Group–Walter Gardiner Photography 13, 14, 18, 20, 21, 28, 30, 99, 100, 101, 103, 104, 105, 106, 108, 109, 110, 111, 112, 114, 115, 116, 117, 118, 119, 120, 123, 127, 128, 131, 137, 138, 141, 144, 145; Hamlyn Group Picture Library 2, 3, 4, 19, 26, 27, 29, 31, 35, 45, 51, 61, 62, 63, 64, 66, 67, 77, 78, 89, 90, 91, 92, 121, 122, 125, 126, 130, 133, 134, 135, 136, 139, 140, 143; Merseyside County Museums, Liverpool 23, 75, 76; Museum of London 10, 11; Nottingham Castle Museum 68, 70; Royal Scottish Museum, Edinburgh 6, 34, 72; Royal Worcester Spode, Worcester 124; Victoria and Albert Museum, London 9, 15, 37, 38, 39, 40, 42, 43, 47, 48, 49, 52, 55, 56, 57, 59, 71, 74, 79, 94, 97, 102, 113, 142, 146; Josiah Wedgwood and Sons, Barlaston 1, 7, 80, 81, 82, 83, 84, 85, 86, 87, 88, 93, 95, 96, 98, 137.

Marks
The following marks are reproduced with the permission of the publishers W. Foulsham & Co. Ltd. from their Identification Guide, *English Pottery and Porcelain Marks* by S. W. Fisher:
1. Bow china works: Anchor and Dagger Mark, painted, c. 1760-76; mark in underglaze glue, c. 1760-76; early incised marks. 2. Bristol marks. 3. Chelsea-Derby marks. 4. Coalport Porcelain Works: mark in enamels or in gold, c. 1851-61; an early painted mark, c. 1805-15. 5. Longton Hall works. 6. New Hall porcelain works. 7. Plymouth porcelain works. 8. Minton. The Doulton and Martin ware marks are reproduced from *The Encyclopedia of British Pottery and Porcelain Marks* by Geoffrey Godden, Barrie and Jenkins, 1964; the Wedgwood marks from the catalogue of the Wedgwood Museum, Barlaston; the Royal Crown Derby marks from *The Story of Royal Crown Derby China* by John Twitchett FRSA. The remaining marks are all taken from *The Handbook of British Pottery and Porcelain Marks* by Geoffrey Godden, Herbert Jenkins Ltd., 1968.

The author and publishers would also like to thank Penguin Books Limited for permission to quote from *The Travels of Marco Polo* translated by R. E. Latham, 1958, © Ronald Latham 1958. The letters of Père d'Entrecolles are reproduced by kind permission of B. T. Batsford Limited, from *Burton's Porcelain, its Art and Manufacture*, published in 1906.

The line drawings are by The Hayward Art Group.

GLASS

All the photographs were provided by the author with the exception of the following:
British Museum, London 3, 13; Bridgeman Art Library, London 122; Fitzwilliam Museum, Cambridge 6, 10; Hamlyn Group–Thomas Photos 17, 18, 20, 100, 103, 114, 116, 117, 118, 124, 125, 126, 127, 128, 130, 139, 142, 143, 145, 146, 147; Hamlyn Group Picture Library 19, 123, 132, 140; Museum of London 9, 58; National Portrait Gallery, London 11, 12; Pilkington Glass Museum, St Helens 14, 34, 40, 97, 129; Science Museum, London 4, 5; Sotheby Parke Bernet & Co, London 7, 8, 24, 35, 66, 67, 68, 101, 102, 108, 109, 110, 111, 115; Victoria and Albert Museum, London 90, 98, 104.

The line drawings are by The Hayward Art Group.

PEWTER, COPPER AND BRASS

The author and publishers are grateful to the following for allowing us to photograph:
Jack Casimir Ltd, The Brass Shop, 23 Pembridge Road, London W.11, Robin Bellamy Ltd, 97-99 Corn St. Witney and Key Antiques, 11 Horsefair, Chipping Norton.

Photographs
Author 2, 3, 12, 19, 20, 34, 46, 52, 53, 56, 57, 58, 60, 62, 64, 83, 98, 105, 134; Brighton Museum 90, 109; Hamlyn Group Picture Library 78, 79, 80, 81, 82, 103, 114, 116, 118, 120, 126; Hamlyn Group–Thomas Photos 1, 10, 13, 16, 22, 23, 25, 30, 35, 36, 37, 38, 41, 43, 45, 47, 49, 65, 72, 73, 74, 75, 77, 85, 89, 93, 97, 100, 101, 102, 110, 111, 113, 115, 119, 121, 129, 133, 135, 136, 139; Hamlyn Group–John Webb 5, 6, 7, 18, 21, 24, 26, 31, 32, 33, 39, 40, 51 66, 67, 70, 71, 76, 88, 92, 95, 96, 104, 112, 117, 128, 137, 138; Robert Perry 107; National Museum of Antiques, Edinburgh 9; Sotheby Parke Bernet, London 8, 11, 14, 15, 17, 27, 28, 29, 42, 44, 48, 50, 54, 55, 59, 61; Cyril Staal 63, 87, 94, 99, 106, 108, 122, 130; Victoria and Albert Museum, London 84, 86, 91, 123, 124, 125, 127, 131, 132.

SILVER

The photographs were all provided by the author with the exception of the following:
James Charles, London 69, 97, 103, 117, 148, 162; Christie Manson and Woods, London 31, 71; Colonial Williamsburg Foundation, Williamsburg, Virginia 2, 3, 4, 5, 6, 7, 8, 9; Worshipful Company of Goldsmiths, London 26, 27, 29, 32, 33, 34, 35, 37, 38, 42, 47, 55, 56, 66, 73, 74, 77, 83, 109; Hamlyn Group Picture Library 28, 57, 92, 93, 106, 107, 108, 111; Los Angeles County Museum of Art, California 30; Thomas Lumley Ltd., London 62, 153, 154; Sotheby's, Belgravia, London 121, 123, 125, 141, 142, 146, 155; Sotheby Parke Bernet, London page 835 top; C. J. Vander (Antiques) Ltd., London 156; Victoria and Albert Museum, London 124.

The line drawings are by The Hayward Art Group.

CLOCKS

The following kindly allowed their clocks to be illustrated or gave invaluable help in the preparation of the book:
Mrs M. W. Arnold, Mr K. Aspinall, Mrs Christine E. Barker, Mr·Granville Barrett, Mr Nelson Bestwick, Miss Rani Butt, Mr David Bovingdon, Mr Donald Cowbourne, Mrs Lynne Finnegan, Mr Don Finney, Mr Robert Foster, Mr Christopher Gilbert, Mrs Claire Greaves, Mr Frederick Hodgson, Miss M. Lawson, Leeds City Museums, Leeds Art Galleries, Mr Brian Loomes, C. Lumb and Sons, Ltd., Mrs Janice Lumb, Museum of Lincolnshire Life, Lincoln, Mr Roy M. S. Precious, Mr Paul Rodgers, Mr Wilfred Scatchard, Mr Norman Whitfield, The Yorkshire Archaeological Society.

The photographs of items in Abbey House Museum, Kirkstall and Temple Newsam House are reproduced by courtesy of Leeds City Art Gallery, those in Townley Hall Art Gallery and Museum by courtesy of Burnley Borough Council, illustrations number 3, 62 and 103 by courtesy of the City of Bradford Metropolitan Council Museums Department, Bolling Hall Museum, number 46 by courtesy of Spalding Gentlemen's Society, numbers 57, 58 and 59 by courtesy of the Archives Department, Westminster City Library.

All the photographs were taken for The Hamlyn Group by David Griffiths with the exception of those listed below:

James Arnfield, Stockport 2, 6, 7, 8, 9, 10, 12; David Barker, Keighley 13, 15, 22, 23, 24, 27, 28, 29, 30, 31, 32, 38, 40, 45, 47, 49, 63, 64, 68, 69, 75, 80, 83, 89, 92, 93, 101, 102, 104, 107, 121, 123, 124, 135; British Museum, London 20, 21, 79, 120; Christie Manson and Woods, London 91; Hamlyn Group Picture Library 87, 110, 111, 113, 114, 116; Hamlyn Group–East Midlands Photographic Services 46; Hamlyn Group–John Webb 57, 58, 67; National Maritime Museum, London 117; Royal Commission on Historical Monuments (England) 16.

The line drawings were made by Samuel McMurran with the exception of those on pages 928, 955 and 967 which were made by David Barker and those on pages 848 and 850 which were made by Bob Mathias and The Hayward Art Group.

JACKET PHOTOGRAPHS

front top left: Hamlyn Group Picture Library
front bottom left: Hamlyn Group–Robert Du Pontet
front right: Hamlyn Group–David Griffiths
back top left: Christie Manson and Woods, London
back bottom left: Hamlyn Group–Thomas Photos
back right: Hamlyn Group Picture Library
back flap: Hamlyn Group–Michael Plomer